Footprint
Caribbean Islands

Sarah Cameron
17th edition

*Out past the swellin' chest, all blue and green,
the sea stretch 'e arm way up along the hills.
Past Arnos Vale, Culloden, Moriah and Castara.
Every time it heave, the arm ripple and, far far away,
white waves wash over rocks, silent.
Long white fingernails stretching out,
clawing and scratching at the cliffs.*

Tide Running, Oonya Kempadoo

1 Havana
The capital city that never sleeps, rumba and salsa are its life blood, page 84.

2 Santa Clara
Tomb and monument to revolutionary hero Che Guevara, page 128.

3 Trinidad
A colonial city in a time warp, with cobbled streets and horse-drawn transport, page129.

4 Little Cayman
A diver's paradise with virgin walls and reefs and excellent visibility, page 197.

5 Blue Mountains
Home of great coffee and forest hikes, page 228.

6 La Citadelle
Mountain-top fortress, symbol of the only successful black slave revolution, page 407.

7 Pico Duarte
The tallest mountain in the Caribbean and a mecca for hikers, page 330.

8 Bahía de Samaná
Great whale watching when humpbacks migrate, page 353.

9 British Virgin Islands
A sailors' playground; dozens of protected bays and islands, page 499.

10 Saba
A tiny Dutch outpost with glorious views and diving, page 562.

11 Barbuda
The world's largest breeding colony of frigate birds, page 597

Caribbean Islands Highlights

See colour maps at back of book

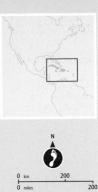

Atlantic Ocean

Turks & Caicos
Islands
North Caicos
Middle Caicos
East Caicos
Grand Turk

Hispaniola

⑦ Santo ⑧
Domingo

Dominican Isla
Republic Saona Isla
Mona
Isla Beata

Greater Antilles

British
Virgin
Islands

San
Juan

Anegada ⑨
Tortola Virgin
Gorda
St Thomas
Vieques

Sombrero
Anguilla
Saint-Martin
St Barthélémy

Leeward Islands

St Croix Sint Eustatius ⑩ Saba ⑫ St Kitts Barbuda ⑪

US Virgin Nevis
Islands Redonda Antigua
Montserrat ⑬

Puerto
Rico

Lesser
Antilles

Guadeloupe ⑭
Les Saintes

Marie-
Galante

Windward Islands

Dominica ⑮

Martinique

St Lucia

Lesser Antilles

Aruba ㉑
Curaçao Bonaire
㉑ ⑳

Islas Los
Roques

Islas Cayo Cayo
Las de Sal Grande
Aves

Isla La Orchila

Isla La Tortuga

Caracas

St Vincent
The Grenadines ⑯ Bequia
Canouan

Barbados ⑰
Mustique
Mayreau
Carriacou

Grenada

Los Testigos

Isla de Margarita

Tobago
Basin

Tobago

Port of Spain

⑲ Trinidad

Gulf of
Paria

VENEZUELA

1

4

Contents

Cuba's colonial heritage is there to see in the city of Trinidad, a UNESCO World Heritage Site.

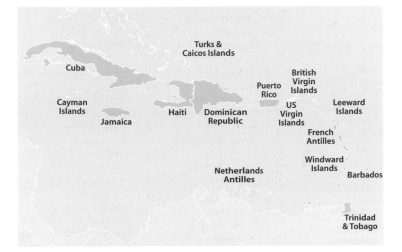

Willemstad's pastel-painted architecture evokes the Dutch colonial heritage of Curaçao.

Sun, sea and sand
A Holy Grail to divers, the Caymans also offer a wide choice of accommodation, all manner of watersports, and great beaches.

A foot in the door

Swaying palm trees, golden beaches, a hammock at siesta time, sunset rum cocktails… The heat of the tropical sun induces lethargy and all the conditions for a relaxing holiday. Sun, sea and sand are offered in abundance in the Caribbean and it is easy to adapt to the unhurried pace of island living. After dark, when it is cooler, everyone comes out to play, to promenade, to sing and dance. This is the time to turn up a different sort of heat. Take hold of a partner and gyrate your hips in time with the local music, whether it be salsa, reggae, merengue or any other local dance. The people of the islands will be delighted to give you some hands-on tuition.

The Caribbean islanders are a diverse mix and their cultures vary according to their ethnic blend. Starting with the different Amerindian tribes, the melting pot has been added to by colonizers: the Spanish, French, English, Dutch, American, Danish, Swedish, followed by their slaves of various African tribes, indentured labourers from India or China and immigrants from Arab countries. Skin colour and features can differ greatly even within families, depending on their ancestors. Despite the huge US influence everywhere (except Cuba), most islands have kept their own identities and traditions based on their own experience of immigration: enjoy Carnival in Trinidad; dance salsa in Cuba; stay in the highest hotel in the Kingdom of the Netherlands, in Saba; dive a sunken Russian frigate off Cayman Brac; worship in the oldest synagogue in the Western Hemisphere in Curaçao; watch African big drum music in Carriacou; immerse yourself in reggae in Jamaica; be initiated into the rites of voodoo in Haiti; ride the sugar train in St Kitts. And, in addition to all that, you can sit back and sample the local rum – everywhere.

10 More than a game

International sporting events are held throughout the year in one island or another and are frequently the catalyst for parties and other entertainment. Whether you participate as a competitor or spectator, plenty of fun can be had by all. Some major events, such as the 2007 Cricket World Cup, hosted by the West Indies, or the 2003 Pan American Games, held in Santo Domingo, attract thousands of visitors – athletes, coaches, fans and media – to the islands. The most popular sport locally is football, followed by cricket in the English-speaking Caribbean and baseball in the Spanish-speaking islands. Interest in cricket has waned along with the fortunes of the West Indies team, but the introduction of the Stanford 20/20 cricket tournament in 2006 pulled in the crowds. Island rivalry, which is a constant hazard in getting a cohesive West Indies team, was harnessed for the benefit of the spectators, who witnessed some exciting matches. In Cuba, the Dominican Republic and Puerto Rico, everything stops for baseball, with a season running through the winter months. It is every boy's dream to become a baseball star – a realisable dream, given the number of talent scouts and the high proportion of Latin players in the US leagues.

Bowled over
Cricket is still king in the English-speaking Caribbean, despite the West Indies team's slump in form.

HiHo, HiHo, it's off to race we go...

A large number of sporting competitions take place in the waters surrounding the islands and the list of regattas is endless. Stanford Antigua Sailing Week has been held annually since 1968 and has grown from an informal collection of 17 boats to the current entry of over 200. It is now one of the top five regattas in the world and the biggest in the Caribbean. Sailors know how to enjoy themselves and the accompanying parties are some of the biggest too. Other major annual sailing events are the Heineken Regatta in Sint Maarten, the International Rolex Regatta in the USVI and the BVI Spring Regatta and Sailing Festival, among many races held in the Virgin Islands. Windsurfers also compete in races around the Virgin Islands, with the annual Highland Spring HiHo one of the most exciting as the competitors cover anything from 100 to 200 miles with the accompanying fleet of catamarans stopping en route at different beaches for meals and parties. Chosen for its stunning location and great waves, Barbados' Silver Rock Beach hosts the annual Windsurfing World Cup Championships. Attracting windsurfers from all over the world, this is a great competition with plenty of other beachside entertainment laid on for both competitors and spectators.

Surf's up
Cabarete is a mecca for top-class windsurfers honing their skills in the Dominican Republic.

1 Humpback whales migrate to the islands to breed and can be seen on whale-watching trips from January to March. ▶▶ See page 356.

2 Vendors at Bridgetown market, Barbados, sell hats to offer shade against the tropical sun. ▶▶ See page 845.

3 Haitans sell what they can to eke out a living on the western portion of Hispaniola. ▶▶ See page 402.

4 Relaxation and pampering have always been an essential part of a Caribbean holiday. ▶▶ See page 816.

5 Don't take on the locals at dominoes in Jamaica; they'll knock the spots off you. ▶▶ See page 206.

6 Trails through the forest are ideal for hiking and biking on St Lucia and are an adrenaline-fuelled antidote to lazing on the beach. ▶▶ See page 755.

7 The first cathedral in the New World was built in Santo Domingo in the in the Dominican Republic and dedicated in 1542. ▶▶ See page 313.

8 High-quality cigars are as essential to the Cuban experience as rum, revolution and rusty old American cars. ▶▶ See page 90.

9 The Culebra National Wildlife Refuge, in Puerto Rico, protects large colonies of sea birds. ▶▶ See page 459.

10 Freshly caught lobster is served up as a Friday night treat in fishing villages around St Lucia. ▶▶ See page 738.

11 Nelson's Dockyard, Antigua, is as busy with sailing boats as it was in its 18th-century heyday. ▶▶ See page 593.

12 Colourful coral gardens attract fish and divers to explore hidden depths throughout the Caribbean. ▶▶ See page 941.

14 Party piece

The huge popularity of Carnival in Trinidad has led many islands to develop new festivals to attract visitors; it is worth considering what events are planned when you are deciding where and when to go. Every island celebrates Carnival in some form or other, mostly as a pre-Lenten event, but several countries, including St Lucia, schedule it for later in the year, partly to spread out the revelries. The biggest and best is still in Trinidad. It's more spontaneous than its rival in Rio and is famous for its music, parades and lavish costumes. Jamaica hosts Carnival around Easter, recycling many of the Trinidadian songs and even the costumes, as well as incorporating much original material. Carnival in Santiago de Cuba is in July, taking in the anniversary of the Moncada rebellion as further cause for celebration. Barbados' Carnival celebrates the end of the sugar harvest, so Crop Over is in July, running into the beginning of August on Kadooment Day, with lots of calypso, soca and other live music. The common theme of all the carnivals is the masquerade, where masked and elaborately costumed dancers 'rush' through the streets, usually in the early hours of the morning on 'J'ouvert' or Carnival Monday. Their disguises can be traced back to legends from Africa and colonial times and vary from country to country depending on their own histories. In the Dominican Republic revellers dress up as devils, piglets or bulls, with battles between rival factions, while in Carriacou, in the Grenadines, they celebrate Shakespeare Mas, where masked characters from Shakespeare's plays recite long speeches until they forget their lines and are beaten over the head by their rivals.

arnival is a spectacular event, famous for its music, parades and extravagant nd for its hedonistic excess.

Traditional music can be heard on any street and in every bar in Havana and in other Cuban towns and villages.

Rhythm of life

Even if you're not around for Carnival, you're sure to catch some other festivity. Each town celebrates its patron saint's day, often with a street party incorporating traditional food and drink, music and dance. Music festivals, particularly jazz, are popular and usually a sell-out. Many are planned in low season, to try and spread the flow of tourists throughout the year. The St Lucia Jazz Festival in May is worth going out of your way for (most neighbouring islands lay on extra transport and package deals for that week). Most performances are open air, although fringe events can be found anywhere. Grenada follows it with a *Spice Jazz Festival* in May or June, which is increasing its international standing, but doesn't yet ha' quite the reputation of St Lucia. Cuba's *Jazz Plaza* Festival is in Dece' conveniently timed so that you can take in the Film Festival as w' Jamaica puts on Reggae Sumfest, in July, when, for five days ' to local and international reggae artists until your head is t' Santo Domingo, in the Dominican Republic, hosts a fes' July with dancing in the streets late into the night.

A more highbrow cultural event is the Holder' March, where you can catch drama, opera and all over the world, held in a plantation hous' fairy lights.

Essentials

Footprint features

Planning your trip

Where to go

Holiday companies and travel agents tend to market the Caribbean as a homogenous tropical destination, but in reality each island has its own personality and what suits one person will not suit another. You have a choice between British, Spanish, French, American and Dutch islands, so language might be a consideration. Some islands are more difficult to get to than others. How much time do you want to spend travelling to your destination? Do you want to stay in one place or indulge in a spot of island-hopping? Do you like company and organized activities or would you prefer an empty mountain or deserted beach? Do you want to take it easy and relax or are you an active person who needs to face challenges?

One-week trip

With only one week to spare it is best to stay on one island and take things easy. If you are basing yourself on an island with good links by ferry then a day trip to a neighbouring island would be plenty. For example, you could stay on Anguilla and hop across to the shops on St-Martin; base yourself on Providenciales and go sightseeing on any of the Caicos Islands; go to Antigua and fly or sail over to Barbuda to see the frigate bird sanctuary or fly to Montserrat to see the volcano.

Two-week trip

Two weeks gives you time to explore two or three small islands or a large one in depth. You need more than two weeks to see everything the Dominican Republic has to offer, for example, and you could see quite a lot of Cuba in a fortnight, too. You will probably have exhausted all there is to do on a small island in a week, so choosing a split destination is a good idea. For transport and immigration reasons this is usually easier if you choose places like Antigua and Barbuda, St Kitts and Nevis, Trinidad and Tobago, which are one country. Alternatively you could explore the British Virgin Islands or St Vincent and the Grenadines with a week ashore and a week on a yacht.

One month

A month gives you serious time to get to know parts of the region. You could visit all the French islands, or all the Dutch islands; cover Cuba from top to toe; investigate both sides of Hispaniola: the Dominican Republic and its neighbour, Haiti.

Two months

The Caribbean is your oyster and where you go will be determined by the size of your budget. You could sail through the arc, stopping in where you felt like it and spending nights on shore at whim. There are those who have spent a couple of months cycling through the islands. Alternatively, set yourself a task: learn Spanish in the Dominican Republic and then put your skills to the test on any of the Spanish-speaking islands, or enrol on a salsa dancing course in Cuba and once you've mastered the art, you'll be in demand at all the bars and clubs as you travel around.

The condensed Caribbean

Finding your way around the Caribbean can seem like a daunting task – so many islands to choose from. Which one or which group would suit you? Here's a handy A-Z trip around them all to help you decide where to start, finish, or just lounge.

Anguilla Anguilla is known for its luxury hotels and extensive sandy beaches. It is
one of the safest islands and consequently one of the most relaxing, but is not a
low-budget option. Visitors amuse themselves in the water during the day and visit
restaurants, bars and weekend beach parties at night. There's not much else to do on
this low-lying coral island, but that's why people come here.

Antigua A family holiday destination with great beaches, watersports and safe
swimming. Direct, non-stop flights from Europe and North America make this island
ideal for introducing children to the Caribbean. Good transport links with other
islands facilitate two-centre holidays or more extensive island hopping. English
Harbour is particularly picturesque, with yachts filling a historic bay that has been a
popular staging post for centuries.

Aruba Aruba is only 25 km north of Venezuela and was closely linked with the oil
industry for most of the 20th century, but when times were hard the island diversified
into mass tourism. The coast on the leeward side of the island with the best beaches
is now wall-to-wall hotels; all those with more than 300 rooms are allowed to have a
casino. A wide range of watersports are on offer, including world-class windsurfing.

Barbados Barbados hasn't got the best beaches in the Caribbean, there are no
volcanoes, no rainforest, but visitors of all ages and budgets come back time and
time again to stay in a luxury hotel room or a moderate apartment. You can play golf,
tennis, squash and any number of other sports, or you can watch cricket, horseracing
or polo. There is lovely walking along the rugged north and east coasts on the Atlantic
side, while beaches are best along the more protected west and south coasts. There
are more sights than you can fit in a two-week holiday: fortifications, plantation
houses, museums, rum distilleries and gardens.

Bonaire The diving on this Dutch island is among the best in the Caribbean, with
pristine reefs and wonderful visibility as there are no rivers to muddy the waters and it
is out of the hurricane belt. Windsurfing is also excellent. The climate is dry and the
vegetation little more than scrub and cactus but It is prized by birdwatchers.

British Virgin Islands These islands have excellent sailing and there are many
charter companies offering crewed or bareboat yachts. Regattas attract competitors
of international standard. Races are accompanied by lots of parties and related
activities typical of the yachtie fraternity. There are plenty of hotels, and a few really
special places – popular with newly weds or the seriously rich.

Cayman Islands These three low-lying little islands south of Cuba are green with
pine and mangroves, while underwater the reefs and walls offer some of the world's
most thrilling dive sites. Grand Cayman is busy with its offshore financial sector as
well as tourism and Seven Mile Beach is wall-to-wall hotels. Cayman Brac and Little
Cayman are quiet, unhurried places where you can escape the crowds and relax
without giving up your creature comforts.

Cuba The largest island in the Caribbean, Cuba is blessed with varied and picturesque
scenery, from the rolling green sugar cane land or flat cattle plains to forested
mountains, lakes, caves, beaches and swamps. Travellers come for the vibrant
culture, music, dance, art and the people who make it. The island's turbulent political
past and its current Communist stability is of interest to many. Colonial towns and
cities are unspoilt by advertising or neon and American influence is minimal: Cuba is
Cuban. You can laze on a beach, hike up a mountain, cycle the deserted roads, or
wander around fortresses, historical monuments and museums.

Curaçao Curaçao has some very fine Dutch colonial architecture painted in a variety of pastel colours. It also has one of the most important historical sites in the Caribbean: a synagogue dating back to 1732, the oldest in continuous use in the Western Hemisphere. An underwater park to preserve the reef has made diving popular and there are dive sites (and hotels) all along the leeward side of the island.

Dominica Dense forests, volcanic hills, rivers, waterfalls and the Boiling Lake provide good hiking and birdwatching opportunities. It is also a highly regarded diving destination and you can see whales and dolphins offshore. Hotels around the island are small, intimate and low-key, greater development being deterred by the lack of beaches. It is the only island where Caribs have survived and they still retain many of their traditions such as canoe carving.

Dominican Republic This is the Hispanic side of Hispaniola, with some stunning scenery: the highest mountain in the Caribbean and some of the most beautiful beaches. The capital, Santo Domingo, was the first city in Spanish America and it boasts the first cathedral and the first university. Hotels sprawl along the coast for sun, sea and sand worshippers, but for anyone wanting action, you can go mountain biking, whitewater rafting, hiking, canyoning or horse riding. If you've still got any energy after all that for nightlife, the discos are throbbing with merengue.

Grenada Grenada is known as the spice island because of the nutmeg, mace and other spices it produces. It has a beautiful mountainous interior and several national parks. Many different ecosystems are found, from dry tropical forest and mangroves on the coast, through lush rainforest on the hillsides, to elfin woodland on the peaks. St George's, now recovering from Hurricane Ivan in 2004, is widely acknowledged as the prettiest harbour city in the West Indies, blending French and English architectural styles with a picturesque setting on steep hills overlooking the bay.

Guadeloupe This is France in the tropics: coffee, croissants, baguettes and delicious, spicy Créole food, which you can wash down with some very fine rum. Guadeloupe is really two islands: the western Basse-Terre, which is mountainous and forested, with a huge national park popular with hikers, and Grand-Terre, to the east, which is smaller, flatter and more densely populated with good beaches. The outer islands of Les Saintes, La Désirade and Marie Galante are easily reached from Guadeloupe but are quiet and untouched by mass tourism.

Haiti The only country successfully to have carried out a slave rebellion, Haiti's religious beliefs, music, dance and art stem directly from Africa with French influences from colonial days. French Créole is nearly everybody's first language. The most impressive fortification is the massive La Citadelle, built on top of a 900-m peak to deter any French re-invasion. Haiti has suffered decades of civil unrest, it is the poorest country in the Western Hemisphere and tourism is minimal. Poverty has led Haitians to cut down all their trees for fuel, leaving the hillsides bare.

Jamaica A beautiful island with rolling hills and steep gullies, the spectacular Blue Mountains overlook a coastline indented with bays and coves. Rain falls freely, water is abundant, the vegetation is luxuriant and colours are vibrant. The people have a culture to match, from reggae and rastafarianism to English plantation houses and cricket. Music is everywhere and Jamaica is a hub of creativity in the Caribbean. Every conceivable watersport is on offer in the resort areas on the north coast, where the beaches are safe for swimming.

Martinique Like Guadeloupe, this is a piece of France in the tropics, where

: How big is your footprint?

The Travel Foundation, www.the travelfoundation.co.uk, provides the following tips:

→ Consider helping to compensate for the environmental impact of your flight. See www.climatecare.org.uk, www.futureforests.com and www.foc-uk.com.

→ Avoid overt displays of wealth, such as wearing expensive jewellery. Carry your camera discreetly.

→ Minimize waste by re-using plastic bags and by taking your used batteries home with you. Take home anything which can be recycled, such as shampoo bottles, as most islands do not have the facilities to process them. Waste disposal is a sensitive issue.

→ Always carry a bag to take waste away with you, and never litter.

→ Use local taxis, and go with local guides when possible, rather than relying on big businesses, as this supports the local economy.

→ Hire a car only when you need to. Use alternatives such as public transport, bicycles and walking, which means you're more likely to meet local people, too.

→ Always, always, ask permission before taking photographs of people or their homes. Don't be offended if they decline, or expect to be paid.

→ Don't pick flowers and plants, or remove pebbles and sea shells.

→ Buy locally made products. Shop, eat and drink in locally owned outlets, rather than international chains. This brings enormous benefits to local people.

→ Always bargain with humour, and remember that a small cash saving to you could be a significant amount of money to the seller.

→ In your hotel, turn off/down air conditioning when it's not required. Switch off lights when leaving the room, and turn the TV off, rather than leaving it on standby.

→ Take quick showers instead of baths, and let staff know you're happy to reuse your towels rather than having them replaced daily.

Other useful websites for tips and inspiration: **Tourism Concern**, www.tourismconcern.org.uk, and **Responsible Tourism Awards**, www.responsibletourism awards.info.

language and customs have adapted to the climate. There is something for everybody: a variety of hotels; good beaches; watersports; historical attractions; beautiful scenery; hiking; birdwatching and countless other activities. Tourism is well-developed in the south, but a large part of the more mountainous north is taken up by protected rainforest. The volcano, Pelée, last erupted in 1902, when it destroyed the former capital, St-Pierre, killing all but one of its 26,000 inhabitants.

Montserrat The 'Emerald Isle', with its Irish influences, is learning to live with an active volcano, which has been erupting since 1995. Volcano watching is now a tourist attraction, with a strategically placed observatory where scientists monitor activity. The southern part of the island, including the capital, Plymouth, is under a blanket of ash and uninhabited. Priority was given to building houses in the north, but now economic and cultural needs are being satisfied, with a new airport and cricket pitch.

Puerto Rico Puerto Rico's inhabitants are descended from Taíno Indians, their Spanish colonial masters and African slaves. San Juan, the island's capital, was founded in 1510 and the lovely old city stands on a spit of land jutting out to sea. The sprawling, hideous new city is US-influenced, with shopping malls, industrial zones

⦂ Hurricane season

June too soon
July stand by
August it must
September remember
October all over

In recent years there have been several late storms and the 'October all over' proved a myth. There was little hurricane activity in the region from the 1950s until the late 1980s. Many of the islands were not affected by hurricanes and residents thought little of them. Homes were not built to withstand severe storms. In 1989 this all started to change when several violent storms roared through the islands and Hurricane Hugo did untold damage in the US Virgin Islands. The next few years were relatively quiet but 1995 struck with a bang (three names were 'retired' in deference to the dead and injured) and was the start of a ten-year period that has gone down in history as the most active stretch on record for hurricanes. Analysts expect that this active hurricane era will last another two or three decades. Storms are now increasing in intensity and 2004 was a bad year. There were 15 named storms, nine hurricanes and six intense hurricanes, of which four reached Florida after sweeping through the islands. Long-term averages are an annual 9.6 tropical storms, 5.9 hurricanes and 2.3 major storms. Ivan was the most destructive in 2004, killing over 100 people in the Caribbean and the USA and flattening both Grenada and Grand Cayman with winds in excess of 130 mph.

In the daily weather forecasts, a **tropical depression** is an organized system of clouds and thunderstorms with a defined circulation and maximum sustained winds of 38 mph (33 knots) or less; a **tropical storm** is an organized system of strong thunderstorms with a defined

circulation and maximum sustained winds of 39 to 73 mph (34-63 knots); a **hurricane** is an intense tropical weather system with a well-defined circulation and maximum sustained winds of 74 mph (64 knots) or more.

A hurricane develops in warm waters and air, which is why the tropics are known for hurricanes. Powered by heat from the sea they are steered by the easterly trade winds and the temperate westerly winds, as well as their own ferocious energy. In the Atlantic, these storms form off the African coast and move west, developing as they come into warmer water. Around the core, winds grow to great velocity, generating violent seas. The process by which a disturbance forms and strengthens into a hurricane depends on at least three conditions: warm water, moisture and wind pattern near the ocean surface that spirals air inward. Bands of thunderstorms form and allow the air to warm further and rise higher into the atmosphere. If the winds at these higher levels are light, the structure remains intact and allows for further strengthening. If the winds are strong, they will shear off the top and stop the development. If the system develops, a definite eye is formed around which the most violent activity takes place; this is known as the eyewall. The centre of the eye is relatively calm. When the eye passes over land those on the ground are often misled that the hurricane is over; some even abandon safe shelter, not aware that as the eye passes the other side of the eyewall will produce violent winds and the other half of the hurricane. At the top of the eyewall (around 50,000 ft), most of the air is propelled outward, increasing the air's upward motion. Some of the air however, moves inward and sinks into the eye and creates a cloud-free area.

The word 'hurricane' is derived from the Amerindian 'Hurakan', both the Carib god of evil and also one of the Maya creator gods who blew his breath across the chaotic water and brought forth dry land. In the north Atlantic, Gulf of Mexico, Caribbean and the eastern Pacific they are called hurricanes, in Australia, cyclones or 'willy willy', and in the Philippines, 'baguio'. In the Western North Pacific tropical cyclones of hurricane force are called typhoons. The first time hurricanes were named was by an Australian forecaster in the early 1900s who called them after political figures he disliked. During World War II US Army forecasters named storms after their girlfriends and wives. Between 1950-52 they were given phonetic names (able, baker, charlie). In 1953 the Weather Bureau started giving them female names again. Today individual names (male and female) are chosen by the National Hurricane Center in Miami (www.nhc.noaa.gov/) and submitted to the World Meteorology Organization in Geneva, Switzerland. If approved these become the official names for the upcoming hurricane season. As a system develops, it is assigned a name in alphabetical order from the official list.

There is very good information before hurricanes hit any land, thanks to accurate weather data gathered by the Hurricane Hunters from Keesler Airforce Base in the USA. During the storm season they operate out of St Croix in the US Virgin Islands, where they are closer to storms. This elite group of men and women actually fly through the eye of a hurricane in C130 airplanes gathering critical information on the wind speeds and directions and other data. This is sent to the Miami Hurricane Center where a forecast is made and sent to all islands in the potential path so they can prepare for the storm. Most of the island governments are now well prepared to cope with hurricanes and have disaster relief teams in place, while many of the island resorts, especially the larger ones, have their own generators and water supplies.

While a hurricane can certainly pose a threat to life, in most cases if precautions are taken the risks are reduced. Some of the main hazards are storm surge, heavy winds and rains. There is usually disruption of services such as communications, internal transport and airline services. Ideally, if a hurricane is approaching, it is better for the tourist to evacuate the island. During the hurricane, which is usually 6-36 hours, you have to be shut up inside a closed area, often with little ventilation or light, which can be stressful. Some tourists think a hurricane will be 'fun' and want to remain on island to see the storm. This is not a good idea. If you do remain you should register with your local consulate or embassy and email home as soon as the warning is given to alert your family that communications may go down and that you will follow the rules of the emergency services. You should be prepared to be inconvenienced and to help out in the clearing up afterwards. Team work in the aftermath of a disaster can be tremendous.

When potentially violent weather is approaching, the local met office issues advisories:

Tropical storm watch be on alert for a storm (winds of 39-73 mph) which may pose threats to coastal areas within 36 hours.
Tropical storm warning the storm is expected within 24 hours.
Hurricane watch hurricane conditions could be coming in 36 hours.
Hurricane warning the hurricane is expected within 24 hours.

One of the best internet sites for information and data during an actual hurricane is www.stormcarib.com. The website of the Hurricane Hunters (www.hurricanehunters.com) has a virtual reality flight into the eye of a hurricane.

and wide highways. Large resorts, casinos, marinas and golf courses line the coast, but inland there are mountains, rainforest, caves and archaeological sites. The islands of Vieques and Culebra are quiet and relaxing.

Saba This tiny Dutch island rises out of the sea, green and lush. An extinct volcano, its peak is aptly named Mount Scenery. Underwater, the landscape is equally spectacular and divers treasure the marine park, noted for its 'virginity'. Ancient trails weave their way around the island, the most stunning being the 1,064 irregular steps up Mount Scenery through different types of tropical vegetation according to altitude.

St-Barthélemy Tiny St-Barths is easily reached by boat or a short air hop from St-Martin. It has gained a reputation as the place to go for the rich and famous. It is chic and expensive and its many beautiful beaches are dotted with luxury hotels and villas, designed for those who appreciate privacy. Gourmet French restaurants and Créole bistros can be found all over the island. This is a place to indulge yourself and be a part of the jet set.

Sint Eustatius Only 2,100 people live on this Dutch outpost. It has a rich colonial history and a prosperous past, when there were 8,000 inhabitants and some 3,500 ships visited each year. Having made its fortune in the 18th century out of the slave trade and commerce in plantation crops, it lost it in the 19th century with the abolition of slavery. There are walking trails up into the rainforest of the extinct volcano, the Quill, and diving is good in the marine park.

St Kitts and Nevis St Kitts is the new hotspot for tourism development since the closure of the sugar industry and subsequent unemployment freed up land and labour for golf courses, villas and other tourist resorts. The island has long been developing its southern peninsula where there are golden sandy beaches, but most of the island has until now been untouched by tourism. Rugged volcanic peaks, forests and old fortresses and sugar mills produce spectacular views and hiking is very rewarding. Two miles away, the conical island of Nevis is smaller, quieter and very desirable. Here, plantation houses have been converted into some of the most romantic hotels in the Caribbean. Cycling or hiking along the old goat trails affords panoramic views.

St Lucia Very popular as both a family holiday destination and a romantic paradise for honeymooners. Its beaches are golden or black sand and many are favoured by turtles as a nesting site. The mountainous interior is outstandingly beautiful and there are forest reserves to protect the St Lucian parrot and other wildlife. Sightseeing opportunities include sulphur springs, colonial fortifications and plantation tours. St Lucia has a rich cultural heritage, French, English and African, and has produced two Nobel prize winners.

Sint Maarten/St-Martin Shared amicably between Holland and France, this island offers you two (or three) cultures. Good international air transport links have encouraged the construction of large, Americanized resort hotels with casinos and duty-free shopping in the Dutch part. The French part is considered more 'chic' and crowded with restaurants dedicated to the serious business of eating well. Both sides have good beaches, harbours and marinas and are popular with the sailing crowd. Heavily populated, this is not a place to come to get away from it all.

St Vincent and the Grenadines St Vincent is green and fertile and very pretty, with its fishing villages, coconut groves, banana plantations and volcanic interior. However, it is widely known for the superb sailing conditions provided by its 32 sister islands and cays and most visitors spend some time on a yacht, even if only for a day. The Grenadines have a certain exclusivity, some of them are privately owned and Mustique is known for its villas owned by the rich, royal and famous.

Trinidad and Tobago Trinidad has a rich culture, largely a mixture of the traditions of African slaves and Indian indentured labourers, brought together so spectacularly in the world's best carnival. Tobago is a laid back island where visitors appreciate the clear, calm sea, the sandy beaches, the diving and snorkelling and the small, friendly hotels and guest houses. The two islands together are home to more species of birds than any other island in the Caribbean and birdwatchers have long been attracted to the forests and swamps.

Turks and Caicos Islands These flat, coral islands have miles of sandy beaches and are a water playground. Diving and snorkelling are superb among coral gardens, wrecks and walls which drop dramatically to the floor of the ocean. Most hotels are on the island of Providenciales, spread along Grace Bay on the north shore. Grand Turk is the seat of government but is a quiet, unhurried place with a few small hotels and a new cruise ship dock. Other inhabited islands, North Caicos, Middle Caicos, South Caicos and Salt Cay have tiny populations – good places to escape the crowds.

US Virgin Islands The three US Virgin Islands are very American. St Thomas attracts cruise ships and when several are in port the streets of town are heavily congested with shoppers. St John is dominated by the Virgin Islands National Park, which has been in existence since 1956 and has some excellent trails for walkers. St Croix is the poorest of the three but has a great deal to offer in the way of tourist attractions. All three have good hotels and are popular with sailors.

When to go

The climate everywhere in the Caribbean is tropical, with variations in rainfall. The volcanic, mountainous and forested islands attract more rain than the low-lying coral islands, so you can expect frequent showers in St Lucia but not on Bonaire. The driest and coolest time of year is usually December-April, coinciding with the winter peak in tourism as snow birds escape to the sun. However there can be showers, which keep things green. Temperatures then can fall to 20°C during the day, depending on altitude, but are normally in the high 20's, tempered by cooling trade winds. The mean annual temperature is about 26°C. At other times of the year the temperature rises only slightly, but greater humidity can make it feel hotter if you are away from the coast, where the northeast trade winds are a cooling influence. The main climate hazard is hurricane season (see page 22), which runs from June to November, although storms are rare before September. Islands south of Grenada are outside the hurricane belt although they can still receive storms and heavy rain at times. Tropical storms can cause flooding and mudslides.

Sport and activities

The crystal clear waters of the sunny Caribbean combined with the constant northeast trade winds make the islands a paradise for watersports enthusiasts. The great increase in tourism in the area has brought corresponding development and every conceivable watersport is now available. Some of the best islands to head for are Barbados, Jamaica, Antigua, Martinique, the Bahamas, Cayman Islands, Puerto Rico and the Virgin Islands. On these islands you can find hobie-cats and sunfishes for rent, windsurfing, kitesurfing, waterskiing, glass-bottomed boats plying the reefs, charter yachts and booze cruises, scuba diving, snorkelling and deep-sea fishing. And for something a bit more animal-friendly, there are numerous opportunities for whale and dolphin spotting.

It's not all about watersports, however. Many of the islands offer excellent hiking and mountain biking. Those who prefer to watch from the sidelines rather than participate are also in for a treat. In the former British colonies, British dependencies and even the US Virgin Islands, **cricket** is more than just the national game; it's a symbol of achievement and a unifying factor (see pages 10 and 27). **Baseball** and **basketball** serve much the same function in the Dominican Republic, Cuba and Puerto Rico, and if you are interested in the game, or just want to watch the crowd, it is worth finding out the dates of the season in advance of your trip.

Cycling

You can rent bikes on almost every island and because of the mountainous terrain and cool breezes, it is quite a comfortable way to get around. Some of the islands have mountains as high as 3000 m towering above the ocean, making the Caribbean one of the most exciting new mountain bike destinations in the world. Some islands are flat, but most have plenty of hills and some fantastic scenery. However, away from the main tourist areas on each island, the tourist infrastructure is not well developed and the potential for crime is high. Most people will be genuinely friendly and interested in your chosen mode of transport but, at times you can feel vulnerable on a bicycle in relatively remote areas.

Antigua
Antigua has good bike shops and great single track, in addition to a local bike club. However the roads are generally flat, traffic moderately heavy and cycling is not as interesting as on some other islands.

Barbados
On Barbados mountain biking on back-country roads with bike rental is available. The east coast is best but elsewhere there is constant heavy traffic. Rush hour starts at 1600 everywhere.

Cuba
Cuba offers mountain bike tours and good terrain. Charity sponsored tours frequently organized. The west is the more popular part For touring, with gentle hills and plenty of places to stop. The centre can be flat and boring with miles of sugar cane or cattle lands. The Sierra Maestra in the east is demanding and very hot. Distances are huge, always start early and take a long lunch break. Roads are good and empty but poorly signed. Get to your destination before dark as street lighting is poor to non-existent.

Dominica
Cycling is a new attraction, with bike rental and tours offered. Roads are good for cycling, traffic is generally light with the exception of the stretch between Layou and Roseau. Canefield to Pont Casse is very steep, twisty and challenging. This is one of the most enjoyable islands to cycle due to the friendliness of the people, there are plenty of natural sites to visit and the coast roads are quite easy even with gear (ie not so steep).

Dominican Republic
Known as the mountain bike mecca of the Caribbean, the DR has a bicycle club with over 300 members with both mountain bike and road bike races held monthly. Bike shops throughout the island. **Iguana Mama** for tours. The north coast, the Cordillera Septentional and the slopes of the Cordillera Central are great places for scenery and challenging cycling. Exhilarating downhills.

Grenada
Bike rental and spare parts are available. Accommodation is strategically placed for cyclists. The cycle between Sauteurs and Victoria is a peaceful ride with spectacular views. The ride through the Grand Étang is rewarding but difficult, five to six hours with some steep hills but the beauty of the forest

⦂ Cricket in the Caribbean

Cricket in the Caribbean is a game played to a backdrop of rapturous music, stomach-tingling food, fervent politics and joyous partying. It is played in front of the most knowledgeable spectators in the world, who will stop you in the street to provide a breakdown of tactics and techniques (or their absence) in West Indian batting. It is played in the sun (mostly). It is played to laughter.

The six first-class teams are: Jamaica, Trinidad and Tobago, Barbados, Guyana, Windward Islands and Leeward Islands. Inter-island matches are hugely entertaining, with a one-day competition before Christmas and the four-day Carib Beer Cup from January to March. Unless the West Indies side is on tour, all the international players are required to play in the competition, so the standard is high. Consult www.caribbeancricket.com, www.windiescricket.com, www.cricinfo.com, or call the West Indies ticket line T1-800 744-GAME/T1-268-481-2490.

The West Indies hosted the six-week **Cricket World Cup** in 2007, with matches played in Antigua and Barbuda, Barbados, Grenada, Guyana, Jamaica, St Kitts and Nevis, St Lucia and Trinidad and Tobago, while warm-up matches were also played in St Vincent. All these islands now have superb facilities with totally new or completely refurbished grounds and there is a wealth of choice of venues for Test Matches, One-Day Internationals or other world-class cricket.

The development of cricket and of the West Indies team in the English-speaking Caribbean during the 20th century reflected the political struggle for Independence. The best cricketers became respected role models. Learie Constantine, a barrister and advocate of cricketers' rights, paved the way in the 1920s and 1930s. Lightning fast bowler, cavalier batsman, the finest fielder in the world, he was loved and revered from Trinidad to England. He captained the Dominions cricket team that played against England in the series immediately following World War II; a massive recognition at that stage of the 20th century for a black man in a white-dominated team.

The great Jamaican batsman, George Headley, became the first black person to captain the West Indies side in 1948. He paved the way for Frank Worrell, another believer in players' rights, who was the first fully appointed black captain of the West Indies a decade later. The first West Indies win in England brought joyous acclaim in 1950 and new respect in the English-speaking world. Worrell, with his two seminal series as captain in Australia in 1960-1961 and England in 1963, brought a unity to the Caribbean and a consistency to the team that lasted for over 35 years. Sir Garry Sobers remains arguably the greatest cricketer yet born. The dominance of Clive Lloyd and Viv Richards in the 1970s and '80s, both in batting and captaincy, took the West Indies to a new level. The bowling of Roberts, Garner, Holding, Marshall, Ambrose and Walsh struck both fear and admiration into many an armchair spectator, let alone the batsmen who faced them. For a decade, West Indies cricket has been in decline. Only the batting brilliance of Brian Lara kept the side from complete annihilation but he retired in 2007 after the World Cup.

reserve and the small friendly communities are well worth it. **Carriacou** has great cycling. Many of the roads are in very poor repair giving it the semblance of off-road cycling. Traffic is light. Beware flat tyres in the dry season when the trail is overgrown with cactii.

Jamaica

Has bike rental and tour operators offering trips, excellent terrain, mountains, coastal routes, rolling hills. However, beware fast drivers on hairpin bends.

Martinique

Do not attempt to cycle from the airport to either Fort-de-France or Trois-Ilets as the only route is via the main highway, four lanes each way with fast, heavy traffic and the shoulder is narrow to non-existent.

Montserrat

The east coast is scenic with only light traffic to the former airport, which is the furthermost point you can travel.

Puerto Rico

Has bike touring companies and rentals throughout the island, excellent terrain. Avoid the highways around San Juan, where traffic is very heavy.

St Croix

Cycling tours of the forest or beach are offered by **St Croix Bikes & Tours**, while **VI Cycling** organize weekly rides and races.

St Kitts and Nevis

Bike rental and tours are available, and traffic is light. Goat trails on Nevis.

St Lucia

The best way to cycle round the island is anti-clockwise. This will ensure long but gradual uphills and steep, fast downhills. Be extremely careful between Dennery and Castries. This is a drug-growing area and the locals are not particularly friendly. Those that are friendly will warn you not to stop. Castries to Soufrière is enjoyable with a fairly demanding but scenic section through the rainforest. Has the potential be to quite wet! Soufrière to Vieux Fort is another good ride and not so hard physically.

St-Martin/Sint Maarten

Bike rental and tours are available on the island but traffic is heavy on Sint Maarten and you need someone to show you how to get off the beaten track.

St Vincent and the Grenadines

There is good cycle shop in Kingstown, which also offers tours. The cycle between Layou and Richmond is a strenuous four hours one way, an absolutely spectacular ride, not to be missed, but expect long, steep hills and lots of them. The northern part of St Vincent is notorious for being a drug producing area, travel with caution. **Bequia** has really enjoyable cycling, lots of hills but not too steep and not a lot of traffic, great views and beaches scattered over the island.

Trinidad and Tobago

Geronimos, in Port of Spain, is an excellent bicycle shop, owned by a retired professional cyclist. Repairs and parts at **Número Uno** in Carnbee, can put you in touch with local Tobagan riders for road riding. A mountain bike is recommended for the road between L'Anse Fourni and Charlotteville on Tobago.

Diving

The Caribbean is a scuba diver's paradise, with a conglomeration of islands surrounded by living reefs providing different types of diving to suit everyone. The numbers of divers has increased dramatically in recent years, with the result that some of the islands have become 'diving circuses', particularly in some of the more developed northern Caribbean islands where 30 or 40 divers are herded onto large dive boats and dropped on somewhat packaged dive sites where 'tame' fish come for handouts. However, other islands in the region are still virginal in the diving sense, which can lead to an exciting undersea adventure. On the more remote islands facilities are often unavailable and diving can be more difficult and basic. Do not assume you can dive wherever you like even if you have all your own tanks and equipment. Several islands require divers to go with a local dive group and it is best to contact a local dive shop for advice. Many dive operators have special rates and packages for yachtie divers and will pick you up from your yacht. Not all diving shops in the Caribbean adhere to the recommended safety standards, so it is important to enquire what level of training an instructor has and request to see certificates of instructor training if they are not displayed.

ABC Islands
Just off the South American coast **Bonaire** has long been known as a 'hot spot' for diving, and is one of the few islands (like the Caymans) which has devoted itself to scuba diving. A far-sighted government established a marine park way back in 1979 when conservation was not even being discussed by most diving destinations. Bonaire, being very experienced in offering diving, has a wide selection of about a dozen dive operations, including photo and marine life education facilities. Diving sites are also varied with reef, wreck and wall dives. In fact, the Marine Park Guide for Bonaire lists over 50 dive sites. The town pier, right off the capital, has long been a favourite night dive and the pilings are covered in soft sponges and invertebrate life. Neighbouring **Curaçao** is also building a reputation for conservation, with an expansion of diving facilities and exciting diving sites including reefs and a couple of wreck dives of interest. The freighter, *Superior Producer* (rather deep at 100 ft) is intact and has a variety of growth including beautiful orange tubastera sponges. **Aruba** is not likely to equal her sister islands as she lacks the reefs which surround Bonaire and Curaçao, although diving is available. There is an interesting wreck site, with which few other sites around the island compare in marine life. The *Antilla*, a 400 ft German ship, is in 70 ft (and less) of water. Her massive hull has provided a home for an amazing variety and size of fish life and night dives are truly a thrill. More wrecks have been sunk to create an artificial reef.

Barbados
Among the more developed islands in the Caribbean and the surrounding reef life is not as pristine as on some of the less developed islands. However, there are some thriving reefs and within the last few years the island has become known as a wreck diving destination. Five shipwrecks have been intentionally sunk as diving sites,

offering interesting underwater photography.

British Virgin Islands
With some 50 coral islands, these islands are well worth a mention as the diving is exciting and varied. Both liveaboard and land-based operations are available with well-developed facilities for divers. Popular diving sites include the wreck of the *HMS Rhone*, a 310-ft British mail ship sunk in 1867 in a hurricane. She was the site for the Hollywood movie *The Deep*. Many sites lie in the string of islands to the south between Tortola and Virgin Gorda.

Cayman Islands
These are among the most developed for scuba diving and there is a fine organization of over 20 dive operations, including liveaboard boats. There is also a well-run decompression facility on Grand Cayman, which is an added safety factor. The Caymans are very conservation minded and it is a criminal offence to take ANY form of marine life while scuba diving. In fact, it is illegal on Cayman Brac, the smaller sister island, even to wear gloves while scuba diving. This helps ensure that divers will not hold or damage the delicate coral formations and other marine life.

Dominica
'The Nature Island', or 'The Water Island', is a lush, mountainous island with rugged topside and underwater terrain. It is diving for the adventurous and not for the diver who wants it easy, although there are a few beginner sites. This is one of few islands left where black coral abounds along the wall drop-offs starting at 60 ft. For the more experienced the Atlantic east coast offers some spectacular wall dives.

Grenada
Grenada and tiny sister island of **Carriacou** have several interesting sites, including a wrecked Italian cruise liner and an underwater volcano. Most of the islands have a dive shop or two, usually attached to a hotel.

Saba
A tiny Dutch island, only 5 miles long, is truly one of the most protected places for divers.

The entire reef surrounding the island was established as a marine park in 1987 and this conservation effort has led to an abundance of 'tame' fish. Saba diving is known for several deep pinnacles including Third Encounter, Twilight Zone and Shark Shoal. For the less adventurous and experienced, sites like Diamond Rock and Tent Reef offer the thrill of seeing large French angels swimming up to you. Land-based and liveaboard diving boat facilities are available, as well as a recompression chamber facility.

St Vincent and the Grenadines
Lying in the South Eastern Caribbean these islands offer pristine diving, although facilities are limited.

Tobago
An unspoiled destination well worth visiting. This small island is close to the South American coast and large marine life is encouraged by the flow of plankton-rich water from the continent's rivers. Manta ray are especially attracted by the plankton and at Speyside (also called Manta City) where currents meet they are seen frequently. Most diving is along the west and north coast.

Turks and Caicos Islands
They consist of over 40 lovely sand islands and cays and are located on the Turks Island Passage, a 22-mile channel which is 7000-ft deep connecting the Atlantic Ocean and the Caribbean Sea. This contributes to the abundance of marine life and large pelagic fish seen in these waters and spectacular wall diving in the channel. The islands are surrounded by coral reefs that cover over 200 sq miles. Visibility is usually 100 ft or more and marine life plentiful. There are several dive shops on Providenciales and Grand Turk, mostly catering for small groups of divers, and there are three or four liveaboard boats in the islands' waters at any one time.

Fishing

Sportfishing is excellent in many of the islands of the North Caribbean. Almost every variety of deep-sea game fish: marlin, swordfish, tuna, mackerel and dorado abound in the waters. In the reefs and shallows there are big barracuda, tarpon and bonefish. There are areas for all methods of fishing: surf fishing, bottom fishing or trolling. Spearfishing, however, is banned in many islands. Although most fish seem to run between Nov and Mar, there is no real off-season in most islands and local captains will know where to find the best fishing grounds.

Fishing is very well organized in such islands as Puerto Rico, especially in the area which has become known to the enthusiasts as Blue Marlin Alley. Fishing is also very good off the Cayman Islands, Jamaica and the US Virgin Islands. Hemingway made fishing off Cuba famous and it remains an exciting sport there. In many islands there are annual fishing tournaments open to all. Deep-sea fishing boats can be chartered for a half or full day and some are available on a weekly basis. Anglers can also pay individually on split charters. When arranging a charter, be careful to clarify all details in advance.

Hiking

The Caribbean provides ideal conditions for medium-distance walking in the tropics. Small islands avoid the very high temperatures which are common in India, Africa or the South American mainland. Distances are manageable; a hard day's walk will take you from coast to coast on the smaller islands, and a few days is enough for a complete circuit. The scenery is varied; mountain streams and waterfalls are perfect for bathing, and the sea is never far away. Road transport, comfortable accommodation and restaurants are always to hand, though the illusion of remoteness can often be very real.

Barbados
Barbados has very safe and pleasant walking, especially on the east coast, but little wild scenery. **Barbados National Trust** (T246-4262421) organizes hikes.

Cuba
Cuba boasts wonderful mountain scenery with several ranges in the east, centre and west of the island. There are trails and waterfalls to cool off in, but in the Sierra Maestra in the east the mountains are usually closed for security reasons except in a few areas for organized tours. Seek local advice.

⋮ Hiking tips

→ Start early, preferably just before sunrise. This will give several hours walking before the sun becomes too hot or before rain sets in during the wet season. Walk west in the morning and east in the afternoon to avoid strong sun on the face.

→ Wear lightweight cotton clothing, with a wide-brimmed hat. Shorts and short-sleeved shirts are comfortable, but can leave the legs and arms exposed to sunburn or sharp razor grasses.

→ Carry a large thermos to keep water ice-cold. Refilling from mountain streams is generally safe with purification tablets, but be careful of streams below villages especially in islands like St Lucia and Martinique where there is some bilharzia, and of springs in cultivated areas where generously applied pesticides may have leached into the groundwater.

→ Snakes are a worry only on Trinidad, Martinique and St Lucia. Trinidad has several dangerous species, and also has African killer bees. All three islands have the venomous fer de lance, which prefers bush country in dry coastal areas. The snake is usually frightened off by approaching footsteps, so snakebites are rare, but they can be fatal. Some other islands have boa constrictors, which can bite but are not poisonous. In Trinidad, beware of the coral snake, which looks like a colourful bracelet coiled on the ground. Ask for local advice on where to go and stick to well-marked trails.

→ Marijuana farmers can be a problem in remote mountain areas, where people are likely to assume that outsiders have come either to steal the crop or as police spies. The best way to avoid them is to keep to well-marked trails and ask local advice about where to go.

Dominica
Probably has the best unspoiled mountain scenery in the Caribbean. Some of the long-distance trails are hard to follow, though. Guides are readily available. Try the path via Laudat to the Boiling Lake.

Dominican Republic
Home to the two highest peaks in the Caribbean (Pico Duarte and Pico La Pelona) in addition to many smaller mountains, it is one of the great places for hiking. A guide is mandatory in all national parks. For information contact **Dirección Nacional de Parques**, Av Máximo Gómez, Santo Domingo, Apto Postal 2487, T4724204.

Grenada
Has very accessible mountain and rainforest scenery. Good network of signposted trails linking Grand Étang, Concord waterfall, and other points. The mountains to the southeast of the Grand Étang Forest Reserve are less well marked, particularly since Hurricane Ivan, and

you may need a local guide, but the walking is spectacular with marvellous views.

Guadeloupe
Has a network of waymarked trails on the mountainous half (Basse-Terre) in the Parc Naturel and up La Soufrière. Contact the **Organisation des Guides de Montagne de la Caraïbe** (Maison Forestière, 97120 Matouba, T590-800579) for a guide and/or the booklet, *Promenades et Randonnées*.

Haiti
Walking is the normal means of transport in rural areas of Haiti, so there are masses of well-trodden trails, but it is better to walk with a group. Maps are rudimentary and small scale. Few people speak French in remote areas – try to pick up some Créole. Make sure you carry basic supplies, particularly water. Hiring a guide should be no problem.

Jamaica
Has spectacular scenery especially in the Blue

Mountains and in the Cockpit country. Marijuana growers are a real problem in the remote areas, but the main trails in the Blue Mountains are safe. **Jamaica Camping and Hiking Association** and Ministry of Tourism have a useful *Hikers Guide to the Blue Mountains*.

Martinique

The **Parc Naturel Régional** (9 Blvd Géneral-de-Gaulle, T596-731930) organizes group hikes, usually on Sun, and publishes a useful *Guide des Sentiers Pedestres à la Martinique*. Good trails on Mont Pelée and along the north coast.

Puerto Rico

Although it has some lovely mountain scenery and several trails through forest reserves, this island is designed for the driver rather than the hiker. Long-distance hiking is difficult as far as food and lodging is concerned and accommodation is expensive when you get there.

St Lucia

There's a very well-marked east-west trail through Quillesse forest reserve with excellent bird- watching. Other walks organized by the Forestry Department. See St Lucia chapter for details.

St Vincent

Spectacular but sometimes difficult trail across the Soufrière volcano from Orange Hill to Richmond. Guide advisable. North coast trail past Falls of Baleine is spectacular, but hard to follow. Marijuana growers.

Trinidada and Tobago

Tobago has safe and pleasant walking, and distances are not too great. The scenery is varied: hills, woodland and unspoilt beaches. **Trinidad** has some fine scenery, but marijuana growers are a problem, particularly in the Northern Range and you are advised always to walk in a group. Well-marked trails are safe. Those at the Asa Wright Nature Centre are recommended (T868-667 4655). **Trinidad Field Naturalists Club** (PO Box 642, Port of Spain,

T868-6248017, evenings only) organizes long-distance hikes, and visits to caves, etc.

Useful addresses

For groups organizing a serious hiking/camping expedition in the Caribbean, contact the **Duke of Edinburgh's Award Scheme**, Bridge House, Cavans Lane, Bridgetown, Barbados, T246-436 9763, who may be able to provide advice and to supply the address of a local organization on most islands with expedition experience. In the UK the **Ramblers Association** has a subsidiary company **Ramblers Holidays** (T+44 1707-331133, www.ramblersholidays.co.uk) offering walking holidays in Barbados, Cuba and St Lucia.

Maps

Good large scale maps (1: 25,000 or 1: 50,000) are available for all the British Commonwealth islands. These can be obtained from the local Lands and Surveys department on each island; and usually from **Stanfords** (see page 43) or the **Map Shop**, 15 High St, Upton-upon- Severn, Worcestershire, WR8 0HJ, T01684-593146, www.themapshop.co.uk. The UK **Ordnance Survey**, Romsey Rd, Southampton, T01703-792763, publishes a series of colourful tourist maps including some holiday destinations. Relevant titles are: Barbados, St Lucia, Cayman Islands, British Virgin Islands, St Vincent, Dominica. There are also good large scale **Serie Bleu** maps of Guadeloupe and Martinique (1:25,000, seven maps of Guadeloupe, No 4601G-4607G) issued by the **Institut Géographique National**, Paris, which include all hiking trails. Footpath information on maps is not always reliable, however.

Sailing

Sailboat races of all types are held throughout the Caribbean during the entire year. Spectator boats may go out to watch the races, there may be crew sign-up lists for those who would like to sail and best of all, there are usually parties and other activities on shore. Most regattas have various

Fishermen should beware of eating large predators (eg grand barracuda) and other fish which accumulate the ciguatera toxin.

different types of classes, even including liveaboard classes. For details of yacht charters and other sailing information, see Getting around, page 40.

Surfing

Good breaks for surfing and boogey-boarding can be found on the north shores of Puerto Rico, the Dominican Republic, Tobago and in Barbados. In both Puerto Rico and Barbados, custom-built surfboards can be bought and several competitions are organized every year. There are several good surf spots in Puerto Rico and the most consistent break in Barbados is at Bathsheba. In the Dominican Republic and Tobago, the sport is less developed. Waves tend to be bigger and more consistent in winter.

Swimming

If all you want is sea and sand, these abound on nearly every island. The coral islands have the white postcard-perfect beaches and some of the islands of the Grenadines are nothing more than this. Swimming is safe on almost all Caribbean coasts, but do be careful on the exposed Atlantic coasts in the east where waves are big at times and currents rip. Swimming in the Atlantic can be dangerous and in some places it is actually forbidden.

Waterskiing

This is usually available in developed resort areas and beginners are looked after well. If you are a serious waterskier it is worth bringing your own slalom ski as many boats only cater for beginners. Most islands have protected marine areas where waterskiing and other motorized watersports are forbidden.

Windsurfing and kitesurfing

Whether you are an accomplished windsurfer or merely wishing to give it a try, the Caribbean offers warm clear water, trade winds and a wealth of locations to choose from. Throughout the Caribbean there are hundreds of pristine windsurfing and

kitesurfing locations, many undeveloped. Bring your own gear and have an adventure, or sail with the many schools across the islands. The strongest, steadiest winds are in June and July when the trade winds are at their most constant. Winter brings either howling winds or flat calm and is unpredictable. In summer the gentle breezes provide good learning conditions. Each island has different winds and conditions, there is something for everyone, even if you just want to sit on the beach and watch. **Kitesurfing** is a hugely exciting activity both to watch and do, but it is often limited to certain times of the day so that you don't clash with windsurfers or mow down swimmers. Barbados, the Dominican Republic and Aruba have good facilities; operators are given in the listings for individual islands.

ABC Islands
Aruba is well-known as a centre for great windsurfing and kitesurfing, flat waist deep water on the leeward side with strong wind make this an ideal location for learners and advanced windsurfers, the perfect family windsurf vacation. Best winds: May to Jul. **Bonaire** has good winds and locations for all levels of sailors from flat water to gentle waves. Best winds: Dec to Aug. Windsurfing takes place in the east, while kitesurfing is organized in the southwest.

Antigua
Has steady winds and good locations. At present there is only one dedicated school, although hotels often have learner boards. Best winds: Nov to Feb and Jun/Jul.

Barbados
Sun, sand, wind and waves make Barbados one of the favourite locations for many pro windsurfers on the World Tour. For those not willing to try the waves, flat water can be found at Oistins Bay. Best wind and wave conditions: Dec/Jan and Jun. Kitesurfing is also well-developed here, taking place along the south coast by the airport, further east from the windsurfers.

British Virgin Islands
This is the centre for windsurf cruising, with over 50 small islands scattered within 40 miles and steady trades, the islands are perfect for

flat water cruising and blasting. Already a popular yachting centre, the two sports fuse with international events such as the Hi Ho (hook in and hold on), a week long windsurf race and yacht cruise. Good sailing for all levels. Best winds: Dec/Jan and Jun/Jul.

Dominican Republic
Voted by many top sailors as one of the most exciting places to sail in the Caribbean. Cabarete, on the north coast, offers everything a windsurfer could want: flat water for beginners and great wavesailing on the outside with thermally affected winds that mean you can take the morning off. Lots of windsurfing and kitesurfing schools and hotels on the strip of beach and some of the best gear in the Caribbean. Best winds: Jan to Mar and Jun to Aug.

Grand Cayman
Famous for its diving, Grand Cayman also offers good windsurfing, the east end is popular for beginners to advanced and everything in between, flat water on the inside and bump and jump further out. Best winds: Nov to Mar.

Grenadines
A great location but with no facilities, take your own gear and hire a yacht out of Grenada or St Vincent, or visit **Bequia**, a beautiful island with the only rental centre in the area. Although the wind blows and the sun shines, there is only one windsurf school run by Basil, a Bequian with a big smile. Good location for learners or advanced sailors with flat water and wave sailing, well off the beaten track. Best winds: Nov to Feb and Jun/Jul.

Nevis
Windsurfer's paradise waiting to be discovered, good flat water and wavesailing, definitely no crowds, the island is small enough to offer all conditions for every skill level. Best winds: Dec/Jan and Jun/Jul.

Puerto Rico
A great wave-sailing spot – the Caribbean's answer to Maui. The location is The Shacks at Isabela on the northwest point of the island. Thermal winds make this a winter spot for the committed wave sailor; gentler sailing is offered in the San Juan area in the summer. Best waves

and winds: Dec to Apr; slalom Jul to Sep.

St Barts
Small, exclusive island with some good windsurf spots for beginners and advanced, and it is quiet. Best winds: Dec to Feb.

St Croix
Great sailing spot. The guys here are good wave sailors and slalom racers as the island boasts all conditions at many locations. Best winds: Jan/Feb and Jul.

St Lucia
Beautiful destination and offers uncrowded sailing for windsurfing and plenty to do when not windy. Bring your own gear if you are an advanced sailor. Kitesurfing is good in the southeast, where there is a dedicated school with good equipment. Best winds: Dec to Jun.

St-Martin
Orient Bay (Baie Orientale) has good winds and plenty of facilities. St-Martin offers good learning and advanced slalom sailing. Best winds: Dec/Jan and Jul.

Trinidad and Tobago
In the prime trade wind zone, **Tobago**'s Pigeon Point is the place to go, beautiful with some excellent sailing spots. You will probably need to take your own gear. Best winds: Dec to May.

Turks and Caicos
Has flat turquoise waters and steady winds, making this an ideal learner and intermediate destination, perfect for a family diving and windsurf vacation. Best winds: Feb to Mar intermediate, Oct to Nov for beginners.

US Virgin Islands
St Thomas has everything you could expect from a Caribbean windsurf vacation, with shopping malls. St Thomas boasts a lively local windsurfing community, flat water and lots of events to attend. Best winds: Dec/Jan and Jul, when the Caribbean Team Boardsailing Championships take place.

Whale and dolphin watching

Whale and dolphin watching, long popular around North America, is starting to take off in the Caribbean too. There are three main attractions: the **humpback whales**, who come to the Caribbean during the winter to mate, raise their calves and sing; **sperm whales**, which are resident in various spots around the Caribbean but are easiest to see along the west coast of Dominica; spotted and other **dolphin** species, which travel in large herds and are resident around many of the reefs, mangrove forests and offshore fishing banks. It is possible to see whales and dolphins from land and on some regular ferries, and even on air flights between the islands, but the best way to encounter them close-up is on boat tours. Some of these are general marine nature or even birding tours that include whales and dolphins. Others are specialized tours offered by diving, sportfishing or new eco-tourism ventures. Following is a guide to the best of whale and dolphin watching in the waters covered by this book.

Dominica
Eight to 12 resident sperm whales delight visitors. You can also see spinner and spotted dolphins, pilot whales, false killer whales, and pygmy sperm whales. Occasional sightings are made of bottlenose, Risso's and Fraser's dolphins, orcas, dwarf sperm whales and melon-headed whales. The tours are are three to four hours and are run out of the **Anchorage Hotel & Dive Centre**, PO Box 34, Roseau, T767-448 2638. Hydrophones are used to find and listen to the whales. Tours are also offered by a well-equipped diving operator, Derek Perryman at **Dive Dominica Ltd**, next to the Anchorage at the Castle Comfort Lodge, PO Box 2253, Roseau, T767-448 2188. For land-based whale watching of sperm whales and others, Scotts Head, at the southwest tip of Dominica, overlooking Martinique Passage, is good most of the year.

Dominican Republic
The most popular and most established whale watching in the Caribbean is found here. The industry is centred on humpback whales but pilot whales and spotted dolphins can also be seen in Samaná Bay, and bottlenose, spinner, and spotted dolphins, Bryde's and other whales on Silver Bank. The season for both locales is January to March, with whale-watching tours in Samaná Bay from 15 Jan to 15 Mar. For whale watching from land from January to March, but especially in Feb, try Cabo Francés Viejo, east along the coast from Puerto Plata, near Cabrera, as well as Punta Balandra light and Cabo Samaná (near Samaná). At Cueva de Agua there is a volunteer land-based whale-watching project.

In recent years, more than 32,000 people a year have gone whale watching in the 20,000-sq-km marine sanctuary, most of them to **Samaná Bay** where the trips last two to four hours. There are about 40 registered boats; some specialize in speed, some in mass tourism and some in education and information. You will get a better view of the whales from a big boat, as the smaller ones can get dwarfed by the waves. **Whale Samaná**, contact: Kim Beddall, Victoria Marine, Samaná, T/F809-5382494, www.whalesamana.com, is the oldest tour operator in the region and highly rated. Another operator, Miguel Bezi at **Transporte Marítimo Minadiel**, Samaná Bay, T809-538 2556, has 5 boats of different sizes. The national parks whale watch co-ordinator in Samaná can be contacted at T809-538 2042, dnpballenas@yahoo.com.

The tours to see humpbacks on **Silver Bank**, some 50 miles north of Puerto Plata, are more educational and are usually arranged by specialist groups, including **Oceanic Society Expeditions**, Fort Mason Center, Bldg E, San Francisco, CA 94123-1394 USA, T415-441 1106, www.oceanic-society.org; **Wild Oceans**, International House, Bank Rd, Kingswood, Bristol BS15 8LX, UK, T0117-984 8040, www.wildwings.co.uk; and **Bottom Time Adventures**, PO Box 11919, Ft Lauderdale, FL 33339-1919, USA, T831-884 0122, www.bottomtimeadventures.net.

Grenada
From St George's Marina, Mosden Cumberbatch of **First Impressions Ltd**, T/F473-440 3678, www.catamaranchartering .com, offers year-round 4-hour whale-watching trips for up to 35 people. Humpbacks are often sighted from Jan to

When referring to dolphins, use the word 'porpoises', since, in most parts of the Caribbean, the word 'dolphin' means the dolphin fish.

Mar. Other whales in the area from Nov to Mar include Cuvier's beaked whale, killer whales and the dwarf sperm whale, amongst others. The rest of the year you can see sperm whales, pigmy right whales, long and shortfinned pilot whales and others, as well as various dolphins.

Guadeloupe
Caroline and Renato Rinaldi of **Associacion Evasion Tropicale Courbaril**, 971125 Bouillante, T590-571944, www.evasiontropicale.org, offer year-round half-day tours to see sperm and pilot whales and spotted dolphins. Naturalists on board talk to passengers and collect scientific data. The whale watch runs from the dive centre **Les Heures Saines**, Rocher de Malendure, about 4 km north of Bouillant, 97132 Pigeon, Basse-Terre, T590-988663, www.heures-saines.gp.

Petit Nevis
Off Bequia, 9 miles (15 km) south of St Vincent is the site of the old whaling station, once the hub of Caribbean whaling in this century. Access can only be arranged locally.

Puerto Rico
Humpbacks and dolphins can be seen from land and on occasional tours, particularly out of Rincón on the west coast of the island. Best lookouts are Aguadilla and from an old lighthouse near Punta Higuera, outside Rincón.

St Kitts and Nevis
From the island of Nevis, trips to see bottlenose dolphins and sometimes humpback whales can be arranged through dive boat operator Ellis Chaderton through **Scuba Safaris Ltd**, Oualie Beach, T869-469 9518, www.scubanevis.com.

St Lucia
Sperm whales and various dolphins can be seen, as well as humpback, pilot and Bryde's whales and orcas, on occasion. The **St Lucia Whale and Dolphin Watching Association**, c/o PO Box 1114, Castries, T758-452456, www.geocities.com/RainForest/Vines/1106, is helping to organize and field enquiries for tours and to make sure that the whale watching is conducted with appropriate regulations. **Captain Mike's Sport Fishing, Pleasure Cruises and Whale Watching**, PO Box GM617, Sunny Acres, T758-452 7044, www.captmikes.com, offers 3-hour morning trips all year round on board the 60-ft *Free Willy* but Nov to Jun is best, when sperm whales and sometimes humpbacks are seen. Trips can also be arranged through the **Soufriere Water Taxi Association**, Bay St, Soufriere, St Lucia, T758- 459 7239.

St Vincent
Off the west coast, large herds of spinner and spotted dolphins are seen regularly. Sometimes bottlenose dolphins and pilot whales are also found and, sporadically, sperm and humpback whales. Tours are run by **Sea Breeze Tours/Guesthouse**, contact: Hal Daize, Arnos Vale Post Office, T784-458 4969, seabreezetours@vincysurf.com, aboard the 36-ft sloop, *Sea Breeze*, or on a 28-ft power boat. Trips cost US$30-40 and depart from Calliaqua Lagoon on Indian Bay, southeast of Kingstown and Arnos Vale Airport. Snorkelling and a trip to Baleine Falls can also be included. Tours are almost year-round but are best Apr to Sep when there is an 80% success rate; avoid windy weather months of mid-Dec to mid-Feb.

Turks and Caicos Islands
Humpbacks can be found offshore late Jan to early Apr with bottlenose and other dolphins sometimes seen close to shore. For trips, contact **Blue Water Divers**, Grand Turk, T649-946 2432, www.grandturkscuba.com; **Sea Eye Diving**, T649-946 1407, www.seaeyediving.com, and **Oasis Divers**, T/F649-946 1128, www.oasisdivers.com.

US Virgin Islands and British Virgin Islands
There are periodic trips to see the 60 to 100 humpback whales that winter north of the islands, from January to March. There are also spinner and other dolphins to be seen. For a full-day catamaran sail contact Grethelyn Piper of the **Environmental Association of St Thomas and St John** (EAST), PO Box 12379, St Thomas, USVI 00801, T340-776 1976. In the BVI, **Paul Knapp, Jr**, PO Box 185, Road Town, Tortola, T284-494 3463, runs humpback whale-listening tours from 30 Dec to 15 Apr on a 13-ft motor cruiser or a 30-ft sloop close to shore. The whales are rarely seen and

never close-up, but their sounds fill the boat. Excellent tapes and CDs of whale songs are also sold. Departure is from Brewers Bay Campground, Tortola.

Conservation

By watching whales and dolphins in the Caribbean, you can actually contribute to saving them. Many dolphins are still killed, mainly by fishermen, for food or fish bait, while pilot whales and even rare beaked whales are commonly harpooned, particularly in the eastern Caribbean. Almost every winter, over the past few years, two humpbacks have been killed off Bequia, nearly always a precious mother and calf, who have very high site fidelity to their mating and calving grounds; local whalers are effectively removing what could be a healthy whale-watching industry.

Your support of whale watching may have the biggest impact in countries of the eastern Caribbean: Dominica, Grenada, St Lucia and St Vincent and the Grenadines. Over the past few years, Japan has contributed to the development of these nations, by helping to build airports and adding fish docks and piers. In exchange, Japan has counted on the support of these four governments, all members of the International Whaling Commission (IWC), in its attempt to re-open commercial whaling.

You can help conservation simply by saying you enjoy seeing whales and dolphins in local waters. If you see whales and dolphins being killed at sea, report the incident to local and national tourism outlets of the country concerned. For more information contact the **Whale and Dolphin Conservation Society**, T0870-870 5001, www.wdcs.org.

Dolphins (and orcas) are also being captured for use in dolphinariums, where they are isolated from their pods (families), fed a diet of frozen fish and antibiotics and taught to perform tricks for tourists. This is big business, despite the advertising literature in which the owners allege they are carrying out scientific research into 'understanding' dolphins. There is a high mortality rate and captive dolphins suffer mental and physical stress, often with behavioural problems. However, there are more entertainment facilities opening all the time, with governments bowing to pressure for attractions to pull in the cruise ships. Whale and dolphin watching out at sea provides local people with another way to look at these intriguing animals – as well as a potentially more sustainable source of income. For more information or to offer support, contact **The Marine Connection** T+44 (0)20-7499 9196, www.marineconnection.org.

Getting there

Air

Operating from Madrid, **Iberia Airlines** (iberia.com) has non-stop flights to Cuba, while **Air France** (www.airfrance.com) and **KLM** (www.klm.com) have weekly departures to the Caribbean. **British Airways** (www.britishairways.com) has direct flights from London to Antigua, Barbados, Cayman Islands, Grenada, Jamaica, St Lucia, Trinidad and Tobago, and Turks and Caicos. From the USA, **American Airlines** (www.aa.com) and **Continental Airlines** (www.continental.com) have an extensive route network across the Caribbean. **Virgin Atlantic** (www.virgin-atlantic.com) is also worth checking out.

In addition to the scheduled flights, there are a great many charter flights from Europe and North America. For details on both types of service, you are advised to consult a good travel agent. An agent will also be able to tell you if you qualify for any student or senior citizen discount on offer. From the USA, Puerto Rico and Antigua are the only islands to which student fares are available; it is worth checking these out since it may be cheaper to take a student flight then continue to your destination rather than flying direct to the island of your choice. If buying tickets routed through the USA, check that US taxes are included in the price. At certain times of the year, **Air**

France have flights at very advantageous prices from several southern French cities and Paris to Guadeloupe and Martinique. A good way to save money is to keep an eye on website special offers. BA and Virgin Atlantic often have a bit of a price battle early in the year with discounts on flights to the Bahamas and Caribbean. See also under Getting there for each island.

... and leaving again

Many islands insist that visitors have an air ticket to their home country before being allowed to enter; for non-US citizens travelling to the Caribbean from the USA, this means a ticket from the USA to their home country, not a ticket back to the USA. Tickets to other countries will not suffice. This becomes a problem if you are not going home for 12 months since airline tickets become void after a year. Some airlines sell tickets on the six- to 12-month extended payment plan; these can be credited when you have left the islands with restrictive entry requirements. Even if you propose to take some boat trips between islands, we recommend that you purchase flights in advance and refund those that have not been used later. For departure taxes, see Touching down sections for each island.

Sea

Cruise lines and cargo ships

The most popular way of visiting the Caribbean by ship is on a cruise liner. It is possible to break your journey for a few days if you want to stay on an island but you will have to check with the company to see whether they can pick you up later. There are also sailing cruisers (eg the Windjammer and Star Clipper fleets) which allow flexible itineraries for cruising between the islands. **Windjammer Barefoot Cruises** ① T305-6726453 in the USA, www.windjammer.com, which operates five tall-masted ships (Flying Cloud, British Virgin Islands; Legacy, US and British Virgin Islands; Mandalay, Leeward and Windward Islands; Polynesia, French West Indies; Yankee Clipper, Grenadines) and a supply ship (Amazing Grace), can be contacted direct in Florida. The supply ship, MV Amazing Grace, sails every month from West Palm Beach, picking up southbound passengers in Freeport, Bahamas and visiting lots of islands as it meets up with the Windjammer tall ships, delivering monthly supplies, before turning round in Trinidad after two weeks and stopping at different ports from the southbound trip. For a budget option, **Easy Cruise**, www.easycruise.com, started cruising the islands from Barbados in the 2005/2006 winter season, allowing you to get on and off the ship anywhere along the route as long as you stay on board at least two nights. The route may vary in future winter seasons, but included St Vincent, Martinique, Bequia, Grenada and St Lucia, with rates starting from US$32 per cabin, including port taxes but no meals. There are few guest houses to compare with those rates and certainly no air fares.

For cargo ships carrying passengers, it is recommended that you enquire in your own country. In general, it is very difficult to secure a passage on a cargo ship from Europe to the Caribbean without making full arrangements in advance. Round trips are easier to organize than one-way passages, although some companies are now offering a flight home. Fares range from about US$70-130 per person per day; cheaper than a passenger cruise, but without the continuous entertainment.

Further information

For full details on this type of travel consult, *The Internet Guide to Freighter Travel*, (www.geocities.com/freighterman.geo/main menu.html), and the following specialists:

In the UK
Cargo Ship Voyages Ltd, Hemley, Woodbridge, Suffolk, IP12 4QF, T/F01473-

736265, www.cargoshipvoyages.co.uk.
Cruise People, T020-7723 2450,
http://members.aol.com /CruiseAZ/
freighters.htm.
Strand Voyages, London, T020-7766 8220,
www.strandtravel.co.uk.

In Europe
SGV Reisezentrum Weggis, Switzerland,
T041-390 1133, www.frachtschiffreisen.ch.

In the USA
Travltips Cruise and Freighter Association,
T800-872 8584, www.travltips.com.

Sailing

From Europe to the Caribbean For boats crossing the Atlantic along the trade wind route, Barbados is the first landfall. Boats have the option of going on to Venezuela and Central America or through the Windward Islands of Grenada, St Vincent and the Grenadines. The **Atlantic Rally for Cruisers**, www.worldcruising.com/arc, offers support and entertainment for any sailors contemplating an Atlantic crossing in their own boat. Departure is from Gran Canaria at the end of November and the yachts arrive in St Lucia to a warm welcome for Christmas.

From the USA to the Caribbean There are two routes from the USA to the Caribbean: from New England or Norfolk directly to the US Virgin Islands with the possibility of a stop in Bermuda; or island-hopping from Florida through the Bahamas across the 'Thornless Path' to windward described by Bruce Van Sant in his book *Passages South*. The **Caribbean 1500 Rally** organizes cruisers wishing to travel in a group to the Caribbean and depart from Newport, Rhode Island or Norfolk, Virginia, in late October arriving in St Thomas in the US Virgin Islands. To visit the USA from the Caribbean by yacht, many yachts leave Trinidad after Carnival in late February; boat deliveries back to the USA are also possible.

‡ *For those with 1000 miles offshore sailing experience, a cheap way to get to the Caribbean is by crewing on a yacht being delivered from Europe or the USA.*

Getting around

In general, you will not find a remote hideaway on islands like Antigua and Sint Maarten, which receive transatlantic charter flights. However, they are useful jumping-off points for smaller islands. If you have a tight budget, it is worth investigating where cheap flights go to from your country and then finding out which islands can be easily reached from there. For example, there are often cheap charter flights to Antigua, Sint Maarten or St Lucia from Europe, which connect with flights to the British Virgin Islands and all the Leeward and Windward Islands. Connections are good between France and Guadeloupe and Martinique, which could combine with a visit to Les Saintes and Dominica. There are lots of flights from the USA to Puerto Rico, which again has links with nearly all the other Caribbean Islands. **Air Jamaica** uses Montego Bay as its regional hub and is increasing the number of flights to other islands, including the Dutch Antilles. Only Cuba has rather poor inter-island links, both by air and by sea, but then there is enough to keep you busy on such a large island for you not to need to combine it with anywhere else.

Transport links between islands are fine if you want to fly everywhere, but after several hours in an aeroplane getting to the Caribbean from Europe, South or North America, you may prefer to travel by sea, which is usually cheaper but takes longer and can be either fascinating or unpleasant if you suffer from seasickness in rough weather. In the Windward Islands there is a ferry between Dominica, St Lucia and the French islands of Martinique and Guadeloupe, well used by local shoppers as well as tourists, offering you the chance of combining the nature tourism of Dominica and the beach resorts of St Lucia with the flavours of France in the Caribbean. You can travel from St Vincent down through the Grenadines to Grenada by mail boat, fishing boat and hovercraft, a cheaper alternative to chartering a yacht and doing it yourself. A car ferry links the Dominican Republic with Puerto Rico and there are ferries between the US and British Virgin Islands letting you visit a number of islands without having the work of sailing your own yacht. In the Leeward Islands, Sint Maarten/Saint-Martin is a useful hub for transatlantic flights from where ferries go out to Anguilla, St-Barts and Saba like spokes of a wheel, allowing you to sample English, French and Dutch islands. A few days on each island would be plenty, as they are small and compact. Links with Venezuela tend to come and go, but there is a ferry from Trinidad to Güiria.

Air

The most extensive links between islands are by air, either with the scheduled flights on the regional and international carriers, or by chartered plane. If you are in a group, or family, the latter option may not cost very much more than a scheduled flight. It often has the advantage of linking the charter direct to your incoming or homeward flight. The regional carriers with most routes in the Caribbean are **LIAT/Caribbean Star** (www.liatairline.com), **Caribbean Airlines** (www.caribbean-airlines.com), and **Air Jamaica** (www.airjamaica.com). There are also several smaller airlines such as **Winair, Air Caraïbes** or **Dutch Antilles Express**, which cover smaller areas with smaller planes.

❣ *Departure tax is payable on leaving each island; make sure you know what this is in advance.*

Sea

Island-hopping by boats with scheduled services is fairly limited. Boat services are more common between dependent islands, eg St Vincent and the Grenadines, Trinidad and Tobago. Again, full details are given in the relevant sections below. There are also good connections by sea in the French Antilles and with their neighbours, Dominica and St Lucia.

Irregular passenger services on cargo boats (with basic accommodation, usually a hammock on deck, no meals supplied) and schooners, and crewing or hitching on yachts can only be arranged by asking around when you are in port. Crewing on yachts is not difficult in winter (in the hurricane season yachtsmen stay away). If you are looking for a job on a yacht, or trying to hitch a ride, it will be easier to make contact if you are living at the yacht harbour. Boat owners often advertise bunks for rent, which is a very cheap form of accommodation (US$10-30); ask around, or look on the bulletin boards. If arriving by sea, make sure you are aware of the island's entry requirements before setting out.

Yachting

Exploring the Caribbean by boat has never been easier. New marinas and local communities near popular anchorages are catering to the increasing number of yachts which have made the Caribbean their home. The Caribbean islanders have coined the name 'yachties' to refer to those people who live and travel on their own boats as contrasted with those who visit the islands on chartered boats and cruise ships or spend their vacation at landbased resorts. While this information is directed toward the yachties, bareboat charterers will also find it useful.

Ports of entry Arrive during weekday working hours to avoid overtime fees. Have the sun at your back to navigate through reefs, sand bars or other water hazards even

Customs and immigration Yachties cross many countries and have to deal with more officials and procedures than tourists aboard cruise ships or travelling to resorts. No matter how many guidebooks are available, there will be at least one country with a change in procedures. Be careful to clear immigration on arrival as there are heavy fines for failing to do so. Plan to pay fees and to fill out paperwork in all countries. Occasionally, there are no fees. Different fees are often charged for charter boats and cruisers on their own boats who may wish to stay for a longer period of time. ▸▸ *For further details, see page 54, and the Touching down boxes in the individual island chapters.*

Q Flag and courtesy flags Fly your 'Q' or quarantine flag until paperwork is completed. The captain should take ship's papers, passports and a list of the places you wish to stop and visit as in some countries you must be given specific clearance to stop and anchor. All crew should remain aboard until they have received clearance from the port authorities. Even though many of the islands are still a part of the British Commonwealth, they prefer to see their country's courtesy flag flown. (Be sure to fly it the right way up!)

Liveaboard community anchorages with a good, well-protected anchorage, provisions, water and laundry are available in Luperón, Samaná and Puerto Plata in the Dominican Republic, Boquerón in Puerto Rico, Phillipsburg in Sint Maarten, Bequia in the Grenadines, Secret Harbour and Prickly Bay in Grenada, Chaguaramas in Trinidad, and at Porlamar, Margarita and Puerto la Cruz in Venezuela. Cruisers Net in Puerto la Cruz, Venezuela VHF 72 0745, during hurricane season in Porlamar, Margarita VHF 72 0800. Radio nets provide information about social activities, including Ladies' Lunches and especially Carnival activities in Trinidad, that might be of interest to tourists with extra time as well as cruisers.

Yacht charters Charter fleets operate from the US and British Virgin Islands, Antigua, Sint Maarten/St-Martin, Martinique, Guadeloupe, St Lucia, St Vincent and Grenada. One-way charters can often be arranged for an additional fee. Yachts can be chartered on a daily or term basis, either bareboat or with skipper and crew. Skippered day charters are now found in almost any area where there are landbased tourists.

Marinas Dry dock facilities for long-term boat storage are found in the Turks and Caicos, Puerto Rico, the Virgin Islands, St Martin, St Lucia, St Vincent, Antigua, Grenada, Trinidad and Venezuela. Marinas with slips of different types (slips, stern-to, pilings) are found in the majority of the islands and new ones are opening frequently. Most marinas will hold mail addressed to yachts for pick-up.

Crewing Hitching and working on yachts is another way to see the islands for the adventurous person with time on his/her hands. Many yachts charter in the Caribbean in winter and go north to the USA or Mediterranean for the charter season there. Other yachts are cruisers passing on their way around the world. Yachties are friendly people and if you ask in the right places, frequent the yachtie bars and put up a few notices, crew positions can often be found. Bulletin boards are found in Turtle Cove Marina (Turks and Caicos), Dock Maarten and Bobby's Marina in the Lagoon (Sint Maarten), Fort-de-France, Trois-Ilets and Le Marin (Martinique), Rodney Bay and Marigot Bay (St Lucia), English Harbour (Antigua), Admiralty Bay (Bequia) and Anchorage (Union Island) in the Grenadines, Secret Harbour and Spice Island Marina (Grenada), Porlamar (Margarita), any of the marinas in El Morro complex in Puerto la

Cruz (Venezuela) where foreign yachties hang out, and any marina or yacht club in Chaguaramas in Trinidad. If you want to crew, check you have all necessary visas and documentation and confirm with the skipper that your paperwork is in order (see also Customs and immigration, above). Puerto Rico and the US Virgin Islands require visas for boat travellers as though you were travelling to the USA.

VHF nets In those areas where there are a substantial number of liveaboard sailors, VHF nets seem to spring up with volunteers taking turns providing weather information, arrivals and departures, information about services and announcements about local activities, sharing taxis or tours; guests returning home often offer to take mail back to the USA or Europe. **Email** access can be obtained by boats staying in a marina.

Marine conservation The Caribbean islands are becoming more ecoconscious. They are interested in preserving their natural resources and beauty and have established parks, marine preserves or national trust foundations. Some have mooring buoys, no-anchoring or anchoring limitations. Most prohibit the taking of coral or live creatures in shells; many prohibit the taking of shells. Don't anchor in areas where coral may be growing. Don't dispose of rubbish in enclosed anchorages. Rubbish is a problem on many of the smaller islands; don't give rubbish to boat boys as they often just take the money and throw the waste into the water. Try to dispose of edible waste at sea while travelling between islands in deep water; take paper, cans and bottles ashore to the town dump or a marina where they have waste disposal facilities.

Weapons Some countries want weapons and ammunition checked in ashore until you are ready to depart. Others will let you keep them locked on board and others don't really ask questions. Make sure clearance papers have the correct serial numbers and ammunition counts to avoid confusion when it comes to picking up the weapons that were checked ashore. Some areas even consider spearguns weapons and require them to be turned in until you leave.

Guidebooks

Steve Dodge Yachtsman's Guide to the Bahamas and Turks and Caicos; Cruising Guide to Abaco.

Chris Doyle Guide to the Leeward Islands; VIP Cruising Guide (Sint Maarten area); Guide to the Windward Islands; Guide to Venezuela, Trinidad & Tobago; Guide to Trinidad and Tobago.

Bruce Van Sant Yachtsman's Guide to the Virgin Islands; Southern Waterway Guide (covers Bahamas and Turks and Caicos); Passages South.

Donald Street Donald Street's Guides to the Caribbean (Volumes I, II, III, IV).

Julius Wilensky Cruising Guide to the Abacos (2nd edition). Good sketch charts that are still useful even if not updated.

There are several 'yachting newspapers' that are distributed free around the Caribbean that have things to do, reports on regattas, tourist and sailing events:

Nautical Scene (St Thomas to Venezuela); The Compass (Bequia and southern Caribbean); All at Sea (northern Caribbean); The Boca (Trinidad and Tobago).

Land

Buses These are cheap, but services tend not to be very convenient, and often involve a night away from the point of departure, even on small islands. This is because buses start in outlying towns in the early morning and return from the capital in the afternoon. Many smaller islands do not even have a bus service. The larger islands, such as Cuba, the Dominican Republic and Jamaica have good,

Car hire Renting a car gives the greatest flexibility, but is also hardest on the pocket. You can expect to pay more than in the USA or Europe. A number of islands require drivers to take out a temporary, or visitor driver's licence (these are mentioned in the text). Some places will not issue a licence to those over 70 without a medical certificate. The minimum age for rental is usually 25. In small places, renting a motorcycle, scooter or bicycle is a good idea.

Taxis Taxis are plentiful, but generally not cheap. Some islands, eg Trinidad, have route taxis, which are inexpensive and travel only on set routes. On many islands, taxi fares are set by the tourist office or government.

Train Cuba is the only country in the Caribbean with a passenger rail service. St Kitts has a scenic railway using the sugar industry network, which runs in a circular route around the island.

Maps
An excellent source of maps is **Stanfords**① *12-14 Long Acre, Covent Garden, London WC2, T020-7836 1321, as well as 29 Corn St, Bristol, BS1, and 39 Spring Gardens, Manchester, M2, www.stanfords.co.uk.*▸ *For hiking maps, see Hiking, page 32.*

Sleeping

Your budget is likely to be the key determining factor in where you stay, but this will stretch further in some islands than others. The codes used in this book (see page 44) are for the price of a double room (rack rate) and take no account of the facilities offered. In some places a hotel in category **B** will be clean and simple, but in others it will represent the height of luxury. In many islands there are no hotels at all in the **F** category and those in **E** will be hard to find, often only on special offer. Youth hostels are non-existent, while camping is not a viable option in general although some islands, such as Puerto Rico or the French Antilles, have well-organized campsites; however, on many islands camping is actually forbidden.

The cheapest accommodation can be found in **guesthouses**, small, privately run establishments which sometimes offer breakfast but do not rely on a full restaurant service. Many of these are not registered with the local tourist office and therefore difficult to find until you get there. They may be perfectly adequate if you are not very demanding, or they may be flea pits. You will soon find out why they have been left off the list.

Turning up at a cheaper place may not always yield a room because competition is great. Note also that, if booking ahead, tourist office lists may not include the cheapest establishments, so you may have to reserve one or two nights at a mid-price hotel for when you arrive and then ask around for cheaper accommodation if that is what you want. The longer you stay the better deal you will get, so negotiation is recommended. Remember also that high season runs from mid-December to mid-April and everything is more expensive then as well as being more heavily booked. The best deals can be found in – you guessed it – hurricane season.

The Dominican Republic and Cuba have the most hotel rooms in the Caribbean, so there is no real problem in finding a space there. The most popular form of accommodation for independent travellers in Cuba is to stay with a registered family in their home, a *casa particular*. In Havana they cost around US$25-40, but elsewhere they are about US$15-30. Food and lodging with families is far better value and much

⦂ Accommodation price codes

LL over US$200	over €150	C US$31-45	€23-35
L US$151-200	€111-150	D US$21-30	€16-22
AL US$101-150	€76-110	E US$12-20	€10-15
A US$66-100	€51-75	F US$11 and under	€9 and under
B US$46-65	€36-50		

Prices are for a double room in high season, based on two people sharing.
A service charge and tax are often added on to hotel bills.

more rewarding than staying in a hotel, although it is not legal in the beach resorts of Varadero of Guardalavaca and not available in remote places such as Cayo Coco.

In Jamaica there are places costing less than US$20 but they are not to be recommended, the **D** range is more possible and **C** will be comfortable. Haiti is surprisingly expensive with most of the guesthouses charging rates in our **A** range unless you get right off the beaten track. The Dominican Republic, on the other hand, has a far greater range and **D** hotels can be found in fairly decent areas, although not beachfront properties. In the eastern Caribbean cheap places can be found in the **C-D** ranges in the capital cities, from where you can use public transport to get out to beaches and places of interest, but you will have to pay more if you want to be on the beach. Further south, Trinidad and Tobago have lots of good value places to stay, either in town or close to the beach.

We assume that most of our readers are not interested in the **all-inclusive resorts**, although we include details of a few, partly to alert you if they predominate, such as in Ocho Rios in Jamaica or Playa Dorada and Punta Cana in the Dominican Republic. We also include the super-luxury hotels, although we do realise that few readers will be able to afford Richard Branson's Necker Island at US$25,000-42,000 a day. Some, however, are within range for a special occasion, such as a honeymoon, and our **LL** range takes in everything from US$200 a night up to the stars.

Eating and drinking

As you might expect of islands, there is a wide variety of **seafood** on offer which is fresh and tasty and served in a multitude of ways. Fish of all sorts, as well as lobster and conch, are commonly available and are usually better quality than local **meat**. Beef and lamb are often imported from the USA or Argentina, but goat, pork and chicken are produced locally. There is no dairy industry to speak of, so cheeses are also usually imported. There is, however, a riot of tropical **fruit** and **vegetables** and a visit to a local market will give you the opportunity to see unusual and often unidentifiable objects as well as more familiar items found in supermarkets in Europe and North America but with ten times the flavour. The best bananas in the world are grown in the Caribbean on small farms either organically or, at least, using the minimum of chemicals. They are cheap and incredibly sweet and unlike anything you can buy at home. You will come across many of the wonderful tropical fruits in the form of juices or ice-cream. Don't miss the rich flavours of the soursop, the guava or the sapodilla. Mangoes in season drip off the trees and those that don't end up on your breakfast plate can be found squashed in abundance all over the roads. Caribbean oranges are often green when ripe, as there is no cold season to bring out the orange colour, and are meant for juicing not peeling. Portugals are like tangerines and easy to peel. Avocados are nearly always sold unripe, so wait several days before

Top rum cocktails – author's addictions

There is nothing better at the end of a busy day than finding a pleasant spot overlooking the sea with a rum in your hand to watch the sunset and look out for the green flash. The theory is that the more rum you drink, the more likely you are to see this flash of green on the horizon as the sun goes down.

There are hundreds of different rums in the Caribbean, each island producing the best, of course. The main producers are Jamaica, Cuba, Barbados, Guyana, Martinique and the Dominican Republic, but other islands such as Grenada also produce excellent brands. Generally, the younger, light rums are used in cocktails and aged, dark rums are drunk on the rocks or treated as you might a single malt whisky. Cocktails first became popular after the development of ice-making in the USA in 1870, but boomed in the 1920s partly because of prohibition in the USA and the influx of visitors to Cuba, the Bahamas and other islands, escaping stringent regulations. People have been drowning their rum in cola ever since the Americans brought bottled drinks in to Cuba during the war against Spain at the end of the 19th century, hence the name, Cuba Libre. You can in fact adapt any cocktail recipe to substitute other spirits and incorporate rum. It makes an excellent Bloody Mary, for example.

One of the nicest and most refreshing cocktails is a **Daiquirí**, invented in Santiago de Cuba in 1898 by an engineer in the Daiquirí mines. The natural version combines 1½ tablespoons of sugar, the juice of half a lime, some drops of maraschino liqueur, 1½ oz light dry rum and a lot of shaved ice, all mixed in a blender and then served piled high in a wide, chilled champagne glass with a straw. You can also have fruit versions, with strawberry, banana, peach or pineapple, using fruit or fruit liqueur.

Another Cuban favourite, drinkable at any time of the day or night, is the **Mojito**, once popular with Ernest Hemingway and his friends in Havana. Put half a tablespoon of sugar, the juice of half a lime and some lightly crushed mint leaves in a tall glass. Stir and mix well, then add some soda water, ice cubes, 1½ oz light dry rum and top up with soda water to taste. Garnish with mint leaves and serve with a straw.

Everybody has heard of the old favourite, **Piña Colada**, which can be found on all the islands and is probably the most popular of the fruit-based cocktails. Combine and blend coconut liqueur, pineapple juice, light dry rum and shaved ice, then serve with a straw in a glass, a pineapple or a coconut.

Many Caribbean hotels offer you a welcome cocktail when you stagger out of the taxi, jet-lagged from your transatlantic flight. This is often a watered-down punch, with a poor quality rum and sickly fruit juice. You are more likely to find something palatable in the bar, but it always depends on which blend of juice the barman favours. In Grenada, rum punch is improved enormously with the addition of nutmeg sprinkled on top. The standard recipe for a **rum punch** is: 'one of sour, two of sweet, three of strong and four of weak'. If you measure that in fluid ounces, it comes out as 1 oz of lime juice, 2 oz of syrup (equal amounts of sugar and water, boiled for a few minutes), 3 oz of rum and 4 oz of water, fruit juices, ginger ale, or whatever takes your fancy. You could add ice and a dash of Angostura Bitters from Trinidad, use nutmeg syrup from Grenada or Falernum from Barbados instead of sugar syrup, and garnish it with a slice of lime. Delicious.

Essentials Eating and drinking

Restaurant price codes

¶¶¶¶ US$31 (€22) and over	Prices refer to the cost of a two-
¶¶ US$15-30 (€11-22)	course meal for one person,
¶ US$14 (€10) and under	excluding drinks, tax or service
	charges.

attempting to eat them. Avocado trees provide a surplus of fruit so you will be doing everyone a favour if you eat as many as possible. Many vegetables have their origins in the slave trade, brought over to provide a starchy diet for the slaves. The breadfruit, a common staple, rich in carbohydrates and vitamins A, B and C, was brought from the South Seas in 1793 by Captain Bligh, perhaps more famous for the mutiny on the *Bounty*. The slaves were needed for work in the sugar plantations and sugar cane is still grown on some islands today, often ending up as **rum**, see page 45.

Restaurants range from gourmet eateries to cafés but all make the most of local ingredients. If you are economizing, find a local place and choose the daily special, which will give you a chance to try the typical food. **Fast food** is also available, but you will be better off going to a local place serving chicken and chips or burgers, rather than the international chains. Trinidad has some of the best food around, drawing on the cultures of its many immigrants: Indian, African, Chinese, Syrian, etc, and fast food there is almost an art form. The *roti*, a thin chapatti wrap filled with spicy or curried meat, fish or vegetables is hugely popular and its success has spread to many other islands. Each island has its own specialities and these are described in the following chapters.

Entertainment

Nightlife varies between the islands. Some, such as Nevis or Saba, are quiet most of the time with occasional live music in restaurants, while others, such as Cuba or Jamaica seem to exist on a diet of music. Restaurants, bars and clubs all host bands from time to time and are the best places to catch live music. A huge variety of styles can be found: merengue in the Dominican Republic, salsa in Puerto Rico, reggae in Jamaica, calypso in Trinidad, timba in Cuba, zouk in Martinique. Music festivals are popular and provide the opportunity to listen to live artists day and night at events such as the **Reggae Sumfest** in Jamaica or the **St Lucia Jazz Festival**. There is a lively drama and dance scene in Jamaica, significant state encouragement of the arts in Cuba and lots of visiting performers in the Dominican Republic and Puerto Rico, as well as a successful arts festival in Barbados: the Holders Season. Cuba is the only island to have a significant film industry, but nearly all the islands have good cinemas and show a range of movies and video releases. ▸▸ *For details of Caribbean festivals, see A foot in the door, page 14, and listings in the individual island chapters.*

Essentials A-Z

Business hours

See Touching down section for each individual island.

Children

Some islands are more geared to children than others. Families are particularly welcome in Antigua, St Lucia and Barbados, but several exclusive resorts around the Caribbean limit the age of children allowed. Some of the all-inclusive resorts are geared towards couples and therefore kids are not accepted. At the cheaper end of the market there will be no restrictions. In the resort hotels there is a standard reduction for children or they go free if sharing a room with two adults. Several hotels offer kids' clubs which amuse the children all day and allow adults to go off and do their own thing. Babysitting services are usually available. If your children are young it might be best to pick a destination you can fly to direct, maybe flying on to a second island after a week when they have acclimatized.

Food is not usually a problem as fast food staples are available for fussy eaters. Bananas and avocados are safe, easy to eat and nutritious; they can be fed to young babies and most older children like them too. Buy what you can when you see it from farmers at the market or roadside stalls. If you are not in self-catering accommodation, there are many hotels with a kitchenette in the room so you can prepare snacks or light meals. It is advisable to take all your own baby food and nappies/diapers if travelling with babies, as in some islands, eg Cuba, you cannot rely on them being available.

Health A little more preparation and care is necessary for babies and children as they can become more rapidly ill than adults. Diarrhoea and vomiting are the most common problems, so take the usual precautions, but more intensively. Breastfeeding is most convenient for babies, but powdered milk is generally available and so are baby foods. Children get dehydrated very quickly in hot countries and can become drowsy and uncooperative unless cajoled into drinking water or juice plus salts. Upper respiratory infections, such as colds, catarrh and middle ear infections are also common so, if your child suffers from these normally, take some antibiotics against the possibility. Outer ear infections after swimming are also common and antibiotic eardrops will help.

Customs

See Before you travel section for each individual island.

Disabled travellers

Pick your hotel carefully. The large, modern hotels will usually have a couple of specially adapted rooms to meet the needs of wheelchair users, but smaller hotels do not. It is worth checking whether the whole hotel is wheelchair friendly, or whether you will have to make a long detour to get to the restaurant or beach to avoid steps. Most activities are designed for able-bodied participants, but there are a few dive operators who will take you underwater, such as in the Cayman Islands. Transport also has to be organized well in advance so that you can get a vehicle which is wheelchair accessible. One taxi company offering this service is *Dial-A-Ride* in St Thomas, T(340)7761277, F7775383. Streets and pavements can be difficult to negotiate as they are often made with storm drains. Potholes and loose paving stones compound the difficulties. However, don't be discouraged, disabled people have been travelling around the Caribbean for years, see *Touch the Happy Isles* by Quentin Crewe, for a first-hand account.

Drugs

See Touching down section for each individual island.

Embassies and consulates

See Before you travel section for each individual island.

Emergency

See Touching down section for each individual island.

Gay and lesbian travellers

Several islands have in the past been homophobic, such as Cuba, where homosexuals were sent to labour camps to be 'rehabilitated' after the Revolution. However, times have changed and the tourist dollar is king. Although Grand Cayman turned away a gay cruise ship a few years ago, gay couples are accepted in hotels. Several hotels are openly gay friendly, such as **Delfina** in St Maarten, but most prefer discretion and no open displays of affection. In 2003 **Sandals** hit the news when it became clear that their Couples resorts were for heterosexuals only, but the company declared that gays and lesbians were welcome at their other resorts. Jamaica has also been in the news for the homophobic content of the lyrics of some of its major music artistes and violence towards Jamaican gays, but this has not, so far, been extended to foreigners.

Health

See your GP or travel clinic at least six weeks before departure for general advice on travel risks and vaccinations. Try phoning a specialist travel clinic if your own doctor is unfamiliar with health in the region. Make sure you have sufficient medical travel insurance, get a dental check, know your own blood group and if you suffer a long-term condition such as diabetes or epilesy, obtain a Medic Alert bracelet/necklace (www.medicalalert.co.uk).

Vaccinations
Polio and Tetanus jabs are recommended if you have not been immunised in the last 10 years; five doses of Tetanus vaccine provides lifetime innoculation. Hepatitis A is also recommended. BCG is recommended for stays exceeding one month. The islands of the Caribbean have no Yellow fever and want to keep it that way; if you arrive from an infected country almost all the islands will want to see a yellow fever certificate. Malaria is limited to Haiti, parts of the Dominican Republic and parts of Jamaica, exclusively in the malignant (Pfalciparum) form (see below). See also under Before you travel for each individual island.

Health risks
The major risks posed in the region are those caused by insect disease carriers such as mosquitoes and sandflies. The key parasitic and viral diseases are malaria and Dengue Fever. Be aware that you are always at risk from these diseases, Dengue Fever is particularly hard to protect against as the mosquitoes can bite throughout throughout the day as well as night (unlike those that carry malaria); try to wear clothes that cover arms and legs and also use effective mosquito repellent. Mosquito nets dipped in permethrin provide a good physical and chemical barrier at night. Some form of diarrhoea or intestinal upset is almost inevitable, the standard advice is to be careful with drinking water and ice. Always buy bottled water and ask from where any water that is served in a restaurant came from. Food can also pose a problem, be wary of salads if you don't know whether they have been washed or not. There is a constant threat of tuberculosis (TB) and although the BCG vaccine is available, it is still not guaranteed protection. It is best to avoid unpasteurised dairy products and try not to let people cough and splutter all over you.

Further information
www.btha.org British Travel Health Association.
www.cdc.gov US government site that gives excellent advice on travel health and details of disease outbreaks.
www.fco.gov.uk British Foreign and Commonwealth Office travel site has useful information on each country, people, climate and a list of UK embassies/consulates.
www.fitfortravel.scot.nhs.uk A-Z of vaccine/health advice for each country.
www.travelscreening.co.uk Travel Screening Services gives vaccine and travel

health advice, email/SMS text vaccine reminders and screens returned travellers for tropical diseases.

Insurance

Take out some form of travel insurance, wherever you're travelling from and to. This should cover you for theft or loss of possessions and money, the cost of medical and dental treatment, cancellation of flights, delays in travel arrangements, accidents, missed departures, lost baggage, lost passport and personal liability and legal expenses. Also check on the inclusion of 'dangerous activities' such as climbing, diving, horse riding, even trekking, if you plan on doing any.

There are many insurance companies and policies to choose from, so it's best to shop around. Reputable student travel organizations often offer good value policies. Travellers from **North America** can try the **International Student Insurance Service** (ISIS), which is available through **STA**, T800-777 0112, www.sta-travel.com. Other recommended travel insurance companies include **Access America**, T800-284 8300, **Travel Insurance Services**, T800-937 1387. Companies worth trying in the **UK** include **Direct Line**, T0845-2468744, www.directline.com, the **Flexicover Group**, T0870 990 9292, www.flexicover.net.uk, and **Columbus**, T020-7375 0011. Note that some companies will not cover those over 65. The best policies for older travellers are offered by **Age Concern**, T01883 346964, or **Saga**, www.saga.co.uk.

Internet

Internet availability is increasing all the time; most countries now have cybercafés and many hotels have business centres with terminals which can be used by their guests and are often open to the public. Often the local telephone office or post office will have a terminal you can use to send emails, but don't rely on it actually working.

Language

In the majority of cases, English is widely spoken and understood. In the French Antilles and Haiti, French is the main language. However, in these last, and on those English-speaking islands that once belonged to France, Créole is spoken and the population is bilingual. On Créole- and English-speaking islands, the English- speaking traveller will have no problems with communication; on the French islands, knowledge of French is a great benefit. The Netherlands Antilles speak Dutch, English and Papiamento. English and Spanish are both spoken on Puerto Rico. The principal language in the Dominican Republic, Cuba and the Venezuelan islands is Spanish. Language courses in Spanish, plus volunteer programmes and travel advice, are run in Puerto Rico and the Dominican Republic by **AmeriSpan**, 117 South 17th St, Suite 1401, Philadelphia, PA 19103, T+1 215-751 1199, T+1-800-879 6640 in N America, www.amerispan.com. Spanish courses with dance and cultural programmes are offered in Cuba and the Dominican Republic by **Càlédöniä Languages Abroad**, The Clockhouse, Bonnington Mill, 72 New Haven Rd, Edinburgh EH6 5QG Scotland, T0131-6217721, www.caledonialanguages.co.uk. Other courses are available with other companies; the universities run programmes in Cuba.

Money

On islands, such as Puerto Rico, the US and British Virgin Islands, the US dollar ($) is the legal tender. In some places, the US dollar is accepted alongside local currency (make sure you know which currency prices are being quoted in). In others, only the local currency is accepted. On the French islands the euro (€) is the official currency, although dollars are often accepted. Most of the Eastern Caribbean uses the EC dollar.

Credit cards and ATMs

Credit cards are widely used and ATMs can be found at banks in all the main towns. Keep your money, credit cards, etc, either safely on your person, or in a hotel safe. If your guesthouse has no safe in which to store money, passport, tickets, etc, try local banks.

⚏ Exchange rates (May 2007)

Country	Currency	Abbreviation	Exchange rate (US$1)
Anguilla	East Caribbean dollar	EC$	2.70
Antigua and Barbuda	East Caribbean dollar	EC$	2.70
Aruba	Aruban florin	Afl	1.79
Barbados	Barbados dollar	B$	2.00
Bonaire	Netherlands Antillies (NA) guilder	Naf	1.78
British Virgin Islands	US dollar	US$	1.00
Cayman Islands	Cayman dollar	CI$	1.22
Cuba	Cuban peso	CP$	26.5
	Cuban peso convertible	CUC$	1.00
Curaçao	NA guilder	Naf	1.78
Dominica	East Caribbean dollar	EC$	2.70
Dominican Rep	Dominican peso	RD$	34
Grenada	East Caribbean dollar	EC$	2.70
Guadeloupe	Euro	€	0.73
Haiti	Gourde	HTG	38
Jamaica	Jamaican dollar	J$	68
Martinique	Euro	€	0.73
Montserrat	East Caribbean dollar	EC$	2.70
Puerto Rico	US dollar	US$	1.00
Saba	NA guilder	Naf	1.78
St Barthélémy	Euro	€	0.73
St Kitts and Nevis	East Caribbean dollar	EC$	2.70
St Lucia	East Caribbean dollar	EC$	2.70
St Martin	Euro	€	0.82
St Vincent and the Grenadines	East Caribbean dollar	EC$	2.70
Sint Eustatius	NA guilder	Naf	1.78
Sint Maarten	NA guilder	Naf	1.78
Trinidad and Tobago	Trinidad dollar	TT$	6.35
Turks and Caicos	US dollar	US$	1.00
US Virgin Islands	US dollar	US$	1.00

Essentials A-Z

Some people recommend setting up two bank accounts before travelling. One has all your funds but no debit card; the other has no funds but does have a debit card. As you travel, use the internet to transfer money from the full account to the empty account when you need it and withdraw cash from an ATM. That way, if your debit card is stolen, you won't be at risk of losing all your capital. Also, by using a debit card rather than a credit card you incur fewer bank charges.

Exchange

There are plenty of banks in the main towns where you can exchange foreign currencies. On islands with very small populations, such as South Caicos, a bank may open only once or twice a week, so take sufficient funds before travelling there. In general, the US dollar is the best currency to take, as cash or traveller's cheques. The latter are convenient and can be replaced if lost or stolen. On the most frequently visited holiday islands, euros and sterling can be exchanged without difficulty but at a poor rate, and US dollars are preferred.

Cost of visiting

The Caribbean is not a cheap area to visit. Transport is expensive (unless you are staying in one place and using only buses), but if you book your flights in advance, taking advantage of whatever air pass or stopovers are suitable, that expenditure, at least, will be out of the way. Accommodation is generally expensive, too, even at the lower end of the market. In a number of instances you can book all-inclusive packages which are often good value and let you know in advance almost exactly what your expenditure will be. However, you will not see much of your chosen island outside your enclave and organized excursions can be costly. To find cheaper accommodation you need mobility, probably a hired car. One option is renting a self-catering apartment, villa or house, the range of which is also vast, and here the advantage is that a group of people can share the cost (not so economical for single travellers).

Post

There are post offices in all the main towns but you can often buy stamps in hotels. Islands like Montserrat, the Cayman Islands and Nevis pride themselves on their philatelic issues, which are collectors' items. Postal services are not very efficient, so a courier service is recommended for sending packages or parcels.

Safety

The Caribbean is a relatively safe part of the world in which to travel. The visitor usually only needs to worry about petty theft such as bag snatching on the beach. Certain countries such as Jamaica and Trinidad have a high murder rate, but this does not generally involve tourists and shootouts between gangs happen in urban areas that no one visits. Political disturbances and rising crime, including kidnappings of foreigners by gangs, in Haiti have led the FCO to advise

against all but essential travel there. Normal security precautions are adequate: do not flaunt jewellery, cameras or other valuables, keep an eye on your belongings and do not wander around poorly lit areas downtown after dark. See also Touching down section for each individual island.

Student travellers

If you are in full-time education you will be entitled to an **International Student Identity Card** (ISIC), which is distributed by student travel offices and travel agencies in 77 countries. The ISIC gives you special prices on all forms of transport (air, sea, rail, etc), and access to a variety of other concessions and services. If you need to find the location of your nearest ISIC office contact: The **ISIC Association**, Herengracht 479, 1017 BS Amsterdam, the Netherlands, T+31 20-421 2800, www.istc.org.

Telephone

Many airport lounges and phone companies in the region have **AT&T**'s USA Direct telephones by which the USA and Canada may be called using a charge card (which bills your home phone account), or by calling collect. The service is not available to Europe, but the **BT** chargecard, for example, can be used on many of the islands (check with your phone company). Public card phones have been introduced by **Cable and Wireless** on those islands where it operates. This company offers discounts on evening rates for IDD calls from cardphones: 1800-2300 15%, 2300-0500 40%. Discounts do not apply to credit card calls (1-800-877-8000). Phone cards come in several denominations, with a tax added, and can be useful for local and international calls, as you avoid the extra charges made by hotels.

Time

See Touching down section for each individual island.

Tipping

Tipping is recommended, even in Communist Cuba. Practices vary according to each island, but you should usually tip in restaurants, even if a service charge is added to the bill, and also leave something for the woman who has cleaned your hotel room. Tipping taxi drivers varies; porters usually expect US$1-2 per bag. Guides and other staff on day trips welcome tips and often have a pot to put them in. See also Touching down section for each individual island.

Tourist information

Each country has its own websites, listed in the relevant chapter in this guide and in the box, page . In addition, the **Caribbean Tourism Organization** (CTO) has an umbrella site with links to individual islands: www.onecaribbean.org, or www.doitcaribbean.com. Useful general websites and search engines for the Caribbean include www.caribbean-on-line.com, which has maps of most countries and cities. www.caribbeannetnews is a daily summary of news from around the Caribbean.

Tours and tour operators

In the UK
Discovery Initiatives, The Travel House, 51 Castle St, Cirencester, Gloucestershire, GL7 1QD, T01285-643333, enquiry@discoveryinitiatives.com, are pioneers in special wildlife, marine and conservation interest groups and tailor-made ecotours.
Exodus Travels, 9 Weir Road, London SW12 0LT, T020-87723822, www.exodus.co.uk.
Interchange, Interchange House, 27 Stafford Rd, Croydon, Surrey CR0 4NG, T020-86813612, www.interchange.uk.com, specializes in Haiti, Cuba and Aruba.
Journey Latin America, 12-13 Heathfield Terrace, Chiswick, London W4 4JE, T020-8747 8315, and in Manchester, T0161- 832 1441, www.journeylatinamerica.co.uk, is good for Cuba and for tailor-made holidays combining Latin America and the Caribbean. Also offers flight options.
Progressive Tours, 12 Porchester Pl, Marble Arch, London W2 2BS, T020-74865704.
Regent Holidays, 15 John St, Bristol BS1

2HR, T0117-9211711.
South American Experience, 47 Causton St, Pimlico, London SW1P 4AT, T020-79765511, www.southamerican experience.co.uk.
Trips Worldwide Ltd, 14 Frederick Place, Clifton, Bristol, BS8 1AS, T0117-311 4400, T0117-311 4494, www.tripsworldwide.co.uk, offers tailor-made trips to the 'Alternative Caribbean'.

In the Americas
Mila Tours, 100 S Greenleaf, Gurnee, Il 6003-3378, USA, T1-800-3677378, www.milatours.com. Latin America and the Dominican Republic.
Wilderness Explorers, 176 Middle St, Georgetown, Guyana, T592-2277698, www.wilderness-explorers.com.

Specialists in upmarket destinations include **ITC Classics/Caribbean Connection**, www.itcclassics.co.uk; **Caribtours**, T020-7751 0660, www.caribtours.co.uk; **Kuoni**, T01306-747000, www.kuoni.co.uk; **Elegant Resorts**, www.elegantresorts.co.uk; **Hayes and Jarvis**, www.hayesandjarvis.co.uk; **Virgin Holidays**, www.virginholidays.co.uk.

Visas and immigration

Since the clampdown on security in 2006-07, all travellers need a passport except in cases

■ *Overseas diplomatic representatives and individual entry requirements for each country are given in the relevant chapter.*

such as Americans visiting the US Virgin Islands, which are a US territory. Anyone (including US citizens) travelling from the Caribbean requires a passport to enter the USA so, while you may get into an island with alternative proof of identity, you will need a passport if travelling on to any US territory. If intending to visit Puerto Rico or the US Virgin Islands, or making connections through Miami or another US gateway, a visa for the United States will not be necessary if your home country and the airline on which you are travelling are part of the US Visa Waiver Program. A US consulate will supply all relevant details. Australians and New Zealanders should note that many islands impose strict entry laws on holders of the above passports. Satisfying visa and other requirements, if not done at home, can take at least a day, usually involves expense, and passport photographs will be needed: be prepared. On all forms, refer to yourself as a 'visitor' rather than a 'tourist'. If asked where you are staying and you have not booked in advance, say any hotel (they do not usually check), but do not say you are going to camp and do not say that you are going to arrange accommodation later. You should carry your passport in a safe place about your

Essentials A-Z

person, or if not going far, leave it in the hotel safe. If staying in a place for several weeks, it is worth registering at your embassy or consulate. Then, if your passport is lost or stolen, it will be replaced quicker. It is also a good idea to keep photocopies of essential documents, as well as additional passport-sized photographs.

Voltage

See Touching down section for each individual island.

Weights and measures

See Touching down section for each individual island.

Women travellers

Lots of women travel around the Caribbean on their own or in pairs without problems. However, be aware that men in many of the islands will consider you fair game and may even believe that you have travelled there specifically to find a gigolo. Many men make their living out of prostitution, just like women. Hassling is unpleasant in Havana and a nuisance in the Dominican Republic, Jamaica and sometimes Tobago, but it can happen anywhere. Single women on the beach are a prime target. A drink in a bar may seem harmless, but your new male friend may be expecting it to lead to something more.

Background

Pre-Columbian civilizations

The recorded history of the Caribbean islands begins with the arrival of Christopher Columbus' fleet in 1492. Our knowledge of the well-developed Amerindian society that inhabited the islands before and at the time of his arrival is largely derived from the accounts of contemporary Spanish writers and from archaeological examinations.

Tribes

The Amerindians encountered by Columbus in the Greater Antilles had no overall tribal name but organized themselves in a series of villages or local chiefdoms, each of which had its own tribal name. The term 'Arawak' was used, at the time, by the Indians of the Guianas, some of whom had spread into Trinidad, but their territory was not explored until nearly a century later. The use of the generic term 'Arawak' to describe the Indians Columbus encountered, arose because of linguistic similarities with the Arawaks of the mainland. It is therefore surmised that migration took place many centuries before Columbus' arrival, but that the two groups were not in contact at that time. The timing of the latest migration from the mainland and, consequently, the existence of the island Arawaks, is disputed, with some academics tracing it to about the time of Christ (the arrival of the Saladoids) and others to AD 1000 (the Ostionoids).

The inhabitants of the Bahamas were generally referred to as **Lucayans**, and those of the Greater Antilles as **Taínos**, but there were many sub-groupings. The inhabitants of the Lesser Antilles were, however, referred to as **Carib** and were described to Columbus as an aggressive tribe which sacrificed and sometimes ate the prisoners they captured in battle. It was from them that the Caribbean gets its name and from which the word cannibal is derived.

The earliest known inhabitants of the region, the **Siboneys**, migrated from Florida (some say Mexico) and spread throughout the Bahamas and the major islands. Most archaeological evidence of their settlements has been found near the shore, along bays or streams, where they lived in small groups. They were hunters and gatherers, living on fish and other seafood, small rodents, iguanas, snakes and birds. They gathered roots and wild fruits, such as guava, guanábana and mamey, but did not cultivate plants. They worked with primitive tools made out of stone, shell, bone or wood, for hammering, chipping or scraping, but had no knowledge of pottery. The Siboneys were eventually absorbed by the advance of the Arawaks migrating from the south, who had made more technological advances in agriculture, arts and crafts.

The people now known as **Arawaks** migrated from the Guianas to Trinidad and on through the island arc to Cuba. Their population expanded because of the natural fertility of the islands and the abundance of fruit and seafood, helped by their agricultural skills in cultivating and improving wild plants and their excellent boat-building and fishing techniques. They were healthy, tall and lived to a ripe old age. It is estimated that up to eight million may have lived on the island of Hispaniola alone.

Society

Arawak society was essentially communal and organized around families. The smaller islands were particularly egalitarian but in the larger ones, where village communities of extended families numbered up to 500 people, there was an incipient class structure. Each village had a headman, called a *cacique*, whose duty it was to represent the village when dealing with other tribes, to settle family disputes and organize defence. However, he had no powers of coercion and was often little more than a nominal head. The position was largely hereditary, with the eldest son of the eldest sister having rights of succession, but women could and did become *caciques*, too. In the larger communities, there was some delegation of responsibility to the senior men, but economic activities were usually organized along family lines, and power was limited.

The division of labour was usually based on age and sex. The men would clear and prepare the land for agriculture and be responsible for defence of the village, while women cultivated the crops and were the major food producers, also making items such as mats, baskets, bowls and fishing nets. Women were in charge of raising the children, especially the girls, while the men taught the boys traditional customs, skills and rites.

Food and farming

The Taínos hunted for some of their food, but fishing was more important and most of their settlements were close to the sea. Fish and shellfish were their main sources of protein and they had many different ways of catching them – from hands, baskets or nets to poisoning, shooting or line fishing. Cassava was a staple food, which they had successfully learned to leach of its poisonous juice. They also grew yams, maize, cotton, arrowroot, peanuts, beans, cocoa and spices, rotating their crops to prevent soil erosion. It is documented that, in Jamaica, they had three harvests of maize annually, using maize and cassava to make bread, cakes and beer. Cotton was used to make clothing and hammocks, while the calabash tree was used to make ropes and cords, baskets and roofing. Plants were used for medicinal and spiritual purposes, and for face and body paint. Also important, both to the Arawaks and later to the Europeans, was the cultivation of tobacco, as a drug and a means of exchange.

Arts and crafts

They had no writing, no beasts of burden, no wheeled vehicles and no hard metals, although they did have some alluvial gold for personal ornament. The abundance of food allowed them time to develop their arts and crafts and they were skilled in woodwork and pottery. They had polished stone implements, but also carved shell tools for manioc preparation or as fish hooks. Coral manioc graters have also been found. Their boat-building techniques were noted by Columbus, who marvelled at the canoes of up to 75 ft in length, carrying up to 50 people, made of a single tree trunk in one piece. It took two months to fell a tree by gradually burning and chipping it down, and many more to make the canoe.

Religion

The Arawaks had three main deities, evidence of which have been found in stone and conch carvings in many of the Lesser Antilles as well as the well populated Greater Antilles, although their relative importance varied according to the island. The principal male god was Yocahú, yoca being the word for cassava and hú meaning 'giver of'. It is believed that the tribes associated this deity's power to provide cassava with the mystery of the volcanoes, since all the carvings are conical. The Yocahú cult was wiped out in the Lesser Antilles by the invading Caribs and, in the Greater Antilles, by the Spaniards, but it is thought to have existed from about AD 200.

The main female deity was a fertility goddess, often referred to as Atabeyra, but she is thought to have had several names relating to her other roles as goddess of the moon, mother of the sea, the tides and the springs, and the goddess of childbirth. In carvings she is usually depicted as a squatting figure with her hands up to her chin, sometimes in the act of giving birth.

A third deity is a dog god, named Opiyel-Guaobiran, meaning 'the dog deity who

takes care of the souls of the immediately deceased and is the son of the spirit of
darkness'. Stone and shell carvings of a dog's head or whole body have been found, many with holes and Y-shaped passages that would have been used to snuff narcotics and induce a religious trance in the shaman or priest, who could then ascertain the status of a departed soul for a recently bereaved relative.

Sport

One custom which aroused interest in the Spaniards was the ball game, not only for the sport and its ceremonial features, but because the ball was made of rubber and bounced, a phenomenon which had not previously been seen in Europe. Catholicism soon eradicated the game, but archaeological remains have been found in several islands, notably in Puerto Rico, but also in Hispaniola. Excavations in the Greater Antilles have revealed earth embankments and rows of elongated upright stones surrounding plazas or courts, pavements and stone balls. These are called *bateyes, juegos de indios, juegos de bola, cercados* or *corrales de indios*. Batey was the aboriginal name for the ball game, the rubber ball itself and also the court where it was played. The word is still used to designate the cleared area in front of houses in the country.

The ball game had religious and ceremonial significance but it was a sport and bets and wagers were important. It was played by two teams of up to 20 or 30 players, who had to keep the ball in the air by means of their hips, shoulders, heads, elbows and other parts of their body, but never with their hands. The aim was to bounce the ball in this manner to the opposing team until it hit the ground. Men and women played, but not usually in mixed sex games. Great athleticism was required and it is clear that the players practised hard to perfect their skill, several, smaller practice courts having been built in larger settlements. The game was sometimes played before the village made an important decision, and the prize could be a sacrificial victim, usually a prisoner, granted to the victor.

Invaders

In 1492 Arawaks inhabited all the greater islands of the Caribbean, but in Puerto Rico they were being invaded by the Caribs who had pushed north through the Lesser Antilles, stealing their women and enslaving or killing the men. The Caribs had also originated in South America, from around the Orinoco delta. In their migration north through the Caribbean islands they proved to be fierce warriors and their raids on the Arawak settlements were feared. Many of their women were captured Arawaks, and it was they who cultivated the land and performed the domestic chores. Polygamy was common, encouraged by the surplus of women resulting from the raids, and the Arawak female influence on Carib culture was strong.

Despite rumours of cannibalism reported to Columbus by frightened Arawaks, there appears to be no direct evidence of the practice, although the Spaniards took it seriously enough to use it as an excuse to justify taking slaves. After some unfortunate encounters, colonizers left the Caribs alone for many years. The Arawaks, on the other hand, were soon wiped out by disease, cruelty and murder. The Spanish invaders exacted tribute and forced labour while allowing their herds of cattle and pigs to destroy the Indians' unfenced fields and clearings. Transportation to the mines resulted in shifts in the native population which could not be fed from the surrounding areas and starvation became common. Lack of labour in the Greater Antilles led to slave raids on the Lucayans in the Bahamas, but they also died or committed collective suicide. They felt that their gods had deserted them and there was nowhere for them to retreat or escape. Today there are no full-blooded Arawaks and only some 2,000 Caribs are left on Dominica (there has been no continuity of Carib language or religious belief on Dominica). The 500 years since Columbus' arrival have served to obliterate practically all the evidence of the Caribbean's indigenous civilization.

Flora and fauna

For many travellers, a trip to the Caribbean offers a first glimpse of the tropics, complete with luxuriant vegetation and exotic wildlife. Images of untouched beaches and rainforest form a major selling point of many travel brochures. In fact there is very little 'untouched' wilderness left and what visitors see is an environment that has been affected by the activities of man. Forestry, agriculture, fisheries and increasingly tourism have all helped to mould the modern landscape and natural heritage of the Caribbean. However, there is still much of interest to see, and it is true to say that small islands can combine a variety of habitats within a limited area. On many islands, it is possible to move between the coastal reefs and beaches through thorn scrub and plantation into rainforest within a matter of miles. Increasingly, the complexity and fragility of island ecosystems is being appreciated and fortunately most countries have recognized the value of balancing development and the protection of the natural environment and have begun to develop national parks and protected areas programmes. Many islands also have active conservation societies or national wildlife trusts (see page).

Over long periods of time, islands tend to develop their own unique flora and fauna. These endemic species add to the interest of wildlife and natural history tours. The St Lucia parrot and Dominica's sisserou have become a regular part of the tour circuit of these islands, and have undoubtedly benefited from the interest that tourists have shown in their plight. Details of National Parks and wildlife are included under the specific island chapters (flora and fauna). This section provides a broad overview of the range of animals, plants and habitats that are to be found in the region.

Mammals

Mammals are not good colonizers of small islands and this has resulted in a general scarcity of species in the Caribbean. Many of the more commonly seen species (mongoose, agouti, opossum, and some of the monkeys) were introduced by man. Bats are the one exception to this rule and most islands have several native species. Mongoose were introduced to many islands to control snakes; they have also preyed on birds, reptiles and other animals, causing a devastating effect to native fauna. The green monkeys of Barbados, Grenada and St Kitts and Nevis were introduced from West Africa in the 17th century. Similarly, rhesus monkeys have been introduced to Desecheo Island off Puerto Rico. The red howler monkeys on Trinidad are native to the island as are several other mammals including the brocket deer, squirrel and armadillo. These species have managed to colonize from nearby Venezuela.

Sailors may encounter marine mammals including dolphin, porpoise and whales. Between November and December humpback whales migrate through the Turks and Caicos Passage on their way to the Silver Banks breeding grounds off the Dominican Republic. The manatee, or sea cow, can still be seen in some coastal areas in the Greater Antilles (especially Jamaica, Cuba – Zapata Peninsula – and Puerto Rico) although it is becoming increasingly uncommon.

Birds

It is the birds, perhaps, that excite the most interest from visitors. Many islands have their own endemic species such as the Guadeloupe woodpecker, Grenada dove, yellow-billed parrot and 24 other species in Jamaica. The islands also act as important stepping stones in the migration of many birds through the Americas. As a result, the region is highly regarded by ornithologists and there are several important nature reserves. Trinidad and Tobago demonstrate the influence of the nearby South American mainland. While they have no endemic species they still support at least

Many of the endemic species have become rare as a result of man's activities. Habitat destruction, the introduction of new species (especially the mongoose) and hunting for food or the international pet trade have all had an effect. Parrots, in particular, have suffered. Fortunately, measures are now being undertaken to protect the birds and their habitats on Jamaica, Dominica, Puerto Rico and St Lucia.

Reptiles

Lizards and geckos are common on virtually all the islands in the region and may even be seen on very small offshore islets. There are also a number of species of snakes, iguanas and turtles scattered throughout the region. Many are restricted to one island and Jamaica has at least 27 island endemics including several species of galliwasp. Many species of reptile are now protected in the region and reserves have been specifically established to protect them. The Maria Islands Nature Reserve on St Lucia is home to the St Lucia ground lizard and grass snake. The latter is one of the rarest snakes in the world with an estimated population of 150 individuals.

The vast majority of reptiles found in the region are completely harmless to man although there are strong superstitions about the geckos (*mabouya*) and, of course, the snakes. The skin and fat of boa constrictors (*tête chien*) are used for bush remedies on some of the Windward Islands. The fer de lance snake (St Lucia, Martinique and also South America) deserves to be treated with extreme caution (see page); although the bite is not usually lethal, hospitalization is required.

Iguanas are still found on many islands although they have declined as a result of hunting throughout the region. In spite of their fearsome appearance, they are herbivorous and spend much of their time in trees and low scrub feeding on leaves and trying to avoid man.

Marine turtles including the loggerhead, leatherback, hawksbill and green turtles are found throughout Caribbean waters and they may occasionally be seen by divers and snorkellers. Females come ashore on isolated sandy beaches between the months of May and August to lay eggs. There may be opportunities for assisting natural history and wildlife societies (St Lucia Naturalists Society, Fish and Wildlife Dept in the US Virgin Islands) in their turtle watches, to record numbers and locations of nests and to protect the turtles from poachers. There is a large commercial breeding programme for green turtles in the Cayman Islands. Freshwater turtles are also found on some islands including Jamaica. Caiman have been introduced to Puerto Rico and are also found on Cuba and the Dominican Republic.

Amphibians

Frogs and toads are common in a variety of shapes and colours. There are generally more species on the larger islands. The Cuban pygmy frog is described as the world's smallest frog, while at the other end of the scale, the mountain chicken of Dominica and Montserrat is probably the largest frog in the region. Its name relates to its supposed flavour. The call of the piping frogs (*eleutherodactylus spp*) is often mistaken for a bird and these small animals are common throughout the Lesser Antilles, becoming especially vocal at night and after rain. The largest and most visible amphibian is probably the marine toad which has been introduced to islands throughout the region in an attempt to control insects and other invertebrate pests. The male toads use flat exposed areas from which to display, often roads. Unfortunately, they have not evolved to deal with the car yet and as a result many are killed.

Invertebrates

This group includes the insects, molluscs, spiders and a host of other animals that have no backbones. It is estimated that there are at least 290 species of butterfly in the Caribbean. No one knows how many species of beetles, bugs or mollusc there are on the islands.

Of the butterflies, the swallowtails are the most spectacular, with several species found in the Greater Antilles (especially Cuba). The other islands also have large colourful butterflies including the monarch and flambeau which are present throughout the region. Another insect of note is the hercules beetle, reportedly the world's second largest beetle with a large horn that protrudes from its thorax, occasionally found in the rainforests of the Lesser Antilles.

Land and freshwater crabs inhabit a range of environments from the rainforest (eg bromeliad crab from Jamaica) to the dry coastal areas (many species of hermit crab). Tarantulas are also common, although they are nocturnal and rarely seen. Their bite is painful but no worse than a bee sting. Of far more concern are the large centipedes (up to 15 cm long) that can inflict a nasty and painful bite with their pincers. They are mostly restricted to the dry coastal areas and are most active at night. Black widow spiders are also present on some of the islands in the Greater Antilles. Fortunately they are rarely encountered by the traveller.

Environment

Coral reef

A diving or snorkelling trip over a tropical reef allows a first hand experience of this habitat's diversity of wildlife. There are a number of good field guides to reef fish and animals; some are even printed on waterproof paper. Alternatively, glass-bottomed boats sail over some sites (Buccoo Reef, Tobago), and there are underwater trails which identify types of corals and marine habitats.

Amongst the commonest fish are the grunts, butterfly, soldier, squirrel and angel fish. Tiny damsel fish are very territorial and may even attempt to nip swimmers who venture too close to their territories (more surprising than painful).

There are over 50 species of hard coral (the form that builds reefs) with a variety of sizes and colours. Amongst the most dramatic are the stagshorn and elkhorn corals which are found on the more exposed outer reefs. Brain coral forms massive round structures up to 2 m high and pillar coral forms columns that may also reach 2 m in height. Soft corals, which include black corals, sea fans and gorgonians, colonize the surface of the hard coral adding colour and variety. Associated with these structures is a host of animals and plants. Spiny lobsters may be seen lurking in holes and crevices along with other crustaceans and reef fish. The patches of sand between outcrops of coral provide suitable habitat for conch and other shellfish. Some islands now restrict the collection and sale of corals (especially black corals) and there are legal restrictions on the sale of black corals under CITES. Overfishing has also affected conch and lobster in places.

The delights of swimming on a coral reef need to be tempered by a few words of caution. Many people assume the water will be seething with sharks, however these animals are fairly uncommon in nearshore waters and the species most likely to be encountered is the nurse shark, which is harmless unless provoked. Other fish to keep an eye open for include the scorpion fish with its poisonous dorsal spines; it frequently lies stationary on coral reefs. Moray eels may be encountered, a fearsome looking fish, but harmless unless provoked at which point they can inflict serious bites. Of far more concern should be the variety of stinging invertebrates that are found on coral reefs. The most obvious is fire coral which comes in a range of shapes and sizes but is recognizable by the white tips to its branches. In addition, many corals have sharp edges and branches that can graze and cut. Another common group of stinging invertebrates are the fire worms which have white bristles. As with

⁝ Disasters

Hurricanes are the most frequent sources of natural disaster, not only for the winds which can uproot trees, rip roofs from buildings and tear down power lines and telephone cables, but also for the rain, which often brings flooding and mudslides (see Hurricane season, page 22). Even without a hurricane, the weather has been extreme recently, not only in the rainy season, but during the normally dry months as well. In November 2004 18 landslides cut roads in Dominica, while in January 2005 Trinidad's north coast road was blocked for several days, The Cibao Valley in the Dominican Republic suffered frequent flooding in 2005 and 2006, with crops, bridges, power cables and houses washed away. The east of Cuba, on the other hand, has suffered from an extended period of devastating drought.

A chain of dormant and active **volcanoes** runs down the eastern Caribbean all the way from Mt Liamuiga in St Kitts to the mud volcanoes of Trinidad. On 6 May 1902, the Soufrière volcano on St Vincent erupted, killing nearly 2,000 people and ruining farming in the area (see page 798). Far worse was the eruption on Martinique when Mt Pelée burst into life on 8 May in the same year (see page 686). The pyroclastic flow swallowed up the chic and cultured city of St-Pierre, killing nearly 30,000 and leaving only one survivor, an inmate in the prison cells. More recently, the Soufrière Hills volcano in Montserrat began erupting in July 1995 and within two years the southern part of the island was covered in ash and lava and uninhabitable (see page 645). The volcano that has erupted most frequently in the region, however, is Kick 'em Jenny, an underwater volcano 8 km north of Grenada, which is known to have erupted 11 times since 1939.

The seismic activity of the region has caused a number of **earthquakes**. According to some, the 'sinful' town of Port Royal in Jamaica, known for its pirates and prostitutes, got its just deserts on 7 June 1692, when an earthquake and subsequent fever epidemic killed some 5,000 inhabitants (see page 219). In 1843 a massive earthquake struck the eastern Caribbean, affecting islands all down the chain from St Kitts to Dominica. The disaster was worst in Guadeloupe, where 5,000 people were killed but there were also 30 dead in Antigua, where much of English Harbour sank. The most recent earthquakes to have caused significant material damage were felt in the southern Caribbean, particularly Trinidad and Tobago, in April and July 1997.

the fire coral, these can inflict a painful sting if handled or brushed against. Large black sea urchins are also common on some reefs and their spines can penetrate unprotected skin very easily. The best advice when observing coral reefs and their wildlife is to look, not touch.

Sea cliffs

Some islands, especially those in the southern part of the Caribbean, have spectacular cliffs and offshore islets. These are home to large flocks of sea birds including the piratical frigate bird which chases smaller birds, forcing them to disgorge their catch; another notable species is the tropic bird with its streamer-like tail feathers. The cliffs may also provide dry sandy soils for the large range of Caribbean cacti, including prickly pear (*opuntia sp*) and the Turks head cactus.

Wetlands include a wide range of fresh and brackish water habitats such as rivers, marsh and mangroves. They are important for many species of bird, as well as fish. Unfortunately they are also home to an array of biting insects, including mosquitoes which are unpleasant and a serious problem where malaria or dengue are present.

Important coastal wetlands include the Baie de Fort de France (Martinique), the Cabrits Swamp (Dominica), Caroni and Nariva Swamps (Trinidad), Negril and Black Morass (Jamaica). These sites all support large flocks of migratory and resident birds including waders, herons, egrets and ducks. In addition, some of the mangroves in the Greater Antilles also provide habitats for manatee, and the Negril and Black Morass has a population of American crocodiles. Large freshwater lakes are less common although Grenada, Dominica and St Vincent all have volcanic crater lakes and these are used by migratory waders and ducks as well as kingfishers.

Thorn scrub, plantations, rainforest

There is little if any primary rainforest left in the Caribbean Islands, although there may be small patches in Guadeloupe. Nevertheless, many of the islands still have large areas of good secondary forest which has only suffered from a limited amount of selective felling for commercially valuable wood, such as gommier, balata and blue mahoe.

Martinique has some of the largest tracts of forest left in the Caribbean (eg rainforest at Piton du Carbet, cloud forest on Mt Pelée, dry woodland in the south). In Dominica, the Morne Trois Pitons National Park is a UNESCO World Heritage Site for its rare combination of natural features: volcanoes, fumaroles and hot springs, freshwater lakes, a 'boiling lake' and the richest biodiversity in the Lesser Antilles. Many other islands also have accessible forest, although you should always use a local guide if venturing off the beaten track.

The Caribbean rainforests are not as diverse as those on the South and Central American mainland, however they still support a large number of plant species many of which are endemic (Jamaica has over 3,000 species of which 800 are endemic). The orchids and bromeliads are impressive in many forests and it is not unusual to see trees festooned with both these groups. The wildlife of the rainforest includes both native and introduced species, although they are often difficult to see in the shady conditions. Agouti, boa constrictor, monkeys and opossum may be seen, but it is the bird life that is most evident. Hummingbirds, vireos, thrashers, todies and others are all found along with parrots, which are perhaps the group most associated with this habitat. Early morning and evening provide the best times for birdwatching.

Plantations of commercial timber (blue mahoe, Caribbean pine, teak, mahogany and others) have been established in many places. These reduce pressure on natural forest and help protect watersheds and soil. They are also valuable for wildlife and some species have adapted to them with alacrity.

Closer to the coasts, dry scrub woodland often predominates. The trees may lose their leaves during the dry season. One of the most recognizable of the trees in this woodland is the turpentine tree, also known as the tourist tree because of its red peeling bark! Bush medicines and herbal remedies are still used in the countryside although less so than previously. Leaves and bark can be seen for sale in markets.

Books

History

James Ferguson, *A Traveller's History of the Caribbean* (1998), The Windrush Press. Concise and easy to dip in to.
J H Parry, **P M Sherlock** and **Anthony Maingot**, *A Short History of The West Indies* (1987), Macmillan. Accessible but academic.
E Williams, *From Columbus to Castro: The History of the Caribbean 1492-1969* (1970).

Geography

James Ferguson, *Far from Paradise, An Introduction to Caribbean Development* (1990), Latin American Bureau.
Mark Wilson, *The Caribbean Environment* (1989), OUP. A fascinating text book.

Field guides

P Bacon, *Flora and Fauna of the Caribbean*, Key Caribbean Publications, PO Box 21, Port of Spain, Trinidad.
J Bond, *Birds of the West Indies*, Collins.
C C Chaplin, *Fishwatchers Guide to West Atlantic Coral Reefs*, Horowood Books. Some are printed on plastic for use underwater.
Raffaele et al, *A Guide to the Birds of the West Indies*, (1998) Princeton University Press.

Economics

Polly Pattullo, *Last Resorts, The Cost of Tourism in the Caribbean* (new edition 2005), Cassell and Latin American Bureau. A study of Caribbean tourism and its impact.
Clive Y Thomas, *The Poor and the Powerless, Economic Policy and Change in the Caribbean* (1988), Latin American Bureau.

Literature

There is no room to detail all the authors whose fiction has been inspired by aspects of the Caribbean, such as **Robert Louis Stevenson**, **Graham Greene**, **Ernest Hemingway** and **Gabriel García Márquez** but for an introduction to Caribbean writers and writers on the Caribbean, with extracts from numerous literary works, try **James Ferguson**, *Traveller's Literary Companion to the Caribbean*, with chapters on Cuba and Puerto Rico by Jason Wilson (1997), In Print. Highly recommended.

The work of a many English-speaking poets is collected in *The Penguin Book of Caribbean Verse in English*, edited by **Paula Burnett** (1986). See also *Hinterland: Caribbean Poetry From the West Indies and Britain*, edited by **E A Markham** (1990), Bloodaxe, and *West Indian Poetry*, edited by **Kenneth Ramchand** and **Cecil Gray** (1989), Longman Caribbean.

For a French verse anthology, see *La Poésie Antillaise*, collected by **Maryse Condé** (1977), Fernand Nathan. There are a number of prose anthologies of stories in English, eg *The Oxford Book of Caribbean Short Stories*, **Stewart Brown** and **John Wickham** (1999); *Stories from the Caribbean*, introduced by **Andrew Salkey** (1972), Paul Elek; or *West Indian Narrative: an Introductory Anthology*, **Kenneth Ramchand** (1966), Nelson.

Heinemann's **Caribbean Writers** series publishes works of fiction by established and new writers. *The Story of English*, by **Robert McCrumb**, **William Cran** and **Robert MacNeil** (1986), Faber and Faber/BBC. Has an interesting section on the development of the English language in the Caribbean.

Travel

Recommended travel writing on the Caribbean includes **Patrick Leigh Fermor**, *The Traveller's Tree*; **Quentin Crewe**, *Touch the Happy Isles*; **Anthony Trollope**, *Travels in the West Indies and the Spanish Main*; **Alec Waugh**, *The Sugar Isles*; and **James Pope-Hennessy**, *West Indian Summer*.

General

A generally excellent series of Caribbean books is published by **Macmillan Caribbean** (www.macmillan-caribbean.com). This includes island guides, natural histories, food and drink, sports, and pirates.

Essentials Background

Cuba

⦂ Footprint features

Introduction

Cuba's charms are as varied as they are fascinating. Most people spend some time relaxing and enjoying the sun and sand on Cuba's sandy beaches and cays, but there is so much more to do. Go before Castro dies and see one of the last bastions of Communism and a culture which has denied itself the influences of the USA for so long. From the Indians who refused to give in to the Spaniards in the 15th and 16th centuries, the African slaves who rebelled against their masters in the 17th and 18th centuries, the Independence fighters in the 19th century, to the revolutionaries in the 20th century, Cuba has a defiant history. The plots to depose Fidel Castro are legendary, but despite ill-health El Jefe stands firm while most of his detractors now live in Miami. Cuba continues to stand up to the most powerful country in the world even though Castro has temporarily stood down from office. Visit the cities, where the Spanish colonial architecture is being beautifully preserved. Stroll along Havana's seafront drive, the Malecón, or explore the narrow streets of the old city with its elegant hotels and bars made famous by American celebrities escaping Prohibition. Trinidad is a time capsule where little has been touched since the 19th century, while Santiago de Cuba roasts in the shelter of the Sierra Maestra and is a hot place to savour Carnival in the summer. Go hiking or cycling and see rural life in Cuba, take a ride in one of those famous 50s cars, go birdwatching or scuba diving, the list is endless. No one will leave the island without being affected by the pulsating rhythms of the music and dance and the racial mixture which has produced such creativity and exuberance in the arts and entertainment.

★ Don't miss...

1 Havana One of the great cities of Spanish colonial times, page 84.

2 Viñales A pretty rural town nestled in lush countryside and surrounded by dramatic mountains; the heart of the tobacco-growing region, page 113.

3 Che Guevara mausoleum The last resting place of the world's greatest revolutionary icon, Che Guevara, and his comrades in arms from the Bolivia campaign, page 129.

4 Trinidad The town that time forgot, charming and tranquil, but with numerous music venues and lively night time entertainment, page 129.

5 Santiago de Cuba Sandwiched between imposing forested mountains and the Caribbean Sea, this is the venue for the legendary Carnival, page 148.

6 Baracoa A small town at the eastern tip of the island, within easy reach of some of the prettiest beaches, as yet untouched by hotel development, page 151.

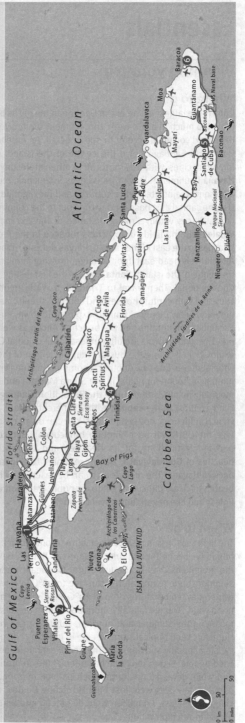

Essentials

Planning your trip

Where to go

Cuba is the largest island in the Caribbean (nearly as big as England) so don't expect to do too much in a two-week trip. If time is limited you should decide which end of the island you would prefer to see in detail. An excellent road runs all the way from Havana to Santiago down the centre of the island, passing through many of the important cities, with side roads off to other interesting places. The old colonial city of **Havana** is unmissable with its palaces, mansions, museums and plazas. There are also some major sites in the suburbs and the nightlife is best in music-mad Vedado. Use the capital as a base for day trips out to the countryside or the beaches along the coast. Places within striking distance of Havana include the lush green valley of **Viñales** and the fields of top-class tobacco in the Province of **Pinar del Río**, or the beaches to the east of the capital, **Playas del Este, Jibacoa** and the resort of **Varadero**. Alternatively head east into the sugar-growing farmlands and forested mountains in the centre of the island. **Santa Clara** is the last resting place of Che Guevara; visit the Che memorial. Then travel to **Trinidad**, a World Heritage Site with its single-storey 18th- and 19th-century houses and cobbled streets, making it a must-see on anyone's itinerary. Allow plenty of time to explore the town, the Valley of the Sugar Mills, the **Escambray mountains** and the beach at **Ancón** as well as enjoy the nightlife.

The central towns are often missed, but colonial **Camagüey** is well worth a day's exploration. If taking the bus or train the length of the island, make sure you break your journey in this city. Another recommended break in the journey is at **Bayamo**, the jumping-off point for hiking in the Sierra Maestra and a visit to Castro's atmospheric mountain headquarters during the Revolution. **Santiago de Cuba**, the second city, is a lively contrast to the capital, with a different culture, more Afro-Caribbean but with French influences, hotter and drier. You can do an easterly round trip to **Guantánamo** (see the US Naval base through binoculars), **Baracoa** (currently one of the most popular destinations for its beaches and laid-back lifestyle), **Holguín** and the beaches of **Guardalavaca**, before returning to Santiago through the mountains or back to Havana. The main towns can be reached by bus or train, but places off the beaten track are difficult to get to on public transport and it is advisable to rent a car unless you like negotiating travel by truck.

When to go

The high season is mid-December to mid-April, when there are more dry days and less humidity. It is hotter and drier in Santiago than in Havana, and wetter and cooler in the mountains than in the lowlands. Northeast trade winds temper the heat, but summer shade temperatures can rise to 33°C in Havana, and higher elsewhere. In winter, day temperatures drop to 20°C and there are a few cold days, 8°-10°C, with a north wind. Average rainfall is from 860 mm in the east to 1730 mm in Havana; it falls mostly in the summer and autumn, but there can be torrential rains at any time. Hurricanes and tropical storms begin in June and can go on until the end of November causing flooding and damage. The deadliest hurricane was Flora in 1963 which killed 1200 people. Since then Cuba has been at the forefront of hurricane defence systems and while devastating storms, such as Ivan in 2004, caused millions of dollars of damage, few lives were lost until Hurricane Dennis, in July 2005. Ten people were killed in the east, 1.5 million were displaced and tens of thousands of homes were ruined in 149 mph winds.

Useful websites

www.dtcuba.com Lots of details and addresses of hotels, tour companies, car hire, etc. They also have a weekly online newsletter, *Boletín Semanal DTC News*. There is a section, *Cocoweb*, where they will answer questions by email; extremely useful and recommended. www.cubaweb.cu News, travel, politics, business, internet and technology, health, science, art and culture, festivals and events. www.cubaism.com Cuba flights, hotels, travel and information, with offices in the UK, Canada and Havana, and a visitor centre in the Bacardí building.

www.travelnet.cu A Cuban travel agency in Spanish, Italian and English. www.cubalinda.com In English and run by former CIA agent, Philip Agee, particularly helpful for travellers from the USA. www.cubaccommodation.com Lists of *casas particulares, paladares*, bars, all with photos, general information. http://casaparticularcuba.org Details of hundreds of *casas particulares* throughout the country with links to other websites giving information on hotels and travel.

Language

Spanish, with local variants in pronunciation and vocabulary. English, German, Italian and French are spoken by those in the tourist industry. There are **language courses** available at the universities of Havana and Santiago. They generally start on the first Monday of the month and you study Monday to Friday 0900-1320. Different levels of study and Cuban cultural courses are also available. At the **Faculty of Modern Languages** at the **University of Havana**, latest prices are US$200 for two weeks. Contact Tamara Proenza Díaz MSc, Calle J 556, entre 25 y 27, Vedado, T7-8324245, www.uh.cu.dpg@uh.cu. Two-week Spanish courses with Cuban dance and a cultural programme are offered by **Càlédöñiâ Languages Abroad** ① *The Clockhouse, Bonnington Mill, 72 New Haven Rd, Edinburgh EH6 5QG Scotland, T0131-6217721, www.caledonialanguages.co.uk*. Their Cuban Summer School in Santiago is timed to coincide with Carnival in July.

Before you travel

Visas and immigration

Visitors from the majority of countries need only a **passport**, return ticket and 30-day **tourist card** to enter Cuba, as long as they are going solely for tourist purposes. Tourist cards may be obtained from Cuban embassies, consulates, airlines, or approved travel agents (price in the UK £20 – agencies sometimes charge more – some other countries US$20-35). You have to fill in an application form, photocopy the main pages of your passport (valid for more than six months after departure from Cuba), submit confirmation of your accommodation booking and your return or onward flight ticket. Immigration in Havana Airport will only give you 30 days on your tourist card, but you can get it extended for a further 30 days at **Immigration** in Nuevo Vedado, ① *Factor esq Final, open 0830-1200*. Go early, it gets busy and there are queues.

The **US** government does not normally permit its citizens to visit Cuba. US citizens should have a US licence to engage in any transactions related to travel to Cuba, but tourist or business travel are not licensable, even through a third country such as Mexico or Canada. For further information on entry to Cuba from the USA and customs requirements, US travellers should contact the **Cuban Interests Section**, an office of the Cuban government ① *2630 16th St NW, Washington DC 20009, T202-7978518*. Many travellers conceal their tracks by going via Mexico, the Bahamas, or Canada, when only the tourist card is stamped, not the passport. On your return be careful to destroy any evidence of having been in Cuba as US Immigration authorities frequently stop people at the border and threaten them with massive fines. A useful website for information and advice is at www.cubalinda.com.

Austria Himmelhofgasse 40 A-C, A-1130, Vienna, T43-1-8778198/8778159, F8777703.

Canada 388 Main St, Ottawa, Ontario, K1S 1E3, T1-613-5630141, embacuba@embacuba.ca.

France 16 rue de Presles 75015, Paris, T33-1-45675535, F45658092.

Germany Stavangerstraße 20, 10439 Berlin, T049-30-91611811, embacuba-berlin@t.online.de.

Italy Via Licinia No 7, 00153, Rome, T39-06-5742347/5755984, F5745445.

Netherlands Scheveningseweg 9, 2517 KS The Hague, T31-70-3606061, F3647586.

Portugal Rua Pero Da Covilha No 14, Restelo, 1400, Lisbon, T351-1-3015318, F3011895.

South Africa 45 Mackenzie St, Brooklyn 0181, Pretoria, PO Box 11605, Hatfield 0028, T27-12-3462215, F3462216.

Spain Paseo de La Habana No 194 entre Calle de la Macarena y Rodríguez, Pinilla, 28036, Madrid, T34-91-3592500, F3596145.

Sweden Sturevägen 9, 182 73 Stocksund, Stockholm, T46-8-6630850, F6611418.

Switzerland Gesellsschaftsstrasse 8, CP 5275, 30112, Berne, T41-31-3022111/3029830 (tourist office), F3022111.

UK 167 High Holborn, London WC1 6PA, T44-0207-2402488/8367886, F78362602.

Duty-free allowance Personal baggage and articles for personal use are allowed in free of duty; so are one carton of cigarettes and two bottles of alcoholic drinks. Visitors importing new goods worth between US$100 and US$1000 will be charged 100% duty, subject to a limit of two items a year. No duty is payable on goods valued at under US$100. You may take in up to 10 kg of medicine. It is prohibited to bring in fresh fruit and vegetables. On departure you may take out tobacco worth US$2000 with a receipt, or only 23 cigars without a receipt, up to six bottles of rum and personal jewellery. To take out works of art you must have permission from the Registro Nacional de Bienes Culturales de la Dirección de Patrimonio del Ministerio de Cultura. More information is available at www.aduana.islagrande.com.

What to take

Bring all medicines you might need as they can be difficult to find. Even painkillers are in very short supply. Many other things are scarce or unobtainable in Cuba, so take in everything you are likely to need other than food: razor blades; medicines and pills; heavy-duty insect repellent; strong sun protection and after-sun preparations; toilet paper; tampons; disposable nappies; photographic supplies; torch and batteries.

Insurance

Asistur ① *Paseo del Prado, entre Colón y Trocadero, Habana Vieja, for 24-hour service T7-8668527,* linked to overseas insurance companies, can help with emergency hospital treatment, robbery, direct transfer of funds to Cuba.

Money

Currency Cuba operates a dual currency system with a domestic peso and a convertible peso. The ***peso cubano*** (CP$) has notes for 1, 3, 5, 10, 20, 50 and 100 pesos, and coins for 5, 20 and 40 centavos and 1 peso. You must have a supply of coins if you want to use the local town buses (20 or 40 centavos). The 20 centavo coin is called a *peseta*. Cubans are paid in *pesos cubanos* and pay for most of their goods in the same currency. The ***peso convertible*** (CUC$) has a different set of notes and coins. It is fully exchangeable with authorized hard currencies such as euros, sterling and Canadian dollars. Foreigners are expected to pay for their accommodation, meals, transport and other items with the *peso convertible*. In some tourist enclaves, such as Varadero, Guadalavaca or the cays, the euro is accepted as well. Remember to spend or exchange any *pesos convertibles* before you leave as they are worthless outside Cuba.

Exchange In 2004 Cuba introduced a 10% tax on exchange transactions involving the US dollar and in April 2005 an 8% revaluation/tax was introduced for all currencies such as the euro, sterling or the Canadian dollar. While the peso convertible was formerly fixed at US$1 = CUC$1, you now get 18% less when you exchange dollars and 8% less when you exchange euros etc. There are **banks** and CADECAS (*casas de cambio*) for changing money. The exchange rate at official *casas de cambio* fluctuates around 24 *pesos cubanos* (CP$) to the *peso convertible* (CUC$). There is no black market. Food in the markets (*agromercados*), at street stalls and on trains, as well as books and popular cigarettes (but not in every shop), can be bought in *pesos cubanos*. You will need *pesos cubanos* for the toilet, rural trains, trucks, food at roadside *cafeterías* during a journey and drinks and snacks for a bus or train journey. Visitors on pre-paid package tours do not need *pesos cubanos*. Euros are accepted in Varadero, Cayo Coco, Cayo Largo, Cayo Santa María and at El Colony, Isla de la Juventud. **Traveller's cheques** expressed in US or Canadian dollars, euros or sterling are valid. Traveller's cheques issued on US bank paper are not accepted. Commission ranges from 3-5%. Don't enter the place or date when signing cheques, or they may be refused.

Credit cards The following credit cards are acceptable in most places: **Visa, MasterCard, Access, Diners, Banamex** (Mexican) and **Carnet**. No US credit cards are accepted so a Visa card issued in the USA will not be accepted. This includes, for example, a Virgin MasterCard issued by MBNA. **American Express**, no matter where issued, is unacceptable. You can obtain cash advances with a credit card at branches of the **Banco Financiero Internacional** and several other banks, but it is best to bring plenty of cash as there will often be no other way of paying for what you need. You will need to show your passport. Most financial institutions require a US$100 minimum withdrawal. It is usually quicker and easier to queue at a bank to get a cash advance on your credit card than to trail around looking for a working ATM. There are no toll free numbers to call if your card is stolen, so bring a number from home for you to call. If you get really stuck and need money sent urgently to Cuba, you can get it transferred from any major commercial bank abroad direct to **Asistur** (see page 70) for a 10% commission.

Getting there

Air

The frequency of **scheduled** flights depends on the season, with twice-weekly flights in the winter reduced to once a week/month in the summer. Most international flights come in to Havana, but the international airports of Varadero, Holguín (for Guardalavaca beaches), Santiago de Cuba, Ciego de Avila (for Cayo Coco), Cayo Largo, Santa Clara (for Cayo Santa María) and Camagüey (for Santa Lucía beaches) also receive flights. The state airline, **Cubana de Aviación** (www.cubana.cu), flies to Europe, Canada, Central and South America and to many islands in the Caribbean. It is cheaper than competitors on the same routes but the service is worse, seats are cramped and some travel agents do not recommend it. Scheduled flights are run by operators such as **Virgin Atlantic, Air France, Air Jamaica, Iberia, Air Europa, Spanair, Martinair, LTU, Condor** and **Aeroflot** from Europe, **Mexicana, Aerocaribe, Aeropostal, Lacsa, Tame, Copa** and **Lan Chile** from Latin America, **AeroCaribbean** and **Air Jamaica** from the Caribbean. There are **charters** from London, Manchester, Brussels, Frankfurt, Toronto, Vancouver, Montréal, Quebec, Halifax, Buenos Aires, Cancún and other cities to all the international airports in Cuba, and between Santiago de Cuba and Montego Bay, Jamaica. Regular charters also fly between Cayo Largo and Grand Cayman and occasional charters between Providenciales, Turks and Caicos Islands and Santiago de Cuba. The Cuban air charter line **AeroCaribbean** has an arrangement

⁞ Touching down

Hours of business
Banks 0830-1200, 1330-1500
Mon-Fri.
Government offices Mon-Fri
0830-1230, 1330-1730. Some offices
open on Sat morning.
Shops 0830-1800 Mon-Sat
0900-1400 Sun. Hotel tourist shops
open 1000-1800 or 1900.
Country code +53.

Official time Eastern Standard
Time, 5 hrs behind GMT; Daylight
Saving Time, 4 hrs behind GMT.
Voltage 110 Volts, 3 phase 60
cycles, AC. Plugs are usually of the
American type.
Weights and measures The
metric system is compulsory, but
exists side by side with American
and old Spanish systems.

with **Bahamasair** for a (nearly) daily service Miami-Nassau-Havana, changing planes
in Nassau; the Cuban tourist agency **Amistur** organizes the service. **AeroCaribbean**
flies from Montego Bay, Santo Domingo and Port-au-Prince, Haiti, to Santiago.

Touching down

Airport information

On arrival Immigration can be very slow if you come off a busy **Iberia** DC10 flight but
speedy off smaller **Cubana** aircraft. Cuba has several airports classified as
international, but only Havana is of any size. Havana now has three terminals, the
third and newest one being for international flights, with exchange facilities, snack
bars, shops, etc. There is an ATM on the ground (arrivals) floor of Terminal 3.

On departure Remember to reconfirm your onward or return flight 48 hours before
departure, otherwise you will lose your reservation. The airport departure tax is
CUC$25. The seating in Havana Airport is uncomfortable. The restaurant is poor to
awful, but this will be your last chance to hear a live Cuban band while eating. The
selection of shops is limited but there is lots of rum, cigars and coffee, a few books
and magazines on sale. It is better to buy before you get to the airport, particularly if
there is a certain brand of cigar or rum which you want. The specialist cigar shops
have more knowledgeable staff and a superior range of stock.

Tourist information

A network of tourist information offices in Havana called **Infotur** (www.infotur.cu) can
be found in Old Havana, at Obispo y San Ignacio, T7-863 6884, Obispo y Bernaza,
T7-866 3333, and the Terminal de Cruceros. In Playa at Av 5 y 112, T7-204 7036. At the
airport at Terminal 1, T7-558734, Terminal 2, T7-558733, and Terminal 3, T7-266 4094.
There is also an office serving the Playas del Este, at Av Las Terrazas entre 11 y 12,
Santa María del Mar, T7-971261, Monday-Saturday 0830-1630.

Local tours Several state-owned tour companies offer day trips or excursion
packages including accommodation to many parts of the island, as well as tours of
colonial and modern Havana. Examples (from Havana, one day, except where
indicated): **Viñales**, including tobacco and rum factories,

⁞ For Havana tour
operators, see page 108.

CUC$44; **Guamá**, CUC$44; **Cayo Coco** (by air), CUC$143
overnight; **Soroa**, CUC$29; **Varadero** CUC$35 without lunch;
Cayo Largo (by air), CUC$119 daytrip, CUC$170 overnight all-inclusive;
Cienfuegos-Trinidad overnight CUC$115; **Santiago de Cuba** (by air) and **Baracoa**,
CUC$159 including one night's accommodation, recommended, you see a lot and

cover a lot of ground in two days. Tours can also be taken from any beach resort. Guides speak European languages; the tours are generally recommended as well organized and good value. Actual departure depends on a minimum number of passengers (usually six). Always ask the organizers when they will know if the trip is on or what the real departure time will be. Lunch is usually a poor-quality set meal.

Sex tourism Cuba had a reputation for prostitution before the Revolution and after a gap of some decades it has resurfaced. Behind every girl there is a pimp. In 2001 a German tourist was murdered by a pimp in Santiago for not paying the girl US$20 for sex. Despite government crackdowns and increased penalties, everything is available for both sexes if you know where to look. Be warned, you are likely to be fleeced. The age of consent is 18 in Cuba, so if you are introduced to a young girl you are in danger of being led into a blackmail trap. Hotels are not allowed to let Cubans enter the premises in the company of foreigners, so sexual encounters now often take place in *casas particulares*, private homes where there is little security and lots of risk. If you or your travelling companion are dark skinned, you may suffer from the exclusion policy in hotels as officials will assume he/she is Cuban until proved otherwise. If you are a man out alone at night in Havana you will find the market very active and you will be tugged at frequently, mostly by females.

Cubans who offer their services (whether sexual or otherwise) in return for dollars are known as jineteros, or jineteras ('jockeys', because they 'ride on the back' of the tourists).

Safety

In general the Cuban people are very hospitable but the crime rate is increasing and certain precautions should be taken. Visitors should never lose sight of their luggage or leave valuables in hotel rooms (most hotels have safes). Do not leave your things on the beach when swimming. Guard your camera closely. Pickpocketing and bag-snatching are quite common in Havana and Santiago. It is best to carry valuables under your clothing. Street lighting is poor so care is needed. Some people recommend walking in the middle of the street. Muggings in Havana have been reported to us, particularly in the dark, narrow streets of Chinatown at night. You must carry your passport and tourist visa everywhere. Never leave it in Havana with a *casa particular* owner while you visit other areas, this is a scam to get you to return to their house. Report all thefts to the police and insist on a crime report. You may get one, you may not, it depends on the officer. Some travellers report extreme helpfulness, while others say that it was like banging your head against a brick wall.

Getting around

Air

There are **Cubana de Aviación** services from Havana to most of the main towns: Camagüey, Holguín, Trinidad, Baracoa, Guantánamo, Manzanillo, Moa, Nueva Gerona/Isla de Juventud, Bayamo, Ciego de Avila, Las Tunas, Santa Clara, Santiago, Cayo Largo, Cayo Coco, Varadero, all have airports. Some places with airstrips are reached by **Aerotaxi**. Havana to Santiago costs CUC$108 one way; it is advisable to prebook flights at home as demand is very heavy, although you can get flights from hotel tour desks as part of a package. It is difficult to book flights from one city to another when you are not at the point of departure, except from Havana; the computers are not able to cope. Delays are common. **Cubana** flights are very cold, take warm clothes and possibly some food for a long flight. **Aerotaxi** flights can also be cold; they are flying buses and you often get wooden bench seating in an old Soviet aircraft.

For people who really want to explore the country in depth and independently, cycling is excellent, although you should bring your own bike and spare parts. **Iberia** and **Cubana** airlines accept bicycles as normal luggage as long as you do not take more than 20 kg, but some charters, such as **Martinair**, charge extra. A good-quality bicycle is essential if you are going to spend many hours in the saddle. However, it does not have to be very sophisticated; most of Cuba is flat, the road network is good and there is little traffic. In cities there are *parqueos bicicletas*, where you can store your bike while walking around. Cycling can get very hot, so try to do long distances early in the morning.

Organized cycling tours
Blazing Saddles Travels, in the UK, T020-84240483, saddles100@aol.com. Also offers bike hire, ATB (mountain bikes) with 21 gears and pannier rack, CUC$12/day including puncture repair kit for a pre-arranged hire period. The bikes will be delivered to your hotel or *casa particular*. **Havanatour UK**, 3 Wyllyots Pl, Potters Bar, Herts EN6 2JD, T01707-646463, F01707-663139.
Fietsvakantiewinkel, Spoorlaan 19, 3445 AE

Woerden, Holland, T31-3480-21844, F31-3480-23839.
You may also be able to join a group of Cuban bikers (mostly English-speaking) through the **Club Nacional de Cicloturismo** (National Bike Club), Transnico Internacional, Lonja del Comercio Oficina 6D-E, Plaza San Francisco, La Habana Vieja, T7-8669944, www.cubafortravel.com, contact Johan Dorssemont, johan@transnico.co.cu. They run tours of 1-28 days in all parts of the country, some with political themes.

Bus

Local The local word for bus is *guagua*. In Havana there are huge double-jointed buses pulled by a truck, called *camellos* (camels) because of their shape, also irreverently known as 'Saturday night at the cinema' because they are full of 'sex, crime and alcohol'. In the rush hours they are filled to more than capacity, making it hard to get off if you have managed to get on. There are plans to buy 400 articulated buses and smaller urban transit buses in 2007 to replace the *camellos*. These more modern vehicles will be more comfortable and, it is hoped, less prone to pickpocketing and other unsavoury behaviour on board. The urban bus fare throughout Cuba is 20 centavos for *camellos* and 40 centavos for all others; it helps to have the exact fare.

Long distance The purchase in 2006 of hundreds of Chinese a/c buses with TVs and good suspension have improved inter-city travel. For bus transport to other provinces from Havana there are two companies theoretically offering services to foreigners. The first is **Astro** ① *ticket office in the Terminal de Omnibus Nacional, Boyeros y 19 de Mayo (third left via 19 de Mayo entrance), T7-703397, open 24 hrs*. You don't have to book in advance but it is wiser to do so. Foreigners are encouraged to use **Víazul (Viajes Azul)** ① *Av 26 y Zoológico, Nuevo Vedado, T7-8811413, www.viazul.cu, 0900- 2300*. You have to pay in *pesos convertibles*, it is more expensive than Astro, and you will travel with other foreigners, but it is an efficient, punctual and comfortable service. The terminal is a long way from the centre so take a taxi. In other cities Víazul and Astro use the same bus terminal. In 2007 **Víazul's** routes were: Havana-Santiago, Havana-Varadero, Havana-Viñales, Havana-Holguín, Havana-Trinidad, Varadero-Trinidad, Varadero-Santiago, Trinidad-Santiago and Baracoa-Santiago, stopping at all major towns along the way. More destinations and routes are being added. There is a weight limit for luggage of 20 kg on all long-distance bus journeys and the bus-hoverfoil to Isla de la Juventud.

Car

Car hire Rental companies are at the airport and most large hotels. Minimum CUC$40 a day (or CUC$50 for air conditioning) with limited mileage of 100 km a day, and CUC$8-20 a day optional insurance, or CUC$50-88 per day unlimited mileage; cheaper rates over seven days. Credit cards accepted for the rental, or cash or TCs paid in advance, guarantee of CUC$200-250 required; you must also present your passport and home driving licence. In practice, you may find car hire rates prohibitively expensive when small cars are 'unavailable' and a four-door sedan at CUC$93, unlimited km, insurance included, is your only option. It pays to shop around, even between offices of the same company. Cubans are not allowed to hire cars (although they may drive them), so even if you have organized a local driver you will have to show a foreign driving licence. If you want to drive from Havana to Santiago and return by air, try **Havanautos**, www.havanautos.cubaweb.cu. They will charge at least CUC$80 to return the car to Havana, but most companies will not even consider it. **Vía Rent-a-Car (Gaviota)**, www.gaviota.cubaweb.cu, charges CUC$160, calculated at CUC$0.18 per km on a distance of 884 km from Santiago to Havana, but this is reduced to CUC$0.09 if the car is hired for more than 15 days. If you hire in Havana and want to drop off the car at the airport, companies will charge you extra, around CUC$10, although this is sometimes waived if you bargain hard. Check what is required concerning fuel, you don't always have to leave the tank full, but make sure the tank is really full when you start. Fly-and-drive packages can be booked from abroad through **Cubacar**, part of the Grupo Cubanacán, www.cubacar.cubaweb.cu, who have a wide range of jeeps and cars all over the country and can even arrange a driver, pmando@cubacar.cha.cyt.cu. Watch out for theft of the radio and spare tyre; you will have to pay about CUC$350 if stolen unless you take out the costly extra insurance. Check the state of the tyres, which are usually in terrible condition and you can expect lots of punctures. Always remember to carry the rental agreement and your driving licence with you. Otherwise, you face an on-the-spot CUC$30 fine if you are stopped by the traffic police and a fine by the hire company when you return the vehicle. There is more information at www.dtcuba.com. Rental cars are likely to be stopped by the police for any minor traffic violation and fined CUC$30. Ask for evidence of the offence, they will often let you go if they cannot prove you are at fault. **Moped** rental at resorts is around CUC$8-10 per hour, cheaper for longer, CUC$25-30 per day, CUC$80 per week.

Taxi

There are three types of taxi: tourist taxis, Cuban taxis and private taxis (*particulares*). With dollar tourist taxis you pay for the distance, not for waiting time. On short routes, fares are metered. From the airport to Havana (depending on destination) costs CUC$12-18 with **Panataxi**, to Playas del Este CUC$30, to Varadero CUC$90. Cuban taxis, or *colectivos*, also operate on fixed routes and pick you up only if you know where to stand for certain destinations. Travelling on them is an adventure and a complicated cultural experience. Cubans are not allowed to carry foreigners in their vehicles, but they do; private taxis, *particulares*, are considerably cheaper than other taxis, for example airport to Havana centre CUC$8-12, from Santiago to the airport CUC$5. A *particular* who pays his tax will usually display a 'taxi' sign, which can be a hand-written piece of board, but have a private registration plate. Some have meters, in others you have to negotiate a price. If not metered, 10 km should cost around CUC$5. For long distances you can negotiate with official taxis as well as *particulares*, and the price should be around CUC$10 per hour. As a general rule, the cost will depend on the quality of your Spanish and how well you know the area.

Train

Travel between provinces is usually booked solid several days or weeks in advance and foreigners are frequently turned away. If you are on a short trip you may do better to go by **Víazul** bus or on a tour with excursions. Long delays and breakdowns must be expected. Be at the station at least one hour before the scheduled departure time.

There is a ticket office in every station. Alternatively, the tourist desks in some of the larger hotels sell train tickets. Long-distance trains allow only seated passengers, they are spacious and comfortable, but extremely cold unless the air-conditioning is broken, so take warm clothes. A torch is useful for the toilet. All carriages are smoking areas. Bicycles can be carried as an express item only and often cost more than the fare for a person. Food service is inadequate so it is advisable to take food with you; if you are 15-16 hours late you will be glad you took snacks and drinks. One hundred new Chinese locomotives are being purchased in 2007-2009, which should improve services. ▶▶ See also Transport, page 110.

Sleeping

Casas particulares

Tourists to Cuba often stay in rooms or apartments in private houses, known as *casas particulares*. Cubans are allowed to rent out only two rooms sleeping two people plus one child in each. Rates in private houses (CUC$15-35 per night) are per room, not per person. You pay in *pesos convertibles* for accommodation and food, but prices are considerably less than in hotels while the service is more friendly and the food better quality and more plentiful. The *casas* must be registered to pay taxes for whatever services they offer. All legal *casas particulares* should have a yellow registration book you have to sign, and a sticker on their door of two chevrons on a white background with *Arrendador Inscripto* written across. There are thousands of *casas particulares* but only 40% of them are licensed. Taxes and licences are high at CUC$130-200 per room per month, depending on the region (Vedado is one of the highest), plus 10% of earnings to be paid at the end of each year, so profit margins are tight. Cubans have to buy another licence, CUC$30 per month, so that they can offer food (*servicios gastronómicos*), whether they want to or not. Private homes vary and can be extremely comfortable or very basic. Because of shortages things often don't work, there may be cold water only, once a day, and the lights often go off. A torch is useful. Rates can often be bargained down if you go directly to the owners, negotiate a package of bed, breakfast and evening meal, or stay for several nights. The owners pay CUC$5 per night per room for each client brought to them by a tout (who does not pay taxes) or recommended by another *casa* owner; this will inevitably end up on your bill. If you are given a business card for a *casa* by someone selling bus tickets or a taxi driver, they will get their commission if you stay at that *casa*. All *casa* owners have an address book full of owners in other towns; they will happily ring up a 'friend' and book a room for you. This may be a useful service but you will pay an extra CUC$5 in commission.

Hotels

All hotels are owned by the government, solely or in joint ventures with foreign partners. Many new hotels have been built since 1990 and these are mostly four star, either in Havana or on the beach in Varadero, Guardalavaca or the north coast cays. Some of the nicest places to stay are in recently renovated colonial mansions converted to boutique hotels in city centres. These can be found in Old Havana and in the old provincial towns such as Baracoa, Bayamo, Holguín or Remedios. The older hotels built in the Soviet era are mostly dated and not very comfortable, although there are plans to renovate them. These were often built on the edge of town and are not very convenient. A three-star hotel costs CUC$30-50 bed and breakfast in high season, CUC$25-35 in low season, while a four-star hotel will charge CUC$80-90 and CUC$60-70 respectively. In remote beach resorts the hotels are usually all-inclusive.

Eating

Food

State-owned 'dollar' restaurants, recognizable by the credit card stickers on the door, serve meals for about CUC$10-25. Generally, although restaurants have improved in the last few years, the food in Cuba is not very exciting. There is little variety in the menu and menu items are frequently unavailable. Always check restaurant prices in advance and then your bill. Discrepancies occur in both the state and private sector. At the cheap end of the market you can expect poor quality, limited availability of ingredients and disinterested staff. For a cheap meal you are better off trying the Cuban version of fast-food restaurants, such as **El Rápido**, or **Burgui**, or one of **Cubatur**'s *cafeterías*. As well as chicken and chips or burgers, they offer sandwiches: cheese, ham, or cheese and ham. A sandwich in a restaurant or bar in Havana costs around CUC$3, a coffee CUC$1. In a provincial town you can pay as little as CUC$2 for a sandwich and beer for lunch. All towns and cities have (Cuban) peso street stalls for sandwiches, pizza and snacks.

Paladares are private houses operating as restaurants, licensed and taxed and limited to 12 chairs. A three-course meal in Havana is CUC$15-25 per person, less than that outside the capital. If someone guides you to a *paladar* he will expect a commission, so you end up paying more for your food. The cheapest way of getting a decent meal is by eating in a *casa particular*. This is generally of excellent quality in plentiful, even vast, portions, with the advantage that they will cook whatever you want. They usually charge CUC$5-7 for a meal, chicken and pork are cheaper than fish, while some *casa* owners seem to have access to all sorts of delicacies (illegal of course). Breakfast is usually CUC$2-3 and far better value than in a state hotel. You will get fresher food in a *casa particular* than in a restaurant or *paladar*, both of which have the reputation of recycling meals and reheating leftovers.

For vegetarians the choice is very limited, normally only cheese sandwiches, spaghetti, pizzas, salads, bananas and omelettes. Even beans (and *congrís*, see below) are usually cooked with meat or in meat fat. If you are staying at a *casa particular* licensed to serve food, or eating in a *paladar*, they will usually prepare meatless meals for you with advance warning. Always ask for beans to be cooked in vegetable oil.

The national dish is *congrís* (rice mixed with black beans), roast pork and yucca or fried plantain. Rice with kidney beans is known as *moros y cristianos*. Pork is traditionally eaten for the New Year celebrations. Seafood is largely found in the export and tourist markets. Most food is fried and can often be greasy and bland. Spices and herbs are not commonly used and Cubans limit their flavourings to onions and garlic. Salads are mixed, slightly pickled vegetables and not to everyone's taste. Cuba's range of tropical fruit and vegetables is magnificent. At the right time of year there will be a glut of avocados, mangoes, guavas or papaya. Cubans are hooked on ice cream, although it usually only comes in vanilla, strawberry or chocolate flavours. The ice cream parlour, **Coppelia**, can be found in every town of any size.

Drink

Rum is the national drink and all cocktails are rum based. There are several brand names and each has a variety of ages, so you have plenty of choice. The locally grown **coffee** is good, although hotels often manage to make it undrinkable in the mornings. The most widely available **beer** throughout the island is *Cristal*, made by Cervecería Mayabe, in Holguín. From the same brewery is *Mayabe*, also popular, and *Bucanero*. *Tínima* is from Camagüey. *Hatuey*, made in Havana, is named after an Indian chief ruling when the Spanish arrived. Cuba now also produces **wines** under the *Soroa* label, grown and produced in Pinar del Río, but you are better off buying something imported.

Entertainment

Of all the islands in the Caribbean, Cuba has the best and most varied nightlife with a great music scene including Latin, jazz, folk and rock. There are theatres for drama and ballet, concert halls for classical music or touring bands, discos, nightclubs, bars, cinemas showing Cuban and foreign movies, and indoor and outdoor music venues around the country. Most of the action is concentrated in Havana, but every town has a *Casa de la Trova* for traditional music and a *Casa de la Cultura* for cultural events, art exhibitions and concerts, as well as a theatre and cinema in the larger towns. Santiago is no poor relation and has its own regional variations in music and culture.

♟ Smoking is banned in theatres, shops, buses, taxis and other enclosed public areas including restaurants and government offices.

Festivals and events

New Year is celebrated all over Cuba as the anniversary of the **Revolution**, so expect speeches as well as parties. Throughout the year there are lots of excuses for music and dancing in the street, washed down with quantities of rum and local food. Some towns even do it weekly, called a **Noche Cubana**. In contrast with other Latin American countries, there are no national religious festivals, although you will find some patron saints' days celebrated in churches (often linked to *Santería*) and Easter is an important time. Processions are usually limited to taking place within the church itself and not all round the streets of the town. **Christmas Day**, was reintroduced as a public holiday in 1997 (having been banned after the Revolution) prior to a visit from the Pope and has become a regular event with Christmas trees and tinsel, but a whole generation missed out on celebrating it and there is little awareness of what it signifies. Public holidays are political and historical events and are marked by speeches, rallies and other gatherings, often in each town's Plaza de la Revolución. **Carnival** has recently been resurrected, taking place in July in Santiago. Havana's Carnival (not such an exciting affair) is moved around a lot, sometimes August, sometimes October or November. These events are colourful, energetic and have a raw vibrancy. Parades are accompanied by music, drumming, dancing and competitions involving children and adults and requiring lots of stamina. There are many cultural and sporting festivals and events held throughout the year, see www.cubameeting.co.cu or www.loseventos.cu.

Jan New Year is celebrated around the country with great fanfare, largely because it coincides with **Liberation Day** (1 Jan, public holiday) marking the end of the Batista dictatorship. There is lots of music and dancing, outdoor discos and merriment, washed down with copious quantities of rum. **Birth of José Martí**, 1853 (28 Jan).

Feb Anniversary of Renewal of War of Independence, 1895 (24 Feb). The **Havana**

International Book Fair is held at **La Cabaña**; a commercial fair in new, purpose-built convention buildings. Look out for new book launches. Pedro Pérez Sarduy launched his novel, *The Maids of Havana*, there in 2002. Contact Iroel Sánchez, T7-8628091, presidencia@icl.cult.cu. The **Cigar Festival** is for true aficionados of *Habanos*. Held at the Palacio de las Convenciones, you can learn about the history of cigars and there are opportunities for visits to tobacco

● The family firm of Bacardí was the largest in Cuba for nearly 100 years. After the 1959
● Revolution, when the sugar industry and distilleries were taken over by the state, the family left the island and took the Bacardí name with them. The Bacardí rum, now found worldwide, is not distilled in Cuba.

plantations and cigar factories. Contact Silvia Hernández, T7-2040513, shernandez@habanos.cu.

Mar International Women's Day (8 Mar). Anniversary of 1957 **Attack on Presidential Palace in Havana** by a group of young revolutionaries (13 Mar). **Festival Internacional de la Trova 'Pepe Sánchez'** held at the **Casa de la Trova** in Santiago with concerts, roving musicians, conferences and other events, organized by the legendary Eliades Ochoa Bustamante, with the **Centro Provincial de la Música 'Miguel Matamoros'** and the **Centro Nacional de Música Popular**, www.loseventos.cu.

Apr Anniversary of defeat of mercenaries at **Bay of Pigs**, 1961 (19 Apr).

May May Day (1 May, public holiday). Huge parades in the Plaza de la Revolución and speeches. **May Theatre** every two years at the Casa de las Américas with workshops and performances. Contact Juan Mesa, T7-552706, teatro@casa.cult.cu.

Jun International Ernest Hemingway White Marlin Fishing Tournament is one of the major events at the Marina Hemingway. Contact José Miguel Díaz Escrich, T7-2046653, yachtclub@cnih.mh.cyt.cu. **International Boleros de Oro Festival** for aficionados of *boleros*, dedicated in 2004 to Brazil. Contact Dirección Promoción y Eventos UNEAC, T7-553113, www.uneac.com.

Jul Cuballet de Verano is a summer dance festival. Contact Lourdes Bermejo, T7-2650848, prodanza@cubarte.cult.cu. The **Festival del Caribe** is held in the first week of Jul in Santiago with theatre, dancing and conferences, continuing later in the month to coincide with the Moncada celebrations on 26 Jul. **Carnival** in Santiago (18-27 Jul) is a week- long musical extravaganza taking in the city's patron saint's day, 25 Jul, but it traditionally stops for **Revolution Day** (26 Jul, public holiday), a day of serious political celebrations. **Martyrs of the Revolution Day** (30 Jul).

Aug Que Siempre Brilla el Sol baseball tournament is always a popular event. Contact Jackeline, T7-2040945, agenciac2@cubadeportes.cu.

Sep International Blue Marlin Fishing Tournament at Marina Hemingway. The marina fills up with mostly US fishermen eager to pit their strength against marlin and their fellow competitors, with lots of après-fishing social events. Contact José Miguel Díaz Escrich, T7-2046653, yachtclub@cnih.mh.cyt.cu.

Oct Death of Che Guevara, 1967 (8 Oct). Beginning of War of Independence (10 Oct, public holiday). **Death of Camilo Cienfuegos**, 1959 (28 Oct). **Festival Internacional del Son 'Matamoros Son'** at Teatro Heredia, Santiago. Music and dancing to celebrate *son* and famous *soneros*. Contact Adalberto Alvarez Zayas, www.loseventos.cu. **Havana International Ballet Festival** held every other year in the second half of the month at the Gran Teatro, Teatro Nacional and Teatro Mella. Run by Alicia Alonso, head of the Cuban National Ballet, T7-8352948, bnc@cubarte.cult.cu. **Fiesta de la Cultura Iberoamericana**, in Holguín, celebrating all things Spanish and Latin American at the Casa de Iberoamérica. Contact Alexis Triana, www.loseventos.cu.

Nov Death by firing squad of 8 medical students by Spanish colonial government, 1871 (27 Nov). **International Tournament of Wahoo Fishing** at the Marina Hemingway. Contact José Miguel Díaz Escrich, T7-2046653, yachtclub@cnih.mh.cyt.cu. **Marabana**, Havana's marathon. Contact Mario Peláez Sosa, T7-2040945, agenciac@ cubadeportes.cu. For other events contact Jacqueline, agenciac2@ cubadeportes.cu. **Festival Internacional de Teatro** held at the university in Santiago. Contact Luisa García Miranda, www.loseventos.cu.

Dec Death of Antonio Maceo in battle, 1896 (7 Dec). **Christmas** (25 Dec, public holiday). **International Festival of New Latin American Cinema** shows prize-winning films (no subtitles) at cinemas around Havana. This is the foremost film festival in Latin America with the best of Cuban and Latin

American films along with documentaries and independent cinema from Europe and the USA. See the stars as well as the films, as the festival attracts big-name actors and directors. Contact Alfredo Guevara, head of the **Cuban Institute of Cinematographic Art and Industry** (ICAIC), T7-552854, www.habanafilmfestival.com. **International Jazz Plaza Festival** follows the film festival every other year at theatres and the Casa de la Cultura de Plaza. It is one of the world's major jazz festivals with the best of Cuban and international jazz. Venues for jazz at the festival and at other times are La Casa de la Música Playa, the theatres Amadeo Roldán, Nacional and Mella, the Jazz Café, La Zorra y el Cuervo and Jazz Club O'Farrell. Information from the **Instituto de la Música**, 15 452 entre E y F, T8323503-6, ask for schedule from Manuel Sanoja, msanoja@icm.cu or roger@icm.cu. There are masterclasses and workshops available (contact Alfredo Muñoz, T8327920, cnmc13@cubarte.cult.cu) and the event is organized by Grammy winner Jesús 'Chucho' Valdés. **Happy End of Year Regatta** at the Marina Hemingway for 3 days with social events that always accompany the racing fraternity. Contact José Miguel Díaz Escrich, T7-2046653, yachtclub@cnih.mh.cyt.cu.

Shopping

Compared with much of Latin America, Cuba is expensive for the tourist, but compared with many Caribbean islands it is not. Shopping centres are springing up and the materialist culture is creeping in.

There is very little you can buy in *pesos cubanos* apart from some food in some areas. Shoes, clothing, cosmetics, toiletries, camera film, imported food and drink are all available in *pesos convertibles*. Throughout the country, dollar stores (selling imported goods priced in *pesos cubanos*) are surprisingly busy, despite the small proportion of the population having direct access to foreign currency. All bags and receipts are checked on leaving a dollar store.

The main souvenirs to take home with you have to be **rum**, **cigars** and maybe **coffee**. The street price of a bottle of rum ranges from CUC$2-8 depending on its age. Cigars can cost whatever you are prepared to pay, but they are still the best in the world. Remember that all the best tobacco leaves go into cigar making rather than cigarettes. Make sure you buy the best to take home and don't get tricked into buying fakes, you may not get them through customs. You are only allowed to take 23 cigars out of the country without a receipt. If you are buying any souvenirs to take home, remember to keep the official receipt in case you have to show it at customs on departure.

Handicrafts are now being developed for the tourist market and there are *artesanía* markets in Havana and Varadero which hold an overwhelming amount of stock. Wooden carvings, inlaid wooden boxes for cigars, jewellery, key rings, baseball bats, model sailing ships, ceramics, Che Guevara hats and innumerable T-shirts will be offered to you. There is a considerable amount of **art work** of varying degrees of worth, but you may pick up a bargain. If you are a serious collector, skip the markets and go straight to the galleries in Havana. Taking art out of the country requires a special licence (see Shopping, page 106).

Sport and activities

Trekking, **hiking**, **rafting** and **birdwatching** are elements of adventure or nature travel which are still in their infancy in Cuba but are sure to be heavily promoted in the near future. The island's plentiful fauna and flora, its mountains, cays and wetlands, and its expanding system of national parks and other protected areas, are perfect for getting close to nature. Hunting and sport fishing are available, but in the last few scuba diving. The state travel agencies' specialist operations offer organized tours, with expert staff on hand to advise on biology, botany or forestry.

Cycling

Cuba has an extensive network of tarmac and concrete roads, covering nearly 17,600 km. This impressive infrastructure means that nearly all the country is accessible to the cyclist, and there are some dramatic roads to climb and descend. There is total freedom of movement and the rewards can be immense. However, many of the roads are in poor condition, particularly in the rural areas. See page 74.

Diving

Cuba's marine environment is pristine compared with many Caribbean islands. The majority of coral reefs are healthy and teeming with assorted marine life. The government has established a marine park around the **Isla de la Juventud** and much marine life is protected around the entire island, including turtles, the manatee and coral. There are three main marine platforms, the **Archipiélago del Rey** (Sabana-Camagüey), the **Archipiélago de la Reina** and the **Archipiélago de los Canarreos**. The first has the greatest diversity of marine species and is being explored and classified with the aim of making it a protected zone. There are believed to be some 900 species of fish, 1400 species of mollusc, 60 species of coral, 1100 species of crustacean, 67 species of shark and ray and four types of marine turtles around the island, as well as the manatee.

The main dive areas are Isla de la Juventud, Varadero, Faro de Luna, María La Gorda, Santa Lucía and Santiago de Cuba.

Fishing

Cuba has been a fisherman's dream for many decades, not only for its deep-sea fishing, popularized by Ernest Hemingway, but also for its freshwater fishing in the many lakes and reservoirs spread around the island. **Freshwater fishing** is mostly for the largemouth bass (*trucha*), which grow to a great size in the Cuban lakes. **Horizontes** is the travel company to contact for fishing packages, which can be arranged all year round. The main places are Maspotón, in Pinar del Río; Laguna del Tesoro in the Ciénaga de Zapata; Presa Alacranes in Villa Clara province; Presa Zaza, in Sancti Spíritus and Lago La Redonda, near Morón in Ciego de Avila province. **Deep-sea fishing** can be organized at most marinas around the island, although most of the tournaments and the best facilities are at the Marina Hemingway, just west of Havana. The waters are home to marlin, swordfish, tarpon, sawfish, yellowfin tuna, dorado, wahoo, shark and a host of others. Varadero is a good point from which to go fishing and take advantage of the Gulf Stream which flows between Key West in Florida and Cuba, but records have been broken all along the northern coast in the cays of the Archipiélago de Sabana and the Archipiélago de Camagüey. There is also good fishing off the south coast around the Isla de la Juventud and Cayo Largo. **Bonefishing** is best done off the south coast in the Archipiélago de los Jardines de la Reina, or off Cayo Largo.

Equipment can be hired, but serious fishermen will prefer to bring their own and large quantities of insect repellent.

Sailing

There are marinas around the country offering moorings, boat rental and a variety of services, see www.cubanacan.cu. The largest is the Marina Hemingway in Havana, see page 95. Before arriving in Cuban territorial waters (12 nautical miles from the island's platform), you should communicate with port authorities on channel HF (SSB) 2760 or VFH 68 and 16 (National Coastal Network) and 2790 or VHF 19A (Tourist Network). Not many 'yachties' (people who live and travel on their own boats) visit the island because of the political difficulties between Cuba and the USA. The US administration forbids any vessel, such as a cruise ship, cargo ship or yacht from calling at a US port if it has stopped in Cuba. This effectively prohibits anyone sailing from the US eastern seaboard calling in at a Cuban port on their way south through the Caribbean islands, or vice versa. It is better to rent a bareboat yacht from a Cuban marina and sail around the island, rather than include it in a Caribbean itinerary. Recommended is *The Cruising Guide to Cuba*, by Simon Charles (Cruising Guide Publications, 1017, Dunedin, FL 34697-1017, USA, T813-7335322, F813-7348179) before embarking.

Hiking

The three main mountain ranges are excellent for hill walking in a wide range of tropical vegetation, where many national parks are being established and trails demarcated. The highest peaks are in the **Sierra Maestra** in the east, where there are also many historical landmarks associated with the Wars of Independence and the Revolution. Unfortunately this area is often closed off for security reasons, so you should check locally before setting out. In any case you will need a guide to accompany you in any National Park. A three-day walk will take you from Alto del Naranjo up the island's highest peak, **Pico Turquino**, and down to the Caribbean coast at Las Cuevas, giving you fantastic views of the mountains and the coastline. The **Sierra del Escambray**, in the centre of the island, is conveniently located just north of the best-preserved colonial city, Trinidad, and there are some lovely walks in the hills, along trails beside rivers, waterfalls and caves. The mountains of the west of the island, the **Sierra del Rosario** and the **Sierra de los Organos**, have some of the most unusual geological features, notably the large number of caves and the limestone *mogotes* – straight sided, flat-topped hills – rising from the midst of tobacco fields and looking almost Chinese, particularly in the early morning mist.

Health

Cuba has a high-quality national health service and is one of the healthiest countries in Latin America and the Caribbean. There are international clinics in tourist areas (credit cards accepted). Visitors requiring medical attention will be sent to them. Emergencies are handled on an ad hoc basis. Check your insurance on coverage in Cuba and take a copy of your insurance policy with you. You cannot dial any toll-free numbers abroad so make sure you have a contact number. Take all prescription medicines and other remedies you might need as they may not be available in Cuba. The most common affliction of travellers is probably diarrhoea. Bottled water is widely available. Doctors will advise you to get hepatitis A and typhoid inoculations. Use plenty of insect repellent, dengue fever has been reported although the authorities spray regularly to keep mosquitos under control. Always carry toilet paper with you. Local health facilities are listed in individual town directories See also main Health section page 48.

Keeping in touch

Internet

Cubans are not generally allowed to access the internet, so facilities are limited. You will be asked for your passport. The large, international four- or five-star hotels have business centres with computers for internet access, and there are a few cybercafés around the country in tourist areas. The telephone company, **Etecsa**, sells prepaid cards which give you an access code and a password for when you log in and these

❖ *Facilities are now more widespread, but expect long queues.*

cost CUC$6 for one hour. **Etecsa** is installing mobile cabins (large blue telephone boxes) with international and national phone services and a computer for internet access, but there will be no internet access in small towns off the beaten tourist track. **Telecorreos** sells a different prepaid card for use in post offices, where you can send emails but not surf the internet. You will not be able to access your inbox via the internet and you will have to set up a new account. The Government plans to install computers in every post office soon.

Telephone

IDD code: +53. Cuba's communications are improving but numbers and codes are frequently changing. In 2007, **Etecsa** added a prefix of 6 to all numbers south of Havana (Boyeros, Arroyo Naranjo, 10 de Octubre) and 7 to those to the east (Guanabacoa) to make them 7-digit numbers. Many public phones take prepaid cards (*tarjetas*) which are easier than coins and are sold for 5, 7 and 10 Cuban pesos. The furthest distance, Pinar del Río to Baracoa, costs 1 peso per minute. **Etecsa** also sells a prepaid card called *Propia*, either in *pesos cubanos* or *pesos convertibles*, in denominations of 5, 7, 10 and 30 pesos (sometimes rechargeable), which can be used to make calls from a private phone. Call the operator and follow the instructions. They can also be used in cabins, dialling a personal code on the upper part of the card. To phone abroad, dial 119 followed by the country and regional codes and number. Many hotels and airports have telephone offices where international calls can be made. Look for the **Telecorreos** or **Etecsa** signs. No 'collect' calls allowed and only cash accepted. In a few top-class hotels you can direct dial foreign countries from your room. Phonecards are in use at **Etecsa** callboxes, in different denominations from CUC$10-50, much cheaper for phoning abroad, eg CUC$2 per minute to USA and Canada, CUC$2.60 per minute to Central America and the Caribbean, CUC$3.40 to South America, CUC$4 to Spain, Italy, France and Germany and CUC$4.40 to the rest of the world. Mobile phones are commonly used in Cuba.

Media

Newspapers *Granma*, mornings except Sunday and Monday; *Trabajadores*, Trade Union, weekly; *Tribuna* and *Juventud Rebelde*, also weekly. *Opciones* is a weekly national and international trade paper. *Granma* has a weekly edition, *Granma International* (in Spanish, English, French and Portuguese) and a monthly German edition, both on the Internet, www.granma.cu, Avenida General Suárez y Territorial, Plaza de la Revolución, La Habana 6, T8816265, F335176.

Television There are four national channels: *Cubavisión, Tele Rebelde* and two educational channels: *Canal Educativo 1* and *2*, which broadcast morning and evening. The Sun Channel can be seen at hotels and broadcasts a special programme for tourists 24 hours a day. Some of the upmarket hotels also have satellite TV.

Havana → *Phone code: 7. Colour map 1, A2. Population: 2,204,300.*

Of all the capital cities in the Caribbean, Havana has the reputation for being the most splendid and sumptuous. Before the Revolution, its casinos and nightlife attracted the megastars of the day in much the same way as Beirut and Shanghai, and remarkably little has changed (architecturally) since then. There have been no tacky modernizations, partly because of lack of finance and materials. Low-level street lighting, relatively few cars (and many of those antiques), no (real) estate agents or Wendyburgers, no neon and very little advertising (except for political slogans), all give the city plenty of scope for nostalgia. Restoration works in the old part of the city are revealing the glories of the past, although most of the city is fighting a losing battle against the sea air and many of the finest buildings along the seafront are crumbling.

Havana is probably the finest example of a Spanish colonial city in the Americas. Many of its palaces were converted into museums after the Revolution and more work has been done (with millions of dollars of foreign aid and investment) since the old city was declared a UNESCO World Heritage Site in 1982. Away from the old city, there is some stunning early 20th-century architecture. ▸▸ *For Sleeping, Eating and other listings, see pages 96-111.*

Ins and outs

Getting there The José Martí international Airport is 18 km from Havana. **Taxi** fares range from CUC$15-20, but CUC$18 is commonly asked to the old city. No bus goes near the international terminal, but **Víazul** operates a transfer service from some hotels for CUC$4. The **Astro bus** terminal is very near the Plaza de la Revolución in Vedado, central and convenient for accommodation. **Víazul** dollar buses stop much further out and a taxi will be needed, CUC$5 to Habana Vieja or Centro. The **train** station is at the southern end of the old city, within walking distance of any of the hotels there or in Centro Habana, although if you arrive at night, take a taxi.

Getting around **Buses** involve complicated queuing procedures and a lot of pushing and shoving. *Camellos* are articulated double buses which cover the main arteries. Regular buses (blue) are being improved but all are hot and crowded. *Bicitaxi*, bicycle taxi, rates are negotiable but generally less than you would pay a normal taxi. Havana is very spread out along the coast. Those with really good walking boots can cover much of the city on foot, but the average visitor will be content with one district at a time, eg Habana Vieja one day, Vedado the next, and still feel well exercised. Car hire is not recommended in Havana. ▸▸ *See also Transport, page 109, for further details.*

Orientation The centre is divided into five sections, three of which are of most interest to visitors: **Habana Vieja** (Old Havana), **Habana Centro** (Central Havana) and **Vedado**. The oldest part of the city, around the **Plaza de Armas**, is quite near the docks. Here are the former **Palace of the Captains-General** and **Castillo de La Real Fuerza**, the oldest of all the forts. From Plaza de Armas run two narrow and picturesque streets, Calle Obispo and Calle O'Reilly (there are two old-fashioned pharmacies on Obispo with traditional glass and ceramic medicine jars and decorative perfume bottles on display in shops that gleam with polished wood and mirrors). These two streets go west to the **Parque Central**, with its laurels, poincianas, almonds, palms, shrubs and gorgeous flowers. To the southwest rises the golden dome of the **Capitol**. From the northwest corner of Parque Central a wide, tree-shaded avenue with a central walkway, the **Paseo del Prado**, runs to the fortress of **La Punta**. At its north seaside end is the **Malecón**, a splendid highway along the coast to the west residential district of Vedado. The sea crashing along the seawall here is spectacular. On calmer days, fishermen lean over the parapet, lovers sit in the shade of the small pillars, and joggers sweat along the pavement. On the other side of the six-lane road, buildings which from a distance look stout and grand, with arcaded pavements, balconies, mouldings and large entrances, are salt-eroded, faded and decrepit inside. Restoration is progressing, but the sea is destroying old and new alike and creating a huge renovation task.

Further west, Calle San Lázaro leads directly from the monument to **General Antonio Maceo** on the Malecón to the magnificent central stairway of **Havana University**. A monument to **Julio Antonio Mella**, founder of the Cuban Communist Party, stands across from the stairway. Further out, past **El Príncipe** castle, is **Plaza de la Revolución**, with the impressive monument to **José Martí** at its centre and the much-photographed, huge outline of Che Guevara on one wall. The large buildings surrounding the square were mostly built in the 1950s and house the principal government ministries. The long, grey building behind the monument is the former Justice Ministry (1958), now the headquarters of the Central Committee of the Communist Party, where Fidel Castro has his office. The Plaza is the scene of massive parades (May Day) and speeches marking important events.

La Habana Vieja and Centro

Castillo del Morro

① *T8637941, daily 0830-1900, CUC$1 for the parque, CUC$4 for the Castillo, CUC$5 with a guide, CUC$2 for the lighthouse.*

Built between 1589 and 1630, with a 20-m moat, but much altered, it was one of the major fortifications built to protect the natural harbour and the assembly of Spain's silver fleets from pirate attack. The flash of its lighthouse, built in 1844, is visible 30 km out to sea. It now serves as a museum with a good exhibition of Cuban history since the arrival of Columbus. On the harbour side, down by the water, is the **Battery of the 12 Apostles**, now a restaurant, and **El Polvorín**, now a bar and disco.

Access to the Castillo del Morro is from any bus going through the tunnel (20 or 40 centavos or 1 peso), board at San Lázaro and Av del Puerto and get off at the stop after tunnel, cross the road and climb following the path to the left. Alternatively take a taxi, or a 20-minute walk from the Fortaleza de la Cabaña.

Havana orientation

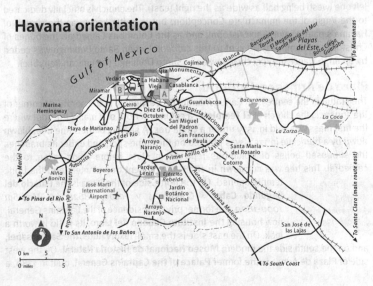

ⓘ *T8620617, daily 1000-2200, CUC$4 before 1800, CUC$6 after 1800, CUC$1 extra for a guide, photography free.*

Fronting the harbour is a high wall; the ditch on the landward side, 12 m deep, has a drawbridge to the main entrance. Inside are **Los Fosos de los Laureles,** where political prisoners were shot during the Cuban fight for Independence. Every night the cannon are fired at 2100 (*El Cañonazo*) in a historical ceremony recalling the closing of the city walls in the 17th century to protect it from pirates; this starts at 2045 so that the walls are closed at 2100. There are two museums here, one about Che Guevara and another about fortresses with pictures and models, some old weapons and a replica of a large catapult and battering ram.

The fortress stands on a bold headland, with the best view of Havana and is illuminated at night.

The **National Observatory** ⓘ *left-hand ferry queue next to the Customs House, opposite Calle Santa Clara, 10 centavos*, and the old station for (Hershey line) trains to Matanzas are on the same side of the Channel as the forts, at **Casablanca**. This charming town is also the site of a statue of a very human Jesus Christ, erected during the Batista dictatorship as a pacifying exercise. Go up a steep, twisting flight of stone steps, starting on the other side of the plaza in front of the landing stage, and you can walk from the statue to the Fortaleza (10 minutes) and then on to the Castillo del Morro. Access as for Castillo del Morro or via Casablanca.

Castillo de la Real Fuerza

ⓘ *O'Reilly y Av del Puerto, T8615010.*

This is the second oldest fort in the New World, built in 1558 after the city had been sacked by buccaneers and rebuilt in 1582. It is a low, long building, with a picturesque tower from which there is a grand view. In 2007 it was undergoing major renovation work and had been closed for some years.

Cathedral

ⓘ *ll Empedrado 156, T8617771, Mon-Fri 1030-1500, Sat 1030-1400, Sun 0900-1200, Mass at 1030.*

Construction of a church on this site was begun by Jesuit missionaries at the beginning of the 18th century. After the Jesuits were expelled in 1767, the church was converted into a cathedral. On either side of the baroque façade are bell towers, the left one (west) being half as wide as the right (east). The church is officially dedicated to the Virgin of the Immaculate Conception, but is better known as the church of Havana's patron saint, San Cristóbal, and as the Columbus Cathedral. The bones of Christopher Columbus were sent to this cathedral when Santo Domingo was ceded by Spain to France in 1795; they now lie in Santo Domingo (Dominican Republic).

Plaza de Armas and around

The statue in the centre is of Carlos Manuel de Céspedes. In the northeast corner of the square is the church of **El Templete**; a column in front of it marks the spot where the first mass was said in 1519 under a ceiba tree. A sapling of the same tree, blown down by a hurricane in 1753, was planted on the same spot, and under its branches the supposed bones of Columbus reposed in state before being taken to the cathedral. This tree was cut down in 1828, the present tree planted, and the Doric temple opened. On the north side of the Plaza is the **Palacio del Segundo Cabo** ⓘ *O'Reilly 4 y Tacón, T8628091, Mon-Sat 1000-1800*, the former private residence of the Captains General, now housing the **Instituto Cubano del Libro**. Its patio is worth a look. On the east side is the small luxury hotel, the **Santa Isabel**, and on the south side the modern **Museo Nacional de Historia Natural**. On the west side of Plaza de Armas is the former **Palace of the Captains General**, built in 1780, a

In the Plaza de Armas there is a small, second-hand book market Wed-Sat 0900-1800.

charming example of colonial architecture with a beautiful courtyard with arcades and balconies and Royal palms. The Spanish Governors and the Presidents lived here until 1917, when it became the City Hall. It is now the **Museo de la Ciudad** ① *Tacón 1 entre Obispo y O'Reilly, T8615779, daily 0900-1800, CUC$3; guided visit CUC$4; charge for photos CUC$2, video CUC$10*, the Historical Museum of the city of Havana. The 19th-century furnishings illustrate the wealth of the Spanish colonial community. The building was the site of the signing of the 1899 treaty between Spain and the USA. The **Casa de la Plata** ① *Obispo entre Mercaderes y Oficios, T8639861, Tue-Sat 0900-1645, Mon 0900-1300, free, donations accepted*, has a fine silverware collection, jewellery and old frescoes.

Close by is the **Museo de Automóviles** ① *Oficios 13 entre Jústiz y Obrapía (just off Plaza de Armas), T8639942, Tue-Sat 0900-1630, Sun 0900-1200, CUC$1, free for children under 12, camera CUC$2, video CUC$10*, the vintage car museum with vehicles going back to the 1920s, which is due to be relocated. There are a great many museum pieces, pre-Revolutionary US models, still on the road especially outside Havana, in among the Ladas, VWs and Nissans. Opposite, **Casa de los Arabes** ① *Oficios 16 entre Obispo y Obrapía, T8615868, Tue-Sat 0900-1700, Sun 0900-1300, free*, is a lovely building with vines trained over the courtyard for shade, and includes a mosque, jewels and rugs (as well as a bar and restaurant, **Al Medina**). A few blocks west is **Casa de Africa** ① *Obrapía 157, entre San Ignacio y Mercaderes, T8615798, africa@cultural.ohch.cu, Tue-Sat 0900-1700, Sun 0900-1300, free*, which contains carved wooden artefacts and handmade costumes, sculpture, furniture, paintings and ceramics from sub-Saharan Africa, including gifts given to Fidel by visiting African Presidents. There's also an exhibit of elements of African-Cuban religions.

La Plaza Vieja and around

Many of the buildings around the 18th-century plaza have elegant balconies overlooking the large square with a fountain in the middle. The former house of the Spanish Captain General, **Conde de Ricla**, who retook Havana from the English and restored power to Spain in 1763, can be seen on the corner of San Ignacio and Muralla. Known as **La Casona** ① *Muralla 107 esq San Ignacio, T8634703, www.galeriascubanas.com, Mon-Sat 0800-1730, free*, modern art exhibitions are held upstairs in the beautiful blue and white building. Note the friezes up the staircase and along the walls. There is a great view of the plaza from the balcony and trailing plants in the courtyard enhance the atmosphere.

One block away is the **Church and Convent of San Francisco** ① *T8629683, daily 0900-1800, CUC$2 for museum and CUC$1 extra for bell tower (under repair in 2007), photos CUC$2, video CUC$10, guide CUC$1*. Built in 1608 and reconstructed in 1730, this is a sombre edifice suggesting defence, rather than worship. The three-storey belltower was both a landmark for returning voyagers and a lookout for pirates. The Basílica Menor de San Francisco de Asís is now a concert hall and the convent is a museum containing religious pieces. Beside the church and convent is the **Museo del Ron** ① *Av del Puerto 262 entre Sol y Muralla, T8618051, www.havanaclubfoundation.com, Mon-Thu 0900-1700, Fri-Sat 0900-1600, Sun 1000-1600, tours on demand, CUC$5 including use of camera or video, under 15s free, multilingual guides included*. Belonging to the **Fundación Distilería Havana Club** it offers displays of the production of rum from the sugar cane plantation to the processing and bottling, with machinery dating from the early 20th century. Tours are available in several languages. There is a wonderful model railway which runs round a model sugar mill and distillery, designed and made by prize-winning Lázaro Eduardo García Driggs. At the end of the tour you get a tasting of a six-year-old Havana Club rum in a bar which is a mock up of the once-famous **Sloppy Joe's**. There is also a restaurant (excellent shrimp kebab) and bar (see below), a shop and an art gallery where present-day Cuban artists exhibit their work.

La Habana Vieja & Centro

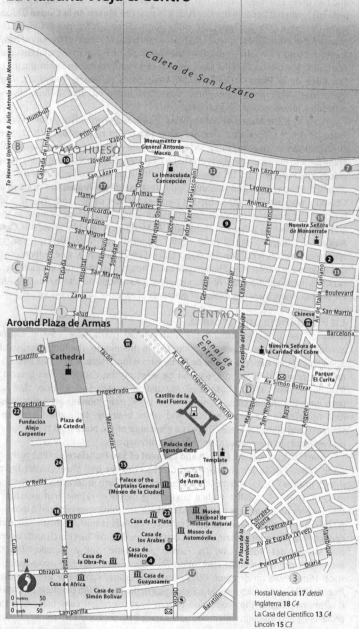

Caleta de San Lázaro

To Havana University & Julio Antonio Mella Monument

Humboldt

25

Príncipe

Vapor

CAYO HUESO

Jovellar

10

San Lázaro

Hamel

Concordia

Neptuno

San Miguel

San Rafael

San Francisco

Espada

Hospital

San Martín

Aramburu

Soledad

Zanja

Salud

1

CENTRO

2

Monumento a General Antonio Maceo

La Inmaculada Concepción

37

16

Ánimas

Virtudes

Marqués González

Lucena

Padre Varela (Belascoaín)

Oquendo

32

San Lázaro

Lagunas

Ánimas

9

Perseverancia

Nuestra Señora de Monserrate

15

4

2

33

Gervasio

Escobar

Lealtad

Boulevard

San Martín

Chinese

Av de Italia (Galiano)

Barcelona

7

Around Plaza de Armas

Tejadillo

14

Cathedral

Tacón

Empedrado

14

Castillo de la Real Fuerza

Canal de Entrada

Av CM de Céspedes (Del Puerto)

To Castillo del Príncipe

Nuestra Señora de la Caridad del Cobre

Av Simón Bolívar

Parque El Curita

D

Empedrado

22

17

Fundación Alejo Carpentier

Plaza de la Catedral

Mercaderes

Palacio del Segundo Cabo

El Templete

24

O'Reilly

15

Palace of the Captains General (Museo de la Ciudad)

Plaza de Armas

19

E

Monte

San Nicolás

Rayo

Ángeles

18

Obispo

23

Casa de la Plata

Museo Nacional de Historia Natural

Corrales

Gloria

Esperanza

27

Casa de los Árabes

Casa de México

Museo de Automóviles

3

4

Av de España (Vives)

Alambique

Cuba

San Ignacio

Casa de la Obra-Pía

Casa de África

Casa de Simón Bolívar

Obrapía

Casa de Guayasamín

17

Oficios

Baratillo

To Plaza de la Revolución

Corrales

Puerta Cerrada

Diaria

3

Lamparilla

0 metres 50
0 yards 50

N

0 metres 200
0 yards 200

Sleeping

Caribbean **2** B4
Carlos Luis Valderrama Moré **4** C3
Casa Federico **1** B4
Conde de Villanueva,
  Hostal del Habano **25** C6
Deauville **7** B3

Dr Alejandro Osés **8** B4
Florida **3** C5
Gustavo Enamorado
  Zamora–Chez Nous **6** D5
Jesús y María **12** D5
Hostal del Tejadillo **14** detail
Hostal El Comendador **17** detail

Hostal Valencia **17** detail
Inglaterra **18** C4
La Casa del Científico **13** C4
Lincoln **15** C3
Marilys Herrera González **16** B1
NH Parque Central **5** C4
Orlando y Liset **20** D5
Residencia Santa Clara **22** D5
Rosa Artiles Hernández **23** B4
Santa Isabel **19** detail
Sevilla **24** C4

Castillo del Morro

CASABLANCA

Castilla de la Punta

Fortaleza de San Carlos de la Cabaña

Canal de Entrada

Av CM de Céspedes

Malecón
San Lázaro
Cárcel

Monumento a Máximo Gómez

El Santo Ángel Custodio
Palacio de la Artesanía

Museo de la Revolución

Cuarteles

Cathedral

Castillo de la Real Fuerza

Tejadillo

Empedrado
Fundación Alejo Carpentier

Plaza de Armas

San Juan Dios

O'Reilly

Obispo

Obrapía

LA HABANA VIEJA

Museo Nacional Palacio de Bellas Artes

Lamparilla

Amargura

Church & Convent of San Francisco

Santo Cristo del Buen Viaje

Teniente Rey (Brasil)

La Plaza Vieja

Museo del Ron

Capitolio

Partagas Cigar Factory

Muralla

La Casona

Museo Humboldt

Sol

Compostela

Porvenir

Convento de Santa Clara

Santa Clara

Luz

Acosta

Jesús María

Espíritu Santo

Merced

La Merced

Leonor Pérez

San Isidro

Central

Desamparados

Ensenada de Atarés

La Coubre

To Casablanca (Passenger Ferry)

To Regla (Passenger Ferry)

Telégrafo 21 C4

Eating 🍴

Al Medina 3 detail
Bellomar 1 C4
Burgui 2 C3
Café París 18 detail
Cafetería Torre La Vega 4 detail
D'Giovanni 14 detail
Dominica 15 detail
Don Lorenzo 6 D5

Doña Blanquita 5 B4
El Castillo de Farnés 11 C4
El Floridita 19 C4
El Patio 17 detail
Gentiluomo 28 C4
Hanoi 21 D4
La Bodeguita
 del Medio 22 detail
La Dichosa 7 C5
La Divina Pastora 8 A6
La Guarida 9 C2

La Mina 23 detail
La Moneda Cubana 24 detail
La Tasquita 10 B1
La Zaragozana 25 C4
Los XII Apóstoles 12 A5
Los Nardos 29 D4
Puerto de Sagua 30 D5
Torre de Marfil 27 detail

Bars & clubs 🍸

Cabaret Nacional 31 C4

Callejon de Hamel 37 B1
Casa de la Trova 32 B2
Casa del Tango
 Edmundo Daubar 33 C3
Dos Hermanos 13 D6
Fundación Distilería
 Havana Club 34 D6
Lluvia de Oro 35 C5
Monserrate 36 C4
Sociedad Yoruba 20 D4

Convento de Santa Clara

ⓘ *Cuba 610 entre Luz y Sol, T8613335, Mon-Fri 0800-1700. CUC$2 for guided tour in Spanish or French.*

Founded in 1644 by nuns from Cartagena in Colombia, Santa Clara was in use as a convent until 1919, when the nuns sold the building. Restoration began in 1982, and is still continuing. The convent occupies four small blocks in Old Havana, bounded by Calles Habana, Sol, Cuba and Luz, and originally there were three cloisters and an orchard. You can see the cloisters, the nuns' cemetery and their cells. The first cloister has been carefully preserved; the ground floor is a grand porticoed stone gallery surrounding a large patio packed with vegetation, in it are the city's first slaughterhouse, first public fountain and public baths. The Sailor's House in the second cloister, reputedly built by a sailor for his love-lorn daughter, is now a *Residencia Académica* for student groups (and independent travellers if room, see page 97).

El Capitolio

ⓘ *T8610261, visitor entrance is currently on Industria because of repairs, tours available daily 0900-1900, but often shuts early, café has same opening hours, CUC$3, CUC$4 with a guide; camera and video charge CUC$2 for non-professionals.*

Opened in May 1929, the Capitol has a large dome over a rotunda. At the centre of its floor is set a 24-carat diamond, zero for all distance measurements in Cuba. The interior has large halls and stately staircases, all sumptuously decorated. El Capitolio is to the north of **Parque Fraternidad**. At its centre is a ceiba tree growing in soil provided by each of the American republics. Also in the park is a famous statue of the Indian woman who first welcomed the Spaniards: *La Noble Habana*, sculpted in 1837.

‼ *This is a copy, on a smaller scale, of the US Capitol in Washington DC.*

Cigar factory

ⓘ *Industria 520 entre Dragones y Barcelona, behind El Capitolio, T8635766, 30-min tours, every 15 mins 0900-1100, 1200-1500, Mon-Fri, CUC$10, buy tickets at Hotels Inglaterra, Saratoga and Parque Central, shop open daily 0900-1900.*

The tour of **Partagas** is interesting but pricey. English-, Spanish- or French- speaking guides available. You are taken through the factory and shown the whole production process (explanation in Spanish only). Four brand names are made here; *Partagas*, *Cubana*, *Ramón Allones* and *Bolívar*. These and other famous cigars (and rum) can be bought at the shop. No photography allowed.

Parque Central

A very pleasant park with a monument to **José Martí** in the centre. On its west side are the upmarket *Hotel Telégrafo*, the regal *Hotel Inglaterra* (built 1875, many famous foreign guests) and the **Gran Teatro de la Habana**, a beautiful building with tours of the inside. The north side is entirely occupied by the **Hotel Parque Central**, while the *Hotel Plaza* is in the northeast corner. On the east side of the park is the **Museo Nacional Palacio de Bellas Artes** ⓘ *T8613858, www.museonacional.cult.cu, Tue-Sat 1000-1800, Sun 1000-1400, CUC$5 entry to each museum for foreigners, entrance to both sites CUC$8 (on different days if you wish), CUC$2 extra for guide which has to be booked in advance, no photography permitted inside, café and small shop.* After a five-year closure and extensive refurbishment estimated at US$14.5 million, Fidel Castro inaugurated this fantastic museum on 19 July 2001. There are two separate buildings: the 1954 Fine Arts Palace (at Trocadero entre Zulueta y Monserrate) houses the collection of **Arte Cubano**, from colonial to the 1990s including a section on the post-Revolution Art Schools; the former Centro Asturiano (at San Rafael entre Zulueta y Monserrate) houses European and ancient art, **Arte Universal**. The collection of European paintings, from the 16th century to the present, contains works by Gainsborough, Van Dyck, Velázquez, Tintoretto, Degas, et al. The museum also has

There are paintings from private collections left behind by rich Cuban families (including the Bacardí and Gómez Mena families) and members of the former dictator Fulgencio Batista's government who fled Cuba soon after the 1959 Revolution.

Museo de la Revolución

① *Refugio entre Monserrate y Zulueta, facing Av de las Misiones, T8624091, daily 1000-1700, CUC$5, with a guide CUC$7, photography free, explanations mostly in Spanish; café and small shops for souvenirs.*

This huge, ornate building, topped by a dome, was once the Presidential Palace, but now contains the Museo de la Revolución. The history of Cuban political development is charted, from the slave uprisings to joint space missions with the ex-Soviet Union. The liveliest section displays the final battles against Batista's troops, with excellent photographs and some bizarre mementoes from the Sierra Maestra campaign. The yacht *Granma*, from which Dr Castro disembarked with his companions in 1956 to launch the Revolution, has been installed in the park facing the south entrance, surrounded by planes, tanks and other vehicles involved, as well as a Soviet-built tank used against the Bay of Pigs invasion and a fragment from a US spy plane. Allow several hours to see it all.

Vedado and Plaza de la Revolución

Vedado is largely a residential area with some wonderful houses from the early 20th century, reflecting the opulence of life when wealth came from supplying the USA with sugar during the First World War. However, many of the magnificent staircases are now crumbling, wrought-iron work is twisted and stained-glass windows are broken and patched. Most government offices are in Vedado or around Plaza de la Revolución, which looks like a huge car park but is the place to be for any demonstration, political rally or festive occasion, the scene of most of Castro's marathon speeches. The University straddles the divide between Vedado and Centro and the area is full of students, helping to make it a lively and happening part of town. It was where the Mafia and mobsters spent their money before the Revolution and it is still the place to come for nightlife, with all the hottest clubs, bars, concerts and floor shows.

In the base of the **Memorial José Martí** ① *Plaza de la Revolución, T592347, Mon-Sat 0900-1630, CUC$3, lookout CUC$2 extra*, is a beautifully restored and impressive museum. The tower is the highest point in the city with good panoramic views of Havana. The **Museo Postal Cubano** ① *T8828255, Mon-Fri 0900-1700, CUC$1*, Ministry of Communications, tells the history of the postal service and stamps and the story books of José Antonio de Armona (1765).

Museo Napoleónico ① *San Miguel 1159 esq Ronda, T8791460, Tue-Sat 0900-1630, Sun 0900-1230, CUC$3, or CUC$5 with a guide, CUC$2 for camera, CUC$10 for video*, near the university, houses 7000 pieces from the private collection of sugar baron, Julio Lobo. There are paintings and other works of art, a specialized library and a collection of weaponry. Check out the tiled fencing gallery.

Further west, in a beautiful 1926 former mansion with gardens, the **Casa de la Amistad** ① *Paseo 406, entre 17 y 19, T8303114, daily 1200-2400; entertainment Tue Noche de Chan Chan, 2100-0100, CUC$5, Sat Noche Cubana, 2100-0200*, is now operated by ICAP (Cuban Institute for Friendship among the Peoples) and houses the *Amistur* travel agency (see page 108). It has a reasonably priced bar, cafetería (same hours) and tourist shop (entrance on Calle 19, 0930-1800). Cuban music nights are CUC$5 or more if a top band is playing; good traditional music in a nice setting. Lots of Cubans go there too, but there is no soliciting. About four blocks away, the **Museo de Artes Decorativas** ① *C17 502 entre D y E, T8320924, Tue-Sat 1030-1730, Sun 0930-1200, CUC$3*, houses European and Oriental art from the 16th-20th centuries in a

Vedado & Plaza de la Revolución

Sleeping

Adita **1** A5
Alicia Horta **7** B5
Armando Gutiérrez **3** B6
Carmen y Ramón
 Fonseca Díaz **4** B4
Familia Villazón **5** B5
Gisela Ibarra y Daniel
 Rivero **12** A4
Martha Vitorte **17** B5

Mercedes González **33** B5
Nacional de Cuba **20** B6
Natalia Rodés León **21** C5
Pedro Mesa López & Tobias
 López Márquez **22** C5
Presidente **23** A4
Sol Meliá Tryp
 Habana Libre **10** C5
St John's **9** C6
Teresa Naredo **25** B4

Vedado **27** C6
Victoria **29** B5
Villa Babi **34** C3

Eating

1830 **2** B1
Amor **1** C4
Burgui **3** C5
Calle 10 **12** B1
Coppelia **4** B5

El Conejito **6** *B5*
Gringo Viejo **9** *B4*
Hurón Azul **7** *C6*
La Tasquita **20** *C6*
La Torre **11** *B6*
Nerei **13** *B5*
Pain de París **14** *B3,D4*
Pekin **8** *C2*
Primavera **5** *B3*
Trattoria Marakas **17** *B6*

Bars & clubs 🍸
Cabaret Las Vegas **21** *C6*
Café Cantante Mi Habana
  28 *D4*
Café El Gato Tuerto **22** *B6*
Callejón de Hamel **16** *C6*
Casa de la Cultura
  de Plaza **30** *B3*
Club Almendores **18** *D1*
Club Atelier **23** *B3*

Copa Room (Hotel
  Riviera) **15** *A3*
El Delirio Habanero **28** *D4*
El Río Club (Johnnie's Club)
  10 *B1*
Habana Café (Hotel Meliá
  Cohiba) **24** *A3*
Imágenes **25** *A4*
Jazz Café **19** *A3*
La Zorra y El Cuervo **26** *B6*

Salón Rojo (Hotel Capri)
  32 *B6*
Scherezada **27** *B6*
Tikoa **29** *B3*
UNEAC **33** *B5*

French Renaissance-style mansion originally designed by Alberto Camacho (1924-27) for José Gómez Mena's daughter. Most of the building materials were imported from France. In the 1930s the mansion was occupied by Gómez' sister, María Luisa, Condesa de Revilla de Camargo, who was a fervent collector of fine art and held elegant society dinners and receptions for guests including the Duke of Windsor and Wallace Simpson. The countess's valuable collections were found in the basement after the family fled Cuba following the Revolution in 1959. The interior decoration was by House of Jansen and her furniture included a desk that had belonged to Marie Antoinette. There are 10 permanent exhibition halls with works from the 16th-20th centuries including ceramics, porcelain (Sèvres, Chantilly and Wedgwood), furniture (Boudin, Simoneau and Chippendale) and paintings. The Regency-inspired dining room is recommended viewing. The attendants are knowledgeable and informative about the exhibits, but only in Spanish. Two blocks further north, the **Museo de la Danza** ① *Línea 265 esq G (Presidentes), T8312198, Tue-Sat 1100-1830, CUC$2, guided tour CUC$3*, contains items from Alicia Alonso's personal collection and from the Ballet Nacional de Cuba. Alongside Casa de las Américas, **Galería Haydée Santamaría** ① *G esq 5, T552706, closed 2007 for renovation*, is a good representation of mostly 20th-century styles by Latin American artists. Also worth visiting is the **Cementerio Colón** ① *entrance on Zapata y 12, T8304517, 0900-1700, CUC$1, camera and video CUC$1*, the second largest cemetery in the world, which has a wealth of funerary sculpture, including Carrara marbles; Cubans visit the sculpture of Amelia de Milagrosa and pray for miracles.

Miramar

Miramar is some 16 km west of the old city on the west side of the Río Almendares. There are many beautiful art nouveau and other early 20th-century houses, and most of the embassies are here. It is being developed into a modern city with glossy hotels for business people alongside fitness and business centres. Some of the best restaurants are in Miramar and there are good places to go at night, including the internationally famous **Tropicana** cabaret show. **Maqueta de la Ciudad** ① *Calle 28 113 entre 1 y 3, Miramar, T2027322,Mon-Sat 0930-1700, CUC$3, children and pensioners CUC$1*, is a scale model of Havana and its suburbs as far out as Cojímar and the airport. Colonial buildings are in red, post-colonial pre-Revolution buildings in yellow and post-Revolution buildings in white.

Havana suburbs

San Francisco de Paula

Hemingway fans may wish to visit his house, **Finca La Vigía** ① *Ctra Central Km 12.5, Finca Vigía, San Francisco de Paula, T910809, Wed-Mon 0900-1630, CUC$2, CUC$3 with a guide, CUC$5 for camera, CUC$25 video camera, no toilets, Hemingway tours are offered by hotel tour desks for CUC$35*, 11 km from the centre of Havana, where he lived from 1939 to 1960 (called the **Museo Ernest Hemingway**). The signpost is opposite the post office, leading up a short driveway. Visitors are not allowed inside the plain whitewashed house, which has been lovingly preserved with all Hemingway's furniture and books, just as he left it, but you can walk all around the outside and look in through the windows and open doors. Since the end of 2002, US and Cuban researchers have been collaborating in going through the 9000 books on the walls and thousands of photographs, manuscripts and letters in the cellar, all of which have been gathering dust where Hemingway left them in 1960. The garden is beautiful and tropical, with many shady palms. Next to the swimming pool (empty) are the gravestones of Hemingway's pet dogs. Finca La Vigía is currently undergoing renovation and visitors should expect scaffolding and possible closure of the sight.

Botanic Gardens

① *Km 3.5, Ctra Rocío, Calabazar, T6547278 (reservations), daily 0900-1700, but you may not be allowed in after 1530, CUC$1, children CUC$0.50 to explore on your own, CUC$2 if you use your own transport, CUC$3 for the train ride with guide.*

South of the city in Arroyo Naranjo, beyond Parque Lenin, the **Jardín Botánico Nacional de Cuba** is well maintained with excellent collections, including a Japanese garden with tropical adaptations. A multilingual guide will meet you at the gate, no charge. You can take a 'train' tour along the 35 km of roads around the 60-ha site. This is an open-sided, wheeled carriage towed by a tractor, enabling you to see the whole garden in about two hours. Several interconnected glasshouses are filled with desert, tropical and subtropical plants, well worth walking through. There are only a few signs and so not as informative as it might be. There is a good **organic vegetarian restaurant** using solar energy for cooking. Only one sitting for lunch, but you can eat as much as you like from a selection of hot and cold vegetarian dishes and drinks for CUC$12. Water and waste food is recycled and the restaurant grows most of its own food. To get there, Camello M6 and omnibus 88 every 30-40 minutes; many hotel tour desks now organize day trips including lunch for CUC$25, better value than going independently and probably less effort; taxi from Old Havana CUC$15-18 one-way.

Marina Hemingway

Off Avenida 5, 20 minutes by taxi from Havana, is the Marina Hemingway tourist complex, in the fishing village of **Santa Fe**. In May and June the marina hosts the annual **Ernest Hemingway International Marlin Fishing Tournament**, and in August and September the **Blue Marlin Tournament**. There are 140 slips with electricity and water and space for docking 400 recreational boats. The resort includes the hotel **El Acuario** (Cubanacán, 248 y Av 5, Santa Fé, T2047628, F2044379), restaurants, bungalows and villas for rent, shopping, watersports, facilities for yachts, sports and a tourist bureau.

Playas del Este

This is the all-encompassing name for a string of beaches within easy reach of Havana. East of the city is the pleasant little beach of **Bacuranao**, 15 km from Havana. At the far end of the beach is a villa complex with restaurant and bar. Then come **Tarará**, **El Mégano** and **Santa María del Mar**, with a long, open beach which continues eastwards to the beach at **Boca Ciega** and **Guanabo** (several train departures daily from La Coubre terminal, Estación Central, Havana, and from Matanzas), a pleasant, non-touristy beach 27 km from Havana, but packed with Habaneros at weekends. Cars roll in from Havana early on Saturday mornings, line up and deposit their cargo of sun worshippers at the sea's edge. The quietest spot is **Brisas del Mar**, at the east end. As a general rule, facilities for foreigners are at Santa María del Mar and for Cubans at Guanabo. The latter is therefore cheaper and livelier in the summer months. Tourism bureaux offer day excursions (minimum six people) for about CUC$15 per person to the Playas del Este, but for two or more people its worth hiring a private car for the day for CUC$20-25. The 400 bus (40 centavos) from Ejido near the Estación Central de Trenes can get you to Bacuranao, Santa María and Guanabo (watch your pockets and possessions), but getting back to Havana is problematic the longer you stay. The standard private taxi price is CUC$15 (fix the price before you set off), but getting a return taxi is more difficult. Cycling is a good way to get there. Use the *ciclobus* from Parque El Curita, Aguila y Dragones, to go through the tunnel under Havana Bay, or the 20-centavo ferry to Regla from near the Aduanas building, and cycle through Regla and Guanabacoa.

La Habana Vieja and Centro *p85, map p88*

LL-L NH Parque Central, Neptuno entre Prado y Zulueta, on north side of Parque Central, T8606627, www.nh-hotels.com. 278 rooms of international standard, excellent bathrooms, separate shower and tub, business centre, 2 restaurants, plush cigar-smoker's lounge, 2 bars, sweeping views of Havana from pool on top floor, fitness centre, charming and helpful multilingual staff.

LL-L Santa Isabel, Baratillo 9 entre Obispo y Narciso López, Plaza de Armas, T8608201, F8608391. Renovated mansion, 17 rooms and 10 suites, busy with groups, height of luxury, very well-equipped bathrooms, rooms on 3rd floor have balcony overlooking plaza, restaurant, central patio with fountain and greenery and lobby bar, great location.

L Conde de Villanueva, Hostal del Habano, Mercaderes 202 esq Lamparilla, T8629293, reserva@cvillanueva.co.cu. 6 rooms and 3 suites around peaceful courtyard, attractive red and green colour scheme, cigar theme with cigar shop, café, bar, good restaurant, highly regarded, friendly staff, named after Claudio Martínez del Pinillo, Conde de Villanueva (1789-1853), a notable personality who promoted tobacco abroad and helped to bring the railway to Cuba.

L-AL Hostal del Tejadillo, Tejadillo 12 esq San Ignacio. T8637283, F8638830. Great location, comfortable rooms, high ceilings, tall wooden shuttered windows, fridge, good breakfast included inside or in the courtyard, lively bar with entertaining barmen and music in the afternoon/evening.

L-AL Hostal El Comendador, next door to Hostal Valencia (below), is a small hotel on 2 floors, same lobby, using the facilities of the Valencia.

L-A Florida, Obispo 252 esq Cuba, T8624127, F8624117. Restored building dates from 1885, cool oasis, elegant restaurant, bar just off the street, serves great daiquirís, marble floors and pillars in courtyard, beautiful rooms with high ceilings, some balconies, some singles, overpriced and poor buffet breakfast, parking.

L-A Telégrafo, Prado 408 esq Neptuno, T8611010, F8614844. On the Parque Central and a great location. Reopened in 2001 after a luxury refit, the original building dates from 1860 but the 63 hotel rooms are modern, stylish and spacious with opulent bathrooms and soundproofing.

AL-A Hostal Valencia, Oficios 53 esq Obrapía, T8671037, reserva@habaguanexhvalencia.co.cu. Joint Spanish/Cuban venture modelled on the Spanish *paradores*, suites and rooms named after Valencian towns, tastefully restored building, nicely furnished, pleasant courtyard with vines, music, good restaurant (see Eating, below).

AL-A Inglaterra, Prado 416 entre San Rafael y San Miguel, T8608595/7, F8608254. Built in 1875 next to the Teatro Nacional, famous former foreign guests included Sara Bernhardt in 1887 and the authors Federico García Lorca and Rubén Darío in 1910. 83 rooms, colonial style, regal atmosphere, some single rooms have no windows, reasonable breakfast, lovely old mosaic tiled dining room, 1 of 4 cafés or restaurants with a variety of services and cuisines.

AL-A Sevilla, Trocadero 55 entre Animas y Zulueta, T8608560, F8608582. Recently restored, 178 rooms of 1937 vintage on edge of La Habana Vieja. Most have no view, noisy a/c, used for package tours, inviting pool open to non-guests, shops, sauna and massage, tourism bureau, elegant restaurant and bar on top floor with great night time views of Centro and the Malecón, huge windows are flung open to let in the breeze.

B Caribbean, Paseo Martí (Prado) 164 entre Colón y Refugio, T8608210, F8609479. Remodelled, good security, convenient for the old town, 38 rooms, try for one on 5th floor, fan and TV, popular with budget travellers, avoid noisy rooms at front and lower floors at back over deafening water pump, internet. Cheap Café del Prado at street level for spaghetti, pizza and snacks, daily 0700-2400.

B Deauville, Galiano y Malecón, Centro, T8668812. 144 rooms, noise from Malecón but great view, balconies overlooking sea and fortress, renovated 1999, breakfast included, pool, helpful *buró de turismo*. Restaurant Costa Norte offers dinner 1900-2200, followed by a cabaret Wed-Sun 2200-0230, CUC$3. The pool is open to non-guests for CUC$6 including drinks worth CUC$5, children under 6 free, snack bar.

B-C La Casa del Científico, Prado 212 esq Trocadero, T8624511, F8600167. Beautiful colonial building with amazing original features, charmingly old-fashioned, shared or private bathroom, cheap breakfast, luxurious dining room and lounge in classic style, very pleasant atmosphere, friendly staff, reservations essential, often booked by groups, best budget option in old city, Asistur office on site.

B-C Lincoln, Virtudes 164 esq Galiano, Centro, T8628061. 135 mostly refurbished and good-value rooms, convenient location, friendly, TV with CNN, a/c, clean, price includes breakfast.

C-D Gustavo Enamorado Zamora – Chez Nous, Teniente Rey (Brasil) 115 entre Cuba y San Ignacio, T8626287, cheznous@ ceniai.inf.cu. 2 spacious double rooms, shared bathroom with original 1904 shower, hot water, fan, a/c, TV, fridge, balcony overlooking street, street noise, nice patio, parking, warm atmosphere, Gustavo (radio cultural correspondent) and Kathy (artist) are kind and helpful, French and English spoken, reservations essential.

C-D pp Residencia Santa Clara, Cuba 610 entre Luz y Sol, T8613335, reaca@ cencrem.cult.cu, see page 90. Colonial convent building dating from 1644, great value, spacious suites with colonial furnishings or double rooms, or dormitories. Lovely atmosphere, spotless, can be noisy early morning, nice café, poor breakfast. Group discounts.

D Carlos Luis Valderrama Moré, Neptuno 404 entre San Nicolás y Manrique, 2nd floor, Centro, T8679842. Carlos and Vivian are former teachers, he speaks English, 1940s apartment above a shop, 2 rooms, balcony overlooking street, good bathrooms, hot water but very small beds.

D Casa Federico, Cárcel 156 entre San Lázaro y Prado, Centro, T8617817, llanesrenta@yahoo.es. Excellent location just off the Prado and the Malecón, but 64 stairs to the apartment on the 3rd floor. Large rooms with tiled floors, extra bed on request, bathroom, a/c, CD player, phone, desk, safe box in each room, run by Federico and Yamelis Llanes, a pleasant young couple, formerly lawyers, some English spoken, good breakfast with lots of fruit and juice and delicious supper.

D Dr Alejandro Osés, Malecón 163, 1st floor, entre Aguila y Crespo, Centro, T8637359. Best view in city from balcony of entire Malecón, from El Morro to **Hotel Nacional**, nice place to stay although the interior rooms can be stuffy, shared bathrooms, breakfast, helpful family, book ahead, always full.

D Jesús y María, Aguacate 518 entre Sol y Muralla, T8611378. Upstairs suite above the family and very private, a/c bedroom with twin beds, bathroom, living room and kitchenette with fan, fridge, also small outside sitting area, comfortable, clean. Breakfast and dinner available.

D Marilys Herrera González, Concordia 714 altos entre Soledad y Aramburo, Centro, T8700608, maguel200220002@yahoo.es. Independent apartment above the family apartment. Bathroom with warm water, kitchen, fridge, a/c, fan, TV, all modern, clean and comfortable, laundry offered, terrace, Marylis is very kind and caring, family atmosphere.

D Orlando y Liset, Aguacate 509 Apto 301 y 102 entre Sol y Muralla, T8675768, lisettesobrino@yahoo.es. Lovely clean apartments, the second one belongs to Liset's mother, great view over La Habana Vieja from the terrace, garage, elevator, own entrance to guest room. Liset is a university maths teacher.

E Rosa Artiles Hernández, Crespo 117 bajos entre Colón y Trocadero, Centro, T8627574. Excellent place, very clean and friendly, 2 rooms, shared use of fridge, a/c, fan, radio, separate entrance, own key, sitting area, beautiful car on ground floor, structural adjustments made to building to house it, breakfast and dinner offered, her children speak English, German or Italian.

Vedado and Plaza de la Revolución *p91, map p92*

LL-AL Nacional de Cuba, O esq 21, T8733564-7, www.hotelnacionaldecuba .com. 426 rooms, including 29 suites, a presidential suite and a royal suite, good bathrooms with lots of bottles of goodies, some package tours use it at bargain rates, generally friendly and efficient service, faded grandeur, dates from 1930, superb reception hall, steam room, 2 pools, restaurants, bars, shops, business centre, exchange bureau, gardens with old cannon on hilltop overlooking the Malecón and harbour entrance.

LL-AL Sol Meliá Tryp Habana Libre, L entre 23 y 25, T8346100, www.solmeliacuba.com. The **Havana Hilton** opened 1958, but became the Revolution headquarters for 3 months. In 1959 it was renamed. 572 rooms in huge block, 25 floors, prices depend on the floor number, most facilities are here, eg hotel reservations, excursions, Polynesian restaurant, buffet, 24-hr coffee shop, Cabaret Turquino 2230-0300, pool, shopping mall includes bank, airlines.

AL-A Presidente, Calzada 110 y G (Presidentes), T551801, www.hotelesc.com. Oldest hotel in Havana with a Mafia heritage, refurbished, 158 rooms and 2 suites, 2 rooms are fully adapted for the disabled, ask for a room on the 10th floor (the Colonial Floor) which has sumptuous antiques, 2 restaurants, pool. Popular with Italian tour groups.

AL-B Victoria, 19 y M, T8333510, www.hotelvictoriacuba.com. Good location, 31 standard rooms, 3 junior suites, small, quiet, intimate and pleasant, tasteful if conservative, good bathrooms, small pool, parking, good cooking, in good order. Business oriented, internet for guests.

A-B St John's, O 206 entre 23 y 25, T8333740. Convenient location steps away from Vedado nightlife, recently remodelled with sparkling new rooms and good bathrooms. Get a room on floors 9-12 for great views over either Habana Vieja or Vedado and Miramar. 24-hr internet access in lobby. Rooftop pool and nightclub daily 2200-0300.

A-B Vedado, O 244 entre 23 y 25, T8364072. Great location with good facilities, 194 basic rooms, a/c, TV, pool, gym and health centre with CUC$10 massages, restaurant, nightclub daily 2230-0200, admission CUC$10 then open bar.

C Gisela Ibarra y Daniel Rivero, F 104 altos, entre 5 y Calzada, T8323238. Straight out of the 1950s, marble staircase, balconies, wonderful old rooms with original furnishings, a/c, fans, fridge, TV, safe box, friendly hosts, speaking Spanish is a help but not essential, huge breakfast for CUC$5.

C Martha Vitorte, G 301 Apto 14, 14th floor, entre 13 y 15, T8326475. High-rise building near corner with Línea, 1 apartment on each floor, referred to as 'horizontals', beautiful modern building, very spacious, en suite bathroom, a/c, security safe in bedroom, balcony on 2 sides for views of Havana, sea and sunsets, Martha is a retired civil servant and speaks some English and French.

D Adita, 9 257 entre J y I, T8320643. Large double rooms, bathroom for each, warm family home full of antiques. The building is dilapidated but the eclectic apartment is clean and a great place to stay.

D Alicia Horta, Línea 53 entre M y N, Apto 9, T8328439. Friendly doctor, daughter speaks English, rooms cleaned daily, long stays possible, good view from 9th floor, popular so call in advance.

D Armando Gutiérrez, 21 62 entre M y N, Apto 7, 4th (top) floor, T/F8321876. Large a/c room with 2 beds and balcony, bathroom, separate entrance, Armando and his wife, Betty, and mother, Teresa, speak English and French and are knowledgeable on history and culture.

D Carmen y Ramón Fonseca Díaz, G 301 esq 13, Apto 13, T8324021, amazingtrece@yahoo.com. Great view from balcony on 13th floor, 2 bedrooms, bathroom, English, French and German spoken, they offer their services as tour guides, translators and Spanish teachers.

D Familia Villazón, 21 203 entre J y K, T8321066. Old colonial home with amazing high ceilings, antiques including antique swing chairs on front veranda, a/c, fridge, kitchen, son speaks some English.

D Mercedes González, 21 360 Apto 2A, entre G y H, T8325846, mercylupe@hotmail.com. 2 rooms, a/c, fan, each with good bathroom, 24-hr hot water, TV and fridge, airy rooms, one has balcony, smart, lots of tropical plants, helpful and friendly, English spoken, breakfast and dinner available, good location, near park.

D Natalia Rodés León, 19 376 p11B, entre G y H, T8328909. Room with sea view, 1 bathroom, fridge, TV, friendly lady, fought with Fidel in the Sierra Maestra.

D Pedro Mesa López y Tobias López Márquez, F 609 Apto 12 entre 25 y 27, T8329057. Quiet area except for rooster, 2 rooms with attached bathrooms, fridge, a/c, only Spanish spoken by friendly couple in their 60s.

D Teresa Naredo, 15 605 entre C y D, Apto 1, T8303382. Ground floor of low-rise block,

balcony, clean and tidy, en suite facilities, a/c, quiet embassy residential neighbourhood, often booked for extended periods.
D Villa Babi, 27 965 entre 6 y 8, T8306373, www.villababi.com. Although the downstairs rooms occupied by the second wife of the late Tomás Gutiérrea Alea, famed director of the movie, **Fresas y Chocolate**, are no longer available as she is out of the country, there are rooms upstairs with private bathrooms, managed by Doris Quesada. Breakfast available, reservations accepted via the website.

Playas del Este *p95*
D Casa Alex, 486 7B07 entre 7B y 9, Guanabo, T960060, mob T2635240. Alex and his mother Prieta have rooms with a/c, kitchen, TV, music. People who stay there can use the pedalos for free at Recreación Náutica. Parking.
E Norma Martín, 472 1A06 entre 3 y Playa, Guanabo, T966734. 2 rooms in small house with a/c and hot water. This place is a stone's throw from the beach.

● Eating

At state restaurants food tends to be greasy, although there does seem to be a tourist-oriented swing towards grilling, with a greater awareness of nutritional content.
There is a rapidly growing number of fast food outlets in all parts of the city:
Pain de París has several locations including Línea entre Paseo y A, next to **Teatro Trianón** and inside the Terminal de Omnibus, Plaza de la Revolución, 24-hr service, good coffee, *café cortadito* or *café con leche* CUC$0.65, croissants CUC$0.55 and *señoritas de chocolate* (custard slices) CUC$1.25, pizzas from CUC$1.25, take-out boxes provided.
El Rápido, red logo, clean with fast service and numerous locations.
Burgui, currently a handful of outlets, 23 entre G y H, Vedado, next to **Riviera** cinema, and Av de Italia (Galiano) esq Neptuno, Centro Habana, near to **Teatro América**, selling fast food (hamburger, fried chicken, fries, pizza, soft drinks and beer), freezing a/c. All **Burguis** are 24 hrs except for the one at Av 5 esq118, Miramar (1100-2300).
DiTú, prefabricated units springing up all over the city selling fried chicken by weight.

El Rapidito, red logo, not to be confused with **El Rápido** chain.
Cadena Imágenes and **Doña Yulla** serve fried chicken, pizzas, soft drinks and beer. There are many **street stalls** and places where you can pick up snacks, pizza, etc. Note that their prices are listed in *pesos cubanos* even though there is a $ sign posted. These can work out very cheap and are good for filling a hole at lunchtime, but don't expect a culinary masterpiece. Make sure you eat pizza fresh from the oven, 6 pesos a piece for cheese, 10 pesos for extra cheese or meat toppings. They are usually very greasy, so take plenty of napkins. Very sweet juice drinks for 2 pesos per glass.

La Habana Vieja and Centro *p85, map p88*
♥♥♥ **El Floridita**, Obispo 557 esq Monserrate, next to the Parque Central, T8671299. 1200-2400. A favourite haunt of Hemingway, it is a very elegant bar and restaurant reflected in the prices (CUC$6 for a daiquirí), but well worth a visit to see the sumptuous decor and 'Bogart atmosphere'.
♥♥♥-♥♥ **D'Giovanni**, Empedrado entre Tacón y Mercaderes, T867102736. 1200-2400. Lovely building with patio and terrace, Italian, overpriced, often cold, pizza and spaghetti.
♥♥♥-♥♥ **El Castillo de Farnés**, Monserrate 361 y Obrapía, T8671030. Restaurant 1200-2400, bar open 0800-0200. Tasty Spanish food, reasonable prices, good for *garbanzos* and shrimp, Castro came here on 9 Jan 1959 at 0445 with Che and Raúl.
♥♥♥-♥♥ **La Bodeguita del Medio**, Empedrado 207 entre Cuba y San Ignacio, near the cathedral, T8671374. Restaurant 1200-2400, bar 1030-2400. Was made famous by Hemingway and should be visited if only for a drink (*mojito* – rum, crushed ice, mint, sugar, lime juice and carbonated water – is a must, CUC$4), food poor, expensive but very popular.
♥♥♥-♥♥ **La Divina Pastora**, Fortaleza de la Cabaña, Casablanca, T8608341. 1200-2300. Expensive, fish and seafood restaurant, food praised.
♥♥♥-♥ **Dominica**, O' Reilly esq Mercaderes, T8602918. 1200-2400. Italian, very smart, set menus, pasta, pizza , vegetarian options, outdoor seating nice for lunch, poor service, credit cards.

¶¶-¶ El Patio, San Ignacio 54 esq Empedrado, Plaza Catedral, T8671034. Restaurant 1200-2400, snack bar open 24 hrs. Expensive, small portions, appalling service, but has national dishes, lovely location.

¶¶¶-¶ La Mina, Obispo esq Oficios, Plaza de Armas, T8620216. 1200-2400, bar open 24 hrs. Expensive, traditional Cuban food, sandwiches, liqueur coffees, tables and chairs outside with live Cuban music.

¶¶¶-¶ La Zaragozana, Monserrate entre Obispo y Obrapía, T8671040. 1200-2400. Oldest restaurant in Havana, international cuisine, good seafood and wine, good service but food nothing special.

¶¶ Don Lorenzo, Acosta 260, entre Habana y Compostela. T8616733. 1200-2400. Not cheap, but one of the most extensive *paladar* menus, with over 50 dishes offered, all types of meat and fish, including farmed crocodile and turtle (internationally protected – don't eat it) with a huge variety of sauces. Good vegetarian options. An entertaining night when it is full.

¶¶ La Guarida, Concordia 418 entre Gervasio y Escobar, Centro, T8669047, www.laguarida .com. 1200-1600, 1900-2300. Film location for *Fresa y Chocolate*, good food, international menu, fish a speciality, light lunches, more formal dinners, always busy, 'street guides' may not take you here because the *paladar* owners do not pay commission to them. Reservations recommended.

¶¶ Los XII Apóstoles, nearby on Vía Monumental, Casablanca, T638295. 1200-2300. International style, as well as fish and good *criollo* food, good views of the Malecón. With it is the **Polvorín** disco, CUC$5 including a drink, 2100-0300, and bar, 1600-2100.

¶¶-¶ Al Medina, Oficios 12, entre Obrapía y Obispo, T8671041. 1200-2400. Arab food in lovely colonial mansion, try chicken in sesame, huge vegetarian combo, lovely fresh fruit juices CUC$1.50, good coffee, some seating on large cushions, trios play during opening hours, also Mosque and Arab cultural centre off beautiful courtyard.

¶¶-¶ Bellomar, Virtudes 169A esq Amistad, Centro, T8610023. 1200-2300. Good unassuming Cuban cooking in this *paladar*, CUC$10 for fish, salad and rice. Friendly and obliging. Quirky festive setting with *bodeguita*-style scribbles.

¶ Doña Blanquita, Prado 158 entre Colón

y Refugio. A *paladar* run by English-speaking lawyer, simple but good food, pork, chicken or eggs, upstairs, inside with fan or on balcony.

¶¶-¶ Gentiluomo, Bernaza esq Obispo, T8671300. 1200-2400. Pasta, pizza, CUC$3-8 reasonable food but don't expect them to have everything on the menu, friendly service, nice environment, a/c.

¶¶-¶ La Julia, O'Reilly 506A, T627438. 1200-2400. Traditional, popular *paladar* with Creole food, large portions, great rice and beans. Few tables so reserve or arrive early.

¶¶-¶ La Moneda Cubana, San Ignacio 77, entre O'Reilly y Empedrado. T8673852. 1230-2200. Limited choice *paladar*, grilled fish with salad, congrí with fried banana and usually good salads prepared for vegetarians. More notable for the decor of wall-to-wall currency and business cards from all over the world.

¶¶-¶ La Tasquita, Jovellar (27 de Noviembre) entre Espada y San Francisco, Centro, T8734916. 1200-2400. Wonderful food, great family atmosphere, traditional *paladar* setting, mammoth portions served with delicious rice and beans, plus good salads. Great cocktails.

¶¶-¶ Los Nardos, Paseo del Prado 563 entre Dragones y Teniente Rey, opposite the Capitolio, T8632985. 1200-2400. Dining room upstairs lined with cabinets containing old football trophies while the heavy wooden furniture is reminiscent of a rancho. Not an option for vegetarians, plenty of fish and meat, pork, lamb or Uruguayan steak, large, filling portions, popular with Cubans and foreigners, background music is limited to golden oldies played 2-3 times during the meal. Above the restaurant is another, smaller, cheaper and less luxurious restaurant run by the same society, Juventud Asturiana, called **El Asturianito**.

¶¶-¶ Puerto de Sagua, Bélgica (Egido) 603 esq Acosta, T8671026. Nautical theme with chrome 1950s-style bar serving great cocktails, a cheap canteen-style restaurant serving good value, well-prepared food such as pasta, pizza and prawns in tomato sauce, or a more upscale, overpriced restaurant with same kitchen, serving fish, seafood, crab and frogs' legs accompanied by live music.

¶ Café París, Obispo y San Ignacio, no phone. 0800-0300. Serves good chicken, beer CUC$1.50, snacks and pizza, live music, lively in evenings, pity about the hassling from harmless but irritating *jineteros*.

♥ Cafetería Torre La Vega, Obrapía 114, next to the Casa de México, no phone. 0900-2100. Cheap breakfast, *platos combinados* CUC$3, better value spaghetti CUC$1.05, beer CUC$1 for national brands, CUC$1.50 imported.

♥ Chinese market, Zanja and Rayo, 1 block west of Galiano, has several *paladares* in a small street, some open until 2400. Tables inside or outside, menus on view, you will be pestered for your custom. Don't expect authentic food. Chop suey or chow mein is about as Oriental you'll get.

♥ Hanoi, Brasil 507 y Bernaza, T8671029. 1200-2400. Cuban food, 3 courses for CUC$6, *combinados* for CUC$2-3, *mojito* for CUC$2, plenty of food, live music, nice atmosphere.

♥ La Dichosa, Obispo esq Compostela. 0800-2300. Good place for breakfast or a snack, CUC$2-5.

♥ Torre de Marfil, Mercaderes, entre Obispo y Obrapía, T8671038. 1200-2400. Good, inexpensive Cantonese menu. Better than anything in Chinatown. Chinese medicine shop open 1000-1800.

Vedado and Plaza de la Revolución *p91, map p92*

Near La Rampa there are some cheap *pizzerías* and self-service restaurants.

♥♥♥ 1830, Calzada y 20, T553090. 1200-2400. Wonderful setting at the mouth of the river, popular for weddings and *quinceañera* celebrations, international food at international prices, cabaret at 2200, themed nights, something different every night, admission price depends on who is playing.

♥♥♥ La Torre, 17 y M, at top of Edif Focsa, T553088. Restaurant and bar 1200-2400. Renovated and reopened in 2005 with every luxury. French and international cuisine, about CUC$40 per person but worth it, great views over Havana, a/c.

♥♥♥-♥♥ El Conejito, M esq 17, T8324671. Restaurant 1200-2400, bar 0900-0200. Specializes in rabbit in several different sauces, other meat options available, quite expensive but worth it.

♥♥♥ Hurón Azul, Humboldt 153 esq P, T8791691. 1200-2400. International menu, works by local artists and photos of celebrity diners adorn the walls of this *paladar*, a/c.

Creative menu, Mediterranean influences.

♥♥ Nerei, 19 110 esq L, T8327860. 0900-2400, breakfast, lunch and dinner. Good food, not everything is fried, lamb with pepper, chicken and beer, grilled squid, main course with salad and rice around CUC$14-18, porch dining, English spoken.

♥♥-♥ Cafetería La Rampa, at the Habana Libre, L entre 23 y 25, T8346100, www.solmeliacuba.com, with access from the street as well as the hotel. Open 24 hrs. Breakfast, sandwiches, pizza (CUC$3.50-10) and pasta (CUC$3.50-6), burgers (CUC$4.50-6.50) and main meals.

♥♥-♥ Casa de la Amistad, Paseo entre 17 y 19 (see page 91). 1100-2300. Chicken, snacks and pizza. Inside the main building is **Restaurant Primavera**, 1200-2400, elegant furniture, antiques, good table service.

♥♥-♥ Trattoria Marakas, O entre 23 y 25, T8333740. 1200-2400. Good Italian, great pizzas, CUC$3.95-5.75, pasta around CUC$5, even has mozzarella and olive oil. Plastic furniture, canteen atmosphere.

♥ Amor, 23 759 entre B y C, T8338150. 1200-2400. Welcoming atmosphere, a *paladar* with large eating area, elegant furniture, great food, good portions for CUC$8-10, fried chicken, peanut sauce, rice, salad and beer. Try and go on the first Sun in the month when they have a musical gathering on the rooftop, the **Azotea de Elda Peña**, 1400-1800. Local artists perform, great fun, entrance by donation to the local hospital.

♥ Gringo Viejo, 21 454 entre E y F, T8311946. 1200-2300. Nice atmosphere with cinema memorabilia around the *paladar*, good portions, fruity or spicy sauces.

♥ Pekin, 12 y 23, T8334020. Close to Cementerio Colón. Also at Calzada entre D y E. 1200-2200. An unprecedented selection of 50 vegetable dishes. Clean, friendly and cheap, with informative run downs of the health benefits of veg. The catch is that it is all cold, tepid at best, there are normally huge queues except on Sun, the service can be slow and by dinner time the options are limited.

Ice cream parlours

A visit to the **Coppelia** open-air ice cream parlour, 23 y L, Vedado, can be a mixed experience. The parlour found movie fame in *Fresas y Chocolate*. The building, which occupies a whole block, has a capacity for 707 seated ice cream lovers. There are several separate outdoor areas to eat in, each with its own entrance and queue in the surrounding streets, or inside in La Torre. Tue-Sun 1100-2230, if you pay in *pesos cubanos*, you will almost certainly have to queue for an hour or so. Pay in *pesos convertibles* to avoid the queue, open 24 hrs. Bring your own plastic spoons for the tubs as they invariably run out. CUC$1-1.50 for one scoop. Disappointed visitors have complained about being segregated from Cubans by chains and forced to sit in a dingy area with a choice of only four flavours of ice cream.

Several street stalls specialize in ice cream, 21 esq K, near to **Coppelia** but no queues, CP$3 per cone.
Bim Bom, 23 y Calzada de Infanta, Vedado, open daily 1000-2400.

Miramar *p94*
🍴🍴🍴 El Tocororo (national bird of Cuba), 18 302 y Av 3, T2042209. Mon-Sat 1200-2400. Excellent food at CUC$40-60 a head although there is a cheaper executive lunch, old colonial mansion with nice terrace, great house band, no menu, ostrich steak, prices fluctuate widely but one of the best restaurants in town. Also has **Sakura**, sushi bar and saki.
🍴🍴🍴-🍴🍴 La Cecilia, 5 entre 110 y 112, T2041562. 1200-2400. Good international food, mostly in open-air setting, a septet plays while you are eating.
🍴🍴 El Aljibe, 7 entre 24 y 26, T2044233. 1200-2400. Open framework design, nice and breezy, friendly atmosphere, popular with Cubans, chicken the house speciality, try *pollo al Aljibe*, CUC$12 and you can have second helpings, other dishes more expensive, delicious black beans, very generous portions.
🍴🍴 La Esperanza, 16 105 entre 1 y 3, T2024361. Mon-Sat 1900-2300. Small sign, very popular with Cubans and foreigners, traditional Cuban food, meal and drinks around CUC$25 per person, potent mango daiquirís, reservations advisable, run by Hubert and Manolo in their living room surrounded by their paintings.
🍴🍴 La Fontana, 3-A 305 esq 46, T2028337. 1200-2400. Good Cuban food, *paladar* extremely popular with Cubans, tourists

and diplomats, ask for *menú de la casa* for non-inflated prices, arrive early or make a reservation.
🍴🍴-🍴 La Cocina de Lilliam, 48 1311, entre 13 y 15, T2096514. Sun-Fri 1200-1500, 1900-2200, closed 20 Dec-5 Jan. *Paladar* serving good Cuban food with tables outside in lovely garden, fish, crab, popular with locals, reservations recommended, main course plus beer CUC$20, good service.
🍴 Calle 10, 10 314 entre 3 y 5, near Teatro Karl Marx, Miramar, T2053970. 1500-2400. A *paladar* in a mansion setting, good service, English spoken, main course plus beer CUC$10.50. Outdoor seating with open-air grill, tiki bar, strolling musicians expect hefty tip.

Havana suburbs *p94, map p85*
🍴🍴 Las Ruinas, 100 esq Cortina de la Presa in Parque Lenin, T6578286. Tue-Sun 1200-1800. One of the best restaurants in Havana, the ruined plantation house has been incorporated into a modern structure, mosquitoes at dusk, great resident pianist, tours of Parque Lenin often include a meal here, otherwise take a taxi, CUC$15, try to persuade the driver to come back and fetch you, as otherwise it is difficult to get back.

Playas del Este *p95*
There are many *paladares* in Guanabo and elsewhere along the coast, reasonable prices. If you are self-catering, there is an excellent farmers' market in Guanabo selling fresh fruit and vegetables 6 days a week and a supermarket. Hotels in Guanabo have cheap food, with live music.
🍴 Pizzería Al Mare, Av 5 y 482, Guanabo. A variety of pizzas. Charges in *pesos cubanos*, CP$4 for a small pizza, CP$21 for a family-sized pizza.

🕐 Bars, clubs and cabarets

Havana clubs are late night/early morning affairs with most Cubans arriving around midnight and staying late. Queues at the weekends. Cubans dress up for club nights and most clubs have a smart dress code, strictly enforced by the door staff. No one under 18 is admitted. The emphasis is on dancing, be it *salsa* and Latin styles, R and B, hip hop or rock. Many places are frequented by *jineteros/as* and lone travellers have reported feeling uncomfortable with unwelcome attention. Several venues now feature early shows, aimed at young Cubans, with entrance in pesos.

All the main hotels have their own cabarets, eg **Parisien** at Hotel Nacional, T8733564 ext 136, excellent show for CUC$35, lasts longer than **Tropicana** and of equivalent standard, 2100-0200, make a reservation on the day or the day before, the main show is 2200-2400 with dancers and cabaret artistes, from 2400-0200 live music with soloists and bands.

La Habana Vieja and Centro *p85, map p88*

Musicians in most bars. Many play a few songs, then come round with the collecting bowl trying to sell their CDs, and move on, to be replaced by another band who do the same thing.
Bar Dos Hermanos, Av del Puerto esq Sol, opposite the ferry terminals, T8613514. 0900-2400. Good, down to earth bar, bohemian atmosphere, popular with Cubans, just off the tourist circuit so lower prices, chicken CUC$3, *mojito* CUC$3, local *son* band any time between 1200-2300, ask the barman who's playing.
Bar Monserrate, Monserrate y Obrapía. 1100-0100. Beer CUC$1.50, cocktails CUC$3, food not recommended, interesting to sit and watch comings and goings, bar staff seem to have unwritten agreement whereby girls are allowed in with a foreigner, or if they buy a drink, but if girl-to-punters ratio gets too high, some of the girls have to leave.
Cabaret Nacional, San Rafael y Prado, entrance to the side of Gran Teatro, Centro, T8632361. A cheap version of the **Tropicana**, 2200-0200, couples only, CUC$10 per couple includes drinks of up to CUC$5. Shows with taped music, occasionally with an orchestra but not top class. If there is a good orchestra the entry fee rises. On Thu **Peña de Yoruba Andabo** for AfroCuban music, 1600-1930, CUC$3 per person including drinks of CUC$1.50. Wed, Sat **Peña del Danzón**, 1600-1930, CP$10.
Callejón de Hamel, Hamel entre Aramburu y Hospital, Centro Habana, T8781661. A fast, kicking *rumba* show with invited guests and community artists every Sun from 1200-1500, a good audience and electric jam

sessions make this a recommended venue. Children's entertainment the first and third Sat of each month 1000-1200 and the last Fri of each month traditional Cuban music 2100-2300.
Casa de la Trova, San Lázaro 661, entre Belascoaín y Gervasio, T8643373. Thu-Sun 1900-2200, where locals go to hear traditional Cuban music, thoroughly recommended.
Casa del Tango Edmundo Daubar, Neptuno 309 entre Aguila y Italia, T8630097. Daily 1000-2000. A museum to tango and dance academy with memorabilia from the 1940s; octogenarians perform heart-wrenching tango. Every Mon there is a tango show and dancing.
Fundación Distilería Havana Club, Av del Puerto 262 entre Sol y Muralla, T8618051. Rum museum, shop, art gallery, courtyard restaurant and 2 bars, 1 with nightly music, 1000-2400, good *cuba libre* and sometimes showcase quality live bands.
La Bodeguita del Medio, the bar not to miss in the old town for Hemingway fans (see Eating, also for **La Floridita**), it is a favourite for tour parties.
Lluvia de Oro, Obispo esq Habana. 0800-2400. Good place to drink rum and listen to loud rock music or *salsa* (full pelt in the afternoon), also food.
Sociedad Yoruba, at the Asociación Cultural Yoruba, Prado 615 entre Monte y Dragones, T8635953, www.cubayoruba.cult.cu. Fri 2100-2400 they hold an event called **Peña del Tambor a la Poesía** with the female percussion, singing and dancing group, Obiní Batá; Sun 1700-2000 *boleros*; second Sun in each month 1100-1200 Peña Infantil with the group Folklórica Optica Obbi; last Sun of the month 1100-1200 Peña Infantil with Proposiciones.

Vedado and Plaza de la Revolución *p91, map p92*
Cabaret Las Vegas, 25 104 esq Calzada de Infanta, Vedado, T8367939. 2200-0300. Show with dancers and taped music, CUC$3 *consumo mínimo*, matinee on Thu-Sun 1600-2000 with the group Yoruba Andabo on Sat.
Café Cantante Mi Habana, downstairs from El Delirio Habanero, side entrance, T8735713. Open nightly from 2200-0300, top live bands, CUC$5, sometimes it is CUC$15, depending

Cuba Havana Listings

on the band, well regarded and popular with Cuban musicians and other personalities. They also hold late afternoon (Tue-Sun 1600-2000) *peñas*, **Tardes de Mi Habana**, sometimes with live local bands, entrance CUC$5-10, very popular with young Cubans.

Café El Gato Tuerto (One-eyed Cat), O entre 17 y 19, T552696. 1200-0300, CUC$5 *consumo mínimo*. *Son*, *trova* and *boleros* performed 2400-0500. Bohemian people and post-modern decor, funky, good restaurant on 1st floor, eat on balcony overlooking Malecón and **Hotel Nacional**.

Casa de la Amistad, Vedado, see p91. Entry free. Dancing on the veranda or in the gardens after the show. You are very unlikely to be hustled. Very limited toilet facilities.

Casa de la Cultura de Plaza, Calzada y 8, Vedado, T8312023. Concerts and shows, different artistes, different times. Known for the **Jazz Plaza Festival** in Dec and **Joven Jazz** in November when local and foreign jazz musicians aged 16-30 compete. Regular events include: **Peña de Tango**, the second Sat in the month, free, 1700-2100; **Peña de pop-rock**, the first Fri in the month1900-2100; drama evenings the second and third Fri of the month with different theatre companies 2000-2200; traditional music the third and fourth Sat of the month 1500-1700; hip hop the last Sun of the month 1700-1900; **Latin show**, with music, singing, dancing, last Sun of the month 1700-1900.

Club Atelier, 17 esq 6, corner of Parque John Lennon, T8306808. Daily 2200-0200, CUC$2 per couple. Small L-shaped dance floor, karaoke and music videos on a large screen, pool table, Cuban beer CUC$1.

Copa Room, at the Riviera, Paseo entre Malecón y 1, Vedado, T8364051, Susana@gcrivie.gca.tur.cu. Wed-Mon 2030-0300. Show 'De Cuba Traigo *Salsa*' with dancers, soloists and orchestra 2200-0030, followed by taped music 0030-0300. Sometimes jazz sessions in the **Hotel Riviera** bar off the lobby, entrance after Copa Room, phone first to check listing. Recommended.

El Delirio Habanero, at the Teatro Nacional, Paseo y 39, Plaza de la Revolución, T8735713, upstairs on the 6th floor (lift sometimes not working). A piano bar where you can hear quality music from small groups, *nueva trova*, *bolero*, etc, 2200-0600, CUC$5-15 depending on who is playing. Resident band **Los Tres de

la Habana**. Great views of floodlit José Martí monument and Plaza de la Revolución. Take the big red sofa seats under the windows. Busy at weekends with a mostly Cuban crowd. Recommended.

Habana Café, the trendy place to go in the **Meliá Cohiba**, T8333636, which is now a 1950s theme place with old cars, Cubana plane hanging from the ceiling, memorabilia on the walls, Benny Moré music and large screen showing brilliant film of old Cuban musicians and artistes, entrance to the left of the main hotel entrance, 2000-0230, live music at weekends 2230-0200, cover charge CUC$10 or more depending on who is playing, when top local bands draw the crowds. On other days there are dancers and soloists.

Habana Libre Turquino Sala de Fiestas, L entre 23 y 25, www.solmeliacuba.com, is on the 25th floor of the hotel, T8334011. Amazing views, the roof opens and you can dance to live music under the stars, CUC$10, if you are in a group 1 person needs a passport, drinks expensive. Top bands often play live, open every night 2230-0300.

Imágenes, Calzada 602 esq C, T8333606. 2200-0200. Different comedians every night followed by taped music. Mon-Thu CUC$5 *consumo mínimo*, Fri-Sun CUC$5 for drinks of CUC$3. Weekend matinee 1530-2030, karaoke and varied taped music.

Jazz Café, Galerías de Paseo, Primera entre A y Paseo, T553556, top floor of blue glass building. Live jazz 2400-0200, including Oscar Valdés and sometimes Chucho Valdés as well as other top jazz bands, CUC$10 *consumo mínimo*, bar and restaurant, very popular, good atmosphere, can be hard to get a table, recommended.

La Zorra y el Cuervo (Fox and Crow), 23 y O, T8332402. Entrance through a very good reproduction British telephone box, CUC$10 with CUC$5 for drink, opens 2200, first set 2300, second set 0010, closes at 0200, very popular with locals and tourists, great jazz every night, get there before 2300 if you want a table with a good view of the stage, gets packed later. Good-quality jazz club, Cuban bands often feature visiting US musicians, weekly listings at the entrance, highly recommended, beer, *cuba libre*, *mojito* all CUC$2.

Salón Rojo at Hotel Capri, T8333747, for reservations. Daily show with taped music, karaoke, games with audience participation and sometimes a dance show. From 0100-0300 live bands, then 0300-0400 taped music, price depends on the band. Matinée on Sun.

Scherezada, Edificio Focsa, M y 19, next to Teatro Guiñol, T8323042. Daily 2200-0200. Matinée 1600-2000. Night club with comedians, live and taped music, CUC$4 per couple, snacks and drinks available.

Tikoa, 23 entre N y O, T8309973. Daily 2200-0200. CUC$6 per couple or CP$150 cover charge, at lower end of La Rampa along with several other similar-style discos, popular with tourists and young Cubans, playing varied music, karaoke and music videos.

UNEAC, Av 17 entre G y H, outside in the Hurón Azul, T553113. Bar, tables, chairs and small stage. *Rumba* (resident band **Clave y Guaguancó**) and *trova* bands play alternate Wed 1700-2000, called **Peña del Ambia** and **Trova sin Trava**. Crowded and can be difficult to get a drink from the bar. Sat, **Noche de Boleros**, 2000-0200. On the second Thu of each month there is jazz, **Tardes del Jazz**, 1700-1900. CUC$5 entrance. Good atmosphere, friendly, popular with Cuban artists. Events listed at entrance.

Miramar *p94*

Casa de la Música Miramar, Sala Te Quedarás, 20 esq 35, in Miramar, T2040447. 1100-0300. A great place with a solid *salsa* disco and live bands on stage in a beautiful old house. Entrance CUC$10-20 depending on which bands are playing, 2300-0300. The latest Cuban bands play here and there is a well-stocked CD/music shop open 1100-2300. Afternoon *peñas* daily 1700-2100, popular with young Cubans, CUC$5-10. **Piano Bar Diablo Tun Tún** on the 2nd floor, live music and disco, Cuban and international styles, daily 0300-0600, CUC$5-15. *Parrillada* 1000-2200.

Club Almendares, Márgenes del Río Almendares, 49C y 28, T2044990, estrella@club.co.cu. A complex including a restaurant, **El Lugar**, 1200-2400, has a lovely view and a trio plays music; the **Salón Chévere** night club, 2300-0400, CUC$6; **Pizzería La Pérgola** and swimming pool, 1000-1800, CUC$5, children under 4 free.

Club Ipanema, Hotel Copacabana, Av 1 entre 44 y 46, T2041037. Tue-Sun 2300-0300, Tue-Thu CUC$3, Fri-Sun CUC$5, 1 cocktail

included. Gets very busy at weekends, large dance floor, *salsa* and western disco, taped music, entry to over-25s only.

El Río Club, A entre 3 y 5, T2093389. Mon-Sat 2200-0300, Sun 1800-0300, CUC$5pp. Recently reopened, locals still refer to it as **Johnnie's Club**, its name before the Revolution. Daily programme changes with soloists, duets and septets.

Salón de Boleros 'Dos Gardenias', 7, esq 26, Miramar, T2042353. Daily 2200-0300, CUC$5. Upmarket *bolero* venue, live shows every night, 2 shows on Fri-Sat, elegant, well-dressed crowd. There are 3 restaurants here: Chinese, Italian self-service and criollo (Cuban and international), all open 1200-2400, each with bar.

Salón Rosado Beny Moré, **La Tropical**, Av 41 y 46, T2035322. Drinks are charged in *pesos convertibles* or *pesos cubanos*. Rock music Tue 2100-0100, CUC$5, techno music with videos Wed 2000-0030, **Tarde de la Rumba**, CUC$5. Fri-Sat 2100-0130, live *salsa* with top bands, CUC$5. Sun 0900-1200 children's activities, free. Sun 1300 onwards, **Peña de los abuelos**, for older people, live bands, CUC$5. Tue-Sun, with live *salsa* bands including top names on Fri-Sun 2100-0200, CUC$5, outdoor location, very popular, mostly Cuban crowd.

Tropicana, 72 No 4504 entre 43 y 45, Marianao, T2670110. Daily 1200-0100. Reservations are recommended between 1300 and 2000. Cabaret 2030-2400, show starts at 2200, followed by taped music. Internationally famous and open-air (entry refunded if it rains). 3 price levels, CUC$70, CUC$80, CUC$90, including a welcome drink, snack, Coca Cola and ¼ bottle of *Havana Club*, but the more you pay the older your rum and the better your seat. If you book through a hotel you can get dinner there for CUC$10 extra. Best to take a tour, which will include transport, as a taxi from La Habana Vieja costs CUC$12.

Havana suburbs *p94, map p85*

Macumba, 222 esq 37, La Coronela, La Lisa, in **La Giraldilla** tourist complex in the western suburbs, T2730568. Sun-Fri 1700-2300, Sat 1700-2400, reservations important. Small floor show, open-air, rated as a top Havana disco, very popular with Cubans and foreigners, queues, 2 large

dance floors for *salsa*, *merengue* and R&B.
Mon fashion show, Tue and Wed variety
show, Thu small live bands, Fri **Noche de
Fantasía** fashion show, reggaeton and
comedians 2300-0200, Sat top-class live
bands, Sun matinee 1700-2300. Mon-Thu
CUC$5, but for good bands CUC$10-15.

● Entertainment

Havana *p84, maps p85, p88, and p92*
Cinema
Observe queuing procedures to buy tickets.
Comprehensive weekly listings of all films
from Thu-Wed are posted in cinema
windows. Most have a/c.
Acapulco, 26 entre 35 y 37, Nuevo Vedado,
T8339573. Showings at 1630, 1830, 2030, Sat
and Sun at 1400, CP$10.
Chaplin, 23 entre 10 y 12, T8311101. Arty
films at 1400, 1700 and 2000.
Payret, Prado 503, esq San José, T8633163.
Films shown continuously from 1230. Thu
Peña Juvenil with the alternative music
group, Balance, free; Fri **Rincón del Feeling**
2000-2400, CUC$5, Sun **Peña 'Algo Contigo'**,
varied musical show, CUC$5.
Riviera, 23 entre Presidentes y H, Vedado,
T8309564. Films shown from 1630.
Yara, opposite **Habana Libre** hotel,
T8311723. Renovated in 2006. From 1230,
last showing after 2100, late showings at the
weekends, 2 video lounges show recently
released US films, 40 seats in each salon, but
several are broken and sound quality is
sometimes poor in Salon B. Often sold out at
weekends. Also 2 galleries for exhibitions
and shop for souvenirs and posters.
Annual Film Festival in Dec (overlaps with
Jazz Festival) in all cinemas. International
films, no translations into English.
Information in **Hotel Nacional**.

Theatre
Amadeo Roldán, Calzada 512 y D, Vedado,
T8324521. Renovated concert hall which is
the base for the Orquesta Sinfónica Nacional,
concerts Sun 1700. 2 auditoriums, la sala
Amadeo Roldán and la sala Alejandro García
Caturla, which is for chamber music, price
varies CUC$5-20 depending on the event.
Gran Teatro de la Habana, Prado y San
José, on Parque Central next to **Hotel
Inglaterra**, T8617391,

dirgth@cubarte.cult.cu, CUC$20. More
traditional programmes, claims to be the
oldest working theatre in the world, opened
in 1837, building seats 1500. The **Conjunto
Folklórico Nacional** and **Danza
Contemporánea** dance companies
sometimes perform here. Highly
recommended.
**Palacio del Teatro Lírico Nacional de
Cuba**, Zulueta 253 entre Animas y Neptuno,
T8665430. Sat 2200, first and third Fri of each
month at 1800, CUC$10. The Compañía del
Teatro Lírico Nacional offers a variety of
concerts: opera, operetta and Spanish and
Cuban zarzuela.
Teatro Karl Marx, Av 1 entre 8 y 10,
Miramar, T2030801. Renovated in 2000 and
now famous for hosting the first gig by a
Western band, Manic Street Preachers, who
played 2001 in front of Fidel Castro. The
main auditorium seats 4800 and changes its
programme every month. The smaller **Sala
Atril** is used for soloists and small cultural
groups, Tue-Sun from 2200. Prices depend
on the artiste but generally CUC$5.
Teatro Mella, Línea 657 entre A y B, Vedado,
T8335651, tmella@cubarte.cult.cu. Thu-Sat
2030-2200, Sun 1700-1900, tickets
CUC$5-10. Specializes in modern dance.
Several international festivals are held here
but other programmes change frequently.

O Shopping

Havana *p84, maps p85, p88, and p92*
Shopaholics, be aware that Cuba is not
going to satisfy your urges. There is little to
spend your money on without a great deal
of effort. Large stores or supermarkets will
ask you to leave your bags at the entrance
and sometimes try and charge you for their
return.

Art and handicrafts
Fin de Siglo, San Rafael entre Aguila y
Galiano. Tue-Sun 1000-1700. Vendors who
used to be at the Feria del Malecón, an
outdoor market are now in this building with
access from three streets. Busy, lots of
homemade products, including shoes,
jewellery, lamps and the ubiquitous
booksellers. Che Guevara and religious
Santería items lead the sales charts. Illegal
cigar sellers operate here.

Galería del Grabado, at the back of the Taller Experimental de Gráfica de la Habana, Callejón del Chorro 62, Plaza de la Catedral, T8620979. Mon-Fri 0930-1630. Original lithographs and other works of art can be purchased or commissioned directly from the artists. You can watch the prints and engravings being made and specialist courses are available.

La Joya, Monserrate esq Teniente Rey (Brasil), T8638364. Mon-Sat 0900-1800, Sun 0900-1300. Arts and crafts, clothing, stamps, all Cuban products with a Cuba logo. You need documentation to take works of art out of the country or you may have them confiscated at the airport; galleries will provide the necessary paperwork and even vendors in the market can give you the necessary stamp.

Palacio de la Artesanía is in the Palacio Pedroso (built 1780) at Cuba 64 entre Peña Pobre y Cuarteles (opposite Parque Anfiteatro), a mansion converted into boutiques on 3 floors with musicians in the courtyard. A large selection of Cuban handicrafts is available. It also has things not available elsewhere, such as American trainers, as well as clothing, jewellery, perfume, souvenirs, music, cigars, restaurant, bar and ice cream. Visa and MasterCard accepted, passport required.

Taller de Serigrafía, Cuba 513, T8623276, www.galeriascubanas.com. Mon-Fri 0900-1700. Another big workshop; again, you can watch the screen prints being made and buy things.

Open-air markets Feria del Tacón, Av Tacón entre Chacón y Empedrado, Habana Vieja, Plaza de la Catedral end. Wed-Sat 0800-1900. Havana's largest craft market, a multitude of products and if they don't have what you want someone will know someone who does, tourist souvenirs, clothing, paintings, the list is endless. Also sold here are carvings, crochet, ceramics, boxes, jewellery, T-shirts, baseball bats and black coral (illegal to bring in to many countries, so avoid).

Bookshops

There are second-hand bookstalls outside on the Plaza de Armas where you can pick up a treasure if you know what to look for.
El Navegante, Mercaderes 115 entre Obispo y Obrapía, T8613625. Mon-Fri 0930-1800, Sat

0830-1230. Maps, guides and nautical charts, both national and regional, also prepaid phone cards, disposable cameras and film.
El Siglo de las Luces, Neptuno esq Aguila, near Capitolio. Books sold in CUC$, postcards, posters and stationery.
Fernando Ortíz, L 160 esq 27, T8329653. Quite a wide selection, mostly in Spanish, and some beautiful postcards.
Instituto Cubano del Libro, Palacio del Segundo Cabo, O'Reilly 4 y Tacón, and 3 bookshops: **Librería Grijalba Mondadori**, excellent selection of novels, dictionaries, art books, children's books from around the world, all in Spanish, sold in CUC$; **Librería Bella Habana**, T8628091-3, Cuban and international publications, sold in CUC$; and **Librería Fayad Jamís**, charges in CP$.
La Moderna Poesía, Obispo 527 esq Bernaza, T8616983. Mon-Sat 1000-1800. Modern design, literature, sciences, art materials, CDs, posters, cards, café.

Food

Caracol chain, in tourist hotels (eg **Habana Libre**) and elsewhere, sells tourists' requisites and other luxury items such as chocolates, biscuits, wine, clothes, require payment in CUC$ (or credit cards: MasterCard, Visa). Bread is available at the French bakery on 42 y 19 and in the Focsa complex on 17 entre M y N.
Focsa Supermarket, or the **Amistad**, on San Lázaro, just below Infanta.
Isla de Cuba supermarket on Máximo Gómez entre Factoría y Suárez, has the best selection of food in Centro.

Food markets Farmers are allowed to sell their produce (root and green vegetables, fruit, grains and meat) in free-priced city *agromercados*. You should pay for food in *pesos cubanos*. There are markets in Vedado at 19 y B and a smaller one at 21 esq J; in Nuevo Vedado, Tulipán, opposite Hidalgo; in the Cerro district at the Monte and Belascoaín crossroads; and in Centro, the **Chinese market** at the junction of Zanja and Av Italia, where you can eat at street food stalls (avoid Mon). The last Sun of every month there is a large and busy food market held in Paseo, between Calzada de Zapata and the Teatro Nacional.

Music and souvenirs

Artex shop on L esq 23, T553162, has

excellent music section. Mon-Sat 1000-2100, Sun 1000-1900.

Casa de la Música EGREM shop, 20 3308 esq 35, T2040447 (see Bars and clubs above). A good selection of CDs and other music.

▲ Activities and tours

Havana *p84, maps p85, p88, and p92*
Dance
Folkcuba, 4 103 entre 5 y Calzada, Vedado, T303939, www.folkcuba.cult.cu. School of dance and percussion, 2 weeks of classes beginning the third week in January or the first week in July, taught in Spanish and English, with extra-curricular activities such as trips to dance venues to practise what you have learned. Course includes popular dance, santería dances and chants, rumba, percussion and Cuban culture, US$500 per participant or US$150 for an observer.

Marinas and diving
Agencies specializing in marinas and diving, including packages with accommodation and transfers, are:
Centro de Buceo La Aguja, dive centre takes up to 8 divers on the boat.
Club Náutico Internacional 'Hemingway', Av 5 y 248, Playa, T/F2046653.
Cubamar Viajes (see below).
Ecotur, Av Independencia esq Santa Catalina, Cerro, T6491055. Specializes in ecotourism, Cuban style, hunting, fishing, diving, birdwatching.
Marlin, C184 123, Reparto Flores, Playa, T2736675, F2737020. Marinas and sailing.

Tour operators
There are bureaux in all the major hotels. Tours can be arranged all over Cuba by bus or air, with participants picked up from any hotel in Havana at no extra charge. Prices vary between agencies and you can negotiate a reduction without meals.
Amistur, Paseo 406 entre 17 y 19, T8301220, amistur@amistur.cu. Agency of the Instituto Cubano de Amistad con los Pueblos, offering socio-political package tours. Specialized visits for groups to factories and schools as well as places of local historical or community interest.
Cuba Deportes, C20 710 entre 7 y 9, Miramar, T2040945, F2041914. All-inclusive sporting holidays.

Cuba Select Travel, Bacardí Building, of 310, Monserrate 261, Habana Vieja, T8664221, www.cubaselecttravel.com. European- owned and managed tour operator offering travel and tour arrangements, also tailor-made itineraries and alternative activities, art and cultural events, student travel, fishing, birdwatching, yacht charters and architectural tours.
Cubamar Viajes, 3 esq A, Malecón, Vedado, T8332523, www.cubamarviajes.cu. Specialize in student groups for adventure tourism, nature and socio-cultural exchanges, villa and campsite rentals and exclusive rental of motorhomes in Cuba.
Cubanacán, 17a entre 174 y 190, Siboney, Playa, T2089920, www.cubanacan.cu. Birdwatching and scuba diving tours, hunting and fishing tours, sailing, hiking and horse riding.
Gaviota Tours, hotels **Kohly, Panorama, Sevilla, Occidental Miramar** in Havana, T2044781, operacion@gavitur.gav.tur.cu, and at all the Gaviota hotels. Specializes in marinas, diving and packages with accommodation and transfers.
Havanatur, Edif Sierra Maestra, Av 1 entre 0 y 2, Miramar, T2042056, F2042877. Also branches in many hotels and separate offices in some towns, recommended for independent travellers who want tailor-made but reasonably priced tours.
Sol y Son, C23 64, La Rampa, Vedado, T8333271, F8365150. The travel company of **Cubana** airlines.

Watersports
Club Náutico Internacional 'Hemingway', Residencial Turístico 'Marina Hemingway', Av 5 y 248 Playa, T/F2041689.
Marlin, same address, part of Marinas y Náuticas Marlin in Reparto Flores, T2045088 (marina open 24 hrs), T2046848 (boat rental 0800-1700), F2045280, VHF 16 and 77. Open 0800-1700, boat trips, sport fishing, CUC$450 ½ day, motorized sports (waterskiing, banana boat), catamarans, sailing lessons in dinghies, windsurfing, diving and snorkelling.
Marina Tarará, Vía Blanca Km 19, VHF16, 19, 08, 72. Has moorings for 20 boats, VHF communications and provisioning, yacht charters, deep-sea fishing (CUC$280-450 per day depending on type of boat) and scuba diving, all of which can be arranged through the hotel tour desks or at the marina.

❷ Transport

Havana *p84, maps p85, p88, and p92*
Air
For information on flights to Cuba, see Getting there, page 71.

Airlines Cubana, www.cubana.cu, 23 64, esq Infanta, T8344446, information .cliente @cubana.avianet.cu; 5 y 110, Playa, T2029367, cubana.5y110 @cubana .avianet.cu; Edif Barcelona, Centro de Negocios, 5 y 76, Miramar, T2040171, cubanaenridan@enridan.mtc.co.cu; Centro de Negocios 3 y 78, Miramar, T2046679 ext 1017; Hotel Occidental Miramar, Room 185, T2049647, cubanaenridan@miramarco.cu; Hotel Habana Libre (Solcaribe Tours), T554600, boletos@solcaribetours.com; Terminal 3 Aeropuerto (24 hrs), T6490410, ventat3@hav.cubana.avianet.cu.
Aerocaribbean, 23 esq P, T8704965, F8365016, Mon-Fri 0830-1600, Sat 0830-1200, or at the airport, T6497340. **Air Europa**, 23 y P, Vedado, T8366917, Mon-Fri 0830-1630 and at Edif Santiago, Centro de Negocios, 5 y 78, Miramar, T2046904, F2046905, Mon-Fri 0830-1630, Sat 0900-1300. **Air France**, 23 y P, Vedado, T8332642, Mon-Fri 0830-1630, at the airport, T6499708, F8332634. **Air Jamaica**, 23 esq P, T8332447, F8332449, Mon-Fri 0830-1600, Sat 0830-1200, and at airport, Terminal 3, T6497340. **Iberia**, Centro de Negocios Miramar, edif Santiago de Cuba, 5 y 76, T2043444, F2043461, Mon-Fri 0900-1600, at the airport T6495234. **LTU**, 23 64 esq Infanta, T8333524, F8333590, Mon-Fri 0830-1200, 1300-1600. **Martinair Holland**, 23 esq E, T8333730, F8333732, Mon-Fri 0900-1600, Sat 0900-1300, at the airport T2664906.
Mexicana de Aviación, 23 esq P, T8333532, F8333077, Mon-Fri 0830-1630, Sat 0830-1200, at the airport F6495051.

Boat
There are ferries from Habana Vieja to **Casablanca** and **Regla**, which depart from San Pedro opposite Santa Clara. If you are facing the water, the Casablanca ferry docks on the left side of the pier and goes out in a left curve towards that headland, and the Regla ferry docks on the right side and goes out in a right curve.

Bus
Local There is a regular service on the *camellos*, long articulated buses on a truck bed, 20 centavos. They cover the main suburbs, M1 Alamar-Vedado, M2 Centro Habana-Santiago de las Vegas, M3 Alamar-Ciudad Deportiva, M4 Centro Habana-San Agustín, M5 Vedado-San Agustín, M6 Calvario-Vedado, M7 Centro Habana-Cotorro. Ask for the right queue. Other buses cost 40 centavos.

Long distance Terminal de Omnibus Interprovinciales, for **Astro** services, Av Rancho Boyeros (Independencia) by the Plaza de la Revolución, T8703397. **Víazul**, leaves from Av 26 entre Av Zoológico y Ulloa, Nuevo Vedado, T8811413, www.viazul.cu, but usually passes through the Astro terminal. **Astro** is cheaper, but **Víazul** is a better service. See below under individual towns for details.

Cycle
Check the bicycle carefully (take your own lock, pump, a bicycle spanner and puncture repair kit; petrol stations have often been converted into bicycle stations, providing air and tyre repairs). Cycling is a good way to see Havana, especially the suburbs; some roads in the Embassy area are closed to cyclists. The tunnel under the harbour mouth has a bus designed to carry bicycles and their riders. Take care at night as there are few street lights and bikes are not fitted with lamps.
Tienda El Orbe, Monserrate 304 esq Ignacio Agramonte, Manzana de Gómez, Habana Vieja, T8602617. Mon-Sat 0900-1630. Sales and rental of bicycles and equipment.

Taxis
Taxis are plentiful, see page 75. **Habanataxi**, **Panataxi** and **Taxi OK** all charge the same rates. Beware of private moonlighters (yellow licence plates, often identifiable by their harassment); they could charge you over the odds, generally are not paying any taxes and you have no come-back in the case of mishaps.
Panataxi is a call-out service, T555556. **Panataxis** also wait just outside most hotels and at the airport, or ask your hotel to call one. They are yellow Citröen cars, so they are the most comfortable, reliable and the cheapest, at under CUC$15 from the airport to Vedado.

Habanataxi is a good call-out taxi service, T539086. **Taxi OK**, T2040000, and **Fénix**, T8666666, a bit more expensive.

The cheapest taxis are the very smallest. Ask for the *oferta especial* or *servicio económico* and you will be charged less per km. For longer trips some companies charge by the hour and some by the km with a meter.

In Habana Vieja and Vedado, **bicycle or tricycle taxis** are cheap and readily available, a pleasant way to travel. A short journey will cost CUC$1, Old Havana to Vedado CUC$3, or pay around CUC$5 per hr, bargaining is acceptable. There is also the **cocomóvil**, quick and readily available if you can handle being driven around in a bright yellow vehicle shaped like a coconut shell on a 125cc motor bike. They take 2 passengers. The fare is fixed in dollars, but agree the fare before the journey. A typical fare from the Hotel Nacional to Old Havana is CUC$3. Less conspicuous are the **Rentar una fantasía** vehicles, using the same 125cc engine but designed as a pre-1920s motor car. **Gran Car**, T555456. For the real thing, Gran Car rent classic cars (including Oldsmobiles, Mercury '54, Buicks and Chevvy '55) with driver, maximum 4 passengers, CUC$25 per hr or CUC$30 per hr for cars without roofs (go for the Oldsmobile '52).

Train
Trains leave from the Estación Central on Ejido (Av de Bélgica) y Arsenal, Havana, to the larger cities. Get your tickets in advance as destinations vary, the departure time is very approximate. Tickets are easily purchased from the ticket office in the central station open 0900-1700 daily, T8614259. The Estación Central has what is claimed to be the oldest engine in Latin America, 'La Junta', built in Baltimore in 1842.

There are 2 services to **Santiago de Cuba** and 3 trains per day. They travel overnight and take 12-20 hrs, or so. Trains have to give way for a goods train, so there are always delays. The *Especial*, uses French-built trains, freezing a/c, reclining seats, folding tables, snacks, clean toilets and comfortable with good lighting. The *Especial* runs every other day, CUC$62 to Santiago with stops in Santa Clara, CUC$21, and Camagüey, CUC$40. The *Regular* train to Santiago (CUC$30) stops at all the provincial

capitals, eg Sancti Spíritus (CUC$13.50), Holguín (CUC$26.50, substituted in 2006 by a/c bus), Bayamo (CUC$25.50), Manzanillo (CUC$27.50), and on to Guantánamo (CUC$32). Take food and a torch as the toilets usually have no light. A coche motor (54-56 seats) runs to Camagüey on alternate days, CUC$27, currently the best service with a/c, TV, video, reclining seats etc. It continues to Santiago, CUC$42, and anywhere else by prior reservation if there is a group of tourists. Another *coche motor* without TV/video goes to Morón on alternate days.

There are also daily trains to **Pinar del Río**, 2205 arrives 0550, CUC$6.50, to Cienfuegos, CUC$8.20 and **Matanzas**, several from 0940, CUC$3, with intermediate stops. The *coche motor* to Cienfuegos, CUC$11, is better but leaves every other day, 1845, arrives 0020. A long-distance bus or dollar taxi may well do the same journey in a fraction of the time, eg Havana-Pinar del Río, 2 hrs or less by taxi, 7-8 hrs by train. It is not unusual for the trains to break down, in fact Cubans refer to this as 'normal service'. It will be fixed and carry on, but be prepared for a serious amount of time travelling. The 'Hershey' electric train with services to **Matanzas** starts from Casablanca, 0444, 0835, 1239 and 1721, buy tickets at booking office an hour before departure, CUC$2.80 one way.

ⓘ Directory

Havana *p84, maps p85, p88, and p92*
Banks For credit card withdrawals, TCs and exchange, Banco Financiero Internacional, 1 esq B, T8333423, F8332190, Mon-Fri 0800-1500, last day of the month until 1200, in Old Havana at Teniente Rey esq Oficios, a branch in Habana Libre complex, T554520, same times, and another branch in Miramar, 18 111 entre 1 y 3, T2042958. **Exchange bureau** in Hotel Nacional, 0800-1200, 1230-1930, credit card cash advances. **Buró de Turismo** in Tryp Habana Libre also gives credit card cash advances. Banco Metropolitano, Línea 63 y M, T553116, Mon-Fri 0830-1500, Sat 0830-1200, weekday commission on TCs is 3.5%, rising to 4% on Sat. Credit card advances from exchange houses, *cadecas*, incur a standard 1.5% handling charge. **Embassies and consulates** All in Miramar, unless stated otherwise. **Austria**, 5A 6617, esq 70, T2042825, F2041235, Mon-Fri 0900-1200. **Belgium**, 8 309

entre 3 y 5, T2042410, F2041318, Mon-Thu 0900-1200. **Canada**, 30 518, entre 5 y 7, T2042516, F2041069. **France**, 14 312 entre 3 y 5, T2013131, F2013127, Mon-Thu 0900-1230. **Germany**, B 652 esq 13, Vedado, T8332569, F8331586, Mon-Fri 0900-1200. **Italy**, 5 402 esq 4, T2045615, F2045661. **Japan**, Av 3 esq 80, Centro de Negocios 5th floor, T2043508, F2048902, Mon-Fri 0900-1230, 1430-1700. **Mexico**, Consulate 7 1206 entre 12 y 14, Embassy 12 518 entre 5 y 7, both T2042498, F2042294, Mon-Fri 0900-1100. **Netherlands**, 8 307 entre 3 y 5, T2042511/2, F2042059, Mon-Fri 0830-1130. **Spain**, Cárcel 51 esq Zulueta, Habana Vieja, T8668029, F8668015, Mon-Fri 0900-1300. **Sweden**, 34 510 entre 5 y 7, T2042831, F2041194, Mon-Fri 0930-1130. **Switzerland**, Av 5, 2005 entre 20 y 22, Miramar, T2042611, swissem@enet.cu, Mon-Fri 0900-1200. **UK**, 34, 702 entre 7 y 17, Miramar, T2041771, F2048104, embrit@ceniai.inf.cu; Commercial Section, Mon-Fri 0800-1530. **US**, **US Interests Section** of the Swiss Embassy, Calzada entre L y M, Vedado, T333551, 334401.

Internet Access is available at the cybercafé in the **Capitolio**. Go in the main entrance and it is diagonally opposite to your right. There are 9 terminals, CUC$3 for 30 mins, CUC$5 per hr. 0900-1800. You may have to wait up to 45 mins for one to be free. The large, 4- or 5-star hotels such as the **Habana Libre**, **Nacional**, **Parque Central**, **Meliá Cohiba**, all have business centres with computers for internet access, also telephone, fax and telex facilities, but they charge a lot more, eg CUC$3.50 for 15 mins, CUC$12 per hr at the **Nacional** and CUC$7 for 30 mins, CUC$12 per hr at the **Parque Central** (business centre on 1st floor, ext 1911, 1833, 0800-2000). The **Hotel Plaza**, Parque Central, also has internet in the lobby, at CUC$6 per hr, 24 hrs. Prepaid Etecsa cards can be used in the **International Press Center** on La Rampa, Vedado, where there are long queues. Several post offices have computers for the **Telecorreos** prepaid cards of CUC$4.50, including the post office at Línea y Paseo (8 terminals, good equipment, email only, not internet), T8334744, 24 hrs. **Medical services** The Cira García Clinic, 20 4101 esq 41, Miramar, T2042811/14, F2041633, payment in dollars, also the place to go for emergency dental treatment; the pharmacy (T2042880, open 24 hrs) sells prescription and patent drugs and medical supplies that are unavailable in other pharmacies, as does the nearby **Farmacia Internacional**, Av 41, esq 20, Miramar (T2042051, 0900-1900). **Clínica Internacional Habana del Este**, Av de las Terrazas, between Aparthotel Las Terrazas and Hotel Tropicoco in Santa María del Mar. **Post** Oficios 102, opposite the Lonja, and in the **Hotel Nacional** and **Hotel Habana Libre** building. Also on Ejido, next to central railway station and under the Gran Teatro de La Habana. **Radio** Radio Taíno FM 93.3, English and Spanish language tourist station, gives details of range of venues and Cuban bands playing, particularly in the programme **El Exitazo Musical del Caribe** from 1500-1800 presented by Alexis Nargona. Radio Ciudad de la Habana, 94.9 FM, 820 AM, in Spanish. Latest salsa programmes.

Telephone Empresa Telecomunicaciones de Cuba (Etecsa): the public telephone division is on Av 33 1427 entre 18 y 14, Miramar, T2061094; the international division is in the Centro de Negocios, Av 3 y 78, Miramar, T2045065; at the same address but in the Edif Barcelona is the mobile phone division, T8800566.

West from Havana

The west of Cuba is blessed with an exotic landscape of limestone mogotes, caves and mountains, forested nature reserves and tobacco plantations. This is where you will find the world's best dark tobacco, which is hand-processed into the finest cigars. There is world-class scuba diving and there are good beaches and wetlands for migrant water fowl. The Sierra del Rosario contains the Biosphere Reserve at Las Terrazas, as well as the orchidarium at Soroa. The capital of the province, Pinar del Río, can be a good base for excursions as transport starts from here, while María La Gorda is a diver's dream, low key, laid back and friendly. The small town of Viñales attracts thousands of visitors. Its position beside the mogotes provides spectacular views and good walking opportunities. Its beauty has been internationally recognized and the Viñales Valley has been declared a UNESCO world cultural landscape.

A dual carriage highway runs to Pinar del Río, the major city west of Havana. It takes two hours to get to there on the autopista, with virtually no traffic except horse-drawn buses to nearby villages. The autopista passes through flat or gently rolling countryside, with large stretches of sugar cane, tobacco fields and some rice fields, scattered royal palms and distant views of the Cordillera de Guaniguanico. An alternative route is to leave the autopista at Candelaria or Santa Cruz de los Pinos for the Carretera Central, quite a good road which adds only 20 minutes to the journey. It passes through citrus and other fruit trees. Villages straggle along the road, with colonnaded single-storey traditional houses and newer post-Revolution concrete block structures. ▶▶ *For Sleeping, Eating and other listings, see pages 114-118.*

Las Terrazas → *Phone code: 8. Colour map 1, B2.*

On the autopista, 51 km west of Havana, the Sierra del Rosario appears on the right and a roadside billboard announces the turning to **Las Terrazas/Moka**, 4 km north of the autopista. However, after that there is little signposting. The **Biosphere Reserve** ① *admission CUC$7, unless you have a reservation at the hotel*, covers 260 sq km of the eastern Sierra del Rosario. Las Terrazas was built in 1971 as a forestry and soil conservation station. It is a settlement of houses overlooking the lake of San Juan. In Las Terrazas there is a *paladar*, craft workshops, a gym, a cinema and a museum which sometimes holds *canturías* or folk music sessions. After the death in a car accident of the popular singer, Polo Montañez in 2002, his house was also opened as a museum, run by his brother. In nearby San Cristóbal, a clay statue of the singer has been put on display. Once a woodcutter, he rose to fame as a singer/songwriter with many hits in the three years before his death, touring Latin America and Europe. The hills behind the hotel rise to the **Loma del Salón** (564 m). There are easy hiking trails of 3-8 km or more demanding whole-day hikes. The cost of a day hiking with a professional guide is CUC$33-41 for one person, falling to CUC$14-18 with six people. Other activities include riding (CUC$6 per hour), mountain bikes (CUC$1), rowing (CUC$2 per hour) and fishing.

Soroa → *Phone code: 8. Colour map 1, B1.*

If travelling by car, you can make a detour to Soroa, a spa and resort in the Sierra del Rosario, 81 km southwest of the capital, either by continuing 18 km west then southeast from Moka through the Sierra del Rosario, or directly from the autopista, driving northwest from Candelaria. As you drive into the area from the south, a sign on the right indicates the **Mirador de Venus** and **Baños Romanos**. Past the baths is the **Bar Edén** (open till 1800), where you can park before walking up to the Mirador (25 minutes, on foot, free or CUC$3 on a horse) for fine views of the southern plains, the forest-covered Sierra and Soroa itself. There are lots of birds, butterflies, dragonflies and lizards around the path, and birdwatching is very popular here too.

Further north is a **Jardín Botánico Orchidarium** ① *guided tours daily 0830-1140, 1340-1555, CUC$3, birdwatching, hiking and riding CUC$3 an hr*, with over 700 species of orchids, of which 250 are native to Cuba, as well as ferns and begonias. There's a reataurant, **Castillo de las Nubes** (1200-1900, CUC$5-6). An excursion is possible to **El Brujito**, a village once owned by French landlords, where the third and fourth generations of slaves live.

Pinar del Río → *Phone code: 82. Colour map 1, B1.*

The capital of Pinar del Río province is lively and attractive, and it gives a good taste of provincial Cuba. The centre consists of single-storey neoclassical houses with columns, some with other interesting architectural detail.

There is a **cigar factory** ① *Maceo 157, T723424, Mon-Sat 0800-1700, CUC$5 for a short visit*, one of the town's main tourist attractions, which reputedly makes the best cigars in Cuba. Avoid the youngsters selling cigars outside; buy from the shop opposite, **Casa del Habano,** and you'll get the genuine article, even if it is pricey. The **rum factory (Fábrica de Guayabita)** ① *Isabel Rubio 189 entre Ceferino Fernández y Frank País, Mon-Sat 0800-1700, CUC$2, tour and stop at the tasting room,* makes a special rum flavoured with miniature wild guavas, Guayabita del Pinar, which comes in either dry or sweet varieties. Between the two is the cathedral of **San Rosendo** ① *Maceo 2 Este esq Gerardo Medina.* The **Museo Provincial de Historia** ① *Martí 58 entre Isabel Rubio y Colón, T754300, Mon-Sat 0800-1700, CUC$0.25,* details the history of the town and displays objects from the wars of Independence. The **Casa de la Cultura Tito Junco** ① *Martí esq Rafael Morales, Mon-Sat 0800-1800, evening activities according to scheduled programmes,* is in a huge, recently renovated colonial house and includes an art gallery, a hall for parties and seven classrooms for teaching dancing, painting, singing, etc. Another renovated building on Martí opposite the Wedding Palace, is the **Palacio de Computación** ① *Martí esq Gozález Coro, Mon-Sat 0800-2100,* with theatre, cafeteria and classrooms, inaugurated by Fidel Castro in January 2001. The **Teatro José Jacinto Milanés** was reopened in 2006 after restoration works that began in the 1990s. Well-known Cuban personalities such as Silvio Rodríguez, Pablo Milanés, Rosita Fornés, Rita Montaner, Brindis de Sala and Alicia Alonso, among others, have performed there. Originally a wooden building with a tiled roof, it was inaugurated in 1845. Restoration works included improvements to modernize the stage machinery, although the building still has a tiled roof, and it is hoped that drama and dance in the west will be promoted by its reopening.

Viñales→ *Phone code: 8. Colour map 1, B1.*

North of Pinar del Río, the road leads across pine-covered hills and valley for 25 km to Viñales, a delightful, small town in a dramatic valley in the **Sierra de los Organos**. The valley has a distinctive landscape, with steep-sided limestone mountains called *mogotes* rising dramatically from fertile flat-floored valleys, where farmers cultivate the red soil for tobacco, fruits and vegetables. An area of 132 sq km around Viñales has been declared a National Monument. There is a visitors' centre near **Hotel Los Jazmines**. Viñales itself is a pleasant town, with trees and wooden colonnades along the main street, red-tiled roofs, a main square with a little-used church and a **Casa de Cultura** with an art gallery. There are several bars and restaurants along the main street, Salvador Cisneros, but hardly of the quality to warrant the thousands of visitors who come here every year. On the edge of town is **Caridad's Garden** ① *turn left at the gas station at the end of Salvador Cisneros; admission free, tips welcome,* first planted in the 1930s and now a beautiful collection of fruit trees

> ⁑ As in so much of rural Cuba, horses, pigs, oxen, zebu cattle and chickens are everywhere, including on the main road.

and flowers from Cuba and around the world. A guide will show you around and let you try the various fruits. The garden is suffering a bit from the volume of visitors it now receives, but it is still worth seeing. The **Mural de la Prehistoria**, 2 km west, was painted between 1959 and 1976 by Lovigildo González, a disciple of the Mexican Diego Rivera. It is generally disliked as a monstrous piece of graffiti. You can see the paintings from **Restaurant Jurásico** (bar open 0800-1630), 100 m before the mural, and there is a swimming pool nearby. The **Cueva del Indio**, 6 km north of Viñales, is a very beautiful cave which you enter on foot, then take a boat (CUC$5 for foreigners) with a guide who gives you a description. There is a restaurant nearby where tour parties are given a lunch of *lechón* (suckling pig). About 100 m before the entrance, on the right side of the road, is a sign for a 2-hr walk through the **Cueva del Cable**. The path leads you down hundreds of steps into the cave. There are no guides, nor entry fee. Take a good torch and spare batteries – you're on your own! You can also visit the **Cueva de San Miguel**, to the west, which has been converted to a disco. More caves in a 25-km system are in the Valle de Santo Tomás, where you can visit the **Gran Caverna Santo Tomás** in a community called **El Moncada** 17 km southwest of Viñales.

The coast north of Viñales is worth a visit. The best and closest beach, 50 km, is at **Cayo Jutías** ① *CUC$5 entrance, beach bar 1000-1800 for drinks, 1300-1800 for food*, near Santa Lucía. A reef offshore protects the white sand beach and there is snorkelling gear for hire. The 6.7-km cay is reached by a causeway. Further east is **Cayo Levisa**, with a long, sandy beach and reef running parallel to the shore, with good snorkelling and scuba diving. Cayo Levisa is 15 minutes by boat from Palma Rubia. The jetty is on the south side and you follow a boardwalk through the mangroves to get to the hotel on the north side. Take insect repellent. Day trips or longer stays (20 cabins on the beach) are organized; you can even visit by helicopter.

Península de Guanahacabibes → *Phone code: 8. Colour map 1, B1.*

The Península de Guanahacabibes, which forms the western tip of Cuba, is a Natural Biosphere Reserve. It is made up of very recent limestone, with a rocky surface and patchy soil cover. There are fossil coastlines, caves and blue holes; but with dense woodland on the south coast and mangrove on the north, the peninsula is uninviting for the casual hiker. There are 12 amphibian species, 29 reptiles including iguana species, 10 mammals (including *carabalí* and *jutia conga*) and 147 bird species, including nine of the 22 which are endemic to Cuba. Permits are required for entering the 1,175-sq-km reserve. There is a scientific station at La Bajada. The Science Academy, T84-3277, offers a Safari Tour with an English-speaking guide, Osmani Borrego, for CUC$6 per person. You can climb to the Radar for CUC$1 for a good view of the forest and the sea.

María La Gorda → *Phone code: 8. Colour map 1, B1.*

In the middle of nowhere, and reputedly the best diving centre in Cuba, María La Gorda is an idyllic spot for relaxing or doing nothing but **diving**. Packages are offered including accommodation, food, diving (CUC$100 per person a day, minimum two people) and transfers from Havana (CUC$70 each way, four or five hours). The sea is very clear, very warm and calm, even when it is too rough to dive anywhere else in Cuba. There is good snorkelling too with small coral heads close to the white-sand beach, or you can go out on the dive boat. Unfortunately we have had reports of divers being allowed by the dive masters to touch and even break off coral, a practice which cannot be condoned.

● Sleeping

Las Terrazas *p112*
A-B Hotel Moka, above the village, T/F335516. 26-room hotel run in co-operation with the Cuban Academy of Sciences as an ecotourism centre, breakfast CUC$5, other meals CUC$15, transfer from Havana CUC$32, a/c. The hotel complex is beautifully designed and laid out, in Spanish colonial style with tiled roofs, gardens behind the hillside site have a tennis court and a pleasant swimming pool. This is an opportunity to stay in a nature reserve with tropical evergreen forests, 850 plant species, 82 bird species, an endemic water lizard and the world's 2nd smallest frog.
E Villa Juanita, La Pastora 601, Cayajabos, Artemisa, 3 km from Las Terrazas. 2 rooms, small kitchenette, meals available, good

food, very welcoming, no English but expressive, slow Spanish spoken.

Soroa *p112*
B-C Horizontes Villa Soroa, T852122. 49 cabins and 10 self-catering houses, a/c, phone, radio, some have VCR and private pool, restaurant **El Centro** (quite good), lunch CUC$8, dinner CUC$10, disco, bar, Olympic-sized swimming pool, bike rental, riding nearby and handicrafts and dollar shop. A peaceful place. The hotel runs 1-day, gently paced hikes around the main sights of the area with picnic for CUC$10, to caves for CUC$12.
D Casa Azul, 300 m outside Soroa next to a primary school. 1 big room with private bath, hot water, balcony overlooking a huge

garden, fruit trees, coffee bushes and mountains, free parking, meals available, daughter speaks some English.

Pinar del Río *p112*

A mafia of youths offer their assistance in taking you to the casa. They are after a commission and sometimes say that they are from Formatur, the tourism school.

E **Bertha Báez**, Pedro Téllez 53 entre Ormani Arenado e Isidro de Armas, T754247. 2 rooms, the 2nd floor is reserved for guests, hot and cold shower, a/c, fans, garage CUC$1.

E **Eloína Arteaga**, Isabel Rubio 18, Apto 4, opposite the Baptist church. 1 room, meals available, Eloína lives with her 2 daughters and 3 grand daughters.

E **Hospedaje Torres**, Adela Azcuy 7 entre Gerardo Medina y Isabel Rubio, no phone. Run by nice lady, room with fan or a/c, clean and safe, excellent breakfast and dinner.

E **José Antonio Mesa**, Gerardo Medina 67 entre Adela Azcuy y Isidro de Armas, T753173. Attractive colonial building, spacious, nice family but involved in paying commissions so unpopular with other renters.

E **Noelia Pérez Blanco**, Gerardo Medina 175 entre Ceferino Fernández y Frank País, T753660. Run by elderly lady, most of the house is used by tourists although there is only 1 bedroom, 2 beds, fan or a/c, TV, hot water, garage CUC$2, roof with table and chairs, a little English spoken.

E **Salvador Reyes** , Alameda 24 entre Volcán y Avellaneda, opposite phone company, T773145. 1 room, a/c, fan, hot shower, attractive terrace, English and German spoken, nice family and atmosphere.

E **Traveller's Rest**, Primero de Mayo 29 entre Isidro de Armas y Antonio Rubio, Apto 16, sign outside, T751792, http://geocities.com/travellers_rest_pinar/. 2 rooms with 2 beds, hot shower, a/c or fan, fridge, good meals available, book exchange, garage CUC$1 a day.

E **Zunilda Rodríguez Hernández**, Acueducto 16 entre Méndez Capote y Primera, Rpto Celso Maragota, T754639. 2 a/c rooms, private bath, hot water, breakfast and dinner, garage. Her husband Julio fought with Che and Fidel.

Viñales *p113*

There are a huge number of registered *casas particulares* and people meet you off the buses.

B **La Ermita**, Ctra de la Ermita Km 2, 3 km from town with magnificent view, T8-893204. 62 rooms, a/c, phone, radio, shop, tennis court, wheelchair access, pool (not always in use), nicer public areas and food better than at **Los Jazmines**, breakfast included, lunch CUC$10, dinner CUC$12.

B **Los Jazmines**, Ctra de Vinales Km 23.5, 3 km before the town, in a superb location with travel brochure view of the valley, T8-936205, F8-936215, in Havana, T7-334042, F7-333722. 62 nice rooms and 16 *cabañas*, nightclub, breakfast buffet CUC$5 if not already included, lunch CUC$10, dinner CUC$12, restaurant, bar with snacks, shops, swimming pool (CUC$5 including towels for day visitors and CUC$5 in vouchers for bar drinks), riding, transport.

C **Rancho San Vicente**, Valle de San Vicente, near Cueva del Indio, T8-893200. 40 a/c *cabañas*, bar, restaurant, breakfast included, lunch CUC$8, dinner CUC$10, nightclub, shop, tourist information desk, pool, open to day visitors, spa with sulphurous waters, mud baths, full-body massage.

E **Caridad Naveda**, Salvador Cisneros 8, no phone. Opposite **Caridad's Garden**, private room, a/c, fan, garage US$1, meals.

E **Casa Maura**, Salvador Cisneros 131, opposite **Don Tomás**. Big breakfast, dinner US$5, hot water, bikes US$3 a day.

E **Doña Inesita**, Salvador Cisneros 40, T8-793297. Energetic and friendly Inés Núñez Rodríguez and her husband, both in their 80s, offer an upstairs apartment with own entrance, 2 bedrooms each sleep 3, sitting room, aged bathroom, cold water, balcony, terrace, a/c, but cheaper without, substantial breakfast CUC$5, vast dinner CUC$8, fruit, eggs and meat from their own garden, even coffee is home-grown and roasted.

E **Estevan Orama Ovalle**, Orlando Nodarse 13, T8-793305. Very knowledgeable and friendly hosts, big room, clean and safe, excellent breakfast and dinner, good *mojitos*.

E **Silvia Guzmán Collado (Berito)**, Camilo Cienfuegos 60A, T8-793245. 1 large room, fans, private, hot shower, garden, English spoken, meals available, try 'Berito's chicken', drinks (beer, *mojito*).

E **Villa Blanca**, Salvador Cisneros, Edif Colonial 2 Apto 12, T8-793319. Friendly couple, 2 bedrooms, fans, shared bathroom, balcony, breakfast and dinner.

E Villa Chicha, Camilo Cienfuegos 22. Charming single-storey house with rocking chairs outside, 1 adequate room, a/c, private bathroom, good-value accommodation and meals, entertaining family.

E Villa Mirtha, Rafael Trejo 129. Run by Martha Fernández Hernández, double room with 2 double beds, bathroom, hot water, breakfast included, dinner CUC$6 for fish, beans, rice and salad, son David speaks French.

E Villa Neyda, Camilo Cienfuegos 41. Comfortable rooms, wonderful hospitality, good food, Neyda's sister, at Camilo Cienfuegos 42, also rents rooms, same quality.

E Villa Yolanda Tamargo, Salvador Cisneros 186, T8-793208. 1 large room, hot and cold shower, fan, colonial architecture, parking CUC$1, terrace overlooking garden with fruits and orchids, nice place, meals available.

E Yolanda y Pedro Somonte Pino, Interior 7A (behind the Secundaria), no phone. Nice family, quiet, relaxing, little garden, 1 room with 2 beds, fan, bathroom, hot water, simple but clean, good breakfast with fruit from the garden, dinner available.

María La Gorda *p114*

B-D María La Gorda, T/F84-78131. Jul-Aug are most expensive, Nov-Easter high season, 3 meals CUC$31 per person, nowhere else to eat, package of accommodation, meals and 2 dives daily is CUC$100. Rooms open onto the beach, hammocks between palm trees, great value, nicely decorated, simple, comfortable, a/c, hot water, minibar, TV. 20 new *cabañas* have been built inland in the forest, but these attract mosquitoes. Good service, friendly, buffet meals, bar, shop, Telecorreos.

● Eating

Pinar del Río *p112*

♥♥♥ **Pinar Café**, Gerardo Medina, opposite Coppelia. 1800-0200. Expensive restaurant, CUC$5 for soft drink, beers, bottle of rum and potato chips, also a show at 2130, Afro-Cuban show Tue. Beware of theft here.

♥ **Doña Neli**, Gerardo Medina 24. 0700-1900 for bread, 0830-2300 for pastries and cakes. Good bakery, pay in CUC$. The best CP$ pizzas are on Gerardo Medina opposite Doña Neli bakery, CP$6-10, Mon-Sat 0900-1700.

♥ **El Mesón**, Martí, opposite the Museo de Ciencias Naturales, T752867. Mon-Sat 1100-2400. A *paladar* run by Rafael, a former teacher, nice place, lunch or dinner CUC$6-7, the only place outside a *casa particular* where you can get a decent meal.

♥ **La Taberna**, Coro 103 opposite La Paquita amusement park for children. Daily from 1800. CP$ only, very cheap, dinner around CP$50-60, beer CP$8-10, bar and patio.

♥ **Mar Init**, José Martí, opposite Parque de la Independencia, T754952. Tue-Sun 1930-2130. Pay in CP$, fish is the speciality of the house.

♥ **Terrazina**, Antonio Rubio y Primero de Mayo. 1130-1500, 1800-2200. Pay in CP$, pizza, spaghetti, beer, eat for less than CUC$1.

♥ **Vueltabajo**, Martí y Rafael Morales. 0930-2000. Food available, also bar selling rum, beer, soft drinks.

Viñales *p113*

♥♥ **Casa de Don Tomás**, Salvador Cisneros. The oldest house in Viñales (1879), state-owned. Food very average, eggs the only option for vegetarians, cocktails are good and it is pleasant to sit on the veranda and listen to live music with a Ron Collins or Mary Pickford. Most cocktails are CUC$1.50, but the house special, *Trapiche*, is CUC$2 (rum, pineapple juice, honey, sugar cane syrup).

♥ **Casa Dago**, Salvador Cisneros. Popular restaurant/bar with good jazz *salsa* band, run by extraordinary character with impressive 1927 Ford Chevrolet, food indifferent, but once the music gets going and the rum starts flowing you could be dancing all night.

♥ **Las Brisas**, formerly **Valle Bar**, T8-93183, on the main street. Small, friendly, recommended, *pollo frito* CUC$4, spaghetti CUC$2.50, steak, or just have a beer, CUC$1, and listen to the live music in the evening, talk to Osmany Paez Arteaga who plays percussion in the band, advice on local attitudes and information.

● Bars and clubs

Pinar del Río *p112*

Pinar del Río is very lively on Sat nights, and to a lesser extent on Fri. There is live music everywhere, *salsa*, *son*, Mexican music, international stuff. During the day in Parque Roberto Amarán you can hear traditional music (*mambo, rumba, cha-cha-cha, danzón*) Wed and Sat 1400-1520, Sun 0900.

Artex, Martí 36, opposite **Photo service.** Daily 0900-0200.

Bar La Esquinita, on Isabel Rubio. 2000-0200. Has live music, usually guitarist.

Casa de la Cultura, Rafael Morales esq Martí. Band plays every Sun evening with a dance contest for the elderly, fantastic, free, photos allowed.

Disco Rita, on González Coro, is an open-air venue popular with teenagers, where they play loud, US-style disco music, entry CP$2, the only drink on sale is neat rum at CP$25 a bottle.

Hotel Pinar del Río, see Sleeping, above. Thu-Sun, 2000-0400. CUC$1. Classy disco, very popular, full every night, young crowd. Next door is the **Cafét D'Prisa**, open 24 hrs, rowdy, frequent fights, avoid.

La Picauala, at the back of the Teatro Milanés. Sat, Sun 2100 for the best bands and a fashion show, CP$10.

Rumayor, 2 km on Viñales road. Restaurant 1200-2200, closed Thu. A **Tropicana**-style show, Fri, Sat, Sun CUC$5, very good, lots of security. Starts 2300, but get there before 2200 to get a table, and lasts about 1½ hrs, followed by disco until 0300 or so. Held in small amphitheatre with proper sound and lighting system. No photography or videos allowed. The complex is in a pleasant garden with lots of trees. Don't bother with mid-week **Noche Cubana**, held on a different stage, the show is no good and the place is full of *jineteros*.

Viñales *p113*

Artex, Salvador Cisneros. Bar open 24 hrs, shop 1000-2200, live music.

Bar Viñalero, Salvador Cisneros, next to the museum. Live music in evenings, inside and outside seating. Varied music from traditional to rock, then move on to Artex.

Los Jazmines, see Sleeping, above. Disco 2000-0300. CUC$5.

Palenque de los Cimarrones, 4 km north of Viñales at Km 32 Ctra a Puerto Esperanza. Show Mon-Sat 2230-2400, followed by recorded music, CUC$5 for foreigners.

▲ Activities and tours

Viñales *p113*

Tour operators

Cubanacán, Salvador Cisneros 63C, next to the bus terminal, T8-936262, vinales@ cimex.com.cu. 0800-1700. Motocross rental, CUC$30 per day, phone cards, lodgings, car rental.

Havanatur, beside **Cubanacán**. Tours, reservations and ticket sales.

Ysobel Reyes Crespo, Camilo Cienfuegos, CUC$5/hr. Ysobel does a 5-hr horse riding tour taking in the Cueva del Indio, good way of seeing the countryside.

⊙ Transport

Pinar del Río *p112*

Air

The airport is on the road to La Coloma, 8 km from town, T755545. To **Isla de la Juventud**, Tue and Thu 1240, CUC$22 1-way, rather like a flying bus, DC3 taking 20 Cubans and 10 foreigners.

Bus

The bus station is on Colón, north of José Martí, near Gómez. **Víazul**, T752571, 755255, daily from Havana to **Viñales** at 0900. It stops on request at **Las Terrazas** (CUC$6) and **San Diego de los Baños** (CUC$8), and gets to Pinar del Río (CUC$11) at around 1120 with no stops. The return bus leaves Viñales at 1330, stopping in Pinar del Río around 1400 and getting to **Havana** at 1645. There is also a daily **Astro** bus **Havana**-Pinar at around 1700, which is cheaper at CUC$7 but unreliable. Pinar del Río to **Viñales** in a state taxi is CUC$10, although locals can hire a taxi for the same distance for about CUC$5. To **Viñales** by bus CP$1 on route for Bahía Honda, La Palma or Puerto Esperanza, but your name has to be on the list. Víazul runs a minibus from Pinar del Río to **María la Gorda**, timed to leave after the bus from Havana has arrived in Pinar del Río, returning 1500, max 8 passengers, CUC$80 for whole bus. Unreliable in low season. Visitors come on package tours with CUC$70 transfers from Havana or rented car.

Car

Distances from Pinar del Río are 157 km to

Havana, 159 km to María La Gorda, 103 km to Las Terrazas, 88 km to Soroa, 25 km to Viñales. For car hire, **Havanautos** and **Transautos** both have offices in Hotel Pinar del Río.

Boat

For visitors arriving by yacht, María La Gorda is a port of entry. There are 4 moorings, maximum draft 2 m, VHF channels 16, 19, 68 and 72.

Train

The railway station in Pinar del Río is on Av Comandante Pinares, T752106. From **Havana** at 2140, arriving at 0310. Take a torch, hang on to your luggage, don't sleep, noisy, train stops about 29 times, very slow. Trains to Havana leave at 0900 on alternate days, and cost CUC$6.50.

Viñales *p113*

Bus

Bus terminal at Salvador Cisneros 63A. **Víazul** daily from **Havana** via Pinar del Río at 0900, CUC$12, arrives 1215, returns 1330, arrives in Havana at 1645 depending on the number of stops. **Astro** from **Havana** 0900 via Pinar del Río, returns 1430, arrives in Havana 1820, CUC$10. Local buses from **Pinar del Río** to **Puerto Esperanza**, **La Palma** and **Bahía Honda** all pass through Viñales.

Car

MiCar, Havanautos, both at the end of Salvador Cisneros by the gas station. Deals can be negotiated for long term rental.

Cycle and scooter

It is now illegal for local people to rent out bikes; they will be confiscated at checkpoints. Scooters, CUC$20-24 per day plus fuel.

Taxi

Several companies, but **Beta**, who works for **Cubataxi**, is the only driver who speaks any English. Look out for him in his green Peugeot, he is of Jamaican origin. An official taxi to Cayo Jutías is US$60-70, they charge by distance and for waiting time, with a surcharge later in the afternoon. A private car costs US$35-40, but you have to avoid patrols, which may mean walking certain sections.

⊕ Directory

Pinar del Río *p112*
Banks Banco Financiero Internacional (BFI), Gerardo Medina, opposite Coppelia, T778183, F778213, Mon-Fri 0800-1500. **Cadeca**, Gerardo Medina, next to Coppelia, 0830-1800, also on Martí 50 next to Artex bar. **Banco Popular de Ahorro**, Martí 113, Mon-Fri 0800-1700, cash on credit cards. **Internet** Etecsa, Av Alameda, CUC$15 for 5 hrs with *tarjeta*. **Post office** Martí esq Isabel Rubio, Mon-Sat 0800-1700. **Telephone** Etecsa, Av Alameda IIA, Parque de la Independencia, T754585-7. A 24-hr phone centre is at Gerardo Medina esq Juan Gualberto Gómez, domestic and calls abroad, phone cards for sale.

Viñales *p113*
Banks Bandec, Salvador Cisneros 58, does card transactions. **Banco Popular de Ahorro**, Salvador Cisneros 54A, does not do credit cards, Mon-Fri 0800-1200, 1330-1630. **Cadeca**, Salvador Cisneros 92, Mon-Sat 0800-1800.

Matanzas province

Matanzas province, to the east of Havana, is mainly associated with the mega-resort of Varadero. This tourist enclave incorporates some 14,000 hotel rooms squeezed onto a finger of land stretching out into the Caribbean. The white sand, palm trees and inviting sea with plenty of watersports make it a popular holiday spot, but for all it represents of Cuba it might as well be another country. Close to Varadero and in contrast to it are the low-key provincial towns of Matanzas and Cárdenas where there is no engineered tourism. The second largest province in the country also has a southern coast with one of Cuba's most notable geographic features, the Ciénaga de

Zapata, a huge marsh and nature reserve, protecting many endemic species of flora and fauna as well as numerous migrating birds. Also here, in the Bay of Pigs, the disastrous American-backed invasion is remembered in two museums. ▶▶ *For Sleeping, Eating and other listings, see pages 122-127.*

Matanzas → *Phone code: 52. Colour map 1, A2. Population: 115,000.*

Matanzas is a sleepy town with old colonial buildings and a busy, ugly industrial zone. Both the rivers Yumurí and San Juan flow through the city. Most of the old buildings are between the two rivers, with another colonial district, Versalles, to the east of the Río Yumurí. This area was colonized in the 19th century by French refugees from Haiti after the Revolution there. The newer district, Pueblo Nuevo, also has many colonial houses. The industrial zone runs along the north shore of the bay, with railways running inland and around the bay.

The town dates from 1693, but became prosperous with the advent of sugar mills in the 1820s, followed by the railway in 1843. Most of the buildings date from this time and by the 1860s it was the second largest town in Cuba after Havana. The **Galería de Arte Provincial** ① *Plaza de la Vigía, daily 0900-1700*, has displays of contemporary Cuban art. Next door is **Ediciones Vigía** ① *daily 0900-1600*, where you can see books being produced. These are all handmade and in first editions of only 200 copies, so they are collectors' items. Also on Plaza de la Vigía is **Teatro Sauto** ① *daily 0830-1600, CUC$2*, a magnificent neoclassical building dating from 1862 to 1863 and seating 775 people in three-tiered balconies. 14 performances are staged a month (ticket prices vary according to the event). The floor can be raised to convert the auditorium into a ballroom.

> ‼ *The Hershey Railway runs inland from Havana and is an interesting way to get to Matanzas. It was built by the Hershey chocolate family in 1917 to service their sugar mill, at what is now the Central Camilo Cienfuegos.*

On the south side of the Parque Libertad is the **Museo Farmacéutico** ① *Milanés 4951 entre Santa Teresa y Ayuntamiento, T223197, Mon-Fri 1000-1800, Sun 0800-1200, CUC$3, camera charge CUC$1 per picture*, which contains the original equipment, porcelain jars, recipes and furnishings of the **Botica La Francesa**, opened in 1882 by the Triolet family. It was a working pharmacy until 1964, when it was converted into a fascinating museum, believed to be unique in Latin America. The **Museo Provincial** ① *Milanés entre Magdalena y Ayllón, T243195, Tue-Fri 1000-1800, Sat 1300-1900, Sun 0900-1200, CUC$1*, is a large museum in the former **Palacio del Junco**, built by a wealthy plantation owner and dating from 1840. The historical exhibits include an archaeological display and the development of sugar and slavery in the province.

Varadero → *Phone code: 5. Colour map 1, A2.*

Cuba's chief beach resort, Varadero, is built on the Península de Hicacos, a 20-km sandspit, the length of which run two roads lined with dozens of large hotels, some of which are hideous. Development of the peninsula began in 1923 but the village area was not built until the 1950s. The Du Pont family bought land, sold it for profit, then bought more, constructed roads and built a large house, now the **Xanadú** clubhouse for the new golf course. Varadero is still undergoing large-scale development with the aim of expanding capacity to 26,000 rooms by 2010. Despite the building in progress it is a good place for a family beach holiday. The beaches are quite empty, if a bit exposed, and you can walk for miles along the sand, totally isolated from the rest of Cuba but not from other tourists.

The **Museo Municipal de Varadero** ① *57 y Av de la Playa, daily 1000-1900, CUC$1*, has some indigenous artefacts and history of Varadero with several unusual exhibits including a two-headed baby shark washed up on the shore. The house itself is interesting as an example of one of the first beach houses. Originally known as Casa Villa Abreu, it was built in 1921, with a lovely timber veranda and wooden balconies all round, designed to catch the breeze and restored in 1980-1981 as a museum. At the far end of the peninsula the land has been designated the **Parque Natural de Varadero** ① *visitors' centre at entrance to Hotel Paradisus Varadero, T613594, 0900-1630.* It is an area of scrub and cactus, with a lagoon where salt was once made, and several kilometres of sandy beach. Towards the end of the peninsula, halfway between Marina Chapelín and Marina Gaviota, are caves. **Cueva de Ambrosio** ① *30 mins' walk from the main road, 0900-1630, CUC$3,* contains dozens of indigenous drawings discovered in 1961. **Cueva de Musulmanes** ① *0900-1630, CUC$3,* contains aboriginal fossils.

Beaches and activities Varadero's sandy beach stretches the length of the peninsula, broken only occasionally by rocky outcrops which can be traversed by walking through a hotel's grounds. Some parts are wider than others and as a general rule the older hotels have the best bits of beach. However, the sand is all beautifully looked after and cleaned daily. The water is clean and nice for swimming, but for good **snorkelling** take one of the many boat trips out to the cays. There are three **marinas** (see below), all full-service with sailing tours, restaurants, fishing and diving. All their services can be booked through the tour desks in hotels. There are **sailing tours** to the offshore cays around CUC$70 including lunch and open bar, several stops for snorkelling or beaches. **Cayo Mono** lies five nautical miles north northeast of Punta de Morlas. During the nesting season in mid-year it becomes a seagull sanctuary for the gaviota negra (*Anous stolidus*) and the gaviota monja (*Sterna fuscata* and *Annaethetus*), during which time you can watch them through binoculars. Other cays visited by tour boats include Cayo Blanco, Cayo Romero and Cayo Diana.

The *Mundo Mágico* submarine (T668063) goes down to a depth of 35 m with 46 passengers for 55 minutes. It leaves from the Dársena Marina. You can also see underwater by taking a trip on a glass-bottomed boat, which does three-hour tours over the reef, including open bar and snorkelling equipment.

> ‼ You can indulge in almost any form of watersports, including windsurfing, parasailing, waterskiing, jet skiing and non-motorized pedalos and water bikes.

Cárdenas

Cárdenas is usually visited as a day trip from Varadero. It was founded in 1828 and is attractive, in the traditional 19th-century Spanish colonial style of houses with tall windows, intricate lattices, high ceilings inside, ceramic-tiled floors and interior gardens. Cárdenas was a wealthy sugar town in the 19th century. The Cuban flag was first raised here in 1850 by the revolutionary **General Narciso López**, a Venezuelan

Varadero

Sleeping 🛏
Aparthotel Izlazul Varazul **7**
Islazul Dos Mares **2**
Islazul Pullman **5**

Mansión Xanadú
& Restaurant **1**
Mercure Coralia Cuatro
Palmas **3**
Varadero Internacional **6**

Eating 🍴
Casa de Al **1**
Castelnuovo **2**
Deportivo Kiki's Club **3**
El Criollo **4**

who tried unsuccessfully to invade Cuba by landing at Cárdenas with an army of 600 men (only six of whom were Cuban). **Plaza Molokoff** has a decaying 19th-century iron market building (Avenida 3 oeste y 12). It was built in the shape of a cross and the two-storey building is surmounted by a 15-m dome made in the USA. Most visitors tour the new museum, opened in 2003 by Fidel Castro, the **Museo Municipal Oscar de María Rojas** ① *Calzada 4 entre Echeverría y José Martí, CUC$2*, also known as the Museum for the Battle of Ideas. The museum, named after a Cuban patriot, houses several exhibitions of history, the arts, natural sciences, archaeology and weaponry, but it is popular for the room devoted to the return of the boy, Elián, see page 170, who now lives with his father in Cárdenas. **Víazul** will drop you in Cárdenas on request on their Trinidad-Varadero route. Alternatively, **Astro** from Havana via Matanzas and Varadero.

Península de Zapata and around → *Phone code: 459. Colour map 1, B2.*

The whole of the south coast of Matanzas province is taken up with the Zapata Peninsula, an area of swamps, mangroves and beaches. It is the largest ecosystem in the island and contains the **Laguna del Tesoro**, a 9.1 sq km lagoon over 10 m deep, an important winter home for flocks of migrating birds. There are 16 species of reptile, including crocodiles. Mammals include the jutia and the manatee, while there are over 1000 species of invertebrate, of which more than 100 are spiders.

There is a **crocodile farm** ① *0900-1630, CUC$5, children CUC$2.50*, in Boca de Guamá, where they breed the native Rhombifer (*cocodrilo*). They also have turtles (*jicotea*), *jutía* and what they call a living fossil, the *manjuari* fishalligator. There are shops, a bar and restaurant, occasional live bands and a ceramics factory. It's all a bit touristy; hotels and tourist agencies from Varadero, Havana and other places organize day excursions including lunch, a multilingual guide and a boat ride on the lagoon through the swamps to a replica Indian village, **Villa Guamá** ① *the big boats leave 1000-1200, 45 mins, speed boats keep running 0900-1800 if there is demand, life jackets are on board*. On one of the islets a series of life-size statues of Indians going through their daily routines has been carved by the late Cuban sculptor Rita Longa. Birdwatchers will see most at dawn before the tour buses arrive. Take insect repellent.

The road south across the peninsula meets the coast at **Playa Larga**, at the head of the world-famous **Bahía de Cochinos** (**Bay of Pigs**). For Cuba the bay signifies a great victory; for the USA a failure of monumental proportions. The US-backed invasion force landed here on 17 April 1961 but was repelled. There is a small monument but most of the commemorative paraphernalia is at Playa Girón (see below). The beach is open and better than that at Playa Girón. The **Laguna de las**

La Cabañita **5**
La Casa del Queso Cubano **6**
La Vega **7**
La Vicaria **8**

Bars & clubs 🍸
Cabaret Cueva del Pirata **10**
La Patana **11**
Mambo Club **12**
Palacio de la Rumba **13**

Salinas ① *tours go from the Hotel Playa Larga, Mon and Wed mornings, CUC$15*, 25 km southwest, is the temporary home of migratory birds from December-April. The rest of the year it is empty.

West of Playa Larga, a track leads to **Santo Tomás** ① *T7249, admission fee CUC$10 per person as well as find a guide (obligatory), about CUC$50*, where, in addition to waterfowl, you can see the Zapata wren, the Zapata rail and the Zapata sparrow. The park also runs a number of rare bird- (Cuban parrots and Cuban parakeets), turtle- and fish-breeding programmes. Not far from the **Hotel Playa Larga** there is a good site for watching birds such as hummingbirds and the Cuban trogon. Park headquarters are near the **Hotel Playa Larga** in the **Empresa Municipal Agropecuaria**, where you can get permission to enter and pay the fee. Insect repellent is essential.

The resort at **Playa Girón** is isolated and small. The beach is walled in and therefore protected, but the sea is rocky. The **diving** and **snorkelling** is excellent and you can walk to the reef from the shore. There is a **museum** ① *T4122, 0900-1700. CUC$2, plus CUC$1 for guide, video show CUC$1, use of camera CUC$1, video camera CUC$1*, at the site of national pilgrimage where, in 1961 at the Bay of Pigs, the disastrous US-backed invasion of Cuba was attempted.

● Sleeping

Matanzas *p119*
Although you will now find numbers written on the streets, locals still refer to names. Streets running north-south in the old town have even numbers, while streets running east-west have odd numbers.
B Casa del Valle, Ctra de Chirino, Km 2.5, Valle de Yumurí, T/F253300. Gorgeous setting in woodland in the Valle del Yumurí in the 1940s house and grounds of the former police chief of the area. 40 rooms, 6 bungalows, 8 apartments. Pool, bowling alley, gym, billiards, tennis, massage and mud treatments, riding, good walking.
C Villa Lila, 127 21011, entre 210 y 212, Reparto Playa, T262176, lila_cuba@yahoo.com. One bedroom and bathroom with private entrance. No meals offered at present but various restaurants and cafés in walking distance. Patio doors open on to a great view of Matanzas Bay, garden goes down to the sea and you can swim off the rocks or walk to a nearby beach. Run by English-speaking Dr Maria Elena Alonso de la Rosa and Wilfredo Rodríguez Reyes.
C-D Canimao, Km 4.5 Ctra Matanzas a Varadero, T261014, F262237. 120 rooms on hill above Río Canímar, good views, modern hotel on outskirts of town opposite the **Tropicana** cabaret. Pool, nightclub, excursions on the river or to caves.
D Enriqueta y Exposito, Contreras 29016 entre Sta Teresa (290) y Zaragoza (292), T245151. 2 pleasant rooms although 1 is up a precarious staircase, a/c, fan, use of fridge. Often full, phone in advance.
D Hostal Alma, Milanés 29008 Altos entre Sta Teresa (290) y Zaragoza (292), T247810, alberto@tuisla.cu. Huge, grand 19th-century house with beautiful stained-glass windows, terrace and fabulous roof view. 2 rooms on 2nd floor, private bathroom, a/c, fridge, hot water, minibar, breakfast CUC$3, dinner CUC$6.
D Hostal Azul, Milanés 29012 entre Santa Teresa y Zaragoza, T2442449. Run by helpful Sr Yoel Baez, well-preserved 1870s mansion with the original tiles.
D Luis Alberto Valdés, Contreras (79) 28205 entre Jovellanos y Ayuntamiento (288), T243397, luis.alberto@tuisla.cu. 2 rooms, shared bathroom in 1st-floor flat, a/c, fans available, breakfast and dinner offered.
D Luis Felipe Pilotz, Cuba esq Manzanera. 1882 house with beautiful tiles. Use of fridge, washing machine, 2 shared bathrooms, large patio, 2 rooms, fan, breakfast and dinner, parking available 30 m away.

Varadero *p119, map p120*
Many hotels offer all-inclusive rates, these can be disappointing with lack of variety in food and drinks. Private accommodation is not legal in Varadero but it exists.

The building and renovation of hotels is continuing all along the Varadero peninsula, with several encroaching on the edge of the nature reserve at the extreme end. Unless you want an all-inclusive beach holiday in an international hotel (**Sandals**, **Superclubs**, **Club Med** and others are all here), it is best to stay in the mid-town area, where restaurants, bars and shops are within walking distance, hotels are smaller and more intimate and the beach is just as good.

L Mansión Xanadú, T668482, www.varaderogolfclub.com. The beach house built for the Du Pont family in the 1920s is now the clubhouse for the golf course, with 5 double and 1 single rooms for guests, each with balcony. Furnished with period pieces and very prettily decorated, golf is usually included in the package. Restaurant and bar. Away from the hustle and bustle of the beach resorts.

AL-A Mercure Coralia Cuatro Palmas, Av 1 entre 60 y 64, T667040, www.accorhotels.com. Good rates with internet booking, hotel code 2986. 343 a/c rooms, also in bungalows and villas hacienda style, on the beach, opposite Centro Comercial Caimán and good for shops and restaurants, very pleasant, pool has built-in sunbeds just under the water, lots of services. Definitely one of the more attractive places to stay.

AL-A Varadero Internacional, Av Las Américas, T667038, www.gran-caribe.com. Formerly the **Hilton**, renovated 1999-2000 when many of its period features were obliterated and instead of the garish pink it is now painted in tasteful but characterless shades of cream. Most rooms are sold on an all-inclusive basis. Tennis, pool, sauna, massage, watersports, restaurant, cabaret, Cuban art gallery, and best bit of beach on the whole peninsula.

A Islazul Dos Mares, Calle 53 y Av 1, T612702, www.islazul.cu. 1 of the oldest hotels, dating from 1940, small, friendly and full of character, across the road from the beach, breakfast included, rooms adequate, some good-sized bathrooms, others small, low water pressure, a/c, TV (CNN), safe, bar, restaurant with average food.

A Islazul Pullman, Av 1 entre 49 y 50, T612702, www.islazul.cu. Small, not directly on the beach, but low key, 15 rooms with fans, restaurant, bar, cambio, parking. Known for its turret and style of a castle.

A-B Aparthotel Islazul Varazul, Av 1 y 13, T667132, www.islazul.cu. 69 1-bedroom apartments, living room, fridge, TV, grocery store, quiet part of town, can use restaurant and other facilities of **Acuazul**.

Península de Zapata and around *p121*

Playa Larga

All the *casas particulares* are in Barrio Caletón, west of the public park. Take an immediate right in front of the park and swing round the edge until you get to the residential area.

B Playa Larga, T7294, F7167. Sometimes fully booked with tour groups, 50 a/c spacious rooms in basic 1- or 2-bedroomed bungalows with bath, TV, pool, restaurant, bar, nightclub, shop, tour desk, birdwatching, watersports.

D Josefa Pita Cobas (Fefa), T7133, yosvanyps@correodeaba.com. Small but pleasant house with sea view but the water laps at the back wall so there is no access to the beach. A/c, hot water, shared bathroom, 2 beds in room.

D-E Fidel Silvestre Fuentes, Caletón, T7233, yosvanyps@correodeaba.com. A/c, hot water, shared bathroom, access to beach from patio, friendly family, *comida criolla*.

E Roberto Mesa Pujol, Barrio Caletón, Playa Larga, T7307. Double room, a/c, bathroom, hot water, garage, marvellous waterfront location, garden opens onto white-sand beach where you can swim, palm trees, volleyball net.

Playa Girón

There are 15 *casas particulares* in houses and 2 blocks of apartments in Playa Girón. Coming from Cienfuegos, the 1st block is edif 2, the one behind, at an angle, is edif 1. Note that there are roosters behind the blocks for early morning wake-up call.

A-B Playa Girón, T4110, F4117. 292 rooms in bungalows or blocks of rooms, a/c with shared bathrooms, all-inclusive with buffet meals, bar, pool, diving, disco opposite, tourist information desk, shop, car rental (gas station opposite museum, open 24 hrs).

D José García Mesa (Tito) y Yaquelín Ulloa Pérez, Frente al edif 2, T4252 (neighbour Hortensia's phone). Room with bathroom, hot and cold water 24 hrs, parking, secure, very nice people, purple plastic furniture.

E Hostal Luis, Ctra a Cienfuegos esq Ctra a Playa Larga, T4121. Owned by Luis A García Padrón, house has blue and green gates wit

lion-topped columns, 1 bedroom, a/c, hot water, parking, very clean and friendly.
E Miguel A Padrón y Odalys Figueredo, behind edif 1, T4100. New house, exceptionally clean, fan, helpful.

● Eating

Matanzas p119
The best food is in the *casas particulares*. Restaurants are largely cafés, serving pizza, sandwiches and snacks.

₸₸-₸ La Ruina, Calle 101 just past Puente Calixto García. Open 24 hrs. Very attractive restaurant converted from sugar warehouse, delicious pastries, great ice cream, live music at weekends.

₸ Café Atenas, 83 y 272 on Plaza La Vigía. 1000-2200. Modern design, strong lighting, snack food, pizza, spaghetti, chicken and fish.

Varadero p119, map p120
Food is very mediocre quality although some hotel restaurants are good.

₸₸₸ Mansión Xanadú, Ctra Las Américas Km 8.5, T668482, www.varaderogolfclub.com. 1900-2230. The mansion was built in the 1920s by the Du Pont family as their beach holiday home, but is now attached to the golf club. Restaurant serves up mouthwatering delights such as octopus with paprika and mango, shrimps in sherry. Also 2 rooms with sea view (**AL**, including green fees).

₸₸₸-₸₸ Casa de Al, Villa Punta Blanca, Reparto Kawama, T668050. A stone building with blue trimmings which used to belong to Al Capone. Quiet spot for a sunset drink with outdoor tables on the terrace, or a meal of Mafia Soup, Godfather Salad, Filet Mignon 'Lucky Luciano' and cold blood ice cream. The service is a little slow, but worth a visit.

₸₸₸-₸₸ La Casa del Queso Cubano, Av Playa y 63. 1200-2300. A variety of fondues including lobster fondue and chocolate fondue as well as breaded pork, chicken and grilled fish. Smart tables, strong a/c.

₸₸₸-₸₸ La Vega, Av Playa entre 31 y 32, T611430. 1200-2300. Charming wooden restaurant with baskets hanging from the staircase and outdoor seating on wooden decking. Large range of seafood including squid, paella and crêpes for pudding. Gorgeous giant leaf sculpture outside.

₸₸ Castelnuovo, Av 1 y 11, T667794.

1200-2345. Italian with indoor or outdoor eating, massive pizzas, efficient service.

₸₸ El Criollo, Av 1 y 18, T614794. 1200-2330. Thatched-roof bar with ambient Cuban music and efficient service. Beef, shrimp, roast pork.

₸ Deportivo Kiki's Club, Av 1 y 8, T614115. 1200-2345. Sports theme, Italian food in partially open-air restaurant.

₸ La Cabañita Camino del Mar esq 9, T616764. 1900-0100. Right on the beach under a thatched roof with a lovely bit of sand, good combos, CUC$5 for chicken or fish, rice, fries and a drink.

₸ La Vicaria, next to Los Delfines hotel. A part thatched restaurant which, apart from doing chicken like everywhere else, serves salads, which are hard to come by.

Península de Zapata and around p121
Ask at *casas particulares* about eating in private homes. Lobster and crocodile on the menu.

₸ La Casa del Mar, on the road to Playa Larga. Bar and grill, 1000-1800. There's a place to swim nearby.

● Bars and clubs

Matanzas p119
Centro de Promoción y Publicidad Cultural, Independencia (85) entre Ayuntamiento (288) y Santa Teresa (290) has a *cartelera* in the window displaying all entertainment fixtures. The Plaza Vigía is the place to go in the evenings; locals congregate here to chat, play dominoes or draughts, or make music.
Sala de Conciertos José White de Matanzas, C79 entre 288 y 290. Formerly the Lyceum Club and famous for being the place where *danzón* was danced for the first time in 1879; music is performed here and all events are free.
Teatro Sauto, Plaza de la Vigía. Usually has live performances at the weekends.
Tropicana Matanzas, Autopista Varadero Km 4.5, T265555, reserves@tropimat.co.cu. Daily 2030-0230, show Wed-Sun 2200-2330. CUC$35 includes a cocktail, ¼ bottle of rum and a mixer. The Matanzas version of the famous cabaret is in a spectacular outdoor setting opposite the Hotel Canimao. Discounts for hotel guests.

Varadero *p119, map p120*

Every hotel has several bars to choose from and it can be fun to work your way through the barman's list of cocktails during your holiday. Even here, however, you may be told '*no hay*', with tomato juice and other mixers often unavailable. Stick to the traditionally Cuban and you won't be disappointed.

Bar Mirador Casa Blanca, top floor of **Mansión Xanadú** at the Golf Club. 1000-2345. Worth a visit for the view and relaxed atmosphere, if not for the prices.

Cabaret Continental at **Hotel Internacional**, T667038. Tue-Sat from 2200. CUC$25. Called **El Ritmo del Tambor**, one of the longest running shows in Cuba, on Sun there is a smaller event.

Cabaret Cueva del Pirata, Autopista Sur Km 11, T61389. Mon-Sat 2200-0300. Show in a cave.

La Patana, Canal de Paso Malo, T667791. 2100-0300. Floating disco at the laguna.

Mambo Club, Ctra Las Morlas Km 14, next to **Club Amigo Varadero**. 0900-1600. CUC$10. The **Orquesta Tarafa** – famous in the 1950s – plays here.

Palacio de la Rumba, Av Las Américas, Km 4, T668210. 2200-0300. CUC$10 Mon-Thu, CUC$15 Fri-Sun, also 1600-2100 Sun, CUC$5. Includes bar, live *salsa* bands at weekends, Popular with Cubans and foreigners.

☻ Entertainment

Varadero *p119, map p120*

Cine Varadero, Av Playa entre 42 y 43. Shows Cuban and foreign films.

☉ Shopping

Varadero *p119, map p120*

Handicraft markets offer all manner of souvenirs, from elaborately decorated wooden *humedores* to keep your cigar temperature controlled, to T-shirts and key rings which are easier to pack. There are several stalls lining the road to the Museo Municipal, but the main market area is in the Parque Central and on the other side of the road around **Coppelia** in the Parque de las Mil Taquillas. Do not buy black coral. It is protected by CITES and it is illegal to take it into your home country.

▲ Activities and tours

Varadero *p119, map p120*

Diving

Barracuda, Av 1 entre 58 y 59, T611852, ventas@aqwo.var.cyt.cu. 2 dives CUC$60. Excursions to Bay of Pigs, CUC$45, also night diving, cave diving, wrecks and lessons. ACUC Open Water Diver CUC$365. Multilingual staff.

There's also diving at **Marina Gaviota**, T667755, and **Marina Dársena**, T668063.

Fishing

Deep-sea fishing costs around CUC$300 for 4 people for half a day, but prices vary according to what exactly is on offer. Available from the marinas, www.aquaworldvaradero.com. Wahoo Oct-Feb, dorado Apr-Sep, sailfish Apr-May, tuna Apr-Sep, barracuda all year, grouper all year, snapper May-Jul best, Aug-Apr good, tarpon and yellow jack best Feb-Apr.

Golf

Varadero Golf Course on Av Las Américas Km 8.5, T667788, www.varaderogolfclub. Upgraded in 1996-1998 to 18 holes, par 72. The original 9 holes were set out by the Du Ponts around their mansion, built in 1928-1930, which is now the **Xanadú Club House**, and the new ones extend along the **Sol Meliá** resorts. Golf lessons are offered and there are 2 putting greens and a driving range. 3-8-day packages are available with accommodation in the clubhouse. Pro-shop and equipment rental at **Caddie House**. Bookings can be made, 24 hrs in advance, direct or through hotel tour desks, green fee CUC$60, golf carts compulsory.

Marinas

Marina Chapelin is at Ctra Las Morlas, Km 12.5, T667550, VHF 16 and 72. Moorings for 20 boats, maximum draft 30 m, boat rental, laundry, fishing, snorkelling trips, safari to Cayo Blanco, sailing trips.

Marina Dársena de Varadero, is at Ctra de Vía Blanca Km 31, T63730, VHF 16, 19, 68, 72. Moorings for 70 boats, maximum draft 5 m, boat rental, showers, laundry, restaurants, bars, fishing, shops, day charters, diving, liveaboard for 20 people.

Marina Gaviota Varadero, Península de Hicacos Km 21, T667550/565, VHF 16. 10

moorings, 3 m draft, showers, laundry, restaurant, bar, seafaris, yacht rental, fishing, dolphinarium, diving.

Tour operators
Most hotels have a tour agency on site offering local and national excursions, boat trips, multilingual guides, transfers, booking and confirmation of air tickets, air charters, car rentals, reception and representation service. A day trip to Havana is usually CUC$55, Guamá CUC$53, Matanzas, riding in the Yumurí Valley and snorkelling in the Saturno Cave CUC$31, to Elguea via the Che Memorial in Santa Clara with mud baths and lunch CUC$45.

Península de Zapata and around p121
Birdwatching
EMA, Playa Larga, T7249, emavg@enet.cu. Daily 0800-1630. Trips to the Río Hatiguanico, Las Salinas, Los Arrollones, Los Sábalos, Bermejas and Santo Tomás. Each trip costs CUC$10 and includes food, drink and *lancha*. The guides are all bird specialists and some speak English. Visitors need their own transport and tips are not included. EMA can also arrange visits to a fish, turtle and bird breeding centre, CUC$2.

Diving
Hotel Playa Girón has a dive centre: CUC$25 each dive, 4 dives and you get 1 free. Courses and dive packages with accommodation.

⊖ Transport

Matanzas p119
Bus
The long-distance bus station is at 131 y 272, Calzada Esteban esq Terry, T291473, while the interprovincial terminal is at 298 y 127, both in Pueblo Nuevo. **Víazul**, T916445, passes through on its Havana-Varadero route. **Astro** from Havana at 0910 arrives around midday, CUC$4.

Train
The 3-4-hr journey via the **Hershey Railway**, the only electric train in Cuba, is memorable and scenic if you are not in a hurry. Those who wish to make it a day trip from Havana can do so, long queues for return tickets, best to get one as soon as you arrive. 4 trains

daily, CUC$2.80 one way, from Casablanca Station to a station north of the Río Yumurí in Versalles. The station south of the town at 181, Miret, T292409, receives regular and *especial* trains from Havana to Santiago.

Varadero p119, map p120
Air
The **Juan Gualberto Gómez Airport** (VRA), T613016, 23 km from the beginning of the hotel strip, receives international scheduled and charter flights and domestic flights from Havana and Santiago. Bus from airport to hotels CUC$10 per person.

Bus
The interprovincial bus station is at Autopista Sur y 36, T663254. **Víazul**, T614886, has 3 daily buses Havana-Varadero via Matanzas and Varadero Airport, 0800, 0830, 1600, 3 hrs, CUC$10 (returning 0800, 1600, 1800), and there is a regular **Astro** bus twice a day (0805 and 1600) from Havana to Varadero, via Varadero Airport, CUC$8, reserve 1-2 days in advance. **Víazul** Varadero-Trinidad 0730, 6 hrs, CUC$20, with stops in Cárdenas CUC$6, Coliseo CUC$6, Jovellanos CUC$6, Jagüey CUC$6, Santa Clara CUC$11 and Sancti Spíritus CUC$16, returns from Trinidad 1430.

There is a tourist bus, an open-topped red double decker, which runs along the peninsula every hour with clearly marked bus stops. CUC$5 for a day ticket, you can get on and off all day.

Car
Hire a car rather than jeep to avoid having your spare wheel stolen, insurance covers 4 wheels, not the spare (see p74). Hire is available through most of the hotels. **Cubacar** main office T667341. **Transtur**, Av 1 y 55. **Nacional** at 13 entre Av 2 y Av 4, T667663.

Cycle and moped
Moped rental: CUC$9 per hr, CUC$15 for 3 hrs, extra hrs CUC$5, a good way to see the peninsula but you will have no insurance and no helmet. **Bicycle-hire** from hotels, CUC$1 per hr.

Taxi
Horse-drawn vehicles act as taxis, usually just for a tour around town. **Taxis** (cars) charge CUC$0.50 per km. They usually wait

at hotels for fares. **Transgaviota**, T619761; **Turistaxi**, T613763; **Taxi OK**, T612827. Beware of being fleeced on arrival at the bus station. A 2-min taxi ride can cost CUC$3 or more for the innocent newcomers.

Península de Zapata and around *p121*

Bus
In high season, **Víazul** runs a daily bus Varadero-Guamá-Girón-Cienfuegos, CUC$16, 4½ hrs, departing Varadero 0830, returning from Cienfuegos 1400. **Astro** to Havana, Fri, Sat, Sun, passes through Playa Larga. Guagua to Playa Larga from edif 2, 0630, 30-40 mins, CP$1.45.

● Directory

Matanzas *p119*
Banks Bandec, 85 y 282, for exchange facilities and cash advances on credit cards. Banco Nacional at 83 (Milanés) y 282. **Medical services** Facilities for foreigners are available in Varadero, but there is a pharmacy here, open 24 hrs, at 85 y 2 de Mayo. **Post office** 85 entre 290 y 288, 24 hrs. **Telephone/internet** Telepunto, Milanés y 282, daily 0830-2130, phone service and internet.

Internet also at **Infotur** on the plaza.

Varadero *p119, map p120*
Banks Banco Financiero Internacional, Av Playa y 32, cash advance service with credit cards available 0900-1900, office open Mon-Fri 0900-1500, last working day of month 0900-1200. **Immigration and police** 39 y Av 1, T116. Immigration is open Mon-Fri 0900-1200, 1350-1630, for visa extensions. **Medical services** Policlínico Internacional, Av 1 y 61, T668611, clinica@clinica.var.cyt.cu. International clinic, doctor on duty 24 hrs, a medical consultation in your hotel will cost CUC$50. The clinic has an excellent **pharmacy**, T667226. Recompression chamber at the **Centro Médico Sub Acuática** at the **Hospital Julio M Arístegui**, just outside Cárdenas. **Post office** Most hotels have post offices. Phone and fax services usually available. **Telephone/internet** The Centro Internacional de Comunicaciones is at 64 entre Av 1 y Av 3, T612103, F667020. Etecsa is at 18 y Av 3, T667070, F667050, with *cabinas* in other locations such as the corner of Av 1 y 30 and Av 1 y 54, where computers for internet with prepaid cards are being introduced.

Centre west

From the early Spanish settlements and sugar plantations built on slavery to magnificent 19th-century merchants' mansions and opulent theatres, this region is generously endowed with architectural delights. The three provinces of Cienfuegos, Villa Clara and Sancti Spíritus in the centre west share the lush, forested Montañas de Guamuhaya, their boundaries meeting close to the highest point, Pico San Juan, in the legendary Sierra del Escambray. Unfortunately the three provinces were also where Hurricane Dennis crashed ashore in July 2005 with winds of 149 mph before going on to flood the east. The forests of the mountains offer great hiking, river bathing and birdwatching. The coastal city of Cienfuegos is known for its 19th-century architecture, particularly the theatre and the Palacio de Ferrer. The 1958 battle for the city of Santa Clara was crucial to the outcome of the Revolution and this lively university city is now a shrine to the Argentine guerrillero and icon, Che Guevara. The provincial capital of Sancti Spíritus was one of the seven towns founded by Diego Velázquez in 1514, but the star attraction is the colonial town of Trinidad, awarded UNESCO World Heritage site status to protect its cobbled streets, single-storey, pastel-coloured houses with red-tiled roofs, its churches and its planters' mansions.

▸▸ *For Sleeping, Eating and other listings, see pages 131-138.*

Cienfuegos and around → *Phone code: 432. Colour map 1, B3.*
Cienfuegos, on the south coast, is an attractive seaport and industrial city, sometimes described as the pearl of the south, and there is a Caribbean feel to the place. French immigrants at the turn of the 19th century influenced the developme

and architecture of the city, which is a fascinating blend of styles. The main street, running north-south, is Calle 37, called the Prado in the north and the Malecón in the south where it runs beside the water, with a central promenade down the middle where people stroll or sit.

There are interesting colonial buildings around the Parque José Martí. On the east side on Calle 29 is **La Catedral Purísima Concepción** ⓘ *Mass is at 0730 and the church is open until 1200*, built in 1868, which has a neo-Gothic interior with silvered columns. On the north side, on Avenida 56, is the **Teatro Tomás Terry** ⓘ *T513361, daily 0900-1800, CUC$1 including guided tour*, built in 1889 after the death of the Venezuelan Tomás Terry, with the proceeds of a donation by his family. It was inaugurated in 1890 with an audience of 1200. The lobby has an Italian marble statue of Terry and is decorated with fine paintings and ornate gold work. The interior is largely original with wooden seats. Note the ceiling with exquisite paintings. On the west side is the **Palacio de Ferrer**, now the **Casa de Cultura Benjamín Duarte** ⓘ *T516584, Mon-Sat 0830-1900, Sun 0830-1400, CUC$0.50 (including the tower, great views), guided tours in Spanish, English and French*, a beautiful building dating from 1894, with a magnificent tower on the corner designed to keep an eye on the port and shipping. Worth seeing for the marble floor, staircases and walls, carved in Italy and assembled at the palace.

Outside town is the **Jardín Botánico de Cienfuegos** ⓘ *Pepito Tey, 23 km east of Cienfuegos between Antón and Guaos, daily 0800-1700, CUC$2.50, children CUC$1, Spanish-speaking guide*, a national monument, founded in 1901 by Edwin F Atkins, the owner of a sugar plantation called Soledad, now called **Pepito Tey**. The gardens started as a research station for sugar cane, later introducing other trees and shrubs that could be used as raw materials for industry. After the Revolution the State decided to preserve and develop the many tropical species found there. Different sections of the gardens are devoted to medicinal plants, orchids, fruit trees, bamboos and one of the world's most complete collections of palm trees. There's a bar for drinks. If driving, look out for two rows of palm trees leading to the garden from the entrance at the road. The bus from Cienfuegos stops outside (20 centavos).

Playa Rancho Luna is about 14 km from Cienfuegos, near the **Hotel Rancho Luna**. The beach is quite nice but nothing special. The **Centro de Buceo Faro Luna** runs the diving here. If you continue along the road past the beach you get to the **Hotel Pasacaballo**, where there is a jetty, and there's another further along a rough track to the left, from where you can get a little ferry (CUC$1) across the mouth of the Bahía de Cienfuegos to the village on the western side, site of the **Castillo de Jagua** ⓘ *Mon-Sat 0900-1700, Sun 0900-1300, CUC$1, guides are available*. The castle was built at the entrance to the bay in 1733 to 1745 by Joseph Tantete, of France. There is only one entrance via a drawbridge across a dry moat. The view would be better without the eyesore of the Hotel Pasacaballo and the housing project of **Ciudad Nuclear**, built for a nuclear power station which was abandoned before completion. Other ferries leave from Avenida 46 entre 23 y 25, in Cienfuegos harbour (CUC$0.50, 0800, 1300, 1730, 45 minutes, returning 0630, 1000, 1500).

Santa Clara → *Phone code: 42. Colour map 1, B3. Population: 200,000. 300 km from Havana.*

Santa Clara is a pleasant university city in the centre of the island best known for being the site of the last and definitive battle of the Revolution and the last resting place of Che Guevara. The northern coast is low lying and there are mangroves and swamps, but it is fringed with coral cays with sandy beaches and crystal clear water.

In December 1958, before Castro entered Havana, Batista sent an armoured train with military supplies including guns, ammunition and soldiers, to Santiago de Cuba to counter-attack the revolutionaries. However, **Che Guevara** and his troops were hiding in the outskirts of Santa Clara, waiting for the train. On 28 December 1958 it was ambushed in the afternoon. The soldiers on the train surrendered quickly and the fighting for the train was soon over. However, the battle for the city lasted nearly four days, until 1 January 1959 when news spread that Batista had fled the country.

Heading east on Calle Independencia towards Camajuaní, between Río Cubanicay and the railway line, is the **Monumento a la Toma del Tren Blindado** ① *T202758, Tue-Sat 0800-1830, Sun 0800-1200, CUC$1*, where four of the carriages of Batista's troop train are preserved. There is a museum inside the wagons showing weapons and other things carried on the train. There is also a monument on top of **El Capiro**, the hill where Che and his troops waited to attack the train. You can get an excellent view of the city from here, just as Che did in 1958.

A monument to Che has been built in the **Plaza de la Revolución Ernesto Guevara**, with a bronze statue of Che on a large concrete plinth, a bas-relief scene depicting Che in battle and an inscription of a letter from him to Fidel. Underneath is a **Mausoleum**. The remains of Che and his comrades who fell in Bolivia have been interred here. Beside the mausoleum is the **Museo Histórico de la Revolución** ① *T205985, Tue-Sat 0800-2100, Sun 0800-1700, free*, with good displays in Spanish and sometimes a video about Che's life and role in the Revolution, as well as displays of the battle in Santa Clara. Recommended. The museum is on Prolongación Marta Abreu after the Carretera Central forks to the north; look out for La Victoria service station, entrance on Rafael Tristá, which runs parallel. A *bicitaxi* costs CUC$1 from the centre.

Sancti Spíritus → *Phone code: 41. Colour map 1, B4. Population: 80,000.*

Sancti Spíritus, the provincial capital, is about 80 km northeast of Trinidad and 90 km southeast of Santa Clara. Like Trinidad, the town was founded by Diego Velázquez in 1514 and is one of Cuba's seven original Spanish towns and has a wealth of buildings from the colonial period. The **Iglesia Parroquial Mayor del Espíritu Santo** ① *Jesús Menéndez 1 entre Honorato y Agramonte, Tue-Sat 0900-1100, 1400-1700*, on Plaza Honorato, dates from 1522 when it was a wooden construction. Fray Bartolomé de las Casas gave his famous sermon here, marking the start of his campaign to help the indigenous people. The present building, of stone, replaced the earlier one in 1680, but it is acknowledged as the oldest church in Cuba because it still stands on its original foundations and is a National Monument. The **Puente Yayabo** is considered a particular feature of Sancti Spíritus and is the only one of its type left on the island. The bridge was built in 1815 with five arches made of lime, sand and bricks. It is now also a National Monument. The river itself has given its name to the *guayaba*, or guava, which grows along its banks, and also to the *guayabera*, a loose man's shirt worn outside the trousers and without a tie. The former **Teatro Principal** next to the bridge was built in 1839 and was the scene of all the major cultural, social and political events of the city.

Trinidad → *Phone code: 41. Colour map 1, B3. Population: 60,000.*

Trinidad, 133 km south of Santa Clara, is a perfect relic of the early days of the Spanish colony: beautifully preserved streets and buildings and hardly a trace of the 20th century anywhere. It was founded in 1514 by Diego Velázquez as a base for expeditions into the 'New World' and Cortés set out from here for Mexico in 1518. The five main squares and four churches date from the 18th and 19th centuries and the whole city, with its fine palaces, cobbled streets and tiled roofs, is a national monument and since 1988 it has been a UNESCO World Heritage site.

On the Plaza Mayor is the cathedral, **Iglesia Parroquial de la Santísima Trinidad** ① *1030-1300 for sightseeing and photos; mass Tue-Fri at 2000, Sat at 1600 and Sun at 0900. Casa Parroquial at Fco J Zerquera 456, opposite the church, T993668, F996387*, built between 1817 and 1892. It is the largest church in Cuba and is renowned for its acoustics. The choir, called Piedras Vivas, composes and sings religious music with a Cuban rhythm, wonderful to hear on Sundays and holidays. On the left of the altar is a crucifix of the brown-skinned Christ of Veracruz, who is the patron of Trinidad. The **Museo Romántico** ① *Hernández 52, T994363, Tue-Sun 0900-1700, CUC$2, cameras CUC$1, videos CUC$5*, next to the church of Santísima

Trinidad on the main square, has an excellent collection of romantic-style porcelain, glass, paintings and ornate furniture, which belonged to several families from the area. The Conde de Brunet family, who made their money from cattle and sugar produced by slaves lived here from 1830 to 1860 during what is known as the Romantic period. **Museo Municipal de Historia** ① *Simón Bolívar 423, T994460, Sat-Thu 0900-1700, CUC$2*, is an attractive building but with rather dull displays in eight rooms of scientific, historical and cultural exhibits; walk up the tower for a good view of Trinidad. Other museums worth visiting include the **Museo de Arqueología Guamuhaya** ① *Simón Bolívar 457, esq Villena, Plaza Mayor, T993420, Sat-Thu 0900-1700, CUC$1*, a general view of developments from pre-Columbian to post-conquest times. The **Museo de Arquitectura Colonial** ① *Desengaño (Ripalda) 83, T993208, Sat-Thu 0900-1700, CUC$1*, has exhibits specifically on the architecture of Trinidad. The **Museo Nacional de Lucha Contra Bandidos** ① *Hernández esq Piro Guinart, T994121, Tue-Sun 0900-1700, CUC$1*, housed in the old San Francisco de Asís convent, has exhibits related to the 1960s counter-revolutionary campaign in the Escambray mountains.

Around Trinidad

Inland from Trinidad are the beautiful, wooded Escambray mountains, whose highest point is **Pico San Juan**, also known as **La Cuca**, at 1140 m. Rivers have cut deep valleys,

Trinidad

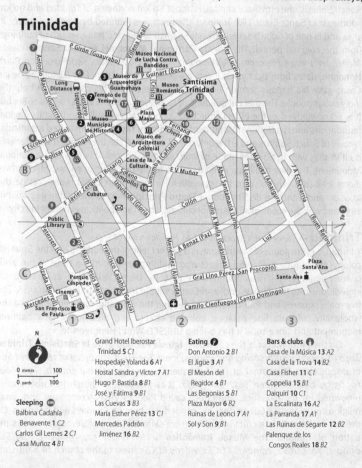

N

0 metres 100
0 yards 100

Sleeping
Balbina Cadahía
Benavente 1 *C2*
Carlos Gil Lemes 2 *C1*
Casa Muñoz 4 *B1*

Grand Hotel Iberostar
Trinidad 5 *C1*
Hospedaje Yolanda 6 *A1*
Hostal Sandra y Víctor 7 *A1*
Hugo P Bastida 8 *B1*
José y Fátima 9 *B1*
Las Cuevas 3 *B3*
María Esther Pérez 13 *C1*
Mercedes Padrón
Jiménez 16 *B2*

Eating ①
Don Antonio 2 *B1*
El Jigüe 3 *A1*
El Mesón del
Regidor 4 *B1*
Las Begonias 5 *B1*
Plaza Mayor 6 *B2*
Ruinas de Leonci 7 *A1*
Sol y Son 9 *B1*

Bars & clubs ①
Casa de la Música 13 *A2*
Casa de la Trova 14 *B2*
Casa Fisher 11 *C1*
Coppelia 15 *B1*
Daiquirí 10 *C1*
La Escalinata 16 *A2*
La Parranda 17 *A1*
Las Ruinas de Segarte 12 *B2*
Palenque de los
Congos Reales 18 *B2*

some of which, such as the Caburní and the Guanayara, have attractive waterfalls and pools where you can swim. The **Parque Natural Topes de Collantes**① *CUC$6.50*, is a 110 sq km area of the mountains which contains many endemic species of fauna and flora. There are several paths in the area and walking is rewarding with lovely views and lush forest. There is no public transport but day trips are organized to Topes de Collantes by tour agencies by jeep or truck, which take in swimming in a waterfall. You can see lots of wildlife, butterflies, hummingbirds and the tocororo. It makes a great day out. Private tours do not go to the same places as jeep tours, whatever anybody tells you.

There are also trips to the **Torre de Manaca Iznaga**① *0900-1600 or 1700, CUC$2*, in the village of the same name about 15 km from Trinidad on the road to Sancti Spíritus, or you can hire a private car to take you for about CUC$10. Alternatively, you can ride on a 1907 steam train, daily in high season, to Manaca Iznaga (0930, CUC$10; it's best to buy ticket at an agency. The tower, built between 1835 and 1845 is 43.5 m high, has seven floors and 136 steps to the top. It was built as a lookout to watch the slaves working in the valley at the sugar mills. It has UNESCO World Heritage status alongside Trinidad city. There is a great view of the surrounding countryside, including the **Valle de los Ingenios**, (Valley of the Sugar Mills) and the Escambray Mountains as well as the rooftops of the village below.

The best beach resort near Trinidad is **Playa Ancón**, not a town as such, just three resort hotels of varying quality. The beach is white sand and clean turquoise water, but sand flies appear after 1600. The best part of the beach is right in front of the **Hotel Ancón**, where there are straw sunshades and beach loungers. The rest of the beach has little shade. People are sometimes disappointed when they come here and expect something more spectacular, but it is very pleasant for a day trip out of Trinidad. There is good **diving** and **snorkelling** less than 300 m offshore, see Activities and tours, page 136. A return taxi fare is about CUC$12-16, but bargain hard and don't pay any money until the driver returns to collect you.

● Sleeping

Cienfuegos *p127*

AL La Unión, Av 31 esq 54, T/F551020, comercial@union.cfg.cyt.cu. Built in 1869, newly restored, upmarket, attractive, 36 double rooms and 13 suites, breakfast included, a/c, safe box, satellite TV, business centre, car rental, gym, lovely pool open to non-guests for CUC$5, restaurant and bars.

A Jagua, Punta Gorda, 37 y 0, T551003, reserves@jagua.co.cu. 147 a/c rooms with view over bay, singles, doubles and triples available, 2 suites and 1 room for the handicapped, 4-star, comfortable, small pool, DHL office in hotel, shop, internet access, restaurant and 24-hr café. Cabaret Wed-Mon, 2200, CUC$5 per person includes a cocktail, very colourful, good.

A-C Faro Luna, Ctra Pasacaballo Km 18, Playa Faro Luna, T548030, aloja@fluna.cfg.cyt.cu. 46 rooms, 3-star, nice, clean, hot water, TV, some staff friendly, aimed at individual travellers who want to dive and sail, beach 100 m away by the enormous **Rancho Luna** hotel.

B-C Villa Guajimico, Ctra a Trinidad Km 42, Cumanayagua, T541205, best to book through **Cubamar**, in Havana, see p108. Overlooks mouth of Río La Jutía, surrounded by cliffs, caves, coral reefs and beaches accessible only by boat. 3-star, 54 cabins, some triples, a/c, bathroom, pool, restaurant, bar, parking, hobicats, good for excursions, a great dive resort, 3 (average) meals CUC$31, diving CUC$25, sailing CUC$10.

D-E Jerónimo García Escoriza, 35 5806 entre 58 y 60, T516549. 1 room with a/c, wardrobe, private bathroom with very large bath. Neoclassical interior with columns and tiled floors. Son-in-law speaks English. Kind and helpful household with excellent food.

D-E Margarita Jiménez Marín, 60 3503 entre 35 y 37, T555185, isidroherrera@ correosonline.co.cu. Royal-blue colonial house with 2 rooms and small patio. Only 1 room has natural light. Only couples get their own key to the house. Kind and friendly family.

E Andrés Haro Cuéllar, Av 62 3922 entre 39 y 41, T527078. 1 room in a colonial apartment above a busy street, although room faces the other way, massive bathroom, large wardrobe, fan, small dining area. Andrés has a very sweet dog.

E Casa de la Amistad – Armando y Leonor Martínez, 56, 2927 entre 29 y 31, T516143, amistad@correosonline.co.cu. Delightful and knowledgeable elderly couple, English-speaking. Armando fought at the Bay of Pigs and is an economist, providing frank and informative conversation. Large, 2nd floor of a colonial house, with 2 rooms, private bathroom, very popular, essential to book, good food.

E Isabel Martínez Cordero y Pepe, Av 52 4318 entre 43 y 45, T518276. 2 a/c rooms with little natural light, private bathroom, fridge, car park nearby, very good vegetarian option.

E María Núñez Suárez, Av 58 3705 Altos entre 37 y 39, T517867. 2 a/c rooms with fan sharing adjoining bathroom (the red plastic loo seat makes a welcome change). Meals served on the balcony. Ask her husband, Oscar, and friends to tell you stories about when they were young, fighting with Che in the Sierra Maestra, at the Bay of Pigs or working in Ethiopia.

E Villa Lagarto, 35 entre 0 y Litoral, apto 4B, T519966, villalagarto@yahoo.es. Tony and Maylin have 2 rooms with open balcony, 1 has 2 beds, fridge and a/c, the other has double bed and fridge. Pretty patio with fabulous views of the water and to the mountains. Small salt-water swimming pool also home to 2 turtles. Welcome cocktail on arrival.

Santa Clara *p128*

Private homes are nicer places to stay than the state hotels on offer in the centre of town. Beware *jineteros* outside who may tell you the house is full and offer to take you somewhere else, or concoct some other story. Ring the bell and get the facts from inside. Most *casas* offer breakfast CUC$3, dinner CUC$7-8, recommended, better than restaurants.

B Villa La Granjita, outside town at Km 2.5 on Maleza road, T218191, aloja@granjita.vcl.cyt.cu. 75 rooms in thatched *cabañas* among fruit trees, cable TV, a/c, ▪hone, pool, bar, shop, buffet restaurant, ▪rses, night-time entertainment around the

pool, Sala de Fiestas, CUC$6, free bar 2200-0130, 24-hr medical services, massage.

C Los Caneyes, Av de los Eucaliptos y Circunvalación, T218140. Thatched public areas with 90 cabins designed to look like Indian huts, a/c, hot showers, TV, facilities for disabled people, pool, disco, evening entertainment by the pool, good buffet, supper CUC$12, breakfast CUC$4, excellent value, car rental, internet access, medical services, shop, tourism bureau, hairdresser, game shooting and fishing can be arranged, popular hotel for tour parties and hunters.

D-E Casa Mercy, San Cristóbal (Machado) 4 entre Cuba y Colón, T216941, omeliomoreno@yahoo.com. Run by Omelio y Mercedes Moreno, 2 good rooms, 1 bathroom, upstairs separate from the rest of the house, private but noise from road, double bed, a/c, fan, stocked fridge, towel and soap provided, iron, hearty food served on roof terrace or in ante-room, several languages spoken by friendly family with dog, very central, parking.

D-E Hostal Florida Center, Candelaria (Maestra Nicolasa) 56 entre Colón y Maceo, T208161. Delightful colonial house with 2 rooms opening on to verdant garden where there are parrots, a dog and cats. Rooms have double bed with extra single bed, basin in room, private bathrooms, a/c, TV, fridge and minibar, antique furniture, hospitable host Angel Martínez is an excellent cook and speaks some English, French and a little Italian.

D-E Martha Artiles Alemán, Marta Abreu 56 altos, entre Villuendas y Zayas, T205008, martaartiles@yahoo.es. Central but quiet, colonial house with balcony views towards Parque Vidal, parking, large rooms, sofa, a/c, fan, bathrooms, laundry, clean, own key to house.

D-E Orlando García Rodríguez, Buen Viaje 7 entre Parque y Maceo, T206761. 2 rooms, a/c, fan, shared fridge, shared bathroom, lovely house, eating area on the roof, guitar/singer, excursions arranged.

E Eduardo Alvarez Chaviano (Casa Suiza), Colón 170 entre Nazareno y San Miguel, T206190. Eduardo is a geography teacher, a good cook, an expert on Santa Clara and speaks English. The room is clean, a/c, private bathroom, fridge, kitchenette, parking.

E Ernesto y Mireya, Cuba 227 altos entre Pastora y Síndico, opposite Iglesia La Pastora,

T273501. Large clean room with bathroom, a/c, fridge. Ernesto is funny and helpful, will arrange collection from bus station if you pay for taxi. Excellent food, huge meals.

Trinidad *p129, map p130*
L-AL Grand Hotel Iberostar Trinidad, José Martí y Lino Pérez, T996070, www.iberostar.com. 35 rooms and 4 suites with view from balcony of plaza, no pool, nowhere to sit outside, no children under 15, a/c, TV, minibar, room service, laundry, safety box, internet, international phones, 24-hr cambio, gourmet restaurant with international cuisine, good buffet breakfast, smokers' bar with cigars and rums available.
B Las Cuevas, Finca Santa Ana, T996133, reservas@cuevas.co.cu. On a hill 10 mins' walk from town (good road), with caves in the grounds and a caving museum, view of the sea. 109 comfortable rooms and mini suites in chalets and apartments with a/c, phone, radio, hot water, very clean, 2 swimming pools, bar with excellent daiquirís and great view, disco 2200-0200 in cave below reception, entrance CUC$10, dollar shop, post office, exchange facilities, restaurant with poor buffet meals, breakfast CUC$5, evening meal CUC$11.
C Casa Muñoz, José Martí 401 entre Fidel Claro y Santiago Escobar, T/F993673, trinidadjulio@yahoo.com. Very friendly, English-speaking, run by Julio César Muñoz Cocina and Rosa Orbea Cerrillo, 2 children and 2 splendid dogs. Great house, built in 1800, 2 rooms with 2 double beds, new bathrooms, a/c and fans, roof terrace, parking, very popular so book in advance. Julio is a photographer and can arrange workshops and study groups, www.casa.trinidadphoto.com.
C Hostal La Rioja , Frank País 389 entre Simón Bolívar y Fco J Zerquera, T994177, tereleria@yahoo.com.mx. Run by friendly and helpful Teresa Leris Echerrí, 2 rooms with bathrooms, 1 with cooking facilities, noisy a/c, fan, hot water, garage, dachshund, some French and English spoken.
C Hostal Sandra y Víctor, Maceo 613 entre Piro Guinart y Pablo Pichs, T996444, hostalsandra@yahoo.com. Family lives downstairs, 2 guest rooms upstairs, privacy and security, well-cared-for property, good bathrooms, a/c, fan, fridge, balcony to the

front off the dining room, spacious and comfortable with friendly hosts who provide delicious and hearty meals.
C María Esther Pérez, Francisco Cadahía 224 (Gracia) entre Colón y Lino Pérez, T993528. Nice extension with 2 rooms attached to old colonial house, antique beds in both, 1 communal bathroom, a/c or fan, fabulous fish meals, run by herbalist, using plants from her own garden, parking 5 doors away.
C Villa de Recreo Ma Dolores, Ctra Circuito Sur, T996481, 1½ km from Trinidad on the road to Cienfuegos. Garden setting near Río Guaurabo, 12 brick *cabañas* and 26 bungalows with kitchen, a/c, shower, clean, restaurant, shop, pool bar, quiet spot but noisy in the evening as it is an all-dancing, all-singing tour group destination, horse riding, volleyball, basketball, fishing, river excursions.
D Balbina Cadahía Benavente, Maceo 355 entre Lino Pérez y Colón, T992585. Very nice family, old colonial house, hot water shower, will arrange trips, friendly, good reports.
D Carlos Gil Lemes, José Martí 263 entre Colón y Fco J Zerquera, T993142, next to library. Beautiful late 19th-century house with sumptuous tile decoration, English spoken, 2 rooms with shared bath, hot water, fans, garden courtyard, neighbour has a garage for rent, CUC$1 per night.
D Gisela Borrell Bastida, Frank País (Carmen) 486 entre Fidel Claro y Santiago Escobar, about 200 m from bus station, T994301. Bedroom with double and single bed on ground floor, bathroom with hot shower, use of own dining room, sitting room, own entrance, lots of space.
D Hospedaje Yolanda, Piro Guinart 227 entre Izquierdo y Maceo, opposite the bus station. Very nice rooms in enormous colonial house including 1 up a spiral staircase with 2 double beds, terrace and views of sea and mountains, hot water shower, a/c.
D Hostal La Candelaria, Antonio Guiteras (Mercedes) 129 entre P Zerquera y A Cárdenas, T994239. Run by Elvira and Eddy, both teachers but no English spoken, friendly and generous, humble accommodation, but spotlessly clean, 2 rooms, hot water, a/c, fans, nice garden, great food, cheap.
D Hugo P Bastida, Maceo 539 (Gutiérrez), entre Santiago Escobar (Olvido) y Piro

Guinart (Boca), T993186. Name above the door, typical dark colonial home with high ceilings, nice room, a/c, bathroom, hot water, very friendly dog, Sr Bastida speaks good English and his wife is an excellent cook.

D José y Fátima, Fco J Zerquera 159 entre Frank País y Fco Petersen, T993898. Upstairs rooms, 1 with double bed, the other with double and single bed, a/c, fan, new private bathrooms, hot water, door and windows open onto balcony for lots of fresh air, table on the patio for meals, roof terrace with laundry facilities and washing machine and a great view over the rooftops.

D Mercedes Padrón Jiménez, Manuel Solano 7 (Pimpollo), T993068. 2 rooms, 1 with own bathroom, more privacy than some, owner is former teacher and speaks the kind of Spanish that even people who don't speak Spanish can understand, phone ahead, popular.

D Pedro Aliz Peña, Gustavo Izquierdo 127 (Gloria) entre Piro Guinart y Simón Bolívar, T993776/993025, just by bus station. Old house with high ceilings, patio, quiet, 2 spacious rooms, fans, simple but clean, new bathrooms, hot water, Pedro and Teresa are sociable and helpful, only Spanish spoken.

● Eating

Cienfuegos *p127*
₩₩₩-₩₩ Palacio de Valle, by **Hotel Jagua**. Tue-Sun 1000-2200. The building dates from 1894 in a mixture of architectural styles but with Arab influences predominating, very ornate ceilings and decorations. The place to go for its style, if not for the food. Speciality seafood, including paella, lobster and shrimp.

₩₩ 1869, Hotel La Unión, T551020. 0700-2145. Good service and handsome decor but food sometimes second rate, particularly the chicken dishes.

₩₩ La Verja, Boulevard (Av 54) entre 33 y 35, T516311. 1100-1500, 1800-2400. Lovely dining room with dark wood carved features, scarlet tablecloths and curtains. Bar and patio dining. Note the bronze chandelier and blue tiles on the floor. Fried fish, breaded shrimp, goulash and salads or just a *bocadito*, good service.

₩₩-₩ Covadonga, on 37 opposite **Hotel Jagua**, T516949. 1230-1530, 1800-2200.

Large restaurant in seaside setting, lobster and fish.

₩ El Criollito, 33 5603 entre 56 y 58, T515540. 1200-2400. Meals include salad, chips, rice and coffee, tasty fish, chicken and beef in this front-room *paladar*.

Santa Clara *p128*
The best food is in the *casas particulares* although some of the *paladares* are worth trying. Begging can be persistent if you eat outside at a street café.

₩₩₩ 1878 Colonial, Máximo Gómez 8, near the Boulevard, T202428. 1000-1100 for snacks, 1200-1445 for lunch, 1900-2245 for dinner. Offers a variety of *criollo* dishes, mainly pork in different styles, bar in the patio, long trousers required for men at night.

₩ Bodeguito del Centro, Villuendas 264 entre San Miguel y Nazareno, T204356. 1200-2300. A *paladar* run by Soledad and José, this bohemian restaurant with graffiti-covered walls recalls Havana's Bodeguita del Medio.

₩ Casa del Gobernador, Boulevard. In old, colonial building, not very hygienic, open daily for lunch 1200-1500, *merienda* (tea/snacks) in the patio 0900-2300, dinner 1900-2245, night club Tue-Sun 2100-0100.

₩ El Alba, Rolando Pardo (Buen Viaje) 26 entre Maceo y Parque. 1200-1500, 1900-2030. Standing counter only catering mainly for Cubans, takeaway food also available. Meals mostly pork dishes with *congrí* and green salad, cheap and practical.

₩ La Casona, Ctra Central 6 entre Padre Chao y Marta Abreu, just by Río Bélico, T205027. 1200-2400. Nice old house with beautiful tiled floor but no tables or chairs, tasty food served at standing counter to avoid *paladar* regulations, like a takeaway service, friendly hosts.

Trinidad *p129, map p130*
Most people eat in *casas particulares* where the food is excellent. Breakfast is usually CUC$2-3 and dinner CUC$5-10. The price of beer in some restaurants drops from CUC$2 to CUC$0.60 after 1700 when the day tours leave, but the state-run places shut then too.

₩₩-₩ Plaza Mayor, Villena 15, just off Plaza Mayor, T996470. 1200-2130. Elegant setting with pink tablecloths, live music, lobster CUC$19, steak and seafood, buffet CUC$8, pleasant courtyard and a couple of internet terminals although they don't both always work.

El Jigüe, Real 69 esq Guinart, T996476. 0900-2230. Live music, good food and atmosphere.

El Mesón del Regidor, Simón Bolívar 426 entre Ernesto V Muñoz y Villena, opposite Toro, T996572/3. Daily 0900-2200. Also a bar, internet terminal and 4 rooms to rent.

Las Begonias, Maceo esq Simón Bolívar. 0900-2200. The only café in town with 6 computer terminals for internet access. Fast food, ice cream parlour opposite.

Restaurante Don Antonio, Izquierdo 118 entre Piro Guinart y Simón Bolívar, T996548. 1130-1700. A colonial house with ornate columns and tiled floor, meals around CUC$6-8.

Ruinas de Leonci, Gustavo Izquierdo 106 entre Simón Bolívar y Piro Guinart, T996498. Bar and restaurant 0900-2300, cosy small garden, pleasant wooden tables and chairs inside.

Sol y Son, Simón Bolívar 283 entre Frank País y José Martí. 1200-1500, 1900-2300. Run by English-speaking ex-architect Lázaro, in 19th-century house, nice decor, courtyard, mixed reports, vegetarian special, excellent pork, tasty stuffed fish around CUC$10 with drinks.

● Bars and clubs

Santa Clara *p128*
Cartelera is a pamphlet with what's on locally.

Bar Club Boulevard (Carishow), Independencia 225 entre Maceo y Unión, T216236. 1300-1900, 2100-0330. CUC$2. Nightclub, trendy, small, also used for social occasions (birthdays etc), open bar, music and show with different acts, singers, comedians.

Club Mejunje (mishmash), 2½ blocks west from Parque Vidal, Marta Abréu 107 entre Alemán y Juan Bruno Zayas, T282572. Open weekdays at variable hours, Sat 2100-0200, Sun 1600-2100. CUC$1 for foreigners. Cultural centre in a backyard full of trees, ruins, artefacts and graffiti-covered walls. Composers, singers, musicians and friends sing, play and drink together. Friendly, welcoming, enjoyable. Rock night Tue, **Trovuntivitis** Thu with very good *trovadores*,

both young and traditional, Fri is **Viernes de la Buena Suerte**, traditional Cuban music, Sat is the night for gays with a show, and Sun there is dancing 1600-2100. Larger events are staged in the courtyard, wide variety ranging from concerts to theatre, from shows for kids to transvestite shows for gays.

El Bosque, Centro Cultural, Av Sandino y Ctra Central, Vigía, 1 km from Parque Central, T204444. An outdoor venue for live and taped music and nightlife, cabaret, CUC$5, including bottle of rum and 4 colas and table for the show, after midnight it becomes a disco. Heady atmosphere and good dancing. 24-hr patio bar.

Hotel Santa Clara Libre, Parque Vidal. In the basement is **El Sótano Sala de Fiesta**. Tue-Sun 2100-0200. *Consumo mínimo* CUC$3 per couple, 1-hr show and taped music afterwards. On the roof is **El Topet, Bar La Terraza**, from 2100 onwards, open-air bar and disco with a bird's eye view of Santa Clara. On the ground floor is the **Cine Camilo Cienfuegos**, T203005. This is the only cinema and entering is like stepping back in time. Seriously cheap, 2 pesos, check billboard outside for what's on when.

Piano Bar, Luis Estévez 13 entre Independencia y Parque, T215215. Restaurant 1000-2145, *comida criolla*, Piano Bar 1200-1900 for drinks and snacks and 2100-0100, live music with the pianist Freyda Anido and band, invited singers, national and international music, couples only.

Trinidad *p129, map p130*
Lots of people offer 'unofficial' *salsa* lessons for about CUC$4 an hr; Trinidad is a good place to learn and you'll soon be dancing with Cubans in local bars.

Bar Daiquirí, Lino Pérez entre Cadahía y José Martí. 0800-2400. Fast food, beer CUC$1, mojito CUC$2, zombie CUC$4.

Bar Las Ruinas de Segarte, Alameda entre Márquez y Galdós, in ruined courtyard. 1000-2400. Fried chicken for CUC$1.50 or other fast food, traditional music, live bands play in the day, Afro-Cuban dance, amazingly energetic and incredible to watch, variety show at 2100.

Casa de la Música, up the steps past the church in Plaza Mayor. 1000-0200. Full of tourists and Cubans, *salsa*, live performers at weekends, show at 2200, restaurant with expensive snacks 1000-2200, internet, shop selling CDs, cassettes, music magazines.

Casa de la Trova, 1 block from the church. 0900-0100. Entry free during the day, CUC$1 at night. Excellent live traditional Cuban music and *trova*, with a warm, vibrant atmosphere. There are mostly Cubans here, of all age groups, and it's a great place to watch, and join in with, the locals having a good time.

Casa Fisher (Artex), Lino Pérez 306 entre Cadahía y José Martí. In colonial house built in 1870, outdoor bar 0900-0100, CUC$1 for show at 2130 with dance, live music and karaoke.

Coppelia, Martí, opposite the public library. Still open after everything else is closed, music, popular with Cubans. Open for breakfast at 0700, restaurant food 1000-2100, disco at 2200, special show Sat, Sun at 2300, CUC$1 for show and disco.

La Escalinata, on the terrace leading up the steps next to the church before you get to the **Casa de la Música**. 1000-2000. Live bands all the time except when it rains.

La Parranda, Villena 59 in the patio of the Templo de Yemaya, just off Plaza Mayor. 0900-2400. An outdoor bar/music venue, very ad hoc farmyard atmosphere, but excellent live music every night, good place to learn *salsa*, watched from semi-circle of seats, cocktails CUC$2, dancing.

Las Cuevas (see Sleeping page133). From 2200. CUC$10. Good disco, dance *merengue* and *salsa* with Cubans between the stalactites in a cave below reception.

Palenque de los Congos Reales, Fernando H Echerri entre **La Escalinata y Casa de la Trova**. Bar 0900-0100. During the day there are sometimes groups playing and at 2200 there is an Afro-Cuban show.

▲▲ Activities and tours

Cienfuegos *p127*
Diving
There are 40 dive sites in the area and 2 dive operators.
Villa Guajimico, see Sleeping, p131. Dive packages with accommodation and meals.
Whale Shark Scuba Center, at Hotels Faro Luna and Rancho Luna, see Sleeping, above. 5 dives CUC$116, night dives CUC$40, courses available with multilingual staff.

Sailing
Club Cienfuegos, 37 entre 8 y 12, T512891, contacto@club.cfg.cyt.cu. Daily 1000-0100, until 0200 Sat. A white Parisian-style mansion built in 1920 is now a sailing club/marina with shop selling sporting and fishing equipment, restaurant, car and moped hire, mini golf, billiards.

Trinidad *p129, map p130*
Diving
Puertosol, by Hotel Ancón, Playa Ancón. Diving and underwater photography, CUC$30 for 1 dive, CUC$50 for 2, CMAS certification course CUC$300.

Fishing
Fly fishing, deep-sea fishing, liveaboards, sea safaris to Cayo Blanco, snorkelling, sunset sails with dinner etc available at the marina (see below). A boat for a party of 4 to go deep-sea fishing all day costs around CUC$250, while fishing from a launch is CUC$50 per day.

Marina
Marina Cayo Blanco, Península Ancón, T996025, VHF 16, 19, 68, 72. 6 moorings, 1.8 m draft, showers, laundry.
Sunsail Cuba, at the marina, T996290, sunsailcuba@syc.co.cu. For sailing and yacht hire, 0800-1230, 1300-1800.

Tour operators
Excursions are all much the same price, for example: CUC$15 for a city tour including the Valley of the Sugar Mills *mirador*, the tobacco and ceramics factories, museums and a bar; CUC$65 for a trip to the Zapata Peninsula, minimum 8 people; CUC$25 for a sea safari from Playa Ancón marina to Cayo Blanco with snorkelling, CUC$32 with seafood lunch; CUC$45 to Guanayara including lunch and jeep (0900-1600, 2 km walk); CUC$28 to Caburní (0900-1400, 3 km walk down, 3 km struggle up); CUC$20 by horse to El Cubano including entrance to National Park, drink and transport (0900-1400).

Bicycles and horses are for hire. Try and use the legal operators as you will be better covered in case of emergency, although your *casa particular* owner may know the person the agencies subcontract who will be able arrange it cheaper.

● Transport

Cienfuegos *p127*

Bus

Bus Terminal at 49 (Gloria) esq Av 56, T515720. Tickets may be purchased 1 hr or so in advance from the small office with a brown door, next to the Salón Reservaciones. Víazul, T518114. 0800-1700. Buses pass through here on the Havana-Trinidad route. To **Pinar del Río**, 0945, 5½ hrs, CUC$35. To **Matanzas** and **Varadero**, 1015, 4½ hrs, CUC$20, minibus, reservations required at least a day in advance. In high season, **Víazul** runs a service Varadero-Guamá-Girón-Cienfuegos, CUC$16, leaving Varadero 0830, 4½ hrs, returning from Cienfuegos 1400. **Astro** to **Havana**, 5 daily, 5 hrs, CUC$14, bus with a/c CUC$17. To **Santiago de Cuba**, every other day, 1600, CUC$25.50, or with a/c CUC$31. Plenty of services to other towns.

Car

Havanautos and Servi Cupet Cimex is at 37 y 20, T451154, also **mopeds** CUC$22/day. RentaCar is in Hotel Jagua car park.

Coaches

Horse-drawn carriages charge around CP$2.

Train

Terminal at 49 esq Av 58, T513403. Services generally slow and uncomfortable.

Santa Clara *p128*

Air

Abel Santa María International Airport on Ctra de Malezas Km 11, north of Santa Clara, T209138. Charter flights come in from Canada taking tourists to the cays.

Bus

Town buses charge 20 centavos. The interprovincial bus station for long distances is 1 km further out on Ctra Central (Av Cincuentenario) 483 entre Independencia y Oquendo, T292114, a/c, snack bar. **Víazul** buses on the **Varadero-Trinidad** route stop here, also buses **Havana-Santiago**. Astro to most towns, cheaper, slower and less frequent. The provincial bus station for destinations within Villa Clara is on Marta Abreu esq Pichardo, T206284, 1 km from centre.

Taxi

Bicitaxi costs CUC$1 to most places in town, fix a price first or they will overcharge you; lots of complaints. The best taxi company is **Cubataxi**, T202691, 206903, good drivers, reasonable prices, about CUC$60 for a whole day's tour to the cays and Remedios.

Train

The **Martha Abreu** railway station is north of Parque Vidal on Estévez at Parque Mártires and is much more central than either of the bus stations. The ticket office is across the square, T202895, reservations T200854. Daily trains to **Havana** and to **Santiago**; the *especial* stops here every other day, heading east at 2205 (CUC$41 first class, CUC$33 second class, 10 hrs), and west at 0205 (CUC$21 first class, CUC$17 second class, 4 hrs). There are trains to **Bayamo**, **Manzanillo**, **Camagüey**, **Sancti Spíritus**, **Holguín** and other towns, timetables are unreliable and the train may not even appear at all.

Trinidad *p129, map p130*

Air

No regular flights, only charters.

Bus

Terminal entrance on Gustavo Izquierdo, near the corner with Piro Guinart, office, T994448, 0600-1700. Víazul from Havana 0815, 1300, via Cienfuegos, arriving 1400, 1800, CUC$25, returning 0700, 1515; from Varadero via Santa Clara and Sancti Spíritus or Cienfuegos at 0730, arriving 1405, CUC$20, returning 1440. Víazul also runs Trinidad-Santiago 0815, 12 hrs, CUC$33, via Sancti Spíritus, Jatibonico, Ciego de Avila, Florida, Camagüey, Sibanicú, Guáimaro, Las Tunas, Holguín, Bayamo and Palma Soriano, returning from Santiago at 1900 overnight. **Astro** daily services to Havana, Sancti Spíritus, Cienfuegos, Santa Clara, cheaper, slower, less comfortable. Ticket office daily, 0800-1200, 1330-1700.

Car

Transtur, Maceo esq Zerquera, T995314, cars and buses. **Havanautos**, at ServiCupet on the way out of Trinidad towards Casilda, T/F996301. Cupet station on Frank País esq Zerquera.

Taxi

Cubataxi, T992214, at the bus station. Taxi OK, T996302.

Train

The station is south of the town, walk south straight down Lino Pérez until you get to the railway line and turn left. The old building once used for the trains has been renovated as the School of Art; the office is now about 100 m to the right, T993348. Local services only.

ⓘ Directory

Cienfuegos *p127*

Banks Banco Financiero Internacional, Av 54 esq 29, Mon-Fri 0800-1500, cash advances on credit cards. **Cadeca**, Av 56 entre 33 y 35, Mon-Sat 0830-1800, Sun 0800-1230. **Internet** Cibercafe Enmi Cuba, 0800-2400, CUC$3/hr, fast service. Etecsa/Telepunto, 31 entre 54 y 56, phone, fax and internet, CUC$6/hr, daily 0830-2130. **Medical services** International Clinic, Punta Gorda on 37 202, opposite the Hotel Jagua, T551622, offering 24-hr emergency care, consultations, laboratory services, X-rays, pharmacy and other services. **Pharmacy** On Prado esq Av 60, open 24 hrs.

Santa Clara *p128*

Banks The **Cadeca** office for changing currency and TCs (4% commission) is at Parque Vidal on the corner of Rafael Tristá and Cuba, T205690, Mon-Sat 0830-1800, Sun 0830-1230. **Bandec**, Vidal esq Cuba, Visa and MC, Mon-Fri 0800-1500. **Banco Financiero Internacional**, Cuba 6 entre Tristá y E Machado, just down from Parque Vidal, T207450, F208115, Mon-Fri 0800-1500, also Visa and MC. **Internet** Several places on Martha Abreu for internet access, prices vary. No printing service anywhere. At **Cubatur**, Martha Abreu 10 entre Máximo Gómez y Villuendas, T208980, US$6/3 hrs. At **Palmares** snack bar next door, US$5/1 hr,

0900-1800. **CITMA** (CIGET), Martha Abreu 55 entre Villuendas y Zayas, CUC$0.10/1 min. **Post office** Colón 10 entre Parque y E Machado, just off Parque Vidal, opposite Coppelia ice cream parlour, T202203, Mon-Sat 0800-2200, email service with prepaid cards. **DHL** at Telecorreos, Cuba 7 entre Tristá y E Machado, T214069, Mon-Fri 0800-1600. **Telephone** Etecsa has a cabina Cuba esq Machado (San Cristóbal), T217898, daily 0900-2100, for domestic, foreign calls and internet access CUC$0.10 per min.

Trinidad *p129, map p130*

Banks Bandec, José Martí 264 entre Zerquera y Colón, T992405, Mon-Fri 0800-1700, Sat 0800-1600, cash advances on credit cards. **Cadeca**, Martí 164, T996262, half a block from Parque Céspedes, Mon-Sat 0830-1800, Sun 0830-1200. There are *cambios* in Hotel Las Cuevas, Hotel Ancón and Hotel Costa Sur. **Internet** Las Begonias, Maceo entre FJ Zerquera y Simón Bolívar, 6 terminals, CUC$1 for 10 mins, CUC$5 per hr, passport required, Mon-Fri 0900-1300, 1500-2100, Sat-Sun 0900-1300. Etecsa, on Parque Céspedes, email facilities using the prepaid card system, 6 terminals, fax, phones and cards. Restaurante Plaza Mayor, see Eating, above, 2 terminals which don't always both work, CUC$0.10 per min. **Medical services** Clínica Internacional, Lino Pérez 103 esq Anastasio Cárdenas, T996492, F996240, modern, with out-patient consultations, laboratory tests, X-rays, pharmacy, dentistry, massage and 24-hr emergency care. A consultation fee is CUC$25, a call out fee CUC$50. After 1600 prices rise. **Post office** Antonio Maceo 418 entre Zerquera y Colón, also for international telephones, Mon-Sat 0900-1800, Sun 0900-1700. Another small post office and Etecsa telephone/fax/internet office on Gral Lino Pérez, Parque Céspedes, beside Iglesia San Francisco, 0700-2300.

Centre east

The three provinces of Ciego de Avila, Camagüey and Las Tunas make up a large area of mostly flat, agricultural land with few natural features of outstanding beauty, although the landscape is pleasing with livestock grazing in the meadows. The city of

Ciego de Avila has little to recommend it and it is not a tourist attraction. North of the city, however, is one of the island's main beach resorts: Cayo Coco. Its extensive beaches of pale sand are now a magnet for the all-inclusive tourist market. Many other cays in the Jardines del Rey archipelago are being developed for tourism, either with hotels or as destinations for scuba diving or deep-sea fishing. The only city of note in the region is Camagüey, which is an ideal place to stay a few days if travelling from one end of the island to the other. The old colonial heart of the city has been restored to its former splendour while the shopping area is full of magnificent 19th-century buildings which have stood the test of time better than in seaside cities such as Havana or Santiago. North of the city is the long-established beach resort of Playa Santa Lucía, with hotels now starting to show their age, but the diving is superb, especially if you like sharks.

The countryside of Holguín province is attractive, hilly and covered with luxuriant vegetation. There are picture-book views of hillsides dotted with Royal palms, towering over thatched cottages, called bohíos, while the flatter land is green with swathes of sugar cane. The city of Holguín is unassuming and pleasant, with a huge central square. The local people take pride in the tourist developments of Guardalavaca, which now include the largest hotel in Cuba, but unlike Varadero there is no wall-to-wall strip. The north coast is indented with pretty horseshoe-shaped bays and sandy beaches, protected by a coral reef. The province of Granma occupies the western end of the Sierra Maestra and the flatlands and swamps to the north of the mountains. It was named after the boat that brought Castro and his comrades to Cuba to launch the Revolution. The area is studded with memories of the guerrilla struggle and the hills are full of evocative plaques commemorating the events immediately after their landing in 1953, but it has been largely neglected as far as tourism is concerned. The capital of the province is Bayamo, which has good transport links and from where hiking into the mountains is organized.▶▶ *For Sleeping, Eating and other listings, see pages 142-148.*

Ciego de Avila → *Phone code: 33. Colour map 1, B4. Population: 85,000.*

Ciego de Avila was founded in 1849, and is an agricultural market town with a large thermal electricity plant. The main road from Havana to Camagüey passes straight through the middle of town; most people just keep going. The main square is the **Parque Martí**, with a church and the former town hall, **Ayuntamiento**, built in 1911, and now the provincial government headquarters. There are a couple of basic hotels, *casas particulares*, and the usual crop of low-quality state-run restaurants if you have to spend the night. There is an airport at **Ceballos**, 24 km north of Ciego de Avila, Aeropuerto Máximo Gómez (AVI), but it is being replaced by the new international airport on Cayo Coco to get holiday-makers out to the resort hotels on the island.

Cayo Coco → *Phone code: 33. Colour map 1, B4.*

Cayo Coco is a large island, 374 sq km, of mostly mangrove and bush, which shelter many migratory birds as well as permanent residents. The island is connected to the mainland just north of Morón by a 27-km causeway across the Bahía de Perros. The Atlantic side of the island has excellent beaches, particularly **Playa los Flamencos**, with some 5 km of white sand and shallow, crystalline water. At certain times of the year you will see flamingos, after whom the beach is named. A nature reserve, **El Bagá** ① *T301064*, opened in 2002 and great emphasis is placed on preserving the wide variety of flora and fauna species, many of which are endemic to the zone. There is an Indian village, a lookout, farms to raise *jutías*, bats, crocodiles, butterflies and flamingos, a dock, a museum on piracy and cafeterias. Most of Cayo Coco is very isolated and nearly all foreigners are here on an all-inclusive package of a week or so and do not go far. **Marina Puertosol** offers deep-sea fishing and there is good diving. There are large, luxury resorts and plans to build an average of 1000 hotel rooms a year, all four or five star, until Cayo Coco has 16,000 and the other cays have a further 6000, up from around 5000 in 2005. A golf course and marina for 400 yachts are also in the works.

Cayo Guillermo, a 13-sq-km cay with 5 km of beach, is connected to Cayo Coco by a causeway and there are plans to build a 35-km causeway to link it with Cayo Santa María to the west. Cayo Guillermo is protected by a long coral reef which is good for diving with many fish and crustaceans, while on land there are lots of birds. Sand dunes, covered in vegetation, are believed to be the highest in the Caribbean.

Only tour buses go to Cayo Coco, there are no public buses and a checkpoint at the beginning of the causeway effectively prevents Cubans without permission from visiting the cay. The **Jardines del Rey** international airport was inaugurated in December 2002, the eleventh international airport in the country.

Camagüey → *Phone code: 32. Colour map 1, B4. Population: 772,000.*

Camagüey has been politically and historically important since the beginning of the 16th century and still has a lot of well-preserved colonial buildings, most dating from the 18th and 19th centuries. Many generations of revolutionaries have been associated with Camagüey and several key figures are commemorated, the most notable being Ignacio Agramonte, who was born here in 1841 and killed in action in 1873.

‡ Until 9 June 1903, the town was called Puerto Príncipe.

The village of **Santa María de Puerto del Príncipe** was first founded in 1515 at Punta del Guincho in the Bahía de Nuevitas but moved several times until it was finally established between the Río Tínima and the Río Hatibonico. Moving inland was no protection against pirate attacks. It was the target of the Englishman Henry Morgan in 1668 and of French pirates led by François Granmont in 1679. Architects took the precaution of designing the layout to foil pirate attacks. No two streets run parallel, to create a maze effect, which is unlike other colonial towns built on the grid system.

Nuestra Señora de la Merced, a National Monument on Avenida Agramonte on the edge of the Plaza de los Trabajadores, was built in 1747 as a church and convent, the catacomb can still be seen. The original wooden cross on the bell tower was moved into the catacombs in 1999. On the walls are 17th- and 18th-century paintings, but the most important treasure in the church is the Santo Sepulcro constructed in 1762 with the donation of 23,000 silver coins. **Nuestra Señora de la Soledad**, on República esquina Agramonte, is the oldest church in town. In 1697 to 1701 a hermitage was built. In 1733 the current church was started, although construction was not finished until 1776. **San Juan de Dios**, another National Monument, was built in 1728 as a church with a hospital attached, the first hospital in the village for men which also contained a home for the aged. Apparently this is the only church in Latin America which has the Holy Trinity as its central image. **Nuestra Señora del Carmen**, on Plaza Carmen, was started in 1732 but soon demolished for being too far out of town. It was later the site of the women's hospital of Nuestra Señora del Carmen, which was finished in 1825. A church was built alongside the hospital, with a second tower added in 1846, making it the only two-towered church in Camagüey. Part of the church collapsed in 1966 but restoration started in January 2001. The whole of the Plaza del Carmen is being renovated, a task which will include housing as well as smart new restaurants and tourist shops.

Playa Santa Lucía → *Phone code: 32. Colour map 1, B5.*

Santa Lucía is a beach resort 112 km northeast of Camagüey, where the sand stretches some 20 km along the northern coast. You can sometimes see dolphins and there are flamingos in the salt flats (*salinas*) inshore. This is a beautiful beach, protected by a reef which contains over 50 species of coral and is much sought after by divers. There are 37 dive sites at depths of 5-40 m in the area including a daily shark-feeding site where up to 20 sharks congregate; some of them swim in between the divers. Contact **Shark's Friends Dive Centre** ① *T336404*, who charge CUC$70. It is a lovely place to come and relax but it is remote, there is no real town, and people who stay here are on all-inclusive package tours.

Playa Los Cocos, 8 km from Santa Lucía, is even better than Santa Lucía. There is a broad beach with a fishing village, **La Boca**, at one end and beach bars at the other end by the channel which leads to Nuevitas. There are coconut palms from which the beach gets its name. The sand is very white and the water crystal clear. Across the channel, west of Playa Los Cocos, is Cayo Sabinal, reached by road from Nuevitas or by boat from Santa Lucía. There are beaches of white sand which are practically deserted and the cay is a wildlife reserve housing the largest colony of pink flamingos in the Caribbean, plus many other birds which are rare or endangered elsewhere. It is possible to stay in *casas particulares* at Playa Santa Lucía and Playa Los Cocos, but they are illegal.

Holguín→ *Phone code: 24. Colour map 1, B5. Population: 250,000.*

Holguín was founded in 1545, but most of the architecture dates from the 19th and 20th centuries. It is known as the 'city of the parks', four of which, **Parque Infantil**, **Parque Carlos Manuel de Céspedes** (also known as Parque San José), the **Plaza Central** (Plaza General Calixto García) and **Parque José Martí**, lie between the two main streets, Antonio Maceo and Libertad (Manduley). There is a statue of **Carlos Manuel de Céspedes** in the park named after him. He is remembered for having freed his slaves on 10 October 1868 and starting the War of Independence. **General Calixto García Iñiguez** (statue in the centre of Plaza Central) was born in Holguín in 1839 and took part in both wars of Independence. He captured the town from the Spanish in 1872 and again occupied it in 1898 after helping the US forces defeat the colonial power in Santiago de Cuba. His birthplace, one block from the plaza, is now a National Monument and a museum, **Casa Natal de Calixto García** ① *C Miró 147, Mon-Fri 0800-1700, Sat 0800-1300, CUC$1*. On the north side of the square is the **Museo Provincial** ① *Mon-Fri 0900-1700, Sat 0900-1300, CUC$1, CUC$3 with camera*, built between 1860 and 1868 and now a National Monument. The most important item on display here is the *Hacha de Holguín*, a pre-Columbian axe head carved with the head of a man, found in 1860 on one of the hills around the city and believed to be about 500 years old. It has become the symbol of Holguín. Renovation work is taking place to restore the **Plaza de la Maqueta** southwest of the Plaza Central between Mártires and Máximo Gómez. The old market building is being reconstructed in the centre to become a theatre and shops, galleries and a hotel are in progress around the outside.

Above the city is **La Loma de la Cruz**, a strategic hill which used to have a cross on top until Hurricane Georges blew it down in 1998. On 3 May 1790, a Franciscan priest, Antonio de Alegría, came with a group of religious people and put up the cross. In 1929 stone steps were begun up the hill, which were finished 3 May 1950. Every 3 May locals celebrate the Romerías de la Cruz de Mayo. They light candles and offer coins.

Guardalavaca and around → *Phone code: 24. Colour map 1, B6.*

Guardalavaca has been developed as a tourist resort along a beautiful stretch of coastline, indented with horseshoe bays and sandy beaches. The resort is in several sections: the older part is rather like a village, with apartments for workers, a few shops, discos, bank, restaurant and bus stop, while newer, all-inclusive hotels further west on the beaches **Estero Ciego** (also referred to as Playa Esmeralda), **Playa Pesquero Viejo** and **Playa Pesquero Nuevo** are very isolated and there is nothing to do outside the hotels. There is a reef offshore for diving, which is very unspoilt.

The lagoon in the **Bahía de Naranjo** has a small marina, where sailing trips and fishing expeditions can be arranged. Near the mouth of the lagoon is an aquarium, 10 minutes by boat from the dock, with dolphins and a sea lion, and a restaurant. At the mouth of the bay on the west side, is **El Birancito**, a replica of where Fidel Castro was born. A few kilometres from Guardalavaca on a hill with a wonderful view, is the

Museo Aborigen Chorro de Maita ① *Mon-Fri 0900-1700, Sun 0900-1300, CUC$2 entrance, CUC$1 per photo, plus CUC$5 per film, CUC$5 video*, a small but well-presented museum displaying a collection of 56 skeletons dating from 1490-1540, exactly as they were found. One is of a young Spaniard of about 22 years of age with his arms crossed for a Christian burial, but the rest are Amerindians, buried in the Central American style, lying flat with their arms folded across their stomachs. Also here is a replica of a **Taíno village** ① *CUC$5*, with statues of Indians going about their daily activities. In the town of **Banes**, the **Museo Indocubano Bani** ① *Gen Marrero 305 y Av José Martí, Tue-Sat 0900-1700, Sun 0800-1200, CUC$1*, has a good collection of pre-Columbian artefacts, probably the best in Cuba. The town itself was originally the site of the Bani chieftancy.

Bayamo → *Phone code: 23. Colour map 1, B5.*

Bayamo is the capital of the province of Granma. It was the second town founded by Diego Velázquez in November 1513 and has been declared a Ciudad Monumento Nacional. It was burned to the ground in 1869 as an act of rebellion against the colonial Spanish, so there is little early colonial architecture. The **Iglesia de Santísimo Salvador** in the Plaza del Himno Nacional is a 16th-century church which was damaged by the 1869 fire. A ten-year restoration programme was completed in 2007, see the baroque gold laminated altar in the Capilla de los Dolores and the painting of the 8 November 1868 ceremonies marking the start of the war of Independence. **Casa Natal de Carlos Manuel de Céspedes**, ① *Maceo 57 entre Donato Mármol y José Joaquín Palma, T423864, Tue-Sat 0900-1700, Sun 0900-1200, CUC$1*, is a museum dedicated to the life of the main campaigner of the 1868 Independence movement, who was born here.

> ❂ *Hurricane Dennis left eight dead in Granma and two in Santiago de Cuba when it passed through in July 2005, the deadliest hurricane since 1963.*

Parque Nacional Sierra Maestra

All trips to the Parque Nacional Sierra Maestra have to be fully guided, so if you want to arrange a few days' hiking you should book it in advance. A private driver will cost about CUC$40 from Bayamo, with the advantage that he will take you direct to the National Parks office, just uphill from **Villa Santo Domingo**, in time to arrange a guide before the tours start at 0900. There is a day trip, taking you by truck from Villa Santo Domingo, 20 km south of Bartolomé Masó, up an exceptionally steep road to the car park at **Alto de Naranjo**, then a 3-km walk (steep in parts and frequently muddy) to the **Comandancia de la Plata**, Castro's mountain base prior to the Revolution. This is a highlight of any visit to Cuba. The camp is very evocative and atmospheric; you see a small museum and other wooden buildings including Castro's bedroom, campbed and kitchen, in a beautiful mountain setting where you can see the trogon and other forest birds. Photographs are not allowed here and cameras have to be left at a half way rest stop. **Pico Turquino** can also be visited from Alto de Naranjo. To the Comandancia de la Plata costs CUC$11 per person (take water and snacks, there is no lunch), while to Pico Turquino it is CUC$33 for a two-day hike. There are other walks available on demand, depending on your abilities and interests. Guides are knowledgeable but only speak Spanish.

◉ Sleeping

Camagüey *p140*
Rooms in *casas particulares* cost CUC$15-20, depending on commission, breakfast usually CUC$2-3, dinner CUC$5-7 if available.
B-C Gran Hotel, Maceo 67, entre Ignacio Agramonte y General Gómez, T292093-4,

comazul@teleda.get.cma.net. Colonial style, built 1939, renovated 1997, very smart now, central, breakfast included, a/c, fan, cable TV, fridge, good bathroom, best rooms with balcony overlooking Maceo, security box rental, car hire, small swimming pool with kids' area, restaurant on top floor, good view, also piano bar, snack bar (see Bars and clubs, below).

C Colón, República 472 entre San José y San Martín, T283346. Old style built in 1920s, beautifully painted blue and white, marble staircase, long thin hotel on 2 floors round central well, rocking chairs overlook patio bar and restaurant, rooms with 1 or 2 beds, a/c, phone, good bathroom, TV, lobby bar, friendly.

D América Avellaneda at the intersection with San Martín, T282135. Small, cosy hotel, a/c, variety of dishes in the restaurant, bar.

D-E Hospedaje Colonial Los Vitrales, Avellaneda 3 entre Gral Gómez y Martí, T295866. Run by English-speaking Rafael Requejo, an architect, and his family, 2 rooms, high ceilings, a/c, fan, fridge, big bathroom, hanging space for laundry, good water pressure, garage. Good traditional meals are served, with beans and rice cooked the way they have been for centuries.

E Caridad García Valua, Oscar Primelles 310 A entre Bartolomé Masó y Padre Olallo (Pobres), T291554. 2 rooms with private bathrooms, a/c or fan, fridge, garden, clean and nice.

E Casa Blanca, San Ramón 201 altos, entre Heredia y Santa Rita, T293542. Run by Blanca Navarro Castro and very welcoming, chatty family. 1 large room with double and single bed covered with bright pink shiny bedspread, private bathroom, a/c, fan, no view, dark but comfortable, tiled floors and high ceilings, laundry service, English spoken plus a little of other languages. Breakfast and dinner about CUC$10.

E Casa Manolo, Santa Rita 18 (El Solitario) entre República y Santa Rosa, T294403. Run by Migdalia Carmenates y Manolo Rodríguez, 2 rooms, a/c, fan, hot shower, patio, laundry CUC$2, garage CUC$2, nice house, positive atmosphere, extremely helpful landlady.

E Casa Rosello, Carlos M de Céspedes 260 (Hospital) entre Hnos Agüeros y San Ramón, T292143/296879, ask for Pedro. 2 beautiful rooms, bathroom, owner practises *Santería* and will show you some interesting things, garage opposite, CUC$1 per night.

E Jorge Rovirosa, Cristo 2C entre Cisneros y Lugareño, T298305. Right by the cathedral and very central. Fabulous 1910 house, cavernous entrance hall with wrought-iron gates inside the front door, marble staircase,

grand but dark and dilapidated. Apartment upstairs, 1 room, light and bright, lots of air, open windows, tiled floors, high ceilings, view over city. Jorge and/or his wife speak English, German and French, but his mother does not. Breakfast CUC$3, dinner CUC$6-7.

E-F Jorge Saéz Solano, San Ramón 239 entre San Martín y Heredia, T286456. 2 rooms each with double and single bed, shared good bathroom between them, communicating doors, a/c, fan, bedside light, nylon sheets rather small, hot water if turned on 15 mins in advance, laundry on request, friendly family, no *chicas* allowed, don't touch the Dobermann. Good food, not greasy, no beans.

Holguín *p141*

C El Mirador de Mayabe, outside the town, T422160, T/F425347. 24 rooms in cabins under the trees, tiled floors, a/c, TV, wooden furniture, fridge, hot water, adequate bathroom, quiet, also a suite (**C**) and 4 rooms in a house at the top of the hill with a fantastic view. Popular for a day trip, for lunch and to see Pancho, the beer-drinking donkey.

C Villa El Bosque, T481012, just off Av Jorge Dimitrov. 69 rooms in spread out villas, patio garden, fridge, basic shower room, TV, a/c, also 2 suites (**C**), good security, car rental, large pool, El Pétalo disco, popular.

C-E Villa Liba, Maceo 46 esq 18, T423823, villaliba@yahoo.es. A very special place run by Jorge Mezerene and his wife Liba, who between them speak some English, Italian and a little French. Liba is super-efficient and can sort out any difficulty for you. She is also a walking information bureau and knows what is going on and where. Modern house in quiet residential area within walking distance of the centre. 2 rooms with double and single bed, a/c, fan, bedside lights, good wardrobe, phone interconnects with kitchen for room service, TV and video if you want it, patio with tables and rocking chairs under *mariposa* flowers and grapevines. Excellent food, good for vegetarians.

E Antonio Ochoa Ochoa, Morales Lemus 199 entre Martí y Frexes, T423659. Spanish-style house with courtyard, 2 rooms with bathrooms, one has independent access through garage, 3 generations live here, English spoken by Antonio's sons, welcoming family, discounts for long stays,

a/c, fan, hot water, towels, laundry.
E Evaristo Bofill and Mirtha Lago, Luz Caballero 78 Altos entre Miró y Morales Lemus. 2 large rooms, very clean, private bathroom, a/c, terrace, friendly and helpful family who make you feel at home.
E Luis Turbay y Marya Ferrás, Agramonte 68 entre Progreso y Río Marañón, T461000. The whole of the first floor is to let, including 2 bedrooms, huge kitchen, 2 bathrooms, a/c, TV, VCR, great place but often booked by long-stay guests, welcoming owners, good breakfast, laundry service.
E Regina Aracelis Arias, Morales Lemus 140 entre Martí y Frexes, T423204. 1 room with own sitting room, fridge, fan, bathroom, area for drying clothes, very private and huge.

Bayamo *p142*
C-D Royalton, on Maceo 53 y Joaquín Palma, very central location, T422290. The building dates from the 1940s and has been elegantly renovated as a 3-star hotel. 33 rooms, a/c, private bathrooms, phones, restaurant, lobby bar and terrace bar open each night, toilets just beyond reception.
E Ana Martí, Céspedes 4 entre Macel y Canducha Figueredo, T425323. 2 rooms, although one is a bit difficult to get up to, clean and good.
E Olga Celeiro Rizo, Parada 16 (altos) entre Martí y Mármol, above **Cubana** office, T423859. Olga and her husband José Alberto are most hospitable and helpful in arranging excursions. 2 bedrooms share bathroom, extra bed on request, comfortable, balcony off sitting room for watching the world go by in the plaza below. Good food, excellent sweet potato chips, substantial breakfast.
E Ramón Enrique Alvarez Sánchez, Pío Rosado 22 entre Ramírez y Av Fco Vte Aguilera, T423984. Enormous rooms, a/c, private bathroom, wife Carolina is a good cook.

Parque Nacional Sierra Maestra *p142*
C-D Villa Santo Domingo, Santo Domingo, Bartolomé Masó, T LD-375. 20 rooms in cabins, some of which are damp, 1 star, a/c, TV, bar, restaurant, barbecue, games room, parking, credit cards accepted. There is good walking in the area along paths and trails and it is a great place to get close to nature with lovely views up in the mountains.

● Eating

Camagüey *p140*
Restaurants have a reputation for reheating leftovers, *paladares* can be expensive, *casas particulares* are best for fresh, wholesome cooking. State-run restaurants offer fairly mediocre food but in very nice locations.
ᵀᵀᵀ-ᵀᵀ El Ovejito, at the entrance to Plaza del Carmen, T292524. Lunch and dinner. Quite elegant and lovely situation, but overpriced with *moros y cristianos* at CUC$4.50 and *mojito* an extortionate CUC$5.50, equivalent to the upper level of Havana prices.
ᵀᵀᵀ-ᵀ Don Ronquillo, at the back of Cubanacán Galería Colonial, Ignacio Agramonte esq República. 1100-1500, 1800-2200. Used by tour parties with set lunch and live music for CUC$10, reasonably priced, most dishes CUC$5-10, beer CUC$1, *mojito* CUC$1.
ᵀ El Paradero, near the railway station. Cafetería, bar and bakery open 24 hrs.
ᵀ Parador de los Tres Reyes, Plaza de San Juan, T295888, and the **Campana de Toledo**, Plaza San Juan, T295888. Lunch and dinner. 2 small colonial-style state restaurants serving Spanish food, live music. The latter has tables overlooking the square or in the courtyard and both are very busy with tour parties at lunchtime, chicken/fish CUC$5-6, *moros y cristianos* CUC$1.50.

Holguín *p141*
ᵀᵀᵀ-ᵀ 1720, Frexes esq Miró. Nicely restored blue and white building, with restaurant, bar, shows, information, souvenirs. The restaurant, on the right as you go in, is called **Les Parques**, and is gloriously elegant with tablecloths, white china and roses on the table, but you don't need to dress up. The food is average but the service OK. Menu ranges from chicken, pork and lamb at CUC$5-6 to beef at CUC$8 and lobster at CUC$22.
ᵀ Casa del Cheff, Luz Caballero entre Máximo Gómez y Mártires, close to Plaza de la Maqueta. 1230 until everyone stops eating. Good, simple seafood place with a good reputation.
ᵀ El Tocororo, Parque Central, T468588. Open 24 hrs. Cheap toasted sandwiches, wooden sculpture above the door.
ᵀ Jelly Boom, on Martí 180, near the cemetery, T424096. 1200-2300 but lunch on

request only, phone ahead. Supposed to be one of the best *paladares* in town; usual *criollo* food.

¶ **La Begonia**, Plaza Central. Outdoor cafeteria under a flowering creeper, very pretty, good for a Mayabe beer, meeting place.

¶ **La Malagüeña**, Martí entre Maceo y Mártires. 4 tables, can get very busy at night and at weekends, long queue, accepts CP$ or CUC$.

¶ **Pico Cristal**, corner of plaza with Libertad, T425855. 1200-1500, 1830-2245. On 3 floors, restaurant on top floor, international and Cuban food, chicken, some fish, cafeteria open 24 hrs, usual range of fastish food, disco **Diskaraoke** on 1st floor, 2100-0100.

¶ **Ramón**, Rastro 57 entre Frexes y Pérez Zorilla, next to the telephone *cabina*. Ramón is the owner, good food, specializes in seafood.

Guardalavaca and around *p141*

♦♦♦-¶ **Pizza Nova**, Centro Comercial, Guardalavaca, T30137. 1100-2300. In garden looking down to sea, nice location, dining outside on circular terrace under a roof or small indoor seating if a/c preferred. Good pizza. Prices range from CUC$4.85-19.60, for basic, small cheese and tomato to large lobster pizzas. There is also chicken, meat, fish, lobster tail (CUC$25), pastas (with lobster) with a similar range of prices.

♦♦-¶ **Compay Gallo**, 3 km out of Holguín on the way to Guardalavaca, on the right, T30132. Spanish *quinta* style, *típico*, in the countryside, pleasant surroundings, traditional music. Good for lunch, but also open for dinner.

Bayamo *p142*

Paladares and bars along General García, charge in pesos.

¶ **1513**, Gen García esq Gen Lora, T425921. 1200-2200. Small but recommended by Bayameses. Cuban cuisine.

¶ **La Casona**, Plaza del Himno Nacional, behind the church. 1300-2200. Nice wooden bar, cheap pizzas or spaghetti, courtyard at the back completely covered with flowering vine, lots of green lizards, delightful.

♦ Bars and clubs

Camagüey *p140*

Every Sat night a **Noche Camagüeya** is held

along República, when the street is closed to traffic and there is music everywhere and traditional food. On Sun morning there are activities in **Parque Casino Campestre**, including live music.

Bar El Cambio, northeast corner of Parque Ignacio Agramonte. This one-time gambling den now has lottery artwork on the walls, *mojito* CUC$2. You can expect to be approached here with offers of private restaurants. Good view of the cathedral.

Casa de la Trova, on the west side of Parque Agramonte between Martí and Cristo, closed Mon. Folk music is played here. It has a courtyard and bar, while at the entrance is a souvenir shop where you can buy music.

Disco Café, Independencia entre Martí y Plaza Maceo. Good late night place.

Disco Labarra, República entre O Primelles (San Estéban) y Santa Rita, opposite the Cadeca. Popular with younger crowd.

Galería Colonial, Ignacio Agramonte y República. Has cabaret 3 times a week. Can be rented for private functions.

Gran Hotel, has several bars with entertainment: **Piano Bar Marquesina**, CUC$5 for 2 people Mon-Fri, CUC$10 per couple on Sat, Sun, includes 2 meals and beer or rum; **Bar Piscina 1920**, CUC$3 per person (CUC$1 entrance, CUC$2 drinks), or CUC$10 Sat, Sun per couple including meal, beer/rum, with *ballet acuático* at 2130; **Bar El Mirador**, CUC$1 per person.

Holguín *p141*

Cabaret El Bariay at the end of Frexes beyond the river. Show with live performers and taped music, dancing.

Cabaret Nocturno, on road to Las Tunas, Km 2.5, T425185. Wed-Mon 2100-0200. Show with different Latin American music followed by disco with *salsa* and dance music.

Café Cantante, Frexes esq Libertad. Live traditional music, *trova*, beer.

Casa de la Trova on Plaza Calixto García between **Casa de la Cultura** and **La Begonia**. Tue-Sun. Good music and dance, notice board outside announcing what's on that night, small stage, bar, salón, you can hear it all from the plaza outside.

Casa del Tango, Maceo esq Arias on Parque Céspedes. Operates like a **Casa de la Trova** but there is only tango.

Bayamo *p142*

Every Sat there is a **Noche Cubana**, when the whole of Gen García fills with stalls, ad hoc bars, pigs on spits, and the restaurants all put tables on the road, selling food and drinks in CP$, accompanied by music.
Amor Bayamés, Hotel Royalton, T422290. Night club, 2100-0100.
Casa de la Trova on the corner of Maspote and José Martí. Shows during the afternoon and every night, quite touristy in high season.

⊚ Entertainment

Camagüey *p140*
Ballet
Ballet de Camagüey, ranked 2nd in the country after Havana's ballet company, often performs at the **Teatro Principal**, on Padre Valencia 64, T293048.

Cinema

There are 3 cinemas: **Casablanca**, T292244, **Guerrero**, T292874, and **Encanto**, T295511.

Holguín *p141*
UNEAC, Libertad entre Martí y Luz Caballero. Open until late, depending on the event. A magnificent restored colonial building with tables and chairs in central courtyard and now the major cultural venue in town. Art exhibitions, video shows daily except Mon, cultural and artistic events.

▲ Activities and tours

Playa Santa Lucía *p140*
Diving
At Playa Santa Lucía there are 37 dive sites at depths of 5-40 m in the area including a daily shark feeding site in the channel between Playa Los Cocos and Cayo Sabinal about 20 m offshore. Up to 20 sharks congregate at a depth of some 26 m by the wreck of a Spanish galleon. Some of them swim between the divers; no one wears any protection.
Shark's Friends, Playa Santa Lucía, T365182. Dive centre charging CUC$70 for shark feeding, CUC$162 for 5-dive package, CUC$365 for open water certification.

Snorkelling

Catamarans leave twice daily at 1000 and 1400 from the pier just north of Escuela Santa Lucía, for the reef. CUC$20 including all gear and soft drinks on board, great snorkelling trip.

Tour operators
Cubatur, 5ta Paralela 417, Florat, Camagüey, T261668; also an office on Ignacio Agramonte, opposite Cine Casablanca, T254785. Daily 0900-1200, 1300-1700. Tours for individuals all start from Playa Santa Lucía, nothing available from Camagüey.
Havanatur, Monteagudo entre Ctra Central y Cuba, Alt Casino, Camagüey, T281564. Also a desk in the **Gran Hotel**, contact Jorge Omar Miranda Sánchez, T283664. He is very knowledgeable but out on tours most of the time. He should be at his desk daily 0730-0930, 1630-2000.

Guardalavaca and around *p141*
Diving
Lots of dive shops on the beaches at Guardalavaca serving the hotels. Dive sites are mostly 5-40 m deep on the reef offshore, can be rough at times.
Scuba Cuba, Playa Guardalavaca. CUC$35 for 1 dive, CUC$69 for 2, less for more. ICUC Open Water certification course CUC$350. No jetty so you have to swim and carry tank and gear out to boat.
Sea Lovers Diving Centre, Playa Esmeralda. Has 2 daily dives, 0900, 1400, CUC$30 for 1 dive, CUC$140 for 5 dives, equipment rental, snorkelling trips CUC$13 including equipment.

Tour operators
The tour desks in the hotels have lots of excursions on offer along the coast or inland, even to Santiago de Cuba. Alternatively you can hire a car, scooter or bike, or contract a local private driver to take you wherever you want. Private operators cannot pick you up from a hotel in Guardalavaca, so meet in the Centro Comercial or on the main road. Negotiate a price before setting out, *paladar* meals can be included.
Cubatur, Hotel Guardalavaca, Room 626, T30171, holguin@cubatur.cu. Tours and excursions for hotel guests and other tourists.
Havanatur, Frexes 172 entre Morales Lemus y Narciso López, T468438. Mon-Fri

0830-1630. Excursions, minibus rental, transfers, guides, hotels.

● Transport

Camagüey *p140*
Air

Ignacio Agramonte International Airport (CMW) is 9 km from the centre on the road to Nuevitas, T261000. **Cubana** flies daily from Havana. There are also charter flights from Toronto and Europe depending on the season.

Bus

The Interprovincial bus station is southwest of the centre along the Ctra Central Oeste, esq Perú. **Víazul**, T272346, stops here on its **Havana-Santiago** and **Trinidad-Santiago** routes. **Astro**, T271668.

Car

There are Servi Cupet gas stations by the river on Ctra Central y Av de la Libertad; a couple of blocks further south on the other side of the Ctra Central; and at the junction as you arrive at Playa Santa Lucía.

For **rental**, Havanautos is at Hotel Camagüey, T272239. and at airport, T287068. At Playa Santa Lucía there are rental desks at or near hotels.

Taxi

Cubataxi, T281247/298721, in Playa Santa Lucía, T336196. *Bicitaxis* charge about CUC$1 per person, fix price in advance.

Train

Railway station, T292633/281525. Train ticket agency, T283214. Trains to/from **Havana** daily, usually in the night.

Holguín *p141*
Air

Frank País International Airport (HOG) is 8 km from Holguín, T425271. It receives flights from Havana and abroad to take visitors out to the beach at Guardalavaca.

Bus

The interurban bus terminal is on Av de los Libertadores opposite the turning to Estadio Calixto García. The interprovincial bus terminal is west of the centre on the Ctra

Central. You can walk along Frexes from the centre, but it is hot with luggage. A *bicitaxi* costs CUC$2. **Astro** and **Víazul** (T422994) buses stop here. Daily services on the Havana-Santiago route. **Víazul** runs buses to Guardalavaca beach daily at 0830, 1 hr, CUC$6, returns 1900 be there 30 mins before departure and check in advance that it is running.

Taxi

Cubataxi, Miró, entre Aguilera y Frexes, T423290. Good service, not expensive.

Bayamo *p142*
Air

Carlos Manuel de Céspedes Airport is 4 km from town; flight to Havana twice a week.

Bus

The terminal is on the corner of Ctra Central and Jesús Rabi, T424036. **Víazul**, stops here for 5 mins on its Havana-Santiago and Trinidad-Santiago routes.

Car

Havanautos in Cupet Cimex gas station next to the bus station, on road to Jiguaní, T423223.

Train

The station is at Saco y Línea. Daily trains to **Santiago** and **Havana**.

● Directory

Camagüey *p140*

Banks Banco Financiero Internacional, Plaza Maceo, T294846. There is a **Cadeca** on República entre Primelles y Santa Rita, T295220. **Bandec**, Plaza de los Trabajadores, Mon-Fri 0800-1400, Sat 0800-1200, Visa accepted. **Internet** Cubatur (see above) has 3 terminals for internet access with CUC$5 prepaid card for 3 hrs, slow and inefficient service. The hotels have internet access for guests. **Medical services** 24-hr **pharmacy**, Avellaneda esq Primelles. In Playa Santa Lucía, **Clínica Internacional**, T365292.

Holguín *p141*

Banks Bandec, Arias 159, Mon-Fri 0800-1500. **Cadeca**, just south of Cristal building on Libertad, Visa, MasterCard.

Banco Financiero Internacional, on Libertad just north of the Plaza Central, Mon-Fri 0800-1500, last working day of the month 0800-1200, MasterCard, Visa, Tran$card. Bancrédito, on south side of Parque Céspedes, Mon-Fri 0800-1500, Visa, MasterCard. **Post office** Maceo, opposite Parque Céspedes. Small post office with telephones and DHL on Libertad, Plaza Central, Mon-Fri 1000-1200, 1300-1600, alternate Sat 0800-1500.

Bayamo *p142*
Banks Banco Nacional de Cuba, Saco y Gen García. **Bandec**, Gen García 101. Visa and Mastercard, Mon-Fri 0800-1500. **Medical services** Farmacia Principal Municipal, 24-hr at Gen García 53.

Santiago de Cuba and around

→ *Phone code: 226. Colour map 1, B6.*
This is the most mountainous part of the country, dominated by the Sierra Maestra, which runs along the foot of the island with several protected areas and National Parks, providing a habitat for many rare creatures. The highest point is Pico Turquino, 1974 m. The Sierra Maestra also provided shelter for Castro and his band of guerrillas during the Revolution. Santiago de Cuba, the second most important city in the country, is one of the oldest towns on the island, protected from the sea in an attractive bay surrounded by mountains. It is a lively city with plenty of music and other cultural activities and the place to come for carnival in July, a raw, ebullient celebration. There is a very Caribbean feel to life here, hot and steamy, both during the day and in the discos and bars as you dance the night away. Sleepy Guantánamo came to the world's attention in 2002 when the US naval base on the coast nearby was chosen to incarcerate prisoners from the conflict in Afghanistan. The crowd-puller in this most easterly province, however, is Baracoa, a laid-back, friendly place, hemmed in by pine-clad mountains. It is one of the best places to come for beaches, rivers, hiking, coconuts, chocolate and seafood, topped off by an active nightlife scene with lots of traditional and contemporary music.
▸▸ *For Sleeping, Eating and other listings, see pages 154-162.*

Ins and outs

Getting there and around Santiago is the end of the line for the main road and rail links from Havana and has domestic and international air services. There are several daily buses, trains and flights from the west end of the island and good connections if you want to fan out to Guantánamo, Baracoa and other towns in the region. International and domestic **Cubana** flights arrive at the **Antonio Maceo Airport** (SCU), 8 km south of the city on the coast. Taxis around CUC$5-8, depending on the company and the distance. The long-distance bus terminal is to the north of the city, by the Plaza de la Revolución. Outside are taxis, *colectivos*, trucks, buses and horse-drawn *coches*. The new railway station is more central, opposite the rum factory on Av Jesús Menéndez, and within walking distance of many *casas particulares* and some hotels.

Urban buses cost 20 centavos. There are also *coches*, 1 peso, motorbikes, CUC$1, and *bicitaxis*, CUC$0.50, for short journeys around town. Plaza Marte is a central hub for lots of local transport. ▸▸ *See also Transport, page 160.*

History

Santiago de Cuba was one of the seven towns (*villas*) founded by Diego Velázquez. It was first built in 1515 on the mouth of the Río Paradas but moved in 1516 to its present location in a horseshoe valley surrounded by mountains. It was Cuba's capital city until replaced by Havana in 1553 and was capital of Oriente province until 1976. During the 17th century Santiago was besieged by pirates from France and England, leading to the construction of the Castillo del Morro, still intact and now housing the piracy museum. Because of its location, Santiago has been the scene of many migratory exchanges with other countries; it was the first city in Cuba to receive African slaves, many French fled here from the slaves' insurrection in Haiti in the 18th century and Jamaicans have also migrated here. Santiago is more of a truly ethnic blend than many other towns in Cuba. It is known as the *Ciudad Héroe* (heroic city) or *Capital moral de la Revolución Cubana*. One of Cuba's foremost revolutionaries of the 19th century, **General Antonio Maceo**, is honoured in the **Plaza de la Revolución**, to the northeast of the centre, with a dramatic monument made of galvanized steel in searing, solid Soviet style, and a gargantuan bronze statue of the general on horseback surrounded by huge iron machetes.

Sights

Parque Céspedes is in the centre of town and everything revolves around it. Most of the main museums are within easy walking distance. The **Hotel Casa Granda** flanks the east side of the small park. The **Cathedral** ① *daily, 0800-1200*, Santa Iglesia Basílica Metropolitana, is on the south side, entrance on Félix Pena. The first building on the site was finished in 1524, but four subsequent disasters, including earthquakes and pirate attacks, meant that the cathedral was rebuilt four times. The west side of the park is occupied by an ugly bank, next to the beautiful 16th-century **Casa de Diego Velázquez** (the oldest house in Cuba, started in 1516, completed 1530), now one of the best museums in the city, the **Museo de Ambiente Histórico Cubano** ① *northwest corner of Parque Céspedes, Félix Pena 612, T652652, Sat-Thu 0900-1700, Fri 1400- 1700, CUC$2, with guided tour in English, French or German, camera fee CUC$1 per photo*. Velázquez lived on the top floor, and the ground floor was a contracting house and a smelter for gold. Each room has a particular period, featuring furniture, porcelain and crystal.

The **Museo Provincial Emilio Bacardí** ① *2 blocks east of the Parque, opposite the Palacio Provincial, entrance on Pío Rosado esq Aguilera, T628402, Tue-Sat 1000-2000, Sun 1000-1800, Mon 1200-2000, guided tour in English, CUC$2*, was named after industrialist Emilio Bacardí Moreau, its main benefactor and collector of much of the museum's contents. This was the second museum founded in Cuba and has exhibits from prehistory to the Revolution downstairs, one of the most important collections of Cuban colonial paintings and the archaeology hall has mummies from Egypt and South America. The **Museo del Carnaval** ① *on Heredia esq Pío Rosado, T626955, Tue-Sat 0900-1800, Sun 0900-1200, CUC$2, daily dance show 1545, CUC$1*, exhibits a dusty collection of instruments, drums and costumes from Santiago's famous July carnival. If you are not going to be there in July, this is the best way to get a flavour of the celebrations. Every afternoon except Sat you can feel the beat of the *bata* drums when the folklore group, **19 de Diciembre**, perform in the courtyard. The **Museo de la Lucha Clandestina** ① *at the top of picturesque Padre Pico (steps), Gen Rabí 1 entre Santa Rita y San Carlos, T624689, Tue-Sat 0900-1900, Sun 0900-1700, CUC$2*, highlights the support given by the local urban population during the battle in the Sierra Maestra. Exhibits revolve around Frank País, from his early moves to foment a revolutionary consciousness to his integration into the Movimiento 26 de Julio under Fidel Castro. The **Museo Casa Natal de Frank País** ① *Gen Banderas 226 y Los Maceos, T652710*, is in the birthplace of the leader of the armed uprising in Santiago on 30 November 1956, who was shot in July 1957. The **Casa Natal de Antonio Maceo** ① *Mon-Sat 0900-1700, CUC$1, Los Maceo 207 entre Corona y Rastro, T623750*, built between 1800 and 1830, was the birthplace, on 14 June 1845, of Antonio Maceo y Grajales, one of the greatest military commanders of the 1868 and 1895 Wars of Independence. The museum houses his biography and details of his 32 years' devotion to Independence.

Plaza Marte, a short walk up Aguilera from Parque Céspedes, is a pick-up and drop-off point for most urban transport. Sometimes musicians play and there's an ice

Cuba Santiago de Cuba & around

150   cream stand. North of Plaza Marte, the **Museo Histórico 26 de Julio** ① *Av Moncada esq Gen Portuondo, T620157, Tue-Sat 0900-2000, Sun 0900-1300, CUC$2, guided tour in English, French, Italian, camera fee CUC$1, video camera CUC$5*, formerly the Moncada Garrison, was attacked (unsuccessfully) by Castro and his revolutionaries on 26 July 1953. When the Revolution triumphed in 1959, the building was turned into a school. To mark the 14th anniversary of the attack, one of the buildings was converted to a museum, featuring photos, plans and drawings of the battle. Bullet holes, filled in by Batista, have been reconstructed on the outer walls.

The junction of Victoriano Garzón and Avenida Las Américas, where the hotels **Santiago** and **Las Américas** are situated, is known locally as **Ferreiro**, after the family that owned a large part of the surrounding area and emigrated to the USA after the Revolution. To the east of Ferreiro off Avenida Manduley, in Reparto Vista Alegre, are several interesting museums. The **Casa del Caribe** ① *off Av Manduley on 13 esq 8, T642285*, is a world-renowned cultural centre. If you are interested in *Santería* (see page 174) there is a musical and religious ceremony at 0930 on Wednesdays. The **Museo de la Religión** ① *13 206, esq 10, Mon-Sat 0830-1700, free, CUC$2 for English-speaking guide*, displays religious items particularly concerning *Santería*, but there are no written explanations of the exhibits, best to ask for a guide.

The **Cementerio Santa Ifigenia** ① *Av Crombet, Reparto Juan G Gómez, CUC$1, extra CUC$1 to take pictures, price includes guided tour in Spanish and English*, northwest of the city, features **José Martí's mausoleum**, a huge structure with a statue of Martí inside, designed to receive a shaft of sunlight all morning. Martí is surrounded by six statues of women, representing the six Cuban provinces of the 19th century. Also in the cemetery is the grave of **Frank País**, a prime mover in the revolutionary struggle and other notable figures such as Céspedes, the Bacardí family and the mother and widow of Maceo. There is a monument to the Moncada fallen and the tomb of Cuba's first president, Tomás Estrada Palma. Well worth a visit.

Around Santiago

South of Santiago The Ruta Turística runs along the shore of the Bahía de Santiago to the **Castillo del Morro**, a clifftop fort with the **Museo de la Piratería** ① *T691569, CUC$4, cameras CUC$1*, a museum of the sea, piracy and local history, charting the pirate attacks made on Santiago during the 16th century. Pirates included the Frenchman Jacques de Sores and the Welshman Sir Henry Morgan, and you can see many of the weapons used in both attack and defence of the city. From the roof you can admire the thrilling views over the Bay of Santiago and Cayo Granma and you can follow some 16th-century steps almost down to the waterline. There's a restaurant on a terrace with a great view (main dish CUC$6). To get there, take a **Turistaxi** to El Morro, CUC$10 round trip with wait. Bus 212 from Plaza Marte or opposite the cinema Rialto, Parque Céspedes, stops in front of embarkation point for Cayo Granma.

East of Santiago Excellent excursions can be made to the **Gran Piedra** ① *CUC$1 to climb* (26 km east) a viewpoint from which it is said you can see Haiti and Jamaica on a clear day; more likely their lights on a clear night. It is a giant rock weighing 75,000 tonnes, 1234-m high, and reached by climbing 454 steps from the road (only for the fit). The view is tremendous and buzzards circle you. There are no buses but a private car will charge you about CUC$15 there and back (hotel tour desks will arrange, good value).

Some 2 km before La Gran Piedra are the **Jardines de la Siberia**, on the site of a former coffee plantation, an extensive botanical garden; turn right and follow the track for about 1 km to reach the gardens. The **Museo La Isabelica** ① *Tue-Sat 0900-1700, Sun 0900-1300, CUC$2*, is at Carretera de la Gran Piedra Km 14, a ruined coffee plantation once owned by French emigrés from Haiti, the buildings of which are now turned into a museum housing the former kitchen and other facilities on the ground floor with farming tools and archaeological finds. Upstairs is the owners' house in 19th-century style.

Cuba Santiago de Cuba & around

On the Carretera Siboney at Km 13.5 is **La Granjita Siboney** ① *T639836, Tue- Sun 0900-1700, CUC$2*, the farmhouse used as the headquarters for the revolutionaries' attack on the Moncada barracks on 26 July 1953. It has a museum of uniforms, weapons and artefacts used by the 106 men who gathered here the night before, as well as extensive newspaper accounts of the attack.

Siboney, 16 km east of the city, is the nearest beach to Santiago with a reef just offshore which is great for snorkelling but gets very crowded at weekends. To get there, take bus 214 from near the bus terminal or a truck from Avenida de los Libertadores outside the maternity hospital (1 peso). At Km 24 is the **Valle de la Prehistoria** ① *T639239, CUC$2, extra CUC$1 to take photos*, a huge park filled with life-size carved stone dinosaurs and stone age men. Great for kids but due to the total absence of shade it is like walking around a desert. Take plentiful supplies of water and try to go early or late.

West of Santiago El Sanctuario de Nuestra Señora de la Caridad del Cobre ('El Cobre'), 10 km west of Santiago and home to the shrine of Cuba's patron saint, the Virgen de la Caridad del Cobre, is built over a working copper mine. The story goes that in the 17th century, three fishermen were about to capsize in Nipe Bay, when they found a wooden statue of the Virgin Mary floating in the sea. Their lives were saved and they brought the statue to its current resting place above the altar. Downstairs there are many tokens of gratitude left by Cubans who have been helped by the Virgin in some way. There is a pilgrimage here on 7 September, the eve of the patron saint's day. There is no bus, so either hire a car and driver (about CUC$8), or get on a truck at the bus station for a few pesos. Cover your shoulders or hire a coverall. **Note** Watch out for the touts; probably best to offer 50 cents or some pesos, otherwise they will be waiting for you when you leave the church.

Guantánamo → *Phone code: 21. Colour map 1, B6. Population: 205,000.*

Guantánamo is the most easterly and most mountainous province on the island. The range of the Montañas de Nipe-Sagua-Baracoa runs through the province, ending in the Atlantic Ocean on the northern coast and the Caribbean Sea to the south. The area is notable for its many endemic species of fauna and flora. Guantánamo, the provincial capital, had a large influx of Haitian, French and Jamaican immigrants in the 19th century. The architecture has much less of a Spanish colonial feel; the narrow, brightly coloured buildings with thin, wooden balconies and wrought ironwork are more reminiscent of New Orleans than Madrid. This is also reflected in the local musical rhythms, notably the *tumba francesa*.

The **US naval base** of Guantánamo (which cannot be easily visited from Cuba) was established at the beginning of the 20th century in the area known as Caimanera. The base is so little a part of the town that you will not come across it unless you make a specific trip to Mirador de Malones to view it through binoculars. In 2002, al-Qaida and Taliban prisoners were transferred there from Afghanistan under heavy guard to await military trial. Huge metal cages were built to incarcerate the prisoners and security at the base has since been tighter than ever.

The **Zoológico de Piedra** ① *Ctra a Yateras Km 18*, is an outdoor museum of stone animals, just outside of town, set in a beautiful hillside location with tropical vegetation. Many are bizarre, from tiny stone lizards to huge bison. All are carved directly from the rocks in their natural setting and you can buy miniature replicas from the sculptor on the way out.

Baracoa → *Phone code: 21. Colour map 1, B6.*

Close to the most easterly point of the island, Baracoa is an attractive place surrounded by rich, tropical vegetation and the perfect place to come and spend a few relaxing days on the beach. It was the first town founded in 1511 by Diego

Santiago de Cuba

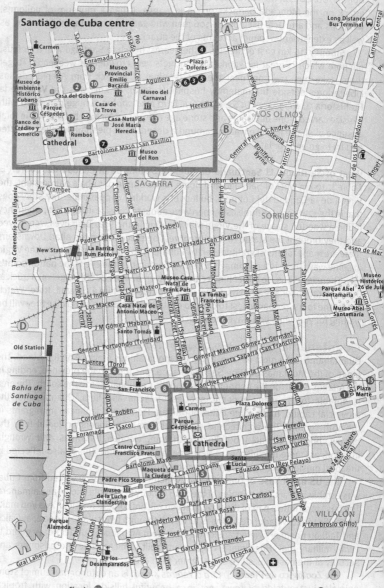

Santiago de Cuba centre
Carmen
Felix Peña
San Pedro
San Félix
Enramada (Saco)
Pío Rosado (Carnicería)
Calvario
Plaza Dolores
Museo Provincial Emilio Bacardí
Aguilera
Museo de Ambiente Histórico Cubano
Casa del Gobierno
Museo del Carnaval
Casa de la Trova
Heredia
Parque Céspedes
Casa Natal de José María Heredia
Banco de Crédito y Comercio
Rumbos
Cathedral
Bartolomé Masó (San Basilio)
Museo del Ron
Av Los Pinos
Estrella
Hdez Mayares
LOS OLMOS
General Pérez
Capdevila
Andrés
Bonifacio Byrne
Av Patricio Lumumba
Av de los Libertadores
Long Distance Bus Terminal
Carretera Central
SAGARRA
Julian del Casal
General Miró
SORRIBES
Av Crombet
San Magín
To Cementerio Santa Ifigenia
S Cisneros
Enrique José
Paseo de Martí
Padre Calles
(Santa Isabel)
(San Fermín)
(Rastro)
Gonzalo de Quesada (San Ricardo)
New Station
La Barrita Rum Factory
Corona
Vargas
Narciso Lópes (San Antonio)
Paseo de Martí
Museo Casa Natal de Frank País
General Moncada
Porfirio Valiente (Calvario)
Mayía Rodríguez (Reloj)
Barnada
Saturnino Lora
Museo Histórico 26 de Julio
Parque Abel Santamaría
Museo Abel Santamaría
Hernán Cortés
Peralejo (Factoria)
Sao del Indio
(San Mateo)
La Tumba Francesa
Los Maceo
Casa Natal de Antonio Maceo
Félix Peña
Hartmann (San Félix)
General Lacret (San Pedro)
General Banderas
Pío Rosado (Carnicería)
Donato Mármol
Jobito
J M Gómez (Habana)
Santo Tomás
Old Station
General Portuondo (Trinidad)
General Máximo Gómez (S Germán)
Juan Bautista Sagarra (San Francisco)
L Fuentes (Toro)
Sánchez Hechavarría (San Jerónimo)
(San Agustín)
Plácido
Plaza Marte
Bahía de Santiago de Cuba
San Francisco
Carmen
Plaza Dolores
Cornelio Robén
10 de Octubre (Gallo)
Aguilera
Parque Céspedes
Heredia
Enramada
(Saco)
Cathedral
(San Basilio)
(Santa Lucía)
Centro Cultural Francisco Prats
Av 24 de Febrero (Trocha)
Bartolomé Masó
Santa Lucía
Eduardo Yero (Rey Pelayo)
Maqueta de la Ciudad
J Castillo Duany
Padre Pico Steps
C Padre Quiroga (Clarín)
Museo de la Lucha Clandestina
Diego Palacios (Santa Rita)
Av Jesús Menéndez (Alameda)
Carlos Dubois (Barracones)
Rafael P Salcedo (San Carlos)
VILLALÓN
Parque Alameda
Desiderio Mesnier (Santa Rosa)
PALAU
A (Ambrosio Grillo)
José de Diego (Princesa)
E Tamayo (Corte)
Gral T Prado
Jesús Rabí
Eduardo Martín
Padre Pico
Colón
C García (San Fernando)
De los Desamparados
Av 24 Febrero (Trocha)
Gral Lahera

Sleeping

Aída Morales Valdés **1** *E4*
Amparo Hernández **15** *F2*
Belkis Rodríguez & Dr Eduman Bell **21** *F2*
Casa Granda **17** *detail*
Dinorah Rodríguez Bueno & William Pérez **2** *E3*
Dr Javier Berdion Sevilla **3** *E2*
Félix Corroso **4** *D2*
Flor María González **20** *B6*
Gran **18** *detail*
Hostal Islazul **19** *detail*
Irma y Umberto **5** *E3*
La Casona Colonial **21** *D2*
Las Américas **13** *B6*
Liliam **7** *E2*
Lourdes de la Gómez Beaton **8** *E2*
Manrique Nistal Bello **9** *F3*
Marta Franco **11** *F2*
Meliá Santiago de Cuba **12** *B6*
Orestes González Campos **6** *D3*
San Juan **10** *D6*

Eating

Isabelica **4** *detail*
La Casa de Don Antonio **3** *detail*
Las Enramadas **6** *detail*
Las Gallegas **9** *detail*
La Taberna de Dolores **5** *detail*
Santiago 1900 **7** *detail*

N

0 metres 200
0 yards 200

Velázquez, and for three years it was the capital of Cuba. Up until the 1960s it was really only accessible by sea until La Farola was built. This is a spectacular road, 30 km long, joined to the mountain on one side and supported by columns on the other. It is well worth the trip from Santiago (150 km, four hours' drive) for the scenery of this section of road, which winds through lush tropical mountains and then descends steeply to the coast.

The area is a UNESCO biosphere, with more than 10 rivers, including the **Río Toa**, 120 km long and the widest river in Cuba. Whitewater rafting is possible down the Río Toa, with different levels of difficulty. The **Río Yumurí**, 30 km east of Baracoa, is the most spectacular of Baracoa's rivers, running through two deep canyons. You can take an organized tour (CUC$28), rent a private car (CUC$10) or take a *colectivo* taxi or truck to the Río Yumurí where the road ends. A canoe will ferry you across or you can hire one to take you upriver for CUC$2. You can continue walking upriver and swim; it's very quiet and peaceful.

Christopher Columbus arrived in Baracoa on 27 November 1492. He planted a cross, now housed in the church, **Iglesia de la Asunción**, and described a mountain in the shape of an anvil (*yunque*) which was thereafter used as a point of reference for sailors. The first maps of Cuba drawn by an Englishman showed the **Yunque de Baracoa** mountain, copies of which can be seen in the museum. Between 1739 and 1742, Baracoa's three forts were built. The oldest, **El Castillo**, was destroyed in 1752 by the French. The others were **Fuerte de la Punta**, now restaurant **La Punta**, and **Fuerte Matachín** ① *daily 0800-1800, CUC$2*, now the Museo Municipal.

Baracoa has 56 archaeological sites, with many traces of the three indigenous groups who lived there: the Siboney, the Taíno and the Guanahatabey. There is one surviving community of 300 members, called the **Yateras**, dating back to the arrival of the Spaniards. They are integrated with the rest of society but only marry among themselves and maintain their traditions. They live in an isolated region along the shores of the Río Toa, but a visit can be organized through the Museo Municipal.

● Sleeping

Santiago de Cuba *p148, map p152*
It is increasingly common for *casas particulares* to offer a package of dinner, bed and breakfast for around CUC$30-40 for 2 people.

L-A Casa Granda, Heredia 201 entre San Pedro y San Félix, on Parque Céspedes, T686600, F686035. Elegant building opened in 1914 and patronized by many famous people. 4-star, a/c, laundry, car hire, satellite TV, pool, post office, 1 room for handicapped people, **Havanatur** and **Asistur** offices. Terrace bar and café overlooking park, 5th floor bar with even better views over city (CUC$2 to go up 2000-0100 if you are not staying at the hotel, but that buys your first cocktail), restaurant and café open 0800-2400, good. Disco (karaoke) at the side of the hotel, CUC$1.

A Meliá Santiago de Cuba, Av Las Américas entre 4 y M, Reparto Sueño, T687070, www.meliasantiagodecuba.solmelia.com. 5-star, 302 rooms and suites on 15 floors built 1991, landmark modern design in red, blue and white, good service, excellent breakfast buffet CUC$9, lots of bars and restaurants, good view of city from roof top bar, swimming pools open to day visitors for CUC$10, tennis, sauna, car hire, has business centre with internet access, post office, will change almost any currency, staff exceptionally helpful and friendly. Good value internet bookings.

B Hotel San Juan (Islazul), Km 4½ Ctra a Siboney, T687156, hotel@sanjuan.scu.cyt.cu. Out of town but nice location, *turistaxi* CUC$3-4, private car CUC$2-3. A complex with cabins, 110 very nice rooms, large, clean, hot water, large pool, bar, restaurants, good breakfast, queues at weekends and during festivals, car hire.

B Las Américas(Islazul), T642011, F687075, Av de las Américas esq Gen Cebreco, easy bus/truck access to centre, taxis around bus stop opposite hotel. 68 rooms, 2 mini-suites, lively, high-quality restaurant, variety of dishes, non-residents may use pool where they have cultural shows every night, nice reception staff, safety deposit, **Cadeca**, shop, car and bicycle hire.

C Flor María González, J314 entre Av Las Américas y 6, Reparto Sueño, upper floor, T645568, fmgc@cnt.uo.edu.cu. Price for dinner, bed and breakfast, 1 large room with en suite bathroom, hot water, a/c, fan, TV, desk. Flor María is a very knowledgeable professor at Oriente University and her husband speaks English and Russian.

C Gran Hotel, Enramada 312 entre San Félix y San Pedro, T653020, www.granhotelstgo.cu. Training school for tourism workers (**Formatur**), 2 star, very central and newly rebuilt on a shopping street. 15 rooms, a/c, TV, hot water, mini bar, restaurant and cafeteria.

C Orestes González Campos, Gral Portuondo (Callejón de Trinidad) 651 ¼ esq Moncada, T626305, norka@ncm.uo.edu.cu. Price is for dinner, bed and breakfast for 2 people, excellent value. Pink colonial house with white columns, high ceilings. 2 bedrooms, no proper windows, but effective a/c and fan, good beds, private bathroom, good food and plenty of it. Within walking distance of Parque Céspedes or Museo 26 de Julio, but quiet with no traffic noise.

C-D Hostal Islazul, San Basilio 403 entre Calvario y Carnicería, T651502. A new hotel in baby blue, close to the historical centre, nice decor with lots of plants and stylish pieces of furniture. 8 large and very comfortable rooms, a/c, fridge, private bathroom, hot water, satellite TV, security box, minibar, 24-hr restaurant serving *criollo* and international food.

D Dinorah Rodríguez Bueno and William Pérez, Diego Palacios (Santa Rita) 504 entre Reloj y Clarín, T625834. Dinorah speaks a little English, independent room with en suite bathroom, a/c, good food, patio, William and Dinorah are excellent sources of information and very helpful, 10-min walk from Parque Céspedes.

D-E Aída Morales Valdés, Enramada 565

entre San Agustín y Barnada, T628612. Room with private bathroom, a/c, good food, friendly, central, only 1 block from Plaza Marte.

D-E Amparo Hernández, Santa Rita 161 entre Corona y Padre Pico, T623208. Extremely pleasant place and nice woman who also cooks really well. Well known and always full.

D-E Belkis Rodríguez y Dr Eduman Bell, Corona 854 entre San Carlos y Santa Rosa, T651472. English, French, Italian speaking tour guide lives in the house. Large room, clean and well decorated, a/c, fan, bathroom, large patio with lots of vegetation, pleasant family of 3, large breakfast for CUC$3.

D-E Dr Javier Berdion Sevilla, Corona 564 Apto B entre Enramadas y Aguilera, T622959. 2 rooms, double bed, a/c, hot water, shared bathroom, fridge, balcony, terrace, great view of the bay. The neighbours also have rooms, a/c, breakfast included.

D-E Emilia Brooks, 6 110 entre 3 y 5, Reparto Vista Alegre, T643195. Good location close to Las Américas hotel, 2 rooms on upper floor as small independent apartment, a/c, fridge, quiet, pleasant host.

D-E Félix Corroso, San Germán 165 entre Rastro y Gallo, T653720. Known as Garden House, 2 rooms, a/c, fan, nice garden, breakfast CUC$3, dinner CUC$6-8.

D-E Irma y Umberto, Santa Lucía 303 entre San Pedro y San Félix, T622391, close to Parque Céspedes. Brother and sister, live in huge house with their respective families, large room sleeps 3, private bathroom, patio. Umberto has a private taxi although he used to be a radiologist, hospitable, caring people.

D-E La Casona Colonial, San Francisco 303 (Sagarra) entre San Bartolomé y San Félix, T622517, arlexjorge@yahoo.com. Run by Alex Rojas Cruz and Jorge and their gorgeous sausage dog, Bebé. 2 rooms with shared bathroom in a lovely colonial house with an internal patio. Little natural light but large and comfortable rooms. Breakfasts are good.

D-E Lourdes de la Gómez Beaton, Félix Pena 454 entre San Jerónimo y San Francisco, T654468. Large old house with patio, excellent accommodation in 2 rooms, bathroom, hospitable hostess.

D-E Manrique Nistal Bello, Princesa 565 entre Carnicería y Calvario, T651909, abarreda@abt.uo.edu.cu. 1 room with 1 bed,

another with 2 beds, bathroom, fridge, good food in large portions, some English spoken.

D-E Marta Franco, Corona 802 bajos entre San Carlos y Santa Rita, T651882. Very central, about 100 m west of Cathedral, apartment on ground floor of fairly modern block. 2 rooms, 1 with a/c, bathroom between them, hot shower, breakfast CUC$3, dinner CUC$6, meals taken in family room, very good food, helpful and friendly family.

D-E Rita María, 3 102 entre Av Manduley y Ctra del Caney, Vista Alegre. Colonial house (Villa Victoria), good location near Las Américas hotel, 2 large bedrooms, a/c, private bathrooms, hot water. Beautiful courtyard where very tasty food is served.

D-E Rubén Rodes Estrada, 10 410 entre 15 y 17, Vista Alegre, T642611. Run by great (gay) couple, house painted red and yellow, giant cactus outside and inside, hot water, good food, CUC$5 huge breakfast and CUC$10 evening meal even bigger.

Guantánamo *p151*

C Islazul Caimanera, Loma Norte, Caimanera, T91414, F99520. On a slight rise overlooking the sea, 3-star, 17 basic rooms and cabins but pleasant location, a/c, TV, bar, restaurant, pool. The closest you'll get to the US base.

D Casa de Los Ensueños, Ahogados esq 15 Norte, Reparto Caribe, T326304. 3 rooms, a/c, TV, bar, 24-hr room service.

D Villa La Lupe, Ctra del Salvador Km 2, T382612. 2-star but much nicer than Islazul Guantánamo which is currently only available for Cubans anyway, a bit far out of town on the Río Bano in pleasant countryside with lots of trees, peaceful atmosphere, 50 a/c rooms in blocks, decent pool, squash court, restaurant, bar.

D-E Elsye Castillo Osoria, Calixto García 766 entre Prado y Jesús del Sol. Rooms with a/c, TV, fridge, sitting room, private and secure in central location.

D-E Lisette Foster Lara, Gen Pedro A Pérez 664 entre Jesús del Sol y Prado. Central, close to plaza, a/c, hot water, secure.

Baracoa *p151*

There are alleged to be 200 *casas particulares* in Baracoa now.

A El Castillo (Gaviota), Calixto García, Loma del Paraíso, T45165, www.hotelelcastillocuba.com.

156

35 a/c rooms with bath, phone, TV in lobby lounge, pool (CUC$2 for use by non-residents), parking, friendly staff, food OK, excellent views, very good breakfast.

A Hostal La Habanera (Palmares), Maceo esq Frank País, T45273, www.hostallahabanera .com. Glorious pink building converted to a hotel in 2003. Stylish, central, internal patio and balconies, 10 rooms, a/c, bath, satellite TV, minibar, room service, internet access, massage room, snack bar with best food in Baracoa, drug store, car hire, friendly service.

A Porto Santo (Gaviota), T45106, 45105, www.hotelportosantocuba.com. 53 rooms, 3 suites, a/c, bath, TV, restaurant, bar, shop, beautiful swimming pool, car hire, next to airport, beach, peaceful atmosphere, friendly.

A-C La Rusa (Islazul), a bright yellow building on the Malecón, Máximo Gómez 13, T43011, www.hotellarusa.com. Named after the Russian woman, Magdalena Menasse, who used to run the hotel and whose photos adorn the walls; famous guests have included Fidel Castro. Accommodation now basic, 12 a/c rooms, food average, nice location, good *paladar* opposite.

D-E Arquimedes, Rubert López 87 entre Limbano Sánchez y Ramón López, T43291. Run by Arquimedes and Bárbara, a/c, hot water, great food with lots of fish in coconut and other local dishes, room has own entrance off the street or you can come in through the house.

D-E Casa Colonial Lucy, Céspedes 29 entre Rubert López y Maceo, T43548. One of the nicest places to stay, Lucy has a delightful colonial house with lovely views over the town and the sea from the roof terrace, 2 rooms with high ceilings, private bathroom, fridge, a/c, hot water, great food, organizes trips.

D-E Casa Ernesto, Libertad 13 entre 1 Abril y M Grajales, 5 mins' walk from Plaza Independencia towards **Hotel Porto Santo**. Room with a/c, big breakfast included, dinner CUC$3-4, traditional food from the region (fish in coconut milk), bike rental CUC$2 per day.

D-E César Labori Balga, Martí 81 entre 24 de Febrero y Coliseo, T433227. A very welcoming and delightful family with a separate apartment with its own off-street entrance. 2 double bedrooms, bathroom,

hot water, a/c, small porch overlooking lush courtyard garden with chatty parrot. Eldest son, César, runs this *casa* and mother Concepción cooks lovely local dishes: fresh fish in coconut milk, lamb and excellent coffee from her father's farm.

D-E Daniel Pérez Carcasses, Coroneles Galana 6 entre Flor Crombet y Martí, T43274. Near the sea, private roof and room with new shower and a/c, nice family, good cooking.

D-E María Magdalena Cardoza Rodríguez, República 7-A entre Moncada y Abel Díaz, T43424. Extremely clean, 2nd floor, big room, a/c, private bathroom, balcony, terrace, wonderful food.

D-E Maritza Delgado, Coliseo 32 (Alto), entre Martí y Maceo, T42129. Room with fan, a/c, TV, fridge stocked with fresh orange juice, private bathroom, very friendly family, great breakfast, local specialities for dinner, excellent food.

D-E Neida Cuenca Prada, Flor Crombet 194 esq Céspedes, T43178. Upstairs rooms better than the one downstairs, kind and generous family, wonderful food and reasonably priced.

D-E Nelia y Yaquelín, Mariana Grajales 11 entre Julio A Mella y Calixto García, T42652. 3 generations of a delightful family offer a simple but comfortable place to stay, sea views, new private bathroom, small room, breakfast CUC$2, dinner CUC$5, both delicious and more than you can eat.

D-E Tatiana Borges, Rodney Coutin 46 entre Abel Días y Moncada, T43674. Nice room with balcony and your own entrance, friendly hosts, dinner available.

D-E Williams Montoya Sánchez, Martí 287, T42798. Very hospitable, a/c, car parking, CUC$1, car cleaning CUC$2, available to non-guests.

D-E Yamilet Selva Bartelemy, Frank País 6 entre Máximo Gómez y Flor Crombet, T42724, yamito2002@yahoo.es. Despite being a seaside town, this is one of the few houses to have a sea view from 2 light and bright rooms. 1 room has 2 beds, the other is smaller with 1 bed and bigger bathroom, hot shower, sea breezes, a/c, fan, in hospitable household with charming couple, secure, comfortable, dinner CUC$5-7, breakfast CUC$2-3, excellent.

Cuba Santiago de Cuba & around Listings

❶ Eating

Santiago de Cuba *p148, map p152*

Street stalls are usually only open until early evening, some only at lunchtime. Snacks sold in pesos. Most things cost 1 peso. Avoid *fritos*, they are just fried lumps of dough; most reliable thing is cheese, pork or egg sandwich; pizza is usually a dry bit of dough with a few gratings of cheese. Lots of stalls along 'Ferreiro' or Av Victoriano Garzón, these are open later than others, especially up near **Hotel Las Américas**. Also lots around bus station on **Libertadores** and a few along the bottom part of **Aguilera**, between Parque Céspedes and Plaza Dolores.

All the hotels have restaurants, some of which are very good, such as in the **Meliá Santiago de Cuba**. In local restaurants the main dish is chicken, usually fried but sometimes with a garlic and onion sauce. A half chicken with fried green plantain (*tostones*), sweet potatoes (*boniato*) or chips costs 25 pesos, rice and beans (*congrí*) 2 pesos, salad 3 pesos, beer 10 pesos. You can find this sort of meal at the **Doña Yuya** chain, where they also serve things like smoked pork chops (*chuletas de cerdo ahumado*), veal (*ternera*) or thin steak (*bistec de palomilla*), costing around 25 pesos. There are only 2 legal *paladares*, although you may get approached in the street by touts offering unofficial/illegal places to eat.

♥♥-♥ La Casa de Don Antonio, Aguilera entre Calvario y Reloj, Plaza Dolores, T652205. 1200-2400. Nice decor, bar inside serving all kinds of Cuban cocktails, complimentary welcome cocktail, tasty *criollo* food, range of dishes with prices up to CUC$28.

♥♥-♥ Sito de Compay Segundo, Montenegro s/n, Siboney, T39325, 1200-2100. The house where the late musician, Compay Segundo, was born is now a restaurant serving international and *criollo* food, with dishes from CUC$1.50 to CUC$28.

♥♥-♥ Pizza Nova, Hotel Meliá Santiago, T687070, outside by the shops, 1100-2400. Open air but under cover, serving surprisingly good pizzas. Prices range from CUC$4.85 for a small cheese and tomato pizza to CUC$19.60 for a large one with lobster. Pastas cost from CUC$5.75 to CUC$11.95 with lobster. You can also have chicken, meat or fish dishes if you are not seeking a pizza fix.

♥♥-♥ Tropical, Fernández Marcane entre 10 y 9, upper floor, Tue-Sun 1800-2400. Open-air *paladar*, well decorated, excellent food, international style.

♥ Isabelica, Aguilera esq Plaza Dolores, open 24 hrs. A café where you can only get coffee, CUC$0.85, cigars rolled, Bohemian hangout, watch out for hustlers. Ask here for the local speciality, Rocío de Gallo, coffee and rum.

♥ Las Enramadas, Búlevar (Plaza Dolores), T652205. Good atmosphere, cheap, basic food, nice setting, open 24 hrs.

♥ Las Gallegas, San Basilio entre San Pedro y San Félix, upper floor. The only other legal *paladar*, but with unexciting food, uncomfortable and negligent service.

♥ La Taberna de Dolores, Aguilera esq Reloj, T623913, 1900-2400. Spanish food, reasonable prices.

♥ Santiago 1900, San Basilio entre San Félix y Carnicería. Basic but excellent meals at bargain price of around CUC$4 including drinks, CP$ and CUC$ accepted.

Guantánamo *p151*

♥ Mirador de Malones, Ctra de Boquerón, T41386, 1200-2200. If you are visiting the Mirador, you can get something to eat here. Cuban food.

♥ Trattoria Italiana El Coliseo, Hotel San Juan, upstairs above Leningrado restaurant, daily 1000-2200. Specialized Italian food, pasta, seafood, meat and Italian desserts, good prices.

Baracoa *p151*

Lots of *paladares*, most offer pork, chicken, fish, turtle (endangered, don't eat), some offer lobster. The isolation of Baracoa has led to an individual local cuisine, mostly featuring coconut milk and fish. 80% of Cuba's coconuts are grown here. Don't miss the *cucurucho*, also known as *pastel de coco* or *coco con chocolate*, a delicious mixture of coconut, fruit and sugar served in a cone of palm leaves and sold at roadsides, 2 for about CUC$1. They also sell coco balls the size of a tennis ball, 3 for CUC$1, which are delicious for making hot chocolate or using in cakes.

♥ Baracoa, Maceo 129. Old colonial house with large dining room serving basic *criollo*

food in CP$ with chicken and pork costing less than CUC$1. Side dishes, like *congrí* or *plátano* cost only CP$3, cucumber CP$1.
♥ **Fuerte La Punta**. The fort at La Punta, which juts out into the bay west of the town, has been converted to a pleasant, breezy, open-air restaurant, with rustic tables and chairs inside the fort looking out through the cannon holes to the sea. Nice setting, reasonably priced food, fish in coconut milk CUC$6, chicken CUC$1.20, sandwiches CUC$2, spaghetti CUC$1.20, ice cream CUC$0.70.
♥ **La Colonial**, José Martí 123, T45391. Excellent candlelit subdued atmosphere. Extensive menu.

Casa de Chocolate, José Martí, near bus terminal. Local version of hot chocolate with water, sugar and salt. Not to everyone's taste but worth trying, only CP$0.30 a cup. Snacks available.

⊙ Bars and clubs

Santiago de Cuba *p148, map p152*
Ballet Folkórico Cutumba, Enramada, at Museo del Carnaval, 2 blocks west of Plaza Céspedes. There is a superb show Sun 1030, CUC$3.
Baturro, Aguilera esq San Félix. Snacks, bar, nice atmosphere, reliable prices.
Cabaret San Pedro del Mar, Ctra del Morro Km 7.5, T691287. Taxi CUC$5, entrance CUC$5, reasonable food.
Casa del Caribe on 13 154 esq 8, T642285. Tue-Sun 2200-0200. CUC$2 entrance. Open-air show, great, authentic, Afro-Cuban music and dance at weekends, recommended if you like *folklórico*.
Casa de los Estudiantes, Heredia, near Casa Granda. Live music Sun 1330, always popular CUC$1. 2 daily shows of music, morning and evening, traditional, acoustic *son* music, open until 2400, CUC$1 and worth it, nice venue in beautiful building with patio where excellent bands play at night, also bar. Very friendly and welcoming, dancing is encouraged, particularly at night when you can expect hassle from locals wanting to dance with you.
Club La Iris, Hotel San Juan. Wed-Mon 2200-0300. Admission CUC$3 per person. Dancing.
Club Tropicana Santiago, Autopista

Nacional Km 1.5, T687020. Restaurant 1200-2200. Taxi CUC$8-10. Local show with emphasis on the Caribbean and Santiaguerans, different from Havana's version and considered one of the best shows in Cuba, disco after the show, Tue-Sun 2000-0300, CUC$50. Limited menu in restaurant, drinks are not cheap.
Disco Bar/Club 300, Aguilera entre San Félix y San Pedro, T653532. Daily 1900-0300. Live and recorded music, snack bar.
El Patio de Artex, Heredia 304 entre Carnicería y Calvario, T654814. Daily 1600-1800 free, 2200-0100 CUC$2. Home of painters, Félix and José Joaquín Tejada Revilla, often live music with fantastic local bands, lots of dancing, friendly.
El Ranchón, Autopista Km 1.5, 1 km before the airport. Run by the Cuban Civil Flying Company Catering. Good place for dancing, drinking and swimming in a rather small pool. Downstairs there is a restaurant with tasty Cuban food at reliable prices, while upstairs there is a bar.
Grupo Folklórico del Oriente, San Francisco y San Félix. Folk groups play daytime till lunchtime, then again in the evening.
Las Américas Tri-Continental Cabaret, to the side of **Hotel Las Américas**. Thu-Tue 2230-0200. CUC$7 per couple including a drink. A show with ballerinas, singer and recorded music.
Las Columnitas, 1 block from Enramada, San Félix y Callejón del Carmen. Outdoor bar and café, beware of double measures here, guaranteed to get you *salsa-ing* before the end of the evening.
Libertad, Aguilera 658 entre Pizarro y Plácido, Plaza de Marte. Daily 1000-1800 free, 1800-0200 CUC$2. Great view from the rooftop bar, traditional live and recorded music, pay at the desk for admission.
Los Dos Abuelos, Pérez Carbo 5 Frente a Plaza de Marte, T623302. EGREM agency, rocks with live traditional *son* and *boleros* from 2130 until dawn and encourages visitors to join in, CUC$2. Also snack bar with tasty small meals, the *daiquirís* are a winner.
Patio Centro Cultural Fernando Ortiz, Av Manduley 106, Vista Alegre. Thu-Sun 1800-2400. Admission CUC$3. Performances by local folk groups.
Sala de Fiesta Café Santiago, Meliá Santiago Hotel side entrance. Daily

2200-0200. Entrance CUC$5 per person includes 2 national drinks. American disco music, hardly any *salsa*, *jinetera* pickup place, lively.

Baracoa *p151*

Artex El Patio, in the Fondo de Bienes Culturales, Maceo 120, T43627. Bar with live music, outdoor seating. Snack bar open all day until 2300, beer.

Cafetería & Night Club El Parque. Open 24 hrs, CUC$1. Traditional live music at night by Grupo Polimitas, lively atmosphere.

Casa de la Cultura, Maceo 124, T42364. Live music on the patio. Programme varies from day to day, with young local talent given the chance to shine. Nightly show of Afro-Cuban music by Barrarumba, which is highly recommended, CUC$1, very interesting to see all the costumes and instruments.

Casa de la Trova, Félix Ruenes esq Ciro Frías. Traditional music, Tue-Sun from 2100, CUC$1 entry, CUC$2 for a *mojito* or *cuba libre*. Good *son* and friendly atmosphere. Seats around the edge but many people stand on the street and look through the windows. Dancing in the centre, foreign women always in demand by Cuban partners.

Cuatro ochenta cinco (485), Félix Ruenes. Bar with live band every night, CUC$1, great fun, everyone gets up to dance. Disco playing western music next door.

Dancing Light on Maceo just before Parque Central. Disco for young Cubans although tourists will not feel out of place, small but lively, check out breakdancing show nightly by local youths.

El Ranchón, up the hill above Calixto García. All the young people move up here after the Casa de la Trova and other places close. Open-air disco with live and taped music, 2100-0300, although it doesn't really get going until after 2400. Great view over Baracoa and out to sea. Watch out for all the steps if you've been hitting the rum.

⊛ Festivals and events

Santiago de Cuba *p148, map p152*
15-19 May The Festival de Baile is a vibrant street festival celebrating dance.
1st week Jul The Festival del Caribe begins in the first week with theatre, dancing and

conferences, and continues later in Jul.
18-27 Jul Carnival is already in full swing by the Moncada celebrations on 26 Jul (as it was in 1953, the date carefully chosen to catch Batista's militia drunk and off-guard and use the noise of the carnival to drown the sound of gunfire). Carnival always lasts 1 week, taking in Santiago's patron saint's day on 25 Jul but traditionally stops for a day of more serious Moncada celebration, then continues on 27 Jul. This Carnival is well worth seeing. Wear no jewellery, leave all valuables behind. Each *municipio* organizes different activities, music, dancing, cabaret, etc, in different parts of the city, even in the sea, with beer, food and kiosks. There are competitions and parades, with rivalry between the *comparsas* (congas) and *paseos* (dance groups). The whole city is covered in lights and all the doors are decorated. The parades and floats are judged from 2100 and pass down Garzón where there are seats for viewing. To get a seat go to the temporary office behind the seating area on the south side of the road between 1800-2000. It starts at 2100, CUC$2 for a tourist seat. Good views are possible if you queue early.
Sep Festival del Pregón, also known as Fruta del Carey, a festival of song when people dress up in traditional costumes and sell fruit in the street while singing.
Sep/Oct Festival de la Trova, a festival of folk music, the date depends on funding.
Dec On New Year's Eve *son* bands play in Plaza Marte and surrounding streets. Just before midnight everyone moves toward Parque Céspedes and sings the National Anthem. On the stroke of midnight the Cuban flag is raised on the Casa de Gobierno, commemorating the anniversary of the first time it was flown in 1902 when the Republic of Cuba was proclaimed. Then there's all-night drinking and dancing on the streets and in local bars.

❍ Shopping

Santiago de Cuba *p148, map p152*
Arts and crafts
Casa de la Artesanía, under the cathedral in Parque Céspedes, T623924. 0800-1730. Also on Lacret 724 entre San Basilio y Heredia, T24027. Cubartesana, on Félix Pena esq Masó under the cathedral. Salón Artexanda,

Heredia 304 entre Pío Rosado y Calvario.
Handicrafts are sold on the street on **Heredia**
entre Hartmann and Pío Rosado.

Food

Doña Neli, Aguilera at Plaza Marte, is a good
bread shop. **Panadería El Sol**, Plaza Marte
entre Saco y Aguilera. **Casa de Miel**, Gen
Lacret, sells honey. **La Bombonera**, near
Parque Céspedes on Aguilera entre Gen
Lacret y Hartmann, Mon-Sat 0900-1800, Sun
0900-1200. Imported food, priced in CUC$.
There's a **food market** on Ferreiro opposite
Hotel Las Américas.

Music

Casa de la Trova, Heredia y San Félix, sells
CDs and tapes. **Artex**, Heredia 304. Music
and videos as well as postcards and cultural
items. **Enramadas** and **Siglo XX**, both on
Enramada, are stores with stalls selling
records, books, clothes, jewellery, ornaments
etc in pesos.

▲ Activities and tours

Santiago de Cuba *p148, map p152*
Havanatur main office is near La Maison on
Av Manduley, T43603, with another office
under the Hotel Casa Granda, offering city
tours with guide, also day trips to all
destinations around Santiago. Prices vary
according to season and number of people.
Cubatur, Victoriano Garzón y 4, is very
helpful with knowledgeable guides and
excellent value. All the main hotels have tour
agencies.

Guantánamo *p151*
There are *burós de turismo* in the hotels that
can arrange tours to Mt Malones, where you
can view the US base through Soviet
binoculars. There is also a day tour taking in
Guantánamo City, La Tumba Francesa,
Zoológico de Piedra and Changüí (a
traditional form of music played on a farm a
short distance from the city to accompany
your lunch), organized by **Havanatur**, with
guide in a/c minibus, daily during high
season, Tue and Sat in low season, 0900
outside Hotel Guantánamo, CUC$30.
Another trip, with the same sights, goes on
to Baracoa the same day.

Baracoa *p151*
Tours
Havanatur, from **Casayara** handicraft shop
on Maceo (David Laffita). **Cubatur**, from
Cubana office or Hostal La Habanera
(T45306, Erick Barrabia, or T45155, Antonio
Mas). Baracoa city tour CUC$4, Saltadero
(35-m waterfall) CUC$8, El Yunque CUC$18,
Playa Maguana CUC$7, Toa CUC$8, Duaba
CUC$8 (Rancho Toa and Finca Duaba,
peasant farms and boat trips including
kayaking on River Toa), Yumurí CUC$12
(fishing village, cocoa plantation and boat
trip).

Taxi drivers will also take you to Playa
Maguana and Río Yumurí via cocoa and
coffee plantations. A battered **Víazul** minibus
leaves Parque Independencia daily at 1000,
returning 1700, CUC$2 one way. **Cocotaxi**
charges CUC$14 return or CUC$15 if they
wait for you. A normal taxi charges
CUC$17-20. Alternatively hire a private car
for about CUC$12-13, 1 hr on an unpaved
road.

● Transport

Santiago de Cuba *p148, map p152*
Air
Airport Antonio Maceo (SCU) is 8 km from
town, T691014. Daily flights to Havana. Also
connections with other domestic airports
and international flights from Haiti, Jamaica
and the Dominican Republic.

Bus
Terminal near Plaza de la Revolución at the
top of Av de los Libertadores/Ctra Central.
Buy ticket in advance at **Astro** office on
Yarayo (the 1st street on the left going north
from the terminal), daily 0600-1400. **Víazul**,
T628484, is in an office to the left of the bus
departure area, with a blue door, daily
0700-2100, closed Sun pm but if you turn up
30 mins before departure you can buy a
ticket. For an overnight journey wear
trousers and a sweater if you have one, as
the a/c is very cold and even **Víazul** is not
comfortable at night. To **Havana**, 1500,
2000, arrive 0720, 1130, CUC$51, from
Havana 1500, 2000, arrive 0650, 1130. To
Baracoa 0730, via El Cristo, La Maya,
Guantánamo, San Antonio and Imías,
arriving 1215, CUC$15, returning from

Baracoa 1415, arriving Santiago 1900. Note that the buses to Baracoa are only 9-seater minibuses and demand can be great in high season. Get your ticket the day before (or Sat for a Mon journey). Once a busload of tickets has been sold no more will be sold that day but if you turn up at 0500 the next morning they usually put on more buses depending on demand. On your return the number of seats depends on how many buses have come from Santiago, but queue early. **Trucks** are available outside terminal to most destinations, drivers shout destination prior to departure, pay in pesos. For a long journey avoid trucks without any kind of cover. Local buses, 20 centavos, run to the suburbs and outskirts. If there is no sign of a bus, catch a truck, ask driver the destination, pay flat rate 1 peso. Horse-drawn *coches* are also 1 peso.

Car
Car hire At the airport: Transautos, T692245; Havanautos, T651056, also has an agency at La Punta service station, T639328; Vía Rent a Car T687278. On return beware of CUC$10 charge for dirty exterior, CUC$20 for dirty interior and CUC$16 for scratches on the paint work caused by flying stones. These and other agencies in main hotels.

Taxis
There are 3 types: **Turistaxi** most expensive, eg CUC$8 from airport to town centre; **Taxis OK** also expensive; **Cubataxi**, T651038/9, cheapest (name on windscreen), eg airport to town CUC$5. You can also get a private taxi, lots of them hanging around Parque Céspedes and Plaza Marte, but they will charge about the same as a **Cubataxi**. For a longer journey, you can negotiate a price. However, get a written quote if possible as even Cubataxis have been known to renegue on their agreements. **Motorbike** transport can be arranged at Plaza Marte for about CUC$1. *Bicitaxis* cost CUC$0.50.

Train
The station is opposite the rum factory on Av Jesús Menéndez. Book tickets in advance from office northeast of new terminal. Train travel is not as reliable or comfortable as bus travel. Take sweater for Havana journey, freezing a/c.

Guantánamo *p151*
Air
Aeropuerto Mariana Grajales (GAO) is 16 km from Guantánamo, off the Baracoa road. Scheduled flight Mon, Wed, Fri, Sat at 0530 from **Havana**, returning 0845, plus Sun 0840 (1155).

Bus
The bus terminal, T326016, is 5 km southwest from the centre. Taxis run from the train and bus station to Hotel Guantánamo/town centre, CUC$1. Daily bus to **Havana**, 4 buses to **Santiago**, 1 bus to **Baracoa**. Víazul stops here on its Santiago-Baracoa route.

Car
Havanautos office is at Cupet Cimex gas station at Prado esq 6 Este, the beginning of the Baracoa road.

Train
The station is in the centre on Calixto García. Daily trains to **Santiago** and **Havana**.

Baracoa *p151*
Air
Airport 100 m from Hotel Porto Santo. There are 2 scheduled **Cubana** flights a week from **Havana**, on Thu (0645) and Sun (0620), with the Sun flight via Santiago (0925). All times subject to frequent change.

Bus
Main bus terminal at the end of Martí near Av de los Mártires, T43880, for buses to Havana, Santiago, Guantánamo. Reserve in advance or queue early at busy times and ensure your name is on the list (*plano*) otherwise your reservation will not be valid. Trucks to Guantánamo, Moa and other destinations from 2nd bus terminal on Coroneles Galano, T42367.

Car
24-hr hire **Servi Cupet** station, near Matachín Museum.

---

❶ Directory

Santiago de Cuba *p148, map p152*
Banks Banco Financiero Internacional, Parque Céspedes at Santo Tomás 565 entre

Enramada y Aguilera, T22101, Mon-Fri 0800-1600, cash on Visa, change foreign currency and TCs. **Banco de Crédito y Comercio**, Parque Céspedes, Santo Tomás entre Aguilera y Heredia and Lacret esq Aguilera, efficient service for changing TCs in European currencies, CUC$2.5% commission. **BICSA**, Enramada opposite Plaza Dolores, for changing foreign currency and TCs. **Banco Popular de Ahorro**, Plaza Dolores, 0800-1500, Visa and MasterCard, ATM, prompt service, also a newly built branch on Victoriano Garzón esq 3. In the **Asistur** office under Casa Granda you can get cash advance on all major credit cards including American Express and Diners Club; they will also change American Express TCs, the only place who will do so in all Cuba.

Immigration Inmigración y Extranjería, Calle 13 entre 4 y Ctra del Caney, Mon, Fri 0900-1200, 1330-1630, Tue, Wed, Thu 0900-1200, in summer holiday mornings only. Go to **Bandec** on Parque Céspedes y Aguilera and buy special stamp (*sello*) for CUC$25, then return to Immigration for paperwork (15 mins). **Internet** Etecsa has an office under the cathedral on the corner of Parque Céspedes, Félix Pena y Heredia, daily 0700-2300. 3 terminals using prepaid cards, 2 international and 2 domestic phone booths. **Hotel Las Américas**, 2 terminals in the lobby, CUC$2 for 30 mins. Bar alongside if you have to wait your turn. **Meliá Santiago de Cuba**, business centre off the entrance. The best place in terms of quality and

quantity of machines, 6 terminals, CUC$5 per hr, connection usually good. **Medical services** Clínica Internacional, Av Raúl Pujol esq 10, T642589. Outpatient appointments, laboratory, dentist, 24-hr emergencies, international pharmacy, especially for tourists, everything payable in dollars, CUC$25 per consultation, the best clinic to visit to be sure of immediate treatment. **Post office** Main post office is on Aguilera y Clarín, 0700-2000, where you can make phone calls within Cuba and buy international phone cards. There is email service but no internet access.

Telephones Etecsa is on Aguilera, just before Plaza Dolores, open 24 hrs. For calls outside Santiago, Centro de Comunicaciones Nacional e Internacional, Heredia y Félix Pena, by the cathedral. **Tourist assistance** Asistur, Hotel Casa Granda, Heredia esq San Pedro, T686600, for all health, financial, legal and insurance problems for foreign tourists.

Guantánamo *p151*
Banks Banco de Crédito at Calixto García esq Ctra. **Cadeca**, Calixto García esq Prado, Mon-Sat 0830-1800, Sun 0800-1300.

Baracoa *p151*
Banks Banco Nacional de Cuba, on Maceo, will change only TCs, you cannot get cash advance on credit cards. **Porto Santo** and **El Castillo** hotels both change TCs.

The islands

The Isla de la Juventud, or Isla – as it is known – was once a lair for French and British pirates, then a prison island for notable revolutionaries such as José Martí and Fidel Castro. This history has led to very little development and what there is has been concentrated around Nueva Gerona, its main town, and the port area. There are few reasons to stay here if you are not interested in diving, as the swimming is not as good compared with other Cuban beaches. It is a good place to go for a weekend out of Havana, although if you plan to see the whole island you will need more than one weekend. There is exceptional diving off the west coast which keeps scuba divers occupied for some time. Cayo Largo is a sun, sea and sand destination, where all-inclusive is the order of the day and you are totally isolated from the rest of Cuba. It is so little a part of Cuba that euros and dollars are the accepted currencies and Cuban pesos are invisible. Everyone comes here on a package deal, for one day, two days or a week, for no other reason than to enjoy the idyllic beaches with pale golden sand and perfect conditions for watersports. ▶▶ *For Sleeping, Eating and other listings, see pages 164-166.*

Isla de la Juventud → *Colour map 1, B2.*

There are three good reasons for visiting the Isla de la Juventud: diving, birdwatching and checking out Cuban provincial life away from tourist resorts. In recent decades its population has been swelled by tens of thousands of Cuban and Third World students, giving rise to the modern name of Isle of Youth.

Nueva Gerona → *Phone code: 61.*

The capital, Nueva Gerona, dates from the 19th century and remains the only substantial settlement. Surrounded by small hills, it is a pleasant country town with a slow pace. As most development has taken place post-1959, there are few historical buildings. The **Río Las Casas** runs through the town heading northwards out to sea, and this has always been the main route to the Cuban mainland. The boat which served as a ferry from the 1920s until 1974, *El Pinero*, has been preserved by the river at the end of Calle 28. It ferried Castro off the island when Batista's amnesty secured his release.

The **Museo Municipal** ① *C30 entre 37 y Martí (39), T323791, Mon-Fri 0900-2200, Sun 0900-1300, CUC$1*, was once the Casa de Gobierno, built in 1853, one of the oldest buildings on the island. It is on the south side of the Parque Central and has a small collection of historical items. The **Museo de la Lucha Clandestina** ① *C24 entre 43 y 45, Tue-Sat, 0900-1700, Sun 0800-1200*, near **Coppelia**, has a collection of photos and other material relating to the Revolution. The **Planetario y Museo de Historia Natural** ① *C414625 y 54, T323143, Tue-Thu 0800-1900, Fri 1400-2200, Sat 1300-1700, Sun 0900-1300, CUC$2*, has exhibits relating to the natural history, geology and archaeology of the island. Outside the town, 3 km west just off the road to La Demajagua, is **Museo Finca El Abra** ① *Tue-Sat 0900-1630, Sun 0900-1300, CUC$2, CUC$1 for camera, Spanish-speaking guide*. This is where José Martí came on 17 October 1870, to spend nine weeks of exile and labour quarrying marble in the Sierra de las Casas before being deported to Spain. You can see the contents of the house and kitchen and some of Martí's belongings.

The **Presidio Modelo** (Model Prison) ① *T325112, Tue-Sat 0900-1630, Sun 0900-1300, CUC$2, cameras CUC$1*, 4 km east of Nueva Gerona in Reparto Chacón, was built by the dictator Machado to a high-security 'panopticon' design first developed by Jeremy Bentham in 1791 to have total surveillance and control of inmates. It is a sinister and impressive sight; wander around the guard towers and circular cell blocks, and see the numbered, tiered cells. Inmates have included many fighters in the Independence struggle, Japanese Cuban internees in the Second World War, and Fidel Castro and fellow Moncada rebels imprisoned from 1953 to 1955. Castro closed the prison in 1967.

The **Cueva del Punta del Este** ① *59 km southeast of Nueva Gerona, transport by hired car or organized excursion*, contains paintings attributed to the original Siboney inhabitants. They were discovered in 1910 by a shipwrecked French sailor and comprise 235 pictures on the walls and ceilings, painted long before the arrival of the Spanish. They are considered the most important pictographs in the Caribbean and have been declared a national monument. It is believed that they might represent a solar calendar.

The **Cocodrilo** ① *NCUC$3*, crocodile farm is a one-hour drive south and west from Nueva Gerona, including much on dirt road. There are guided tours (in Spanish) of the hatchery and breeding pens where the crocodiles stay for four or five years until release.

Cayo Largo → *Phone code: 5. Colour map 1, B2.*

Cayo Largo is at the eastern end of the Archipiélago de los Canarreos, 114 km east of Isla de la Juventud and 80 km south of the Península de Zapata. It is a long, thin, coral

Cuba The islands

island, 26 km long and no more than 2 km wide. There are beautiful white sandy beaches protected by a reef, all along the southern coast which, together with the crystal-clear, warm waters of the Caribbean, make it ideal for tourism. A string of all-inclusive hotels lines the southern tip of the island. The northern coast is mostly mangrove and swamp, housing hungry mosquitoes as well as numerous birds (pelicans being the most visible) and iguanas. Turtles lay their eggs at Playa Tortuga in the northeast, and there is a turtle farm at Combinado northwest of the airstrip.

The best beach on the island is the 2-km white-sand **Playa Sirena**, which faces west and is spared any wind or currents which sometimes affect the southern beaches. Snorkelling and scuba diving can be done here, 10 minutes' boat ride from the hotels and at **Playa Los Cocos**, which you can reach by bicycle. **Scuba diving** is good around the island. There is an extensive reef with gorgonians, sponges and lots of fish, while north of the island you will find large pelagics. There is **deep-sea fishing** for marlin and other big fish, with international fishing tournaments held here. **Sailing** is popular and there is a bareboat yacht charter fleet. The **Marina Cayo Largo del Sur** at Combinado has 50 moorings for visiting yachts. You don't have to buy a tourist card to come here if you are not going on to anywhere else in Cuba, because the island is a free port. To clear customs, call the marina on VHF 6, or maritime security (*Seguridad Marítima*) on VHF 16.

♣ Watersports include windsurfing, kayaking, jet skis, catamarans, and banana rides.

You can only get to Cayo Largo del Sur by air or yacht. There are several charters and scheduled international flights as well as domestic flights from Aeropuerto Playa Baracoa, a former military air base outside Havana, and from Varadero. Package tours from Havana might fly you on a 60-year-old Antonov biplane, at an altitude of 3500 ft.

● Sleeping

Isla de la Juventud *p163*

Hotels can be booked through **Amistur**; many are not advertised in tourist literature and it can be difficult to book or verify whether they are open.

A El Colony, T398282. 40 mins by road from Nueva Gerona's small airport. Very isolated, diving centre with access to 56 buoyed diving locations. Swimming and snorkelling not great because of shallow water and sea urchins, you have to wade a long way before it is deep enough to swim, but beach is white sand. Price for half board. 77 a/c rooms in main block and *cabañas*, in need of renovation, single and triple available, discounts for stays of over a week, TV. Lovely setting, pool, 3 restaurants, snack bar, store, basket ball, volleyball, tennis and squash courts, horse riding, disco Sat 2100-0600, excursions, busy with package tourists, accommodation can be hard to find.

C-D Villa Gran Caribe Isla de la Juventud on the outskirts of Nueva Gerona on the road to La Fé beside the river, T323290. 20 rooms, single and triple available, extra cots for children, a/c, fridge, TV, phone, pool where national swimming team trains, good service

at poolside bar, restaurants, squash court and gymnasium, disco Thu-Sun 2130-0400, techno music, cave-like atmosphere, young crowd, dance and aerobics classes advertised, the nicest hotel if you are not diving or on a package, despite the ugly foyer.

E Villa Chave, 45 3406 entre 34 y 36, T324292. Run by the kind family of Isabel and Inil. Good breakfasts and enormous suppers. Bathroom is shared between the 2 rented rooms.

E Villa Niñita, 32 4110 entre 41 y 43, T321255, zerep@web.correosdecuba.cu. Run by the friendly Viviana y Alina Pérez Castanedo. Excellent self-contained apartment above family home with separate entrance and kitchen and terrace with great views.

● Eating

Isla de la Juventud *p163*

There are very few *paladares*. The best bet is to eat in your *casa particular*, where you can get an excellent meal for CUC$5-6. At the Mercado Agropecuario at Calles 24 y 35, you can get fresh fruit and vegetables and there are a few basic places to eat in this area where you can pay in CP$.

♥♥♥ Cabaret El Dragón, 39 y 26. Mon-Thu 1600-2200, Fri-Sun 1600-0030. Chinese and Cuban food, restaurant and bar, cabaret at weekends, deluxe atmosphere, upscale crowd.

♥♥♥ La Insula, 22 y 39. Sun-Fri 1530-2230, Sat 1530-2100, café Sun-Fri 1200-0130, Sat 1200-2100. Probably the most upmarket place in town and popular with travellers. The food is of a high standard and the staff are friendly. You might want to avoid the karaoke nights as the staff will try and get you to join in.

♥ Día y Noche, 39 entre 24 y 26. Open 24 hrs. *Bocaditos* for CUC$1 and fried chicken for CUC$1.10.

♥ El Cochinito, 39 y 24. State-run, 1400-2200. specializes in pork with dishes ranging from CUC$1-9. Airy dining room but food displayed in a cabinet at the entrance looks really unappetizing. You can sit on real cowskin chairs.

● Bars and clubs

Isla de la Juventud *p163*
Cabaret El Patio, 24 entre 37 y 39. 2100-0200, cabaret, 2 shows nightly at weekends, at 2200 and 0100, entry CUC$3, CUC$10 Fri-Sun, lots of Cubans and popular.
Casa de la Cultura, 37 y 24. Check the schedule posted outside for dance events.
Casa de los Vinos, 20 y 41. Mon-Wed 1400-2200, Fri-Sun 1400-2400. Popular CP$ drinking spot with grapefruit, melon, tomato and grape wines in earthenware jugs, drink orders finish at 2300, advisable to take glasses, avoid the snacks.
La Movida, Calle 34 entre 18 y 20. Outdoor disco, CUC$3, young student crowd, starts at 2200.
Taberna Gerona, 39 y 22. Daily 1100-2100. Cuban food and pub atmosphere, very friendly, strictly CP$.

▲ Activities and tours

Isla de la Juventud *p163*
Diving
Centro Internacional de Buceo El Colony has excellent facilities including underwater photography and there is a recompression chamber. All dives are boat dives and, as most of the sites are quite a long way from the marina, lunch is usually on board before your second dive. The area around Punta Francés in the west is probably the best, with caves, tunnels and all manner of sea creatures including turtles, which are protected. There are over 40 different corals and innumerable fish. The area is a marine reserve, you may only dive with an official operator. Fishing is not allowed in the marine reserve.

Marina
Marina El Colony has mooring for 15 boats, maximum draft 2.5m, VHF channels 16, 19, 68 and 72, a liveaboard, *Sondylus*, with a capacity for 10 divers and other facilities. Watersports are available, such as catamarans, CUC$10 per hr, a 2-person kayak, CUC$6 per hr and a single kayak, CUC$4 per hr.

Tour operators
Ecotur, 26 entre 39 y 41, T327101, www.cayolargodelsur.cu/ecotur/home.htm. Daily 0800-1700. Trips to the south of the island include La Cañada, Los Indios, El Cocodrilo, Punta del Este, Rincón del Guanal, Jacksonville, with chances to see chocolate-scented wild orchids and the tocororo bird plus deer. Guides speak English, Italian, French and German and are all naturalists. Prices are CUC$12.50-15 per person if you have a car or they can hire you a car for CUC$65 a day. If more than 4 people a minibus needs to be hired. All trips must be booked at least 1 day in advance because permits must be secured for visits to the southern part of the island. Also sells tours for **Hotel Colony**, seafari, snorkelling, diving and you can take advantage of the hotel's bus service, CUC$3. Internet CUC$5 per hr. Flights arranged.

● Transport

Isla de la Juventud *p163*
Air
The **Rafael Cabrera Airport (GER)**, T322690, is nearly 5 km from town and there are 2 or 3 scheduled 40-min flights a day from Havana so you could do a day trip if you wanted. Fare CUC$32 1-way, book in advance. Long queues to get tickets off the island,

so best to book your return flight in Havana before you visit.

Airlines Cubana at 39 1415 entre 16 y 18, Nueva Gerona, T324259, Mon-Fri 0800-1600, closed 1300-1400.

Boat

From the side entrance of the **Astro** bus station in Plaza de La Revolución, Havana, there is a little booth for the company **Viajero**. Phone for instructions T7-8781841; it's advisable to check times and to find out whether you need to go on the day or several days beforehand because of availability problems (in Batabanó, T62-83845). If you turn up on the departure day you will need to be there at 0900 to collect a valueless ticket for which you must have your passport. Then you need to return to the office window for a bus pass at 1140. The bus leaves at 1230 and arrives at Surgidero de Batabanó on the south coast at 1330. You can not turn up at Batabanó and expect to get on the ferry; you will be turned away without a reservation. The scheduled ferry/ catamaran departure is at 1400. You may or may not need to pay the CP$2 bus fare there and back depending on the driver. At the port, there are some small buildings to the right of the waiting room area where you need to go to buy your passage, CUC$11, one way. From there you and everyone else will be checked, rechecked, checked and checked again. There is a 20-kg baggage allowance and they are fairly strict about it. You will also have to pass your stuff through an X-ray machine. Bring all food and drink as the Cuban cafeteria will not sustain you should you suffer delays because of the boats, which is common. If you have not organized your return trip, which is highly inadvisable, you need to go to **Agencia Sta María**, Oficina de Correo, 53 entre 39a y 8, Mercado de Abel, in Nueva Gerona, T322270. This is where boat tickets are sold in CUC$ but only from 1400. There is a return ferry (with cold a/c but a film showing to pacify you) or catamaran at 0700 and 1200. Because of hijackings of planes security is tight on all transport. This adds to delays.

Bus

Buses run to **La Fe**, the Hotel Colony, **Playa Bibijagua**, and bus marked 'Servicio Aereo', between the airport and the cinema, but don't rely on any of these to run on a regular basis.

Car

Car hire Havanautos 32 y 39, T324432, but the hotels also have car hire desks. Rates CUC$70-87 a day with insurance.

❶ Directory

Isla de la Juventud *p163*
Banks Banco de Crédito y Comercio, 39 y 18, Mon-Fri 0800-1500. **Cadeca**, 20 y 39, Mon-Sat 0830-1800, Sun 0830-1200. Best to bring enough cash from the mainland.
Medical services Pharmacy at 39 y 24, Mon-Fri 0800-2200, Sat 0800-1600. Take plenty of insect repellent, particularly for the Ciénaga or the Hotel Colony.

Background

History

Spanish conquest Cuba was visited by Cristóbal Colón (Christopher Columbus) during his first voyage to find a westerly route to the Orient on 27 October 1492, and he made another brief stop two years later on his way from Hispaniola to Jamaica. Columbus did not realize it was an island when he landed; he hoped it was Japan. He arrived on the north coast of 'Colba', but found little gold. He did, however, note the Indians' practice of puffing at a large, burning roll of leaves, which they called 'tobacos'. Cuba was first circumnavigated by Sebastián de Ocampo in 1508, but it was Diego de Velázquez who conquered it in 1511 and founded several towns, called *villas*, including Havana. The first African slaves were imported to Cuba in 1526. Sugar was introduced soon after. Tobacco was made a strict monopoly of Spain in 1717. The coffee plant was introduced in 1748. The British, under Lord Albemarle and Admiral Pocock, captured Havana and held the island from 1762 to 1763, but it was returned to Spain in exchange for Florida. Towards the end of the 18th century Cuba became a slave plantation society. By the 1860s Cuba was producing about a third of the world's sugar and was heavily dependent on slaves to do so, supplemented by indentured Chinese labourers in the 1850s and 1860s. An estimated 600,000 African slaves were imported by 1867.

Independence movement Independence from Spain became a burning issue in Cuba as Spain refused to consider political reforms which would give the colony more autonomy. The first War of Independence was in the eastern part of the island between 1868 and 1878, but it gained little save a modest move towards the abolition of slavery; and complete abolition was not achieved until 1886. One consequence of the war was the ruin of many sugar planters. US interests began to take over the sugar plantations and the sugar mills, and Cuba became more dependent on the US market.

From 1895 to 1898 rebellion flared up again in the second War of Independence under the young poet and revolutionary, José Martí, together with the old guard of Antonio Maceo and Máximo Gómez. José Martí was tragically killed in May 1895 and Maceo in 1896. Despite fierce fighting throughout the island, neither the Nationalists nor the Spanish could gain the upper hand. However, the USA was now concerned for its investments and its strategic interests. When the US battleship *Maine* exploded in Havana harbour on 15 February 1898, killing 260 crew, the USA declared war on Spain. American forces were landed, a squadron blockaded Havana and defeated the Spanish fleet at Santiago de Cuba. In December peace was signed and US forces occupied the island for four years.

❧ Many national heroes of this period have become revolutionary icons in the struggle against domination by a foreign power.

The Republic of Cuba was proclaimed in 1902 and the Government was handed over to its first president. However, the Platt Amendment to the constitution, passed by the US Congress, clearly made Cuba a protectorate of the USA. The USA retained naval bases and reserved the right of intervention in Cuban domestic affairs but, to quell growing unrest, repealed the Platt Amendment in 1934. The USA formally relinquished the right to intervene but retained its naval base at Guantánamo on a 99-year lease.

Dictatorship Around two-thirds of sugar exports went to the USA under a quota system at prices set by Washington; two-thirds of Cuba's imports came from the USA; foreign capital investment was largely from the USA and Cuba was effectively a client state. Yet its people suffered from grinding rural poverty, high unemployment, illiteracy and inadequate health care. Politics was a mixture of authoritarian rule and corrupt democracy. From 1924 to 1933 the 'strong man' Gerardo Machado ruled Cuba. He was elected in 1924 on a wave of popularity but a drastic fall in sugar prices in the late 1920s led to strikes; nationalist popular rebellion was harshly repressed. The USA tried to negotiate a deal but nationalists called a general strike in protest at US interference, and Machado finally went into exile. The violence did not abate, however, and there were more strikes, mob attacks and occupations of factories. In September 1933 a revolt of non-commissioned officers including Sergeant Fulgencio Batista, deposed the government. Batista then held power through presidential puppets until he was elected president himself in 1940. He pursued nationalist and populist policies, set against corruption and political violence. In 1940 a new Constitution was passed by a constituent assembly dominated by Batista, which included universal suffrage and benefits for workers such as a minimum wage, pensions, social insurance and an eight-hour day. In 1944 Batista lost the elections but corruption continued. Batista, by then a self-promoted general, staged a military coup in 1952. Constitutional and democratic government was at an end. His harshly repressive dictatorship was brought to a close by Fidel Castro in January 1959, after a three-year campaign, mostly in the Sierra Maestra, with a guerrilla force reduced at one point to 12 men.

Revolution Fidel Castro, the son of immigrants from Galicia and born in Cuba in 1926 saw José Martí as his role model and aimed to follow his ideals. In 1953, the 100th anniversary of José Martí's birth, Castro and a committed band of about 160 revolutionaries attacked the Moncada barracks in Santiago de Cuba on 26 July. The attack failed and Castro and his brother Raúl were later captured and put on trial. Fidel used the occasion to make an impassioned speech denouncing corruption in the ruling class and the need for political freedom and economic independence. In 1955 the Castros were given an amnesty and went to Mexico. There Fidel continued to work on his essentially nationalist revolutionary programme, called the 26 July Movement, which sought radical social and economic reforms and a return to the democracy of Cuba's 1940 constitution. He met another man of ideas, an Argentine doctor called Ernesto (Che) Guevara, who sailed with him and his brother Raúl and a band of 82 like-minded revolutionaries, back to Cuba on 2 December 1956. Their campaign began in the Sierra Maestra in the east of Cuba and, after years of fierce fighting, Batista fled the country on 1 January 1959. Fidel Castro, to universal popular acclaim, entered Havana and assumed control of the island.

Communism and the 1960s From 1960 onwards, in the face of increasing hostility from the USA, Castro led Cuba into socialism and then communism. Officials of the Batista regime were put on trial in 'people's courts' and executed. The promised new elections were not held. The judiciary lost its independence when Castro assumed the right to appoint judges. The free press was closed or taken over. Trade unions lost their independence and became part of government. The University of Havana, a former focus of dissent, and professional associations all lost their autonomy. The democratic Constitution of 1940 was never reinstated. In 1960 the sugar *centrales*, the oil refineries and the foreign banks were nationalized, all US property was expropriated and the Central Planning Board (Juceplan) was established. The professional and property-owning middle classes began a steady exodus which drained the country of its skilled workers. CIA-backed mercenaries and Cuban emigrés kept up a relentless barrage of attacks, but failed to achieve their objective.

1961 was the year of the **Bay of Pigs** invasion, a fiasco which was to harden Castro's political persuasion. Some 1400 CIA-trained Cuban émigrés landed in the Bahía de Cochinos (Bay of Pigs), but were stranded on the beaches when the Cuban air force attacked their supply ships. Two hundred were killed and the rest

surrendered within three days. In his May Day speech, Fidel Castro confirmed that the
Cuban Revolution was socialist. The US reaction was to isolate Cuba, with a full trade
embargo. Cuba was expelled from the Organization of American States (OAS) and the
OAS imposed economic sanctions. In March 1962 rationing had to be imposed.

In April 1962, President Kruschev of the USSR decided to send medium-range
missiles to Cuba, which would be capable of striking anywhere in the USA. This
episode, which became known as the 'Cuban Missile Crisis', brought the world to the
brink of nuclear war, defused only by secret negotiations between John F Kennedy
and Kruschev. Without consulting Castro and without his knowledge, Kruschev
eventually agreed to have the missiles dismantled and withdrawn on condition that
the west would guarantee a policy of non-aggression towards Cuba.

Economic policy during the 1960s was largely unsuccessful in achieving its aims.
The government wanted to industrialize rapidly to reduce dependence on sugar.
However, the crash programme, with help from the USSR, was a failure and had to be
abandoned. The whole nation was called upon to achieve a target of 10 million tonnes
of sugar by 1970 and everyone spent time in the fields helping towards this goal. It
was never reached and never has been. Rationing is still fierce, and there are still
shortages of consumer goods. However, the Revolution's social policies have largely
been successful and it is principally these achievements which have ensured the
people's support of Castro and kept him in power. Education, housing and health
services have improved and the social inequalities of the 1940s and 1950s have been
wiped out.

1970s Soviet domination Cuba became firmly entrenched as a member of the
Soviet bloc, joining COMECON in 1972. The Revolution was institutionalized along
Soviet lines and the Party gained control of the bureaucracy, the judiciary and the
local and national assemblies. A new Socialist Constitution was adopted in 1976.
Cuba's foreign policy changed from actively fomenting socialist revolutions abroad
(such as Guevara's forays into the Congo and Bolivia in the 1960s) to supporting other
left-wing or third-world countries with combat troops and technical advisers including
Angola, Ethiopia, Nicaragua, Jamaica and Grenada. In September 1979, Castro
hosted a summit of the non-aligned nations in Havana, a high point in his foreign
policy initiatives.

1980s dissatisfaction By the 1980s, the heavy dependence on sugar and the USSR,
coupled with the trade embargo, meant that the expected improvements in living
standards were not being delivered as fast as hoped and the people were tiring of
being asked for ever more sacrifices. In 1980, the Peruvian embassy was overrun by
11,000 people seeking political asylum. Castro opened the port of Mariel for a mass
departure of some 125,000 by sea in anything they could find which would float.

Before the collapse of the Soviet system, aid to Cuba from the USSR was
estimated at about 25% of GNP. Cuba's debt with the USSR was a secret; estimates
ranged from US$8.5 bn to US$34 bn. Apart from military aid, economic assistance
took two forms: balance of payments support (about 85%), under which sugar and
nickel exports were priced in excess of world levels, and assistance for development
projects. About 13 million tonnes of oil a year were supplied by the USSR, allowing
three million to be re-exported, providing a valuable source of foreign earnings. By the
late 1980s up to 90% of Cuba's foreign trade was with planned economies. The
collapse of the Communist system in Eastern Europe, followed by the demise of the
USSR, nearly brought the end of Castro's Cuba.

1990s crisis and change Economic difficulties in the 1990s brought on by the loss
of markets in the former USSR and Eastern Europe, together with higher oil prices
because of the Gulf crisis, forced the Government to impose emergency measures

and declare a special period in peace time. Rationing was increased, petrol became scarce, the bureaucracy was slashed. In 1993, Cuba was hit by a storm which caused an estimated US$1 bn in damage. In mid-1994, economic discontent flared and Cubans began to flee for Florida in a mass exodus. It was estimated that between mid-August and mid-September 30,000 Cubans had left the country. The crisis forced President Clinton into an agreement whereby the USA was committed to accepting at least 20,000 Cubans a year, plus the next of kin of US citizens, while Cuba agreed to prevent further departures.

As the economic crisis persisted, the government adopted measures which opened up many sectors to private enterprise and recognized the dependence of much of the economy on dollars. The partial reforms did not eradicate the imbalances between the peso and the dollar economies, and shortages remained for those without access to hard currency. Cuba intensified its economic liberalization programme, allowing farmers to sell at uncontrolled prices once their commitments to the state procurement system were fulfilled. Importantly, the reforms allowed the middlemen to operate.

US pressure in the 1990s Before the Revolution of 1959 the USA had investments in Cuba worth about US$1 bn, covering nearly every activity from agriculture and mining to oil installations. Today all American businesses have been nationalized; the USA has cut off all imports from Cuba, placed an embargo on exports to Cuba, and broken off diplomatic relations. Prior to the 1992 US presidential elections, President Bush (Senior) approved the Cuban Democracy Act (Torricelli Bill) which forbade US subsidiaries from trading with Cuba. Many countries, including EC members and Canada, said they would not allow the US bill to affect their trade with Cuba and the UN General Assembly voted in favour of a resolution calling for an end to the embargo.

In 1996, US election year, Cuba faced another crackdown by the US administration. In February, Cuba shot down two light aircraft piloted by Miami émigrés allegedly over Cuban air space and implicitly confirmed by the findings of the International Civil Aviation Organization (ICAO) report in June. The attack provoked President Clinton to tighten and internationalize the US embargo on Cuba and on 12 March he signed into law the (Helms-Burton) Cuban Freedom and Democratic Solidarity Act. This legislation allows legal action against any company or individual benefiting from properties expropriated by the Cuban government after the Revolution. It brought universal condemnation: Canada and Mexico (Nafta partners), the EU, Russia, China, the Caribbean Community and the Río Group of Latin American countries all protested that it was unacceptable to extend sanctions outside the USA to foreign companies and their employees who do business with Cuba.

Recent events 1997 was the 30th anniversary of the death of Che Guevara, whose remains were returned from Bolivia to Cuba in July. During a week of official mourning for Che and his comrades in arms, vast numbers filed past the remains in Havana and Santa Clara, where they were laid to rest on 17 October. In December 1998 the remains of 10 more guerrillas killed in Bolivia in 1967 were also interred in the Che Guevara memorial in Santa Clara.

In January 1998 the Pope visited Cuba for the first time and held open-air masses around the country. The Pope preached against Cuba's record on human rights and abortion while also condemning the US trade embargo preventing food and medicines reaching the needy. The visit was a public relations success for both Castro and the Pope. Shortly afterwards, 200 prisoners were pardoned and released.

In November 1999 a six-year-old boy, Elián González, was rescued from the sea off Florida, the only survivor from a boatload of illegal migrants which included his mother and her boyfriend. He was looked after by distant relatives in Miami and quickly became the centrepiece of a new row between Cuban émigrés – supported by right-wing Republicans – and Cuba. The US Attorney General, Janet Reno, supported the decision by the US Immigration and Naturalization Service (INS) on 5 January 2000, that the boy should be repatriated and reunited with his father in Cuba by 14 January, but she postponed the deadline to allow for legal challenges. Mass demonstrations were held in Havana in support of Elián's return but legal manoeuvres by US politicians stalled progress and caused further disputes. Amid enormous controversy, the US authorities seized Elián on 22 April and reunited him with his father, who had travelled to the USA earlier in the month with his second wife and baby. The family finally took him home, amid celebrations in Cuba, where the boy had become a symbol of resistance to the USA.

The election of George W Bush to the US presidency was bad news for any prospects of a thaw in relations with the USA. A crackdown on spies was ordered and in June 2001, five Cubans were convicted in a US Federal Court in Miami. Castro referred to them as 'heroes', who he said had not been putting the USA in danger but had been infiltrating Cuban-American anti-Castro groups and defending Cuba. However, 2001 did see the first commercial export of food from the USA to Cuba, with a shipment of corn from Louisiana and the debate on the lifting of sanctions was fuelled by the visit of former US President Jimmy Carter in 2002.

Towards the end of 2002 lobbying intensified in the USA for an end to the embargo and travel restrictions while farmers enthusiastically embraced trade with Cuba. However, the thaw came to a grinding halt in 2003 when Castro had three ferry hijackers executed and imprisoned 75 journalists, rights activists and dissidents, many of whom had allegedly been encouraged by the head of the US Interests Section in Havana. Amid universal condemnation, the EU announced a review of its relations with Cuba and curtailed high-level governmental visits.

In 2002, Osvaldo Paya, leader of the dissident Varela project (Félix Varela was an Independence hero), delivered a petition with 11,020 signatures to the National Assembly demanding sweeping political reforms, but it was dismissed. Undeterred, Paya submitted a second petition in October 2003 with 14,384 signatures, calling for a referendum on freedom of speech and assembly and amnesty for political prisoners. At the same time, the US administration announced a clampdown on its citizens travelling to the island. Immigration and Customs officers were ordered to carry out the letter of the law, with thousands of baggage searches and the first prosecutions were announced. In January 2004, the USA cancelled semi-annual migration talks as relations deteriorated. With 2004 being another presidential election year in the USA, Cuba knew it was in for a rocky ride, but this time Bush hit out at ordinary Cubans as well as their government. Remittances were sharply curtailed and Cuban Americans were limited in their travel to the island, with only one trip permitted every three years to see a close relative, even if they were dying.

In August 2006 Fidel Castro had his 80th birthday. The occasion was to have been marked by national celebrations, parades and speeches, but shortly beforehand Castro made the surprise announcement that he was about to undergo major abdominal surgery and that he was handing over the reins of power to his brother, Raúl. The nature of his illness, operation and subsequent condition was shrouded in secrecy, with rumours of terminal illness and even his death circulating in Cuba and in Miami. Coinciding with Fidel dropping out of the limelight, in the USA the Democrats won control of both houses of Congress and there were moves towards closer relations. Raúl made conciliatory noises to the USA, which the Bush administration rebuffed. By May 2007, Fidel was well enough to receive foreign dignatories and write articles on world issues.

Government

In 1976 a new Constitution was approved by 97.7% of the voters, setting up municipal and provincial assemblies and a National Assembly of People's Power. The membership of the Assembly is now 609, candidates being nominated by the 169 municipal councils, and elected by direct secret ballot. Similarly elected are members of the 14 provincial assemblies, both for five-year terms. In the latest elections, in January 2003, 8.1 million of the 8.2 million registered voters cast ballots and support for the candidates reached 97% of votes cast. All Cubans over 16 may vote. The number of Cuba's provinces was increased from six to 14 at the First Congress of the Communist Party of Cuba in December 1975. Dr Fidel Castro was elected President of the Council of State by the National Assembly and his brother, Major Raúl Castro, was elected First Vice-President. There are five other vice-presidents. Since August 2006, Raúl Castro has been acting President, aided by a committee of six: Vice President Carlos Lage, José Ramón Machado Ventura, José Ramón Balaguer, Esteban Lazo, Francisco Soberón, Felipe Pérez Roque.

Economy

Following the 1959 Revolution, Cuba adopted a Marxist-Leninist economic system. Almost all sectors of the economy were state controlled and centrally planned, the only significant exception being agriculture, where some 12% of arable land was still privately owned. The country became heavily dependent on trade and aid from other Communist countries, principally the USSR (through its participation in the Council of Mutual Economic Aid), encouraged by the US trade embargo. It relied on sugar, and to a lesser extent nickel, for nearly all its exports. While times were good, Cuba used the Soviet protection to build up an impressive, but costly, social welfare system, with better housing, education and health care than anywhere else in Latin America and the Caribbean. The collapse of the Eastern European bloc, however, revealed the vulnerability of the island's economy and the desperate need for reform. A sharp fall in GDP of 35% in 1990-1993, accompanied by a decline in exports from US$8.1 bn (1989) to US$1.7 bn (1993), forced the Government to take remedial action and the decision was made to change to a mixed economy.

Transformation of the heavily centralized state apparatus has progressed in fits and starts. The Government initially encouraged self-employment to enable it to reduce the public sector workforce. Some small businesses were registered, particularly in tourism, but numbers of tax payers have fallen. Free farm produce markets were permitted in 1994 and these were followed by similar markets at deregulated prices for manufacturers, including goods produced by state enterprises and handicrafts. The US trade embargo and the associated inability to secure finance from multilateral sources led the Government to encourage foreign investment, principally in joint ventures. However, Castro gradually returned to a more centralized economy. Numbers of joint ventures have fallen steadily from 412 in 2002 to 236 at end-2006 and free trade zones have been scrapped. Major foreign investors include Sherritt International (Canada) in nickel, oil and gas, Pernod Ricard (France) in rum, Altadis (Spain-France) in tobacco, Nestlé (Switzerland) in bottled water and soft drinks, and Sol Meliá (Spain) in hotels. Cuba has encouraged its current western partners to increase their investment rather than look for new investors. Since 2004, Cuba has given priority to key sectors such as energy and mining, and has looked to Venezuela and China for investment. In 2007 Cuba and Venezuela announced 16 new joint ventures. The two largest, with a US$1.1 billion investment, are a steelworks to be built in Venezuela and a ferro-nickel plant to be built at Camariocas in western Cuba.

Sugar is the major crop, but the industry has consistently failed to reach the targets set, with output falling from 8 million tonnes in 1990 to 3.2 million tonnes in 1998, the lowest for 50 years. Poor weather and shortages of fertilizers, oil and spare parts cut output. In 2002, 71 of the country's 156 sugar mills were closed and the land under production cut by 60%, with consequent severe job losses. **Tobacco** has also suffered from lack of fuel, fertilizers and other inputs. Production is recovering with the help of Spanish investment and credits and importers from France and Britain.

Diversification away from sugar is a major goal, with the emphasis on production of **food** for domestic use because of the shortage of foreign exchange for imports. The supply of food for the capital has greatly improved, partly with the introduction of city vegetable gardens, *agropónicos*, but the main staple, rice, is still imported to make up a shortfall in domestic production caused by inefficiencies. However, severe drought in the east of the country in 2004-2005 as well as hurricanes and flooding elsewhere put a brake on the improvement and agriculture is still in crisis.

The sudden withdrawal of **oil** supplies when trade agreements with Russia had to be renegotiated and denominated in convertible currencies, was a crucial factor in the collapse of the Cuban economy. Although trade agreements involving oil and sugar remain, Cuba has had to purchase oil from other suppliers with limited foreign exchange. As a result, Cuba has stepped up its own production: foreign companies explore for oil on and offshore and investment has borne fruit, with over 92% of electricity generated by domestic oil and gas and half of all consumption met by domestic production, but shortages of fuel remain. A new agreement has been negotiated with Venezuela, which meets domestic needs in return for a steady supply of Cuban doctors and teachers who are in the process of eradicating illiteracy and improving basic health care in Venezuela.

Mining is attracting foreign interest and in 1994 a new mining law was passed. Major foreign investors include Australian (nickel), Canadian (gold, silver and base metals) and South African (gold, copper, nickel) companies. About half of nickel and cobalt production comes from the Moa Bay plant, a Canadian/Cuban joint venture.

Tourism is now a major foreign exchange earner and has received massive investment from abroad with many joint ventures. New hotel projects are coming on stream and many more are planned. By 2006 Cuba had 44,000 hotel rooms available, of which a quarter were managed by Sol Meliá, of Spain. Despite political crises, numbers of visitors rose steadily from 546,000 in 1993 to 2 million in 2004. Arrivals dipped slightly in 2006 to 2.2 million from 2.3 million in 2005, as the industry was hit by the revaluation of the peso (see below), making holidays in Cancún and the Dominican Republic better value. The target is for 7 million tourists a year by 2010, bringing earnings of about US$11.8 bn. It is estimated that if the travel ban were lifted in the USA, some one million American tourists would immediately book holidays in Cuba.

The rise in importance of tourism and the opening of the economy to the US dollar led to a huge gap between those who had access to dollars and those who lived in the peso economy, which encouraged highly skilled professionals, such as doctors, to give up their training and become waiters or tourist guides. At the end of 2004, the government moved to redress the imbalances emerging in the economy, by introducing a 10% tax on the US dollar, making it more expensive to exchange than any other currency. While it is still legal for Cubans to hold dollars, they can no longer spend them in shops and businesses and all foreign currency now has to be exchanged for *pesos convertibles*. The resulting rush to exchange dollars before the tax took effect led to a sharp increase of US$1.5 bn in foreign reserves. In 2005 Castro went further and revalued the *peso convertible* by 8% against all currencies, making the country more expensive for visitors and Cubans holding foreign exchange. He also raised the minimum wage to halt growing poverty and social differences from 100 to 225 *pesos cubanos* a month, while putting up pensions from 55 to 150 pesos. Health care and education remain free and a basic food ration, utilities and services are subsidized. The measure was criticized as potentially inflationary.

Geography

The island of Cuba, 1250 km long, 191 km at its widest point, is the largest of the Caribbean islands and only 145 km south of Florida. Old coral reefs have been brought to the surface, so that much of the northern coast consists of coral limestone cliffs and sandy beaches. By contrast the southern coastline is being gradually submerged, producing wetlands and mangroves. Limestones of various types cover about two-thirds of the island. In most areas, there is a flat or gently rolling landscape. There are three main mountain areas in the island. In the west, the Cordillera de Guaniguanico is divided into the Sierra del los Organos in the west, with thick deposits of limestone which have developed a distinctive landscape of steep-sided flat-topped mountains; and the Sierra del Rosario in the east, made up partly of limestones and partly of lavas and other igneous rocks. Another mountainous area in central Cuba includes the Escambray mountains north of Trinidad, a double dome structure made up of igneous and metamorphic rocks, including marble. The Sierra Maestra in east Cuba has the country's highest mountains, rising to Pico Turquino (1,974 m) and a rather different geological history, with some rocks formed in an arc of volcanic activity around 50 million years ago. Older rocks include marble, and other metamorphics. Important mineral deposits are in this area; nickel is mined near Moa.

Culture

Religion Church and State were separated at the beginning of the 20th century. The domination of the USA after that time encouraged the spread of Protestantism, although Catholicism remained the religion of the majority. Nevertheless, Catholicism was not as well supported as in some other Latin American countries. After the Revolution relations between the Catholic Church and Castro were frosty. Most priests left the country. By the late 1970s the Vatican's condemnation of the US embargo helped towards a gradual reconciliation. A ban on religious believers joining the Communist Party has been lifted and Protestant, Catholic and other Church leaders have reported rising congregations. In 1996 Fidel visited Pope John Paul II at the Vatican and the Pope visited Cuba in January 1998. Castro has stated in the past that there is no conflict between Marxism and Christianity and has been sympathetic towards supporters of liberation theology in their quest for equality and a just distribution of social wealth.

Afro-Cuban religion From the mid-16th century to the late 19th, hundreds of thousands of African slaves were brought to Cuba. The most numerous and culturally most influential group were the Yoruba-speaking agriculturalists from southeast Nigeria, Dahomey and Togo, who became known collectively in Cuba as *lucumí*. It is their pantheon of deities or *orishas*, and the legends (*pwatakis*) and customs surrounding these, which form the basis of the syncretic Regla de Ocha cult, better known as Santería. Though slaves were ostensibly obliged to become Christians, their owners turned a blind eye to their rituals. The Catholic saints thus spontaneously merged or syncretized in the *lucumí* mind with the *orishas* whose imagined attributes they shared. Some two dozen regularly receive tribute at the rites known as *toques de santo*. Santería is non-sectarian and non-proselytizing, co-existing peacefully with both Christianity and the Regla Conga or Palo Monte cult brought to Cuba by *congos*, slaves from various Bantu-speaking regions of the Congo basin. Indeed many people are practising believers in both or all three. The Abakuá Secret Society is not a religion but a closed sect. Open to men only, and upholding traditional *macho* virtues, it has been described as an Afro-Cuban freemasonry, though it claims many non-black devotees. Also known as ñañiguismo, the sect originated among slaves brought from the Calabar region of southern Nigeria and Cameroon, whose Cuban descendants are called *carabalí*.

Literature The Cuban Revolution had perhaps its widest cultural influence in the field of literature. Many now-famous Latin American novelists (like Gabriel García Márquez, Mario Vargas Llosa and Julio Cortázar) visited Havana and worked with the Prensa Latina news agency or on the Casa de las Américas review. Not all have maintained their allegiance, just as some Cuban writers have deserted the

London in 2005, whose most celebrated novel was *Tres tristes tigres* (1967). Other
established writers remained in Cuba after the Revolution: Jorge Lezama Lima
(*Paradiso*, 1966); Edmundo Desnoes (*Memorias del subdesarrollo*); and Alejo
Carpentier, who invented the phrase *lo real maravilloso* (marvellous realism) to
describe the different order of reality which he perceived in Latin America and the
Caribbean and which influenced many other writers from the region (his novels
include *El reino de este mundo, El siglo de las luces, Los pasos perdidos*, and many
more). Of post-revolutionary writers, the poet and novelist Miguel Barnet is worth
reading, especially for the use of black oral history and traditions in his work. After
1959, the black writer Nicolás Guillén was adopted as the national poet; his poems of
the 1930s (*Motivos de son, Sóngoro cosongo, West Indies Ltd*) are steeped in popular
speech and musical rhythms. In tone they are close to the work of the *négritude*
writers (see under Martinique), but they look more towards Latin America than Africa.
The other poet-hero of the Revolution is the 19th-century writer and fighter for
freedom from Spain, José Martí.

Music and dance Cuban music, famously vibrant, is, again, a marriage of African
rhythms, expressed in percussion instruments (*batá drums*, *congas*, *claves*, *maracas*,
etc), and the Spanish guitar. Accompanying the music is an equally strong tradition of
dance. There are four basic elements out of which all others grow. The *rumba*
(drumming, singing about social preoccupations and dancing) is one of the original
black dance forms. By the end of the 19th century, it had been transferred from the
plantations to the slums; now it is a collective expression, with Saturday evening
competitions in which anyone can partake. Originating in eastern Cuba, *son* is the
music out of which *salsa* was born. *Son* itself takes many different forms and it gained
worldwide popularity after the 1920s when the National Septet of Ignacio Piñeiro
made it fashionable. The more sophisticated *danzón*, ballroom dance music which
was not accepted by the upper classes until the end of the 19th century, has also
been very influential. It was the root for the *cha-cha-cha* (invented in 1948 by Enrique
Jorrin). The fourth tradition is *trova*, the itinerant troubadour singing ballads, which
has been transformed, post-Revolution, into the *Nueva Trova*, made famous by
singers such as Pablo Milanés and Silvio Rodríguez. The new tradition adds politics
and everyday concerns to the romantic themes. There are many other styles, such as
the *guajira* (the most famous example of which is the song *Guantanamera*), *tumba
francesa* drumming and dancing, and Afro-Cuban jazz, performed by internationally
renowned artists like Irakere and Arturo Sandoval. Apart from sampling the
recordings of groups, put out by the state company Egrem, the National Folklore
Company (Conjunto Folklórico Nacional) gives performances of the traditional music
which it was set up to study and keep alive.

The international explosion of Cuban music, old and new, has led to a trend in
Cuban musical documentaries. The film that has made the greatest impact in recent
years is without a doubt Wim Wender's documentary *Buena Vista Social Club*
(Cuba/Germany, 1998), a nostalgic reconstruction of the lives and times of the band
of the same name, whose original members are now in their eighties and nineties or
dead. Rubén González's piano playing, Ibrahim Ferrer's crooning, accompanied by Ry
Cooder on guitar (with his son Joaquín Cooder, on drums) practising for two gigs in
Amsterdam (April 1998) and New York (July 1998) and – above all – the stunning
colour photography are quite unforgettable. Two Grammy Award winning CDs are
available: *Buena Vista Social Club* (WCD050) and *Buena Vista Social Club Presents
Ibrahim Ferrer* (WCD055).

Flora and fauna

When the Spanish arrived at the end of the 15th century more than 90% of Cuba was covered with forest. However, clearance for cattle raising and sugar cane reduced this proportion: 75% of the land is now savannah or plains and 4% swamps. A reforestation programme aims to increase Cuba's forests to 27% of the total area. Besides semi-deciduous woodland, vegetation types include rainforest, coastal and upland scrub, distinctive limestone vegetation found in the Sierra de los Organos and similar areas, savannah vegetation found on nutrient-deficient white silica sands, pine forests, xerophytic coastal limestone woodland, mangroves and other coastal wetlands. Cuba has extraordinarily high rates of biodiversity and endemism, particularly in four regions: the Montañas de Moa-Nipe-Sagua-Baracoa, which have the greatest diversity in all the Caribbean and are among the highest in the world, and 30% of the endemic species on the island; Parque Nacional Sierra de los Organos, the Reserva de la Biósfera Sierra del Rosario and the Reserva Ecológica del Macizo de Guamuhaya.

There are over 7000 plant species in Cuba, of which around 3000 are endemic and 950 are endangered, rare, or have become extinct in the last 350 years. Oddities in the plant world include the *Pinguicola lignicola*, the world's only carniverous epiphytic plant; the cork palm (*Microcycas colocoma*), an endemic living fossil which is a threatened species; and the *Solandra grandiflora*, one of the world's largest flowers, 10 cm across at the calyx and 30 cm at the corolla. There are around 100 different palm trees in Cuba, of which 90 are endemic. The Royal palm is the national tree and can be seen throughout the island. Cubans use the small, purple fruits to feed pigs, as they are oily and nutritious. There is one tiny orchid, *Pleurothallis shaferi* which is only 1 cm, with leaves measuring 5 mm and flowers of only 2 mm.

Animal life is also varied, with nearly 14,000 species of fauna, of which 10% could be on the verge of extinction. There are no native large mammals but some genera and families have diversified into a large number of distinct island species. These include mammals such as the hutia, bats and the protected manatee with more than 20 breeding groups, mostly in the Ciénaga de Zapata and north of Villa Clara. Reptiles range from 3 types of crocodiles including the Cuban crocodile now found only in the Ciénaga de Zapata (although they are farmed) to iguanas and tiny salamanders. Cuba claims the smallest of a number of animals, for example the Cuban pygmy frog, 12 mm long, the almiquí, a shrew-like insectivore, the world's smallest mammal, the butterfly or moth bat and the bee hummingbird, 63 mm long, called locally the *zunzuncito*. The latter is an endangered species, like the *carpintero* real woodpecker, the *cariara* or caracara, the pygmy owl, the Cuban green parrot and the *fermina*, or Zapata wren. Less attractively, there is also a dwarf scorpion, 10 mm long.

The best place for birdwatching on the island is the Zapata Peninsula, where 170 species of Cuban birds have been recorded, including the majority of endemic species. In winter migratory waterbirds, swallows and others visit the marshes. The national bird is the forest-dwelling Cuban trogon, the *tocororo*, partly because of its blue head, white chest and red underbelly, the colours of the Cuban flag.

Protected areas cover 30% of Cuba including its marine platform. There are 14 national parks and 4 UNESCO biosphere reserves: Guanahacabibes in the extreme western tip of the island; the Sierra del Rosario, 60 km west of Havana; Baconao in the east and Cuchillas del Toa. However, not all legally established conservation areas have any infrastructure, personnel or administration in place.

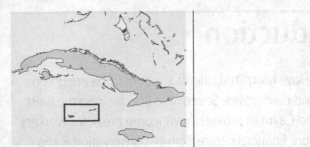

Cayman Islands

Introduction

These three low-lying little islands south of Cuba are green with pine and mangroves. Seven Mile Beach along the west side of Grand Cayman provides a welcome break for workers in the offshore financial centre. Nature conservation is top priority here, both on land and under water and there are a number of sanctuaries in the ponds and wetlands. The sister islands of Cayman Brac and Little Cayman are quiet, unhurried places where you can escape the crowds and relax without giving up your creature comforts. A dive destination ranked among the world's best, the islands offer a variety of thrilling dive sites. Famous for their underwater scenery, there are tropical fish of all kinds in the waters surrounding the islands, especially in the coral reefs, and green turtles are now increasing in numbers, having been deliberately restocked by excess hatchings at the Cayman Turtle Farm.

In September 2004 Grand Cayman experienced the full force of Hurricane Ivan with winds of around 155 mph and an 8-ft storm surge resulting in waves exceeding 23 ft. Grand Cayman became two islands for a while, as waters coming across the North Sound collided with surge generated from the South Sound. The force of the hurricane sent boats floating through villages, flooded the airport and destroyed or damaged the majority of buildings. Inhabitants were left without communications, power or water. By 2005, however, the trees were beginning to green up again and tourist facilities were mostly open for business, but the island remained a building site as repairs or rebuilding works continued. There was some reef damage, particularly to sponges, but a clean-up by dive operators soon removed the evidence. Little Cayman and Cayman Brac were not so badly hit by Ivan, but some hotels took the opportunity to upgrade their buildings while carrying out repairs.

★ Don't miss ...

1 *MV Captain Keith Tibbetts* A Russian frigate deliberately sunk in 1996 30m off Cayman Brac. Now a well-established wreck dive site and good snorkelling site 9-35m deep, with lots of coral and fish, page 183.

2 **Pedro St James** The oldest stone structure still standing in the Cayman Islands and a national landmark because it was here the decision was made in 1831 to introduce democracy to Grand Cayman, page 187.

3 **Queen Elizabeth II Botanic Park** Beautiful gardens in a 65-acre park, with trails, lakes, forest and swamps, page 188.

4 **Little Cayman** Quiet and peaceful, with a tiny population and a handful of small hotels, this is the place to come to get away from stress and do nothing but dive, or nothing at all, page 198.

5 **Cayman Brac Parrot Reserve** The sanctuary protects about 400 endangered Cayman Brac parrots in dry woodland up on the bluff on rocky terrain and the endemic birds fly in and out at dusk and dawn, page 204.

Cayman Islands

Caribbean Sea

Cayman Islands

GRAND CAYMAN
North Sound
Rum Point
West Bay
George Town
Savannah
Bodden Town
Gun Bay

LITTLE CAYMAN
Bloody Bay
Owen Island
South Town

CAYMAN BRAC
Stake Bay
Spot Bay
West End

N

0 km   20
0 miles   20

Essentials

Before you travel

Documents A passport or birth certificate and photo ID (but not voter registration card) are required for citizens of Canada, UK and British Dependent Territories; visas are not required. Passports are required for visitors of all other countries including the USA. Everyone needs a return or onward airline ticket. Visas are not required for citizens of Commonwealth countries, Andorra, Argentina, Austria, Bahrain, Belgium, Brazil, Chile, Costa Rica, Denmark, Ecuador, El Salvador, Finland, France, Germany, Greece, Guatemala, Iceland, Irish Republic, Israel, Italy, Japan, Kuwait, Liechtenstein, Luxembourg, Mexico, Monaco, Netherlands, Norway, Oman, Panama, Peru, Portugal, San Merino, Saudi Arabia, Spain, Sweden, Switzerland and Venezuela. If you are from any of these countries you may be admitted to the Cayman Islands for a period of up to six months. Resident aliens of the USA who show a valid US Alien Registration Card (Green Card) may enter and remain in the Cayman Islands for 30 days. Visas are required by all countries not included in the above list and should be applied for at the nearest British Consulate or High Commission Office. Temporary work permits are available for business people on a short visit; these can be obtained in advance from the Department of Immigration, PO Box 1098 GT, Grand Cayman, T9498052. If you want to work in the country you may not accept a job unless you have a government-issued work permit.

Tourist offices overseas

Canada, 234 Eglinton Av East, Suite 306, Toronto, Ontario, M4P IK5, T416-4851550, info-canada@caymanislands.ky.
UK, 6 Arlington St, London, SW1A 1RE, T020-74917771, www.caymanislands.co.uk.
USA, 8300 NW 53rd St, Suite 103, Miami, FL 33166, T305-5999033; One Lincoln Centre, 18W140 Butterfield Rd, Suite 920, Oakbrook Terrace, IL 60181, T 630-7050650; 2 Memorial City Plaza, 820 Gessner, Suite 170, Houston, Texas 77024, T713-4611317; 3 Park Av, 39th Floor, New York, NY 10016, T212-8899009, info-usa@caymanislands.ky.

Money

The legal **currency** is the Cayman Islands dollar (CI$). The **exchange rate** is fixed at CI$1 to US$1.20, or CI$0.80 to US$1, although officially the exchange rate is CI$0.84 to US$1. US currency is readily accepted throughout the islands (although all change will be returned in CI$) and Canadian and British currencies can be exchanged at all banks. There is no exchange control. **Credit cards** are accepted nearly everywhere. Personal cheques are not generally welcome. Traveller's cheques are preferred. Most of the major international **banks** are represented in George Town, Grand Cayman but not all offer normal banking facilities. Commercial banking hours are Monday-Thursday 0900-1600 and Friday 0900-1630.

Getting there

Air All international flights land in Grand Cayman. **Cayman Airways** and **Island Air** connect the sister islands, Cayman Brac and Little Cayman.

From Europe British Airways flies from London via Nassau, so two-centre visits are possible. There are also daily **BA** flights to Miami, which connect with **Cayman Airways** and only take an hour longer.

From North America The number of routes and destinations increases in winter, when there are also lots of charter flights, but the following are year-round: the national flag carrier, **Cayman Airways**, has regular services to Grand Cayman from Chicago, Fort Lauderdale, Houston, Miami and Tampa in the USA and a direct flight

from Miami to Cayman Brac. **American Airlines** flies from Miami. **US Airways** flies from
Charlotte. **Continental** flies from New York (Newark). **Delta** flies from Atlanta.
Northwest flies from Detroit. **Air Canada** flies from Toronto. **Sunworld** from Cincinnati.

From the Caribbean Air Jamaica and **Cayman Airways** share a service from
Kingston and Montego Bay. **Isleña (Grupo Taca)** flies from La Ceiba, Honduras.
Cubana and **Cayman Airways** fly to/from Havana, Cuba (contact **Lily Tours**, T9450871,
or **Cayman Airways**, T9492311).

Airport information Air communications are good and there are two
international airports, the **Owen Roberts International Airport** on Grand Cayman and
the **Gerrard Smith Airport** on Cayman Brac. Owen Roberts International Airport is
situated less than 2 miles from the centre of George Town and only 10 minutes' drive
from most of the hotels on Seven Mile Beach. In a plaza outside the terminal there are
car hire companies and a café, open 0600-1800.

Airlines Cayman Airways, T9492311 on Grand Cayman, T9481221 on Cayman
Brac, www.camanairways.com. **Island Air**, T9490241 (charters), T9495252
(reservations), F9497044, online reservations can be made at http://.islandair.ky. **Air
Jamaica**, T9492300. **American Airlines**, T9490666. **Northwest Airlines**, T9492955/6.
US Air, T9497488.

Boat The islands are not served by scheduled passenger ships but they are a
popular port of call for cruise ships and there are cargo services between the islands,
Kingston in Jamaica, Honduras and Costa Rica and Miami and Tampa in the USA.
There are three cruise ship terminals in George Town. The port at Creek, Cayman Brac,
can handle the same vessels but Little Cayman only has a small facility.

Touching down
Tourist information Information may be obtained from the **Cayman Islands
Department of Tourism** ① *Leeward 2, Regatta Business Park, West Bay Rd, Grand
Cayman, KY1-1102, BWI, T9490623, toll free 1800-3463313, www.caymanislands.ky,
0830-1700*. The **Department of Tourism** publishes a **Travel Planner** annually, giving
hotel prices as well as other useful information. The **Cayman Islands National Trust**
① *Dart Park, 588 South Church St, www.nationaltrust.org.ky*, has a lot of historical
and environmental information.

The **Cayman Islands Government Information Services** ① *The Pavilion, Cricket
Sq, Grand Cayman, T9498092, F9498487*, publishes a series of booklets including
Marine Parks Rules and Sea Code in The Cayman Islands and several on banking,
captive insurance, company registration, residential status, work permits, living in
the Cayman Islands, etc.

Getting around
Air Cayman Airways Express provide inter-island services from Grand Cayman to
Cayman Brac and Little Cayman and return (see Airlines above). There are several
flights a day from Grand Cayman to Cayman Brac and Little Cayman. You can have a
full day on either sister island. Fares are US$132.60 day trip Grand Cayman to Little
Cayman or Cayman Brac (US$50.30 day trip Cayman Brac to Little Cayman).

Sleeping
Accommodation is plentiful and varied, ranging from resort hotels on the beach to
small, out of the way, family-run guesthouses, but it is not cheap and you will not get a
double room for less than US$60 on any of the islands. There is also a wide variety of
cottages, apartments (condominiums) and villas available for daily, weekly or
monthly rental, which can work out more economical if you are in a group. Most
hotels offer watersports, scuba diving and snorkelling, and many have tennis courts,
swimming pools and other facilities. A government tax of 10% is added to the room

▮ Touching down

Business hours **Banks**: Mon-Thu 0900-1600, Fri 0900-1630; **Offices**: 0830-1600; **Shops**: 0900-1700.
Currency Cayman Islands dollar (CI$). US currency is readily accepted (although all change will be returned in CI$). Credit cards are accepted nearly everywhere.
Departure tax US$25/CI$20 for all visitors aged 12 and over included in the price of your airline ticket.
Emergency numbers T911.
Country code +345.

Official time Eastern Standard Time, 5 hours behind GMT.
Safety The Cayman Islands are safe to visit and present no need for extra security precautions. However, drugs-related offences have increased. The islands remain a major trans-shipment point. Care must be taken when walking on roads, especially at night; they are narrow and vehicles move fast.
Voltage 110 voltage, 60 cycles.
Weights and measures Imperial.

charge and most hotels also add a 10-15% service charge to the bill in lieu of tipping. The winter season, running from 16 December to 15 April, is the peak tourist season. Visitors intending to come to the islands during this period are advised to make hotel and travel arrangements well in advance. There are substantial reductions during the rest of the year, with cut rates or even free accommodation for children under 12.

Eating

The range of restaurants is wide and all styles are available from fast food to gourmet. Check your bill as gratuities are sometimes added. Cayman-style fish is sautéed with tomato, onion, pepper and piquant seasoning. Conch is available as chowder, fritters or marinated. Try Caymanian rum cake for dessert. The **Tortuga Rum Company** ① *T9497701, bakery daily 0730-1700*, has many outlets plus a 2,500-sq ft bakery, where up to 5,000 rum cakes are baked daily for shipment worldwide. While the recipe remains a family secret, a key component is the use of *Tortuga Gold Rum*, which is not sold to the public. You can visit and sample the varieties of rum cake, purchase the rum blends or other locally made items such as fudge, hot pepper sauce, steak sauce or flavoured coffee. The **Cayman Islands Brewery Ltd** ① *(formerly the Stingray Brewery), Red Bay, east of George Town, T9476699*, has had a multimillion dollar investment to install German technology and will eventually produce up to 13,000 barrels of beer for island consumption and export, every year. **Icoa Chocolates** ① *Seven Mile Shops, George Town, T9451915, Mon-Fri 0900-1700, Sat 1130-1700*, makes delicacies blended with local ingredients such as Caribbean spice, Cayman honey and coconut.

Festivals and events

Jan New Year's Day.
Mar/Apr Ash Wed, Good Fri Easter Mon.
3rd Mon in May Discovery Day.
Jun Mon after the Queen's official birthday.

1st Mon in Jul Constitution Day.
Nov Mon after Remembrance Sun.
Dec Christmas Day and Boxing Day.

Shopping

As a free port, there is duty-free shopping and a range of British glass, crystal, china, woollens, perfumes and spirits are available. US citizens are entitled to a US$400 exemption after being away from the USA for 48 hours. Black coral carvings and jewellery are widely available. Note that since the 1978 **Cayman Islands Marine Conservation Law** prohibited the removal of coral from local waters, manufacturers turned to Belize and Honduras for their supply. All the Central American countries are now members of CITES, so if you must buy it, check the source in case it has been procured illegally. Caymanite is a semi-precious gem stone with layers of various colours found only in the Cayman Islands. Local craftspeople use it to make jewellery.

Sport and activities

Diving and snorkelling Since 1986, a Marine Parks plan has been implemented to preserve the beauty and marine life of the islands. Even before then, however, a moorings project was in place. This has been highly successful in marine conservation and critical in protecting Cayman's fragile coral reefs and marine life from destruction by boat anchors. Permanent moorings have been installed along the west coast of Grand Cayman where there is concentrated diving, and also outside the marine parks

❦ *The best months for diving are April to October.*

in order to encourage diving boats to disperse and lessen anchor damage to the reefs. Make sure you check all rules and regulations as there have been several prosecutions and convictions for offences such as taking conch or lobsters. The import of spearguns or speargun parts and their use without a licence is banned. Divers and snorkellers must use a flag attached to a buoy when outside safe swimming areas. For further information call **Natural Resources (Department of Environment)** ① T9498469.

Although boats take snorkellers to many sites, you can snorkel quite happily from the shore. However, each island has a wall going down to extraordinary depths: the north wall of Cayman Brac drops from 60 to 14,000 ft, while the south wall drops to 18,000 ft. The deepest known point in the Caribbean is the **Cayman Trench**, 40 miles south of Cayman Brac, where soundings have indicated a depth of 24,724 ft. The *Dive Sites of the Cayman Islands*, by Lawson Wood (latest edition published by McGraw-Hill in 2001), describes 260 dive and snorkel sites around the islands, together with beautiful underwater photographs mostly taken by the author. One site is the **Russian frigate** (a Brigadier Type II Class), brought from Cuba and deliberately sunk in 1996 to provide good wreck diving off Cayman Brac. The 330-ft relic of the Cold War was sunk on a sloping bed of sand 27-72 ft deep and only 90 ft from the shore,

❦ *Many of the better reefs and several wrecks are found in water shallow enough to require only mask, snorkel and fins; the swimming is easy and the fish are friendly*

good for snorkellers as well as divers. It has been renamed the *MV Captain Keith Tibbetts*, after a popular resident of Cayman Brac, and its sinking was supervised by Jean Michel Cousteau, who stood on the bridge and 'went down with the ship'. Mounted underwater cameras will monitor the growth of coral, etc.

The dive-tourism market is highly developed in the Cayman Islands and there is plenty of choice, but it has been often described as a cattle market with dive boats taking very large parties. Many companies offer full services to certified divers as well as courses designed to introduce scuba diving to novices; there are many highly qualified instructor-guides. There is a firm limit of a depth of 100 ft for visiting divers, regardless of training and experience and the 69 member companies of the CIWOA will not allow you to exceed that. A complete selection of diving and fishing tackle, underwater cameras and video equipment is available for hire. The tourist office has a full price list for all operators. There is also the liveaboard *Cayman Aggressor IV*, which accommodates 18 divers and cruises around Grand Cayman, Cayman Brac and Little Cayman, depending on weather conditions. Contact **Aggressor Fleet Limited** ① T9495551, www.aggressor.com.

Health

Grand Cayman is sprayed frequently though it is advisable to bring insect repellent to combat mosquitoes and sandflies. Little Cayman is sprayed every two weeks.

Medical care on Grand Cayman is good and readily available. There is a 128-bed

Cayman Islands Hospital ① *George Town, T9498600*, with accident and emergency unit. For 24-hour **ambulance and paramedic service** on Grand Cayman, T911. A two-person, double-lock **recompression chamber** is located by the hospital and supervised by a physician experienced in hyperbaric medicine. Outpatients pay a fixed charge per visit. The **Chrissie Tomlinson Memorial Hospital** ① *George Town, T9496066*, is private, with 18 beds and outpatient clinics. There is a 12-bed hospital in **Cayman Brac** ① *T9482243/2245*, and a clinic on **Little Cayman** ① *T9480072, Mon, Wed,Fri 0900-1300, Tue, Thu 1300-1700, or on call 24 hrs*, staffed by a registered nurse. A doctor visits every Wednesday.

Keeping in touch

Communications Post The **Philatelic Bureau** releases six stamp issues a year. Stamps are sold separately or as a First Day Cover from CI\$0.10 to 2.00. Airmail postal rates are divided into three groups. **Group A:** the Caribbean, USA, Canada, Central America and Venezuela, first class CI\$0.75, second class, post cards, airletters CI\$0.20. **Group B:** Europe, Scandinavia, West Africa, South America, first class CI\$1. **Group C:** East Africa, the Arabian sub-continent, Asia and the Far East, first class CI\$1.

  Telephone and internet IDD code: +345. The Cayman Islands have a modern automatic telephone system. Public international telephone booths are at **Cable & Wireless** ① *Anderson Sq, Mon-Thu 0815-1700, Fri 0815-1600, Sat 0815-1300*. **Communication Station** ① *Fort St, George Town, Mon-Sat 0830-1700*, there are 32 telephones, five internet kiosks, a photocopier, fax machine and phone cards for sale. Many hotels offer internet access for guests. The international code is followed by a 7-digit local number. For overseas credit card calls (Visa and Mastercard) dial 0 for operator and follow instructions.

Media The *Caymanian Compass*, www.caycompass.com, is published Monday-Friday with a circulation of 25,000. For news and information visit *Cayman Net News* at www.caymannetnews.com.

Grand Cayman → *IDD code: 345. Colour map 1, C2. Population 52,466.*

Grand Cayman is a prosperous island with a British feel despite the huge American influence on tourism. The island is green with luxuriant vegetation, especially at the East End where there are pastures and grazing cows. North Sound is a 40-square-mile lagoon with mangroves, although dredging schemes and urban growth threaten the mangrove habitat and the reefs. Some low-key but sophisticated development has taken place along the north coast around Cayman Kai, which has lovely beaches and good swimming and snorkelling. Most of the tourist development is along Seven Mile Beach on West Bay, where there are hotels, clubs, sports facilities, banks, restaurants and supermarkets. ▶▶ *For Sleeping, Eating and other listings, see pages 189-196.*

Ins and outs

Getting there and around See page 180 for details of flights from London, Toronto and US cities as well as from neighbouring islands. Driving is on the left and the roads are in good order. The Public Transportation Board offers a recorded information service at T9455100, giving details on buses, taxis, limousines and tour buses, including routes and fares. There is a bus service all over the island with marked stops. If you stand by the road minibuses will toot their horns to see if you want a ride. Be careful of buses whose doors open into the centre of the road. Island tours can be arranged at about US\$60 for a taxi, or US\$10 per person on a bus with a minimum of 20 people. Check with your hotel for full details. ▶▶ *See Transport, page 196 for more details.*

⁝ Heritage One passport

Interesting places to visit in Grand Cayman are included in a Heritage passport, with discounts of 25% to the National Museum, Turtle Farm, Pedro St James and Queen Elizabeth II Botanic Garden. The green and blue passports are stamped at each site but have no expiry date. They are available at each attraction, CI$19.95 adults, CI$10.95 children.

George Town → *Population: over 18,000.*

The largest town and capital of the islands is George Town, which is principally a business centre dominated by modern office blocks. However, many of the older buildings are being restored and the government is trying to promote museums and societies to complement beach and watersports tourism. When cruise ships come in the town can be exceptionally crowded, but at other times it is a quiet place where people work rather than live.

The **Cayman Islands National Museum** ① *renovated and reopened 2007, T9498368, www.museum.ky, Mon-Fri 0900-1700, Sat 1000-1400, closed first Mon of every month for exhibit maintenance, US$5, children 6-18 US$2.50, children under 6 or in school uniforms, college students with ID and senior citizens free*, in the restored Old Courts Building, has exhibits portraying the nation's seafaring history, an audiovisual presentation and a natural history display, as well as temporary exhibitions. There is a CD-ROM interactive exhibit, where you can access nearly 400 images of traditional sand yards, provision gardens and other features of typical Caymanian life as it used to be. There are also audio segments where you can hear accounts by older Caymanians about backing sand, caboose cooking, tending provision gardens, making grounds and sharing the harvest with neighbours. There is a museum shop and The Cool Caboose for refreshments.

Four of the older buildings which are being preserved are the work of a local boat-builder, Captain Rayal Brazley Bodden, MBE, JP (1885-1976). He was called upon to build the **Elmslie Memorial Church** (Presbyterian, on Harbour Drive, opposite the docks) in 1923. He put in a remarkable roof, with timbers largely salvaged from shipwrecks. Admiration was such that he was asked to design the **Town Hall**, a peace memorial for the First World War. It now looks tiny, but when it was opened in 1926 it was considered a grandiose folly, far too big for the island. Then came the **Public Library** nearby, with its hammer-beam roof and painted British university heraldic

Grand Cayman

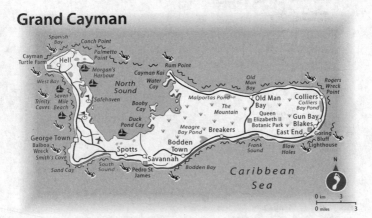

shields. Lastly came the **General Post Office,** 1939, which once housed all the colony's departments of government. Bodden surrounded the main façades of the building with art deco tapered columns. All his buildings have an inter-war flavour. They are one-storey, made of shaped concrete blocks, poured to give a rustic, deep-grooved effect.

An archaeological dig on the waterfront on the site of **Fort George** has been sponsored by the **Cayman National Trust** ① *T9490121*. Unfortunately only a small part of the walls remain, much was demolished in 1972 by a developer who would have destroyed the lot if residents had not prevented him. The National Trust has designed a walking tour of George Town to include 28 sites of interest, such as Fort George, built around 1790, the Legislative Assembly, the war and peace memorials and traditional Caymanian architecture. A brochure and map (free) is available from the National Trust, or the tourist office. Walking tours are also available for West Bay and Bodden Town.

There is a duty-free shopping mall close to George Town harbour containing a 12,000-gallon saltwater aquarium, stocked with colourful fish.

The **butterfly farm** ① *Lawrence Blvd, opposite the cinema, T9463411, www.thebutterflyfarm.com, daily 0830-1600, last tour at 1530, US$15 adults, US$9 children, 3 and under free, admission includes guided tour, reusable ticket during your stay on the island*, is a tropical garden containing 34 different species of butterflies from around the world, best in the morning and in full sun when the butterflies are most active although afternoons are better for photography. Wear bright colours to attract them; they also like citrus-based perfume.

Around the island

The **Cayman Turtle Farm** ① *Boatswain's Beach, Northpoint West, PO Box 645GT, T9493893/4, www.turtle.ky, daily 0830-1700, adults US$75 including lagoons and snorkel programme, US$50 without, children 2-12 US$35 and US$25, transport from certain hotels US$10-15, days vary*, houses over 11,000 green turtles and is the only commercial turtle farm in the world. Most of the turtles are used for meat locally since the USA banned the import of turtle meat, but some 30,000 turtles have been released into the wild to replenish native stocks. They are released as yearlings weighing 3-6 lbs. Those at the farm range in size from 2 oz hatchlings to breeding stock and old-timers weighing up to 600 lbs. They are kept in overcrowded, murky

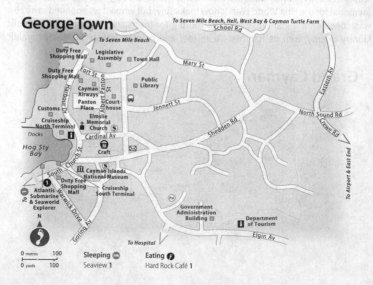

George Town

To Seven Mile Beach, Hell, West Bay & Cayman Turtle Farm

To Seven Mile Beach

School Rd

Mary St

Duty Free Shopping Mall
Legislative Assembly
Town Hall
Duty Free Shopping Mall
Fort St
Public Library
Cayman Airways
Panton Place
Court-house
Jennett St
Customs
Elmslie Memorial Church
Cruiseship North Terminal
Cardinal Av
Docks
Hog Sty Bay
Craft
Cayman Islands National Museum
Duty Free Shopping Mall
Cruiseship South Terminal
Atlantis Submarine & Seaworld Explorer
N
Government Administration Building
Department of Tourism
Harbour Dr
Albert Panton St
South Church St
Warwick Drive
Goring Av
Shedden Rd
North Sound Rd
Eastern Av
Crewe Rd
Elgin Av

To Airport & East End

To Hospital

0 metres 100
0 yards 100

Sleeping
Seaview 1

Eating
Hard Rock Café 1

Stingray City

Stingray City is a popular local phenomenon, where it is possible to swim with and observe large groups of extremely tame rays in only 12 ft of water. They come for food and it is an entirely unnatural concentration of fish. Stingray City is better dived but half a mile away is the sandbar where stingrays also congregate, usually over 30 at a time, although there are thought to be around 250 in the area. The water here is only 1-3 ft deep and crystal clear, so you hop out of your boat and the rays brush past you waiting to be fed.

Their mouths are beneath their head and the rays, 3 ft across, swim into your arms to be fed on squid. They can give your arm quite a suck if they miss the food in your hand. Unfortunately the sandbar can get too popular. Thousands of cruise ship passengers crowd into a small area and there are no limitations on the number of boats allowed to visit. There are lots of options, with motor boats, sailing boats and glass-bottomed boats offering wading, snorkelling or diving at varying prices.

concrete pools with no landscaping or features to stimulate the turtles, which may be up to the standards of a slaughterhouse, but do not adhere to aquarium standards. Polished turtle shells are sold here for about US$100, but their import into the USA is prohibited. International trade in turtle products is prohibited under CITES international legislation. In November 2001, a surge storm associated with Hurricane Michelle seriously damaged the farm's sea walls allowing 275 breeding turtles to escape. A few were recovered but it was decided that relocation was essential to prevent it happening again. **Boatswain's Beach** (pronounced Bo'sun's Beach) expansion was completed in 2005, with a snorkel lagoon, research facility, predator tank, aviary, iguana sanctuary, shops, restaurants and nature trail.

In a further conflict with Cayman's policies to protect the environment and natural resources, two separate dolphin entertainment facilities have been granted planning permission: one at the old turtle farm in West Bay as part of Boatswain's Beach, and the other south of Calypso Grill in Batabano, West Bay, by the North Sound. Dolphin Discovery (Cayman) Ltd is to import eight dolphins from Mexico for the former while Dolphin Cove Cayman will stock the latter with dolphins caught in the wild by Cuba. These highly controversial proposals for the entertainment of cruise sh   isitors have received local and international opposition. So far, only one cruise company Regent Seven Seas Cruises, has taken the bold step of not promoting dolphinarium   on their cruises. For further information, see www.marineconnection.org.

West Bay is a colourful area with houses dating back to the seafaring days. The National Trust has a self-guided walkers' booklet of the area, directing you along lanes and paths with illustrated information about the district. The **Pink House**, built in 1912, is included in tour itineraries as a typical Caymanian home. Originally home to the Bothwell family, it is now open to the public. **Hell**, situated near West Bay, is a rock formation worth visiting. There's a gift shop and you can have your cards and letters postmarked at the **sub-post office** ⓘ *Mon-Fri 0800-1700, Sat 0830-1130*.

On the south coast at Savannah, just off the main coastal road, **Pedro St James** ⓘ *T9473329, www.pedrostjames.ky, daily 0900-1700, US$10, children under12 free*, has been developed into a national landmark. On 4 December 1831 a historic meeting was held here at which it was decided to split the island into districts with representation, and democracy was introduced. The site has the oldest known existing stone structure in the Cayman Islands. The original building is believed to have been built of quarried native rock around 1780 by William Eden, a plantation owner, and are the only known remains of a late 18th-century residence on the island. The upper floors are of mahogany with a fine balcony. There are a number of outbuildings and traditional activities which recreate plantation life. An impressive Visitors' Centre offers the opportunity to learn about the history of the site before beginning the tour. A state-of-the-art, interactive multimedia theatre features a 20-minute show (1000-1600, every hour on the hour) that brings to life the people, their dramas and the conditions in which they struggled, including a storm.

There are caves in **Bodden Town**, believed to have been used by pirates, where you can see bones and stocks, and a line of unmarked graves in an old cemetery on the shore opposite, said to be those of buccaneers. Bodden Town was once the capital of the island and all shipping came here. Continuing east just after Half Moon Bay you will see blowholes: waterspouts that rise above the coral rock in unusual patterns as a result of water being funnelled along passages in the rock as the waves come rolling in.

The **Queen Elizabeth II Botanic Park** ① *Frank Sound Rd, T9473558 (information line), 9479462, www.botanic-park.ky, daily 0900-1830, 1730 in winter, last admission one hour earlier, US$7.50, children 6-12 US$5, separate charge for the iguana facility, taxi from cruise ship dock US$50 one way, bus from town on North Side route CI$2*, was officially opened by the Queen in 1994. A mile-long woodland trail has been cleared and an entrance garden created. In 1997 a second phase brought a Floral Colour Garden and a Heritage Garden, with endemic plants, within the park. The trees and gardens took a beating from Hurricane Ivan and were closed until end-April 2005, but regeneration was swift. Orchids bloom in May and June and there are breeding areas for the Grand Cayman parrot, the Cayman rabbit and the Cayman anole lizard. In 2005 a new Cayman Blue Iguana Facility was opened (www.blueiguana.ky), where visitors can see the iguanas up close, learn about them and about the conservation efforts to save them from extinction. There are many wild blue iguanas now running through the Botanic Park so you will see them even if you don't go to the Iguana Facility. There are special events, which are sometimes held, such as an orchid show, in February, and a mango morning in August. There is a Visitor Centre, café and giftshop and a typical Caymanian cottage and garden has been built.

At the east end of the island there is a good viewing point at the **Goring Bluff lighthouse**. A trip to **Gun Bay** at the east end of the island will show you the scene of the famous 'Wreck of the Ten Sails', which took place in 1788 (see page 202).

A drive along the north coast to **Rum Point** (see below) is picturesque, with views of the sea through the vegetation. There are lots of villas and plots of land for sale along the coast and all development is upmarket. The return journey can be made via Frank Sound and the Botanic Park (see page 188) to complete a circular trip.

The National Trust organizes guided village walks and has opened a nature trail, the **Mastic Trail**, a two-mile walk through a variety of habitats: black mangrove wetland, stands of royal palms and silver thatch palms, abandoned agricultural land and extensive ancient dry forest. It starts near the south coast and ends near the north coast, from where a van will carry you back to the start. It takes about 2½ hours, moderate fitness recommended, US$50 per person (see Hiking, page 195).

For a pleasurable day's outing, arrange a boat trip to **North Sound** for US$35 or so. This will include snorkelling, fishing and a good look at marine life on a barrier reef. Your guide will cook fish, fresh marinated conch or lobster, for you, delicious and highly recommended. You can also take a moonlit cruise aboard the *Jolly Roger* or the *Valhalla*, T9498988 (sunset buffet dinner cruise US$60; cocktail cruise US$40, daily, weather permitting).

Beaches and activities

West Bay Beach, now known as **Seven Mile Beach**, has dazzling white sand and is lined by hotels, tall Australian pines and silver thatch palms, the national tree.

Beaches on the east and north coasts are equally good, and are protected by an offshore barrier reef. On the north coast, at **Cayman Kai**, there is a superb public beach with changing facilities; from here you can snorkel along the reef to **Rum Point**. The beaches around Rum Point are recommended for peace and quiet, with shallow water safe for children. **Red Sail Sports** at Rum Point also ensure lots of entertainment, with wind surfers, sail boats, wave runners and waterskiing as well as glass-bottomed boat tours to see the stingrays and scuba diving. There are hammocks, sunbeds, lockers, changing rooms, showers, restaurants, bar and Thomas the tabby cat. Around Rum Point at Water Cay and Finger Cay there are picnic sites on the lagoon. Take insect repellent. South of George Town there are good beaches for swimming and snorkelling at **Smith's Cove** and **Sand Cay**. In Frank Sound, **Heritage Beach**, just west of Cottage Point, is owned by the National Trust.

Diving Snorkelling and dive sites abound all round the island and include shallow dives for beginners as well as highly challenging and deeper dives for the experienced. Off the west coast there are three wrecks, arches, tunnels, caves, canyons and lots of reef sites close to shore which can be enjoyed by snorkellers and divers. Along the south coast the coral reefs are rich and varied with depths ranging from 15 ft to thousands of feet. The **East End wall** has pinnacles, tunnels and a coral formation known as **The Maze**, a 500-ft coral formation of caverns, chimneys, arches and crevices. There are several wrecks here also. Snorkelling is good near the **Morritt's Tortuga Club** at the East End, also all along **Seven Mile Beach**, **North Sound**, **Smith Cove** in South Sound and off **Eden Rock**, near George Town. Along the north coast you can dive the **North Wall**. Near **Rum Point Channel** experienced divers can dive the Grand Canyon, where depths start at 70 ft. The canyons, collapsed reefs, are 150 ft wide in places. Other sites in this area towards **Palmetto Point** include the aptly-named **Eagle Ray Pass**, **Tarpon Alley** and **Stingray City**.

The popular and accessible dive sites are off South Sound or North West Point, where the wall or mini walls are close to shore. Boat dives go to the many sites along Seven Mile Beach or the North Wall, which is much more dramatic but generally a little rougher. Prices for a certification course start at US$300, rising to US$500; for qualified divers, a two-tank dive costs US$50-75 and a Stingray City dive US$40-60, depending on how far the boat has to come. Snorkelling trips are also available, US$20-40.

Grand Cayman is host to a revolutionary product for youngsters under 12 who are too young to use standard scuba equipment. Children as young as 4 can now snorkel with a **SASY** (approved by **PADI** and **NAUI**). **Supplied Air Snorkelling for Youth** (SASY) is a scuba unit customized to fit children, allowing the child to float safely on the surface and view the marine world below without danger of being submerged. SASY units are available at all **Red Sail Sports** ① *www.redsail.com*, locations in Grand Cayman. ▸▸ *See also pages 183 and 194.*

● Sleeping

Grand Cayman *p184, map p185 and p186*
There are about 50 hotels along Seven Mile Beach; almost all of the major US chains are represented, including **Marriott**, **Hyatt** and **Westin**, offering all types of luxury accommodation. There are guesthouses catering for divers in the suburbs south of George Town.
LL Beach Club Colony, T9498100, www.caymanresortsonline.com/beachclub/. 41-room beachfront hotel reopened

mid-2005, the only all-inclusive resort on Seven Mile Beach, 3 miles from George Town, tropical in ambiance and decor, full range of facilities including bar, restaurant, a/c, internet access, TV, watersports and dive shop.
LL Cobalt Coast Resort & Suites, north of Seven Mile Beach, past Turtle Farm on Boatswains Bay, T9465656, www.cobaltcoast.com. Built in the style of a Great House, small and intimate, 18 rooms in 1-2 bedroom suites and villas sleeping up to

6, kitchens, **Duppies** restaurant, pool, jacuzzi, dock, dive shop on site.

LL Royal Reef Resort, East End, Colliers Bay, T9473100, www.royalreef.com. 90-room beachfront hotel, tranquil setting in the less crowded East End, full facilities including beauty salon, floodlit tennis courts, pool and dive shop.

LL-L Comfort Suites and Resort, West Bay Rd, just south of the **Marriott**, Seven Mile Beach, T9457300, www.caymancomfort.com. On the beach side of the road but not beach-front, about 300 ft from sea behind condos, 110 suites, studios and spacious 1-2 bedroom suites with full kitchens, some accessible for wheelchair guests, phones, restaurant, **Stingers** bar, meeting room, fitness centre, child care facilities, pool, scuba and watersports rental on site, dive packages available.

LL-L Grand Caymanian Beach Club and Resort, North Sound, T 9493100, www.grandcaymanian.ky. 5-star, full-service resort, studios, 1 to 2-bedroom suites, grand villas, all with lots of luxury facilities, kitchens, jacuzzis, pool, barbecues, children's playground, Kid's Club, fitness centre, gift shop, concierge, watersports.

LL-L Sunset House, south of George Town, T9497111, www.sunsethouse.com. 59 rooms, no smoking, dedicated dive hotel on rocky shoreline, good shore diving, a bronze statue of a mermaid called Amphitrite (Poseidon's wife, queen of the sea) has been sunk in 50 ft of water for snorkellers and divers to enjoy.

L-AL Turtle Nest Inn, Bodden Town, T9478665, www.turtlenestinn.com. On a quiet, protected beach with excellent snorkelling, 8 smart 1-bedroom apartments with sofa beds, TV, phone, a/c, fans, laundry room, maid service, gas barbecue, pool, internet access.

AL Annie's Place, 282 Andrew Drive, Snug Harbour, Seven Mile Beach, behind Grand Pavilion, T9455505, www.anniesplace.ky. 2 bedrooms, breakfast included, a/c, fan, TV, fridge, no smoking, 2 sitting rooms, 1 with TV and library, beach chairs and towels.

AL Eldemire's Guest House, South Church St, T9495387, www.eldemire.com. A friendly 'home away from home' atmosphere, room, studio or apartment, 1 mile from town, ½ mile from beach, bicycles, hammocks, wheelchair accessible, Wi-Fi on property, free

snorkelling trip to Stingray City, water surcharge US$5 pp.

A Wild Orchid Inn, 120 Northward Rd, Bodden Town, T/F9472298, orchidin@candw.ky. Breakfast included, a/c, kitchen, TV, jacuzzi, internet access.

Self-catering

Basic cottages may cost US$900-1,000 per week per house. For those wishing to stay longer, 2-bedroom, furnished houses can be found away from the tourist areas in places such as **Breakers** or **Bodden Town** for US$700-1,000 a month.

Cayman Villas, T9454144, www.caymanvillas.com. Luxury villas, apartments and beachfront properties all round the island, along Seven Mile Beach and North Side, including the exclusive resort area of Cayman Kai.

Eating

Grand Cayman *p184, map p185 and p186*
There are about 200 restaurants on Grand Cayman ranging from gourmet standards, to smaller places serving native dishes, see www.caymangoodtaste.com or www.bestofcayman.com for partial lists. In George Town, many cater for the lunchtime trade of office workers. Eating out is not cheap, but you pay for what you get, and food is usually excellent. For dinner, main courses range from about US$10 to US$60 or more for a full meal including wine. Lunch prices can be around US$7-15 and breakfast from about US$5. Excellent Sun brunch buffets, all you can eat, with orange juice and sparkling wine, at the **Hyatt** (T9491234, recommended for meat and spit roasts) and the **Westin** (T9453800, recommended for fish and sushi, but it also has pasta, spit roast, oyster and seafood bar, salads, fruit and cheese, you can stay there from 1100 to 1400 and visit the buffet as many times as you want) for about US$55 per person. All-you-can-eat lunch buffets are good value at the **Thai Orchid**, Queen's Court, West Bay Rd, T9497955 (Tue, Thu, 1145-1430), and **Gateway of India**, T9462815 (Mon-Fri, 1130-1430), both on West Bay Rd.

During the high season it is advisable to reserve tables for dinner. People tend to eat early so if you reserve a table after 2000 you are likely to finish with the restaurant to yourself, although many restaurants have adjoining bars that stay open until later. Most bars have a Fri happy hour with free food.

Fine Dine-In, T9463463, ken@candw.ky, is a restaurant delivery service which you can call daily 1730-2300 (all sorts of cuisines from a choice of over 22 restaurants). They also do video rental, drinks, etc, for a real night in.

♥♥♥ Bamboo Bar & Lounge, at the **Hyatt**, West Bay Rd, T9491234. Mon-Fri 1730-0100, Sat 1730-2400. Not your normal hotel restaurant. By far the best sushi on the island, sashimi, riqiri and specials, also vegetarian menu, Japanese chef with flair, creative, generous portions, intimate and relaxing atmosphere, staff professional and friendly, popular with locals and visitors. Jazz on Tue. Sushi lessons Mon-Thu 1730.

♥♥♥ Brasserie, Cricket Sq, George Town, T9451815. www.brasseriecayman.com. Mon-Fri 1130-1430, daily 1800-2200. Off the beaten path, undiscovered by many visitors, sophisticated menu, excellent wine selection, tapas bar daily, excellent value Sun dinner menu for 2.

♥♥♥ Grand Old House, 648 South Church St, George Town, T9499333, www.grandoldhouse.com. Mon-Fri 1145-1400, daily 1800-2200. Restored waterfront home, top-notch service and seafood specialities, good wine list.

♥♥♥ Kaibo Bar & Grill, at Cayman Kai, north coast, T9479975, www.kaibo.ky. 1100-2300. Pasta, steak, fresh local seafood always on the menu.

♥♥♥ The Lighthouse at **Breakers**, on the south coast, T9472047, www.lighthouse.ky. 1130-1630, 1730-2200. 20 mins' drive east of George Town, seafood and Italian cuisine, idyllic setting with a stunning ocean view, one of the finer spots to dine on the island.

♥♥♥ Pappagallo, Barkers, in the northwest, T9491119. 1800-2230. Italian cuisine, expensive, on 14-acre bird sanctuary overlooking natural lagoon, eat in the haphazardly thatched building or in screened patio, excellent food and extensive wine list, reservations essential.

♥♥♥ Pirate's Buffet at the **Marriott**, T9490088. Fri 1800-2100. All you can eat, music, fire eater, limbo dancer, book ahead.

♥♥♥ Ragazzi, Buckingham Sq, off West Bay Rd, T9453484, www.eragazzi.com. 1130-2300.

Generally agreed to be the best Italian on the island, extremely popular. Daily specials including a pizza. Singles can eat at the bar rather than alone at a table.

♥♥♥ Reef Grill, at **Royal Palms Beach Club**, T9456358, www.reefgrill.com. Sun-Fri 1100-1500, Mon-Sat 1730-2200. One of the hottest dining and entertainment spots, dinner inside or out on the patio or upstairs, wheelchair- accessible, American bistro, live bands Wed-Sat in May-Nov, Mon-Sat in Dec-Apr and special occasions at the **Royal Palms**, also watersports centre and beach facility open daily.

♥♥♥ The Wharf, 43 West Bay Rd, on the outskirts of George Town on the way to Seven Mile Beach, T9492231, www.wharf.ky. Bar open Mon-Fri 1500-0100, Sat-Sun 1500-2400, restaurant daily 1130-1430 (15 Dec-15 Apr), 1800-2200 (all year), beautiful water- front setting, tarpon feeding nightly at 2100.

♥♥♥-♥♥ Calypso Grill, Morgan's Harbour, T9493948, www.calypsogrillcayman.com. Tue-Sun 1130-1500, 1800-2200. 3-tiered dining area with panoramic view of North Sound, seafood and beef or salads and pasta, good desserts.

♥♥♥-♥♥ Casanova Restaurant, 65 North Church St, T9497633, www.casanova.ky. 1100-2300. Excellent, Italian, on the waterfront, family-run, friendly service.

♥♥♥-♥♥ Cracked Conch, Northwest Point Rd, T9455217, www.crackedconch.com.ky. Mon-Sat 1030-1500, 1730-2200, Sun 1100-1600, 1730-2200, Macabuca Oceanside Tiki Bar 1000-late. Near Turtle Farm, popular stopping place for excursions, very nice setting and atmosphere, lively, conch is the speciality, takeaways very popular.

♥♥♥-♥♥ Decker's, West Bay Rd, opp Hyatt, T9456600, www.deckers.ky. Dinner 1700-2230, Bar open till 0100. Built around a double decker bus, which serves as the bar, moderate prices, bistro style, nightly music, daily happy hours.

♥♥♥-♥♥ Edoardo's, Coconut Place, West Bay Rd, T9454408, www.edoardos.ky. Mon-Sat 1130-1430, daily 1730-2230. Upmarket Italian, extensive wine list to accompany home made pasta, fresh seafood, a range of entrées and gourmet pizzas, lunch menu includes sandwiches.

♥♥♥-♥♥ Neptune's, Trafalgar Sq, West Bay Rd, T9468709. 1130-1430, 1730-2200. Chefs from India and Italy, good and varied menu, welcoming atmosphere, popular locally, booking advisable.

††† -†† Pirate's Den, Galleria Plaza, T9497144. Mon-Fri 0700-0100, Sat-Sun 1100-2400. Popular with ex-pats, breakfast, lunch and dinner, pub grub, great Sun brunch buffet.

†† Champion House, 43 Eastern Av, George Town, T9497882. Mon-Sat 0630-2400, Sun 0800-2400. Caribbean breakfast buffet followed by buffet or à la carte lunch and dinner, local food, stewed conch, cowfoot, ackee and codfish.

†† Chicken! Chicken!, West Shore Centre, T9452290, www.chicken2.com. 1100-2200. Tasty spit-roasted chicken with assorted accompaniments, US$20 for whole chicken plus 'fixin's', eat in or takeaway.

†† Durty Reids Palace, Red Bay Plaza, Red Bay Rd, near Savannah, T9471860. 1000-2200, bar open until 0100 weekdays, midnight at weekends, depending on demand. With possibly the most amusing menu of all time, this bar is reminiscent of the US Midwest, and a popular beer-drinking, football-watching, local hangout. Wed and Fri all you can eat buffet, happy hour 1630-1900 with free snacks.

†† Hard Rock Café, 43 South Church St, by South Terminal, T9452020, www.hardrock.com. 1030-late. A pink Cadillac from 1960 is suspended from the ceiling and the decor includes John denim hat as well as memorabilia from the likes of Madonna, Justin Timberlake, Slash of Guns'n'Roses, Elvis Presley, the Beatles and U2. Serves the usual American food, deep fried with fries, burgers are popular followed by hot fudge brownie with trimmings. The bar serves frozen cocktails, souvenir glasses, cold beer including local Stingray Beer.

†† Welly's Cool Spot, 110 North Sound Rd, T9492541. Mon-Thu 1000-2100, Fri 1000-2300, Sat 1000-2200, Sun 0700-1900. Native food at reasonable prices, stewed conch, curry goat, popular with residents. Looks rather rough but isn't.

† Azzurro Café, Buckingham Sq, opposite *The Hyatt*, T9467745, www.azzurro.ky. Mon-Sat 0630-1800, Sun 0630-1600. Italian coffee, sandwiches on freshly baked focaccia, grilled pannini, crêpes, salads, wraps and delicious handmade pastries, wireless laptops for internet access.

† Breadfruit Tree & Garden Café, 50 Eastern Av, T9288990. Sun-Thu 0600-2400, Fri 0600-0330, only place open that late, Sat 0600-0100. Best spot for local delicacies, no alcohol, busiest very late, serves cowfoot, fish tea, curry goat, jerk pork, jerk chicken, etc, quaint, garden-like atmosphere in decor, best prices in town.

† Full of Beans, Passadora Place, off Smith Rd, George Town, T9432326, www.fullofbeans.ky. Mon-Fri 0700-1700, Sat 0700-1600. Eclectic mix of dishes for breakfast and lunch, smoothies, frappuccinos and organic fair trade coffee.

† Seymour's Jerk Centre, in the parking lot of Roy's Boutique on Shedden Road, George Town, T9451931. Mon-Thu 1130-0100, Fri 1130-0300, Sat 1130-0100. Sells Mannish Water, a local concoction of goats' parts rumoured to give a man extra potency, not sold to women, popular Fri, Sat night, couples line up to get a taste and eat great jerk pork and chicken.

◑ Bars and clubs

Grand Cayman *p184, map p185 and p186*
Due to licensing laws, the vast majority of bars are attached to restaurants that stay open until 0100, or 2400 Sat. **Bamboo** has one of the most popular bars and all have live music at least twice a week. The opening hours of clubs are subject to frequent change due to difficulty with licensing laws, but usually close earlier at weekends than during the week. For information on what's on, look at **www.partysurfers.ky**.

Aqua Beach, Seven Mile Beach, T9466398, www.aquabeach.ky. Mon-Fri 1100-0100, Sat-Sun 1100-2400. Restaurant and bar, lively clientele, large screens for sporting events, casual, good food with salads, appetizers, wraps, entrées and children's dishes. Thu night take your own instrument for a jam session, DJ some nights, lots of drinks specials.

Coconut Joe's, Seven Mile Beach, near Comfort Suites, T9435637, www.coconutjoes.com.ky. International food, from nachos and quesadillas to burgers, soup, salads, ribs and oriental dishes. Fun staff, welcoming atmosphere, lively bar, popular.

Fidel Murphy's, Seven Mile Beach, T5495189. Irish pub and restaurant, good value.

Hammerheads, waterfront, North Church St, George Town, T9493080. 1000-late. Nelson Dilbert makes Old Dutch beer on the premises, 1 of only 2 breweries on the island. Paul 'The Hammer' Wammer runs the bar, with signature drinks such as *Green Hammer* or *Hammer Lemonade*. You sit on hammerhead bar stools to drink your hammer cocktail. Harold 'Bull' Powell is in charge of food, a range of seafood and turtle stew.

Legendz, by **Westin Hotel** on Seven Mile Beach, T9451590, www.legendz.ky. Mon-Fri 1130-0100, Sat-Sun 1130-2400. Sports bar with 11 TVs including 2 huge screens for all major events and concerts, also live bands, DJs and comedy nights. Snacks and full meals.

Lone Star Bar and Grill, next to the **Hyatt Hotel**, West Bay Rd, T9455175. Favourites with sports fans, showing international sporting events nightly, Tex-Mex food, happy hour Mon-Fri 1700-1830 but particularly known for its Fri happy hour.

Matrix, Lawrence Blvd, in the Islander Complex, West Bay Rd, T9497169. From 2000-late. Themed nights at this club, Thu Reggaeton, Sat Dance Hall.

Next Level, on West Bay Rd opposite the Marriott, T9466398, www.nextlevel.ky. Mon free Ladies night, US$10 for men, open bar 2200-0100. Club and lounge, 2 VIP lounges, different music styles Mon-Sat, dance hall, retro, remixes, hip hop.

Peppers, above Mitzi's Jewellery on Seven Mile Beach. 2100-0300, US$5. A range of themed nights, dance hall, reggae, international club hits and local live music.

Rackham's Pub, North Church St, T9453860. Good rum-based drinks, light meals, view of harbour, food good value.

❸ Entertainment

Grand Cayman *p184, map p185 and p186*
Cinema
There is a cinema on West Bay Rd with 2 screens, 2 showings a night Mon-Sat, US$8.5 adults, US$4.50 children, US$6.75 senior citizens, T9494011.

Theatre
Cayman National Cultural Foundation, T9495477, puts on plays and musicals at the Harquail Theatre on West Bay Rd. The Cayman Drama Society uses the **Prospect Play House**, a small theatre on the road to Bodden Town.

❸ Festivals and events

Grand Cayman *p184, map p185 and p186*
Mar Annual Rooster Shootout Fishing Tournament is a long weekend (16-18 Mar 2007) of fishing with lots of prizes for wahoo, yellowfin tuna and dolphin fish.

Apr/May Batabano, www.caymancarnival .com, is Grand Cayman's costume carnival weekend, with street parades, music and dancing, which takes place in the last week of Apr or beginning of May. **Cayfest**, the islands' national arts festival, takes place through most of Apr, with exhibitions, displays, dance and drama.

May International Fishing Tournament, with big prizes for catches of blue marlin, yellowfin tuna, wahoo and dolphin fish, contact tournament HQ T9453131, www.fishcayman.com, for details.

Jun The Queen's Birthday is celebrated in mid-Jun with a full-dress uniform parade, marching bands and a 21-gun salute.

Nov The Cayman Islands Restaurant Association holds an annual food festival: the Taste of Cayman, with lots of food and outdoor activities, T9498522.

Nov Pirates' Week (9-19 Nov 2007) is the islands' national festival and takes place in the last week of Oct. Parades, regattas, fishing tournaments, treasure hunts, historical and cultural 'district days' in Grand Cayman's 5 districts and on Little Cayman, are all part of the celebrations, which commemorate the days when the Cayman Islands were the haunt of pirates and buccaneers (T9495078, www.piratesweekfestival.com).

Dec Christmas brings the Parade of Lights by boat on the waterfront, the Rotary Club's Annual Christmas Tree Lighting and Radio 3-99's Wacky House Light Tour. Gimistory is an international storytelling festival with traditional Caribbean themes told through calypso, mime and dance. Contact the Cayman National Cultural Foundation, T9495477, marketcncf@candw.ky. Jazz Fest is an annual jazz festival, contact Shomari Scott, T9490623.

O Shopping

Grand Cayman *p184, map p185 and p186*
Art and crafts
Craft Market, George Town. Vendors are only allowed to sell goods produced in the Cayman Islands, nothing imported. Crafts include goods made from the silver thatch palm, the national tree, Cayman sea salt and rum cake.

Caribbean Charlie's, Northside, near Rum Point, T9479452. A wide assortment of tropical crafts with handmade, custom-designed and signed work.

Churchill's Cigar Store, T9456141. Cuban seed tobacco, rolled and packaged in the Cayman Islands so it can be legally imported into the USA, look for **Cayman Crown** and **Cayman Premium**.

Kennedy Gallery, in the West Shore Centre off West Bay Rd, T9498077. Mon-Sat 1000-1800. Exhibits all types of art including functional sculpture.

National Gallery of the Cayman Islands, Harbour Place, George Town, T9458111, www.nationalgallery.org.ky. Mon-Fri 0900-1700, Sat 1100-1600. Work for sale by local artists and craftsmen, as well as crafts from around the world. Comprehensive 'Art Trail' map with the location of artists' studios, galleries, craftsmen's homes and retail outlets, related establishments and points of interest in the Cayman Islands. The National Gallery will be moving to a new home on the Esterly Tibbetts Highway in 2008.

National Museum, on the waterfront, George Town, T9498368, www.museum.ky. Mon-Fri 0900-1700, Sat 1000-1400. Has a popular, well-stocked gift shop for prints, posters, books and crafts.

Pure Art, South Church St, T9499133. Daily 0900-1700. Sells the work of over 100 local artists and craftsmen and women; paintings, prints, sculptures, crafts, rugs, wallhangings, etc.

Books
The Book Nook, Galleria Plaza, West Bay Rd, T9454686. Mon-Sat 0900-1800. Also at the Anchorage Centre, T9497392, PO Box 1551, F9455053. Mon-Fri 0900-1600. Sells books, toys, gifts and games.

Hobbies and Books, Elgin Av and at Grand Harbour, T9490707, www.cayman.com.ky/com/hobbook. Sells books for children and adults, educational materials and postcards.

▲ Activities and tours

Grand Cayman *p184, map p185 and p186*
Children's play centres
Scholars Park, on Stadium Drive opposite the Stadium in West Bay. Daily 0700-1900. Offers a large outdoor play area. Each district has its own community park with play areas.

Smyles, at the Islander complex just off the Harquail Bypass, T9465800. Tue-Thu 0900-2000, Fri 0900-2200, Sat 1000-2200, Sun 1100-2000 CI$5.50. An indoor play centre with more than 3,200 sq ft of tunnels, ball pit, snack bar, soft play area, arcade, games.

Cricket
Matches are played at the **Smith Road Oval** near the airport (although location may change with extension of runway); there are 5 teams in the **Cayman Islands Cricket Association's** league.

Diving and snorkelling
See also page183 and page189.
The tourist office lists 32 dive operations on Grand Cayman, offering a wide range of courses and dive sites. For a full list, see www.divecayman.ky. Many are at more than 1 location, attached to hotels; all are of a high standard but you may want to make your choice according to the number of divers per boat.

Atlantis submarines, T9497700, www.atlantisadventures.com. Operate a submarine with room for 48 passengers, which dives to 100 ft along Cayman Wall; fares are US$79 for a 1-hr day or night dive (teenagers US$69, children 4-12 US$49).

For US$34 (children US$19) you can take a 1-hr ride in *Seaworld Explorer*, an underwater observatory for 35 people, down 4 ft. A diver attracts fish within view by feeding them (Don Foster's – *Subsee* – Ltd, T9498534). The *Nautilus Semi-Submersible* is a 110-ft hulled vessel, which seats 60 people 5 ft below the surface.

Fishing
There are at least 14 companies on Grand Cayman offering fishing. The tourist office can give you a full list with prices, which depend on the type of boat you choose. Deep-sea fishing boats can be chartered for a half day (US$350-700) or full day

(US$500-1,500). Reef and bone fishing is about US$400-700 for a full day, all equipment, bait and lunch included. **Angling Club**, call Donna Sjostrom, T9497099, fishing@candw.ky.

Golf
Blue Tip, at the Ritz Carlton. A 9-hole course designed by Greg Norman, but it is available only to guests.
Britannia Golf Course, designed by Jack Nicklaus for the **Hyatt-Regency Grand Cayman Resort & Villas**, T9498020. There is a 9-hole Championship course, an 18-hole Executive course and an 18-hole Cayman course played with a special short-distance Cayman ball, but it can only be laid out for 1 course at a time; the Executive has 14 par 3s and 4 par 4s, so it is short, while the short-distance ball with local winds is a tourist gimmick. To play the Executive course with hire of clubs and compulsory buggie will cost you about US$75, the Regulation course US$90 for 18 holes.
The Links, Safehaven, T9495988, F9495457. The 18-hole championship golf course was still closed at end-2006. Check for an opening date.

Hiking
Silver Thatch Excursions, T9456588, www.earthfoot.org/places/ky001.htm. The only tour operator offering the National Trust escorted hikes along the Mastic Trail (see page 188) and is highly recommended.

Horse riding
Horse riding with **Nicki's Beach Rides**, T9455839, on trails and beaches in the northwest; with **Pampered Ponies**, T9452262; or with **Coral Stone Stables**, T9164799, estones@candw.ky.

Motorsports
Motorsports are popular in Grand Cayman. A new 30-acre racetrack, with a 20-acre family recreation area and 15-acre nature reserve is being built at Breakers and is partially open, T9497135. Races on Sat night. No alcoholic beverages allowed.
Eagles Nest Cycles runs the **Harley Davidson Club**, T9494866, specializing in HD motorcycles and souvenirs.

Rugby
The Cayman Rugby Union at South Sound, T9497960. Founded in 1971 as the Cayman Rugby Football Club, the Cayman Islands compete locally and internationally at many age grades and levels and in many competitions throughout the year. Visiting teams are welcome, contact Richard Adams, the technical director of rugby at T9497960, techdir@candw.ky. There are five senior men's teams, several junior sides and a women's team. The national team has a wide range of international players, many of whom played in their respective countries before emigrating to Cayman. Some played in the newly-formed West Indies team which has toured the UK.

Sailing
Aquanauts at Morgan's Harbour, T9451990, F9451991. 15 slips accommodating boats of 6½ ft draft and the usual facilities.
Cayman Islands Yacht Club, Grand Cayman, T9454322, F9454432. With docking facilities for 154 boats, 7 ft maximum draft.
Grand Cayman Sailing Club, Red Bay Estates, T9477913. A social sailing club.

Squash
Cayman Islands Squash Racquets Association, South Sound, T9499469, www.squash.ky. 7 a/c international squash courts including two coloured courts.

Tennis
Most of the larger hotels have their own tennis courts.
Cayman Islands Tennis Club, next door to the squash courts at South Sound. Has 6 floodlit tennis courts and a club pro.
For match information contact Scott Smith, T9499464.

Tour operators
Native Safari Tours, T3244778. Offers tours of the Botanic Park and other sites. Their 4-hr west side tour costs US$62.50 pp, and their 7-hr east side tour costs US$80 pp, some admission fees included.
Reality Tours, T9477200, www.realitytourscayman.com. Offers tours of the Botanic Park and other sites. Daily tours from CI$29-98 with hotel pick-up.

Silver Thatch Excursions, T9456588, www.earthfoot.org/places/ky001.htm. An eco-friendly tour operator offering birdwatching and nature walks, US$50-55 pp.

Windsurfing

Windsurfing at the East End is highly rated for people of all abilities. Beginners are safe within the reef, while outside the reef experienced sailors can try wave jumping or wave riding. Winds are brisk nearly all the year, with speeds of 15-25 knots. Lots of hotels' watersports operators offer windsurfing, sunfish, wave runners and other equipment.

Cayman Windsurf, a BiC Centre, is at **Morritt's Tortuga Club**, East End, T9477492, cawin@candw.ky. A full range of BiC boards and UP sails and instruction available.

Surfside Aquasports, Seven Mile Beach, T/F9491068, windsurf@candw.ky. Rental and instruction, this is a Mistral certified school.

● Transport

Grand Cayman *p184, map p185 and p186*
Air
See page 180.

Bus

Public buses, hotline T9455100, run on 8 colour-coded routes from the terminal next to the Public Library on Edward St, George Town. All routes run Sun-Thu 0600-2300, Fri-Sat 0600-0100. Route 1 (yellow) and 2 (lime green) to **West Bay** every 15 mins 0600-1800, then every 30 mins, CI$1.50. Route 3 (blue) to **Bodden Town** runs hourly, same price. Route 4 (purple) to **East End** and Route 5 (red) to **East End** and **North Side**, every hr, CI$2. Route 6 (dark green) North Side to **West Bay**. Route 7 (green, white numbers) around **George Town**. Route 8 (orange) to **North Side**.

Car

The minimum hiring age is 21 at some places, 25 at others; ask around. **Avis**, **National** and **Hertz** are represented and there are a number of good local companies

as well, many of which are at the airport. Rental firms issue visitors with driving permits on production of a valid driving licence from the visitor's country of residence. Most car hire firms have boxes in the airport departure lounge where you can drop off your car keys prior to departure, having left the car in the company's car park. **Ace Hertz**, T9492280, F9490572. Compact car US$25-52.

Andy's Rent A Car Ltd, West Bay Road, opposite **Marriott**, T9498111, F9498385. Cheapest automatic car US$35 in winter, US$25 in summer, weekly rates US$210 or US$150.

Cico Avis, T9492468, F9497127. Smallest standard car US$46/37 winter/summer, jeeps and automatics available.

Coconut Car Rentals Ltd, T9494037, F9497786. From US$50/35 a day winter/summer or US$295/195 a week, jeeps US$50/55, US$320/250. Collision damage waiver US$14 a day.

Taxi

Taxis are readily obtainable at hotels and restaurants. In George Town there are always lots of taxis at the dock when the cruise ships come in, otherwise hailing a taxi is most easily done in the vicinity of the post office. Fares are based on a fixed place-to-place tariff rather than a meter charge and vary according to how many people there are and how much luggage there is. For going a long distance (ie across the island) they are expensive. From the airport to George Town is US$12, based on up to 4 passengers with 2 pieces of luggage each; to West Bay US$23-29; to East End, US$49; to Rum Point US$60. **Burton's Taxi Service**, T9472274, and **AA Chauffeur and Transportation Services**, T9497222, F9455823, offer standard taxi service plus island tours.

● Directory

Grand Cayman *p184, map p185 and p186*
For Health and communications, see pages183 and 184.

Cayman Brac and Little Cayman

→ *Phone code: 345. Colour map 1, C3. Population 1,822.*

Settlement on Cayman Brac has been determined by the Bluff, which rises from sea level at the west end to a sheer cliff at the east end. Most building first took place on the flatter land in the west, where the sea is a little calmer, and then spread along the north coast where the Bluff gives shelter. A number of Heritage Sites, linked by hiking trails, are being promoted, including bat caves, the old lighthouse and a place to watch the sunset. Cayman Brac is blessed with spectacular reef and wall diving with excellent visibility. Hurricane Ivan was not as destructive here as it was in Grand Cayman and all the nature trails remained open. The tourist office can be contacted at PO Box 194, Stake Bay, T9481649, F9481629.

Little Cayman is small and low lying with large areas of dense mangrove swamps, ponds, lagoons and lakes. The diving is excellent. Underwater visibility averages 100-150 ft all year. Bloody Bay wall, a mile-deep vertical drop, is one of the major dive sites worldwide and is highly rated by marine biologists and photographers.

▶▶ *For Sleeping, Eating and other listings, see pages 199-201.*

Cayman Brac

The recently introduced Heritage Sites and Trails include 35 attractions and hikes to entice visitors away from the water and discover what is on land. It is not possible to drive all round the island because of the Bluff. The road linking the north and south coasts is roughly halfway along the island. There are three roads running east-west, one along the north shore, one along the south coast and a third (unpaved) in the middle which runs along the top of the Bluff to the lighthouse. Although lots of roads have been built up on the Bluff, they are to service houses which have not yet been built, and do not lead anywhere. There are several, rather poor farms, and cows wander on the road. At the top of the Bluff it is sometimes possible to spot various orchids and there is a 197-acre **Parrot Reserve** (see page 204). A hiking trail has been cleared by the Cayman Brac National Trust, only for the able bodied as it is rocky, but there is a great view from the Bluff at the end of the path. You are only likely to see parrots at dawn or dusk, but it is a nice walk anyway through the bush.

✿ www.naturecayman.com, for information on birdwatching and nature tourism.

Cayman Islands Cayman Brac & Little Cayman

Cayman Brac

Sleeping 😴
Almond Beach
Hideaways 1

Brac Caribbean
Beach Village 2
Brac Reef Beach Resort 3

Carib Sands 4
La Esperanza 6
Walton's Mango Manor 7

From the airport the north shore road leads to **Cotton Tree Bay**, where in 1932 a hurricane flooded the area, killing more than 100 people and destroying virtually every house. The coconut groves were devastated and many people left the island at this time. Demand for turtle shell went into decline as the use of plastic increased and many men found that the only opportunities open to them were as sailors, travelling around the world on merchant ships.

Stake Bay is the main village on the north coast and it is well worthwhile visiting the small, but interesting **Cayman Brac Museum** ① *T9482622, Mon-Fri 0900-1200, 1300-1600, free.* Further east at Creek, **La Esperanza** is a good place to stop for refreshment, in a glorious setting with good views and welcome sea breeze. At **Spot Bay** at the extreme east, follow a track up towards the lighthouse. Here you will find Peter's Cave and a good viewpoint. From the end of the north coast road you can walk through the almond trees to the beach, for an excellent view of the Bluff from below.

Bat Cave and Rebecca's Cave are in the southeast and can be visited. When you get to the end of the road, walk along the ironshore to the end of the island. There is a blow-hole, lots of beachcombing opportunities and if you look for stripes in the cliff you may find caymanite, which is only found here and at the east end of Grand Cayman. Holiday homes have been built along this coast. Tourism is now the mainstay of the economy but construction of homes for foreigners has pushed up the price of land out of the reach of many local families.

> ❢ Rock climbing is popular along this coastline. There are 66 climbing sites.

Beaches and activities

Most of the sites are around the west end, with both shallow reef snorkelling, with beautiful coral gardens and lots of fish, and diving and deeper wall diving a bit further out. There are also a few wrecks among the 40 or so named dive sites including a newly-sunk Russian frigate (see page 183), which is within snorkelling distance of the beach and rises to about 10 ft from the surface. On the north coast road, go west past the airport turning to Robert Foster Lane, which leads to the sea. You can locate the wreck by the buoys for dive boats.

Along the south coast, the best beaches are at the west end, where there are two dive resorts. There is a pleasant public beach with shade and toilets at **South East Bay**.

Little Cayman → *Phone code: 345. Colour map 1, C3. Population: 115.*

Little Cayman's swamps, ponds, lagoons and lakes make an ideal habitat for red-footed boobies and iguanas. **Booby Pond Nature Reserve** ① *T9481010*, attracts about 3,500 nesting pairs of red-footed boobies and 100 pairs of frigate birds. On the edge of the pond, the other side of the road from the museum, is the **National Trust House** ① *Mon-Sat 1500-1700; you can use the veranda any time*, where you can look through a telescope or strong binoculars to watch the birds. Further east is **Tarpon Lake**, another good spot for seeing wildlife. A boardwalk has been built out into the lake and if you are lucky you might see some tarpon.

Blossom is by the airstrip, and there you will find the **post office** ① *Mon-Fri 0900-1100, 1300-1500, Sat 0900-1100*, car hire, a grocery and hardware store, bank (open Wednesday) and the **Little Cayman Museum** ① *T9481072, Mon-Fri 1500-1700, free*. The museum is in a typical wooden house and has a small, but nicely presented, collection of local artefacts and antiques. **Little Cayman Baptist Church** ① *services Sun 1100, 1930, Wed 1930*, is the only church.

Diving and marine life

There are dive sites all round the island, but the most popular spot is in the Marine Park in **Bloody Bay**, a two-mile stretch between Spot Bay and Jackson's Point off the about 65 ft and drop down about a mile, the Bloody Bay wall begins at 15-20 ft, meaning you can snorkel over the drop-off. This is spectacular, with coral canyons and caves before you get to the outer reef. There is also a Marine Park off the south coast opposite the airport, with **Pirate's Point Dive Resort** at one end. Snorkelling is good just to the west of **Pirate's Point Resort,** where the water is shallow just within the reef. Shore diving from **Jackson's Point** is also superb, with coral heads rising from a 40-ft sandy bottom to within about 10 ft of the surface.

The beaches by the hotels on the south coast are good, with fine sand, but the swimming is marred by huge swathes of sea grass in the shallow water. Many of the other beaches around the island are more gritty, but you will have them to yourself. The best beach for swimming and snorkelling is at **Sandy Point** at the east tip of the island. Look for a red and white marker opposite a pond, a sandy path leads down to the beach. Other beaches are at **Jackson's Point** on the north side and on **Owen Island** in South Hole Sound. This privately owned island, 200 yd offshore, is freely used by residents and visitors and is accessible by row boat or kayak.

⊜ Sleeping

Cayman Brac *p197, map p197*
Accommodation is mostly self-catering in condos and villas, check www.thebrac.com.
LL-L Brac Caribbean Beach Village, south coast, West End, T9482265, www.866thebrac.com. A condominium development, a/c, fans, on beach, reef protected, credit cards accepted, 16, 2-bedroom condos, restaurant **Captain's Table**, pool, dive packages, laundry, maid service available, satellite TV, child and teenage discounts.
LL-L Carib Sands, T9481121, www.866thebrac.com. 34, 1-4 bedroom condos, nicely furnished, in 2 pink blocks by the sea, full kitchens, balconies, pool, bicycles, dive packages, pier for pick up by dive boat.

L Almond Beach Hideaways, Spot Bay, T9480470, www.almondbeachhideaways .com. On beach, good snorkelling, villas with 2 bedrooms, 2 bathrooms, sofa bed in living room, a/c, fans, hammocks and sunbeds.
AL Brac Reef Beach Resort, West End Point, T9481323, www.bracreef.com. 40 rooms, packages available, comfortable, nice beach, some sea grass, lovely dock with lookout tower, conference centre for large and small groups, internet access.
AL B La Esperanza, Stake Bay, T9480531, www.candw.ky/users/cay06865. Condos and houses on north side, sea view, access to private beach, meal plans available, good restaurant, snorkelling on reef just offshore, hammocks, bicycles, car hire, airport transfers, grocery store in walking distance.

Little Cayman

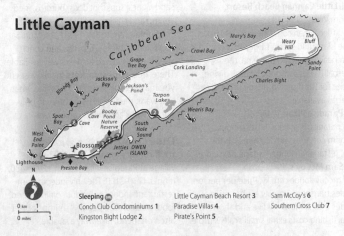

Sleeping 🛏
Conch Club Condominiums 1
Kingston Bight Lodge 2
Little Cayman Beach Resort 3
Paradise Villas 4
Pirate's Point 5
Sam McCoy's 6
Southern Cross Club 7

0 km 1
0 miles 1

A Walton's Mango Manor, Stake Bay, T/F9480518, www.waltonsmangomanor .com. Bed and breakfast, 5 rooms, antiques, veranda, hammocks, a/c, fans, TV, kitchenettes, great snorkelling.

Little Cayman *p198, map p199*
Accommodation consists of small hotels, diving lodges, a few private cottages and homes.

LL Conch Club Condominiums, Blossom Village, T9481033, www.conchclub.com. 8 privately owned townhouses with 2 or 3 bedrooms, beachfront, 2 pools, jacuzzi, restaurant, Conch Club Divers offer diving, snorkelling.

LL Southern Cross Club, T9481099, www.southerncrossclub.com. Includes all meals, packages for scuba and/or fishing, luxury cabins on sandy beach, view of Owen Island, friendly, excellent staff, good food served in dining room, on pool deck or on the beach, indoor and outdoor bar, pool, internet access, Island Moon Massage spa with choice of massages, run by Terry Thompson, a retrained former dive master at SCC, one of the nicest places to stay, relaxed, laid back, barefoot elegance.

LL-L Pirate's Point, Sefton Bay, T9481010, www.piratespointresort.com. Rooms in cabins, simple luxury, lovely big bathrooms, all-inclusive with or without diving, 42-ft dive boat, 5 instructors, fishing, a/c, fan, TV, phone, small deep pool and 10-person jacuzzi, bar decorated with driftwood signs made by guests, owned by a cordon bleu chef, very relaxing, friendly.

LL-AL Little Cayman Beach Resort, Blossom Village, T9481033, www.littlecayman.com. The only real hotel on the island and seems huge, 40 rooms, a/c, TV, on beach, dock facilities, spa, tennis, basketball, volleyball, pool, jacuzzi, diving, facilities for the disabled, all-inclusive dive packages available.

L-AL Paradise Villas, T9480001, www.paradisevillas.com. Small, duplex, 1-2-bedroom cottages with kitchens, on the shore, restaurant Hungry Iguana next door.

L-AL Sam McCoy's, T9480026, www.mccoyslodge.com.ky. Price per person. Includes transport, 3 meals, higher price includes 2-tank morning dive and shore diving, fishing costs extra, small scale, simple

and low key, 8 rooms, tiny pool with jacuzzi jets, hammocks, small beach, internet access.
AL Kingston Bight Lodge, T9481015, kblodge@candw.ky. A small personal lodge with 4, 4-bedroom units, snorkelling, diving, fishing, bar and restaurant.

Eating

Cayman Brac *p197, map p197*
The Captain's Table, at Brac Caribbean Beach Village, T9481418. Lunch 1130-1500, dinner 1800-2200, bar 1200-2400. The best on the island, lobster, seafood and steaks.
La Esperanza, Stake Bay, T9480531. Mon-Sat 0800-2100, Sun 0900-2100. Seafood, jerk chicken, conch fritters, 1 of the nicest restaurants, tables at water's edge as well as a/c dining room, music, bar, active at weekends, bar busy most nights, transport available.
Aunt Sha's Kitchen, T9481581. 0730-2300. Ocean view, island style, local dishes, conch fritters, key lime pie, breakfast, lunch, dinner, also takeaway, TV, billiards, darts, Coral Isle, next door, is 1 of the few nightspots on the island.
Blackie's, at the Youth Centre, South Side, T9480232. Good home-made ice cream, fried chicken, lunch only.
Cozy Kitchen, West End. Casual, local lunch only, eat in or takeaway.
G&M Diner. Thu-Tue 0730-1430 and 1830-2030. Breakfast, lunch and dinner, local dishes and seafood, no alcohol.
Martin's Pizzeria and Grill, West End at airport entrance. Sun-Thu 0900-2200, Fri 0900-0100, Sat 0900-2400. Pizza, burgers, sandwiches, subs, hot dogs, burritos, fried shrimp and chicken, milk shakes, casual.
Sonia's, White Bay, T9481214. Mon-Sat 0830-1330. Chicken, fish, ribs and conch, special diets catered for, takeaway available. There are 3 **supermarkets** in the west end, you may need to shop at all 3 to find what you want, the supply boat comes in only once a week and things can run out.

Little Cayman *p198, map p199*
Hungry Iguana, T9480007, in the village at Paradise Villas. Lunch 1200-1430, dinner 1730-2100. The only independent restaurant, indoor or outdoor dining, good food, pizza on Sat, popular, shrimp, lobster often on menu, takeaway available.

⦿ Shopping

Cayman Brac *p197, map p197*

Joe Tourist, T9465638. 'Made in Cayman'
casual wear and accessory line. Kid'srange is
decorated with stingrays, blue iguanas and
green sea turtles. Joe Tourist products are
available only in the Cayman Islands; you can
order them on-line at www.joetourist.com.
NIM Things, Spot Bay at east end of the Main
North Side Rd, T9481296. Usually open
0900-1900. Sells items made locally, including
caymanite jewellery, straw bags and crochet.

⊛ Festivals and events

Cayman Brac *p197, map p197*

Jun Cayman Brac has a celebration similar
to Batabano, known as **Brachanal**, which
takes place in Jun. Everyone is invited to
dress up and participate, and there are
several competitions. See also page 182.

▲ Activities and tours

Cayman Brac *p197, map p197*
Diving
Brac Aquatics, T9481429,
www.candw.ky/users/Cay3931. Charges
US$70 for a 2-tank dive.
Reef Divers, T9481642, www.bracreef.com.
Offers diving at both Cayman Brac and Little
Cayman sites, certification and resort
courses, photo/video services and
equipment rental. A 2-tank dive costs US$75,
snorkelling trips are US$10-15.

Little Cayman *p198, map p199*
Diving
Diving can be arranged with **Pirate's Point**,
Conch Club, **Sam McCoy's** (at the west end
of Spot Bay) or **Southern Cross Club** (always
winning awards), usually a package deal
with accommodation, dive computers are
required, available for hire or bring your own.

Fishing
Bonefishing around Little Cayman is some of
the best. The 15-acre Tarpon Lake is home to
the game fish from which the pond gets its
name. Fishing is offered at **Sam McCoy's** and
at **Southern Cross Club**. Rates on request, but
generally US$100/half day, US$300/full day for
bonefishing, twice that for deep-sea fishing.

⦿ Transport

Cayman Brac *p197, map p197*

There are no buses on the island, so taxis or
car hire or walking are the only options.

Air
Cayman Airways Express fly from Grand
Cayman and Little Cayman. There is no
inter-island ferry service, so you have to
catch a small plane, used like a bus service.

Car
Brac Rent-A-Car, T9481515.
CB Rent-A-Car, at the airport, T9482424,
www.cbrentacar.com. 0800-1800. Compact
car US$25 winter/summer, also jeeps and
vans.
Four D's, T/F9481599, fourds@thebrac.com.
About US$35-40 per day for a car.

Cycle and moped
B&S Motor Ventures, T9481646,
www.bandsmv.com. For rental.

Taxi
An island tour by taxi costs about CI$15, **Elo's
Taxi and Tours**, T9480220, recommended;
Hill's Taxi and Tours, T9480540; **Maple
Edward's Taxi and Tours**, T9480448.

Little Cayman *p198, map p199*

There is no public transport, a 25 mph speed
limit and frequent signs for iguana or duck
crossings.

Air
Cayman Airways Express has small planes
for island hopping from Grand Cayman and
Cayman Brac (see page 181). The airport
consists of a wooden shack and a grass
runway.

Car
Roads are unpaved around the east half of
the island but the main road goes all the way
round the edge. You cannot always see the
sea because of seagrape and other
vegetation lining the shore.
   Jeep and compact car hire (US$50-75 per
day) is available here with **McLaughlin
Rentals**, T9481000, F9481001, daily and
weekly rates, prices vary due to length of
rental. The office is 100 yd from the airport.

Background

History

The islands were first sighted by Columbus in May 1503 when he was blown off course on his way to Hispaniola. He found two small islands (Cayman Brac and Little Cayman) which were full of turtles, and he therefore named the islands Las Tortugas. A 1523 map of the islands referred to them as *Lagartos*, meaning alligators or large lizards, but by 1530 they were known as the Caymanas after the Carib word for the marine crocodile which also lived there. The first recorded English visitor to the Caymans was Sir Francis Drake in 1586, when he reported that the *caymanas* were edible. But it was the turtles which really attracted ships in search of fresh meat for their crews. Generations of sailors stocked up on turtle meat here, keeping the creatures alive on board ship for later use. The islands were ceded to the English Crown under the Treaty of Madrid in 1670, after the first settlers came from Jamaica in 1661 to 1671 to Little Cayman and Cayman Brac. The first settlements were abandoned after attacks by Spanish privateers, but British privateers often used the Cayman Islands as a base and in the 18th century they became an increasingly popular hideout for pirates, even after the end of legitimate privateering in 1713. In November 1794, a convoy of 10 ships was wrecked on the reef in Gun Bay, on the East End of Grand Cayman, but with the help of the local residents there was no loss of life. Legend has it that there was a member of the Royal Family on board and that in gratitude for their bravery, King George III decreed that Caymanians should never be conscripted for war service and Parliament legislated that they should never be taxed.

From 1670, the Cayman Islands were dependencies of Jamaica, although there was considerable self-government. In 1832, a legislative assembly was established, consisting of eight magistrates appointed by the Governor of Jamaica and 10 (later increased to 27) elected representatives. In 1959 dependency ceased when Jamaica became a member of the Federation of the West Indies, although the Governor of Jamaica remained the Governor of the Cayman Islands. When Jamaica achieved Independence in 1962 the islands opted to become a direct dependency of the British Crown.

The first three families of settlers arrived on Cayman Brac in 1833, followed by two more families in 1835. These five families, Ritch, Scott, Foster, Hunter and Ryan, are still well represented on the island today. They made a living from growing coconuts and selling turtle shells and from the 1850s started building boats to facilitate trading. In 1886 a Baptist missionary arrived from Jamaica and introduced education and health care.

The first inhabitants of Little Cayman were turtlers who made camp on the south shore. After them, at the beginning of the 20th century, the population exploded to over 100 Caymanians living at Blossom on the southwest coast and farming coconuts. Attacks of blight killed off the palms and the farmers moved to the other two islands. In the 1950s, some US sport fishermen set up a small fishing camp on the south coast known as the **Southern Cross Club**, which is still in operation today as a diving/fishing lodge. A handful of similar small resorts and holiday villas have since been built but the resident population remains tiny.

In 1991 a review of the 1972 constitution recommended several constitutional changes to be debated by the Legislative Assembly (see Government, below). The post of Chief Secretary was reinstated in 1992 after having been abolished in 1986 and members of the executive committee are called ministers.

Government

A Governor appointed by the British Crown is the head of Government. The present Constitution came into effect in 1993 and provides for an Executive Council to advise the Governor on administration of the islands. The Council is made up of five Elected

and three Official Members and is chaired by the Governor. The former, called
Ministers from February 1994, are elected from the 15 elected representatives in the
Legislative Assembly and have a range of responsibilities allocated by the Governor,
while the latter are the Chief Secretary, the Financial Secretary, and the Attorney
General. The Legislative Assembly may remove a minister from office by nine votes
out of the 15. There is no Chief Minister. There have been no political parties since the
mid-1960s but politicians organize themselves into teams. There are three teams, the
National Team, Team Cayman and the Democratic Alliance Group. The Chief Secretary
is the First Official Member of the Executive Council, and acts as Governor in the
absence of the Governor.

Economy

The original settlers earned their living from the sea, either as turtle fishermen or as
crew members on ships around the world. In 1906 more than a fifth of the population
of 5,000 was estimated to be at sea, and even in the 1950s the government's annual
report said that the main export was of seamen and their *The Cayman Islands is the largest offshore financial centre and the fifth largest financial centre in the world.*
remittances the mainstay of the economy. Today the standard of
living is high, with the highest per capita income in the
Caribbean. The islands' economy is based largely on offshore
finance and banking, tourism, real estate and construction, and
a little local industry. Apart from a certain amount of meat, turtle,
fish and a few local fruits and vegetables, almost all foodstuffs and other necessities
are imported. The cost of living therefore rises in line with that of the main trading
partners. The economy is highly dependent upon the fortunes of the US economy,
with interest rates rising and falling according to those of US instruments. Tourism
revenues have risen sharply in recent years although income still fluctuates according
to the strength of the US economy. In the 1990s cruise ship visitors soared with the
introduction of calls by the cruise liner *Ecstasy* which carries 2,500 passengers. Cruise
ship passengers outnumber stayover visitors by two to one, but the latter account for
90% of revenues. Nearly three quarters of all stayover visitors are from the USA.

Geography

Grand Cayman, the largest of the three islands, lies 150 miles south of Havana, Cuba,
about 180 miles northwest of Jamaica and 480 miles south of Miami. Grand Cayman
is low-lying, 22 miles long and four miles wide, but of the total 76 sq miles about half
is swamp. A striking feature is the shallow, reef-protected lagoon, North Sound,
40 miles square and the largest area of inland mangrove in the Caribbean. None of
the islands has any rivers, but vegetation is luxuriant, the main trees being coconut,
thatch palm, seagrape and Australian pine. George Town, the capital of the islands, is
located on the west side of Grand Cayman. **Cayman Brac** (Gaelic for 'bluff') gets its
name from the high limestone bluff rising from sea level in the west to a height of
140 ft in the east. The island lies about 89 miles east northeast of Grand Cayman. It is
about 12 miles long and a little more than a mile wide. **Little Cayman** lies five miles
west of Cayman Brac and is 10 miles long and just over a mile wide with its highest
point being only 40 ft above sea level. **Owen Island**, an islet off the southwest coast of
Little Cayman, is uninhabited but visited by picnickers.

People

The total population of mixed African and European descent is estimated at 36,500,
of whom around a third are foreigners on work permits. Nearly *District days during Cayfest in April and Pirates' Week in October are good times to meet local people.*
everyone lives on Grand Cayman, most of them in George Town,
or the smaller towns of West Bay, Bodden Town, North Side and
East End. The population of Cayman Brac is only 1,200. Little
Cayman is largely undeveloped with only about 120 residents.

The Cayman Islands are very exclusive, with strict controls on who is allowed to settle. Consequently the cost of living is extremely high. On the other hand, petty crime is rare and the islands are well looked after (described as 'a very clean sandbank'). Although Caymanians have considerable affection for Britain and do not seek Independence, their way of life is Americanized. Higher education and advanced health care are usually sought in the USA and their geographical proximity influences travel choices.

Flora and fauna

Around 200 species of bird inhabit the islands. These include the Antillean grackle, the smooth-billed ani, the green-backed heron, the yellow-crowned night heron and many other heron species, the snowy egret, the common ground dove, the bananaquit and the Cayman parrot. The endangered West Indian whistling duck can be seen on Grand Cayman and Little Cayman. If you are interested in birdwatching, go to the mosquito control dykes on the West Bay peninsula of Grand Cayman, or walk to the Cistern at East End. A former Governor was a keen birdwatcher and in 1993 he set up a fund to establish the **Governor Michael Gore Bird Sanctuary** on 3½ acres of wetland on Grand Cayman, where you can see 60 local species. There are nesting colonies of the red-footed booby and the magnificent frigate bird on Little Cayman. There is a parrot reserve on Cayman Brac on 197 acres of land donated to the National Trust by Donald Pennie. The **Brac Parrot Reserve** is the nesting ground for the endangered endemic Cayman Brac parrot, numbering about 400 birds. The reserve covers pristine ancient woodlands on a very rough and rocky terrain with a diversity of native trees, including species not present on Grand Cayman or Little Cayman. A 1-mile nature trail has been established through part of the reserve. The trail forms a loop which passes through several different types of terrain, from old farm land now under grass, past mango trees on red soil and through thickets and mature woodlands, a startling mixture of hardwoods and cacti. Signs and information boards are placed at strategic points along the trail and a brochure is available. *Birds of the Cayman Islands*, by PE Bradley (published by the British Ornithologists Union; £35), is a photographic record. **Cardinal D's Park** ① *T9498855, Mon-Fri 1000-1800, Sat-Sun 1200-1800, US$ 6, children US$3*, on the outskirts of George Town, and the beginning of Seven Mile Beach, has 4 acres of natural lakes and woodlands. The bird sanctuary includes parrots, macaws, whistling duck and turtles.

Indigenous animals on the islands are few. The most common are the agouti, non-poisonous snakes, iguana and other small lizards, freshwater turtle, the hickatee and two species of tree frog. Several animal sanctuaries have been established, most of which are RAMSAR sites where no hunting or collecting of any species is allowed. On **Grand Cayman** there are sanctuaries at Booby Cay, Meagre Bay Pond and Colliers Bay Pond; on **Cayman Brac** at the ponds near the airport and on **Little Cayman** at Booby Road and Rookery, Tarpon Lake and the Wearis Bay Wetland, stretching east along the south coast to the Easterly Wetlands. The **National Trust** ① *T9490121, ntrust@candw.ky*, has set up a Land Reserves Fund to buy environmentally sensitive land and protect natural resources.

Oncidium calochilum, a rare orchid, indigenous to Grand Cayman with a small yellow flower about ½ in long, is found only in the rocky area off Frank Sound Drive. Several other orchid species have been recorded as endemic but are threatened by construction and orchid fanciers. There is protection under international and local laws for several indigenous species, including sea turtles, iguanas, Cayman parrots, orchids and marine life. For a full description of the islands' flora see George R Proctor, *Flora of the Cayman Islands* (Kew Bulletin Additional Series XI, HMSO, 1984, 834 pages), which lists 21 endemic plant taxa including some which are rare, endangered or possibly extinct.

Jamaica

☝ Footprint features

Introduction

Jamaica has been called the Island of Springs, and Xaymaca, the name used by its pre-Columbian inhabitants, the Taínos, meant 'land of wood and water'. It is indeed an extravagantly beautiful island, with rolling hills and steep gullies, and the spectacular Blue Mountains overlooking a coastline indented with bays and coves. Rain falls freely, water is abundant, the vegetation is luxuriant and colours are vibrant. The people have a culture to match, from reggae and Rastafarianism to English plantation houses and cricket. The place lives and breathes rhythm: music is everywhere and Jamaica is a hub of creativity in the Caribbean. The cultural impact of reggae and its contemporary offshoot, dancehall, is now a global phenomenon.

Kingston is a busy capital city, the centre of commercial activity with a lively arts and entertainment scene including theatre, live music, clubs, bars and restaurants. It is where everything happens, albeit constrained and overshadowed by a reputation of gang-related crime and violence. Montego Bay is the tourist capital of the island, offering entertainment for holidaymakers in huge all-inclusive resorts or smaller hotels, whether they are wealthy celebrities seeking exclusivity in a boutique hotel or students looking for a good time on a budget. Every conceivable watersport is on offer in the resort areas on the north coast, where the beaches are safe for swimming. The south coast, though having fewer beaches, is richly endowed with natural attractions such as Black River Safari and YS Falls and is fast becoming the destination for nature lovers and people wanting to get off the beaten track. Away from the coast you find the other Jamaica, of mountains and forests for birdwatching and hiking, rivers tumbling over boulders and small farms clinging to hillsides where the exquisite Blue Mountain coffee grows in the mist.

★ Don't miss...

1 Devon House Built in 1881 by Jamaica's first black millionaire along the lines of a Great House, page 217.

2 Spanish Town The former capital with a wonderful central square surrounded by historical government buildings, page 220.

3 Blue Mountains A beautiful forested area rising to a peak of 2256 m with spectacular views in all directions, page 228.

4 Port Antonio Charming old buildings on the waterfront and some of the most picturesque beaches on the island nearby, page 232.

5 Rose Hall Great House An 18th-century plantation house with majestic gardens giving a view to the sea, page 239.

6 Royal Palm Reserve Part of a huge wetland sanctuary. Royal palms tower above walkways and birds and butterflies flit around the forest, page 246.

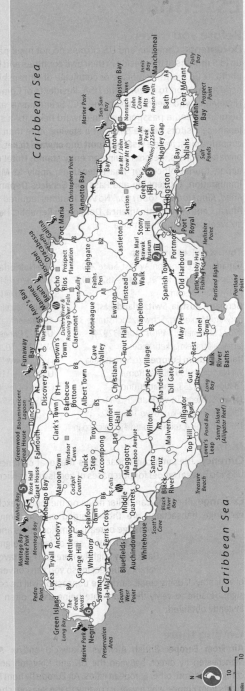

Jamaica

Essentials

Before you travel

Documents Canadian and US citizens do not need passports or visas for a stay of up to 6 months, if they reside in their own countries and have proof of citizenship with photo ID (ie a birth certificate or certificate of citizenship), although Americans now need a passport to return to the USA. Residents of Commonwealth countries (except Nigerians, who need a visa), the EC, Scandinavia and Switzerland, Turkey and Germany, need a passport and an onward ticket for a stay not exceeding 6 months. Japanese visitors need a passport if staying more than 30 days. Citizens of all other countries must have a **visa**, **passport** and **onward ticket**. Immigration may insist on an onward address, before issuing an entry stamp. Hotel rooms can be booked at the airport tourist office. For visa extensions, apply to **Ministry of National Security, Immigration, Citizenship and Passport Services Department** ① *25 Constant Spring Road, Kingston 10, T9061304*. No vaccinations required unless you have visited Asia, Africa, Central or South America, Dominican Republic, Haiti, Trinidad or Tobago within six weeks of going to Jamaica.

Tourist offices overseas

Canada, 303 Eglington Av East, Suite 200, Toronto, Ontario M4P 1L3, T416-4827850, jtb@jtbcanada.com.

Germany, **Austria**, **Switzerland**, Fast Forward Marketing, Schwarzbachstrasse 32, 40822 Mettmann, T49(0) 2104 832974, jamaica@travelmarketing.de.

Italy, **Southern Europe**, c/o Sergat Italia, Via Nazionale 230, 00184 Roma, T3906-48901255, sergat@rmnet.it.

Japan, Strategic Tower Bldg 2F, 2-11-1 Shibuya, Shibuya-ku, Tokyo 105-0002, T813-34002974, tourist-board@jamaica.co.jp.

The Netherlands, Postbus 2073, 3441 DB Woerden, T31-348430829, Jamaica.tb@12move.nl.

Spain, Barcelona, T34-934140210, sergat@sergatspain.com.

UK, 1-2 Prince Consort Rd, London SW7 2BZ, T020-72240505, jamaicatravel@btconnect.com.

USA, Suite 1101, 1320 South Dixie Highway, Coral Gables, Miami, FL 33146, T305-6650557, jamaicatrv1@aol.com.

Money

Currency The Jamaican dollar (J$) is the local currency but foreign currency up to US$100 is legal tender for purchases of goods and services, with change given in J$.

Exchange The Jamaican dollar floats on the foreign exchange market. The only legal exchange transactions are those carried out in commercial banks, or in official exchange bureaux in major hotels and the international airports. It is illegal to buy, sell or lend foreign currency without a licence. Banks pay slightly more for US$ travellers' cheques than for cash. Retain your receipt so you can convert Jamaican dollars at the end of your stay. If using credit cards the transaction will be converted into US$ before you sign; be sure to verify the exact rate being used, often a 5-10% adjustment can be instantly obtained.

❧ Rates in Negril can be worse than in Montego Bay.

Getting there

Air From Europe: **British Airways** (Gatwick) and/or **Air Jamaica** (Heathrow and Manchester) fly direct, between the UK and Kingston and Montego Bay with lots of connections from other European cities. **Air Europe** fly from Milan. There are many charter flights from Europe which vary according to the season, check with a travel agent.

From North America: **Air Jamaica** has services to Kingston and/or Montego Bay from Atlanta, Baltimore, Boston, Chicago, Fort Lauderdale, Houston, Los Angeles, Miami, New York, Orlando, Philadelphia. **Air Canada** and **Air Jamaica** fly from Toronto to Kingston and Montego Bay. **American Airlines** flies to Kingston and/or Montego Bay from Dallas, Houston, New York and Miami, with lots of connections from other cities through Miami. **US Air** flies to Montego Bay from Charlotte, New York, Philadelphia and Pittsburg. **Northwest Airlines** from Memphis and New York to Montego Bay.

From the Caribbean: regional airlines have services to Kingston from Antigua, Barbados, Curaçao, Grand Cayman, Havana, Nassau, Port-au-Prince, Port of Spain, St Maarten and Santo Domingo, and to Montego Bay from Barbados, Bonaire, Curaçao, Grand Cayman, Grenada, Havana, Holguín, Nassau, Port-au-Prince, Providenciales, Punta Cana, St Lucia and Santo Domingo. Flights are timed to connect with intercontinental arrivals and departures.

Boat It is extremely difficult to book a passage by ship to other Caribbean islands. About seven cruise lines call at Ocho Rios or Montego Bay weekly from Florida ports: **Carnival Cruises** (www.carnivalcruises.com), **Costa Cruises** (www.costacruises.com), **Norwegian Cruise Line** (www.ncl.com), **Royal Caribbean** (www.royalcaribbean.com), **Celebrity Cruises** (www.celebrity-cruises.com), **Princess Cruises** (www.princesscruises.com) and **Holland America** (www.hollandamerica.com). Others include from New York: **Royal Olympic Cruises** (T800-4686400); from Piraeus, Greece: **Festival Cruises** (www.festivalcruises.com, T30-210-6598500); from Hamburg, Germany: **Hapag Lloyd** (www.hlk.de, T49-40-30014600); from Manchester, UK: **Sun Cruises** (www.airtours.co.uk).

Touching down

Airport information There are two international airports: the **Norman Manley** in Kingston and **Donald Sangster** in Montego Bay. Montego Bay airport is the only one really within walking distance of most hotels. The Kingston domestic airstrip is at **Tinson Pen**, 3 km from the centre of town on Marcus Garvey Drive; those at Ocho Rios and Port Antonio are a long way out of town. At Kingston's Norman Manley Airport you can change back excess Jamaican dollars into US dollars at the bank in the departure lounge. ❧ See pages 216 and 238 for further details. There are also several reasonable shops there which will accept Jamaican currency (except for duty-free goods). Allow three hours to check in for a flight; there are four separate security, baggage or documentation checks.

Airlines

Air Canada, at the airports, T9248211.
Air Jamaica, passenger information and reservations, Kingston office, 72 Harbour St, Kingston, T9223460, or frequent flyer at 4 St Lucia Av, Kingston 5, T1888-9913733, ticket office and sales in Montego Bay at 9 Queens Drive, T9524100, other offices in Negril, T9575151, Ocho Rios, T7261344. Montego Bay is its regional hub.

Air Jamaica Express, reservations and information, 9 Queens Drive, T9525401.
American Airlines, 26 Trafalgar Rd, Kingston 10, T1800-7440006 (Montego Bay, T888-3592247).
British Airways, in The Towers, 25 Dominica Drive, Kingston 5, T1800-2479297.
Caribbean Airlines, 33 Tobago Av, Kingston 5, T800-7442225 (information and reservations too free).

Tourist information **Tourist office** Helpline ⓘ *T1888-995-9999 (free if outside Jamaica), www.jamaicatravel.com.* Head office at **Pan Caribbean Merchant Bank Building** ⓘ *64 Knutsford Blvd, Kingston 5, T9299200, info@visitjamaica.com,* circulates detailed hotel lists and plenty of other information. **Other offices in Jamaica** ⓘ *at the Cornwall Beach Complex, Montego Bay, T9524425, F9523587; City Centre*

Plaza, Port Antonio, T9933051, F9932117. The 'Meet the People' programme can introduce you to Jamaicans with your interests and hobbies, T1888-2666328. For Tour operators, see page 227.

Maps The *Discover Jamaica* road map (American Map Corporation) is widely available free from tourist offices. It has plans of Kingston, Montego Bay, Negril, Mandeville, Ocho Rios, Port Antonio and Spanish Town. Good clear series of 1:50,000 maps covering Jamaica in 20 sheets from Survey Department, National Land Agency, 23½ Charles St, Kingston, T9224278.

Security

The vast majority of Jamaicans welcome tourists and want to be helpful but the actions of the minority can leave you with the impression that tourists are not wanted. There are frequent military patrols to reinforce security in tourist areas. Harassment of tourists in downtown Montego Bay has been greatly reduced as a result of increased police patrols on bikes, and community involvement. Still, exercise caution when shopping and especially at nights.

The per capita crime rate is lower than in most North American cities, but there is a lot of violent crime. This is particularly concentrated in sections of downtown Kingston (90% of violent crime takes place in four Kingston police districts). While most incidents are community and turf related, crime can be encountered anywhere. Do not walk about in downtown Kingston after dark. There are large areas of west Kingston where you should not go off the main roads even by day. The motive is robbery so take sensible precautions. Gang warfare has been exacerbated by the US policy of deporting Jamaican criminals back to Kingston. Beware of pickpockets and be firm but polite with touts. Do not wear jewellery. Do not go into the downtown areas of any towns at night. Avoid arriving in a town at night. Take a taxi from bus stations to your hotel. Travellers have reported being threatened for refusing to buy drugs, as well as incidents where Jamaicans have become aggressive over traffic accidents, however minor. Take the obvious precautions and you should have no problem.

> *While most areas are generally safe, advice should be sought on the most appropriate routes and means of travel. If possible, travel in groups.*

Getting around

Air Air Jamaica Express (T1-888-FLYAIRJ, www.airjamaica.com/express) flies to the two international airports, **Boscobel Aerodrome at Ocho Rios**, Negril, T7261344, and **Tinson Pen Aerodrome** in Kingston, T9236664. Charges are reasonable but using this method of travel is not very satisfactory unless you can arrange to be met at your destination. Fares Kingston-Montego Bay, US\$61.50 adults US\$34 children one way, US\$123 adult US\$67 children return.

> *All fares attract US\$2.50 stamp duty.*

Bus Public road transport is mostly by minibus. The transportation system was reorganized in 2001 and is now more convenient and safe for travel. This form of travel is cheap and fast as buses operate on a schedule enforced by the transport authority officials located at bus terminals. Help may be obtained from the uniformed conductor or conductress on the bus. In the Kingston area the bus fare is US\$0.60; in Montego Bay the base fare is US\$0.22 for the first km and US\$0.04 per km thereafter.

Car Distances and driving times of major routes: Kingston to Montego Bay 193 km (3½ hours), to Ocho Rios 86 km (two hours), to Port Antonio 98 km (two hours); Montego Bay to Negril 83 km (one hour), to Ocho Rios 107 km (two hours); Ocho Rios to Port Antonio 108 km (2½ hours); Negril to Treasure Beach 107 km (1¾ hours). New highways in the north (North Coastal Highway) and south (Highway 2000) are being

☷ Touching down

Boat information Port Antonio Marina opened in 2002 with 24-hour Customs and Immigration, 32-slips for yachts of up to 100 m, as well as facilities for fishing boats. Fuel, provisioning, power and 3 phone lines for each berth, restaurant, bar, pool, internet access, laundry, showers and storage. Full-service boatyard for repairs and maintenance, haul-out for vessels up to 80 tons, 50-bay storage for vessels up to 15 m across the harbour from the marina.

Business hours Banks: Mon-Fri 0900-1500 or 1530 (some local variations). Offices: Mon-Fri 0830-1630. Shops: Mon-Sat 0830 or 0930-1600 or 1730, depending on area; half-day closing (1200) on Wed in Down Town Kingston, on Thu in uptown Kingston and Montego Bay, and on Fri in Ocho Rios.

Clothing Light summer clothing is needed all the year round and up in the mountains, with a sweater for cooler evenings. Some hotels expect casual evening wear in their dining rooms and nightclubs, but for the most part dress is informal. Bathing costumes, though, are only appropriate by the pool or on the beach.

Departure tax J$1000 (US$15), payable in Jamaican or US dollars for stays of 24 hrs or more. Cruise ship passengers pay US$15.

Drugs Marijuana (*ganja*) is widely grown in remote areas and frequently offered to tourists. Cocaine (not indigenous to Jamaica) is also peddled. Possession of either drug is a criminal offence. On average over 200 foreigners are serving prison sentences in Jamaica at any given moment for drug offences. The police stop taxis, cars, etc in random road checks. Airport security is tight with sniffer dogs, scans, etc.

Emergency Fire/Ambulance 110, Police 119.

Country code +876.

Official time Eastern Standard Time, 5 hours behind GMT and 1 hour behind the Eastern Caribbean.

Tipping Hotel staff, waiters at restaurants, barmen, taxi drivers, cloakroom attendants and hairdressers get 10-15% of the bill. When service is included, personal tips are often still expected. In some areas you may be expected to tip when asking for information.

Voltage 110 volts, 50 cycles AC; some hotels have 220 volts.

Weights and measures Metric.

Jamaica Essentials

built to improve travel times and comfort. Highway 2000 will connect Kingston with Montego Bay and Ocho Rios. Some parts are already completed. It is a 4-6-lane toll road (speed limit 110 kmph) with charges of US$2.80 (J$180) for cars and US$3.50 (J$230) for SUVs and minibuses. The Northern Coastal Highway is being done in stages with Negril-Montego Bay complete and Falmouth-Ocho Rios due to be completed in Dec 2007. Ocho Rios-Port Antonio is planned for 2008, so expect roadworks and delays for some time. Montego Bay-Rose Hall will have four lanes, but the rest will be two lanes. The speed limit is 80 kmph in unrestricted areas and 50 kmph or less in townships and other built-up areas. A North American driving licence is valid for up to three months per visit, a British licence 12 months and a Japanese licence one month. Try to avoid driving outside towns at night. Roads are often poorly lit, twisty and potholed, especially in mountainous areas, where there are no guard rails. Plan ahead because it gets dark early. Breath tests for drunk driving and speed traps are now in effect. Traffic congestion is to be expected in all large towns and jams are the norm in rush hour. Traffic is particularly slow and heavy

☷ *Drive on the left. Most petrol stations open on Sunday. There are a few 24-hr stations, but most close at 2200.*

between Kingston, Portmore and Spanish Town.

Car hire Undoubtedly a rented car is the most satisfactory, and most expensive, way of getting about. All the major car rental firms are represented both at the airports and in the major resort areas. There are also numerous local car rental firms which are mostly just as good and tend to be cheaper. The tourist board has a list of members of the **Jamaica U-Drive Association** ① *31 Hope Rd, Kingston 10, T9202872*. Be prepared to pay considerably more than in North America or Europe (starting from about US$49 per day (US$299 per week) for the smallest vehicle, US$58 (US$349) for a mid-sized car and US$73 (US$435) for a large vehicle, plus CDW of US$25 and tax of 15%). Many companies operate a three-day minimum hire policy. **Island Car Rentals** ① *www.islandcarrentals.com, airport office, Kingston, T9248075, airport office, Montego Bay, T9525771, Kingston T9268861, head office, 17 Antigua Av, Kingston 10, T9265991, 1-800-8924581, Main St, Ocho Rios, T9742666*, is a well-known firm with several offices around the island. **Praise Travel Ltd** ① *72 Half Way Tree Rd, Kingston 10, T9290215, F9296962*, good deals on longer rentals, no trouble with refunds, airport transfers, recommended. Clients must be 23 years old and have had a valid driver's licence for a minimum of a year.

Taxi There are taxis, with red **PPV** (Public Passenger Vehicle) licence plates, in all the major resort areas and at the airports. Some have meters, most do not. Only the **JUTA** taxis have officially authorized charges to all destinations. With others, the important point is to find out the fare before you get in. The police are a good source of information on fares. It can be around US$4-5 for a short hop, US$6-7 from New Kingston to Down Town, US$8-10 from Down Town to Mona Campus. All taxis should charge the same to the airport, US$18-23 from New Kingston. The tourist information centres should also be able to help in this respect. Some 'non-tourist' taxis, called 'robot taxis', operate like minibuses, that is, they have a set route and can be flagged down at the bus stop or anywhere along their route. They will carry up to four passengers, usually in a Nissan or Toyota, and charge about US$1 per person, but if you do not want to share you can hire it all for yourself at a higher cost. Negotiate the fare in advance. Be careful when taking 'robot taxis'. Avoid overcrowded vehicles as they may be stopped by the police for road code violations; a clean and well-maintained vehicle says volumes about the operator and the likelihood of having a safe and comfortable trip. To take a taxi for a long distance is expensive; a **JUTA** taxi from Kingston to Ocho Rios for example could cost US$125-145, rather more than a day's car hire, although you could negotiate a fare of less than half that with a smaller taxi company.

Sleeping

All-inclusive resorts are extremely popular in Jamaica, and include **SuperClubs** ① *www.superclubs.com*, **Sandals** ① *www.sandals.com*, **Couples Resorts** ① *www.couples.com*, and **Riu** ① *www.riu.com*, with hotels mainly along the north coast; some allow children but most are for couples only. As a result of their popularity, other hotels have been forced to discount their rates. Chris Blackwell's **Island Outpost** ① *www.islandoutpost.com*, now has several luxury hideaways, popular with the rich and famous.

❦ *Larger hotels have introduced strict security to prevent guests being bothered by hustling.*

Aim to arrive at Montego Bay rather than Kingston because the former is the island's tourism capital with a greater variety of affordable accommodation. However, if you can arrange to fly out from Kingston you will have a chance to get the flavour of the Jamaican experience in both cities. Get hold of the tourist board's list of hotels and guesthouses offering rates and addresses, and also a copy of **Jamaica Vacation Guide** (both free). Many small hotels and inns have grouped themselves as the **'Insider's Jamaica'** ① *www.insidersjamaica.com*. The tourist board has their brochure.

The **Jamaica Association of Villas and Apartments (JAVA)** ⓘ *Pineapple Place, Ocho Rios, Box 298, T9742508, F9742967*, represents over 300 private houses, villas and apartments. Renting a **villa** ⓘ *www.villasinjamaica.com*, may be an attractive option if you do not intend to do much travelling and there are four to six of you to share the costs (about US$1800-2000 per week for a nice villa with private swimming pool and fully staffed). You will, however, probably have to rent a car as you will have to take the cook shopping, etc. You can go even more upmarket and pay US$3000-14,000 a week for a fully staffed luxury villa.

> ❖ Accommodation is subject to a 16.5% General Consumption Tax, check whether it is included in room rates.

Cultural **homestays** can be arranged if you want to experience local hospitality with professional or retired professional hosts. Contact Hilary Burke, T613-2374658, hilary.burke@pointtopointbooks.com. English-language tuition is also offered.

Eating

Food There are many unusual and delicious vegetables and fruits such as sweetsop, soursop, starapple and naseberry. National specialities include saltfish (salt cod) and ackee, saltfish fritters and curried goat. Jerked pork is highly spiced pork which has been cooked in the earth covered by wood and burning coals. Chicken is cooked in the same way. Watch out for the scotch bonnet chillies which will give you an instant suntan. Festival is a very popular finger-shaped sweetened dough usually eaten with fried fish, bammy is pancake-shaped cassava bread also usually eaten with fried fish. Patties, sold in specialist shops and bars, are seasoned meat, vegetables or lobster in pastry, and very good value. Curried lobster is a delightful local speciality. The closed season for lobster fishing is April to June, so if lobster is on the menu during those months check where it has come from. Stew peas is chunks of beef stewed with kidney beans and spices and served with rice. Along the coast, fish tea is a hotch potch of the day's catch made into a soup, US$1-1.50 a cup. Jamaicans tend to 'marry' one food item to another and being able to order the appropriate combination from the menu is to demonstrate a mastery of local cuisine.

Drink Local rum is combined with local fruit juices to create cocktails, or mixed with *Ting*, a local carbonated grapefruit soft drink. *Red Stripe* lager, with which, the locals say, no other beer compares, is about US$1.50 at roadside bar, considerably more in a hotel. If you want any other beer you will have to specify the brand, otherwise you will automatically be given Red Stripe. *Irish Moss* is made from red algae mixed with herbs and roots and considered an aphrodisiac. All rums are very cheap duty free, typically US$13 for a three-pack.

Festivals and events

The tourist board publishes a calendar of events which covers arts and sports festivals, www.jamaicatravel.com/events. There is also www.whatsonjamaica.com, a guide to events, sports, entertainment and theatre. Cultural events are organized by the **Jamaica Cultural Development Commission (JCDC)**, 3 Phoenix Av, Kingston 10, T9265726, www.jcdc.org.jm. They publish a full calendar of national and local cultural events. **Jan** New Year's Day. Rebel Salute is held mid-Jan on the lawns of the Port Kaiser Sports Grounds in St Elizabeth, organized by reggae stalwart and Rastafarian, Tony Rebel. It features live performances by legendary reggae musicians and is patronized by a wide cross-section of Jamaicans who enjoy the sounds of the 1970s and 1980s in a spirit of oneness. The grounds become a huge encampment when fans descend from home and abroad.

Feb 6 Feb is **Bob Marley Day**, a celebration of the singer's earthday (birthday) held at the Bob Marley Museum, Kingston, and several other locations. A Fi Wi Sinting, Portland's Heritage Fest is held at Nature's Way Recreational Centre, Buff Bay, Portland, and features some of the best of local cultural traditions in food, crafts, poetry, music and dance, including folk forms such as Kumina,

Nyabinghi drumming, Mento and other rhythms. It is organized by Sister P (Pauline Petinaud, T7153529, www.fiwisinting.com), a cultural icon in the parish, who promotes authentic Jamaican culture through the lives of ordinary people.

Mar Fun in the Son is an annual gospel spring festival held in Ocho Rios for 4 days, packed with events including street jams, worship, sporting events and concerts with performances by top local and overseas gospel singers. Misty Bliss is an annual cultural event held on the last Sun in Mar at Holywell Park in the Blue Mountains, with live entertainment, traditional Jamaican food and authentic craft markets.

Mar/Apr Ash Wed, Good Fri, Easter Sun, Easter Mon are all local holidays when everyone on the island goes to church and congregations spill out on to the streets. On Easter Mon the popular Trelawny Yam Festival is held in Albert Town, Trelawny.

Carnival (www.jamaicacarnival.com) is held around Easter time, at various locations around the island, attended by thousands. Parades are made up of different groups in costumes, marching and dancing for the whole day through the streets. Upon reaching their destination there is a competition between the different groups, judged on stage according to their energy, creativeness and design. You can choose to be a part of the competition, by dressing in the costumes of a particular group, or you can simply march along with them in regular clothes as a supporter. Byron Lee, the leading Jamaican calypsonian, spends a lot of time in Trinidad over Carnival period and then brings the Trinidadian calypsonians and their music back to Jamaica.

May Calabash Literary Festival, www.calabash.org, includes literary performances by top local and overseas artistes over a 3-day weekend at the end of May in Treasure Beach. There are also live post-show musical performances on each night. Events leading up to the festival are held in Kingston, with film festivals and workshops. Calabash was founded in 2001 by the novelist Colin Channer and is the only international literary festival in the English-speaking Caribbean.

23 May Labour Day, a local holiday when you can find various activities.

Jul Red Stripe Reggae Sumfest, www.reggaesumfest.com, runs for a week and is possibly the greatest reggae show on earth. Certainly Jamaica's leading annual reggae music festival, at Catherine Hall Entertainment Complex in Montego Bay, it attracts all the most popular musicians from Jamaica and overseas, with each night themed according to types of artistes performing. The Portland Jerk Festival is held in the first week of Jul, bringing lovers of spicy food from all over the island to enjoy finger-licking pork, chicken, fish and more.

Aug The celebrations around Emancipation Day, 1 Aug, and Independence Day, 6 Aug, last a week, ending with a street dance at Half Way Tree. Reggae Sunsplash has returned after several years' absence, with great acts from the 1970s, held around Independence Day.

Oct The weekend leading up to National Heroes Day (3rd Mon in Oct) is packed with parties on the north coast and crowds of people gather from all over the island for non-stop partying, day and night.

Nov Jamaica Film and Music Festival (www.jamericanfilmfest.com) is held at the Wyndham Rosehall, Montego Bay. Film makers, musicians and artistes gather for discussions. It ends with an awards ceremony.

Dec East Fest is an annual reggae stage show held in St Thomas, hosted by the top local reggae group, Morgan's Heritage. Lively but also reflective, it is relaxing and good entertainment.

25-26 Dec Christmas Day, Boxing Day. The Greatest One Night Reggae Show on Earth is held on Boxing Day at the Jamworld Entertainment Centre, Portmore, St Catherine. It is the grand finale of dance hall acts for the year, a meeting place for the top artists of the genre.

Shopping

In the craft markets and stores you can find items of wood (by Rastafarians, Maroons and other craftsmen), straw, batik (from a number of good textile companies) and embroidery; the hand-knitted woollen gold, red, green Rasta caps (with or without black dreadlocks affixed) are very cheap. Blue Mountain coffee is excellent, cheaper at airport duty-free shop than in supermarkets or tourist shops.

Check with legislation (and your conscience) before buying articles made from tortoiseshell or crocodile skin, and certain corals, shells and butterflies. Many of these creatures are protected and should not be bought as souvenirs. It is illegal to take or possess black or white coral in Jamaica; sea turtles are protected and you should refuse to buy products made from their shells.

> ❖ Some shopkeepers offer a 10-15% discount on all goods and there is a 16.5% tax added to all goods (never added by street vendors).

Sport and activities

Diving and marine life There are marine parks in Montego Bay, Port Antonio and Negril. The **Montego Bay Marine Park** ① *T9795221*, stretches from the east end of the airport to the Great River and contains three major ecosystems: seagrass bed, mangroves and coral reefs. Non-motorized watersports such as diving, snorkelling and glass-bottom boat tours are permitted, but you are not allowed to touch or remove anything. There are several conservation groups involved in marine ecology. In St Ann, *Friends of the Sea*, Shop 5, Pineapple Plaza, Ocho Rios, T9747811, is a non-profit, non-governmental organization, which concentrates on education and public awareness and draws attention to what is happening on land that might affect what happens underwater. The **Northern Jamaica Conservation Association** (NJCA), also in St Ann, actively promotes conservation along the northern coast. The **Negril Coral Reef Preservation Society**, T9573735, has installed permanent mooring buoys for recreational boats and works on educational programmes with schools. The Negril marine park set up in conjunction with protected coastal and terrestrial habitats, aims at protecting the coral reefs and improving fish stocks.

Around Negril there are many reef sites and a huge variety of marine life: coral, sponges, invertebrates, sea turtles, octopus, starfish and lots of fish. Off Montego Bay and Ocho Rios there is wall diving quite close to shore and a few wrecks. Off Port Antonio fish are attracted to freshwater springs which provide good feeding grounds. The best wreck diving is off Port Royal and Kingston where you can also explore the city that slid into the sea in the 1692 earthquake. You will need a permit and to be escorted if diving the lost city.

Dive centres Nearly all dive operators are based at hotels along the north coast. The **Jamaica Association of Dive Operators** (JADO) offers courses at all levels. Contact the tourist board for a full list of operators and map of dive sites. Diving can be included in a hotel package. A two-tank dive costs on average US$65. Dives are limited to 30 m. There is a hyperbaric chamber at Discovery Bay.

Fishing Deep-sea fishing for white marlin, wahoo, tuna and dolphin fish can be arranged at north coast hotels. A half-day charter costs US$400 for up to six people, plus a 10% tip for the crew, who will expect to keep half the catch. There is a blue marlin tournament at Port Antonio and others at Montego Bay, Falmouth and Discovery Bay, as well as a James Bond Oracabessa Marlin Tournament. For details contact the **Montego Bay Yacht Club** ① *Montego Freeport, T9798038, mbyc@infochan.com*.

Health

In general, health care is good with average life expectancy of 75 years. Declining government spending on health and social programmes has led to falling standards and a rise in private hospitals and clinics with rising costs. The growing rate of HIV infection among Jamaicans is a serious concern. St James parish, which includes Montego Bay, has the highest incidence of AIDS in the country, with 198 cases per 100,000 population, compared with the national average of 83 per 100,000.

Communications **Internet** Additional phone lines have been installed and internet access is now available in several post offices and internet cafés around the country.

Post There are post offices in all main towns. The central sorting office on South Camp Road, Down Town Kingston, T9229430, has a good philatelic bureau.

Telephone Country code: 876. Cable, telephone, fax and cellular services are operated by **Cable & Wireless Jamaica Ltd** ① *47 Halfway Tree Rd, Kingston 5, T9269700, www.cwjamaica.com*. 'Time and charge' phone calls overseas cost the same in hotels as at the phone company, but there is a 16.5% tax and a service charge that varies. In fact, making an international call is often easier from a hotel. Phone cards may be obtained from Cable & Wireless, gas stations, supermarkets and various stores, available in J$50, J$100, J$200, J$500 and J$1000 denominations, plus 20% tax. Check that the year is valid for use. Other telecommunications companies have entered the cellular service market: **Digicel** ① *10-16 Grenada Way, Kingston 5, T5115000, www.digiceljamaica.com, Mon-Fri 0800-1700*, and **Mi Phone** ① *30 Knutsford Blvd, Kingston 5, T7541319, www.oceanicdigital.com, Mon-Fri 0800-1700*.

Newspapers The daily paper with the largest circulation is *The Daily Gleaner*, which also publishes an evening paper, *The Star*, and the *Sunday Gleaner*. The *Jamaica Herald* is a livelier daily than *The Gleaner*, also the *Sunday Herald*. The other daily is the *Observer*. *Mandeville Weekly* is a weekly community newspaper covering the parish of Manchester. *Money Index* is a financial weekly, in Montego Bay. *The Western Mirror* is weekly. *Lifestyle* is a monthly glossy magazine, *Jamaica Journal* is a quarterly with interesting but academic articles.

Kingston → *Phone code: 876. Colour map 1, C5. Population: 850,000.*

Jamaica's capital since 1870 and the island's commercial centre, Kingston has the seventh best natural harbour in the world. Following the earthquake of 1907 much of the lower part of the city (Down Town) was rebuilt, replacing red bricks with concrete. The old racecourses have been redeveloped: the Kingston Race Track was converted to the National Heroes Park after independence in 1962 and the Knutsford Track was redeveloped in the 1960s as the New Kingston commercial district, which contains most of the big hotels and many banks and financial institutions. Kingston and the adjoining parish of St Andrew (Corporate Area) are busy traffic-clogged urban areas. The Corporate Area is dominated by commerce and central government, but Kingston is the cultural and intellectual hub of the island, offering a diversity of attractions and activities unmatched by any other parish. A city tour could extend as far as Devon House and the nearby Blue Mountains and beaches at Hellshire, Lime Cay and other cays off Port Royal, followed by several nightclubs. Reggae lovers should visit the Bob Marley Museum and the Tuff Gong recording studios, but music can be heard anywhere with frequent blasts from buses, bars and cars. There are several art galleries, institutes and museums worth paying a visit. The Jamaica National Heritage Trust is a good source of heritage, www.jnht.com. ▸▸ *For Sleeping, Eating and other listings, see pages 220-228.*

Ins and outs

Getting there The international airport for Kingston is the **Norman Manley** (restaurant, shops), 17 km away, up to 30 minutes' drive, on the peninsula opposite Kingston across the bay. There is also an airstrip for domestic flights at Tinson Pen Aerodrome, Marcus Garvey Drive, Kingston 11, 3 km from the centre. If you have flown in to Montego Bay on the north coast you can get to Kingston by air or overland by frequent bus. ▸▸ *See also Transport, page 227, for further details.*

Travelling by bus is safe and convenient as the transport system is now operated by
the Government and monitored by the **Transport Authority**
① *T9294642*. **Crossroads, Pechon Street** and **Half Way Tree**
are the main bus stops. Addresses in the Parish of St Andrew

⁑ *It's best to go to a hotel to order a taxi.*

have a numbered zone, eg Kingston 10, while those in the Parish of Kingston have no
zone number and the address is just Kingston. **Jamaica Tourist Board** ① *Pan
Caribbean Merchant Bank Building, 64 Knutsford Blvd, Kingston 5, T9299200.*

Sights

Among older buildings of note in the Down Town area are **Gordon House** ① *81 Duke
Street, T9220200*, which dates from the mid-18th century and houses the Jamaican
legislature. Visitors are allowed into the Strangers' Gallery but must be suitably
dressed. There is also the early 18th-century Kingston Parish Church south of Parade,
where Admiral Benbow is buried. **Parade** (Sir William Grant Park, named in honour of
the 1938 labour leader who was an associate of Sir Alexander Bustamante) is at the
heart of the city centre; it is an open oasis amid the densely packed surroundings. The
name derives from the British soldiers' parades here during colonial rule. There are
several monuments, chief of which is of Queen Victoria, after whom the park was
originally named until independence. To the north is the statue of National Hero
Norman Manley and to the south the statue of Sir Alexander Bustamante. The park is
at the junction of the main east-west route through the Down Town area (Windward
Road/East Queen Street-West Queen Street/Spanish Town Road) and King
Street/Orange Street, which runs north to Cross Roads. At Cross Roads, the main
route forks, left to Half Way Tree, the capital of St Andrew, and straight on up Old Hope
Road to Liguanea. These two roads encompass New Kingston.

The Parish Church at St Andrew at **Half Way Tree** dates from 1700. Half Way Tree
was a half-way stage on the road between Spanish Town, the then capital, and the hills.
Half Way Tree is conspicuously marked by an old clock tower and a public park (recently
renamed Nelson Mandela Park). It is a busy junction which takes some negotiating in a
car. The two parishes of Kingston and St Andrew together form the **Corporate Area**
(Kingston being that section of the Corporate Area south of the National Heroes
Circle/Park) and St Andrew being to the north. Most of the new shops and offices are in
the Parish of St Andrew, although visitors and even locals are often not aware of where
one parish ends and the next begins. Crossroads and Half Way Tree (St Andrew) are
referred to as midtown areas. Many shopping plazas are further north again along the
Constant Spring Road and east along **Old Hope Road** to Liguanea. Just a few minutes'
drive to the east of Half Way Tree along Hope Road is **Devon House** ① *Waterloo and
Hope roads, Mon-Sat 0930-1630, US$5 adults, US$2 children under 12, for a guided
tour, T9260829*, built like a 'great house' by Jamaica's first negro millionaire in the
1880s. Now renovated, it has a museum of antique furniture. The craft shops and
restaurants in the grounds are well worth a visit. Not far away is **King's House** ① *corner
of Hope Rd and East King's House Rd*, the official residence of the Governor-General,
and, nearby is **Jamaica House** ① *Hope Rd*, the office of the Prime Minister.

About 10 blocks east of Devon House is the **Bob Marley Museum** ① *56 Hope Rd,
T9279152, Mon-Sat, 0930-1600, US$8 adults, US$6 13-18 years, US$3 children 4-12
years, including obligatory 1-hr guided tour and 20-min audio
visual presentation*. The house where Marley used to live traces his
story back to the time of his childhood and family, with paintings,
newspaper cuttings, posters and other memorabilia. He died
tragically of brain cancer in 1981 at the age of 36, having survived a
controversial assassination attempt (the bullet-holes in the walls have been left as a

⁑ *Photography is allowed outside but cameras must be left at reception during the tour.*

reminder). There is a gift shop selling Jamaican and African artefacts. Marijuana plants grow profusely throughout the grounds and ganja is smoked openly by staff.

Further east, along Old Hope Road, are the **Hope Royal Botanical Gardens** ① *0600-1800, free*. The land was first acquired by Major Richard Hope in 1671 and 200 years later the Governor of Jamaica, Sir John Peter Grant, bought 81 ha and created the gardens. In 1961 a **zoo** ① *T9271257, daily 1000-1600. US$0.30 adults, US$0.15 children*, was opened alongside the gardens, now a showcase for the different habitats of Jamaica and its indigenous animals. The gardens have lost much of their former glory because of a lack of government financial support. Private civic bodies are now combining their resources to manage and restore both facilities.

West of downtown Kingston, near the May Pen Cemetery, is the **Bob Marley Culture Yard**, a project started by the **Trench Town Development Association (TTDA)** ① *6 Lower*

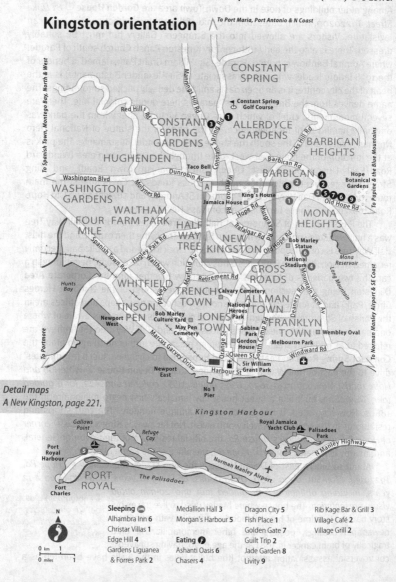

Kingston orientation

Detail maps
A New Kingston, page 221.

Sleeping	Medallion Hall 3	Dragon City 5	Rib Kage Bar & Grill 3
Alhambra Inn 6	Morgan's Harbour 5	Fish Place 1	Village Café 2
Christar Villas 1		Golden Gate 7	Village Grill 2
Edge Hill 4	Eating	Guilt Trip 2	
Gardens Liguanea	Ashanti Oasis 6	Jade Garden 8	
& Forres Park 2	Chasers 4	Livity 9	

First St, Trench Town, Kingston, T9484455, and 18 Collie Smith Drive, Kingston 12, T7576739, a community-based NGO, to boost the inner-city community of Trench Town, concentrating on the reggae heritage of Bob Marley and other great musicians who came from the area. Culture Yard is an attraction in the making, based on restoring the home and belongings of the reggae superstar to be opened for visitors.

On the waterfront there are some notable modern buildings including the **Bank of Jamaica**, **Nethersole Place**, the **Jamaica Conference Centre**, **Duke Street**, **The Institute of Jamaica**, **The National Library**, **East Street**, and the **National Gallery of Jamaica** ① *12 Ocean Blvd, T9221561*.

Beaches

The swimming at Kingston is not good and the sea at Gunboat beach, near the airport, is dirty. Swim at Port Royal (see below) and the cays offshore instead. 'Hellshire', south of Port Henderson, is a locals' favourite, but is about 15 to 20 minutes out of Kingston depending on traffic. *Bammy* (made from cassava root) and *festival* (a Jamaican appetizer) with fish are prepared along the beach strip.

Around Kingston

Port Royal → *Population: 2000.*

① *Beyond the international airport, some 24 km by excellent road; it can also be reached by boat from Victoria Pier (7 daily, 20 mins, US$0.30).*

Port Royal, the old naval base, lies across the harbour from Kingston. It was founded in 1650, captured by the English and turned into a strategic military and naval base. Merchant shipping developed under naval protection and the town soon became prosperous. It also attracted less reputable shipping and in 1660-1692 became a haven for pirates such as Henry Morgan, with gambling and drinking dens and brothels protected by the six forts and 145 guns. The 'wickedest city on earth', with a population of 8000, soon provoked what was thought to be divine retribution. On 7 June 1692 an earthquake hit east Jamaica, coursing along the Port Royal fault line and bringing with it massive tidal waves. The port, commercial area and harbour front were cut away and slid down the slope of the bay to rest on the sea bed, while much of the rest of the town was flooded for weeks. About 5000 people died (of drowning, injuries or subsequent disease) and the naval, merchant and fishing fleets were wrecked. The town was gradually rebuilt as a naval and military post but has had to withstand 16 hurricanes, nine earthquakes, three fires and a storm (which in 1951 left only four buildings undamaged).

Nelson served here as a post-captain from 1779 to 1780 and commanded **Fort Charles**, built in 1655, key battery in the island's fortifications. The former British naval headquarters now house the **Fort Charles Maritime Museum** ① *Mon-Thu 1000-1700, Fri 1000-1600, US$1*, with a scale model of the fort and ships. Part of the ramparts, known as **Nelson's Quarterdeck** ① *US$2*, still stands. The **Giddy House** was the Royal Artillery store, built in 1888 but damaged by the 1907 earthquake, which caused it to tilt at an angle of 45°. The Victoria Albert battery complex was a boiler house and underground armoury with late 19th-century guns to protect the harbour and tunnels. The old naval hospital was built in 1819 of prefabricated cast-iron sections brought all the way from England, one of the earliest constructions of this type and built on a raft foundation. The old gaol can also be seen. This dates from the early 18th century and was used as a women's prison in the 19th century. **St Peter's Church** is of historic interest, though the restoration is unfortunate. The **National Museum of Historical Archaeology** ① *US$0.30*, is little more than one room and the Fort Charles remains are more informative and substantive.

Boats may be hired for picnics on the numerous nearby cays or at Port

Henderson. **Lime Cay** (about the size of a football pitch) is the most popular, offering a white-sand beach and crystal clear water. A seafood restaurant and bar provides tasty fried fish and chicken meals. There is a full service marina at **Morgan's Harbour** with customs clearance, 24-hour security and fishing boats for hire.

Spanish Town

Spanish Town, the former capital, founded in 1534 and some 23 km west of Kingston (bus from Half Way Tree and from Orange Street), is historically the most interesting of Jamaica's towns and in desperate need of funds for renovation. Some money has been secured and restoration has started on sections of the fine Georgian main square, from where the proclamation ending slavery in 1838 was read. Its English-style architecture dates from the 18th century. Well worth seeing are the **Cathedral Church of St James**, the oldest in the anglophone West Indies, dating back to 1714. The square houses the ruins of the **King's House**, built in 1762 (Governor's residence until 1872 when Kingston became the capital) and burnt down in 1925. The façade has been rebuilt and beside it is the **Jamaican People's Museum of Craft and Technology** ① *Mon-Thu, 0930-1630, Fri 0930-1530, US$1.50, children US$0.60*. Also on the square are a colonnade (paint peeling off) and statue commemorating Rodney's victory at the Battle of the Saints, the **House of Assembly** (now local government offices)and the **Courthouse** (in ruins). The **park** in the centre is overgrown with weeds and the gates are padlocked. Outside town, on the road to Kingston is the **Taíno Museum** ① *Mon-Thu 0830-1630, Fri 0830-1530, US$1.50, children US$0.60; it's kept locked, ask in Spanish Town museum for permission to visit.*

⊙ Sleeping

Kingston *p216, maps p218 and p221*

LL Christar Villas, 99A Hope Rd, Kingston 6, T9783933, www.christarvillashotel.com. 32, 1- or 2-bedroom suites and studios with kitchenettes, pool, spa, sports bar, restaurant, small gym, conference facilities and business centre, free airport shuttle 0800-1700.

LL Hilton Kingston, 77 Knutsford Blvd, Kingston 5, T9265430, www.hiltoncaribbean .com. 303 comfortable, well-equipped rooms, usual **Hilton** facilities with fine dining, conference facilities, fitness centre, gaming room, swimming pool, tennis court, high speed internet access, complimentary cellular phone use. For nightlife, **Jonkanoo** night club and Kingston's first (expensive) Japanese restaurant.

LL Strawberry Hill, up in the hills of Irish Town overlooking Kingston Bay, T9448400, www.islandoutpost.com. Now a 14-villa luxury retreat but formerly a coffee and fruit plantation house, sadly destroyed by Hurricane Gilbert in 1988. Elegant, traditionally furnished rooms, enchanting gardens, breathtaking views. Gourmet dinners, brunches, lunches and tea, also sophisticated entertainment. Recommended weekend brunch of real Jamaican dishes

such as jerk meats, ackee and salt fish, washed down with strawberry bliss, blended champagne and strawberries, US$38.50, reservations recommended. Full service spa, conference, banquet and wedding facilities.

LL-AL Courtleigh Hotel and Suites, 85 Knutsford Blvd, Kingston 5, T9299000, www.courtleigh.com. 126 luxury 1- and 2-bedroom suites, spacious rooms, fully equipped business centre and meeting facilities, internet access in rooms, multilingual staff, gym, pool, magnificent view of city, harbour and mountains, **Alexander's Restaurant** and **Mingles Pub** on site.

L Jamaica Pegasus, 81 Knutsford Blvd, Kingston 5, T9263690, www.jamaica pegasus.com. 350 well-appointed rooms with balcony, state-of-the-art conference facilities, very good local and international cuisine, 2 flood-lit tennis courts, swimming pool and children's wading pool, enclosed jogging trail, gaming room, fitness centre.

L Terra Nova, 17 Waterloo Rd, Kingston 10, T9262211, www.terranovajamaica.com. 35 rooms, popular with business travellers, conference facilities and business centre, pool, bar, café and restaurant with excellent cuisine on the terrace or in the **Regency**

Room. Live entertainment by the pool bar.
AL Altamont Court, 1-5 Altamont Terrace, Kingston 5, T9294497, www.altamontcourt .com. 55 comfortable rooms, pool, restaurant, a/c, TV, facilities for the disabled, meeting rooms, multilingual staff.
AL Knutsford Court, 16 Chelsea Av, Kingston 10, T9291000, F9607373. Formerly **Sutton Place**, now refurbished and re-branded. 177 deluxe rooms and suites around a courtyard, a/c, TV, balcony, smoking or non-smoking floors, breakfast included, room service, restaurant, pool, business centre and meeting rooms,

laundromat or laundry service.
A Alhambra Inn, 1 Tucker Av, Kingston 6, T9789072, F9784338. Relaxing hotel with lots of greenery and climbing plants, wood panelling restaurant, bar, conference facilities, pool, good location.
A Four Seasons, 18 Ruthven Rd, Kingston 10, T9297655, www.hotelfourseasonsja.com. Run by Mrs Stockhert, German, long-time knowledgeable resident, in a converted Edwardian house and gardens, 75 a/c rooms, most with balcony, pool, 3 bars, gym, internet access, conference room, business centre, restaurant with average food.

New Kingston

To Spanish Town, North Coast & West

King's House

Sandhurst

Bob Marley Museum

Jamaica House

King's Mall

W King's House Rd

Springs Mall

Courtney Walsh Drive

Village Mall

St Andrew's Church

Nelson Mandela Park

To Spanish Town

Devon House

Hope Rd

Lady Musgrave Rd

To Hope Botanical Gardens, Papine, University & Blue Mountains

British High Commission

Western Union

New Kingston Mall

British Airways

Trafalgar Rd

Braemar Av

Worthington Av

Dominica Dr

Old Hope Rd

Oxford Rd

Belmont Rd

Central Rd

To Crossroads

To Crossroads, (Carib Cinema) & Downtown

N

Not to scale

Sleeping
Altamont Court 1
Courtleigh & Suites
& Mingles Pub 11
Four Seasons 2
Hilton Kingston 3
Indies 9
Jamaica Pegasus 5
Johnson Holborn Manor 9

Knutsford Court 10
Mayfair 6
Sandhurst 4
Terra Nova 8

Eating
Akbar 1
Bob's Café 6
Chelsea Jerk Pork
Centre 5
Dragon Court 12
Gaucho's Grill 13
Golden Bowl 19

Heather's Garden 2
Hot Pot 3
Island Grill 4
Lyn's Vegetarian 7
Norma on the Terrace
& I Scream 17
Red Bones Blues Café 8
Sugardaddies 20
Susie's Bakery &
Coffee Bar 21
TGI Friday 22
Thai Gardens 18
Up On D'Roof 23

Bars & Clubs
Asylum 9
Caesar's Night Club 10
Countryside Club 24
Cuddy'z 25
Jamrock Sports Bar
& Grill 9
Palais Royale Exotic
Nightclub 14
Platinum Dance
Club 15
Priscilla's Night Club 11
The Quad 16

A The Gardens Liguanea and Forres Park, 23 Liguanea Av, Kingston 6, T9278275, www.forrespark.com. Town houses, with 2 rooms, private bathrooms and shared living and dining room downstairs, rent a room or the whole house, breakfast included, pool, TV, internet access, homely service, convenient location within walking distance of Sovereign Shopping Mall and the bus route, also close to the university. The **Forres Park** is in the shadow of Blue Mountain Peak, offering accommodation, birdwatching, hiking and a paradise for photographers.
A Indies, 5 Holborn Rd, Kingston 10, T9262952, indies@discoverjamaica.com. 15 rooms, phone, cable TV US$6 extra, internet access, 2 restaurants, comfortable, pleasant patio, garden, helpful owners, relaxed family atmosphere.
A Johnson Holborn Manor, 3 Holborn Rd, Kingston 10, next door to **Indies**, T9293070. Breakfast included, fan, clean, safe and quiet, very convenient for business in New Kingston, 3 good places to eat within 50 m, luggage storage available, friendly, new annex.
A Mayfair, 4 West King's House Close, Kingston 10, T9261610, mayfairhotel @cwjamaica.com. Beautiful setting (adjoining the Governor General's residence), balconies look towards mountains, 32 rooms and suites, also 8 houses with gardens, restaurant, poolside buffet, barbecue Wed, Sat, Sun, spa, conference room.
A Medallion Hall, 53 Hope Rd, Kingston 6, T9275721, F9275866. 22 elegant a/c rooms with Victorian-style furniture, wheelchair access, conference rooms, restaurant, central.
B Sandhurst, 70 Sandhurst Cres, Kingston 6, T9277239. 35 rooms, a/c or fan, pool, restaurant, good food, excellent hospitality and convenient location.
B-C Edge Hill, 198 Mountain View Av, Kingston 6, T9784879, www.discoverjamaica. com/edge. Beautifully laid out small hotel, very cosy with friendly staff. 12 self-contained studios with kitchenette, fridge, TV, a/c, 9 standard rooms with TV, 2 top of the line suites. Indoor and patio dining, 2 bars, sun deck and view of the harbour, airport and business district.

Port Royal *p219, map p218*
AL Morgan's Harbour at Port Royal, T9678075, mharbour@kasnet.com. Near the airport, transport there and back. A favourite holiday centre, 40 rooms, 5 suites, sea view, seminar rooms, fresh and saltwater swimming pools, beach cabins, good seafood restaurant, and dancing, closest hotel to airport.

🍴 Eating

Kingston *p216, maps p218 and p221*
There are many places, plush and modest, to eat in **Downtown Kingston**, **New Kingston**, **Half Way Tree** and the **Liguanea** area. For the impecunious, meat patties can be bought for US$0.80 each from **Tastee**, **Juici Patties**, **Sugar & Spice** or **Mother's**, various locations but mostly in **Liguanea**, **Half Way Tree**, **New Kingston**, **Cross Roads** or **Manor Park**. Also a wide range of lovely cakes and pastries. On Knutsford Blvd there are lots of vans selling a satisfying lunch for about US$2.50, often less, depending on what you eat.
♥♥♥ Norma's on the Terrace, Devon House (see page 217), 26 Hope Rd, Kingston 10, entrance on Waterloo Rd, T9685488. Plush, expensive restaurant. Also at Devon House are a reasonably priced snack bar and delicious ice cream at **I Scream**.
♥♥♥-♥♥ Jade Garden, Shop 54, Sovereign Centre, 106 Hope Rd, Kingston 6, T9783476 for reservations or takeaway. Mon-Sat 1200-2200, Sun 1000-2100. Very elegant and sophisticated Chinese restaurant with a taste of the Orient, also a more relaxing and comfortable cocktail lounge, private dining room and conference room.
♥♥♥-♥♥ Red Bones Blues Café, 21 Braemar Av, Kingston 10, T9786091. Mon-Fri 1200-2300, Sat 1800-2300. 'Nouvelle Jamaican cuisine', quite expensive but lovely garden and blues music.
♥♥ Akbar, 11 Holborn Rd, Kingston 10, T9263480. Very good authentic Indian food, Georges Duboeuf fine wines, good service, nice atmosphere, US$20 for 3-course dinner and drinks for 2, also delivery service.
♥♥ Bamboo Village, Shop 15, Village Plaza, 24 Constant Spring Rd, Kingston 10, T9268863. Daily 1200-2200. Chinese food, comfortable and pleasant, courteous staff.
♥♥ The Fish Place Limited, 136 Constant Spring Rd, Kingston 8, T9244063. Jamaican restaurant, the best place in town for fish in all styles, prices around US$10-15, easy-going, relaxed atmosphere, popular after-work dining and weekend stop for families and friends, live music sometimes.

¶ **Gaucho's Grill**, 20A South Av, Kingston 10, T7541380. Ribs, steak and seafood. Great service, inspiring menu.

¶ **Golden Gate**, 14 Northside Drive, Northside Plaza, Kingston 6, Liguanea, T9777552. Mon-Sat 1130-2100, Sun 1400-2100. Good Cantonese food, cosy dining room, eat in or takeaway.

¶ **Guilt Trip**, 20 Barbican Rd, Kingston 6, T9775130. Lovely garden setting, Italian-influenced menu and delicious pastries.

¶ **Heather's Garden Restaurant**, 9 Haining Rd, Kingston 5, T9262826. Middle Eastern and Jamaican dishes, US$3.25-9.

¶ **Lillian's**, in the grounds of the University of Technology at Papine, T9702224. Staffed by trainees, good cheap lunch for about US$3, comfortable atmosphere.

¶ **Real Jamaican Jerk**, very tasty fast foods, affordable prices, several branches now appearing, including at the international airports in Kingston, T9248818, and Montego Bay, T9714288. Jerk chicken and fish are popular, side orders include seasoned fries, festivals, callaloo rice and pumpkin rice.

¶ **The Rib Kage Bar & Grill**, 149 Constant Spring Rd, Kingston 8, entrance on Saxthorpe Av, T1-888-7425243, or 9051858 for takeaway and reservations. Mon-Sat 1100-2300. Laid-back and relaxed, friendly staff, serving the best ribs in the Caribbean as well as other tasty specialities. Will delivery to some areas.

¶ **Thai Gardens**, 11 Holborn Rd, Kingston 10, next to Akbar, T9063237. Mon-Fri 1200-1530, Sun 1430-2230. Reservations recommended, Thai cuisine.

¶ **Up On D'Roof**, 73 Knutsford Blvd, Kingston 5, T9298033. Mon-Fri 1800-2330, Sat 1600-2330. Great food, Jamaican cuisine at its best, with lots of fish and vegetarian options as well as jerk meats to bring on a sweat. Pleasant service and atmosphere, cheerful décor and good music.

¶-¶ **Dragon City**, 17 Northside Drive, Northside Plaza, Kingston 6, Liguanea, T9270939. Mon-Sat 1130-2100, Sun 1400-2100. Good, authentic Cantonese food, eat in or takeaway.

¶-¶ **Dragon Court**, Dragon Centre, 6 South Av, Kingston 10, T9208506, 1-888-9913388 for reservations. Mon-Sat 1200-2200, Sun 1000-1400. Elegant Chinese restaurant offering large variety of Chinese dishes as well as Dim Sum and barbecue. Takeaway service available.

¶ **Ashanti Oasis**, Hope Gardens, Old Hope Rd. Vegetarian meals and cool jazz on Sun afternoons. Daily from 1300.

¶ **Bob's Café**, 56 Hope Rd, Kingston 6, T9782627. Mon-Sat 1100-2300.

¶ **Chasers Restaurant & Lounge**, 29 Barbican Rd, Kingston 6, T7022702. Lots of Jamaican favourites are served for lunch.Popular.

¶ **Chelsea Jerk Pork Centre Limited**, 7 Chelsea Av, Kingston 10, T9266322. Jerk chicken and pork with festivals, popular with locals.

¶ **Eden Vegetarian Restaurant**, Shop 24, Central Plaza, Kingston 10, T9263051. Variety of vegetarian cuisine, including patties and pastries and also provides natural supplements. Eat in, takeaway or delivery service.

¶ **Golden Bowl**, 7 Cargill Av, T9298556, Mon-Thu 1100-2100, Fri-Sat 1100-2130, Sun 1200-1900. Good Chinese. Elegant dining room or efficient takeaway service.

¶ **Hot Pot**, 2 Altamont Terr, Kingston 5, T9293906. Very cheap, serves good Jamaican food in a pleasant patio, also a take-out box for just over US$1; difficult to find.

¶ **Island Grill**, Shop 28, Twin Gates Plaza, 25½ Constant Spring Rd, Kingston 10, T9262807, and Sovereign Centre (Shopping Mall), Shop 16, 106 Hope Rd, Kingston 6, T9783535. Tasty Jamaican meals to go.

¶ **Livity Gourmet Vegetarian Restaurant**, 166½ Old Hope Rd, Kingston 6, T9775433. Delicious, original vegetarian recipes and a cool atmosphere.

¶ **Lyn's Vegetarian Restaurant**, 7 Tangerine Place, Kingston 10, T9683487. Tasty vegetarian and fish dishes, tuna casserole, stewed gungu peas and sweet and sour tofu.

¶ **Prendy's on the Beach**, Putt and Play, Kingston 10, T8819689, prendysonthebeach@ yahoo.com. Wed, Fri, Sat 1800-2300. Hellshire Beach, T3936181. Mon-Wed 0900-2100, Thu 0900-2200, Fri, Sat 0900-2300, Sun 0800-2400 party on the beach. Tasty Jamaican seafood meals.

¶ **Sonia's Homestyle Cooking and Natural Juices**, 9 Lane Plaza, Kingston 10, T9686267. Mouthwatering Jamaica dishes and very friendly staff.

¶ **Sugardaddies**, 19 Hillcrest Av, Kingston 6, Liguanea, T9461063. Lunch, dinner and Sun brunch. Modern Caribbean soul food, serves up good local and Caribbean favourites such as fried and barbecued chicken, pizzas, salads and natural juices, also catering services.

¶ **Susie's Bakery and Coffee Bar**, Shops 1 and 2, Southdale Plaza, 40 Constant Spring Rd, Kingston 10, T9262791, and in the Orchid Village, 20 Barbican Rd, Kingston 6, T9704645. Recommended for light lunches, pastry and coffee, cosy atmosphere, wholesome aroma, friendly service.

¶ **Village Café**, Orchid Village, 20 Barbican Rd, T9704861, robsvillage@hotmail.com. Delicious finger foods with alternative live entertainment, often referred to as 'Kingston's living room' because of its relaxed atmosphere.

¶ **Village Grill**, Orchid Village, 20 Barbican Rd, under the same roof as **Village Café**, T9704861. Tue–Sun 1800 until late, finger food such as Ma Lou's wing dings (chicken wings), fries and sandwiches.

Spanish Town *p220*
Miami, Cumberland Rd, near the market area; food is delicious, especially the pumpkin soup. In the Spanish Town Shopping Centre there are fast food restaurants, some serving real Jamaican dishes.

⊙ Bars and clubs

Kingston *p216, maps p218 and p221*
Most hotels have dancing at weekends. Unless they have Jamaican friends, tourists are strongly advised not to probe too deeply into real Jamaican nightlife. The *Jamaica Vacation Guide* (at hotels, tourist offices) has the latest information. There is always a party going on every weekend in Kingston, and almost every night during any of the holiday seasons. The fliers are well circulated and the light posts full of billboards promoting the respective parties, informing the public of dates and venues. These parties boast loud, lively music from mostly Jamaican and North American culture, with some carrying themes. The gates of the venue usually open around 2200, although the locals don't arrive until about midnight, and the fun stops around 0400. The cost may range between US$5-10 not including drinks.

Asylum, 69 Knutsford Blvd, Kingston 5, T9061828, asylumja@hotmail.com. Sat-Thu 2100-0400, Fri 1700-0400, US$5 (Wed US$2). The number one young adult disco, closed Mon, Ladies' Night Tue (ladies free); Lazy night Wed; Dance Hall night Thu with Stone Love Disco and various performers, after-work jam and disco Fri (free 1700-1900), international music Sat and after-party, Vibes night Sun.

Countryside Club, 7 Courtney Walsh Drive, Kingston 10, T9206645. Wed-Sat 1200-late, Sun 1700-late. A little tropical paradise in the heart of Halfway Tree, relax under palm trees and huts while enjoying local dishes and live entertainment.

Cuddy'z, Shops 4-6, New Kingston Shopping Centre, Kingston 5, T9208956. Mon-Thu 1130-2300, Fri-Sat 1130-0100, Sun 1800-2300, happy hour 1700-2000. Sports bar owned by former West Indies bowler Courtney Walsh, TVs everywhere, computers on the tables, long modern bar. Food ranges from saltfish and ackee to chicken quesadillas, good callaloo dunk, dishes named after Jamaican sports heroes. Fri nights lots of events. Favourite spot for sports personalities and fans.

Devon House is a good place for a quiet evening drink under the trees. Grounds are well kept and there are several benches to sit and enjoy a night under the stars while eating delicious ice cream.

Jamrock Sports Bar & Grill, 69 Knutsford Blvd, downstairs from **Asylum**, T7544032. Young crowd, music, TV, pool, sports fans, can get loud, place to hang out and enjoy good food and company.

Jonkanoo Lounge, **Hilton Hotel**, 77 Knutsford Blvd, Kingston 5, T9297439. Popular venue for relaxation and fun. Wed-Sun 1800-late. Thu Latin night, Fri, Sat party nights with happy hour always packed, US$5.

Mingles Pub and Pool Bar, **Courtleigh Hotel**, 85 Knutsford Blvd, Kingston 5, T9299000, www.courtleigh.com. Every night from 2000. US$3-4. Nightclub and disco, with food and drink. Regular hangout for consultants and young professionals, wide variety of alcoholic and non-alcoholic mixed drinks, karaoke on Thu, barbecue and jive on the terrace Mon, Fri, Latin night on Sat (free) including dance lessons from 1900, popular with cross-section of party goers.

Palais Royale Exotic Night Club, 14 Ripon Rd, Kingston 5, T9291113. Nightly 2100-late, and **Caesar's Night Club**, 5 Balmoral Av, Kingston 10, T9296273, Wed-Sun 1800-late, are both wild and exciting if you like dancing girls in costumes that leave as much to the imagination as hair on a turtle's shell, but safe and comfortable and an interesting aspect of Jamaican culture.

Platinum Dance Club, Dominica Drive, Kingston 5, T9081143, exotic dancers from Russia, closed Sun.

Polo Lounge, Jamaica Pegasus, 81 Knutsford Blvd, Kingston 5, T9253690. Sophisticated, indoor and outdoor seating, tables in cosy nooks and corners for intimacy, poolside bar, live entertainment. Daily 1700-late. US$8-9.

Priscilla's Night Club, 103 Constant Spring Rd, Kingston 8. Favourite for after-work professionals, laid-back atmosphere and great city views. Mostly R&B music, also a Latin night.

The Quad, 20-22 Trinidad Terrace, New Kingston, Kingston 5, T754QUAD. Jamaica's only multi-level night club, each with its own atmosphere and type of music:

Christopher's Jazz Café is on the ground floor, very relaxed and soothing, where lounge seating and sweet jazz music set the tone. There may be live entertainment. Good wine cellar. Mon, Tue, Thu 1100-2400, Wed, Fri, Sat 1100-late.

Oxygen is on the 1st floor and has a high energy atmosphere with mostly North American top 40 mixes by popular DJs Alric and Boyd. Wed 2100-0300, US$8-9. Fri, Sat 2200-late, US$10. Wed is retro night with music from the 1980s and 1990s. Good lighting and an excellent sound system, choice of bars.

Voo Doo Lounge is on the top floor, comfortable, only retro music played here. Outdoor deck with good view of Kingston. Wed (60s and 70s music) 2100-0300, US$8-9. Fri, Sat (70s, 80s, 90s music), 2200-late, US$10.

Rae Town, just east of downtown Kingston, is primarily a fishing community on the coast, but it is a very popular inner-city hangout for locals and visitors, especially on Sun nights, offering a secure experience of street dance urban entertainment 'ghetto style', with typically heavy Dance Hall music from huge sound systems, and a variety of Jamaican food and drink from roadside bars and restaurants.

Red Bones Blues Café, 21 Braemar Av, Kingston 5, T9786091. 1200-0100. Great food, see Eating page 225, excellent service and an upscale ambiance in a garden setting. Jazz and blues, indoors or outdoors, entry US$8-9, also ongoing art exhibition and a gift shop.

The Village Café, see Eating page 224. Tue-Sun 1800 until late. Exciting events every night. Tue Be a DJ for a night, enjoy

snow cover, Wed **Dream's Ultimate Calendar Girl Competition**, also an electric mix with international music and snow cover (ladies enter free), Thu the fashion village, where clothes from top local designers are modelled, also the best music from the 80s and 90s (ladies enter free), Fri party night, with entertainment from the 'village duppy' (2 Appleton mixed drinks for the price of 1, ladies enter free), Sat college night (ladies free), Sun 'tantra'; chic, sexy, divine Sun (also 2 for 1 Appleton drinks and free entry for all).

Weekenz, 80 Constant Spring Rd, Kingston 8, T7554415. Sells itself as the Caribbean's Finest Entertainment Centre and host to a number of events such as parties, poetry readings, singing and drama as well as relaxing and drinking with friends.

● Entertainment

Kingston *p216, maps p218 and p221*
Cinema
Carib Cinema, in the heart of Crossroads, Kingston 5, T9266106.
The Cineplex, in Sovereign Centre, Shop 47a, 106 Hope Road, Kingston 6, T9783522.

Theatre and dance
Edna Manley School for the Visual and Performing Arts produces graduates of a very high standard in art, music and dance. There are several very active theatre and dance companies such as the **Ashe Creative Arts group**, **Dance Theatre Xaymaca**, the **Wolmer's Dance Troupe** and **Praise Academy of Dance Troupe**. **National Dance Theatre Company** is well known internationally. All have shows annually or biannually.

Ward Theatre Foundation, North Parade, T9220453.
Little Theatre Movement, 4 Tom Redcam Av, Kingston 5, T9266129.
The Center Stage Theatre, 18 Dominica Drive, Kingston 5, T9687529.
The Barn Theatre, 5 Oxford Rd, Kingston 5, T9266469.
The Pantry Playhouse and Dinner Theatre, 2 Dumfries Rd, Kingston 5, T9266469.
Phillip Sherlock Centre for the Creative Arts (PSCCA), on the grounds of the University of the West Indies, Mona, Kingston 7, T9271047. Watch the press for details of performances.

⊙ Shopping

Kingston *p216, maps p218 and p221*
Most shops are in the plazas along Constant
Spring Rd, in Manor Park and in Liguanea.
There is a smart shopping centre in New
Kingston with duty-free concessions for visitors.

Arts and crafts

Jamaica Crafts Market, downtown
Kingston, at the corner of Ocean Blvd and
Port Royal St and many shops at west end of
Port Royal St have local crafts. The market is a
must for souvenir hunters, craft items are
reasonably priced and there is a wide range
of traditional Jamaican handicrafts.

Other shops for great local crafts are the
Craft Cottage Limited, in The Village Plaza, 24
Constant Spring Road, Kingston 10, T9260719,
Carby's Craft Village and **Souvenirs Discount
Centre**, shop 4, Twin Gates Plaza, 25 ½
Constant Spring Rd, Kingston 10, T9264065.
Chelsea Galleries, Chelsea Rd, **Gallery 14, Old
Boulevard Gallery, Grosvenor Galleries**, 1
Grosvenor Terrace, Kingston 8, T9246684,
Contemporary Art Gallery, 1 Liguanea Av,
Kingston 6, T9279958. **Things Jamaican**, Devon
House, 26 Hope Road, Kingston 10, T9261961,
and also at both the Norman Manley
International Airport in Kingston, T9248556,
and the Donald Sangster International Airport
in Montego Bay, T9710775.

Books

Kingston Bookshop, at 70B King St,
T9224056, the Pavilion Shopping Mall, 13
Constant Spring Rd, T9605376, and at The
Springs Plaza, 15-17 Constant Spring Rd,
T9201529.
Bookland 53 Knutsford Blvd, Kingston 5,
T9264035, has a wide range of US magazines
and newspapers and also *The Times*.
Sangster's Book Stores, 15 Constant Spring
Rd, Kingston 10, T9207589, www.sangsters
books.com, and at several other locations
has a wide variety of books and stationery.

Market

The market off West Queen St is an
interesting local market, selling fish, fruit and
general produce. Downtown is where
Jamaicans shop for bargains, but be careful,
particularly in the market, it can be
dangerous, even if you don't get robbed.

Music

Reggae music shops can be found close
together along Orange St, just north of
Parade. Others are in the shopping plazas.

▲▲ Activities and tours

Kingston *p216, maps p218 and p221*
For diving and fishing, see page215.

Golf

Putt 'n' Play Mini Golf Park, 78 Knutsford
Blvd, Kingston 5, T9064814. Tue-Fri
1700-2300, Sat-Sun 1600-2400. 18 holes and
an artificial turf with streams and bridges,
sand patches, and greens, giving players a
real golf experience. There are instructors on
hand to give lessons or pointers. The
environment is very relaxed with a snack bar,
lounge chairs, a pool table and background
music. There are also rides for children which
operate on Sat and Sun until 2200, good
family night out.
The Constant Spring Golf Club, 152 Constant
Spring Road, Kingston 8, T7552066. Daily 0800-
2200, 18 holes, green fee US$38 weekdays and
US$46 weekends and public holidays.
Caymanas Golf Club, Mandela Highway,
T9223386. 18 holes, green fee US$42
weekdays and US$54 weekends, open
Mon-Fri 0830-1600, Sat-Sun 0630-1630; golf
cart rental US$23 and US$15.50 for the
caddy. There is also a pro shop, a restaurant,
2 bars and a pool.
The Jamaica Golf Association, Constant
Spring Rd, Kingston 8, T9252325,
jamaicagolf@cwjamaica.com, has
information on tournaments.

Spectator sports

Basketball has become increasingly
popular in Jamaica over the last decade, with
the sport becoming more and more
competitive and exciting each year. Contact
the **Jamaica Basketball Association**, and get
information on the newly formed and very
popular National Basketball League (NBL), as
well as the Division 2 League, and the
Women's League.
Cricket is the island's main spectator sport,
although it was overtaken by football
(soccer) in 1998 when Jamaica qualified for
the World Cup. Test matches are played at
Sabina Park. For details on matches ring

Jamaica Cricket Association, T9228423-4, 39 South Camp Rd, Kingston 4. Jamaica hosted the opening ceremony for the Cricket World Cup 2007 and West Indies' first round matches as well as some of the semi-finals.

Football For information on national team matches as well as the very popular National Premier League matches, contact the Jamaica Football Federation, 20 St Lucia Crescent, Kingston 5, T7547976-8.

Horse racing At Caymanas Park, T7045042, every Wed and Sat and most public holidays.

Polo International tournaments are held at Caymanas Polo Club.

Tennis

Try the Eric Bell Tennis Centre.

Tour operators

Apollo Travel Services, 14 Dominica Drive, Kingston 5 , T9298483, F9687214, and Shop 3, Spanish Town Shopping Centre, 17 Burke Rd, Spanish Town, T9845040, IATA members. For scheduled or charter flights to neighbouring islands.

Caribic Vacations, Providence Drive, Rose Hall, T9532600, reservations T9532565.

JUTA Jamaica, Marvins Park, Ocho Rios, T9742292, Claude Clarke Av, Montego Bay, T9520813, F9525355 and Norman Manley Blvd, Negril, T9579197.

Sun Venture Tours, 30 Balmoral Av, Kingston 10, T9606685, 4694444, www.sunventuretours.com. Activities for nature lovers away from the beach, hiking, caving, safaris, birdwatching, downhill Blue Mountain bicycle tours and educational tours, managed by Robert Kerr.

⊖ Transport

Kingston *p216, maps p218 and p221*
Bus
Fares from Kingston are: US$3 to **Mandeville**, US$5 to **Montego Bay**, US$1.50 to **Negril**, US$2.80 to **Ocho Rios**, US$3 to **Port Antonio**. The buses are invaded by touts as they approach the bus station.

The local Government bus service, Jamaica Urban Transit Company (JUTC), has largely replaced the old bus franchise services with a fleet of newly acquired buses and a much more efficient service, significantly improving travel times and comfort around the Corporate Area. Tickets are US$0.50. Buses and shared taxis to/from North Parade for the airport, US$0.85. The buses and timetabling have been upgraded and improved, but allow waiting time during rush hour. The buses are well marked with destinations and numbers. To get to New Kingston by bus, change bus (to No 83) downtown. The recognized service between town and airport is JUTA, taxi/minibus, which charges US$21 to New Kingston (taxi dispatcher gives you a note of fare before you leave, can be shared). Alternatively, if travelling light, taxi to Port Royal, US$13, ferry to Kingston (see below, Port Royal) and then taxi to New Kingston, US$6-7.

⊙ Directory

Kingston *p216, maps p218 and p221*
Banks National Commercial Bank of Jamaica, The Atrium, 32 Trafalgar Rd, Kingston 10, T9299050, and branches in New Kingston, Half Way Tree, Downtown, Manor

Jamaica Kingston Listings

Park, Liguanea and all over the island; **Bank of Nova Scotia Jamaica Ltd**, head office: Duke and Port Royal Sts, Kingston, T9221000, other branches in the corporate area include Cross Roads, Half Way Tree, Liguanea, New Kingston and Downtown; **RBTT Bank Jamaica Ltd**, 17 Dominica Drive, Kingston 5, T9602340, with other branches in Cross Roads, Half Way Tree, Liguanea, New Kingston and Downtown, as well as branches out of town. **Citibank**, 63-67 Knutsford Blvd, Kingston 5, T9263270, with another branch in Montego Bay. There are several other local banks. ATMs are widespread. Immediate money transfers such as the **Western Union Bank**, 2 Trafford Place, Kingston 5, T9262454, behind the **National Commercial Bank** at the top of Knutsford Blvd, with several branches throughout the corporate area and out of town.

Embassies and consulates Australia (High Commission), 9263550. **Canada** (High Commission), 3 West Kings House Rd, Kingston 10, T9261500, kngtn@international.gc.ca. **Cuba**, 9 Trafalgar Rd, Kingston 10, T9780931. **Denmark**, T9235051. **Dominican Republic**, 32 Earls Court, Kingston 8, T7554154. **France**, 13 Hillcrest Av, Kingston 6, T9780210, www.ambafrance-jm.org. **Germany**, 10 Waterloo Rd, Kingston 10, T9266728. **Haiti**, 2 Munro Rd, Kingston 6, T9277595. **Israel**, T9268768. **Italy**, T9202673. **Japan**, 2 Oxford Rd, NCB Towers, north Tower, 6th floor, Kingston 5, T9293338. **Netherlands**, 53 Knutsford Blvd, Kingston 5, T9262026. **Norway**, T9235541. **Spain**, 25 Dominica Drive, Kingston 5, T9296710. **Sweden**, T9225860. **Switzerland**, T9787857. **UK** (High Commission), 26 Trafalgar Rd, T9269050, bhckingston@cwjamaica.com. **US**, 142 Old Hope Rd, 3rd floor, Kingston 6, T7026000.

Blue Mountains and the east

The Blue Mountains are synonymous with the greatest coffee in the world, sold at premium prices because of its exquisite flavour acquired during its slow growth on the cool, misty slopes where methods of cultivation, harvesting and roasting are the same as they have been for 200 years. It is also the most beautiful part of Jamaica, with forests, trails, birds and flowers for all nature lovers and the hike up to the highest point, Middle Peak, to see the dawn inspires a huge sense of achievement and wonder. It has been nominated as a UNESCO World Heritage Site. The coast around Port Antonio is also attractive and unspoilt, being quite a distance from either of the main airports. Pretty bays, sandy coves, banana plantations, waterfalls and rafting on the Rio Grande characterize this end of the island. ›› *For Sleeping, Eating and other listings, see pages 233-235.*

North from Kingston

Behind Kingston lie the **Blue Mountains**, with Blue Mountain Peak rising to a height of 2256 m. This is undoubtedly one of the most spectacular and beautiful parts of Jamaica and an absolute must for keen birdwatchers and botanists and also for those who like hiking. It is possible to explore some of the Blue Mountains by ordinary car from Kingston via **Papine**. After leaving Papine and just after passing the **Blue Mountain Inn** (good restaurant and nightclub), turn left to Irish Town and thence to **Newcastle**, a Jamaica Defence Force training camp at 1219 m with magnificent views of Kingston and Port Royal. The road to **Catherine's Peak** (1585 m) directly behind the camp is about an hour's climb for the moderately fit.

Holywell National Park

ⓘ *Entry US$5, children US$2, Jamaicans J$100. Oately Mountain Trail is a commercial trail within the Holywell Park for which there is a separate user fee of US$10, children* the JCDT, 29 Dumbarton Av, Kingston 10, T9208278, jcdt@kasnet.com.

Beyond Newcastle lie **Hardwar Gap** and **Holywell National Park**, a recreational area within the Blue and John Crow Mountains National Park. Managed by the **Jamaica Conservation and Development Trust (JCDT)**, the park offers nature trails, campsites and picnic areas.

The picturesque little community of **Section** is an old Maroon lookout point at the junction of three roads and is a travel halt. There the road from Holywell intersects with the Silver Hill to Buff Bay Road. A left turn from Holywell takes you to Buff Bay and a turning off to the right to Silver Hill Gap. The road from Section to Buff Bay is prone to landslides and blockages so before setting out make enquiries about the road.

Section is the most popular spot on the north side of the Blue Mountains for purchasing genuine Blue Mountain coffee. A coffee tour is offered which includes a demonstration of the traditional way of growing, preparing and roasting Blue Mountain coffee, as it has been done for 200 years. **The Old Tavern Coffee Estate** ① T/F9242785, dtwyman@colis.com, run by Alex Twyman is a small family farm on the cool, northern slopes of the Blue Mountains where coffee is grown at about 1200 m and considered by many connoisseurs to be the finest in the world.

> ‡ *This whole area is full of mountain trails with innumerable birds, some unique to Jamaica.*

The road from Silver Hill Gap to the left turn-off to Clydesdale (about a 4-km drive) has mostly been repaired and the route is passable. The road to Clydesdale and the **Cinchona Botanical Garden** is unpaved and very steep between Clydesdale and Cinchona (4WD required, or walk, about two hours uphill but well worth it). The route from Silver Hill Gap continues past the turn-off to Clydesdale to **Content Gap**. Content is a three-road junction; coming from Clydesdale the right turn goes to Gordon Town and Kingston whereas the left goes to Mavis Bank and Blue Mountain Peak.

Blue Mountain

To go towards **Blue Mountain Peak** from Kingston (Corporate Area) via Papine, drive straight on at **Blue Mountain Inn** (instead of turning left), through Gordon Town and on through **Mavis Bank** for 6.5 km to **Hagley Gap**, if the Mahogany Vale ford is passable. The community and the national park have constructed a flat bridge that has made passage more secure even during the rainy season. However, you will almost certainly not be able to get a car up to the starting point for the walk to the peak. Public transport up the Blue Mountains is infrequent. There are some buses to Mavis Bank from the square in Papine, US$1, but you will need to ask. Taxis from Papine to Mavis Bank are about US$7.50. Only 4WD vehicles are advisable after Mavis Bank (no shortage of people offering to take you), and there are no petrol stations en route. There are two options for getting to the start of the trail at Abbey Green/Penlynecastle area; walking from from Mavis Bank or taking a 4WD. The two hiking routes are the short cut (5.5 km uphill through villages), or along the road (6.5 km) from Mavis Bank. A guide is recommended for both options but

> ‡ *You should avoid all major rivers whenever flood warnings have been issued or during very heavy rains.*

especially if taking the short cut. Local guides are available and the Mavis Bank Police are always willing to assist in locating one. Ask for **Whitfield Hall** or **Wildflower Lodge** (see below), the turning is just beyond Penlynecastle School, by the post office. Land Rovers are available from **Whitfield Hall** (John Allgrove, T9270986) and **Wildflower Lodge** (Dudu, T5804226). **Sun Venture Tours** (see page 227) provide complete tour services for Blue Mountain Peak, with transfers from anywhere on the island to Penlynecastle, meals, accommodation and guides.

Climbing the peak The Blue Mountains play a symbolic role for Jamaicans. Jamaican poet Roger Mais (1905-1955) wrote a moving poem called *All Men Come to the Hills* about men's desire to rest finally in the hills, wherever or however they have spent their lives. The walk to **Blue Mountain Peak** (10.5 km from Whitfield Hall) takes three or four hours up and two or three hours down. The first part is the steepest. Some start very early in the morning in the hope of watching the sunrise from the peak. The thrill of victory takes on new meaning once you've climbed Jacob's Ladder and posed atop the Trig Station on the highest point, **Middle Peak** (2256 m), waiting anxiously ... braving the bitter cold ... to catch that first faint glow of sunlight. As often as not, though, the peak is shrouded in cloud and rain in the early morning; a disheartening experience. You can leave in early daylight and almost certainly reach the top before it starts clouding over again (mid to late morning). In this case you do not need a guide, as the path is straightforward. Short cuts should be avoided at all costs. The trail winds through a fascinating variety of vegetation: coffee groves and banana plantations on the lower, south slopes, to tree ferns and dwarf forest near the summit (with some explanatory and mileage signposts). The doctor bird – a beautiful swallow-tailed hummingbird, the national bird of Jamaica – is fairly common. It's quite hard to spot, at first recognizable by its loud buzz, especially near the many flowering bushes. Take your own food and torch (spare set of batteries and bulb), sweater and raincoat if you set out in the darkness. There is one hut on the peak (an empty concrete building with no door) where you can stay overnight in some discomfort. However, the National Park authorities discourage overnighting at the peak due to the absence of proper facilities and inadequate waste disposal. There is a campsite with cabins (bunk beds and floor space rental), pit latrines, water and a shower at Portland Gap, about one hour up.

Another trail, to **Mossman Peak**, starts at Portland Gap, but is currently overgrown after 15 minutes, not having recovered from Hurricane Gilbert. At holiday times, especially in the summer, scores of people walk up Blue Mountain Peak every day, while in low season there will be only a handful. Considering the numbers, it is remarkably unspoiled and the views are spectacular.

Southeast coast

The A4 road runs east out of Kingston, all along the south coast through Bull Bay, Yallahs, Morant Bay and Port Morant, before turning up on to the north coast to Port Antonio, Buff Bay and Annotto Bay, where it ends at the junction with the A3 running directly north from Kingston. Just beyond **Bull Bay** on the way to Yallahs, there is a plaque in memory of **'Three-Finger Jack'**, Jack Mansong, one of Jamaica's legendary highway men and a folk hero-villain in the mould of Robin Hood. From the marker you get a magnificent view of Kingston harbour to the southwest, while to the north are the dry forested hills of the Port Royal Mountains, once the territory of Jack. He fought a guerrilla war single-handedly against the British military and the plantocracy. It is not known whether he was born in Africa or Jamaica in 1780-1781. He is thought to have lost two fingers in a battle with a maroon called Quashie who later killed Jack in another fight, whereupon he cut off his head and three remaining fingers as trophies. Legends about Jack proliferated, books about him became popular and then came a musical, or pantomime. *Obi-* or *Three-Fingered Jack* had a run of some nine years at the Covent Garden, Haymarket and Victoria Theatres in London. (Further reading: L Alan Eyre, *Jack Mansong, 'Bloodshed or Brotherhood'*.)

About 300 m from the junction of the A4 with the roads to Easington and Yallahs at Albion are the overgrown ruins of the **Albion Great House and Aqueduct**, often referred to as **Albion Castle**. Of the remaining structures the great house and the waterwheel are the most impressive. Descendants of those who worked on the estate as slaves still occupy the 'slave house' today. In colonial times the estate was the leading producer of sugar in Jamaica and its crystal sugar was known as 'Albion Sugar'. On emancipation in 1838 there were about 450 slaves at Albion producing

400 hogsheads of sugar and more than double that quantity of rum was being produced at the end of the century. Its waterwheels were supplied by a large aqueduct transporting water from the Yallahs River several kilometres away. One of the wheels had a diameter of 9.6 m and supported 88 buckets. These and other innovations in the milling and drying process made Albion Estate a leader in sugar production technology. Access to the property is through the estate gate just up the road. There is usually a caretaker in the old 'slave house' or someone to help you gain access.

Yallahs is one of the major towns in St Thomas. No one is quite sure where the town got its name, but it may have been named after a privateer, or buccaneer, called Captain Yhallahs, who operated in the area around 1671. On the other hand it may have been a corruption of Hato de Ayala, the name of one of the large cattle ranches run by the Spanish when they occupied the island. **Yallahs Salt Ponds** stretch for about 5 km, providing an outstanding landmark. Legend has it that two brothers argued over the sub-division of a piece of land and the argument became so fierce that the two plots of land sank, forming two of the three salt ponds. The hyper-saline ponds have created a unique ecosystem and several scientific discoveries have been made here. They are also good spots for birdwatching.

Yallahs is famous for jerk chicken (drum roasted) and its main street must have more jerk chicken stands than anywhere else.

A 4WD vehicle is recommended for visiting the beach side of the ponds, ask directions in town, best at **Miss Johnson's A&I Bar and Restaurant** in the centre, or contact the **Yallahs Community Development Fund** ① *T9825021/7063035*. The dumping of wrecked cars spoils the first part of the journey but beyond that it is great going.

Morant Bay, the capital of St Thomas, has a colourful and legendary past. On 11 October 1865, it was the scene of the Morant Bay Rebellion. A group of farmers and other disaffected citizens led by farmer and Baptist Deacon, Paul Bogle, marched to the Courthouse to complain about high taxes, the collapse of the sugar industry and the economic downturn, which had been exacerbated by drought and outbreaks of smallpox and cholera. The Government was not sympathetic to the views of the people, the Courthouse was burned down and the uprising assumed dangerous proportions. The military rounded up the protestors and killed or sentenced to death hundreds of men and women who had allegedly taken part, burned nearly 1000 homes and flogged members of the surrounding communities. Today there is a statue to Paul Bogle at Morant Bay, and the monument is in remembrance of Bogle, George William Gordon and 437 martyrs who fought and died for justice. Both Paul Bogle and George William Gordon are National Heroes. The artist was Edna Manley, the wife of former Prime Minister and National Hero Norman Washington Manley, and mother of the Hon Michael Manley, also a former Prime Minister.

North of Port Morant at the east end of the island, is **Bath**, another place from which to access the **John Crow Mountains** (named after the ubiquitous turkey buzzards). There is a modest but cheap hotel, **Bath Fountain Hotel** (T7034345), dating from 1727, where the main attraction is the natural **hot water spring baths** ① *daily 0800-2200, US$5 single, US$6.70 double for the baths, US$8.40 single and US$10 double for the jacuzzis; J$100 entry fee is later deducted if you use the baths and jacuzzis*, which are most relaxing at the end of a long day. Two passes above Bath, the **Cuna Cuna Pass** and the **Cornpuss Gap** lead down to the source of the Rio Grande River on the north slopes of the mountain range. Both are tough going particularly the Cornpuss Gap. It is absolutely essential to take a local guide. The north slopes of the mountain range are the home of the unique and extremely rare **Jamaican butterfly**, *Papilio humerus*, a large black and yellow swallowtail. It is the second-largest butterfly in the world and the largest in the Americas, and is protected under international law (CITES) regulating the trade in endangered species. This butterfly is very spectacular in flight and easily recognizable because of its size. It can best be seen in May and June.

East of Port Morant, but not easily accessible, is the magnificent **Pera** beach between Port Morant and Morant Lighthouse. Near the lighthouse is another good beach. Just before reaching Manchioneal a road off to the left leads to the **Reach Falls** or **Manchioneal Falls** (about 5 km). Well worth a visit if you have a car or are prepared to walk (45 minutes with views of rolling forested hills) from the main road. Pretty tiers of smooth boulders, the highest fall about 4.5 m, tumble through a lush, green gorge. Buses from main road to Port Antonio are infrequent, every one or two hours. Taxis are a better option and more frequent. Since the government acquired the Falls they have been closed temporarily, so check with local people about entry and be prepared to pay for their services. Further along the coast from Manchioneal to Long Bay cottages and guesthouses have been built on the beach.

> ✱ Nearly all the beaches along the east coast round to Port Antonio have a dangerous undertow in certain spots.

Port Antonio → *Population: 14,000. Colour map 1, C5.*

Once the major banana port, where many of the island's first tourists arrived on banana boats, Port Antonio dates back to the 16th century. Its prosperity has for many years been in gentle decline and it is now run-down, but it has an atmosphere unlike any other town in Jamaica, with some superb old public buildings. It is an excellent base from which to explore inland or along the coast. **Boston Bay**, **Fairy Hill Beach** (also known as Winnefred Beach), **San San Beach**, the **Blue Lagoon** (also known as the Blue Hole) and **Frenchman's Cove Beach** are notable beauty spots to the east of the town. **Boston Bay** is renowned for its local jerk food pits; several unnamed places by the roadside serve hot spicy chicken, pork or fish, chopped up and wrapped in paper, cooked on planks over a pit of hot coals, very good and tasty.

> ✱ For information on Port Antonio Marina, see page 211.

The **tourist office** ① *upstairs in City Centre Plaza on Harbour Street, T9933051, F9932117*, is quite helpful, with timetables for local buses ('soon come'), which leave regularly when full, but at uncertain hours, from seafront behind Texaco station.

Also worth visiting are **Somerset Falls** ① *T8731198, daily 0900-1700, US$5*. To get there take a bus to Buff Bay (any westbound Kingston bus) and walk for five minutes. You can hike along trails, swim in the pools or take a boat ride into a cave, set in a deep gorge covered in rainforest. About 30 minutes' walk around the bay from town are the **Folly Ruins**, an elaborate, turn-of-the-century mansion built in the style of Roman and Greek architecture, now in ruins (partly because the millionaire American's wife took an instant dislike to it). It is a ghostly, crumbling old mansion in an open field with lovely views shared with grazing cows. To find it, fork right off the path before going into a clump of trees on the peninsula (leading towards the lighthouse inside the military camp). At **Nonsuch Cave** ① *daily 0900-1600, US$5*, a few kilometres to the southeast, there are fossils, stalactites and evidence of Taíno occupation. There's a gift shop and lunch area too, but no public transport (return taxi fare US$10 including waiting time).

> ✱ The rainfall in this part of the island is very high and in consequence the vegetation very lush.

Navy Island

In the harbour you can visit the 28-ha Navy Island (ferry 0700-2200 daily, US$3 return), at one time owned by Errol Flynn, which has beaches (one nudist) and a moderately expensive restaurant. 'Errol Flynn Gallery' has display of movie stills and screenings of his golden oldies. The beaches on the island all belong to the resort (closed) but are open to non-guests. Snorkelling available (at the nudist beach), US$2 for half-day hire, but there are strong currents and not many fish.

Rafting on the Rio Grande

① T9935778, reservations essential, 0900-1700, last raft at 1600, US$50 per raft, takes a couple and child under 10; private captains are cheaper, US40-45, but they are illegal and have no insurance.

Flynn saw the bamboo rafts which used to bring bananas down the Rio Grande as a potential tourist attraction. If you turn up at Berrydale there are now always expert rafters ready and willing to take you down the river. The trip takes 2½ hours (depending on the river flow, it can take four hours, take sunscreen and a hat) through magnificent scenery and there is an opportunity to stop en route. A driver takes your car down from the embarkation point to the point of arrival, **Rafter's Rest**, on the main coastal road (US$15), recommended as a place to have a pleasant, moderately priced lunch or drink, even if you are not proposing to raft. Otherwise, the return taxi fare is US$10; there are also buses, US$0.25, back to Berrydale, the setting-off point, though infrequent. Returning from St Margaret's, downstream, is easier as there are plenty of buses passing between Annotto Bay and Port Antonio.

The Maroons

The Rio Grande valley is also well worth exploring, including a trip to the Maroons (descendants of escaped slaves) at **Moore Town**, but the roads are rough and public transport minimal. **Grand Valley Tours** ① T9934116, run by Veronica Saxter, who arranges tours of the town with Colonel Harris, the leader of the Maroons, and is recommended for guided tours, US$30-35, by reservation only. For accommodation call Lynette Wilks, T3955351, cabins sleep 3 (C). Guided trail tours US$31 per day, meals US$4-7, entertainment such as traditional live music US$123-153, lectures on Maroon history US$77. To the west of the Rio Grande lie the north slopes of the Blue Mountains. **Nanny Town**, the home of the Maroons, was destroyed by the British in 1734 and then 'lost' until the 1960s. There is recent archaeological evidence at Nanny Town to suggest that the Maroons originally took to the mountains and lived with (and possibly later absorbed) Taíno peoples. There have been some dramatic discoveries of Taíno wooden carvings which are now on display at the National Gallery.

Port Antonio to Buff Bay

Between Port Antonio and the Buff Bay area there are several roads into the interior from places such as Hope Bay and Orange Bay. Just to the east of Buff Bay is **Crystal Springs**, and from there the road goes on to Chepstow and thence to **Claverty Cottage** and **Thompson Gap**; spectacular scenery, waterfalls in the valleys and very remote. It was possible to walk from Thompson Gap over the Blue Mountains via Morces Gap and down to Clydesdale, but the trails have been extensively damaged by storms and are no longer passable.

● Sleeping

Holywell National Park p228
A Starlight Chalet & Health Spa, T9693116, Kingston office T9603070, www.starllightchalet .com. A hideaway in the Blue Mountains, good for relaxing, birdwatching and hiking. Spa, TV, bar and restaurant serving local and international dishes, transport on request, children under 11 stay free.
B **Silver Hill Gap**. 3 log cabins, 2 sleep 4 and 1 sleeps 6 people.

Blue Mountain p229
Mountain lodges
LL **Lime Tree Farm**, Tower Hill, Mavis Bank, T8818788, www.limetreefarm.com. Charlie and Suzie Burbury run this working coffee farm with glorious views down into Cedar and Yallus valley and across the Blue Mountains. Three cottages, each individually furnished with a large, comfy bedroom which can sleep a family, bathroom and terrace. Price includes full

board and transfers from Kingston. Suzie cooks excellent Jamaican dishes using local ingredients and lots of herbs. Good hiking on nearby trails, friendly staff, internet access, honour bar, environmentally aware, funding for local school and community projects.

A-B Foress Park Guest House, on the main road near the Mavis Bank Coffee Factory, T9278275, www.forrespark.com, see Sleeping in Kingston, above. Run by Jennifer Lyn. Rooms in main house, a Swiss-style chalet, 4 cabins nearby, all with private bathroom and balcony. In middle of coffee plantation, excellent birdwatching, many trails for hiking. 4WD transport can be arranged with a guide to the Blue Mountain Peak. The family also owns another coffee farm, Abbey Green, higher up at 1500 m, with a small lodge which can be used as a base before hiking up the Peak.

E Whitfield Hall Hostel, close to where the Blue Mountain trail begins (c/o John Algrove, 8 Amon Jones Crescent, Kingston 6, T9270986). A large wooden lodge with no electricity but paraffin lamps, capacity 40, hostel or private room, cold showers only. No meals unless you order them in advance, but kitchen with gas stoves and crockery, for guests' use. Very peaceful and homely with comfortable lounge, log fire and library (visitors' books dating back to the 1950s), friendly and helpful staff. If the hostel is full, camping is permitted.

E Wildflower Lodge, just before **Whitfield Hall**, near the start of Blue Mountain trail, known locally as the **White House**, T9295394/5 (or c/o Dudu, Penlyncastle PA, St Thomas). Same prices as **Whitfield Hall**, but a bit more modern and better food, breakfast US$5, evening meals US$7, substantial and excellent vegetables from the garden. Both lodges will arrange 4WD transport from Mavis Bank (**Wildflower Lodge** will also arrange transport from Kingston and the airport) and offer guides and mules for walking and carrying bags.

Port Antonio *p232*

Port Antonio has a **Guesthouse Association** offering good-value lodging, excursions and transfers, www.go-jam.com.

L Trident Villas and Hotel, T9932602, www.tridentvillas.com. 26 rooms/suites with sea view, meals included, antique furniture,

tennis, croquet, pools, restaurants.

AL Jamaica Palace, Drapers, T9937720, www.jamaicapalace.com. 10 mins from Port Antonio, 65 rooms, a/c, beach, pool, wheelchair accessible, watersports.

A Bay View Villas, Anchovy, Port Antonio, T/F9933118, www.caribicvacations.com. Beautiful cottages amidst lush coconut plantation, overlooking Turtle Harbour; relaxing atmosphere with pool, restaurant and bar, breakfast included.

A Demontevin Lodge, 21 Fort George St, Titchfield Hill, T9932604, demontevin@ cwjamaica.com. Breakfast included, shared bath, more expensive rooms have private bath, old Victorian house, restaurant serves set meals, US$5-10, good value.

A Jamaica Crest Resort and Villas, Fairy Hill, T9938400, crest@discoverjamaica.com. A Christian Resort with 52 luxurious rooms and 14 villas, pool, tennis court, horse riding, restaurant and a lovely view of the sea. They offer a shuttle service to Boston.

B-C Ivanhoe's Guest House, 9 Queen St, T9933043. Some rooms with shared bath, patio with bay view. Several nearby private houses take guests.

C Triff's Inn, 1 Bridge St. Modern, clean, 17 rooms, restaurant, bars.

Around Port Antonio

LL Goblin Hill Villas at San San, T9937443, reservations c/o 11 East Av, Kingston 10, T9258108, F9256248. 44 rooms in 1- or 2-bedroomed villas, kitchen, restaurant or housekeepers available, cheaper with no sea view, tennis, short walk to beach, pool, car hire, bar, TV room.

LL-L Mocking Bird Hill, Frenchman's Cove, Port Antonio, T9937267, www.hotelmockingbirdhill.com. 15 mins from town, 5 mins' walk from beach, 10 rooms in Caribbean-style villa in 3 ha of parkland, pool, gardens, nature trail, restaurant with Jamaican and international cuisine, Gallery Carriacou and gift shop exhibits owner's art, German, French, English and Spanish spoken.

LL-A Fern Hill Club, Fern Hill, San San, Drapers, T9937375, www.fernhillclub.com. 31 rooms and spa suites, cottages, all-inclusive available including tours, 4 pools, jacuzzi, restaurant, golf, tennis, windsurfing, sailing, diving, snorkelling, horse riding.

AL Moon San Villa, San San, Drapers, at the

Blue Lagoon, T9937600, www.portantonio-onestop.com/moonsan/msmain.htm. A cosy 3-floor villa with a choice between 1-4 bedrooms, complimentary breakfast, and free access to the Blue Lagoon and San San beach. 5% surcharge for credit cards.

❶ Eating

Holywell National Park p228
♨♨♨ **The Gap Café**, Hardwar Gap, Newcastle, T9973032. Long drive but has spectacular views. Breakfast, lunch, high tea and dinner, and serves fresh Blue Mountain coffee.

Port Antonio p232
♨♨♨-♨ **Blue Lagoon**, Fairy Hill. Built over the water, great swimming in the deep blue water, under new ownership 2007 and temporarily closed.

♨♨♨ **The Best Kept Secret**, on road coming into Port Antonio from the west, little blue and yellow shack with banana leaves hanging from it, perched on a cliff, T8096276. Alvin Dickie Butler and his wife Joy offer fine dining with beautiful view of Port Antonio, reservations only, breakfast, lunch and high tea, great home cooking and flavours, Dickie's famous clientele have included Errol Flynn, the Duke of Edinburgh, Winnie Mandela and Princess Margaret.

♨♨-♨ **Barracudas Restaurant and Lounge**, 1 Bridge St, T7156111. Mon-Sat 1130-2130. Variety of seafood and Jamaican cuisine at affordable prices, central and easily accessible.

♨ **Coronation Bakery**, near Musgrave Market, 18 West St, T9932710. Good for cheap patties and spice buns.

♨ **Cream World**. Good for ice cream, cakes and cheap snacks.

♨ **Stop Group Jerk Centre** on the bay out of town towards the Folly. Bar and jerk pork, chicken and fish, also music and dance until late.

❶ Bars and clubs

Port Antonio and around p232
Roof Club, 11 West St. Disco and night spot where everything happens, with sign outside saying 'no drugs, no firecrackers, don't destroy furniture'. Popular with all types, melting pot of excitement, advisable for women to be escorted or in a group, weekends best nights.

Renny, also known as *Old Hits Corner*, on Somers Town Rd, near police station. Popular at weekend with locals and visitors, its selection of 'oldies' offers an alternative from the dance hall and hip hop rhythms.

The north coast

The north coast attracts the majority of visitors to Jamaica, with thousands arriving by cruise ship in Ocho Rios and thousands more staying in all-inclusive resorts along the coast, principally at Montego Bay, the site of the international airport. There are well-known attractions such as Dunn's River Falls, but also less infamous places to visit away from the crowds: the fine Georgian town of Falmouth, caves in the Cockpit Country, or the Rocklands Feeding Station, a delightful garden where the doctor hummingbird is tame enough to drink sugar syrup from a bottle in your hand. Montego Bay is brash and fun-loving, attracting the party crowd, but away from the hip strip there are some architectural and anthropological sights worth exploring.
▶▶ For Sleeping, Eating and other listings, see pages 240-246.

Port Maria to Oracabessa
The Kingston to Port Maria road (the Junction Road) passes through **Castleton Botanical Gardens** (T9271257, in a very tranquil setting, well worth a visit). The journey takes about two hours and there are plenty of minibuses. **Port Maria** itself is a sleepy and decaying old banana port not without charm and with lots of goats.

A few kilometres northwest of Port Maria is **Firefly**① *Sat-Thu 0830-1700, US$10,*

Noel Coward's Jamaican home, now owned by the **Jamaica National Heritage Trust**. It is evocative of a stylish era and a highlight if you are interested in the theatre or film stars of that period and the view is magnificent. Noel Coward's other property, **Blue Harbour**, is about 1 km away; this is where he used to entertain film stars, royalty etc. It is now a guesthouse (see Sleeping page 240).

Oracabessa is another old banana port with a half-completed marina and **Golden Eye**, the house where **Ian Fleming** wrote all the James Bond books. The house is now a luxurious retreat owned by Chris Blackwell's **Island Outpost**, www.islandoutpost.com. The James Bond beach is in front of the house, it is small but highly recommended, as safe and child-friendly. Bars and fish meals available.

To the west of Oracabessa is **Boscobel**, where the airstrip for Ocho Rios is located. Opposite the airstrip there are numerous houses for rent.

Ocho Rios → *Colour map 1, C5.*

The journey from Kingston to Ocho Rios follows a spectacular route, up the gorge of the **Rio Cobre**, then across Mount Diablo. **Faith's Pen**, right on the top, is an enormous collection of huts selling food and drink, mostly jerk chicken, pork or fish, festival, boiled or roasted corn, soup and natural juices or sodas, and great for a stop. The last section of road whizzes round a series of blind corners as you go through **Fern Gully**, a marvel of unspoilt tropical vegetation. Driving time is one hour 50 minutes by bus. Alternatively, take a minibus from the Texaco petrol station on Da Costa Drive, Ocho Rios (US$0.30 to Fern Gully). There are lots of minibuses for the return journey.

Ocho Rios stands on a bay sheltered by reefs and surrounded by coconut groves, sugar cane and fruit plantations. The town has become very popular, with many cruise ships making a stop here. It is 103 km east of Montego Bay and claims some of the best beaches on the island. The beach in town, safe and well organized with facilities, is 200 m from Main Street where most of the shops and vehicle hire companies can be found. A landscaped and paved boardwalk, the 'One Love Trail', leads from Ocho Rios and Island Village shopping and entertainment complex adjacent to the cruise ship pier (food, music, cinema, art, beach, casino and gaming) to the surrounding attractions of Dunn's River Falls and Dolphion Cove. Recommended are the **Shaw Park Gardens** ① *T9742723, daily 0800-1700. US$10*, an easy walk from the town centre, up the hill on the edge of town.

The scenery of the surrounding area is an added attraction. Most spectacular are the beauty spots of **Roaring River Falls**, and **Dunn's River Falls** ① *T9744767, daily 0830-1600, US$15 adults, US$12 children, locker US$5, bath shoes US$5 (rental) but not necessary if you move with care*, tumbling into the Caribbean with invigorating salt- and freshwater bathing at its foot. Get there early before the coach parties arrive; it's a five-minute bus ride (US$0.20) from Ocho Rios, or one-hour drive from Montego Bay (beware of pseudo guides who hang around and take you somewhere totally different, then try to sell you marijuana). Opposite the entrance to Dunn's River Falls is **Dolphin Cove** ① *T9745335, www.dolphincovejamaica.com, 0830-1730, US$45.00 entrance with tour, including interacting with stingrays and other activities, US$67 to touch the dolphins, US$119 to hold, feed and swim with sharks, US$129 to swim with one dolphin, US$195 to swim with 2 dolphins, entrance included in all programmes*, a large dolphinarium where captive dolphins are taught tricks for the entertainment of tourists.

Harmony Hall art gallery ① *T9754222, www.harmonyhall.com, Tue-Sat 1000-1800*, just east of Ocho Rios, is worth a visit. There are frequent exhibitions of paintings and sculpture in a classic gingerbread house, as well as crafts, clothes and other gifts to buy. There is also an Italian restaurant, **Toscanini's** (T9754785, Tue-Sun 1200-1415, 1900-2215). If you have your own transport you could combine a visit to Harmony Hall with some time on **Reggae Beach**, 2 km east of White River Bridge in a

little cove between Little Bay and Frankfort Bay. A bright sign on the seaward side of
the main road marks a somewhat inconspicuous entrance leading to a long, shaded
driveway and then a beach hideaway bustling with activity. It
is an easy going spot with clean water and a nice beach, but
you also get jerk chicken, roasts at festivals, reggae music,
dominoes and Red Stripe beer to complete the picture.

> ‡ *There are numerous plantation tours, see page 245.*

Ocho Rios to Falmouth

Sevilla Nueva, some 14.5 km to the west of Ocho Rios, is the place where the Spanish
first settled in 1509. The ruins of the fort still remain. The Great House and property is
now called the **Seville Great House and Heritage Park** ① *T9729407, daily 0900-1700,
last tour 1600, US$4, children US$2,* managed by the **Jamaica National Heritage Trust**
as a museum. Guided tours are professional and informative and give you a good
understanding of the island's heritage. Offshore, marine archaeologists are
investigating the **St Ann's Bay** area for sunken ships. Salvaged timbers are believed
to have come from two disabled caravels, the *Capitana* and the *Santiago de Palos*,
abandoned at Sevilla Nueva probably in 1503 during Columbus' last visit to Jamaica.
Mammee Beach, is beautiful and is much less crowded than Ocho Rios, though there
is no shade.

Continuing west along the coast is **Runaway Bay**, an attractive and friendly
resort. It is named for the Spanish governor Ysasi, who left quickly for Cuba in a canoe
when he saw the English coming. The **Green Grotto Caves** ① *T9732841,
www.greengrottocaves.com, US$20/J$500 adult, US$10/J$200 child, 0900-1600,
45-min tour,* formerly known as the Runaway Bay Caves, were once a haven for
runaway slaves and smugglers, a labyrinthine limestone cave with stalagmites and
stalagtities extending for 1525 m with chambers, light holes and a subterranean lake.
Tours are of two caves, Runaway and Green Grotto. Only 8 km away is **Discovery Bay**
where Columbus made his first landing. The **Columbus Park**, an outdoor museum,
has exhibits and relics of Jamaican history.

Falmouth

Falmouth is a charming small town about 32 km east of Montego Bay. It is the best
example of a Georgian town and the **Jamaica National Heritage Trust** has declared the
whole town a National Monument. It has a fine colonial courthouse, a church, some
18th-century houses with wrought-iron balconies, and **Antonio's**, a famous place to buy
beach shirts. There is good fishing (tarpon and kingfish) at the mouth of the Martha
Brae, near Falmouth, and no licence is required. It is possible to go rafting from **Martha
Brae** village ① *T9520089, www.jamaicarafting.com, 0830-1630. US$42 on 2-person
raft.* Expert rafters guide the craft very gently for the one-hour trip to the coast. To get
there, take a local bus from Montego Bay to Falmouth (US$0.50), hitchhike or walk 9.5
km to upper station; end station is about 5 km from Falmouth. **Jamaica Swamp Safaris**
① *US$6 for adults,* is a crocodile farm where you can see lazy crocodiles with equally
laid-back guides. There's a bar and restaurant. Some 10 miles inland, the 18th-century
plantation guesthouse of **Good Hope** ① *T6105798,* set among coconut palms offers
deluxe accommodation, as well as day tours and horse riding – daily 0800-1630,
US$40, some of the best riding in Jamaica – and its own beach on the coast.

A little-known but exciting attraction, 2.5 km east of Falmouth, is a bioluminescent
lagoon, known locally as the **Luminous Lagoon**, where the water comes alive at night
with sparkling blue-green lights from marine micro-organisms
called dinoflagellates. The lagoon is said to be the most active
bioluminescent lake in the world. A dark, moonless night, a
local guide with typical Jamaican sense of humour, and a small
power launch, all of which can be booked through **Fisherman's
Inn**, are all that you need. Alternatively, the **Glistening Waters Restaurant** next door,

> ‡ *Collect some of the water from the lagoon in your hand and shake it to see it sparkle for several seconds.*

Jamaica The north coast

offers regular boat tours after dark (see page 243). Less than five minutes out, the pitch-black water behind the boat begins to illuminate, leaving a blue-green-white trail in its wake. When the boat stops, streaks of light flash intermittently in every direction, caused by small fry jumping out of the water. Larger fish tunnelling through the water carry a wake of luminescence with them.

Cockpit Country

This is a strange and virtually uninhabited area to the south of Falmouth. It consists of a seemingly endless succession of high bumps made of limestone rock. The tourist office and some hotels in Montego Bay organize day trips (about US$60) to **Maroon Town** and **Accompong**, the headquarters of the Maroons who live in the Cockpit Country area. An annual festival is held here on 6 January with traditional music and dance, to commemorate the treaty with the British giving the Maroons lands and autonomy. Older locals can accurately describe what happened at the last battle between the Maroons and the British forces. ① *For tours in the Cockpit Country call the Southern Trelawny Environmental Agency, T6100818/6101676. Various tours available, the Quashi tour US$70, Dromily US$57, Clear River picnic US$58, Bunthill nature walk US$55 and Barbeque Deep Bush US$55. Kenneth Watson is a tour guide, T9524546.* Ask to see the **Wondrous Caves** at Elderslie near Accompong. If you have a car take the road on the east side of the Cockpit Country from Duncans (near Falmouth) to Clark's Town. From there the road deteriorates to a track, impassable after a few kilometres even for 4WD vehicles, to **Barbecue Bottom** and on to Albert Town. The views from Barbecue Bottom are truly spectacular (the track is high above the Bottom) and this is wonderful birding country. If you wish to walk in the Cockpit Country make your way (no public transport) to the **Windsor Caves** due south of Falmouth. They are full of bats which make a spectacular mass exit at dusk. There are local guides. The underground rivers in the caves run for miles, but are only for the experienced and properly equipped potholer. A locally published book called *Jamaica Underground* details the many caves and good walks in the area. It is possible to walk from the Windsor Caves across the middle of the Cockpit Country to Troy on the south side (about eight hours). It is essential to have a local guide and to make a preliminary trip to the Windsor Caves to engage him. Make sure that he really does know the way because these days this crossing is very rarely made even by the locals. It is also vastly preferable to be met with transport at Troy because you will still be in a pretty remote area.

Montego Bay → *Population: 92,000.*

About 193 km from Kingston, on the island's northwest coast, Montego Bay is Jamaica's principal tourist centre with all possible watersports amenities. Known familiarly as Mo' Bay, it has superb natural features, sunshine most of the year round, a beautiful coastline with miles of white sand, deep blue water never too cold for bathing and gentle winds that make sailing a favourite sport. **Doctor's Cave** is the social centre of beach life, while **Gloucester Avenue** is one of the busiest streets for tourists, lined with duty-free shops, souvenir arcades, hotels and restaurants.

The **Donald Sangster International Airport** is only 3 km from the town centre, taxi US$7, or 20-minute walk to Doctor's Cave. **JUTA** and **JCAL** are licensed taxi service providers. The **tourist office** ① *T9524425*, is on Cornwall Beach, Gloucester Avenue. ▸▸ *See also Transport, page 245 for further details.*

Sights

Of interest to the sightseer are the remaining battery, cannons and powder magazine of an old British fort, **Fort Montego**, with landscaped gardens and crafts market (free), and the 18th-century church of **St James** in Montego Bay, built in 1778 and restored after earthquake damage. There are a few Georgian buildings, such as the **Town House Restaurant** ① *16 Church St* (local art gallery next door), and the Georgian Court at the corner of Union and Orange streets. The centre of town is **Sam Sharpe Square**, named after the slave who led a rebellion, now a National Hero. The Burchell Memorial Church, established by the Baptist missionary, Thomas Burchell, was where Samuel Sharpe served as a deacon. The recently opened **Museum of St James** ① *T9719417, Tue-Fri 0900-1700, Sat, Sun by reservation, US$3 adults, US$1 children*, displays the history of the parish from pre-Columbian times to the present in the restored Old Courthouse in the civic centre on Sam Sharpe Square.

> ● *Mosquitoes are a problem at certain times of the year; take repellent and coils.*

Beaches

Doctor's Cave Beach ① *Gloucester Av, daily 0830-1730, US$5, children under 12 half price*, has underwater coral gardens, so clear that they can be seen without effort from glass-bottomed boats. It is relaxed and you can sunbathe quietly. **Cornwall Beach** is undergoing development and there are currently no facilities. The **Walter Fletcher** beach has been converted to the **Aqua Sol Theme Park** ① *T9799447, daily 0900-1700, US$5*, the latest addition to the list of attractions, offering rides and sports facilities. **Margaritaville** ① *US$10* (see Bars and clubs, page 244) offers a mix of beach, bar, restaurant, rides, slides and various forms of entertainment. Scuba diving can be arranged through about a dozen operators, several of which have outlets at more than one hotel (single dive, US$45, a snorkelling trip US$25).

If you are staying in town, rather than at the hotel strip, there are beaches close by, either public with no services or private (US$0.50-2), with food, drinks, tennis, boat hire, snorkelling, shower, changing rooms, etc. Walk from the traffic circle in the middle of town towards the hotels and the beach will be on your left.

Around Montego Bay

Out of town, to the east, are two great houses. **Greenwood** ① *T9531077, daily 0900-1800, US$12*, was built in 1780 1800 by the forefathers of the poet Elizabeth Barrett Browning. It has a colourful avenue of bougainvillea and mimosa and a panoramic view over the coast from the veranda. **Rose Hall** ① *T9539982, daily 0900-1800. US$15 adults, US$10 children*, was started in 1770 by John Palmer. A lively legend of witchcraft surrounds the wife of one of his descendants, Annie Palmer.

> ● *Southeast of Montego Bay is the Taíno rock carving at Kempshot.*

Southwest of Montego Bay is the unmissable bird sanctuary at **Anchovy**, **Rocklands Feeding Station** ① *T9522009, daily 1230-1730; no children under 5, adults US$10, children US$5*, where the doctor bird humming birds hover to eat sugar syrup from a little bottle and other birds will even perch on your finger. The road to Anchovy is too rough for ordinary cars. Five kilometres west of Anchovy is **Lethe**, the starting point for rafting down the Great River. Sixteen kilometres from Montego Bay on the Savanna-La-Mar road is the **Montpelier Great House**, on the site of the old Montpelier sugar factory, destroyed during the 1831 rebellion. South of Anchovy, about 40 km from Montego Bay, is **Seaford Town**, which was settled by Germans in the 1830s. About 200 of their descendants survive (write to Francis Friesen, Lamb's River Post Office). **Tamarind Lodge** serves excellent Jamaican food.

Continuing along the island's west end, the road passes through **Green Island** before reaching Negril (29 miles from Lucea, a charming spot on the north coast), where there are several pretty fishing villages, such as Cousins Cove, with small guesthouses and seaside cottages for rent.

Port Maria to Oracabessa *p235*

L-AL Golden Seas Beach Resort, Oracabessa, T9753251, www.goldenseas.com. Price includes 3 meals. 79 colourful rooms in lush gardens, spa, restaurant, beauty salon, fitness centre, pool table, tennis, swimming pool, private beach and a river running through the resort.

AL Blue Harbour Villas, northwest of Port Maria, T5861244, www.blueharb.com. Price per person per day including meals. Three villas on property which once belonged to Noel Coward. Accommodation for 2-20 guests in the **Villa Grande** (2 bedrooms), the **Villa Chica** (1 bedroom) and the **Villa Rose** (3-4 bedrooms), all much as Coward left it, including his library. Saltwater pool, coral beach, good snorkelling and scuba, gardens, lovely views.

AL-D Sonrise Beach Retreat, Robin's Bay, 3 km from village, T9997169, www.in-site.com/sonrise. Standard or 'deluxe' cabins (sleep 5-6) with private or shared bath,mini spa suite sleeps 2, bamboo hut, tent sites and tent rental, bath house, transport essential or arrange pick-up with resort, meal plans and ecotour packages available, restaurant, nature trails, trampoline, volleyball, ping pong. Good for family or special interest groups, Jamaican family fun days at weekends with barbeque, music and singing.

B Casa Maria, Castle Gardens, Port Maria, T7250156, www.nwas.com/casamaria. 20 rooms, beach, pool, restaurants, bars. Relaxing, private, also used for weddings, seminars and parties.

Ocho Rios *p236*

The coast is dominated by many huge, all-inclusive resorts, usually booked from abroad.

LL Jamaica Inn, T9742449, www.jamaicainn.com. Award-winning hotel, top of its league since it opened in 1950, casually elegant but unpretentious. 47 spacious and comfortable suites and cottages, all with balconies, meal plans available, room service, pool, private beach, Kiyara Ocean Spa, facilities for the disabled, Winston Churchill used to stay here and Noel Coward drank here.

LL-AL The Crane Ridge Resort, 17 DaCosta Drive, Ocho Rios, T9748050, www.craneridge.net. No frills hotel in pleasant gardens on a Bluff, overlooking Ocho Rios. Rooms and suites in blocks, TV, private balconies, swimming pool, tennis courts, beach shuttle, restaurant and spa. The 2 bedroom suites feature a jacuzzi in the master bedroom.

AL Hibiscus Lodge, 83 Main St, T9742676, mdoswald@cwjamaica.com. 26 rooms in gardens overlooking sea, man-made beach, pool, jacuzzi, tennis, **Almond Tree** restaurant.

AL-A Fisherman's Point, Main Street, Ocho Rios, T9745318, www.fishermanspoint.net. A beachfront condominium resort adjacent to Margaritaville, with 74 a/c 1 and 2 bedroom apartments, complete with kitchenette, TV and private balcony, maid service, adult and kids pool, restaurant and bar.

C La Penciano Guest House, 3 Short Lane, T9745472, run by Lloyd Thomas. Rooms with shared or private bath, fan, TV, in centre and noisy, but clean and safe, friendly, bar (open Fri and Sat night) has views over Ocho Rios.

Camping

E-F Milford Falls, about 1.5 km from town centre, by the waterfall. Take Kingston road out of Ocho Rios, turn right at sign to Shaw Park Gardens then fork left up Milford Rd, stop at **George Barnes'** shop on right, he will take you there and provide you with information, food and drink, he has a tent or a rustic cabin with 1 bed to rent.

Ocho Rios to Falmouth *p237*

L Runaway Bay HEART Hotel, T9736671, runaway.heart@cwjamaica.com. Has an adjoining hotel training centre and overlooks the golf club.

Falmouth *p237*

LL-AL Silver Sands Villas and Beach Club, Silver Sands Estates, Duncan's, call **Jamaican Villa Vacations**, T9542001 for bookings, www.silversandsjamaica.com. Private, homely villas, each with its own style. Most have a/c rooms, TV, phone, private swimming pool, and friendly maid service (mainly for cooking). Easy access to the beach, snack shop, bar, games room, commissary and nightclub.

AL-A Fisherman's Inn, Rock, Falmouth, T9543427 (rooms with 2 single or 2 double beds), on the main road, heading to St Ann. You can have an excellent seafood sunset dinner on the deck followed by a 25-min lake tour.

Montego Bay *p238, map below*
There are over 40 all-inclusive hotels, guest-houses and apartment hotels listed by the tourist board and many more which are not.
L El Greco, 11 Queens Drive, T9406116, www.elgrecojamaica.com. 64, 1-bedroom

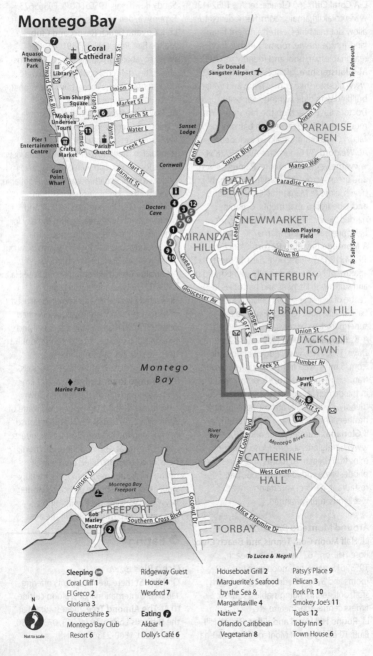

Montego Bay

Sleeping
Coral Cliff **1**
El Greco **2**
Gloriana **3**
Gloustershire **5**
Montego Bay Club
  Resort **6**

Ridgeway Guest
  House **4**
Wexford **7**

Eating
Akbar **1**
Dolly's Café **6**

Houseboat Grill **2**
Marguerite's Seafood
  by the Sea &
  Margaritaville **4**
Native **7**
Orlando Caribbean
  Vegetarian **8**

Patsy's Place **9**
Pelican **3**
Pork Pit **10**
Smokey Joe's **11**
Tapas **12**
Toby Inn **5**
Town House **6**

Not to scale

Jamaica The north coast Listings

and 32, 2-bedroom suites with balconies on hillside overlooking bay, breakfast included, direct elevator access to Gloucester Av and Doctor's Cave Beach, grocery store, internet access, pool, beach towels, tennis, laundry, cook and nanny on request.

L-A Coral Cliff, 365 Gloucester Av, T9524130, www.coralcliffjamaica.com. Remodelled to allow slot machines, entertainment fantasy-land, jungle theme, rooms variable, food reasonable, bar, pool and friendly service.

AL Gloustershire, Gloucester Av, T9524420, www.gloustershire.com. Cream and white building with blue awnings opposite Doctor's Cave Beach on the hip strip. 95 a/c rooms, phone, TV, most with balcony, pool, Jacuzzi, restaurant, breakfast included.

AL Wexford, 39 Gloucester Av, T9522854, www.thewexfordhotel.com. Painted violet and green, across the road from the public beach, close to Margaritaville. Pink rooms and 1-bedroom apartments, ocean or garden view, tiled floors, TV, phone, a/c, balconies, restaurant open 0700-2300.

A Montego Bay Club Resort, Gloucester Av, T9524310, F9524639. Dominant 12-storey apartment hotel with privately-owned studios and suites with kitchens and balconies in centre of tourist area overlooking Doctor's Cave Beach, pool, tennis, beauty salon, supermarket, maid service.

A-B Ridgeway Guest House, 34 Queen's Drive, T9522709, www.ridgewayguesthouse.com. 5 mins' walk from airport, free airport transfer, 10 rooms, bath, a/c or fan, fruit trees in the garden for guests' to help themselves, friendly, clean, family atmosphere, run by brothers Christopher and Colin Tatem.

B Gloriana, 1 Sunset Boulevard, T9790669, www.hotelgloriana.com. Close to airport, 10 mins from beach, 75 rooms and suites, TV, phone, some with balcony, pool, bar, restaurant, garden, entertainment at weekends, tours arranged.

Around Montego Bay p239

LL Half Moon Golf, Tennis and Beach Club, Rose Hall, on 162 ha adjoining beach, T9532615, www.halfmoon.com.jm. 340 rooms and 5- to 7-bedroomed villas with staff, golf, tennis, riding stables, squash, fitness centre, spa, theatre etc.

LL Round Hill Hotel and Villas, Round Hill Bluff, 10 mins west of Montego Bay on 40-ha peninsula, T9567050, www.roundhilljamaica.com. Originally a coconut and pineapple plantation, it opened in the 1950s with the help of Noel Coward. Celebrity villa owners include Paul McCartney and Ralph Lauren.

LL Tryall Golf Tennis and Beach Club, Sandy Bay, Tryall, T9565660/5, F9565673. Expensive, deluxe villas, 1-2 beds.

LL-L Coyaba Beach Resort and Club, Mahoe Bay, Rose Hall, T9539150, www.coyabaresortjamaica.com. 50 rooms and suites, gardens, pool, jacuzzi, private dock, tennis, fitness room, hammocks on the shore, family-owned.

AL Royal Reef, east of Mo'bay, opposite turning for Greenwood, T9531700, www.royalreefjamaica.com. 19 rooms, standard to super deluxe, some with sea view, others look on to road with patio, TV, a/c, bright white tiled bathrooms, price negotiable in low season, Jamaicans pay less than foreigners. Cool lounge area with TV and games, piano. Quiet area, go into Mo'bay for nightlife. Salt and fresh water pools, man-made sandy cove safe for kids, sea shallow out to the reef, sea grass and mangroves.

A Cariblue Beach Hotel, Ironshore, Rose Hall, T9532022, www.caribluehotel.com. A dedicated dive resort with its own beach, east of Mo'bay past **Sandals Royal**, sandwiched between main road and the sea. Small and pink, lots of packages, 24 a/c rooms, pool, deep-sea fishing, sailing, snorkelling, windsurfing, glass-bottom boats, day sails.

B-E Orange River Lodge, Inland, 1 km from Montego Bay off the Maroon Town road (turn off east 1 km before the village of Johns Hall), T9792688. An old great house overlooking the Orange River Valley, guest rooms, hostel accommodation with bunk beds, and camping (bring own tent), beautiful location, excellent food, friendly staff, excursions, shuttle service to Montego Bay. Good walking, river swimming, canoeing and birdwatching, in the area.

Eating

Ocho Rios p236

On **Main St** there are restaurants offering Jamaican, international or seafood cuisine.

The Almond Tree, the restaurant at the **Hibiscus Lodge**, T9742813. 0730-1030, 1200-1430, 1800-2130.

♥♥-♥ The Lobster Plate, lobster, fish and chicken.

♥ Café Aubergine, near Moneague T9730527. 1200-2230. An upmarket and tasteful restaurant in an 18th-century house, about US$25 per person.

♥♥-♥ The Little Pub, 59 Main St, T7953169. Jamaican food and entertainment.

Ocho Rios to Falmouth *p237*

♥♥-♥ Ultimate Jerk Centre, Main St, Runaway Bay, T9732054. 2000-late. Good, affordable food, with an oldies night on the last Sat of every month.

♥ Scotchies Jerk Centre, Drax Hall at the intersection of the St Ann's Bay to Ocho Rios main road and Chalky Hill road. An authentic Jamaican Jerk haunt, popular, the food and service are outstanding. Rustic but nicely landscaped eating areas, absolutely delicious fish, pork and chicken meals.

Falmouth *p237*

♥♥-♥ Glistening Waters Restaurant, Rock, Falmouth, T9543229. Mon-Sat 0900-2130, Sun 1200-2130, boat tours are nightly every 30 mins, 1900-2100, US$17 adult, US$8.50 children under 12, 50% discount if you eat in the restaurant. On Thu and Sat evenings a local Mento band plays delightful Jamaican folk songs.

Montego Bay *p238, map p241*

Most restaurants are happy for guests to bring wine and will provide chillers and glasses. Rum is cheaper here than at airport duty-free shops. Service at restaurants can be begrudging but the food is excellent. On the way into town from the airport there are several reasonably priced restaurants.

♥♥-♥ Houseboat Grill, Southern Cross Blvd, Montego Freeport, T9798845, houseboat @cwjamaica.com. Tue-Sun dinner. Lovely location, houseboat on the lagoon, pontoon ferry to board it, glass-bottom section fascinating for kids, lobster tank, tasty appetizers, vegetarian dishes such as gnocchi in an apple hazelnut cream sauce, entrées mostly steak, lobster, fish and shrimp, international wine list. Move upstairs on deck for dessert and comfortable chairs to watch rays, tarpon and snook around the boat, romantic but insect repellent essential.

♥♥-♥ Ma Lou's, Coral Cliff Hotel, Gloucester Av. Gourmet restaurant owned by Miss Lou, a Jamaican of Chinese origin whose parents came from Bermuda and Isla Margarita, her culinary influences come from all round the islands. Lots of seafood, lobster and meat, try a starter of chicken kebab with tropical fruit or peanut sauce, wine from around the world, reservations essential, only seats 25 people in Jamaican-style chattel house, cheerful colours.

♥♥-♥ Tapas, Cornice Rd, T9524130, tapas45@hotmail.com. Take road to left of Coral Cliff up hill, take first left turn and restaurant is on the right. Romantic and delicious, with a sample of any 3 dishes on the menu, recommended are snapper camembert, lamb tzatziki and other Middle Eastern recipes.

♥♥-♥ Town House, 16 Church St (see page 239), T9522660, 1130-2300. The house is covered in bougain-villea overlooking Church Sq, dining on lower ground floor, very smart, dimmed lighting, linen napkins. Mildly pungent, tasty stuffed lobster US$42, other dishes also good, US$17-27.

♥ Akbar, 71 Gloucester Av, T9790113. Delicious, authentic Indian food.

♥ The Native, 29 Gloucester Av, T9792769. 0730-2230. Opposite **Aqua Sol**, upstairs to catch the breeze, very pleasant, lunch specials, local dishes, curried goat, brown stew pork, stewed peas, or try coconut crusted chicken with cinnamon banana, also salads, sandwiches, soups, seafood and vegetarian dishes. Parking.

♥♥-♥ Dolly's Café, 1-2 Sunset Blvd, **Hotel Gloriana Plaza**, T9790045. Breakfast, lunch and dinner. Great for Jamaican breakfast if just off the plane, ackee and saltfish, US$8, juices US$2, very good Jamaican dishes, also sandwiches, eat indoors or by the street.

♥♥-♥ Marguerite's Seafood by the Sea, Gloucester Av, T9524777, on the seafront. 2 restaurants, one posh with a/c and **Margaritaville** next door on a patio, T9529609. Sports bar and grill.

♥♥-♥ The Pelican, Gloucester Av, west of Coral Cliff, T9523171. Excellent breakfasts and dinners, good value, comfortable, popular, varied menu, vegetarian selection.

♥♥-♥ Rum Jungle Café and Bar, Coral Cliff Hotel, Gloucester Av. 24 hrs. Tropical jungle decor, pirate climbing down a rope over the bar, lots of realistic plastic greenery. All-day

Jamaica The north coast Listings

breakfast American or Jamaican style, snacks such as potato skins, jerk fries, rotis, nachos, pizzas, vegetarian options, sandwiches, burgers, or main meals of ribs, steak and roasts. Great place to come for Sun brunch, 1000-1400, where you can try unusual Jamaican fruit, jackfruit, otaheite apple (purple skin, white flesh, pear-shaped) or star apple (purple and white).

¶ **Baba Joe's** (Barbara Joe's), Kent Av, near airport on way to Whitehouse Village, just past **Sandals**. Excellent fish, local style, about US$8 for meal with beer.

¶ **Pork Pit**, 27 Gloucester Av, T9403008. Jerk chicken, pork and ribs sold by weight, service basic, they often give the best bits to locals and the fat to foreigners.

¶ **Orlando Caribbean Vegetarian Restaurant**, 71 Barnett St. 1000-1600. Tidy, comfortable, low prices, rather out of the way.

¶ **Patsy's Place Sunset Bar and Restaurant**, 35 Gloucester Av, T9520738. Small, good local dishes, excellent curried goat, cheap.

¶ **Scotchie's**, Coral Gardens Villas, Rose Hall, near the **Holiday Inn**, T9533301. 1100-2300. Just about as good as jerk gets; pork, chicken and fish available with just the right amount of spice, served wedded to roasted breadfruit, potato, yam or festival.

¶ **Smokey Joe's**, 19 ½ St James St, T9521155. Good local restaurant, also caterers, about US$6 for soup, main course, beer.

¶ **Toby Inn**, 1 Kent Av, T9524370. Very good for cheap barbecued chicken and pork, cheap drinks, live band, romantic atmosphere.

◑ Bars and clubs

Ocho Rios *p236*

Late night action usually takes place in the resorts and along James St also known as the reggae strip. Usually on Thu at 1900 the street comes alive with fire entertainers and booths offering local cuisine.

The Acropolis nightclub. Lively and fairly safe.

Amnesia Night Club, 70 Main St, T9742633.

Jamaica Me Crazy, Renaissance Jamaica Grande. One of the top nightspots.

Lion's Den, T9746768. A friendly club frequented by Rastafarians; rooms available, good food, clean.

Montego Bay *p238, map p241*

Harassment of tourists has reduced, still exercise caution when shopping and at night. Lots of hotels have discos and clubs.

The Brewery, Shop 4, Miranda Ridge Plaza, Gloucester Av, T9402433, thebreweryja@hotmail.com. 1100-0200. Bar with draught Red Stripe, pub atmosphere, food available, hamburgers, salads and lunchtime buffet, also takeaway, sit on patio overlooking the sea. Happy hour daily 1600-1800, live entertainment Wed, Sat, Sun nights, popular locally, particularly if a reggae star is performing, karaoke Tue, Fri, sports TV in bar.

Coral Cliff Gaming Room, Gloucester Av, T9524130. 24 hrs. Montego Bay has no casino, but here there are about 100 slot machines, big screen sports TV and live music or other shows on the stage.

The Garage, Unit 29, Central Point, 2 Union St, close to Sam Sharpe's Sq, T9403098. Sports bar and grill, the place to be, entertaining music.

Margaritaville Caribbean Bar and Grill, Gloucester Av, T9524777. Now quite an institution, very popular with students if pricey, 52 flavours of Margaritas and 32-oz 'bong of beer', food available, sport on big TVs, Nintendo and kids' menu, waterslide from roof to sea, wet T-shirt competitions, DJ at night, dancing. Daily from 1000, cover charge US$10 Fri-Sat.

Pier One, on the waterfront, junction of Howard Cooke Blvd and Barnett St in River Bay, T9522452. Look out for live concerts on Fri night with well-known Jamaican reggae stars attracting an audience of up to 1000 people, loud and energetic, dancing. Good food, everything from sandwiches to curry, eat indoors or outside, Fri buffet 1200-1500, fast and friendly service. Bar serves variety of tropical drinks.

Witches Nightclub, Holiday Inn SunSpree Resort, T9532485. 1800-0200. One of the most popular places for dancing, US$50 cover for all-inclusive eating, drinking and nightlife.

◉ Shopping

Ochos Rios *p236*

Wassi Art pottery workshop, Back St, Great Pond, T9748097, is delightful; there is a good selection in the salesroom and you can visit each artist. Ask your taxi driver to wait as it is several kilometres away.

▲ Activities and tours

Ochos Rios *p236*
Golf
Sandals Golf & Country Club, Upton, T9750119/22. 18 holes, green fee US$100, golf free for Sandals guests.

Horse riding
Riding lessons and trail rides are available at Chukka Cove, which has probably the best facilities.

Polo is played on Sat afternoons at Drax Hall Estate, St Ann's Bay, near Ocho Rios, T9729331, and at the Polo and Equestrian Club of Oakbrook, T9228581 for match details. International tournaments are held at Chukka Cove, Richmond Llandovery, St Ann's Bay, T9722506.

Tour operators
Blue Mountain Bicycle Tours, Shop 15, Santa Maria Plaza, Main St, T9747075, www.bmtoursja.com. Tours include a 29-km downhill trip through the forest to a waterfall, but don't expect much from the bikes.
Circle B, just southwest of St Ann's Bay, T9134511, owned by former senator, Bob Miller. Very good tour of working plantation with a welcome drink and sample fruits of Jamaica; lunch can be included.
Prospect Plantation Tour, east of Ocho Rios nearly opposite the Sans Souci Lido, T9941058, www.prospectplantationtour.com. Probably the most attractive and informative, and certainly the most accessible of the plantation tours. Daily 1030, 1400, and 1530, US$12. Ride on an open jitney or ride horses on scenic trails.

Ocho Rios to Falmouth *p237*
For diving and fishing, see page 215.
Golf
Breezes Golf Beach Resort, T9737319. 18 holes, green fee US$58, free for guests at Breezes Runaway Bay.

Spectator sports
A magnificent multi-purpose stadium

seating 25,000 was opened in 2007 at Greenfields, Trelawny, just east of Falmouth. Built with Chinese help for the Cricket World Cup, it hosted the opening ceremony on 11 March and four warm-up matches beforehand.

Cockpit Country *p238*
Tour operators
For **caving**, contact Mike Schwartz of **Windsor Great House**, T9973832, windsor@cwjamaica.com, where there is rustic accommodation.
Sun Venture Tours (see page 227) offer tailor-made tours of the Cockpit Country Crossing (Troy to Windsor the preferred route, or for a less arduous hike, St Vincent to Clarks Town).

Montego Bay *p238, map p241*
Golf
Half Moon Golf Club, T9532560, advance booking necessary for this championship course, 18 holes, green fee US$130, mandatory cart US$35 and caddy US$25, also tennis and squash.
Ironshore Golf and Country Club, a Sandals course, free for guests, 18 holes, green fee US$45.
Wyndham Rose Hall Golf Club, east of Montego Bay, T9532650, 18 holes, green fee US$125 for outsiders, US$80 after 1300.

Horse riding
Hotels can arrange riding with local stables and there are good facilities at the Equestrian Centre at Half Moon Club. A 3-hr beach ride costs about US$55.

Tour operators
JUTA Tours, Claude Clarke Av, T9520623, or airport T9712857, offer 12-hr day trip to Kingston via Dunns River Falls and Ocho Rios, US$250 in a/c car; also 9-hr tour to Negril, US$150, with sunset drink at Rick's Café.

⊖ Transport

Montego Bay *p238, map p241*
Air
Donald Sangster International Airport is Air Jamaica's regional hub and there are good connections with lots of airlines landing here. There is a transfer service to Kingston by

Martins minibus, 5 hrs. To get to the **Norman Manley Airport**, Kingston, take the minibus from the town centre to Pechon St, Kingston, from where the airport buses leave.

Bus

The bus station for Kingston and Ocho Rios is behind **Courts** (Electrical). The bus station for Negril is off Barnett St (beware pickpockets). Buses get crowded. They depart when full. They are fast, very frequent and cheap, about US$2 to **Negril** with a 30-second transfer in Lucea. There are more buses Montego Bay-Lucea than Lucea-Negril, which often causes a bottleneck. Buses from Kingston depart from Pechon St, roughly every hr

from 0600 to 1500, US$4.50. It is possible to get to Montego Bay from **Port Antonio** all along the north coast, a scenic journey involving changes in Annotto Bay (then shared taxi, US$1 per person, mad rush to squeeze into clapped-out Ladas, the locals giving no quarter to slow tourists), **Port Maria** US$1, and **Ocho Rios**. Ochos Rios-Montego Bay by bus takes 2 hrs, US$2.

Taxi

JUTA are usually found outside hotels. JCAL, 80B Queen's Drive, T9527574, charges US$25 to Gloucester Av from **Sandals Montego Bay**, US$30 from **Wyndham**. Lucea-Negril about US$35. See also Tour operators, above.

The southwest

Negril, the main tourist town in the west, earned a reputation in the days of hippies and is still considered more laid back than other destinations. Its seven-mile beach attracts families, couples and students on their spring breaks and accommodation is equally varied, from basic cabins to boutique luxury hotels. Long ignored by all except fisherman, the south coast is gradually attracting attention from visitors. Treasure Beach has a few small hotels, of which Jake's has a number of celebrity devotees, but in 2005 Sandals opened a large resort at Whitehouse. Unfortunately, hurricanes also came calling in 2004 and 2005, causing flooding and other damage in their wake, but the area's attractions remained undimmed, from the crocodiles in Black River to the rum factory at the Appleton Estate. ➤ For Sleeping, Eating and other listings, see pages 249-254.

Negril and the south coast

Negril, on a seven-mile stretch of pure white sand on the west end of the island, is far less formal than other tourist spots but is still a one-industry town. The town is at the south end of Long Bay; at the north is the smaller Bloody Bay, where whalers used to carve up their catch. The **Negril Environmental Protection Trust (NEPT)** ① *Norman Manley Blvd, T9573115*, is an NGO charged with managing the Negril Environmental Protection Area, which includes a marine park managed by the **Negril Coral Reef Preservation Society (NCRPS)** ① *T9573735*. The main part of the town has resorts and beaches but no snorkelling and you have to take a boat. In the West End of the town are beautiful cliffs and many fine caves, with great snorkelling but no beaches. In between is an area with neither beaches nor cliffs. Behind the bay is the **Great Morass**, which is being drained for development but remains a protected area as a natural wetland. The **Royal Palm Reserve** ① *T9573736 (office), T3647407 (reserve), www.royalpalmreserve.com, 0900-1800, birdwatching by appointment from 0600, adult US$10, children US$5*, is well worth a visit, a little way out of Negril on the south coast road to Sheffield. The **Jamaican Petroleum Corporation** mined it for peat in the late 1970s, but they gave up and left the resulting pond and forest for ecological purposes. The reserve, at 289 acres, is part of the 6000-acre wetland protected by the NEPT, on and offshore. Apart from a wonderful collection of palms, you can see the

West Indian whistling duck and blue herons on the water, with red tilapia and tarpon in the pond, as well as Jamaican boa and crocodile, which are less visible.

Hawkers ('higglers'), pushing their drugs, hair braiding, aloe, etc, on the beach, are annoying and reported to be worse than at Montego Bay. Politely decline whatever they are offering (if you do not want it). Fruit is readily available although not ready to eat; ask the vendor to cut it up and put it in a bag for you. To avoid the worst of the higglers go to the end of the beach near the crafts market where there are no stalls or bars.

Kool Runnings ① *Norman Manley Blvd, opposite Beaches Hotel, T9575400, www.koolrunnings.com. US$28 adult, US$19 children, family US$80*, is a water park with amusement and entertainment facilities. The park promises the 'greatest chill' under the sun and there is a variety of chutes and slides, rafting and tubing, a climbing wall, bungee trampolining, go-karting, etc.

By the **Poinciana Beach Resort** is the **Anancy Park** ① *Tue-Sun 1300-2200, US$1-3*, with boating lake, minigolf, go-karts, fishing pond, nature trail, and historical exhibitions.

Savanna-la-Mar

About 29 km east of Negril, on the coast, is Savanna-la-Mar, a busy, commercial town with shopping and banks, but no major attractions for tourists. Regular concerts are held at **St Joseph's Catholic Church** ① *20 Luis St, T9552648*. Local musicians play under the auspices of Father Sean Lavery, formerly a professor of music at Dublin University. Easily reached by minibus from Negril, there are hourly buses from Montego Bay (US$2). The **Frome sugar refinery**, 8 km north of Savanna-la-Mar, will often allow visitors to tour their facilities during sugar cane season (November-June). Another interesting outing is to the 9.5-km **Roaring River** and the organic **Ital Herbs and Spice Farm**, owned by an American, Ed Kritzler. There is a cave at Roaring River and the farm is about half a mile on, 3 km north of Petersfield, from where it is well signposted. It is a scenic area

> There is clothes- optional bathing at certain hotels, quite rare in the Caribbean There are toilets and showers (US$0.30).

with interesting walks and streams suitable for bathing. A restaurant serves fish and vegetable dishes at the farm, and it is best to order lunch before exploring. Basic hut accommodation is available and popular, but try to look before you book.

Bluefields

Outside Savanna-la-Mar, the main south coast road (A2) passes by Paradise Plantation, a private estate with miles of frontage on **Bluefields Bay**, a protected anchorage with reefs and wetlands teeming with birds. At Ferris Crossroads, the A2 meets up with the B8 road, a well-maintained north-south connection and about 40 minutes' drive to Montego Bay via Whithorn and Anchovy. For the next 6.5 km the A2 hugs the coast along the road to Bluefields, where there is a white-sand beach mainly used by locals. There is no mass tourism either in Bluefields or in the adjacent village of **Belmont**.

The south coast is known as the best part of Jamaica for deep-sea fishing and boat trips go out from Belmont to the reefs or to offshore banks. Snorkelling is also good because the sea is mainly calm in the morning. The **Bluefields Great House**, now privately owned, was the place where Philip Gosse lived in the 1830s and wrote his book, *Birds of Jamaica*. It reportedly contains the first breadfruit tree planted in Jamaica by Captain Bligh after his expedition to the South Pacific. The next 9.5 km of coast southeast of Bluefields covers a beautiful, unspoiled coastal stretch.

Black River

Black River is one of the oldest towns in Jamaica. It had its heyday in the 18th century when it was the main exporting harbour for logwood dyes. Along the shore are some fine early 19th-century mansions, some of which are being restored. In the town there several lovely old wooden buildings and a yellow brick parish church, low, squat and solid. At Black River, you can go by boat from across the bridge up the lower stretches of the Black River, the longest river in Jamaica. You should see crocodiles, mostly at midday basking on the river banks, and plenty of birdlife in tranquil surroundings. To avoid large tour parties, go with a local, whose boats are through the fish market. The boats are smaller, slower, quieter and go further up river. They stop at a 'countryside bar' rather than the one the large tour companies use (see Tour operators, page 254).

Treasure Beach

On the south coast past Black River is Treasure Beach, a wide dark-sand beach with body-surfing waves, in one of the most beautiful areas on the island. It is largely used by local fishermen as it is the closest point to the Pedro Banks. There is one small grocery shop and a bakery. A van comes to the village every day with fresh fruit and vegetables. This area is quite unlike any other part of Jamaica and still relatively unvisited by tourists. The local people are very friendly and you will be less hassled by higglers than elsewhere. Frenchman's Beach is the best for swimming, then Calabash Bay. You can take a daytime or moonlight tour to **Sunny Island** (Alligator Reef) from **Jake's Hotel**. Hire a fishing boat to go to **Pelican Bar**, run by Floyd, on a sand bar 1 km out to sea, entirely rebuilt on stilts of timber and thatch after Hurricane Ivan swept through in 2004. To the east of Treasure Beach lies **Lovers' Leap** ① *T9656577, daily 1000-1800, no entry fee but visitors are expected to patronize the restaurant and bar*, a beauty spot named after the slave and his lover (his owner's daughter) who jumped off the cliff in despair. East of Alligator Pond is **Gut River**, where you can sometimes see alligators and manatees. Boat and fishing trips can be made to **Pigeon Island**, with a day on the island for swimming and snorkelling.

❧ *The first car imported into Jamaica was landed here.*

Bamboo Avenue

Inland on the A2 is Middle Quarters, on the edge of the Black River Morass, hot pepper shrimp are sold by the wayside, but make sure they are today's catch. Just after Middle Quarters is the left turn which takes you to **YS Falls** ① *T9976360, www.ysfalls.com, Tue-Sun 0930-1530, closed public holidays, US$13, children US$7, 15-min walk from car park* (pronounced Why-Ess), in the middle of a large private plantation where they produce beef cattle and breed race horses. River bathing is popular with local families as well as tour parties and there are changing rooms and composting toilets. A walkway follows the course of the river and up the tiered falls to the top pool where there is a rope for swinging (gloves provided and life jackets when the river is full). The natural pool, surrounded by decking, is fed by a nearby spring and is always clear even when the river and falls are in full spate. A cool spot for non-swimmers. Further along the A2 is the impressive 2½-mile long Bamboo Avenue. North of Bamboo Avenue is **Maggotty**, on the (closed) railway line from Montego Bay to Kingston and close to the **Appleton Estate** ① *T9639215, www.jamaica-southcoast.com (distillery), www.appletonrum.com (product), Mon-Sat 0900-1530, US$15 adults, US$12 children*, where tours of the rum factory are offered and there is good rum tasting. A buffet lunch is offered with advance reservation, vegetarian or other special requirements catered for. Opposite the Maggotty train depot is the **Sweet Bakery**, run by Patrick and Lucille Lee, who can arrange accommodation in a great house (**D**) or at a rustic campsite, very friendly and helpful, local trips organized.

Mandeville → *Colour map 1, C5. Population: 50,000.*

After Bamboo Avenue, the A2 road goes through Lacovia and Santa Cruz, an expanding town on the St Elizabeth Plain, and on up to Mandeville, a peaceful upland town with perhaps the best climate on the island. It is very spread out, with building on all the surrounding hills and no slums. In recent years, Mandeville has derived much of its prosperity from the bauxite/alumina industry (outside the town). There are lots of expensive homes and the town is congested.

The town's centre is the village green, now called **Cecil Charlton Park** (after the ex-mayor, whose opulent mansion, Huntingdon Summit, can be visited by prior arrangement). The green looks a bit like New England; at its northeast side stands a **Georgian courthouse** and, on the southeast, **St Mark's parish church** (both 1820). By St Mark's is the **market** area (busiest days Monday, Wednesday and Friday) and the area where buses congregate. West of the green, at the corner of Ward Avenue and Caledonia Road, is the **Manchester Club** ① *T9622403*, one of the oldest country clubs in the West Indies (1868) and the oldest in Jamaica. It has a nine-hole golf course (18 tee boxes, enabling you to play 18 holes) and tennis courts (you must be introduced by a member).

Around Mandeville

Although some way inland, Mandeville is a good place from which to start exploring both the surrounding area and the south coast. In fact, by car you can get to most of Jamaica's resorts, except those east of Ocho Rios or Kingston, in two hours or less. Birdwatchers and those interested in seeing a beautiful 'great house' in a cattle property should contact Ann Sutton at **Marshall's Pen** ① *T9045454, US$10 for great house tour by appointment only*. Also around the town you can visit the **High Mountain Coffee** ① *Main Rd, Williamsfield, T9634211, Mon-Fri, 0800-1700, free*, **Pioneer Chocolate Company** ① *T9634216*, the Alcan works, and local gardens.

From Mandeville it is about 88.5 km east to Kingston on the A2, bypassing May Pen, through Old Harbour then on to Spanish Town and Kingston. Before the May Pen bypass, a road branches south to **Milk River Bath** ① *May Pen, Clarendon, T9024657, daily 0700-2100, US$2, 15 mins, restaurant and hotel*, the world's most radioactive spa. The baths are somewhat run-down, but the medical properties of the water are among the best. Five kilometres from the baths is a marine conservation area, **Alligator Hole**. Local boatmen will take you on tours.

● Sleeping

Negril *p246*
This whole beach is lined with hotels, bars and clubs and can be noisy. The northern end is the more expensive part of town, but there are a few cheap cabins. None of the cabins has any services, nor do they provide blankets, but they are on the beach. When choosing a cabin check to see whether it has a fan, whether there is a mesh or screen to keep out mosquitoes, and whether it looks safe (many get broken into). Locals living along the beach will often let you camp on their property. There are several large all-inclusives which are not listed below.
LL The Caves, Lighthouse Rd, West End, T9570269, www.islandoutpost.com. All-inclusive luxury, 12 rooms and 2, 2-bedroom villas, all different with lots of privacy, minibar, CD player, CDs, books, huge bath tub with shower, some have outdoor

shower, no children under 16 unless you hire the whole property with nanny. Lots of private areas on the cliffs with sundecks, little nooks, steps down to the sea through limestone rock. Private dining room in cave lit by candles for romantic dining. Sauna and massage, spa with sea view.
LL Sunset at the Palms (Negril Cabins), Norman Manley Blvd, on Bloody Bay, across the road from the beach, T9575350, www.sunsetatthepalms.com. All-inclusive, deluxe rooms and suites in wooden cabins on stilts, rustic elegance, light and airy, Asian-inspired furnishings, pool, swim-up bar, private beach, tennis, internet access, restaurants, fruit from the 10-acre garden, piano bar, children's programme, security guards keep away 'higglers'.
LL-L Tensing Pen, Lighthouse Rd, West End, T9570387, www.tensingpen.com. Tensing is

the dog, a Ridgeback, wait until staff arrive before getting out of car. Well-established upmarket hotel but unpretentious and sociable. 16 rooms in lush, leafy gardens, some adjoining can be suites, rooms on stilts with open showers downstairs, no a/c, no TV, supremely relaxing, breakfast included 0730-1100, get your own lunch in kitchen, dinner 5 nights. All the advantages of a hotel but with independence of a villa. Yoga hut, massage, hammocks, lots of private areas for sunbathing.

LL-AL Charela Inn, Norman Manley Blvd, on the beach, T9574648, www.charela.com. 40 rooms around pool, access for wheelchairs, 3 rooms for the less able, family-owned and run, wide beach, kayaks, Sunfish, sailboards, restaurant, bar, meal plans, French chef, wine brought from France, own bakery on site, old-fashioned dining room, dress code for dinner.

LL-AL Negril Escape Resort and Spa, West End, T9570393, www.marinersnegril.com. On cliffs, rooms and apartments, yoga, spa, PADI and NAUI instructors for diving at Negril Scuba Centre on site or at sister property, Mariner's Negril Beach Club, to where there is a regular beach shuttle, kayaking, riding, volleyball.

LL-AL Rockhouse, Lighthouse Rd, T/F9574373, www.rockhousehotel.com. On cliffs at Pristine Cove, just north of Rick's Café, 11 octagonal villas by the sea with fans, indoor bathrooms, outdoor showers, built of timber, stone and thatch, or 17 studios in thatched blocks in the garden, cliff-edge pool, restaurant above the water serving 'new Jamaican cuisine', 0700-2300, no beach but steps down to sea, snorkelling and kayak rental, quiet, restful, Australian-owned, no children under 12 because of potentially dangerous cliffs.

LL-AL Rondel Village, Norman Manley Blvd, T9574413, www.rondelvillage.com. 40 rooms in 1-3 bedroom villas on 3 floors, some have jacuzzis off master bedroom, all have TV, fridge, a/c, fan, light, bright colours but a bit cramped with a lot of rooms in a small lot. Irie beach restaurant and bar, good bit of beach, plenty of sand, sun beds. Garden rooms across the road are cheaper.

LL-A Seasplash, Norman Manley Blvd, T9574041, www.seasplash.com. A **Green Globe** resort, rooms and suites cheapest in May-Jun and Sep-Oct, when very good value, spacious, comfortable, homely, good fittings and furnishings, everything you could need.

L-AL Firefly Beach Cottages, Long Bay, on the beach and therefore not very private, T9574358, www.jamaicalink.com. From a basic cabin for 2 or studios, to 1- to 3-bedroomed cottages or luxury villas, clothes optional, gymnasium, Wi-Fi internet access, minimum 1-week rental in winter, 3 nights in summer.

AL-B Heart Beat Seaside Retreat, West End Rd, T9574329, www.heartbeatjamaica.com, on West End cliffs. 9 rooms, 1- 2- or 3-bed cottages and efficiencies, run by Valerie Brewis, cafés and music nearby, great sunset watching from veranda, Wi-Fi internet access.

B-C Gloria's Sunset, Norman Manley Blvd, T9574741. Jamaican family-run, clean, friendly, helpful, security guards at night, variety of accommodation, bar, restaurant.

B-D Tigress 1 Cottages, West End Rd, T9570697, **Tigress 2**, T9574249 . Cheaper rooms with fan, no hot water, shared bathrooms, higher-priced rooms with a/c, hot water, private bath, all with kitchen facilities, good security, bar and pool in gardens, 20 mins' walk to beach and walking distance from town centre, friendly, clean, lots of repeat business.

Bluefields *p247*

A 360-room **Sandals** resort opened in 2005, occupying 50 acres of beach front at Whitehouse, Bluefields Bay.

B Casa Mariner, in Cave, 3.2 km from Bluefields, T9558487. Friendly owner Manley Wallace, restaurant, private pier and gazebo.

Black River *p247*

A-C Ashton Great House, up hillside, Luana, just outside Black River to the west, T/F9652036. Lovely old plantation house with balconies and fretwork detail. Pool, restaurant, free ride from Bluefields, 24 rooms.

B-C Port of Call Hotel, 136 Crane Rd, 3 km east of Black River T9652410. A bit spartan but on the sea, a/c, pool.

B-C Waterloo Guest House, 44 High St, T9652278. A Georgian building, the first house in Jamaica with electric light. Old rooms in the main house, or more expensive in the new annex, all with showers, very good restaurant (lobster in season).

D-E Bridge House Inn, 14 Crane Rd, T9652361, F9652081. 14 comfortable rooms, a/c, fan, kitchen facilities, shady garden with hammocks leads down to beach, restaurant, good Jamaican food, US$8-10 for a meal, staff friendly, bar, TV, lounge, ask for odd-numbered room at front to avoid noise from club on the beach.

Treasure Beach *p248*

LL-A Jake's, Calabash Bay, T9650635, www.islandoutpost.com. Part of **Island Outpost** chain, run by award-winning Jason Henzell. One of the loveliest places to stay in the Caribbean. Intimate, friendly, a great place. Rustic rooms in small, brightly painted cottages, all different with themed designs. Also honeymoon suites in individual buildings on the shore, like iced cakes in pretty blue or pink with rooftop sun deck where you can have room service. Games room/library with TV/VCR, **Dougie's** bar by salt water pool looking out to sea. Boat trips, riding, cycling and hiking can be arranged, yoga and massage, music. 2 restaurants, very good food, lovely banana pancakes for breakfast.

L-AL Treasure Beach Hotel, Frenchman's Beach, T9650110, www.treasurebeachjamaica .com. 36 rooms, restaurant, good view, used for groups and package tours.

AL-A Sunset Resort, Treasure Beach next to Jake's, T9650143, www.sunsetresort.com. Rooms and suites, flexible accommodation, Jamaican decor, good for family groups, view from cliff top down to beach with fishing boats and pelicans, US and Jamaican owned, lots of flags, keen fisherman, Astroturf around the pool. Bar and restaurant, unlimited buffet Fri night.

Mandeville *p248*

AL-B Mandeville Hotel, 4 Hotel St, T9622460, www.mandevillehotel.com. TV, spacious, pool, restaurant, excursions arranged, good.

B Kariba Kariba, Atkinson's Drive, near New Green roundabout on Winston Jones highway, first right off New Green Rd, 45 mins' walk from centre, on bus route, T9628006, www.karibaholidays.com. Bath, fan, 5 rooms or suites, breakfast included, TV lounge, bar, dining room. The owners,

Derrick and Hazel O'Conner, are friendly, knowledgeable and hospitable, they can arrange for you to meet local people with similar interests and offer tours. Derrick is developing a 5-ha farm at Mile Gully and plans to develop a small campsite, bar, accommodation and other facilities there.

● Eating

Negril *p246*

Eating cheaply is difficult but not impossible. The native restaurant-food stalls are good and relatively cheap; the local patties are delicious. Street hawkers will sell you jerk chicken for US$4-5.

♥♥♥-♥ **Norma's**, at **Seasplash** hotel, see above, T9574041. Breakfast, lunch and dinner. On decking with steps down to sea, by pool and bar, sun beds on narrow strip of sand. Breakfast US$4-8, lunch of burgers, seafood, jerk meats, pasta up to US$12, pizza US$14-18, dinner main courses more elegant, up to US$23. Very good food, smoked marlin a speciality for any meal.

♥♥♥-♥ **Rick's Café**, T4570380. Lunch 1200-1600, dinner and entertainment 1800-2200. Full ocean view from clifftop setting, famous for the local divers who throw themselves off the rocks and trees into the sea for tips. Food ranges from surf'n'turf down to coco bread chips and salsa dip, Cuban and Jamaican cigars, live music in evenings on small stage, lively place and a must for a sunset drink.

♥♥-♥ **Cosmos**, on the beach, north of **Sandals Beaches**, T9574330. 0900-2130, food from 1100. Wide area of sand under palm trees, seating at benches on sand or at tables under roof by bar. Day pass US$3. Local food at local prices, popular with Jamaicans, red pea soup, curry goat, stews, fish, conch, with local accompaniments, rice and peas, steamed or fried bammy, hearty and filling.

♥♥-♥ **Hungry Lion**, Lighthouse Rd, West End, T9574486. 1100-2300, Sat until 0200. Small, colourful and arty crafty, art on the walls, gift shop. Lunch downstairs in lounge-style restaurant, dinner upstairs on roof terrace or indoors, open from 1700, healthy eating, natural foods, salads, sandwiches, fish for lunch, crab backs, shrimp, vegetarian options, pasta for dinner. Bar and occasional night time entertainment with screen for

showing unusual DVDs and documentaries.
♟-♟ **The Office**, on the beach, open 24 hrs,
provides a good choice of Jamaican food,
reasonably priced and friendly service, a
good place to meet the locals.
♟-♟ **Pirates Cave Bar and Grill**, on cliffs at
West End, 1100-2300. Film location for the
films *20,000 Leagues Under the Sea* and
Papillon. Circular thatched hut on top of cliffs
with tables round edge in shade or full sun.
Snorkelling and raft for rent US$5/hr, cave
and water entrance, wet dollars accepted
from those who arrive by sea and swim
ashore. Cliff jumping has been going on here
since before 1973 when owner Tom Martin
arrived. Food ranges from sandwiches and
burgers to snapper fillet.
♟-♟ **Sun Beach**, Norman Manley Blvd, south of
Margaritaville, T9579119. 0730-2200, later at
weekends. Restaurant and bar on beach,
sunbeds on sand, snacks and salads, fish,
ginger curry chicken, sauteed snapper, 2-for-1
lobster special Sun nights, live music on Sun.
♟ **Pete's Seafood**, just off the beach in the
main part of town, is a restaurant as well as a
market and serves good, local, filling meals
for about US$4.
The Bread Basket, next to the banks at the
mall in town, is recommended, as is
Fisherman's Club supermarket, just off the
beach in the main part of town near **Pete's
Seafood**.

Black River *p247*
♟-♟ **Fish Pot Bistro**, on the river by the
boats, Lunch and dinner (mosquitoes at
dusk), serving fish at US$6 per lb, lobster,
garlic crab.
♟ **Bayside**, 19 High St, near bridge, T9652537.
Excellent steamed fish with rice and peas for
US$6, usually all gone by 1300.
♟ **Carib**, Chambers Plaza, near bus station,
T9652645. Very good steamed fish and
curried goat for US$6 with beer.
♟ **Riverside Dock**, water's edge, Morass,
T6343333. Just up Black River from the coast,
exquisite Japanese, Chinese and
international seafood dishes, outside bar,
pool tables, swings and slides for children,
karaoke and local music. Safari rides up the
Black River can be arranged through the
restaurant with one of the local tour
operators.
♟ **Superbus**, an old bus near bus station.

Good cheap food, eg fried chicken with
trimmings and beer for US$3.

Treasure Beach *p248*
♟-♟ **Little Ochie**, Alligator Pond, on the
beach, T9654449, www.littleochie.com.
1100-2300, later at weekends, depending on
customers. Blackie's fish restaurant is
legendary, everything freshly caught, sit at
wooden tables under thatch, some made
out of old fishing boats with benches for
tables, raised on stilts above the sand.
Choose your fish or seafood from the fridge
and they'll cook it however you want, very
fresh and tasty, garnished with spicy onion
(pickled), carrot and scotch bonnet chillies,
accompanied by festival or bammy.

Mandeville *p248*
♟-♟ **Bloomfield Great House**, 8 Perth Rd,
T9627130, bloomfield.g.h@cwjamaica.com.
Originally a coffee estate, part of its land was
used to build the town, 200 m above
Mandeville, panoramic views. The Georgian
great house has also been used as a hotel, a
dairy, a private home and more recently, **Bill
Laurie's Steak House**, now owned by Ralph
Pearce (Australian) and his wife Pamela
Grant (Jamaican). Open for lunch and dinner,
varied menu, fish 'n' chips, filet mignon,
beer-batter shrimp, homemade pasta,
smoked marlin, cheesecakes are a speciality.
♟ **Hungry Jack's**, 45 Manchester Rd,
T9620648. Cheap, excellent food and service
(owner, Fay, grew up in England).
♟ **International Chinese Restaurant**, 117
Manchester Rd, T9620527.

✪ Bars and clubs

Negril *p246*
Live reggae shows in outdoor venues most
nights, featuring local and well-known stars.
Entrance is usually US$5-7, good fun, lively
atmosphere, very popular. Nice bars are
located along the beach, usually with music.
For beautiful surroundings try the bar at the
Rock Cliff Hotel on the West End Rd, friendly
barman who mixes great fruit punches and
cocktails.
Alfred's, at Ocean Palace, Norman Manley
Blvd. Nightly entertainment, live music,
varied programme, reggae some nights, on
the beach, open air.

The Jungle, Norman Manley Blvd, across from Rondel Village, T9573283. Daily from 2200 until dawn, queues start at 1100, gets going 2400, noise abatement rules kick in at 0200 but club doesn't close until 0400-0430. Entry around US$5-6, depending on night. Used to be a bank and still looks like it, with vault doors. Ladies' Night Thu, Dance Hall Night Fri, restaurant and bar, lots of high spirits, gaming room open from 1500 until the club closes, sports bar, pool tables, ATM, snacks and stage for comedy and other entertainment, occasionally live music, but mostly DJs. Plenty of security on gate, vendors outside to increase traffic jam.

Margaritaville, Norman Manley Blvd, T9579396. Restaurant and well-stocked bar on the beach specializing in margaritas. Several TV screens showing sports. Stage for live music but mostly taped, foam nights, all you can drink US$12 1100-1600 if you want to get drunk early. Pretty at night with fairy lights around tree trunks. Trading Post shop selling T-shirts etc.

Treasure Beach p248
Pelican Bar, 30 mins out to sea on a sandbank. Reached by fishing boat, Floyde Forbes' bar is built of wood and thatched with palm fronds, a precarious stilted construction furnished with mismatched wooden tables and bench seating, while underneath hover sting rays waiting for scraps and pelicans sit on the roof. Floyde will cook fish and rice, whatever he has caught that day, and serve up drinks from a cooler. Tours of the Black River sometimes stop by for daytime drinks, while guests at Jake's come out at sunset or for a full moon.

Mandeville p248
Jerky's Restaurant, near the Greenvale roundabout en route to Spur Tree Hill, T9628138. Pool bar with karaoke on Sun and music and entertainment during the week. Speciality jerk pork and chicken.

O Shopping

Negril p246
Times Square, for jewellery, perfume and gifts. The mall in downtown Negril offers much the same but at slightly higher prices. The Craft Market is overwhelming, with 200 stalls of sarongs and wood carvings, not much in the way of variety and everyone wants your attention.

▲ Activities and tours

Negril p246
Diving
Sundivers, a PADI 5-star facility at Negril Beach next to Footprints and at Point Village Resort, T9579943, www.sundiversnegril.com. Free pick-up, 2-tank boat dive US$60, plus US$20 for equipment, Open Water course US$300.
Negril Scuba Centre is at Negril Beach Club, Norman Manley Blvd, T9574425, neg.scuba.centre@toj.com.
Marine Life Divers, Samsara Hotel, West End, T9573245, www.mldiversnegril.com. Boat and shore diving, 1 tank US$40, 2 tanks US$70, night dive US$50, 3 dives (1 shore, 2 boat) US$150, Open Water course US$305.

Golf
Tryall Golf, Tennis and Beach Resort, Sandy Bay, between Montego Bay and Negril, T9565660, pro shop T9565681. Par 71, 6328 m in 890-ha resort complex, probably the best known and hosts the annual Johnny Walker World Championship. Advance bookings are essential.
Negril Hills Golf Club, Sheffield, inland, up in the hills near Negril, T9574638, F9570222. Par 72, 5790 m, 18-hole course with clubhouse, restaurant, pro shop and tennis. Green fees US$58.

Horse riding
Babo's Horseback Riding Stable and Country Western Riding Stables have facilities for riding and tennis, daily 0800-1700, US$30-35.

Road races
The Reggae marathon and half marathon starting at the Negril UDC playing field to Green Island and return, www.reggaemarathon.com. An annual event in Dec, starting at 0515. Well-supported marathon and half marathon, begins and ends at Long Bay Beach Park.

Tour operators

Charles Swaby's South Coast Safaris, 1 Crane Rd in Black River, T9652513. Takes up to 250 people per tour, looking for crocodiles, 1½ hrs, 5 times a day, from east side of Black River bridge.

Irie Safari, T6344232, lintonirie@ hotmail.com. Takes a maximum of 35 passengers, using several different sizes of boat, US$40 for 2 people, less for more, wheelchair access. The captain is a guide, giving a rounded tour, educational, not just watching crocodiles but spotting birds and crabs and other wetland creatures.

Mandeville p248

Golf

Manchester Club, Wint Rd, T9622403, 9-hole, green fee US$16.

Road races

High Mountain Coffee, one of several races during the year. 10-km and 5-km races at Williamsfield, Manchester, which usually attract around 450 runners.

◉ Transport

Negril p246

Licensed, unmetered taxis have red licence plates with PP before the numbers. Avoid unlicensed taxis. Route taxis charge US$1 for locals but up to US$4 for tourists into town. A taxi will also cost US$4 into town from the beach hotels. Local buses operate between Negril and Montego Bay stopping frequently. JUTA-operated tour buses typically charge US$250 for 1-4 people between **Montego Bay** and Negril. From the **Donald Sangster Airport** minibuses run to Negril; you must bargain with the driver to get the fare to US$5-7. Lots of companies do bike rental.

Black River p247

To get to Black River from **Mandeville** by bus involves a change in Santa Cruz.

◉ Directory

Negril p246

Banks National Commercial Bank and Scotiabank and several *cambios* in town including one at the Hi-lo-Supermarket.

Background

History

When Columbus landed on Jamaica in 1494 it was inhabited by peaceful Taíno Indians living in over 200 villages, most of them on the south coast, especially around what is now Old Harbour. Under Spanish occupation, which began in 1509, the race faced harsh slavery and virtual extinction. Most died but some escaped into the mountains. Gradually African slaves were brought in to provide the labour force. In 1655 an English expeditionary force landed at Passage Fort and met with little resistance other than that offered by a small group of Spanish settlers and a larger number of African slaves who took refuge in the mountains, co-existing with the remaining Taínos. The Spaniards abandoned the island after about five years, but the slaves and their descendants, who became known as Maroons, waged war against the new colonists for 80 years until the 1730s although there was another brief rebellion in 1795. Some of their descendants still live in the Cockpit Country, where the Leeward Maroons hid, and around Nanny Town where the Windward Maroons hid.

After a short period of military rule, the colony was adopted with an English-type constitution and a Legislative Council. The great sugar estates were planted in the early days of English occupation when Jamaica also became the haunt of buccaneers and slave traders. In 1833 slave emancipation was declared and modern Jamaica was born. The framework for Jamaica's modern political system was laid in the 1930s. Norman W Manley formed the People's National Party (PNP) in 1938 and his cousin, Sir Alexander Bustamante, formed the Jamaica Labour Party (JLP) in 1944. These two parties had their roots in rival trade unions and have dominated Jamaican politics since universal adult suffrage was introduced in 1944. In 1958, Jamaica joined the West Indies Federation but withdrew following a national referendum on the issue in 1961. On 6 August 1962, Jamaica became an independent Commonwealth member.

After 23 years as leader of the PNP, eight of them as Prime Minister in the 1970s and three as Prime Minister from 1989, Michael Manley, son of the party's founder, retired in March 1992 because of ill health. During Manley's first two terms in office between 1972 and 1980 he endorsed socialist policies at home and encouraged South-South relations abroad. He antagonized the USA by developing close economic and political links with Cuba. Manley's government focused on state-led income distribution to the poorer classes at the expense of private sector support and increased productivity. Failure to deliver economic stability and growth led to his defeat in the 1980 elections. The conservative Edward Seaga (JLP), held office for the next nine years. By 1989 however, Manley's political thinking had changed dramatically and he was re-elected with policies advocating the free market. He was succeeded by the Party Chairman, former Deputy Prime Minister and Finance Minister P J Patterson. Patterson promised to maintain Manley's policies and to deepen the restructuring of the economy.

General elections were held early, on 30 March 1993, and the incumbent PNP was returned for a second term. Despite a landslide victory, the elections were marred by violence that led to 11 deaths, malpractices and a turnout of only 58%. The JLP boycotted parliament for four months while it demanded electoral reform and an inquiry into the election day events. It also refused to contest by-elections. Concessions were made by the Government, including a reorganization of the police force and the postponement of local government elections pending electoral reform. The reform drafted by the Electoral Advisory Committee was completed in time for general elections in December 1997.

The 1997 elections gave the PNP a third consecutive term in office. When he was sworn into office, Prime Minister PJ Patterson promised that it would be the last time that the Government would swear allegiance to the British monarchy. The PNP proposes an executive president but the JLP advocates a ceremonial president with a Prime Minister.

The 2002 general elections resulted in the ruling PNP winning 35 seats and the JLP 25. Massive expenditures on infrastructure projects, involving island-wide road repairs and construction in the months leading up to the elections, secured victory in a keenly contested poll. The other minor parties made insignificant showings, receiving less than 1% of the vote in each case. Politically motivated violence was considerably reduced and the elections were judged well run and markedly free from corruption. In 2005 PJ Patterson stood down as leader of the PNP and the party elected its first female leader, who became Prime Minister, Mrs Portia Simpson-Miller. Elections were due in 2007, with the incumbent party seeking its fifth consecutive victory. Both parties fielded new leaders and many new legislative candidates.

Economy

Once one of the more prosperous islands in the West Indies, Jamaica went into recession in 1973 and output declined steadily throughout the 1970s and 1980s. At the core of Jamaica's economic difficulties lay the collapse of the vital bauxite-mining and alumina-refining industries. Jamaica is the world's third-largest producer of bauxite after Australia and Guinea, but despite rising production of bauxite and alumina, earnings have slumped because of lower prices.

Manufacturing and mining contribute over 28.5% to GDP, while agriculture accounts for only 7%. Garments exported to the USA and other miscellaneous manufactured articles have seen considerable decline due to competition from

⁝ Dreadlocks to reggae

Followers of the Rastafarian cult are non-violent, do not eat pork and believe in the divinity of the late Emperor of Ethiopia, Haile Selassie (Ras Tafari). Haile Selassie's call for the end of the superiority of one race over another has been incorporated into a faith which holds that God, Jah, will lead the blacks out of oppression (Babylon) back to Ethiopia (Zion, the Promised Land). The Rastas regard the ideologist Marcus Garvey (born 1887, St Ann's Bay) as a prophet of the return to Africa (he is now a Jamaican national hero). In the early 20th century, Garvey founded the idea of black nationalism, with Africa as the home for blacks, whether they are living on the continent or not.

The music most strongly associated with Rastafarianism is reggae. According to OR Dathorne, "it is evident that the sound and words of Jamaican reggae have altered the life of the English-speaking Caribbean. The extent of this alteration is still unknown, but this new sound has touched, more than any other single art medium, the consciousness of the people of this region" (*Dark Ancestor*, page 229, Louisiana State University Press, 1981). The sound is a mixture of African percussion and up-to-the-minute electronics; the lyrics a blend of praise of Jah, political comment and criticism and the mundane. The late Bob Marley, the late Peter Tosh, Dennis Brown and Jimmy Cliff are among Jamaica's most famous reggae artists. Irie FM radio station is devoted entirely to reggae.

Over the last few years, traditional reggae has been supplanted by dancehall reggae, which has a much heavier beat. Recently dancehall has drawn adverse international attention for the homophobic lyrics of some songs, with artists such as Beanie Man, Capleton, Buju Banton, Sizzla and Bounty Killer having concerts cancelled abroad. This has not affected their popularity at home and has drawn them closer to the fundamentalist church groups and to the bobo Ashanti variety of Rastafarianism favoured by Sizzla and Capleton, among others.

One of the most influential films to come out of the Caribbean was *The Harder They Come* (1972, Perry Henzell), starring Jimmy Cliff. The reggae soundtrack helped to bring the island's culture to international attention and raised awareness of the Rastafarian way of life as well as the poverty in the slums of Kingston. The film acquired cult status, remaining constantly in circulation and in 2006 was adapted as a musical in London.

Also closely related to reggae is dub poetry, a chanted verse form that combines the musical tradition, folk traditions and popular speech. Its first practitioner was Louise Bennett, in the 1970s, who has been followed by poets such as Linton Kwesi Johnson, Michael Smith, Oku Onora and Mutabaruka. Many of these poets work in the UK, but their links with Jamaica are strong. The dancehall culture has spawned its own genre of poets, as some young and upcoming artists give vent to their feelings on the growing social divide. One such group is the popular Twins Of Twins, Paul and Patrick Gaynor, song writers and poets whose talented writings bring the painful experience of the ghetto to their audiences through humorous but deeply reflective social commentary.

Two novels which give a fascinating insight into Rasta culture (and, in the latter, Revival and other social events) are *Brother Man*, by Roger Mais, and *The Children of Sysiphus*, by H Orlando Patterson. These writers have also published other books that are worth investigating, as are the works of Olive Senior (eg *Summer Lightning*), and the poets Mervyn Morris, the late Andrew Salkey and Dennis Scott (who is also involved in the theatre).

Mexico and other NAFTA member states, and from imports due to market liberalization. Sugar is the main crop, and most important export after bauxite and alumina, but production costs are high and the industry insolvent. Other export crops include bananas, coffee, cocoa and citrus fruits. Jamaica is famous for its Blue Mountain coffee, first produced in 1757, which commands a high premium in the world market.

Tourism is the second largest foreign exchange earner, contributing about 18% of GDP. The island recorded its best tourism year ever in 2005 with just over 2.6 million combined stopover and cruise arrivals. Remittances from Jamaicans abroad remain the largest source of foreign exchange income, with over US$3.3 billion transferred privately to Jamaica through remittance companies, commercial banks and building societies during 2001-05. The support, whether in cash, clothing, food or cars, is a significant source of welfare income, especially for those in the lower economic and social strata.

The Government turned to the IMF for support in 1976 and was a regular customer until 1995. In compliance with IMF agreements, the Government reduced domestic demand commensurate with the fall in export earnings, by devaluing the currency and reducing the size of its fiscal deficits. Jamaica rescheduled its debt to creditor governments and foreign commercial banks. Some debt forgiveness was granted. The foreign exchange market was deregulated, and interest rates and credit ceilings kept high to reduce consumption, close the trade gap and rebuild foreign reserves.

Debt servicing remains a heavy burden, with external debt amounting to 60% of GDP. The worldwide recession in the wake of the 11 September terrorist attacks had an adverse effect on the Jamaican economy and even though it recovered partially in 2003-04, there are still long-term problems. The floating exchange rate puts a heavy burden on the budget because of the government's debt servicing obligations and economic growth has been stifled. It was hoped that the construction boom and subsequent revenue from the 2007 Cricket World Cup would help revenues, but the forthcoming elections in 2007 meant that any further investments were in limbo.

Geography

Jamaica lies some 145 km south of Cuba and a little over 160 km west of Haiti. With an area of 10,992 sq km, it is the third-largest island in the Greater Antilles. It is 235 km from east to west and 82 km from north to south at its widest, bounded by the Caribbean. Like other West Indian islands, it is an outcrop of a submerged mountain range. It is crossed by a spectacular range of mountains which rises to 2256 m at Blue Mountain Peak in the east and descends towards the west, with a series of spurs and forested gullies running north and south. The luxuriance of the vegetation is striking. Tropical beaches surround the island. The best are on the north and west coasts, though there are some good bathing places on the south coast too.

People

With a population 2.5 million, the island is a fascinating blend of cultures from colonial Britain, African slavery and immigrants from China, India and the Middle East. Reggae and Rastafariansim have become synonymous with Jamaica, and Bob Marley and Peter Tosh are just two of the greats to have been born here. Over 90% of Jamaicans are of West African descent. Because of this, Ashanti words still figure very largely in the local dialect (patois). There are also Chinese, East Indians and Christian Arabs as well as those of British descent and other European minorities. There is considerable poverty on the island, which has created social problems and some tension, although Jamaicans are naturally friendly, easy-going and international in their outlook (more people of Jamaican origin live outside Jamaica than inside).

The predominant religion is Protestantism, but there is also a Roman Catholic community, as well as followers of the Church of God, Baptists, Anglicans, Seventh

Day Adventists, Pentecostals, Methodists and others. The Jewish, Moslem, Hindu and Bahai religions are also practised. Jamaicans are a very religious people and it is said that Jamaica has more churches per square mile than anywhere else in the world. To a small degree, early adaptations of the Christian faith, Revival and Pocomania, survive, but the most obvious local minority sect is Rastafarianism (see box above).

Flora and fauna

‼ *The national flower is the dark blue bloom of the lignum vitae.*

The 'land of wood and water' is a botanist's paradise. There are reported to be about 3000 species of flowering plants, 827 of which are not found anywhere else. There are over 550 varieties of fern, 300 of which can be found in **Fern Gully**. There are many orchids, bougainvillea, hibiscus and other tropical flowers. Tropical hardwoods like cedar and mahogany, palms, balsa and many other trees, besides those that are cultivated, can be seen. Cultivation, however, is putting much of Jamaica's plant life at risk. Having been almost entirely forested, an estimated 6% of the land is virgin forest. A great many species are endangered.

This is also a land of hummingbirds and butterflies (see page 231). Sea cows and the Pedro seal are found in the island's waters, although fewer than 100 sea cows, or manatee, survive. There are crocodiles, but no large wild mammals apart from the hutia, or coney (an endangered species), the mongoose (considered a pest since it eats chickens) and, in the mountains, wild boar. There are, however, lots of bats, with 25 species recorded. Most live in caves or woods and eat fruit and insects, but there is a fish-eating bat which can sometimes be seen swooping over the water in Kingston Harbour. The Jamaican iguana (*Cyclura collei*) was thought to have died out in the 1960s, but in 1990 a small group was found to be surviving in the Hellshire Hills. There are 5 species of snakes, all harmless and rare, the largest of which is the yellow snake (the Jamaican boa), which can grow up to 3 m.

Good sites for birdwatching are given in the text; the 3 main areas are the **Cockpit Country**, the **Blue Mountains** and **Marshall's Pen**. The national bird is the red-billed streamertail hummingbird (*Trochilus polytmus*), also known as the doctor bird or swallow tail hummingbird. The male has a long, sweeping tail much longer than its body, and is one of Jamaica's endemic species. Other endemic birds are the yellow-billed parrot and the black-billed parrot, found in the Cockpit Country or Hope Zoo. There are 25 species and 21 subspecies of endemic land birds which are found nowhere else. A good place to see Jamaica's birds is the **Rocklands Feeding Station**, near Montego Bay. On weekday evenings you can watch the birds being fed and even offer a hummingbird a syrup and get really close. Many migratory birds stop on Jamaica on their journeys north or south. One of the best references is *Birds of Jamaica: a photographic field guide* by Audrey Downer and Robert Sutton with photos by Yves-Jacques Rey Millet Cambridge University Press (1990).

In 1989 the Government established two pilot national parks under the Protected Areas Resource Conservation (PARC) project. The **Blue Mountain/John Crow Mountain National Park** encompasses almost 81,000 ha of mountains, forests and rivers. Efforts are being made to develop the area for ecotourism and provide a livelihood for local people. The **Montego Bay Marine Park** aims to protect the offshore reef from urban waste, over-fishing and hillside erosion leading to excessive soil deposition. Several initiatives on protected areas are under way, including the Negril Environmental Protection Area and the Negril Marine Park, Ocho Rios, Port Antonio Marine Park along the northern coast and the Portland Bight Protected Area and the Canoe Valley National Park along the south coast. All coral reefs are now protected. Hunting of the American crocodile, the yellow- and black-billed parrot and all species of sea turtle is banned. See Shopping, page 214.

Turks and Caicos Islands

⁑ Footprint features

Introduction

Similar to the southern Bahamas, to which they are geographically linked, these flat, coral islands are a British Overseas Territory. Miles of sandy beaches attract sun-loving tourists from North America to a water playground, for there is little of interest on land to tempt them away from the sea. Diving and snorkelling are superb among coral gardens, wrecks and walls which drop dramatically to the floor of the ocean. Whales migrate through the deep Turks Passage and dolphins can be seen following boats and even swimming with divers, while fishermen wrestle with huge game fish out in the ocean.

Most accommodation is on the island of Providenciales (also known as 'Provo'), where 12-mile Grace Bay on the north shore is now wall-to-wall hotels providing package tourism and the condo lifestyle. There are lots of facilities for sailing, diving and fishing as well as golf or just enjoying the beach. Grand Turk is the seat of government but is a quiet, unhurried place with a few small dive lodges and some pleasant colonial buildings. Its residents are uncertain about the merits of the cruise ship pier built in 2004 and the arrival of cruise passengers in large numbers in the winter season. Other inhabited islands, North Caicos, Middle Caicos, South Caicos and Salt Cay, have tiny populations, although each has its own distinctive character, and they are good places to escape the crowds. Island hopping is easy and recommended.

Turks & Caicos Islands

★ Don't miss...

1 **Cockburn Town** The seat of government but the atmosphere is of a quiet back-water; tourism is low key; the emphasis is on diving and doing nothing, page 267.

2 **Salt Cay** With the salt industry long closed, the windmills are still and the warehouses empty, as are the beaches; snorkelling and diving are excellent, page 269.

3 **South Caicos** Much loved by fishermen, sailors and divers, this outpost benefits from a naturally protected harbour and miles of deserted beach, page 270.

4 **Crossing Place Trail** This 12-mile path takes in beaches, cliffs and caves huge and beautiful with stalactites, stalagmites and underground salt lakes, page 272.

5 **Princess Alexandra Marine Park** Diving and snorkelling are spectacular in this park. Look out for dolphins playing in the wake of the dive boats, page 281.

Map labels:

Atlantic Ocean

Columbus passage

Caicos passage

Caicos Bank

GRAND TURK

Cockburn Town

Gibbs Cay

Martin Alonza Pinzon Cay (East Cay)

Long Cay

Penniston Cay

Cotton Cay

SALT CAY

Balfour Town

Big Sand Cay

Endymion Rock

South Rock

EAST CAICOS

Drum Point

SOUTH CAICOS

Cockburn Harbour

Long Cay

Six Hill Cay

Fish Cays

Big Ambergris Cay

Little Ambergris Cay

Bush Cay

Seals Cay

White Cay

MIDDLE CAICOS

Lorimers

Bambarra

Conch Bar

Big Pond

NORTH CAICOS

Whitby

Bottle Creek

Kew

Sandy Point

Parrot Cay

Pine Cay

Water Cay

Little Water Cay

Five Cays

Blue Hills

The Bight

PROVIDENCIALES

WEST CAICOS

French Cay

West Sand Spit

N

0 km   10
0 miles   10

Essentials

Before you travel

Documents Canadian citizens need only a birth certificate and photo ID such as a driving licence to enter the Turks and Caicos, but Americans need a passport to return to the USA. Other nationalities need a valid passport; a visa is not necessary except for nationals of former eastern bloc. An onward ticket is officially required. Visitors are allowed to stay for 30 days, renewable once only for a fee of US$50.

Tourist offices overseas

Canada, RR 2 Bancroft, Ontario, K0L 1C0, T613-3326472, rwilson.tcitourism@allstream.net.
UK, 42 Westminster Palace Gardens, 1-7 Artillery Row, London, SW1P 1RR, T020 72222669, shankland@tcilondon.org.uk.

USA, Suite 2817, The Lincoln Building, 60 East 42nd Street, New York, NY 10165, T646-3758830, ehiggs@tcigny.com; Chicago, T708-720.9999, tc_islands@yahoo.com; Miami, T305-6713414, TCItourismMiami@cs.com.

Money The official **currency** is the US dollar. Most banks will advance cash on **credit cards**. Most hotels, restaurants and taxi drivers will accept travellers' cheques, but personal cheques are not widely accepted. There are **banks** on Grand Turk and Providenciales (and South Caicos on Wed) but not on the other islands. Take lots of cash and small denomination US dollars when visiting an island without a bank, as it is often difficult to get change from big notes. As well as domestic banking there is a growing offshore banking industry, regulated by the UK.

Getting there

Air Ports of entry for aircraft are Providenciales, South Caicos and Grand Turk, but the major international airport is on Providenciales (PLS). There are also airstrips on North Caicos, Middle Caicos, West Caicos, Pine Cay and Salt Cay. Flights from Miami, New York, Boston (**American Airlines**), Philadelphia and Charlotte (**US Airways**), Fort Lauderdale (**Spirit Airlines**), Atlanta (**Delta**), Toronto (**Air Canada**), Montréal (**West Jet**), Kingston/Montego Bay, Puerto Plata/Santiago and Cap Haitiën/Port-au-Prince (**Air Turks and Caicos, Sky King**), Bahamas (**Bahamas Air, Sky King**), and the UK (**British Airways**) come in to Providenciales and then, if you are not staying on Provo, you get a connecting flight to your destination on a small plane. See each island's Transport section for details.

> *There are weekly BA flights to Provo from London via Nassau. Other flights from Europe connect with AA in the USA.*

Boat There is no scheduled passenger service (cargo comes in regularly from Florida). A pier and Cruise Center have been built on Grand Turk to receive cruise ships, www.grandturkcc.com. No port on Providenciales is deep enough to take cruise ships although some occasionally stop outside the reef and shuttle in passengers for half a day.

Ports of entry (British flag) Providenciales: Turtle Cove Marina, Caicos Marina & Boatyard, Leeward Marina, South Dock/Sapodilla Bay; Grand Turk; South Caicos; Salt Cay. Clear in and out with customs and immigration, VHF 16. On arrival, customs will grant seven days immigration clearance. Go to town to the Immigration Office (closed 1230-1430) to obtain a US$50 30-day extension. Fuel and alcoholic drink may be purchased duty free with clearance to leave the country. The Customs Office is at Airport Rd, Provo, and there are Customs Officers at the airport all day too.

> *Evening weather report on VHF radio from Blue Water Divers on Grand Turk; Mystine on SSB. There are no bareboat charters.*

⠿ Touching down

Business hours (On Provo) **Banks**: Mon-Thu 0900-1600, Fri 0900-1630; **Offices**: 0830-1600; **Shops**: 0900-1700. On other islands hours are more erratic.

Currency The official currency is the US dollar.

Clothing Dress is informal and shorts are worn in town and on the beach, but some restaurants are more formal, ask when making a reservation. Nudity is illegal although topless is condoned by Club Med on Grace Bay. The islanders find it offensive and flouting local protocol may elicit stares and remarks.

Departure tax US$25.50 including US$2.50 US security tax. All but the US$2.50 is included in the price of your ticket.

Emergency numbers T999/911.

Country code +649.

Official time GMT minus 4 hours.

Safety Providenciales is not as safe as it was before it became a tourist and offshore banking destination, but it is still safer than most Caribbean islands. It is definitely not advisable to walk around alone at night or on deserted beaches. On Provo, take precautions about leaving valuables in your room or on the beach. Traffic is fast and aggressive, causing many accidents. Personal security is much better on Grand Turk and the other islands.

Useful addresses Chief Secretary: (Grand Turk) T9462702, (Provo) T9464258, T9415123; **Harbour Master**: (Grand Turk) T9462993/4, (Provo) T9464214; **Customs Dept**: (Grand Turk airport) T9462345, (Provo Airport) T9464906; **Immigration**: (Grand Turk) T9462939, (Provo) T9464233.

Voltage 110 volts, 60 cycles, as in the USA.

Weights and measures Imperial.

Marinas On Provo, **Leeward Marina** at Leeward Going Through, T9465553, www.leeward.com, gas/diesel sales only, restaurant; **Turtle Cove Marina**, Sellar's Pond, T9413781, www.tcmarina.com, full service, all-weather anchorage, 7.5-ft draft, 100 new slips, RO, water and ice, premium prices, Wi-Fi internet access, diving, hyperbaric chamber; **South Side Marina**, T9464747, dockside T9464200, hamilton&pratt@tciway.tc, diesel, gas, oil, water, 4½ ft controlling depth, call for reservations; **Caicos Marina & Boatyard**, Long Bay, T9465600, www.caicosmarina.com, SSB 4143.6 (fuel, ice, dry storage, machinist/diesel mechanic). South Caicos also has a marina.

Touching down

Airport information Scheduled service airlines are **American Airlines** (T1-800-4337300, T9415700); **US Airways** (T1-800-6221015, T9415837, Provo office hours 1115-1530 Monday, Wednesday, Friday, Saturday); **British Airways** (on Provo T1-800-2479297); **Sky King** (T9461520 on Grand Turk, T9415461/4 on Provo, King@tciway.tc); **Air Turks and Caicos** (Provo T9415481, Grand Turk T9461667, www.airturksandcaicos.com) and **Bahamas Air**. Charter airlines are **Global Airways**, run by the Gardiner family (T9413222 on Provo, T9467093 on North Caicos, www.globalairways.tc); **Provo Air Charter** (T9465578).

> ⠿ *It is worth checking in early when returning to Miami from Provo, to avoid long queues.*

Tourist information Local tourist office: Turks and Caicos Islands Tourist Board, Grand Turk, Turks and Caicos Islands, T9462321, www.turksandcaicostourism.com. On Provo the tourist office is at Stubbs Diamond Plaza, on the low road leading to *Sibonné*, T9464970. Various maps and guidebooks have been published including

Where, When, How, Providenciales; Your Monthly Entertainment Guide, distributed in hotels and selected shops, free of charge; *Times of the Islands; International Magazine of the Turks and Caicos*, quarterly, US$4. Useful websites with lots of information on lodgings, particularly on the smaller islands are **www.tcimall.tc** and **www.wherewhenhow.com**.

Local tour operators: **Marco Travel Services**, Town Centre Mall, Down Town, T9464393, www.marcotravel.com, for reconfirmation of tickets, emergency cheque cashing, travel services, TC sales, Amex representative. **Provo Travel Ltd**, run by Althea Ewing, at Central Sq, Leeward Highway, T9464035, helpful. On Grand Turk: **T & C Travel Ltd**, Duke St, T9462845.

Getting around

Air Several airlines provide flying bus services between the islands. The main ones are **Air Turks and Caicos**, www.airturksandcaicos.com, **SkyKing**, www.skyking.tc, and **Global Airways**, www.globalairways.tc. Flight time from Grand Turk to the furthest island (Provo) is 35 minutes. Sample round-trip fares: Provo to North Caicos is US$70, to Middle Caicos US$90, to South Caicos US$110, to Grand Turk US$120 and to Salt Cay US$150. Grand Turk to South Caicos US$70. Private charters are readily available within the island group and can easily be arranged by asking around at Grand Turk or Provo airport, as charter pilots meet incoming international flights and wait to see if they can fill a plane in the mornings. They often hold up boards showing which island they are flying to. If you pre-book you may sit for two or three hours waiting for a particular plane; similarly if travelling to the outer islands, do not buy a return ticket, whatever the airlines tell you, as you may have to pay twice if you come back with someone else. Your hotel or guesthouse can help you arrange your return flight when you are ready to leave (this does not include package tours). **TCA** does not fly on Sunday.

❗ Taking a small plane between islands is a delightful experience as you fly low over the coral cays, reefs and sea.

Bus Numerous cramped mini-vans serve as buses on Provo. There are also shuttle services between the hotels and restaurants.

Car Rental cars are available on Grand Turk, North and South Caicos and Provo, although demand often exceeds supply on Provo. Most roads are fairly basic, although those on Provo have been upgraded and paved, and all parts are easily accessible. Leeward Highway, the main road on Provo is now 4 lanes. Maximum speed in urban areas is 20 mph and outside villages 40 mph, but on Provo driving is erratic and no one (except visitors) pays heed to speed limits, not even the Traffic Department. Local drivers do not dim their headlights at night. Pedestrians and cyclists should be careful on the roads because of the speeding drivers and heavy construction vehicles.

❗ Drive on the left. Watch out for donkeys on Grand Turk.

Cycle Bicycles and motor scooters can be rented from some hotels but can be relatively expensive compared with cars. Helmets are not mandatory but should be worn. Tourists invite trouble riding in bathing suits and bare feet and at night.

Taxi Taxis can be found at the airport or at the cruise ship terminal on Grand Turk, otherwise call for one. Taxis can be hired for island tours, agree the price beforehand.

Sleeping

Hotels on Provo are aiming for North American standards and so they are expensive.

● *The islands were named after the Turk's Head 'fez' cactus found growing here. The name*
● *Caicos comes from the Lucayan, caya hico, meaning 'string of islands'.*

Rack rates will not include tax and service, so be sure to check what you are quoted. Most hotels on Provo are all-inclusive or condominium-style. Grand Turk, Salt Cay, South Caicos and North Caicos are better bets for inexpensive, charming, more 'islandy' lodgings. **Camping** is possible on beaches on most islands but not encouraged (no water or sewage facilities). Contact the District Commissioner's office on each island for permission. If planning to stay on a deserted island take everything with you and leave nothing behind.

> ● There is a 10-15% service charge and 10% bed tax added to the bill.

Eating

Expensive to mid-range meals in restaurants and bars will usually be of good quality. Watch out for specials with no posted prices. Wine by the glass is US$4.50-8.50 while beer ranges from US$3.50-6. With over 50 restaurants and delis on Provo alone, prices are mainly expensive but local restaurants with native cuisine are reasonable. Many restaurants feature vegetarian meals and low-fat cooking. All food is imported (except seafood) from Miami, occasionally from the Dominican Republic, and therefore not cheap. Many restaurants charge a 10% gratuity in addition to the 10% government tax. Restaurants owned and operated by the islanders, or 'Belongers', do not have to charge tax because they serve the local market. Some do not charge for service. Check your bill carefully and tip, or not, accordingly.

> ● Seafood, lobster, conch with peas 'n' rice is standard island fare.

Entertainment

There are a few night spots on Providenciales, but on the other islands you will find only occasional live music after dinner at a restaurant. Local bands play mostly calypso, reggae and the traditional island music with its Haitian and African influences. Bands from the USA and UK are sometimes invited in high season. On Provo, ask hoteliers and residents when and where live bands are playing. Latin influence in discos, featuring soca, reggae and latino, loudly! Check cover charges before you go. Nightlife does not start until 2200-2300.

Festivals and events

Jan New Year's Day.
Mar Commonwealth Day.
Mar/Apr Good Fri and Easter Mon.
End-May National Heroes Day.
2nd week in Jun Queen's birthday.

Early Aug Emancipation Day.
End Sep National Youth Day.
Oct Columbus' Day and International Human Rights' Day.
Dec Christmas Day and Boxing Day.

Sport and activities

Diving and marine life The islands have become one of the most highly regarded diving locations in the region, with excellent visibility, unspoilt reefs, unpolluted waters and uncrowded dive spots. The best months for diving are April to November. Some of the best diving is off the wall at Northwest Point, West Caicos and French Cay. Great care has been taken in the past to conserve the reefs and the coral is in very good condition. However, the new cruise ship dock in Grand Turk is predicted to damage much of the famous wall on the west side of that island. Marine life is varied and beautiful and can be enjoyed by snorkellers and sailors as well as scuba divers. Colourful fish and grouper can be seen on the coral, and close to the shore there are green and loggerhead turtles and manta and spotted eagle rays. Beyond the reef are the game fish such as tuna, blue marlin, wahoo, snapper, bill fish and barracuda. Dolphins are commonly seen playing in the wake of dive boats and there is a friendly bottlenose dolphin named **Jo Jo**, which has been declared a National Treasure. He visits the Princess Alexandra Marine Park often coming in very close to shore. For

> ● The sea is often rough between February and March.

more information contact Jo Jo's warden, Dean Bernal, at VHF 'Sea Base' channel 68 or 73, or T/F9415617, www.marinewildlife.org. From January to March, humpback whales migrate through the deep Turks Island Passage on their way south to the Silver and Mouchoir Banks breeding grounds north of the Dominican Republic (see box page 356). Whale watching is co-ordinated by the Department of Environmental Heritage and Parks, which has drawn up rules to protect the whales, and several dive operators offer whale-watching tours in the season, January to March.

Fishing is popular, both for bonefishing and deep sea fishing. November-April is the season for wahoo and May-September is the season for blue marlin while you can also catch white marlin, sailfish, dorado and yellowfin tuna at any time. Provo and Pine Cay have the best bonefishing though it is also possible at South Caicos, Middle Caicos, North Caicos and Salt Cay. A US$30 sport fishing licence is required from the **Fisheries Department** ① *Grand Turk, T9462970, or South Caicos, T9463306, or Provo, T9464017.* Ask your guide whether the fishing licence is included in his package. Spear fishing is not allowed. ▶▶ *For more information on fishing as well as diving and other activities, see individual islands and page 265.*

Health
There are no endemic tropical diseases and no malaria, no special vaccinations are required prior to arrival. See main Health section on page 48.

Keeping in touch
Internet There are two internet cafés on Provo: **TCI Online** in Ports of Call, Grace Bay area, T9414711, and **The Computer Guy's Internet Café**, Leeward Highway, Central Provo, T9464152. Most hotels offer their guests internet access and Wi-Fi is widely available.

Post On Grand Turk the post office is on Front Street near **FirstCaribbean International Bank**, T9462801. **Federal Express**, T9462542 (Grand Turk), T9464682 (Provo); **DHL**, T9464352 (Provo); **UPS** agent, T9462030, incoming only package delivery, Cee's Building, Pond St, Grand Turk and on Provo through **Provo Travel**, T9464080.

Telephone The IDD code is T649. Grand Turk, Provo and South Caicos have a modern local and international telephone service, with **Cable & Wireless** offices in Grand Turk and Provo. Telephone services on the North and Middle Caicos and Salt City are improving. There are five exchanges, 946 and 941 for land lines, 231 for post pay cell phones and 241 and 242 for prepaid cell phones. Local directory assistance T118, international operator T115; credit card calls T111, 1-800-8778000, 3 mins minimum. The small volume of international calls means that costs are higher than in the USA. The local phone book has a list of charges to anywhere in the world. Pay phones take phone cards, which are available from Cable & Wireless and from many outlets including Provo Airport in US$5, US$10 and US$20 denominations plus 10%. The Cable & Wireless Public Sales Office in Grand Turk and Provo has a public fax service, F9462497/4210. Paging service is popular among businesses and cell phones are widely used. Many visitors bring their own cell phones, or you can rent one while on the islands. There is a telephone directory published by **Olympia Publishing**, saunders@tciway.tc, with lots of useful information about the TCI, more useful than the Cable & Wireless directory.

Grand Turk → *Phone code: 649. Colour map 2, A2. Population: 4,000.*

Grand Turk is not a resort island although there are a few hotels and dive operations that concentrate mostly on the wall just off the west coast. It is a wonderfully laid-back place to come for a holiday but the atmosphere may change with the advent of cruise ships to the new dock in the south which started in 2004 with the signing of a 30-year contract with Carnival. Several times a month a cruise ship dwarfs Cockburn Town and disgorges the equivalent of the island's population to visit the sights. The vegetation is mostly scrub and cactus, and wild donkeys and horses roam freely. Behind the town and around the island are old salt pans, with crumbling walls and ruined windmills, where pelicans and other waterbirds fish. The east coast is often littered with tree trunks and other debris which have drifted across from Africa, lending credence to the claim that Columbus could have been carried here, rather than further north in the Bahamas chain. There are great sea views from the 1852 lighthouse at the extreme north of the island. Grand Turk is the seat of government and the second-largest population centre, although it has an area of only 7 square miles. ▶ For Eating, Sleeping and other listings, see pages 273-279.*

Ins and outs
Getting there Airlines and schedules tend to change often. Most visitors arrive in Provo and then shuttle over on a small aircraft. There are frequent inter-island flights and it is possible to turn up on the day you want to travel and catch the next flight. If coming by yacht, the harbour is in North Creek. ▶ *See also Transport, page 278, for further details.*

Getting around
Taxis are the only form of public transport. Jeeps, cars and bicycles can be rented. Distances are not great and if you are based in Cockburn Town you may not need a vehicle.

Cockburn Town
Cockburn Town, the capital and financial centre, has some attractive colonial buildings, mostly along Duke Street, or Front Street, as it is usually known. The government offices are in a small restored square with cannons facing the sea. The post office and government buildings are painted in blues, ranging from deep turquoise to almost white, nicely matching the ocean.

The oldest church on Grand Turk is **St Thomas' Anglican church** (inland, near the water catchment tanks), built by Bermudan settlers. After a while it was considered too far to walk to the centre of the island and **St Mary's Anglican church** was built in 1899 on Front Street. This is now a pro-Cathedral with the southern Bahamas and is the first cathedral in the islands. The **Victoria Library**, built to commemorate 50 years of Queen Victoria's reign, is also an interesting building. **Odd Fellows Lodge**, opposite the salt pier, is thought to be one of the oldest buildings on the island and was probably the place where the abolition of slavery was proclaimed in 1832.

The **Tourist Board office** is in a renovated town customs building and warehouse, built in the old Bermudan architectural style. It sits on the water at the north end of Cockburn Town and is a pleasant place to stop off.

The **Turks and Caicos National Museum** ① *T9462160, www.tcmuseum.org, Mon-Fri 0900-1600, Sat 0900-1300. US$5 for non-residents, US$2 residents, US$0.50 students*, is in the beautifully renovated Guinep Lodge. The exhibition on the ground floor is of the early 16th-century wreck of a Spanish caravel found on the Molasses Reef between West Caicos and French Cay in only 20 ft of water. The ship is

⁞ The Battle of Waterloo

Former Governor John Kelly was a keen golfer and when he took over the Governor's residence, Waterloo, in 1996, he soon had designs on the 20 acres of wilderness surrounding his new home. The overgrown land was attacked by a battalion of volunteer kindred spirits to create a nine-hole course. The acacia thorn bushes and vines fought back as trees not seen for years were exposed and park land appeared. The wilderness was finally dominated by a team from Her Majesty's Prison and some heavy equipment operators who uprooted the big thorn trees. The opening of the golf club was planned for June 1997, the anniversary of the Battle of Waterloo, but actually took place in January 1998, with 43 players in the Governor's Trophy competition. Visitors may pay their green fee of US$25 per day at the Governor's office – a slightly unusual arrangement, T9462308. Numbers of players are limited to 36 at any one time because of the small size of the course. There are some rental clubs, but bring your own if you have them.

believed to have been on an illegal slaving mission in the islands, as evidenced by locked leg irons found on the site. A guided tour is highly recommended although not essential. Upstairs there is an exhibition of local artefacts, photos, stamps, coins, a few Taíno beads, figures and potsherds. A local historian, the late Herbert Sadler, compiled many volumes on the theory of Columbus' landfall and local history. A **Science Building**, has been completed beside the museum, which houses a conservation laboratory, the only one of its kind in the English-speaking Caribbean. One recent find was a Taíno paddle buried in the peat bottom of North Creek, which has been carbon dated to AD 1100. A new Space Gallery was opened in 2002 at the museum, including photos, a starry night sky, space toys from the 1960s and personal recollections from John Glenn and Scott Carpenter's splashdown just off the shores. Also beside the museum is a new and delightful garden of native plants. The original building on the site was destroyed by fire, but the oven from the old slave kitchen and the water catchment tank have been renovated and preserved as garden features. The museum is involved in the survey work being carried out on a wreck off East Caicos believed to be that of the slave ship Trouvadore, which sank in 1841. Its cargo of 193 Africans, captured to be sold into slavery, miraculously survived the wrecking and were freed in the Turks and Caicos Islands.

Around the island

The Governor's residence, **Waterloo**, south of the airport, was built in 1815 by a Bermudan salt merchant as a private residence and acquired for the head of government in 1857. Successive governors and administrators have modified and extended it, prompted partly by hurricane damage in 1866 and 1945, and by the Queen's visit in 1966. In 1993 the building was again renovated and remodelled; the works were so extensive they constituted a near rebuilding of the residence. Governor's Beach is one of the nicest beaches and excellent for snorkelling, with isolated coral heads rising out of the sand and a wide variety of fish and invertebrates.

Further south is an ex-USAF base, known as **South Base**, which is now used as government offices, and beyond some nice beaches on the south coast, with good snorkelling at White Sands beach by the point. US Navy, NASA and Coast Guard bases were once important for the economy of Grand Turk; John Glenn, the first American to orbit the earth, splashed down off Grand Turk in the 1960s. However, the south of the island is now dominated by the Grand Turk Cruise Center,

Grand Turk

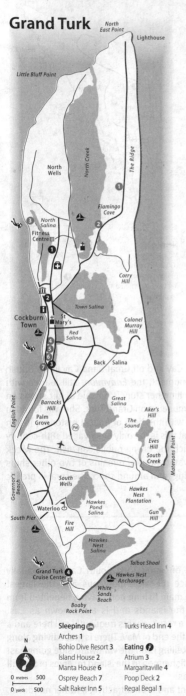

Sleeping 😴
Arches 1
Bohio Dive Resort 3
Island House 2
Manta House 6
Osprey Beach 7
Salt Raker Inn 5
Turks Head Inn 4

Eating 🍴
Atrium 3
Margaritaville 4
Poop Deck 2
Regal Begal 1

0 metres 500
0 yards 500

The cays southeast of Grand Turk are a land and sea national park, sheltering Turks Head cacti on **Martin Alonza Pinzon Cay**, frigate birds on **Penniston Cay** and breeding sooty terns, noddy terns and other seabirds on **Gibbs Cay**. The lagoons and red mangroves of South Creek are also a national park, with a nursery for fish, crabs and other sea life, as well as a reserve for birds.

Beaches and activities

The highlight of **diving** is the wall off Cockburn Town, which drops suddenly from 40 ft to 7,000 ft only a quarter of a mile offshore. There are 25 moored sites along the wall where you can find coral arches, tunnels, canyons, caves and overhangs. A mile east of Grand Turk is **Gibbs Cay**, where snorkellers are taken for a great day trip, suitable for all the family. As well as a pristine sandy beach and beautifully clear water, there are friendly sting rays which will come right up to you and nose around. Picnics are usually provided and conch is often caught along the way to make a really fresh conch salad. There are three very experienced dive organizers who have been diving these waters for decades and can offer a range of courses, full accommodation and diving packages, as well as whale watching in season. All three have retail outlets and offer photographic services with equipment rental. Rates are US$40-50 for a single-tank dive, US$70-80 for two tanks, depending on whether you have pre-booked, although there are extra charges for long distance trips such as to South Caicos, which is an hour there and two hours on the way back.

Salt Cay → Phone code: 649. Colour map 2, A2. Population: 208.

Seven miles south of Grand Turk, Salt Cay is out of the past, with windmills, salt sheds and other remnants of the old salt industry and little else. The island was first visited by the Bermudans in 1645;

they started making salt here in 1673 and maintained a thriving salt industry until its collapse in the 1960s. Production ceased all together in 1971. Plant life was curtailed during the salt raking days to prevent rainfall. Look into some of the ruined houses and you will find salt still stored in the cellars. The main village is **Balfour Town**, divided into North Side and South Side, noted for its Bermudan buildings and pretty cottages with stone walls around the gardens. The **White House**, which dominates the skyline, was built in the 1830s of Bermudan stone brought in as ballast by the Harriott family during the height of the salt industry. The **Methodist Church** nearby, one of several churches on the island, is over 130 years old. Snorkelling is good and diving is excellent; there are 10 moored dive sites along the wall, with tunnels, caves and undercuts. Between January and March you can often see the humpback whales migrating through the channel as they pass close to the west coast. The island has been designated a UNESCO World Heritage Site.

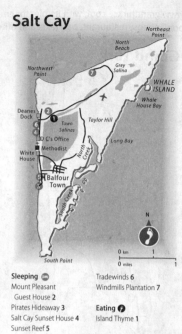

Salt Cay

Sleeping
Mount Pleasant Guest House 2
Pirates Hideaway 3
Salt Cay Sunset House 4
Sunset Reef 5

Tradewinds 6
Windmills Plantation 7

Eating
Island Thyme 1

Beaches and activities

There are seven moored dive sites off Salt Cay and off Great Sand Cay lies a British shipwreck from 1790, now a National Monument, the *Endymion*, still loaded with cannon. A wall chart telling her story is on sale at gift shops on the islands and at the museum on Grand Turk. She was found in 1991 by Brian Sheedy with the help of a local historian, Josiah Marvel. It is thought that this is the only unsalvaged 18th-century wreck in the world which the diving public can visit. The wreck lies in about 25 ft of water with the remains of two other ships nearby: a Civil War steamer and a ship dating from around 1900. The coral is prolific and the fish are plentiful.

☛ *The beaches going east and north are totally deserted. You can walk for miles beachcombing along the east shore.*

South Caicos

→ *Phone code: 649. Population: 1,198.*

The nearest Caicos island, 22 miles west of Grand Turk, South Caicos (originally named Guana by the Lucayans) was once the most populous and the largest producer of salt in the region. It is now the main fishing port, having benefited from the most naturally protected harbour in the islands and is also known as East Harbour, or the 'rock', or 'the big south'. As a result, yachts frequently call here and a popular annual Big South Regatta is held at the end of May. There is great diving along the drop-off to the south and the best snorkelling is on the windward side going east and north. Boat trips can be organized with fishermen to the island reserves of **Six Hill Cays** and **Long Cay**, where there are iguanas.

Cockburn Harbour is the only settlement and is an attractive, if rather run-down, little place with lots of old buildings, a pleasant waterfront with old salt warehouses and boats. The District Commissioner's house, currently unoccupied, stands atop a hill southeast of the village and can be recognized by its green roof. The **School For Field Studies** is in the 19th-century *Admiral's Arm Inn*, and attracts undergraduate students from abroad to the island to study reef ecology and marine resources, but otherwise there are very few visitors. Wild donkeys, cows and horses roam the island and several have made their home in an abandoned hotel construction site along the coast from the Residency. The **salinas** dominate the central part of the island and there is a 'boiling hole', connected to the sea by a subterranean passage, which was used to supply the salt pans. It makes an interesting walk and you may see flamingos.

‡ *Don't be alarmed if you meet sharks; there have been sightings of black tip, reef, bull, tiger and hammerhead sharks as well as manta rays.*

On the west side of the Columbus Passage the wall along the east shores of South Caicos and Long Cay drops gradually or steeply from a depth of about 50 ft, with many types of coral and a variety of fish of all sizes. Snorkelling is rewarding with several shallow reefs close to the shore, but the diving is really for advanced divers, as it is best on the windward side where there are strong currents and surges.

Ambergris Cay

Further south are the two **Ambergris Cays**, Big and Little, where there are caves and the diving and fishing are good. Uninhabited for nearly five centuries, (Big) Ambergris Cay has now fallen victim to tourism development. Villas, a 5-star hotel and spa, yacht club, deep water marina and airstrip for corporate jets are all part of the development plan, www.ambergriscay.com.

East Caicos

East Caicos has an area of 18 sq miles which makes it one of the largest islands, and Flamingo Hill, at 156 ft, is the highest point in the Turks and Caicos. A ridge runs along the north coast, but the rest of the island is swamp, creeks, mangrove and mudflats. Jacksonville, in the northwest, used to be the centre of a 50,000-acre sisal plantation and there was also a cattle farm at the beginning of the 20th century. The island is now uninhabited except for mosquitoes and wild donkeys. There is an abandoned railway left over from the plantation days and feral donkeys have worn paths through the scrub and sisal. Caves near Jacksonville, which were once mined for bat guano, contain petroglyphs carved on the walls and there is evidence of several Lucayan settlements. Splendid beaches include a 17-mile stretch on the north coast. Off the north coast, opposite Jacksonville, is **Guana Cay**, home to the Caicos iguana. There is no official transport to East Caicos, although people occasionally sail there.

Middle Caicos → *Phone code: 649. Population: 275.*

Also known as **Grand Caicos**, this is the largest of the islands, with an area of 48 sq miles. Its coastline is more dramatic than some of the other islands, characterized by limestone cliffs along the north coast, interspersed with long sandy beaches shaded by casuarina trees or secluded coves. The south part of the island is swamp and tidal flats. There are three settlements linked by the paved King's Road: **Conch Bar**, where there is an airstrip, a primary school, beach and guesthouses, **Bambarra** and **Lorimers**. A visit to the caves between Bambarra and Lorimers is a must. Originally

● *According to legend, the rock formation at the entrance to Cockburn Harbour is a sea*
● *monster, Sassy Sam, who guarded pirates' treasure on the island and was turned to stone.*

used by Amerindians as dwelling places, they were later mined for guano. They are huge, complex and beautiful with bats, stalactites, stalagmites and underwater salt lakes with pink shrimps. Day tours are available from Provo, including transport from Leeward, lunch, drinks, snorkelling and beachcombing. Archaeological excavations have uncovered a Lucayan ball court and a settlement near Armstrong Pond, due south of Bambarra, but these are not easily accessible. Evidence of the Lucayan civilization dates back to AD 750. Loyalist plantation ruins can also be explored. Bambarra beach is an empty, curving sweep of white sand, fringed with casuarina trees. Middle Caicos regatta is held here, but there are no facilities. A sand bar stretches half a mile out to **Pelican Cay**, which you can walk on at low tide. A pretty and popular cove is **Mudjeon Harbour**, just west of Conch Bar, protected by a sand bar and with shade under a rocky overhang. The reef juts out from the land here, and this can be spectacular in the winter months with the crashing waves. South of Middle Caicos is a nature reserve comprising a frigate bird breeding colony and a marine sinkhole with turtles, bonefish and shark. The blue hole shows up on the satellite photo of the islands on display in the museum in Grand Turk.

The **Crossing Place Trail** was a path worn by Lucayan Indians and later by slaves travelling between plantations. It is well marked and runs for 12 dramatic and beautiful miles (seven can be cycled) along the north coast, connecting Lorimers, Bambarra and Conch Bar. Developed by the National Trust to encourage ecotourism, the trail takes in beaches, coastal cliffs, Conch Bar, Indian Caves and the Blowing Hole. Tours from Provo and Grand Turk are available.

> ‡ For tour information; District Commissioner's office, T94661000. Wear strong walking shoes.

North Caicos → Phone code: 649. Population: 1,400.

The lushest of the islands, North Caicos has taller trees than the other islands and attracts more rain. As on Middle and East Caicos, the south part of the island comprises swamp and mangrove.

There is one nature reserve at **Dick Hill Creek** and **Bellefield Landing Pond**, to protect the West Indian whistling duck and flamingos, and another at **Cottage Pond**, a fresh/saltwater sinkhole, about 170 ft deep, where there are grebes and West Indian whistling duck. **Pumpkin Bluff Pond** is a sanctuary for flamingos, Bahamian pintail and various waders. Flocks of flamingos can also be seen on **Flamingo Pond**, but take binoculars. There is a viewing point at the side of the road, but at low tide they can be a long way off. There is good snorkelling at **Three Mary's Cays** (a sanctuary for flamingos and an osprey nesting site) and **Sandy Point beach** to the west is lovely. The rough road to Three Mary's Cays is suitable for jeeps. The beaches are good along the north coast where the hotels are, although the best is a seven-mile strip west of Pumpkin Bluff, where there has been no development so far. It can be reached by walking along the beach or via a dirt road past the **Club Vacanze** (an Italian all-inclusive) car park. A cargo ship foundered on the reef in the 1980s, and is still stuck fast, making it of snorkelling interest. Construction of a new deep-water harbour has begun and when finished it will extend from Pine Cay to Bellefield Landing and over Dick Hill Creek.

Kew, in the centre, is a pretty little village with neat gardens and tall trees, many of them exotic fruit trees, to provide shade. There are three churches, a primary school, a shop and two bars. A lookout tower has been built to give 360° views. **Bottle Creek**, in the east, has a high school, clinic and churches. The paved road ends here and a rough road requiring 4WD continues to Toby Rock. **Whitby**, on the north coast, is rather spread out along the road, and this is where the few hotels are. Several expatriates have built their homes along Whitby Beach. **Sandy Point**, in the west, is a fishing community. North Caicos is the centre of basket making in the islands and there are several women and designs. Prices do not vary much from those in the shops in Providenciales. **Wades Green Plantation,** just to the west of Kew, is the best example of a Loyalist plantation in the islands, with many ruins, including a courtyard and a prison.

Parrot Cay and Dellis Cay

Cotton used to be grown on Parrot Cay and there are the remains of a plantation house, protected wetlands and mangroves. A luxury resort has been built, so exclusive that Ben Affleck chose to get married here in 2005.

Dellis Cay is currently uninhabited but due to be developed with a hotel and spa to be run by the Mandarin Oriental Hotel Group on the southwest shore of the island. The Cay is frequently visited for its shells. You can be dropped off there for the day for shelling by a local charter boat out from Leeward Marina, on Providenciales.

Pine Cay

Pine Cay is an 800-acre private resort owned by a group of homeowners who also own the exclusive 12-room **Meridian Club** (see Sleeping, below). Day trippers are not encouraged although visitors may come for lunch at the restaurant by prior reservation as long as they do not use the facilities; the homeowners value their privacy and put a ban on visitors if they feel there have been too many. Pine Cay benefits from a few freshwater ponds and wells, so water is no problem and it is greener than Provo. On the other hand mosquito control is a constant problem. Nature trails have been laid out around the ponds and through the trees and there are tennis courts. There is an airstrip for guests who charter a flight, and a dock if they prefer to come in with the **Meridian Club's** exclusive shuttle boat.

> ❖ A hurricane in 1969 left Pine Cay 5 ft under water for a while and since then houses have been built back from the beach and many are on stilts.

Water Cay and Little Water Cay

Water Cay is a nature reserve and, although classified as a separate island, is joined to Pine Cay by sand dunes created during the 1969 hurricane.

Little Water Cay, the nearest island to Provo is inhabited by iguanas. The endangered Turks and Caicos rock iguana is now protected from threatening human presence by boardwalks, which protect their burrows and nesting chambers, and by strict rules that stop visitors feeding them. A visitor's fee is charged to support the protection programme. (Most tour operators have day trips, see page 281.)

ⓔ Sleeping

Grand Turk *p267, map p269*
All hotels offer dive packages with local dive companies.
LL The Arches, on North Ridge, T/F9462941, www.grandturkarches.com. 4 townhouses each with 2 bedrooms, 2 bathrooms, balconies with views east and west for sunrise and sunset, can sleep 6 if you're good friends or family, a/c, fan, kitchen, pool, bicycles, dive gear storage and washing area, housekeeping and food available, new, clean, spacious, but some way from the beach.
LL Bohio Dive Resort, Pillory Beach, T9462135, www.bohioresort.com. Opened in 2005 on the site of the old **Guanahani hotel**. 16

rooms, 4 of them suites with kitchenettes, a/c, fans, fridges, TV, all right by the beach with sea views and balconies. Dive shop on site, dive packages offered. **Guanahani restaurant** with French, Italian, Asian and West Indian influences, Canadian chef Zev Beck uses whatever is fresh that day. **Bohio Bar** for all-day snacks. Pool Bar for sunset cocktails.
LL Grand Turk Inn, Front Street, T9462829, www.grandturkinn.com. Converted in 2005 from the historic Methodist Manse to a luxury guest house with 5 suites, all with kitchens, breakfast in your suite, Wi-Fi, sundeck upstairs with sea view or shady lounge downstairs with fountain. No children.

LL Turks Head Mansion, Duke St, T9462466, www.turksheadmansion.com. Built in 1869 by Jonathon Glass first as a private house and later used as a doctor's dispensary, the American Consulate and a guesthouse for the British Government, then an inn and now for private rental, it is set back from the beach surrounded by tall trees. Renovated and decorated in period style, 5 rooms, with wooden floors, 4-poster beds and balconies, it is designed to attract the rich and famous seeking luxury and exclusivity and was used as a location for 10 movies in 2006. Included are all meals, drinks, snacks, bartender, concierge, maid service, security guards on request.

LL-AL Osprey Beach, T9462666, www.ospreybeachhotel.com. 27 beachfront rooms, those on ground floor open directly onto the sand, suites available with kitchenette, a/c, TV, fan, fridge, pool, also 12 standard rooms in the Atrium without sea view, lots of packages available for divers or non-divers, breakfast, lunch and dinner at Michael's Atrium restaurant across the road from the beach, good Jamaican and local dishes, or poolside/beachside dining with a tapas menu and barbeque twice a week when Mitch and the High Tide Band plays and sings poolside (CD available).

L-AL Island House, north of town on Lighthouse Road, T9461519, www.islandhouse-tci.com. Price includes tax and service, golf cart and airport transfers for stays of 4 nights, 8 different suites or studios with kitchen and barbecue, spacious, fully equipped, TV, phone, a/c, fan, on edge of North Creek, pool, free laundry facilities, maid service, bicycles available, fishing can be arranged, popular with people who like to spend a month or 2 on the island in the winter, attentive and welcoming management, contact Colin Donna Brooker.

L-A Salt Raker Inn, Duke St, T9462260, www.hotelsaltraker.com. An old Bermuda-style building, built by Bermudan shipwright Jonathon Glass in the 1840s, facing the beach. It is very friendly, relaxed and unpretentious. 10 rooms, 3 suites, sea or garden view, balconies or patios, a/c, fan, fridge, TV. Secret Garden restaurant serving locally-caught fish, conch and lobster.

A Manta House, Duke St, T9461111, www.grandturk-mantahouse.com. 2 self-contained bungalows, with optional breakfast services and a main guest house with 3 bed & breakfast suites, sea view, steps from the beach. Run by Canadian sisters Katya and Tonya Vieira, who have decorated their guesthouse with a young, fresh feel and touch of fun, offering excellent value. Also Dive packages and flight.

Salt Cay *p269, map p270*

All hotels can arrange dive packages.

LL Windmills Plantation on a 2½ mile beach, T9466962, www.windmillsplantation.com. The most expensive and exclusive hotel and it appeals to people who want to do nothing undisturbed, 8 suites, including all food and drink, meals taken family style, local recipes, saltwater pool, no children.

LL-L Sunset Reef, T9417753, www.sunsetreef.com. 1 or 2-bedroom villa with en suite bathrooms, on the beach with wonderful view from the deck, look out for whales in season, all amenities, well-equipped and comfortable, golf cart or bicycle rental.

L-L Pirates Hideaway, Victoria St, T/F9466909, www.saltcay.tc/index. 4 rooms in cottage, 'Blackbeard Quarters', or rent whole house, or 2 suites, 'The Crow's Nest' upstairs with sea views, balcony, and 'African Suite' downstairs, fans, meals on request, pool, complimentary bikes and kayaks, boat trips, ask about the workshops held here by eminent international artists if you are keen on painting.

L-AL Mount Pleasant Guest House, T9466927, www.mtpleasant.tc. House dates from 1832, 4 standard rooms share bathroom or 2 deluxe with private bath and a/c, video/TV, library, bicycles, outdoor bar, breakfast included, dive packages, cheerful, very laid-back, relaxed, now run by Diane and Wayne Russell.

L-AL Tradewinds, Victoria St, T9466906, www.tradewinds.tc. 5, 1-bedroom suites each sleep 4, new, kitchenettes, on the beach surrounded by casuarina trees, screened patios, deck for whale watching, hammocks, barbecue, walking distance from the dock, bicycles.

South Caicos *p270*

LL-L South Caicos Ocean & Beach Resort, in town, T3311800, www.southcaicosoceanbeachresort.com. Newly renovated site of old hotel, 12 ocean view and 12 garden view rooms in 2007, with 36 more being built for 2008. Also 2-bedroom condos for rent. A clean, quiet dive lodge, a top location for diving and world-class bonefishing, diving packages available, pool, ocean kayaks, windsurfing. **A Mae's Bed & Breakfast**, Forth St, T9463207. 3 rooms, laundry service, no credit cards.

Middle Caicos *p271*

LL Dreamscape Villa, Bambarra beach, T802-2952652 in the USA, T9466175 in the TCI (Ernest Forbes Jr), www.middlecaicos.com. 3 bedrooms, 2 bathrooms, outside shower, large veranda, 80 ft from water, hammock on deck.

LL-L Blue Horizon Resort above Mudjeon Harbour beach, T9466141, www.bhresort.com. 1- or 2-bedroomed cottages, screened porches, well equipped, light and airy, on 50 acres (land for sale), weekly rental available, bicycles, fishing, tours arranged, bring your own groceries or ask for accommodation to be stocked with your requirements.

B Arthur's Guesthouse, in Conch Bar next to Arthur's Store, T9466122. Stacia and Dolphus Arthur run 1 double, 1 twin-bedded room, private bath, kitchen.

North Caicos *p272*

All accommodation is in the Whitby Beach area on the north coast. Sandflies can be a problem, particularly if there is not enough wind; take insect repellent.

LL Datai Villa, T9467755, www.datai-villa .com. On beach, 2 separate buildings open on to patio with large deck, master bedroom in 1, 2 further bedrooms in the other, sleep 2-6 people. Kayaks, bicycles provided.

LL Hollywood Beach Suites, Whitby, T2311020. 4, 1-bed units with kitchen on the beach, transportation, fishing, diving arranged, bring your own food. Bicycles, kayaks and snorkelling gear provided.

LL St Charles Resort, T9467042, www.stcharlesnc.com. Rather different from the other places to stay, newly built and glitzy, studios, suites and apartments with kitchens on 4 floors, pool, hot tub, children's pool, dive shop, tiki huts on the beach, Wi-Fi internet access, fitness room, snorkelling equipment and water toys, fishing.

LL-L Pelican Beach Hotel, T9467112, www.pelicanbeach.tc. Friendly, few facilities, 14 rooms, 2 suites, the older rooms face the beach, restaurant and bar, packages available, run by Clifford and Susan Gardiner. Complimentary bicycles, car hire arranged.

LL-AL Ocean Beach, T9467113, www.oceanbeach,tc. 10 units in condominiums, room only or suites, with up to 3 bedrooms, freshwater swimming pool, diving on site and excursions with Beach Cruiser Charters. Meal plans available at Silver Palm restaurant and bar.

LL-A Jo Anne's Whitby Plaza Bed & Breakfast, T/F9467301, www.tcimall.tc/Joannesbnb/index.htm. Large rooms or suites with bath, hot water, fans, king, queen or twin beds, private entrances and veranda, also 4-room housekeeping unit, condos and villas, short walk to Whitby Beach, bicycle, kayak and canoe rental, **Papa Grunt's** on premises.

L Bottle Creek Lodge, Belmont, T9467080, www.bottlecreeklodge.com. Run by Capt Jay and Sandy Johnson, who have 3 children, West Indian style cabins. Breakfast, lunch and dinner offered in **Bottle Creek Restaurant and Bar** in main house on top of small ridge on northeast side of Flamingo Pond, sea views, fans, kayaks, bicycles, snorkelling equipment, windsurfers. Fishing packages available.

Parrot Cay *p273*

LL Parrot Cay Resort, T9467788, http://parrotcay.como.bz. A luxury 56-room hotel, opened in 1998 on this 1,300-acre private island. It has attracted the rich and famous, with a guest list that includes Paul McCartney and Bruce Willis, and it is frequently featured in glossy magazines and TV travel shows. It has beautiful landscaping and the largest freshwater pool in the TCI. The furniture is Indonesian, some of the staff are Asian and the food is Asian-influenced. You can have a Thai, Balinese or Swedish massage at the award-winning **Shambala Spa**, and there are tennis courts.

Pine Cay *p273*

LL Meridian Club (Nov to Jun, **Premier Resorts Management Group**, T866-7463229 or 770-5001134, locally T/F9465128, http://meridianclub.com). Children under 6 years are not allowed to stay in the hotel and there are lots of restrictions on where they are allowed if brought to a villa. The homes, which are very comfortable, with spectacular views, can be rented. There is a fairly well-stocked commissary or you can eat in the hotel; golf carts are used to get around the island.

❷ Eating

Grand Turk *p267, map p269*
The best restaurants and bars are at the hotels.

¶-¶ Michael's Atrium Restaurant, in the courtyard of the **Osprey Beach**, T9462878, breakfast, lunch and dinner. Across the road from the beach, surrounded by trees. Local and Jamaican food served under the arches in the open air.

¶-¶ Salt Raker Inn, Duke St. Recommended for good food and pleasant company. It is a popular meeting place with live music and a sing-along some nights.

¶-¶ Touch of Class on the road south out of town. Local food and lunch specials, a/c, TV, bar, filling, tasty portions.

¶-¶ Water's Edge, Duke St, T9461680. Offers a very cheerful, informal atmosphere for lunch and dinner with ample portions served and a reasonably priced menu, lots of conch, burgers and pizza. Scooter rental available.

¶ Peanut's snack bar at the airport. Hot snacks, peanuts and drinks.

¶ Poop Deck, a tiny bar set back from the road in the centre of town by the sea. Local food and hamburgers at lunchtime, chicken and chips in the evenings.

¶ Regal Begal, on the road north of town on the west side of North Creek, T9462274. Serves local food, conch, a favourite lunch place.

Salt Cay *p269, map p270*
See the **Blue Mermaid Sunset Café**, page 269, and **Mount Pleasant Guest House**, page 274.

¶¶-¶ Island Thyme, T9466977, www.islandthyme.tc. Usually closed Wed, depending on the ferry schedule. Complimentary coffee from 0700, breakfast by reservation 0730-0900, lunch 1200-1400, cocktails 1830-1930, dinner by reservation 1930-2100. A pleasant, screened restaurant

and bar run by Porter and Haidee Williams. Mostly seafood, some chicken, pasta, steaks, lots of cocktails US$7-8, corkage US$15, make your choices for dinner by 1500, breakfast US$11-18 on request, takeaway meals for picnics, lunch of soups, salads, sandwiches and burgers.

South Caicos *p270*
¶-¶ Dora's Lobster Pot, at the airport, T9463247.

¶-¶ Love's. Local dishes.

¶-¶ Muriel's, Graham St, T9463535. Native dishes.

¶-¶ Pond View, T9463276. Native dishes.

Middle Caicos *p271*
Canned foods and sodas are available from the few small stores in **Conch Bar** and fresh food arrives weekly on the ferry from Provo. However, it is advisable to bring your own food. **Annie Taylor** is known for her cooking and runs a restaurant on demand in her house.

¶-¶ Daniel's Café, Middle Caicos Co-Op, T9466132. Serves native specialities for breakfast, lunch and dinner.

¶-¶ Shanique's Kitchen, Conch Bar, T9466128. Reservations only, catering service for breakfast, lunch and dinner.

¶ Elshaadi's, at the airport, T9466136. Snacks, burgers, conch fritters and drinks.

¶ T&J Boutique in Conch Bar. Has ice creams, cold drinks and fried chicken on Fri.

North Caicos *p272*
¶¶-¶ Silver Palm, at Ocean Beach condos, Whitby, T9467113. Breakfast, lunch, dinner at 1900. Cheerful dining room, colourful linens. Simple fare of steak, lobster, fish, chicken or conch served in various ways.

¶-¶ Papa Grunt's Restaurant, T9467301, Whitby Plaza. Mon-Sat from 0830, Sun 1100-1400 for lunch. Credit cards accepted, indoor or screened veranda dining, native and American cuisine, fresh seafood, lots of conch, sandwiches with home-made bread US$5.75, pizza, salads, vegetarian platter.

¶-¶ Pelican Beach Hotel, T9467112, www.pelicanbeach.tc. Good food but only open if there are guests at the hotel.

¶ Club Titter's Restaurant and Bar, T9467316. Simple local restaurant near the airport.

¶ Super D's, in the airport itself. Local food.

🍸 Bars and clubs

Grand Turk *p267, map p269*

Grand Turk is not an island where you will find lots of nightlife. Most evening activity takes place when people get together for meals and drinks at the small inns and restaurants, with live music some nights, usually provided by Mitch Rolling, a guitarist/singer and the High Tide band. Don't expect a lot of action. **Margaritaville**, at the cruise ship centre, www.margaritaville.com/grandturk.php. Jimmy Buffett's Margaritaville is the largest stand-alone Margaritaville Café in the Caribbean seating 500 for 'cheeseburgers in paradise' and other typical dishes. In addition to the retail shop and restaurant, a 3-ft deep swimming pool winds it way throughout offering a swim up bar, slide, and infinity edge view. 52 flavours of margaritas on offer or their own Latitude beer.

Middle Caicos *p271*

🍴 **Johnson's Bar** is open in Conch Bar most afternoons and evenings for cold beer, dominoes and music.

North Caicos *p272*

Taylor's Bar and **Big Josh's** in Kew (beer US$2). **The Anchor Inn**, T2434441, and **Bernie's** in Bottle Creek.

⚜ Festivals and events

Jan New Year's Day is celebrated with a **Junkanoo Jump-Up** from midnight to sunrise on most of the islands, with lots of noise and masquerades. Most events are linked to the sea, and land-based activities are tacked on to regattas or fishing tournaments.

Grand Turk *p267, map p269*

Jun Conch Carnival with island music and dancing, competitions, snorkelling treasure hunts, lots of conch fritters, etc.
Aug Heineken Game Fishing Tournament, with beach parties every evening, and the **Cactus Fest**, with competitions for sports, costumes, bands and gospel, a float parade, dancing and an art exhibition.
5 Nov Guy Fawkes Bonfire Night.
End Nov Museum Day, celebrating the anniversary of the opening of the museum with music, choral singing, children's events.

Dec 1st week Run Turks and Caicos; 2nd week **Christmas Tree-lighting Ceremony**; mid-Dec **Anglican Church Bazaar** a week before Christmas. The Methodist Church holds a fair on **Boxing Day**.

South Caicos *p270*

24 May The oldest festival in the islands, the **Regatta**, with power boat and sail boat races and associated activities, takes place on the weekend closest to 24 May.

Middle Caicos *p271*

Jul Festarama.

North Caicos *p272*

Aug Expo, with traditional sailboat races and a procession along the Crossing Place Trail.

🏔 Activities and tours

Grand Turk *p267, map p269*
Diving

The 3 dive shops on **Grand Turk** also offer whale watching in season. See Whale and dolphin watching, page , and Diving and marine life, page 265.
Blue Water Divers Ltd, Front St, next to the museum, T/F9462432, www.grandturkscuba .com. The only PADI 5-star operation on the island, owned by Mitch Rollings.
Oasis Divers, T9461128, www.oasisdivers.com. Run by Everette Freites (see whale watching, page) and Dale Barker, taking small groups aboard 28-ft dive boats.
Sea Eye Diving, T/F9461407, www.seaeyediving.com. Run by Cecil Ingham and Connie Rus, has a range of watersports on offer. They have NAUI and PADI instruction, frequent cay trips.

Fishing

Fishing can be arranged through Ossie (Oswald) Virgil, of **Virgil's Taxis** at the airport, T9462018. Ossie also arranges an annual game fishing tournament in Aug. The record catch is a 460-lb marlin caught in 1998 by Art Pickering of Provo.

Golf

The former Governor created a 9-hole golf course on Grand Turk in the grounds of his residence (see box page 268).

Salt Cay *p269, map p270*
Diving
Reef Runners, T9417753, www.reefrunnerssc
.com. Have a 24-ft Carolina skiff and a 27-ft
Dusky V-hull which take you to the main
dive site in 5 mins. A 1-tank, 1-day dive
package is US$80, but most people take a
7-night, 5-days diving package for US$999
including accommodation, transfers, 3 meals
and 3 dives a day.
Salt Cay Divers, T9466906, www.saltcaydivers
.tc. Have 3 Carolina skiffs and a yacht for
non-diving activities, accommodation and
diving packages.Five days of 2-tank diving is
US$350. Daily whale watching trips Jan-Mar,
US$65 for divers (can be included in diving
package), US$75 for non-divers.

South Caicos *p270*
Diving
South Caicos Diver, T3311800,
www.southcaicosdiver.com. Offers excellent
diving and snorkelling with eagle rays about
10 mins offshore, airplane wreck, caves, large
pelagics, whalewatching, packages available.
US$95 for 2-tank morning dive, US$50 for
single afternoon dive, US$65 for night dive.

Middle Caicos *p271*
Fishing
Cardinal Arthur, Conch Bar, T9466107, VHF
16, www.tcimall.tc/middlecaicos/
cardinalarthur. Can take you to catch
grouper, barracuda, grunt or snapper.
Cardinal also runs a taxi service, tours on land
and at sea. He is extremely knowledgeable
about the islands, having spent most of his
life here while being able to trace his family
back 6 generations on Middle Caicos.

North Caicos *p272*
Watersports
Beach Cruiser at the Ocean Beach Hotel,
T9467113, www.oceanbeach.tc/diving. A
charter operation, 20-ft pontoon 'flat top'
boat offering diving (US$240 for 1-tank
dive, 1-4 people, US$480 for 2-tank dive,
packages and equipment hire available),
snorkelling 1-4 people US$160 for 1hr,
US$280 for 2 hrs, beach trips and excursions
to other cays US$480-600. Bonefishing
charters US$600-800, other fishing
excursions US$550 half day, US$750 full day
1-4 people.

⊖ Transport

Grand Turk *p267, map p269*
Air
Sky King (T9461520 on Grand Turk) has
scheduled flights from Provo and South
Caicos and will fly to Cuba, the Dominican
Republic, Bahamas and Haiti on request. **Air
Turks and Caicos**, T9461667, has scheduled
services throughout the Turks and Caicos (6
daily flights to Provo, 3 a week to Salt Cay
and South Caicos) and chartered flights to
Cuba, Cap Haïtien, Puerto Plata and other
Caribbean destinations.

Boat
There is a safe harbour and marina at
Flamingo Cove, North Creek, T9462227.

Car
If you rent a bicycle, jeep or car, note that the
islanders completely ignore the 25 mph speed
limit, particularly on Pond St, recommended
to stay on Front St/Duke St route through
town and exercise caution elsewhere. Fatal
accidents have occurred. **Tony's**, at the
airport, T9461879, www.tonyscarrental.com,
cars from US$70 a day, jeeps from US$95,
scooters US$60, bicycles US$20 and
snorkelling gear for US$30 a day can be
rented, or scooter tours are offered. **Dutchie's
Car Rental**, Airport Rd, T9462244.

Salt Cay *p269, map p270*
Air
There is a paved airstrip for small aircraft,
around which a fence has been erected to
keep out the donkeys. A day trip is possible
from Grand Turk or Provo. The island is
served by **Air Turks and Caicos** from Grand
Turk Mon, Wed, Fri, 0900 and 1650, returning
0920 and 1700. They fly from Provo daily.
Alternatively, charter a flight, or get a seat on
someone else's charter, which costs the
same if you can fill the aircraft.

Car and taxi
Salt Cay Riders, T9466989, www.saltcay.org
/golfcart, contact Nathan Smith for golf cart
rental, single seater US$40 a day, twin seater
US$60, US$100 deposit required. Nathan also
runs the taxi van, T9466920, for airport pickup
and tours. There are very few vehicles of any
sort and no other public transport.

Boat

Contact the District Commissioner's Office on Salt Cay (or **Mount Pleasant Guest House**, who cross regularly to do shopping) for details of ferries.

South Caicos *p270*

See Getting around, page 264. There are a few **taxis** on the island.

Middle Caicos *p271*
Air
See Getting around page 264.

Boat

A ferry service for cargo and passengers runs between Middle and North Caicos on Sat (Fri evening and Sun by appointment), starting from Middle at 0800, 30 mins, until early afternoon. The ferry carries 2 cars or 1 truck, US$20 per vehicle round trip, passengers US$2 round trip.

Cycle
Sports Shack, in Conch Bar, sells, rents and repairs bicycles.

Taxi
You have to take a taxi from the airport to where you are staying. **Carlton Forbes** runs a taxi service or contact **Cardinal Arthur**, see above, Fishing.

North Caicos *p272*
Air
See Getting around, p264. Flight from Provo is 12 mins, US$40 one way with Global Airways. The return flight leaves at 0600, allowing time

to make connections in Provo for onward morning flights to Miami. North Caicos is a port of entry and private aircraft can clear customs here by prior arrangement. Normal Customs office hours 0800-1630.

Car
Pelican Car Rental, T2418275, or **Safe Car Rental**, T9467770.

Taxi
Taxis at the airport for transfers and tours, the drivers are friendly and knowledgeable but some run their own errands while working.

● Directory

Grand Turk *p267, map p269*
Banks FirstCaribbean International Bank, T9462831; **Turks & Caicos Banking Co Ltd**, Grand Turk, T9462368; **Scotiabank** at Harbour House, T9462506. **Medical services** There is a small, understaffed hospital on the north side of town, T9462333, and a **government clinic** in town, T9462328, 0800-1230, 1400-1630. The other islands organize emergency air evacuation to Grand Turk hospital.

South Caicos *p270*
Banks FirstCaribbean International Bank, opens on Wed.

North Caicos *p272*
Banks You are advised to bring small-denomination US dollar notes as there is no bank and it is difficult to cash US$50 or US$100, TCs or money orders around the island.

Providenciales → *Phone code: 649. Population: over 10,000.*

'Provo' is 25 miles long and about 3 miles wide. A surge of building work since the early 1990s has changed Grace Bay, on the north shore, beyond all recognition, but despite the many hotels and condominiums you can still walk along the beach and snorkel without feeling crowded. Away from the smart hotels, condos and villas, however, the island is dry, scrubby and nothing like as pretty as the underwater world surrounding it. The reef is superb and attracts thousands of divers every year. ►► *For Sleeping, Eating and other listings, see pages 282-288.*

Ins and outs
Getting there Provo has the main airport for the islands and international flights come in here. There are no scheduled boat services and cruise ships do not call.

Getting around Most roads are paved, contributing to fast, erratic driving by residents; speed limits (40 mph highway, 20 mph in town) are not observed, dangerous overtaking is common. Hired cars are generally not well serviced, and may have to be exchanged for another. Taxis are very expensive; complaints have not lowered the rates. There are usually taxis at the large hotels. The Gecko shuttle bus is a convenient and cheaper option if you are staying in the Grace Bay area, or there are the 'jitneys', vans which you flag down, used like buses. ▸▸ *See page 262 for international air services and other transport details.*

Around Providenciales

Development of the island began in 1967 although it had been settled in the 18th century and there were three large plantations in the 19th century growing cotton and sisal. The three original settlements, **The Bight** (meaning Bay), **Five Cays** and **Blue Hills**, are fragmented and have not grown into towns as the population has increased. Instead shopping malls and offices have been built along the Leeward Highway (**Market Place, Plantation Hills, Central Square, Provo Plaza**). The Office of the Chief Secretary, Customs Office, banks, law firms, supermarkets and travel agents are **Down Town. Turtle Cove** calls itself 'the heart of Provo', with a couple of hotels, a marina, dive operators, boat charters, deep-sea fishing, restaurants and the tourist office.

On the south side of the island, **South Dock** is the island's commercial port and

Providenciales

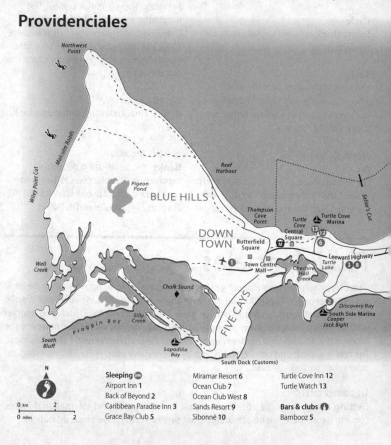

Sleeping 🛏
Airport Inn **1**
Back of Beyond **2**
Caribbean Paradise Inn **3**
Grace Bay Club **5**

Miramar Resort **6**
Ocean Club **7**
Ocean Club West **8**
Sands Resort **9**
Sibonné **10**

Turtle Cove Inn **12**
Turtle Watch **13**

Bars & clubs 🍸
Bambooz **5**

0 km   2
0 miles   2

N

here you will find the Harbourmaster. The **Caicos Marina and Boatyard** on the south coast is many miles from shopping supplies. Also on the south side is the small **South Side Marina**. To the west, **Sapodilla Bay** offers good protection for yachts in all winds west through southeast. It is open to the south through southwest. **Chalk Sound**, a national park inland from Sapodilla Bay, is a shallow lagoon of marvellous turquoise colours, dotted with rocky islets.

Northwest Point, a marine park offshore, has good beaches, diving and snorkelling. In 1993 a French television company shot a series of underwater game shows here and a treacherous road was bulldozed through to the beautiful beach. They left several tiki huts which offer much-needed shade for a day on the beach. Two good places to snorkel in the **Grace Bay** area are just to the east of Turtle Cove, where grouper rays and turtles can be seen on Smith's Reef near the entrance to the marina, just west of **Treasure Beach Villas**, and in front of **Coral Gardens Resort**. The **Princess Alexandra Marine Park** along Grace Bay incorporates the reef offshore. At the northeast end, a deep channel known as **Leeward Going Through** is a natural harbour and a marina with fuel, water and ice, and a restaurant has been built here. The **Caicos Conch Farm** ① *near Leeward, T9465643, www.caicosconchfarm.com. Hatchery tours Mon-Fri 0900-1600, Sat 0900-1400, US$6, children under 12 US$3, gift shop*, is worth visiting and children love being able to hold the molluscs. Most of the restaurants on the islands buy their conch from among the 2mn conch being reared here in onshore ponds and offshore pasture.

Inland, along Seasage Hill Road in Long Bay, is **The Hole**, a collapsed limestone, water-filled sinkhole next to a house called **By the Hole**. A tunnel to the right-hand side gives access to the main pool. Do not attempt to descend. Ruins of Loyalist and Bermudan settlers' plantations and houses can be seen at **Cheshire Hall**, Richmond Hills and along the Bight road. On the hill overlooking the **Mariner Hotel** (closed) at Sapodilla Bay a pole marks the location of stones engraved with initials and dates in the 17th century possibly by shipwrecked sailors or wreckers. The view, even with the commercial dock in the foreground, is quite lovely, and it is free.

Beaches and activities

Grace Bay is the longest stretch of sand, at 12 miles, and despite the hotels it is possible to find plenty of empty space, but no shade. There is rarely any shade on the beaches except umbrellas supplied by resorts, usually for their guests only. Most watersports can be arranged through the hotels or tour operators.

Several tour operators represent all **day sails**, **scuba dives** or **snorkelling trips** or you can contact the captains direct or through your hotel.

> 230 miles of white-sand beaches and coral surround the islands.

BET Soundstage &
  Gaming Lounge **2**
Bonnie's **7**
Calico Jack's **6**
Club Med **1**
Club Sodax **3**
Danny Buoy's Irish Pub **4**
Where It's At **8**

Diving There are many land-based dive operations offering courses (resort course approximately US$130, full certification US$400) and dive packages. The standard cost of a two-tank dive is US$100. ▸▸ *For dive centres, fishing trips and parasailing, see page 285.*

West Caicos

Rugged and uninhabited for 100 years but visited for its beach on the northwest coast and diving offshore. Parcels of this island are being developed as a luxury hotel and villa resort with a dredged marina to accommodate mega-yachts. An airstrip is under construction to serve the Ritz Carlton resort being built there. Access is currently by launch from the private dock at Split Rock, Provo, or by light aircraft. See www.westcaicosreserve.com. The east shore is a national marine park. Inland there is a saltwater lake, **Lake Catherine**, which rises and falls with the tides and is a nature reserve, home to migrant nesting flamingos, ducks and waders. The ruins of **Yankee Town**, its sisal press and railroad are a surface interval destination for scuba divers and sailors.

Once frequented by pirates, there are many wrecks between here and Provo.

French Cay

An old pirate lair, now uninhabited, but with exceptional marine life, and on the diving circuit (see page 265), French Cay has been designated a sanctuary for frigate birds, osprey and nesting seabirds. There is no official transport but tour and dive operators will go there on demand.

● Sleeping

Providenciales *p280, map p280*
When confirming rates and availability, check whether tax and service are included. There are plenty of self-catering condos and villas around the island. There is still a lot of construction in progress. Most hotels offer diving packages and many offer golf too.
LL Grace Bay Club, on beach, T9465050, www.gracebayclub.com. Luxury accommodation, 22 elegant condos renovated 2007, a/c, phone, TV, watersports, tennis, pool, jacuzzi, all amenities, French restaurant, beach bar. Also **The Villas at Grace Bay**, 38 newly constructed ocean-front suites with spa and fitness centre.
LL Ocean Club and Ocean Club West , T9465880, www.oceanclubresorts.com. Two resorts less than a mile apart, shared facilities. From studios to 3-bedroom condos, on the beach, comfortable, well-equipped, balconies, some with good views the length of Grace Bay, spacious deck around pool with daytime snack bar, next to **Provo Golf Club**, packages available, free transport to airport, bike rentals.
LL The Sands Resort, T9465199, www.thesandsresort.com. On the beach, 116

suites and rooms in 5 buildings, 2 pools, spa, extensive landscaping.
LL-L Turtle Watch, Turtle Cove area, 2 mins' walk to north shore beaches, T9464362, www.turtlewatchvilla.com. Linda and Mike St Louis rent out The Carriage House and The Guest House, each of which is a separate building and private, with 1 bedroom, the latter has a kitchen. Sit on the dock and watch the turtles swim by. Pool and patio, close to beach, several restaurants only a short walk away. Kayaks and glass bottom rowing boat available.
LL-AL Back of Beyond, Venetian Rd, Discovery Bay, T9414555, backofbeyond@tciway.tc. 9-bedroom adobe-style guesthouse with bar and restaurant on the south side of the island.
LL-AL Caribbean Paradise Inn, T9465020, www.paradise.tc. 200 m from beach, by **Grace Bay Club**, 15 rooms, ocean or pool view, breakfast buffet included, snacks available, new, popular, dive gear storage, German-owned and managed.
LL-AL Sibonné, T9465547, www.sibonne.com. The first hotel to be built on Grace Bay, with a prime bit of beach but not as luxurious as some. 28 rooms and

☷ The Turks and Caicos National Trust

The National Trust is a non-profit, non- governmental conservation organization, working in co-operation with the Government, the World Wildlife Fund, The Nature Conservancy and local people to preserve the natural and historical heritage of the islands and develop sustainable tourism to keep the Turks and Caicos Islands 'beautiful by nature'. Projects completed include: an exhibition on national parks, endangered animals and the islands' history in the departure terminal at Provo Airport; a historically oriented public park around the Cheshire Hall plantation ruins near downtown Provo; public access to the 100-acre Bird Rock Point Natural Area on the northeast tip of Provo for walking and birdwatching; a fund-raising campaign and work with the Government on a financial framework for the long-term management of the national parks. For information or to become a member or volunteer, contact Ethlyn Gibbs-Williams, the National Trust of the Turks and Caicos Islands, Providenciales, T9415710, www.nationaltrust.tc.

apartments, beachfront restaurant, lovely bougainvillea in the courtyard, pool.

LL-A Turtle Cove Inn, T9464203, www.turtlecoveinn.com. 30 rooms and apartments, special weekly packages, car park, poolside or ocean view, smallish rooms but comfortable, suite with kitchenette available, not on beach but you can use the beach at the sister hotel, Sibonné, all watersports at the marina, cable TV, 2 restaurants.

L-AL Miramar Resort (formerly Erebus Inn), on hillside overlooking Turtle Cove, T9464240, www.miramarresort.tc. 10 rooms overlooking Turtle Cove and 10 overlooking the pool, larger than those in other hotels, dive packages available, all watersports at the marina, shuttle to White House reef for snorkelling, gym and fitness centre on site, tennis, Wi-Fi internet access, massages in your room.

AL Airport Inn, T9413514, www.airportinntci.com. 2 mins to airport, close to banks, groceries, restaurants, 25 rooms, 24-hr service, shops and restaurant on site, a/c, TV, special rates for pilots, 15% discount on rental car for guests.

❶ Eating

Providenciales *p280, map p280*
Dinner with wine at an expensive restaurant can easily cost US$200 for 2.

Turtle Cove

Aqua Bar and Terrace, T9464763. Daily breakfast, lunch and dinner. 'Creative' conch, seafood, tables on deck overlooking the Pond and the yachts.

Baci Ristorante, T9413044. Fine Italian dining indoors and on the terrace overlooking the Pond, 1200-1430, 1800-2200, pizza until 2300, bar until late.

Magnolia Restaurant and Bar, at the Miramar Resort overlooking Turtle Cove, T9415108, www.miramarresort.tc /Magnolia.htm. 0730-1030, 1800-2200, bar from 1500, closed Mon. Spectacular view, serving New Age Asian and Caribbean cuisine to popular acclaim.

Banana Boat, dockside at Turtle Cove marina, T9415706, www.turksandcaicos.tc /bananaboat. Daily 1100-late. Caribbean bar and grill, colourful, cheerful. Fri happy hour 1700-1900. Internet kiosk, slot machines, karaoke Sat.

Tiki Hut, at the Turtle Cove Marina landspit, T9465341, www.tikihuttci.com. Daily lunch and dinner until 2200, weekend breakfast from 0700. Mon West Indian curry night, chicken, goat or beef. Wed night chicken or ribs, popular with ex-pats, brunch on Sun, kids menu, several good vegetarian options, lots of fish, burgers, pizza, pasta.

Sharkbite Bar and Grill, Admiral's Club, on the water, T9415090, www.thesharkbite.com. 1100-0200, food until 2200, happy hour Fri 1700-1900, nightly specials and events, Wed fish'n'chips US$8 with live music from 2000. Sports bar, darts, slot machines.

Down Town

Down Town and on Airport Rd you'll find the least expensive (but not necessarily cheap) meals, catering to islanders and office workers.

Hole in the Wall, Williams Plaza on Old Airport Rd, T9414136, www.holeinthewall-provo.com. Mon-Sat 0800-late. Native food with Jamaican twist, try the jerk chicken. Sports bar.

Tasty Temptations, Butterfield Sq next to the dry cleaners, T9464049. Daily 0630-1500. French pastries, breakfasts, sandwiches, fresh salads for lunch, good coffee, deli.

Blue Hills settlement

Smokey's On the Bay, T2414343. Mon-Sat 1030-2300, but hours can vary. Not to be missed, indoor or tiki hut dining on the beach, great native dishes, lobster, conch, buffets, sometimes live band.

Three Queens Bar and Restaurant, Wheeland, off Blue Hills Rd, T9415984. Mon-Sat 1130-2100, Sun 1130-1600. Excellent, reasonably priced, local seafood lunches and dinners, overlooking the water, dominoes.

Da Conch Shack, on the beach. Daily lunch and dinner. Great conch salad, conch fritters, catch of the day, fish and seafood, all very fresh and tasty, wash it down with a rum punch. Variety of rums at the rum bar.

Leeward Highway

Restaurant hours change with the season so call first to avoid disappointment.

Hey José Cantina, near the Tourist Shoppe, Central Square Shopping Centre, T9464812. Mon-Sat 1200-late. Great food, Mexican/ American, tacos, huge pizza, etc, takeaways.

Pizza Pizza, T9413577. Tue-Thu 1130-2130, Fri-Sat 1130-2200, Sun 1700-2130. New York-style pizza, eat in or takeaway, recommended.

Angela's Top O' The Cove Deli, next to Napa auto at Suzie Turn, T9464694. Mon-Fri 0630-1700, Sat 0630-1500, Sun 0630-1400. 'Little bit of New York-style deli', subs, bagels, beer, wine, picnic food.

Chinson Jade Garden, opposite Do-It Centre, T9413533. 0800-2100. Jamaican and Chinese, variety of pastries, in house bakery, lunch buffet.

Gilley's at Leeward, Leeward going through, at the east end of Providenciales, T9465094, www.provo.net/Gilleys/. 0800-1900. By the marina, breakfast, lunch specials, good food, friendly, superb service, meet local fishermen, arrange outings, boat trips.

Mackie's Café, At Market Pl, T9413640. Mon-Sat 0900-2100. Native-style, stewed fish and Johnny cake, fresh seafood.

Where It's At, Leeward Hwy opposite PPC power station, T9464554. Lunch daily. Jamaican specialities by Yvette, curried goat and *Presidente* beer, generous portions, daily specials, seafood buffet Tue, Fri, nightclub next door.

Grace Bay

Hotel restaurants are open to all, but visitors to all-inclusives must have a day/evening pass.

Anacaona restaurant and bar on the beach at **Grace Bay Club**, T9465050. Daily1200-1500, 1900-2100. Thatched roof elegance, nouvelle cuisine with Caribbean flair, exclusive and expensive, live music some evenings, reservations recommended. No children under 12.

Bay Bistro, at Sibonné, T9465396. Wed-Mon 0700-2200. Ocean-front dining, international cuisine, very nice, live music Mon dinner.

Bella Luna Ristorante, in the Glass House, west of Allegro, T9465214. Tue-Sun 1830-2200. Nightly specials, Italian with a Caribbean twist, reservations recommended.

Coco Bistro, past Caicos Café, east of Allegro near Club Med, behind Sunshine Nursery in palm trees, T9465369. Tue-Sun 1800-2130, closed Sep-Oct. Indoor dining/bar, or jazz outdoors under the palms, Mediterranean cooking, specials every night reservations advised, expensive, congenial hosts and service.

Coyaba at Coral Gardens, T9465186, www.provo.net/Coyaba. Wed-Mon 1800-2200. The name means 'heavenly' in Arawak and so is the food, try the dessert martinis.

Mango Reef, in Royal West Indies Resort, T9468200, www.mangoreef.com. Breakfast, lunch and dinner. Indoor and poolside dining, great food, good service.

₶₶-₶₶ Caicos Café and Grill, next to **Ports of Call**, T9465278. Daily Jan-Apr 1200-1530, 1800-2200, May-Aug and Nov-Dec closed Sun dinner, closed totally Sep-Oct. Homemade pasta, grilled fish and seafood, lots of conch, own bakery, go early or late to avoid crowds, open-air.

₶₶-₶₶ Fairways Bar and Grill, opposite **Ocean Club**, **Provo Golf Course Clubhouse**, T9465991. Daily 0700-1500 and Tue-Sat 1800-2200, Wed lunch specials, Fri happy hour, lobster nights a couple of times a week in season, Fri pub night.

₶₶-₶₶ Hemingway's, at The **Sands Resort**, T9465199. Ocean-view dining, good service.

⊕ Bars and clubs

Providenciales *p280, map p280*
Provo is not a party place, people come here for relaxation and to enjoy the water, not for the nightlife. There's a Latin influence in discos such as **Club Latino**, Down Town, and **Caribbean Mack**, in Blue Hills, featuring soca, reggae and latino, loudly! Live entertainment, Fri nights, Ports of Call courtyard.
Bambooz, The Saltmills. American-style bar with pool tables, food and drink, karaoke.
BET Soundstage & Gaming Lounge, Leeward Hwy, T9414318. Music every night, late-night disco, often live bands, huge plasma TVs, casino, a place for gaming, dining and entertainment.
Bonnie's, Lower Bight Rd, Grace Bay, on the road to Sibonné, T9418452, www.bonniesrestaurant.com. Happy hour 1700-1900, all beers US$3. Local favourite for sports events and movie nights. Island food, lots of conch, served outside on the deck under palm trees surrounded by conch shells, or in a/c bar, slot machines, pool table, Wi-Fi internet access.
Calico Jack's, Ports of Call, T9465129. Pizzas and other food upstairs, great outdoor deck, indoor bar, live music on Fri night and most Sats, happy hour specials, lively crowd.
Club Med, T9465500. Arrive 1830-1930 to get in. Has nightly dinner/show for guests and visitors who phone for reservations. Night club has a DJ playing very loud music and foam party once a week.
Club Sodax, off Leeward Highway next to **Where It's At**, T9414540. Nice sports bar and restaurant, serves jerk chicken and pork, large

screen TV, pool tables, gaming room, dominoes.
Danny Buoy's Irish Pub, Grace Bay Rd, The Saltmills, T9465921. Weekly events, Tue quiz night, Fri live music, Sat Calypso, lots of British football on TV. Bottled beer US$5.
Dora's, on Leeward Highway near PPC power station, T9464558. 0730-late. Local restaurant, eat in or takeaway, bar, jukebox, live band sometimes on Thu and Fri.
Where It's At, on Leeward Highway, T9415475. 1600-0100. Loud 'island' music, DJ, drinks, Fri night specials.

⊙ Entertainment

Providenciales *p280, map p280*
Cinema
Village Cinemas, T9414108, is a 2-screen movie theatre complex which will seat 370 people, tickets US$10 adults, US$7 children under 12.

⊛ Festivals and events

Providenciales *p280 map p280*
Two international billfishing tournaments are held annually, T9413781; they are big events with lots of parties.
Jan **New Year's Day** is celebrated with a **Junkanoo Jump-Up** from midnight to sunrise on most of the islands, with lots of noise and masquerades. Most events are linked to the sea, and land-based activities are tacked on to regattas or fishing tournaments.
Jul **Provo Day Summer Festival**, held over a weekend at the end of the month; sees the crowning of Miss Turks and Caicos.
Oct **Annual Amateur Open Golf Championship**; tourists are welcome to participate.

▲ Activities and tours

Providenciales *p280, map p280*
Diving
Do not remove live coral, sea fans or other marine life. The use of spearguns is prohibited. See also Diving and marine life, page265. There is a recompression chamber at **Associated Medical Practice**, T9464242, DAN insurance is accepted. There are lots of land-based dive operations offering courses (resort course approximately US$230, full certification

US$500) and dive packages. The standard cost of a 2-tank dive is US$100-110. Prices are higher here than in other islands and pre-paying a number of dives is the best value.

The Turks and Caicos Aggressor II, T2311322, or contact the **Aggressor Fleet Limited**, T800-3482628, www.turksandcaicosaggressor.com. Based at Turtle Cove, this luxury liveaboard travels around the waters of the Turks and Caicos visiting all the best dive sites depending on local conditions. There are also humpback whale watching trips in season in the TCI and to Silver Bank, Dominican Republic, where you can snorkel with the whales.

Big Blue Unlimited, Leeward Marina, T9465034, www.bigblue.tc. Eco-award-winning company, specializes in small groups, private charters. Their catamarans take 4, 6, or 9 divers. Also eco-tours, kayaks, boat trips including lunch with an island family, snorkelling, marine ecology classes, trips to North Caicos for off-road biking and kayaking, on to Middle Caicos for hiking and biking, trips to West Caicos, French Cay and West Sand Spit, a sand bar on the Caicos Bank.

Caicos Adventures, South Side Marina, Turtle Cove, T/F9413346, www.tcidiving .com. Has 3 comfortable motor catamarans for dive trips to West Caicos, French Cay for small groups, NAUI/CMAS.

Dive Provo, T9465029, www.diveprovo.com. Has 3 boats, wind-surfing, kayaks, shop in Ports of Call.

Flamingo Divers, next to the Marine Biology Center on Venetian Rd, T/F9464193, www.flamingodivers.com. Caters for small groups, PADI instruction, diving French Cay, West Caicos and Northwest Point.

O2 Technical Diving, Port of Call, T/F9413499, www.o2technicaldiving.com. The latest in hi-tech diving, offering rebreather training, DPV specialties, mixed gas training up to trimix and instructor training.

Ocean Vibes, Turtle Cove Marina, T2316636, www.oceanvibes.com. Does small dive groups and other watersports. Run by Wayne Hall, a native islander. Also operates Eagle Parasail on Grace Bay Beach.

Provo Turtle Divers, Turtle Cove, T9464232, www.provoturtledivers.com. Art Pickering's outfit at Turtle Cove Marina and at Ocean Club Resort, and **Ocean Club West**, Grace Bay, is recommended for small groups of experienced divers. This is the longest-established dive shop in the TCI, with a wealth of experience. Dive computers required. With Kristi Vestal, Art also runs **After 5 Concierge**, www.after5.tc, for private dive charters or instruction, excursions, fishing, kiteboarding, parasailing, or anything else you fancy.

Silver Deep, Leeward Marina, T9465612, www.silverdeep.com. Private charters only with dive master Arthur Dean, a native islander, Tanks and weights Included, rental equipment available. Also excursions in one of 12 boats and fishing.

Fishing

Bite Me Sportfishing, Turtle Cove Marina, T2310366, www.fishingtci.com, run by Chris 'Fineline' Stubbs, a native islander. Half and full day charters for up to 5 people, no experience necessary.

Gwendolyn Fishing Charters, Turtle Cove, T9465321, www.fishtci.com. 45-ft Hatteras sportfisher, experienced crew, beginners welcome.

Hook 'em Fishing Adventures, T2313586, www.hookem.tc. Capt Wing Dean and crew can take you deep sea, light tackle trolling, bottom fishing or bone fishing. Deep sea fishing from US$950 full-day charter.

Silver Deep (see Diving, above) includes bone, fly, light tackle and night fishing in its itinerary.

Golf

An 18-hole championship course (black tees 2,928 m, white tees 2,620 m), owned by the water company, T9465991, www.provogolfclub.com, is located within walking distance of the **Club Med**, **Grace Bay Club** and **Ocean Club**. US$160 for 18 holes, including cart, while a 3-round pass is US$375 and a 5-round pass is US$550. Competitions include the Bob Graham Classic in Mar, the Rizzoli Cup in Apr, the President's Open in Jun, the Turks & Caicos Amateur Open in Oct and the Provo Ryder Cup in Nov.

Horse riding

Provo Ponies, T9465252, www.provo.net/ ProvoPonies. On quiet roads and Long Bay Beach. Suitable for novice or experienced riders, very popular, the only tuition is for kids on Sat.

Sailing, watersports

Atabeyra, Sun Charters, T2310624, www.suncharters.tc. A traditional 77-ft trading schooner now retired from carrying cargo between the islands and taking visitors on excursions instead, anchored at Leeward Marina, offers Pirates Cay full- and half-day sails and private charters, cold drinks and snorkelling gear included.

Beluga, Leeward Going Through, T/F9464396, VHF 68, www.sailbeluga.com. 37-ft catamaran, private, full- and half-day sails.

Caicos Tours Undersea Explorer, Turtle Cove Marina, T2310006, www.caicostours .com. Semi-submersible for diving without getting wet. Adults US$49, children 12 and under US$39. Private charters US$600 per hr for up to 16 passengers. Daily tours at 1000, 1200, 1400.

Catch the Wave Charters, Leeward Marina, T/F9413047, www.tcimall.tc/catchthewave. Has a 26-ft Bowrider, comfortable and roomy, and a 27-ft World Cat, both with shade tops. Specialize in private charters and offer bonefishing, flyfishing, waterskiing, beach cruising, reggae sunset cruises.

J & B Tours, Leeward Marina, T9465047, www.jbtours.com. Offers beach and snorkelling excursions, barbecues, waterskiing, island getaways, trips to Conch Farm, caves on Middle Caicos, glo-worm cruises, fishing.

Sail Provo, T9464783, www.sailprovo.com. Catamaran excursions and private charters, sailing and snorkelling, trips to Iguana Island.

Silver Deep (see Diving, above) offers similar beach cruises, glo-worm charters, secluded getaways, trips to Middle and North Caicos.

Turtle Parasail, Turtle Cove Inn, T9415389, parasail@tciway.tc.

Windsurfing Provo at Ocean Club, Grace Bay, T2411687, www.windsurfingprovo.tc. Hobie waves, hobie cats, small motor boats and kayaking as well as windsurfing and kiteboarding, waterskiing and wakeboarding. Owner Mike Rosati is an expert and an excellent teacher.

Jetskis are banned from any of the marine parks, although they may be used in parts of Leeward Channel and on the Banks.

Tennis

There are courts at several of the larger hotels. A small but active **squash** community welcomes visitors and can be contacted at **Johnston Apartments**, Kings Court, T9465683.

⊝ Transport

Providenciales *p280, map p280*
Bus

The Gecko, T9417433, www.thegecko.tc, Mon-Sat 1000-2230, Sun on call, every 30 mins starting from the IGA Supermarket and stopping at various locations along Grace Bay including The Sands, Grace Bay Plaza, Ports of Call, Club Med, up to the Golf Course, returning via Caicos Plaza, Turtle Cove Marina and Central Square, back to the supermarket, one-way token US$4, US$11 for a one-day ticket, US$22 for 3 days, US$33 for 7 days, discounts for children, family tickets available, get token or pass in advance, no cash on bus.

Car and bike hire

Be careful on the roads; Leeward Highway is especially risky. A valid driver's licence from your own country is required. A tax of US$15 is levied on all hired cars and US$5 on motor scooters. Remember to drive on the left.

Avis at airport and Bayview Motors, Leeward Highway, T9464705, at Club Med, T9469730, www.avis.tc, affiliated with **Sunrise Auto Rental**, jeeps and scooters, Leeward Highway and Club Med, T9469730. **Budget**, Down Town, Town Centre Mall, Mon-Sat 0800-1700, Sun 1000-1600, T9463709, worldwide reservations T800-5270700, www.budget .com, Suzukis, Mitsubishis, 1 day free for weekly rental. **Hertz**, Central Leeward Highway, T9413910, www.hertztci.com. **Provo Fun Cycles** at Ports of Call across from Allegro, single scooters US$25 per day, doubles US$39, packages, can take them to North Caicos on the ferry, Honda motorcycles, also bicycles and jeeps, T9465868, Provofuncycles @Provo.net. **Provo Rent A Car**, T9464404, rentacar@provo.net, at the airport, T9465610, a/c vehicles, jeeps, vans, recommended. **Rent-a-Buggy**, Leeward Highway, T9464158, Suzuki jeeps, and VWs. **Scooter Bob**, Turtle Cove Marina, T9464684, vans, scooters and bicycles, Mon-Sat 0900-1700, Sun 0900-1200.

Tropical Auto Rental, Tropicana Plaza at Grace Bay, T9465300. **Turks and Caicos National Car Rental**, Airport Rd, T/F9464701.

Taxi
Island's Choice Taxi, T9410409; **Nell's Taxi**, T9413228; **Paradise Taxi Co**, T9413555; Provo Taxi Association, T9465481.

❶ Directory

Providenciales *p280, map p280*
Banks FirstCaribbean International Bank, Butterfield Sq, Provo, T9464245; **Scotiabank**, Town Centre Mall, T9464750. **Medical services** MBS Group Medical Practice,

Leeward Highway, Jon Delisser Building, Mon-Fri 0830-1700, Sat 0830-1200, recompression chamber; **Grace Bay Medical Clinic** is a private clinic in the plaza on the road to the Allegro from Leeward Highway, Dr Sam Slattery, T9415252, T2310525 (mob). The government clinic on Provo is **Myrtle Rigby Health Complex**, Leeward Highway, near Down Town, T9413000, open daily. **Ambulance** services available and emergency medical air charter to USA or Nassau, full life support can be arranged, T999 or any doctor. There is no anaesthetist on Provo so surgery is done on Grand Turk, in Nassau or Miami. **Island Pharmacy**, T9464150.

Background

History The islands' first dwellers were the peaceful Taínos, who left behind ancient utensils and little else. By the middle of the 16th century not one Lucayan, as Columbus named them, remained. Like the Lucayans in the Bahamas islands, they were kidnapped for use as slaves or pearl divers, while many others died of imported diseases. The discovery of the islands, whether by Columbus in 1492 or later by Ponce de León, is hotly disputed. There is a very convincing argument that Columbus' first landfall was on Grand Turk, not Watling Island in the Bahamas, now officially named San Salvador. The infamous Caicos Banks, south of the Caicos group, where in the space of 1 km the water depth changes from 1,830 m to 9 m, claimed many of the Spanish ships lost in the central Caribbean from the 16th to the 18th century.

The Bermudan traders who settled on the islands of Grand Turk, Salt Cay and South Caicos in the 17th century used slaves to rake salt for sale to British colonies on the American mainland, and fought pirates and buccaneers for over 200 years. During the American Revolution, British loyalists found refuge on the islands, setting up cotton and sisal plantations with the labour of imported slaves. For a while, cotton and sisal from the islands were sold in New York and London, solar salt became the staple of the economy, and the Turks and Caicos thrived, but all these products encountered overwhelming competition from elsewhere. The thin soil was an added disadvantage and a hurricane in 1813 marked the demise of cotton plantations.

Following an alternation of Spanish, French and British control, the group became part of the Bahamas colony in 1766. Attempts to integrate the Turks and Caicos failed, rule from Nassau was unpopular and inefficient, and abandoned in 1848. Links with Jamaica were more developed, partly because London-Kingston boats visited frequently. The Turks and Caicos were annexed to Jamaica in 1874. After Jamaica's Independence in 1962, they were loosely associated with the Bahamas for just over 10 years until the latter became independent. At that point, the Turks and Caicos became a British Crown Colony (now a Dependent Territory). The Anglican Church maintained its links with the Bahamas, which is where the Bishop resides.

The main political parties were established in 1976: the People's Democratic Movement (PDM) and the Progressive National Party (PNP). From time to time Independence is raised as a political issue but does not have universal support.

The isolation of the Turks and Caicos and the benign neglect of the British government led to increasing use of the islands as refuelling posts by drug smugglers en route from South America to Florida. Constitutional government was suspended in

1986 after it was discovered that several Ministers were involved and direct rule from the UK was imposed while investigations continued into malpractice by other public officials. The Chief Minister and the Minister of Development were imprisoned for accepting bribes to allow drugs planes to refuel on South Caicos. The islands are still being used for trans-shipment of cocaine and other drugs.

In 1988, general elections restored constitutional government. These were won by the PDM. The April 1991 elections brought the PNP back to power, but economic austerity measures and civil service job cuts cost the PNP its mandate. The PDM, under the leadership of Derek Taylor, held power from 1995 until 2003. Declining popularity of the government led to hotly contested elections in April 2003. Initial results gave the PDM seven seats and the PNP six, but three seats were contested in court and there were rumours of illegal dealings. By-elections for two seats were held in August 2003 and were awarded to the PNP, giving them eight seats to the PDM's five. In the February 2007 elections, the PNP won 60% of the vote, gaining 13 seats against 2 for the PDM. The Premier (formerly Chief Minister) is Michael Misick, of the PNP, while Floyd Seymour is the leader of the opposition.

Only eight islands are inhabited.

Geography The Turks and Caicos comprise about 40 low-lying islands and cays covering 193 sq miles, and surrounded by one of the longest coral reefs in the world. The islands are separated by the Columbus Passage, a 22-mile channel over 7,000 ft deep, which connects the Atlantic and the Caribbean, contributing to the area's profusion of marine life. Generally, the windward sides of the islands are made up of limestone cliffs and sand dunes, while the leeward sides have greener vegetation. The south islands of Grand Turk, Salt Cay and South Caicos are very dry, having had their trees felled by salt rakers long ago to discourage rain. The other islands have slightly more rain but very little soil and most of the vegetation is scrub and cactus. The islands lie directly east of Inagua at the south tip of the Bahamas and north of Hispaniola.

Government The Turks and Caicos are a British Overseas Territory. The British monarch is Head of State, represented by a Governor. The Cabinet consists of the Governor, the Premier, six ministers appointed by the Governor from among the members of the House of Assembly, and the Attorney General. The unicameral House of Assembly has 21 seats, of which 15 are popularly elected members, who serve for four years. In 2006 a new constitution created the post of Premier, abolishing the role of Chief Minister.

Economy The traditional economic activity, salt production, ceased in 1964, and for two decades there was little to generate legal income apart from fishing, government employment and some tourism. Natural resources are limited, even water has to be strictly conserved. Agriculture is almost non-existent. Practically all consumer goods and most foodstuffs are imported. The lack of major employment activities led in the 1960s and 1970s to thousands of local people emigrating to the nearby Bahamas or the USA to seek work. This trend has now been reversed as the economy has improved and the population is rising. Belongers have returned to work in the tourist industry and professionals trained abroad are returning to work as lawyers, accountants, etc. Poorly paid skilled and unskilled labour, much of it illegal, comes from Haiti and the Dominican Republic.

There is no income tax, company tax, exchange control or restriction on the nationality or residence of shareholders or directors. New legislation and the creation of the Offshore Finance Centre Unit (OFCU) were designed to regulate the growth of offshore finance and encourage banking, insurance and trust companies.

Turks & Caicos Islands Background

People The main islands of the Turks group, Grand Turk and Salt Cay, shelter 20% of the colony's 7,901 'belongers', as the islanders call themselves, but only 15% of the total resident population of 20,000-25,000, which includes many Haitians, Dominicans and ex-pat North Americans and Europeans. The rest of the population is scattered among the larger Caicos group to the west: South Caicos, Middle Caicos, North Caicos and Providenciales, the most populous, known locally as 'Provo'.

Flora and fauna The islands support 175 resident and migrant species of birds, including flocks of greater flamingos, frigate birds, ospreys, brown pelicans, the ruby-throated humming bird, the belted kingfisher, white-billed tropic birds, black-necked stilts, snowy plovers, peregrine falcons, red-tailed hawks, northern harriers, Baltimore orioles and scarlet tanagers, and many others. *Birds of the Turks and Caicos*, by Richard Ground (Chief Justice in 2003), is available through the **National Trust office** ① *T9415710, www.nationaltrust.tc*. There are lizards, iguanas, two species of snake, including a pygmy boa, and two species of bat. The south parts of North, Middle and East Caicos have been designated an internationally important wetland under the Ramsar Convention for the protection of waterbirds, lobster, conch, flora and a fish nursery.

‡ *The islands have 11 national parks, four sanctuaries, 10 nature reserves and seven historical sites; entrance to sanctuaries by permit only.*

The **National Environment Centre**, in the Bight, Provo, is open to the public. It is also home to the **Coastal Resources Management Project** ① *T9415122*.

Dominican Republic and Haiti

Footprint features

Introduction

One island shared by two very different nations. Hispaniola was the island where Columbus first brought Spanish settlers, wiping out the Amerindians who lived there within a generation. At the end of the 17th century, the island was divided between France and Spain and from then on their paths diverged. The French colony, Saint Domingue, was highly profitable but based on the untenable basis of slavery. The Spanish colony, Santo Domingo, was less profitable, having been abandoned by Spain in favour of richer colonies in South and Central America. Nowadays the position is reversed. Having carried out a successful slave rebellion at the beginning of the 19th century, Haiti's new rulers never managed to achieve the former level of prosperity and gradually the country declined to become the poorest in the Western Hemisphere. The former Spanish colony, which called itself the Dominican Republic, remained impoverished under the rule of ruthless dictators until the 1960s, when the last of the oligarchs was assassinated and the first steps were taken towards democracy and prosperity.

Today, the Dominican Republic welcomes foreign visitors to its beach resorts and millions come each year to enjoy the sun, sea and sand, while others seeking more adventurous pastimes head into the mountains and the national parks for mountain biking, hiking, whitewater rafting and other sports. Athletes come from around the world for windsurfing and kiteboarding competitions, while in 2003 the country hosted the Pan American Games. Haiti, on the other hand, receives aid workers and peace-keeping troops and only a handful of tourists. Despite its rich Afro-French culture, its people are torn apart by political rivalries and gang warfare, while the countryside is ravaged by poverty and the hillsides are stripped bare of trees.

Dominican Republic & Haiti

★ Don't miss...

1 Santo Domingo The first European city to be built in the Western Hemisphere; packed with museums and places of historical interest as well as some lovely boutique hotels and atmospheric restaurants and bars, page 311.

2 Pico Duarte The tallest mountain in the Caribbean, covered in flourishing forests and a haven for fauna and flora. Birdwatching is rewarding in the national park, but the thrill of hiking to the top can't be beaten, page 330.

3 Cabarete Famous for world-class windsurfing and kiteboarding, Cabarete's extensive beaches and bays attract the fit and active, page 341.

4 Bahía de Samaná Humpback whales migrate here in January-March to mate and give birth, page 353.

5 La Citadelle An immense hilltop fortress overlooking the northern plain, built by Roi Henri Christophe in the 19th century, page 407.

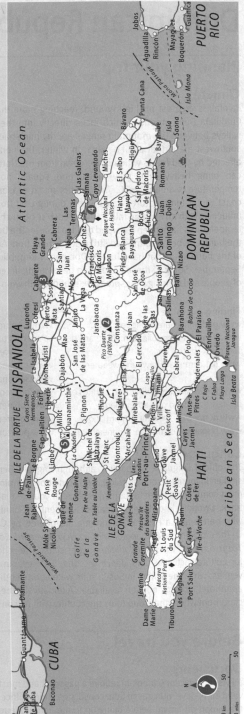

Dominican Republic

Planning your trip

Climate

Rainfall is greatest on high ground, reaching more than 2500 mm in parts of the Cordillera Septentrional, which faces directly into the northeast trade winds. The valleys between the mountain ranges are dry rain-shadow areas; some parts of the southwest are virtual semi-deserts. In winter, the northern parts of the island are affected by cold fronts which move down from the North American continent; these can bring heavy rain, grey skies, and squally northern winds. The average temperature is around 25°C. There is not much seasonal variation, although north coast winter temperatures can be cool during cold fronts. Altitude is an important influence, with an average fall of 6°C for each 1000 m above sea level. Below-freezing temperatures have been recorded on Pico Duarte. The Dominican Republic lies within the hurricane belt. Storms can strike at any time from August to November, but 60% of the hurricanes that have hit the Dominican Republic since 1871 have done so in September. Some of these have been devastating in recent years, killing thousands of people and causing widespread disruption, with wind speeds of close to 200 kph.

Finding out more

www.godominicanrepublic.com, www.dominicanrepublic.com Secretaría de Turismo websites.
www.dr1.com Daily news and weather service.
www.thedominicanrepublic.net Listings of businesses with no paid advertising.
www.domrep.ch News and information.
www.hispaniola.com A good general site.

www.DRpure.com Great for adventure sports with background information too. There are a few other local sites, such as:
www.samana.net,
www.samanaonline.com,
www.activecabarete.com,
www.cabaretekiteboarding.com,
www.cabaretewindsurfing.com,
www.puertoplataguide.com.

Language

The official language is Spanish, although English, German, French and Italian are spoken in tourist resorts by guides and some hotel employees. English is the language most commonly taught to tourism workers. If you are planning to travel off the beaten track, a working knowledge of Spanish is essential. Spanish courses of one-four weeks with dance and a cultural programme are offered by **Càlédöniâ Languages Abroad** ① *The Clockhouse, Bonnington Mill, 72 New Haven Rd, Edinburgh, EH6 5QG, Scotland, T0131-6217721, www.caledonialanguages.co.uk.* The school in Santo Domingo is best for cultural activities and dance lessons, with evening excursions to local dance venues, while the school in Sosúa suits watersports enthusiasts better. Homestays or aparthotel accommodation available. Alternatively there is a two-week travelling classroom where the group tours the country with lessons en route.

Before you travel

Documents

All visitors (except Canadian) require a **passport** and most need a **tourist card**, US$10, valid for 15 days, purchased from consulates, tourist offices, airlines on departure, or at the airport on arrival before lining up in the (long) queue for immigration. Additional charges for longer stays are US$9.30 for up to 90 days, US$15 for up to nine months, US$62 for up to a year. Canadian citizens may enter with a birth certificate or voter registration card and photo ID, but will need a passport to cash traveller's cheques, hire a car or make large credit card purchases. Citizens of Argentina, Chile, Ecuador, Iceland, Israel, Japan, Liechtenstein, Peru, South Korea, Uruguay do not need a tourist card to enter. The time limit on tourist cards is 90 days, but if necessary extensions are obtainable from **Immigration** ① *Av George Washington, Centro de Los Héroes, Santo Domingo, T8095082555, www.migracion.gov.do.* The easiest method of extending a tourist card is simply to pay the fine (variable) at the airport when leaving. You should have an outward ticket, although not always asked for.

Tourist offices overseas

Argentina, Arenales 1101 Esq Cerrito (C1061AAI), Buenos Aires, T5411-43122203, argentina@sectur.gov.do.

Belgium, Louizalaan 271, 8th floor, 1050 Brussels, T322-6461300, repdomtur@skynet.be.

Brazil, Av Sao Luis 50, Conjunto 91E-9 Andar, Edif Italia/Cantro, CEP 01046-926 Sao Paulo, T5511-21892403, andrea@republicadominicana.tur.br.

Canada, 2080 rue Crescent, Montréal, Québec, H3G 2B8, T514-4991918, montreal@sectur.gov.do; 26 Wellington St East, Suite 201, Toronto, Ontario M5E 1S2, T416-3612126, toronto@sectur.gov.do.

Chile, Augusto Leguia Sur 79, Of 1105, Las Condes, Santiago, 1562-9520540, chile@sectur.gov.do.

Colombia, Oficina 513 de la Torre A Edif, Teleport Business Park, Calle 114 7-21, Bogotá, T571-6291818, colombia@sectur.gov.do.

France, 11 rue Boudreau, Paris 75009, T331-43129191, otrepdom@aol.com.

Germany, Hochstrasse 54, 60313 Frankfurt am Main, T49-69-91397878, domtur@oal.com.

Italy, Piazza Castello 25, 20121 Milan,

T3902-8057781, italia@sectur.gov.do.

Japan, Kowa 38 Building 904, 4-12-24 Nishi-Asabu, Minaro-Ku, Tokyo 106-0031, T813-34996020. masatoshinagami@yahoo.com.

Puerto Rico, Av Ashford 890, Local C-3, Condado, San Juan, PR 00907, T787-7220881, opt_pr@yahoo.com.

Russia, C Shpalernaya 54, Of A12, 191015 St Petersburg, T812-3330952, optdom-ru@mail.ru.

Spain, General Yagüe 4, Puerta 12, Madrid 28020, T3491-4177375, espana@sectur.gov.do.

UK, 20 Hand Court, High Holborn, London, WC1V 6JF, T44-20-72427778, inglaterra@sectur.gov.do.

USA, 136E 57 St Suite 803, New York, NY 10022, T212-5881012/4, drtourismboardny@verizon.net; 561 West Diversey Building, Suite 214, Chicago, IL 60614-1643, T773-5291336/7, chicago@sectur.gov.do; 848 Brickell Av, Suite 405, Miami, Florida 33131, T305-3582899, miami@sectur.gov.do.

Venezuela, Calle Villaflor con Av Casanova, Edif Offimaker piso 1, Oficina 1-3, Sabana Grande, Caracas, T58212-7611956, oficinadeturismord@cantv.net.

Vaccinations

You should be up to date with your typhoid, tetanus and polio inoculations. The vaccine against infectious hepatitis is a good idea. Malaria prevention is recommended, as it is present in the southwest and the west of the country and unusually there was an outbreak in Punta Cana in 2004. There is also dengue fever: the Aedes mosquito breeds in urban areas and is more prevalent when there has been lots of rain. There is no cure, so prevention against bites is essential. There is rabies, so if you are at high risk get yourself vaccinated before you travel. In any case, if you are bitten seek medical help immediately.

Customs

Duty-free import permitted of 200 cigarettes or one box of cigars, plus two litres of alcoholic liquor and gift articles to the value of US$1000. Military-type clothing and food products will be confiscated on arrival. Currency in excess of US$10,000 may not be taken out of the country without special permission. Airport police are on the lookout for illegal drugs. It is illegal to bring firearms into the country.

Money

Currency The Dominican peso (RD$) is the only legal tender. The peso is divided into 100 centavos. There are coins in circulation of 25 and 50 centavos, 1, 5, 10 and 25 pesos, and notes of 10, 20, 50, 100, 500, 1000 and 2000 pesos.

Exchange The exchange rate fluctuates against the dollar and was trading at around RD$32-35=US$1 in April 2007. Banks and exchange houses (*casas de cambio*) are authorized to deal in foreign exchange. Cambios often give better rates than banks. You will be given a receipt and, with this, you can change remaining pesos back into dollars at the end of your visit (maximum 30% of dollars changed; cash obtained against a credit card does not count). There is sometimes a buyback charge. Do not rely on the airport bank being open. The US dollar is the best currency to bring. Sterling and Euro can be changed at **BanReservas**. If stuck at weekends, most hotels will change money; cash only. ATMs are an easy way to get cash and you will get close to the market rate, plus a commission of up to 5%. They are sometimes out of action at weekends and holidays and in small places they suffer from lack of maintenance and often do not work. Travellers' cheques should be denominated in US dollars; you may have difficulty changing them other than in Santo Domingo and tourist places. In Santiago, only the **Banco Popular** on Calle del Sol is authorized to change traveller's cheques.

❧ *In the countryside away from major centres, it can be difficult to change anything higher than a 100-peso note.*

Credit cards Nearly all major hotels, restaurants and stores accept most credit cards. Several banks will give cash against Visa, Mastercard or American Express cards, usually with 5% commission. It is advisable to inform your bank or credit card company before you use your card in the Dominican Republic. Some companies will put a stop on your card after you have used it twice. This is for your own protection as the Dominican Republic has a high rate of credit card fraud.

Banks The commercial banks are: **Scotiabank** (Santo Domingo and other cities), **Banco León** (Santo Domingo and other cities), **Citibank** (Santo Domingo and Santiago), **BanReservas**, **Banco Popular**, **Banco Central**, **Banco BHD**, **Banco del Progreso** and others. Money can be sent via **Western Union**, which operates through **Vimenca** but the exchange rate is up to 20% more than banks.

Getting there

Air

The main gateways are Santo Domingo, Puerto Plata, La Romana, Santiago and Punta Cana although there are other international airports with limited services. Punta Cana and La Romana are only worth flying to if you are staying at one of the all-inclusive hotels along the eastern coast. If you want to start your travels on the south coast, including the capital, then fly to Santo Domingo. For the north coast use the airport outside Puerto Plata. It is possible to fly in to one and out of the other, although that will obviously cost a little more. A new international airport opened at El Catey on the Samaná peninsula at the end of 2006, which will improve access to Las Terrenas and Samaná. ▶▶ *For details of airlines see Transport sections.*

Boat

Many passenger cruise lines from the USA, Canada and Europe call at the Dominican Republic on itineraries to various ports on Caribbean islands or the mainland. **Ferries del Caribe** has a car and passenger ferry between the Dominican Republic and Puerto Rico, with a capacity for 250 vehicles and 550 passengers. The **Millennium Express** (known as *El Ferry*) ① *in Santo Domingo, T8096884400, F8096884963; in Puerto Rico, T787-8324800, F8311810, www.ferriesdelcaribe.com*, departs Mayagüez Monday, Wednesday, Friday, 2000, 10-12 hours, departs Santo Domingo Tuesday, Thursday, Sunday, 2000, prices from US$189 return for passengers, Monday-Friday, including port tax each way, sleeper cabins available for up to four people, US$250 for a car. Discounts are available. You can arrange onward transport by bus from Mayagüez to San Juan and from Santo Domingo to **Terrabús** destinations in the Dominican Republic and Haiti.

Ports of entry Santo Domingo, Luperón, Puerto Plata, Samaná, La Romana, Punta Cana (with 24 hours' notice). **Boat documents** You must show your boat registration and documents received from the captain's port of origin, a list of passengers aboard and their passport numbers, immigration fees of US$60 for the yacht and tourist cards of US$10 per passenger. Thirty days' immigration clearance. Declare weapons and check in with Customs officials ashore at each port of entry. Do not depart from anchorage before sunrise after picking up weapons. You have to clear Customs, Agriculture and Immigration at each port. The port captain will come on board with a group of officials, each of whom have been reported by yachties to ask for 'tips' of US$20-25 to expedite the paperwork.

Travel to Haiti

Air **Caribair**, T8095426688, www.caribair.com.do, has 2 daily scheduled services between Santo Domingo and Port-au-Prince. The travel agency, **Takeoff**, T8095521333, www.takeoffweb.com, offers flights to Port-au-Prince from Santo Domingo (Joaquín Balaguer, US$150), Punta Cana (US$249), Samaná (Arroyo Barril, US$215). **Vol Air**, www.volair-dr.com, has flights from Santo Domingo and Santiago to Cap Haitien Mon, Wed, Fri, for US$130 one way.

Bus The easiest way is with **Terrabús** (T8094721080, terminal at Av 27 de Febrero esq Anacaona, Plaza Criolla), **Caribe Tours** (T8092214422, terminal at Av 27 de Febrero esq Leopoldo Navarro) (both Dominican) or **Capital Coach Line** (Haitian). They all charge US$40 one way, US$75 return, child reductions, daily service. They deal with all immigration and other formalities so all you have to do is get off the bus to take care of Dominican customs. Excellent service, efficient, comfortable a/c buses, snacks and drinks provided, recommended.

There are cheaper options but they take longer and are less comfortable. A syndicate of Dominican operators runs 30-seat buses from outside the Haitian embassy, 33 Av Juan Sánchez Ramírez, just off Av Máximo Gómez between Independencia and Bolívar. 3-4 leave every morning Mon-Fri 1100-1200 and take about 7 hrs or longer to Port-au-Prince, depending on the amount of merchandise to be inspected by Customs at the border. They return next day. Your passport must be processed in the embassy before boarding the bus. Be quick on arriving at the embassy, get through the gates, ignoring hangers on and cries of 'passport', unless you want to wait in the street and pay someone else US$10 to take your passport in. All the passports are processed together. Payments may be required. Do not wear shorts. Alternatively, take a minibus to Jimaní from near the bridge over the Río Seco in the centre of Santo Domingo, 6-8 hrs; get a lift up to the Haitian border and then get overcharged by Haitian youths on mopeds who take you across 3 km of no-man's-land for US$3. From Haitian immigration take a lorry-bus to Port-au-Prince, 3-4 hrs, very dusty. You can also take Dominican public transport to Dajabón, cross to Ounaminthe and continue to Cap Haïtien. If driving to Haiti you must get a vehicle permit at the Foreign Ministry (T8095331424). Hire cars

> ‡ *Remember there is a 1-hr time difference between Haiti (GMT-5) and the Dominican Republic (GMT-4).*

are not allowed across the border. The drive from Santo Domingo to Port-au-Prince takes about 6 hrs. Buy gourdes from money changers outside the embassy, or at the border, but no more than US$50-worth, rates are much better in Haiti. Also take US$25 for border taxes, which have to be paid in dollars cash.

Touching down

Airport information

There are several airports: **Las Américas**, Santo Domingo, T8095490450/80, **Dr Joaquín Balaguer**, at El Higuero/La Isabela, Santo Domingo, T8098264003, **Gregorio Luperón**, Puerto Plata, T8095860331, **Arroyo Barril**, Samaná, T8092482566, the new **Prof Juan Bosch (El Catey)** airport, Samaná, www.elcatey.com, **Cibao**, Santiago, T8095751140, **La Romana International Airport**, T8098139000, **Punta Cana**, Higüey, T8099592376, and **María Montéz**, Barahona, T8095244144).

Tourist information

The head office of the **Secretaría de Estado de Turismo** ① *Edificio de Oficinas Gubernamentales, Av México esq 30 de Marzo, Ala 'D', T8092214660, F8096823806, sectur@verizon.net.do*, near the Palacio Nacional, but there are no facilities for dealing with the general public. There are small tourist offices in most towns, though, and there are offices at **Las Américas International Airport**, in Santo Domingo in the colonial city on the first floor of the Palacio Borgella near the Cathedral (T8096863858), **Gregorio Luperón Airport** at Puerto Plata, in Puerto Plata (Av El Teleférico, T8099700501), in Santiago (Ayuntamiento, T8095825885), Barahona (T8095243650), Jimaní (T8092483000), Samaná (T8095382332), Boca Chica (T8095235106), San Pedro de Macorís (T8095293644), La Romana (T8095506922), Baní (T8095226018), San Cristóbal (T8095283533), Pedernales (T8095240409), Higüey (T8095542672), El Seíbo (T8095523402), Sosúa (T8095712254), Cabarete (T8095710962), Gaspar Hernández (T8095872485), Río San Juan (T8095892831), Nagua (T8095843862), Las Terrenas (T8092406363), Luperón (T8095718303), Monte Cristi (T8095792254), La Vega (T8092421289), Bonao (T8095253941), Constanza (T8095392900).

Guides The Asociación de Guías de Turismo de la República Dominicana (Asoguiturd) ① *Calle Vicente C Duarte 3, Apdo Postal 21360, Santo Domingo, T8096820209*. Nearly all their members speak English and other languages. A two-hour tour of colonial Santo Domingo will cost about US$15, or US$50 for a full day, depending on the number of people and what they want to do. Outside the historic buildings in Santo Domingo, on the beaches and at other tourist attractions, visitors will be approached by unofficial English-speaking guides, sellers of rum, women or drugs. The only value in taking an unofficial guide is to deter others from pestering you. Unofficial guides often refuse to give prices in advance, saying 'pay what you want' and then at the end, if they are not happy, they make a scene and threaten to tell the police that you had approached them for drugs, etc. ▶▶ *See also Tour operators, page 325.*

Local customs and laws

It is advisable to take at least one smart outfit with you so that you can dress up in the evening. Shorts are not permitted in the cathedral in Santo Domingo. It is polite to ask before taking photos of people. Normally they will agree cheerfully, but some may ask for a payment. **Note** Swim wear is for the beach only.

Safety

On no account change money on the streets. Banks and *cambios* offer the market rate and are safer. Be careful with 'helpers' at the airports, who speed your progress through the queues and then charge US$15-20 for their services. Single men have complained

Touching down

Business hours Offices: 0830-1230, 1430-1630; some offices and shops work 0930-1730 Mon-Fri, 0800-1300 Sat. **Banks:** 0830-1500 Mon-Fri. Government offices 0730-1430. **Shops:** normally 0800-1900, some open all day Sat and mornings on Sun and holidays. Most shops in tourist areas stay open through the siesta and on Sun.

Clothing Light clothing, preferably cotton, is best all year round. It is recommended to take one formal outfit since some hotels and night-clubs do not permit casual dress.

Currency The Dominican peso (RD$) is the only legal tender.

Departure tax US$20.

Emergency numbers T911.

Official time Atlantic Standard Time, four hours behind GMT, one hour ahead of EST.

Tipping In addition to the 10% service and 16% VAT charge in restaurants, it is customary in the nicer, sit down restaurants to give an extra tip of about 10%, depending on service. Porters receive US$0.50 per bag; taxi drivers, público drivers and garage attendants are not usually tipped.

Voltage 110 volts, 60 cycles AC current. American-type, flat-pin plugs are used. There are frequent power cuts, often for several hours, so take a torch with you when you go out at night. Many establishments have their own (often noisy) generators.

Weights and measures Officially metric, but business is often done on a pound/yard/US gallon basis. Land areas in cities are measured by square metres, but in the countryside by the tarea, one of which equals 624 sq m.

of the massive presence of pimps and prostitutes. Be prepared to say 'no' a lot. These problems do not occur in rural areas and small towns, where travellers have been impressed with the open and welcoming nature of the Dominicans. Violent crime against tourists is rare but, as anywhere, watch your money and valuables in cities at night and on beaches. The streets of Santo Domingo are not considered safe after 2300. Purse snatchers on motorcycles operate in cities. Keep away from anything to do with illegal drugs. You may be set up and find yourself facing an extended stay in a Dominican prison. Beware of drug-pushers on the Malecón in Santo Domingo and near the Cathedral in Puerto Plata.

Politur, the Tourist Police, has a toll-free phone 1-200-3500, or at the office in Santo Domingo T8092222036/8096896464. There are also Politur offices in Puerto Plata, Luperón, Sosúa, Cabarete, Río San Juan, Las Terrenas, Samaná, Jarabacoa, Barahona, Boca Chica, Juan Dolio, La Romana, Bávaro, and Las Américas international airport. If you have anything stolen go to a police station to report the crime and get a signed, stamped declaration for your insurance company.

Getting around

Air

Several companies offer internal air taxi or charter services, all based at Dr Joaquín Balaguer International Airport at Higuero/La Isabela, Santo Domingo.

Air Santo Domingo, Av 27 de Febrero 272, esq Seminario, T8096838006, has regular flights between Santo Domingo (Dr Joaquín Balaguer, T8096834535, and Las Américas, T8095491110) and Puerto Plata (US$56, daily, T8095860385), Punta Cana (US$56, daily, T8092211170), Arroyo Barril and El Portillo, Samaná (US$55, Mon-Sat,

T8092406571); also flights from Puerto Plata to Punta Cana (US$66, daily). Fly drive available from US$100.

Caribair, T8095426688, www.caribair.com.do, has offices in all national airports and a fleet including air ambulance and helicopters. They fly to Barahona, Constanza, Dajabón, Higuey, La Romana, Monte Cristi, Pedernales, Puerto Plata, Samaná (El Portillo), Samaná (Arroyo Barril), San Isidro, Santiago, Santo Domingo (Joaquín Balaguer), Santo Domingo (Las Américas). If there isn't a proper airport they will get you there by helicopter. They also fly to Port-au-Prince twice a day and to Aruba twice a week.

Air Century, T8095676778, www.aircentury.com.

AERODOMCA, T8095671195, www.aerodomca.com. Charter flights by plane or helicopter all over the country and 3 daily flights from Santo Domingo to El Portillo, US$75.

Vol Air, T8095488686, www.volair-dr.com, flies between Santo Domingo, Punta Cana, El Portillo and Cap Haitien.

Coturisca, T8095677211. Operates a fleet of helicopters and planes.

Road

Bus Services between most towns are efficient and inexpensive. In rural areas it can be easy to find a *guagua* (minibus or pick-up) but they are usually filled to the point where you cannot move your legs and luggage is an uncomfortable inconvenience. There are also cars (*carros/públicos*) on some of these routes, which are equally dilapidated and crowded. It is possible to buy an extra seat in a *carro* or *guagua* to make yourself more comfortable. Long-distance bus services are very good, with a wide network and several different companies. The three most comfortable and reliable are **Metro, Caribe Tours** and **Terrabús**.

Bus services

Metro Expreso, first class (T8092270101 in Santo Domingo, T8095866062 in Puerto Plata, T8095829111 in Santiago, www.metrost .com) operate from Calle Hatuey esq Av Winston Churchill, near 27 de Febrero and have buses to Santiago (US$8) and Puerto Plata (US$9).

Caribe Tours (T8092214422) operates from Av 27 de Febrero esq Leopoldo Navarro; the bus terminal, with ticket office, café, information desk, ATM (Visa, Electron, Plus), cambio and waiting area with TV; most of their services are in a/c buses, with video and toilet, punctual, good service, no smoking (US$3.50 to La Vega, US$5.30 to Jarabacoa, US$6 to Santiago, US$6 to Barahona, US$8 to Dajabón, Puerto Plata, Monte Cristi, Sosúa, Sánchez, Samaná or Río San Juan); they run to all parts except east of Santo Domingo.

Terrabús, Plaza Criolla, Anacaona 15, T8094721080, is an international company with services to Haiti and Puerto Rico (via the ferry, see above), but it also has linked domestic routes to Santiago (T8095873000), Puerto Plata (T8095861977) and Sosúa (T8095711274). Their buses are comfortable, offering TV, snacks, pillows and blankets, while their terminals have food shops, toilets, television and children's play area.

Transporte del Cibao, Caracas 112, San Carlos, after the Plaza Lama parking lot, T8096857210, to Puerto Plata, cheaper at US$5.60, Sosúa US$5.90, Santiago US$3.85.

Transporte Espinal, Paris 69, T8095601363, US$4.85 to Santiago.

La Covacha buses leave from Parque Enriquillo (Av Duarte and Ravelo) for the east: La Romana, Higüey, Nagua, San Pedro de Macorís, Hato Mayor, Miches, etc.

Astrapu does the same routes.

Expresos Moto Saad, Av Independencia near Parque Independencia runs 12 daily buses to Bonao, La Vega and Santiago.

Línea Sur (T8096827682) runs to San Juan, Barahona, Azua and Haiti. Offices in other towns, see text.

Car A valid driving licence from your country of origin or an international licence is accepted for three months. Dominicans drive on the right. Many of them do not have licences. The Autopista Duarte is a good, four-lane highway between Santo Domingo and Santiago, but dangerous. It is used by bicycles and horse-drawn carts as well as motorized vehicles, while drivers switch from one lane to the other without warning.

Lots of shopping opportunities by the roadside contribute to the hazards, with vehicles swerving on and off the road. The **Autovía del Este** is an excellent road from Santo Domingo out to the east, with good access roads to Higüey, Punta Cana Airport, Hato Mayor and Sabana de la Mar. A new road is being built from Santo Domingo to Samaná, which should be completed by end-2007 and cut driving times dramatically. Minor roads and many city streets are in poor condition with lots of potholes. The speed limit for city driving is 40 kmph, for suburban areas 60 kmph and on main roads 80 kmph. Service stations generally close at 1800, although there are now some offering 24-hour service. Gasoline prices are around US$4.30 for super unleaded, US$3.15 for diesel. Most police or military posts have 'sleeping policemen', speed humps, usually unmarked, outside them. In towns there are often 'ditches' at road junctions, which need as much care as humps. At night look out for poorly lighted, or lightless vehicles. Many *motoconchos* have no lights. There are tolls on all principal roads out of the capital: RD$30 (US$0.90), exact change needed. The toll (peaje) is paid once for a round trip. Road signs are very poor: a detailed map is essential, plus a knowledge of Spanish for asking directions. Expect to be stopped by the police at the entrance to and exit from towns (normally brief and courteous), at junctions in towns, or any speed-restricted area.

❢ *Local drivers can be erratic; be alert. Hand signals mean only 'I am about to do something', nothing more specific than that.*

Car hire Avoid the cheapest companies because their vehicles are not usually trustworthy. Prices for small vehicles start at US$40 per day but can be as much as US$90. Weekly rates are better value. Credit cards are widely accepted; the cash deposit is normally twice the sum of the contract. The minimum age for hiring a car is usually 25, although some companies will rent to 20 year olds; maximum period for driving is 90 days. Mopeds and motorcycles are everywhere and are very noisy. Most beach resorts hire motorcycles for US$15-35 a day. By law, the driver of a motorcycle must wear a crash helmet; passengers are not required to wear one.

Taxi If travelling by private taxi, bargaining is very important. In Santo Domingo, **Apolo Taxi**, T8095370000, is recommended, cheap, friendly and efficient. Motorcyclists (*motoconchos*) also offer a taxi service and take several passengers on pillion. In some towns, eg Samaná, *motoconchos* and cyclists pull four-seater covered rickshaws. During the day a short distance costs US$0.45 for one passenger. For longer journeys negotiate fare first. During the night fares double. There are usually fixed *público* rates (see under Santo Domingo) between cities, so inquire first. They can take two passengers in front and four on the back seat, regardless of the size of the car, so the ride is often uncomfortable, but friendly.

❢ *Motoconchos can be found on all the main streets and near the beaches.*

Maps **Berndtson & Berndtson** publish a good road map, 1:600,000, with detail on Santo Domingo, Puerto Plata and Santiago, available locally for US$5. **Scheidig** publishes the *Mapa Geográfica de la República Dominicana*, which is approved by the Instituto Geográfico Universitario and available for US$7 at **Gaar** ① *Arzobispo Nouel esq Espaillat, Santo Domingo, Mon-Fri 0830-1900, Sat 0930-1500.*

Sleeping

There is a wide range of accommodation, from the four- or five-star, all-inclusive beach resorts run by international companies, to simple lodgings for local travelling salesmen. The cheaper all-inclusive hotels usually offer buffet food and local alcoholic drinks (rum and beer), which can get boring after a few days; you get what you pay for. In Santo Domingo the string of four- or five-star hotels along the Malecón are designed to cater for businessmen, diplomats and politicians and are of international standard, with business centres, elegant restaurants, casinos and conference centres. Note that five-star hotels charge an average of US$140 room only, plus 26% tax. In aparthotels, the average price is US$130 for two, but this can be negotiated down for long stays.

‼ *All hotels charge the 26% tax; made up of 16% VAT and 10% service.*

There are plenty of nice places to stay in the **A** range, which offer peace and quiet, good food and comfortable rooms in pleasant locations. In more modest guesthouses, a weekly or monthly rate, with discount, can be arranged. Hotels with rooms for less than US$30 will be basic with erratic plumbing and electricity; check the lock on the door.

Eating

Food

Like most Caribbean cooking, local food tends to be calorific and spicy. The usual starches, rice, yams and plantains, underpin most meals, while chips/fries are usually also available. Dominicans like their food well seasoned, so sauces include a good deal of garlic, pepper and oregano. Strangely, the staple of *comida criolla* (Creole cooking) is the dish known as *bandera dominicana* (the Dominican flag), a colourful arrangement of stewed beef, rice, plantains and red beans, which is actually rather unspicy. More exotic and challenging is the legendary *sancocho* or *salcocho prieto*, a hearty stew made of six or seven different types of meat as well as vegetables. Even traditional Dominican breakfasts can be a serious affair. The dish *mangú* is mashed plantain, drizzled with oil and accompanied by fried onions. Goat meat is a great favourite and usually comes either as roast (*chivo asado*) or stewed (*chivo guisado*). A *locrio* is a rice dish, accompanied by meat, chicken or sausages, and the formidable *mondongo* is a tripe stew. Another local speciality is the *asopao*, somewhere between a soup and a pilau-style rice dish (sometimes unappetizingly translated as soupy rice) that is served with fish, shrimp or chicken. The ubiquitous street snacks such as *pastelitos* (pasties or turnovers filled with minced beef, chicken or cheese) are fried according to demand, as are *quipes* (cracked-wheat fritters with a meat filling) or *platanitos* (hot plantain crisps). *Tostones*, or twice-fried slices of plantain, are often served as a side dish.

Most Dominican restaurants assume their customers to be carnivorous and the number of vegetarian restaurants is still limited. Fresh fruit is plentiful all year round and changes according to season. *Lechoza* (papaya) is commonly served at breakfast, as is *guineo* (sweet banana), *naranja* (orange), *piña* (pineapple) and mango. More unusual are *jagua* (custard apple), *caimito* and *mamey*. Many *cafeterías* serve delicious fresh milk shakes (*batidas*), made out of any of these fruits, water and milk (optional, *con leche*).

Drink

Statistics reveal that Dominicans account for one of the world's highest per capita consumptions of alcohol, and a look around any *colmado* (corner store) will confirm this fact. The Presidente brand of lager beer comes in two sizes (*pequeño* or *grande*) and seems to enjoy a near monopoly. Other beers such as Quisqueya and Bohemia are much less visible. *Mamajuana* is a home-made spiced rum mixed with honey and sweet wine, sold in markets and on street corners, frequently called the Dominican viagra. There are many rums (the most popular brands are Barceló, Brugal and Bermúdez). Light rum (*blanco*) is the driest and has the highest proof, usually mixed with fruit juice or other soft drink (*refresco*). Watch out for cocktails mixed with 151° proof rum. Amber (*amarillo*) or gold (*dorado*) is aged at least a year in an oak barrel and has a lower proof and more flavour, while dark rum (*añejo*) is aged for several years and is smooth enough, like a brandy, to be drunk neat or with ice and lime. **Brugal** allows visitors to tour its bottling plant in Puerto Plata, on Av Luis Genebra, just before the entrance to the town, and offers free daiquiris. In a discothèque, *un servicio* is a ½ litre bottle of rum with a bucket of ice and *refrescos*. In rural areas this costs US$3-4, but in cities rises to US$15. Despite being a major coffee-producer, the country does not always offer visitors good coffee, and much of what is served in hotels is either American-style watery instant or over-stewed and over-strong. Good coffee is available in small *comedores*, *cafeterías* and even from street vendors, who sell a small, dark shot for a few pesos.

Festivals and events

Each town's saint's day is celebrated with several days of festivities known as *patronales*.

1 Jan New Year is celebrated in the capital on Av Francisco Alberto Caamaño Deñó (formerly Av del Puerto) beside the river. The major bands and orchestras of the country give a free concert, which attracts thousands of people. The celebration ends with fireworks and the whole area becomes a huge disco.

6 Jan Epiphany.

21 Jan Day of the Virgen de la Altagracia, spiritual mother of the Dominicans, is celebrated with *velaciones*, or night-long vigils, and African-influenced singing and music, found in many towns. Higüey is the site of a mass pilgrimage and huge all-night party.

26 Jan Duarte Day.

27 Feb Independence Day.

End Feb Carnival (www.carnaval.com.do) is notable in Santo Domingo for the parade along the Malecón. Carnival in Santiago de los Caballeros is very colourful; its central character is the piglet, which represents the devil.

On Sun in Feb at Monte Cristi there are the festivals of the Toros versus the Civiles. La Vega also celebrates for several Sun prior to Lent.

Mar/Apr Holy Week is the most important holiday time for Dominicans, when there are processions and festivities such as the *guloyas* in San Pedro de Macorís, the mystical-religious *ga-ga* in sugar cane villages and the *cachúas* in Cabral in the southwest.

Apr/May Santo Domingo International Book Fair held in the Plaza de la Cultura, with free concerts and other cultural events. 2.5 million people visited in 2007.

1 May Labour Day.

May/Jun Corpus Christi.

Jul Merengue Festival (see Culture, page 379), includes festivals of gastronomy, cocktails, and exhibitions of handicrafts and fruit.

16 Aug Restoration Day parades.

24 Sep Our Lady of Las Mercedes.

Last week Sep Sosúa's annual Merengue Festival.

Nov Puerto Plata has an annual Merengue Festival on the Malecón La Puntilla.

25 Dec Christmas Day.

Shopping

The native amber is sold throughout the country. Do not buy amber on the street, it will as likely as not be plastic. Real amber fluoresces under ultra violet light (most reputable shops have a UV light); it floats in saltwater; if rubbed it produces static electricity; except for the very best pieces it is not absolutely pure, streaks, bits of dirt, etc, are common. Larimar, a sea-blue stone found only in the Dominican Republic, and red and black coral are also available (remember that coral is protected). Other souvenirs are leather goods, basketware, weavings and onyx jewellery. The ceramic muñeca sin rostro (faceless doll) has become a sort of symbol of the Dominican Republic. Paintings and other art work are on sale

If you are taken into a shop by a guide you can expect to pay a premium so that he gets his commission.

everywhere, but beware of the mass-produced Haitian-style naive art. Thousands of these brightly coloured, low-quality paintings are churned out for sale to tourists. Good Dominican art is for sale in the Santo Domingo galleries or you can buy direct from artists in Jarabacoa. There are excellent **cigars, rum** and **coffee** at very reasonable prices. Bargaining is acceptable in markets but rarely in shops. You will not get much of a discount but it is worth a try, particularly if you are buying in bulk.

Sport and activities

Cycling

The Dominican Republic has miles of dirt roads and endless mule trails, making it a paradise for mountain bikers. There is also some good road biking if you don't mind sharing the roads with trucks, mules, motorbikes and *guaguas*. There are hundreds of great rides in the mountains and along coastal routes. These can change after hurricanes and rain storms. You can bike all year round. It is hottest from 1200-1500, so if you want to cover large distances get an early start and take a long lunch break. In the mountains it is hot during the day, but gets cool at night, so dressing in layers and having warm clothing for after sunset is important. Good rain gear is also recommended. Carry at least two water bottles and make sure you drink more than you think you need.

> ❣ The scenery is breathtaking and the locals are so friendly that you may have a hard time making any great distance in one day, due to constant photo stops and invitation for coffee.

Bike rental There are only a few places to rent mountain bikes, including **Iguana Mama** based in Cabarete, and **Rancho Baiguate** in Jarabacoa. Sometimes some of the local bike shops have bikes to rent. Equipment at hotels is often not well maintained; this doesn't mean that they are not great bikes for a coastal cruise, but anyone wanting a real mountain bike adventure should not be fooled into thinking that they have a suitable bike at their hotel.

Beaches and watersports

According to UNESCO, the Dominican Republic has some of the best beaches in the world: white sand, coconut palms and many with a profusion of green vegetation. They vary enormously in development, cleanliness, price of facilities, number of hawkers and so on. Boca Chica and Juan Dolio, for instance, are very touristy and not suitable for anyone seeking peace and quiet (except mid-week out of season). The best-known beaches are in the east of the Republic, including: Boca Chica, Juan Dolio, Guayacanes and Villas del Mar in San Pedro de Macorís; Minitas (**Casa de Campo**, La Romana), Bayahibe, Macao, Bávaro and Punta Cana in the far east, all taken up by resort hotels. Cayo Levantado, an islet with one hotel where the beach is used by day-trippers, Las Terrenas, Playa Bonita, Playa Rincón, Playa Portillo and Las Galeras, are all on the Samaná peninsula and hardly ever crowded. On the north coast, Playa Diamante at Cabrera, Playa Grande and Laguna Grí-Grí at Río San Juan, where you can also visit the lovely beaches of Puerto Escondido, Punta Preciosa in

the Bahía Escocesa and Cabo Francés Viejo. East of Puerto Plata, recommended,
although fully developed, beaches include Cabarete, Sosúa and Playa Dorada. West
of Puerto Plata are Costambar, Cofresí, and several smaller beaches. Towards the
northwest and the Haitian border there are uncluttered beaches at Bahía de Luperón,
Playa El Morro, Punta Rucia, Cayos los Siete Hermanos and Estero Hondo. In the
southwest the best beaches are Las Salinas, Monte Río, Palmar de Ocoa, Najayo,
Nigua, Palenque, Nizao and those south and west of Barahona, including the
fabulous Playa las Aguilas. This area is rather neglected as far as tourism is concerned
but popular with people from Santo Domingo and at weekends the beaches can get
busy and noisy with those escaping the capital.

Watersports are available on most beaches east of Santo Domingo and along the
north coast, but you are less likely to find facilities in the southwest except in certain
places like Las Salinas, where windsurfing is popular.

Windsurfing/Kiteboarding Cabarete, near Sosúa, is one of the best windsurfing
and kiteboardingplaces in the world, attracting international competitors to
tournaments there. Other centres are Playa Salinas (Baní), Boca Chica and Puerto
Plata, while most beach hotels offer windsurfing facilities. Cabarete is the place to
be in June, when the town is taken over by serious competitors for the annual
Kiteboarding World Cup ① www.cabaretekiteboarding.com and then **Cabarete Race
Week** ① www.cabaretewindsurfing.com. The winds are at their best at this time of year
attracting both professional and amateur racers. There are lots of competitions, fiestas
and other events, contact **Vela** ① T8095710805, for information. Although the strength
of the wind varies throughout the year, windsurfing/kiteboarding is nearly always
possible. Generally the mornings are calm, but by the afternoon the bay is full of sails
flitting about like butterflies on a puddle. The schools are all good, with excellent
equipment. They do not all stock the same, so if you have a preference it is worth
contacting them in advance to see what they can supply. Most of them stock other
watersports equipment too, such as surf boards and kayaks.

Surfing Guibia is a great surfing beach, but it is full of garbage and oil from the ships
going to Ozama. Other surf beaches include Baoruco and Playa Pato in Barahona, La
Preciosa, La Pasa and Playa Grande in Río San Juan, El Encuentro and El Canal in
Cabarete, Sosúa Bay and La Boca in Sosúa, La Puntilla in Puerto Plata, Cofresí west of
Puerto Plata, and El Macao near Bávaro in the east.

Diving
There is good diving all round the island despite there being relatively few underwater
parks. The coral in most places is in good condition and the underwater landscape is
varied and interesting. Offshore, the tropical reef provides a
diversity of wildlife which you can see by scuba diving,
snorkelling or taking a glass bottomed boat trip. There are over
50 species of hard coral (the form that builds reefs) with a variety
of sizes and colours. Among the most dramatic are the staghorn and elkhorn corals
which are found on the more exposed outer reefs. Brain coral forms massive round
structures up to 2 m high, while pillar coral forms columns which reach a similar
height. Soft corals, which include black corals (protected by CITES), sea fans and
gorgonians, colonize the surface of the hard coral adding colour and variety.
Associated with these structures is a host of animals and plants. The quantity of fish
varies from place to place, depending on the local fishing industry, as some areas
have depleted stocks because of spearfishing. Nevertheless, in Dominican waters
you can see whales, dolphins, grouper, barracuda and other large pelagics, as well as
lots of colourful reef fish, turtles and invertebrates.

In the Puerto Plata area of the north coast, the diving is best around Sosúa. It is

Snorkelling is good and many dive boats offer snorkelling excursions.

particularly good for first time divers, with sandy spots, reefs and interesting rock formations, while for more experienced divers there are tunnels, chimneys, overhangs and walls. Some sites are virgin, but many are fished out. In places the coral has been badly damaged and broken by overdiving. The best time of year is usually May to September, when the sea is calm and the visibility good. In high season, December to April, there can often be winds and rain which stir up the sand, reduce visibility and bring in a lot of rubbish which litters the dive sites. More

From Puerto Plata to Cabarete there are 16 or 17 dive operations, but you need to ask lots of questions to establish their safety record, standard of equipment and teaching ability.

conservation-minded divers should head further east to Río San Juan, where there are plans to make the area offshore of the Laguna Grí Grí an underwater park. There are varied dive sites for beginners or intermediate divers and the coral is in good condition. Lots of reef fish can be seen, and if you go over the wall you are likely to spot larger life such as barracuda. At the beginning of the year whales are sometimes seen, usually humpbacks during their migration and breeding season. The Samaná peninsula offers rewarding diving on its north side and there are several dive shops at Las Terrenas and at Las Galeras. In season some of them offer whale watching as well as diving. There are dive sites all around the bays and headlands, including wrecks, caves, drop-offs and reefs.

Bayahibe on the southeast coast is good for independent divers as there is reasonable, cheap accommodation and a good, German-run dive shop offering tailor-made programmes into the national park. There are also several all-inclusive resorts with their own dive shops if you want to stay in more upmarket lodgings. The National Park offers some of the best diving in the country; the reef is in good condition, and although local fishermen are still going in and spearfishing, it is not overfished. There are nice dive sites all along the coast to Saona island, in the park, with plentiful and colourful underwater life. Catalina island, with its wall and coral gardens, is a big attraction here but there is also Catalinita, north of Saona island, about one hour by boat from Bayahibe, where you can find sharks and rays, while dolphins will accompany you on your route. Nearer to Santo Domingo is La Caleta underwater park which has good reef and wreck diving, with two deliberately sunk boats close to each other. There are no dive shops at La Caleta, most divers come on trips from nearby Boca Chica or from Santo Domingo.

Dive operators Most dive operations in the Dominican Republic offer tuition in a variety of languages. PADI is the most widely offered instruction, although CMAS and others are available. A PADI Open Water certification can cost anything from US$300 to US$400, while a two-tank boat dive for qualified divers varies from US$60 to US$75, so it is worth shopping around. In case of emergencies, those with DAN insurance will be flown out to Miami. There is a recompression chamber at the Hospital Dario Contreras in Santo Domingo, but there is no one to operate it, so the nearest is in Puerto Rico. A chamber is planned for the new hospital in the Punta Cana/Bávaro area.

Fishing

Several international billfish tournaments are held each year, including ESPN's Billfish Xtreme Tournament at Punta Cana Resort Club. Several world records have been broken in the waters surrounding the country. Off the north coast, white marlin is abundant May-August; blue marlin and tuna in July-August; and sailfish in November-April. Wahoo, king mackerel and dorado (mahi mahi) can be found year-round. Off the south coast, white and blue marlin, dolphin fish and barracuda visit June-December, while sailfish and wahoo come October-January. There is also freshwater lake and river fishing. One of the best locations is Lake Hatillo, a reservoir near Cotui which contains large quantities of bass. Deep sea fishing charters in the Punta Cana area can be arranged with **Punta Cana Fishing Charters**, full day, up to 10 people and 7 fishing lines, or US$590 for a half day; **Mike's Marina Fishing Charters**, www.mikesmarina.info, based at El Cortecito, Bávaro, with full-day charters from the dock at Punta Cana Marina, same prices, or US$90pp split charter for four hours. Fishing charters are available at all the marinas (see below, Sailing).

Golf

There are over two dozen golf courses with more being built or renovated, many more than any other country in the Caribbean. All the biggest and newest resorts have a golf course attached and golf is included in many package holidays. The three most famous golf courses are the **Teeth of the Dog**, at Casa de Campo, **Playa Grande**, near Río San Juan, and **Playa Dorada**, near Puerto Plata. The first is a Pete Dye-designed masterpiece with eight holes right on the sea and judged one of the most beautiful par 72 championship courses in the world. Next to it is **The Links**, par 71, and the **Romana Country Club** (members only, par 72) and a new par 72 course at **Altos de Chavón**. **Playa Grande** was designed by Robert Trent Jones Sr and has 10 of its holes along the coast on top of cliffs but none is far from the sea. **Playa Dorada** was also designed by Robert Trent Jones Sr as part of a complex of all-inclusive hotels outside Puerto Plata. There are many courses around Santo Domingo, of the country club variety, offering tennis and swimming and social activities for their members. Other 18-hole courses include **Las Aromas** in Santiago, which is hilly, with lovely views of the Cibao valley, wide fairways and lots of trees. In the **Bávaro** area there are several courses at the resort hotels and at **Punta Cana** a Pete Dye course runs between the **Punta Cana Beach Resort** and the **Club Med** (www.puntacana.com). More are being built, including one on the Samaná peninsula and three at the AtlanticA development at Luperón on the north coast.

Golf is big business here, with swathes of the coast east of Santo Domingo and along the north coast devoted to the sport.

The **Dominican Golf Association** organizes tournaments all year round, T8094764898. For information about courses, tournaments, holidays, tours, pros, club membership, etc, T8092485263, F8092482287.

Hiking

The Dominican Republic provides ideal conditions for medium-distance walking in the tropics. Distances and temperatures are manageable. Road transport, accommodation, restaurants and rum shops are all within convenient reach. Nevertheless, the illusion of remoteness can sometimes be complete. The two highest peaks in the Caribbean are here: **Pico Duarte** (3087 m) and **La Pelona** (3082 m), side by side in the Cordillera Central. Hiking up Pico Duarte is now a major attraction. Although most people start from the park entrance at La Ciénaga, there are other, longer routes you can take. There is a fee of US$1.50 to enter any national park in the Republic and you must always be accompanied by a guide, who will bring food and water and mules to carry your bags and the provisions. The guides are well trained and highly experienced, but they only speak Spanish. Other areas for rewarding hiking are around **Jarabacoa**, **Constanza** and in the **Valle Nuevo National Park**, while easy climbs can be done up **Pico Yaque**, **Mt Isabel de Torres** outside Puerto Plata, or in the **Sierra de Bahoruco** in the southwest. Wherever you are in the country you will be able to find walking opportunities in the many ranges of hills and mountains, or even along the beach for a few kilometres. In rural areas farms and villages are reached by dirt tracks, rather than roads, which are proving popular with mountain bikers, horse riders and hikers. You may be greeted as a curiosity by local children but everyone will be pleased to see you and refreshments can usually be sought at a *colmado*, the village shop and bar. There are no large scale, reliable maps for walkers, although you can pick up regional

Walking sticks are advised, particularly if it has been raining and the tracks are slippery or muddy.

maps from people like **Iguana Mama** in Cabarete (see page 349). You will need to carry plenty of water. Do not drink from the rivers unless you have a purification system with you. Information can be found at www.DRpure.com, www.hispaniola .com/ whitewater, and www.rancho baiguate.com.

Horse riding

Riding is available in several places, but like cycling, the mountains descending to the north coast are especially rewarding. No previous experience of riding is necessary as

> ‼ *No one wears a hard hat, so check your insurance policy before setting out along mountain trails. It's not far to fall, but rocks are hard from any height.*

Dominican horses are placid and well behaved. Complaints from tourists have led to improvements in their care, but you still need to keep an eye out for a healthy horse and check there are no sores, particularly in the saddle area. You should also make sure that your saddle is well made and comfortable, for your own benefit as much as the horse's. If you are going to be in it for hours, you will suffer on a wooden saddle with no padding. Riding is western style, with a raised pommel on the saddle to hang on to.

River sports

Jarabacoa is the centre for adventure sports, being blessed with three main rivers, the Río Yaque del Norte, the Jimenoa and the Baiguate, and their many tributaries. There are three companies active in watersports: **Aventuras del Caribe, Get Wet** and **Máxima Aventura**. **Canyoning** is done on the Río Jimenoa amidst beautiful scenery, unless the river is too full, as you can't do it at high water. Advanced level athletes can also go canyoning at La Damajagua near Imbert. **Cascading** is done at El Salto de Jimenoa and El Salto de Baiguate, elsewhere it can be done at the Cascada Ojo de Agua near Gaspar Hernández. The Río Yaque del Norte is a Class 3 or 4 river for **rafting**. There are several short rapids in gorges with lots of rocks and boulders to negotiate, followed by calmer sections of river. The rainy season (November and May) is more exciting than the dry season because the more water there is the faster it flows. The rainy season is also the favoured time of year for **tubing**, the best rivers being the Río Yaque del Norte, the Río Jamao and the Río Isabela. **Kayaking** is offered for beginners and advanced level by **Aventuras del Caribe**, which has all the equipment for Class 5-6 rivers, found on the tributaries of the Río Yaque del Norte. Beginners are taken to the lower Yaque del Norte, the Río Yasica and the lower Río Bao, which are Class 2.

Sailing

For renting boats and yachts, contact the **Secretaría de Turismo**. There are no charter fleets at present. Most beach resorts have small craft for rent by the hour or the half day. For independent yachtsmen the Dominican Republic is an excellent place to reprovision if cruising the islands. There are several marinas and many more being built. On the south coast, the waterfront and seaport of Santo Domingo is being redeveloped, with a new marina for 500 ships built between the obelisk, across from the Parque Eugenio María de Hostos and the Montesinos monument. Further east at La Romana, **Casa de Campo Marina**, www.marinacasadecampo.com, is a full-service marina accommodating 350 yachts including 30 slips for megayachts of up to 250 ft. There is also a sailing school with instructors from the Costasmeralda Yacht Club in Italy. **Club Nautico de Santo Domingo**, www.clubnautico.org, has marinas at Boca Chica, San Cristóbal and Monte Cristi, which host fishing tournaments and regattas. On the north coast, **Puerto Blanco Marina** at Luperón, west of Puerto Plata, is a fully enclosed marina with mooring space for 200 yachts with drafts of up to 8 ft. Popular with the yachting fraternity, the mangroves provide shelter during storms. The hurricane hole has attracted investors and there are other marinas under construction: **Marina Luperón**, www.marinatropical.com, which will have 250 slips for yachts of 30-80 ft and seven for boats of over 100 ft; **AtlanticA**, www.atlanticadr.com, with a deep water harbour, will have 450 marine slips, 260 super yacht hangars and a cruise ship terminal as well as hotels, villas, three golf courses and other services. **Ocean World**, www.oceanworld.net, west of Puerto Plata, is building a marina with 83 slips and capable of taking megayachts to expand its existing services around the dolphinarium. On the Samaná peninsula marinas are being built at Playa Bonito, Las Terrenas and in the Bahía de Samaná. In the east, **Punta Cana Resort Club Marina**, www.puntacana.com, is a full-service marina with two docks and mooring for 43 yachts up to 70 ft. Popular with big game fishermen, several billfish tournaments are held here. Along the coast a new marina is being built, **Cap Cana Harbour and Marina**, www.capcana.com, which will be the largest in the Caribbean with 500 slips and a host of man-made waterways including a 200-ft wide Grand Canal. The master plan includes hotels, villas, a casino, spa, five 18-hole golf courses and a nature reserve. North of Punta Cana at El Macao another marina is being built, **Roco Ki**, www.rocoki.com, which will have a Westin hotel, four golf courses and lagoon for watersports and sailing lessons as well as fishing charters.

Spectator sports

The national sport is **baseball**. The Dominican Republic has produced a phenomenal number of great players and the game has become known as a way out of poverty, with thousands of boys hoping to be plucked out of obscurity by team selectors and paid a fortune to play their favourite game. The best players are recruited by US and Canadian teams who maintain feeder academies in the Republic; about half of the 300 professional Dominican players in the USA come from San Pedro de Macorís. The regular season starts on the last Friday in October and runs until the end of December, with national and big league players participating. At the beginning of January for three weeks, round robin semi-final matches are held, after which the two best teams compete in the Serie Final in the last week of January.

Basketball is the second sport, played on an amateur basis in the Félix Sánchez (formerly Olympic) centre, the Palacio de los Deportes, and in sports clubs around the country, also matches at the Club San Lázaro and Club San Carlos. Every town has a good outdoor court where they play every evening and anyone can join in. The talent is good, there are a lot of Dominicans in the NBA.

Keeping in touch

Communications

Internet **Verizon** offices in most towns have a free computer for brief internet access (testing their service, a quick email home), but don't expect it to work. **Tricom** has internet access at Las Américas Airport and a few centres in Santo Domingo (RD$8.99 15 minutes, RD$0.55 additional minutes). **Cyber Café** is a franchise at three of the most popular shopping malls in Santo Domingo: Plaza Universitaria, T8095324743, Plaza Central, T8095658937 (US$0.60 for 15 minutes). Cybercafés are opening in tourist areas such as Cabarete, Boca Chica, Bayahibe and Las Terrenas, but, again, service is often down.

Post Don't use post boxes, they are unreliable. The postal system as a whole is very slow. A letter to Europe is RD$15; to North America and the Caribbean, RD$10; to South and Central America, Australia and Asia, RD$28. It is recommended to use *entrega especial* (special delivery, with separate window at post offices), for RD$2 extra, on overseas mail, or better still a courier service (see under Santo Domingo).

Telephone To phone from abroad you now have to dial the IDD code 809 in front of the local number which also begins with 809. Operated by the **Verizon** (T8092201111, www.verizon.net.do), or **Tricom** (T8094766000 in Santo Domingo, T8094718000 in

Santiago). Call centres usually open 0800-2200. Through **Verizon** you call abroad either person-to-person or through an operator (more expensive, but you only pay if connected). Calls and faxes may be paid for by credit card. Pre-paid calling cards are available and are the preferred choice for long distance calls. They are sold in supermarkets, shops and by vendors on the streets. For phone boxes you need two, one-peso coins. Phone calls to the USA cost RD$9.40 per minute, to Europe RD$23.80, to Australia RD$25.90, Puerto Rico RD$7.80, Haiti RD$10.90 and the rest of the Caribbean RD$12.90.

Media

Newspapers There are six daily papers in all, four in the morning, two in the afternoon. *Listín Diario* (www.listin.com.do) has the widest circulation; among the other morning papers are *El Caribe* (www.elcaribe.com.do), *Hoy* (www.hoy.com.do), *Diario Libre* (www.diariolibre.com.do). In the afternoon, *Ultima Hora* (www.ultimahora.com.do) and *El Nacional* (www.elnacional.com.do) are published. *Primicias* is a Sunday paper. *Touring* is a multilingual tourist newspaper with articles and adverts in English, German, French, Spanish and Italian. *La Información*, published in Santiago on weekdays, is a good regional paper carrying both national and international stories. **Radio and television** There are over 170 local radio stations and seven television stations. Cable television is available. *Cadena de Noticias* and *RNN* transmit news programmes 24 hours a day. *Caribbean Travelling Network* (CTN) has news of tourist sites, good for visitors.

Dominican Republic

Santo Domingo

→ *Phone code: 809. Colour map 2, B3. Population: 4,000,000.*

Travellers have been marvelling at this city since the beginning of the 16th century, when its streets, fortresses, palaces and churches were the wonder of the Caribbean and conquistadores set off from the port on the river to discover new territory for Spain in the Americas. Santo Domingo, the first European city in the Western Hemisphere, is now the capital and business centre of the Dominican Republic. Busy and modern, it sprawls along the Caribbean coast and inland along the banks of the Río Ozama. Restoration of the old city on the west bank of the river has made the area very attractive, with open-air cafés and pleasant squares near the waterfront. Those who have wealth flaunt it by building ostentatious villas and driving German cars, but the slums are some of the worst in the Caribbean. ➤➤ *For Eating, Sleeping and other listings, see pages 319-328.*

Ins and outs

Getting there Aeropuerto Las Américas, east of Santo Domingo, is the main international airport for the capital, receiving flights from North and South America and Europe. **Aeropuerto Internacional Dr Joaquín Balaguer**, at El Higuero/La Isabela opened in 2005. See Airport for details of taxis and buses. If you are arriving in the capital by bus, you will come in to that company's bus terminal. There is no central bus station. Taxis wait outside to take you to your hotel or other destination.
➤➤ *See Getting there, page 296.*

Getting around If you are limiting yourself to the colonial city, you will be able to walk around all the places of interest. Further afield, however, distances are great. Public transport is varied: there are government-run buses on the arterial routes in and out of town for commuters; shared or privately hired taxis called *públicos*, radio taxis and motorcycle taxis, known as *motoconchos*. Car hire is not recommended for the capital. There is a **tourist office** ① *in the colonial city in the Palacio Borgella, Isabel la Católica, near Plaza Colón, T8096863858, and at Las Américas Airport, T8095491496.* ➤➤ *See Transport, page 326 for further details.*

History

The first wooden houses were built in 1496 by Christopher Columbus' (Cristóbal Colón) brother Bartolomé on the eastern bank of the Río Ozama after the failure of the settlement at La Isabela on the north coast. In 1498 the Governor, Nicolás de Ovando, moved the city to the other side of the river and started building with stone, a successful

Dominican Republic Santo Domingo

move which was continued by Diego Colón, Christopher's son, when he took charge in 1509. It then became the first capital city in Spanish America. For years the city was the base for the Spaniards' exploration and conquest of the continent. Santo Domingo holds the title 'first' for a variety of offices: first city, having the first Audiencia Real, cathedral, university, coinage, etc. In view of this, UNESCO has designated Santo Domingo a World Cultural Heritage Site. However, Santo Domingo's importance waned when Spain set up her colonies in Peru and Mexico with seemingly limitless silver and gold to finance the Crown. Hurricanes managed to sink 15 ships in 1508, 18 in 1509 and many more in later years. 1562 brought an earthquake which destroyed much of the town; 1586 brought Sir Francis Drake, who attacked from inland where defences were vulnerable, looted and pillaged and set the city alight. He was the first of many British and French pirates and privateers who attacked in

‼ *Little remains of the original interior decoration, because when Drake sacked the city in 1586 his men removed everything of value.*

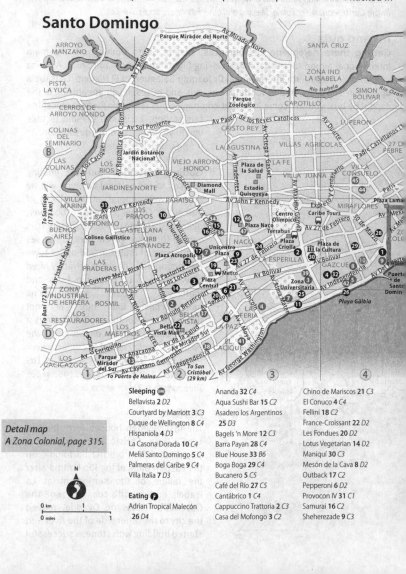

Santo Domingo

Dominican Republic Santo Domingo

Detail map
A Zona Colonial, page 315.

0 km   1
0 miles   1

Sleeping 🛏
Bellavista **2** *D2*
Courtyard by Marriott **3** *C3*
Duque de Wellington **8** *C4*
Hispaniola **4** *D3*
La Casona Dorada **10** *C4*
Meliá Santo Domingo **5** *C4*
Palmeras del Caribe **9** *C4*
Villa Italia **7** *D3*

Eating 🍴
Adrian Tropical Malecón
   26 *D4*

Ananda **32** *C4*
Aqua Sushi Bar **15** *C2*
Asadero los Argentinos
   25 *D3*
Bagels 'n More **12** *C3*
Barra Payan **28** *C4*
Blue House **33** *B6*
Boga Boga **29** *C4*
Bucanero **5** *C5*
Café del Río **27** *C5*
Cantábrico **1** *C4*
Cappuccino Trattoria **2** *C3*
Casa del Mofongo **3** *C2*

Chino de Mariscos **21** *C3*
El Conuco **4** *C4*
Fellini **18** *C2*
France-Croissant **22** *D2*
Les Fondues **20** *D2*
Lotus Vegetarian **14** *D2*
Maniquí **30** *C3*
Mesón de la Cava **8** *D2*
Outback **17** *C2*
Pepperoni **6** *D2*
Provocon IV **31** *C1*
Samurai **16** *C2*
Sheherezade **9** *C3*

the 16th and 17th centuries and rebuilding works were continually in progress.

In the 1930s, the dictator Rafael Leonidas Trujillo renamed the city Ciudad Trujillo and embarked on a series of public works. After his assassination in 1961 the city immediately reverted to the title of Santo Domingo, but his successor, Joaquín Balaguer, continued to build on a monumental scale. Prestigious projects such as the Faro a Colón took pride of place over social spending on education, health and housing for the poor. Governments since the 1960s have been criticized for concentrating on the capital and ignoring the provinces. As a result, migration to the capital has surged and little has been done to prevent the growth of slums and poor *barrios*. However, tourism is booming and it is a lively and vibrant place to spend a few days.

Zona Colonial

The colonial city is now only about 1% of the total area of Santo Domingo but it is the first port of call for visitors, holding almost all the sights of historical interest. **Calle Las Damas**, which runs alongside the Fortress, is the oldest paved (cobbled) street in the New World and is where the wife of Diego Colón and the ladies of the court would take their evening promenade. **Plaza España** lies at the end of Calle Las Damas and has lovely views over the river. At night time there are often cultural events laid on, such as music, folk dancing or theatre. **Calle El Conde** runs the length of the colonial city from the entrance gate, **Puerta El Conde** in the west, to the Fortaleza Ozama and the river in the east. It is a pleasant pedestrian boulevard with shops, bars and cafés.

Fortification of Santo Domingo began in 1503, with the construction of a tower to protect the entrance to the port. The city walls, only partially restored, were started in 1543 by the architect, Rodrigo de Liendo. All along the walls they built 20 defensive positions, six of them gates to the city and the others forts or bastions reserved for the military. The most important and largest fort was the **Fortaleza Ozama** ① *Mon-Sat 0900-1900, Sun 1000-1500. US$1*, or Fortaleza de Santo Domingo, overlooking the river and now bounded by the Avenida Francisco Alberto Caamaño Deñó, or Avenida del Puerto, running beneath it at the water's edge. It is the oldest fortress in America, constructed 1503-1507 by Nicolás de Ovando.

Just to the west, is the **Catedral Basílica Menor de Santa María** ① *Primada de América, Isabel La Católica esquina Nouel, Mon-Sat 0900-1630, Sun for services; no shorts allowed*, the first

Spaghettíssimo **19** *C2*
Sully **10** *C2*
Vesuvio del Malecón **11** *D3*
Vesuvio II **24** *C3*
Yatoba **23** *C3*

Bars & clubs 🍸
Alta Copa **37** *D2*
Beer House **35** *C2*
Blanc Dance & Lounge **36** *C2*
Club 60 **39** *C3*
El Rincón Habanero **45** *B4*

Etnia Disco **43** *B5*
Guácara Taína **13** *D1*
Jet Set **38** *D2*
Loft Lounge &
 Dance Club **46** *C3*
Maunaloa Night Club **41** *D3*
Montecristo Café & Club
 34 *C2*
Praia Café Lounge **47** *C3*
Salón La Fiesta
 (Jaragua Hotel) **42** *C4*
Secreto Musical **44** *B4*
TGI Friday **7** *C2*

⫶ The mystery of Columbus' bones

After his death in 1506, Columbus was buried in Valladolid, Spain. In 1509 his body was apparently removed to Sevilla, then together with that of his son Diego to Santo Domingo sometime in the 1540s. When France took control of Hispaniola in 1795, Cuba (still part of Spain) requested Columbus' remains. An urn bearing the name 'Colón' was disinterred from beneath the altar, sent to Havana and then back to the cathedral in Sevilla in 1898, when Cuba became independent. In 1877, however, during alterations and repairs in Santo Domingo cathedral, the cache of urns beneath the altar was reopened. One casket bore the inscription 'Almirante Cristóbal Colón', both outside and in. Experts confirmed that the remains were those of Columbus; the Spanish ambassador and two further experts from Spain were dismissed for concurring with the findings. A second pair of Spanish experts denied the discovery, hence the confusion over where the admiral's bones lay. The urn that was opened in 1877 is that which is now given pride of place in the Faro a Colón. Further research in Spain in 2002-05 cast further doubts on the bones. DNA analysis suggested that Christopher Columbus might be buried in Spain after all, or at least part of him. DNA material was extracted from three sets of bones: the one Spain claims is Christopher, the one researchers believe is his brother, Diego and a third from Christopher's son, Hernando, whose bones were never moved after his death in 1539. DNA testing on the bones held in the Faro a Colón is planned to complete the picture. It is possible that Columbus' bones lie at either end of his exploratory journey to the Americas.

cathedral to be founded in the New World. Its first stone was laid by Diego Colón in 1514 (although there is some dispute and some people think it was after 1520); the first architect was Alonzo Rodríguez, but there were several. It was finished in 1540 and dedicated in 1542. The alleged remains of Christopher Columbus were found in 1877 during restoration work. In 1892, the Government of Spain donated the tomb in which the remains lay, a neo-Gothic wedding cake of a monument, behind the high altar, until their removal to the Faro a Colón (see below). The cathedral was fully restored for 1992, the 500th anniversary of Columbus' first voyage, with new gargoyles and sculptures at the gates showing the indigenous people when Columbus arrived. There are 14 chapels with multilingual boards explaining each one.

Parque Colón is outside the Cathedral, on its north side, next to Calle El Conde. A statue to Christopher Columbus (Cristóbal Colón) is in the middle, with a Taíno woman at his feet, a symbol now considered rather politically incorrect. The **Museo de Ambar** ① *El Conde 107 on Parque Colón, T8096864471*, is upstairs, with a shop on the ground floor selling amber, larimar, protected black coral, local gold and pearls. There is also a **Museo de Larimar** ① *Isabel la Católica, T8096896605, Mon-Fri 0830-1800, Sun 0900-1300, free*, where you can see examples of this lovely pale blue stone found only in the Dominican Republic.

A cluster of historical buildings lies either side of Las Damas running north from the Fortaleza Ozama. The first is the **Casa de Don Rodrigo de Bastidas/Museo Infantil** ① *T8096855151, www.trampolin.org.do, Tue-Sun 0800-1700, Sat 0900-1800, US$2, children US$1*, built in to the city wall on Calle Las Damas in 1510. This was the house of the royal tax collector and mayor, who went on to colonize Colombia. It is built around an inner courtyard with arches around all four walls and enormous caucho trees. In 2004 it was remodelled as a children's museum, with rooms encompassing the themes of universe, family, ecology and interactive games. Beside it is the **Casa de Ovando**, the home of the man who did most to build the city. It has been restored and developed into a splendid hotel, the **Hostal Nicolás de Ovando**, see Sleeping.

The **Casa de Francia**, opposite the **Hostal Nicolás de Ovando**, was built in the early 16th century and occupied by Hernán Cortés before he went off to conquer Mexico, later housing numerous government and private occupants. Next door is the **Convento de San Ignacio de Loyola** ① *Las Damas between Mercedes and El Conde, Tue-Sun 0900-1630, free*, a Jesuit monastery and church. Finished in 1743, it has been the **Panteón Nacional** since 1958. The central nave forms a cross with the lateral chapels and a bronze lamp donated by the Spanish government (General Franco)

Zona Colonial

Dominican Republic Santo Domingo

N

0 metres 100
0 yards 100

Sleeping
Aída 1
Antiguo Hotel Europa 10
Aparthotel Condo-Parque
& Venus Bar 8
Conde de Peñalba 2
El Beaterio 12

El Palacio 3
Hodelpa Caribe Colonial 5
Hostal Nicolás Nader 6
Independencia 11
Mercure Comercial 7
Saint-Amad 9
Sofitel Francés 4
Sofitel Nicolás de Ovando
& La Résidence 14

Eating
Alfatori 13

Anacaona 6
Coco's 4
La Atarazana 7
La Briciola 5
La Cafetería Colonial 3
La Crêperie 7
La Panadería 14
Mesón de Barí 2
Mesón La Quintana 7
Museo de Jamón 7
Palmito Gourmet 1
Pat'e Palo 7

Rita's Café 7

Bars & clubs
Abacus 9
A-Club 15
Atarazana 9 12
Fusion Rose 10
Hard Rock Café 17
Llegó 6
Pop Lounge 11
XXO Bar & Lounge 8

hangs in the intersection. It contains the tombs of, or memorials to, many of the country's presidents, heroes and an ornate tomb built before his death for the dictator Trujillo, the 'Benefactor of the Fatherland', but after his assassination he was not given the honour of being buried here. Cross the street again for the **Capilla de Nuestra Señora de Los Remedios**, built in the early 16th century as the private chapel of the Dávila family. By its side the Reloj de Sol (sundial) was built in 1753, near the end of Las Damas, so that court officials could tell the time.

One of the most significant historical buildings in this area is the **Museo de las Casas Reales** ① C *Las Damas, T8096824202, daily 0900-1700, US$1*, in a reconstructed early 16th-century building which was in colonial days the Palace of the Governors and Captains-General, and of the Audiencia Real and Chancery of the Indies. The Audiencia Real was a supreme court made up of three judges, designed to check the power of the Governor, and its power extended to the rest of the Caribbean and the mainland coast around the Caribbean basin. It is an excellent colonial museum (often has special exhibits), with many items salvaged from ships sunk in local waters as well as furniture, art and military items.

Calle Las Damas opens out into the Plaza España, a paved open space surrounded by historical monuments with a statue of Nicolás de Ovando in the middle. It has lovely views over the river and many cafes. At night there are often cultural events, such as music, folk dancing or theatre. The **Alcázar de Colón** at the end of Las Damas and Emilio Tejera, is a fortified house constructed without any nails by the first Viceroy, Diego Colón, in 1510-1514 to house his court and his wife, María de Toledo. It was the seat of the Spanish Crown in the New World until the family left for Spain in 1577 and in 1770 the building was abandoned. Now completely restored, it houses the interesting **Museo Virreinal** ① *Mon-Sat 0900-1700, Sun 0900-1600, US$1.50*, (Viceregal Museum), with religious art and colonial artefacts. **Las Atarazanas**, the Dockyards, near the Alcázar, are a cluster of 16th-century buildings which served as an arsenal, warehouses and taverns for the sailors in port, now restored to contain shops, bars and restaurants. The **Museo Naval de las Atarazanas** ① *T8096825834, daily 0900-1700, US$0.60*, at the end, contains recovered treasure from several shipwrecks, namely the *Concepción*, *Nuestra Señora de Guadalupe* and *Conde de Tolosa*. There are accounts of the many attempts to raise numerous 17th- and 18th-century ships which sank around the island and exhibits show what life was like on board ship at that time.

Near the end of Isabel La Católica lies the only joint church and fort in Santo Domingo, the **Iglesia de Santa Bárbara**, just off Avenida Mella. Built in 1574 on the site of the city quarry, it was sacked by Drake in 1586, and destroyed by a hurricane in 1591. It was reconstructed at the beginning of the 17th century. Its design is rather lopsided and haphazard, its two towers being of completely different size and style and bearing little relation with the main entrance with its triple arches. Behind the church are the ruins of its fort, where there are good views and photo opportunities. Santa Bárbara is the patron saint of the military.

‡ Just outside the old city walls is Chinatown, on Benito González entre José Martí y Duarte, newly renovated as a visitor attraction.

Don't miss the **Museo Mundo de Ambar** ① *Arzobispo Meriño 452, esquina Restauración, T8096823309, Mon-Sat 0800-1800, Sun 0800-1300, US$1.20*, in a restored 17th-century building, which has a fascinating display of scorpions, butterflies and plants fossilized in amber, with microscopes and videos. A guided tour is recommended but not essential. The staff are informative and will teach you how to tell real from fake amber. Craftsmen also polish and shape raw amber for sale here.

Round the corner and up the hill, the **Monasterio de San Francisco** (ruins), Hostos esquina E Tejera, was the first monastery in America, constructed in the first half of the 16th century, although dates vary. Sacked by Drake and destroyed by earthquakes in 1673 and 1751, it was repeatedly repaired or rebuilt. For about 50 years until the 1930s it was used as an asylum for the insane, and there are still metal brackets in places where patients were restrained with leg chains. A hurricane closed it down for good and the ruins are now used for cultural events.

Walk south down Hostos to the **Hospital-Iglesia de San Nicolás de Bari** (ruins), Hostos between Mercedes and Luperón, begun in 1509 by Nicolás de Ovando, completed 1552, was the first stone-built hospital in the Americas. In a cruciform plan, the three-aisled Gothic-vaulted church was used for worship while two-storey wings were used for wards to cure the sick. Also plundered by Drake, it was probably one of the best-constructed buildings of the period, it survived many earthquakes and hurricanes. In 1911 some of its walls were knocked down because they posed a hazard to passers-by; also the last of its valuable wood was taken. It is now full of pigeons.

The **Museo de la Familia Dominicana** has a collection of furniture, antiques and memorabilia from the 19th century. It is housed in the **Casa de Tostado** ① *C Padre Billini esq Arz Meriño, T8096895000, Mon-Sat 0800-1600, US$0.90*, an early 16th-century mansion with a Gothic-Isabelline double window on its northern façade. The house was the home of the writer, Francisco de Tostado, the first native professor at the university, who was killed when Drake set about destroying the city in 1586. One block further down Padre Billini is the **Convento de los Dominicos**, built in 1510. Here in 1538 the first university in the Americas was founded.

East of the Río Ozama

Sans Souci, the eastern bank of the Río Ozama, is the site of a massive redevelopment project. Formerly the docks, commercial shipping was moved some years ago to Haína and a marina was constructed. In 2005 a new project was initiated to develop the mouth of the Ozama and part of the Malecón to make Santo Domingo more attractive for large cruise ships. A seven-year plan calls for the construction of malls, high-rise apartments, hotels and a new marina on the east side of the river. The **Monumento de Caña** by the river is a reminder of the origins of the country's wealth, a huge statue of a bullock cart laden with sugar cane. Of historical importance, the Capilla de La Virgen del Rosario is on the site of the first church constructed in America, restored in 1943.

The **Faro a Colón** ① *Parque Mirador del Este, T8095911492, daily 0900-1700, US$0.90, children, US$0.45* (Columbus Lighthouse), built at great cost (and not without controversy), is in the shape of a cross. Where the arms of the cross intersect is the mausoleum containing the supposed remains of Columbus. Spotlights project a crucifix of light into the night sky, spectacular on a cloudy night. One of the rooms in the lighthouse is a chapel, in others, different countries have mounted exhibitions (the British exhibit concentrates on the entries for the competition to design the lighthouse: the competition was won by a British design). Slums were cleared and some of the 2000 families evicted received a paltry sum of US$50 before losing their homes. Some 100,000 people are thought to have been affected by the construction work, road building and slum clearance. In the light of the controversy the King and Queen of Spain declined an invitation to attend the 1992 celebrations and the Pope withdrew his acceptance to officially open the building. Two days before the ceremonies were to begin, President Balaguer's sister, Doña Emma, to whom he was devoted, inspected the Faro and, hours later, she died, inspiring further belief that Columbus brings bad luck and that there was a curse, or *fukú* on the building. Balaguer, who had been held responsible for the whole enterprise and who was criticized for his megalomania, also stayed away from the ceremony, while he mourned his sister. Photography inside permitted, but no photos in the museums, no smoking, eating, drinking or pets; guides are free, but tip; shorts above the knee not allowed.

East of the Lighthouse in the **Parque Mirador del Este** are the *cenotes* (limestone sinkholes) **Tres Ojos** ① *daily, US$1.10 adults, US$0.60 children and students, ferry to the furthest lake US$1.50*

At the entrance to Tres Ojos vendors sell artesanías made from stalactites (light colour) and stalagmites (dark colour), an ecological horror.

Dominican Republic Santo Domingo

adults, children US$0.60, toilets (Three Eyes), a popular tourist attraction. They used to be public bathing pools in the times of the Taínos, and Anacaona, the wife of Enriquillo, would bathe here, but now 'Tarzan' is the only person allowed to swim. A local man, he has been doing it since 1958 and is a tourist attraction in himself. Take the *guagua* from Parque Enriquillo.

West of the Río Ozama

Gazcue is a quiet, attractive residential area with expensive homes built in the 1930s and 1940s, stretching west of the Zona Colonial as far as Avenida Máximo Gómez. The **Palacio Presidencial** ① *T8096958000*, with a neoclassical central portico and cupola, built by Trujillo, is at the intersection of Doctor Delgado and Manuel María Castillo. It is used by the President, but guided tours of the richly decorated interior can be arranged. Opposite the Palacio's grounds are the government offices (Avenida México y 30 de Marzo). The 1955/1956 World's Fair (Feria de Confraternidad) buildings now house the Senate and Congress.

The modern city to the west is very spread out because, until recently, there was no high-rise building. Avenida George Washington (also known as the **Malecón**) runs parallel to the sea; it often becomes an open-air discothèque, where locals and foreigners dance the *merengue*. The annual merengue festival is held here in July. The **Plaza de la Cultura**, founded by Presidente Joaquín Balaguer on Avenida Máximo Gómez, contains the country's major museums alongside the national library and the ultra-modern, white marble **National Theatre** ① *T8096873191*. You will have to go to the ballet or opera to see the lavish interior, although you can go to the restaurant at the back of the building for a wonderful buffet at lunchtime). The **Museo del Hombre Dominicano** ① *T8096873622, Tue-Sun 1000-1700, US$0.90*, traces the development of the modern Dominican, from the Amerindians, in pre-Columbian times, who were hunters and gatherers, to the Spanish conquerors and the African slaves. There were about 400,000 Taínos on the island in 1492, but only 60,000 in 1508 and they had nearly all died by 1525. Despite their rapid annihilation their influences live on in Dominican life today, all explained here. There is a large display of carnival costumes. The **Museo de Arte Moderno** ① *T8096852154, Tue-Sun 0900-1700, US$0.90*, contains a huge amount of 20th-century Dominican art on four floors. The **Museo de Historia Natural** ① *T8096890106*, was renovated and reopened in 2007 after a four-year closure. It has seven main areas and halls: earth, minerals, ecology, biogeography, marine giants, birds and the Santo Domingo planetarium. The **Museo de Historia y Geografía** ① *T8096866668, Tue-Sun 1000-1700. US$0.90, children US$0.45*, has a few Taíno exhibits, but most of the displays are from the 19th and 20th centuries, starting with the Haitian invasion and following on to the American occupation. A great deal of space is taken up by artefacts belonging to Trujillo, illustrating his wealth and vanity. The museum organizes ecological excursions to different parts of the country.

Parks

Among the attractive parks are the **Centro Olímpico**, now renamed after the world champion hurdler, **Félix Sánchez**, JF Kennedy and Máximo Gómez, in the city centre, **Parque Mirador del Este** (Autopista de las Américas, a 7-km-long alameda), almost entirely taken up by the sports facilities built for the PanAmerican Games, and **Parque Mirador del Sur**. The Centro Félix Sánchez is a public park, but the sporting facilities are technically only for Dominicans. The Paseo de los Indios at Parque Mirador del Sur is a 7-km-long trail, popular for walking, jogging, cycling and picnics. Avenida Anacaona runs along the north side and many desirable residences overlook the park. On Avenida José Contreras are many caves, some with lakes, in the southern cliff of Parque Mirador del Sur. Along this cliff is the Avenida Cayetano Germosén, giving access to a number of caves used at one time by Taíno Indians. Caves are also the setting for the **Mesón de la Cava** restaurant and the **Guácara Taína** nightclub. The road, lined with gardens, links Avenidas Luperón and Núñez de Cáceres. **Parque Mirador del Norte** ① *Tue-Sun 0900-1800, US$0.30*, has been constructed on the banks of the Río Isabela, near Guaricano and Villa Mella. There is a boating lake, picnic areas, restaurants, jogging and cycling trails.

The **Jardín Botánico Nacional** ① *Av República de Colombia, Urbanización Los Ríos, T8093852611, daily 0900-1700, US$2, children US$0.40*, has a full classification of the Republic's flora. Plants endemic to the island are grown here. There are 300 types of orchid and a greenhouse for bromeliads and aquatic plants, highly recommended, especially the beautifully manicured Japanese Garden; a small trolley bus tours the extensive grounds.

⊜ Sleeping

Prices listed are high season rates and do not include taxes, normally 26%.

Zona Colonial *p313, map p315*
LL Sofitel Nicolás de Ovando, C Las Damas, T8096859955, www.sofitel.com. The conversion of the **Casa de Ovando** has provided the most luxurious hotel in the country, a haven of cool elegance with stone walls and high, dark wooden ceilings. 104 rooms and 3 suites, spacious and comfortable, with marble bathroom, TV, a/c, safe box, phone and data port. The pool overlooks the river, as do many of the rooms, small well-equipped gym, massage on request, billiards and books in the lobby bar, gourmet restaurant open for all meals.
L Sofitel Francés, Las Mercedes esq Arzobispo Meriño, T8096859331, H2137@accor-hotels.com. A restored colonial mansion with 19 luxury rooms and lovely furnishings. The restaurant is in a beautiful courtyard and serves superb French food, expensive but recommended. Buffet breakfast and tax/service included.
AL-A El Palacio, Duarte 106 y Ureña, T8096824730, www.hotel-palacio.com. A colonial mansion with new extension at the rear, swimming pool, heavy wooden furniture and tiled floors. No restaurant.
AL-A Hodelpa Caribe Colonial, Isabel La Católica 159, T8096887799, www.hodelpa .com. 54 rooms and suites in art deco style with a/c, TV and fridge. A smart hotel in a good location. Bar, restaurant, internet access.
A Antiguo Hotel Europa, Arzobispo Meriño esq Emiliano Tejera, T8092850005, www.antiguohoteleuropa.com. Built at the turn of the 20th century and lovingly restored to its former glory, complete with

elegant wrought iron balconies and fabulous tiled floors from the era. 52 rooms and suites with mahogany furniture. Internet centre, travel agency and sushi bar. Meals are served in the **La Terraza** bar on the top floor, which has a wonderful view of the San Francisco monastery ruins and the sunset. Great value introductory rates.
A Conde de Peñalba, El Conde esq Arzobispo Meriño facing Parque Colón, T8096887121, www.condepenalba.com. Great location with bar and restaurant. Newly decorated rooms with TV, suites with balcony, interior rooms have no windows, US$10 for an additional person.
A El Beaterio, Duarte 8, T8096878657. 16th-century guesthouse with 11 rooms set around a courtyard with palm trees and potted plants, roof terrace and patio. Breakfast is included. A wonderful renovation with antique furniture, exquisite tiles in the bathrooms, a/c and ceiling fan. Taxi service from airport, to be booked when you make your room reservation.
A Hostal Nicolás Nader, Duarte y Luperón, T8096876674, www.hostalnader.com. 10 rooms in a pleasant colonial mansion, beautifully furnished with lots of modern art for sale. Friendly, personal service. Includes taxes.
A Mercure Comercial, El Conde esq Hostos, T8096885500, www.mercure.com. Renovated by the French group, **Accor**, to a high standard. 96 rooms with good bathrooms, phone, TV and fridge. Buffet breakfast and tax/service included. Good for business travellers with business centre and internet connection.
A Saint-Amad, Arzobispo Meriño 353, T8096871447, F8096871478. 14 rooms in a colonial house with a/c and TV. Charming

restaurant and bar area, room service, internet, all beautifully renovated.

C Aída, El Conde 464 y Espaillat, T8096857692. Very pleasant family-run accommodation. A/c rooms have no windows, rooms with fan have balcony, some rooms sleep three. No smoking. Fairly quiet at night, but record shop below may be noisy during the day. Popular, central location, and so often full. Amex accepted.

C-D Aparthotel Condo-Parque & Venus Bar, Palo Hincado 165, T8093336713, www.condo-parque.ch.vu. Rooms, studios and penthouse with fan or a/c, small kitchenettes with fridges, cheap and cheerful, short or long stay available, popular meeting place, Wi-Fi, restaurant/bar on first floor, good goulash, snacks and breakfast, run by multilingual Walter Rüfenacht, who also runs tours to National Parks including Pico Duarte and Lago Enriquillo.

D Independencia, Estrella y Arzobispo Nouel, near Parque Independencia, T8096861663. Clean, convenient location. Price is for a single room. Soap and towels provided. Some rooms don't have windows. Also has a club, bar (noisy all night), language school (across the street) and art exhibitions.

West of the Río Ozama *p318, map p312*
LL-L Meliá Santo Domingo, Av George Washington 365, T8092216666, www.solmelia.com. One of the top hotels in the city. International style for business travellers with the advantage of being on the Malecón. Lots of facilities including restaurants and nightlife. Good service.

AL Courtyard by Marriott, Av Máximo Gómez 50-A, Gazcue, T8096851010, www.marriott.com/SDQCY. Within walking distance of many places of interest. 142 very comfortable rooms and 4 suites sleeping up to 4. Breakfast is included. Free access to the internet in the lobby or in the rooms. 5 rooms are wheelchair accessible and have a connecting room for a carer. The restaurant serves breakfast and dinner, but there is a snack machine and delivery from outside restaurants. 24-hour gym, pool, self-service laundry, safe box, fridge, coffee maker, iron and spotless bathrooms. Friendly atmosphere.

AL Hispaniola, Av Independencia y Abraham Lincoln, near the university, T8092217111, F8095350976. Very clean with good service, but the bedrooms and corridors are showing

their age. Pleasant public areas, a pool, disco and noisy, glitzy casino.

A-B La Casona Dorada, Independencia 255 y Báez, Gazcue, near Jaragua, T8092213535, casonadorada@verizon.net.do. 25 rooms, some of which sleep 3, with a/c and TV. Facilities include a laundry and dry cleaning, small pool, 24-hour room service and secure parking. Staff are courteous.

B Duque de Wellington, Av Independencia 304, Gazcue, T8096824525, www.hotelduque .com. Conveniently located with 28 budget rooms with TV and fridge. Bar and restaurant.

B Villa Italia, Av Independencia 1107 casi esq Alma Mater, near the university, T8096823373, hotel.villa@verizon.net.do. 25 rooms, 3 suites and 1 apartment, equipped with a/c, phone and TV; a fridge is available for extra charge. The terrace has a jacuzzi and sea view. Attractive but the service is lacking.

C Bellavista, Dr F Defilló 43, Ens Bella Vista, near Parque Mirador del Sur, T8095320412, hotelbellavista@verizon.net.do. Rooms are good, clean and have plenty of space.

D Palmeras del Caribe, Cambronal 1, Gazcue, T8093335510. Rooms are nice but small, with use of a fridge. There is a pleasant garden and adjoining café.

Eating

Zona Colonial *p313, map p315*
Coco's, Padre Billini 53, T8096879624. Tue-Sat 1830-2400, Sun 1200-1500. Excellent food and service, menu changes daily.
La Briciola, Arzobispo Merino 152, T8096885055. 1800-late. Italian cuisine in courtyard of colonial house. Dine by candlelight under the brick arches or in the open air. The piano bar has live music.
La Résidence, C Las Damas, T8096859955. 1200-1500, 1900-2330. The restaurant is at Sofitel Nicolás de Ovando and is as upmarket as the hotel, with elegant wicker furniture and beautifully presented meals. Mediterranean-style gourmet food, served to music. Very romantic.
La Atarazana, La Atarazana 5, T8096892900. 1200-2400. Popular for Creole and international cuisine, good seafood.
Mesón de Barí, Hostos esq Arzobispo Nouel, T8096824973. 1200-0100. Great place for typical Dominican dishes, merengue music at weekends, unusual collection of art.

Museo de Jamón, La Atarazana 17, Plaza España, T8096889644. 1100-late. Not a museum but a pleasant Spanish restaurant with live music. Ceiling covered with hams. Delicious selection of tapas.

Pat'e Palo, La Atarazana 25, T8096878089. 1200-late. Named after the pirate, Peg Leg, who presumably liked eating and drinking after work. The first tavern in the New World was on this site, dating from 1505, although the brasserie is in a later colonial building. Meat, seafood, salads, pasta and imported cheeses and a tasting menu if you can't decide. Bar serves international cocktails and several foreign beers.

Alfatori, Arzobispo Meriño 115, T8092212109, www.alfatori.com. 1200-late. Exquisite menu, live music, excellent service and valet parking.

Anacaona, El Conde 101 esq Isabel La Católica, T8096828253. 1000-2400. Excellent location and menu, outdoor seating.

Mesón La Quintana, La Atarazana 13, T8096872646. Tue-Sun 1200-2400. Spanish and some Italian dishes. One of several bars and restaurants in this area.

Palmito Gourmet, Arzobispo Portés esq Santomé, T8092215777. 1200-late. Restaurant and bar, mix of Dominican and Italian dishes, good atmosphere.

Rita's Café, La Atarazana 27, T8096889400, ramaup@aol.com. Open from 1000. International and Dominican food in colonial setting, paella, Mexican, meat and seafood, overlooking river, credit cards accepted.

La Crêperie, La Atarazana 11, Plaza de España, T8092214734. 1530-late. Nice outdoor seating on the plaza.

La Cafetería Colonial, El Conde 253, T8096827114. 0730-2200. Good for fresh coffee after a meal elsewhere.

La Panadería, Isabel La Católica 251. Mon-Fri 0630-2030, Sat 0700-1700, Sun 0800-1300. A good place for snacks and drinks and excellent freshly ground Dominican coffee.

West of the Río Ozama *p318, map p312*
Fellini, Roberto Pastoriza 504 esq Av Winston Churchill, T8095405330. 1900-late. Mediterranean and Italian cuisine. Fine dining.

Mesón Iberia, Miguel Angel Monclus 165, Mirador Norte, T8095317694. Tue-Sun 1130-2400. Spanish cuisine. Great food and service.

Outback, Av Winston Churchill 25, Acrópolis Center, T8099550001. 1200-2400. Australian franchise. Serves good steaks and salads. Free soda drink refills.

Spaghettíssimo, Paseo de los Locutores 13, entre Av Abraham Lincoln y Av Winston Churchill, T8095653708. 1200-2400. Italian, fish, seafood, meat, pasta, open-air jazz on Wed, home delivery.

Vesuvio del Malecón, Av George Washington 521, T8092211954, www.restaurantvesuvio.com. Lunch and dinner. Established in 1954, the place to go in Santo Domingo for an expensive meal. Elegant dining, Italian cuisine with seafood and pasta, as well as Caribbean specialities. Wheelchair accessible, valet parking.

Yatoba, Av Abraham Lincoln 615, T8095624222. 1200-2400. Eclectic, nice food and atmosphere. Beautiful outdoor decoration to enjoy a moonlight dinner or if preferred there is an a/c dining area.

Adrian Tropical Malecón, Av George Washington, T8092211764. (Also at Av John F Kennedy 82, Plaza Safari T8095668373; Av Independencia, Plaza Atala II, T8095080025; Av 27 de Febrero 429, esq Núñez de Cáceres, T8094721763; soon to open at Av Abraham Lincoln 809.) 1200-2300. Good, reliable place to try local specialities such as *mofongo*, but international dishes are also available. Perched on the waterfront on the Malecón, you can dine outdoors with the sea breeze and the waves crashing beneath you, particularly attractive at night when the rocks are lit up.

Asadero los Argentinos, Av Independencia entre Av Abraham Lincoln y Máximo Gómez, T8096864060. 1200-late. Excellent Argentine food.

Pepperoni, Av Sarasota esq Winston Churchill, Plaza Universitaria, T8095321464. Sushi, great salads and gourmet dishes. Delicious desserts.

Sheherezade, Roberto Pastoriza 226, T8092272323. 1200-late. Arabian and Mediterranean food, with Mediterranean architecture and design.

Sully, Av Charles Summer 19 y Calle Caoba, Los Prados, T8095623389. Tue-Sun 1200-1500, 1900-2400. Lots of seafood in Dominican, French and Italian styles.

Aqua Sushi Bar, Av Abraham Lincoln esq Gustavo M Ricart, Plaza Rosa, T8095633030. 1200-2400. Japanese and other international dishes. Baskets of orchids as part of the oriental-style decoration.

Boga Boga, Plaza Florida, Av Bolívar 203, T8094720950. 1100-0100. Spanish, good *jamón serrano* and *chorizo*, US$15-20 for a meal.

Cantábrico, Av Independencia 54, T8096875101, www.restaurantcantabrico. com.do. 1100-2400. Recommended fresh fish and seafood, Spanish and *criollo*. Good reputation for more than a decade.

Cappuccino Trattoria and Restaurant, Av Máximo Gómez 60, T8096898600. 0800-2400. Italian-owned restaurant and café, great Italian food, suave, prices to match, Italian murals.

Chino de Mariscos, Av Sarasota 38, T8095335249. 1200-late. Very good Chinese seafood, long-standing business in operation for over a decade.

El Conuco, Casimiro de Moya 152, Gazcue, T8096860129, www.elconuco.com.do. 1100-1500, 1800-2400. Good-value buffet at lunch time and a more extensive buffet in the evening. You can also eat à la carte and try more exotic items such as *mollejitas fritas en salsa de mango* (chicken's stomachs in mango sauce), *mondongo* (tripe) or *patica* (pigs' knuckles). A show of typical dancing is laid on at lunch and in the evening from 1900.

Les Fondues, Av Winston Churchill, esq Roberto Pastoriza, Plaza de las Américas I, T8096835233. Lunch and dinner. All types of fondue including chocolate, run by Swiss.

Lotus Vegetarian Restaurant, Av 27 de Febrero y Carmen Mendoza, T8095353319. 1100-1530, 1900-2200. Chinese. One of the few vegetarian restaurants in the country.

Maniquí, Pedro Henríquez Ureña in the Plaza de la Cultura, T8096882854. From 1200. Busy at lunch time, try the crab in coconut, vegetarian dishes.

Mesón de la Cava, Parque Mirador del Sur, in a natural cave, T8095332818. 1130-1700, 1730-2400. Good steaks, live music, dancing, great experience, very popular, reserve in advance.

Noa Noa, Miguel de Jesús Troncoso 5B, esq Fco Prats Ramírez, Piantini, T8095405038. From 1200. Serves international dishes, nice eclectic restaurant with VIP lounge, sushi bar and terrace for outdoor dining by candlelight or indoor restaurant with a/c.

Samurai, Seminario 57, Ens Piantini, T8095651621. Mon-Sat 1200-1500, 1800-2400; Sun 1200-1600.Very good Japanese, try the Sun brunch.

Vesuvio II, Av Tiradentes 17, Naco, T8095626060, www.vesuviotiradentes.com. 1200-1500, 1800-2300. Italian and international cuisine, better value than **Vesuvio I**. Bar, private dining room, home delivery, Italian family business, well thought of.

Ananda, Casimiro Núñez de Moya 7, Gazcue, T8096827153. 1000-2200. *Cafetería* style, excellent vegetarian restaurant.

Bagels'n More, Fantino Falco, T8095402263. From 0800. New York bagel sandwiches, soups, salads and muffins. The only bagel place in the Dominican Republic.

Casa del Mofongo, 27 de Febrero y Calle 299, T8095411121. 0900-late. A long way from the centre, but famous for its *mofongo* (balls of mashed plaintain and pork) and other local specialities.

Barra Payan, 30 de Marzo 140, T8096896654. Open 24 hours. Sandwiches and tropical juices, an all-time Dominican favourite.

France-Croissant, Av Sarasota 82 y Dr Defilló. From 0800. French bakery, tastiest pastries in the country, unsweetened wholemeal bread available, small café.

Provocon IV, Santiago 253, Gazcue, T8092212233. 1200-2300. The best place for *pollo al carbón* with *waza-kaca* sauce. Also other locations around the city.

East of the Río Ozama p317, map p312

Blue House, Autopista San Isidro 1, T8095914242. 1130-2400. International cuisine, specializes in meats and seafood.

Bucanero, Av España, Puerto Turístico Sans Souci, T8095922202. 1200-2400. Famous for their seafood.

Café del Río, Plaza la Marina, overlooking the Ozama River. 1200-2300. Good place for a cold beer, near the Sugar Cane Monument on eastern side of river.

Bars and clubs

Santo Domingo p311, maps p312 and p315

There are **casinos** in several of the hotels and **Maunaloa Night Club**, Centro de los Héroes.

Bars

Abacus, Hostos 350 esq Luperón, Zona Colonial, T8093337272, www.abacus.com. A great place to gather with friends for a drink. Low couches, soft lighting, good mix of cocktails, DJ music.

Alta Copa, Pedro A Bobea, Bella Vista, T8095326405. Former wine shop, now the place to gather with friends for a nice glass of wine or cocktails. Decorated as a *cava*.

Atarazana 9, La Atarazana 9, Zona Colonial, T8096880969. Colonial building, very historic, nice place, good drinks.

Bar Phoenix, Polvorín 10, Zona Colonial, Santo Domingo, T8096897572. Neighbourhood bar, gay-friendly, British-run.

Beer House, Gustavo Mejía Ricart esq Winston Churchill, T8096834804. From 1700. Stocks about 30-40 beers from around the world, live bands (often jazz) mid-week, decent, casual ambience.

Fusion Rose, El Conde 54 esq Las Damas, Zona Colonial, T8094492346, www.fusionrose.com. Hip-hop electronic music. Wed hip-hop crazy nights (US$2). Popular with the young crowd.

Hard Rock Café, El Conde 103, T8096867771. Right in front of the Cathedral and the biggest in Latin America with a dance floor and salons for private receptions or activities. The usual pop memorabilia with items which once belonged to the very famous, such as Mick Jagger, Juan Luis Guerra, Madonna and John Lennon.

Pop Lounge, Arzobispo Nouel esq Hostos, Zona Colonial, T8096865176, www.pop.com.do. 2100-late. European design influences with pop art for decoration. Multicoloured cocktails and coloured ice. House and European dance music. Latest activities are posted on the website.

Praia Café Lounge, Av Gustavo Mejía Ricart, Naco, T8097320230. Exotic decoration, good cocktails, popular place for social activities among Dominican people.

TGI Friday, Av Winston Churchill, Plaza Acropolis, 3rd floor. 1200-late. Good food. Bar area has floor-to-ceiling windows, large crowd for happy hour.

XXO Bar and Lounge, Hostos esq Emiliano Tejera, T8096858103. Weekly activities such as hip-hop and ladies' night.

Clubs

A-Club, Arzobispo Nouel entre Hostos y Duarte, Santo Domingo, from 2100. Shows on selected nights frequented by *bugarones* or *sankipankies* with the pick-up-and-pay mentality. No cover charge.

Atlantis Disco, Av George Washington 555, Zona Colonial, Santo Domingo, T8096852011, www.atlantis-disco.com. Thu-Sun from 2300. Different gay shows every night with male strippers, transvestites and drag queens. Large dance floor, 2 bars.

Blanc Dance and Lounge, Av Abraham Lincoln esq Gustavo M Ricart, Plaza Andalucía, 2nd floor, T8095632043. New in 2005 and immaculate, one of the fanciest night spots in the capital.

Club 60, Máximo Gómez 60. Fri-Sun from 2100. Rock, merengue and ballads. On Fri and Sat they play merengue and pop music, on Sun they play Cuban *son*. Appeals to the older crowd, most clients are over 30. US$1.

El Rincón Habanero, Sánchez Valverde y Baltazar de los Reyes, Villa Consuelo. Enthusiasts of Cuban *son* dance to records of the 1940s and 1950s.

Etnia Disco, Av Venezuela, Ens Ozama, from 2100. No cover charge. Merengue and salsa for Latin lovers.

Guácara Taína, Paseo de los Indios, Av Cayetano Germosén, T8095330671. 2100-0200. Shows of Taíno dancing in the spectacular setting of a huge natural cave with stalactites and indigenous pictographs. Also a disco with all types of music, 2 dance floors, happy hours and fashion shows. Capacity for 2000 guests. US$4-12. For daytime tours of the cave T8095302662 (0900-1700), or T8095331051 (1700-2100), reserve 24 hours in advance.

Jet Set, Independencia 2253, Centro Comercial El Portal, T8095354145. www.jetsetclub.net, 2200-late.The place for good Latin dance music. Dress casual. Live merengue bands on a schedule basis but mostly on Mon. Livens up after midnight.

Llegó, José Reyes 10 esq Arzobispo Nouel, Zona Colonial, T8096898250. From 2100. No cover charge.

Loft Lounge & Dance Club, Tiradentes 44, Naco, T8097324016, www.loft.com.do. The website lists activities and events such as live merengue, salsa and pop. Dress casual.

Maunaloa Night Club, in the Centro de los

Héroes, T8095332214. 2200-late. Live music and comics, dancing to Dominican music. Only open when there are scheduled activities.

Montecristo Café & Club, Abraham Lincoln esq José Amado Soler, T8095425000. Happy hour 1700-1900. Café turns into a dance floor after midnight. Dress casual. No cover charge.

Salón La Fiesta, in the Jaragua Hotel, Av George Washington 367, also Jubilee, T8096888026, www.empresasee.com. From 2100. One of the top international-style hotels in the city where you can combine gambling with a little exercise on the dance floor. Dominican music.

Secreto Musical Bar, Baltazar de los Reyes and Pimentel. Cuban music, headquarters of **Club Nacional de los Soneros**, rock, merengue, salsa and ballads.

Seven to Seven, George Washington 165 (El Malecón), T8092211919, seventosevenritmo@ hotmail.com. Nice, fun place, with merengue, salsa and pop music. Dress casual.

Entertainment

Santo Domingo *p311, maps p312 and p315*

Cinema

Ticket prices are around US$5. Some cinemas have discounts Mon-Wed at the earlier showing. Performance times are around 1700-2200 in most cinemas. New releases come out on Thu.

Broadway Cinemas, Plaza Central Mall, 3rd floor, Av 27 de Febrero esq Winston Churchill, T8098720272.

Caribbean Cinemas, Diamond Plaza Mall, Av de Los Próceres, T8095658866, also at Plaza Acrópolis, Av Winston Churchill, T8099551010, www.caribbeancinemasrd.com.

Cinemacentro Dominicano, Av George Washington, T8096888710.

Hollywood Diamond Cinemas, Av Abraham Lincoln, Diamond Mall, T8096831189.

Palacio del Cine Cinemas, Bella Vista Mall, Av Sarasota, T8092550921.

Theatres

Teatro Nacional, Plaza de la Cultura, Av Máximo Gómez, T8096873191, for tickets. Used for drama, dance and opera, lectures and presentations.

Casa de Teatro, Arzobispo Meriño 110, T8096893430. Small drama workshop.

Shopping

Santo Domingo *p311, maps p312 and p315*

Duty-free at Centro de los Héroes, La Atarazana, shops in large hotels; departure lounge at airport; all purchases must be in US dollars.

Art and crafts

Galería de Arte Nader, Calle Rafael Augusto Sánchez 22, Torre Don Roberto, Ens Piantini, T8095440878. The best gallery. The Nader family are hugely influential and stock collecters' items of Haitian, Dominican and other Latin American works of art, see also Sleeping above and Haiti, page 396.

Centro de Arte Cándido Bidó, Dr Báez 5, T8096855310.

Boutique del Fumador, El Conde 109, T8096856425, www.caobacigars.com. This is a factory outlet for Caoba cigars on the Plaza Colón. You can have a tour of the works.

The shop at the **Museo del Hombre Dominicano** sells ceramics, Taíno reproductions and works of anthropological interest.

Street sellers of Haitian or Dominican copies of Haitian naif art are not representative of what is going on in the Dominican art world and are merely gaudy paintings for tourist consumption. For details on contemporary Dominican painters, consult **Arte Contemporáneo Dominicano**, by Gary Nicolás Nader.

Bookshops

Tienda Macalé, Calle Arzobispo Nouel 3, T8096822011, near cathedral. Open daily. Has a wide selection of books, especially on the Republic's history.

New Horizons Book Shop, Av Sarasota 51, T8095334915, and 3rd floor of Bella Vista Mall, T8092550676.

Centro Cuesta del Libro, 27 de Febrero esq Lincoln. Mon-Sat 0900-2100, Sun 0900-1500.

Thesaurus, Av Abraham Lincoln esq Sarasota, T8095081114. Sofas, reading areas, café, play area, cultural events with Dominican authors, some English-language books.

Jewellery

Go to the shops in the amber and larimar museums (see above) for the best selection with good explanations.

Markets

Calle El Conde, now reserved for pedestrians, is the oldest shopping sector in Santo Domingo; Av Mella at Duarte is good for discount shopping.
Mercado Modelo, Av Mella esq Santomé. Open Mon-Sat 0900-1230, 1430-1700. GFift shops, handicrafts, paintings, foodstuffs; bargain to get a good price, most prices have been marked up to allow for this. Guides appointed to assist tourists get a 5-10% commission from the vendor.
Mercado de las Pulgas, a flea market, operates on Sun in the Centro de los Héroes and at the Parque Mirador del Sur at Av Luperón.

Music

Music Box, Los Jardines, Arroyo Hondo, T8095403055.
Tiagos, Calle El Conde, T8096896154.
Musicalia Outlet, El Conde, T8092218445, also Tiradentes esq Gustavo Mejía Ricart, T8095622878.
CD Mania, Av Venezuela 104, T8095915698.
CD Stop, Plaza Central, T8095495640.
Karen Records, El Conde 251, T8096860019.

Shopping malls

There are some 20 shopping malls, including **Plaza Naco**, Av Tiradentes y Naco, www.plazanaco.com; **Unicentro Plaza**, Av 27 de Febrero esq Av Abraham Lincoln; **Plaza Caribe**, Av 27 de Febrero esq Leopoldo Navarro; **Multicentro Churchill**, Av Winston Churchill esq Gustavo Mejía Ricart, www.gruporamos.com; **Acropólis Mall**, Av Winston Churchill esq Julio A Aybar, www.acropolisdr.com; **Bella Vista Mall**, Sarasota 64 entre Dr Defiló y Winston Churchill, www.bellavistamallrd.com; **Diamond Mall**, Los Próceres, Arroyo Hondo, all offering a variety of shops, food halls, restaurants, cinemas, banks and offices.

▲ Activities and tours

Santo Domingo *p311, maps p312 and p315*
Diving
GUS Dive Center, Santo Domingo, T8095660818, gusdive@verizon.net.do. SSI certification. Possibly the best dive centre in the capital with rental gear and scheduled dive trips.

Mark Goldsmith, Santo Domingo, T8096977996, ddbconsultants@verizon.net.do. British, gives PADI certification, classes in English, very professional.
Mike's Dive Center, Santo Domingo, T8095663483, dive@verizon.net.do. A small dive shop renting scuba gear and arranging miscellaneous trips to different dive sites on demand. Dive master, Emiliano García, is very friendly and professional.

Spectator sports

Boxing Boxing matches take place frequently in Santo Domingo at the **Gimnasio-Coliseo de Boxeo** (with a capacity to seat 7000 but capable of holding 10,000 spectators) next to the baseball stadium, at the **Carlos Teo Cruz Coliseum**, at hotels and at sports clubs, where you can also see fencing, judo, karate and table tennis.
Horse racing Horse racing takes place at the **Hipódromo V Centenario** at Km 14.5 on the Autopista de las Américas, T8096876060, grandstand ticket US$1.
Polo Polo matches are played at weekends at Sierra Prieta, 25 mins from Santo Domingo, and at Casa de Campo, T8095233333, see below.

Tour operators

Coco Tours, T8095861311, www.cocotours.com. City tour Thu US$49 including lunch, shopping tour Sat US$25.
Espeleogrupo Santo Domingo, T8096821577, is an educational organization working to protect many anthropological and geological sites, to which they also arrange technical and non-technical excursions, specifically **Las Cuevas de Pomier** in San Cristóbal and the **Cuevas de las Maravillas** in La Romana.
Museo de Historia y Geografía in Santo Domingo organizes archaeological and historical tours in the Republic. Tours are announced in the newspapers. The co-ordinator is Vilma Benzo de Ferrer, T8096886952.
Turinter, T8096864020, www.turinter.com. City tour US$41 not including lunch, Santo Domingo by night, US$39 starting at **Museo del Jamón** and moving on to **Guácara Taína**.

Other sports

Bowling Sebelén Bowling Centre (Bolera), Av Abraham Lincoln, esquina

Roberto Pastoriza, T8095400101, in a large commercial plaza in Santo Domingo. Built to host the 1997 Panamerican Bowling Games, it is said to be the world's most hi-tech bowling alley. Open 1000-0200.

⊜ Transport

Santo Domingo *p311, maps p312 and p315*

Air

From North America Boston, Ft Lauderdale, Miami, New York (JFK and Newark) and Philadelphia with connections from other US cities, with **American Airlines**, **USAirways**, **Continental** and **Delta**. 2 low-cost airlines are **JetBlue** from New York and **Spirit Airlines** from Ft Lauderdale.

From Europe Amsterdam (**Martinair**), Madrid (**Iberia**) with connecting flights from most European and Spanish cities, (**Air Europa**), Milan (**Lauda Air**), Paris (**Air France**).

From the Caribbean Direct flights from Aruba, Barbados, Curaçao, Fort-de-France, Havana, Kingston, Mayagüez, Montego Bay, Pointe-à-Pitre, Port-au-Prince, St Maarten, San Juan and Santiago de Cuba, and connections with other islands with a variety of regional and international airlines.

From Central America Copa from Panama City, San José, Guatemala City, Managua.

From South America From Caracas, **Aserca** and **Aeropostal**; other capital cities are connected through Miami or Panama City.

Airport Aeropuerto Las Américas, 23 km out of town, T8095491253, very clean and smart. Immediately on arrival there is a tourist office on your right (helpful, will make bus reservation if you want to go straight out of Santo Domingo), and next to that an office selling tourist cards, a blackboard indicates who needs a card. Check if you need a card, or else the long queue to get through immigration will be wasted. **BanReservas** for currency exchange is in the customs hall open Sun and at night, while ATM machines are outside the customs hall in the food court area. **Car hire offices** are numerous as you come out of the customs hall. On departure, the queue for check-in can be long and slow, allow plenty of time.

Leaving the airport on the ground floor, you find the expensive, individual taxis. (Upstairs, outside departures, *colectivo* taxis cram up to 6 passengers into the vehicle; much cheaper.) The drive from Las Américas International Airport to Santo Domingo should take no more than 30 mins (but allow 1 hr), and cost no more than US$20 during the daytime although it varies between companies and US$25 is usual. From the capital to the airport for the return journey prices range from US$15 (**Alex Taxi**) to US$20 (**Apolo Taxi**). Most large hotels have a taxi or limousine service with set fares throughout the city and to the airport. Alternatively you can get from the airport to the colonial city for about US$1 if you walk, or take a *moto- concho* (motorcycle taxi), to the *autopista* (main road) and then catch a *guagua* (minibus) to Parque Enriquillo. On your return, catch any bus to Boca Chica or towns east and get a *motoconcho* from the junction; only really feasible if you are travelling light. If arriving late at night it may be better to go to Boca Chica (see page363), about 10 km from the airport, taxi about US$20. Various tour agencies also run minibuses to the airport; check with your hotel.

Airline offices Air Europa, Av Winston Churchill 459, T8096838020. **Air France**, Av Máximo Gómez 15, Santo Domingo, T8096868432, Las Américas International Airport, T8095490309, Punta Cana Airport, T8099593002. **Air Jamaica**, F P Ramírez 159, Santo Domingo, T8098720080. **Air Santo Domingo**, Av 27 de Febrero 272 esq Seminario, Santo Domingo, T8096838006, information and reservations, T8096838020, at Las Américas, T8095491110, at La Romana airport, T8098139144, at Puerto Plata airport, T8095860391, at Punta Cana, T8092211170, at Puerto Plata, T8095860385, at El Portillo, Samaná, T8092406571. **American Airlines**, Edif IN TEMPO, Av W Churchill, Santo Domingo, T8095425151, La Romana airport, T8095565786, Punta Cana airport, T8099597002. **American Eagle**, Las Américas, Santo Domingo, T8095492339, Puerto Plata airport, T5860325. **Caribair**, Av Luperón, Santo Domingo, T8095426688, La Romana, T8092218076, Puerto Plata, T8096829855, Punta Cana, T8096885542, caribair.sa@verizon.net.do. **Condor**, Av George Washington 353, T8096853125. **Continental**, Av Winston Churchill, Santo Domingo, T8095626688. **Copa**, 27 de Febrero,

Santo Domingo, T8094722233. **Coturisca**, Av Luperón 49, Santo Domingo, T8096833435. **Cubana**, Av Tiradentes, Santo Domingo, T8092272040, ventascuba@verizon.net.do. **Iberia**, Lope de Vega 63, Santo Domingo, T8095080188. **Lufthansa**, Av George Washington 353, Santo Domingo, T8096899625. **Martinair**, M Gómez y Juan S Ramírez, Santo Domingo, T8096886661. **Mexicana de Aviación**, Av G M Ricart 54, Santo Domingo, T8095411016. **Sky King**, Puerto Plata international airport, T8095860342. **United Air Lines**, G M Ricart 54, Santo Domingo, T8095418072. **US Airways**, G M Ricart 54, Santo Domingo, T8095400505.

Bus
OMSA buses run along the main corridors (*corredores*), Avs 27 de Febrero, Luperón, Bolívar, Independencia, John F Kennedy, Máximo Gómez and the west of the city, US$0.30. For information on long-distance buses, see Essentials page 299.

Car
Car hire There are many places at the airport, on the road to the airport and on the Malecón. **MC Auto Rent-A-Car** (Av George Washington No 105, T8096886518, F6864529, www.mccarrental.com), branches also at Las Américas Airport (T8095498911) and Boca Chica (T8095234414); **Nelly** (Av Independencia 654, T8096877979, www.nellyrac.com, from US$45 a day); **Dollar** (Av Independencia 366, T8092217368, www.dollar.com.do, from US$47 a day); **Europcar** (Av Independencia 354,T8096882121, www.europcar.com.do); **Payless** (Gustavo Mejía Ricart 826, T8095634686).

Taxi
Carros públicos, or *conchos*, are shared taxis normally operating on fixed routes, 24 hrs a day, basic fare US$0.30. *Públicos* can be hired by one person, if they are empty, and are then called *carreras*. They can be expensive (US$3-4, more on longer routes); settle price before getting in. Fares are higher at Christmas time. *Públicos/conchos* also run on long-distance routes; ask around to find the cheapest. You can get to just about anywhere by bus or *público* from Parque Independencia,

but you have to ask where to stand. *Conchos* running on a shared basis are becoming scarcer, being replaced by *carreras*.
Radio taxis charge between US$3-5 on local journeys around Santo Domingo (US$10 per hr) and are safer than street taxis, call about 20-30 mins in advance: **Taxi Anacaona**, T8095304800; **Apolo Taxi**, T8095370000; **Taxi Express**, T8095377777; **Taxi Oriental**, T8095495555; **Alex Taxi**, T8095403311; **Taxi Hogar**, T8095682825; **Tecni Taxi**, T8095672010; **Maxi Taxi**, T8095440077; **Taxi Raffi**, T8096877858.
Motorcycle taxi service, *motoconchos*, US$0.20, sometimes illegally take up to 3 passengers on pillion. Drivers are supposed to wear a helmet, but none of the regulations are respected. Take care.

❶ Directory

Santo Domingo *p311, maps p312 and p315*
Banks Many along Isabel La Católica, but check which banks accept which TCs, see page 296. **Casa de Cambio La Catedral**, Sánchez, off El Conde, gives a slightly better rate than banks. **Embassies and consulates** Canada, Capitán Eugenio de Marchena 39, Ens La Esperilla, T8096851136, sdmgo@dfait-maeci.ge.ca. **Denmark**, Torre Panamericana, Piso 10, Av Abraham Lincoln 504, T8095495100. **France**, Calle Las Damas 42, Zona Colonial, T8096954300, ambafrance.sd@verizon.net.do. **Germany**, Gustavo M Ricart, Torre Piantini, T8095428949, embal@verizon.net.do. **Haiti**, Juan Sánchez Ramírez 33, Zona Universitaria, Santo Domingo, T8096868185, amb.haiti@verizon.net.do. **Italy**, Manuel Rodríguez Objío 4, Gazcue, T8096820830, ambital@verizon.net.do. **Netherlands**, Max Henríquez Ureña 50 esq Abraham Lincoln, Ens Piantini, T8092620320, std@minbuza.nl. **Spain**, Independencia 1205, T8095356500, embesp.do@mail.mae.es. **UK**, 27 de Febrero 233, Edificio Corominas Pepín, 7th floor, T8094727111, brit.emb.sadom@verizon.net.do. **USA**, César Nicolás Penson esq Leopoldo Navarro, (embassy) T8092212171, (consulate) 8092215511,

www.usemb.gov.do. **Internet** Centennial Dominicana offices allow you to walk in and use their internet computer stations for free. Offices at corner of Winston Churchill and Gustavo Mejía Ricart (Edificio Grouconsa), corner of Máximo Gómez and Av Bolívar (Plaza de los Libertadores), and Ctra Mella Km 8.5 next to the Ferretería Haché. Mon-Sat 0800-1900. Reserve in advance to use the internet service at the **Verizon** offices in Unicentro Plaza, T8092204721, Cacique, T8092207411 and Oficina Torre Cristal, T8092205312. Verizon is among the cheapest, at US$0.75 for 15 mins, US$2 per hr. **Cyber Café**, Plaza Universitaria, Av Winston Churchill T8095324743, 15 mins US$0.45, 30 mins US$0.75, 45 mins US$1.10. Also at Av Máximo Gómez 49, T8096872888. In the Zona Colonial: **Abel Brown's Internet World**, El Conde 359, T8093335604, 0900-2100 Mon-Sat, Sun 1000-1600; **Servir**, El Conde 351 esq José Reyes, T8096228537, Mon-Sat 0800-2200, Sun 0800-2000; **Verizon**, El Conde 202, T8092201111, Mon-Sat 0800-2000, Sun 0800-1400. **Medical services Hospitals** Clínica Abréu, Av Independencia y Beller 42, T8096884411, and adjacent **Clínica Gómez Patiño** are recommended for foreigners needing treatment or hospitalization. Fees are high but care is good. 24-hr emergency department. For free consultation and prescription, **Padre**

Billini Hospital, Calle Padre Billini y Santomé, Zona Colonial, efficient, friendly. **Pharmacies Farmacia San Judas Tadeo**, Independencia 57 esq Bernardo Pichardo, T8096858165, open 24 hrs all year, home delivery. **Post Correo Central** is in La Feria, Calle Rafael Damirón, Centro de los Héroes. Mon-Fri 0800-1600, Sat 0800-1200. **Lista de correo** (poste restante) keeps mail for 2 months. There are post offices in **Hotel Embajador**, T8092212131, **Plaza Central**, T8094726777, **Isabela La Católica**, Zona Colonial, T8096894721, and Av George Washington, T8096823439. To ensure the delivery of documents worldwide, use a **courier service**: **American Airlines** (T8095490043); **DHL Dominicana**, T8095437888; **Universal Courier Services**, T8095497398; **UPS Dominicana**, T8095665177; **Federal Express**, T8095653636; **Internacional Bonded Couriers**, T8095425265. **Telephone** International and long distance, also fax: **Verizon**, Av 30 de Marzo 12, near Parque Independencia, and 11 others throughout the city (Mon-Fri 0730-1800, Sat 0800-1300). Cheaper for phone calls is the **Tricom** office on Av Máximo Gómez between Bolívar and Independencia. In the Zona Colonial: **Verizon**, El Conde 202, T8092201111, **Tricom**, El Conde, T8094766000.

North to Santiago

The Autopista Duarte, a four-lane highway, runs northwest from Santo Domingo to Santiago de los Caballeros, with the Cordillera Central on one side and the Cordillera Septentrional on the other. From there it reduces in size and follows the length of the Cibao Valley alongside the Río Yaque del Norte to its outlet on the coast at Monte Cristi. This is the main artery through the country, used by cars, trucks, motoconchos, cows, horse-drawn vehicles and others. The first town of any size just west of the Autopista Duarte is Bonao, 85 km from the centre of Santo Domingo and surrounded by rice paddies. To the east is the Falconbridge ferronickel mine, a large employer and major contributor to the region's economy. After Bonao on the Autopista Duarte, on the left, is the main road to Constanza. ➤ For Eating, Sleeping and other listings, see pages 332-337.

Constanza → *Population: 80,000. Altitude: 1300 m.*

● *The Garlic Festival is held in June.*

High up in the mountains, set in a circular valley formed by a meteor, is Constanza. Dubbed the Alps of the Dominican Republic, the mountains provide a spectacular backdrop for what is a fairly ordinary town with no buildings of note. The scenery is some of the best in the country, with rivers, forests and waterfalls and there are lots of good hikes in the area. In winter, temperatures can fall to zero or lower and there may be frosts at night, but during the day it is pleasant and fresh. In the 1950s, the dictator, General Trujillo brought in 200 Japanese families to farm the land and the valley is famous for food production, potatoes, garlic, strawberries, mushrooms and other vegetables, and for growing ornamental flowers. The main street is Calle Luperón, which runs east to west. Most of the cheap hotels and restaurants are here or nearby. La Isla gas station is at the east end, where taxis and *motoconchos* congregate. The local **tourist office** ① *www.constanza.net*, is beside Radio Constanza on Matilde Viñas esquina Abreu.

With a good, tough, 4WD you can visit the **Parque Nacional Valle Nuevo**, via the very poor but spectacular road from Constanza to San José de Ocoa, see below. The views are wonderful and you pass the geographical centre of the island, marked by four small pyramids at the Alta Bandera military post about 30 km south of Constanza. The park's alpine plateau is at an altitude of about 2640 m and has a large number of plants which are unique to the island in pine and broadleaf forests. There are also thermal springs, three Amerindian cemeteries and the **Aguas Blancas** waterfall about 15 km south of town, so you can walk it if you want. The waterfall falls in three stages with a maximum drop of 87 m to a large pool at the bottom. At weekends or holidays it is very busy and lots of litter accumulates.

La Vega → *Population: 200,000.*

Further north up the Autopista Duarte is La Vega, a quiet place in the beautiful valley of La Vega Real. After the declaration of Independence on 27 February 1844, La Vega was the first place to raise the national flag, on 4 March. It was also the first town to embrace the Restoration Movement in 1863. The town is nothing special and most people only come here to change *guaguas* or buses or to visit the local archaeological sites (see below), which can be reached by hiring a taxi in the Parque Central or at the bus stations.

La Vega's **carnival** is one of the most colourful pre-Lenten festivities in the country, with elaborate masks (*caretas*) of limping devils (*diablos cojuelos*), made mostly of papier mâché. It is also the oldest carnival, having been celebrated here since 1510, when a Spanish priest organized a re-enactment of the Spanish 'Moors and Christians' tradition. Activities are held on six Sundays in February and March, in the afternoons from 1500-1800. On the first Sunday there is an inaugural parade and on

> ‡ *Watch out for the local custom of hitting people with vejigas, balls on ropes, traditionally made from cows' bladders.*

subsequent Sundays there are 'runs' by the devils. There is also a Children's Day, held in the Diablodromo. *Comparsas*, sponsored music groups, compete and there are competitions for the best costumes. Materials are brightly coloured and hundreds of little bells are sown into the costumes. There are currently over 90 'groups' of between five and 40 members, and it is estimated that some 1500 people dress up every Sunday. Traditional groups include Las Broncos, Las Mazones, Las Fieras, Las Hormiguitas, Las Panteras, Los Cavernarios, Los Bestias, Los Tigres, Las Plagas, Los Pieles Rojas and Los Rocky. It is a huge, rowdy affair. There are also performances by leading merengue and bachata groups. A collection of masks can be seen in the **Casa de la Cultura** ① *Calle Independencia, Mon-Fri 0930-1200, 1400-1700, free*, which also puts on temporary art exhibitions. See also www.dominicanmasks.com.

About 5 km north, the other side of the Autopista, is the turn for **Santo Cerro**, an old convent where the image of Virgen de las Mercedes is venerated and pilgrims come every 24 September to pray to Nuestra Señora de las Mercedes. Legend has it that Columbus raised a cross on the summit of the hill in 1494. Inside the brick church on the hill is a hole in which the cross is supposed to have stood. If you continue along the road to the other side of the hill and into the valley, 6 km north of La Vega on the road to Moca, the ruins of **La Vega Vieja** ① *Mon-Sat 0900-1200, 1400-1700, US$2* (Old La Vega), can be seen. It was founded by Columbus in 1494 but destroyed by an

Dominican Republic North to Santiago

earthquake on 2 December 1562. Bartolomé de las Casas said the first Mass here and the first baptisms of Taínos took place here, on 21 September 1496. The first protest against the treatment of Indians was also made here in 1510, by Fray Pedro de Córdoba. La Vega Vieja is now a National Park and the foundations of the fortress, church and a few houses can be seen.

Conuco

At Conuco, 5 km east of Salcedo, just before Tenares on the main road towards San Francisco de Macorís, is the **Museo Hermanas Mirabal** ① *T8095772704, daily 0930-1700, US$0.25*. The house of the Mirabal sisters, is one of the most popular museums in the country. It was built in 1954 by their mother Doña Chea, and was the second family home. The gardens are immaculately kept, with beautiful orchids in the trees and lots of other flowers and fruit. The sisters and their husbands were active in the resistance movement in the late 1950s, but Patria, Minerva and María Teresa were ambushed and murdered in 1960 on their return from visiting their husbands in prison, and are now icons for both liberty and the rights of women. The day of their assassination, 25 November, is remembered in many Latin American countries as the International Day Against Violence Towards Women. Their murder helped to lead to the downfall of General Trujillo, who was himself assassinated in May 1961. The fourth sister, Dedé, is still alive as she did not go with them that day. The bodies of the three sisters and Minerva's husband, Manolo, are buried in the garden, which has been declared an extension of the Pantéon Nacional, where national heroes are buried.

Jarabacoa

The road from the Autopista Duarte to Jarabacoa winds through some beautiful pine forests. The climate is fresh, with warm days and cool nights. It is an important agricultural area, growing coffee, flowers, strawberries, watercress and other crops. The town itself is quite modern. Everything is in walking distance and most things can

❗ *Jarabacoa is the place to come for adventure sports.*

be found along the main street, **Calle Mario Nelson Galán**. Several notable artists and sculptors live in the area and are willing to receive visitors to their studios or give classes.

The three main rivers are the **Río Jimenoa**, the **Río Baiguate** and the **Río Yaque del Sur**. The Baiguate flows into the Jimenoa and the Jimenoa then flows into the Yaque. There are several other tributaries which are being explored for new whitewater rafting locations. The Jimenoa waterfalls, **Salto Jimenoa** ① *0800-1800, US$0.50*, are worth seeing, 10 km from town, although they are often crowded with tour parties. Hurricane Georges wreaked havoc in 1998, washing away the power plant and bridge by the falls. A new walkway has been made, with wobbly suspension bridges (avoid too many people on them at any one time). The falls are large, with a tremendous volume of water and consequent noise. The last wall is used for canyoning. There is

❗ *Mountains, rivers and waterfalls are spectacular features in this area.*

another waterfall dropping 75 m over a cliff on the Río Jimenoa, which is more difficult to get to and unsigned, off the road to Constanza, so you will have to ask for directions locally or go with a group. Closer to town, off the Constanza road, are the Baiguate

falls, **Salto Baiguate**, 3½-4 km, an easy walk, there is a signpost to the falls, fourth turn on the right after **Pinar Dorado**. A path leads from the road around the hillside, hugging the side of the gorge, until you get to some steps down to a sandy river beach and the rocks beneath the falls. There are usually lots of tours to the falls by jeep or horse. The local **tourist office** is on Parque Duarte.

Pico Duarte

In the Cordillera Central near Jarabacoa and Constanza is Pico Duarte, at 3087 m the highest peak in the Caribbean, but only just. Its neighbour, La Pelona, is only 5 m lower at 3082 m. During the Trujillo dictatorship, when Pico Duarte was inevitably named Pico Trujillo, one of his geographers erroneously added to the height of the mountain, allegedly to impress his *jefe* (boss). To this day, most maps have Pico Duarte at 3175 m. There are several popular hiking routes, requiring differing degrees of stamina. Some of the routes take in other mountains as well. You will see a wide selection of native flora and birds, rainforest and pine forest, and pass through several different ecosystems. It is very beautiful landscape and a great experience. If you are not shrouded in cloud there is a fantastic view looking down on clouds and other mountain peaks. The most popular routes are the 46-km trail from La Ciénaga near Jarabacoa, and the 90-km trail from Mata Grande near San José de las Matas. Whichever route you take you will have to pay a US$2 National Park fee (passport or copy required) and hire a guide, US$5 per day, and mules, US$3 per day for baggage, US$4 for riding. Mules are definitely recommended for the average hiker, you can carry all your gear and water if you want, but the guide will want a mule for his gear. Guides speak only Spanish and you must pay them as well as feed them and tip them. You are not allowed to set off on your own. Allow US$60 for park entry fee, guide and mule hire for three days. There are other walks in the Parque Nacional Armando Bermúdez and the adjoining Parque Nacional José del Carmen Ramírez, but they all involve some steep climbing. Guides are available at the park entrance.

> **?** *The driest time is December-February, but March-November is still good.*

La Ciénaga route At La Ciénaga the DNP has set up a nice little camp ground. You can sleep here and there is a tap in the yard for washing but facilities are very basic. The hike is moderate, for intermediate to advanced hikers, but very hard indeed for those who are not in regular training for hill climbing. Allow three days (or more if it rains, the paths turn to mud). Guagua from Jarabacoa to La Ciénaga US$3, or hitch (very little traffic). On your return, the last carro for Jarabacoa leaves at 1600. **Iguana Mama**, in Cabarete and **Rancho Baiguate** in Jarabacoa (see page 330) both offer tours of three to nine days, or a custom-designed trek is possible if they have nothing else arranged. Walking sticks/hiking poles are recommended, particularly for the journey down, which can be hard on the knees and dangerous if wet and muddy. Take adequate clothing with you; it can be cold (below 0°C) and wet; also take a torch and matches.

Santiago de los Caballeros → *Population: 690,000.*

Santiago de los Caballeros is the second largest city in the Republic and chief town of the Cibao valley. The streets of the centre are busy, noisy, with lots of advertising signs; east of the centre it becomes greener, cleaner and quieter. The Río Yaque del Norte skirts the city with Avenida Circunvalación parallel to it. There are few sites of tourist interest, this is a modern, working city, although there are some old buildings. In the colonial part look out for tiles on the walls at street corners, with the old names of the streets, put there in 1995 to mark the 500th anniversary of the founding of the city.

Ins and outs
Getting there and around There are good links by road from Santo Domingo (4-lane highway all the way) and Puerto Plata on the coast. Several bus companies have services to the city. There is also an airport for domestic flights.

The long-distance bus terminals are scattered around the city and you will probably have to get a taxi to your destination. You can walk round the centre of the city but suburbs and outlying areas are best reached by bus or *carro público*. Calle del Sol is the main commercial street, with both vendors and the main shops. In the newer part of the town, Avenida Juan Pablo Duarte and Avenida 27 de Febrero have shopping plazas, banks and fast food restaurants, very much in the US style.
→ *See also Transport, page 336, for further details.*

There is a **tourist office** in the basement of the Town Hall (Ayuntamiento), Av Juan Pablo Duarte; it has little information available, only Spanish spoken.

Sights

On **Parque Duarte** are the **Catedral de Santiago Apóstol**, a neoclassical building (19th-century) containing the tombs of the tyrant Ulises Heureux and of heroes of the Restauración de la República; the **Centro de Recreo** (one of the country's most exclusive private clubs) with Moorish-style arches and the **Palacio Consistorial** (1895-1896), now the **Casa de Cultura de Santiago** ① *Calle del Sol, T8092765625, Mon-Sat 0800-1800*, which holds cultural and art exhibitions. **Fortaleza San Luis**, overlooking the Río Yaque del Norte, was inaugurated in 2005 as a cultural plaza and lots of artists now have their work on exhibition. Repair works in 2004 uncovered 18th- and 19th-century weapons and artefacts and it was decided to convert the building from an active military base to a museum. The fort, where Dominican Independence was approved in 1844, was the scene of battle in 1863 in the War of Restoration. The clock tower dates from 1885.

Other places worth visiting are the **Pontífica Universidad Católica Madre y Maestra** (founded 1962) and the **Monumento a los Héroes de la Restauración**, at the highest point in the city (panoramic views of the Cibao valley, commissioned by Trujillo in his own honour and remodelled in 1991 to include a mirador). You can climb up to the top of the monument for a panoramic view of the city, the valley and the mountains. Behind the monument is a **theatre** built by Balaguer in the 1980s, a rather impenetrable rectangular block with lots of Italian marble. This area is popular at weekends and fiestas and there are lots of bars and restaurants around the park. At carnival or any other outdoor celebration, this is the place to come. Rum shops sprout all over the open spaces and parades and parties occupy roads and squares. Along Avenida 27 de Febrero is the **León Jiménez tobacco factory**, established in 1903. As well as 18 mn **Marlboro** cigarettes a day, the workers turn out 20,000 hand-rolled cigars, which you can watch being made. Each cigar maker has a target of 100 cigars a day and earns about US$70 a week. The free tour is interesting and ends with a free drink and shopping opportunities if you like cigars. Next to the factory is the **Centro Cultural Eduardo León Jiménez** ① *Av 27 de Febrero 146, T8095822315, www.centroleon.org.do, exhibitions, café and shop open Tue-Sun 1000-1900, US$1, children under 12 US$0.50; guided visits US$2 in Spanish, US$2.50 in English, French or German*. The state-of-the-art cultural centre opened in 2003 in celebration of the 100th anniversary of the founding of the tobacco group. There is a visual arts collection, an anthropological collection with some priceless archaeological and ethnological pieces and a bibliographical collection.

⊜ Sleeping

Bonao *p328*

D-G Rancho Wendy, Los Quemados, Bonao, T8094048330, www.ranchowendy.com. Rural backpacker's hostal in the mountains with rooms, dormitories and camp site, owned by American Marshall Zipper. Good, cheap food available, breakfast US$3. Lots of activities, hiking, mountain biking, horse riding, white water rafting, kayaking, also immersion language courses and volunteering. Motoconcho from Bonao US$2.50.

Constanza *p328*

AL-A Rancho Guaraguao, T8095393333, www.ranchoguaraguao.com. On hillside overlooking the town, rooms, villas, cabins and campsite, lots of facilities including restaurant 1100-2300, snack bar 0700-2100, pool bar 0800-late, disco from 2100, games room, gym, pool, thermal jacuzzi, playground, picnic area, barbeques and chapel. Meal plans available, lots going on. **A-D Mi Cabaña**, Ctra Gen Antonio Duvergé, Colonia Japonesa, T8095392930, www.micabana.bizland.com. At entrance to Hotel Nueva Suiza on the road to San José de Ocoa, rooms, suites and small townhouses which sleep up to 6, kitchenettes, pool, bar, volleyball court, loud music, breakfast included, cheapest rates are mid-week.

B-D Hotel Rancho Constanza and Cabañas de la Montaña, Calle San Francisco de Macorís 99, Sector Don Bosco, east of town towards Colonia Kennedy, T8095393268, http://ranchoconstanza.tripod.com/. Modern, rustic, Alpine-style hotel, 11 rooms or suites with kitchens, also 12 dark, basic cabins, good for families, sleep up to 5, meal plans available, cheapest rates mid-week, playground and volley ball, lovely setting, tours arranged to waterfalls and hikes up into the mountains behind the hotel.

B-E Alto Cerro, east of town, T8095391553, www.altocerro.com. Highly thought of, camping, 10 hotel rooms and 30 2-bedroom villas, strung along a rise, great view of fields in valley, excursions on horse back, quad bike rental, very popular at weekends, cheaper during the week, grocery, restaurant remodelled 2007 serving home-grown meat, fruit and veg, playground.

E Mi Casa, Luperón y Sánchez, T8095392764. 7 single rooms, 3 double rooms, 1 suite sleeps 4, hot water, restaurant/*comedor*, great strawberry juice and strawberry jam.

La Vega *p329*

Some basic hotels (**E**) on Calle Cáceres, but they are not recommended; slightly better accommodation (**D**) is along the highway.

D El Rey, Restauración 3, T8095739797, rey.Fernandez@verizon.net.do. Rooms with 1 or 2 beds for 2-4 people, new, a/c, phone, TV, central, good standard, clean and safe.

Jarabacoa *p330*

L-B Gran Jimenoa, out of town on Av La Confluencia, Los Corralitos, T8095746304, www.granjimenoa.com. 28 rooms and suites in lush countryside beside the river, safe for bathing when there isn't too much water, great location, new and in good condition, comfortable, pool, jacuzzi, indoor games, TV, room service, good restaurant with river view, local meats, packed with Dominicans at weekends. Rates include breakfast and taxes.

A-B Rancho Baiguate, T8095744940, www.ranchobaiguate.com. Price per person,

including meals. Owned and managed by Omar and Estela Rodríguez. Lovely countryside setting beside river, extensive gardens, 27 rooms from standard to luxury, or small, medium and large, hot water, good bathrooms. Also 2 dormitories with 9 bunk beds in each for students/groups (the hotel started out as a summer camp). Bracing unheated pool, soccer and basketball court, quad bikes, horse riding and **Maroma's Parcours**, an adventure playground for adults, helpful staff and management, friendly, English spoken, good place for buffet lunch, lots of tour parties come for the day. Free transport into town until 2200, if there are not many guests you eat supper at the **Rancho Restaurant**.

D California, on road to Constanza, Calle José Durán E 99, T8095746255. 10 simple rooms opening onto patio area with arches giving shade over the doors, big room sleeps 5, bathroom, hot water, fan, breakfast US$5, other meals on request, bar, small pool, popular, friendly, tours arranged to Pico Duarte, horse riding, rafting.

E Brisas del Yaque, Luperón esq Peregrina Herrera, T8095744490. Small rooms but new, with good furnishings and good bathrooms, excellent value, small balcony, TV, a/c, brick and wood decor, tiled floors, no food but in town and close to places to eat.

Santiago de los Caballeros *p331*

AL-A Hodelpa Gran Almirante Hotel and Casino, Av Estrella Sadhalá 10, Los Jardines, on road north, T8095801992, www.hodelpa.com. 156 rooms and suites with a/c, mini bar and 24-hr room service. Popular with business visitors, quite good, pool, fitness centre, internet access, casino, Spanish restaurant and tapas bar.

AL-B Aloha Sol, Calle del Sol 150, T8095830090, www.alohasol.com. 66 rooms and suites, a/c, TV, breakfast included, smart, upmarket, cool, restaurant **D'Manon** with local and international food.

A Hodelpa Centro Plaza, Calle Mella 54 esq del Sol, T8095817000, www.hodelpa.com. 86 rooms and suites with a/c, phone, TV, minibar, fitness centre and massage parlour. Smart, modern, good restaurant overlooking the city, disco club **Tarari** next door, no parking facilities.

D-E Colonial, Av Salvador Cucurullo 115,

T8092473122. Small clean rooms with a/c and/or fan, good bathrooms, very hot water, fridge, TV, cheap restaurant serving good Dominican food, friendly, luggage store, internet access, currency exchange. Better option than the other hotels on this street.

❶ Eating

Constanza *p328*
All the food here is wonderfully fresh, with local ingredients such as guinea fowl and rabbit.
♥ **Aguas Blancas**, Rufino Espinosa 54, T8095391561. 1000-until everybody goes home. Like most of Constanza, casual dining and family dining serving typical Dominican dishes. Try the *Guinea a la salsa roja*.
♥ **Comedor Gladys**, Luperón, T8095393625. 0700-2230, *menú del día* US$2.25, plenty of food and freshly cooked, fish, goat or ask for something different, pastry counter popular with kids after school.
♥ **Exquiteses Dilenia**, Gaston F Deligne 7, T8095392213. 1000-late. Specializes in lamb, guinea fowl and rabbit dishes. For a little variety, try the mixed grill or the *cocido*.
♥ **Lorenzo's**, Luperón 83, T8095392008. 0800-2300. Excellent Dominican food, try the guinea fowl or rabbit cooked in wine, also sandwiches, pizza and pasta, most dishes under US$5, open for breakfast, lunch and dinner, TV.
♥ **Los Niveles**, town centre, upstairs. 1100-1600, 1800-2300. The poshest restaurant in town, serving steak, rabbit, guinea fowl, goat and fish, most dishes US$4-6.50, wine by the glass or bottle, special events held here.
♥ **Pizzería Antojitos d' Lauren**, Duarte 16 beside the Red Cross, T8095392129. 0800-2300. Casual, plastic tables, plastic cups, chicken, sancocho, local specialities, popular at night for pizza.

Jarabacoa *p330*
Buy strawberries beside the road, locally grown, but restaurants hardly ever have them.
♥ **Rancho Restaurant**, opposite Esso station. Open for lunch and dinner. Criollo and international, good food using locally grown ingredients, belongs to **Rancho Baiguate**. The walls are lined with the work of several local artists (who often dine there with the owners).

♥ **El Jalapeño**, Calle Colón next to **Banca Sport**. 1200-late. Run by a Puerto Rican family, this funky place specializes in Mexican food and snacks. At night a small disco on the roof can help you digest.
♥ **La Herradura**, Independencia esq Duarte. 1200-2300. Probably the best place to eat in town with most dishes around US$4-6. Soup, sandwiches, pasta, fish and meat on the menu. Rustic decor in keeping with rancho style. Live music from 2100 on Fri, Sat, Sun, with variety of local singers performing until the early hours, particularly if the *gaucho* owner and his cowboy friends are there.
♥ **Pizza & Pepperoni**, Calle Gastón next to the elementary school, T5744348. 1100-2400. Small restaurant with a covered outdoor terrace, pizzas and *calzones* hit the spot late at night.
♥ **Vistabella Club Bar & Grill**, off road to Salto Jimenoa, 5 km from town, also part of **Rancho Baiguate**. Open for lunch and dinner. Pleasant setting overlooking valley and Hipólito Mejía's new country mansion, pool, bar and excellent food, specialize in goat, guinea fowl, pigeon, duck, US$5-9, or for a snack ask for a plate of mixed *longaniza*, *carne salteada* and *tostones*, great with a cold beer, popular for lunch at weekends but often quiet at night.

Santiago de los Caballeros *p331*
There are several restaurants around the monument on Av Francia and Calle del Sol, popular on Sun.
♥♥♥-♥♥ **El Café**, Av Texas esq Calle 5, Jardines Metropolitanos, T8095874247. Lunch and dinner. The favourite of businessmen and the wealthy, at the upper end of the price range with white linen on the tables. Good for sea bass and rack of lamb.
♥♥ **Camp David Ranch**, Ctra Luperón Km 7, the turn-off is on the right, unsigned, before the **El Económico** supermarket, T8096260578. Lunch and dinner. A 10-min drive up a winding, paved road to the ranch. The food quality is erratic, but the view is breathtaking across the Cibao Valley.
♥♥ **Pez Dorado**, Calle del Sol 43 (Parque Colón), T8095822518. 1200-2400. Chinese and international, good-quality food in generous portions, very popular for Sun lunch, excellent wine list.
♥♥-♥ **Ciao Ciao**, Av María R Sánchez, Los

Jardines 13, T8095831092. Lunch and dinner. Fresh homemade Italian food. Run by an eccentric, entertaining Italian.

♥♥♥ Il Pasticio, behind the Supermercado Nacional. Lunch and dinner. Eclectic Italian place, great for late night drinks, a time when the owner, Paolo, is frequently there for conversation.

♥♥♥ Kukara Macara, Av Francia 7 esq Calle del Sol, T8092413143. 1100-0200. Rustic decor, cowboy style, lots of steak including Angus, prices up to US$20 for a huge, top-class piece of meat, also seafood, tacos, sandwiches and burgers.

♥ Los 3 Café, Calle R, César Tolentino 38, T8092765909. 1200-late. Specializes in comida criolla.

♥ Olé, JP Duarte esq Independencia. 1200-late. Restaurant serving Dominican criollo food and American-style pizzería. Outdoor dining under thatched roof.

♥ Puerta del Sol, Calle del Sol 12, T8092417588. 1200-late. Cheap and popular with a slightly younger crowd.

🍷 Bars and clubs

Santiago de los Caballeros p331

Alcázar, Gran Almirante Hotel, Estrella Sadhalá esq Calle 10, 2200-late. A popular disco which doesn't get going until 0100 but stays full until 0700. Dress to kill. US$1 cover charge.

Ambis, Autopista Duarte Km 2, T8095810854. 2300-late. A long-established disco and one of the biggest in the area. Lots of girls looking for men with money to spend on them.

Bar Code, Cuba 25. Popular courtyard bar with live music. A pleasant place to chill with friends.

Daiquiri Loco, JP Duarte esq Oeste. Outdoor, lively bar with snack food, including toasted sandwiches and burritos. Try one of their great frozen daiquiris.

El Callao, in the carnavalesque-area of the Monument, Santiago. This is the oldest gay bar in Santiago. Having no walls, everyone seems to be on display. This bar has never been closed down as there is no place to hide any activity suspicious to authorities and conservatives.

Francifol, Del Sol esq Parque Duarte. Pub atmosphere with ice cold beer. Good for conversation, you can hear each other.

Metropolis Billards, Estrella Sadhalá, in front of the PUCMM University in Plaza Alejo. Bar

with several pool tables, a students' local.

Me Voy Corriendo, 27 de Febrero, Santiago. A lesbian hang-out favoured by the younger crowd. It is more of a colmado or bodega as its bar is very tiny. Without the stigma of a gay bar, patrons tend to sit on chairs on the sidewalk relaxing, talking, and enjoying a few drinks watching the city pass by.

Tailú Bar & Grill, Sabana Larga 166, Santiago, T8095820233. Like El Callao, close to the Monument, gay-friendly and gay-frequented, but it's is a bit more discreet and upmarket. It is big on Fri as the starter bar of the night.

Tarari Disco Club, Calle Mella esq del Sol, next to Hodelpa Centro Plaza, T8095817000, www.hodelpa.com. Mon-Fri 1800-dawn, Sat from 1900, Sun from 1600. Dancing all night until everyone goes home, live shows Tue, Thu.

Tin Marín, Estrella Sadhalá esq Argentina. Lively outdoor bar popular with the young rich of Santiago.

🎭 Entertainment

Santiago de los Caballeros p331

Santiago is the home of perico ripiao (see Music and dance, page 380), a folk style of merengue, which can be heard in bars and clubs alongside more modern merengue, salsa, bachata and US disco music. Things start late and go on until dawn. The monument is always a great place to hang out.

Theatre

The Gran Teatro del Cibao, T8095835011. Seats 15,000 in its main auditorium, sometimes shows opera, while merengue concerts and plays are put on in the smaller concert hall.

🎉 Festivals and events

Jarabacoa p330

Feb Carnival, similar to that in La Vega, but on a smaller scale, rather chaotic with lots of music and rum all month.

Santiago de los Caballeros p331

Feb-Mar Santiago's carnival is a pagan celebration surrounding Independence and Easter. Working-class barrios, particularly La Joya and Los Pepines, have developed rival themes of Los Lechones and Los Pepines and there is much competition between them. The *lechones* have papier mâché masks of stylized pigs, while the *pepines* have pointed horns on their masks, often hugely decorated. The Carnival Queen is crowned the first Sun in Feb, with 'warm-ups' the first 3 Suns in Feb. Parades start the weekend before **Independence Day** (27 Feb), moving off from Las Carreras and ending up at the Monumento a los Héroes de la Restauración.

▲ Activities and tours

Jarabacoa *p330*
Whitewater rafting, canyoning, tubing, kayaking, rock climbing, horse riding, mountain biking, quad bikes, jeep safaris, paragliding and hiking are all on offer here. It is one of the starting points for climbing Pico Duarte.

Adventure sports
Aventura Máxima, Rancho Baiguate (see page 333), is the biggest adventure sports centre and has a small army of Dominican and international specialist guides and instructors for each activity. They have also taken over **Get Wet**, still run as a separate operation, which offers river activities. **Aventuras del Caribe/Dominican Canyon Club**, based at Rancho Jarabacoa, T/F8092420395, www.dr-canyon.com, is run by Franz Lang, an Austrian. He deals with small groups, is recommended for canyoning, canyon trekking, rafting and kayaking and is very safety conscious.

Paragliding/parapenting
Fly Vacher, Jarabacoa, off the road to Rancho Baiguate, T8098821201, www.simonvacher.com. Owned by French instructor Simon Vacher, and the first paragliding school in the country. Tandem flights, parapenting/paragliding, US$60 off Alto de Guayabo, above Jarabacoa, or from Manaclita, US$29 at the Mantúa flying site, Km 22 off the Autopista Duarte. Courses cost US$500 for groups, US$600 for individual tuition and take 7-10 days, all gear provided. Accommodation available at the school.

◉ Transport

Constanza *p328*
Bus
There are direct buses from **Santo Domingo**, Línea Cibao, San Martín 197 esq Máximo Gómez, T8095657363, and **Línea Gladys**, San Martín 194, T8095651223, US$4.50, 0500, 0600, 1300. The last direct bus back to Santo Domingo leaves at 1200. Also buses from **Santiago**, **La Vega** and **Bonao**. Expreso **Dominicano**, Av Independencia, 100 m west of Parque Independencia, Santo Domingo, to **La Vega** every hr 0700-1800, get off at junction for Constanza. You can get to/from the Autopista Duarte by taking a *público* or *guagua* (US$1.50) to/from Constanza.

Car
There is a poor, part-paved, part-dirt road from **Jarabacoa** to Constanza, passable with an ordinary car in dry weather, but 4WD recommended for safety, 1½-2 hrs. Constanza can also be reached from the south coast via **San José de Ocoa**. Sturdy 4WD essential, with 2 spare tyres, food, drink and warm clothing in case you break down. Much of the road has been washed away by Hurricane Georges and other storms, leaving huge holes and cracks.

La Vega *p329*
Caribe Tours, T8095733488, Metro, T8095737099, and Vegano Express, T8095737079, are on Ctra La Vega, the road coming in to town from the autopista, but *guaguas* can be found on the corner of 27 de Febrero y Restauración.

Jarabacoa *p330*
Bus
No transport anywhere after 1800, very little after 1500. *Conchos* in town US$0.60. *Motoconcho* to **Rancho Baiguate** US$1.20. Jarabataxi, opposite Esso, beside **Rancho** restaurant, T8095744640. To **Santo Domingo**, Caribe Tours, T8095744557, from its own terminal off the main street, 0700, 1000, 1330, 1630, arrive 30 mins in advance (even earlier for the 0730 Mon bus), tickets sold only on day of departure, US$4.66, 2½ hrs. To **La Vega** by *guagua*, US$1.20; if you want to go to the capital or **Santiago**, they will let you off at the right

place to pick up the next *guagua*. To **Constanza**, you can get a 2-cabin pick-up truck via a very poor road over the mountains, but most people go back down to La Vega and up the Constanza road 10 km before Bonao. All transport can be found opposite the gas station.

Santiago de los Caballeros *p331*
Air
American Airlines and **Jet Blue** fly daily from Miami and New York. **North American Airlines** and **Continental** also fly from New York. **Delta** flies from Atlanta. **American Eagle** flies from San Juan, Puerto Rico and **Vol Air**, from Cap Haitien. **Sky King** flies from the Turks and Caicos Islands. See page 299, for domestic flights.

Bus
OMSA buses on main routes, as in Santo Domingo. All *carros públicos* have a letter indicating which route they are on; *carros* cost US$0.25, *guaguas* US$0.25. Many congregate at La Rotunda de las Pinas at the intersection of Estrella Sadalhá and Av 27 de Febrero.

Caribe Tours (Av 27 de Febrero, Las Colinas, T8095760790) bus to **Puerto Plata**, US$2.66, every hr; it is easier to take **Caribe Tours** than **Metro** to Puerto Plata or the capital because **Metro** only takes passengers on standby on their Santo Domingo-Puerto Plata route. **Metro** terminal, Maimón y Duarte, T8095829111, a block or so towards the centre on Duarte from the roundabout at Estrella Sadhalá (opposite direction from Verizon); 6 buses daily Santo Domingo-Santiago. **Terrabus** has its terminal at the junction of Calle del Sol and Av Francia by the monument. Service to **Santo Domingo** with connections for the ferry to **Puerto Rico** or the bus to **Haiti**. Other companies from the capital with good, a/c buses include **Cibao** and **Transporte Espinal**. To **Samaná**, go to Puerto Plata and take **Caribe Tours** from there. *Guaguas* to **San José de las Matas** leave from the Puente Hermanos Patiño, by the river not far from the centre. *Guaguas* for **La Vega**, US$1.20, go from the park at the corner of Restauración y Sabana Larga. Many other *guaguas* leave from 30 de Marzo with Salvador Cucurullo, average US$1.30, eg Puerto Plata 2 hrs, not recommended if you

have lots of luggage. **Transporte del Cibao**, Restauración almost with the corner of J P Duarte, runs buses up to **Dajabón** in the northwest near the Haitian border, 2½ hrs.

🅞 Directory

Constanza *p328*
Banks There is an **ATM** (Plus, Visa).

La Vega *p329*
Banks There is an **ATM** on the Parque Central. **Telephone** The Verizon office is also on the Parque Central

Jarabacoa *p330*
Banks Banco de Progreso by the Palacio Municipal near the bus stop. 5 banks on Mario Galán. No ATMs in town. **Internet and telephone** Verizon about ½ km on the road to La Vega beyond the gas station. In town. **Tricom** is at Sánchez y Libertad. Televimenca and **Western Union** are at Herrera e Independencia, Mon-Sat 0900-1200, 1400-1700. The **Centro de Copiado y Papelería**, a stationery shop on Calle Duarte 53, T8095742902, has 6 computers for internet access, US$2.30 per hr, open 0800-1300, 1400-1900. **Medical services** Clínica César Terrero, at the junction, T8095744397. Farmacia San Miguel, 16 de Agosto y Libertad, T8095746536, Mon-Sat 0900-1200, 1400-1700.

Santiago de los Caballeros *p331*
Banks Scotiabank, Parque Duarte, others on Calle del Sol between San Luis and Sánchez include Banco Popular (ATM), Banco León (ATM), Banco del Progreso, and BanReservas (ATM). There are also a BanReservas, Banco León and Banco del Progreso on Av 27 de Febrero. The only place you can change traveller's cheques is the Banco Popular on Calle del Sol esq Mella. **Post office** On the corner of Calle del Sol and San Luis. **Telephone** Verizon is at San Luis between Restauración and Independencia, and further out at the junction of Estrella Sadhalá and J P Duarte; take Carro A from the Parque. **Tricom** is on San Luis between Restauración and Beller, also on Av 27 de Febrero next to Banco León.

North coast

Along the north coast is a stretch of shoreline of immense beauty, with sandy beaches, cliffs, coves and mangroves sandwiched between clear, blue sea and picturesque green mountains. It is home to the historic port of Puerto Plata, fishing villages, all-inclusive resorts and guesthouses. To the west the climate is dry and the vegetation predominantly scrub and cactus, while to the east it is wetter and the vegetation lush, with the ubiquitous coconut palms towering above the beaches and greener than green golf courses. ▸▸ For Sleeping, Eating and other listings, see pages 343-352.

Puerto Plata → *Colour map 2, B3. Population: 200,000.*

Puerto Plata, sandwiched between Mount Isabel de Torres and the sea, is the main gateway on the northern coast, but the town itself is not much visited. The old town centre comprises dilapidated wooden houses and other colonial buildings behind warehouses and the power station alongside the docks. A large renovation project was approved for 2007 to restore the old world charm of the historical core. This may include the restoration of 21 Victorian houses, the conversion of the former Sánchez chocolate factory into a cultural centre and the creation of several museums. The seafront drive, the **Malecón**, sweeps along the beach for about 5 km, between the San Felipe fortress to the west on the point protecting the harbour and Long Beach to the east. Following a World Bank sponsored sewage water project for the town, in 2006 Long Beach was renovated and erosion was countered by bringing in tonnes of sand from Río San Juan. The seafront area was further enhanced by evicting brothels and other seedy establishments, while there are plans to build a boardwalk where open air restaurants and bars will attract visitors.

Ins and outs

Getting there and around Domestic and international flights use the Gregorio Luperón International Airport, 15 minutes by road from town. Taxis are for hire at the terminal, or you can walk to the main road if you have not much luggage and hail a *guagua*. **Caribe Tours, Metro** and many other bus companies pass through or terminate at Puerto Plata and transport links are good.

The old city and the fortress can be toured on foot as it is quite compact. For longer distances you can hop on a *motoconcho* or take a safer taxi. There are buses if you've got plenty of time and know where you are going.

The **tourist office** ① *T8095865000, F8095863806, 0830-1530*, is at the far east end of the Malecón at Playa Long Beach, in the little park in the same building as the tourist police.

History

Puerto Plata, was founded by Nicolás de Ovando in 1502, although Columbus had sailed past the bay and named it the silver port because of the way the sun glistened on the sea. For many years it was used as a supply stop for the silver fleets on their way from Mexico to Spain, but it was prone to pirate attacks and it was eventually supplanted by Havana. Buccaneers then roamed the hills hunting wild cattle and pigs and selling the hides and meat. After the War of Restoration in the 1860s, tobacco became the supreme commodity. The profitable trade attracted merchants, many of them from Germany, and they built luxury mansions, some of which still stand. Tobacco waned at the beginning of the 20th century, but by 1910 Puerto Plata was experiencing a boom in sugar prices and more building. Boom turned to bust with the

Great Depression in the USA in the 1930s. In the 1960s investment in tourism and the construction of the **Playa Dorada** all-inclusive complex, provided thousands of jobs and is the mainstay of the region's economy.

Sights

The old city is contained within Avenida Colón, the Malecón and Calle José Ramón Torres. The hub of the old town is the **Parque Central**. In the centre is an early 20th-century gazebo, or bandstand, and on the south side, the **San Felipe Cathedral** is worth a visit. Also on the Parque Central is the **Patrimonio Cultural** in a majestic building dating from 1908 where there are interesting art exhibitions. The **Museo del Ambar** ① *Duarte 61 esquina Emilio Prud'home, T8095862848, www.ambermuseum.com, Mon-Sat 0900-1800, US$1.50*, (Amber Museum), houses a collection of rare amber in a renovated house built by a German tobacco merchant in 1918. The main museum is on the second floor containing amber from the Cordillera Septentrional, the mountains behind Puerto Plata, which contain the world's richest deposits of amber. For the **Amber Museum Shop** see Shopping, page 348.

A visit is recommended to the **Fortaleza de San Felipe** ① *US$0.60, guided tours available but not really necessary*, the oldest colonial fortress in the New World, on a promontory at the west end of the Malecón. Once the era of pirates and privateers was ended the fortress was long used as a prison. Juan Pablo Duarte was locked up here in 1844. The museum contains rusty armoury and photos of the excavation and renovation of the fortress, which was built in 1540. The museum is not especially interesting but if you climb the turrets you get a wonderful view of the coast and ships coming into the harbour. Outside there is a statue and monument to General Gregorio Luperón on a prancing horse. Nearby is the restored iron **lighthouse**, first lit on 9 September 1879, now surrounded by bits of fortress walls and cannon.

Just 1 km past Puerto Plata, a *teleférico* (cable car) runs to the summit of **Loma Isabel de Torres** ① *daily except Wed 0830-1700, US$5 round trip*, an elevation of 779 m. A statue of Christ looks out over all of Puerto Plata, rather like the one in Rio de Janeiro; it also houses craft shops, a restaurant and there are beautifully manicured botanical gardens with a lovely view of the coast and mountains. Entrance is south of the Circunvalación del Sur on a paved road marked teleférico. Hiking tours up the mountain can be arranged with **Iguana Mama**, in Cabarete. Hiking alone is not recommended. It is a moderate to hard hike, being quite steep in parts, and takes about three hours to get up to the top.

Playa Dorada

Just 6 km east of Puerto Plata, 4 km from the airport, is the beach resort of **Playa Dorada** with an exceptional golf course, and other sporting facilities. The Playa Dorada Resort is an umbrella name for a complex of 14 large all-inclusive hotels with over 4000 rooms, offering similar services, eg pool, tennis, golf, best booked as part of a package from abroad. Not all of them are beachfront. There is a central shopping mall, the **Playa Dorada Centro Comercial**, and lots of nightlife. The beach is a glorious sweep of golden sand around the promontory on which stand most of the hotels, while the golf course weaves in and out of the hotels not on the beach.

West of Puerto Plata

To the west of Puerto Plata and within easy striking distance of the city, is **Costambar**, which has a long stretch of sand with few waves, making it perfect for children. There are restaurants beside the beach and supermarkets if you want to cater for yourself. This is the best place to look for self-catering accommodation, there are lots of villas and condos, some for as little as US$100 a week, excellent value if you are in a group.

Cofresí and around

Cofresí beach has several hotels, villas and cabins and is busy at weekends. **Ocean World Adventure Park** ① www.oceanworld.net, an enormous dolphinarium, has been built here despite opposition from conservationists and environmentalists (see also Anguilla, Cayman Islands chapters). A huge hotel and marina come as part of the investment package, changing the character of the village entirely. If you want to swim with dolphins it will cost you US$145. However, bear in mind that the dolphins have been captured against international treaties, removed from their pods (families) and fed on a diet of frozen fish and antibiotics.

Further west, **Luperón** is a typical Dominican village, with several markets selling fish, meat and vegetables, basic restaurants and baseball field. The jetty in the village is in a lagoon surrounded by mangroves and is a safe harbour for yachts and other boats. 3 km from the village is **Puerto Blanco Marina** ① T8092994096, surrounded by more mangroves providing a pretty setting and good protection for yachts. *Motoconchos* charge less than US$1 from the village, and taxis US$3. The marina is the place to be. The bar is popular, with a happy hour at 1700-1900 and live music some nights. The restaurant is known for its seafood and the food is cheap. Rooms are available (E) with a/c and hot water. Watersports include snorkelling, fishing and scuba diving. Catamaran tours are recommended as a great way to see the coast and snorkel in some lovely secluded spots where the coral is alive and healthy. **Cat's Sailing Adventure** (T/F2612046, catsail@hotmail.com) charges US$75 per person for its daily catamaran trips.

A massive development is to be constructed on 445 ha at Luperón, called AtlanticA, www.atlanticadr.com, which will include a large marina, villages, luxury hotels, restaurants and three golf courses, the first of which opens in 2007. Designed to be built in stages over ten years, there will eventually be 3000 homes around the marina or golf courses, 450 slips for yachts, 260 super yacht hangars, five shipyards and a cruise ship terminal as well as all the usual watersports, tennis, polo and a spa. Mangrove areas are to be protected by the **Luperón Mangrove National Monument**.

La Isabela

① *Daily 0800-1745, US$1.20; there is a small museum with labels in Spanish and a brief description in English, a café, toilets and small gift shops selling artesanías. Guides are available.*

15 km west of Luperón is La Isabela, now a **Parque Nacional Histórico**. Here, on his second voyage, on 29 May 1493, Columbus landed with 1500 men on 17 ships. He founded the first European town in the Americas, with the first *ayuntamiento* and court, and here was said the first mass on 6 January 1494 by Fray Bernardo Boil. Only the layout of the town is visible. The story goes that Trujillo ordered the place cleaned up before an official visit, but his instructions were misunderstood and workers bulldozed the whole site, pushing the ruins into the sea. The restoration and archaeological excavation of La Isabela has uncovered a variey of ruins as well as Taíno and Macorix pottery and the first Hispanic ceramics. The Guayacán tree found growing around La Isabela was there before Columbus landed. The wood is very hard and the Guayacán is used to carve replicas of Taíno artefacts. To get there, take a tour from Puerto Plata, or a *carro público* from Villanueva y Kundhard, Puerto Plata, to La Isabela village, US$3.50, then a *motoconcho* to the ruins, US$5 return including wait at ruins, a lovely trip.

❧ Bring lots of insect repellent.

Monte Cristi → *Colour map 2, B2. Population: 22,000.*

At the far northwestern tip of the Dominican Republic is Monte Cristi, a 19th-century town with a Victorian feel to it, while the sea around it is believed to hold the treasures of 179 sunken galleons. Carretera Duarte runs from Santiago to Monte Cristi, passing first through rice paddies and tobacco plantations in the valley, but about 50 km from the town the area becomes arid, with cactus and other desert plants, home to a multitude of goats. A large land and marine park stretches either side of the town along the coast, protecting the mouth of the Río Yaque del Norte, with mangroves, a lagoon and lots of channels. Its proximity to the Haitian border means that transport links are good and a new airfield opened in 2006. There are several lovely old wooden houses in sore need of renovation. Just beyond the **BanReservas**, on Calle Duarte (which was the first theatre), is a large old house formerly the home of one of Trujillo's mistresses. Another, called Doña Emilia's house, is huge, with lovely fretwork and verandas. Both are due to be renovated. The town has an interesting, big old clock on the **Parque Central**, or Parque Reloj, made in France, but brought here on the train *Lavonia* on 11 March 1895. You can visit the house of **Máximo Gómez** ① *Av Mella, opposite Helados Bon, 0900-1200, 1500-1900*, the Dominican patriot who played an important role in the struggle for Cuban Independence and in the Dominican Restoration. Inside are pictures and mementoes of Máximo Gómez, a library with a detailed atlas of Cuba and a lot of books relating to Cuba, but very few about the Dominican Republic. Between the town and Playa Juan de Bolaños there is a monument to **José Martí** (a rather lugubrious head of Martí on a stick), the Cuban poet and Independence fighter who came here in September 1892 before sailing with Máximo Gómez to liberate Cuba. The beach is nothing special and backs on to salt pans, but the coast is dominated by a large flat-topped mountain known as El Morro. Steps have been built up the hillside, making an extremely testing climb to a windy viewpoint.

East of Puerto Plata

The coast east of Puerto Plata has some of the most beautiful beaches in the world, with a green backdrop of mountains descending to a narrow coastal plain, with palm trees, pale sand stretching for miles and sea of all shades of blue. Sosúa, Cabarete and Río San Juan are the main beach destinations, Cabarete being the windsurf capital of the world, having hosted many World Cup events. From all these places you can get quickly up into the mountains for hiking, cycling, horse riding or whatever you fancy away from the beach.

Sosúa

Sosúa (28 km east of Puerto Plata) is a little town with a beautiful and lively 1-km beach. Vendors' stalls and snackbars line the path along the back of the beach and you will be offered anything from sunbeds to toilets. There is a smaller public beach on the east side of town, referred to as the *playita*, or Little Beach, where you will be less bothered by vendors. The main street (correctly named Calle Pedro Clisante, but only ever referred to as Main Street, or Calle Principal in Spanish) is lined with a variety of shops, restaurants and bars. Little or no attention is paid to street names or numbers. The **El Batey** side of town (the side that houses most of the hotels and restaurants) was founded by German-Jewish refugees who settled here in 1941. A synagogue and memorial building are open to the public. The western end of the town is referred to as **Los Charamicos** (the two ends are separated by the beach); this is the older side of town, where the Dominicans themselves generally live, shop and party.

Cabarete

Cabarete, famous for world-class windsurfing and kiteboarding, is 14 km east of Sosúa. Although it has grown considerably since French-Canadian windsurfers first staked their claim on this small fishing village it still maintains its small-town character. There is a wide range of places to stay, eat and dance the night away, with most places along the main road which runs next to the sea. The lagoon behind the main road is good for spotting water birds. The beach is long and sandy with beach bars, romantic dining spots and watersports touting for your business. It is split into two parts, the western end for kiteboarders and the eastern end for windsurfers. Cabarete hosts international windsurfing, kiteboarding and sandcastle competitions; it also offers a variety of other adventure sports: mountain biking, horse riding, whitewater rafting and scuba diving are within easy reach. Close to town is the **Parque Nacional El Chocó**, which has caves believed to be 5 million years old and interesting routes for mountain biking and hiking. There's a local **tourist office** ① *T8095710950*, although an alternative and better place for information is Iguana Mama (see Tour operators page 349).

Activities Cabarete is the place to be in June, when the town is taken over by serious windsurfers for the **Cabarete Race Week** ① *www.cabareteevents.com* or *www.cabaretewindsurfing.com*. The winds are at their best for Race Week, but windsurfing takes place all year round. In summer (mid-June to mid-September) there are constant trade winds but few waves. In winter, there is less wind, but the waves can be tremendous. The mornings are generally calm, but by the afternoon the bay is full of sails flitting about like butterflies on a puddle.

Kiteboarding has taken Cabarete by storm (www.cabaretekiteboarding.com). It takes place about 1 km downwind of the windsurfers at the western end of Cabarete beach on the aptly named **Kite Beach**, where there is flat water for the first 500 m and then a reef with waves. Kiteboarding is the newest and most exciting watersport around the world, and Cabarete is considered by those that know to be the best location for the sport. In the summer, the sea is flat calm, with winds side-onshore, picking up around 1100-1300, making the mornings good for training. The **Kiteboarding World Cup**, is held here annually in June, with top international kiteboarders competing. Alex Soto is the top male Dominican kiteboarder, ranked 19 in the world in 2006, followed by Luis Miguel Martínez at 28 and Luciano González at 40. In 2006 Cabarete was one of the stops in the PKRA World Tour, attracting 156 professional kiteboarders from over 30 countries. Aaron Hadlow, from the UK (www.aaronhadlow.com) confirmed his position as the world's top-ranking kiteboarder.

On the outskirts of town is El Encuentro, a **surfing** beach, with a consistent 'break' off the right and left.

Río San Juan

Further east along the north coast, Río San Juan is a friendly town in an area now quite a tourist attraction. For **tourist information** ① *T8095892831, F8095892964*. One major site of interest is a lagoon called **Laguna Grí Grí**. Boats take visitors through the mangrove forests into the lagoon and to see caves and rocks, notably the **Cueva de las Golondrinas**, formed by an 1846 rockslide. It is several kilometres long and filled with swallows, from which it gets its name. Expect to pay about US$25 per person on a boat trip taking up to 20 people.

The main attraction here is the beach called **Playa Grande**, 5 km east of Río San Juan. Great swathes of pale sand make it one of the most beautiful beaches on the island. It is packed with people at weekends. There is public access to the beach, which is one of the longest white-sand beaches on the north coast. When the swell is up in winter this is the place to be for good surfing and is a seventh heaven for golfers with one of the best courses in the country (see Sport, page 307), designed by Robert Trent Jones Sr with 10 of its tees at the edge of the ocean. On arrival at Playa Grande you will be surrounded by traders looking for your business at their restaurant or stall. Politely decline their offers of help until you have chosen a restaurant.

Playa La Preciosa was so named by surfers who come here to surf because of its beauty. It is a great place for photos and a lot more secluded than Playa Grande. *National Geographic* took one of their cover shots at this beach. It is the next left turn east after Playa Grande at the headland of the **Parque Nacional Cabo Francés Viejo**.

● Sleeping

Puerto Plata *p338*

Cheap hotels can only be found in the centre.

D Aparta-Hotel Lomar, Malecón 8, T8093208555. 18 large rooms, warm water, cable TV, a/c or fan, some rooms with balcony overlooking sea, good value.

D Sofy's Bed & Breakfast, C Las Rosas, T/F8095864111, gillin.n@verizon.net.do. Run by Canadian Noelle Gillin (and Sofy the dog), look for sign of Monte Silva (if you pass El Furgón you've missed the turn) between the baseball stadium and the police station on Av Luis Ginebra, go down that street and the house is the third to last on the left. 3 rooms, great American breakfast on the terrace, popular with ex-pats, airport transfers are included if you stay a week.

D-E Victoriano, San Felipe 33 esq Restauración, T8095869752. Central, a/c, cable TV, fan or a/c, 1 or 2 beds, clean, friendly, own generator, hot water.

D-F Castilla, José del Carmen Ariza 34, near Parque Central, look for the red awning of Sam's Bar & Grill, T8095867267, sams.bar@verizon.net.do. The first hotel in town, dating from 1890s, now showing its age but friendly and very cheap. 1-bedroom furnished apartment or rooms with private or shared bathroom, weekly and monthly rates available, own generator, hot water in the evening, internet access.

Cofresí and around *p340*

A-B pp Luperón Beach Resort, Luperón, T8095718303, www.besthotels.es. All-inclusive, no other hotel close by, on lovely beach, comfortable rooms decorated daily with flowers, a/c, TV, fridge, fan, terrace, some connect to make a suite, 3 restaurants, bars, pools and jacuzzis, lots of watersports, tennis, archery, riding (check horses' condition), bicycles, ping pong, billiards, gym and sauna, children's activities.

E Dally, 27 de Febrero 46, Luperón, T8095718034, F8095718052. On the main road, popular, 8 rooms, clean, fan, hot water, good seafood restaurant, The Moon disco behind. There are lots of Dominican restaurants which are best found by just walking around town. Most serve good, freshly caught fish and seafood for less than US\$10.

Monte Cristi *p340*

A-B Cayo Arena, Playa Juan de Bolaños, T8095793145, F8095792096. 2-bedroomed apartments on the beach, sleep 4, basic bathroom and kitchen, small pool, bar, security, parking.

C Los Jardines, next to Cayo Arena, T8095792091, hotel.jardines@verizon.net.do. Run by Hervé and Dorca, 2 bungalows each with 2 basic rooms, fan or a/c, no food or cooking facilities, good bathrooms, quiet, parking, beach chairs, boat excursions to the mangroves and Cayos Siete Hermanos, English and French spoken, jeep and bicycle hire, owner will collect you from Caribe Tours if you call.

D Chic Hotel Restaurant, Benito Monción 44, T8095792316. 50 rooms sleep 1-4, nice hotel, only Spanish spoken, TV, hot water, phone, shag carpet or tiled, decor different in each room, good food but slow service.

Sosúa *p341*

There are several all-inclusives not listed here including the new luxury Sosúa Bay Hotel at the El Batey end of the beach.

LL Haciendas El Choco, El Choco Rd, T8095712932, www.elchoco.com. A good option for self-catering families or groups. Villas with swimming pool and large thatched verandas. All have telephone, maid, gardener and pool service and 24-hr electricity.

AL-A Sosua-by-the-Sea, Playa Chiquita, T8095713222, www.sosuabythesea.com. Breakfast included, meal plans available, MAP or all-inclusive. Immaculate, beautiful a/c rooms and suites which sleep up to 4, pool and bar. Internet centre. Fireworks on Sat nights during high season. Northern Coast Diving (see page 349) on site offering boogie boards, kayaking, snorkelling and dive lessons. Good location, short walk into town.

A pp Piergorgio Palace Hotel, Calle La Puntilla 1, T 8095712626. Victorian-style building, facing the Atlantic Ocean for a breathtaking sunset. Perched on the cliffs, no beach, steps lead down to the water, good snorkelling among the rocks. Elegant all-inclusive hotel, impeccable decor, all rooms have semi-circular balcony and good bathroom. Romantic outdoor dining but food nothing special.

A-C On the Waterfront, Dr Rosen 1, El Batey, T8095712670, www.hotelwaterfrontdr.com. 30 cabins, quiet, tropical, ocean front pool, on cliff overlooking the sea, 5 mins to the beach, special rates for groups. Some a/c rooms, OK for the price.

B Club Residencial, 32 Main St, T8095713675, www.clubresidencial.com. 54 apartments, some with a/c, restaurant, bar, laundry, swimming pool, internet and cable TV.

B-C Pensión Anneliese, Dr Rosen, T8095712208, www.weblatino.de/pension. 10 large clean rooms with fridge, Wi-Fi, balcony or terrace, shower, fan, breakfast extra, car hire available, bar and restaurant La Roca, short walk to the beach, right by **On the Waterfront** hotel and restaurant.

B-C Voramar, outskirts of Sosúa next to Playa Chiquita. T8095713910, www.voramar-sosua.com. 20 rooms plus several apartments all decorated in Spanish style, fans, some with a/c, TV. Tropical garden, pool, tennis courts, restaurant and a pool bar. German, Swiss management, lots of languages spoken.

Cabarete p341

Low-rise hotels, condos and guesthouses line the 2-km bay. Some of them offer meal plans, but there are certainly plenty of other places to eat. The largest all-inclusive, **Viva Wyndham Tangerine** (www.vivaresorts.com) is to the west of town, while the smaller **Tropical Casa Laguna** (www.tropicalclubs.com) is in town. There are 2 high seasons: Dec-Apr and then mid-Jun to mid-Sep, when the winds are strong and attract the windsurfing and kitesurfing crowd.

LL-AL Bahía de Arena, T8095710370, www.cabaretevillas.com. Managed by Hans-Peter and Gundula, a variety of nice villas and apartments within walking distance from Cabarete. Central area with pool and jacuzzi, tennis court, convenience store, fruit and vegetable market and Swiss restaurant. Spanish, English, French and German spoken.

L Natura Cabañas, Perla Marina, between Sosúa and Cabarete, T8095711507, www.naturacabana.com. 7 thatched cabañas sleeping 2-6, hidden away in gardens, run by Chilean couple with children. Each one is different, hammocks and hammock swings on the porch. Spa for steam bath, massages and beauty therapies.

Rates include airport transfers, breakfast and yoga offered beside or on the beach.

L-A Aparthotel Caracol, T8095710680, www.hotelcaracol.com. A 3-star, 50-room hotel at the western entrance to Cabarete, 5 mins walk from town, with studios, 1- and 2-bedroom apartments and penthouse, all with kitchenette. Reduced rates for long stays. Kiteboarding school on site. Full range of services with Wi-Fi at the beach club, **Tropicoco** restaurantby reception, **Marabu** Italian restaurant and bar at beach club, free newspapers, massage centre, TV room, children's playground and pool and babysitting. Quiet with good service and excellent value, you get more for your money than at other kitesurfing hotels. Price includes breakfast.

L-A Velero Beach Resort, Calle La Punta 1, T8095719727, www.velerobeach.com. 4-star hotel at east end of the beach, rooms and suites can be combined to make apartments or penthouses with kitchens, all with sea view, neat lawns, pretty gardens and small pool giving view of whole bay, eating places in walking distance, excellent value out of season.

L-B Kitebeach, T8095710878, www.kitebeachhotel.com 30 rooms from budget to superior and 8 a/c junior suites or apartments with balconies, buffet breakfast included, good value with special rates for long stays. On Kite Beach, packages including kiteboarding lessons, kite storage, repair and cleaning facilities, pool, beach bar, free Wi-Fi. No credit cards, cash or TCs only.

L-B Palm Beach Condos, T8095710758, www.cabaretecondos.com. Spacious, deluxe condos, 2 bedroom, 2 bathroom, fully equipped kitchens, patios with ocean views, perfect for families, nannies available, studios for couples, pool, on the beach, free internet access, Dominican meals delivered, central but quiet, no traffic noise, close to main restaurants and shops.

AL-A Villa Taína, T8095710722, www.villataina.com. On the beach in town centre, windsurf school alongside, 57 rooms and an apartment, a/c, balcony or terrace, some rooms larger than others, comfortable, phone, breakfast included, restaurant on the beach. **Villa Taína** is environmentally aware and good value.

AL-A Windsurf Resort, T8095710718, www.windsurfcabarete.com. 42, 1- and

2-bedroom spacious apartments, excellent value for money, all with full kitchens and balconies facing the pool, Wi-Fi throughout. Carib Bic windsurf centre has windsurf equipment, surf boards, boogie boards, kayaks and sailboats. Italian restaurant, bar, evening entertainment and outings.

AL-B Cabarete Surfcamp, T8095710733, www.cabaretesurfcamp.com. On the lagoon, quiet and offers every kind of accommodation from camping (bring your own tent, showers in the washhouse), basic cottages and bungalows, to more luxurious apartments with kitchens. Prices from US$25pp for bed, breakfast and evening meal, using facilities in washhouse. Pool, garden, terraces, internet access for laptops.

A-D Kaoba, T8095710300, www.kaoba.com. Good location across the road from the beach and good value. Bungalows, rooms, suites and apartments at a wide variety of prices and level of comfort. Fan or a/c, discounts for stays over 2 weeks, pool, garden, restaurant, bar. Some of the more expensive rooms have 24-hr free ADSL internet connection but there is also an internet café.

B Blue Moon Retreat, Los Brazos, 20 mins from Cabarete on the mountain road to Moca, T8092230614, www.bluemoonretreat.net. Set in 38 acres of peaceful, lush rolling farmland dotted with Royal palms and fruit trees with a stunning view of the sea. 4 simple bungalows with 4 suites, 1 family suite and 1 big apartment with 2 bedrooms, 2 bathrooms and kitchen, all with distinctive decor, fan, spacious living area, small library, patio, laundry service, country breakfast, full service bar, back-up generator. Excellent restaurant, see page 346.

B Extreme Hotel, T8095710880, www.extremehotels.com. Another dedicated kiteboarding hotel with lots of facilities for kiters and their gear and kite school. 20 rooms with a/c and fan, full breakfast included, bar, restaurant, internet access. Skateboarding ramp.

B Wilson's Beach House, T8095710616, www.wilsonsbeachhouse.com. 4 nice rooms with bathrooms upstairs and 1, 3-bedroom apartment downstairs which can be divided into 2 apartments, family atmosphere, best location right on the beach. Guests upstairs share sitting room with fridge and large balcony. Space for storing windsurfing gear. Solar powered electricity and hot water.

B-C Residencia Dominicana, T8095710588, www.residenciadominicana.com. Excellent value, 24 comfortable studios, some with kitchenettes, 3 apartments, balconies, pool, tennis courts across the street, own generator so no power cuts, breakfast buffet, evening restaurant for dinner and snacks, special price for long stays, internet connection in rooms for a fee.

C-E Kitexcite Beach Hotel, T8095719509. 20 spacious rooms on Kite Beach with fans, a/c, cable TV, internet access, full breakfast included with storage lockers for gear. Pool, beach bar, restaurant with lots of vegetarian options.

Río San Juan *p342*

Several large all-inclusives have been built in the area, offering lots of facilities.

D Bahía Blanca, Gastón F Deligne 5, T8095892563. Lovely location right on rocks above the sea, beach 75 m away. 3-floor, well-maintained, white building, 21 rooms open out onto balcony, from where you get a great view of the coast, no pool, no TV, no a/c, restaurant open for breakfast and dinner, meal plans available.

E La Casona, Duarte 6, T8095892597. Small, exceptionally clean, hot water, cable TV, mini fridge, purified water, very friendly, restaurant serves their famous *empanadas*, fresh juices, good value.

● Eating

Puerto Plata *p338*

† **Jardín Suizo**, Malecón 32, T8095869564. Mon-Sat 1100-2300. Lunch and dinner. Run by Swiss James and his Dominican wife, excellent food.

†† † **Aguaceros**, Malecón edif 32, near fire station, T8095862796. 1700 until late. Steaks, seafood, burgers, Mexican, tables on sidewalk, bar.

†† † **Hemingway's Café**, Playa Dorada shopping mall, T8093202230. 1100-late. Predictable nautical, sport fishing theme. Good food and music, a/c, good service, fun at night and during the day, live bands at weekends, karaoke some nights.

†† † **Jungle Bar**, Plaza Turisol 12, T8092613544. 1000-1800, later for event nights. English run with English menu, come here for chip butties, curry or fried breakfast, popular with ex-pats, particularly on quiz nights.

¶¶-¶ **La Parrillada Steak House**, Av Manolo Tavarez Justo, T8095861401. Lunch and dinner. On busy road with outdoor seating but not too noisy or polluted at night. Tasty *churrasco* and plenty of it.

¶¶-¶ **Sam's Bar and Grill**, José del Carmen Ariza 34, near Plaza Central, T8095867267, sams.bar@verizon.net.do. Breakfast, lunch and dinner. American-run, satellite TV, meeting place, notice board, internet, rooms also available, see **Hotel Castilla**, above.

¶ **Comacho**, Circunvalación Norte (Malecón), T8096856348, lunch and dinner. Good Dominican restaurant.

Monte Cristi *p340*

Goat is the local speciality and you will see goats all over the roads. *Chivo picante* (spicy goat) is sold at roadside stands.

¶¶-¶ **Cocomar**, by the monument to José Martí, T8095793354. 0800-2200. Good breakfast, if a little greasy, also lunch and dinner, meals from US$3 per person, with the top price for the *paella marinera* or seafood platter, they will make what you want if they have the ingredients.

¶¶-¶ **Don Gaspar Restaurant & Hotel**, Pte Jiménez 21 esq Rodríguez Camargo, T8095792477, F8095792206. Breakfast, lunch and dinner. Also a disco with a variety of music and requests, good breakfast menu, eggs, *mangú*, juice and coffee for less than US$4, Dominican and Spanish dishes.

¶¶-¶ **El Bistro**, San Fernando 26, 3 blocks from the clock, T8095792091. Mon-Fri 1100-1430, 1800-2400, Sat-Sun 1000-2400. Same ownership as **Hotel Los Jardines**, set in lovely courtyard on a corner with big wooden doors, white furniture and rocking chairs, seating in open air or under cover, seafood, lobster, goat, as well as sandwiches, salads and pasta.

¶ **Comedor Adela**, Juan de la Cruz Alvarez 41, T8095792254. Lunch and dinner. Family atmosphere, lots of choice, good food, parking available.

Sosúa *p341*

There are several restaurants on Main St serving international, French, Italian food, walk around and see what takes your fancy, they change frequently. Also several eating places along the beach, with lobster tanks, OK for lunch. For Dominican food go to **Los Charamicos**, where there are *comedores*.

¶¶¶-¶ **Morua Mai**, Main St by the turning to the beach, T8095712966. 1100-0000. Varied menu that includes meat, fish and sea food dishes as well as pizza, pasta and burgers. Good selection of wines.

¶¶ **On the Waterfront**, C Dr Rosen 1, El Batey, T8095712670, www.hotelwaterfrontdr.com. 0800-2200. Fish, seafood, snacks, excellent food and a spectacular sunset overlooking the sea, all-you-can-eat. Live music at weekends.

¶¶-¶ **La Roca**, Main St, opposite **Morua Mai**, T8095713893. 0700-0000. Speciality seafood and fish with catch of the day, with shrimp sold by the pound, also sandwiches and Mexican food, curry and pasta. Sit inside where there is billiards and a book exchange, or outside on the terrace.

¶ **PJ's**, corner of Main St with Duarte, T8095712091. 24 hours. Burger bar, satisfying breakfasts, chef's salad and schnitzel burger for lunch, outdoor seating for people watching.

Cabarete *p341*

Wide range of places to eat and drink, lots of beach restaurants and bars with great atmosphere.

¶¶¶ **La Casa del Pescador**, on the beach, T8095710760. 1200-2300. Excellent seafood and fish including paella.

¶¶¶ **Miró**, on the beach next to **José Oshay's**, T8095710888. 1500-2300. Excellent dinners in arty atmosphere, on the expensive side. Art exhibitions held regularly.

¶¶¶ **Otra Cosa**, at La Punta, around the eastern point, near **Hotel Velero**, T8095710897. Wed-Mon 1230-2200. Delicious French-Caribbean food, dinner only. The place is pretty small, so book in advance.

¶¶¶-¶¶ **Vento**, on the beach next to **La Casita**, T8095710977. 1800-2400. Owner Julia offers well-cooked Italian food and wine.

¶¶ **Blue Moon**, 20 mins outside town in a village called Los Brazos on the way to Moca, T8092230614, www.bluemoonretreat.net. 1200-2400. Reservations essential. The only authentic East Indian restaurant in the region. Well-known for feasts of up to 30 guests in thatched-roof dining area, or 90+ with buffet. Dinner served with guests on cushions on the floor with banana leaves as plates and the right hand as silverware. A typical feast features vegetable *pacoras*, tandoori or coconut chicken or fish or goat curry, spicy vegetable curries, homemade chutneys, cooling fresh salads, cinnamon- cardomom spiced rice, and a refreshing dessert.

The Castle Club, 20 mins from Cabarete in Los Brazos, T8092230601. 1830-2300. Owned and managed by American couple Doug and Margarite. Gourmet dining experience, private dinner parties for 4-10 guests, reservations required.

La Casita de Don Alfredo, also known as **Papi**, middle of town, beachfront. 1200-2400. Excellent seafood, large portions, don't miss *camarones a la papi*, own recipe with shrimps and spaghetti. Decorated in local style.

Tropicoco, 5 mins west of Cabarete beside Hotel Caracol, T8095710647. 1700-2400. Owned by José and Ute, varied menu at affordable prices. Fantastic Sat night all-you-can-eat barbecue buffet, fabulous Thai food Thu, lots of vegetarian options.

Lax, west side, on the beach, near **La Casa del Pescador**. 1100-0100. A lively place on the beach all day and night. International cuisine including a huge Mexican special and sushi. Good food and prices considering its location on the sand. Meeting place for windsurfers and kiteboarders.

Dick's bakery, west end of town, near **La Casa Rosada** grocery store, T8095710612. 0630-1800. Serves you the best coffee in town and fabulous breakfasts, very popular with locals.

Friends, next door to **Dick's**. Tue-Sun 0700-1800. Another nice option for breakfast.

Mercedes, Callejón de la Loma, T8095710247. 1200-2200. In the Dominican part of town on the way to **Parque Nacional El Chocó**, there are several cheap Dominican restaurants but this is 1 of the best. Try the fish of the day.

Pomodoro, on the beach. 1100-2200. Breakfast, lunch and dinner. Good food at reasonable prices. Pizza a speciality.

Sandros, on the main street on the west side of town, T8095710723. 0830-1700. Rough and ready but nice people, good fun and great Dominican food, a 'small' portion of stew, rice, salad for US$4 is more than enough, beer US$1.50. Good for filling lunch.

☉ Bars and clubs

Puerto Plata *p338*
On Sun nights there is open-air dancing on the Malecón, with huge sound systems on the road and street vendors selling drinks. Most of the nightlife is in **Playa Dorada**, where there are discos and a casino.

The American Casino, in **Jack Tar Village**, Puerto Plata, T8093201046, www.allegroresorts.com. 1600-0400. Free drinks for players and free gaming lessons to get you hooked. 12 table games and 40 slot machines. Live entertainment. Disco 2300-0200, with variety of music and good lighting, but small.

Café Cito, on the roadside on the main road, 5 mins' walk west from the entrance to Playa Dorada. Mon-Sat 1030-2400. Makes a change from the hotel complex, pool table, sports TV, live music and karaoke at weekends, very cold beer, good food.

Crazy Moon, in **Paradise Beach Resort**, T8093203663. 2200-0400. Popular bar and disco offers a mix of merengue, salsa and international pop music. Plenty of Dominicans to teach you how to dance.

Sosúa *p341*
Britannia, Main St. 1000-0000. Very popular bar among residents.

D' Classico, Main St. 2200-0400, gets going after 2300. New, nice big disco, mixing local and international music. From Fri to Sun you will have the chance of meeting more locals and learning how to dance merengue and *bachata*. At weekends they sometimes charge an entry fee of US$2.

D' Latino's Club, Main St. 2200-0400. Disco and bar, smaller than the others, but music is good. Renovated 2004. Sometimes an entry fee of US$1, depending on the day.

High Caribbean Disco, by the casino at the east end of the town. 2200-0500. Renovated 2004. Terrace and small indoor and outdoor swimming pool. Entry fee of around US$2 depending on the day and what's on.

Voodoo Lounge, at the end of Main St. 1900-0300. A nicely decorated cocktail bar and disco with no entry fee. Outdoor terrace.

Cabarete *p341*
Cabarete has quite a reputation for its nightlife. Many of the beach restaurants

double as bars in the evening and are open after the sun comes up. You can dance merengue or listen to international music. Ask any local and they will point you in the direction of the party that night. Live bands play certain nights of the week.

Bambú, close to Onno's. 1100-0600. Comfortable with chairs and sofas where you can have a drink and a large place to dance until sunrise.

José Oshay's Irish Beach Pub, beachfront, T8095710775. 0800-0100. Go through the José Oshay's Shopping Village, near Miró. Serves 1 dish every night, popular drinking spot.

Onno's, town centre on the beach, T8093831448. 1100-0600. Access by Harrison's jewellers, relaxed ambience during the day but completely packed at night.

Village Club, next to Villa Taína, after Dick's Bakery, T8098020914. 2000-0300. If you like jazz, this is your place. Live music at weekends, ask around to check who is playing.

⊙ Entertainment

Puerto Plata p338
Cinema Recently released US films with Spanish subtitles in Centro Comercial, Playa Dorada.

⊛ Festivals and events

Monte Cristi p340
Feb Monte Cristi is famous for its pre-Lenten fiesta. On Sun the *toros* and the *civiles* compete against each other in the streets. The *toros* are people dressed in costumes with elaborate bull masks, wielding whips with a ball.

Cabarete p341
Feb Cabarete hosts an international sandcastle competition, when visitors construct fantastic mermaids, flowers, fruit and even the *Titanic*.
Jun Cabarete Race Week (windsurfing) and a Kiteboarding World Cup event.
Oct Jazz Festival.
Nov International Surf Competition.

⊙ Shopping

Puerto Plata p338
The Mercado Viejo is at Ureña and

reparación and sells mostly hardware and furniture, although there is also a *botánica*, items relating to syncretist religion, witchcraft, voodoo and folk healing. The **Mercado Nuevo**, at Isabela de Torres and Villanueva, sells handicrafts, rum, Cuban cigars, Haitian art and other souvenirs. The Playa Dorada complex has the first real shopping mall on the north coast, called the **Playa Dorada Plaza** or **Centro Comercial**. Prices are slightly inflated, but the quality of all items, especially the locally made ceramics, jewellery and clothing, is superior to most sold by beach or street vendors. The mall includes a **Bennetton**, a selection of Tiffany lamps and some very original jewellery. Cigars, leather goods, amber, larimar, coffee and rum can all be found here.

Amber Museum Shop (see page 339), Playa Dorada Plaza, T8093202215, and at Marien Coral by **Hilton**, Costa Dorada, T8093201515. Daily 0800-2200.

▲ Activities and tours

Puerto Plata p338
Golf
Playa Dorada Golf Course, T8093203472. Designed by Robert Trent Jones. Right in the middle of the resort, see Sport and activities, page 307. If you are staying at one of the resort hotels, green fees with caddy are discounted; outsiders pay US$94 for 18 holes with caddy. The hotels offer lots of sports for their all-inclusive guests, and activities away from Playa Dorada, like horse riding, are easily arranged. Most watersports are also on offer through the hotels, but for scuba diving go to Sosúa.
Playa Grande Golf Course, Km 9, Carretera Río San Juan-Cabrera, T8095820860 ext 21. Wonderful ocean views with 10 holes on the water. Designed by Robert Trent Jones. Reservations essential. Green fees US$120 in high season, US$90 in low season, caddies (compulsory) US$15 for 18 holes. Clubs for rent, lessons US$50/hr.

Monte Cristi p340
Watersports
Scuba diving is excellent in the area, with over 9 shipwrecks to explore, but there is no organized dive operation. **Fishing** is popular. Contact the Club Náutico,

T8095972530. Offshore there are barracuda, tuna, marlin, dorado and carite. If you are **sailing** in the lagoon or channels, be aware that when the tides change the water can rise or fall by about 1½ m. There is one channel in the lagoon, which apparently has some 50 different entrances but only 1 exit.

Sosúa *p341*
Diving
There are lots of dive operations, in town and on the beach, offering tuition and boat dives. There is no jetty and no large dive boats, so you must be prepared to wade out to a small boat, with probably no shade, and be capable of getting back into the boat without a ladder after your dive, which can be tricky if it is rough.
Northern Coast Aquasports/Diving, Pedro Clisante 8, T8095711028, www.northerncoast diving.com. Open daily 0800-1800. A recommended and long-established dive shop. Lots of courses, multilingual staff, boats in Sosúa and Grí Grí, normally taking 4-6 divers, good with novice or experienced divers, probably the most professional operation on this stretch of coast. 2-tank dive US$60, open water course US$350, beginner's course US$60, snorkelling trips US$29 for 1½ hrs, Grí Grí day trip with a cruise, snorkelling and lunch US$85.

Swimming
Columbus Aqua Park, 3 mins from the airport, Km 18, T8095712642, www.aguasosua.com. Closed for renovations early 2007, usually open 1000-1800, US$10 adults, US$3 children, with water toboggans, a water slide where you can reach speeds of 50mph, 3 large pools, a lazy river, children's water play area, diving tower, restaurants, gift shops, bars, discos and parties, etc.

Cabarete *p341*
Horse riding
Rancho Al Norte, Jamao, on the north coast, T8092230660, www.unclebobsranch.com. Weekly rates include all lodging, meals, riding, activities and transport. Small groups, 20 riders max, trails of about 15 km a day, sometimes you swap the horse for tubing down the Río Jamao. 50 criollo and paso fino horses.
Rancho Montana, north coast, 1 hr east of Puerto Plata, just after Sabaneta de Yasica,

T8092485407, www.ranchomontana.com. Run by Canadian, Michel Godin. Riding along river beds and through mountains, swimming in the river, lunch, snacks, drinks, transport, US$67. Half day tours also available, US$49.

Kiteboarding
Kiteclub Cabarete, T8095719748, www.kiteclubcabarete.com. 3-day beginner course US$399, tuition to all levels including private VIP instruction with Jon Dodds, IKO certification, multilingual staff from Europe and the Dominican Republic, accommodation available at Surf Camp.
Laurel Eastman Kiteboarding Centre, Caracol Beach Club, T8095710564, www.laureleastman.com. Offers good equipment and lessons at all levels, including women-only clinics, massage, kite cleaning facilities, storage and sales. 4-day beginner's course US$460 private tuition, US$425 each for a couple.
Dare2Fly, next to **Agualina Kite Resort**, T8095710805, www.dare2fly.com. Good school, owned by **Vela Windsurf Centre**, offering courses for beginners and equipment rental for all levels. Beginner's course 3 days US$390. The centre has many facilities: a bar/restaurant, lockers, shop, parking and restrooms.

Surfing
No Work Team, Calle Principal, next to Plaza Laguna de Don Pepe, Cabarete, T8095710820, www.noworkteamcabarete.com. Daily minisurf course, board rentals, boogie board rentals and surf camps. Wind and wave report, updated twice a week for the Cabarete area. Excellent shop for sports clothing and beach wear.
321 Take-Off, Playa Encuentro, T8099637873, www.321takeoff.com. Surfing school, run by long-time local surfer, Markus Bohm, daily surf lessons, US$40, for all ages and levels. Also 3-day one-on-one kitesurf course, US$350, and personal guide service US$250 per day.

Tour operators
Iguana Mama, Main Street 74, T8095710908, or in the US, toll free, T800-8494720, www.iguanamama.com, is

the only licensed biking tour operator on the north coast. Guided daily mountain biking, hiking and cultural tours as well as several multi-day tours, including Pico Duarte hike and whale watching in Samaná. Also contact them for whitewater rafting, canyoning and cascading, they will put you in touch with the best companies.

Tours Trips Treks & Travel, T8098678884, www.4tdomrep.com. Organizes customized educational, adventure and communitiy service expeditions for small or large groups throughout the Dominican Republic, including all national parks, focusing on anthropology, history and geography.

Windsurfing

The windsurfing schools are all good, with excellent equipment. They do not all stock the same, so if you have a preference it is worth contacting them in advance to see what they can supply. Boards rent for around US$50 per day, US$200 per week, with variations, make sure insurance is available. Schools have international staff able to offer lessons in Spanish, English, German, Italian or French. Walk along the beach and compare equipment and prices. Most of them stock other watersports equipment too, such as surf boards and kayaks.

Carib Bic Center, T8095710640, www.caribwind.com. Excellent windsurfing gear for rent, with professional and experienced instructors, and the nicest surf shop in town. They have a full watersports centre with sea kayaks, boogie boards, surfboards, hobiecats and snorkelling gear for rent. Also laser training and racing and forthcoming kiteboarding school.

Club Mistral, **Pequeño Refugio Hotel**, T8095719791, www.cabaretewindsurfing .com/mistral. Part of an international company with a team of qualified instructors. Caters for beginners to advanced and wave freaks. Instruction in English, Spanish and German. Kayaks and kiteboarding also available.

Club Nathalie Simon, T8095710848, www.cabaretewindsurf.com. French speaking. Tuition for all levels, including children from 5 years old, who can start on the lagoon behind the beach. Also recommended for kiteboarding. Bar and restaurant on the beach.

Fanatic, T8095710861, www.fanatic-cabarete.com. German speaking. Offers equipment rental and courses for adults. They also offer Spanish courses as well as babysitting services. Café Pitu alongside for breakfast, lunch, snacks, pizza and dinner.

Vela, T8095710805, www.velawindsurf.com. Reliable. Equipped with the latest in high performance gear, styled boards available for rent. Beginner courses and free windsurf clinics. Integrated with **Dare2fly** kiteboarding school, so you get a complete watersports service.

● Transport

Puerto Plata *p338*
Air
For domestic flights, see Essentials, page 296.

From North America American Airlines from Miami and New York. Continental also from New York. Delta from Atlanta.

From Europe Martinair from Amsterdam. Condor and/or LTU from Berlin, Düsseldorf, Frankfurt, Leipzig and Munich. There are many charter flights from various airports in the UK, mostly booked by package tour companies, but spare seats are sold on a flight-only basis, see www.charterflights.co.uk/flights/dominican_republic/puerto_plata/.

From the Caribbean TCI Sky King from Providenciales. American Eagle from San Juan. Some flights are seasonal.

Airport Gregorio Luperón International Airport, T8095800219/5860106, serves the entire north coast. It is 15-20 mins from Puerto Plata, 7 mins from Sosúa and 20 mins from Cabarete. Taxi from airport to Puerto Plata or Cabarete US$30, to Sosúa US$20. Small bank for exchange (closed weekends), car hire agencies and a few shops. Tipping for baggage handlers (in overalls) is about US$2 per bag and they will expect something just for picking up a bag.

Bus and taxi
Motoconchos, US$0.60 almost anywhere in town, negotiate a fare for longer distances. *Guaguas*, leave Parque Central, more frequently, from the hospital on Circunvalación Sur to destinations along the north coast. Taxis charge US$5 from Puerto

Plata to Puerto Dorado. They can be found around the Parque Central or on Circunvalación Sur near **Caribe Tours**.

Long distance **Metrobus** (T8095866062, Beller y 16 de Agosto), and **Caribe Tours** (T8095864544, at Caribe Centro Plaza, Camino Real, just off the Circunvalación Sur), run a/c coaches to/from Santo Domingo, 4 hrs, US$6. To Santiago, every hour on the hour, 1000-1800, US$3. **Caribe Tours** also run buses to Samaná (US$6) via Sosúa (US$1.60) and Cabarete, 0700, 1600 daily, 3½ hrs. To La Vega US$4. Alternatively you can use the *guagua* system, changing at each town, but this will take much longer, be more uncomfortable and more costly.

Car
Rental is best arranged at the airport, more choice than in town. **Avis**, airport, T8095860496. **Honda**, Carrera Luperón 2½ km, T8095863136, at the airport, T8095860233. **Puerto Plata Rent a Car**, Beller 7, Puerto Plata, T8095863141. **Nelly Rent a Car**, Puerto Dorada, T8093204888, at the airport, T8095860505.

Cyclo
Rental from **Iguana Mama** (see Tour operators, below) on the main street at the east end of town next to **Fanatic Windsurf School**, rents well-maintained Rock Hoppers, US$25 per day, US$150 per week. All have front suspension. They include helmets, water bottles, repair kit and spare tubes and bike insurance with all bike rentals. A variety of whole-day and half-day tours range from US$55-98. Multi-day tours also available.

Highly recommended are the **Cibao Downhill**, US$74 half-day or US$98 full-day tours. The company is friendly and helpful and the multilingual staff know the country inside out.

Monte Cristi *p340*
Bus and taxi
Taxis and *motoconchos* collect at the corner of Mella and Duarte. For long distance, **Caribe Tours** is on Rodríguez Camargo esq Mella, services to **Dajabón** (34 km, border town opposite Ounaminthe in Haiti, 5 buses daily from Santo Domingo via Monte Cristi) and **Santiago**.

Sosúa *p341*
Bus and taxi
In Sosúa, transport congregates by the Texaco station and the junction of Calle Dr Rosen and the Ctra. *Motoconcho* (motorcycle taxi), US$0.40 (US$0.50 at night) to anywhere in town. A taxi to/from Puerto Plata costs US$20, a *guagua* US$0.60 and a *carro público* US$7 if you take the whole car. **Caribe Tours** (T8095713808) from **Santo Domingo**, US$8.

Car and motorcycle
Rentals are everywhere, shop around for prices. **Asociación de Renta Moto Sosúa Cabarete**, US$28-35 for 1-2 days, US$5-7.25 hourly, depending on type. **Pilar**, Pedro Clisante 1, T8095713281. Friendly.

Cabarete *p341*
Bus and taxi
Cabarete-Sosúa US$8-9, airport US$30, Puerto Plata US$40. Always check price with driver before setting off. *Guagua* to Sosúa US$0.60. *Motoconcho* US$0.60 anywhere in town, negotiate price for anywhere further, price doubles at night.

Río San Juan *p342*
Bus and taxi
Guagua from Sosúa, 1¼ hrs, may have to change in Gáspar Hernández. Transport stops at the junction of Duarte and the main road. **Caribe Tours**, T8095892633, to Puerto Plata US$3, to Samaná 0830 US$4, 3 hrs.

Directory

Puerto Plata *p338*
Banks Banco Popular (24-hr ATM) on José del Carmen Ariza esq Duarte, opposite the cathedral, and Banco del Progreso (T8093200504) on the other side of the square on Separación, either side of Beller. BanReservas, J F Kennedy 16, T8095862518, and at Playa Dorada, T8093204830. At the Centro Comercial, Playa Dorada, are Banco Popular and Banco BHD, both of which have ATMs. **Immigration** Dirección General de Migración, 12 de Julio 33, T8095862364. **Internet** Comp.Net, C 12 de Julio 77, T8095864104, US$3 per hr. Hotel Castilla/Sam's Bar & Grill, US$3 per hr, credit given for time not used. Hot.com C@fé in

the Playa Dorada Plaza, T8093425500, hot.com@verizon.net.do. Tour agencies in the Centro Comercial offer free internet access if you buy a tour, otherwise US$2 for 30 mins. **Medical services** Hospital Ricardo Limardo, J E Kunhardt, T8095862210/ 5862237. There are several doctors with clinics. **Post office** 12 de Julio 42 esq Separación, T8095862377.

Telephone Verizon is on Beller 48 esq Padre Castellanos, T8095863803, and 27 de Febrero, T8095863311, for domestic and international calls. Tricom long-distance call centre is at 27 de Febrero 75, T8094715005. Cheaper is Centennial, on J F Kennedy 40, T8095862660.

Cofresí and around *p340*

Internet Punto Internet Café, at Farmacia Vanessa (see below), Luperón, US$2 per hr. **Medical services** There are 2 pharmacies, Vanessa, T8095718201, Independencia 7 esq Hugo Kunhart, and Alejandra, Duarte 121, Luperón, T8095718135.

Monte Cristi *p340*

Banks BanReservas, Duarte 38, T8095792392. Frías, *casa de cambio*, Duarte 40, T8095792388. **Medical** services Hospital Padre Fantino, J Cabrera, T8095792401. **Pharmacies** Sol, Mella 1a, T8095792404, San Juan Bosco, Benito Monción 49, T8095792327, Clara Nidia, Duarte, T8095791180, and Pueblo, Duarte 41, T8095792394. **Telephone** Verizon, Duarte 56, T8095793021.

Sosúa *p341*

Banks Banco Popular (ATM outside), Calle Dr Martínez and Duarte. Banco León (ATM outside), Duarte, T8095711204. BanReservas, Urb Tavárez, T8095713836, F5713181. Banco del Progreso, Pedro Clisante 12B, T8095712815. Vimenca, Duarte 2, T8095713800. **Internet** On Duarte is an

internet café, @, also **Tricom** on the corner near Banco León. **Post office** E Kunhardt 8, T8095712222. **Medical services** The main hospital for the area is in Puerto Plata, but there are several clinics and pharmacies in Sosúa. **Telephone** Verizon, Calle Dr Alejo Martínez, near corner with Dr Rosen, T8092203697, F5712456 (also in Charamicos, T8095712601, F5712900).

Cabarete *p341*

Banks Banco del Progreso, Ctra Luperón, T8095710625. Banco BHD, Ctra Cabarete, T8095710662. Banco Popular, Plaza Popular, just before Callejón de la Loma, T8095710903. Scotiabank, in front of Iguana Mama on Main Street, T8095710292. All banks have ATMs outside.

Internet Verizon, Plaza Don Pepe, in same office as Western Union, T8095710998, US$2 per hr. Tele-cabarete, in front of Onno's, T/F5710975, calls at US$0.43 per min to Europe, US$0.15 to USA, internet access RD$1 per min, 0900-0400. Internet Gallery, beyond Fanatic, calls to Europe US$0.45 per min, to USA and Canada US$0.30 per min, printer, scanner, USB reader and CD burning available. **Medical services** Servi-Med medical centre, open 24 hrs, Ctra Cabarete 6, T8095710413, close to Helados Bon. **Telephone** Tricom, long distance and local, T8095719757.

Río San Juan *p342*

Banks Agencia de Cambio e Inversiones Río San Juan, Duarte 34, T8095892455. Banco Metropolitano, Duarte 38, T8095892383, F5892493. Banco Popular, Bahía Príncipe, T8092263234. **Medical services** There is a cardiology unit here, Centro de Cardiología y Especialidades, M Alejandro, T8095892807, also 2 clinics and several pharmacies on Billini and Duarte. **Police** T8095892298.

The Samaná Peninsula

The Samaná Peninsula is in the far northeast of the country, geologically the oldest part of the island, a finger of land which used to be a separate island. In the 19th century the bay started to silt up to such an extent that the two parts became stuck together and the resulting land is now used to grow rice. Previously the narrow channel between the two was used as a handy escape route by pirates evading larger ships. A ridge of hills runs along the peninsula, green with fields and forests. There are several beautiful beaches, which have not been overdeveloped or 'improved', fringed with palm trees and interspersed with looming cliffs. They have become popular with Europeans, many of whom were so attracted by the laid-back lifestyle they set up home here, running small hotels and restaurants. Whale watching is a big attraction, January-March, when the humpbacks come to the Bahía de Samaná to breed. This is one of the best places in the world to get close to the whales and a well-organized network of boats takes out visitors to see them. ➤➤ *For Sleeping, Eating and other listings, see pages 356-363.*

Ins and outs

A new road is being built from Santo Domingo to the new international airport, Prof Juan Bosch, at El Catey, on the northern coast of the Samaná peninsula, which should be finished end-2007, and which will cut driving times from the capital from 4½ hours to a little over 1 hour. Flights from Canada, Germany and Italy arrived at end-2006 when the airport opened. **Sánchez** is the gateway town to the peninsula and all road transport passes by here. A good road runs along the southern side of the peninsula to Samaná with a spur over the hills from Sánchez to Las Terrenas on the north side. Another new road is to be built direct from El Catey airport along the northern coast to Las Terrenas. There are good bus services from Santo Domingo and from Puerto Plata and towns along the north coast. You can also get a ferry from Sabana de la Mar, across the bay.

Samaná

The town of **Santa Bárbara de Samaná**, commonly known just as Samaná, is set in a protected harbour, within the Bahía de Samaná. Columbus arrived here on 12 January 1493, but was so fiercely repelled by the Ciguayo Indians that he called the bay the Golfo de las Flechas (Gulf of Arrows). Nowadays two small islets offshore are linked by a causeway to the mainland, providing a picturesque focal point when looking out to sea and added protection for yachts. The town itself is not startling, there are no colonial buildings, no old town to wander around, but the location is most attractive and it is a lively place particularly in whale-watching season.

There is no tourist office in Samaná. **Samaná Tourist Service** (T8095382451), on the Malecón, sells tours but will also provide information; alternatively, call T8095382206 (Ayuntamiento), or 8095382210 (Governor's office).

The present town of Santa Bárbara de Samaná was founded in 1756 by families expressly brought from the Canary Islands. The city, reconstructed after being devastated by fire in 1946, shows no evidence of this past, with its modern Catholic church, broad streets, new restaurants and hotels, and noisy motorcycle taxis. Any remaining old buildings were torn down by Balaguer in the 1970s as part of his grand design to make the Samaná Peninsula into a huge tourist resort. When he was defeated in the 1978 elections his plans were discarded and Playa Dorada was developed instead. His dream is now being revived and the peninsula is witnessing an unprecedented construction boom with new hotels and villas, marina, golf course, airport, etc. There were 2400 hotel rooms on the peninsula at end-2006, with another

5400 planned to be built by end-2011.

In contrast to the Catholic church, and overlooking it, is a more traditional Protestant church, white with red corrugated-iron roofing, nicknamed locally *La Churcha*. It came from England, donated by the Methodist Church. They began the custom of holding harvest festivals, which still take place. The Malecón waterfront road is the main street in the town, lined with restaurants, bars and tour operators. The dock is here, for the ferry to Sabana de la Mar, some whale-watching tours and private yacht services. A causeway links two islands in the bay, where there is a hotel.

Humpback whales return to Samaná Bay at the beginning of every year to mate and calve. Various half-day tours go whale watching, certainly worthwhile if you are in the area then. This is recognized as one of the ten best places in the world to see whales and is very convenient for the average tourist as they are so close to the shore.

▸▸ *See box, page 356 for more details.*

Parque Nacional Los Haïtises

ⓘ *Visits to the Park can be arranged by launch for US$50-60 including lunch, with departures from Sánchez and Samaná on the north side of the bay, and Sabana de la Mar on the south side. Permits must be obtained from the DNP, Sabana de la Mar, T8095567333.*

Across the bay is the Los Haïtises National Park, a fascinating area of 208 sq km of mangroves, humid subtropical forest, seagrass beds, cays, *mogotes* and caves, which were used by the Taínos and later by pirates. The irregular topography of bumpy, green hills was caused by the uplifting of the limestone bedrock and subsequent erosion. There are anthropomorphic cave drawings and other pictures, best seen with a torch, and some carvings. Wooden walkways have been constructed through the caves and into the mangroves in a small area accessible to boats and tourists. The park is rich in wildlife and birds. Many of the caves have bats, but there are also manatee and turtles in the mangroves and inland the endangered solenodon (see Flora and fauna, page 381).

Various companies organize tours (eg Amilka Tours, T8095527664, daily from Sánchez, takes large tour parties and is the most regular). Some include a trip upriver to a village and a swim in the Cristal lagoon (turquoise, cool, sweet water) as well as lunch on a beach near Sánchez. Take hats and lots of sun screen, no shade. It takes longer to get there by boat from Samaná, so it is better to start from Sánchez. Sabana de la Mar is even closer, but excursions are informal.

Cayo Levantado

The offshore island, Cayo Levantado, is a popular picnic place, especially at weekends when the beach is packed and best avoided. The white-sand beach, known as **Bacardi Beach**, is nice, though, and there are good views of the bay and the peninsulas on either side. Unfortunately, a large new hotel (**Gran Bahía Príncipe Cayo Levantado**) has been built and access restricted in some areas.

▸ *Often included as a lunch and swim stop after a whale-watching tour.*

Public boats go there from the dock in Samaná (US$6-8 return, buy ticket at Malecón No 3, not from the hustlers on the pier, lots of boats daily outward 0900-1100, return 1500-1700); alternatively, take a *público* or *motoconcho* 8 km out of town to Los Cacaos (US$3) to where **Transportes José** and **Simi Báez** run boats to the island.

Las Galeras

At the eastern end of the peninsula is **Playa Galeras**. The 1-km beach is framed by the dark rock cliffs and forested mountains of **Cape Samaná** and **Cape Cabrón**, now designated a National Park. The village is popular with Europeans, several of whom have set up small hotels and restaurants. There is a fair amount of weed on the beach and some coral, so rubber shoes are a good idea, but it is 'unimproved', with trees for shade. If you walk east along the beach you come to the biggest hotel so far, **Casa Marina Bay**, set among masses of coconut palms. The beach here is sandy with no coral and very safe for children.

Playa Rincón is 20 mins from Las Galeras by boat, US$10 return journey, or 40 mins by jeep along a paved 8-km road to Rincón village, followed by a 2-km rocky and muddy track through coconut palms. Playa Rincón is dominated by the cliffs of 600-m high **Cape Cabrón** at one end but backed by thousands of coconut palms filling every available space. The sand is soft and there are few corals in the water, which is beautifully clear, but the beach is wild and uncleaned, so coconuts and branches litter the sand. On reaching the beach turn right along a track to get to several beach restaurants at the end where you can get delicious fried fish, caught that morning. They are on a small promontory which gives protection against the waves.

> ❧ There are very few vendors and the beaches are hassle-free.

Playa El Valle is reached by 10 km dirt road from Samaná, 4WD needed, or come by boat from Las Terrenas or Las Galeras. A *guagua* comes a couple of times a day from Samaná, US$1. The drive over the mountain is spectacularly beautiful, with two river crossings where women still wash their laundry and children hitch a ride to school. On the way back you get a wonderful view of the Samaná Bay with a flash of white sand on Cayo Levantado as you come over the top. The beach is undeveloped except for a tiny beach bar, aptly named El Paraíso, see page 360. There is also a beach bar for the sole use of guests from **El Portillo Hotel** in Las Terrenas, who stop here for lunch on a safari trip, but otherwise the beach is usually empty of tourists. The view from the beach is dramatic, with the headlands rising vertically out of the water and a river running into the sea. Coconut palms are everywhere, be careful about sitting underneath one for shade. Check before swimming at deserted beaches where there can be strong surf and an undertow. Drownings have occurred near El Valle. Only go in when the sea is flat calm, ask for advice at the beach bar or at the tiny naval station behind.

Las Terrenas

On the north coast of the peninsula is Las Terrenas, with some of the finest beaches in the country, from which, at low tide, you can walk out to coral reefs to see abundant sea life. The beaches go on for miles, fringed by palm trees under which are hidden a large number of small hotels and restaurants, often run by Europeans, attracted by the lifestyle. It is a quiet, low-key resort and never crowded, although development is in progress and greater numbers of visitors are expected; the beaches are mostly clean and remain beautiful. It is reachable by a 17-km road from Sánchez which zig-zags steeply up to a height of 450 m with wonderful views before dropping down to the north coast. The road Samaná-Las Terrenas via Limón is also a pretty route although perhaps not so spectacular from the top. A new road is planned, which will link Las Terrenas directly with the new airport at El Catey and run along the northern coast behind the beaches.

Where the road reaches the shore, at the cemetery in Las Terrenas village, a left turn takes you along a sandy track that winds between coconut palms alongside the white-sand beach for about 5 km, past guesthouses and restaurants. At the end of the beach, walk behind a rocky promontory to reach **Playa Bonita**, with hotels, guesthouses and restaurants. Beyond the western tip of this beach is **Playa Cosón**, a magnificent 6-km arc of white sand and coconut groves ending in steep wooded cliffs (1½-hour walk or US$3 on *motoconcho*). A large hotel and marina development is being constructed here, while an all-inclusive hotel, Viva Wyndham Samaná, has already opened at the far end of Playa Cosón. A nice trip is to take a *motoconcho*, about US$3, along a very bumpy dirt and sand track and walk back along the beach.

A right turn at the waterfront in Las Terrenas takes you along a potholed road about 4 km to the largest hotel in the area, **El Portillo**, an all-inclusive resort. The

356

Dominican Republic The Samaná Peninsula

Humpback whales

A fully grown humpback whale (Megaptera novaeangliae) measures 12-15 m and weighs 30-40 tonnes. It is dark grey, or black, with a white belly and long white flippers. On its nose and flippers it has large nodules, not perhaps an attractive feature, but the hairs coming out of the lumps on its nose are used like a cat uses its whiskers. All humpbacks can be identified by the markings on their tails, or flukes, as no two are the same, and scientists have recorded thousands of them so that they can trace and monitor them. They even give them names. Humpbacks are famous for their singing. Only the males sing and they all sing the same song, repeating phrases over and over again, sometimes for hours, but each year they have a new refrain, a variation on the theme, which they develop during the journey. Maybe to keep the kids amused along the way, but more likely to attract a

mate. The humpback is a baleen whale, which means that it scoops up huge gulps of water containing small fish or krill, then sieves it, squeezing the water out between the baleens, retaining the food. When they are in the Bahía de Samaná, Banco Navidad (Navidad Bank) or the Banco de Plata (Silver Bank), they do not feed for the three months of their stay. The water is too warm to support their type of food, although a perfect temperature in which to give birth without harming the calf, which is born without any protective fat to ward off the cold. This fat is soon built up, however, in time for the return journey north to the western north Atlantic and Iceland, by drinking up to 200 litres a day of its mother's milk and putting on weight at a rate of 45 kg a day.

The Dominican Republic has the most popular and well established whale watching in the Caribbean.

airstrip is behind it on the other side of the road. **El Limón**, 10 km further on, is a farming village on the road across the peninsula to Samaná. From El Limón you can ride or hike for an hour into the hills to a 40-m high waterfall on the Arroyo Chico and swim in a pool of green water at its foot, a highly recommended excursion. The **Salto de Limón** (or Cascada del Limón) is a National Monument. There are four different access routes to the falls from the Samaná road, from the communities of Rancho Español, Arroyo Surdido, El Café and El Limón, from all of which you can hire horses, buy food and drinks and local produce. If taking a guide to the falls, fix the price in advance (the falls can be deserted, do not take valuables there). Access to the falls is regulated to prevent erosion and other damage; visits are only permitted during the day on foot or horseback. *Motoconcho* from Las Terrenas to El Limón US$2.50, but they will try to charge US$5-10.

Sleeping

Samaná *p353*
LL Gran Bahía Príncipe Cayacoa, Loma Puerto Escondido, T8095383135, www.bahia-principe.com. Reopened 2006 after complete refit. Luxury all-inclusive overlooking the bay of Samaná, just before the causeway. 295 rooms and suites, 4 restaurants, 3 bars, pools, gym, spa, tennis, casino.
LL Gran Bahía Príncipe Samaná, on coast

road 8 km east of town, T8095383111, www.bahia-principe.com. Renovated and reopened 2007. 110 rooms 8 villas, charming, luxury, all-inclusive resort, pool, all facilities available, small beach, good food and service, compact 9-hole golf course, watersports, tennis, horse riding, heliport, shuttle service to Cayo Levantado.
A Tropical Lodge, on Malecón heading east,

The industry is centred on humpback whales, but pilot whales and spotted dolphins can also be seen in Samaná Bay, and bottlenose, spinner and spotted dolphins, Bryde's and other whales on Silver Bank. The season for both locales is January to March with whale-watching tours in Samaná Bay 15 January-15 March. Whale-watching trips in Samaná Bay last 2-4 hours. The trips to Silver Bank are more educational and are usually arranged by specialist groups offering tours of up to a week.

The whole of Samaná Bay, Silver Bank and Navidad Bank is now a National Marine Mammal Sanctuary. The aim is to include the peninsula and Los Haïtises National Park and have it all declared a Biosphere Reserve by UNESCO. During the season the Dirección Nacional de Parques monitors the whale watching and has four vigilantes, recognizable by their green caps, of which three are in Samaná and one at Silver Bank. They can be contacted at the offices of the Centre for the Conservation and Ecodevelopment of Samaná Bay (CEBSE), T8095382042, cebse@verizon.net.do. A set of rules and guidelines has been drawn up by CEBSE, the DNP and the Association of Boat Owners in Samaná to regulate the activities of whale-watching boats, including limits on how close they can get to whales and how long they can remain watching them. Data has been collected on the impact on breeding of whale watching, to see if this new tourist attraction has been affecting the humpbacks. There has, however, been no change since 1987, with mothers and calves and singers still in the same area, although more studies are to be undertaken on dive intervals, to see if they are being forced to stay down longer. For whale-watching tours see Whale and dolphin watching, page 34.

T8095382480, www.tropical-lodge.com. Jean-Philippe and Brigitte have run this hotel for many years. 17 rooms, fan or a/c, some have balconies and cable TV, own generator, pool and jacuzzi, pleasant, not fancy but clean and good restaurant and pizzeria. Breakfast included. Extensive library.
D El Paraíso, Av Francisco del Rosario Sánchez 53, T8095382648. Near rotonda, central but quiet, modern, good and clean, TV, a/c, 12 single and double rooms.
E Bahía View, Av Circunvalación 4, T8095382186, asavachao@aol.com. By the middle traffic circle, new building in walking distance of everywhere with view of bay. 9 clean and newly painted rooms, all different sleeping up to 8 in the biggest, distinguished by a painting on the wall in each. A/c, fans, own generator, parking, rooms facing the harbour have balconies, restaurant on first floor.
E Cotubanamá, T8095382934, go west along the Malecón to the roundabout and turn right, the hotel is one block up on the left. Clean, adequate, fan, bedside light, make sure your bedroom door locks properly, hot water sometimes, doesn't last long.
E Docia, overlooking La Churcha, T8095382041. New, basic lodging, fan, rooms upstairs have bigger windows and are lighter and brighter with more breeze, also great view of harbour from balcony. Free morning coffee, use of communal kitchen.

Las Galeras *p354*
Water is brackish here and you should not drink water from the tap. All hotels have salt-water showers.
L-AL Villa Serena, T8095830000, www.villaserena.com. Plantation house theme with wooden balconies and verandas, overhanging roofs and a charming double staircase to the lobby. View across manicured gardens dotted with palms to the sea, where there is a tiny islet with a few palm trees. 21 elegant rooms, with a/c, ceiling fans. Drinking water is provided. The restaurant offers European-style food, making its own pasta, breakfast is included

in room rate. Tours organized, free bicycles, snorkel gear for hire.

AL-C El Marinique, T8095380262, www.elmarinique.com. 2 deluxe apartments, 3 cottages and 1 room in gardens with a path down to the sea. All have fans, 24-hr electricity, continental breakfast included. Internet access for guests. The room has 2 beds and bathroom, cold water, simple but adequate. Cottages have 1 or 2 beds, a table and chairs, windows on all 4 sides for maximum ventilation and corrugated roofs. Apartments have a full kitchen, sofa bed in the living area and loft room upstairs. Secure parking and Andy's guard dogs deter intruders. Nicole is a wonderful cook, see Eating. Fishing, horse riding and boat trips also offered, meal and activity packages available.

AL-D Plaza Lusitana, T8095380093, www.plazalusitania.com. 10 suites and apartments for self-catering, comfortable chairs, kitchen and dining table, with tiled floors, a/c, fan. Conveniently located above the shops in the centre of the village.

A Todo Blanco, T8095380201, www.hoteltodoblanco.com. Plantation house style, all white, gingerbread fretwork, 8 rooms with balconies overlooking the sea through palm trees, light and airy, good-sized bathrooms, gardens slope down to the beach. Breakfast available in dining room, on terrace or in your room, dinner by reservation only, outside restaurants will deliver. Tours available.

A-B Moorea Beach, T8095380007, www.hotelmoorea.com. 8 rooms, 1 apartment, balcony overlooking sea, 200 m from beach, in palm trees, painted white, pool, quiet but close to village centre, Wi-Fi, bar, restaurant open in high season only, no credit cards.

C Casa ¿Por Qué No?, Main St. Contact is by fax at the Communications Centre around the corner, otherwise just turn up. Bed and breakfast, other meals available on request, specialities are seafood and oriental dishes. 2 small rooms with bathroom using rain water rather than brackish water, set back from the road in pleasant gardens, very peaceful. Open mid-Oct to end-Apr, when the French Canadian owners are in residence.

Las Terrenas p355

Most hotels on the beach have prices up to **C** grade, but in town or behind those on the beach can be cheaper.

AL Las Casitas Playa Perdida, Loma Bonita, at the end of Playa Las Ballenas, T8092406043, www.casitasplayaperdida.com. 4 very nice French-owned bungalows on hillside with sea view, each with a loft, terrace, jacuzzi, hammocks, deck chairs. Pool, patio bar, beach, breakfast included, served pool-side or in your room, children catered for.

AL-A Las Palmas al Mar, about 1 km from town on Portillo road, T8092406292, www.laspalmasalmar.com. Great villas with 2 bedrooms, 2 bathrooms, veranda, rocking chairs, barbecue, all mod-cons and well-stocked kitchens, generous welcome package of fruit bowl, bouquet, and fresh milk and coffee in the fridge. Cheaper the longer you stay. German owned, very clean, lovely setting, pool, just across the road from a nice stretch of beach.

AL-B Playa Colibrí, Francisco Caamaño Deño, west end of Las Terrenas, T8092406434, www.playacolibri.com. 45 studios, 1-bedroom and 2-bedroom apartments, a few sleep 6-8, daily, weekly or monthly rates, kitchenette, internet access in apartments, pool, jacuzzi, parking, all clean and new, comfortable, sea view through the palm trees.

A-B Las Casitas en el Jardín Secreto, behind Casa Nina, T/F8092406668, www.lascasitaseneljardinsecreto.com. 4 adorable restored Dominican thatched houses in a nice garden, painted bright and pretty colours, rustic and romantic, breakfast and taxes included, Spanish and French owners, very quiet.

A-C Kanesh Beach 'Las Cayenas', Francisco Caamaño Deño, T8092406080, www.lascayenas.com. Nice hotel in old plantation house style on the beach, now run by Kanesh Wollenmann, rooms with or without balcony, breakfast included, also large room for 4, good value, restaurant in the garden with comfy lounge chairs. Mini golf course in the garden.

B Casa Nina, Av 27 de Febrero, T8092405490, www.hotel-casanina.com. Turn right for 800 m along the beach in Las Terrenas in the direction of El Limón. Renovated, 15 cosy cabins around pool in gardens. Nice spot facing the sea.

B-C Kari Beach Hotel, at end of west track to beach, T8092406187, www.karibeach.com. Italian-owned, some rooms cheaper, a/c extra, clean, hot water, large rooms with

balconies and sea view, good food, help with excursions. **Stellina Diving** on site.
C Casas del Mar Neptunia, 1 Emilio Prud'homme, Calle del Portillo, T8092406617, www.casas-del-mar-neptunia.com. 8 bungalows in garden with fan and fridge, hot water, run by multilingual Franck and Yves, breakfast US$3.
D Papagayo, Av 27 de Febrero, T8092406131, www.hotel-papagayo.com. On beach road heading to El Portillo. Traditional style building on two floors with latticed balcony. Breakfast included, good, bath, clean, fans, screened windows, small bar and restaurant.
F Fata Morgana, near French school off Fabio Abreu, inland between Las Terrenas and Playa Bonita, T8098365541, www.samana.net/fatamorgana. Budget option, run by Edit de Jong, rooms with bathroom sleep 1-4, kitchen, book exchange, barbecue area, large garden, quiet place away from the beach.

Playa Bonita *p355*
AL-B Atlantis, T8092406111, www.atlantis-hotel.com.do. Veronique and Gérard Prystasz run this beach hotel, known for its excellent French cuisine, chef used to work for President Mitterand. Nice garden under coconut palms, 18 spacious rooms, all different sizes and décor, some with a/c, marble bathrooms, breakfast and taxes included, pleasant beachfront bar with swinging chair.
A Coyamar, 1st hotel at Playa Bonita, T8092405130, www.coyamar.com. German-run, 10 rooms, nice, cosy, beachfront, friendly, helpful, breakfast included. Very nice garden with small pool. Diving with Las Terrenas Divers close by.
A-B Acaya, Playa Bonita, T8092406161, www.hotelacaya.com. 2 buildings on the beach, 24 rooms all with ocean view, hot water, fan, a/c at extra cost, Wi-Fi, terrace, good breakfast included, thatched restaurant, international menu.
A-B Casa Grande, right on beach at Playa Bonita, T8092406349, www.casagrandebeachhotel.com. Friendly, run by French couple with children, pleasant rooms with 1 or 2 beds, sleep 2-4, good kitchen, nice location, lawns with coconut palms running down to the beach.

● Eating

Samaná *p353*
The local cuisine is highly regarded, especially the fish and coconut dishes and *sancocho*.
♦ **Bar Le France**, Malecón, T8095382257. 1130-late. Café style. Open-air and indoors.
♦ **Camilo's**, Malecón, T8095382781. 1100-2300. Local and not-so-local food, reasonable (takes credit cards).
♦ **Chino's**, on hill behind Docia. 1200-2300. Beautiful view, run by immigrants, doing very well.
♦ **La Mata Rosada**, opposite the harbour, T8095382388. 1200-2300. French-run but lots of languages spoken, popular with ex-pats, not always open, seafood, about US$10 per person.
♦ **Le Café de Paris**, Malecón, T8095382488. 0800-2300. Brightly painted, good crêperie, ice cream, breakfast, cocktails, loud rock music, very slow service when busy, can take ages to get the bill.
♦ **L'Hacienda**, Malecón, T8095382383. Thu-Tue 1200-late. Grill and bar open from 1200, the best in town, excellent specials, main dishes US$8-10.

Las Galeras *p354*
Locals eat at the *mini-comedores* on the beach at the end of the road where the *guaguas* stop, not recommended for hygiene but plenty of local colour. You can find boatmen here for trips to other beaches.
♦♦ **El Pescador**, Calle Principal, T8095380052. Daily 1600-late. On your right as you head out of the village, look for the coloured lights and the building painted terracotta, blue and white. Spanish-owned, specializes in seafood, fish, shrimp, lobster and crab accompanied by small salad and rice.
♦♦-♦ **Chez Denise**, T8095380219. 1030-2330. French food, delicious crêpes, shrimp, salads, from US$3.50. Colourful and friendly.
♦♦-♦ **Nicole's Ocean View Restaurant**, El Marinique, T8095380262, www.elmarinique.com. Breakfast, lunch and dinner. Delicious papaya crêpes, seafood caught daily and delicious homemade desserts. Nicole bakes her own bread and pastries. Also good steaks and barbecue lobster, chicken and ribs, all served on shady outdoor veranda by the bar overlooking the sea.

¶ **El Paraíso**, on the beach at El Valle, T8098012246 at the marine guard house behind. Daily until 1800. Owner gets there at 0600 to clean the beach and set up the awning for shade. Small shack on the sand serving the catch of the day, cold beer, rum cocktails, as well as water and soft drinks. Fish or shrimp, caught that morning, fried or baked, served with rice and salad and followed by fresh fruit. Delicious and in an unbeatable setting, see page 355.

Las Terrenas *p355*
The **Pueblo de los Pescadores** (fishermen's village) is a collection of renovated wooden huts on the sand whih have been converted into charming restaurants. They tend to come and go, but it is worth wandering along to see what takes your fancy. In 2007, in addition to those listed below, there were ¶¶¶ **Wasabi**, T8092406337, restaurant and sushi bar open from 1800, and a French restaurant ¶¶¶ **La Terrasse**, T8092406730, with a Mediterranean menu.

¶¶¶ **Casa Boga**, between Salsa and Indiana Café, in the Pueblo de los Pescadores, T8092406321. 1900-2300. Fish and seafood, fresh daily, nice little restaurant right by the sea, friendly, Basque-owned.

¶¶¶ **Hotel Acaya**, Playa Bonita, T8092406161, www.hotelacaya.com. Breakfast, lunch and dinner. Thatched restaurant, international menu, the seafood is excellent.

¶¶¶ **La Salsa**, Pueblo de los Pescadores, on the beach, T8092406805. 1900-2400. French-owned, thatched roof restaurant, expensive.

¶¶¶ **Tropic Banana**, on the beach, T8092406110. Breakfast, lunch and dinner. Good food, you don't have to be a hotel guest to eat here. Fri evenings sushi and sashimi with live music 2000-2400.

¶ **Casa Coco**, Calle El Portillo 42, T8092406095. 1200-2400. The first pizzeria to open in town and still good, with a restaurant or home delivery for an extra charge.

¶ **Casa Delfín**, Calle Francisco Bono, just past Hotel Cacao Beach. Good, cheap lunch, only US$4 for a main course, German-owned.

¶ **Herody**, Calle Principal next to Supermercado Rey. 1200-2100. Cheap and good, noisy but best Dominican food.

¶ **La Capannina**, next to Hotel Aligio, T8098862122. 1200-1400, 1900-2300. Good Italian food with very good pizzas, large garden and nice atmosphere.

¶ **La Llave del Mar**, beachfront, by the police station. Good Dominican meals at low prices, typical of the region, local atmosphere, try the special *pescado al coco*.

¶ **Pizzería al Coco**, Playa Bonita. Lunch and dinner. Good pizzas, Swiss-run, excellent Swiss food, nice atmosphere, also bungalows to rent for 1-3 people.

¶ **Sucresale**, at the main road, T8098661371. French bakery, breakfast and pastries.

◑ Bars and clubs

Samaná *p353*
Outdoor nightlife can be found along the Malecón, where several stalls are set up as bars at weekends and fiestas. There is usually music at one or other of the restaurants, whether live or recorded. Nightclubs open and close sporadically and many are little more than brothels.

Las Terrenas *p355*
At weekends there is quite a lot going on, particularly along the beach road, with street sellers of food and drinks and impromptu drum music, but this is not Ibiza. There is often music at the bars and restaurants for gentle entertainment. There are several bars at the Pueblo de los Pescadores, such as **Café Caraïbes**, T8099942962, a small bar, typically Dominican with good drinks, and **Café Atlántico**, T8092406648, a more expensive lounge bar with good music and nice atmosphere, but these tend to change hands regularly.

El Mosquito, Pueblo de los Pescadores, T8098778374, alexindiana@hotmail.com. 1800-0200. Nice seafront spot with good atmosphere and meeting point. Vero and Alex prepare very good long drinks.

Hotel Cacao Beach has a casino for black jack, poker, roulette etc, open until 0400.

Hotel Palo Coco, on main road, T8092406068. 2000-2300. Spanish-run hotel. No restaurant but the bar serves the best tapas in town.

La Bodega, by the cemetery. A bar with live music every Wed and Sat.

Mambo Social Club, Calle El Portillo, set back off the road by Casa Coco, T8098778374. Bar with nice atmosphere and good music, restaurant with French chef in the back yard.

Nuevo Mundo, Av Duarte. 2100-0200. Popular disco although tourists pay more than Dominicans.

Paco Pasha. Libertad. Nice spot but expensive.

Syroz, Libertad, T8098665577. 1700-0200. Bar and dance floor on the beach with live music at weekends. Run by Michelle (French).

⊛ Festivals and events

Samaná *p353*
Traditional dances, such as *bambulá* and the *chivo florete* can be seen at local festivals.
4 Dec Patron saint's day.
24 Oct San Rafael.

▲ Activities and tours

Samaná *p353*
Whale watching
All tours mid-Jan to mid-Mar, depending on when the whales actually arrive and depart the Bay.
Sunshine Services, T8092406164, www.sunshineservice.ch. Offer tours on the Samaná peninsula and further afield, from hiking to whale watching.
Transporte Marítimo Minadiel, T8095382556. Miguel Bezi is another good operator. Their smaller boats can get closer but have a restricted view of the whales.
Whale Samaná, Victoria Marine, T8095382494, www.whalesamana.com. Kim Beddall runs excellent tours in a large boat giving a good view, US$50. Multilingual naturalist guides explain what is happening

and answer questions. A thrill for anyone, especially children. Seasickness pills offered and recommended.

Las Galeras *p354*
Diving
Dive Samaná, Casa Marina Hotel, T8098407926. Peter Traubel and his multilingual staff run CMAS courses, charging US$340 for the first stage. A single dive costs US$38 including equipment, 6 dives cost US$195, snorkelling US$10. The boat is small, with only limited shade. Peter also offers coastal excursions, boat transfers and whale watching in season.

Las Terrenas *p355*
Diving
See also page305 and page 304.
Diving schools at the **Kari Beach Hotel** (**Stelling Diving**, www.stellinadiving.com), and the **Bahía Las Ballenas** hotel, Playa Bonita (**Las Terrenas Divers**, www.lt-divers.com).

Horse riding
Horse riding can be arranged through **Rancho Isabela** (donde Poncho), behind **Hotel Kanesh las Cayenas**, where they have over 35 horses and offer trips from 1 hr to full-day, or lessons for US$20.

Sailing and windsurfing
Apart from the all-inclusive resorts but equipment can be rented at the **Pura Vida** office, on the Portillo road, Calle Libertad 2, **Pizzería Casa Coco**. Sailing, kiteboarding, windsurfing, surfing, mountain biking, tours, all available with lessons, equipment hire.

Dominican Republic The Samaná Peninsula Listings

Tour operators
La Casa de las Terrenas, Calle Principal,
T/F8092406251, casater.resa@verizon.net.do.
Can also help with information, tours, bookings.
Sunshine Services, Calle del Carmen 151,
T8092406164, www.sunshineservice.ch. For
tourist information, domestic flights and
hotel booking service. Run by Mara
(Argentine) and Urs (Swiss); Spanish, English,
German, French and Italian spoken. Lots of
information and help, also house, car and
motorbike rental, well-run excursions (about
25), fishing and boat trips.

⊖ Transport

Samaná *p353*
Air

The peninsula is now well served with
airports: **Arroyo Barril**, just west of Samaná
on the southern coast and **Prof Juan Bosch**
at El Catey, www.elcatey.com, to the west of
the peninsula on the north coast, are both
international airports. El Catey opened at the
end of 2006 with flights from Germany (**LTU**,
Condor), Canada (**Air Transat**, **Sky Service**)
and Italy (**Neos**). There is also an airstrip east
of Las Terrenas at El Portillo, which is in
regular use by domestic charter planes and
scheduled air taxi services.
Airlines AERODOMCA, T8092406571, in
Las Terrenas, www.aerodomca.com. Has
scheduled flights between Santo Domingo
and El Portillo. **Vol Air**, www.volair-dr.com,
also flies the same route, US$75pp. **Takeoff
travel agency and tour operator**,
T8095521333, www.takeoffweb.com, offers
flights between Arroyo Barril and Punta
Cana, Santo Domingo and Port-au-Prince,
including tour packages if required, eg from
Punta Cana you can include whalewatching,
the Salto de Limón, a tour and lunch.

Boat

There is a ferry across the bay from Sabana de
la Mar to Samaná run by **Transporte Marítimo
Tom Phipps**, T8095382289. Morning crossings
are usually calmer than the afternoon, when
the sea can be choppy. Many yachts anchor at
Samaná. The Port Captain comes on board
when you arrive, with a group of officials, each
of whom may expect a tip to expedite the
paperwork. It can be particularly bad at
weekends and holidays.

Bus and taxi

For short excursions you can take a
motoconcho, some of which have been fitted
with tricycles like rickshaws. There are also
guaguas, or minibuses, for a safer ride. *Concho*
or *guagua* in town US$0.25; *carreras* US$3.50-4.
Guagua to Sánchez from market place US$2.

From the capital either via San Francisco
de Macorís (where **Caribe Tours** has a
terminal, 5 hrs with ½ hr stop), Nagua and
Sánchez, or via Cotui, Nagua and Sánchez
(**Caribe Tours** and **Metro**, 4 hrs). Alternatively
from the capital by bus or *público* to San
Pedro de Macorís, then another to **Sabana
de la Mar** and take the ferry across the bay.
Return to Santo Domingo, **Caribe
Tours**,T8095382229, 5 daily. US$6. **Metro**,
T8095382851, at 0800, 1500, via Sánchez
US$3, Nagua US$3, San Francisco de Macorís
US$4.40, to Santo Domingo US$6. **Caribe
Tours** from Samaná to Puerto Plata (US$6) via
Sánchez, Nagua, Cabrera, Río San Juan, Gáspar
Hernández, Cabarete (US$4) and Sosúa daily
1600, 4 hrs. **Línea Gladys** to Santiago,
US$4.50, from traffic lights west of town.

Car

Rentacar is on the Malecón, next to Mata
Rosada restaurant and opposite Metro.
Fabrizio y Daniele, T8092535727, have
motorbikes and run moto tours.

Las Galeras *p354*

Las Galeras is 1 hr, US$1.75 by *guagua*, from
either the market or the dock in Samaná,
US$4.50 by *motoconcho*. All transport
congregates where the road ends at the
beach, by the *comedores* on the sand.
Guaguas leave when more or less full but you
won't have to wait long. Jeep and motorbike
rental on the road to **Hotel Moorea Beach**.

Las Terrenas *p355*
Bus and taxi

Motoconchos whizz up and down the road
through the village and weave their way
along the beach track, US$1-3, depending
on how far you go.

Caribe Tours stops in **Sánchez**
(T8095527434) on the way to **Samaná**, from
Santo Domingo or Puerto Plata. You will be
met by *motoconchos*, US$3 to the *guagua*
stop, up to US$4.50 to a hotel further along
the beach. A taxi (minibus) Sánchez-Las

Terrenas costs US$20, Samaná-Las Terrenas US$47. Note that *guaguas* which meet arriving **Caribe Tours** buses in Sánchez overcharge for the journey to Las Terrenas (US$4.75-9.50).

Car

Lots of car, jeep, *moto* hire. Motorbikes (US$15-25) and mountain bikes (no brakes) can be hired. Jeep rental US$60. There is a petrol/gasoline station.

○ Directory

Samaná *p353*
Banks Banco del Cambio, behind **Samaná Tours**, changes TCs. **Scotiabank** has ATM inside, gives cash against Visa, 6% commission, open 0830-1500 Mon-Fri. Also Banco de Reservas, but no ATMs.
Internet Compucentro in the same building as **Verizon** but round the corner on Calle Lavandier, has email facilities, T8095383146, compucentro@hotmail.com.

Mon-Fri 0900-1230, 1500-1800, US$2.75 per hr, minimum charge US$1. **Medical services** Clínica Vicente, T8095382535, is the most advanced in Samaná, with ultrasound and X-rays. **Post office** behind Camilo's, just off Parque. **Telephone** Verizon, Calle Santa Bárbara, daily 0800-2200 for phone, fax and email.

Las Galeras *p354*
Telephone Verizon is on the main road next to De Todo Un Poco.

Las Terrenas *p355*
Banks Scotiabank in *centro comercial* in the middle of the village. Banco del Progreso's ATM doesn't always work. **Crediprogreso** in the centre Paseo down by the cemetery. **Agencia de Viajes Vimenca**, Remeses Vimenca, on the main road. **Western Union** for fast money transfers, exchanges money at the best rates in town. **Telephone** Verizon has a phone, internet and fax office, daily 0800-2200, credit cards accepted.

East of Santo Domingo

The eastern end of the island is generally flatter and drier than the rest, although the hills of the Cordillera Oriental are attractive and provide some great views. Cattle and sugar cane are the predominant agricultural products and this is definitely cowboy country. However, much of the sugar land has been turned over to more prosperous activities such as tourism, the Casa de Campo development being a prime example. The main beach resorts are Boca Chica, Juan Dolio, Casa de Campo, Punta Cana and Bávaro, but there are several other smaller and more intimate places to stay. ▸▸ *For Eating, Sleeping and other listings, see pages 367-369.*

Boca Chica

About 25 km east of Santo Domingo is the beach town of Boca Chica, the principal resort for the capital. Its days of being a quiet fishing village are long gone. It is set on a reef-protected shallow lagoon, with a wide sweep of white sand and the water is perfect for families. Tourist development has been intensive and there are many hotels, aparthotels and restaurants of different standards with lots of bars and nightlife. All-inclusive resorts, of which there are several, are best booked as a package if you want a good deal. Vendors line the main road, selling mostly Haitian paintings of poor quality but they are colourful. The main street is closed to traffic at night and the restaurants move their tables on to the road. The local **tourist office** is near **Coral Hamaca** at end of Calle Duarte, upstairs with **Politur**.

Juan Dolio

Guayacanes, Embassy and Juan Dolio beaches, east of Boca Chica, are also popular, especially at weekends when they can be littered and plagued with hawkers (much cleaner and very quiet out of season). The whole area is being developed in a long ribbon of holiday homes, hotels and resorts, and the new highway has improved access. **Guayacanes** has a nice little beach and the village is less overcrowded than Boca Chica. Buses going along the south coast will drop you, and pick you up again, at the various turn-offs to the beaches. **Juan Dolio** village is low key, with hotels, apartments, a few small bars, a tour agency and dive shop. Tourist taxis from the Juan Dolio hotels charge US$44 for a return trip to Santo Domingo with a three-hour wait. Taxi to the airport US$20 one-way (T8095262006). East of Juan Dolio is the resort of Villas del Mar, and the beach area of Playa Real, with eight all-inclusive resorts and several apartment developments.

The **Reserva Antropológica de las Cuevas de las Maravillas** ① T8096961797, www.cuevadelasmaravillas.com, Tue-Sun 1000-1800, adults US$2, children under 12 US$1, at Cumayasa, 15 km after San Pedro de Macorís on the way to La Romana, (signed off main road) is an excellent new development and well worth a detour off the main road when heading east. The huge caves are now managed by the Ministry of the Environment and access is regulated. There are walkways, steps and ramps through the caves and a discreet lighting system works on sensors. The elevator sometimes breaks down, but other than that the attraction works well and is clean and tidy with pleasant gardens planted outside. Inside the caves there are stalactites, stalagmites and Taíno cave drawings. A knowledgeable guide will accompany you on your one-hour tour and answer questions. There's a museum, shop, cafeteria, toilets and facilities for wheelchair users. Photography only by prior arrangement.

La Romana → *Population: 101,350.*

East of San Pedro de Macorís is La Romana. The town is dominated by its sugar factory, which can be seen all along the coast. There are still railways here which carry sugar to the Central La Romana and the trains' horns can be heard through the night. The town is very spread out, mostly on the west bank of the Río Dulce, which reaches the sea here. The Río Chavón area east of La Romana and Casa de Campo is a protected zone to safeguard a large area of red and black mangroves.

Isla Catalina

Off La Romana is Monumento Natural Isla Catalina (also called **Serena Cay**). Although inland the southeast part of the island is dry, flat and monotonous, the beaches have fine white sand. The reef provides protected bathing and excellent diving. Tours for US$30-68 including lunch, supper and drinks. Cruise ships also call, disgorging some 100,000 passengers in a winter season. The island is under the permanent supervision of the Dominican Navy and the Ministry of Tourism. All works that may affect the vegetation have been prohibited.

Casa de Campo

Just east of La Romana on the road to Higüey you pass the entrance to Casa de Campo. This is the premier tourist centre in the Republic. The resort was built in 1974 by Charles Bluhdorn, the founder of **Gulf & Western**, which originally grew sugar cane on the land. After he died the Cuban-American family Fanjul bought it and opened it to paying guests in the 1980s. It is kept isolated from the rest of the country behind strict security. Covering 7000 acres, it is vast, exclusive, with miles of luxury villas surrounded by beautifully tended gardens full of bougainvillea and coleus of all colours. It has won numerous awards and accolades from travel and specialist sporting magazines. A **Marina and Yacht Club** with Customs on site is at the mouth of the Río Chavón, from where you can take boat trips up the river.

Sport is the key to the resort's success. There are lots of activities on offer and they are all done professionally and with no expense spared. The tennis club has 13 courts where you can have lessons with a pro or knock up with a ballboy, the club is busy from early in the morning to late at night. The riding school has some 150 horses for polo, showjumping, trail riding, or whatever you want to do. The polo is of a particularly high standard and international matches are held here. For those with a keen eye, there is a world-class Sporting Clays facility developed by the British marksman, Michael Rose, with trap, skeet and sporting clays. Above all, however, guests come here for the golf. There are two world-class 18-hole courses designed by Pete Dye: 'The Links' and 'Teeth of the Dog'. The latter, ranked number one in the Caribbean, has seven water holes which challenge even the greatest players.

> ‡ Many famous people have stayed here, including Michael Jackson and Lisa Marie Presley when they got married in the Dominican Republic in 1994. Bill Clinton is a regular visitor and Julio Iglesias has a house here.

Altos de Chavón

Altos de Chavón is an international artists' village in mock-Italian style built by an Italian cinematographer, in a spectacular hilltop setting above the gorge through which flows the Río Chavón. Students from all over the world come to the art school, but the village is now a major tourist attraction and is linked to **Casa de Campo**. There are several restaurants of a variety of nationalities, expensive shops and a disco. The **Church of St Stanislaus**, finished in 1979 and consecrated by Pope John Paul II, contains the ashes of Poland's patron saint and statue from Krakow. It is a perfect spot for a wedding with a lovely view of the river and great photo opportunities. An amphitheatre for open-air concerts seating 5500 was inaugurated with a show by Frank Sinatra (many international stars have performed there, from Julio Iglesias to Gloria Estefan and the best Dominican performers). There is also an excellent little **Museo Arqueológico Regional**, with explanations in Spanish and English and lots of information about the Taínos.

Bayahibe

Bayahibe is a fishing village (about 25 km east of La Romana) on a small bay in a region of dry tropical forest and cactus on the edge of the **Parque Nacional del Este**, a great place to stay, with excursions, diving, budget lodgings and cafés. Recent archaeological discoveries have shown that there were groups of hunter-gatherers living in the Bayahibe area around 2000BC and that later immigrants arriving around 1500BC used pottery, made weights for their fishing nets and tools from conch and coral to grate foods. Its proximity to the park and offshore islands has made it popular with divers and it is considered it the best dive destination in the country. Small wooden houses and church of the village are on a point between the little bay and an excellent, 1½ km curving white-sand beach fringed with palms. There are lots of rooms and cabañas to rent and several bars and restaurants for low-budget travellers but all-inclusive resorts now dominate the area. Plenty of fishing and pleasure boats are moored in the bay and it is from here that boats depart for Isla Saona.

Isla Saona is a picture book tropical island with palm trees and white sandy beaches, set in a protected national park. However it is also an example of mass tourism, which conflicts with its protected status. Every day some 1000 tourists are brought on catamarans, speed boats or smaller *lanchas*, for a swim, a buffet lunch with rum on the beach and departure around 1500 with a stop off at the 'swimming pool' a patch of waist-deep water on a sand bank, where more rum is served. The sea looks like rush hour when the boats come and go. If you arrange a trip independently on a *lancha*, a smaller, slower boat, the local association of boat owners assures uniform prices.

Diving Wear shoes when you go in the water as there is broken glass. Some of the best diving in the country is in this area, in the national park, and although local fishermen are still spearfishing, the reef is in good condition and there are plenty of fish, more in some areas than others. Dolphins are often seen from the boat, while underwater you find sharks and rays off Catalinita Island, east of Saona, reef sharks at

La Parguera, west of Saona, the wreck of *St George* close to the *Dominicus* and freshwater caves inland for experienced divers. ▸▸ *For dive operators, see page 368.*

Higüey

The main town in the far east of the island is the modern, dusty and concrete Higüey. The **Basílica de Nuestra Señora de la Altagracia** (patroness of the Republic) can be seen for miles away. It is a very impressive modern building, to which every year there is a pilgrimage on 21 January; the statue of the Virgin and a silver crown are in a glass case on the altar and are paraded through the streets at the end of the fiesta. According to legend, the Virgin appeared in 1691 in an orange tree to a sick girl. Oranges are conveniently in season in January and huge piles of them are sold on the streets, while statues made of orange wood are also in demand. The Basilica was started by Trujillo in 1954, but finished by Balaguer in 1972. The architects were French, the stained glass is French. The Italian bronze doors (1988) portray the history of the Dominican Republic.

Punta Cana

Punta Cana, on the coast due east from Higüey, has some beautiful beaches, good diving, excellent golf courses and an international airport. The area is not particularly pretty, the land is flat and the vegetation is mostly scrub and cactus, except for the palm trees along the beach. For many years there were only two resorts. The **Club Med** opened in 1981, followed by the **Punta Cana Beach Resort** in 1988 and a golf course runs between them. Now there is a construction boom, with several new hotels or villa developments with marinas (see page 309 for details), golf courses (see page 307) and other facilities. There is even a championship bowling alley in the residential area, with 18 lanes, billiards, internet and cafeteria. Independent visitors find it difficult to find a public beach as the hotels will not allow non-residents through their property.

‼ *Julio Iglesias and Oscar de la Renta have built villas in Los Corales.*

Bávaro

Continuing round the coast, there are many other beaches with white sand and reef-sheltered water. The area now known as Bávaro was once a series of fishing villages, but they have disappeared under the weight of hotels which contrast with the shacks still hanging on in places. All the hotels are usually booked from abroad as package holidays and most of them are all-inclusive, run by international companies such as Barceló, Sol Meliá, Occidental (Allegro), Fiesta (Palladium) or Riü.

Playa el Cortecito is a little oasis, a breath of fresh air in amongst the all-inclusives, being the nearest thing to a village that you will find on this stretch of coast. There are several beach bars, restaurants, gift shops, a supermarket, watersports, internet access and tour operators here. It is a lively place and makes a welcome change from the all-inclusive life style. The focal point is the beach restaurant, **Capitán Cook**, famed for its lobster and sea food and the place to be for lunch or dinner.

Bibijagua is more of a craft market than anything else, with restaurants and bars, just along the beach from the **Barceló** complex. The Mercado Artesanal, cleverly signed as BI²JH²O, is a large covered market on the beach where you can buy handicrafts, rum, cigars (likely to be fakes), T-shirts, paintings (copies of Haitian art) and other souvenirs; but don't buy the shell, turtles and stuffed sharks which are for sale, as they are protected by international treaties and should be impounded by customs officials on your return home.

● Sleeping

Boca Chica *p363*

Within easy reach of the capital and the airport visitors tend to stay for short breaks, sometimes only a night. The cheapest guesthouses are away from the beach up by the autopista.

A-C Costalunga, Av del Sur 3, T8095236883, www.costalunga.net. Short walk to beach, Italian-run studios and apartments, clean, a/c, TV, fridge, cooker, wall safe, parking, pool, restaurant, travel agency and internet service, excellent value, security guard at night but no one to check you in if you've had a late flight.

B-C Calypso Beach Hotel, Caracol esq 20 de Diciembre, T8095234666. Not on beach, but close, some of the 40 rooms overlook the small pool, well kept, a/c, TV, pleasant, lots of plants, small bar, restaurant, higher price includes breakfast, billiards.

B-C Mesón Isabela, Duarte at eastern end of town, opposite Neptuno's restaurant, T8095234224. Rooms and studios, with or without a/c, lounge with TV, French-Canadian and Dominican owned, bar, pool, family atmosphere, quiet, personal service, breakfast, light lunches on request, walk round Hamaca to beach, cookers in some rooms.

B-C Villa Sans Souci, Juan Bautista Vicini 48, T8095234461, F8095234136. Includes tax, clean, pool, restaurant, excellent French-Canadian food, bar by pool, rooms with or without a/c, airport transfers with advance notice, 3 blocks to beach.

B-D La Belle, Juan Bautista Vicini 9, on corner of highway, T8095235959, F8095235077. Very nice, a/c, pool, TV, permanent water and electricity (but may be turned off in low season when quiet), bar, restaurant.

D-E Pensión Alemania, Calle 18, 6 blocks from beach, T8095235179. Quiet, clean and good value. English and German spoken, airport transfers, small rooms, double rooms and apartments with kitchen, small pool.

Juan Dolio *p363*

All the large hotels are all-inclusive.

A-B pp Playa Esmeralda, Paseo Vicini, Guayacanes, T8095263434, www.playaesmeralda.com. All-inclusive, 45 rooms in 5 buildings, a/c, fan, fridge, some rooms sleep 3, nice gardens, pool, quiet, low

key, but beach can get busy at weekends with Dominicans from the capital, diving.

B-C Sol-y-Mar, Calle Central 23, Guayacanes, T8095262514. Breakfast included, very clean big rooms, own beach, helpful, French-Canadian-run, overpriced restaurant.

C-F Fior di Loto, Calle Central 517, Playa Juan Dolio, T8095261146, www.fiordilotohotel .com. Guest house with Indian influences, Mara teaches yoga, meditation, martial arts, dance and other spiritual activities, also massage and acupuncture available. Simple rooms, some with kitchenettes, all with bathroom, TV, double bed, casual, laid-back atmosphere.

La Romana *p364*

LL Casa de Campo, 10 km to the east of La Romana, T8095233333, www.casadecampo .cc. Operated by Premier Resorts & Hotels. Hotel, villas, bars, restaurants and country club. Lots of different packages for families, golf, tennis, etc.

Bayahibe *p365*

There are half a dozen all-inclusive hotels along the coast and more are planned. It is more fun to stay in the village. Cabañas for rent, for as little as US$10, ask around, don't expect hot water.

A-B Cabana Elke, Playa Dominicus, T/F 8096898249, www.viwi.it. Behind Wyndham Dominicus Beach, with access to their grounds on purchase of a US$40 day pass. Standard rooms look on to the road, small bathroom, can be joined to make an apartment. Apartments looking onto garden and pool have a large living area with sofa bed, kitchenette, shower room downstairs and loft bedroom upstairs. All have screened porches with chairs. Restaurant and bar. Discounts in low season.

B-E Boca Yate, Av Eladia Bayahibe, T8096886822, h_bocayate@hotmail.com (or in France Daniel.muller69@wanadoo.fr). Priced in euros, with high season in Dec-Feb and Aug, the cheaper rates are for a week's stay. Nicely painted rooms around the central garden in a variety of washed turquoise, blue and pink, spacious, table and chairs, good-sized bathroom, seafood restaurant specializing in lobster and bar on site. Open

1800-0100. Meal plans available. Other side of the road from the all-inclusive resorts, 100 m from the Dominicus beach, day passes are available if you want to use their facilities.

C-E Hotel Bayahibe, T8098330159, M8092245804, hotelbayahibe@hotmail.com. Best in village but it's often full, some rooms have 2 beds, TV, fridge and kitchenette, a bargain if there are four of you, bathroom, hot water, reasonable showers, a/c or fan, balcony, 50 m to the water and dive boats. Internet access in the lobby US$2/hr.

E-F Llave del Mar, T8098330081. Bright pink, blue, green and white, you can't miss it. *Cambio* and phone centre downstairs. Basic but adequate, 25 rooms with 1-2 beds, fan, fridge, a/c and balcony in more expensive rooms, pine furniture, small bathroom but OK for the price, hot water, TV.

⦿ Eating

Boca Chica *p363*
There are beach bars and stalls (*frituras*) all along the beach selling fried fish, *yaniqueques*, sausages, and other local specialities as well as cold beer and soft drinks.

⦿⦿⦿-⦿⦿ Boca Marina, Prolongación Duarte 12A, 1 block east of the Hamaca, T8096886810. Built over the water with a pier full of tables and comfy sofas, old colonial style furniture, lamps made of shells hanging from the palm thatched roof. Nice place to spend a day on the beach listening to good music and having a variety of food, good seafood, also great for sunset watching or a romantic dinner. Reservations strongly recommended, particularly at weekends and holiday times.

⦿⦿-⦿ Neptuno's Club, east of Hamaca, T8095234703, www.neptunosclub.com. Tue-Sun 0900-2230. Built over water, with pier, good fish watching, swimming rafts, seafood, German-owned, menu is German and English, children's menu available, reservations essential, bar in replica of the *Santa María*. Live music Wed and Sat nights.

⦿ Bars and clubs

Boca Chica *p363*
There are numerous small bars all along **Calle Duarte** (closed to traffic at night). Restaurants stay open until around 2300 and

a family atmosphere prevails. From around 0200 hotel and restaurant workers show up and by 0300 everything is in full swing, finally winding down around 0400. The tourist office is trying to clean up under-age prostitution and drug abuse and several bars have been closed.

▲ Activities and tours

Juan Dolio *p363*
Diving
Pirates Cove Dive Centre, Juan Dolio beach, about 500 m from the Juan Dolio Police station in front of the Chocolate Plaza, T8094174257, www.piratescovedivecenter.com. Run by Susanne Heinz and Uwe Rath, English, German and Spanish spoken. US$39 for a single dive, rental equipment available, lots of courses, from beginners to advanced and speciality courses, US$395 PADI Open Water course.

Bayahibe *p365*
Diving
The all-inclusive resorts have their own dive operations.
Scubafun, Calle Principal 28, T8098330003, www.scubafun.info. An independent dive shop run by Germans, Werner and Martina Marzilius. Their clients range from **Casa de Campo** guests to backpackers, beginners to experienced divers. They are very flexible and will do almost anything on request. 2-tank dives with a beach stop cost US$70, a trip to Saona, Catalina or Catalinita, including national park fees, drinks and snacks, costs an additional US$35-59. Day trip to Saona Island costs US$50.

⦿ Transport

Boca Chica *p363*
Bus
Guagua US$1 from either Parque Enriquillo or Parque Independencia, or the corner of San Martín and Av París but not after dark. **Boca Chica Express**, US$1, 30-40 mins, stops running around 2100.

Car
If driving from the capital, look carefully for signposts to whichever part of Boca Chica you wish to go. Numerous parking attendants will offer spots along the beach.

Taxi
Santo Domingo-Boca Chica US$25-30 (can be only US$15 from Boca Chica to Santo Domingo), US$15 from the airport.

La Romana *p364*
Air
La Romana International Airport (LRM), across the road from Casa de Campo, receives **American Airlines, Delta** and US Airways from New York, **American Airlines** flights from Miami and San Juan. **Lauda Air** flies from Milan. Charter transfers can be arranged from Santo Domingo's International Airport, Las Américas.

Bus
Carros públicos from La Romana to **Casa de Campo**, US$0.20.

Altos de Chavón *p365*
Bus and taxi
Free bus every 15 mins from **Casa de Campo**. Taxi from La Romana, US$15-20. Most people arrive on tour buses or hired car.

Bayahibe *p365*
Bus and taxi
Take the road which turns off the highway from La Romana to Higüey. A *carro público*

La Romana-Bayahibe is US$2.50, or take a Higüey bus to the turn-off and take a *motoconcho*, US$1. A taxi from La Romana costs about US$10.

Punta Cana *p366*
Air
Flights vary according to season.
  From North America Lan, American Airlines, US Airways and United Airlines from Miami and American Airlines, US Airways, United Airlines, American West and Delta from New York.
  From Europe Amsterdam (Condor) and ArkeFly, Madrid (Air Europa and (Condor), Paris (Air France), Condor and/or LTU from Berlin, Düsseldorf, Frankfurt, Hamburg, Leipzig, Munich. and **Lauda Air** from Milan. For discount flights from Europe and the USA try www.airninja.com.

① Directory

Boca Chica *p363*
Banks Banco Popular has an ATM and will change TCs at good rates. There are several exchange houses. **Telephone** Phone calls can be made from Televimenca/Western Union, on main street, also Verizon, near Coral Hamaca.

Dominican Republic Southwest

Southwest

The far southwest of the Republic is a dry zone with typical dry-forest vegetation. It also contains some of the country's most spectacular coastline and several national parks. It is a mountainous area with great views and scary roads and the closer you get to the Haitian border the poorer and more deforested the country becomes. This was the major cause of the devastation after heavy rains in 2004. It may never be known how many thousands of people lost their lives in mud slides at Jimaní and across the border in Haiti, where there were no trees to hold the soil in place. Tourism is not big business here yet, although there are some fascinating places to visit, such as Lago Enriquillo, a saltwater lake below sea level and three times saltier than the sea, or the mines for larimar, a pale blue semi-precious stone used in jewellery. The towns and villages are unremarkable and unpretentious but give a fascinating insight into rural and provincial life in the Republic. ▶ For Eating, Sleeping and other listings, see pages 373-375.

San Cristóbal and around
The birthplace of the dictator Rafael Leonidas Trujillo, San Cristóbal is 25 km west of Santo Domingo. Most of the sites of interest are related to his involvement with the town. He was on his way to San Cristóbal to visit a mistress when he was gunned down. Both of Trujillo's homes are now in ruins but can be visited. The **Casa de Caoba** was looted and stripped bare after the dictator's death, but still gives an idea of the

building's former opulence, when it was lined with mahogany. Take the turning off the dual carriageway from Santo Domingo signed to La Toma de San Cristóbal, bypassing the city. Turn right after the purple PLD office and then stop just after the water tank on your left. The 1-km road up to the house is on your left, but a sturdy 4WD is required – it is better to walk. A caretaker will let you in and show you around for a tip. The **Palacio del Cerro** was another luxury residence on top of a hill with a tremendous view. The Palacio is run down, although there are more decorative features than at the Casa de Caoba, including a grand marble staircase, a gold and silver mosaic-tiled bathroom and a heliport on the roof. From the Parque Central follow the Baní road, Av Luperón, and turn left at the Isla petrol station. The house is guarded by the military, for a tip someone will show you around.

The caves at **El Pomier** ① *Mon-Sat 1000-1600, US$2 for tour*, protected by the **Reserva Antropológica de las Cuevas de Borbón**, are some 15 km north out of town (buses from Parque Central) on the road to La Toma de San Cristóbal. The caves are of enormous archaeological value, considered to be as important for the Caribbean Basin as Egypt's pyramids are for the Middle East. The reserve comprises over 6000 pictographs and some 500 petroglyphs. Espeleogrupo de Santo Domingo is working to restore and protect the caves and their drawings with the help of local and foreign volunteers (see www.responsibletravel.com or www.4tdomrep.com). Cave One has been fitted with special lights and ramps, giving access to all. On the local saint's day festival (6-10 June) religious ceremonies take place around the caves, with a mix of supposedly Taíno ritual and African-influenced stick and drum festivals.

South of San Cristóbal, the beaches at **Palenque**, **Nigua** and **Najayo** (*públicos* leave regularly from San Cristóbal's Parque Central) are mostly of grey sand. On a hill overlooking Najayo beach are the ruins of Trujillo's beach house. These beaches are popular as excursions from Santo Domingo and at weekends and holidays can be packed. Lots of beach bars serve finger-licking fried fish and local food, washed down with ice cold beer. The music can be overbearing at times with personal sound systems competing against each other on the beach. At Palenque the dark sand beach is deserted at the far end and you don't have to walk far to get away from the crowds. Good swimming at Palenque, rougher at Najayo but there is an artificial wave breaker.

Baní and Las Salinas

From San Cristóbal the road runs west through sugar cane country to Baní. Baní is the birthplace of Máximo Gómez, the 19th-century fighter for the liberation of Cuba. The **Casa de Máximo Gómez** ① *Av Máximo Gómez, daily 0800-1200, free*, is a museum with a mural in his memory, set in a shady plaza within walking distance of the main Parque Duarte, the centre of the town and a pleasant spot. The small house is at the back of a pretty park marked by a bust of the hero at the entrance and flags flying at either side. There is a great deal on his biography, as well as general history of the period, photos and old documents, but no personal belongings. The lady guardian speaks some English.

Of the two roads west out of Baní, take the one to Las Calderas naval base for **Las Salinas**. There is no problem in going through the base (photography is not allowed); after it, turn left onto an unmade road for 3 km to the fishing village of Las Salinas, passing the sand dunes of the **Bahía de Calderas**, now a national monument and an inlet on the Bahía de Ocoa, shallow, with some mangroves and good windsurfing and fishing. The dunes, the largest in the Caribbean, can be reached from the road, but there are no facilities and little shade. The views are spectacular, however.

❧ *Baní is famous for the small, pink and very sweet, Banilejo mango, in season in April-July.*

Barahona → *Colour map 2, C2. Population: 100,000.*

Barahona is a comparatively young town, founded in 1802 by the Haitian leader, Toussaint Louverture, when he was briefly in control of the whole of Hispaniola. Its economy initially rested on the export to Europe of precious woods, for example mahogany. In the 20th century the sugar industry took over. The large sugar mill at the northern end of town is surrounded by the shanty town district of Batey Central and is currently closed pending privatization negotiations. The main attractions of this rather run-down grid-system town revolve around the seafront **Malecón**, where most hotels and restaurants are to be found. The **Parque Central**, five blocks up, is the commercial hub of the town and a pleasant spot to sit (although tourists are liable to be pestered). The small, public beach at Barahona frequently has stinging jelly fish. It is also filthy, as is the sea, and theft is common. The best beach near town is called **El Cayo** and is reached by passing the sugar mill and surrounding slums and doubling back on to the sandy peninsula with palms (visible from the **Brisas del Caribe** restaurant).

Beaches south of Barahona

Those with a car can visit remote beaches from Barahona (public transport is limited to *públicos*). The coast road south of Barahona, runs through some of the most beautiful scenery in the Republic, mountains on one side, the sea on the other, leading to Pedernales on the Haitian border (146 km). All along the southern coast are many white-sand beaches with some of the best snorkelling in the Republic. The first place is the pebble beach of **El Quemaito**, where the river comes out of the beach, the cold freshwater mixing with the warm sea; offshore is a reef.

At the end of the village of **Las Filipinas**, about 14 km from Barahona, turn right on to a dirt road. Inland about 15 km into the hills along a very poor track (4WD essential, especially after rain, ask directions at the nearby *colmado)* are the open-cast mines where the semi-precious mineral, larimar, is dug. The primitive mines are worth a visit but they will be closed if it rains as the mines flood. Miners or local boys will sell you fragments of stone, usually in jars of water to enhance the colour, for US$5-10, depending on size and colour. When dry, larimar is a paler blue.

‼ *Larimar is mined only in the Dominican Republic and is mostly used for jewellery.*

Back on the main road, you pass through **Baoruco** (see Sleeping) and **La Ciénaga** (small stony beaches and rough tides). The road comes right down to the sea before **San Rafael** natural springs (about 40 minutes from Barahona) where a river runs out onto a stony beach. The forest grows to the edge of the beach. Where the road crosses the river is a *pensión* with a free cold water swimming hole, *balneario*, behind it (the swimming hole is safer than the sea as enormous waves surge onto the beach). At weekends it gets very crowded. There are normally a number of stalls selling drinks and fried fish. It is also possible to climb up the mountain alongside the river, which has small waterfalls and pools. At **El Paraíso**, a medium-sized town 31 km from Barahona, are a popular beach, Texaco station and many *colmados, cafeterías* and bars.

At **Los Patos** another river flows into the sea to form a cool bathing place; a great place to spend the day at a weekend to watch Dominicans at play, with excellent swimming and lots of family groups. **Restaurante Los Patos** has a small pool and good seafood. **La Chorrea** is a man-made pool from a natural spring about 5 minutes' drive up a dirt road on the right-hand side. There are cool, freshwater lagoons behind several of the other beaches on this stretch of coast. **Laguna Limón** is a flamingo reserve. Roads are dangerous at night and impassable without 4WD after rain.

‼ *Note that most of these beaches have domestic animals, so there are droppings on the sand.*

Enriquillo, 54 km south of Barahona, is the last place for fuel until Pedernales, 80 km away, but no unleaded is available. After Enriquillo the road turns inland up to Oviedo and then skirts the Parque Nacional Jaragua as it runs a further 60 km to Pedernales. **Oviedo**, with the atmosphere of a desert settlement, has no hotels or decent restaurants and is one of the hottest places in the country.

Pedernales is the most westerly town of the Republic, on the Haitian border. This is a major crossing point for migrant Haitian workers who come over to work in the sugar cane plantations and in construction. There is no immigration office so in theory only Haitians may enter Haiti here. However, this prohibition is frequently flouted, as border guards are willing to turn a blind eye in return for a small sum (US$10 or so). It is advised, however, that you make yourself known at the Anse-à-Pitres police station on the Haitian side and that you return within a few hours. If there is a change of personnel at the border station, you may find yourself paying another 'tip'. There is no road link, but the crossing can be done on foot if the stream that divides the countries is not too high, or you can hire a *motoconcho*. Every Friday there is an informal market in the no man's land at the border crossing, where Haitians sell cheap counterfeit clothing brands, smuggled spirits and a vast array of plastic kitchenware.

Parque Nacional Jaragua

ⓘ *Ministry of the Environment office just outside Oviedo in Cajuil; daily 0830-1630, entry U$1.50; a boat tour on Laguna Oviedo costs around US$35, for up to 8 visitors.*
Parque Nacional Jaragua is the largest of the Dominican Republic's national parks. This area of subtropical dry forest and inhospitable prickly scrub also contains a marine zone, in which lie the uninhabited islands of **Beata** and **Alto Velo**. The vegetation is largely cactus and other desert plants, but there are also mahogany, frangipani and extensive mangroves. Of particular interest is the **Laguna Oviedo** at the eastern end of the park, which is easily accessible from Oviedo. Here there are the country's largest population of flamingos as well as herons, terns, spoonbills and frigate birds. Animals include the Ricord iguana, the rhinoceros iguana and several species of bat. The lagoon is reached via the National Park office just outside Oviedo where an entrance permit must be bought. Turn right on a rough track after the office to reach a hut, where the park official, Señor Blanco, offers a highly recommended boat trip around the lake. He is a knowledgeable guide (Spanish only), who will point out birds and iguanas and will take visitors to inspect a couple of Taíno cave sites with pictograms.

Also in the national park is **Bahía las Aguilas**, one of the most pristine and virginal beaches in the country. The government is threatening to develop this protected area, so you are recommended to visit before the all-inclusive hotels move in. From Oviedo, continue on Route 44 towards Pedernales. At the intersection of Cabo Rojo, head south towards the Ideal Dominicana, and then on an unpaved road along the coast heading east to the small fishing community called La Cueva. Resourceful members of the community have actually converted the caves into homes. A small Ministry of the Environment shack collects the US$1.50 fee near four outhouses. Primitive camping areas abound, and there is even a small cabin located toward the western end of the bay above the dune. From here boat passage may be negotiated for around US$25 for up to 10 people to make the 30-minute journey to the sandy-white and desolate shores. A dangerous and serious 6-km 4WD road also runs to the beach for the not-so-faint-of-heart. Definitely bring your lunch, water, sunscreen, and appropriate attire for the weather as there are absolutely no services available in the area. Remember to pay your boat driver only after he has picked you up for the return journey.

Parque Nacional Isla Cabritos

ⓘ *Purchase a Dirección Nacional de Parques (DNP) permit (US$1.50) at the ranger station east of La Descubierta (0700-1500) to visit the island; only groups with a guide are permitted to go there. The US$15, 30-min boat trip to the island is offered by various local boatmen, who are recommended by the DNP staff.*
Near the Haitian border, is the 200 sq km **Lago Enriquillo**, whose waters, 30 m below sea level, are three times saltier than the sea. Once linked to the bay of Port-au-Prince

and the Bahía de Neiba, the lake was cut off from the sea by tectonic movements some million years ago and the surrounding beaches and the islands are rich in ancient seashells and coral fragments. Wildlife includes about 500 American crocodiles, iguanas and flamingos. Three islands in the lake, together with the lake and surrounding shoreline, make up the Parque Nacional Isla Cabritos. There are usually one or two boats waiting to take parties over, which leave when full. Isla Cabritos is a flat expanse of parched sand, with cactus and other desert vegetation. It is extremely hot and oppressive around midday (temperatures have been known to rise to 50°C) and visitors are recommended to arrive as early as possible and to take water and precautions against sunburn. This barren island is home to the rhinoceros iguana and the Ricord iguana, both of which have become quite tame, even aggressive, and approach boat parties in search of treats. The two smaller islands are **Barbarita** and **La Islita**. To visit the lake it is best to have your own transport because, even though public transport runs both on the north and south shores, there is no guarantee of travelling on (or returning) the same day. Note that there is a filling station in Duvergé but no fuel elsewhere in this area.

> ‡ There is no accommodation on the lake shore but basic lodging can be found at La Descubierta.

La Descubierta is a pleasant and quiet town. The centre of most activity is at the public *balneario* of **Las Barías**, a pretty spot and cool under the trees. The community area serves local dishes, accompanied by 1.5-litre bottles of hot sauce.

Jimaní

Jimaní, at the western end of the lake (not on the shore), is about 2 km from the Haitian border. The space in between is a no man's land of rocky terrain crossed by an extremely hot road, which fortunately has a constant coming and going of *guaguas* and *motoconchos*. Jimaní is an authorized crossing point for foreigners in general (as is Dajabón) and it is possible to leave the Dominican Republic here and cross into Haiti (see Travel to Haiti, page 297). Customs officers in Jimaní are not above taking items from your luggage. The immigration office closes at 1800 (or before). There is a semi-permanent market in the no man's land, in which Haitian merchants display vast quantities of mostly shoddy and/or counterfeit goods, Barbancourt rum and perfumes. Jimaní itself is a spread-out town of single storey housing which swelters in temperatures of up to 50°C.

● Sleeping

Baní and Las Salinas *p370*
AL-C Hotel Salinas, Las Salinas, Puerto Hermoso 7, Baní, T8093468855. Price per person. Rates at this hotel and restaurant run by Jorge Domenech are all-inclusive but all meals are à la carte. 40 rooms on the waterfront and the other side of the road. Lots of decking, tiled floors, wooden bench seating in the open-air restaurant, all very rustic, but comfortable, with good bathrooms, internet café. Great for windsurfers and kiteboarders (bring your own equipment) and fishermen, many guests arrive in their own boat and tie up at the jetty (where there is also a helipad), diving can be arranged with local boatmen (bring your own gear).
C-D Boca Canasta Caribe Beach Club Hotel, Boca Canasta, T8092230664,

www.boca-canasta-caribe.de. Run by Hans Dieter Riediger, 40-room hotel on the beach, a/c, hot water, café, bar, restaurant, massage room, diving, tennis, basket and volleyball, fishing, horse riding, windsurfing, sailing, waterski, jetski, car hire.

Barahona *p370*
A Pontevedra, Ctra Paraíso in Arroyo, T8093418462. The hotel is new and modern looking. Large rooms have extra sofabed in small living room, a/c, TV, hot water and price includes breakfast and dinner. There is beach access, but the waves are very strong. Two huge pools, large bar, restaurant.
A-B Casa Bonita, Ctra de la Costa Km 16, Baoruco, T8094765059, www.casabonitadr.com. On hillside overlooking coast,

wonderful view from expensive restaurant. 12 rooms in bungalows with gardens, small pool, fan, a/c, no TV or phone. Come here for relaxation rather than for creature comforts. Very popular on Dominican holidays.

B-C Hotel Quemaíto, Ctra Paraíso about 500 m down a dirt road on the left-hand side leaving Barahona, T8092230999. The Swiss-owned hotel sits on a cliff about 30 m above the water and has stunning views of a small inlet below and sprawling green lawns. Some rooms have small terraces and a/c. Breakfast and dinner is included with most room prices.

D Caribe, Av Enriquillo, opposite **Hotel Guarocuya**, T8095244111. All rooms have private bath, telephone, cable TV, fan, a/c, breakfast included. Excellent open-air restaurant (**La Rocca**) next door.

D El Gran Marquíz, Ctra Paraíso 3, T8095246866. Recently opened and very good value, the hotel is large and clean with rooms from 1-3 beds all with private bath with hot water, fan, a/c, telephone and cable TV. Secure parking and a great restaurant. Breakfast included.

D Guarocuya, opposite **Hotel Caribe**, T8095244121. On its own beach near the town centre. Rather gloomy, but good value, with a/c.

E Juan José, Enriquillo, 54 km south of Barahona, T8095248323. One of a couple of small, basic places to stay if you are stuck in the area after a day of drinking rum and eating fish on the beach. Part of a family home and very basic, catering mostly to Dominicans.

Parque Nacional Isla Cabritos *p372*
A-C Casa Maguey, Padre Billini 26, T8094406060. Alex Ramírez is the owner and a major community figure in La Descubierta. Rustic 4-bedroom (all with a/c and bathrooms) house with a big balcony overlooking Lago Enriquillo. Set in a large property, it might require a little spring cleaning and visitors are expected to provide supplies, such as soap, toilet paper, and towels. Basic cabins have been constructed, as has an industrial kitchen for group activities.

E Iguana, Padre Billini 3, T8093014815. 6 very basic rooms for double occupancy. The family will prepare food for guests upon request.

E Plaza Comercial Las Barías, Padre Billini 18, T8097514676. A small, tidy little family *pensión* conveniently located near the centre of town. A small *colmado* is also part of the house.

🍴 Eating

Barahona *p370*
🍴 **Brisas del Caribe**, at northern end of Malecón, T8095242794. 0900-2300. Excellent seafood restaurant, popular at lunchtime, reasonable prices, pleasant setting.

🍴 **El Quemaíto**, Juan Esteban Km 10 on the Barahona-Paraíso road, T8092230999. 0800-1000, 1900-2000. Lunch by reservation only. Dominican and Swiss cuisine in a rustic restaurant overlooking a big garden and the ocean. Quiet ambience with traditional decoration, nice breeze out in the garden.

🍴🍴 **Los Robles**, on the Malecón in front of the port. Excellent for grilled meats, seafood, and *mofongo*, a Dominican specialty prepared with plantains.

🍴 **La Rocca**, next to **Caribe Hotel** on Malecón. Daily all day. Great breakfast menu, inexpensive. Seafood.

🍴 **Punta Inglesa**, Av Enriquillo 21, on the Malecón at **Hotel Caribe**, T8095244111. 0700-2300, closed Mon for lunch. Large Dominican restaurant with a/c inside seating and terrace for great views of the passing action. Specializes in seafood, good-value set menu, friendly place.

▲▲ Activities and tours

Barahona *p370*
Tour operators
The **Barahona Ecological Society** (Soeba) welcomes enquiries from Spanish-speaking visitors and offers ecotourism advice and possibly guides. Contact Roberto Dominici, T8095245081, r.dominici@verizon.net.do.
Eco Tour, Av B Colón 52, Santo Domingo, T8092474310. Customized educational adventure tours to the area's national parks.
Julio Féliz, T8095246570, F8095243929. Is an English-speaking local guide who specializes in ecotourism and birdwatching, fees negotiable.
Tours Trips Treks & Travel, Cabarete, T8098678884, www.4tdomerep.com. Customized educational adventure tours to the national parks in the area.

⊖ Transport

Barahona *p370*
Air
The international María Montéz Airport, opened in 1996 but is little used so far.

Bus
Journey time from **Santo Domingo** is 3 hrs. Minibus fare is US$3.50, *público* US$4.50. Caribe Tours runs 4 buses a day. To **Jimaní**, 2½ hrs, US$3.50. *Concho* or *guagua* in town US$0.30; *carrera* US$0.30.

Pedernales *p372*
Air
The domestic airport of **Cabo Rojo** was refurbished in 2006 after being out of use for 20 years. It is expected to be used by charter planes bringing tourists to the beaches, especially Bahía de las Aguilas.

⊕ Directory

Barahona *p370*
Banks Banco Popular on Parque Central has an ATM (Plus, Visa).
Telephone Verizon, across the square from Banco Popular, daily 0800-2200.

Background

History
The colony Although the Spanish launched much of their westward expansion from Santo Domingo, their efforts at colonizing the rest of the island were desultory. Even Santo Domingo soon declined in importance, overwhelmed by the onslaught of hurricanes and pirate attacks. Drake sacked Santo Domingo in 1586 and the rebuilding costs were more than the fledgling colony could bear. The French invaded in the 17th century from their base on Tortuga and colonized what became known as Saint Domingue in the west. The French colony, the largest sugar producer in the West Indies, soon became the most valuable tropical colony of its size in the world, while the Spanish colony was used mostly for cattle ranching and supplying ships from the Old World to the New.

❧ See page 415 for more on Columbus' colonization of Hispaniola.

By the mid-18th century, the number of Spaniards in the eastern part of the island was only about one-third of a total population of 6000. Since there was little commercial activity or population of the interior, it was easy prey for Haitian invaders fired with the fervour of their rebellion at the turn of the 19th century. Between 1801 and 1805, followers of **Toussaint L'Ouverture** and **Dessalines** plundered the Spanish territory. Sovereignty was disputed throughout the beginning of the 19th century with frequent incursions and occupations by Haitian forces. In 1822, Haiti's army took control for a further 22 years. This occupation lives on in the country's mythology as its lowest point, with the ruthless Haitians expropriating land and raising taxes. It was a very anti-Spanish and anti-white régime and many of the Spanish hierarchy left the island. Santo Domingo descended into poverty.

Independence In February 1844 pro-Independence forces led by three men, the writer **Juan Pablo Duarte**, the lawyer **Francisco del Rosario Sánchez** and the soldier **Ramón Mella**, defeated Haitian troops in Santo Domingo. The independent nation was called the Dominican Republic, supposedly free and independent of all foreign domination. However, the new leaders were not a cohesive group and once in power they soon succumbed to infighting. Duarte was sent into exile and the country underwent yet another period of instability, including more Haitian incursions. In November 1844, the strongman, **Pedro Santana**, assumed the presidency. He wanted to make the Republic a protectorate of France, Spain or Britain, but with no luck. The other leader, or *caudillo*, at this time, Buenaventura Báez, also favoured annexation and the USA was also approached.

A Spanish colony again In 1861, Santana finally achieved re-annexation with Spain in the first and only recolonization in the Americas. Spanish bureaucrats were incompetent, the clergy was once again dominated by reactionary Spaniards and military rule was repressive and contemptuous of the Dominicans. There was a hatred of Spain and an increasing number of guerrillas took to the hills to fight a war of attrition. Spain resented the money it had to spend on suppressing revolts and reinforcing its garrison, depleted by yellow fever.

The Restoration The resurrection in the countryside proved successful and became known as the **War of Restoration** (la Restauración), ending in 1865 when Queen Isabella II abrogated the treaty of annexation and evacuated Spanish officials and troops. The Restoration is remembered as a great moment in Dominican history, but governments still pursued the idea of annexation as the answer to their problems. They wooed the USA, but the US Senate could not muster enough support and a vote for the proposal was defeated. However, Germany became deeply involved in the economy, with its traders and bankers supporting the tobacco crop. German warships were sent on occasion to collect debts and the USA was becoming increasingly apprehensive about Germany's motives.

US intervention The USA intervened to prevent a European power gaining control of the country's customs on behalf of creditors. Roosevelt put the Dominican customs into receivership and under an agreement signed in 1905, the US authorities would collect import and export duties and distribute 55% to the country's creditors and 45% to the Dominican government. In 1907 a formal receivership treaty was signed, heralding the start of the USA's financial leverage in the region. Peace was not assured, however, and in 1916, when the presidency appeared to collapse in chaos, US marines were landed. During the US occupation Dominican finances improved dramatically and the country became creditworthy again, but the American occupiers were deeply resented. Guerrilla fighters were suppressed by US troops. In 1920 the new Land Registration Act dispossessed peasant farmers who had held land communally in traditional holdings known as *terrenos comuneros*, in favour of private ownership, allowing Dominican and US investors to buy up land titles and purchase huge areas on the cheap. Some of the dispossessed small scale farmers formed armed bands, known as *gavilleros*, and waged intermittent guerrilla warfare against the Guardia Nacional and US forces. In 1924 US troops were withdrawn, although the administration of the customs remained under US control.

The Trujillo dictatorship In May 1930 elections were won by the armed forces commander, **Rafael Leonidas Trujillo Molina**, who became president. Thus began one of the most ruthless dictatorships ever seen in the Dominican Republic. With either himself or his surrogates at the helm (Héctor Trujillo, 1947-1960, and Joaquín Balaguer, 1960-1962), Trujillo embarked on the expansion of industry and public works and the liquidation of the country's debts. Nevertheless, his methods of government denied any form of representation and included murder, torture, blackmail and corruption. For 30 years he ruled supreme, dispensing favours or punishment as he deemed appropriate. During his reign, in 1937, an estimated 10,000 Haitian immigrants were rounded up and slaughtered, prolonging the hatred between the two republics. The economy prospered with the expansion of the sugar industry and an influx of US capital, but much of the wealth ended up in the bank accounts of the Trujillos, as the General appropriated companies and land. In 1961 Trujillo was assassinated and another power vacuum was created.

The Balaguer presidencies Joaquín Balaguer had been part of Trujillo's government since 1930 and was nominally president at the time of the murder, although without any real power or legitimacy. He tried to hang on to the presidency, but there was violence and the military intervened. A Council of State was set up in 1962 which, with US approval and finance set the country on the path to some sort of representative democracy. The first free elections for 40 years were held on 20 December 1962 in which Balaguer was defeated by **Professor Juan Bosch** of the Partido Revolucionario Dominicano (PRD). Bosch was a left-wing intellectual who had formed the social democratic PRD in exile. The party's policies for land reform with the redistribution of the vast estates held by the Trujillo family, together with an attack on unemployment and poverty, were overwhelmingly supported by the electorate. He took office in February 1963 but after seven months he was ousted by a military coup and sent into exile. A three-man civilian junta was installed with martial law and new elections were promised, but instability ruled, with several changes of government. With civil war raging in the capital and memories of Communist Cuba still fresh, the USA dispatched 23,000 troops on 28 April 1965 to control the country. The USA supported another provisional government, but there followed several months of fighting with the loss of some 3000 lives. Finally, new elections were held in June 1966. They were won by Balaguer, returned from exile in New York. The economy was in tatters and US aid was crucial in rebuilding the country. The US peace keeping force returned home, calm descended for a while and Balaguer concentrated on imposing austerity and bolstering the country's finances. He retained power in the 1970 elections, and remained in office with the help of a secret paramilitary force known as *La Banda*, the gang, until 1978, forging closer links with the USA, but not without facing coup attempts, right-wing terrorism and left-wing guerrilla incursions.

The PRD boycotted elections in 1970 and 1974, but the declining popularity of Balaguer led it to challenge him in 1978. A PRD President was returned: **Antonio Guzmán**, a wealthy landowner and former minister in Juan Bosch's brief government, whose chief aims were to reduce army power and eliminate corruption. His election was achieved after the intervention of President Carter of the USA, who prevented a military takeover when it became clear that the PRD was winning. Guzmán's successor, **Dr Salvador Jorge Blanco**, also of the PRD, presided over severe economic difficulties which led to rioting in 1984 in which 60 people died. The party split over the handling of the economy, helping Joaquín Balaguer to win a narrow majority in the 1986 elections giving him a fifth presidential term. The 1990 elections were contested by two octogenarians, Dr Balaguer (83) and Dr Juan Bosch (80), now of the Partido de la Liberación Dominicana (PLD). Dr Balaguer won a sixth term of office by a narrow majority, which was subjected to a verification process after Dr Bosch alleged fraud had taken place in the capital. The May 1994 elections had the same outcome, after Balaguer had decided late in the campaign to stand for re-election. His chief opponent was **José Francisco Peña Gómez** of the PRD, who was subjected to blatantly racist campaign abuse because of his dark skin and alleged Haitian ancestry. First results gave Balaguer the narrowest of victories. Peña Gómez, supported by many outside observers, claimed that fraud had taken place and the election was reviewed by a revision committee appointed by the Junta Central Electoral (JCE). The committee found irregularities, but its findings were ignored by the Junta which awarded victory to Balaguer. To defuse the crisis, Balaguer signed a pact with Peña Gómez allowing for new elections in November 1995; Congress rejected this date, putting the new election back six months to 16 May 1996. The PRD selected Peña Gómez again while the PLD chose **Leonel Fernández** as its candidate, to replace Juan Bosch who had retired. Within the PRSC, jockeying for the candidacy was beset by scandals and power struggles, exacerbated by the absence of an appointment by Balaguer himself. Peña Gómez won the first round but in the second round, Balaguer gave his support to Fernández, in an effort to keep Peña from the presidency, and he won 51% of the vote.

The Fernández administration President Leonel Fernández was sworn in on 16 August 1996 and appointed a cabinet largely from his own party, after a cooling of relations with Dr Balaguer. His comparative youth signalled a breath of fresh air despite the continuing influence of the old *caudillos*. He pledged to fight poverty, modernize the economy and fight corruption. In 1997 relations with the PRSC deteriorated rapidly because of investigations into land purchase scandals involving members of the previous administration. Land which was in national parks or in protected areas of special scientific interest, or expropriated under the agrarian reform programme for distribution to small farmers, was found to have been allocated to PRSC officials and sold on for profit, mostly for tourism development. There was also a shake up in the top ranks of the military and police, with some linked to drugs offences, others to unsolved murders and disappearances.

José Francisco Peña Gómez died of cancer in May 1998. Six days later, his party, the PRD, won a landslide victory in the mid-term congressional and municipal elections.

Change in the new millennium Presidential elections in 2000 were keenly fought between the 93-year-old Balaguer for the PRSC, Danilo Medina for the ruling PLD and **Hipólito Mejía** for the PRD. The government was credited with achieving economic growth, but it was perceived that the benefits had not been widely enough distributed and corruption within the administration was alleged. Despite his age, blindness and other infirmities, Balaguer was seen as an influential power broker and a force to be reckoned with. Mejía won 49.87% of the vote, Balaguer 24.6% and Medina 24.9%. As no one achieved the 50% required for an outright win, a second round was technically necessary, but after both other candidates visited Balaguer, both he and Medina pulled out of the race, leaving Mejía the victor. Joaquín Balaguer died in 2002.

Mejía's presidency soon became deeply unpopular and was beset by financial scandals, economic decline, the collapse of the peso and rising inflation, while it was also perceived as deeply corrupt. Inevitably he lost the 2004 elections to former president Leonel Fernández (PLD), who set about restoring the country's economic health. This involved an agreement with the IMF, restructuring the foreign debt and reforming public finances, which soon resulted in an appreciation of the peso and very low inflation.

Government

The Dominican Republic is a representative democracy, with legislative power resting in a bicameral Congress: a 30-seat Senate and a 149-seat Chamber of Deputies. Senators and deputies are elected for a four-year term, as is the President.

Economy

The largest foreign exchange earner is tourism, with annual receipts exceeding US$2 bn. The industry generates 20% of gdp and employs about 5% of the labour force, 50,000 in direct jobs and 110,000 indirectly. The number of hotel rooms is around 55,000, compared with 11,400 in 1987, and more than any other Caribbean country. Nearly half of hotel rooms are sold on an all-inclusive basis.

There are six main agricultural regions: the north, the Cibao valley in the north central area, Constanza and Tiero, the east, the San Juan valley, and the south. Cibao is the most fertile and largest region, while the eastern region is the main sugar-producing area. Sugar was traditionally the main crop and times of prosperity have nearly always been related to high world sugar prices, but diversification out of sugar cane, the conversion of some cane lands into tourist resorts, the expulsion of Haitian cutters and a slump in productivity led to lower volume and value of sugar production. Traditional products grown for export include sugar, coffee, cocoa and tobacco, but they now account of only a third of total exports. Non-traditional products have been gaining in importance. These include fruit and vegetables, plants and cut flowers, marine products, processed foods, cigars and other agroindustrial products. Growth of the cigar industry has put the Dominican Republic in competition with Cuba, with sales of around US$400 million a year.

Since 1975 gold and silver mining has been of considerable importance. Large gold, silver and zinc deposits have been found near the Pueblo Viejo mine, where the oxide ores were running out, and a major gold and silver deposit has been discovered in the Haitian border area, which could mean a joint operation to establish an open cast mine. The country also produces ferronickel, which has overtaken sugar as the major commodity export earner. Reserves are estimated at 10% of total world deposits.

Despite the tourist economy roughly half the population lives in poverty, with a third lacking secure employment. Two thirds of the people live in urban areas and many depend on the informal economy to survive. Remittances from relatives in the USA are the life blood of many families. Inequalities in income are glaring, with the poorest 20% receiving less than 5% of the national income. The rich live in luxury villas driving large cars and the oligarchy continues to dominate the economy as it has since colonial times. From sugar cane and coffee, the powerful families (among them Bermúdez, Barceló and Jiménez) have moved into tourism and export manufacturing.

Geography
The western part of the Dominican Republic is dominated by four mountain ranges which run roughly northwest to southeast. The most impressive is the Cordillera Central, which rises to twin peaks of La Pelona and Pico Duarte, and at 3082 m and 3087 m are the highest mountains in the Caribbean. The eastern half of the country is flatter, bar the hills of the Cordillera Oriental which run roughly parallel to the northeast coast. There is a tropical limestone landscape in part of the Cordillera Oriental, to the south of Sabana de la Mar. The northern boundary of the Caribbean plate lies just north of Hispaniola. The whole island is an active seismic zone, and there have been eight major earthquakes since 1751, the most recent in 1953. The island is moving slowly east, while Cuba and the Bahamas are moving to the west; what is now Hispaniola was attached to southeastern Cuba around 20 million years ago.

Culture
Literature As with all facets of Dominican culture, the US occupation of 1916 to 1924 proved a turning-point in the search for authentic forms of expression. But no sooner had a radical generation of nationalist writers begun to find their voice to protest against the imposition of North American values than the long period of the Trujillo dictatorship was under way. For 30 years the régime tolerated no criticism whatsoever, stamping on any literary originality and encouraging only absurd paeans of praise to 'the Benefactor'. Two of the 20th century's most prominent Dominican writers chose exile. The opposition leader, Juan Bosch, wrote polemics against Trujillo, historical studies and, most readable, two collections of short stories that revealed a formidable grasp of narrative technique. Probably the greatest of the country's poets, Pedro Mir, also lived and wrote abroad until the late 1960s, producing *Hay un país en el mundo* (There's a Country in the World, 1949), an epic poem that tells of an imaginary but recognizable country's history of suffering and exploitation. In 1978, Mir published *Cuando amaban las tierras comuneras* (When They Loved the Communal Lands), a powerful fictional critique of the US occupation and its expropriation of traditional communal land. The conservative Joaquín Balaguer who remained on the island, wrote poetry, historical fiction and a biography of Juan Pablo Duarte. With the assassination of Trujillo in 1961, the exiles were able to return and politically committed writing was again allowed. Authors such as Manuel del Cabral wrote incisively about the social turmoil of the 1960s in books like *La Isla ofendida* (1965), while Freddy Prestol Castillo's *El Masacre se pasa a pie* (1973) was a damning account of the 1937 massacre of Haitians ordered by Trujillo.

Curiously, the dictatorship itself, although stifling literary creativity for three decades, has inspired some of the country's most interesting recent writing. One of the country's most successful writers, Julia Alvarez, situates her *In the Time of the*

Butterflies (1994) around the political assassination of the three Mirabal sisters by Trujillo's henchmen. The brutal methods and bizarre megalomania of the dictator have also caught the imagination of foreign writers, notably the Peruvian Mario Vargas Llosa, whose *La Fiesta del chivo* (The Feast of the Goat) was published in 2000 to great critical acclaim. Dramatizing the worst excesses of the Trujillo period and the build-up to the dictator's assassination, the novel caused unease and controversy in Santo Domingo, where memories are long. Alvarez, together with Junot Díaz, typifies the new generation of Dominican writers, who have been as much shaped by their experience of life in the USA as in their parents' homeland. Both write in English as easily as in Spanish, and Díaz in particular has mastered the tough street-wise vernacular of young Dominicanyorks, the distinctive community of migrant Dominicans in New York and other US cities. His collection of short stories, *Drown* (1996) received rapturous reviews for its unsentimental and sometimes shocking portrayal of alienation and cultural displacement in the Dominican diaspora. Julia Alvarez has also written about the tensions and contradictions experienced by those with double lives. *How the García Girls Lost Their Accents* (1991), looks at a Dominican family in New York and their relationship with *la isla*.

Music and dance The most popular dance is the merengue, which dominates the musical life of the Dominican Republic and has spread across the water with migrants to colonize New York as well. Merengue is believed to have developed in the mid-19th century as a local version of European dances for couples, such as *contredanse*. An Afro-Caribbean flavour was added with lively rhythms and lyrics to reflect social commentary. It was the music of the people, from cane-cutters to dock workers, but, with regional variants it survived as a sort of folk music. There would be four musicians, playing the *cuatro*, similar to a guitar, the *güira*, a cylindrical scraper of African origin but akin to the Indian gourd scraped with a forked stick, the *tambora*, a double-headed drum using male goatskin played with the hand on one head and female goatskin played with a stick on the other, and the *marimba*, a wooden box with plucked metal keys. Despite the regional variations, the merengue of the Cibao Valley around Santiago developed most strongly and became known as the *merengue típico*. In the 1920s, it was played with an accordion, introduced by the Germans, a *güira*, *tambora* and *marimba*, with the accordion being the most important. Over the years, other instruments have been added, such as the saxophone, horn or electric bass guitar. A merengue would have a short introduction, *paseo*, then move into the song, or merengue, followed by a call and response section, the *jaleo*. Although similar to some Cuban or other Latin music and dance, the steps of the merengue have always been simpler, with a basic two-step pattern, but at a fast tempo with a suggestive hip movement.

The other main music style you will find in the Dominican Republic is bachata, which also emerged from the peasant and shanty town dwellers. It was music for the soul, for the poor and downtrodden, the dispossessed farmers who were forced off the land in the 1960s and flooded into the urban slums with their guitar-based *canciones de amargue*, songs of bitterness. The traditional group had one or two guitars, maracas, bongo and *marimba*, with a solo male singer, who sang songs based on the Cuban *son*, Mexican *ranchera*, merengue and boleros. The songs expressed the frustrations of the newly-urban male, a *macho* without a cause, who was often unemployed and often dependent on a woman for his income. The sudden rise in popularity of bachata was principally due to Juan Luis Guerra, who experimented with the romantic, sentimental genre and sensitively created a poetry which appealed to everyone, particularly women. Most bachata songs are similar to boleros, with the guitar, the rhythm and the sentimentality, but faster than usual and with one singer rather than three.

There is a merengue festival in the last week of July and the first week of August, held on the Malecón in Santo Domingo. Puerto Plata holds its merengue festival in the first week of October and Sosúa has one the last week of September. Salsa is also very popular in dance halls and discos (every town, however small, has a discoteca).

People African slaves began to arrive in Santo Domingo from the 1530s. Although the
proportion of slaves in the colony never matched that of Saint-Domingue, blacks
nevertheless formed an important part of the colonial population. As the indigenous
Taíno inhabitants were exterminated within half a century of European colonization,
African slaves and their descendants became the largest non-European group. From the
mixing of Africans and Europeans emerged the mulatto population to which the majority
of Dominicans nowadays belong. Successive governments tried to attract non-African
settlers, especially after Independence, when fears of Haitian territorial ambitions were at
their highest and the 'whitening' of the population was deemed desirable. Some
Canarian and Italian migrants took up the offer of government-assisted
relocation schemes, while an important community from the Middle East,
mostly Syrians but known generically as *turcos*, arrived to establish
businesses. Another group of immigrants, known as *cocolos*, left the
English-speaking Caribbean islands of Tortola, Anguilla and St Kitts to work
in the Republic's sugar plantations. Their descendants still live around San Pedro de
Macorís. Under Trujillo, there was even an attempt to settle Japanese farmers near the
border with Haiti, presumably as a deterrent to would-be smugglers and rustlers. This
racial policy is no longer on the agenda, but it shows how the country's leaders have
traditionally viewed the nation as white, Hispanic and Christian.

About one million legal and illegal Dominican immigrants live in the USA, mostly in New York.

Conventional demographic surveys suggest that about 15% of Dominicans are
white, 15% black and 65% mixed-race or mulatto (the rest being of Middle Eastern or
other origins). The island's indigenous Taíno population was effectively extinct only
50 years after the arrival of the first European colonists. However, recent research into
DNA in the Dominican Republic and Puerto Rico has shown that claims of Taíno
ancestry are not fanciful and that much of the population does indeed carry
Amerindian genes passed down by enslaved Taína women.

Afro-Caribbean religious beliefs have significant numbers of followers in the
Dominican Republic. Mixing reconstructed Taíno rituals, Catholic saints and African
divinities, believers worship archetypal lúas or gods, such as Anaísa, the goddess of love
(based loosely on Santa Ana) or the Barón del Cementario (equivalent to the Christian
San Elías), the guardian of the graveyard. Ceremonies involve music, dancing, trances
and spirit possession, and often take place at what are thought to be holy Taíno sites or
during rural village fiestas. Other well-known venues for *vodú dominicana* are the mostly
black, inner-city barrios of Villa Mella and the western mountain town of San Juan de la
Maguana. A connected phenomenon is the widespread Dominican interest in *brujería* or
witchcraft. *Brujos* are thought to have supernatural powers, both benevolent and
malevolent, and are consulted by a wide cross-section of people in search of cures for
broken hearts, financial problems and the difficulties caused by *mal de ojo* (the evil eye).
Market place stalls and so-called *botánicas* (shops selling religious paraphernalia of all
sorts) testify to the country's fascination with spiritual and supernatural forces.

Flora and fauna

The Dominican Republic offers luxuriant vegetation and exotic wildlife, combining a
variety of habitats within a limited area. It is possible to move between the coastal reefs
and beaches through thorn scrub and plantation into rainforest within a matter of miles.

Varied plant life is found within several tropical zones, from the arid tropical forest
found in the west, where scrub and cactus predominate, to the subtropical forest on the
slopes of the mountains and in the valleys and the mountain forests in the highlands
where pine trees predominate. There is no primary rainforest left, but there are large areas
of secondary forest which have suffered from only a limited amount of selective felling.
There are many palm trees, including the royal palm (*Roystonea regia*) and the coconut
palm (*Cocos nucifera*), as well as other tropical species such as Hispaniolan mahogany
(*Swietenia mahogoni*), West Indian cedar (*Cedrela odorata*) and American muskwood
(*Guarea guidonia*). The most common pine tree is the Creole pine (*Pinus occidentalis*).

The national plant is the *caoba* (mahogany). Along parts of the coast there are red (*Rhizophora mangle*), white (*Laguncularia racemosa*) and button (*Conocarpus erectus*) mangroves which provide a habitat for migrating birds and the manatee as well as fish, shrimp, mosquitoes and other insects. You can see large flocks of sea birds including the frigate bird and the tropic bird with its streamer-like tail feathers.

There is some confusion over which is the national bird. Some have it as the *sigua palmera* or palm chat (*Dulus dominicus*), an olive brown bird in the thrush family with bold streaks of white and brown on its underparts. It usually makes its nest high up in a palm tree in a communal structure with passages to the eggs in an inner chamber. Others name the *cotica* or Hispaniolan parrot (*Amazona ventralis*), which is green, very talkative and a popular pet although it is protected. Among other birds that can be seen are the *periquito* or Hispaniolan parakeet (*Aratinga chloroptera*), which is also green but with some red feathers, the *guaraguao* or red-tailed hawk (*Buteo jamaicensis*), and todies, known locally as *barrancolí*, which behave rather like fly catchers but nest in burrows. There are several hummingbirds (*zumbador*) throughout the country, including the Hispaniolan emerald (*Chlorostilbon swainsonii*), the Antillian mango (*Anthracothorax dominicus*) and the tiny Vervain hummingbird (*Mellisuga minima*). The Hispaniolan trogon (*Temnotrogon roseigaster*) is worth looking out for, with its green upper parts, grey breast, red underbelly and long tail streaked with white. It is known locally as a *papagayo*, or *cotorrita de sierra*, and although it is found chiefly in the mountains, it is also seen in mangroves. The Hispaniolan woodpecker, the *carpintero* (*Melanerpes striatus*) is found only on Hispaniola.

Indigenous mammals are few. There are two, rare and endangered species, however, which you are unlikely to see in the wild. They are both nocturnal. The *jutía*, or hutia (*Plagiodontia aedium*), is a small rodent which lives in caves and tree trunks. The *solenodonte*, or solenodon (*Solenodon pardoxus*), is an insectivore with a long nose, round ears and long tail, with the appearance of a large rat, which grows to about 30 cm and can weigh 1 kg. Similarly in peril is the *manatí*, sea cow or manatee (*Trichechus manatus*), which lives in mangroves and seagrass beds. The Taíno used to eat the manatee, which are slow moving and therefore easy prey, as did the pirates who hid in the waterways where they live. There are also lots of bats, many of which live in the plentiful caves found around the island.

There are two species of iguana found in the Dominican Republic, the rhinoceros iguana (*Cyclura cornuta*) and the Ricord iguana (*Cyclura ricordi*), both found in the hot, dry area in and around Lake Enriquillo where the terrain is rocky and cactus, scrub and thorn bushes such as acacia grow. They are best seen at the hottest time of the day as they disappear when it gets cool. In this area you can also find the American crocodile (*Crocodylus acutus*), one of the largest wild crocodile populations in the world.

National parks The government has adopted six generic categories for environmental protection: areas for scientific research, national parks, natural monuments, sanctuaries, protected areas and wildernesses. The total number of protected areas (including panoramic routes, recreational areas and ecological corridors) is about 70. All are under the control of the Dirección Nacional de Parques (DNP). Armando Bermúdez and José del Carmen Ramírez National Parks, both containing pine forests and mountains in the Cordillera Central, are the only remaining areas of extensive forest in the Republic; since the arrival of Columbus, two-thirds of the virgin forest has been destroyed. The Reservas Científicas include lakes, patches of forest and the Banco de la Plata, to which humpback whales migrate yearly from the Arctic for the birth of their young. It lies some 140 km north of Puerto Plata but there is a proposal to include it in a Biosphere Reserve which would stretch as far as Los Haitises. The reserve protects fish, coral and several species of sea turtles as well as the whales. It is a rather dangerous area for shipping, with depths changing from 20 m to 1800 m giving the wildlife added protection.

Haiti

Essentials

Before you travel

Documents All visitors need **passports** valid for at least six months after your departure date from Haiti. **Visas** are not needed for anyone staying under 90 days, but everyone must have an onward ticket. All visitors, except cruise ship passengers, must complete an embarkation/disembarkation card on the plane; this is valid for 90 days, and may be extended. Don't lose the yellow card (exit visa) because you will need it when you leave. Keep your passport with you as identification for police controls when travelling in the interior. Baggage inspection and drug-enforcement laws are strict. There is no restriction on foreign currency and no export limitations.

Finding out more
Embassy of Haiti, 2311 Massachusetts Av NW, Washington DC 20008, USA, T202-3324090, embassy@haiti.org. Mon-Fri 0900-1400.

Useful websites:
www.haiti-info.org,
www.haititourisme.com,
www.haitiglobalvillage.com,
www.port-haiti.com, www.uhhp.com.

Money

Currency The unit is the gourde (Créole: *goud*), divided into 100 centimes (Créole: Sentim). Coins in circulation are for 5, 10, 20 and 50 centimes, and 1, 2 and 5 gourdes, notes for 10, 25, 50, 100, 250 and 500 gourdes. Businesses often do not provide change for larger notes, but you can break them down at banks, expensive hotels and larger grocery stores.

> ♣ *Try to break down large notes whenever possible.*

Exchange The gourde was tied at 5 to the US dollar during the US occupation. In the 1980s it began to trade at a slightly lower value on a parallel market, but the official rate was kept until 1991, when the Aristide government severed the tie and let the gourde float. From 7.5 to the dollar at the time of the September 1991 coup, it was down to 38 to the dollar in March 2005 but improved to 36 by March 2007. So far, so good; now it gets complicated. Haitians routinely refer to their own money as dollars, based on the old 5 to 1 rate. Thus, 5 gourdes is called a dollar, 10 gourdes is 2 dollars, 25 gourdes is 5 dollars, etc. Prices in shops are usually in Haitian dollars, therefore multiply by 5 to get the price in gourdes. Visitors must always clarify whether the price is in Haitian or American dollars, or gourdes.

The best exchange rate is obtained from money changers, whether those on the street or those working out of offices. It is perfectly legal but not recommended, for safety reasons. The rate in banks is not far behind and it is therefore better to trade with one of the many banks. It is foolish to come to Haiti with any currency other than US dollars. Currencies such as sterling can be changed, but only at a massive loss. Traveller's cheques are not changed in most banks.

Credit cards Visa, MasterCard and American Express are widely accepted. Beware, card users will not get a good rate and are often charged a premium.

Getting there

Air From Europe There are no direct flights, but **Air France** flies from Paris via Guadeloupe and Martinique.

From North America **American Airlines** flies from New York and Fort Lauderdale

❧ Safety

The British FCO is advising against all but essential travel to Haiti because of the increasing threat to personal security. Incidences of violence and kidnappings for ransom, specifically targeting foreigners, are prevalent, mainly in Port-au-Prince. Half of the women kidnapped have been raped. There have also been random shootings of civilians, with robbery usually the motive. British travellers are reminded that there is no British Embassy in Haiti and the British Consulate office in Port-au-Prince has been closed since 2005 because of the security risks. The nearest UK diplomatic representation is in Santo Domingo. Crime is widespread and often violent. You should take precautions against pickpockets. Carry handbags securely and do not leave belongings in sight in a parked car. Travel with car doors locked and windows shut. Armed hold-ups of vehicles take place in busy parts of Port-au-Prince. During any political unrest it is advisable to limit your movements in the daytime and never go out at night. Streets are usually deserted by 2300. The FCO recommends that you use a reliable guide when travelling in the country and advises against using public transport, suggesting instead a hired car from a reputable agency with a local driver, or internal flights. For up-to-date Foreign Office advice, check www.fco.gov.uk.

daily and Miami three times a day. **Air Canada** flies from Montréal weekly.

From Central America Copa flies from Panama City twice a week with connections from neighbouring capitals.

From the Caribbean Air France from Fort-de-France and Pointe-à-Pitre, **Caribair** has two flights daily to Port-au-Prince from Santo Domingo, **Vol Air** flies to Cap-Haïtien from Santo Domingo and Santiago in the Dominican Republic, **Sky King** from Turks and Caicos to Cap-Haïtien and Port-au-Prince twice weekly.

Sea Cruise ships stopped calling at Port-au-Prince years ago, partly because of passenger reaction to begging. One cruise line, Royal Caribbean, leases a peninsula near Cap-Haïtien for one-day stopovers.

Road Travel to the Dominican Republic *Taptaps* (converted pick-ups) and trucks ply the road to the border of the Dominican Republic at Malpasse/Jimaní, one hour from Port-au-Prince. The Ouanaminthe/Dajabón crossing in the north is a three-hour drive on a largely rough dirt road from Cap-Haïtien. On leaving Haiti by bus or car you have to pay US$30 per person. It is US$25 to re-enter Haiti from the Dominican Republic. If you are travelling by bus you pay at the bus terminal. These rates are variable and change frequently. It is advisable to put aside US$60 to cover all taxes both ways. Mopeds ferry you between the Haitian and Dominican border posts for US$1. There are lots of money changers on both sides. The easiest way to get to Santo Domingo is with **Capital Coach Line**, a Haitian company, or **Terra Bus** or **Caribe Tours**, both Dominican companies. They all charge US$40 one way, US$75 return, child reductions. They deal with all immigration and other formalities so all you have to do is get off the bus to take care of Dominican customs. Excellent service, efficient, comfortable a/c buses, snacks and drinks provided, recommended. **Capital Coach Line** ① T5125989, is in Tabarre. **Terra Bus,** is handled by **Chatelain Tours** ① T2232400, in Port-au-Prince. Departs daily 0830, arrives Santo Domingo 1530. Both leave from Tabarre, between Pétion-Ville and the airport, US$20 by

❧ See page 294 and check with the Dominican Consulate to see if you need a visa. There is a one-hour time difference between Haiti and the Dominican Republic.

Touching down

Business hours **Banks**: Mon-Fri 0900-1300; **Government offices**: Mon-Fri 0700-1200, 1300-1600 (Oct-Apr 0800-1200, 1300-1800); **Shops and offices**: May-Sep 0700-1600, Oct-Apr 0800-1700.

Clothing As in most other countries in the Caribbean, beachwear should not be worn away from the beach and poolside.

Departure tax Visitors leaving by air must pay a US$35 departure tax in US currency. Do not buy international flight tickets in Haiti, especially not at the airport. Sales tax is very high and the application of exchange rates may be arbitrary.

Emergency numbers Observe the US Embassy travel warning: Haitian authorities are unlikely to respond to requests for assistance; you are advised to call your consulate in an emergency.

Country code +509.

Official time Eastern standard time, 5 hours behind GMT.

Tipping Budget travellers, particularly outside Port-au-Prince, are a rarity. Expect to be the subject of much friendly curiosity, and keep a pocketful of small change to conform with the local custom of tipping on every conceivable occasion. Even cigarettes and sweets are accepted. Hotels generally add 10% service charge. Baggage porters at hotels usually get US$0.50 per bag. Do not fail to reward good service since hotel and restaurant staff rely on tips to boost their meagre salaries. Nobody tips taxi, *publique*, *camionette* or *taptap* drivers, unless exceptional service has been given.

Voltage 110 volt, 60 cycle AC. Electricity supply is unpredictable as there are insufficient funds to maintain the service. Port-au-Prince neighbourhoods are in blackout most of the time, and many other towns never get electricity. Only the best hotels have powerful generators to make up the deficiency.

Weights and measures Metric.

taxi from town centre. **Capital** shows at least three movies per trip. **Caribe Tours** ① T2579379, is in Pétion-Ville, and departs from the corner of rue Clerveaux and Gabart, daily at 0730, arriving 1530 local time, leaves Santo Domingo at 1100 for the return journey, arriving 1630 or 1700. Haitian travel agencies sometimes offer three- or four-day inclusive bus tours into the Dominican Republic. There are regular buses from the Dominican frontier town of Jimaní to Santo Domingo (six hours) and from Dajabón via Montecristi and Santiago de los Caballeros. Rental cars are not allowed to cross the border, but you could safely leave one at the border for a few hours to visit Jimaní. Cheaper **Dominican buses** ① T4050864, leave Port-au-Prince from the **Hotel Palace**, rue Capois, every morning for their return trip to Santo Domingo via Malpasse. They depart 0800 and 1000, arriving Santo Domingo 1700 and 1900, with more than an hour at the border. US$25 round-trip, a/c, TV, radio, no films or snacks. Buses also leave from rue du Centre, near rue des Miracles, three or four times per day, mostly 25-seater a/c Mitsubishis, US$20.

Touching down

Airport information On arrival at Port-au-Prince and after emerging through Customs, you will be crushed by a throng of porters and taxi drivers eager to take your bags. It is best to have a plan of action before leaving Customs, preferably arrange to be met by a friend or contact. The main departure area has two snack bars, a handicraft shop, a call centre, a flight information desk, and a handicraft shop. Duty-free goods and more crafts are on sale in the area reserved for departing passengers.

Air Canada, T2501115/6/7. **Air France**, T2221700/1086, 11 rue Capois, corner rue Ducoste, near Le Plaza. **American Airlines**, T2460100, 2566803, at Public's Plaza on Delmas 32 and at Chouchoun Plaza in Petion-Ville. **Copa**, 35 Ave Marie Jeanne, T2232326/7.

Tourist information **The Tourism Secretariat** ① *upstairs at 8 rue Légitime, T2232143, F2210161, half a block from the Musée d'Art Haïtien*, has poor information and no maps or brochures. Extra information may be found at the Haitian **Association for the Tourism and Hotel Industry** at Hotel Villa Créole, Pétion-Ville, at the Hotel Montana, or from travel agencies. **ISPAN (Institute for the Protection of the Nation's Heritage)**, ①*corner of Avenida Martin Luther King and Cheriez, Pont Morin, T2453118*, has information on forts and plantation houses. Also at rue 15-B, Cap-Haïtien, T2624948.

Guides Young men and boys offer their services as guides. In some places it's worth taking them up on it – it is easier to get about, you can visit places off the beaten tourist track and avoid some of the frustrations of the public transport system – though generally you can get by without one. Most guides speak English or pidgin English. **Chauffeurs-guides** are cab drivers who cater to foreign visitors. Usually found outside the biggest hotels such as the **Le Plaza**, or at the airport, their cars can be used like regular taxis or hired by the hour, half-day, day or for a tour. The drivers usually speak French, plus a little English. They can be booked for US$80-100 day through the **Association des Chauffeurs-Guides** ①*18 Blvd Harry Truman, T2220330*. You usually have the option of having a driver when hiring a car. Secom's rates are US$15 a day/US$105 a week in Port-au-Prince for an 8-hr day, rising to US$25 a day if you go into the provinces, with an additional US$35 a night for his accommodation and US$15 a day for his meals. Recommended private guides/drivers are **Alfonse Altena** ① *T4014549*, a good-natured driver, guide and translator who works with foreign journalists and speaks French and English; **Makenson Rémy** ① *106 rue de la Réunion, T2228432*, a fun and energetic Radio Megastar reporter who is happy to take newcomers anywhere and bargain aggressively on their behalf. Speaks French and some English. Price negotiable depending on the job and whether you have your own transport. Créole Guides cost about US$40-100 per day, depending where you go, and you should also buy them food and drink. Bear in mind that most guides are 'on commission' with local shops and stall-keepers. If you ask them to bargain for you, you will not necessarily be getting a good price. Nor will they necessarily go where you want to go. If you don't want a guide, a firm but polite *Non, merci* gets the message across. It is best to ignore altogether hustlers outside guesthouses, etc, as any contact only makes them persist.

Getting around

Air Caribintair ① *T2502032*, has regular scheduled services linking Port-au-Prince with Jérémie, Les Cayes, Cap-Haïtien and Santo Domingo. **Tropical Airways d'Haiti** ① *T2563627*, has flights from Port-au-Prince to Cap Haïtien and Port-de-Paix. There are less regular domestic services with **Mission Aviation Fellowship** ① *T5108086*.

Book and pay through travel agents. Flights leave from **Aviation Générale**, a small domestic airport 1 km east of the international airport. **Caribintair** also operates as a charter/air taxi company. **Jean Marc Nouaisser** ① *T5529958*, flies journalists and others anywhere in Haiti.

Bus Fairly conventional-looking buses (Créole: *bis*) or colourfully converted trucks and pick-ups (*taptap*) provide inter-city transport. There are no fixed departure times. Buses leave the 'stations' when they are packed. Roads are bad and journeys are long and uncomfortable. In trucks, it is worth paying more to sit with the driver. Note Foreign travel advisories currently warn against taking public transport because of security concerns.

Car Driving in Haiti is a hazardous free-for-all which some find exhilarating. The streets are narrow, with many sharp bends, and full of pedestrians, potholes, animals and police roadblocks in the towns, with all the same challenges plus speed bumps out of town. In heavy rains, city streets turn to rivers, making driving particularly hazardous for small cars. Haitians use their horns constantly to warn pedestrians of their approach. Vehicles swerve unexpectedly to avoid potholes. Cars often don't stop in an accident, so, to avoid paying the high insurance excess, keep a pen and paper handy to take down a number if necessary. Fuel (leaded, unleaded or diesel) is usually available in the big provincial towns, but power cuts may prevent stations from pumping. For driving to Les Cayes and Jacmel, an ordinary car is fine, but for Jérémie, Cap-Haïtien, Port-de-Paix or Hinche, a 4WD is necessary. Foreigners may use an international driving licence for three months, then a local permit is required. However, it is safer to hire a local driver from a reputable company. For car hire, see page 398.

Hitchhiking Many young Haitian men stick out a thumb asking for a *roue libre*, or *wou lib* in Créole, especially from foreigners. **Note** This is dangerous and not advisable.

Sleeping

Hotels There are a few good hotels in Pétion-Ville, up the hillside from Port-au-Prince, mostly designed for businessmen, and a couple of international-standard beach hotels along the Côte des Arcadins, northwest of the capital. Elsewhere, however, lodgings can be idiosyncratic, poor value, and variable in the quality of furnishings and service. In Port-au-Prince only the most expensive hotels and guesthouses have a/c plus sufficiently powerful in-house generators able to cope with the long electricity blackouts in the city. Some have a generator to give partial power to the bar but not to guest rooms. Water is also rationed, and many of the cheaper, central hotels lack both water and electricity much of the time. Check rooms in advance in the cheaper hotels, where service may be deficient. Tax, service charge and energy surcharge are usually added to hotel bills. These extras have been included in the prices given here, which are very approximate because of exchange rate vagaries. While hotels are accommodating UN and NGO personnel, prices are usually quoted in US dollars and in consequence are high. Where possible, it is cheaper to pay in gourdes. Paying by credit card is more expensive. The **Association Hotelière et Touristique d'Haïti** is at **Hotel Villa Créole**, Pétion-Ville.

Camping This is an adventure in Haiti and not currently recommended for security reasons. The dramatic scenery is very enticing but access to much of it is over rough terrain and there are no facilities. Campers have to take everything, and create or find their own shelter. Peasant homes dot the countryside and it is almost impossible to find a spot where you will be spared curious and suspicious onlookers. It is best to set up camp or lodging before dark. To prevent misunderstanding, it is important to explain to the locals your intentions, or, better still, talk to the local elder and ask assistance or protection, and offer to pay a small amount for use of the land.

Eating

Food Most restaurants offer Créole or French cuisine, or a mixture of both. Haiti's Créole cuisine is similar to that of the Spanish Caribbean, with many dishes accompanied by fried plantains and rice and beans. Specialities include *griot* (deep-fried pieces of pork), *lambi* (conch, considered an aphrodisiac), *tassot* (jerked beef) and rice with *djon-djon* (tiny, dark mushrooms). As elsewhere in the Caribbean, lobster is widely available. Pétion-Ville has many good French restaurants. Some are French-managed or have French chefs. Haiti's wide range of micro-climates produces a large assortment of fruits and vegetables. It is popular to buy these in the regions where they

❧ Bakeries sell French croissants, baguettes, cakes and pastries, together with Créole bread and meat pasties.

Haiti Essentials

grow and are freshest (prices can be bargained). The French influence is obvious in the handful of small pastry shops around Petion-Ville. American influence is felt in the supermarkets, where you can find almost everything. Vegetarians will find Haiti extremely difficult. Haitians cook nearly everything in pig fat, so even beans are to be avoided. One traveller survived on a diet of cornflakes, boiled eggs and fruit. Only the expensive restaurants and hotels will have a vegetarian option on the menu.

Drink Haiti's *Barbancourt* rum is excellent. The five-star is particularly recommended and a bottle sells for only US$7; if you buy it at the airport on departure you can get a case of five bottles for about US$30. The distillery is in Damians and can be visited. Rum punch is popular but often over-sweet. The local beer, *Prestige*, may be too sweet for some palates but is an acceptable alternative to sugary, fizzy drinks. The Dominican beer *Presidente* is the best of the foreign beers sold in Haiti, which all cost around US$2.50-3.00 depending on the brand. Soft drinks include *Séjourne* and *Couronne*.

❖ Haitian coffee is drunk strong and sweet; Rebo is the best brand.

Entertainment

Until the mid-1980s, Haiti was a very good place for nightspots. With the drop in tourism and Haitians hesitating to be out late in uneasy times, many places have had to close or curtail their level of entertainment. The few that survive offer a good night out; evening entertainment starts at about 2030-2100. Nightclubbing starts around 2330.

Shopping

The iron markets normally sell only food items, charcoal, knick knacks, etc, and sometimes paintings. The iron market in Port-au-Prince, which sells a wide variety of arts and crafts, would be a fascinating place to visit but for the hustlers who will latch on to you and make the experience hell. It is also extremely narrow and dirty; it is important to be careful, go with a group and do not carry valuables. Try out your bargaining skills at the iron markets in Jacmel and Cap-Haïtien. Haitians may tell you that many of the items for sale in the few tourist shops can be bought far cheaper in markets. That may be true for them, but market vendors jack up prices for the foreigner, who will have to haggle skilfully to bring them down. See page 422 for best buys, and under towns for individual establishments.

❖ It's normal to ask for a discount in shops, except in food shops.

Festivals and events

The standard of the **Port-au-Prince Carnival** has fallen since the Duvaliers left (see page 416). Nowadays few people wear costumes and the floats are poorly decorated. There is a cacophony of music blaring out from both stands and passing floats. Excitement is provided by the walking bands (*bandes-à-pied*), cousins of the Rara bands that appear after carnival (see below). Circulating on foot, drawing a large, dancing, chanting crowd in their wake, they specialize in salacious lyrics and political satire. When crowds move in different directions there is boisterous pushing. The safest place to watch is from one of the stands near **Le Plaza**. Safer still and more peaceful are the Carnival celebrations in **Pétion-Ville**. **Carnival** climaxes on the three days before Ash Wednesday, but the government lays on free open-air concerts in different parts of the city during the three or four weekends of pre-carnival. Many people prefer the Carnival a week earlier at **Jacmel**, two to three hours from the capital, where the tradition of elaborate, imaginative masked costumes still thrives. If you plan to stay in Jacmel you must book accommodation weeks, if not months, in advance, as it gets packed.

Port-au-Prince Carnival is immediately followed by **Rara**, dubbed the 'peasant carnival.' Every weekend during Lent, including Easter weekend, colourfully attired Rara bands emerge from Vodou societies and roam the countryside. They seek donations,

so be ready with a few small notes. Beating drums, blowing homemade wind
instruments, dancing and singing, some bands may have a thousand or more
members. A good place to see it is the town of Léogâne on Easter
Sunday. Beware, the drinking is heavy and fights are common.

The **Gede** (pronounced gay-day) are *loas* (spirits) who possess
Vodouists on 1-2 November (**All Saints'** and **Day of the Dead**). Seen
in cemeteries or roaming the streets, they dress to look like corpses
or undertakers. The Lords of Death and the Cemetery mock human
vanity and pretension, and remind people that sex is the source of
life by dancing in a lewd fashion with strangers, causing much
hilarity. For pilgrimages, see under **Saut d'Eau**, **Plaine du Nord** and **Limonade**.

> ‡ *Football is the national sport and in 2007 the country erupted with joy when Haiti defeated Trinidad and Tobago's Soca Warriors 2-1 in the final of the Digicel Caribbean Cup.*

Health

Prophylaxis against **malaria** is essential and **dengue fever** has also been reported, so
avoid being bitten by mosquitoes. Tap water is not to be trusted (drink only bottled,
filtered or treated water) and take care when choosing food. The local herb tea can
help stomach troubles; diarrhoea is often known as 'Haitian Happiness'! Hepatitis is
common in some areas. Good professional advice is available for the more common
ailments. Ask at the hotel desk for referrals to a doctor suited to your requirements.
Office hours are usually 0730-1200, 1500-1800. A consultation costs about
US$20-50. Hospital care and comfort varies. See page 398 for hospital listings in
Port-au-Prince. Pharmacies can fill out prescriptions and many prescription drugs
may be bought over the counter.

At around 6%, Haiti has the highest HIV infection rate in the Americas.
Heterosexual transmission is the most common transmission vehicle, followed by
mother-to-child transmission. There are no laws in Haiti to suppress prostitution.
Activity seems to be evident only at night with the commonly known areas being
along the main roads in Carrefour and street corners in Pétion-Ville. After hours the
prostitutes move into the dive-type joints, targeting foreigners.

Keeping in touch

Telephone, internet and post Country code: 509. Always bad, calls often do not go
through on landlines or the two cell phone companies. The Haitian international
operator (dial 09) is hard to raise. However, **Teleco** offices in major cities are central
and easy to use and the operators are helpful. Expect queues. Cell phones can be
rented at the airport and at **Hotel Villa Créole**. Higher end hotels allow direct calls
overseas from the rooms, but all overseas connections can be problematic. Email
service is limited. Higher end hotels have satellite internet, but usage can cost up to
US$6 per hour. There are a handful of cybercafés around Port-au-Prince and
Pétion-Ville, but many suffer from electricity problems. Cheap and reliable is
Netaccess, above Ice Cream on rue Darguin, US$2 for 65 minutes. The postal service
is slow but much improved in recent years.

Media **Newspapers** *Le Nouvelliste* and *Le Matin* are the two daily French-language
newspapers. Three weekly newspapers are published in French.

Radio Radio stations use a mix of French and Créole. **Metropole** and **Tropic** are
best for news. **Radio France Inter** is re-broadcast locally on FM 89.3. The **Voice of
America** is now aired only in Créole.

Television A commercial TV station, **Télé-Haiti**, re-transmits American, French,
Canadian and Latin American stations (including CNN, CBS, NBC, ABC, HBO, etc) to
cable subscribers.

Port-au-Prince

→ *Phone code: 509. Colour map 2, B2. Population: 846,247. Metropolitan area: 2,500,000.*

What Port-au-Prince lacks in architectural grace, it makes up for with a stunning setting. Steep mountains tower over the city to the south, La Gonâve island lies in a horseshoe bay to the west, and another wall of mountains beyond a rift valley plain rises to the north. The city has overflowed its original waterfront location, swollen by a rural exodus, and has climbed into the mountains behind. Most of the city is very poor, but the worst bidonvilles (shantytowns) are in a marshy waterfront area north of the centre. Some of the capital's poorest neighbourhoods have been paralysed by violence since President Jean-Bertrand Aristide was driven from power early 2004. There are crowds of people everywhere, spilling off the sidewalks into the streets, moving to a cacophony of horns and engines. ▸▸ *For Sleeping, Eating and other listings, see pages 393-399.*

> ‼ *Watch out for pickpockets in markets, bus terminal areas and inside buses.*

Ins and outs

Getting there The **airport** ⓘ *T2501120/3/4/5*, is on the northern edge of Delmas, 13 km outside Port-au-Prince. In spite of recent improvements to the arrival terminal that have made entry less chaotic, it is not unusual to wait more than an hour to get your bags. Once through the squash inside you emerge into a squash outside, of taxi drivers and people awaiting friends. A knowledge of French is useful. Porters expect about US$0.50 per bag. A private taxi into town from in front of the airport is US$20-25 depending on how hard you bargain, or walk a few minutes to the main road and flag down a shared taxi for US$0.40 to US$1.20, depending on how far you are going, or, if you know what you are doing, take a seat in a *taptap* (open-backed truck), for US$0.15, extra charged for large bag. You will need to change *taptaps* once or twice to get to most major hotels and this method is not recommended for security reasons. To get to the airport cheaply take a shared taxi from the turning off avenue St-Martin (formerly avenue François Duvalier) for 3-4 km to rue Toussaint Louverture where *taptaps* marked 'Airport' gather; US$0.15 from here, 10 km. For those coming by bus from the Dominican Republic, see page 383.

> ‼ *The so-called 'supervisors' at the airport are in fact taxi drivers touting for business.*

Getting around Shared taxis (called **publiques** or simply **taxis**) are flagged down. They charge a basic fare (Créole: *kous*) of US$0.40 that may double or treble (*de kous, twa kous*) depending on how far you go. A red ribbon tied to the inside rear-view mirror identifies the taxis, which are almost always old, beaten-up cars. The driver might turn you down if you're going somewhere inconvenient. Otherwise he will take you even if the car is full and you have to sit on someone's lap. French is needed. They stop work at about 1930. **Camionettes** (minibuses) and *taptaps* (open-backed pick-ups usually with a brightly painted wooden superstructure) have fixed routes and fares (about US$0.15). They rarely circulate after 2030. They are difficult to manage with luggage. *Camionettes* to Pétion-Ville stop along Av John Brown, US$0.15. ▸▸ *For further details see Transport, page 398.*

> ‼ *Several major thoroughfares have two names, the official one used for maps and the telephone book, and the one commonly used in speech. Often taxi drivers only know the second.*

Safety Shantytown dwellers don't welcome sightseers and people with cameras. The area between the Champs de Mars and the waterfront is deserted after dark and should be avoided. It is safe to go to most places by car or taxi at night, but don't go about on foot. Pétion-Ville is generally considered safer than Port-au-Prince, but you should avoid walking on empty or unlit streets after dark. Remember that frequent power cuts can plunge entire neighbourhoods into darkness. Drivers must always carry a licence as police blocks are common at night. Be careful of traffic when walking around town. Street vendors crowd the pavements, which forces pedestrians into the path of vehicles and many people have been knocked down and injured.

Sights

The commercial quarter starts near the port and stretches inland about 10 blocks. It lacks charm or interest, except the area beside the port that was remodelled for the city's 1949 bicentennial. Known as the **Bicentenaire** (more formally, Cité de l'Exposition), it contains the post office, foreign ministry, parliament, American Embassy and French Institute. It is now very run down. The central reference point is the large, irregularly shaped park called the **Champs de Mars**, which begins to the east of the commercial quarter. The northwest corner is dominated by the white, triple-domed presidential palace. It was built in 1918 on the site of a predecessor that was blown up in 1912 with its president inside. In the 1991 coup, President Aristide made a stand inside the present building. Just to the northeast is the colonnaded, white and gold army high-command building, where soldiers nearly lynched Aristide after dragging him out of the palace. (He was saved by the French Ambassador, the American Ambassador or General Cedras, depending on whose story you believe.) Immediately behind the palace, to the south, is a large, mustard-yellow army garrison that was once the fief of the ill-famed Colonel Jean-Claude Paul, indicted in Miami in 1987 for drug smuggling and poisoned the following year.

Immediately to the east of the palace, on Place des Héros de l'Indépendance, the subterranean **Musée du Panthéon National (MUPANAH)** ① *T2228337, Tue-Thu, Sat 1000-1600, Fri 1000-1800, Sun 1200-1800, closed Mon, US$1.30 adults, US$0.65*

Haiti Port-au-Prince

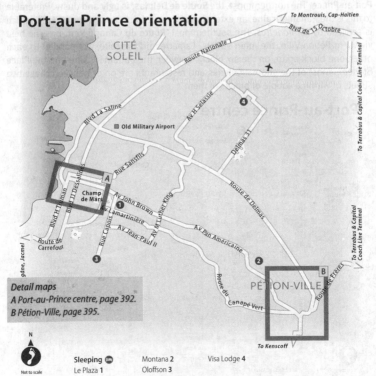

Port-au-Prince orientation

To Montrouis, Cap-Haïtien

Blvd de 15 Octobre

CITÉ SOLEIL

Route Nationale 1

To Terrabus & Capital Coach Line Terminal

Blvd La Saline

Av H. Selassie

Old Military Airport

Rue Sanfils

Delmas 31

④

Blvd H Truman

Blvd J Dessalines

Champ de Mars

A

Av John Brown

Route de Delmas

V Lamartinière

Rue Capois

Av M Luther King

A V Jean-Paul II

A V Pan Américaine

①

To Terrabus & Capital Coach Line Terminal

Route de Carrefour

③

②

Route de Frères

B

PÉTION-VILLE

gdne, Jacmel

Route du Canapé Vert

To Terrabus & Capital Coach Line Terminal

Detail maps
A Port-au-Prince centre, page 392.
B Pétion-Ville, page 395.

N

Not to scale

To Kenscoff

Sleeping 🛏
Le Plaza **1**

Montana **2**
Oloffson **3**

Visa Lodge **4**

students 16-20, US$25 children 6-15, houses historical relics, including the rusted anchor of Columbus' flagship, the *Santa María*. It is not a very big museum, but worth the stop to learn a little about Haitian history and see some art displayed. Don't miss an 1818 oil painting of King Henri Christophe by Welshman Richard Evans, director of Christophe's Fine Arts Academy at Sans Souci. Two blocks north and two west, at the corner of Avenue Mgr Guilloux and the busy rue Pavée, the **Sainte Trinité Episcopal Cathedral** ① *T2230814*, has astounding biblical murals created in 1949 by the greatest naive artists, including Philomé Obin, Castera Bazile and Riguaud Benoit. The adjoining complex has a gift shop and a school whose students give excellent choral and classical music concerts.

At the intersection of rues Capois and Légitime, the **Musée d'Art Haïtien** ① *T2222510, Mon-Fri 1000-1600, Sat 1000-1430, US$0.40*, has Haiti's finest naive art collection, plus a craft shop and a small café in its garden. The collection is not large and there is no recent art. The **Maison Défly** ① *7 Av John Paul II, Mon-Sat 0900-1300*, built by an army commander in 1896, is in the Victorian 'gingerbread' style, characterized by steep roofs and gables, round turrets, high ceilings, balconies and rich fretwork embellishment. Not a distinguished example, it contains a museum with period furniture. The rue Capois has several hotels, restaurants and shops. At the southern end, 1 km from the Champs de Mars, is the **Hôtel Oloffson**, a much more imposing example of a gingerbread. East of rue Capois are leafy neighbourhoods climbing into the foothills where prosperous 19th-century gingerbread house residences abound.

Pétion-Ville

Pétion-Ville was once the capital's hill resort, lying just 15 minutes from Port-au-Prince, but 450 m above sea level and therefore cooler. Now it is considered a middle-class suburb, with restaurants and boutiques. Three roads lead up from Port-au-Prince. The northernmost, the **Route de Delmas**, is ugly and dusty. Preferable to this is the **Panaméricaine**, an extension of Avenue John Brown (Créole: Lali), which is serviced by *camionettes*. The southernmost, **Route du Canapé Vert**, has the best views. In Pétion-Ville, the main streets, Lamarre and Grégoire, are parallel to each other, one block apart, on the six blocks between the Panaméricaine and the Place St-Pierre. Most of the shops, galleries and restaurants are on or between these two streets or within a couple of blocks of them.

Port-au-Prince centre

● Sleeping

Port-au-Prince *p390, maps p391 and p392*

L-B Le Plaza (formerly **Holiday Inn**), 10 rue Capois, central location on Champs de Mars, T2239800. Jungly gardens, pool, tolerable restaurant, though service is extremely slow, own generator, price includes taxes and electricity, children under 18 free if sharing room, all rooms a/c.

AL-A Oloffson, rue Cadet Jérémie at intersection with rue Capois, T2234000, oloffsonram@aol.com. Model for **Hotel Trianon** in Graham Greene's *The Comedians*, and eccentrically managed by Haitian-American musician Richard Morse, this was traditionally Haiti's most charming hotel, but is now shabby and neglected. The smaller rooms were built as a hospital and maternity wing by the US marines. Haunt of writers, journalists and film-makers, the CIA and drug runners, you can meet all sorts at the bar. Thu live music with RAM band, well worth the money. Pool, intermittent a/c, internet, breakfast included.

AL-A Visa Lodge, rue des Nimes, Rte de l'Aéroport, T2501407. Business hotel in industrial zone near airport, pool, good restaurant, own generator.

A La Griffonne, 21 rue Jean Baptiste, Canapé Vert, T2454095/3440. Guesthouse in quiet neighbourhood 5 mins' walk from Av John Brown, own generator, all rooms with private bath and some with a/c, meals included.

A Prince, corner of rue 3 and Av N, Pacot, T2452764. Quiet hillside neighbourhood 15 mins' walk from taxis, Victorian building, own generator, all rooms a/c, clean but a bit musty, Wi-Fi in conference room, pool, restaurant, good breakfast, helpful if slow service, armed security, gate locked at night.

A-B Palace, corner of rue Capois and Champs de Mars. Salsa classes on grand balcony Sat evenings.

A-B Park, 23 rue Capois, near **Le Plaza**, T2224406. Cheaper to pay in gourdes, safe, central, generator.

B May's Villa, 28 Debussy, T2451208. Quiet neighbourhood at top of Av John Paul II, 10 mins' walk from taxis, view, has generator, rooms with bath and fan, breakfast included.

Pétion-Ville *p392, map p395*

Most of the larger hotels with pools will let

non-guests use their facilities for the day for a small charge.

LL-L Montana, rue Cardozo, a turning off the Panaméricaine at the entrance to Pétion-Ville, T2294000, www.htmontana.com. An oasis of luxury, best views over Port-au-Prince, especially from poolside restaurant, phone, a/c, TV, airport transfers, conference facilities, internet, built on hillside with lots of stairs, elevators, non-guests can use the pool for US$3.

LL-L Villa Créole, just beyond **El Rancho** on José de San Martín, T2571570/1, www.villacreole.com. Tennis court, pool, good view, rooms and suites, some connecting, a/c, TV, internet access, superior customer service.

LL-A El Rancho, rue José de San Martín, just off the Panaméricaine, T2572080, www.hotelelrancho.com. Very pleasant, painted white with tiled roofs, a/c rooms and suites, internet access, balconies, beautiful view, 2 pools, fitness centre, tennis, 2 restaurants, bars, casino 1700-0400, nightclub, ballroom dancing classes, sauna, spa, a/c.

AL Le Ritz, corner rue Panaméricaine and rue José San-Martin, T2576520/1, www.hotelkinam .com. Under same ownership as Kinam. Aparthotel, studios, good for business groups, conference facilities.

AL-B Kinam, at the corner of rue Lamarre and rue Moise, facing Place St-Pierre, T2574553/7, www.hotelkinam.com. Mock gingerbread house, 38 rooms, 3 suites, a/c, phone, TV, good restaurant, bar, small pool, handy location.

A Caraïbe, 13 rue Leon Nau, Nerette, T2572524. 12 rooms with large baths, a/c, restaurant, TV lounge, pool, built in 1920s, charming, friendly, helpful, family-run, French, English, Spanish spoken.

B Ife, 30 rue Grégoire, a busy street by the market, T2570737. Some a/c, bed and breakfast.

B Villa Kalewes, 99 rue Grégoire (at the upper, quiet end of the street), T2570817. Bed and breakfast, pool.

C St Joseph's Home for Boys Guest House, Delmas 91, by Caribbean Market Grocery, T/F2574237, US fundraising group www.heartswithhaiti.org. Rates include breakfast and dinner, vegetarian meals on request, laundry, bottled water, money exchange, security. For a fee the boys will escort you or give drum lessons; the home can also provide guides, translators, Créole lessons, airport pick-up. Some of the boys perform in the Resurrection Dance Theatre, self-written dances based on their experiences when they lived on the street. Revenue from guests helps to pay for the boys, aged 8-18, who live and work as a family, running the guesthouse when not at classes. Founder Michael Geilenfeld was a brother with Mother Theresa before starting the home in 1985.

C-D Doux Séjour, 32 rue Magny (quiet street 5 blocks from Place St Pierre), T2571560. Weekly rates, apartments or nice rooms with 2 beds, fan and bathroom, pizza restaurant alongside.

● Eating

Port-au-Prince *p390, maps p391 and p392*
Almost the only decent places to eat out at night in Port-au-Prince are the **Oloffson** or **Le Plaza**, or a row of terrace cafés selling barbecued chicken at the southeast corner of the **Champs de Mars** (starting near Rex theatre). Well-off Port-au-Princiens go up to Pétion-Ville to dine out.

♥♥-♥ Café Terrasse, rear of **Air France** Bldg, 11 rue Capois and rue Ducoste, T2225648/5025. 1130-1600. Excellent lunch, favoured by international aid agency staffers.

♥♥-♥ Les Jardins du Musée, at the Musée d'Art Haïtien. 1130-1600. A small oasis, but a bit pricey, popular with *blancs*, particularly French embassy staff at lunchtime, slow service.

♥♥-♥ Tiffany, Blvd Harry Truman, Bicentenaire 12, north of Télé-Haiti, T2220993. 1130-1600. Haitian, French and American food.

♥ Chez Yvane, 19 blvd Harry Truman, south of Télé-Haiti. 1130-1600. Créole lunch in a/c premises.

♥ La Perle, 80 rue Pavée, between Dessalines and rue des Miracles. 1130-1600. Pleasant, cool, enormous sandwiches, also spaghetti, omelettes.

♥ L'Arc en Ciel, rue Capois. Cheap Créole food, outdoor seating, open at night.

♥ Paradis de Amis, 43 rue Pavée, between Centre and Dessalines. 1130-1600. Club sandwiches, omelettes, ice cream, a/c,

popular with locals, cheap, large portions, spaghetti costs US$2.

♥ Tropical Bar & Grill, 73 Ave Lamartinière, T2458722. Open at night and serving basic Créole cuisine, outdoor seating and occasional live music.

Pétion-Ville *p392, map p395*
♥♥♥-♥♥ Basilic, 12 rue Borno, T5139534. Pricey but very good, grand stone house in jungly setting.

♥♥♥-♥♥ Boukan Gregoire, 89 rue Grégoire, T2578522. Mon-Sat 1800-2330. Belgian-owned, nice atmosphere, reasonable prices, appetizers, such as quiche, ceviche, soup and salad, US$3-9, and main courses, such as grilled steak, rotisserie chicken and *lambi*, US$11-24, good food, Cuban and Dominican cigars, Prestige beer for US$2, rum sour for US$3.95.

♥♥♥-♥♥ Chez Gérard, 17 rue Pinchinat, T2571949. Beautiful setting with outside veranda and lush greenery growing everywhere, only items written on menu board are available, prices relatively high, appetizers US$8.00-12.00, entrées US$17.00-25.00, rum US$3.00, beer US$2.00 for Prestige, US$3.00 for imports.

♥♥♥-♥♥ Hotel Kinam, see above. French/Créole cuisine, very good, lovely ambiance, *lambi* in Créole sauce recommended, prices around US$10-23.

♥♥♥-♥♥ La Souvenance, 48 rue Geffrard, T2574813/3766. Gourmet French cuisine. Recommended. Pricey. Reservations a must Fri and Sat.

♥♥♥-♥♥ Plantation, Impasse Fouchard, turning off rue Borno, T2570979. Excellent French chef, good wine. Recommended, but not cheap. Main courses range from US$13-50.

♥♥ Café Albert, Place Boyer, T5567449. Good Haitian and European food, charming setting inside and out, very popular so reservation advised.

♥♥-♥ Cassagne, at the corner of Louverture and Mettelus. Beautiful old home converted into a restaurant, outdoor and indoor seating, bar, stage, live DJ at weekends with dancing from 2300, very nice owner, Haitian/Créole cuisine, moderate prices, food on grill US$6-10, seafood a bit more expensive.

♥♥-♥ Coin des Artistes, 59 rue Panaméricaine, T2576233. Grilled fish and lobster, moderate prices.

Fabrizio's, 126 rue Louverture, T2578433, fabrizio@haitiworld.com. American-style, Italian restaurant, a/c, wide-screen TV, with large portions and some tasty dishes, meals from US$12-14, desserts, takeaway and delivery available, beer US$2.60, rum US$2.40-6.15 a glass.

Fior Di Latte, Choucounne Plaza, corner of rue Lamarre and rue Chavannes, T2568474. Tue-Sat 1000- 2200, Sun 1300-2200. Excellent, especially thin-crust pizzas, small US$ 8-12.70, medium (for 2 people) US$ 9.45-14.10, home-made ice cream, US$1 per scoop, cappuccino US$2.30, shady outside seating, popular.

La Dolce Vita, 59 rue Geffrard, T2571133. Good Italian, home-made pasta, US$9-17 main course, Italian wine, dinner only.

Le Saint-Pierre, corner of rue Lamarre and rue Chavannes, T2572208. Mon-Sat 1100-2330, Sun 1500-2330. Small outside seating area overlooking street and indoors with 3 TVs for sports fans, Canadian-owned, pizzas, wings, Créole dishes and *poutine* (fries with cheese and gravy, a Canadian speciality).

Anba Tonel, rue Villate, T2577560. Cheap food, atmosphere both camp and romantic, dark courtyard covered with vines and shimmering tinsel, great shish kabobs, nothing for vegetarians.

Dorothy's, rue Darguin, T2579362, 4030525. Hole in the wall, good rotisserie chicken, rice and beans.

Epi D'Or, Delmas 56 and 51 rue Rigaud in Pétion-Ville. Haiti's biggest bakery. Good

Pétion-Ville

To Airport, Cap-Haïtien

To Port-au-Prince

To Kenscoff & Boutilliers Viewpoint, Fort Jaques & Baptist Mission

Haiti Port-au-Prince Listings

N

Not to scale

Sleeping
Caraïbe 1
Doux Séjour 8
El Rancho 2
Ife 6
Kinam 3
Le Ritz 5
Villa Créole 4
Villa Kalewes 7

Eating
Basilic 1
Boukan Gregoire 4
Café Albert 6
Cassagne 2
Chez Gérard 3
Coin des Artistes 5
Fabrizio's 7
Fior Di Latte 8
La Coquille 12
La Dolce Vita 13
La Souvenance 14
Le Saint-Pierre 16
Mun Cheez 19
Pâtisserie Marie
  Beliard 20
Ricky's 21

Bars & clubs
Barak 17
Café Des Arts 23
Extrème 22

baguette sandwiches. Wide assortment of pastries and cakes.

♦ **La Coquille**, 42 rue Lamarre, T2572542. 1230-1800. Buffet place with good food, mainly Créole, US$6.85, Prestige beer US$1.50.

♦ **Mun Cheez**, Av Panaméricaine on the corner of rue Rebecca, T2562177. Daily 0800-2300. Subs, burgers, pizza, salads, egg rolls, fries, also home delivery.

♦ **New Orleans Bar Restaurant**, 10 rue Rigaud, T5584639. Mon-Thu 1100-2200, Fri-Sat 1100-2400, closed Sun. Passable Haitian and international cuisine, main courses US$5.90-US$7.90. Charming staff, balcony seating, bar, live music at weekends.

♦ **Pâtisserie Marie Beliard**, on corner of rue Lambert and rue Faubert. Great bread, cakes, pâtés and French pastries.

♦ **Presse Café**, 28 rue Rigaud. Open for breakfast, lunch and dinner. Nice atmosphere, courtyard seating, regular international breakfast and Haitian lunch and dinner, US$1.15 US$1.30 for an expresso. Very good Créole lunch buffets Mon (US$7.85) and Fri (US$10). Good place to linger, sit and read French language, Haitian magazines and newspapers lying around, Live music Thu and Fri.

♦ **Ricky's Restaurant**, 34 rue Faubert, T2578524. Mon-Sat 1200-1600, and in evening until midnight, with live bands on weekends. Mostly Créole dishes, US$5.70 buffet.

♦ **Station 39**, 39 rue Lamarre. Breakfast from US$1-2.75, sandwiches and pasta dishes for lunch US$1-3.50, meat and seafood for dinner US$4.50-9.

⍟ Bars and clubs

Port-au-Prince *p390, maps p391 and p392*
Vodou beat band RAM performs Thu at the Oloffson, the place to be. Otherwise, the best nightlife is to be found in Pétion-Ville.

Pétion-Ville *p392, map p395*
Barak, rue Grégoire, across the street from Extrème. A New York-style bar that draws a bourgeois and ex-pat crowd.

Café Des Arts, 19 rue Lamarre (same house as Galerie Monnin), T2577979. Has live shows once or twice a month, large bar, beautiful setting.

Casino, at Hotel El Rancho, T2573490. A popular night spot.

Extrème, 64 rue Grégoire. An intimate couples' dance place with black lights and mirrors everywhere, Haitian and Dominican music.

Harry's, 97 Av Panaméricaine in Bagatelle Plaza, T2571885. Food OK, good value. Dance club with DJ music every night from 2000.

Shooter's, 17 rue Gabart, T5558224. A relaxing hang-out on a quiet side street, sit inside in a funky converted living room or outside on the roof of a barber's shop, range of drinks and tasty snacks.

⍟ Entertainment

Port-au-Prince *p390, maps p391 and p392*
Cinemas
The best are **Imperial** (a/c), **Delmas** and **Capitol** (a/c), 53 rue Lamarre. Cheap and interesting. Non-French or non-Créole films are dubbed into French.

⍟ Shopping

Port-au-Prince *p390, maps p391 and p392*
Art and crafts
Some galleries have a near-monopoly on certain artists, so don't expect to see a cross-section of all the major artists in any one good gallery. Mass-produced copies of the Haitian masters are sold cheaply around town. If you want to buy paintings, you are advised to take your time, look around, and be prepared to bargain. You will learn which patterns are imitations or mass-produced just by seeing them repeatedly. The paintings hung at the Oloffson are for sale.

Ambiance, 17 Av M, Pacot, T2452494. Haitian jewellery and pottery.

Comité Artisanal Haïtien, 29 rue 3, Pacot (near Oloffson), T2228440. Mon-Fri 0900-1600, Sat 1000-1200. A co-operative selling handicrafts from all over Haiti at good prices.

Fanal, 124 Av Christophe, corner of rue Waag, T2451948. Mon-Fri 1000-1700, Sat 1000-1400. Antiques, handicrafts, toys. Souvenir sellers also set up close to the Plaza.

Galerie Nader, 18 rue Bouvreuil, T2450565, Croix Desprez. Is now principally a museum. See also Pétion-Ville, below.

Le Centre d'Art, 58 rue Roy, Pacot, T2222018. Mon-Fri 0930-1300, 1430-1600, Sat 0930-1230. In a beautiful but crumbling old house, 2 floors of artwork with stacks of paintings, upstairs, founded 1944.

The Rainbow, 9 rue Pierre Wiener, Bourdon, T2456655/6039. Sells handicraft and paintings.

Pétion-Ville *p392, map p395*
Art and crafts
Aid to Artisans, 30 rue Goulard, Place Boyer, Petion-Ville, T2577212, 5588341, www.ata-haiti.org. Gift shop, excellent selection of crafts made by artisans across the country who receive assistance from this non-profit international organization.
Expressions, 55 rue Mettelus, south of rue Ogé, T2563471, expregal2000@yahoo.com. One of the Nader family galleries, English-speaking owners, beautiful gallery, excellent and large selection of paintings.
Festival Arts Gallery, 1 bis, rue Gabart, T2577956. Mon 1200-1800, Tue-Fri 1000-1800, Sat 1000-1400. Range of Haitian paintings and sculpture.
Fleur De Canne, 34 bis, rue Gabart, T2574266. Good-quality craft in a charming store. Place St-Pierre is a good place to find street vendors selling handicrafts, paintings, carpets, sculptures, plants, flowers, etc, remember to bargain.
Galata, 57 rue Faubert, T2572124. Mainly handicrafts, especially weavings, metalwork.
Galerie Marassa, 17 rue Lamarre, T2571967, galeriemarassa@hotmail.com. Hand-painted boxes, trays, art exhibitions.
Galerie Monnin, 19 rue Lamarre, in same house as **Café des Arts**, T2574430, galeriemonnin@hotmail.com.
Galerie Nader, 50 rue Grégoire, T2570855, www.galeriedartnader.com. The most expensive, but has an exceptional range of naive and other modern Haitian artists, also exhibitions.
Grim Gallerie, rue Clerveaux between rues Gabart and Lambert. Good selection of paintings.
La Galerie, 37 rue Clerveaux, T2575303. Great selection of paintings and cheaper than the other galleries.

Books
Asterix, corner of rue Ogé and rue Grégoire. French and Haitian books, magazines (some in English), stationery. Disorganized but you might find some treasures.
La Pleïade, Complexe Promenade, at the intersection of Grégoire and Moïse (southeast corner of Place St-Pierre),

T5139972. Excellent and well-organized selection of children's books as well as spectrum of themes, including cooking, sports, and psychology. Haitian and international books, newspapers and magazines. **La Promenade** is a garden turned into a small shopping promenade with an outdoor café, 1000-1800.

Food
Apollo, rue Grégoire just north of Place St-Pierre. Best place to buy fresh meat.
Caribbean Supermarket, Delmas 95. The biggest supermarket with the most varieties.
Deli-Cat, rue Clerveaux and Chavanne. Small store carrying snacks, wine, pasta and other imports from around the world.
Foodmax, corner of rue Darguin and rue Lamarre. A supermarket which carries a lot of 'Western' items.
Royal Supermarket, rue Clerveaux, just north of rue Louverture. Also full of imported goods.

▲ Activities and tours

Port-au-Prince *p390, maps p391 and p392*
Tour operators
ABC Tours, 156 rue Pavée, near Sainte-Trinité, T2220335. Courteous and helpful.
Agence Citadelle, 35 Place du Marron Inconnu, T2225900, www.agencecitadelle.com. Mon Fri 0800 1300, 1400 1630, Sat 0830 1230. Also offices in Pétion-Ville and Cap Haïtien. Sightseeing tours in a/c buses, airport shuttle (US$20 per person, min 2 people), travel and tours to Dominican Republic and Cuba, as well as specializing in travel to South, Central America and the Caribbean islands (owner Bobby Chauvet is a leading Haitian ecologist).
Bernard, T5583549. Can arrange custom-made boat excursions to Isle de la Gonâve for groups of up to 15, day trips or over-nights for up to a week, price US$50 per person per day, extra for food and snorkelling.
Voyage Chatelain, rue Geffrard, T2220130, F2225015. Handles **Terra Bus** to Santo Domingo including immigration formalities.

Pétion-Ville *p392, map p395*
Tour operators
Agence Citadelle, branch at Complexe Promenade, Angle rues Grégoire et Moise, T2570944, vppvl@agencecitadelle.com. Mon

and Wed-Fri 0900-1300, 1400-1730, Tue 0800-1530, Sat 1000-1400.

DOABN, T5115580, www.haititravels.org. Provides tours and cultural immersion programs, university study programmes and internships.

Jacqualine Labrom, T5570753, voyageslumiere@haitelonline.com. English-speaking and very nice, Jacqui can book packages to Cap and trips all over Haiti.

Multivision, Angle rues Lambert and Clerveaux, T2579771. English spoken.

Tour Haiti, T5102223, 115 rue Faubert, www.tourhaiti.net. Organizes nature and cultural excursions by boat, horseback, foot, bus and airplane.

Voyages Plus, Complexe Promenade, rue Grégoire, T5100944, F2573586. You can book **Caribe Tour** buses to the Dominican Republic here.

● Transport

Port-au-Prince *p390, maps p391 and p392*
See also page 386 and page 390.

Bus

Pick-up trucks with seats in the back, known as *Publiques* are the common form of public transport. They stop on demand and are usually overcrowded and uncomfortable. The 2 main bus stations for out-of-town destinations are at **Portail Léogâne** and between **Cité Soleil** and **Lasaline**.

Car

A small Japanese car with a/c, rents for about US$70 per day, US$430 per week, including 10% sales tax, unlimited mileage. A basic 4WD starts at US$ 790 per week with US$1800 deposit for damages.

Avis, T2501367. **Hertz**, T2500700, and **Dollar**, T2501800, have bases near the airport. **Avis** is opposite the airport terminal, T2501898. **Hertz** is in the Dynamic Entreprise Building.

Smaller companies include **Secom**, 564 Route de Delmas, T2571913, www.secomhaiti.com, **Easy Car Rental**, T5108246, and **Safety Car Rental**.

Taxis

Family Taxi, T5113100, is the only radio taxi company.

A passing *Publique* that is empty can be persuaded to do a private job (Créole: *flete*). The driver removes the red ribbon.

● Directory

Port-au-Prince *p390, maps p391 and p392*

Banks Promobank, T2998000, corner of Lamarre and Av John Brown, also a branch at Blvd du Quai and rue Eden. Scotiabank, T2993000, Delmas 18 and branch on 360 Blvd Dessalines. Citibank, T2993200, Route de Delmas. Also several Haitian banks such as Sogebank, T2295000, with ATMs at branches and gas stations throughout the metro area, and Banque de L'Union Haïtienne, T2998500. There are long queues in most banks for any kind of service. Street money changers (*cambistes*) can be found on rue Pavée and at the airport (see page 383). Banks or currency dealers working out of offices give almost as good a rate. They rarely take TCs. Many importers and big retailers give a good rate for cash and even personal cheques on US bank accounts. Try Didier Rossard, 22 rue Audan, T2225163.

Embassies Canada, Rte de Delmas, T2499000; Cuba, 18 rue E Pierre Péguy-Ville, Pétion-Ville, T2576626; Dominican Republic, 121 rue Panaméricaine (50 m down rue José de San Martín), Pétion-Ville, T2579215; EC Delegation, Delmas 60, Impasse Bravé 1, rue Mercier Laham, T2490141, F2490246; France, 51 Place des Héros de l'Indépendance, on rue Capois at the southwest corner of the Champs de Mars, near Hotel Palace, T2220951, F2235675; Germany, 2 Impasse Claudinette, Bois Moquette, Pétion-Ville, T2576131; Japan, Villa Besta Vista, Impasse Tulipe 2 Desprez, T2455875, F2458834; Spain, 54 Pacot, T/F2454410; US, Blvd Harry Truman, Bicentenaire, T2220200, F2239665; US Consulate, 104 rue Oswald Durand, T2236424, Mon-Wed, Fri 0730-1400, Thu 0730-1100, emergencies T2230955, acspap@state.gov. **Internet** US$2 per 65 mins at Netaccess, above Ice Cream on rue Darguin. **Medical services** Hospital Canapé Vert, rue Canapé Vert, T2450984. Adventiste de Diquini, Carrefour Rd, T2340521/2384/2732. Hospital Français de Haiti, rue du Centre, T2222323. St François de Salles, 53 rue Chareron, T222/0232.

Pétion-Ville p392, map p395

Banks BUH and **Capital** are on rue Lamarre, Mon-Fri 0900-1700, Sat 0900-1300, very slow and bureaucratic. **Sogébank**, on rue Grégoire and on rue Louverture, gives faster service. **Promobank** is on the corner of rue Rigaud and Faubert. **CitiBank** has an affiliate on rue Louverture between rue Faubert and rue Clerveaux. Street money changers at Place St-Pierre. **Internet** Mail

'n More, 107 rue Louverture, photocopying, email, fax, UPS, calling cards, new and clean building. **Post** DHL is at 21 rue Gabart, T2576192, dhlpickup@pap-co.ht.dhl.com. **Telephone** Téléco is at the corner of rue Magny and rue Rigaud. All calls go through an operator. Faxes can be sent through **Speedy Fax** on rue Louverture, between rues Faubert and Clerveaux.

Around Haiti

Hispaniola is the most mountainous island in the Caribbean, but pressure for the land has led Haitians to cut down all their trees for fuel, leaving the hillsides bare. There is no mass tourism and exploring the country beyond the capital is a rewarding experience for the independent and adventurous of spirit. Fortifications and other historical landmarks dot the countryside, but the most impressive is La Citadelle, built on top of a 900-m peak in order to deter any French invasion.» *For Sleeping, Eating and other listings, see pages 411-414*

East of Port-au-Prince

The asphalt road to Kenscoff, in the mountains behind Port-au-Prince, starts just to the west of the Pétion-Ville police station, on the Place St-Pierre. After 10 minutes, there is a turn-off on the right at **United Sculptors of Haiti**, which sells good wood carvings. It skirts a huge quarry and climbs to **Boutilliers**, a peak topped by radio and television masts that dominates the city. Great view but you will be promptly greeted by handicraft vendors and good-natured pestering. In about 20 minutes, the main Kenscoff road reaches **Fermathe** where the large Baptist Mission has a restaurant selling sandwiches, hot dogs, fries, pizza, ice cream, etc, with fine views south, and a store selling handicraft and souvenirs (*taptaps* and *camionettes* from near the market in Pétion-Ville). There is also a museum of the 'history of this land, of this people and of serving Satan'. Vodou is seen by the museum as the cause of all poverty in Haiti. A turn-off near the Mission leads to **Fort Jacques** and **Fort Alexandre** (10 minutes by car or 45 minutes' walk), two forts on adjoining summits built after the defeat of Napoleon. The views over the Cul de Sac plain are breathtaking. Fort Jacques has been restored.

Kenscoff is a hill resort where, just 30 minutes (15 km) from Pétion-Ville, but 1500 m above sea level, members of the élite retire to their country homes in July and August to escape the heat. A *camionette* from Pétion-Ville is US$0.40. Market day is on Friday. You can drive just beyond **Furcy**, from where you can hike to the summit above Kenscoff (about one hour), or the summit just to the west, called Morne Zombi. The ridge just to the east of the radio mast can be reached by a surfaced road in poor condition. It offers views south over a rugged, dark massif that boasts Haiti's highest peak, the 2674-m **La Selle**.

From the ridge, a four to five-hour hike (at a comfortable pace) along a trail heading towards the village of **Seguin** brings you to **Parc La Visite**, a nature park covering part of the massif. It has pine woods, montane cloud forest at higher altitudes, dozens of big limestone caves (one 10 km long) and strange karst-formation rocks locals call 'broken teeth' (Créole: *kase dan*) (see page 423). A guide is required. Camp at a disused saw mill (Créole: *siri*) by the trail, where water is available from a fountain. Bring thick clothes and sleeping bags; temperatures can fall to freezing at night. A waterfall is a short hike away. For longer hikes and fine views, head east with a guide and climb the 2282-m **Pic Cabaio** or the 2100-m **Pic La Visite** (another camping site). The park keeper, Jean-Claude, rents horses. Seguin lies on a sloping plateau on the massif's southern face, about one hour beyond the park. There's a hostal/guesthouse (C per person with meals), which you'll need to book in advance through the restaurant **Yaquimo** in Jacmel (see below and Eating, page 413). They will send a guide with a mule/horse to carry your luggage and show you the way. You can walk there in less than three hours. From Seguin, a five-hour hike gets you to the south-coast village of **Marigot**, from where you can bus back to Port-au-Prince via Jacmel in four hours.

Lake Saumâtre (see page 423) is at the eastern end of the Cul de Sac plain near the Dominican border. The road from Croix-des-Bouquets to the border crossing at Malpasse skirts the lake's southern side. The northern side offers more chance of seeing its wildlife. On Route Nationale 3, heading northeast from Port-au-Prince towards Mirebalais, fork right at the Thomazeau turn-off to the lakeside villages of Manneville and Fond Pite. It takes 90 minutes.

South of Port-au-Prince

Set off on the Route Nationale 2, the highway heading west toward **Les Cayes**. The lush, densely populated coastal **Léogâne Plain**, 45 minutes west of the capital, offers a look at rural life. East and west of the town of Léogâne, the plain is dotted with small villages and criss-crossed by bumpy lanes. After Léogâne, at the Dufort junction, fork left. The road climbs steeply, winding through the mountains with good views.

The run-down port of Jacmel is Haiti's prettiest city at the head of a 3 km wide horseshoe bay. The name Jacmel derives from an Indian word meaning 'rich land'. A quiet place, Jacmel has changed little since the late 19th century, when it was a booming coffee port and its wealthy merchants built New Orleans-style mansions using cast-iron pillars and balconies imported from France or the United States. Its charming Victorian streets wind down three small hills to a palm-fringed, black-sand beach. A hurricane swallowed up most of Jacmel's beach and what is left is dirty, with pigs rooting around in the debris.

The best views are from the south-facing houses on rue d'Orléans. The main square is pleasant and busy with vendors; the **Hôtel de la Place** restaurant is a good place to have lunch and watch the world go by. One block to the east opposite the church is an iron market built in 1895. Saturday is market day. The street below rue d'Orléans, rue Seymour Pradel, has an art gallery called **Salubria-Brictson Galleries**. Owner Bob Brictson is in residence only a few months of the year, but if you knock you will be shown his collection of worldwide art. Closer to the beach, on rue du Commerce, 19th-century homes have been turned into galleries or handicraft stores. The Boucard family residence at

There are excellent views over Jacmel bay on the way.

the corner of Grand' Rue and Commerce, is especially fine. At the other end of rue du Commerce, near the wharf, note the Vital family warehouse dating from 1865. The nearby prison was built in the 18th century. Jacmel's handicraft speciality are objects painted with colourful parrots or flowers. There are lots of artists painting and selling their work along Portail Léogâne.

A 12-km track into the hills west of Jacmel leads to **Bassin Bleu**, a series of natural pools and waterfalls descending a limestone gorge in tiers. The biggest, deep, blue-green pool is framed by smooth rocks and draped with creeper and maidenhair fern. Jump in for a cool swim. It takes 1½-two hours each way on foot or horseback (horses for hire in Jacmel or in the village up the hill on the other side of the river from Jacmel, about US$6-7, depending on the quality). Take a guide, fixing a price in advance, and water to drink. If it has not rained, the road is fine for a 4WD for three-quarters of the way. The Jacmel guide hands over to a local guide for the last kilometre which is a rough path and, at one point, requires the aid of a rope. This means an additional small fee. Guides here can be a problem, only one with the rope is needed, but you will find that you may be accompanied by others who will later demand payment.

Beaches on the south coast tend to have a slight undertow.

The diver who plunges from the uppermost rock into the pool also expects to be paid for his 'show'. In sum, this is a very rewarding excursion and highly recommended, but you need deep pockets with lots of small change for tips.

A good dirt road leads east to fine white-sand **beaches**. The first is **Cyvadier,**

Atlantic Ocean

Plage Labadie
Plage Cormier
Cap-Haïtien
Caracol
Fort Liberté
100
Limonade
121
Citadelle
Milot Terrier Rouge Dajabon
Dondon
k Raphaël)
Grande Rivière du Nord
Ouanaminthe
nel de Pignon
laye
300
te Rivière Maïssade
Artibonite
Hinche
Thomassique
Thomonde
09
DOMINICAN REPUBLIC
Belladère
aie Mirebalais
305
Lascahobas
300 Etang Saumâtre
Croix-des-
Bouquets
hor Pétionville
Malpasse Jimani
Kenscoff Lago Enriquillo
Massif de la Selle
Marigot Mandàto
Grand Gosier
ayes
cmel Belle Anse
Anse-à-Pitres

Vodou

Seeing a Vodou ceremony or dance during a short visit is likely to get easier since Vodou was recognized as an official religion in 2003. However, they are not announced in newspapers or on the radio. Never go unless accompanied by a Haitian, or someone already known there. Most middle-class Haitians do not attend ceremonies. They won't know where or when they are happening and they may even be discomforted by your interest. Instead, tell poor, working-class Haitians about your interest. You may strike lucky. To increase your chances, time your stay to coincide with 2 November (Day of the Dead), Christmas, New Year or the Epiphany (6 January), when there are many ceremonies. If invited, take a bottle or two of rum or whisky and be ready to give generously if there is a collection. Sometimes, on the contrary, a wealthy *oungan* (priest) or *mambo* (priestess) will insist on lavishing drinks and food on a visitor. Don't refuse. Before taking pictures with a still camera or video, ask permission. You may be asked to pay for the privilege. TV crews are usually asked to pay substantial amounts. An *oungan* may always be consulted in his *ounphor* (temple) even if there is no ceremony; plead poverty if the sum requested seems exorbitant.

Aboudja (T2458476, or through the Oloffson), an English-speaking TV news cameraman and Vodou consultant for visiting journalists and TV crews, has been initiated as an *oungan* although he does not practise regularly.

a tiny cove down a side road at Km 7. The shade around the beach prevents much sunbathing, but the water is clean and pleasant, although the surf can be rough at times. Fishermen cast their nets from the beach. At Km 15, just before Cayes Jacmel, is **Raymond-les-Bains**, a beach alongside the road. No facilities except showers. Just after Cayes Jacmel, at **Ti Mouillage**, the road runs beside two beaches. The first has a basic restaurant. From Marigot, a pretty coastal village 10 km further on, a 4WD can climb a rough trail to the village of Seguin and Parc La Visite (see page 399).

West of Port-au-Prince

The southwestern peninsula is the greenest and most beautiful part of Haiti. Its rugged western tip has forests, rivers, waterfalls and unspoilt beaches. The Route Nationale 2 to Les Cayes is very scenic but is frequently almost non-existent and where there is any surface it is often seriously potholed.

For the first 92 km the Route Nationale 2 runs along the north coast of the peninsula. There are rooms to let near **Grand Goâve** on Taïno Beach (Villa Taina (F), 80 rue Jeanty, T5511153. Meals are US$13.20), sailing and fishing trips can be organized, and there's a good view of Île de la Gonâve. At Km 68 is the town of **Petit Goave** (Créole: Ti Gwav). Visit the **Relais de l'Empereur**, once the residence of Emperor Faustin I (1849-1856). The hotel is no longer operating, but the caretaker will show you around.

Just 2 km down a turn-off at Km 92 is the smugglers' port of **Miragoane**, a town of narrow streets that wind around a natural harbour or climb up a hill capped by a neo-Gothic church. The town is dirty, dusty, crowded and poor, bars and restaurants no longer function and the hotel is for sale. Activity has moved up to the main road where there is a large market. In the centre of the market is a good café with parking space and charging medium prices. A 4WD is needed for the dirt road that continues along the north coast, fording rivers and passing fishing villages, as far as Petit Trou de Nippes. At Petite Rivière de Nippes, 15 km from Miragoane, a three-hour trek inland on foot or horseback (take a guide) brings you to one of Haiti's four great waterfalls, **Saut de Baril**.

After Miragoane, the main road crosses the peninsula's spine and reaches the southern, Caribbean coast at Aquin (Km 138), where you can bathe in several rivers. At **Zanglais**, 6 km further on, there are white-sand beaches. Just beyond Zanglais a ruined English fort is visible on a small offshore island, with the remains of a battery emplacement opposite.

Lying on a wet, coastal plain 196 km west of Port-au-Prince, Haiti's fourth city, **Les Cayes** (Créole: Okay), is quiet but not without charm. The **Fête de Notre Dame** around 15 August is recommended. Spend the day swimming, eating, drinking and watching people, and at night until 0200 the crowd moves to the *musique racine*, which is irresistible. Some people sleep on the beach because hotels are usually packed. Advance booking is necessary at this time. Buses or *taptaps* leave Port-au-Prince in the mornings from the same area as those for Jacmel, on Blvd Dessalines, for the four-hour trip (US$4). Visible from the waterfront is **Île-à-Vache**, a 20 km-long island with a population of 5000 that was Henry Morgan's base for a 1670 raid against Panama. It has Indian remains and good beaches on the southern side near La Hatte, the biggest village. Visit it by renting a motor boat (about US$25 for the day) or take the daily ferry, leaving at around 1600, and pay to sleep in someone's home. Or camp, after asking permission. A more regular service goes to **Port Morgan**, a wonderful small resort/marina run by a French couple, Didier and Françoise Boulard (T4850804, www.port-morgan.com). They have their own boat service to Les Cayes, US$15 round-trip, and offer tours to local villages for markets and other activities. There are some beautiful hikes in the area. As well as accommodation (see below), showers, laundry, fuel and internet access are available for visitors to the marina. They are very knowledgeable and helpful hosts, willing to help with travel arrangements on the mainland.

Fortresse des Platons, a huge ruined fortress built in 1804 at Dessalines' behest on a 600-m summit overlooking the coastal plain, can be visited in a one-day excursion from Les Cayes. Take the coast road southwest out of the city. Just after Torbeck, a rough road heads inland up a river valley via Ducis to the village of Dubreuil (trucks from Les Cayes). From Dubreuil, the fortress is a two- to three-hour hike up a steep trail with great views. Carry on the same trail via Formond to enter the **Macaya National Park**, which has Haiti's last virgin cloud forest surrounding the 2347-m Pic Macaya (see page 423). A University of Florida base at Plaine Durand (two hours beyond the fortress) has basic camping facilities. Hire guides for hikes into the lower montane rainforest. Only the very fit should attempt the hike to the top of the Pic Macaya. It entails climbing a 2100-m ridge and then descending to 1000 m before tackling the peak itself. Allow at least two days each way and take a guide.

Beyond Torbeck, the coast road goes as far as **St Jean du Sud** where a small offshore cay is suitable for camping. Before St Jean du Sud, fork right at L'Acul for **Port Salut**, a 90-minute drive from Les Cayes (two buses a day, also some trucks). This small village (birthplace of President Aristide) has a wild, 800 m-long, palm-lined beach that is one of the most beautiful in Haiti. The town is a haven of paved roads and laid-back people. The beaches are beautiful and totally empty. There is a pleasant waterfall, 10 minutes' drive, 30 minutes' walk away, where you can swim.

The adventurous can take the coastal route from Les Cayes to **Jérémie**, around the peninsula's tip, a remote, rugged, lush region that has changed little in 200 years. It has wild rivers, sand beaches, mountains falling steeply into the sea, and some of Haiti's last rainforest. Allow four days. Les Cayes buses or *taptaps* may go as far as **Les Anglais**, depending on the state of the road. A 4WD may even get to **Tiburon**. Thereafter, you must hike to **Anse-d'Hainault** or even **Dame Marie** before finding a road good enough to be serviced by *taptaps* out of Jérémie. Alternatively, take your life in your hands and try getting a ride on sloops that carry merchandise and passengers along the coast. Villagers all the way will cook meals and rent beds for a few dollars. *Pripri*, rafts made of bamboo lashed together and steered by a pole, ply the rivers. Anse-d'Hainault and Abricots (25 km west of Jérémie) have good beaches.

The scenic, hair-raising, 97-km mountain road from Les Cayes to Jérémie, across the Massif de la Hotte, takes three hours, but it may be impassable after rain and must be done in daylight. One hour's drive brings you to **Camp Perrin**, a hill resort at the foot of Pic Macaya. Here there are several guesthouses. Hire horses for a two-hour ride to **Saut Mathurine**, Haiti's biggest waterfall. There is good swimming in the deep, green pool at its base.

Fork right off the Jérémie road at the Kafou Zaboka intersection for **Pestel**, a picturesque port dominated by a French fort. It is worth seeing especially during the Easter weekend regatta, when many Rara bands come. The town is pretty with old wooden houses and a hotel with nice rooms and a friendly owner. Charter a boat to tour nearby fishing villages such as **Les Basses** (Créole: Obas) on the Baradères peninsula and **Anse-à-Maçon** on the offshore island of **Grande Cayemite** with its splendid view of the Massif de la Hotte. The beaches are very beautiful and totally empty.

With crumbling mansions overgrown by rampant vegetation, **Jérémie** is famed for its poets, eccentrics and isolation. Although the road is bad, some buses are still running from Port-au-Prince, leaving from Jean-Jacques Dessalines near rue Chareron. The 12-hour overnight ferry is not recommended. In February 1993 at least 800 people (maybe as many as 1500) drowned when an overloaded ferry, the *Neptune*, sank on its way to Port-au-Prince. The quickest and easiest way of getting there is to fly with **Caribintair** ① *T2502032*, from Port-au-Prince. They may be booked up to 10 days ahead. **Anse d'Azur**, 4 km west of the town, is a white-sand beach with a rocky headland at one end, and a big cave into which you can swim. The road west continues to the beaches of Anse du Clerc and Abricots (see above).

North of Port-au-Prince

The Gulf of La Gonâve beaches, the only ones that can be reached within an hour's drive, are not particularly good compared to the ones on the north coast of the island, but they're popular for a day trip out of the capital at weekends. The first beaches you get to are rather gritty, but they improve as you go further north. The backdrop is of arid, deforested mountainside but the calm, clear, shallow water is excellent for children.

The seaboard north of the capital is arid or semi-arid most of the way to Gonaïves, and all round the northwest peninsula as far as Port-de-Paix. This area was hit by drought and famine in the 1990s and severe ecological damage has occurred. From Port-de-Paix to the Dominican border, it is quite lush and green. Route Nationale 1 hugs the coast for most of the first 85 km skirting the foot of the Chaine des Matheux mountains.

Cabaret (Km 35) is the former Duvalierville. Its modernistic buildings and pretensions to become Haiti's Brasilia were lampooned in *The Comedians*. **L'Arcahaie** (Km 47) is where Dessalines created the blue and red Haitian flag by tearing the white out of the French tricolor. Outside L'Arcahaie, just before the highway crosses the small Mi Temps river, a road heads east high into the Chaine des Matheux to a region where coffee was grown in colonial times.

‡ RN 1 is asphalted to Cap-Haïtien, but is badly potholed for 65 km between Pont Sondé and Gonaïves.

The **Côte des Arcadins**, a 20-km stretch of beach, begins 60 km north of the capital. The few hotels have bars and restaurants, and charge admission to day visitors. They may be crowded with wealthy Port-au-Princiens or aid agency staff at weekends. There are also public beaches with no hotels. The **Musée Colonial**

Ogier-Fombrun ① *after Montrouis, at Km 77, daily 1000-1700, US$2, students and children US$1*, (see **Moulin Sur Mer**, page 412), in an 18th-century stone plantation building, has a model of the original house and buildings, also museum pieces outside. **The Arcadins** are three uninhabited, sandy cays 3 km offshore, surrounded by reef. The diving is excellent. Isle La Gonâve is also visible and dive boats visit the wall offshore.

Sailboats leave mid-morning from Montrouis (Km 76) for the 22-km crossing to **Anse-à-Galets** (one guesthouse), the main town on barren **Île La Gonâve**. In 1997 a ferry capsized just off Montrouis as it was docking. At least 172 died when passengers all fell to one side, causing the boat to turn over only 50 m from the shore. At Km 96, after the Côte des Arcadins beaches, the Route Nationale 1 reaches the port of **St Marc**. There are several gingerbread houses on streets to the east of the main street. A pretty valley runs inland southeast as far as Goavier.

The highway crosses the Artibonite river at **Pont Sondé**, entering a region of rice paddies irrigated by canals. Fork right at the Kafou Peyi intersection, 2 km north of Pont Sondé, for **Petite Rivière de L'Artibonite** (Créole: Ti Rivyè), a picturesque town built by King Henri Christophe on a steep-sided ridge overlooking the river Artibonite. Its Palace of 365 Doors was Christophe's provincial headquarters. In 1802, there was a key battle at the Crète-à-Pierrot fort (five minutes' walk above the town) in which Leclerc sacrificed 2000 men to dislodge a force of 1200 led by Dessalines.

About 8 km after **L'Estère**, a right turn-off runs southeast 25 km to **Marchand**, a town at the foot of the Cahos mountains that was briefly Dessalines' capital. Hike into the surrounding hills to visit seven big ruined forts built by Dessalines. Near the town is a spring with a natural swimming pool. Dessalines told his soldiers that bathing here made them immune to French bullets. The house of Dessalines' wife, Claire Heureuse, still survives in the town. You can also see the foundations of his own home. After Marchand, the RN1 crosses a semi-desert called Savane Désolée.

Amid salt pans and arid lowlands, **Gonaïves** at Km 171 is an ugly, dusty town of 70,000 (Haiti's third-largest). It is called the City of Independence because Dessalines proclaimed Haiti's Independence here in 1804. The unrest that toppled Jean-Claude Duvalier in February 1986 also began here and there have often been labour disputes here which have had a national impact. More recently, Gonaïves was the scene of rioting and violence primarily motivated by opposition to President Jean-Bertrand Aristide, and in February 2004, a group calling itself the Revolutionary Artibonite Resistance Front seized control of the city, starting the rebellion. In September of the same year, some 3000 people died in Gonaïves when Tropical Storm Jeanne deluged the area, causing mud slides and flooding, which reached the roof of the Hôtel Chachou, formerly the town's biggest hangout for the UN, aid workers, journalists and police. Efforts have been made to shore up defences against such a disaster ever happening again, but people are still wary.

After Ennery at Km 201, the Route Nationale 1 climbs steeply up to the Chaine de Belance watershed and enters the green, northern region. **Limbé** at Km 245, has the **Musée de Guahaba**, created by Dr William Hodges, a Baptist missionary doctor who runs the local hospital and supervises archaeological digs along the north coast (see La Navidad on page 409). The museum is not always open but you can ask for admission from his family who work at the Limbé hospital nearby. **Fort Crète Rouge**, above Limbé, is one of the many fortresses built by Christophe.

A rugged road from Limbé down to **Le Borgne** (Créole: Oboy) on the coast offers spectacular views. The 20 km either side of Le Borgne abound with white-sand beaches. The green mountains behind add to their beauty, but the coast is densely inhabited and the beaches are used as a public latrine. From Le Borgne to St Louis du Nord, the road is bad but passable for 4WD. After Limbé, the highway descends quickly, offering fine views over **L'Acul Bay**, where Columbus anchored on 23 December 1492, two days before his flagship sank.

Northeast of Port-au-Prince

Grandly called the Route Nationale 3, the 128-km dirt road northeast from Port-au-Prince to Hinche requires a 4WD and takes at least five hours (much longer by public transport). It crosses the Cul de Sac plain via Croix-des-Bouquets, where a road branches off southeast through a parched, barren region, skirting Lake Saumâtre (see pages 423 and 400) before reaching the Dominican border at Malpasse (see page 384). On the north side of the plain, the Route Nationale 3 zig-zags up a steep mountainside called Morne Tapion (great views back over Port-au-Prince) to reach **Mirebalais**, a crossroads at the head of the Artibonite valley, and Haiti's wettest town. The road east leads to Lascahobas and the frontier town of Belladère, the least used of Haiti's three border crossings into the Dominican Republic. The road west heads down the Artibonite valley. A left turn-off leads up into the hills to the charming village of **Ville-Bonheur** which has a church built on the spot where locals reported an appearance of the Virgin in a palm tree in 1884. Thousands of pilgrims come every 15 July. The Vodouists among them hike 4 km to visit the much-filmed **Saut d'Eau** waterfall. Overhung by creepers, descending 30 m in a series of shallow pools separated by mossy limestone shelves, the fall seems enchanted. The Vodouists bathe in its waters to purify themselves and light candles to enlist the help of the ancient spirits who are believed to live there.

The Route Nationale 3 heads north out of Mirebalais on to the Central Plateau, where the military crackdown was especially harsh after the 1991 coup because peasant movements had been pressing for change. After skirting the Peligre hydroelectric dam, now silted up and almost useless, the road passes Thomonde and reaches the region's capital, **Hinche**. In Port-au-Prince, buses leave from the station Au Cap at the intersection of Blvd La Saline and Route de Delmas. East of Hinche, **Bassin Zim** is a 20-m waterfall in a lush setting 30 minutes' drive from town (head east on the Thomassique Road, then fork north at Papaye). The cascade fans out over a rounded, sloping, limestone rockface. At its foot is a 60-m wide natural pool with deep, milky-blue water that is perfect for swimming.

Cap-Haïtien

Cap-Haïtien, Haiti's second city, has a dramatic location on the sheltered, southeast side of an 824-m-high cape, from which it gets its name. It was the capital in colonial times, when it was called Cap-Français. Its wealth and sophistication earned it the title of 'Paris of the Antilles'. The colony's biggest port, it was also the commercial centre of the northern plain, the biggest sugar-producing region. It was burned to the ground three times, in 1734, 1798 and 1802, the last time by Christophe to prevent it falling intact into the hands of the French. It was destroyed again by an 1842 earthquake that killed half the population. The historic centre's architecture is now Spanish-influenced, with barrel-tile roofs, porches, arcades and interior courtyards.

✻ *Nowadays it is usually referred to simply as Cap, or Okap in Créole.*

Vertières, an outlying district on the Port-au-Prince Road, is the site of the battle at which Dessalines' army definitively routed the French on 18 November 1803, forcing them to leave the island for good 12 days later. There is a roadside monument.

Cap appears to be more relaxed than Port-au-Prince and you will see people out on the streets at night. It is well worth visiting for its buildings and its surroundings but the people are not accustomed to tourists (*blancs*). The streets are filthy with streams of foul-smelling water running down them. The municipal government functions rarely and its services, such as street cleaning, are moribund.

The rich, alluvial plain to the south and east of Cap boasted a thousand plantation houses during the last years of the colonial period. **ISPAN** ⓘ *rue 15 and rue B in Cap, T2622459*, is a good source of information on these nearby colonial ruins, as well as on Sans Souci and the Citadelle.

The **beaches** in Cap itself are dirty and lack charm, but excellent beaches can be reached in 20 minutes by car from Cap. The first is **Cormier Plage**. Five minutes further west (30 minutes on foot) is **Labadie**, or **Labadee**, a fenced-off sandy peninsula used by **Royal Caribbean Cruise Lines** as a private beach for its cruise ships two days a week. Passengers are taken on snorkelling trips to L'Îlet, renamed by RCCL as Amiga Island, they can jet ski or take a banana boat ride and there is a craft market within the beach compound and a couple of bars. They are not, however, taken beyond the compound to sites in Haiti. In fact they are not even told they are on Haiti, the destination is marketed as the 'private island of Labadee'. On other days the public may use the empty beach and watersports for US$3.

Just beyond this beach, about 30 minutes' walk, are steps down to **Belli Beach**, a small sandy cove with a hotel. Boats, some with outboards, can be rented here to visit nearby Labadie village, dramatically located at the foot of a cliff, and other beaches further along the coast, for example Paradise beach, 30 minutes, US$6, no facilities. Fix a price before boarding. Labadie village (about US$3 by boat, also reachable by scrambling over the rocks) has guesthouses. Excursions can be arranged, ask Arnold at **Kayanol Village Labadee** about going to the Citadelle (see below), beaches and water taxi.

La Citadelle and Sans Souci

ⓘ *US$5 admission to the Citadelle and Sans Souci but they will try and sell it to you for more including guide. Sans Souci closes at 1700; no buses or taptaps back to Cap after 1700.*

At Milot are the ruins of Christophe's royal palace, Sans Souci. More than a palace, it was an embryo administrative capital ranging over 8 ha in the foothills beneath the Citadelle. Christophe sited his capital inland because of the difficulty of defending coastal cities against the overwhelming naval might of France and Britain. The complex included a printing shop, garment factory, distillery, schools, hospital, medical faculty, chapel and military barracks. Begun in 1810, inaugurated in 1813 and ransacked after Christophe shot himself in the heart with a silver bullet in 1820, it was finally ruined by the 1842 earthquake that destroyed Cap.

The mountain-top fortress of La Citadelle was built by King Henri Christophe to deter any French reinvasion (see page 416). It has walls up to 40 m high and 4 m thick, and covers 10,000 sq m. It is perched atop the 900-m Pic La Ferrière, overlooking Cap and the northern plain, and controlling access to the Central Plateau. Its 5000 soldiers (plus the royal family and its retinue) could have held out for a year. Restoration work is ongoing. Behind the fortress, at the end of a 1.5-km level ridge with sheer drops on both sides, is the **Site des Ramiers**, a complex of four small forts which controlled the rear access.

To get to the fortress take the 25-km asphalt road south from Cap to the village of Milot in a *publique* (US$1) or *taptap* (US$0.30). *Taptaps* leave Cap in the morning. Hotels like the Mont Joli offer jeep tours for about US$60 per person, but don't count on the guide's information being correct. From Milot it is a steep 5-km hike through **Sans Souci Palace** and lush countryside up to the fortress (about 1½ hours, start early to avoid the heat; wear stout shoes and protect yourself from the sun). Horses can be rented for about US$7 plus a tip for the man who leads the horse (dangerous in wet weather). Hire a guide even if you don't want one, just to stop others importuning and to make you feel safer (fix the fee in advance, US$10 for two, or more, for the walk). Several speak fluent French and English making the visit more

Haiti Around Haiti

❦ *Haitians call this the eighth wonder of the world. It is indeed impressive, with breathtaking views.*

Shiver me timbers

The buccaneers who settled on the north coast of Hispaniola were a mixed bunch of runaways and renegades. Some were escaped indentured labourers, who fled the gruelling life of the plantation; others were marooned sailors or deserters. Most were European, but there were a few blacks among them. Although some had a background in piracy, this was not their principal means of subsistence. What kept them alive and gave them their name were the cattle that roamed in the deserted northern plains of the island. These they rounded up and slaughtered, cooking the meat over wooden fires known as *boucans*. From these early barbecues came the English word 'buccaneer'.

The disappearance of the indigenous population together with thriving herds of feral cattle and pigs, introduced by the Spanish in the early days of settlement, ensured a viable, if not comfortable, lifestyle. The buccaneers would hunt cattle in the interior, tanning hides and curing meat on their *boucans*. Accompanied by dogs and armed with muskets, they collected enough of their bloody merchandise to return to the coast, where occasional trading exchanges took place with passing pirate or smuggling ships. So covered in blood were the buccaneers after their expeditions that contemporary observers thought they were covered in ship's tar.

In return for meat and hides, the buccaneers wanted alcohol, tobacco and weaponry. These were among the few manufactured essentials in an otherwise rudimentary way of life. They lived in basic stilted shacks with palm roofs, modelled on the indigenous *ajoupa*, and wore rough cotton trousers and shirts with home made caps, belts and shoes of rawhide.

The 'brethren of the coast', as they were called by the French historians Dutertre and Labat, inhabited a world without women. Many entered into same-sex marriages, known as *matelotage*. These relationships probably had legal foundations, ensuring that the surviving member of a pair would inherit the other's assets on his death. Death in the wilds of northern Hispaniola and nearby Tortuga Island was commonplace, through violence, malaria and other tropical hazards.

Although they were not first and foremost pirates, most buccaneers were not averse to a little casual predation. As their numbers grew, they occasionally set out to attack coastal traders, mostly Spanish, in long dugout canoes. After seizing whatever was on board, they would normally throw the crew into the sea before returning to their bases in the captured ship. Loot was scrupulously shared out, with extra quotas going to those who had been injured in the adventure.

Over time, the buccaneers seem to have tired of piratical activity, and many began to farm smallholdings of coffee and sugar cane. As the French staked a claim to the western side of Hispaniola, so the forces of law and order arrived, discouraging brigandage and supporting more sustainable economic pursuits. The buccaneers eventually disappeared as a distinct community, some moving on to other pirate havens such as Port Royal, Jamaica, others remaining in Hispaniola as small farmers and hunters.

interesting. Prices of refreshments at the Citadelle are higher than elsewhere, but then someone has had to carry them up there. Those with a car can drive to a car park two-thirds of the way up, reducing the walk to 1½ km (this last part is the hardest). Horses available here too, US$3.50 plus tip.

Around Cap-Haïtien

Morne Rouge, 8 km southwest of Cap, is the site of Habitation Le Normand de Mezy, a sugar plantation that spawned several famous rebel slaves. Leave Cap by the RN1 and take a dirt road running north from a point about 75 m west of the turn-off to the town of Plaine du Nord. Its ruins include two aqueducts and bits of walls. Vodou ceremonies are held under a giant tree in the village. Among its rebel progeny was Mackandal, an African chief's son who became an *oungan* and led a band of maroons. After terrorizing the entire northern plain by poisoning food and water supplies, he was captured and burned alive in January 1758. **Bois Caiman** was the wood where slaves met secretly on the night of 14 August 1791 to hold a Vodou ceremony and plan an uprising (it is near the Plaine du Nord road, about 3 km south of the RN1; ask locals to guide you once you are in the area.) Their leader was an *oungan* and slave foreman from Le Normand de Mezy called Boukman. The uprising a week later was the Haitian equivalent of the storming of the Bastille. Slaves put plantation houses and cane fields to the torch and massacred hundreds of French settlers. It began the only successful slave revolt in history and led to Haiti's Independence. Little is left of the wood now except a giant ficus tree overgrowing a colonial well credited with mystic properties.

The town of **Plaine du Nord**, 12 km southwest of Cap, becomes a pilgrimage centre on 24-25 July for the Catholic festival of St James, who is identified with Ogou. Vodou societies come from all over Haiti, camp in the streets and spend the two days in drumming and dancing. On 26 July, the feast day of St Anne, they decamp to nearby **Limonade**, 15 km southeast of Cap, for another day and night of celebrations. A dirt road on the northwest side of Limonade leads to Bord de Mer de Limonade, a fishing village where Columbus' flagship, the *Santa María*, struck a reef and sank on Christmas Day 1492. Columbus used wood from the wreck to build a settlement, **La Navidad**, which was wiped out by Taíno Indians after he left. Its location was discovered by American archaeologist William Hodges while digging at the site of Puerto Real, a city founded years later on the same spot. The untrained eye will detect nothing of either settlement now, but the Hodges museum in Limbé, see page 405, has relics.

Fort Liberté, 56 km east of Cap, is a picturesque, French-designed town on a large bay with a narrow entrance. It is dotted with French forts that can be reached by boat. The best is Fort Dauphin, built in 1732. The bay was the site of the Caribbean's largest sisal plantation until nylon was invented. There are direct *taptaps* from Cap to Fort Liberté, but it may be easier to return to Cap from the main road, which is 4 km from the centre of Fort Liberté.

Ounaminthe is northern Haiti's chief border crossing. Accommodation is available at Hotel Paradis on the main street. The Dominican frontier town, **Dajabón**, is just 2 km from the Ounaminthe *taptap* station. *Taptaps* for US\$2 from the Station Nordest in Cap; US\$1.10 from Fort Liberté. The crossing is straightforward and the Haitian border office is very helpful. Buses leave Dajabón for many Dominican cities. The river Massacre, which forms the border, had this name long before the massacre of thousands of Haitians in the neighbouring part of the Dominican Republic under Trujillo in 1937, when the river was said to have been red with blood for days. The bridge across the river is packed with money changers and *motoconchos* (not necessary for transport to Haitian border post, which is about 1 km from Dominican side). The Dominican side of the border has been described as an armed camp, with a heavy military presence controlling the flow of Haitian labour. The Haitian side, on the other hand, is more like a gypsy camp, with a thicket of tents and shacks.

South of Cap-Haïtien

The dirt road forking left 5 km before Milot could be a rugged alternative, two- to three-hour route back to Port-au-Prince via Hinche and the Central Plateau (see page

Haiti Around Haiti

406) by 4WD. By public transport it takes much longer – up to two days. Vehicles tend to be old, it is very dusty and the worst stretch is from near Milot to Hinche. The first town is **Grande Rivière du Nord,** where another of Christophe's fortresses, Fort Rivière, sits atop a ridge to the east. It was used by the Cacos guerrillas who fought the US occupation from 1918-1920. The Americans captured the Cacos leader Charlemagne Peralte near here. **Dondon** has caves inhabited by bats. One is close to the town. The other, 90 minutes away on foot or horseback up a river bed to the west of the village, has heads carved in relief on its walls, presumably created by the original Indian inhabitants. In the rainy season, cars cannot ford the river near St Raphaël, but you can walk, with locals helping for a small fee.

Northwest

Except for Tortuga Island and a coastal strip running east from Port-de-Paix, the northwest peninsula is Haiti's driest, most barren region. In recent years, especially since the 1991 coup, it has teetered on the brink of famine and toppled over in 1997 when international agencies had to bring aid.

The 86-km mountain road from Gonaïves to **Port-de-Paix** via Gros Morne fords several rivers and the trip takes four hours in a 4WD, needed for travel anywhere in the northwest. (Minibuses from Gonaïves, big buses from Port-au-Prince, leaving from beside the station Au Cap.) Port-de-Paix once made an honest living exporting coffee and bananas. Now it specializes in importing contraband goods from Miami. Vendors tout the wares on all its unpaved streets. In 1992-1993, its small freighters also ferried illegal immigrants into Miami. Despite the smuggling, it is safe.

A coast road runs west from Port-de-Paix along the north coast of the peninsula as far as **Môle St Nicolas** and then returns to Gonaïves via the south coast. **Jean Rabel** is a tense town which was the site of a peasant massacre in July 1987. At least 150 died in the clash, said to have been engineered by local Duvalierist landlords seeking to crush the attempts of Catholic priests to organize landless peasants. From Jean Rabel round to Baie de Henne, the landscape is arid, windy and dusty. Old people say they can remember when it was still green and forested.

Columbus first set foot on the island of Hispaniola at Môle St Nicolas. It has several ruined forts built by the English and French. General Maitland's surrender of Môle to Toussaint in 1798 marked the end of a five-year British bid to gain a toehold on this end of the island. Strategically located on the Windward Passage, just 120 km from Cuba, Môle was long coveted as a naval base by the USA. The hinterland has Haiti's lowest rainfall and little grows. The main occupation is making charcoal and shipping it to Port-au-Prince. Because few trees are left, charcoal makers now dig up roots. The peninsula's south side, especially from Baie de Henne to Anse Rouge, is a mixture of barren rock and desert, but the sea is crystal clear. There are few inhabitants. With salt pans on either side, Anse Rouge ships sacks of salt instead of charcoal.

Île de la Tortue → *Colour map 2, B1. Population 30,000.*

A 30-minute drive to the east of Port-de-Paix takes you to **St Louis du Nord,** a pretty coastal town from where sailing boats cross the 10-km channel to **Tortuga Island,** the Caribbean's biggest pirate base in the 17th century. Nearly 40 km long, 7 km wide and 464 m above the sea at its highest point, its smooth rounded shape reminded seafarers of the back of a turtle (*tortuga* in Spanish and *la tortue,* its Haitian name, in French).

The biggest south-coast villages, **Cayonne** and **Basse-Terre,** are less than 1 km apart. A ferry boat leaves Cayonne for St Louis du Nord at 0800 and returns at about 1000, charging locals US$0.50 each way. Foreigners may have to pay up to US$10, depending on their negotiating skills. Boats crossing at other times charge more.

From Cayonne there is a narrow cement road up to **Palmiste** serviced by a single *taptap*, one of the few cars on the island. From Palmiste, the biggest village on the rounded spine, there are spectacular views of the corniche coastline stretching from Cap to Jean Rabel, and the towering mountains behind. The best view is from the home of French Canadian priest Bruno Blondeau (T2685138), the director of a Catholic Church mission who has effectively governed the island since 1977. He runs 35 schools and has built all 55 km of its roads. His order also operates a small, basic hotel (**F**, room only).

The best beach, 2 km long, is at **Pointe Saline**, at the western tip (34 km from Palmiste, two hours by car). This is also the driest part of the island and there is little shade. **La Grotte au Bassin**, 6 km east of Palmiste, is a large cave with a 10 m high pre-Columbian rock carving of a goddess. There are two other big caves: **Trou d'Enfer**, near La Rochelle ravine, and **La Grotte de la Galerie**, 1 km east of Trou d'Enfer. The largest ruin is a 15-m-high lime kiln (*four à chaux*), built at the end of the 18th century. **Fort de la Roche**, 1639, was once Tortuga's biggest fortress (70 m high). Its masonry foundations can be seen at a spring on the hillside above Basse-Terre. Three cannon and a bit of wall remain from **Fort d'Ogeron**, built in 1667.

● Sleeping

East of Port-au-Prince *p399*
B-C The Lodge, Furcy, T4585968, www.thelodgeinhaiti.com. Spacious rooms, good food, run by an American, Stanley Urban, a popular weekend destination in a beautiful setting, reminiscent of a Swiss chalet, built with timber from Canada.
C Hotel Florville, Kenscoff, T2452092. Good food, a beautiful view, and occasional outdoor concerts.

South of Port-au-Prince *p400*
AL-A Cyvadier Plage, on the beach at Cyvadier, T2883323, www.hotelcyvadier. com. A quiet hotel and restaurant offering rooms and 3 meals with ceiling fans, balcony, private bath with water and electricity, mostly seafood, fruit and vegetables, all fresh and local, swimming pool, secure, gates locked at night.
A La Jacmelienne, Jacmel, T2883451. A modern, 2-storey hotel on the beach with pool, meal plans, fans, a/c in some rooms, all rooms with balcony and sea view, restaurant open-air and pleasant at night. Mixed reports on service and cleanliness, but great location.
A-B Hotel Florita, rue du Commerce 29, near the post office, T2882805, www.hotelflorita.com. Charming old 1888 building, polished wooden floors, balconies, balustrades, arched doorways, antique furniture. Breakfast available, cosy living room, 10 rooms, vary in quality and size.

B-C Hôtel de la Place, 3 rue de l'Église, T2882832, overlooks Place d'Armes. Good location, very central with lots to see and interesting people-watching, functional rooms with bathrooms, clean, pleasant restaurant, reasonable food. Lovely troubadour band plays every evening.
D Guy's Guesthouse, 52 Ave de la Liberté, T2883421, www.guysguesthouse.com. 10 rooms, breakfast, 2 rooms with bathroom, fans, clean, popular, good value.

West of Port-au-Prince *p402*
A Village Touristique Morgan, Port Morgan, Ile à Vache, T4460804, www.port-morgan.com. Immaculate bungalows, 3 meals, delicious French food, visit organized as a package custom tailored for client. Scuba diving, snorkelling, windsurfing, sailing excursions, marina, volleyball, hiking, more sports and activities planned, massages, bar with happy hour 1700-1800.
A-B La Cayenne, Presqu'iles des Icaques, Les Cayes, T2860770. By the beach, some rooms with a/c, pool, **La Cayenne Restaurant**, T2860379, in the centre of town.
B Hotel le Meridien, Les Cayes, at entrance to town, T2860331. Basic but comfortable, fans and a/c, decent restaurant with slow service, can call overseas from lobby phone with calling card.
B Pestel. Bungalows for rent by the sea, which are basic but OK, for 2-4 people.

Haiti Around Haiti Listings

Rented by Frenchman and his son who run **Café de la Gare**, 5 mins from Pestel.

C Hôtel La Cabane, rue Bordes, Jérémie, T2845128. On a hill above the town, with a shady garden, meals included.

D Village Touristique, Les Cayes, at the end of the village, BP 118. Comfortable bungalows with shower, big bed, mosquito screens, nice, quiet, right on beach, water but not always electricity, candles supplied, contact Maurice, the caretaker; or rent rooms from locals.

North of Port-au-Prince p404

Côte des Arcadins is popular for overnight stays at weekends; you may need to book ahead; very calm at night, beautiful stars.

LL-L Moulin Sur Mer, Côte des Arcadins, after Montrouis, at Km 77, T2786700, www.moulinsurmer.com. Reached through the extensive gardens of the Musée Colonial Ogier-Fombrun (see page 405), with palms, peacocks, geese and ducks, beautiful setting on sandy beach. 68 rooms including 4 suites, meals included, Haitian furniture and art, a/c, hot water, tiled floors, phones, suites for families, also beach rooms for day use, large restaurant, vegetarian food available, tennis, volleyball, ping pong, pool, mini golf, playground, watersports including pedalos, kayaks, diving arranged. A day pass costs US$9.

AL-A Kaliko Beach Club, Côte des Arcadins, at Km 61, T2984607/9, www.kalikobeachclub .com. All-inclusive, smart blue and white plantation-style resort, popular with French Canadians, this is the noisiest of the resorts with music playing all the time by the pool, but it also has the most facilities to offer, 55 rooms (sleep 4) with fan or a/c, day pass US$20 with 1 meal, US$10 lunch only, good food, lots of fruit for breakfast, pleasant beach but not spectacular, pool, gardens, boat cruises, conference facilities, internet access, excursions.

AL-A Wahoo Bay, Côte des Arcadins, T2983410, www.wahoobaybeach.com. Day pass US$4.30. 22 large, clean rooms, 2 suites, 1 apartment, breakfast included, a/c, upstairs rooms with balcony and view of La Gonâve, good showers, delicious food with generous portions, pool, small but sandy beach, good swimming, loungers and tables with shade, volleyball, kayaking, horse riding, tennis, some new rooms.

A-B Kyona, Côte des Arcadins, T2576850. Basic rooms in bungalows or newer block, breakfast included, cold water, some rooms with a/c. Thatched open-air restaurant, volleyball, hotel dates from early 1960s. Daily admission US$5.70, curved, gritty beach, loungers and tables in shade, lots of trees, locals selling paintings, turtle shells, black coral.

B Ouanga Bay, Côte des Arcadins, at Km 65, T2224422. Day pass US$3.50 until 1900, food and drinks extra, small sandy beach with man-made reef, quiet and private, loungers, restaurant built over the water, 27 rooms and apartments right on beach, large beds, fan or a/c, TV and phones, bathrooms adequate, English-speaking owner, friendly, watersports include snorkelling, windsurfing, pedalos and glass-bottom boats with electric motors, diving arranged.

B-C Le Gouté Auberge Sport Bar, Portail Guêpes, St-Marc, Rte Nationale 1 northbound, T2791497. Owned by Henry Dalencour, pool, a/c.

C Chachou, 145 Ave des Dattes, Gonaïves, T2741888. The town's biggest hangout for the UN, aid workers, journalists and police. The only pool in town, internet access, decent restaurant serving basic Haitian food. During the 2004 floods the water rose up to the roof.

C Hotel Le Paradis, Gonaïves, on a side street farther up Ave des Dattes away from the town centre. Lacking a restaurant and any vibrancy but clean and charming.

E Hotel Belfort, 168 rue Louverture, St Marc, T2791610. Clean but basic.

Northeast of Port-au-Prince p406

E Foyer d'Accueil, Hinche. Is an unmarked guesthouse above a school behind the blue and white church on the east side of the main square, basic, fan, rarely any power (electricity plant).

Cap-Haïtien p406

Do not drink the water, or even use it to clean your teeth.

A Habitation Labadie, Labadie, T2624630. Delicious meals included, 24 rooms, TV, beach, pool, good for lunchtime excursion.

A-B Beck, on the mountainside, residential Bel-Air district, T2620001. Woodland setting, 2 pools, constant water, own generator, private beach at Cormier, German owner, rooms with private bath and fan, meals included.

A-B Hotel Cormier Plage, Cormier Plage, T2621000. Simple chalets or rooms overlooking the sand and sea, meals included, excellent food, freshly caught seafood, own generator turned on 0730-1100 and 1630-2330, airport transfers. Scuba diving with good wrecks and coral reefs. Run by a charming French couple, Jean-Claude and Kathy Dicqueman. Book ahead, because tour groups from Dominican Republic sometimes fill the place up. Take mosquito repellent.

A-B Mont-Joli, on the hillside above town, T2620300, nbussenius@yahoo.com. Includes breakfast and tax, a/c, TV, hot water, rooms have a beautiful view, free internet access in the lobby, pool, tennis court, good restaurant, sandwiches US$10-12, shrimp or lobster meal US$12, bar open 0900-2300, own generator.

B Les Jardins de l'Océan, 90 Blvd de Mer, T5534270, F2622277. Small hotel, nice terrace with sea view, good food à la carte, steak, pizza, lobster, shrimp, friendly atmosphere, cosy rooms all with bathroom, fan.

B Roi Christophe, T2620414, corner of 24 and B. Central location in colonial house first built in 1724 as the French Governor's palace (Pauline Bonaparte stayed here), lush gardens, pool, own generator, more expensive with a/c, cheaper with fan, breakfast included.

B-D Kayanol Village Labadee (Arnold's Place), Labadie, T4316659, www.kayanol .com. 10 rooms on a hill overlooking Labadie, a/c, TV, VCR/DVD, 24-hr electricity, bar, games room, becomes a dance hall at night. There is usually a DJ, but sometimes a live band and folklore show. The restaurant and garden have an ocean view.

D pp Norm's Place, Labadie, T2620400, normsplacelabadee@yahoo.com. An old French fortress, refurbished by an American, Norm, and Angelique, who are very hospitable and run it as a guesthouse, 8 basic rooms, some sleep 2, some sleep 4, no screens but beds have mosquito nets, private shower and toilet, no shower curtains, no hot water, swimming 3 steps down from reception, accessible only by boat. Good food, breakfast

US$8, dinner US$12.50.

E Brise De Mer, 4 Carenage (on waterfront at northern edge of town), T2620821. Friendly but reportedly not very safe, own generator, rooms with private bath and fan.

Tortuga Island *p410*
C Hotel Brise Marina, Port-de-Paix, about 10 mins from town centre northeast along the coast. The best in the area, clean, basic rooms with bathroom, pool, restaurant OK, nice view over the sea.

---

❶ Eating

East of Port-au-Prince *p399*
¶-¶ Le 3 Decks, 3 bis, Fermathe 54, on the Kenscoff road near the Mission, T5103722. Fri-Sat 1200-2100, Sun 1200-1800, Mon-Thu by reservation only. A lovely and very peaceful restaurant in the hills, with a beautiful view, excellent Haitian-French-Asian fusion cuisine, main courses US$9-16.

South of Port-au-Prince *p400*
¶-¶ Yaquimo Nightclub and Restaurant, Jacmel, is 100 m west of the wharf. Fairly good food, good atmosphere, live bands.

West of Port-au-Prince *p402*
¶-¶ Café de la Gare, 5 mins from Pestel. Run by a Frenchman and his son. There's dancing in the evenings and happy hr Sat evening.

North of Port-au-Prince *p404*
¶ Rex Restaurant, rue Louverture, Gonaïves, half a block from the market. Créole food and hamburgers.

---

❶ Shopping

Cap-Haïtien *p406*
Most shops close between 1700-1800.
Ateliers Taggart, T2621931, rue 5 near Blvd (by Cap 2000). Mon-Fri 1000-1700. Handicrafts, especially weavings and metalwork.
Galerie Des Trois Visages, excellent art gallery next to **Ateliers Taggart**. A tourist market by the port has handicrafts and naive paintings. Bargain hard.
Marina Market is a supermarket on the Blvd with rue 13.

▲ Activities and tours

North of Port-au-Prince p404
Diving
Pegasus Diving, just along the beach from the **Kaliko Beach Club**, T5107397, www .kalikobeachclub.com. Snorkelling trips at Les Arcadins, US$30pp, minimum 6 passengers, and La Gonâve, US$ 60. Diving for certified divers to Les Arcadins, US$80 for 2 dives including gear, and the wall at Isle La Gonâve, US$90 for 2 dives, 30 mins on dive boat.

Fishing
US$350 for 4 people half day, US$500 full day, including gear, captain, drinks, fuel and boat rental, also at **Kaliko Beach Club** (see above).

Cap-Haïtien p406
Tour operators
Agence Citadelle, rues 11 and A, T2620484, vpcap@agencecitadelle.com. Mon-Fri 0800-1300, 1400-1600 Sat 0800-1200. **Cap Travel**, 84 rue 23A, T2620517.

⊖ Transport

South of Port-au-Prince p400
Bus In Port-au-Prince, buses leave from the station Jacmel on Dessalines, a couple of blocks the other side of Chareron, 2½-3 hrs, US$1.50, lovely route, very crowded. In Jacmel buses leave from the gas station at the junction of Portail Léogâne and Av de La Liberté.

North of Port-au-Prince p404
Bus
Buses (US$3, 4 hrs) leave Port-au-Prince mornings from the intersection of Blvd La Saline and Jean-Jacques Dessalines.

Taxis
In Gonaïves, mopeds operate as taxis, charging US$0.40 a ride.

Cap-Haïtien p406
Air
Tropical Airways d'Haiti daily from Port-au-Prince and Port-de-Paix. **TCI Sky King** from Providenciales, Turks and Caicos. There are also air taxi services.

Bus
Buses leave Port-au-Prince from the station Au Cap opposite the big Texaco garage at the junction of Delmas and Blvd La Saline between 0630 and 0830, when full. The 274-km trip usually takes 6-7 hrs. Fare US$6. It may be necessary to change in Gonaïves, 3½ hrs, US$2. There are 2 principal *taptap* stations in Cap: **Barrière Bouteille** at southern end of town, for all destinations to Port-au-Prince (*taptaps* go during the morning, buses at night), and **Port Métalique**, at A2, also south end of town, cross bridge for station for all destinations to **Milot** (outside Hôtel Bon Dieu Bon), **Hinche**, **Fort Liberté**, **Ounaminthe** and the border. *Taptaps* US$0.60 to **Labadie** from Cap leave frequently in the morning from Champs de Mars, 10 mins' walk up rue 22 away from the centre and the waterfront towards the mountains, ask if you get confused, it looks a bit rural. *Taptaps* will drop you at the gate to **Coco Beach**.

Car
Hertz, T2500700/2048. Check price quotes very carefully. Don't leave your passport as deposit.

⊕ Directory

South of Port-au-Prince p400
Banks BMH, 60 Grand' Rue, Jacmel, between bus station and Guy's Guest House, good rates, changes TCs. You can also change money at **La Jacmelienne**, but don't expect a good rate.

Cap-Haïtien p406
Banks BNP, changes TCs; also **Banque Union Haïtien** changes TCs, open until 1300. **Internet** Internet café opposite church, US$1.40/hr. **Post office** Av B at rue 17.

Background

History

Hispaniola Columbus visited the north coast of Hispaniola, modern Haiti, on his first visit to the West Indies, leaving a few men there to make a settlement before he moved on to Cuba. He traded with the native Taínos for trinkets, which were to seal the Indians' fate when shown to the Spanish monarchs. A second voyage was ordered immediately. Columbus tried again to establish settlements, his first having been wiped out. His undisciplined men were soon at war with the native Taínos, who were hunted, taxed and enslaved. Hundreds were shipped to Spain, where they died. When Columbus had to return to Spain he left his brother, Bartolomé, in charge of the fever-ridden, starving colony. The latter sensibly moved the settlement to the healthier south coast and founded Santo Domingo, which became the capital of the Spanish Indies. The native inhabitants were gradually eliminated by European diseases, murder, suicide and slavery, while their crops were destroyed by newly introduced herds of cattle and pigs. Development was hindered by the labour shortage and the island became merely a base from which to provision further exploration, being a source of bacon, dried beef and cassava. Even the alluvial gold dwindled and could not compete with discoveries on the mainland. The population of some 400,000 Taínos in 1492 fell to about 60,000 by 1508. In 1512 the Indians were declared free subjects of Spain, and missionary zeal ensured their conversion to Christianity. A further 40,000 were brought from the Turks and Caicos, the Bahamas and Venezuela, but by 1525 the Indian population had practically disappeared. Sugar was introduced at the beginning of the 16th century and the need for labour soon brought African slaves.

Birth of a colony In the 17th century the French invaded from their base on Tortuga and colonized what became known as Saint Domingue, its borders later being determined by the Treaty of Ryswick in 1697. The area was occupied by cattle-hunting buccaneers and pirates, but Governor de Cussy, appointed in 1684, introduced legal trading and planting. By the 18th century it was regarded as the most valuable tropical colony of its size in the world and was the largest sugar producer in the West Indies. However, that wealth was based on slavery and the planters feared rebellion. After the French Revolution, slavery came under attack in France and the planters called for more freedom to run their colony as they wished. In 1791 France decreed that persons of colour born of free parents should be entitled to vote; the white inhabitants of Saint Domingue refused to implement the decree and mulattos were up in arms demanding their rights. However, while the whites and mulattos were absorbed in their dispute, slave unrest erupted in the north in 1791. Thousands of white inhabitants were slaughtered. Soon whites, mulattos and negroes were all fighting, with shifting alliances and mutual hatred.

Toussaint Louverture Out of the chaos rose a new leader, an ex-slave called François-Dominique Toussaint, who created his own roaming army after the 1791 uprising. When France and Spain went to war, he joined the Spanish forces as a mercenary and built up a troop of 4,000 negroes. However, when the English captured Port-au-Prince in 1794 he defected with his men to join the French against the English. After four years the English withdrew, by which time Toussaint was a leader among the black population. He then turned against the mulattos of the west and south, forcing their armies to surrender. Ordered to purge the mulatto troops, Toussaint's cruel lieutenant, **Jean-Jacques Dessalines**, an African-born ex-slave, slew at least 350. Mulatto historians later claimed that 10,000 were massacred. The same year, torrential rain broke the irrigation dams upon which the prosperity of the area depended. They were never repaired and the soil was gradually eroded, creating a wilderness. By 1800 Toussaint was politically supreme. In 1801 he drew up a new constitution and proclaimed himself Governor General for life. However, Napoleon had other plans, which included an alliance with Spain, complicated by Toussaint's successful invasion of Santo Domingo, and the reintroduction of the colonial system based on slavery. In 1802 a French army sent to Saint Domingue defeated Toussaint and shipped him to France, where he died in prison. The news that slavery had been reintroduced in Guadeloupe provoked another popular uprising which drove out the French.

19th-century revolution The new revolt was led by Dessalines, who had risen to power in Toussaint's entourage and was his natural successor. In 1804 he proclaimed himself Emperor of an independent Haiti, naming the country after the Taíno word for 'high land'. Dessalines was assassinated in 1806 and the country divided between his rival successors: the negro **Christophe** in the north, and the mulatto **Pétion** in the south. The former's rule was based on forced labour and he managed to keep the estates running until his death in 1820. He called himself **Roi Henri Christophe** and built the Citadelle and Sans Souci near Milot. Pétion divided the land into peasant plots, which became the pattern all over Haiti and led to economic ruin with no sugar production and little coffee. Revolution succeeded revolution as hatred between the blacks and mulattos intensified. Constitutional government rarely existed in the 19th century.

❧ For a fictionalized account of this period, read Alejo Carpentier's El reino de este mundo (The Kingdom of This World).

US intervention In 1915, the USA intervened for geopolitical and strategic reasons, provoked by the murder and mutilation of a President. Occupation brought order, the reorganization of public finances, health services, water supply, sewerage and education, but there was still opposition to it, erupting in an uprising in 1918-1920 which left 2,000 Haitians dead. By the 1930s the strategic need for occupation had receded and the expense was unpopular in the USA. In 1934 the USA withdrew, leaving Haiti poor and overpopulated with few natural resources. Migrants commonly sought work on the sugar estates of the neighbouring Dominican Republic, although there was hatred between the two nations. In 1937 about 10,000 Haitian immigrants were rounded up and massacred in the Dominican Republic.

Duvalier Dynasty In 1957 **François (Papa Doc) Duvalier**, a black nationalist, was elected President and succeeded in holding on to power. He managed to break the mulattos' grip on political power, even if not on the economy. In 1964 he became President-for-Life, a title inherited by his 19-year-old son, **Jean-Claude (Baby Doc) Duvalier**, in 1971. The Duvaliers' power rested on the use of an armed militia, the **Tontons Macoutes**, to dominate the people. Tens of thousands of Haitians were murdered and thousands more fled the country. Repression eased under Jean-Claude, but dissidence rose, encouraged partly by US policies on human rights. Internecine rivalry continued and the mulatto elite began to regain power, highlighted by the President's 1980 marriage to Michèle Bennett, the daughter of a mulatto businessman. Discontent erupted with the May 1984 riots in Gonaïves and Cap-Haïtien, and resurfaced after the holding of a constitutional referendum on 22 July 1985 giving the Government 99.98% of the vote. Several months of unrest and rioting gradually built up into a tide of popular insistence on the removal of Duvalier, during the course of which several hundred people were killed by his henchmen. The dictatorship of the Duvaliers (father and son) was brought to a swift and unexpected end when the President-for-Life fled to France on 7 February 1986.

Democracy and the army The removal of the Duvaliers left Haitians hungry for radical change. The leader of the interim military-civilian Government, **General Henri**

Namphy, promised presidential elections for November 1987, but they were called off after Duvalierists massacred at least 34 voters early on polling day with apparent military connivance. New, rigged elections were held in January 1988, and **Professor Leslie Manigat** was handed the presidency only to be ousted in June when he tried to remove Namphy as army commander. Namphy took over as military President, but four months later he himself was ousted in a coup that brought **General Prosper Avril** to power. Dissatisfaction within the army resurfaced in April 1989, when several coup attempts were staged in quick succession and lawlessness increased as armed gangs, including disaffected soldiers, terrorized the population. Nevertheless, the USA renewed aid, for the first time since 1987, on the grounds that Haiti was moving towards democratic elections, promised for 1990, and was making efforts to combat drug smuggling. Under General Namphy, cocaine worth US$700 million passed through Haiti each month, with a 10% cut for senior army officers. However, Avril's position was insecure; he moved closer to hardline Duvalierists, and arrests, beatings and murders of opposition activists increased. Foreign aid was cut off in January 1990 when Avril imposed a state of siege and the holding of elections looked unlikely. In March, Avril fled the country. Following his resignation, Haiti was governed by an interim President, Supreme Court judge **Ertha Pascal-Trouillot**.

1990 elections and coup Despite poor relations between Mme Pascal-Trouillot and the 19-member Council of State appointed to assist her, successful elections were held on 16 December 1990. The presidential winner, with a landslide 67% of the vote, was **Father Jean-Bertrand Aristide**, who was sworn in on 7 February 1991. His denunciations of corruption within the government, church and army over the previous decade had won him a vast following. One of his immediate steps on taking office was to start investigations into the conduct of many officials, to seek the resignation of six generals, to propose the separation of the army and police and to garner urgently needed financial assistance from abroad. Aristide's refusal to share power with other politicians, his attacks on the interests of the armed forces and the business elite, and the actions of some of his militant supporters provoked his overthrow by the army on 30 September 1991. Aristide fled into exile. Harsh repression was imposed; at least 2,000 people were said to have died in the first six months, almost 600 during the coup itself. People began fleeing in small boats to the US Guantánamo naval base on Cuba in an exodus that had reached 38,000 by May 1992. The USA brought it to an end by immediately repatriating everyone without even screening claims for political asylum.

International pressure International condemnation of the coup was swift, with the Organization of American States, led by the USA, imposing an embargo. The EU and other nations suspended aid and froze Haitian government assets. The sanctions hurt, but not sufficiently to promote a formula for Aristide's return; this was partly because of Washington's misgivings about his radical populism. The election of Bill Clinton to the US Presidency in 1992, with the prospect of more decisive US action on restoring Aristide to power, prompted UN involvement. With Washington making it clear it was ready to step up sanctions, the UN envoy persuaded the army commander, **General Raoul Cedras**, to agree in February 1993 to the deployment of 250 civilian UN/OAS human-rights monitors throughout Haiti. Further UN pressure was applied in June 1993 with the imposition of an oil embargo and a freeze on financial assets. As a result, an accord was reached in July whereby Aristide would return to office by 30 October, Cedras would retire and Aristide would appoint a new army chief and a Prime Minister.

As the 30 October deadline approached, it became clear that Aristide would not be allowed to return. In mid-October, the Haitian rulers humiliated the USA by refusing to allow a ship to dock carrying a 1,300-strong UN non-combat mission. Aristide supporters continued to be killed and harassed. Aristide's appointed cabinet resigned in mid-December as the regime showed no signs of weakening. As smuggled fuel from the Dominican Republic flowed in, Cedras and his collaborators set their sights on staying in power until the end of Aristide's term of office, February 1996.

Aristide's return Despite the lack of wholehearted support in the USA, an occupation of Haiti by 20,000 US troops began on 19 September 1994. Aristide returned to the presidency on 15 October to serve the remainder of his term, aided first by a 6,000-strong US force, then by 6,000 UN troops who replaced the Americans in March 1995. General Cedras and his chief-of-staff, General Philippe Biamby, were talked into exile in Panama, while the third leader of the regime, police chief Michel François, fled to the Dominican Republic. Aristide set about reducing the influence of the army and police and the USA began to train recruits for a new police force, but by April 1995, the absence of a fully trained police force and of an adequate justice system had contributed to a general breakdown of law and order. Many people suspected of robbery or murder were brutally punished by ordinary Haitians taking the law into their own hands. 'Zenglendo' thugs, often thought to be demobilized soldiers, were involved in the killing of political figures and others.

The fear of violence disrupted preparations for legislative and local elections, held over two rounds in 1995. These gave overwhelming support to Aristide's Lavalas movement in the Senate (all but one of the seats up for election) and the Lower House (71 of the 83 seats), but the turn-out was very low and the results were bitterly contested. Of the 27 competing parties, 23 denounced the election because of irregularities reported by international observers.

Economic reform under Aristide was slow and there was dissent within the cabinet. Progress on judicial reform progressed but investigations into killings stalled. The US Senate consequently blocked disbursement of aid. Mob violence and extra-judicial killings continued, with the new police force unable to cope.

René Préval Presidential elections were held on 17 December 1995. René Préval, a close aide of Aristide's, won a landslide victory with 87% of the vote, although only 25% of the electorate turned out and most opposition parties boycotted the event. He was inaugurated on 7 February 1996. Agreement on a structural adjustment programme was reached with the IMF in May but was hampered by a hostile Congress and not approved until October. Haiti was treated as a political football in the US Senate, which was absorbed in its own presidential race. Aid only dribbled in; civil servants and police were unpaid and there was mounting violence in the streets. The UN Peacekeeping Force was asked to stay for longer as the new police force was unready to take over. Some arrests were made as the Government attempted to move against widespread corruption but nothing could be done about the nationwide violence.

For the first time power was transferred from one elected Haitian President to another.

Rivalries within the ruling coalition, the Lavalas Political Organization, spilled into the open at the end of 1996 when Aristide launched a new group, the Lavalas Family (Fanmi Lavalas), which became a political party in time for the senatorial and local elections, held in April 1997, at which less than 10% of the electorate voted. The major opposition parties boycotted the poll, claiming that the electoral council was controlled by Aristide, and later called for the results to be annulled. The second round of the senatorial elections was postponed indefinitely. It was feared that if the Lavalas Family gained control of the Senate, the reform package would subsequently be blocked.

In November 1997, about 1,200 UN troops began to withdraw, leaving 300 police instructors in place for another year and 400 US troops, who were engaged in construction and health care. Violence and murders continued. The Organisation

Politique Lavalas changed its name to Organisation du Peuple en Lutte (OPL) to distance itself from Fanmi Lavalas (FL), and in February 1998 it dropped its demands to have the April 1997 elections annulled, but other parts of a political deal collapsed within a week. International donors held up millions of dollars of aid with a brake on growth and poverty alleviation.

The new millennium The much-delayed legislative and municipal elections were held in May 2000 and were won overwhelmingly by the FL. Foreign observers described the elections as flawed but credible, but opposition parties denounced the results. Murder and harassment of candidates and their supporters before and during the vote did not prevent the USA and the UN praising the generally peaceful voting process, but certain results were disputed.

Opposition parties boycotted the presidential elections in November 2000 because of the flawed May elections and for the same reason the USA, Canada and the EU refused to send observers. Six candidates were found to stand against Aristide, but none of them campaigned because of pre-election violence. Aristide himself was rarely seen in the years he was out of office, preferring to stay at his walled compound in Tabarre in the north of Port-au-Prince. Official results gave Aristide 92% of the vote and he was inaugurated in February 2001. His party gained 28 of the 29 Senate seats, over 80% of the seats in the Legislature and nearly all the mayoralties and municipalities. Violence did not stop, however. Despite post-election declarations by Aristide for peace and democracy, his supporters continued to carry out violent anti-opposition protests, while the opposition continued to question the legitimacy of the electoral process.

Crisis followed crisis and political instability was accompanied by violence and gang warfare which eventually became a full insurrection. Parts of the country were taken over by rebels, who gradually edged their way towards Port-au-Prince. The USA, France and the Caribbean backed a power-sharing deal, but neither side trusted each other enough to sign. Eventually, under US pressure, Aristide, the country's first democratically elected president, resigned on 29 February 2004 and was flown out of the country on 1 March. Supreme Court Chief Justice Boniface Alexandre was installed as interim President, later replaced by Gerard Latortue, and a Multination Interim Force (MIF) of peace keepers arrived to quell the unrest. The MIF was replaced by a UN Stabilization Force on 1 June and a transitional government was put in place. However, despite the presence of 7000 troops, a year later there were still armed gangs of Aristide supporters who had joined forces with groups of ex-army militia, roaming the streets and terrorizing local people.

Elections for a new government took place on 7 February 2006 and were conducted peacefully. It took ten days for the Provisional Electoral Commission publicly to announce the result, giving René Preval victory with 51.15% of the vote, during which time there were outbreaks of violence. President Preval was inaugurated on 14 May 2006. In the year after he took office improvements were made in the areas of political, economic, and social development, although the main challenges continued to be a lack of security, the fight against extreme poverty, maternal deaths and infant mortality, armed gangs, drug trafficking and the vulnerability of Haitian institutions in general. The United Nations stabilisation mission in Haiti (MINUSTAH) had its mandate renewed at the beginning of 2007 until October 2007 and pursued a policy of action to disperse the criminal gangs by going into the slums and doing battle if necessary.

Geography and people

Haiti is the Caribbean's most mountainous country. Except for a few small, mainly coastal plains and the central Artibonite River valley, the entire country is a mass of ranges. The highest peak is the 2674-m La Selle, southeast of the capital. Little remains of Haiti's once-luxuriant forest cover, cut down for fuel or to make way for farming. With soil erosion and desertification far advanced, Haiti is an ecological disaster. The main regions still regularly receiving abundant rainfall are the southwest peninsula and the eastern two-thirds of the northern seaboard.

About 95% are of almost pure African descent. The rest are mostly mulattos, the descendants of unions between French masters and African slaves, and some are of Arabic descent, who tend to be merchants and shop owners. The Haitian culture is a unique mixture of African and French influences. Haiti was a French colony until 1804

Haiti is a Taíno word meaning 'high ground'.

when black slaves revolted, massacred the French landowners and proclaimed the world's first black republic. Throughout the 19th century Haitians indulged in a succession of bloody, almost tribal wars. Even today African cults, particularly Vodou, play a large part in everyday life like nowhere else in the Caribbean. The country is desperately poor and the standard of living is the lowest in the Americas. According to UNICEF, only 20% of children reach secondary school and, according to a World Bank report, illiteracy was 46% in 2003. Unemployment is believed to be around 80% of the work force. Per capita income is only US$400 a year, with 76% of the population living in poverty. Infant mortality is 80.3 per 1000 live births (2004) and life expectancy is only 51 years. Progress has been made in some areas. The incidence of HIV was running at 6.3% of pregnant women in 2002. Since then the rate has been reduced to less than 4%. Infant mortality has also decreased, but most indicators remain worse than all others in the Americas. The UN has highlighted the deteriorated state of the infrastructure in urban areas, where the roads are very poor and there is a lack of electricity and potable water, as well as a badly degraded environment. Such problems can be largely attributed to political instability and the resulting scarcity of international aid.

Government

Under the terms of the 1993 UN-brokered agreement to restore democracy, Haiti has two legislative houses, a 29-seat Senate and an 83-seat Chamber of Deputies. The parliament, with the elected President as chief of state, came into effect in October 1994. Senators are elected for a 6-year term; Deputies are elected for a four-year term; and the President is elected for a 5-year term.

Economy

Haiti is the western hemisphere's poorest country and among the 30 poorest in the world; 80% of the people fall below the World Bank's absolute poverty level (1998). It is overpopulated. It lacks communications, cheap power and raw materials for industry. Its mountainous terrain cannot provide a living for its rural population.

Until the embargo, the main economic problem was low agricultural productivity, compounded by low world commodity prices. Just 1% of the population controls 40% of the wealth. The average farm size is less than 1 ha. Only a third of the land is arable, yet most of the people live in the country, using tools to grow maize, rice, sorghum and coffee. Deforestation has played havoc with watersheds and agriculture. Only a fraction of the land is now forested, yet charcoal continues to supply 70% of fuel needs. Agriculture generates 30% of the GDP but employs two thirds of the workforce. Coffee is the main cash crop, providing 8% of exports. Sugar and sisal output has slumped as population pressure has forced farmers to switch to subsistence crops. A land reform programme was begun in 1997 in the Artibonite Valley to give land to families in an area where violent land disputes have been common. Agriculture was badly hit by a drought in the northwest in 1997, causing famine in that area. In September 2004 floods from Tropical Storm Jeanne killed more than 3,000 and left some 200,000 homeless in the Artibonite Valley. The devastation was intensified because of the lack of trees and ground cover, which meant flooding and erosion.

Industry and commerce are limited, and heavily concentrated in Port-au-Prince.

Vegetable oils, footwear and metal goods are still produced for domestic
consumption. Manufactured goods make up two-thirds of total exports. Tourism has
all but disappeared, at first because of AIDS, then because of the political instability.

Culture
Although Haiti wiped out slavery in its 18th-century revolution, the country's society
still suffers from slavery's legacies of racial, cultural and linguistic divisions.
Toussaint's tolerant statesmanship was unable to resist Napoleon's push to
reimpose slavery. It took the tyranny and despotism of Dessalines and Christophe.
Haitian despots stepped into the shoes of the French despots. The new mulatto ruling
class considered its French language and culture superior to the blacks' Créole
language and Vodou religion, which it despised. The corruption and despotism of the
black political class created by Duvalier suggest that, despite its profession of
noirisme, it internalized the mulatto contempt for its own race.

Religion Vodou is a blend of religions from West Africa, above all from Dahomey
(present-day Benin) and the Congo River basin. Like Cuba's Santería and Brazil's
Candomblé, it uses drumming, singing and dance to induce possession by powerful
African spirits with colourful personalities. These spirits, called *loas* in Haiti
(pronounced *lwa*), help with life's daily problems. In return, they must be 'served' with
ceremonies, offerings of food and drink, and occasional animal sacrifice in temples
known as *ounphors*. The essence of Vodou is keeping in harmony with the *loas*, the
dead and nature. Magic may be used in self-defence, but those in perfect harmony
with the universe should not need it. Magic in the pursuit of personal ambitions is
frowned upon. The use of black magic and sorcery, or the use of attack magic against
others without just cause, is considered evil. Sorcerers, called *bokors*, exist but they
are not seen as part of Vodou. The *loas* punish *oungans* (Vodou priests) or *mambos*
(priestesses) who betray their vocation by practising black magic. Many Haitians
believe in the existence of *zombis*, the living-dead victims of black magic who are
supposedly disinterred by sorcerers and put to work as slaves.

Vodou acquired an overlay of Catholicism in colonial times, when the slaves
learned to disguise their *loas* as saints. Nowadays, major ceremonies coincide with
Catholic celebrations such as Christmas, Epiphany and the Day of the Dead and
lithographs of Catholic saints are used to represent the *loas*.

The role of attack and defence magic in Haiti's religious culture expanded during
the slave revolts and the Independence War. Many rebel leaders were *oungans*,
including Mackandal, who terrorized the northern plain with his knowledge of
poisons from 1748 to 1758, and Boukman, who plotted the 1791 uprising at a
clandestine Vodou ceremony. Belief in Vodou's protective spells inspired a
fearlessness in battle that amazed the French. As a result, many Haitian rulers saw
Vodou as a threat to their own authority and tried to stamp it out. They also thought its
survival weakened Haiti's claim to membership of the family of 'civilized' nations.
François Duvalier enlisted enough *oungans* to neutralize Vodou as a potential threat.
He also co-opted the hierarchy of the Catholic Church. He had less success with the
Catholic grass roots which, inspired by Liberation Theology, played a key role in his
son's 1986 fall and Aristide's election in 1990. After several ruthless campaigns
against Vodou, most recently in the early 1940s, the Catholic Church has settled into
an attitude of tolerant coexistence. Now the militant hostility to Vodou comes from
fundamentalist Protestant sects of American origin, which have exploited their
relative wealth and ability to provide jobs in order to win converts. In 2003 President
Aristide recognized Vodou as an official religion, thereby allowing *oungans* legally to
accept money for the services they provide as well as to counter the Protestant
missionary zeal.

Language Haitian Créole is the product of the transformation of French in Saint Domingue by African slaves who needed a common language, one that the slave-owners were forced to learn in order to speak to their slaves.

More important is the way in which Créole and French are used now. All Haitians understand Créole and speak it at least part of the time. Use of French is limited to the élite. The illiterate majority of the population understand no French at all. There is almost no teaching in Créole and no attempt is made to teach French as a foreign language to the few Créole-only speakers who enter the school system. Since mastery of French is still a condition for self-advancement, language perpetuates Haiti's class divisions. All those pushing for reform in Haiti are trying to change this. Radio stations have begun using Créole in the last 10 years and musicians now increasingly sing in Créole. The 1987 constitution gave Créole equal official status alongside French and even élite politicians have begun using Créole in speeches. Aristide's sway over the people is due in part to his poetic virtuosity in Créole. A phonetic transcription of Créole has evolved over the last 50 years, but little has been published in the language except the Bible, some poetry and a pro-Aristide newspaper, *Libète*. Créole is famed for its proverbs voicing popular philosophy and reflecting Haiti's enormous social divisions.

❖ Haitian Créole is the only language of 85% of inhabitants. It evolved from French into a distinct language. The other 15% speak Créole and French.

The arts Haitian handicraft and naive art is the best in the Caribbean. Even such utilitarian articles as the woven-straw shoulder bags and the tooled-leather scabbards of the peasant machetes have great beauty. The *rada* (Vodou drum) is an object of great aesthetic appeal. Haiti is famed for its wood carvings, but poverty has pushed craftsmen into producing art from such cheap material as papier maché and steel drums, flattened and turned into cut-out wall-hangings or sculpture. Haitian naive art on canvas emerged only in response to the demand of travellers and tourists in the 1930s and 40s, but it had always existed on the walls of Vodou temples, where some of the best representations of the spirit world are to be found. Weddings, cock fights, market scenes or fantasy African jungles are other favoured themes. Good paintings can range from 100 to several thousand dollars. Mass-produced but lively copies of the masters sell for as little as US$10. Negotiating with street vendors and artists can be an animated experience, offering insights into the nation's personality.

Exposure to white racism during the US occupation shook some of the mulatto intellectuals out of their complacent Francophilia. Led by Jean Price Mars and his 1919 pioneering essay *Ainsi parla l'oncle* (Thus Spoke Uncle) they began to seek their identity in Haiti's African roots. Peasant life, Créole expressions and Vodou started to appear together with a Marxist perspective in novels such as Jacques Romain's *Gouverneurs de la rosée* (Masters of the Dew). René Depestre, now resident in Paris after years in Cuba, is viewed as Haiti's greatest living novelist. Vodou, politics and acerbic social comment are blended in the novels of Gary Victor, a deputy minister in the Aristide Government before the coup.

Music and dance Nigel Gallop writes: The poorest nation in the western hemisphere is among the richest when it comes to music. Its most popular religion worships the deities through singing, drumming and dancing. The prime musical influence is African, and, while European elements are to be found, there are none that are Amerindian. Music and dance can be divided into three main categories: Vodou ritual, rural folk and urban popular. Vodou rituals are collective and profoundly serious, even when the *loa* is humorous or mischievous. The dance is accompanied by call-and-response singing and continuous drumming, the drums themselves (the large *manman*, medium-sized *seconde* and smaller *bula* or *kata*) are regarded as sacred.

During Mardi Gras (Carnival) and Rara (see below), bands of masked dancers and revellers can be found on the roads and in the streets almost anywhere in the country, accompanied by musicians playing the *vaccines* (bamboo trumpets). Haitians also give free rein to their love of music and dance in the so-called Bambouches, social gatherings where the dancing is *pou' plaisi'* (for pleasure) and largely directed towards the opposite sex. They may be doing the Congo, the Martinique or Juba, the Crabienne or the national dance, the Méringue. The first two are of African provenance, the Crabienne evolved from the European Quadrille, while the Méringue is cousin to the Dominican Merengue. Haitians claim it originated in their country and was taken to the Dominican Republic during the Haitian occupation of 1822 to 1844, but this is a matter of fierce debate between the two nations. In remote villages it is still possible to come across such European dances as the Waltz, Polka, Mazurka and Contredanse.

Haitian migrant workers returning from Cuba, the Dominican Republic and elsewhere in the region brought musical influences from elsewhere (as well as exporting its own music to Cuba's Oriente province in the form of the Tumba Francesa). One important external influence was that of the Cuban Son, which gave rise to the so-called 'Troubadour Groups', with their melodious voices and soft guitar accompaniment. Jazz was another intruder, a result of the US Marines' occupation between 1915 and 1934. In the 1950s two equally celebrated composers and band leaders, Nemours Jean-Baptiste and Weber Sicot, introduced a new style of recreational dance music, strongly influenced by the Dominican Merengue and known as Compact Directe (*compas*) or Cadence Rampa. Compas dominated the music scene until the past few years, when it has become a much more open market, with Salsa, Reggae, Soca and Zouk all making big inroads.

A number of Haitian groups have achieved international recognition, notably Tabou Combo and Coupé Cloué, while female singers Martha-Jean Claude and Toto Bissainthe have also made a name for themselves abroad. Also highly recommended is the set of six albums titled *Roots of Haiti*, recorded in the country. Finally, no comment on Haitian music would be complete without reference to the well-known lullaby *Choucounne* which, under the title *Yellow Bird*, is crooned to tourists every night on every English-speaking Antillean island.

Mike Tarr adds: A musical revolution came with 'Vodou beat', a fusion of Vodou drumming and melody with an international rock guitar and keyboard sound. Its lyrics call for political change and a return to peasant values. With albums out on the Island label, and US tours behind them, Boukman Eksperyans is the most successful of these bands. People who have ignored Vodou all their life are seemingly possessed at Boukman concerts. Other 'Vodou beat' bands of note are RAM, Boukan Ginen, Foula, Sanba-Yo and Koudjay, and new bands are springing up all the time RAM remains very popular, as are T-Vice, Sweet Micky, King Posse and Kompa Kreyol.

Flora and fauna

Deforestation and soil erosion have destroyed habitats. Haiti is therefore poor in flora and fauna compared with its eastern neighbour. Lake Saumâtre, 90 minutes east of the capital, is worth visiting. Less brackish than Enriquillo, across the Dominican border, it is the habitat of more than 100 species of waterfowl (including migratory North American ducks), plus flamingos and American crocodiles. The north side of the lake is better, reached via the town of Thomazeau (see page 400).

❖ *There are no poisonous snakes or insects in Haiti.*

Also worthwhile and relatively easy to reach is Parc La Visite, about 5 hours' hike from the hill resort of Kenscoff behind Port-au-Prince. On the high Massif de la Selle, with a mixture of pine forest and montane cloud forest, it has 80 bird species and two endemic mammals, the Hispaniolan hutia (*Plagiodontia aedium*) and the nez longue (*Solenodon paradoxus*). North American warblers winter there. It is also a nesting place for the black-capped petrel (*Pteradoma hasitata*), see page 399. Harder to reach is the Macaya National Park, at the tip of the southwest peninsula, site of Haiti's last virgin cloud forest. It has pines 45 m high, 141 species of orchid, 102 species of fern, 99 species of moss and 49 species of liverwort. Its fauna include 11 species of butterfly, 57 species of snail, 28 species of amphibian, 34 species of reptile, 65 species of bird and 19 species of bat. As well as the hutia, nez longue and black-capped petrel, its most exotic animals are the grey-crowned palm tanager (*Phaenicophilus poliocephalus*) and the Hispaniolan trogan (*Temnotrogan roseigaster*). The endangered peregrine falcon (*Falco pergrinus*) winters in the park. From Les Cayes, it takes half a day to get to a University of Florida base on the edge of the park which has basic camping. Allow two days each way for the 2347 m Pic Macaya (see page 403).

Leaf doctors, Vodou priests and sorcerers have a wealth of knowledge of natural remedies and poisons to be found in Haiti's surviving plant life. They do not share their knowledge readily. In his book *The Serpent and the Rainbow*, Harvard ethnobotanist Wade Davis gives a racy account of his attempts to discover which natural toxins sorcerers are thought to use to turn their victims into *zombis*. Almost any tree is liable to be chopped down for firewood or charcoal; a few very large species are not because they are believed to be the habitat of *loas* (spirits). Chief among them is the silkcotton tree, called *mapou* in Créole.

Books

Fiction

Carpentier, Alejo *El reino de este mundo (The kingdom of this world)*. About Mackandal and Christophe.

Danticat, Edwidge *The Farming of bones*. (1998) Soho Press. A fictional account of the massacre of Haitians in the Dominican Republic in 1937. Also worth reading are *The Dew breaker, Krik! Krak!* and *Breath, eyes, memory*.

Depestre, René *Hadriana dans tous mes rèves*. (1988) Gallimard. Haiti's best-known living writer who grew up in Jacmel where the story is set.

Greene, Graham *The comedians*.

History

Diederich, Bernard and Al Burt *Papa Doc and the Tontons Macoutes*.

James, CLR *The black jacobins*. About Toussaint.

Smartt Bell, Madison *All Souls rising, master of the crossroads*, and *The stone that the builder refused*. An extremely detailed 3-part historical fiction series on the life of Toussaint Louverture.

Travelogue

Thomson, Ian *Bonjour blanc: a journey through Haiti*. (1992) Hutchinson.

Wilentz, Amy *The rainy season: Haiti Since Duvalier*. (1989) Jonathan Cape.

Vodou

Courlander, Harold *The Drum and the hoe.*

Davis, Wade *The serpent and the rainbow.*

Deren, Maya *Divine horsemen.*

McCarthy Brown, Karen *Mama Lola.*

Puerto Rico

ᢒ Footprint features

Introduction

Puerto Rico is a part of the USA and its infrastructure and standard of living is of a higher quality than many other islands. It exhibits an open American way of life yet retains much of the more formal Spanish influences acquired from centuries of Spanish colonial rule. The country is a mixture of the very new and the very old. This is reflected in the architecture, not just the contrast between the colonial and the modern in urban areas but also in the countryside, where older buildings sit side by side with concrete schools and dwellings; it is found in the cuisine, a plethora of fast-food restaurants together with local cooking which has its roots in a hybrid Caribbean culture; and it is found in the music, where rock and salsa are played in beach resorts but where, in the hilly interior, rustic songs of Puerto Rican folklore can still be heard, its music and dance a combination of both Spanish and African rhythms. Huge beach resorts, marinas and golf courses can be found all round the island, while at the other end of the scale there are more campsites on Puerto Rico than in all the rest of the Caribbean islands combined. However, be warned: if you do not stray beyond the tourist areas on the coast, you will have a very one-sided experience of this paradoxical dependent territory. Offshore there are the two sister islands of Vieques and Culebra, laid-back beach retreats well off the beaten track, particularly now there is no US military presence on Vieques and the land it occupied is a national park.

★ Don't miss …

1 San Juan The old walled city sits on a spit of land between the ocean and the bay, its narrow cobbled streets lined with Spanish colonial houses, mansions and churches, all meticulously restored and beautifully painted, page 437.

2 El Yunque Rainforest Hiking trails wind through the forest and up the mountains to waterfalls and pools in what is the largest rainforest in the US forest system; excellent views and birdwatching is rewarding, page 445.

3 Arecibo Observatory The world's largest radio radar telescope is here, operated by Cornell University and open to the public, with a visitor's centre and changing exhibitions, page 451.

4 Culebra National Wildlife Refuge About 40% of the island is park or national reserve, protecting large colonies of breeding seabirds and four species of nesting sea turtles, page 459.

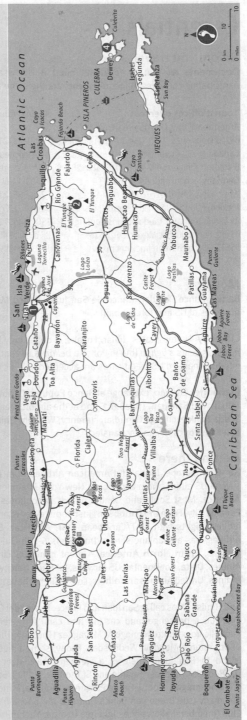

Puerto Rico

Essentials

Before you travel

Documents All non-US residents need a US visa, or a US visa waiver for participating countries. All requirements are the same as for the USA.

Tourist offices overseas

Argentina, Piso 9, Oficina D, Calle Santa Fe 882, Buenos Aires 1059, T(54-11-4) 3144525.

Canada, 6-295 Queen Street East, Suite 465, Brampton, Ontario L6W 4S6, T(416) 5806287.

Germany, Schenkendorfstr 1, 65187 Wiesbaden, T49 611 2676710.

Mexico, Augusto Rodin 299, Desp 1, casi esq Av San Antonio, Col Ciudad de los Deportes, 03710, Benito Juárez, México DF, T(5255) 55632320, ctpr@webtelmex.net.mx.

Spain (France, Italy, Benelux, UK), Calle Serrano, 1-2° izda, 28001, Madrid, T3491-4312128, 00 800 74267426, puertoricoeuro@prtourism.com.

USA, 666 5th Av, 15th floor, New York, NY 10103, T1-800-8667827, 212-5866262, F212-5861212; 901 Ponce de León Blvd, Suite 101, Coral Gables, Fl33134, T305-4459112, F4459450; 3575 W Cahuenga Blvd, Suite 405, Los Angeles, CA90068, T323-8745991, F8747257.

Money

Banks Banco Popular; Banco de San Juan; Banco Mercantil de Puerto Rico; and branches of US and foreign banks.

Currency United States dollar. Locally, a dollar may be called a *peso*, 25 cents a *peseta*, 5 cents a *bellón* (but in Ponce a *bellón* is 10 cents and a *ficha* is 5 cents). Most international and US credit cards are accepted.

Exchange Currency exchange at **Banco Popular; Caribbean Foreign Exchange**, 201B Tetuán, Old San Juan, T7228222, and at the airport; **Deak international** at the airport; **Scotia Bank** exchange Canadian currency; **Western Union**, Pueblo Supermarket, Old San Juan, for cable money transfer.

Getting there

Air From Europe Iberia and **American Airlines** from Madrid; **British Airways** and several US airlines from London via New York, Miami or other US hubs. **From Latin America** Most South and Central American countries are connected via Miami or Panama City. **From the Caribbean** Just about every island is connected with direct or indirect flights with **LIAT/Caribbean Star, American Eagle** and others. **Seaborne Airlines**, has a seaplane service from Piers 6-7 in Old San Juan to St Croix and St Thomas. **From North America** A great many US cities are served by **American Airlines, Delta, Continental, US Airways, Jet Blue, Northwest Airlines, North American Airlines, United Airlines** and others. Lots of flights have connections at JFK and Miami.

Sea Cruise ships call at San Juan and Ponce. **Ferries del Caribe** ① *T8324800, see page 297*, run a passenger and car (no hire cars) ferry service to/from the Dominican Republic from Santo Domingo to Mayagüez (Tuesday, Thursday, Sunday 2000, arrives 0800; returns Monday, Wednesday, Friday, same times) with a bus link across the island to San Juan. There is a weekend passenger launch on the **Caribe Cay** ① *T8608809*, between Fajardo and St Thomas, 1³/₄ hrs, Saturday 0830, US$70 return.

  Anchorages Boquerón, La Parguera, Guánica, Ponce, Fajardo, Vieques, Culebra has many (see Bruce Van Sant's *Guide to the Spanish Virgin Islands*). Ponce Yacht Club (members) allows one night free to other Yacht Club members.

Boat documents Clearance required from Customs, Immigration and
Agriculture. Boats arriving from outside Puerto Rico's territorial waters should contact Customs 24 hours in advance. Foreigners must meet same entry requirements as into USA. Sailors may pick up a free 12-month cruising permit in the USVI. If you don't get one there, you will have to buy one when you arrive in Puerto Rico. The cost is US$37 for non-US ships and US$25 for US ships. This fee exempts sailors from other customs charges for one calendar year. Overtime fees will be charged outside working hours of 0900-1600 Mon-Sat. US citizens must clear into Puerto Rico when coming from the US or USVI. Do not bring in fruit, vegetables or garbage into the USA/Puerto Rico. Boats and firearms must be registered after 60 days.

Marinas There is a liveaboard community at Boquerón. Ponce is a good place to provision, with wholesale houses, **Sears, Walmart,** nearby. Fajardo is headquarters for marinas, boat supplies and haul-out. Puerto del Rey marina has 750 slips, transient rate US$1 per foot per day (includes water, electricity, cable TV); Palmas del Mar, 40 slips, also many houses on the water have space to rent with water and electricity. Small anchorage area has cleaner water than stagnant marina. Nothing nearby, car rental needed.

Ports of entry Mayagüez (Customs T8313368), Ponce (T8413130), Fajardo (T8630950), San Juan (not Boquerón) (T7296850).

Weather VHF weather, VI Radio or local AM station.

Touching down

Airport information There are airport limousines to a number of hotels. Set rates for *Taxi Turístico*: Zone 1, Luis Muñoz Marín Airport to Isla Verde, US$8; Zone 2, airport to Condado/Miramar, US$12; Zone 3, airport to Pier area in Old San Juan, US$16. Between and beyond the zones rates are metered.

Airlines
Air Caraïbes, T877-7721005.
Air St Thomas, T800-5223084.
American Airlines and American Eagle, T800-4337300.
American Trans Air, T800-2252995.
Continental, T800-2310856.
COPA, T800-3592672.

Delta, T800-2211212.
Iberia, T800-7724642.
Isla Nena, T877-8125144.
LIAT/Caribbean Star, T7913838.
Northwest Airlines, T800-3747747.
Seaborne Airlines, T888-3598687.
United Airlines, T800-2416522.
Vieques Air Link, T888-9019247.

Tourist information Local tourist offices The **Puerto Rico Tourism Company** ① *La Princesa Building, 2 Paseo La Princesa, San Juan, T00902-3960, www.gotopuertorico .com*, publishes lots of brochures and booklets including *Travel and Sports Planner* (www.travelandsports.com) and *Qué Pasa!* (www.travelandsports.com/quepasa) which comes out every two months and has a useful tourist directory. Information centres also at the **international airport** ① *T7911014; next to the Condado Plaza Hotel, T7212400, ext 2280;* **La Casita** ① *near Pier One, Old San Juan, T7221709, Mon-Wed 0830-2000, Thu and Fri 0830-1730, Sat and Sun 0900-2000;* **Rafael Hernández Airport** ① *Aguadilla, T8903315;* **Citibank Building** ① *53 McKinley East, facing plaza, Mayagüez, T8315220;* **Casa Armstrong-Proventud** ① *Plaza Las Delicias, Ponce, T8405695.*

Regional tourist offices Adjuntas, T8292590; Añasco, T8263100, ext 272; Bayamón, T7988191; Cabo Rojo, T8517015; Camuy, T8982240; Culebra, T7423291; Dorado, T796-5740/1030; Fajardo, T8634013; Guanica, T8212777; Jayuya, T8285010; Luquillo, T8892851; Naguabo, T8740389; Rincón, T8235024; Vieques, T7415000. Out in the country, tourist information can be obtained from the town halls, usually found on the main plaza. Hours are usually Monday to Friday, 0800-1200, 1300-1430.

⦂ Touching down

Business hours **Banks**: 0830-1430, some have extended hours. **Shops**: mostly Mon-Sat 0900-2100 , Sun 1100-1700.
Currency US dollar.
Emergency numbers Tourist Zone Police, Vieques St, Condado, T7220738, 7245210, can help you settle problems with taxis. Emergency T911.
Country code +787/939.
Language Spanish is the first language with less than 30% of the population speaking English fluently.
Official time GMT minus 4 hours.
Safety We have received several warnings from travellers. Of all crimes 65% are related to drugs trafficking. La Perla is known as San Juan's most dangerous slum and the end of Calle Tanca should be avoided as it is a favourite drinking

and drug-dealing area for residents. Female tourists should avoid the Condado beach areas at night and all areas of San Juan can be dangerous after dark. Take precautions against theft from your person and your car, wherever you are on the island. Hiking on mainland beaches is not a good idea; never stay on a beach if you are alone, beautiful areas such as Carite or Route186 above El Verde look like great hiking spots but do not always attract people with good intentions. Look for safety in numbers and take advice locally.
Tipping Service is usually included in the bill, but where no fixed service charge is included, it is recommended that 15-20% is given to waiters, taxi drivers, etc.
Voltage US system, 110 volts AC.
Weights and measures Imperial.

Maps The *Rand McNally* road map is recommended; the *Gousha* road map is sold at Texaco stations. The tourist office distributes an *Official Transportation Map* with town maps of San Juan, Caguas, Ponce, Mayagüez, Aguadilla and Arecibo.

Getting around

Air Several local airlines operate services within Puerto Rico, including **American Eagle** and **Vieques Air Link,** and have offices either at the **Luis Muñoz Marín International Airport**, or the **Isla Grande Airport.** There are three daily **American Eagle** flights between San Juan and Ponce and several to Mayagüez. Some charter or inter-island flights leave from the Isla Grande Airport.

Bus Bus stops are marked *Parada*, or *Parada de guaguas*. From the terminal near Plazoleta del Puerto in Old San Juan, **B21** goes along the upper road along the ocean (near **Caribe Hilton**) to Condado (Condado Plaza, El Canario) then up Avenida de Diego to stop 18 on Ponce de León, and then to Plaza las Américas Shopping Mall. **A5** goes along to Ponce de León and then down Avenida de Diego to Isla Verde (**El San Juan, Ritz Carlton,** etc) and to Iturregui terminal. To get to the airport by bus from Old San Juan is complicated. Take **A5** bus to Isla Verde terminal, then **C45** or **B40** to the airport. From Condado take **B21** to Avenida de Diego, then **A5,** then as above. **Metrobus 1** (US$0.50) goes from Old San Juan along the upper road along the ocean to Avenida Ponce de León and then to Río Piedras. **Metrobus E** goes to Río Piedras via the express way to Hato Rey. Long-distance buses run to all the major towns, leaving from their own bus stations in San Juan.

⦂ *City buses run to a 30- or 45-minute schedule and cost US$0.25. Many don't operate after 2200.*

Car There are many car rental agencies, including at the airport: **Hertz,** T800-6543131, www.hertz.com; **Budget,** T800-5270700, www.budget.com; **AAA,** T7912609,

T7281447, www.targettrentacar.com), not at airport, among the cheapest, will negotiate rates, Mon-Sat 0900-1900, Sun 0800-1700. **Charlie's Rental**, T800-2891227, www.charliecars.com, in Condado and Isla Verde among the cheapest, 24-hour service. **L & M**, T800-6660807, www.lmcarrental.com, free pick-up, make sure you get it even for day hire, daily 0600-2400. For the less mobile, **Wheelchair Getaway**, T7264023, 800-8688028, has vehicles which can accommodate a wheelchair, daily 0800-2200. A small car may be hired for as little as US$25 (not including collision damage

❖ *This is the best form of transport if you want to see the island; public transport is not always easy and finishes early.*

waiver, US$12.50, insurance is sometimes covered by your credit card) for 24 hours, unlimited mileage (national driving licence preferred to international licence), but rates vary according to company and demand.

A good map is essential because there are few signs to places, but there are frequent indications of Route numbers and intersections. Avoid driving in the San Juan metropolitan area as traffic can be very heavy. Car theft and burglar damage is a major problem in the San Juan area. Make sure you use all the security devices provided by the rental company. Many people actually recommend that you do not stop at red lights after 2200, because of hold-ups; just pause, look and go. Best not to drive at night at all; lock car doors.

Taxi All taxis are metered, charge US$1.75 for initial charge and US$0.10 for every additional 1/19 mile; US$0.50 for each suitcase, US$1 for the fourth and subsequent cases; US$1 reservation charge, surcharge 2200-0600 US$1. Minimum fee US$3. US$36 hourly rental charge. Taxi drivers sometimes try to ask more from tourists, so beware, insist that the meter is used, and avoid picking up a taxi anywhere near a cruise ship. If they refuse, tell them you will call Puerto Rico Tourist Zone Police, T7220738, or the Public Service Commission, T7515050, ext 253. They can revoke a taxi licence. White tourist taxis with a logo on the side offer fixed rates to and from tourist sites, for example airport, San Juan Pier, but outside those areas they are metered. Piers to Old San Juan, US$7; Piers to Condado/Miramar, US$12; Piers to Isla Verde, US$19; Airport to Isla Verde US$10; Airport to Piers/Old San Juan US$19.

Públicos There are also shared taxis, usually Ford minibuses (*carros públicos*) which have yellow number plates with the letters P or PD at the end and run to most parts of the island from one main plaza to the next. They usually carry about 10 people and are not particularly comfortable. The Río Piedras *terminal de públicos* handles all departures to the east. Many *públicos* for the west leave from *puntos* near parada

❖ *Be prepared to wait a couple of hours for the car to fill up.*

18 in Santurce. Also some leave from the main post office and others collect at the airport; elsewhere, ask around for the terminal. They do not usually operate after about 1600 and some connections do not operate after 1500, for example Río Piedras-Fajardo. They are also very scarce on Sunday and public holidays. *Público* to Caguas costs US$1.25; Río Piedras-Fajardo 1½ hours (US$3); to Ponce takes 2 hours (US$6-7). A service referred to as *línea* will pick up and drop off passengers where they wish. They operate between San Juan, and most towns and cities at a fixed rate. They can be found in the phone book under *Líneas de Carros*.

Train An urban elevated rail service has been constructed in San Juan and service began in June 2005 after a few months' trial, 3 years late and US$900 mn over budget. Phase 1 runs along 10 miles of track from Santurce to Guaynabo and Bayamón, stopping at 16 stations, US$1.50.

The summer season runs from 16 April to 14 December and is somewhat cheaper than the winter season. An 11% tax is charged on the room rate in hotels with casinos, 9% in those without casinos, 7% in *paradores* and there is a US$3pp per night city tax in San Juan. There are many large, resort hotels managed by international chains but smaller, more intimate hotels and guesthouses can be found around the island. Cheap hotels are very hard to find, there is nothing under about US$45 double, and single rates are often non-existent. Campsites (see below) are the only budget option, but you will probably need a hired car to reach them, which will increase the cost of your holiday.

There are **Paradores Puertorriqueños** to put you up while touring, some old, most new, some quiet and peaceful (for example **Coamo, Gripiñas, Juanita, Casa Grande**), some used by local families for boisterous entertainment, with prices at US$55-100.The majority are to the west of San Juan; for reservations T7212884 or from the USA T1-800-4430266. Many *paradores* are not what the average traveller wants, so research first. They are convenient when on the road, but lack the old charm of their Spanish counterparts. The cheapest is in motels, but these are generally used by 'couples'.

Camping Camping is permitted in the forest reserves; you usually have to get a permit in advance (see below) although often they are available at the sites themselves. Camping is also allowed on some of the public beaches. Government agencies expect everyone to arrive or call before 1500. You can take *públicos* to some of the camping places, but with difficulty, car rental is advised.

The Government agency **Compañía de Parques Nacionales** (CPNPR) ⓘ T6225200, ext 8700 for reservations, www.parquesnacionalespr.com, administers campgrounds, cabins and balnearios. Two-bedroom cabins and villas are offered on five of their beaches, villas are newer and nicer. They have two rates, depending on the location. 2007 rates for *localización regular* cabins were US$65.40 and for villas US$109, while *localización especial* (on the beach, pool) cabins were US$71 and villas were US$115. Internet bookings can be made for villas and cabins at the **Centro Vacacional de Boquerón** (Cabo Rojo), **Centro Vacacional Punta Guilarte** (Arroyo), **Centro Vacacional Punta Santiago** (Humacao), **Centro Vacacional Villas de Añasco** (Añasco) and the **Centro Vacacional Monte del Estado** (Maricao). Other campsites include **Parque Nacional La Monserrate** (Luquillo), **Parque Nacional Seven Seas** (Fajardo), **Parque Nacional Sun Bay** (Vieques), **Parque Nacional Tres Hermanos** (Añasco), **Parque Nacional Punta Guilarte** (Arroyo), **Parque Nacional Cavernas del Río Camuy** (Camuy), **Parque Nacional Cerro Gordo** (Vega Alta) and **Parque Nacional Monte del Estado** (Maricao), where bare camp sites are usually US$10, with water US$13, with water and electricity, when available US$17 and car parking US$3. The CPNPR also administers 12 balnearios, with parking, lifeguards, showers, toilets, restaurants and other facilities.

The **Negociado del Servicio Forestal** (part of the Departamento de Recursos Naturales y Ambientales – DRNA) ⓘ *PO Box 9066600, Puerta de Tierra, San Juan, Puerto Rico 00906-6600, T7243724, F7215984*, administers eight campgrounds and cabins and trips to Mona Island. You need a permit and reservation, fee US$4 per person per night (prices for cabins may vary), easiest to go to their office at **Club Náutico** by the marina at the Dos Hermanos bridges on the way to Old San Juan. They will also help you plan an itinerary. Permits and changes to reservations can be made at regional offices Their campgrounds are: **Carite Forest** (two campgrounds in the forest, near Lake Carite where there is fishing), **Toro Negro Forest Reserve** (camp site near lakes where you can fish), **Guilarte Forest Reserve** (no camping but basic cabins available in eucalyptus forest, no electricity, barbeque facilities), **Coamo Hot Springs**, **Lago Luchetti**, **Susua Dry Forest** (good hiking and beaches), **Guánica Forest**, **Guajataca Forest** (camping on Lake Guajataca, dozens of trails and footpaths, fly

> ❖ *Forest reserves campsites are safer than beach ones; large groups are recommended.*

fishing, kayaking on lakes and rivers), **Río Abajo Forest** (good campground, caves and
lake nearby), **Cambalache Beach** (camping in the forest reserve in two areas, water,
showers, 8 trails, good mountain biking, beach nearby). **El Yunque rainforest**
ⓘ *www.elyunque.com*, is administered by the **US Forest Service** ⓘ *T8881880,
www.fs.fed.us, and ask for camping information, or get free permit at El Portal, Route
191, north side, before 1600. Take rain gear as you are bound to get wet.* The
Autoridad de Conservación y Desarrollo de Culebra (ACC) ⓘ *PO Box 217, Culebra, PR
00775, T7420700*, administers the Flamenco Beach campgrounds on Culebra (US$10
per tent per night); they often accept walk-in reservations in winter but in summer,
especially at weekends, it is like a zoo. Bus into town, toilets available but no drinking
water, no food, security guards at night. There are also some private campgrounds
listed in Sleeping, below.

Eating
Food Good local dishes are the mixed stew *asopao*, (chicken, seafood, etc).
Mofongo, mashed plantain with garlic served instead of rice, is very filling. *Mofongo
relleno* is the *mofongo* used as a crust around a seafood stew.
Sancocho is a beef stew with various root vegetables, starchy but
tasty. *Empanadillas* are similar to South American *empanadas*
but with a thinner dough and filled with fish or meat. *Pasteles* are
yucca, peas, meat, usually pork, wrapped in a banana leaf and
boiled. *Tostones* are fried banana slices. Rice is served with many dishes; *arroz con
habichuelas* (rice with red kidney beans) is a standard side dish. *Provisiones* are root
vegetables and are worth trying. *Comida criolla* means 'food of the island', *criollo*
refers to anything 'native'.

Mesones Gastronómicos, a network of 42 restaurants outside San Juan, serve Puerto Rican dishes.

Some local fruit names: *china* is orange, *parcha* passionfruit, *guanábana*
soursop, *toronja* grapefruit; juices are made of all these, as well as guava, tamarind
and mixtures. *Papaya* in a restaurant may not be fresh fruit, but *dulce de papaya*
(candied), served with cheese.

Drink Local beers are *Medalla* (a light beer), *Gold Label* (a premium beer) and *Indio*
(a dark beer); a number of US brands and *Heineken* are brewed under licence. Rums
include *Don Q*, the local favourite, *Palo Viejo*, *Ron Llave* and the world-famous *Bacardi*
(not so highly regarded by puertorriqueños). *Ron Barrilito*, a small distillery, has a very
good reputation. *Maví* is a drink fermented from the bark of a tree and sold in many
snack-bars. Home-grown Puerto Rican coffee is very good.

Keeping in touch
Post Inside the post office in Hato Rey, on Avenida Roosevelt is a separate counter
for sales of special tourist stamps. In Old San Juan, the post office is on Cruz and
Fortaleza. Stamps may be bought at hotels and the airport. *Poste restante* is called
General Delivery, letters are held for nine days. For more information, www.usps.com.

Telephone and internet Numbers with area code 800, 888, 877 or 866 are toll free
from Puerto Rico or the USA. Most hotel systems are compatible with dial-up modems
and there are internet cafés in San Juan.
Local calls from coin-operated booths cost US$0.10, or US$0.25 from a private
pay phone, but from one city to another on the island costs more
(for example US$1.25 Ponce-San Juan). Local calls from hotel
rooms cost US$2.60 and often a charge is made even if there is
no connection. Payphones now charge a fee of US$0.25, either
deducted from your prepaid card or with a coin. The cheapest
way to phone abroad is from **Phone Home**, 257 Recinto Sur, Old
San Juan, T7215431, F7215497, opposite the post office by Pier 1, US$0.36 per min to

To call outside San Juan from the metropolitan area dial 1-787 and then the number.

Puerto Rico Essentials

the USA, discounts on all other calls abroad, no 3-min minimum charge, faxes also sent and received. Overseas calls can be made from the **AT&T** office at Parada 11, Avenida Ponce de León 850, Miramar (opposite **Hotel Excelsior**, bus T1 passes outside, a chaotic place), from an office next to the Museo del Mar on Pier One, and from the airport. Three minutes to New York, US$1.50 and to the UK, US$3. For Canada Direct, dial 1-800-4967123 to get through to a Canadian operator.

Media Newspapers: *San Juan Star* is the only daily English paper. There are two Spanish daily papers of note, *El Vocero* and *El Nuevo Día*.

Radio: There are 7 radio stations: WDAC-FM, 105.7FM Alfa Rock 106; WKAQ-FM, 104.7FM KQ105; WIOA-FM 99.9FM Cadena Estereotempo; WMEG-FM, 106.9FM La Mega Estación; WDOY-FM, 96.5FM Y-96; WOYE-FM, 94.7FM Cosmos 94; WOSO-AM, 1030AM Radio Woso.

Festivals and events

Jan New Year's Day (1 Jan), Three Kings' Day (6 Jan), De Hostos' Birthday (11 Jan).

22 Feb Washington's Birthday.

22 Mar Emancipation Day.

Mar/Apr Good Fri.

16 Apr José de Diego's Birthday.

May Every town/city has local holidays for crop-over festivals (pineapple, tobacco, sugar cane, etc) and for celebration of the town's saint. These festivals can be great fun, especially the **Carnival in Mayagüez** (late May). **Memorial Day** (30 May).

May/Jun Another annual music festival in is the **Puerto Rico Heineken JazzFest**, held in the open-air Tito Puente Amphitheatre, T2779200, www.prheinekenjazz.com. Founded in 1990, this also attracts international artists in Latin and contemporary jazz.

Jun St John the Baptist (24 Jun), one of the most important festivals; the capital grinds to a halt the previous afternoon and everyone heads for the beach where there is loud salsa music and barbecues until midnight when everyone walks backwards into the sea to greet the Baptist and ensure good fortune. For lovers of classical music, there is the annual **Casals Festival**, which brings orchestras from all over the world for a couple of weeks of concerts at the Luis A Ferré Performing Arts Center. The festival was founded in 1957 by Pablo Casals, who created the Puerto Rican Symphony Orchestra and the Musical Conservatory. Tickets range from US$20-40, with a 50% discount for senior citizens, while children under 12 are free if accompanied by an adult, T7217727 for information, www.artes-musicales.com.

Jul Independence Day (4 Jul). Muñoz Rivera's Birthday (17 Jul). Constitution Day (25 Jul). Día de la Constitución (weekend near 25 Jul) and it is almost impossible to get a hotel room. Reserve in advance. Dr José Celso Barbosa's Birthday (27 Jul).

1 Sep Labour Day.

Oct Columbus Day (12 Oct). Veterans' Day (11 Nov). Discovery of Puerto Rico (19 Nov). Thanksgiving Day (25 Nov).

26 Dec Christmas Day.

Shopping

Puerto Rico is a large producer of rum, with many different types (see above). Handmade cigars can be found in Old San Juan and Puerta de Tierra. There is a place in the bus station complex in San Juan where cigars are rolled using Dominican leaf, which is better than local leaf. Shopping malls include **Plaza las Américas** in Hato Rey (the largest in the Caribbean with 300 stores, 21 cinemas, restaurants and other services, Monday to Saturday 0900-2100, Sunday 1100-1700), others include **Plaza Carolina** in Carolina, **Río Hondo** in Levittown, **Plaza del Carmen** in Caguas and **Mayagüez Mall** in Mayagüez. There are many souvenir shops in Old San Juan. Local *artesanías* include wooden carvings, musical instruments, lace, ceramics (especially model house fronts, for example from **La Casa de Las Casitas**, Cristo 250), hammocks,

❧ Many of the tourist shops in the old city sell Andean goods.

masks and basketwork. It is more interesting to visit the workshops around Puerto
Rico. Contact the **Centro de Artes Populares** ① *T7246250*, or the **Tourism Company Artisan Office** ① *T7212891*, for details of the 681 artisans on the list.

Sport and activities

Diving The shallow waters are good for snorkelling and while a boat is needed to reach deeper water for most scuba diving, divers can walk in at Isabela. Visibility is not as good as in some other islands because of the large number of rivers flowing out to the sea, but is generally around 70 ft. However, an advantage is that the freshwater attracts a large number of fish. Manatees can occasionally be seen and humpback whales migrate through Puerto Rican waters in the autumn.

There are many companies all round the island offering boat dives, equipment rental and diving instruction. Diving is also available at some of the larger hotels. Companies in San Juan and to the east also dive Culebra and Vieques, but there are dive shops on those islands if you want to avoid long boat rides. Check how many divers are taken on the boats, some companies cater for small groups of six or seven divers, but several of the larger operations take out parties of 40 or 80. Look for instructor's certificate, motor boat operator's licence and coast guard inspection sticker on the boat. If any are missing you will not be insured. The inspection sticker on the boat specifies how many paying passengers are allowed. Also check what sort of diving is offered. Some concentrate on the cruise ship market and quick thrills such as fish feeding, which can upset the balance of fish and encourage the more aggressive species.

Fishing Deep-sea fishing is popular and more than 30 world records have been broken in Puerto Rican waters, where blue and white marlin, sailfish, wahoo, dolphin, mackerel and tarpon, to mention a few, are a challenge to the angler. An international bill fish competition is held in August at the **Club Náutico de San Juan** ① *T7220177*, one of the biggest tournaments in the Caribbean and the longest consecutively held big-game fishing tournament in the world. Fishing boat charters are available: for example **Mike Benítez Fishing Charters Inc** ① *Club Náutico de San Juan, T7232292 (till 2100), 7246265 (till 1700)*. Also **Caribbean Outfitters** ① *T3968346, www.fishinginpuertorico.com*. Others around the island are mentioned in the text below. Contact the **Department of Natural Resources** ① *T7248774, ext 445, for details*.

Golf There are 19 golf courses around the island, many of which are professionally designed championship courses. The **Hyatt Cerromar** and **Hyatt Dorado** hotels ① *T7968915, www.hyatt.com*, in Dorado have four excellent 36-hole championship golf courses; among the 18-hole courses, **Berwind Country Club** ① *T8763056*, accepts non-members on Tuesday, Thursday and Friday; **Palmas del Mar** ① *Humacao, T2852221, www.palmasdelmar.com*, **Westin Riomar** ① *Río Grande, T8886000*, and **Punta Borinquén** ① *Aguadilla, 9 holes, T8902987*, all have golf pros and are open to the public.

Horse riding Riding is a good way to see the island. Puerto Rico also prides itself on its paso fino horses. There are over 7,000 registered paso fino horses on the island and several horse shows are held. The two best known are the **Dulce Sueño Fair**, Guayama, the first weekend in March, and the **Fiesta La Candelaria**, Manatí, the first weekend in February. At **Palmas del Mar**, Humacao, there is an **equestrian centre** ① *T8528888*, with beach rides and riding and jumping lessons. **Tropical Trail Rides** ① *Route 4466, Km 1.8, Isabela, T8729256, www.tropicaltrailrides.com, US$35 for 2 hrs*, Craig Barker has 20 beautiful paso fino horses, about 1½ hours west of San Juan, beach, forest and cliff trails. At the **El Conquistador Resort** complex ① *T8631000*, ask for Richard and the ferry to the horses on Isla Palominos.

Sailing There are marinas at **Fajardo**, **Puerto del Rey**, the **Club Náutico** at Miramar and another at **Boca de Cangrejos** in Isla Verde (both in San Juan) and one at the **Palmas del Mar Resort** near Humacao. There is a marina for fishing boats at **Arecibo**. Sailing is popular, with winds of about 10-15 knots all year round. Craft of all sizes are available for hire. There are several racing tournaments. Power boats appeal to the Puerto Rican spirit and there are a lot of races, held mostly off the west coast from Mayagüez Bay to Boquerón Bay. A huge crowd collects for the Caribbean Offshore Race, with professionals and celebrities participating.

Puerto Rico's coastline is protected in many places by coral reefs and cays which are fun to visit and explore. **La Cordillera** is a nature reserve of cays and rocks off the northeast tip of Puerto Rico, including Icacos, Diablo, Ratones and Las Cucarachas, which have a rich coral reef, clear water and sandy beaches. There is an abandoned limestone quarry on the south side of Icacos. The cays are easily accessible by boat from Las Croabas or Fajardo.There are many sailboat excursions from Fajardo with snorkelling, lunch and drinks, usually US$55 per person on catamarans (also known as cattlemarans taking 49 people), more on the monohulls. Also sailboats from Marina del Rey, San Juan and **La Parguera**.

Snorkelling Luquillo Beach has two snorkelling spots: in town, off the point between the surfers' beach, **La Pared** and **Blue Beach** (the beach in front of the tallest condos), and at the point of the Balneario Luquillo, past the 'no swimming' signs (beware of current, and jet skis at weekends). **Seven Seas Beach** has some good snorkelling right off the beach and there are reefs to the east. **Caribe Kayak Tours & More** ① *near Fajardo, T8897734, www.pinacolada.net/caribekayak*, specialize in small groups for snorkelling and kayaking (ocean and Lagoon) starting from Seven Seas Beach. Many dive shops will also take you snorkelling.

> **‡** *Be aware of jet skis and other motorized craft when snorkelling: they will be oblivious of you.*

Spectator sports **Cockfighting** season is from 1 November to 31 August and is held at the new, a/c **Coliseo Gallístico** ① *Route 37, Km 1.5, T7911557, on Sat 1300-1900, admission from US$4-10*, in Isla Verde, near the Holiday Inn. **Horse racing** at **El Comandante** ① *Route 3, Km 15.3, T8762450*. Canóvanas is one of the hemisphere's most beautiful race courses. Races are held all the year round (Wednesday, Friday, Sunday and holidays 1415-1730; Wednesday is Ladies' Day; children under 12 not admitted). **Polo** is popular and the **Ingenio Polo Club** hosts the Rolex Polo Cup on its 25-acre grounds by the Loiza River in March. Popular sports are **boxing** and **baseball** (at professional level, also a winter league at **San Juan stadium** ① *US$4 for a general seat, US$5 box seat, Tue is Ladies' Night*), **basketball**, **volleyball** and **beach volleyball**.

Surfing The most popular beaches for surfing are the **Pine Beach Grove** in Isla Verde (San Juan), **Jobos** (near Isabela in the northeast, not the south coast bay), **La Pared** in Luquillo, officially listed as dangerous for swimming but used for surfing tournaments, **Surfer** and **Wilderness** beaches in the former Ramey Field air base at Punta Borinquén, north of Aguadilla and **Punta Higuero**, Route 413 between Aguadilla and Rincón on the west coast. Several international surfing competitions have been held at Surfer and Wilderness.

Swimming Swimming from most beaches is safe; the best beaches near San Juan are those at **Isla Verde** in front of the main hotels; **Luquillo** to the east of San Juan is less crowded and has a fine-sand beach from where there are good views of El Yunque (controlled car parking, US$3 per car all day, if arriving by *público* from San Juan, ask to get off at Balneario Luquillo, which is 1 km west of the town). There are showers, toilets and lifeguards, food kiosks and souvenir shops, it is peaceful during the week but noisy at weekends. The north coast

> **‡** *Never leave anything unattended on the beaches in Puerto Rico; if you are alone it is probably best to leave.*

Atlantic sea is rougher than the east and south waters, particularly in winter; some beaches are semi-deserted. There are 13 *balneario* beaches round the island where lockers, showers and parking places are provided for a small fee. Some have cabins, tent sites or trailer sites. *Balnearios* are open Tuesday to Sunday 0900-1700 in winter and 0800-1700 in summer. Some of Puerto Rico's beaches have Blue Flag status.

Tennis Over 100 tennis courts are available, mostly in the larger hotels. There are also 17 lit public courts in San Juan's Central Park, open daily, with tennis pro, T7221646. The **Palmas del Mar** resort, at Humacao, has 20 courts.

Windsurfing The **Condado lagoon** is calm with steady winds and is popular for windsurfing, as is **Boquerón Bay**, off Isla Verde beach, and **Ocean Park beach**. Only experts can cope with conditions on the northeast shore near Aguadilla: **Jobos**, **Wilderness** and **Surfer** beaches, where the winds are good and the waves break with excellent shape. **Rincón** is the same. **La Parguera** is great for slalom conditions, a great sail to Cayo Enrique on waters with lots of wind.

Health

La monga is a common, flu-like illness, nothing serious, it goes away after a few days. Avoid swimming in rivers; bilharzia may be present. There has been dengue fever, so take care not to get bitten by mosquitoes; the northeast coast is particularly risky.
➤➤ *See also Health, page 38.*

San Juan → *Phone code: 787. Colour map 2, B5. Population: about 1 million.*

Founded in 1510, San Juan, the capital, spreads several kilometres along the north coast and also inland. The nucleus is Old San Juan, the old walled city on a tongue of land between the Atlantic and San Juan bay. It has a great deal of charm and character, a living museum, lovingly restored. The narrow streets of Old San Juan, some paved with small grey-blue cobblestones which were brought over as ships' ballast, are lined with colonial churches, houses and mansions, in a very good state of repair and all painted different pastel colours. Although the old city is lovely, the rest of San Juan is modern, sprawling, without a semblance of planning and devoid of attractive features. The beach resorts are massive, high-rise, expensive and international in character. ➤➤ *For Sleeping, Eating and other listings, see pages 441-445.*

Ins and outs

Getting there Getting a taxi from the airport is your best bet; buses from the airport to San Juan and back are complicated. There is a despatch desk for *públicos* at the airport. ➤➤ *See also page 429.*

Getting around Small yellow buses, or trolleys, run around the old city all day 0600-2200, free. They start from La Puntilla and Covadonga public car parks. There is also a trolley service in the Isla Verde beach area from Punta Las Marías. There is a city bus (*guagua*) service with a fixed charge of US$0.25 for standard route, US$0.50 for longer. They have special routes, sometimes against the normal direction of traffic, in which case the bus lanes are marked by yellow and white lines. Bus stops *paradas* have white and orange signs or yellow and black notices on lampposts. Up until the 1950s tramcars ran between Río Piedras and Old San Juan along Avenidas Ponce de León and Fernández Juncos. To this day directions are given by *Paradas*, or tram stops, so you have to find out where each one is.

One of the restored and interesting buildings to visit is **La Fortaleza** ① *T7217000 ext 2211, Mon-Fri 0900-1600, guided tours in English on the hour, in Spanish every 30 mins*, the Governor's Palace, built between 1533 and 1540 as a fortress against Carib attacks but greatly expanded in the 19th century. It is believed to be the oldest executive residence in continuous use in the Western Hemisphere. Access to the official areas is not permitted. The **cathedral** ① *daily 0630-1700*, was built in the 16th century but extensively restored in the 19th and 20th centuries. The body of Juan Ponce de León rests in a marble tomb. The tiny **Cristo Chapel** ① *Tue 1000-1600*, with its silver altar, was built after a young man competing in 1753 in a horse race during the San Juan festival celebrations plunged with his horse over the precipice at that very spot. Next to it is the aptly named **Parque de las Palomas**, where the birds perch on your hand to be fed. This practice is best avoided, however, as we have heard of people contracting a lung virus and ending up in hospital. **San Felipe del Morro** ① *T7296777, www.nps.gov/saju, daily 0900-1700, US$3 for adults or US$5 for both forts, children 15 and under free, annual or senior passes available, tours in English at 1100 and 1500*, was built in 1591 to defend the entrance to the harbour, and the 11-ha **Fort San Cristóbal** ① *T7296777, www.nps.gov/saju, daily 0900-1700, US$3 for adults or US$5 for both forts, valid 7 days, tours in English at 1000 and 1400*, was completed in 1772 to support El Morro and to defend the landward side of the city, with its five independent units connected by tunnels and dry moats, rising 46 m above the ocean. There are good views of the city. Next to El Morro is the **St Mary Magdalene** cemetery, also called the San Juan cemetery, which is beautiful and well worth a visit, though crowded. The **Plaza del Quinto Centenario**, inaugurated on 12 October 1992 to commemorate the 500th anniversary of Columbus' landing, is a modernistic square on several levels with steps leading to a central fountain with hundreds of jets (good view of El Morro, the cemetery and sunsets). The restored **Cuartel de Ballajá**, once the barracks for Spanish troops and their families, was also inaugurated 12 October 1992 to house the **Museum of the**

San Juan orientation

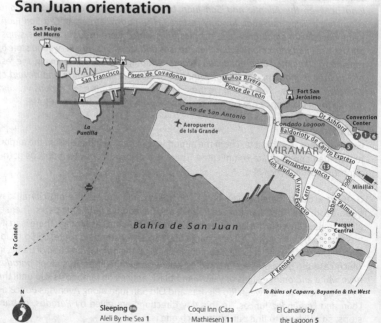

N

Not to Scale

Sleeping 😴
Aleli By the Sea 1
Beach Buoy Inn 2

Coqui Inn (Casa
  Mathiesen) 11
Coqui Inn (Green Isle) 9

El Canario by
  the Lagoon 5
El Canario by the Sea 6

1100-1700, admission charge for some exhibitions; guided tours available Mon-Fri 1030, 1130, 1230 and 1400, on the second floor tracing the cultural development of the history of the New World. The **Dominican Convent** ① T7240700, Wed-Sun 0900-1200, 1300-1630, built in the early 16th century, later used as a headquarters by the US Army, is now the office of the Institute of Culture, with a good art gallery. Cultural events are sometimes held in the patio, art exhibitions in the galleries. The 16th-century **San José church** ① Mon-Sat 0830-1600, Sun mass at 1200, originally a Dominican chapel, is the second oldest church in the Western Hemisphere and once the family church of Ponce de León's descendants. Ponce was buried here until moved to the Cathedral in the 20th century. The early-18th-century **Casa de los Contrafuertes** ① T7245949, Wed-Sun 0900-1630, believed to be the oldest private residence in the old city, now has periodic art exhibitions on the second floor and a small pharmacy museum with 19th-century exhibits on the ground floor. The **Casa Blanca** ① 1 Calle San Sebastián, T7244102, Tue-Sun 0900-1200, 1300-1630, US$2, US$1 children; guided tours Tue-Fri by appointment, was built in 1523 by the family of Ponce de León, who lived in it for 250 years until it became the residence of the Spanish and then the US military commander-in-chief. It is the oldest continuously occupied residence in the Western Hemisphere. It is now a historical museum which is well worth a visit. The **Alcaldía** ① T7247171, ext 2391, Mon-Fri 0800-1600 except holidays, or City Hall, was built between 1604 and 1789. The **Naval Arsenal** ① T7245949, Wed-Sun 0900-1200, 1300-1630, was the last place in Puerto Rico to be evacuated by the Spanish in 1898.

Apart from those in historic buildings listed above, there are the **Pablo Casals Museum** ① T7239185, Tue-Sat 0930-1730. US$1, children US$0.50, in an 18th-century house beside San José church, with Casals' cello and other memorabilia. The **San Juan Museum of Art and History** ① Norzagaray y MacArthur, T7241875, Tue-Sun 1000-1600, built in 1855 as a marketplace, is now a cultural centre with exhibition galleries. The **Casa del Libro** ① T7230354, Tue-Sat 1100-1630 (except holidays), is an 18th-century

Puerto Rico San Juan

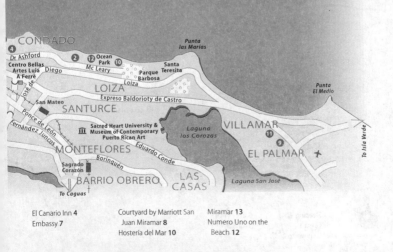

Atlantic Ocean

Related map
A Old San Juan, page 440.

El Canario Inn 4
Embassy 7

Courtyard by Marriott San
Juan Miramar 8
Hostería del Mar 10

Miramar 13
Numero Uno on the
Beach 12

house on Calle Cristo, has a collection of rare books, including some over 400 years old. The **Museum of the Sea** ⓘ , *on Pier One, T7252532, open when the pier is open for cruise ships*, has a collection of maritime instruments and models. The **Indian Museum** ⓘ *Calle San José 109 on the corner of Luna, T7245477, Tue-Sat 0900-1600, free*, concentrates on Puerto Rican indigenous cultures, with exhibits, ceramics and archaeological digs. Another museum in the old city is a military museum at **Fort San Jerónimo** ⓘ *T7245949, Wed-Sun 0930-1200, 1300-1630*.

Metropolitan San Juan

The metropolitan area of San Juan includes the more modern areas of Santurce, Hato Rey, and Río Piedras. In **Santurce**, the **Museo de Arte de Puerto Rico** ⓘ *300 de Diego Av, Santurce, T9776277, www.mapr.org, Tue-Sat 1000-1700, Sun 1100-1800; the gallery is open Wed until 2000 for special interactive and educational programmes, US$6, concessions US$3, free on Wed 1400-2000*, showcases 500 years of Puerto Rican sculpture, painting, drawing, photography and graphic arts. There are also temporary exhibitions, films and classes. The west wing contains the last remnant of the former Municipal Hospital and has a permanent collection in 18 exhibition halls. The east wing is a modern, 5-storey structure, designed by local architects, Otto Reyes and Luis Gutiérrez, containing an atrium, a conservation laboratory, an interactive family gallery and ActivArte, a computer learning centre, as well as studios and workshops, museum shop, restaurant and café. The **Sacred Heart University** with the **Museum of Contemporary Puerto Rican Art** ⓘ *Tue-Sat 0900-1600, Sun 1100-1700. T2680049*, is in Santurce. The **Centro Bellas Artes Luis A Ferré** (Fine Arts Centre) ⓘ *T7244747, www.cba.gobierno.pr, Mon-Fri 0800-1700*, opened in 1981, with theatres and halls at the corner of De Diego and Ponce de León.

Old San Juan

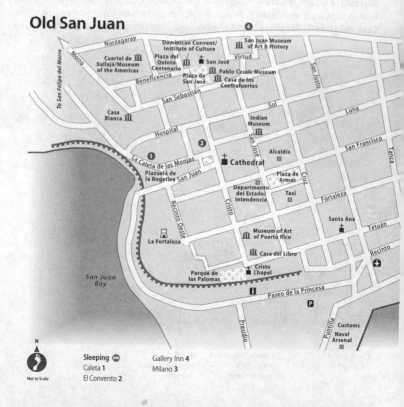

N
Not to Scale

Sleeping		
Caleta **1**	Gallery Inn **4**	
El Convento **2**	Milano **3**	

Río Piedras ① *T7557979, Tue-Sat 0900-1300*, was founded in 1714 but became incorporated into San Juan in 1951. On the edge of Río Piedras, the gardens and library of the former governor, Luis Muñoz Marín, are open to the public, with a museum showing his letters, photos and speeches. The **University of Puerto Rico** at Río Piedras is in a lovely area. The **University Museum** ① *T7640000, ext 2452, Mon-Fri 0900-2100, Sat-Sun 0900-1500*, has archaeological and historical exhibitions, and also monthly art exhibitions. The **Botanical Garden** ① *T7634408, www.upr.clu.edu, daily 0800-1630*, at the Agricultural Experiment Station, has over 200 species of tropical and subtropical plants, a bamboo promenade (one variety can grow 4 ft in a day), an orchid garden (over 30,000 orchids), and an aquatic garden.

Hato Rey is the financial district of San Juan nicknamed 'the Golden Mile'. The **Luís Muñoz Marín Park** ① *Av Jesús T Piñero, Tue-Sun 0900-1700*, covers 35 ha, which can be toured by a 1 km cable car. The residential area **Miramar** has several moderately priced hotels as well as some expensive ones. Miramar is separated from the Atlantic coast by the **Condado lagoon** and the Condado beach area, where the luxury hotels, casinos, nightclubs and restaurants are concentrated. From Condado the beachfront is built up eastwards through **Ocean Park**, Santa Teresita, Punta Las Marías and **Isla Verde** along the narrow strip beyond Isla Verde, between the sea and the airport.

A ferry, Old San Juan (Pier Two) – Hato Rey, Cataño, crosses every 30 minutes, 0600-2200, weather permitting, T7881155, US$0.50, to **Cataño**. In 1999 an enormous statue of Columbus made by a Georgian, Zurab Tsereteli, was assembled in sections here as a major tourist attraction. From Cataño waterfront you can catch a *público* (US$1 per person), or bus C37 to about five blocks from the **Bacardí rum distillery** ① *Route 888, Km 2.6, T7881500, www.bacardi.com, Mon-Sat 0830-1630, every 30 mins, closed for Christmas holidays*, where there are free conducted tours around the plant, travelling from one building to the next by a little open motor train.

On Route 2, shortly before Bayamón, is the island's earliest settlement, **Caparra**, established by Ponce de León in 1508. Ruins of the fort can still be seen and there is a museum, **Museo y Parque Histórico Ruinas de Caparra** ① *T7814795, daily 0900-1600*.

🛏 Sleeping

Most of the large San Juan hotels are in Condado or Isla Verde and overlook the sea, with swimming pools, nightclubs, restaurants, shops and bars. They are mostly part of international chains, such as **Hilton**, **Marriott**, **Radisson**, **Ritz Carlton**, **Wyndham**, and are not listed here. To get value for money, it may be advisable to avoid the luxury hotels on the sea front. There are beachfront apartments at reasonable prices for stays of a week or more, and the further away from the beach you go, the cheaper they will become; look in the local newspaper, *El Nuevo Día* for notices, usually quote monthly rates but available for shorter stays.

Old San Juan *p438, map p440*
Picturesque area, hilly cobbled streets, ocean views but no beach swimming.

LL El Convento Hotel & Casino, a converted Carmelite nunnery at Cristo 100, T7239020, www.elconvento.com. A charming hotel with a Spanish atmosphere and the dining room is in the former chapel, exclusive, very good service, 58 rooms, swimming pool, nice garden in which to have a drink, unfortunately the plaza opposite is a nocturnal campsite for junkies/alcoholics and stray cats.

LL The Gallery Inn at Galería San Juan, Norzagaray 204-206, T7221808, www.thegalleryinn.com. 300-year-old rambling house with inner courtyards, artist's residence and 7 studios, art, antiques, views everywhere, labyrinth, 22 a/c rooms and suites, all different, rates include breakfast and daily happy hour with hosts, popular for private dining and cocktail parties.

L-A Milano, Fortaleza 307, T7299050, www.hotelmilanopr.com. 19th-century building on 3 floors with restaurant and bar on roof giving views of harbour and cruise ships, 30 rooms, breakfast included, most expensive at the front, cheapest in the middle of the building, 2 rooms for the disabled, comfortable, TV, phones, mini-fridge. Wi-Fi at rooftop restaurant and bar.

AL-B The Caleta Balcony Rentals, 11 Caleta de las Monjas, T7255347, www.thecaleta .com. Furnished studios and apartments, some with kitchens or kitchenettes, most have a/c, TV and phone, run by Michael Giessler, minimum 3-night stay, weekly, monthly and long-term rates, coin laundry.

Metropolitan San Juan *p440*
Miramar
Residential area, easy bus to old San Juan, but not great at night.

L Courtyard by Marriott San Juan Miramar, 801 Ponce de León, T7217400, www.marriott.com. Formerly the Excelsior, now renovated and upgraded. 136 rooms, including 10 suites with panoramic views, 2 restaurants, bar, pool, rooms overlooking freeway are noisy, higher up you get a great view of the lagoon, business-type hotel with internet access in rooms but with attention to families, facilities for the handicapped, fitness room, self laundry service.

L Miramar, 606 Av Ponce de León, T9771000, www.miramarhotelpr.com. 'Not chic', but OK, designed for business travellers, a/c, pool, sea view from 5th floor front, large desks, free Wi-Fi, coin laundry, fitness centre, restaurant.

AL-A Olimpo Court, 603 Av Miramar, T7240600, hotelolimpocourt@hotmail.com. 45 rooms and studios with kitchenettes, a/c, TV, phone, **Chayote** restaurant, parking.

Condado
L-AL Best Western Pierre, 105 De Diego, T7211200, www.hotelpierresanjuan.com. Designed for business travellers or families. 154 rooms in 7-floor tower and 30 rooms on 3 floors in Club Pierre, designed for corporate travellers, with free internet access in all rooms.

AL Atlantic Beach Hotel and Embassy Guest House, 1126 Sea View, T7258284, www.embassyguesthouse.com. 58 rooms, good bathroom, TV, a/c, fan, Wi-Fi, pool and jacuzzi on the beach, some rooms have kitchenette.

AL El Canario by the Lagoon, 4 Clemenceau, T7228640, www.canariohotels .com. 44 a/c rooms with balconies, 1 block from beach, B&B, free Wi-Fi in rooms, parking, laundry room, good value.

AL-A El Canario by the Sea, 4 Condado Av, T7228640, www.canariohotels.com. 25 a/c rooms, close to beach behind a block of condos, next to Stellaris Casino, B&B, comfortable, good value.

AL-A El Canario Inn, 1317 Ashford, T7223861, www.canariohotels.com. Near beach, 25 a/c rooms, B&B, simple but comfortable, good value.

A Aleli By The Sea, 1125 Sea View St, T7255313, F7214744. On seafront, 9 rooms, kitchen facilities, no pool, no phones or TVs in rooms, simple accommodation but great location, parking.

AL-A Casa del Caribe, 57 Caribe, T7227139, www.casadelcaribe.net. 1 block from beach, breakfast included, a/c, TV, phone, patio and garden, 13 rooms, some with kitchenettes, convenient for restaurants and nightlife.

Ocean Park
LL-AL Numero Uno on the Beach, 1 Santa Ana, T7265010, www.numero1guesthouse .com. 14 rooms, suites and apartments of different sizes, substantial discounts in low

season, a/c, fan, breakfast included, beachfront restaurant, safe, good beach but not safe after dark, with pool, beach towels, gay friendly.

LL-A Hostería del Mar, 1 Tapia St, T7273302, www.hosteriadelmarpr.com. On the beach, 20 rooms, kitchenettes, a/c, TV, internet access, patio bar and restaurant overlooking the sea.

A Beach Buoy Inn, 1853 McLeary, T7288119, F2680037. Safe behind barred doors and high walls, but on busy road so some traffic noise, 17 comfortable rooms, some with bath and some with shower, 1 equipped for the less able, a/c, TV, continental breakfast but no restaurant, parking, shopping close by, beach towels.

Isla Verde

AL-A Coqui Inn (Casa Mathiesen), Uno 14, T7268662, and (**Green Isle**), Uno 36, T7264330, www.coqui-inn.com, are jointly owned and managed as one hotel, both in same block. Near airport, swimming pools, cooking facilities, standard, value or economy rooms, some with access for the less able, continental breakfast included, friendly, free transport to and from airport, bridge over the road to the beach, free internet access, Asian restaurant at Casa Mathiesen.

A El Patio, Tres Oeste 87, Bloque D 8, Villamar, T7266298. 14 simple rooms, swimming pool, use of kitchen, laundry, short walk to beach via bridge, quiet area, Angela is very welcoming.

● Eating

For breakfast or lunch seek out the *fondas*, not advertised as restaurants but usually part of a private home, or a family-run eating place serving *criollo* meals which are filling and good value. Recommended in San Juan are: **Macumba**, 2000 Loíza; **Casa Juanita**, 242 Av Roosevelt, Hato Rey. Try chicken *asopao* or pork chops *con mangú*. **Cafetería del Parking**, 757 José de Diego. Interior, Cayey (specialities include *mondongo*, and *boronia de apio y bacalao* – cod and celery root). **D'Arcos**, 605 Miramar, Santurce. Speciality is roast veal with stuffed peppers and white bean sauce, also try *pega'o* (crunchy rice).

♥♥♥-♥♥ Al Dente, 309 Recinto Sur, T7237303. Open for lunch and dinner. Posh Italian, live entertainment, reservations required, valet parking.

♥♥ Amadeus Café, 106 San Sebastián, T7216720, amadeuscafé@worldnet.att.net. Lunch and dinner, European cuisine with Caribbean touches, tasty vegetarian options and puddings, popular, lively, friendly, bar, live entertainment, parking.

♥♥ Café Berlin, 407 San Francisco, T7225205. Breakfast, lunch and dinner. Local produce, some organic, vegetarian dishes, also chicken and fish.

♥♥ Ché's, Coaba 35, Punta Las Marías, T7267202. Lunch and dinner. The place for meat lovers, Argentine parrilladas, churrascos and chimichurri, parking.

♥♥ La Danza, corner of Cristo and Fortaleza, T7231642. Fri-Wed 1200-2030. Eat inside or outside, opposite Capilla de Santo Cristo, Puerto Rican food but paella a speciality, live entertainment Tue, Fri, Sat 1430-1700.

♥♥ La Mallorquina, San Justo 207, T7223261. Mon-Sat 1130-2200. The oldest restaurant in San Juan, Puerto Rican food.

♥♥ Yukiyu, Recinto Sur 311, T7221423, www.yukiyupr.com. Mon-Fri 1200-1430, 1730-2230, Sat 1800-2200, Sun 1700-2100, takeaway available daily 1200-1430, also Sat, Sun 1700-2100. Sushi bar, Teppan Yaki and Japanese restaurant.

♥♥-♥ La Bombonera, San Francisco 259, T7220658. Daily 0730-2030. Restaurant, bar and pastry shop, good value breakfast, 1960s atmosphere, antique coffee machine, try the *mallorcas*, a pastry dusted with sugar, sandwiches or full meals.

♥♥-♥ Patio de Sam, 102 San Sebastián on Plaza San José, T7238802. Daily 1100-2400. Facing the plaza, serving everything from burgers to gourmet, kids' menu, live entertainment, bar, very good for local drinks (happy hour 1600-1900).

Metropolitan San Juan *P440*
Hato Rey

♥♥ Frida's, Av Domenech 128, Hato Rey, T7634827, www.letsdine.com/fridas. Dinner only. Mexican, quite upscale, good, parking.

♥♥ Jerusalem, O'Neil St, G-1, T2818232. Lunch and dinner. Middle Eastern food, belly dancing Fri, Sat nights.

There is a huge selection of restaurants in Condado, from the posh to all the fast food chain restaurants.

♥♥♥-♥♥ Ajili Mojili, 1052 Ashford Av, T7259195, www.icepr.com/ajili-mojili. Daily 1145-1500, also Mon-Thu 1800-2200, Fri and Sat 1800-2300. Fine dining, Puerto Rican cuisine, elegant, live music Sun, reservations required, valet parking.

♥♥ Don Andrés, 1350 Ashford Av, T7230223. Tue-Wed 1130-2300, Thu-Sat 1130-2400, Sun 1700-2400. Mexican, live entertainment Thu-Sat evenings, moderate prices, casual, valet parking.

♥♥ José José, 1110 Magdalena Av, T7258546. Tue-Fri 1200-1500, 1830-2300, Sat 1830-2300, Sun 1200-2130. Named after 2 owner chefs, José Garden and José Abreu, international food with Caribbean flair, gourmet, valet parking.

Isla Verde

This area is well served by the fast-food fraternity.

♥♥-♥ Bagelfields Inc, 6070 Isla Verde Av Food Court, T2533663. 0800-1700. Many types of bagels baked daily, lots of deli and healthy fillings, wraps and sandwiches, pastries, coffee bar, wines and beer, good for breakfast, parking.

♥♥-♥ The Hungry Sailor, on the beach, Isla Verde. Bar and grill, sandwiches, tapas, burgers, with a snack bar next door.

Puerto Nuevo

♥♥ Allegro Ristorante, Av Roosevelt esq Duero 1350, T7930190. Tue-Fri 1200-1500, 1800-2200, Sat 1800-2200, Sun 1200-1800. High-class Italian, parking.

♥♥ Aurorita Mexican Restaurant, Av de Diego 303, T7832899. Tue-Thu 1130-2200, Fri-Sun 1130-2230. Authentic Mexican, *mole poblano*, margaritas, mariachi band Wed-Sun, takeaway, parking.

⊙ Bars and clubs

Check age limits, some clubs are for 18 and over but others for 21 and up.

Old San Juan *p438, map p440*

Calle San Sebastián has lots of bars and clubs making it a lively street after dark.

Bachelor's, Av Condado 112, T7252734. Tue-Sun 2300-0500. Gay club, dance and techno music, casual.

Club Lazer, Cruz 251, T7257581. Mon-Sat 2000-0500. Bar on first floor, then above is the dance floor with state-of-the-art light show and above that is the roof terrace, themed nights.

The Gallery Café, Fortaleza 305, T7258676. Open from 2100 onwards. DJs play dance and electronic music, casual.

Jazz at The Place, Fortaleza 154 in old San Juan. No admission charge, drinks about US$2.

Neons Videotech, Tanca 203, T7243426. From 2000 Thu, from 2100 Fri and Sat, from 1900 Sun. Music, dance, live rock Sun.

Rumba, San Sebastián 152, T7254407. Daily from 1930. Live guaracha and salsa Thu-Sat, casual.

Shannons Irish Pub, Bori esq San José de Diego, Condado. Sun-Tue open until 0100, Wed-Sat 0230. Bus from airport passes it, don't miss St Patrick's Day, live music (rock and roll) Wed-Sun, beer US$2.50.

Metropolitan San Juan *P440*
Santurce

Asylum, Av Ponce de León 1420, T7233416. From 2100 onwards Thu-Sat. Converted theatre, invited DJs on Fri, usually drum, bass, trance.

Eros, Av Ponce de León 1257, T7221131. Tue-Sat from 2200, Sun from 2000. Gay club, tribal house music, dress creatively.

Stanley's E-Net Club, Av Ponce de León 1515, T9770770, www.stanleysenc.com. Thu-Sat from 2100 onwards. Unlimited free use of Play Station, Dream Cast and internet as well as invited DJs, live bands, music is varied, pop, lounge, breakbeats, trance, house.

Stargate, Av Roberto H Todd 1, T7254664. Thu, Sat 2130 onwards, Fri, Sun from 1700. House DJs play dance music, smart casual.

Isla Verde

Area 51, or **The Dome**, Av Isla Verde, D-11, T7283780. Fri-Sat 2100-0400. Dance music, electronic and rave, UFO-shaped building, smart casual.

Dunbar's, 1954 McCleary St, Ocean Park, T7282920. Open until 0100. Bar and restaurant with live music weekends, happy hour 1700-1900.

The X Club, Calle Rosa 7, T2533050. Daily

from midnight. DJs playing rock and dance, casual.

▲ Activities and tours

San Juan *p437, maps p438 and p440*
Tour operators
Atlantic San Juan Tours, T6449841, www.puertoricoexcursions.com. Andrés Alicea offers day trips to the Indian ceremonial centre, Guanica Forest, El Yunque, Ponce, Río Camuy Caves, etc.
Aventuras Tierra Adentro, 272B Av Pinero, University Gardens, Río Piedras, PR 00927, T7660470, www.aventuraspr.com. Tue-Sat 0900-1800. Rappelling, rock climbing, body rafting, canyoning, ziplines, outdoor sport shop, caving and team building.
Countryside Tours, 1048 Las Palmas Av, Suite 1101, T7239691, www.freewebs.com/countrysidetourspr. Daily 0800-2000. Customized tours, to the University of Puerto Rico, the first Governor's house in Trujillo Alto and a (hard to find) typical lunch, pointing out typical plants and trees along the way, delightful cultural experience, recommended to get to know Puerto Rico.
Encantos Ecotours, El Muelle Shopping Center, T2720005. Bikes and kayaks, tours and rentals, also surf rafting in Piñones, internet café.

Around Puerto Rico

An interesting round trip through the east half of the island can be done by a series of públicos from San Juan-Río Grande-Luquillo-Fajardo-Humacao-Yabucoa- Guayama-Cayey-Aibonito-Barranquitas-Bayamón-San Juan. If travelling by car, a variant between San Juan and El Yunque takes you on Route 187 from Isla Verde, outside San Juan, to Loíza along a stretch of the north coast, which includes the Piñones State Forest, a sand-blown and palm-lined road. There are some huge resorts and golf clubs in the Río Grande area.

A round trip through the west half of the island would take in Ponce, the second city (reached by motorway from San Juan via Caguas), Guánica, Parguera, San Germán, Boquerón, Mayagüez (the third city), Aguadilla, Quebradillas and Arecibo, with side trips to the Maricao State Forest and fish hatchery, the Río Abajo State Forest and Lake Dos Bocas, the pre-Columbian ceremonial bull-park near Utuado, and the Arecibo observatory. ▸▸ *For Sleeping, Eating and other listings, see pages 453-458.*

East of San Juan

El Yunque
① *Caribbean National Forest, HC-01, Box 13490, Rio Grande, PR 00745-9625, T8881880, www.fs.fed.us/r8/caribbean, daily 0730-1800.*
El Yunque (see also page 466), or **Caribbean National Forest**, is a tropical forest and bird sanctuary, the largest rainforest in the US forest service system. It is divided into north side and south side, with no road connection; after a series of landslides everyone has given up and Route 191 is permanently closed in the middle; you have to drive all the way around to get to the south side or hike (a bit tricky to get past the landslides). There are paved trails to the various peaks: **El Yunque** (The Anvil) itself, **Mount Britton**, **Los Picachos**, as well as to waterfalls and lookout towers giving excellent views. There are 13 trails in all, covering 37 km. The **Baño Grande** is the shortest, taking about 45 minutes and passing a large man-made pool built by the Civilian Conservation Corp in the 1930s. The **Big Tree Trail** is about the most strenuous, taking 1¾ hours and ending at La Mina waterfall. To get to El Yunque take Route 3 from San Juan towards Fajardo, and then turn right on Route 191 at Palmer. The **Palma de Sierra** picnic grounds have parking, tables, water and shelters. **El Portal**

Centro Forestal Tropical ① *at the entrance on Route 191, 0900-1630*, has exhibitions, educational and conservation material, patios where you can relax and admire the view, 100-seat theatre showing a 30-minute documentary film on El Yunque, in Spanish followed by an English version (US$3 adults, US$1.50 children and seniors). The Park Service publishes a good map.

The south side of the forest is approached from Naguabo up Route 191. No facilities have yet been developed. The soil and weather here is different from the north. The north is red clay (and soggy) and the south is almost sandy (fine granite), while it is less humid and cooler. It is also quieter, with no tour buses or parking lots.

Luquillo

Luquillo was founded in 1797 when a group of colonizers led by Cristóbal de Guzmán moved from San Juan to escape frequent British naval attacks. The town was named after the Indian cacique Loquillo, who died a few years after the last Indian rebellion of Boriquén that took place following the seizure of the Spanish settlement of Santiago by the shores of the Río Daguao in 1513. In honour of the anniversary of its founding, in 1997 a new landscaped plaza municipal was inaugurated with a statue of Loquillo. There is a beach in town and a *balneario* west of town (see page 436); just by the latter is a row of restaurants on the slip road off the dual carriageway (Route 3). *Públicos* from San Juan to Luquillo are marked Fajardo, US$3, no return *públicos* after 1500.

Fajardo

Fajardo is a boating centre with several marinas and a public beach at Seven Seas; beyond Seven Seas is Las Croabas beach. Offshore is **Icacos**, an uninhabited but much-visited coral island. **Las Cabezas de San Juan** ① *Wed-Sun US$5, US$2 children. Tours, reservations required. T7225882, or T8602560 at weekends, www.fideicomiso .org*, is a nature reserve on the headlands (three promontories) north of Fajardo on Route 987, Km 6. A 19th-century lighthouse contains a nature centre and its observation deck has a great view of El Yunque and surrounding islands. There are trails and boardwalks, a tour by trolley, guides and explanatory signs of the different ecological habitats. Off Humacao Beach/Balneario is a tiny cay called **Cayo Santiago**, also known as **Monkey Island**. It is inhabited by over 500 tiny monkeys, which are protected. The island is closed to the public although there are sightseeing tours which get you close enough to see the monkeys through binoculars.

The southeast

One of the prettiest parts of Puerto Rico, lies south of Humacao, between Yabucoa and Guayama. Here are the villages of **Patillas** (*público* from Guayama) and **Maunabo** (*público* from Patillas, and from Yabucoa). There are a number of restaurants in this area, especially on the coast, which sell good, cheap food. **Yabucoa** is the east starting point of the Panoramic Route which runs the length of the island. There is an extension to the Route around the Cerro La Pandura and the Puntas Quebrada Honda, Yaguas and Toro; this affords lovely views of the Caribbean coast and Vieques island. **Guayama**, the cleanest town in Puerto Rico, it claims, has a delightful square, on which are the church and the **Casa Cautiño**, built in 1887, now a museum and cultural centre. Route 3, the coastal road around the east part continues from Guayama to Salinas (see below), where it joins Route 1 for Ponce.

Carite Forest

① *Servicio Forestal regional office in Guayama, T8643262.*
The Carite Forest lies west of Yabucoa on the Panoramic Route (see page 451). Covering an area of 2,428 ha, its highest peak is **Cerro La Santa** at 903 m. The Forest Supervisor, (Km 20 Route 184), is very helpful and can tell you what there is to do including kayaks to rent on the lake. Bring permit from San Juan or Servicio Forestal

(the latter closer to the forestry office, phone and supplies) with bathrooms. If you
have a car you will be given a key to get it into the campsite. By *público*, from Río
Piedras terminal, San Juan, occasionally direct to Barrio Guavate, Carite, otherwise
you'll have to go to Caguas and change. The *público* will drop you quite close to the
office where you check in.

West of San Juan

Baños de Coamo

Off the motorway which runs from San Juan to Ponce is Baños de Coamo, which was the
island's most fashionable resort from 1847 to 1958; legend has it that the thermal spring
was the fountain of youth which Juan Ponce de León was seeking. Take Route 153 from
the motorway and then 546. About 45 minutes southeast of Coamo is **Salinas**, a fishing
and farming centre. There are several good seafood restaurants on the waterfront. The
Marina de Salinas ① *T7528484*, offers transport to islands and accommodations.

Ponce

The city (www.ponceweb.org) is now very pleasant to walk around. Much renovation
has taken place in the heart of the city; the Casas Villaronga and Salazar-Zapater have
been restored (the latter to accommodate the Museo de Historia de Ponce), other
houses are being repainted in pastel shades and the large, air-conditioned market on
Vives and Atocho (north of the plaza) has been remodelled. There are two tourist
information centres: **Puerto Rico Tourism Co** ① *Route 1, west of Route 52, south side,
T8430465*, and the **Ponce Tourism Office** ① *1st floor inside Citibank, Plaza Las
Delicias in front of Parque Bomberos, T8418160, Mon-Fri 0800-1630*.

The cathedral is worth a look, and so is the black and red fire station, built for a
fair in 1883. Both buildings stand back to back in the main square, **Plaza Las Delicias**,
which has fountains and many neatly trimmed trees. Also on the plaza and facing the
cathedral is the neoclassical **Casa Armstrong-Poventud** (**Casa de las Cariatides**).
Inside is the **Instituto de Cultura Puertorriqueño** (Región Sur) ① *closed to visitors in
2005, awaiting restoration*, and the tourist information centre (see above). East of the
plaza is the 19th-century **Teatro La Perla**, city's cultural centre, painted cream, white
and gold. It was restored in 1990, as was the Alcaldía on the Plaza.

Ponce has a very fine **Museo de Arte de Ponce** ① *2325 Av de las Américas,
T8480511, www.museoarteponce.org, daily 1000-1700, US$3, children under 12 US$2*,
donated by a foundation established by Luis A Ferré (industrialist, art historian and
Governor 1968-1972) in a modern building designed by Edward
Durrel Stone, with a beautiful staircase, now famous. It contains a
representative collection of European and American art from the
third century BC to the present day. As well as an extensive
Baroque collection and fine examples of pre-Raphaelite painting,

❧ *There are three gardens
here, one Spanish, one
American and one Puerto
Rican.*

there is a small collection of pre-Columbian ceramics and art nouveau glass. Most of
the best Latin American painters are exhibited and there are often special displays.

The **Museo de la Historia de Ponce** ① *Calle Isabela 51-53, near La Perla,
T8447071, Wed-Mon 0900-1700 (Jun-Aug Sat-Sun 1000-1800), US$3, children US$1*,
opened in 1992 and has 10 exhibition halls with photographs, documents and
memorabilia provided by locals, as well as models and other exhibits chronicling the
city's history. Guided tours are available in English, Spanish or French. Next door, the
Museo de la Música Puertorriqueña ① *Calle Isabela 45, T8487016, Wed-Sun
0900-1630, catalogue US$3*, is in the neoclassical former home of the
Serralés-Nevárez family, with music videos and history of local music.

On **El Vigía** hill is the **Observation Tower** ① *Tue-Thu 0900-1800, Fri-Sun*

0930-1830, US$0.50. Also on El Vigía hill, the **Museo Castillo Serrallés** ① *T2591774, Tue-Sun 0900-1800, US$3, children US$1.50, groups must reserve in advance,* is a fine 1930s mansion which has been restored by the Municipio.

Outside the town by the **Yacht and Fishing Club** ① *T8429003,* is a good and lively place to be at the weekend. A wooden broadwalk, La Guancha, has been built along the edge of the harbour. There are kiosks selling *pinchos* and other local treats, simple meals, cold beer and drinks. At one end is an open-air stage for live music or DJs with big sound systems. The music is loud, especially at weekends. A two-storey building houses a restaurant, small theatre, tourist office and police substation. There is also an observation tower you can climb up.

Around Ponce

A short drive away on Route 503, Km 2.1, in the outskirts of the city, is the **Tibes Indian Ceremonial Center** ① *T8402255, http://ponce.inter.edu/tibes/tibes.html, Tue-Sun 0900-1600, US$2, bilingual guides give an informative description of the site and a documentary is shown.* This is an Igneri (AD 300) and pre-Taíno (AD 700) burial ground, with seven ball courts (*bateyes*) and two plazas, one in the form of a star, a replica of a Taíno village and a good museum. The site was discovered in 1975 after heavy rain uncovered some of the stone margins of the ball courts. Under the Zemi Batey, the longest in the Caribbean (approximately 100 m by 20 m), evidence of human sacrifice has been found. Underneath a stone in the Main Plaza, which is almost square (55 by 50 m), the bodies of children were found, buried ceremonially in earthenware pots. In all, 130 skeletons have been uncovered near the Main Plaza, out of a total on site of 187. The park is filled with trees (all named), the most predominant being the *higuera*, whose fruit is used, among other things, for making *maracas* (it's forbidden to pick them up though).

❗ *All the ball courts and plazas are said to line up with solstices or equinoxes.*

Hacienda Buena Vista ① *T7225882 (weekends 8487020), www.gicco.com /19thCentury.htm, Sat-Sun, tours at 0830, 1030, 1330 and 1530; groups of 20 or more admitted Wed and Thu, US$5, children under 12 US$2; reservations are necessary for the 2-hr tour (Spanish or English),* at Km 16.8 on Route 123, north of the city, is another recommended excursion. Built in 1833, converted into a coffee plantation and corn mill in 1845 and in operation till 1937. Now restored as a working coffee farm, all the machinery works (the metal parts are original), operated by water channelled from the 360-m Vives waterfall; the hydraulic turbine which turns the corn mill is unique.

At weekends trips can be made to the beach at **Caja de Muerto** (Coffin Island). The **ferry** ① *(if still running) T8484575, US$5.50 return, children US$3.50,* leaves from La Guancha at 0900, returns 1600. There is a fishing pier, barbecue area, information office and beautiful beach with clear water. A trail to the 1880 lighthouse leads from White Beach where the dock is. The snorkelling is very good.

Guánica

Going west from Ponce is Guánica, the place where American troops first landed in the Spanish-American war. It has an old fort from which there are excellent views. Although Guánica has a history stretching back to Ponce de León's landing in 1508, the first of many colonist landings in the bay, the town was not actually founded here until 1914. Outside Guánica is a *balneario* with a large hotel alongside, **Copamarina**. Scuba diving and other watersports are possible here; the wall is close to the shore and there are drop-offs and canyons. You can get to **Gilligans Island** ① *0900-1700, closed Mon (or Tue if Mon is a holiday)* by 15-minute water taxi (US$16). Go past **Balneario Caña Gorda** on route 333, turn right towards Punta Jacinto and the pier. There is a fishing pier, barbecue area, information office and beautiful beach. ▸▸ *For details on the Guánica Forest, see page 466.*

La Parguera

Further west is La Parguera, originally a fishing village and now a popular resort with *paradores*, guesthouses, fish restaurants, fast food outlets. Noisy on holiday weekends. Fishing, kayaking, mountain biking and other activities are offered. **Phosphorescent Bay** is an area of phosphorescent water, occurring through a permanent population of minescent dinoflagellates, a tiny form of marine life, which produce sparks of chemical light. One-hour boat trips round the bay depart 1930-2230, every 30 minutes, US$5. It is best to go on a very dark night or even when it is raining. Mosquito Bay on Vieques is much better (see page 458).

San Germán

Inland from La Parguera, off the main Route 2, San Germán has much traditional charm; it was the second town to be founded on the island and has preserved its colonial atmosphere. It is an excellent base from which to explore the mountains and villages of southwest Puerto Rico. The beautiful little **Porta Coeli chapel** ① *Wed-Sun 0830-1200, 1300-1630*, on the east plaza contains a small museum of religious art. On the west plaza, **San Germán de Auxerre** is another beautiful church. A university town, it can be difficult to get cheap accommodation in term time.

Boquerón

On the south side of the west coast is Boquerón, in Cabo Rojo district, which has an excellent swimming **beach**① *admission US$1*. It is very wide and long, with camping and changing rooms, but the beach and first 30 m of sea are packed with bodies on holiday weekends. About 1½ km away across the bay is a beautiful, deserted beach, but there is no road to it. The small village is pleasant, with typical bars, restaurants and street vendors serving the local speciality, oysters.

South of the town is **Boquerón Lagoon**, a wildfowl sanctuary; also the **Cabo Rojo Wildlife Refuge**, with a visitors' centre and birdwatching trails. The **Cabo Rojo lighthouse** (Faro), at the island's southwest tip is the most southerly point on the island with a breathtaking view; the exposed coral rocks have marine fossils and, closer inshore, shallow salt pools where crystals collect. The vegetation is dry scrub and you can find the slow growing hard wood, *lignum vitae*. Popular beaches in this area are **El Combate** (miles of white sand, undeveloped, but now a favourite with university students), south of Boquerón, and **Joyuda** (Isla de Ratones, a small island just offshore offers good snorkelling and swimming, but the beach itself is not spectacular) and **Buyé** to the north. At Joyuda you can go fishing, snorkelling or take a trip to Mona Island with **Tour Marine Adventures** ① *T2552525*, on the beach near **Perichi's**.

‡ *This is one of the cheapest spots on the island because it is a centre for the Compañía de Fomento Recreativo providing holiday accommodation for Puerto Rican families.*

Mayagüez

Founded in 1760, Mayagüez is now the third largest city, but crowded with little of interest to the tourist unless you want to go to the **Tropical Agricultural Research Station** ① *T8313435*, or the **zoo**, with its butterfly house and aviary ① *T8348110, www.parquesnacionalespr.com/ofrecimientos_zoologico.asp, Wed-Sun 0830-1600, adults US$6, children 11-17 US$4, 5-10 US$2*. There are some historic buildings around the Plaza Colón, including the City Hall and church. One block away, on Calle McKinley, the **Teatro Yagüez** ① *www.mayaguezpr.gov/turismo/lugares_de_interes/yaguez.htm*, has been restored as the main cultural centre for the west of the island. It is not far to get to beaches or into the hills and is the western end of the Panoramic Route.

Mona Island → *Colour map 2, B/C 5.*

Mona Island, 80 km west of Mayagüez, is fascinating with its turquoise sea and white sand. Originally inhabited by Taíno Indians and then by pirates and privateers, it is now deserted except for its wildlife. Here you can see 1-m iguanas, colonies of seabirds and bats in the caves. Cliffs, 60-m high, are dotted with caves, ascending to a flat table top covered with dry forest. The surrounding waters are teeming with fish, turtles, dolphins and, in the winter, whales, with excellent visibility and great diving. The island can only be reached by boat. There is no fresh water and you must bring all your own food and water and remove all evidence of your presence when you leave.

Rincón

Going north from Mayagüez, you come to Rincón, on the westernmost point of the island. Here the mountains run down to the sea, and the scenery is spectacular. For a great panoramic view visit the **Punta Higuera Lighthouse**, built on a cliff overlooking the surf where the Atlantic and Caribbean meet. The town itself is unremarkable, but the nearby beaches are beautiful and the surfing is a major attraction. The beaches are called **Steps**, **Domes** (named after the nearby nuclear storage dome) and the **Public Beach**, with lifeguard. **Pools**, **Sandy Beach** and **Antonio's** are north of Punta Higuera and popular with winter surfers. **Domes** and **María's** are further south and offer good waves.

Excursions can be arranged to the island of **Desecheo**, 19 km off the coast of Rincón. Desecheo is near Mona Island, but is smaller with terrific diving offshore.

Aguadilla

North of Rincón the road leads to Aguadilla, another good spot for sunset watching. **Crash Boat Beach** is a popular surfing and diving beach just to the north and lots of watersports are on offer. North again are more surfing beaches, **Gas Chamber** and **Wilderness**. Aquatica Dive and Bike Adventures ① *Route 110, Km 10, T8906071, http://premium.caribe.net/~aquatica/menu2.htm*, offers diving, cycling, snorkelling, hang gliding and fishing and trips to Desecheo.

North coast road

Route 2, the main road in the north, runs from Aguadilla through Quebradillas to Arecibo. After Arecibo the coast is more built up, and from Manatí to San Juan it is completely urbanized. South of Quebradillas in the Montañas Aymamón is the **Bosque Estatal de Guajataca**, a dry forest with a large number of bird species, on Route 446. There are over 40 walking trails with 40 km of maintained footpaths through the Karst region, three picnic areas and two camping areas with tent sites (see page 432). South of Arecibo in the Karst country is the **Bosque Río Abajo**, a 2,023-ha reserve off Route 10. It contains 70 trails and dirt roads, ideal for viewing plant and birdlife, 15 commercial plantations (teak, mahogany, maga trees), two natural springwater swimming pools and some amazing bamboo near the end of the road. There is a private campsite at **Dos Bocas**, see Sleeping, page 456.

The Río Camuy runs underground for part of its course, forming the third largest subterranean river in the world. Near Lares, on Route 129, Km 20, the **Parque Nacional Cavernas del Río Camuy** ① *T8983100, www.parquesnacionalespr.com /ofrecimientos_cavernas.asp, Wed to Sun, and holidays 0830-1600, last trip 1545, US$12 for adults, US$7 for children aged 4-12, camping US$5 per person*, is highly recommended and very easy, but entry is limited. Visitors are taken by trolley bus through a cave and two sinkholes. The trip takes two hours and you may have to wait an hour beforehand, so allow plenty of time. There are fine examples of stalactites, stalagmites and, of course, plenty of bats. Keen photographers should bring a tripod for excellent photo opportunities. A recently opened part of the Río Camuy cave system is named **Cathedral Cave Wild Adventure**. You have to rappel down 150 ft into a vaulted cave, where there are lots of pre-Columbian petroglyphs, then exit through interlinked caves to the valley floor before hiking back to the rim of the canyon. Advance reservations essential as the trip is organized only twice a week and depends on the weather. Several caving tour specialists can take you to a different and undeveloped part of the cave system. Offered in three

> ❖ Puerto Rico has some of the most important caves in the western hemisphere.

degrees of difficulty, they explore underground caves, pre-Columbian petroglyphs, rivers and sinkholes. No prior knowledge needed but you need to be in good physical shape as you will have to travel on a hot-line, rappel and body raft, about US$85 for a day's adventure starting at dawn, returning to San Juan by 1800. See page 445 for tour agents. Also close is the privately owned **Cueva de Camuy** ①*daily 0900-1700 (till 2000 Sun). US$1, children US$0.50, Route 486, Km 1.1*; much smaller and less interesting, with guided tours, the area also has a swimming pool and waterslide, amusements, café, ponies, go-karts, entertainments. Nearby is **Cueva del Infierno,** to which two- to three-hour tours can be arranged by phoning T8982723. About 2,000 caves have been discovered; in them live 13 species of bat (but not in every cave), the *coquí* (tiny frog), crickets, an arachnid called the *guavá*, and other species. Contact the **Speleological Society of Puerto Rico** (Sepri) for further details.

Arecibo is famous for the **Observatory** ① *Route 625, T8782612, www.naic.edu, Wed-Fri 1200-1600, Sat-Sun 0900-1600, adults US$5, children and senior citizens US$3*, the world's largest radio radar telescope, south of the town, operated by Cornell University. There is a Visitors' Centre which puts on exhibitions for all ages. The **Arecibo Lighthouse** ① *Arecibo Dock, Route 655, T8807540, www.arecibolighthouse.com, Mon-Fri 0900-1800, Sat-Sun 1000-1900, US$9 adults, US$7 children 2-12 and over 65s*, is also worth a visit, particularly if you have children. It has been fully restored in a recreation park with play area and replica sailing ships, together with museum, restaurant and sports facilities.

If you have the time it is much nicer to drive along the coast then along Route 2. Take Route 681 out of Arecibo, with an immediate detour to the Poza del Obispo beach, by Arecibo lighthouse. Here a pool has been formed inside some rocks, but the breakers on the rocks themselves send up magnificent jets of spray. The bay, with fine surf, stretches round to another headland, **Punta Caracoles**, on which is the **Cueva del Indio** ① *small car park on Route 681, US$1 charge if anyone is around*. A short walk through private land leads to the cave, a sea-eroded hole and funnel in the cliff. There are Taíno/Arawak drawings in the cave. *Públicos* run along Route 681 from Arecibo. Rejoin Route 2 through Barceloneta. The **State Forest of Cambalache** is between Arecibo and Barceloneta. *Cambalache Beach* has two camping areas, La Boba and La Rusa, with water and showers, see page 432.

The coast road is not continuous; where it does go beside the sea, there are beaches, seafood restaurants and some good views. Route 165, another coastal stretch which can be reached either through **Dorado** on the 693 (where there are three large **Hyatt** hotels and several golf courses, www.hyatt.com), or through Toa Baja, enters metropolitan San Juan at Cataño.

Panoramic Route

Heading east from Mayagüez is the Panoramic Route, which runs the whole length of Puerto Rico, through some of the island's most stunning scenery. It passes through the Cordillera Central, with large areas of forest, and there are several excursions to various countryside resorts. Despite the fact that you are never far from buildings, schools or farms, the landscape is always fascinating. In the evening the panoramas are lovely and you can hear the song of the *coquí*. A trip to the interior should take in at least part of the Panoramic Route; but if you want to travel all of it,

❢ *In this part of the island it rains frequently. Get your walking done in the morning as far as possible.*

allow three days. The roads are narrow, with many bends, so drive carefully. From Maricao to Adjuntas there is no accommodation and no public transport. The **Maricao State Forest** ① *T7243724, visitors' areas open 0600-1800*, (Monte del Estado) is the most westerly forest on the Route. It is a beautiful forest with magnificent views, an observation tower and a fish hatchery.

A good three- or four-hour walk is to Las Marías, a cheery little town on a hill north of Maricao. You climb through banana and coffee plantations to a high ridge; views to the east show the degree of deforestation caused by coffee growing and building. For dedicated hikers, six hours of hard walking separates Las Marías from Lares ('captain of the mountains', see below). The countryside is lovely, you pass through forests, up large hills, down deep valleys and across wide rivers.

Adjuntas

South of the Panoramic Route between Sabana Grande and Yauco on Route 371 is the **Bosque Estatal de Susua**, a dry forest with recreational areas, a river, 40 tent sites and showers (see page 432). As it approaches Adjuntas and the transinsular Route 10 (now the 123), the Panoramic Route goes through the **Bosque de Guilarte**, again with fine views, flowering trees, bougainvillaea, banks of impatiens (busy lizzie, *miramelinda* in Spanish), and bird song (if you stop to listen).

Adjuntas is a pleasant town with a picturesque plaza, surrounded by hills. Not much English is spoken at the **tourist office** ① *main square, Plaza Aristides, T8293310, Mon-Fri 0800-1630, Sat 1000-1400*. Roads around Adjuntas are confusing because new roads and road numbers may not be on your map. The old Route 10 to Ponce is now the 123, and there is a new road, Route 6. A big day out from Adjuntas is to climb up **Monte Guilarte** (1,205 m). To walk, leave town on the old Route 10 off the square, turn right on the 518 (unmarked). Three hours' walking, past the lake, brings a park ranger station at the junction with the 131. From here a path takes nearly 30 minutes through eucalyptus trees to the summit, from where there are fantastic, breathtaking views. The path is easy and lovely but can be slippery coming down. If walking, this is what you have come to Puerto Rico for. At the bottom of the path is a small restaurant. Camping is available a few hundred metres away (see Camping, page 432).

> ❦ Officially the coolest place in Puerto Rico, a good place for hikers to rest.

Toro Negro

After Adjuntas, the road enters the **Toro Negro Forest Reserve**, which includes the highest point on the island, **Cerro de Punta** (1,338 m). This is a smaller area than El Yunque, with fewer rivers. There are many very tall eucalyptus trees along the road. Lago El Guineo and Lago de Matrullas are Puerto Rico's highest lakes. The reserve has five trails, one to an observation tower with views of the mountains and lakes. You can see all too clearly the destruction of the forests by house building and coffee planting. A camping area (14 tent sites), has showers and toilets, see page 432.

Jayuya

Just north of the Panoramic Route is Jayuya, overlooked by Cerro de Punta and Tres Picachos in a beautiful mountain setting, but the town is rather ramshackle. It is known as the indigenous capital of Puerto Rico and is named after the Indian cacique Hayuya. Two monuments commemorate the Taíno heritage: a statue of **Hayuya** sculpted by Tomás Batista in 1969, and the **Tumba del Indio Puertorriqueño**, containing a Taíno skeleton buried in the foetal position. A *público* to San Juan, **Línea San Juan**, leaves at 1730 (T7661720, three hours, US$10).

Cañón San Cristóbal

After this high, lush forest with its marvellous vistas, the Panoramic Route continues to **Aibonito**, around which the views and scenery are more open, mainly as a result of deforestation. Thence to **Cayey** and, beyond, to another forest, Carite (also known as Guavate, see page 446). Finally, the road descends into the rich, green valley which leads to Yabucoa. Between Aibonito and Barranquitas is the Cañón San Cristóbal, where you can climb down a mountain trail between steep walls to the bottom, where the temperature is considerably warmer. It's a four-hour trip. Call Félix Rivera (T7355188), for a guide, you will need one to find the way. He usually meets people at **La Piedra** restaurant, on Route 7718, one of Puerto Rico's gastronomic delights.

From various points on the Panoramic Route you can head north or south; for example Route 10/123 goes south from Adjuntas to Ponce, or north to Utuado and then on to **Río Abajo State Forest** ① *0600-1800*, where there's a swimming pool and various picnic spots. It is approached through splendid views of the karst hills and the **Dos Bocas Lake**. Fishing in the lake is good. Free launch trips are offered on this lake at 0700, 1000, 1400 and 1700; they last two hours and are provided by the Public Works Department. Route 10 reaches the north coast at Arecibo.

Caguana Indian Ceremonial Park
① *On Route 111 to Lares, Km 12.3, Wed-Sun 0900-1600, free.*
The Caguana Indian Ceremonial Park, west of Utuado, dates from about AD 1100, and contains 10 Taíno ball courts, each named after a Taíno *cacique* (chieftain). The courts vary in size, the longest being about 85 m by 20 m (Guarionex), the largest 65 m by 50 m (Agueybana). These two have monoliths in the stones that line the level 'pitch', and on those of Agueybana there are petroglyphs. A path leads down to the Río Tanamá. The setting, amid limestone hills, is very impressive. It is believed to be a site of some religious significance and has been restored with a small museum in the 13-acre landscaped botanical park containing royal palm, guava, cedar and ceiba.

⊜ Sleeping

El Yunque *p445*
For camping, see p432.
LL-L Casa Flamboyant, Route 191 through Naguabo, T8746074, www.elyunque.com /flamboy. 3 rooms in main house and 1 suite by the pool, quiet, luxury, great views, no children under 12, heated pool overlooking waterfalls.
AL Casa Cubuy Ecolodge, Route 191 through Naguabo, T8746221, www.casacubuy.com. Fabulous views, built on hillside overlooking forest, close to Río Cubuy, 10 rooms, family-style breakfast at 0900, snack lunch US$7 and dinner on request for minimum 6 guests, Wi-Fi internet access.
C-E Phillips Exotic Fruit Farm, south side above Naguabo, Route 191, a mile from El Yunque forest, T8742138, phillips @east-net.com. Robin Phillips has several rustic cabins and tent sites on his fruit farm. Robin and Sita will guide you through the forest or to the petroglyphs. Terrific views to the sea. Robin is full of information.

Fajardo *p446*
There are several mega resorts in the area: the new **Inter-Continental Cayo Largo Resort**, El Conquistador Resort & Country Club, west of Fajardo on the hill and **Palmas del Mar**, further south.

LL-AL Fajardo Inn, Route 195, Parcelas Beltrán 52, Puerto Real, T8606000, www.fajardoinn.com. 75 rooms, a/c, TV, phone, computer services, lots of packages available, conference centre, restaurant, also guesthouse alongside, **Scenic Inn**, T8635195, both with great views of El Yunque and the coast from on top of the hill.
A Anchor's Inn, Route 987 Km 27, Fajardo, T8637200, www.anchorsinn.homestead.com /anchorsinn.html. Nice rooms, a/c, TV, good facilities but no breakfast, bar/restaurant expensive, part of **Mesones Gastronómicos** programme.
A La Familia, on Route 987, Km 4, Las Croabas, Fajardo, T8631193. 27 rooms, rather small, a/c, bath, TV, breakfast included, pool, restaurant, 2 mins from beach, next to **El Conquistador**.

The southeast *p446*
AL Caribe Playa, Route 3, Km 112, near Patillas, right on the Caribbean, T8396339, www.caribeplaya.com. 32 beachfront rooms, sleep 4, a/c, fan, TV, patio or balcony, comfortable, rather noisy road runs behind rooms, pool and whirlpool, children's pool, open-air restaurant (order dinner in advance), library, sea bathing and snorkelling in a small, safe area, barbecue, hammocks,

massages, boat trips for fishing, diving, snorkelling, very friendly and helpful.

AL-AHacienda Margarita, Route 52, Km 1.7, North of Barranquitas, T8570414, F8571265. 27 rooms, a/c, TV, balcony, pool, restaurant, view of El Yunque, useful for people following the Panoramic Route.

AL-APalmas de Lucía, Route 901 at Route 9911, Yabucoa, T8934423, www.palmasdelucia .com. New *parador*, 29 rooms, balconies with sea view, clean, basketball court, pool, restaurant, waves can be rough at nearby Lucía beach. All-inclusive meal plans available.

BPlaya Emajaguas Guest House, off the Ruta Panorámica, Route 901, Km 2.5, near Maunabo, T8616023. Lovely view, short walk down private path to empty beach (rough sea, currents), owned by Victor Morales and Edna Huertos, 7 apartments with kitchens, friendly, helpful, pool, tennis court, pool table, horses. Good seafood restaurants nearby.

Baños de Coamo *p447*

AL-ABaños de Coamo, at the end of Route 546, Coamo, Puerto Rico 00640, T8252186, www.banosdecoamo.com. Thermal water springs (maximum 15 mins) and an ordinary pool (spend as long as you like), 48 rooms, bar, restaurant with limited hours.

Ponce *p447*

LL-LPonce Hilton & Casino, 1150 Caribe Av, on the beach, T2597676, www.ponce.hilton .com. 153 rooms, convention centre for 1,500, all the business and sporting facilities you expect of a Hilton including golf course, fitness centre, sauna and spa.

L-ALPonce Holiday Inn & Tropical Casino, Route 2, Km 221.2, west of the city on bypass, T8441200, www.hidpr.com. 116 rooms, tennis, pools, golf arrangements made.

ALMeliá, 2 Cristina, just off main plaza, T8420260, www.hotelmeliapr.com. Run by Meliá family since 1920s, 77 rooms, breakfast included, a/c, TV, roof top and garden terraces.

ABélgica, 122 Villa, in old centre, next to Plaza Delicias, on free trolley route for touring city, T8443255, www.hotelbelgica.com. Tasteful, clean, 20 huge, traditional rooms with balcony overlooking city hall, friendly.

Around Ponce *p448*

AL-APichi's, Route 132, Km 204, west of Ponce at Guayanilla, T8353335, www.pichis .com. Next to **McDonalds**. 58 big rooms, a/c, TV, phone, pool, seafood and steak restaurant, bar, meeting rooms and banqueting facilities.

Guánica *p448*

LL-LCopamarina Beach Resort, Route 333, Km 6.5, T8210505, www.copamarina.com. Set in 6.5-ha tropical estate, 106 rooms, also villas sleeping 6, a/c, TV, balcony, packages available, from B&B to all-inclusive, 2 pools, tennis, watersports, PADI dive centre, tour desk, restaurants, on eelgrass beach but good swimming on Gilligans Island.

La Parguera *p448*

L-APosada Porlamar, Route 304, Km 3.3, T8994015, www.posadaporlamar.info. 35 rooms, TV, phone, on the canals, dock, watersports arranged, dive shop on site, dive packages available, restaurant.

ALVilla Parguera, Route 304 Km 3.3, T8997777, www.villaparguera.net. 70 rooms, meal plans available, sea view, by docks, rent boat to get to mangrove canals and cays for good swimming and snorkelling, restaurant, live music and dancing on Sat.

San Germán *p449*

A-BOasis, 72 Luna, T8921175, F8924546. 52 rooms in old colonial mansion, a/c, TV, restaurant, pool, parking, corporate rates.

Boquerón *p449*

LL-ALParador Bahía Salinas, Route 301, Km 11.5, T2541212, www.bahiasalinas.com. Lovely setting, suites and rooms, most with porch for sunset watching, pool, kayaking, sailing, diving, fishing.

LPunta Aguila Resort, Cabo Rojo, T2544954. On shallow eelgrass beach with a bay on either side and good swimming beaches, good hiking area, gazebos with hammocks, jacuzzi, pool, 2-bedroom suites with kitchens, a/c.

AL-ABoquemar, end of Route 100, Int 101, Gil Bouye St, T8512158, www.boquemar.com. 75 rooms, a/c, bar, restaurant, pool, facilities for disabled, parking.

AL-AJoyuda Beach, Route 102, Km 11.7, T8515650, www.joyudabeach.com. *Parador* with 41 rooms, restaurant, discounts for students with university identification, business people, federal employees and senior citizens.

AL-A Perichi's, Route 102,Km 14.3, Playa Joyuda, T8513131, www.hotelperichi.com. 41 rooms, balconies with sea view, well-run, with good award-winning restaurant, walking distance to beach.

A Centro Vacacional de Boquerón, see Camping, page 432, T8511900. Fully self-contained, with barbecues, 200, 2-bedroom basic beach cabins, a/c, fans, basketball, tennis, baseball, life guards and security guards. Foreigners are welcomed, but it is so popular with Puerto Ricans that you may have to make an application up to 3 months in advance.

A Estancia La Jamaca, Route 304, T/F8996162, www.laparguerapuertorico.com. 8 rooms, quiet, inland, country noises at night, gardens, pool, rustic decor, pretty colours in rooms.

Mayagüez *p449*

LL-L Mayagüez Resort & Casino, Route 104, Km 0.3, T8317575, www.mayaguezresort.com. 140 rooms in 20 acres, view of harbour, business hotel and resort of international standard but independently operated, corporate floor, add 11% tax and US$5 per night per room resort fee to rates, tennis, pool.

A-B Embajador, 111 Ramos Antonini, Este, T8333340, F8347664. 29 rooms, central, a/c, phones, TV, restaurant, facilities for wheelchair visitors, laundry room.

B Colonial, Iglesia 14 Sur, T/F8332150, www.hotelcolonial.com. 29 rooms for 1-4 people, breakfast included, TV, Wi-Fi internet access, building dates from 1920s and was once used as a convent.

Camping

Balneario Tres Hermanos, North of Mayagüez at Bahía de Añasco, Route 115 Km 5, T8260996. Campground with beach and pool (**A**) cabins sleep 6, camping with water and electricity see Camping, page 432.

Mona Island *p449*

The island is managed by the **Department of National Resources** (permit required, T7221726), who have cabins to rent with prior permission. **Camping** is allowed at Sardinera Beach, where there are bathrooms. Take all your food and water with you and bring back all your rubbish, see Camping, page 432.

Rincón *p450*

LL Horned Dorset Primavera, Route 429, Km 0.3, T8234030, www.horneddorset.com. Member of Relais & Chateaux, height of luxury, very expensive. No children under 12, no TV, no organized activities, suites in colonial Spanish style, private, good restaurant, beach not good for swimming, pool.

L-AL Villa Cofresí, Route 115, Km 12, T8232450, www.villacofresi.com. 63 rooms in modern blocks, on the beach, TV, kitchens, restaurant, bar, outdoor restaurant, watersports.

AL The Lazy Parrot Inn and Restaurant, Route 413, Km 4.1, Barrio Puntas, T8235654, www.lazyparrot.com. In La Cadena hills overlooking coast, 11 rooms, unusually decorated in cheerful designs, upstairs adjoining rooms for families, a/c, cable TV, fridge, restaurant with vegetarian options.

AL Villa Antonio, alongside it, also at Route 115, Km 12, T8232645, www.villa-antonio .com. 61 rooms, suites and cottages (1 or 2 bedrooms), concrete blocks, basic furnishings, on a good beach for swimming and near good surfing beaches, a/c, volleyball, tennis, pool, kitchen, TV, parking, bar and restaurant close by.

Aguadilla *p450*

L-A La Cima, Route 110, Km 9.2, Barrio Maleza Alta, T8902016, www.lacimahotel .com. 40 rooms in 2-storey block around pool, some apartments sleep up to 8 at a pinch, a/c, TV, phone, exercise room, within reach of 6 beaches and golf.

A Hacienda El Pedregal, Route 111, Km 0.1, T8822865, www.hotelelpedregal.com. 27 rooms, view of ocean and sunsets, attractive rooms, TV, phone, parking, restaurant, bar, pools. Also villas with 2-4 bedrooms.

A Parador El Faro, Route 107, Km 2.1, T8828000, www.farohotels.net. 75 rooms, built 1990, TV, phone, Wi-Fi internet access, 2 pools, Tres Amigos restaurant for Puerto Rican, Mexican and Italian food.

A Parador J B Hidden Village, Route 416, Barrio Piedras Blancas, Aguada, T8688686, F8688701. 36 rooms built in 1990, a/c, bar, restaurant, pool, parking, facilities for disabled.

North coast road *p450*

LL-AL Villa Montana, Route 4466, Km 1.2, near Isabela, T8729554, www.villamontana .com. Nice resort, tranquil spot, miles of sand and surf, protected area for swimming, tennis, spa treatments, riding next door, mountain bikes, kayaks, rock climbing wall, restaurant by pool bar, hotel rooms or villas with kitchens, not much else, lots to do during the day but quiet at night, summer camp for kids.

AL T J Ranch, go over the dam on Route 146, first left straight up to the top, past phone booth, then at intersection turn left (small sign for T J Ranch), T8801217, HC02 Box 14926, Arecibo, PR 00612, tjranch@caribe.net. A coffee farm run by Tony and Juanita, cabins with porches, private, breakfast included, pool.

AL-A Ocean Front Hotel, Route 4466, Km 0.1, near Isabela, T8720444, www.oceanfrontpr.com. Right on the beach with verandas overlooking the sand and the waves lapping feet away. 13 rooms with ocean view and excellent restaurant.

AL-A Villas del Mar Hau, near Isabela, Route 466 Km 8.9, T8722627, www.paradorvillasdelmarhau.com. Beachfront cabins all different colours set in palm and pine trees, a/c, TV, a few tent sites, US$10, private farm on beach, horse riding nearby, bike rental, massage, tennis, pool tables, volleyball, basketball, kayaking, restaurant.

AL-A Vistamar, Km 7.9, Route 113, T8952065, www.paradorvistamar.com. 55 rooms, pool, tennis court, restaurant and bar with view down to ocean, live music Sat.

A El Guajataca, Near Quebradillas, Route 2, Km 103.8, T8953070, http://prwest.com/puertorico/guajatca.htm. Beautifully located on hillside with gardens leading down to beach (dangerous swimming). 38 rooms, under renovation 2007, pool, entertainment, restaurant, bars.

Camping

A-B Punta Maracayo Camping, next to Sardinera beach, Km 84.6 on Ruta 2, T8200274. Owned by Hatillo Municipality, surreal with concrete dinosaurs, elephant, etc next to campsite, small sheltered cove, calm water, good swimming, sand average, pool, villas and **cabins** sleep 6-8, minimum 3 days over a weekend, tent for 4 people US$50 for 2 nights, US$20 additional nights, also caravans and motor homes, guard, fenced in, busy at weekends and in summer.

Panoramic Route *p451*

AL Parador Hacienda Juanita, Route 105, Km 23.5, Maricao, T8382550, www.haciendajuanita.com. 21 modest rooms, some sleep 4-6, full breakfast and dinner included, 24-acre farm, part of an old coffee plantation, bar, restaurant, pool, volleyball, tennis, basketball, gardens, walking trails, parking, facilities for disabled, cool at night.

A-B El Castillo, on the road to San Sebastián, Route 111, Km 28.3, Barrio Eneas, T8962365. Lares has nowhere to stay and this is the closest place. New building, good rooms, a/c, TV, pool, games room, barbecue and kitchen for guests' use, also cabins with jacuzzi, parking.

A-C Gutiérrez Guest House, ½ mile east of town centre perched on top of a hill, Route 119, Km 26.1, T8272087. The only accommodation in Las Marías. Essential to book ahead otherwise it may be closed, 13 rooms, big kitchen, pool, bar.

Adjuntas *p452*

LL-A Parador Villas de Sotomayor, Route 10, Km 36.3, Barrio Garzas, T8291717, www.paradorvillassotomayor.com. In valley west of Adjuntas. Villas sleep 2-6, TV, lots of activities, tennis, volleyball, basketball, barbecue, bicycles, horse riding, hiking, nature trails, badminton, pool.

B Hotel Monte Río, 2 blocks from Plaza in Adjuntas, Calle César González 18, T/F8293705, melo@coqui.net. Pool, economical, convenient, a bit old-fashioned but cheerful, daytime restaurant and bar.

Jayuya *p452*

AL-A Parador Hacienda Gripiñas, Route 527 Km 2.7, T8281717, F8281719. About 1 hr's walk from town, 19 rooms in a coffee plantation, main house built in 1858, set in lovely gardens, friendly, pleasant, meals included, bar, restaurant, pool, parking, facilities for disabled.

AL-B Posada Jayuya, Guillermo Esteves 49, T8287250. The only hotel in town, hideous building, conference facilities, can organize excursions, no food, helpful staff, live music Sat.

Caguana Indian Ceremonial Park *p453*

A Casa Grande, Barrio Caonillas, Utuado, Route 612, Km 0.3, T8943939, www.hotelcasagrande.com. 20 rooms in 5 wooden buildings in attractive mountain setting, surrounded by lush greenery, botanical garden and forest, former coffee plantation, hammock on balcony, no a/c, TV or phone, yoga centre with class at 0800, hiking, **Casa Grande Café** has tables indoors, on the patio or on the veranda with lovely view, meal plans available, vegetarian options, pool. Work/exchange programme.

● Eating

For hotel restaurants, see Sleeping, above.

Ponce *p447*

♥♥♥-♥♥ Mark at the Meliá, 2 Cristina, just off main plaza, T8420260, www.hotelmeliapr.com. The restaurant of the Meliá hotel is good and the award-winning chef, Mark French, is on the Puerto Rican National Team.
♥♥ Canda's, Alfonso XII esq Bonair, T8439223. Menu with seafood Mon-Fri 1100-2200, Sat and Sun 1100-2400.

Boquerón *p449*

Joyuda is famous for seafood restaurants on the beach; inexpensive food, good quality, nice atmosphere, whole, grilled fish is a must, especially snapper (*chillo*).

▲ Activities and tours

East of San Juan *p445*

Lots of companies offer day sails, snorkelling, diving and fishing.

Marinas

Isleta Marina, Playa Puerto Real, T6432180 (**Ventajero Sailing Charters**, T8631871, www.sailpuertorico.com, day sails and overnight charters).
Marina Puerto Chico, Route 987, Km 2.4, T8630834; Marina Puerto Real, Playa Puerto Real, T8632188.
Puerto del Rey Marina, Route 33, Km 51.4, T8601000, www.puertodelrey.com (**Sea Ventures Dive Center**, PADI 5-star, T800-7393483, www.divepuertorico.com, *East Wind* catamaran to islands for snorkelling and

beaches, T8603434, www.eastwindcats.com).
Sea Lovers Marina, Route 987, Km 2.3, T8633762.
Villa Marina Yacht Harbour, Route 987, Km 1.3, T8635131 (**Club Nautico Powerboat Rentals**, T8602400, **Caribbean School of Aquatics**, T7286606, catamaran for cruises and day sails, dive boat for snorkelling and diving).
El Conquistador Marina, 1000 El Conquistador Av, T8636594 (**Palomino Island Divers**, T8631000, **Tropical Fishing and Tournaments**, T2664524, deep-sea sport fishing). Lots of other companies offering day sails, snorkelling, diving and fishing.

Ponce *p447*
Tour operators

A tourist **trolley bus** makes a tour of the city, 0900-2130, 1¼ hrs on eastern route, 1¾ hrs west, 1½ hrs north. Free tour of city and out to La Guancha boardwalk on **Chu Chu Tren**, Sat, Sun 0900-1700, T8418160. There are also **horses and carriages**, Thu-Sun 1000-1800.

La Parguera *p448*
Watersports

Parguera Divers are at **Posada Porlamar**, T8994171, www.pargueradivers.com, for wall diving.
Parguera Fishing Charters, T3824698, www.puertoricofishingcharters.com. Will take you reef fishing or out to catch marlin, dorado and tuna.

● Transport

Ponce *p447*

Several flights daily from San Juan. *Público* from San Juan, US$6-7, 2 hrs. *Públicos* serve outlying districts if you have not got a car. Most *carros públicos* leave from the intersection of Victoria and Unión, 3 blocks north of the plaza. To **Guayama**, either direct or via Santa Isabel, US$3.

Mayagüez *p449*

Públicos leave from a modern terminal in Calle Peral. Bus to **San Juan** US$10. Trolley bus service around town is free.

Mona Island *p449*

Boats from **Boquerón** or **Cabo Rojo** 4 hrs, US$1,200 for 20-person boat, less for 14-person boat, leave before dawn. Contact

Captains **Porfirio Andujar**, T8517359; **Ramón Peña**, T2552031; **Catalino Lallave**, T2855129; **David Rodríguez**, T8511885; **Luis Ortiz**, T8516276. Check with the **PR Forestry Service** or **Vieques Air Link** (Coptco Aviation T7290000 for private charter).

Rincón *p450*

Rincón can be reached by *público* from **Mayagüez** or (less frequent) from **Aguadilla**. Public transport is scarce at weekends.

The islands

Vieques, a peaceful, relaxing, low-key island of rolling hills, is 11 km across the sea from Puerto Rico. It was catapulted into the limelight in 1999 when islanders began a successful campaign for the removal of the US military from their bases at the east and west ends of the island. The island is about 34 km long and the inhabitants are mostly concentrated in the main town of Isabel Segunda. It was named Graciosa by Columbus, after a friend's mother, but was then better known as Crab Island by pirates.

Culebra has a climate and landscape similar to that of the Virgin Islands, with tropical forest on the hills and palm groves near the beaches. It is even better than Vieques, with less petty theft, better accommodation, more peace and more beautiful beaches, though the island is poor, with very high unemployment; most people who have jobs work for the municipality or in construction. The island is about 11 km long and 5 km wide. ➤➤ *For Sleeping, Eating and other listings, see pages 459-462.*

Vieques → *Colour map 2, B6. Population: 9,400.*

Fajardo is the closest sea and airport to Vieques. To reach the islands, catch the ferry or a plane from San Juan or Fajardo. *Públicos* meet you at the airport and ferry dock (posted rates US$2-5, but some drivers will try to overcharge you, ask the price first), or let your hotel/guesthouse arrange transport for you. If you use a *público* to go to the beach you can arrange a time to be picked up later. Car hire is widely available on the island.

There is an excellent historical museum in Isabel Segunda at the beautifully restored fort, **El Fortín Conde de Mirasol** ① *no reservations required to visit the fort but if you want to access the archives, contact Robert Rabin, the historian, T7411717 (7418651 evenings)*, which was the last fort begun by the Spanish in the Western Hemisphere. There is another interesting exhibit at the **Punta Mulas Lighthouse** ① *T7415000, daily 0800-1630*.

The small beach town of **Esperanza** is the main area of guesthouses and restaurants geared at tourists, bars, dive companies (**Blue Caribe Dive Center**, SSI facility, full service, T7412522, PO Box 1574), etc. The town's **museum** ① *T7418850, Tue-Sun 1100-1500*, has archaeological and natural history exhibits.

❖ *The biggest 'action' is on Saturday night in Esperanza. Everyone promenades along the sea front dressed in their finest, talking and flirting, before going to a nightclub or bar.*

The US Military used to own two-thirds of Vieques, but since 2003 the land has been a national park, see page 463. Vieques has over 52 beaches in secluded coves. Public **Sun Bay** has picnic and camping areas (no shade in camping area, lots of petty theft). Small, hardy, island horses, most with paso fino blood lines (that means smooth gaits with no bouncing), are still used as transport, and wild horses roam the island. Renting a horse is an exciting way to explore the island.

Mosquito Bay, also known as **Phosphorescent Bay**, is a large, but very shallow bay, surrounded by mangrove trees and full of bioluminescent organisms. The organisms glow when disturbed. The glow generated by a 13-cm fish is about a 39 cm circle of light brighter than a light bulb. Swimming in this glow is a wonderful experience. Sightseeing trips go at night (see Activities and tours). The beaches here

Mosquito permits camping, but watch out for petty theft.

Culebra → *Colour map 2, B6. Population: 3,500.*

The main village, **Dewey** (called Pueblo by the locals) is attractively set between two lagoons. A visitors' information centre is in the City Hall, and there's a **tourist office** ① *T7423291, F7420111*. About 40% of the land is park or national reserve, including many beaches. The **Culebra National Wildlife Refuge** ① *T7420115*, 600 ha, comprising 23 offshore islands and four parcels of land on Culebra, protects large colonies of sea birds, particularly terns, red-billed tropic birds and boobies, as well as nesting sea turtles: hawksbill, leatherback, loggerhead and green. Volunteers are welcomed (April to August) to help Wildlife Refuge rangers count and protect nests and hatchlings. Contact **Culebra Leatherback Project** ① *PO Box 617, Culebra, PR 00775, T7420050*.

Flamenco Beach is 1½ km long with white sand and exquisitely beautiful clear turquoise water, a reef at one end and waves at the other. It is almost deserted except for a few guesthouses at the far end selling a limited amount of drinks, but it becomes a zoo at summer weekends. **Culebrita** and **Luís Peña** are two small cays offshore with beaches. Both are wildlife sanctuaries.

● Sleeping

Vieques *p458*
www.vieques-island.com.
www.enchanted-isle.com.
LL-L Inn on the Blue Horizon, Route 996, Km 4.2, on the beach west of Esperanza, T7413318, www.innonthebluehorizon.com. Run by Billy Knight and James Weis, from New York, 9 rooms furnished with antiques, original art and billowing drapes, pool, popular bar and restaurant, tennis, children under 14 allowed in low season only.
LL-AL Crow's Nest, inland, T7410033, www.crowsnestvieques.com. 16 rooms with kitchenettes or 2-bedroom suites with living areas, breakfast included, pool, restaurant.
LL-AL Hacienda Tamarindo, inland T7410420, www.haciendatamarindo.com. 16 elegant rooms, suites and a 2-bedroom villa, breakfast included, no children under 15 in high season, none under 8 in low season, sea views, pool, run by Linda Vail, an interior designer before taking on the hotel.
AL-A Amapola, Flamboyan 144, Esperanza, T7411382, www.enchanted-isle.com/amapola. 5 a/c rooms with private baths and 3 studio apartments, all brightly painted and colourful, restaurant.
A Bananas Guest House, Esperanza, T7418700, www.bananasguesthouse.com. Facing the ocean. Some rooms a/c, some with fan, some with fridge, simple but charming.
A Tradewinds, T7418666, www.enchanted-isle.com/tradewinds. Bar,

restaurant, owned by Janet and Harry Washburn.
A Vieques Ocean View, 751 Calle Plinio Peterson, Isabel Segunda, T7413696, F7411793. Concrete block hotel right on water's edge next to ferry dock, 31 rooms with balconies, Chinese restaurant next door under same ownership, car rental for guests.
A-B Sea Gate, Isabel Segunda, near the fort, T7414661, www.seagatehotel.com. 16 rooms, apartments and cottages high up on hill, good views, breakfast served on your balcony, pool, tennis, beach shuttle, horse riding.
C Posada Vistamar, 1 block from Malecón, Barrio Esperanza, Isabel Segunda, T741 8716. 5 rooms, a/c, fan, basic but adequate, helpful and friendly, excellent food, mosquitoes, no sea view.

Culebra *p459*
www.culebra.org.
L Club Seabourne Mini Resort, Fulladoza Bay, T7423169, www.clubseabourne.com. Villas and rooms, breakfast included, range of packages, restaurant, bar, pool, view, 1 mile from town, car hire needed.
L-AL Tamarindo Estates, T7423343, www.tamarindoestates.com. Pool, dock, private bay, 12, 1-2-bedroom cottages with kitchens on 60-acre undeveloped estate, snorkelling, dirt access road with potholes, 2 miles to town, car hire needed.
L-AL Villa Flamenco Beach, on the beach, 2

miles from town, T7420023. 2, 1-bedroom apartments sleep 4, 4 studios upstairs sleep 2, best to get ocean view with balcony rather than at the rear, no a/c, hot water in shower only, nice place to stay, casual and relaxed, right on the sand.

AL Posada La Hamaca, 68 Castelar, T7423516, www.posada.com. Well kept, 6 rooms, private bath, 3 efficiencies with well-equipped kitchenettes, and an apartment which sleeps 8, beach towels, coolers and ice provided for picnics, book in advance, next to Mamacitas on the canal.

AL Villa Boheme, Ensenada Honda, T/F7423508, www.villaboheme.com. On the edge of town, harbour front. Family place, well managed, clean, a/c, fans, 12 rooms, variety of sizes, sleep 2-6, 9 with communal kitchen, 3 with private kitchens, lovely breeze.

A Arynar Villa, T7423145, berniefrancette@cs.com. Run by the very welcoming Francette and Bernie, 2 rooms in lovely house on hillside above the water, breakfast included, hammocks, deck, less than a mile to town, open mid-Oct-mid-May.

A Culebra Beach Resort, T7420319. Run by Max and Esmeralda, next to Villa Flamenco, on the beach, nice, simple, clean rooms with kitchen, pleasant, helpful, lots of repeat business.

A Villa Fulladoza Guest House, T7423576, on the bay. Best value, kitchens, short walk to town, usually booked up.

A-B Mamacitas Guest House, in town on the canal of Laguna Lobinas, T7420090, www.mamacitaspr.com. Also restaurant, bar and gift shop. With or without kitchens, suites have balconies, room for handicapped with adjoining room for carer, a/c, boat dock for guests. Iguanas may join you at mealtimes.

Camping

Culebra Campgrounds are government-run, US$10 per site, up to 6 people per tent, 2-night minimum, 140 tent sites, bathrooms and water provided but that's all. Not crowded during winter months, just turn up, office open 0700-1800, T7420700. To make a reservation (essential Jun-Sep) send US$20 cheque to *Autoridad de Conservación y Desarrollo de Culebra*, attn Playa Flamenco, Apdo 217, Culebra, PR 00775 USA.

🍴 Eating

Vieques *p458*

Almost all of the island's restaurants are part of a hotel or guesthouse, most close by 2100.

♦♦♦ Café Media Luna, 351 AG Mellado, Isabel Segunda, T7412594. In yellow colonial house, food a fusion of Puerto Rican and Indian, run by a Puerto Rican from New York and his wife from Bombay, choose a variety of dishes from a tasting menu, tapas style, allow US$50 per person with wine, live music some nights, reservations recommended.

♦♦♦-♦♦ The M Bar, inland, opposite Wyndham Martineau Bay, on road to airport, T7414000. Closed Mon. Breezy bar and restaurant with very good food, particularly seafood, and music. One of the few places open late with a bar menu from 2200.

♦♦♦-♦♦ Uvas, Main St, Isabel Segunda. Fine dining in the restaurant, Argentine chef, also tapas bar outdoors open late, which is more casual.

♦♦ Island Steak House, at Crow's Nest Inn. Fri-Tue. Eat upstairs, open air, very popular Tue happy hour with finger food and Fri Latin fusion menu, reservations essential.

♦♦ La Sirena, Esperanza, T7414462. Waterfront French Caribbean, delicious 3-course dinner with wine US$30-35, some nights steel band and dancing.

♦♦ Posada Vistamar, Isabel Segunda (see above). Great Puerto Rican food with modern interpretation, full meal with wine around US$30.

♦♦-♦ Bananas, T7418700, Flamboyán St, Esperanza. Food until 2200-2300. Pub food, burgers and pizzas as well as ribs and grilled fish, beachfront, late bar, popular hang-out.

♦♦-♦ Coconuts, Isabel Segunda. Breakfast, lunch and dinner. Popular with residents, particularly Sat nights for paella and steel band music when you'll need a reservation.

♦♦-♦ Scoops, Isabel Segunda. Breakfast, lunch and dinner. Pizza and calzoni, ice cream, fresh fruit and vegetable juices and smoothies.

♦ Café Mar Azul, Isabel Segunda, bar on ocean front, T7413400. 0900-0100, happy hour 1700-1800. Popular, pool table, a place to hang out.

♦ Crabwalk Café, next to Tradewinds, Esperanza. Opens 0800. Sandwiches, salads.

♦ Taverna Española, Isabel Segunda, T7411175. Spanish food, seafood, cheap and

cheerful, around US$15 for meal with wine.
❚ **Tropical Baby**, Isabel Segunda, main street. Breakfast and lunch. Healthy food.

Culebra *p459*

Prices range from US$10-25 for a meal. There are several small restaurants in Dewey, offering local dishes and seafood. Takeaways available.

❚❚❚-❚❚ **Juanita Bananas**, on hill above Dewey, T7423855. Fri-Mon 1800-2200. Good food, nice setting, take your own wine, often full, reservations recommended.

❚❚ **Barbara Rosa's**, Dewey, T3971923. Popular, good seafood, don't miss the crab cakes or shark nuggets.

❚❚ **Coconuts Beach Grill**, Culebra Villas, Flamenco Beach, T7420280. Wed-Sun 1200-2000. Great grilled tiger prawns, sangria with a kick.

❚ **Café Isola**, opposite the ferry dock. Mon, Wed, Fri 1100-2000, Tue, Thu 1100-1530. Tapas served Mon, Wed, Fri from 1730. Draft beer and espresso coffee, also darts.

❚ **Dinghy Dock Restaurant** on the water in the lagoon, T7420581. Breakfast, lunch and dinner. American and Caribbean food, service sometimes lacking, has a rare salad bar. There are also restaurants at the hotels, **Mamacitas** (music Fri, Sat, jazz brunch Sun), **Seabourne**, **Tamarindo**. For those who are self-catering, there are 7 grocery stores; **Culebra Deli** is a fish market and a liquor store. All on the island is imported so prices are high.

▲ Activities and tours

Vieques *p458*
Tour operators

Sightseeing trips go to **Phosphorescent Bay** at night, US$15-18. **Clark**, T7417600. Has a small boat. Sharon Grasso at **Island Adventures**, T741-0717/0720, www.biobay.com, electric boat, naturalist, US$23 for night-time tour. **Blue Caribe Divers**, T7412522. Night-time kayak tours, US$23, and night scuba dives. This is the only dive shop on the island, charging US$90 for a 2-tank dive with equipment rental.

Culebra *p459*
Diving and watersports

There are good, sandy beaches, clear water and a coral reef. Scuba diving is spectacular in the waters around Culebra, where the sea is clear and the pristine reefs provide lots to see. Dive shops are small and friendly, with flexible programmes and other watersports and boat trips on offer.

Culebra Divers, opposite the ferry dock, T7420803, www.culebradivers.com. Run by Walter Rieder (Swiss) and Monika Frei (both instructors).

Culebra Dive Shop, T7420566.

Ocean Safari, T3791973. Kayak rental from Jim and Barbara Peters, US$25 half day, guided expeditions US$45 half day, US$70 full day.

Tour operators

Several people offer boat trips or water taxi, some of whom can also do fishing.

Pat's Water Taxi and glass-bottom boat trips, from the dock by **Dinghy Dock Restaurant**, T5010011. To Culebrita US$40, Luis Peña US$20, glass-bottom tours US$15, snorkelling tours US$20-40.

Culebra Boat Rental, T7873559, hires 6-person skiffs for exploring and transport. **Jack's**, T3977494, offers boat trips for snorkelling or water taxi service to the cays offshore, as do **Tanama Glass-Bottom Boat**, T5010011, **Culebra Divers**, T7420803, and **Guilins Water Taxi**, T7420575.

● Transport

Vieques *p458*
Air

Vieques Air Link (T7413266) have flights from **Fajardo** (on demand, every 1-1½ hrs until 1730, 10 mins, US$23 one way, T8633020), **San Juan International** (30 mins, T7223736), and **Isla Grande**, US$45 one way, and **St Croix** (30 mins, T7789858) many times a day. Isla Nena, T7411577, and the charter airline **Air Culebra**, T2686951, also fly to Vieques.

Boat

In Dec-Apr a private ferry leaves **Old San Juan** at 0800, arriving Culebra at 0945, leaving again at 1030 and arriving in Vieques at 1100, then going back at 1630, departing Culebra at 1730, arriving San Juan at 1915. On Fri, Sat, Sun it leaves Vieques later, at 1830, Culebra at 1930, arriving San Juan at 2115. **Island Hi-Speed Ferry**, T1-877-2283977, www.islandhispeedferry.com. One way ticket to Culebra US$42, to Vieques US$47, round

Puerto Rico The islands Listings

trip Culebra US$68 and Vieques US$78. Vieques to Culebra and back US$33 or US$22 one way (rates reduced for residents and children). From **Fajardo**, the passenger ferries leave Mon-Fri 0930, 1300, 1630, 2000, returning from Vieques 0630, 1100, 1500, 1830. On Sat, Sun and holiday Mon, it departs Fajardo 0900, 1500, 1800, returning from Vieques 0630, 1300, 1630, US$2 one way, 1½ hrs. Cars US$15-19 depending on size, Reservations must be made at least 2 weeks in advance for cars but not required for passengers. **Car/cargo ferries** leave **Fajardo** Mon-Fri 0400, 0930, 1630, returning 0600, 1300, 1800. In Fajardo call the Port Authority office to transport a car, T8630852, in Vieques T7414761, open for reservations 0800-1100, 1300-1500.

Car

There are several car rental companies including **Maritza's Car Rental**, T7410078, www.islavieques.com/maritzas; **Island Car Rentals**, T7411666; or **Vieques Car and Jeep Rental**, T7411037, www.viequescarrental.com.

Cycle

Bicycle rental through **La Dulce Vida Mountain Bike and Adventure Co**, Calle Orquideas 69, T4353557, www.bikevieques .com. Rentals US$25/day including helmet, lock, delivery, or weekly rates and tours starting at US$65.

Culebra *p459*

Public transport consists of vans; if they're not at the airport, walk into town. They also run from town to Flamenco Beach, but for access to other beaches, cars and bicycles can be hired and there is also a taxi service.

Air

There are no direct flights Vieques-Culebra. Flights from **San Juan International Airport** take 30 mins, from **Isla Grande Airport** 30 mins and from **Fajardo** 15 mins. **Isla Nena**, at San Juan International Airport,

T(888)2636213, 7411577, in Culebra, T7420972, flies 4 times a day **San Juan**-Culebra, US$60 one way, US$115 return, also 3 times a day Culebra-**Fajardo**, US$20 one way, and Culebra-**St Thomas**, US$50 on the mail flight Tue and Thu. **Vieques Air Link**, T7420254 (Culebra), T8633020 (Fajardo), T7223736 (San Juan), **San Juan Isla Grande**-Culebra twice a day, US$43 one way, and 3 times a day **Fajardo**-Culebra, US$20. **Air Culebra** is a charter company, T2686951, US$300 one way for up to 5 people.

Boat

At weekends the ferries are usually full; best to fly. See Vieques Boat, above for ferry from **Old San Juan**. The public ferry from Fajardo to Culebra takes about 1½ hrs, and costs US$2 per person each way, cars about US$26 return. Reservations 2 weeks in advance needed for cars. Fajardo ticket and information office is open 0800-1100, 1300-1500, T8630705, 1-800-9812005 (Culebra T7423161). Ferries which take cars are slower and rougher and passengers tend to get seasick. Cars also sometimes get bumped off; it is better to hire a 4WD on Culebra when you get there. A ferry sails weekdays Vieques-Culebra at 0600, returning 1700, US$2 each way.

Car

Cars and jeeps can be rented from **Prestige**, 7423242; **Richard and Kathy's Rentals**, T7420062; **Willy Solis**, T7423537; **R & W**, T7420563; and **Jerry's Jeeps**, T7420587.

Cycle

Bicycle hire is US$12 per day from **Culebra Bike and Beach**, T7420434; **Richard**, T7420062; or **Wille**, T7420563.

Taxi

Taxi service with **Marcelino**, T7420292, or **Cito**, T7422787.

Background

History

Columbus, accompanied by a young nobleman, Juan Ponce de León, arrived in Puerto Rico on 19 November 1493. Attracted by tales of gold, Ponce obtained permission to

colonize Boriquén (or Boriken), as it was called by the natives. Boriquén (later altered 463
to Borinquén in poetry) meant 'land of the great lord' and was called that because of
the belief that the god, Juracan, lived on the highest peak and controlled the weather
from there. The word 'hurricane' is derived from this god's name.

Because of Puerto Rico's excellent location at the gateway to Latin America, it
played an important part in defending the Spanish Empire against attacks from French,
English and Dutch. After the Spanish-American war, Spain ceded the island to the
United States in 1898. The inhabitants became US citizens in 1917, and in 1948 they
elected their own Governor, who is authorized to appoint his Cabinet and members of
the island's Supreme Court. In 1952 Puerto Rico became a Commonwealth voluntarily
associated with the United States.

The island's status is constantly debated for both political and economic reasons
as Puerto Rico is heavily dependent on US funding. The New Progressive Party (NPP)
favours Puerto Rico's full accession to the USA as the 51st state. The Popular
Democratic Party (PDP) favours enhancement of the existing Commonwealth status.
Pro-Independence groups receive less support, the Puerto Rican Independence Party
(PIP) struggles to gain seats in Congress. A referendum on Puerto Rico's future status
was held in 1991 and 1993.

In December 1998 Puerto Ricans voted again in a referendum on the island's
status. 46.5% was in favour of statehood, but 50.2% voted for 'none of the above'
options, which were to continue the present Commonwealth status, enter the USA as a
state of the union, free association, or become independent, with a 10-year transitional
period for any change in status. 'None of the above' was included at the request of the
PDP, which supports the present Commonwealth status but objected to the wording.

The presence of the US Navy on Vieques became an issue after a civilian was
killed in 1999 during bombing practice. Local people on Vieques and Puerto Rico
protested and called for a ban on live ammunition and the return of the land to the
people of Vieques. Exercises using live ammunition were suspended in May 1999.
Governor Rosselló rejected a US presidential panel's recommendation that exercises
should continue for another five years. President Clinton offered to limit operations to
90 days a year instead of the previous 180, and then conceded that live ammunition
would no longer be used, while offering US$40 mn in development aid for the island if
residents accepted the five-year continuation. His proposals were rejected. A revised
proposal from the Pentagon was also rejected and civil disobedience intensified
during 2000. In May 2000 US Navy aircraft resumed bombing practice. Dummy
ammunition was used.

In November 2000, Sila Calderón, of the PDP, a business executive and former
Secretary of State in the previous PDP administration in the 1980s, was elected
Governor on an anti-statehood platform. The PDP won the majority of seats in both
houses, giving it a clear mandate not to become the 51st state of the union. The
victory was also seen as a popular rejection of the agreement with the US
administration to delay until 2003 the withdrawal of the Navy from its bombing range
on Vieques. The Navy refused to transfer 8,000 acres of land on Vieques to the
government, planned for 31 December, until Ms Calderón promised to stand by the
agreement. In May 2003, amid general rejoicing, the Navy finally pulled out of
Vieques and the land became a national park.

The latest elections, in November 2004 were so close that a recount had to be
held for only the second time ever. Victory was given to the PDP, with 48.4% of the
vote, led by Aníbal Acevedo Velá, against 48.2% for the NPP led by Pedro Rosselló.
Governor Acevedo took office at the beginning of 2005.

Geography
Puerto Rico is the smallest of the Greater Antilles. Old volcanic mountains, long
inactive, occupy a large part of the interior, with the highest peak, Cerro de Punta, at

1,338 m in the Cordillera Central. North of the Cordillera is the karst country where the limestone has been acted upon by water to produce a series of small steep hills (*mogotes*) and deep holes, both conical in shape. There is an extensive cave system, much of which is open to the public or can be explored with expert guidance. The mountains are surrounded by a coastal plain with the Atlantic shore beaches cooled all the year round by trade winds. Offshore are the sister islands of Vieques, Culebra and the even smaller Mona Island, where facilities are limited to a camp site.

Government

Puerto Rico is a self-governing Commonwealth in association with the USA (Estado Libre Asociado de Puerto Rico). The chief of state is the President of the United States of America. The head of government is an elected Governor. There are two legislative chambers: the House of Representatives, 51 seats, and the Senate, 27 seats. Two extra seats are granted in each house to the opposition if necessary to limit any party's control to two thirds. Puerto Ricans do not vote in US federal elections, nor do they pay federal taxes, when resident on the island.

Economy

The 'Operation Bootstrap' industrialization programme, supported by the US and Puerto Rican governments, began in 1948, and manufacturing for export subsequently became the most important sector of the economy. Until 1976, US Corporations were given tax incentives to set up in Puerto Rico and their profits were taxed only if repatriated. Industrial parks were built based on labour intensive industries to take advantage of Puerto Rico's low wages. In the mid-1970s, however, the strategy changed to attract capital intensive companies with the aim of avoiding the low wage trap. The agreement between the USA, Canada and Mexico for the North American Free Trade Agreement (NAFTA) also had implications for Puerto Rico because of competition for jobs and investment. Although wage levels were lower in Mexico, Section 936 gave companies in Puerto Rico an advantage in pharmaceuticals and hi-tec industries. In low-skill labour-intensive manufacturing, Mexico had the advantage. Puerto Rico currently employs 30,000 in the clothing industry. Dairy and livestock production is one of the leading agricultural activities; others are the cultivation of sugar, tobacco, coffee, pineapples and coconut. Rum has been a major export since the 19th century and the island supplies 83% of all the rum drunk in mainland USA. Tourism is another key element in the economy although it contributes only about 7% to gdp. Over 4 mn people visit Puerto Rico each year and spend about US$1.9 bn. Large construction projects have recently boosted tourism still further, with several 5-star hotels being built around the country and a massive Convention Center with adjacent 850-room hotel at Isla Grande.

Despite the progress made to industrialize the country, the economy has suffered from US budget cuts. Some 30% of all spending on GNP originates in Washington and high unemployment is possible because of food stamps and other US transfers. Migration is a safety valve, and there are more Puerto Ricans living in New York than San Juan. The economy depends heavily on tax incentives given to US mainland companies and on federal transfers.

Culture

Music and dance One of the oldest musical traditions is that of the 19th-century Danza, associated particularly with the name of Juan Morel Campos and his phenomenal output of 549 compositions. This is European-derived salon music for ballroom dancing, slow, romantic and sentimental. The Institute of Puerto Rican Culture sponsors an annual competition for writers of danzas for the piano during the Puerto Rican Danza Week in May. The peasants of the interior, the Jíbaros, sing and dance the Seis, of Spanish origin, in its many varied forms, such as the Seis Chorreao, Seis

Zapateao, Seis Corrido and Seis Bombeao. Other variants are named after places, like the Seis Cagueño and Seis Fajardeño. Favoured instruments are the *cuatro* and other varieties of the guitar, the *bordonúa*, *tiple*, *tres* and *quintillo*, backed by *güiro* (scraper), *maracas*, *pandereta* (tambourine) and *bomba* (drum) to provide rhythm. One uniquely Puerto Rican phenomenon is the singer's 'La-Le-Lo-Lai' introduction to the verses, which are in Spanish 10-line *décimas*. The beautiful Aguinaldos are sung at Christmastime, while the words of the Mapeyé express the Jíbaro's somewhat tragic view of life. Many artists have recorded the mountain music, notably **El Gallito de Manatí, Ramito, Chuito el de Bayamón, Baltazar Carrero** and **El Jibarito de Lares**.

Puerto Rico's best-known musical genre is the **Plena**, ironically developed by a black couple from Barbados, John Clark and Catherine George, known as 'Los Ingleses', who lived in the La Joya del Castillo neighbourhood of Ponce during the years of the First World War. With a four-line stanza and refrain in call-and-response between the *Inspirador* (soloist) and chorus, the rhythm is distinctly African and the words embody calypso-style commentaries on social affairs and true-life incidents. Accompanying instruments were originally tambourines, then accordions and *güiros*, but nowadays include guitars, trumpets and clarinets. The Plena's most celebrated composer and performer was **Manuel A Jiménez**, known as 'Canario'.

❖ *Each year several music festivals celebrate different styles and forms, including Jazzfest in May and Casals Music Festival in June.*

The only black music in Puerto Rico is the Bomba, sung by the 'Cantaor' and chorus, accompanied by the drums called *buleadores* and *subidores*. The Bomba can be seen and heard at its best in the island's only black town of Loiza Aldea at the Feast of Santiago in late July. Rafael Cepeda and his family are the best known exponents.

Literature The **Jíbaro** is a common figure in Puerto Rican literature. It refers to the *campesino del interior*, a sort of Puerto Rican equivalent to the gaucho, native, but with predominantly hispanic features. The literary Jíbaro first appeared in the 19th century, with **Manuel Alonso Pacheco's** *El gíbaro* emerging as a cornerstone of the island's literature. Alonso attempted to describe and to interpret Puerto Rican life; he showed a form of rural life about to disappear in the face of bourgeois progress. The book also appeared at a time (1849) when romanticism was gaining popularity. Before this, there had been a definite gulf between the educated letters, chronicles and memoires of the 16th to 18th centuries and the oral traditions of the people. These included *coplas*, *décimas*, *aguinaldas* and folk tales. The Jíbaro has survived the various literary trends, from 19th-century romanticism and *realismo costumbrista* (writing about manners and customs), through the change from Spanish to US influence, well into the 20th century.

One reason for this tenacity is the continual search for a Puerto Rican identity. When, in 1898, Spain relinquished power to the USA, many Puerto Ricans sought full Independence. Among the writers of this time were **José de Diego** and **Manuel Zeno Gandía**. The latter's series of four novels, *Crónicas de un mundo enfermo* (*Garduña*, 1896; *La charca*, 1898; *El negocio*, 1922; *Redentores*, 1925), contain a strong element of social protest. For a variety of domestic reasons, many fled the island to seek adventures, happiness and wealth in the United States. While some writers and artists in the 1930s and 1940s tried to build a kind of nationalism around a mythical, rural past, others still favoured a separation from the colonialism which had characterized Puerto Rico's history. For a while, the former trend dominated, but by the 1960s the emigré culture had created a different set of themes against the search for the Puerto Rican secure in his/her national identity. These included the social problems of the islander in New York, shown in some of the novels of **Enrique A Laguerre**, *Trópico en Manhattan* by **Guillermo Cotto Thorner**, or stories such as *Spiks* by **Pedro Juan Soto**, or plays like **René Marqués'** *La carreta*. There is also the Americanization of the island, the figure of the 'piti-yanqui' (the native Puerto Rican who admires his North American neighbour) and the subordination of the agricultural to a US-based, industrial economy. Writers after 1965 who have documented this change include **Rosario Ferré** and the novelist and playwright, **Luis Rafael Sánchez**. The latter's *La guaracha del Macho Camacho* (1976) revolves around a traffic jam in a San Juan taken over by a popular song, *La vida es una cosa fenomenal*, a far cry from the Jíbaro's world.

Flora and fauna

Although less than 1% of the island is virgin forest, there are several forest reserves designed to protect plants and wildlife. At the highest altitude you find dwarf cloud forest, with palms, ferns and epiphytes. On exposed ridges it has a windswept appearance. Below the dwarf forest is the rainforest and below that the subtropical wet forest, with open-crowned trees and canopy trees such as *Cyrilla racemiflora*, which is large with reddish bark. Classifications below this include the lower wet forest (Tabanuco) and the subtropical moist forest zone, which covers most of Puerto Rico, and dry forest, found along the south coast and the eastern tip of the island.

In **El Yunque Tropical Rain Forest** (called **The Caribbean National Forest**) there are an estimated 240 types of tree (26 indigenous), and many other plants, such as tiny wild orchids, bamboo trees and giant ferns. The total area is 11,270 ha and 75% of Puerto Rico's virgin forest is here. Several marked paths (quite easy, you could walk two or three in a day, no guide needed), recreational areas and information areas have been set up. It is also home to the Puerto Rican parrot, but there are only 30 left. The whole forest is a bird sanctuary. (*Las aves de Puerto Rico*, by Virgilio Biaggi, University of Puerto Rico, 1983, US$12.95, and Herbert Raffaele's *Guide to the Birds of Puerto Rico and the Virgin Islands* is recommended.)

Mangroves are protected in **Aguirre Forest**, on the south coast near Salinas, at the **Jobos Bay National Estuarine Research Reserve** ⓘ *Box 1170, Guayama, Puerto Rico 00655, T8640105, or 7248774 in San Juan*, at the west end of Jobos Bay from Aguirre, and at Piñones Forest, east of San Juan. Unlike the north coast mangroves, those on the south coast tend to die behind the outer fringe because not enough water is received to wash away the salt. This leaves areas of mud and skeletal trees which, at times of spring tide, flood and are home to many birds. In winter, many ducks stop on their migration routes at Jobos. Also at **Jobos Bay**, manatees and turtles can be seen. A short boardwalk runs into the mangroves at Jobos, while at Aguirre a man runs catamaran trips to the offshore cays, and there are some good fish restaurants; take Route 7710. For Jobos Bay take Route 703, to Las Mareas de Salinas (marked Mar Negro on some maps). Before going to Jobos, contact the office at Jobos.

The largest number of bird species can be found at the 655-ha **Guánica Forest** ⓘ *T7231770, daily 0900-1700, no admission charge; wear protective clothing and take drinking water*, west of Ponce, which is home to 700 plant species of which 48 are endangered and 16 exist nowhere else. Guánica's dry forest vegetation is unique and the forest has been declared an International Biosphere Reserve by UNESCO. There are 10 marked trails through the forest, but contact the wardens for directions before wandering off. It can be hot in the middle of the day so don't be too ambitious in which trail you choose. The Ballena Trail is quite short and you will see lizards, snakes, birds and a 700-year old *guayacán* tree, very gnarled and not as big as you might expect. If you want to head for the beach, Playa de Ventanas is within the Reserve. The **Punta Ballena Reserve** is next to the Guánica Forest and included in the Biosphere Reserve because of coastal ecosystem. It contains mangrove forest, manatees, nesting sites for hawksbill turtles, and crested toads. Beach access off Route 333.

Other forest reserves, some of which are mentioned above are **Aguirre**, T8640105, **Boquerón**, T8517260, **Cambalache**, T8811004, **Carite**, T7474545, **Casa Pueblo Forest**, T8524440, **Ceiba**, T8524440, **Cerrillos**, T7243724, **Guánicam**, T8215706, **Guajataca** in the northeast, T8721045, **Guilarte**, T8295767, **Maricao**, T7243724, **Mona Island**, T7243724, **Piñones**, T7917750, **Río Abajo**, T8806557, **Susúa**, T7243724, **Toro Negro**, T8673040, **Vega**, T8332240. These can also be contacted through the Central Office in San Juan, T7243724, or at prforests@hotmail.com.

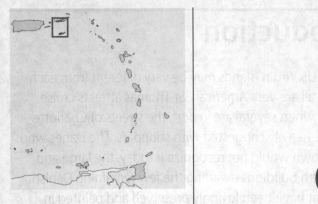

US Virgin Islands

Footprint features

Introduction

The three US Virgin Islands may be very different from each
other, but all are very American. St Thomas attracts cruise
ships and, when several are in port, the streets of Charlotte
Amalie are heavily congested with shoppers. The Danes who
built the town would not recognize it today, the large and
ugly modern buildings dwarfing the few remaining Danish
houses that have been lovingly preserved and painted in
pastel colours. St John is dominated by the Virgin Islands
National Park, which has been in existence since 1956 and has
some excellent trails in the hills for walkers and under the sea
for snorkellers. Compared with St Thomas it is low key, but
even here certain beaches can be packed with day-trippers on
package tours. St Croix is the poorest of the three and perhaps
for that reason has more to offer the visitor who wants to
explore the island without the hassle of crowds. Although
blighted by an oil refinery and dependent on tourism for a
large part of its income, the island is relatively unspoilt, with
some pretty bays, lush rainforest in the west and rewarding
diving. Christiansted can only receive small cruise ships
because of the barrier reef so it is never as crowded as St
Thomas, and there is an active restoration programme for its
colonial Danish buildings, which include forts as well as
red-roofed houses. All three islands have good hotels, a wide
selection of restaurants and bars and are popular with the
sailing fraternity.

★ Don't miss...

1 **Water Island** The smallest, inhabited island was purchased from Denmark by the USA in 1944 for use as a military base, but was relinquished by the Department of Defense in 1952, page 478.
2 **Virgin Islands National Park** Around two-thirds of the island of St John is a national park, page 485.
3 **Christiansted** The red roofs and pastel-painted houses of the former Danish capital overlook Kings Wharf and the waterfront, page 490.
4 **Fort Christiansvaern** The fortress was built by the Danes in 1749 with a commanding view of the bay and is now open to the public, page 490.
5 **Buck Island** The island and reef offshore are a national park, with snorkelling trails, lots of fish and nesting sites of turtles, page 492.

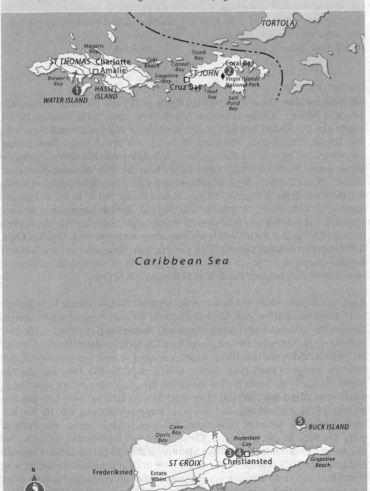

US Virgin Islands

Essentials

Before you travel

Tourist offices overseas

Canada 703 Evans Av, Suite 106, Toronto, Ontario, M9C 5E9, T416-6227600, jsintzel@travelmarketgroup.com.

Denmark Park Allé 5, DK-8000 Aarhus, usvi@danskvestindiskturist.dk.

Italy Via Carlo Pisacane 26, 20129, Milan, T(39)02-33105841, USVI@themasrl.it.

Puerto Rico 60 Washington Street, Suite 1102, San Juan 00907, ncumpiano@usa.net.

UK Molasses House, Clove Hitch Cay, Plantation Wharf, London SW11 3TW, T020-89940978, usvi@destination-marketing.co.uk.

USA Atlanta, Marquis One Tower, Atlanta,

GA 30303, T404-6880906, usviatl@aol.com; **Chicago**, 500 North Michigan Av, Suite 2030, Chicago, IL 60611, T312-6708784, usvichgo@earthlink.net; **Los Angeles**, 3460 Wilshire Boulevard, Suite 412, CA 90010, T213-7390138, usvila@msn.com; **Miami**, 2655 South LeJeune Rd, Suite 907, Coral Gables, FL 33134, T305-4427200, usvimia@aol.com; **New York**, 1270 Av of the Americas, Suite 2108, NY 10020, T212-3322222, usviny@aol.com; **Washington DC**, 444 North Capital St, Suite 305, DC 20001, T202-6243590, usvidc@sso.org.

Getting there

Air From the USA: There are scheduled flights to St Croix and/or St Thomas with **American Airlines** (Baltimore, Boston, Miami, New York), **Delta** (Atlanta, Detroit, Washington DC), **United Airlines** (Chicago, Washington DC), **Continental** (New York), and **US Air** (Philadelphia, Charlotte). There are no direct flights **from Europe**; connections can be made via Miami or Puerto Rico, St Maarten and Antigua. During the winter season there are many charter flights from the USA (**Midwest, Northeast**), Canada, UK and Denmark. **Regional airlines** link the USVI with other Caribbean islands and there are flights to Anguilla, Antigua, St Barthélemy, Puerto Rico (San Juan and Fajardo), St Kitts, Nevis, St Maarten and the BVI. **Bohlke International Airways**, T7789177, has a charter service between St Thomas and St Croix and day trips to Virgin Gorda and Anegada in the BVI with lunch, swimming and sightseeing. **American Eagle, Gulfstream International, Cape Air** (T800 3520714, www.flycapeair.com) and **Seaborne Aviation** (seaplane, T7736442 in St Croix, T7771227 in St Thomas) all run services several times daily between Puerto Rico, St Thomas and St Croix.

Boat Ocean-going ships can be accommodated at Charlotte Amalie in St Thomas and Frederiksted and the South Shore cargo port in St Croix. There are regular services between the USVI and the BVI (passport needed). **Native Son** (T7748685) and **Smith's Ferry** (T7757292) alternate services weekly from Charlotte Amalie to West End, Tortola (45 minutes, US$25 one way, US$45 return), Red Hook to West End (same fares), and Charlotte Amalie to Road Town, Tortola, several daily. Smith's Ferry also sail Red Hook-Cruz Bay-Virgin Gorda (US$60 round trip, Thu, Sun 0800, return 1500, 1hr 45 mins). **Inter Island Boat Services** (T7766597) several daily between Cruz Bay and West End (US$40 round trip); Red Hook-Cruz Bay-Jost Van Dyke, BVI, Fri, Sat, Sun 0800 and 1400, returning 0915, 1500, 45 mins, US$50 round trip. **Ports of entry** Charlotte Amalie, St Thomas; Christiansted and Frederiksted, St Croix; Cruz Bay, St John. **Documents** The USVI are a territory of the USA but constitute a separate customs district. US boats with US citizens have to clear in here when coming from Puerto Rico (can be done by phone on St Croix) and all other islands. For more about custom fees, call Mr Harrigan on T7742510, ext 223. St Croix customs T7731011. When arriving by boat ensure that you have the correct visas for immigration. All vessels must clear in upon arrival from a foreign port and all crew members aboard must go is a pain due to the crowded harbour. **Anchor** If you can find room, try northwest end or just outside harbour. On St Croix, foreign boats or boats with foreign passengers clear customs at Gallows Bay Dock.

Getting around

Air There are lots of flights between St Croix and St Thomas. **American Eagle, Cape Air** and other flights are available. **Seaborne Airlines** (T7736442, www.seaborneairlines.com) has many flights a day between Frederiksted or Christiansted Harbour and Charlotte Amalie, 18 minutes, US$65-105one way depending on the type of ticket. From the seaplanes, the view arriving into St Croix and seeing the coral reef is spectacular. There is a strictly enforced 30-lb baggage weight (US$0.50 per lb overweight but excess baggage may not travel until later).

Car The country speed limit is 35 mph and in towns it is 20 mph. Traffic is heavy so you will be lucky to go that fast. On St John the speed limit is 20 mph everywhere. Driving is on the left, even though the cars are left-hand drive. Be sure to buckle up as there is a seatbelt law for the driver and front seat passenger that the police enforce (US$25 fine).

Ferry St Thomas-St John: Transportation Services of St. John/Varlack Ventures, T7766282, run the ferry from Red Hook to nearby Cruz Bay (daily 0630, 0730, then every hr from 0800 to 2400, returning from Cruz Bay hourly 0600-2300, takes 20 mins, US$5 each way). Also Charlotte Amalie to Cruz Bay, 6 daily, US$11.50 one way, 45 mins. There are 2 car ferries (barges): Republic Barge/Captain Vic, T7794000, US$42 round trip, US$27 one way, no credit cards, 5 daily Mon-Fri, 4 crossings weekends or holidays; Boyson's General, T7766294, US$50 round trip, US$30 one way, no credit cards, departs Red Hook every hour on the half-hour 0630-1830 Mon-Sat, 0730-1830 Sun. On St Thomas, barges arrive and depart from a marine terminal to the left of the passenger ferry dock in Red Hook. Cars and trucks queue up in the parking lot there. On St John, the barges arrive and depart from a terminal between the US Customs Building and the National Park dock. Pay staff once the boat is under way. Ferries between St Thomas/St John and St Croix come and go.

Finding out more

Tourist offices

St Thomas St Thomas' Visitors' Bureau, Havensight Welcome Center at the West Indian Company dock, Mon-Fri 0800-1700, Sat 0900-1300. **Department of Tourism**, PO Box 6400, Charlotte Amalie, USVI 00804, T7748784.

St John There is a **tourist office** next to the post office in Cruz Bay. **Department of Tourism**, PO Box 200, Cruz Bay, USVI 00830, T7766450.

Sr Croix Tourism booth at the airport on St Croix in the baggage claim area and next to it the **First Stop Information Booth**. **Visitors' Bureau**, Queen St, Christiansted, on the corner with King Cross St, Mon-Fri 0800-1700. **Department of Tourism**, PO Box 4538, Christiansted, USVI 00822-4538, T7730495. **Visitors' Centre**, Frederiksted, the

Old Custom House Building, Strand St, USVI 00840, T7720357.

Useful websites

www.usvi.net.
www.usvitourism.vi.
www.usvichamber.com.
www.onepaper.com.

Useful publications

The following publications all have regularly updated tourist information: *Explore St Thomas & St John, The St John Guidebook, Boutique Shopping Guide, St Croix This Week, Destination US Virgin Islands, Virgin Island Playground, What To Do St Thomas and St John, St John Tradewinds and St Thomas This Week*. The free weekly *Island Trader* is also a good source of events and activities.

US Virgin Islands Essentials

Touching down

Boat information St Thomas: Most moorings are privately owned. It is illegal to use a private mooring without permission from the DPNR. The dive companies have placed moorings near some dive locations on Buck Island, Saba Island, Little St James Island and a few others. There are dinghy docks along the waterfront near Coast Guard Dock, Frenchtown Marina, Crown Bay Marina, Water Island Ferry Dock (privately owned). **St John:** The US Park Service has placed moorings to protect reefs and seagrass. A yacht may anchor in the park for no more than 14 days a year. Park moorings on north shore: Caneel Bay, Hawksnest, Cinnamon Bay, Maho, Francis Bay; on south shore: Salt Pond, Little Lameshur and Great Lameshur. Forbidden to anchor on south shore, moorings must be used. There are some private moorings for day charter boats in Maho Bay, Cruz Bay. Great

Cruz Bay and Coral Bay are not within the park territory and have privately owned moorings. **St Croix:** Divers have placed mooring buoys at all dive locations to prevent damage to the reefs while anchoring. Stays are limited to four hours. All moorings in the harbour are privately owned. Buck Island has moorings placed within the snorkelling area for day use only. Overnight anchoring is not allowed and boats must anchor in sand at southwest end of island. Marinas at St Croix Marine, Jones Maritime, St Croix Yachting Club, Green Cay Marina, Salt River Marina. Anchorages at Christiansted, Frederiksted (deep, so very difficult), Green Cay, Teague Bay by St Croix Yacht Club (reciprocates with members of other yacht clubs). **Business hours** Banks: Mon-Fri 0830-1500; **Government offices:** Mon-Thu 0900-1700 (banks, filling stations and government offices close

Sleeping

There is an 8% tax on all forms of accommodation in the US Virgin Islands. Hotels may also charge 10-15% service, but most leave tipping to the individual. High season is mid-December to mid-April, but higher prices can last into May, depending on carnival dates, despite lower hotel occupancy. See individual islands for further information.

Shopping

The USVI are a free port and tourist-related items are duty-free. Shops are usually shut on Sunday unless there is a cruise ship in harbour. If you want to shop seriously, St Thomas is the cheapest island of the three and has the largest selection. Nevertheless it is a good idea to have done your research at home and know what you want to buy. There are several rums available in white or gold, and some interesting fruit-flavoured ones as well. Guided tours of the distillery on St Croix are available with **Cruzan** ① 3 Estate Diamond, Frederiksted, T6922280, Mon-Fri 0900-1130, 1300-1615, but phone in advance; US$4 adults, US$1 children. Locally woven crafts (hats, baskets, brooms, fish traps, bookmarks, Christmas tree ornaments) are made from coconut palms, sabal and wild teyer palm. Baskets are made from wiss and hoop vines. Handmade moco jumbi dolls are works of art. See individual towns for further information.

Festivals and events

1 Jan New Year's Day.
6 Jan Three Kings Day.
15 Jan Martin Luther King Day.

19 Feb Presidents' Day.
Mar/Apr Holy Thu, Good Fri, Easter Mon.
28 May Memorial Day.

for local holidays).

Clothing Bathing suits are considered offensive when worn away from the beach, so cover up. There is a law against it, and you can even be fined for having your belly showing. It is illegal to go topless on Magens Beach.

Currency US dollar. Credit cards are widely accepted.

Departure tax None at the airport (charge is included in the ticket).

Documents Visitors need passports, visas (or waiver for participating countries) and return/onward tickets, as they would for the mainland USA.

Embassies and consulates On St Thomas: Denmark, T7760656. Sweden, T7746845. On **St Croix**: Dutch, T7737100. Norwegian, T7737100.

Emergency numbers T911.

Country code +340.

Official time Atlantic Standard Time, four hours behind GMT, one hour ahead of EST.

Safety Take the usual precautions against crime: lock your car, leave valuable jewellery at home and be careful walking around at night. Do not go to deserted beaches on your own. Couples have been held up at gunpoint and robbed and/or raped on the beach after dark. Youth unemployment is a problem. St John is generally safer than St Thomas, but take the usual precautions, there have been reports of attacks on Cinnamon Bay Beach, while crack cocaine is sold fairly openly on the streets in Cruz Bay.

Tipping As in mainland USA, tipping is 15%; hotels often add 10-15%.

Useful addresses Air Ambulance: Bohlke International Airways, T7789177 (day), 7721629 (night); recompression chamber 7762686.

Voltage 120 volts 60 cycles.

Weights and measures Imperial.

3 Jul Emancipation Day.
4 Jul Independence Day.
Early Sep Labour Day.
Mid-Oct Puerto Rico/Virgin Islands Friendship Day.
1 Nov Liberty Day.
11 Nov Veterans' Day.
Mid-Nov Thanksgiving Day.
25-26 Dec Christmas.

Keeping in touch

Telephone Local telephone calls within the USVI from pay phones are US$0.25-0.35 for each five minutes. Privately owned payphones charge for local calls, even 800 numbers. **Innovative** and **Vitelcellular** do not make extra charges. **Radio Shack** offers pre-paid cellular service, T7775644, 7741314, so does **Cingular**, bring your own phone or buy one of theirs, US$0.52 per minute in USVI and Puerto Rico.

Media The Thursday edition of *The Daily News*, US$0.75, includes the weekend section listing restaurants, nightclubs, music and special events, for all three islands. Also the *St. Croix Avis* US$0.60. The St John newspaper, *Tradewinds*, is published bi-weekly, US$0.50. Funny, informative and free, the *St John Guidebook* and map is available in shops and also at the ticket booth at the ferry dock.

St Thomas → Phone code: 340. Colour map 2, B6. Population: 51,000.

St Thomas is on practically every Caribbean cruise itinerary, and thousands of cruise ship passengers descend daily in winter on Charlotte Amalie, the capital, for the ultimate shopping experience. A beautiful natural harbour, the former Danish town has been a major trading port for centuries and is still popular with visitors seeking duty-free bargains. St Thomas rises out of the sea to a range of hills that runs down its spine. The highest peak, Crown Mountain, is 1,550 ft. On St Peter Mountain, 1,500 ft, is a viewpoint at Mountain Top. There are various scenic roads to drive along, such as Skyline Drive (Route 40), from which both sides of the island can be seen simultaneously, and Mafolie Road (Route 35), which leaves Charlotte Amalie, heading north to cross the Skyline Drive becoming Magens Bay Road, and descends to the beautiful bay. ▸▸ *For Sleeping, Eating and other listings, see pages 479-484.*

Ins and outs

Getting there and around The taxi stand is at the far left end of the terminal at the **Cyril E King Airport** (STT), a long way from the commuter flights from Puerto Rico and other islands. Taxi to town charges US$7 for the first person and US$6 per subsequent person (US$2 for each bag). There are sporadic public buses 0600-1900 from the terminal to the town, US$1. Boats come in to Charlotte Amalie or Red Hook in the east. ▸▸ *See also Transport, page 484.*

St Thomas

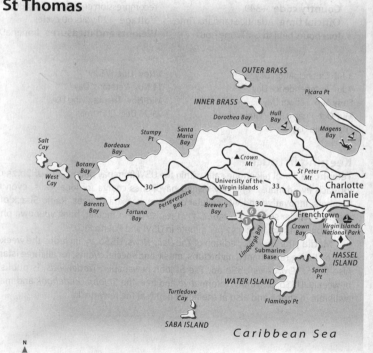

Sleeping 🛏
Best Western Carib Beach Resort **1**
Best Western Emerald Beach Resort **2**

Bluebeard's Castle **3**
Bolongo Bay Beach Club & Villas **4**
Elysian Beach Resort **5**

There is a bus service running west from Charlotte Amalie to the university and east to Red Hook. If you wish to drive yourself, rental firms are plentiful. Parking is difficult, particularly in town and at Red Hook.

Charlotte Amalie → *Phone code: 340. Population: 12,331.*

The harbour at Charlotte Amalie, capital of St Thomas and also of the entire USVI, still bustles with colour and excitement. As the Fort Christian Museum puts it, "oversized, architecturally inappropriate buildings have marred the scenic beauty of the harbour." One could add that by day the streets are congested too if more than eight cruise ships are in. But, as the museum also points out, there are still a number of historical buildings. The town was built by the Danes, who named it after their King's consort, but to most visitors it remains 'St Thomas'. Beautiful old Danish houses painted in a variety of pastel colours are a reminder of the island's history. One recently opened to the public is **Haagensen House** ⓘ *Entrance near top of 99 steps, T7749605, daily 0900-1300, US$8 adults, US$4 children*, the home of a former Danish banker, with a courtyard, gardens and antique furniture. A free shuttle service runs from Emancipation Garden. **Government House**, off Kongens Gade, was built in 1865-1887. The **Enid M Baa Library and Archive** is on Main Street, in another early 19th-century edifice. The former house of the French painter, **Camille Pissaro**, off Main Street, now houses shops and also displays his paintings. One historical building which cannot be visited is the former Danish Consulate, on Denmark Hill, now the Governor's residence. For a good view of the town and the surrounding area, take the **St Thomas Skyride** ⓘ *T7749809, www.stthomasskyride.com, 0900-1700, when cruise ships are in port, later some*

Island Beachcomber **6**
Island View Guest House **11**
Point Pleasant Resort **7**

Sapphire Beach Resort & Marina **8**
Secret Harbour Beach Resort **9**
Villa Blanca **10**

evenings, US$18 adults, US$9 children 6-12 yrs round trip, across the street from the cruise ship dock and Havensight Mall, actually a cable car which takes you on a seven-minute ride up 700 ft to **Paradise Point** where there is an observation deck and a bar and café (① *also open for dinner Thu-Sun 1900-2200, access via the road*), a parrot show, nature walks and shopping. The view of the harbour and lots of neighbouring islands provides some great photo opportunities.

While you are at Havensight Mall, you can visit the new **Butterfly Farm** ① *WICO Dock, Havensight Mall, T7153366, daily 0830-1700, US$15 adults, US$8 for children over 3*, in the same chain as the farms in St-Martin, Aruba and Grand Cayman. The butterflies hatch out in the mornings and are most active then, but in the afternoons there are better opportunities for photography, when they are more lethargic. They are attracted by colourful clothing and will often land on people wearing citrus-based perfume.

There are over 14 historic churches in the USVI dating back as far as 1737. The **Dutch Reformed Church** is the oldest established church, having had a congregation since 1660, although the present building dates from 1846. The **Frederick Lutheran Church** dates from 1820 and its parish hall was the residence of Jacob H S Lind (1806-27). The **Crystal Gade Synagogue** is one of the oldest in the western hemisphere (1833), an airy, domed building, with a sand floor and hurricane-proof

Charlotte Amalie

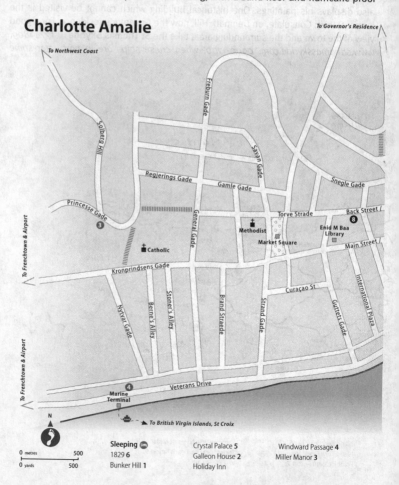

To Governor's Residence

To Northwest Coast

Solberg Hill

Frebun Gade

Savan Gade

Regjerings Gade

Gamle Gade

Snegle Gade

Princesse Gade

3

Torve Strade

Back Street /

General Gade

Methodist

Market Square

Enid M Baa Library

8

Main Street

To Frenchtown & Airport

✝ Catholic

Kronprindsens Gade

Nyval Gade

Berne's Alley

Stoner's Alley

Brand Strade

Strand Gade

Curaçao St

Guttets Gade

International Plaza

To Frenchtown & Airport

Veterans Drive

Marine Terminal **4**

N

To British Virgin Islands, St Croix

0 metres 500
0 yards 500

Sleeping 🛏

1829 **6**
Bunker Hill **1**

Crystal Palace **5**
Galleon House **2**
Holiday Inn

Windward Passage **4**
Miller Manor **3**

US Virgin Islands St Thomas

walls; it has books for sale in the office, iced springwater and visitors are given a free 10-minute introduction. It is worth a visit. The Hebrew Congregation of St Thomas was founded in 1796. The adjacent **Weibel Museum** ① *15 Crystal Gade, T7744312, daily 0900-1600*, charts the history of the Jews on St Thomas. Be careful if walking to the Crystal Gade Synagogue and never walk there at night.

There are many old fortifications within the town. **Bluebeard's Castle Tower** and **Blackbeard's Castle**, the latter allegedly built in 1679 and lived in by the pirate and his 14 wives. The **Virgin Islands Museum** ① *T7764566, Mon-Fri 0830-1630, US$3 adults, children free, donations welcome as much restoration work remains to be done*, is in the former dungeon at **Fort Christian** (1666-1680). There are historical and natural history sections and an art gallery. In contrast to the red-painted fort is the green **Legislative Building** ① *Mon-Fri*, originally the Danish police barracks (1874).

St Peter Great House and Botanical Gardens ① *6A St Peter Mountain Rd, Route 40, T7744999, www.greathouse-mountaintop.com, daily 0900-1630, US$10 adults, US$5 children*, has 500 varieties of plants, an orchid garden, bird sanctuary, nature trail, a stunning view over to Tortola and lots of smaller islands and an art gallery for local artists. At the top of St Peter Mountain at 1,500 ft, is a lookout and duty free shopping mall known as **Mountain Top** ① *T7742400, open daily 0900-1700*. Once known as Signal Hill and of strategic communications importance in the 1940s

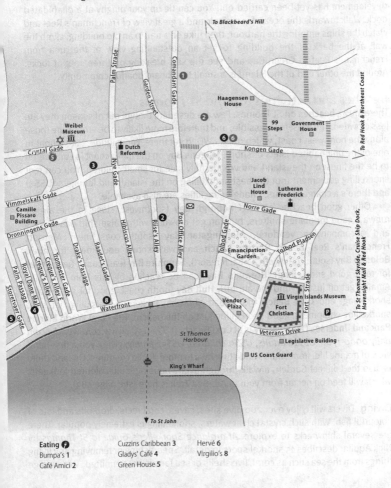

US Virgin Islands St Thomas

against potential German naval activity, it is now very touristy and trades on its secret recipe for banana daiquiris as well as the spectacular view.

Water Island

Water Island, at the west end of St Thomas' main harbour, is the smallest inhabited island and is now known as the fourth USVI. Its name comes from the once plentiful freshwater ponds, now salt ponds. The island was purchased from Denmark by the USA in 1944 to use as a military base during the Second World War. **Fort Segarra** was built as an underground fort and later the island was used to test weapons. It was transferred to the Department of the Interior from Defense in 1952. A year later a 40-year lease of the entire island was given to a developer for construction of a hotel and homes. The hotel closed after Hurricane Hugo in 1989 and is now in ruins. The island's ownership was turned over to the VI Government and private island homeowners in December 1996. Open-air buildings on the beach are available for public use. At weekends the beach is busy with local residents and charter-boat guests. ▶▶ *See also Transport, page 484.*

Hassel Island

Hassel Island is part of US National Parks. There are ruins on the shore but no development has yet been carried out. You can tie up your dinghy at a dilapidated dock. Walk towards the ocean for a picnic and a great view of Frenchman's Reef and watch the ships entering the harbour; then hike on a trail to an old building; climb the wall at the back of the building to get an outstanding view of the area from Frenchman's Reef to Green Cay and see the surf breaking on three sets of rocks. Around the other end of the island is a small liveaboard boating community.

Beaches and activities around St Thomas

There are 44 **beaches** on St Thomas. Few are deserted, though out of season they are less crowded. The most inaccessible, and therefore more likely to be empty, are those along the northwest coast, which need 4WD to get there. For solitude, take a boat to one of the uninhabited islets offshore. **Magens Bay** on the north coast is considered to be the finest on the island and wonderfully safe for small children. You can rent snorkelling equipment (not the best snorkelling on the island) and loungers (US$4) and there's a charge for cars. Changing facilities are also available.

Other good beaches are at **Lindbergh Bay** (southwest, close to the airport runway, good for plane spotters, but can get crowded with cruise ship passengers and accompanying vendors), **Morningstar Bay** (south coast near **Marriott Frenchman's Reef Beach Resort**; beach and watersports equipment for hire), **Bolongo Bay** (south coast with a beach resort), **Sapphire Bay** (east coast, beach gear for rent, good snorkelling), **Brewer's Bay** (can be reached by bus from Charlotte Amalie, get off just beyond the airport), **Hull Bay** (north coast, good for surfing and snorkelling) and **Coki Beach** (northeast, showers, lockers, waterskiing, jet skis, snorkelling equipment, good snorkelling just off the beach). The **Coral World Marine Park and Undersea Observatory** is at Coki Beach ① *T7751555, www.coralworldvi.com daily 0900-1700, US$18 adults, US$9 children, US$52 family*, giving you a first-hand view of marine life, from sharks and sting rays to more docile creatures. On land there is also the Lorikeet Garden, a walk-through aviary housing multi-coloured lorikeets, which will feed on nectar from your hand. **Sea Trek** is here (see page 483).

Diving Divers will enjoy over 200 dive sites, caves, coral reefs, drop-offs and lots of colourful fish. With such crystal clear waters, snorkelling is extremely popular. There are several shipwrecks to explore. *At-a-glance Snorkeller's Guide to St Thomas* by Nick Aquilar describes 15 snorkel spots in detail. Spearfishing or removing any living things from the sea such as coral, live shells or sea fans is not permitted. The average price of a one-tank dive is US$60, but most places only do two-tank dives at US$85. Many of the resorts offer diving packages or courses and there are many dive companies. Complete lists are available from the Tourist Board (*USVI Dive Guide*). Equipment and instruction for underwater photography are available. There are also several liveaboard sail/dive charters. The *Atlantis* submarine dives to 90 ft for those who cannot scuba dive but want to see the exotic fish, coral, sponges and other underwater life. ▸▸ *For dive operators, see page 482.*

Fishing There is deep-sea fishing, with the next world record in every class lurking just under the boat. Game fish include white marlin, kingfish, sailfish, tarpon, Alison tuna and wahoo. No fishing licence is required for shoreline fishing; government pamphlets list 100 good spots (T7756762). ▸▸ *For tournaments, see Festivals and events, page 482.*

Sailing Day sailing of all types is available. Half-day sails from US$60, full-day from US$100 and sunset cruises from US$45 are offered by many boats. Before taking a day trip on any boat, ask about size, any shade awning and the number of passengers. Many day sail boats limit their guests to six passengers, take a stop for snorkelling and provide drinks. A variety of charter yachts is available, more or less luxurious, with or without crew; they can cost the same as a good hotel. You can explore on your own by renting a small power boat.

Whale watching The **Environmental Association of St Thomas-St John (EAST)** organizes whale watching during the migration season at the beginning of the year. Humpbacks are the most commonly sighted, see page 356.

● Sleeping

Department of Tourism website, www.usvitourism.com, is comprehensive. There are many hotels, guesthouses, apartments, villas and cottages on St Thomas with a cluster around the east end. The cheaper places to stay are in town or up in the hills. The newer, top-of-the-range chain hotels are on the beach and include the huge **Marriott**, www.marriott.com, with all sporting and conference facilities. Summer rates are about 20% cheaper than winter. The **Hotel Association** counter at the airport can help you with reservations.

Charlotte Amalie *p475, map p476*
Be cautious around downtown at night.
LL Bluebeard's Castle, on hillside overlooking town, T7741600, www.bluebeards-castle.com. 183 rooms, studios and 1-bedroom villas, lots of facilities and sports, pool, free shuttle to Magens Bay Beach and to Veterans' Drive.
LL-L Holiday Inn Windward Passage, on the waterfront towards the airport, T7745200, www.holidayinn.st-thomas.com. Pool, restaurant, 151 rooms and suites, Wi-Fi, walking distance from shops and ferries,

gaming centre, shuttle to beach.
LL-AL Hotel 1829, on Government Hill, T7761829, www.hotel1829.com. Luxury hotel in lovely old house built for the bride of a 19th century sea captain, designed by an Italian architect in a Spanish motif and constructed with Danish and African labour. Good views over the town. Variety of suites and rooms, bar in former kitchen open Mon-Sat 1500-2300, breakfast available but dining room for private parties only.
L-A Island View Guest House, 11-1C Content, T7744270, www.islandviewstthomas.com. Great place to stay before or after a charter, near airport, pool, gardens, great view, rooms or suite, boat available for snorkelling trips with Captain Ron. Complimentary continental breakfast or pay extra for full breakfast.
AL-A Bunker Hill Hotel, 7A Commandant Gade, T7748056, www.bunkerhillhotel.com. 15 rooms, a/c, TV, the more expensive rooms have a balcony with view of the town, breakfast included, pool, airport transfers.
AL-A Crystal Palace, 12 Crystal Gade, T7772277, www.crystalpalaceusvi.com. Lockhart family home for many generations

now converted to a bed & breakfast guest house and run by Ron Lockhart, 6 a/c rooms, of which 4 share a bathroom and 2 have en suites, antique mahogany furniture in communal areas, view over town and harbour. Beautiful old double-fronted merchant's house, the first on the island to have glass sash windows, which gave the street and the house it's name.

AL-A Danish Chalet Inn, 4 and 5 Gamble Nordsidevej, T7745292. Good value, 15 rooms in 3 buildings with view over harbour, bed and breakfast, a/c, TV, friendly and informative owners.

AL-A Galleon House, 31 Kongen Gade, T/F7746952, www.galleonhouse.com. Swimming pool, veranda, gourmet breakfast, snorkel gear provided, discounts for senior citizens. A variety of rooms, new and old, shared or private bathroom, steep steps up to the hotel from the town.

AL-A Miller Manor, 27 Prinsesse Gade, on the hill behind the Catholic Cathedral, T7741535, www.millermanor.com. Clean, very friendly, a/c, 5 mins' walk to town, microwave and fridge in each room.

Around the island *p478, map p474*
LL Best Western Emerald Beach Resort, 8070 Lindbergh Bay, T7778800, www.emeraldbeach.com. 90 rooms, pool, bar, restaurant, 'The Palms' rooms have ocean and airport view, tennis, watersports.
LL Elysian Beach Resort Cowpet Bay, T7751000, www.elysianbeachresort.net. rooms, suites and villas, timeshare resort, fitness centre, tennis, pool, jacuzzi, watersports centre offering diving, kayaking, parasailing, use of facilities at **Bluebeard's**.
LL Sapphire Beach Resort & Marina, T7756100, www.sapphirebeachstthomas.com. 171 huge rooms with kitchen and sofabed, suites, villas, pool, watersports, tennis, kitchens, restaurant, children 4-12 free when sharing room with paying adult, children's activities.
LL Bolongo Bay Beach Club & Villas, 7150 Bolongo, on the south coast, T7751800, www.bolongobay.com. Room only or all-inclusive family resort, kids' offers, pool, beach, tennis, kitchen facilities, 2 restaurants.
LL Point Pleasant Resort, 6600 Estate Smith Bay, T7757200, www.pointpleasant resort.com. On Water Bay with views to the BVI. Under 21s sharing parents' room free,

128 suites in 15 acres of tropical gardens, 3 pools, 2 beaches, tennis, watersports.
LL-L Secret Harbour Beach Resort, T7756550, www.secretharbourvi.com. 64 rooms, studios and villas, ocean view or beachfront, spread around the bay, popular with honeymooners, watersports, tennis, kitchens, restaurant.
LL-AL Island Beachcomber, Lindbergh Bay, T7745250, www.islandbeachcomber.net. Laid-back hotel, 47 smallish rooms with veranda, a/c, TV, Wi-Fi, coffee makers and fridge, on beach, by airport, free shuttle to town. Hotels on Lindbergh Bay suffer from popularity of cruise ship visitors who crowd the beach during the day and attract vendors.
L-AL Best Western Carib Beach Resort, 70C Lindbergh Bay, T7742525, www.caribbeachresort.com. Sister resort of Emerald Beach Resort. Smaller, with 60 rooms, pool, casual, sheltered beach at end of airport runway, only drawback is aircraft noise, shuttle to town, Wi-Fi.
L-AL Villa Blanca, 2 miles east of town, T7760749, www.villablancahotel.com. 14 rooms with kitchenettes set in 3 acres of gardens, on hillside, view of town and harbour, pool, quiet, family-run, breakfast delivered to room, Wi-Fi.

🍴 Eating

Charlotte Amalie *p475, map p476*
There are many very good restaurants on the island, most of which are listed in tourist brochures, see page 471. The waterfront in Charlotte Amalie is safe in the early evening, but elsewhere you should take a taxi. The area west of the market square is more local, with restaurants and bars.
♦♦♦ Banana Tree Grill at Bluebeard's Castle, T7764050, www.bananatreegrill.com. Open for dinner Mon-Sat. Expensive, but great US-mediterranean cuisine overlooking cruise ships in the bay.
♦♦♦-♦♦ Hervé Restaurant & Wine Bar, Government Hill, T7779703. Tue-Sun dinner only, happy hour 1700-1900. Good variety of specials during happy hour at the bar, patio bar on first floor, good view, seafood, pasta, great desserts, interesting menu with some unusual items, mostly French.
♦♦♦-♦♦ Virgilio's, between Main and Back

streets, up from Storetvaer Gade, T7764920. Lunch 1130-1500, dinner 1700-2200 Mon-Sat. Italian, good food and service, not cheap, reservations requested.

Café Amici, A H Riise's Mall, T7765670. Mon-Sat 1030-1530, Sun 1030-1500. Italian and Mediterranean food, moderate prices.

Green House, on harbour front, Veterans Drive, T7747998. 0800-2200, bar open until 0200, happy hour 1630-1900. Excellent, reasonably-priced restaurant, attracts younger crowd, steak, ribs, burgers, Sun brunch.

Bill's Texas Pit BBQ, T7769579, a mobile truck which shows up Tue-Sat in the Waterfront and Red Hook for dinner, also for lunch at Sub Base, award-winning ribs, the best on the island, very popular with locals, also chicken, brisket and side dishes.

Bumpa's, waterfront, T7765674. Breakfast and lunch. Upstairs, outdoors, small spot overlooking harbour, locally popular and inexpensive, no credit cards, salads, sandwiches, ice cream and cakes.

Cuzzins Caribbean Restaurant & Bar, Back St, T7774711. Open for lunch Mon-Sat, dinner Tue-Sat. Good, large, local meals. West Indian cuisine, conch, fish, also drinks such as sea moss and maubi, vegetarian plates available.

Glady's Café, in Historic Royal Dane Mall, T7740604. Mon-Sat 0700-1530. Local dishes such as salt fish and dumplings, mutton stew.

Around the island *p478, map p474*

Alexander's Café, Frenchtown, T7744349. Mon-Sat for lunch and dinner. Grills, ribs, burgers, chilli and Italian.

Craig and Sally's, Frenchtown, T7779949. Lunch Tue-Sat, dinner Tue-Sun. International influences, new wave of American cuisine, very popular.

Hook, Line and Sinker, Frenchtown, T7769708. Breakfast, lunch and dinner Mon-Sat. American, steak and seafood, pasta and sandwiches, vegetarian options, daily specials.

Lattitude 18, across the water from Red Hook Harbour, T7792495. Dinghy dock. Live entertainment occasionally, good food, varied, steak, seafood and pasta.

Romano's, Smith Bay, T7750045. Open from 1800 Mon-Sat. Italian and continental, lamb, seafood and pasta.

Duffy's Love Shack, Red Hook Plaza, T7792080. Open daily for lunch and dinner. Good lunches, some unusual meals plus burgers, American, hotspot, very busy weekends.

Tickle's Dockside Pub, Crown Bay Marina, T7761595, American Yacht Harbour, T7759425. Open daily for breakfast, lunch and dinner. American, burgers, chicken and ribs.

Bars and clubs

St Thomas *p474, map p474*

St Thomas offers the greatest variety of nightlife in the Virgin Islands. It is best to check a local newspaper: *The Daily News* (on Fri), or the free *Island Trader* (found everywhere on Thu), for the music schedule for the upcoming week. Most hotels and many restaurants offer live music several nights a week. Some hotels offer limbo dancing 3 or 4 nights a week and the ubiquitous steel bands remain a great favourite. Some restaurants in Frenchtown offer live music.

The Green House, on the Waterfront in Charlotte Amalie, T7747998. Daily 1100-0100. Has the best of live local bands several nights a week and DJ dancing several nights a week.

Happy Buzzard, downtown Charlotte Amalie, T7778676. Daily 0800-2200. Happy hour all night and famous daiquiris, food served all day long.

Hard Rock Café, next door to the **Green House** on the waterfront, Charlotte Amalie, T7775555. Daily 1030-2100. Occasional name band concerts.

Iggie's Beach Bar, Bolongo Bay Hotel, T7751800. Lunch 1100-1700, dinner 1700-2230, bar until 2400, happy hours 1600-1800. Mon night live music and home cooking menu, Tue, Sat all-you-can-eat crab legs at US$34 per person, Fri night 'south of the border' margarita specials, Sun night barefoot beach barbecue ribs all you can eat US$25. Karaoke Thu. Occasional live concerts on the beach, beach volleyball, basketball, sports TV.

Lattitude 18, Red Hook, T7792495. Live music several nights a week including an open-mike night.

Offshore Bar, in the Havensight area, T7796400. Mon-Fri 0900-0200, Sat, Sun

0900-0400. DJ dancing Thu and live music at weekends.

Paradise Point, at the top of the Skyride, see p475, T7749809. Bar open 0900-2000, restaurant 1100-2000. Sunset party on Wed with a live band, 1700-2100. The Skyride is not always open that late, so access is via the road most nights.

Room With A View at Bluebeard's Castle, T7742377. Mon-Sat 1700-2400, late dining 2200-2400. Offers free champagne to ladies 2200-0100, midnight menu of pizza or sandwiches.

Sapphire Beach Hotel, T7756100. Beach party with a live local band every Sun afternoon, 1430-1800, free.

SIBS on the mountain, Charlotte Amalie, T7748967. Daily 1700-2200 for dinner, bar until 0400. Offers happy hour, bar, late-night crowds, pool tables.

⊕ Entertainment

St Thomas   *p474, map p474*

Theatre   The **Reichhold Centre for the Arts**, part of the University of the Virgin Islands, has programmes with local or international performers. Concerts are scheduled throughout the winter season. **Tillett Gardens**, T7751929, www.tillettgardens.com. Concerts and other live music are held here with events scheduled throughout the winter season.

⊕ Festivals and events

St Thomas   *p474, map p474*

Mar   The **Rolex Cup Regatta**, www.rolexcupregatta.com, last weekend in Mar at St Thomas Yacht Club, T7756320, www.styc.net.

Apr   **Carnival**, T7763112, www.vicarnival .com, is spectacular. Dating back to the arrival of African slaves who danced *bamboulas* it was originally based on ritual worship of the gods of Dahomey. The festivities have since been redirected towards Christianity with a marked US influence. Parades with costumed bands include the **J'Ouvert Morning Tramp**, the **Children's Parade**, **Mocko Jumbis** on stilts and steel bands. There are beauty queens and groups of baton-twirling majorettes. **Jun**   USVI Fishing Club Tournament.

Jul   Bastille Day Kingfish Tournament. **Aug**   USVI Open Atlantic Blue Marlin Tournament, T7742752.

⊙ Shopping

St Thomas   *p474, map p474*
Arts and crafts
The Native Arts Coop, opposite the Vendors Plaza, Charlotte Amalie. A showcase for locally made goods and souvenirs.
Tillett Gardens, opposite **Four Winds Plaza**, Charlotte Amalie. A good arts and crafts centre, you can watch the craftsmen at work.

Books
Dockside Bookshop, Havensight Mall, Charlotte Amalie, T7778786, dockside @islands.vi. Mon-Thu 0900-1700, Fri 0900-1800, Sat 0900-1700, Sun 1100-1500. Books and other publications on the Virgin Islands and the Caribbean in general, board games and maps.

Food
Gourmet Gallery, Crown Bay Marina, **Plaza Extra** in Tutu Park Mall and **Havensight Deli** in Havensight Mall. Local produce can be bought in the Market Square (most produce brought in by farmers on Sat 0530) and there are some small supermarkets and grocery stores. **Solberg Supermart** on Solberg Hill has a launderette. **Marina Market** in Red Hook is a good gourmet-type deli, opposite St John Ferry Dock. **Pueblo Supermarket**, near Safe Haven Marina, Crown Bay Marina, **K-Mart** and **Cost U Less**.

Shopping malls
Havensight Shopping Mall at the cruise ship dock, www.havensightmall.com, is recommended for people who want to get away from crowds and parking problems. It has a smaller selection than in town, but the same duty free shops, with restrooms, tourist office, banks, ATMs, post office, restaurants, free parking.

▲ Activities and tours

St Thomas   *p474, map p474*
Diving and snorkelling
Snorkelling gear can be rented at all major hotels and the dive shops.

Atlantis Submarine, Building VI, Bay L, Havensight Mall, St Thomas, T7765650 for reservations, or 7760288 for information (also kiosk on waterfront, usually 6 dives daily), www.atlantisadventures.com/stthomas. You have to take a 4-mile launch ride on the *Yukon III* to join the submarine at Buck Island. 1-hr day dives US$84, children 4-17 US$45.

Chris Sawyer Diving Centre, at the American Yacht Harbour (Red Hook), T7777804, Wyndham Sugar Bay, T7777100 ext 2121, and Caneel Bay on St John, T6424214, www.sawyerdive.vi. The largest dive company, specializes in quality service to small groups, great all-day wreck of the *Rhone* trip once a week (dives for locals on Sun), certification classes every 2 weeks.

Coki Beach Dive Centre, T7754220, www.cokidive.com. Cruise ships bring their guests here but separate programme for hotel guests.

VI Ecotours, T7792155, www.viecotours.com. Offer kayaking and snorkelling in the marine sanctuary in the last mangrove lagoon left on the south side of St Thomas. No experience necessary. If there is enough demand they run a night trip, recommended.

Sea Trek, Coral World Marine Park and Undersea Observatory, Coki Beach, T7751555, www.coralworldvi.com. For an undersea walk wearing breathing apparatus helmets, US$50, plus admission to Coral World.

St Thomas Diving Club, at Bolongo Bay Beach Resort, 7762381, www.stthomasdivingclub.com. Offers daily snorkelling trips to Buck Island and complete PADI diver training programs from introductory dives to instructor training.

Fishing

Charterboat Centre, T800-8665714, www.charterboat.vi, also known as **St Thomas Sports Fishing**, T7757990. For sportfishing charters as well as sailboats, motor boats and day charters including trips to the BVI.

Doubleheader Sportfishing, T7777317, www.doubleheadersportfishing.net.

Marlin Prince, T6935929, www.marlinprince.com.

Golf

Mahogany Run, T800-2537103, www.mahoganyrungolf.com. 18 holes, 6,022

yds, green fee varies according to the season, cheaper after 1400.

Parasailing

Caribbean Watersports Tours, T7759360, www.viwatersports.com. A variety of jet skis, etc, to go fast and make a noise, or pedalos to go slowly and peacefully. Parasailing also at some hotels.

Sailing

Limnos, T7753203, www.limnoscharters.com. Small power boats for hire, also day trips to the BVI (take passport) or St John on motor catamarans.

Nauti Nymph, T7755066, www.st-thomas.com/nautinymph. 25-29-ft Fountain Power Boats for hire.

See An Ski, T7756265. 22/24/28-ft makos single/double engines.

VI Charteryacht League, T800-5242061, www.vicl.org.

Virgin Islands Power (VIP), T7761510, 800-5242015. The largest power yacht charter fleet and sportfishing fleet in the Caribbean, bareboat or crewed.

Tennis

There are a few public tennis courts (2 at Sub Base), operating on a first-come first-served basis, but the hotel courts at the major resorts are mostly lit for night-time play and open for non-residents if you book.

Tour operators

There are group tours by surrey, bus or taxi. Island tours in an open bus cost US$20 per person, many leave from Emancipation Garden at about 1200.

Air Center Helicopters, T7757335. Helicopter tours of the islands.

Whale watching

The Environmental Association of St Thomas-St John (EAST), www.eastvi.org. Trips leave from the dock in Red Hook on a 77-ft catamaran, see website for dates or look for adverts in the local paper during Jan-Mar.

Windsurfing

Morningstar, Magens Bay and Secret Harbour, Sapphire Beach. Lessons and rental of equipment.

West Indies Windsurfing, T7756530. Will deliver windsurfing boards, sunfish and kayaks to wherever you are staying. Sunfish sailboats for rent at Morningstar, Magens Bay.

⊖ Transport

St Thomas *p474, map p474*
Air
Cyril E King International Airport is 2 miles, 12 mins from Charlotte Amalie. Seaplanes come in at the Seaplane base (SPB) in the capital's harbour.

Boat
There are many ferry boats to various destinations, see Getting around, page 471. There is also a ferry from downtown to **Marriott Frenchman's Reef Beach Resort** and **Morningstar beach**, free for hotel guests, US$3 each way, leaving every hr 0900-1700, 15 mins. Ferry to **Water Island** runs frequently.

Bus
Vitran bus services (US$0.75 city fare, US$1 country fare, exact change) have 15 a/c buses that run from town to the university (passing near Yacht Haven Marina), to Four Winds Plaza and to Red Hook (past the hospital, K-Mart and Cost U Less).

Car and scooter
Car hire rates range from US$40-80 per day, unlimited mileage, vehicles from small cars to jeeps. **Budget**, T7765774; **Cowpet**, 7757376; **Avis**, 7741468; **Sun Island**, 7743333; **Discount**, 7764858; **VI Auto Rental**, 7763616 (Sub Base). Most have an office by the airport.

Scooters from **Island Scooters**, opposite Havensight Mall, T7147408, US$55 per day.

Taxis
Cabs are not metered but a list of fares is published in *St Thomas This Week* and *What To Do*; a fares list must be carried by each driver. Rates quoted are for 1 passenger and additional passengers are charged extra; drivers are notorious for trying to charge

each passenger the single passenger rate. **Airport** to Red Hook is US$15 for 1, US$11 each extra passenger, town to **Magens Bay** is US$10 for 1, US$8 for extra person. When travelling on routes not covered by the official list, agree the fare in advance. There are extra charges of US$2pp between 2400 and 0600 and charges for luggage. A 2-hr taxi tour for 2 people costs US$50, additional passengers US$25 each. **VI Taxi Association** T7747457, **Wheatley Taxi Service and Tours**, T7751959. *Gypsy cabs*, unlicensed taxis, operating outside Charlotte Amalie, are cheaper but agree fare and route before getting in.

Water Island *p478*
Sea
During the week, the **Kontiki** floating booze cruise makes daily stops; other day-charter boats may also stop when weather is rough. **Water Island Ferry**, www.usvi.net/water /html/ferry.html, runs frequently from Crown Bay Marina (outside Tickles) Mon-Sat 0645-1800, US$3 one way, with night runs Mon, Fri, Sat, US$5 one way, and a reduced service Sun and holidays. Weekly and monthly passes are available and special runs can be arranged with the Captain.

❶ Directory

St Thomas *p474, map p474*
Banks Banco Popular de Puerto Rico, T7767800. Bank of Nova Scotia, T7740037. First Bank, T7744800. **Internet** Little Switzerland Internet Café, Main St, upstairs, T7762010, www.littleswitzerland.com. Jascom, Havensight Mall, building III, upper level, internet access and other services. **Telephone** AT&T calling centre at Havensight and **St Thomas Communications** in Crown Bay Marina at Sub Base. Local and overseas calls, faxes, internet US$3 per 15 mins. **Medical services** St Thomas has a 225-bed hospital, T7768311, and a 24-hr emergency services. Mobile medical units provide health services to outlying areas. **Red Hook Family Practice** is open Mon-Fri 1000-1600, walk in.

St John → *Phone code: 340. Colour map 2, B6. Population: 4,197.*

Much of St John is a national park and it is its protected status that draws visitors. The island is covered with steep hills and is hot. The roads are steep and rocky and 4WD is required to get to many places. The population is mainly concentrated in the little town of Cruz Bay and the village of Coral Bay. A drive from Cruz Bay across to Coral Bay is a worthwhile experience and allows you to appreciate how much land is owned by the park, though there is not much in Coral Bay itself. Only 21 sq miles, St John is about 5 miles east of St Thomas and 35 miles north of St Croix. ▶▶ *For Sleeping, Eating and other listings, see pages 486-489.*

Ins and outs

Getting there and around There is no airport on St John. Visitors arrive by ferry, see page 470 or by private yacht, see page 489.

There are three main roads, though government maps show more roads that are 4WD dirt tracks. It's only 7 miles from Cruz Bay to Coral Bay but the journey takes 40 minutes to drive. Hiking is hot and hilly. You can always start walking and then catch a taxibus. Hitchhiking is easy.

Virgin Islands National Park

ⓘ *T7766201, www.nps.gov/viis, US$4 to enter the park at Trunk Bay and to view the Annaberg ruins.*

The population of St John fell to less than a thousand people in 1950 when 85% of the land had reverted to bush and second-growth tropical forest. In the 1950s Laurance Rockefeller bought about half the island but later donated his holdings to establish a national park which was to take up about two-thirds of the predominantly mountainous terrain. The Virgin Islands National Park was opened in 1956 and is covered by an extensive network of trails (some land in the park is still privately owned and not open to visitors). Several times a week a park ranger leads the **Reef Bay hike**, which passes

> ✦ *There are 22 hikes in all, 14 on the north shore, eight on the south shore.*

US Virgin Islands St John

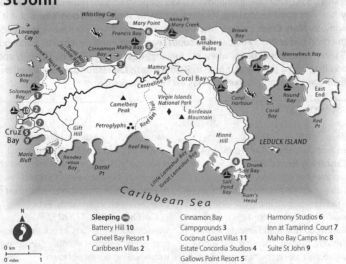

St John

Sleeping ⬤
Battery Hill **10**
Caneel Bay Resort **1**
Caribbean Villas **2**

Cinnamon Bay
Campgrounds **3**
Coconut Coast Villas **11**
Estate Concordia Studios **4**
Gallows Point Resort **5**

Harmony Studios **6**
Inn at Tamarind Court **7**
Maho Bay Camps Inc **8**
Suite St John **9**

through a variety of vegetation zones, visits an old sugar mill (**Annaberg**) and some unexplained petroglyphs, and ends with a ferry ride back to Cruz Bay. The trail can be hiked without the ranger, but the National Park trip provides a boat at the bottom of the trail so you do not need to walk back up the three-mile hill. You should reserve a place on the guided hike at the **Park Service Visitors' Centre** ① *Cruz Bay, T7766201, daily 0800-1630*, on north side of harbour. Here you'll get park information, including informative displays, topographical and hiking trail maps, books on shells, birds, fish, plants, flowers and local history, and you can sign up for activities. The trails are well maintained and clearly signed with interpretative information along the way. Insect repellent is essential. A seashore walk in shallow water, using a glass-bottomed bucket to discover sea life, is recommended. A snorkel boat trip around St John, taking you to five or six reefs not accessible from land (and therefore less damaged), is a good way to see the island even if you do not snorkel. An informative, historical bus tour goes to the remote East End. There are evening programmes at Cinnamon Bay and Maho Bay camps, where rangers show slides and movies and hold informal talks.

Beaches and activities

North shore beaches can go from calm to a surfer's delight in winter when northerly swells roll in from the Atlantic, making the sea rough and dangerous. Go to the south

❧ *Day trippers off cruise ships head for Hawk's Nest, Cinnamon and Trunk bays, so avoid these areas if you want some space.*

for calm beaches and anchorages. **Frett's Maho Bay Shuttle** goes around the north shore coast to any of the beaches, which is easier than trying to reach them by road. In the national park there are snack bars at Cinnamon Bay and Trunk Bay only. Bring water and lunch if you are hiking or going to other beaches which will not be so crowded. Other good beaches include **Hawk's Nest Bay**, **Caneel Bay**, **Cinnamon Bay** (there is a small museum of historical photographs and pictures here), **Maho Bay** (beach is 5 ft from the road, lots of turtles, sometimes tarpon, nice and calm) and **Solomon Bay** (unofficial nudist beach about 30 minutes' walk from the road).

Snorkelling Off **Trunk Bay**, the island's best beach, is an underwater snorkelling trail maintained by the National Parks Service. Not surprisingly, the beach tends to get rather crowded (especially when tour groups come in); lockers for hire, US$2 (deposit US$5), snorkelling equipment US$6 (deposit US$40) return by 1600. **Jumbie Bay** has very good snorkelling, as does the north shore of **Francis Bay**, but if it is choppy, try **Mary Creek** instead, where you can snorkel among the mangroves or out to the coral reef at Anna Point. On the south coast, **Salt Pond** (reached by Vitran bus, US$1 every two hours or so, when it's running, has an excellent beach with good snorkelling and a spectacular hike to Ram's Head), **Lameshur Bay** is reached by a difficult road but worth it. **Reef Bay** has excellent snorkelling.

◉ Sleeping

St John *p485, map p485*
Rates are published at st-john.com/rates.
LL **Caneel Bay Resort**, T7766111, www.caneelbay.com. Lots of packages available in a variety of rooms or cottages, 166-room resort built in the late 1950s by Laurance Rockefeller, since 1993 managed by **Rosewood Hotels and Resorts**, several restaurants, bars, dress smartly after sunset, 11 all-weather tennis courts, complimentary watersports for guests including sunfish, windsurfers, also boat rentals, fishing and diving available, kids' club and exercise club, ferry service between Caneel Bay and downtown St Thomas, also to sister resort of *Little Dix Bay* on Virgin Gorda, BVI.
LL **Caribbean Villas**, T7766152, www.caribbeanvilla.com. 2-bedroom villas, pool, personal service, attentive management, within walking distance of town.

LL Coconut Coast Villas, T6939100, www.coconutcoast.com. Studios and villas, 6 m from water, kitchens, snorkelling.

LL Gallows Point Resort, T7766434, www.gallowspointresort.com. 52 suites, fans, pool, watersports, kitchen facilities.

LL Suite St John, Gallows Point, T7766969, www.gallowspoint.com. 1-bedroom waterfront loft or ground floor condos, sleep 4, luxury, full kitchens, balconies, every convenience, internet access, pool, beach, deck overlooking snorkelling trail, sea views to other islands, walking distance to Cruz Bay.

LL-L Battery Hill, T/F6938261, www.batteryhill.com. 9 apartments, good view, breezy, walk to beach or town.

LL-AL Maho Bay Camps Inc, Maho Bay, 8 miles from Cruz Bay, regular bus service), T7766240, www.maho.org. Maho has expanded and taken over Harmony Studios, Estate Concordia Studios and Concordia Eco-Tents, providing eco-friendly options from camping to condos with all levels of creature comforts. A privately run campground, tent cottages are connected by a raised boardwalk to protect the environment, lots of steps, take a torch to negotiate them at night, magnificent view from restaurant, planned activities, attracts socially conscious, environmentally aware guests and staff, possible to work in return for board.

L-AL The Inn at Tamarind Court, in Cruz Bay, T7766378, www.tamarindcourt.com. Rooms and suites sleeping 2-4, also a block of 6 single rooms with 2 shared bathrooms (A), a/c, fridge, TV. Nothing special, adequate, inexpensive breakfast and dinner (closed Sat night), bar open all the time except Sat it closes at 1700.

L-D Cinnamon Bay Campgrounds, Cinnamon Bay (frequent taxi-buses from Cruz Bay), T7766330, www.cinnamonbay .com. Campground and chalet site run by the National Park Service, usually full so book in advance, maximum stay 2 weeks; bare site (D), or tent provided (A), a few shared showers, food reasonably priced in both the cafeteria and grocery store.

🍴 Eating

St John *p485, map p485*
St John is known for fine dining.

¶¶¶ **Asolare**, Northshore Rd, Cruz Bay, T7794747. Daily, dinner only 1730-2045 last reservation. Euro-Asian cuisine, lovely setting, reservations recommended.

¶¶¶ **Chateau Bordeaux**, Centerline Rd, Bordeaux Mountain, T7766611. Daily, lunch 1100-1500, dinner 1730-2045 last reservation. Fine dining at the highest viewpoint on the island, expensive, reservations advised. Lunch is lighter but with hot dogs, hamburgers and sandwiches.

¶¶¶ **The Lime Inn**, Cruz Bay, T7766425. Mon-Sat lunch 1130-1500, dinner 1730-2130 last reservation. Seafood, steak, excellent lobster and pasta, all-you-can-eat night on Wed, very popular with locals and visitors.

¶¶¶ **Panini Beach**, Cruz Bay, T6939119. Mon-Fri lunch 1130-1500, dinner 1730-2030 for last reservation. Pricey, seafood/Caribbean.

¶¶ **Café Roma**, Cruz Bay, T7766524. Daily 1700-2200. Italian food, also vegetarian dishes. Pizza for take out orders and at the bar only.

¶¶ **Chilly Billy's**, upstairs at the Lumber Yard, Cruz Bay, T6938708. Daily 0800-1400, breakfast all day on Sat and Sun. Serves great Bloody Marys for breakfast or any time.

¶¶ **JJ's Tex Mex**, Cruz Bay ferry dock, T7766908. Daily 0800-1100 for breakfast, 1100-1700 for lunch, dinner 1700-2100. Great for breakfast or at any time, Tex Mex food.

¶¶ **Morgan's Mango**, Cruz Bay, T6938141. Daily 1730-2200. Excellent seafood and steak, also vegetarian, open-air dining, great sauces, reservations recommended.

¶¶ **Paradiso**, at Mongoose Junction, Cruz Bay, T6938899. Daily 1800-2100 for last dinner reservation. American food, has children's menu, eat indoors or on balcony, quite expensive.

¶¶ **Shipwreck Landing**, Coral Bay, T6935640. American cuisine, frozen drinks, nightly specials, open-air dining, live music at weekend.

¶¶ **Zo Zo's**, Gallow's Point, Cruz Bay, T6938490. Lunch and dinner, closed Mon. Continental and seafood.

¶ **Miss Lucy's**, on the way to Salt Pond, Cruz Bay, T6935244. Tue-Sat lunch 1100-1500, dinner 1800-2100, Sun brunch 1000-1400. Locally famous, worth the trip just for the conch chowder, full-moon parties are a tradition, with a pig roast (1800-2100, US$15) and a live band, ferries available from

US Virgin Islands St John Listings

St Thomas. Maho Bay Campground, T7766226, run trips for the occasion, also Fri night steel band, Sat jazz night, Sun brunch with live jazz, closed Sep-Oct.

Skinny Legs (named after the owners), Coral Bay, T7794982, www.skinnylegs.com. Daily 1100-2100. Local hang-out, soup, sandwiches, grills and fish. Lunch and dinner same menu.

Uncle Joe's, opposite the Post Office in Cruz Bay, T6938806. Lunch 1200-1530, dinner 1730-2130. No sign outside, just the barbecue grill. Great barbecued ribs.

Bars and clubs

St John   *p485, map p485*
Up-to-date information on events is posted on the trees around town or on the bulletin board in front of **Connections**. In Cruz Bay, the place to go and dance is **Fred's**, calypso and reggae Wed and Fri. Popular places to 'lime' (relax) are **JJ's** and sitting in Cruz Bay Park, watching the world go by. See **Lucy's**, above, for full-moon hog roast and music. **Quiet Mon Pub**, above **La Tapa**, Cruz Bay, T7794799, www.quietmon.com. 1000-0400. Draft beer, cyber Celtic café, Irish-Caribbean-American bar which celebrates St Patrick's Day and Super Bowl.

Festivals and events

Jan St John Yacht Club Island Hopper Race.
Jul Carnival is in the week of 4 Jul, with lots of events in the 2 preceding weeks.
Nov Thanksgiving Day Regatta.
   Other yacht races include **Coral Bay Yacht Club** (meets at Skinny Legs), **CATS** (programme for children) and **ANTS** (adults).

Shopping

St John   *p485, map p485*
Scattered around **Cruz Bay**, **Wharfside Village** and **Mongoose Junction** are shops selling souvenirs, arts and crafts. Right in the Park is **Sparkey's**, selling newspapers, film, cold drinks, gifts. The **St John Drug Center Inc** is open daily.

Food
Food is expensive (rum is cheaper than water) and the selection is limited.

Starfish Market (the largest) and **Marina Market** in Cruz Bay, **Joe's Discount** near Shipwreck Landing in Coral Bay. **Maiden Apple**, health food store, 1st floor of Boulton Centre, T6938781. Liquor and drinks at **Cases by the Sea**, near Coral Bay Watersports. Grocery near **Shipwreck Tavern**, **Joe's Discount** and **Pickles Deli**. If you are camping it's a good idea to shop at the supermarkets on St Thomas. Fish and produce is sold from boats twice a week at the freight dock.

Activities and tours

St John   *p485, map p485*
Diving and snorkelling
Cinnamon Bay Watersports, T7766330. Also **kayaking** and **windsurfing**.
Cruz Bay Watersports, 3 locations, T7766234. Offers a free snorkel map.
East End Divers, T7794994 or 6937519, Coral Bay.
Low Key Watersports, Wharfside Village, T800-8357718, 6938999. For 1- and 2-tank dives, wreck dives and night dives; personal attention; also **kayaking**.
St John Snorkel Tours, T7766922. Day and night tours, guided Reef Bay hikes.
VI Snuba Excursions, T6938063. You can *snuba* (air in the boat, not on your back) at Trunk Bay.

Horse riding
Carolina Corral, T6935778. Beach rides, sunset and full-moon rides.

Rock climbing
Adventures Unlimited, T6935763. Will take you rock climbing, all equipment provided.

Sailing and fishing
Connections, T7766922. Half-and full-day sails and fishing trips.
Coral Bay Watersports, T7766850, next to Serafina. Rents power boats, sport fishing and tackle, and also offers diving, snorkelling, kayaking and windsurfing.
Noah's Little Arks (Zodiacs), T6939030. Sailing and fishing trips.
Ocean Runner Powerboats, T6938809. Motor boats for hire.
Proper Yachts, T7766256. Sailing trips.

Sadie Sea, T7766421. Good, offering a snorkelling tour around St John.
Wayward Sailor, T6938555. A recommended sailing and snorkelling trip is with Captain Phil, US$85 for the day with a most knowledgeable host, who takes you out to the St James islands between St John and St Thomas.

Tennis
There is tennis at the large resorts and also 2 public courts available on a first-come-first-served basis.

Tour operators
As well as the National Parks Service (see above), **Thunderhawk Trail Guides**, T7741112, offers hikes through the national park.

Windsurfing
Windsurfers can be rented at Cinnamon Bay and Maho Camps, sunfishes at Maho Camp.

⊝ Transport

St John *p485, map p485*
Boat
To **St Thomas**, hourly 0700 to 2200 and 2315 to Red Hook, every 2 hrs 0715 to 1315, 1545 and 1715 to **Charlotte Amalie** (see page 484).

Bus
There are 2 **Vitran** buses, US$1 exact change only, from Cruz Bay to Coral Bay and Salt Pond about every hr. If one breaks down you have to wait for the next.

Car
Vehicles may be rented, but parking is difficult. There are 3 fuel stations, open 0800-1900, in Cruz Bay and Coral Bay, may be closed on holidays. Rental agencies: **Hertz**, T7766695; **Delbert Hill's Jeep Rental**,

T7766637; **Budget**, T7767575; **Avis**, T7766374; **Cool Breeze**, T7766588, **St John Car Rental**, T7766103; rates start from US$50 per day.

Taxi
Official taxi rates can be obtained from St John Police Department or ask the taxi driver to show the official rate card (see page 484 for details). A 2-hr island tour costs US$50 for 1 or 2 passengers, or US$25 per person if there are 3 or more. Taxi from **Cruz Bay** to **Trunk Bay**, US$8; to **Cinnamon Bay** US$9. It is almost impossible to persuade a taxi to take you to **Coral Bay**, so hitch a ride from the intersection by the supermarket deli.

❶ Directory

St John *p485, map p485*
Banks Banco Popular de Puerto Rico, T6932777. Bank of Novia Scotia, T6939932. St John's banking hours are 0830-1500 Mon-Fri. **Internet and telephone** Cyber Celtic Café/Quiet Mon Pub, Cruz Bay town above La Tapa, T7794799, www.quietmon.com. Connections West, Cruz Bay, T7766922, as well as arranging sailing trips and villa rentals, is the place for business services, local and international telephone calls, faxes, Western Union money transfers, photocopying, word-processing, notary, VHF radio calls and tourist information (they know everything that is happening). **Connections East**, T7794994, does the same thing in Coral Bay. **Coral Bay Marine Services** for mail drop, message centre, if you have your own computer you can use their phonepoint to access email.
Laundry Laundromat next to **Raintree Inn**, Cruz Bay, Mon-Fri 0830-1730, Sat 0830-1200. **Medical services** St John has a 7-bed clinic, T7766400 and a 24-hr emergency service.

St Croix → Phone code: 340. Colour map 2, C6. Population: 53,000.

St Croix (pronounced to rhyme with 'boy') is perceived as the poor relation of the main group of islands, but its lack of development is part of its charm and there is more to see here than on St Thomas. Columbus thought that St Croix looked like a lush garden when he first saw it during his second voyage in 1493. He landed at Salt River on the north coast, now a national park encompassing the landing site as well as the rich underwater Salt River drop off and canyon. It had been cultivated by the Carib Indians, who called it Ay-Ay, and the land still lies green and fertile between the rolling hills. Today, agriculture has been surpassed by tourism and industry, including the huge Hovensa oil refinery on the south coast. The east of the island is rocky and arid terrain; the west is higher, wetter and forested. St Croix is the largest of the group with 84 sq miles, lying 40 miles south of St Thomas. People born on the island are called Crucians, while North Americans who move there are known as Continentals. ▶▶ *For Sleeping, Eating and other listings, see pages 493-496.*

Ins and outs

Getting there and around See page 470 for details of flights to **Henry Rohlson international airport**. A taxi dispatcher's booth is at the airport exit. Rates are listed in many publications. ▶▶ *See Transport, page 496 for further details.*

A bus service runs between Christiansted and Frederiksted. The major car rental agencies are represented at the airport, hotels and both cities. A 4WD car is ideal to drive along the scenic roads, for example to Ham's Bay or Point Udall. There is a distinct lack of road signs on St Croix, so if you use a car, take a good map.

Christiansted

The town square and waterfront area of Christiansted, the old Danish capital, still retain the colourful character of the early days. Red-roofed pastel houses built by early settlers climb the hills overlooking **Kings Wharf** and there is an old outdoor market. Many of the buildings are being restored and the dock is being improved to take small cruise ships (the reef prevents large ships entering the harbour), but it is unlikely to be overrun with cruise ship tourism like St Thomas. Old Christiansted is compact and easy to stroll around. The best place to start is the **Visitors' Bureau** ① *corner of King Cross St and Queen St*, where you can pick up brochures.

Fort Christiansvaern ① *T7731460, www.nps.gov/chri, 0800-1645, US$3*, was built by the Danes in 1749 on the foundations of a French fort dating from 1645. See the punishment cells, dungeons, barracks room, officers' kitchen, powder magazine, an exhibit of how to fire a cannon, and the battery, the best vantage point for photographing the old town and harbour. The fort and the surrounding historic buildings are run by the National Parks Service. The old customs house in front of the fort is now its office. The **Steeple Building** ① *Mon-Fri 0900-1600, Sat 0900-1200, entry fee included in the fort entrance*, was built as a church by the Danes in 1734, then converted into a military bakery, storehouse and later a hospital. It is now a history museum. The area here is full of old Danish architecture, and many of the original buildings are still used. The West India and Guinea Co, which bought St Croix from the French and settled the island, built a warehouse on the corner of Church and Company Streets which is now a post office and Customs House.

On King Street is the building where the young **Alexander Hamilton**, who was to become one of the founding fathers of the USA, worked as a clerk in Nicolas Cruger's counting-house. Today the building houses the Little Switzerland shop.

Government House ① *T7731404, 0800-1700*, has all the hallmarks of the elegant and luxurious life of the merchants and planters in the days when 'sugar was king'.

The centre section, built in 1742 as a merchant's residence, was bought by the Secret Council of St Croix in 1771 as a government office. It was later joined to another merchant's town house on the corner of Queen Cross Street and a handsome ballroom (which you can visit, along with the gardens and the Court of Justice) was added. The Governor stays here when he works away from Charlotte Amalie.

A **boardwalk** spans the entire waterfront of Christiansted, providing a wonderful stroll with lively restaurants, cafés and bars along the way. The boardwalk is well lit and security is tight with policemen on duty and security cameras. Between the waterfront and Strand Street there is a fascinating maze of arcades and alleys lined with boutiques, handicrafts and jewellery shops. Just offshore is **Protestant Cay** (just called The Cay), reached by ferry for US$3 return. It has a pleasant beach, and the **Hotel on the Cay**, with restaurants, pool, tennis and watersports.

Frederiksted

Frederiksted, 17 miles from Christiansted, is the only other town on St Croix. Historic buildings such as **Victoria House**① *7-8 Strand St*, and the **Customs House**, have been repaired following hurricane damage. **Fort Frederik** ① *Mon-Fri 0830-1600, free*, (1752) is a museum. This is the place where the proclamation freeing all Danish slaves was read, in 1848. An exhibition of old photos and newspaper articles and other display items shows the destruction caused by hurricanes.

Around the island

Agriculture was long the staple of the economy, cattle and sugar the main activities, and ruins of sugar plantations with their great houses and windmills still remain. You can tour the restored estates several times a year. The **St Croix Heritage Trail**, www.stcroixheritagetrail.com, promotes culture, heritage and communities and was designated one of 50 Millennium Legacy Trails by the White House Millennium Council. There are many attractions to be toured. A good guide is available at www.millenniumtrails.org. Starting in February for six weeks the **St Croix Landmarks Society** ① *T7720598, www.stcroixlandmarks.com*, runs house tours every Wednesday, US$30, in different parts of the island.

Estate Whim ① *T7720598, www.stcroixlandmarks.com, Mon-Sat 1000-1600 Nov-Apr, 1000-1500 Mon-Fri May-Oct, US$8, children under 12 US$4, seniors and students with ID US$5. tours every 30 mins*, has been restored to the way it was under Danish rule in the 1700s. There's a gift shop and candlelight concerts and other functions are held here, including an annual antiques auction, usually in March, which is considered one of the best places to find antique West Indian furniture. The **St Croix Landmark Society** can be contacted here. **St George Village Botanical Garden**① *T6922874, www.sgvbg.org, daily in winter 0900-1700, Tue-Sat in summer 0900-1600. US$6 adults, US$1 children, just off Centreline Road*, has 16 acres (6.5ha) of beautiful gardens amid the ruins of a 19th century plantation village.

The **rainforest** to the north of town is worth a visit. Two roads, the paved Mahogany Road (Route 76) and the unpaved Creque Dam Road (Road 58) traverse it.

Beaches and activities

Good beaches can be found at **Davis Bay, Protestant Cay, Buccaneer** (good snorkelling), **The Reef, Cane Bay** (good snorkelling), **Grapetree Beach** and **Cormorant Beach. Cramer Park** on the east shore and **Frederiksted beach** to the north of the town both have changing facilities and showers. **Rainbow Beach Club**, 1½ km north of Frederiksted, has a spectacular sandy beach, restaurant and beach bar. All beaches are open to the public, but on those where there is a hotel that maintains the beach (Buccaneer, for example), you may have to pay for the use of facilities. Try the isolated beach to the east of the **Buccaneer Hotel** (walk across the golf course), at **The Waves** restaurant at Cane Bay, or explore and find your own. Generally the north coast is best for surfing because there are no reefs to protect the beaches. On the northwest coast, the stretch from Northside Beach to Ham's Bay is easily accessible (but watch out for sea urchins at Ham's Bay beach); the road is alongside the beach. The road ends at the General Offshore Sonorbuoy Area (a naval installation at Ham's Bluff), which is a good place to see booby birds and frigate birds leaving at dawn and coming home to roost at dusk.

Diving Scuba diving is very good around St Croix, with forests of elkhorn coral, black coral, brain coral, sea fans, a multitude of tropical fish, sea horses under the **Frederiksted pier** (great day or night dive for novices, an easy shore dive and one of the best in the USVI), walls and drop offs, reefs and wrecks. The wrecks are varied, some 40 years old and some recent, with marine life slowly growing on the structures and schools of fish taking up residence. They range from 75-300 ft in length and 15-110 ft deep, providing something for beginners and the more experienced. **Butler Bay**, off Frederiksted, is home to six shipwrecks. Nearby in **Truck Lagoon** are the remains of around 25 old truck chassis that were sunk by **Hess Oil** to promote marine growth and create an artificial reef. The wrecks of the *North Wind*, *The Virgin Islander Barge* and *Suffolk Maid* are close together, but usually done as two separate leisurely dives, otherwise you have to swim rather briskly to get round them all. There are also the *Rosaomaira*, the deepest of the wrecks, and the *Coakly Bay*, the newest, while to the south is the *Sondra*, a shallow dive which can even be snorkelled, although there is not a great deal remaining on the site. Just behind the *Sondra* is the wreck of a motor boat. During February, March and April you are likely to see humpback whales near the islands and dive boats sometimes go out to watch them. Diving trips are arranged by several companies all round the island, many of which also charter boats out and offer sailing lessons, see page 495.

Snorkelling At **Buck Island** there are underwater snorkelling trails, the two main ones being Turtle Bay Trail and East End Trail. The fish are superb. The reef is an underwater national park covering over 850 acres, including the island. Hawksbill

St Croix

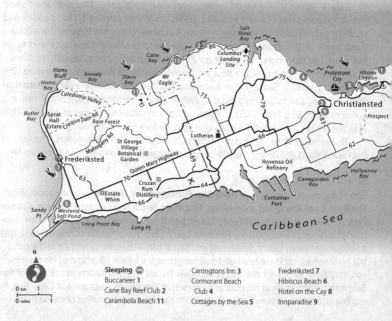

Sleeping
Buccaneer **1**
Cane Bay Reef Club **2**
Carambola Beach **11**

Carringtons Inn **3**
Cormorant Beach Club **4**
Cottages by the Sea **5**

Frederiksted **7**
Hibiscus Beach **6**
Hotel on the Cay **8**
Innparadise **9**

turtles nest on Buck Island and, during a 1993 Buck Island National Monument Sea Turtle Research Programme, Sandy Point leatherbacks were also observed nesting there. Half-day tours to Buck Island, including 1¼ hours snorkelling and 30 minutes at the beach, can be arranged through hotels or boat owners on the waterfront at Christiansted. Only six operators are licensed to take day charters to the island, which means that they are often crowded. Another attraction is the **Salt River coral canyon**.

> ♣ *Anchorage is crowded 1000-1600 with day charters; watch the charter boat's race for the best spots at 1000 and 1600.*

🛏 Sleeping

For hotel rates consult www.usvitourism.vi. For small, intimate places to stay, check out www.gotost croix.com, or www.visitstcroix .com. Hotels often add an energy surcharge in addition to tax and service.

Christiansted *p490, map p495*
L-AL Caravelle, 44A Queen Cross St, T7730687, www.hotelcaravelle.com. 44 good rooms, all well-equipped, price depends on view, good restaurant, **Rumrunners**, pool, diving, transport to other sports facilities, diving packages available.
L-AL Hotel on the Cay, on Protestant Cay, see p, in Christiansted harbour, T7732035, www.hotelonthecay.com. Free 1½ min ferry service, 55 rooms, also timeshare with

kitchenettes, snorkelling, pool, beach, watersports, tennis, Wi-Fi internet access.
L-AL Pink Fancy, 27 Prince St, near shopping centre and waterfront, T7738460, www.pinkfancy.com. 18th-century town-house, a National Historic Trust property, 11 rooms, 2 categories, all include breakfast, honeymoon packages, bar, pool.
A The Breakfast Club, 18 Queen Cross St, T7737383. 7 rooms with bath and kitchenette, one has a/c, new owner but still great breakfast, hot tub on deck.

Frederiksted *p491*
LL-AL Sand Castle On The Beach, ½ mile from town, T7721205. Pool, 20 rooms, suites, villas, kitchenettes, restaurants, serves gay community, lots of privacy.
AL The Frederiksted, 442 Strand St, T7720500, www.frederikstedhotel.com. Modern, 36 rooms, half of which face the water, fridge, TV, a/c, phones, pool, restaurant, bar, dive shop.

Around the island *p491, map p492*
LL Buccaneer, Gallows Bay, north coast, T7122100, www.thebuccaneer.com. 132 luxury rooms and suites, 340 acres, 3 beaches, sports including golf, tennis, fitness centre, watersports centre, restaurants, packages available.
LL Tamarind Reef Hotel, on the northeast coast, T7734455, www.usvi.net/hotel /tamarind. 46 rooms, half have kitchenettes, a/c, fan, TV, balcony, all with seaview, 2 beaches, pool, snorkelling, boardsailing, kayaking at hotel, or diving, fishing, sailing from adjacent Green Cay Marina, croquet and tennis lawn, packages available.
LL-L Carambola Beach, on Davis Bay, north coast, T7783800, www.carambolabeach .com. Soon to become a Renaissance Hotel with US$20mn refurbishment. 146 rooms in

Sand Castle on the Beach **10**
Tamarind Reef **12**
Waves at Cane Bay **13**

25 2-storey villas, tennis, golf, pool, jacuzzis, snorkelling, scuba.

LL-L Cormorant Beach Club and Hotel, near Christiansted, T7788920. 1st class, beach, tennis, pool, deluxe, gay friendly.

LL-L Hibiscus Beach Hotel, west of Christiansted, T7734042, www.1hibiscus.com. 37 beachfront rooms, hammocks on the beach, access for handicapped to beach, pool, restaurant, watersports in all-inclusive packages, special deals.

LL-AL Cane Bay Reef Club, Cane Bay, north coast, T/F7782966, www.canebay.com. 9 suites with balconies over the sea, pool, restaurant, bar, weekly rates cheaper.

LL-AL Cottages by the Sea, 127A Estate Smithfield, south of Frederiksted, T7720495, www.caribbeancottages.com. Beach, watersports, maid service, 19 cottages, 1 villa, in groups or on their own, individual floor plans, each one different, half of them on the sand.

L-AL Carringtons Inn, 4001 Estate Hermon Hill, T7130508, www.carringtonsinn.com. 5 light and airy rooms, each one different, private bathrooms, bed and breakfast, pool.

L-AL Innparadise, 1 Estate Golden Rock on Little Princess Hill overlooking Christiansted, T7139803, innparadise@worldnet.att.net. Run by Paula and Tommie Boradnax, 4 rooms, breakfast included, private or shared bath, microwave and fridge, TV, pool, minimum stay 3 days, no smoking, pets or children under 12, 10% discount for over-50s.

L-A Waves At Cane Bay, Kingshill, T7781805, www.thewavesatcanebay.com. 12 ocean-front studios with balconies, cable TV, natural grotto pool, beach, good snorkelling and scuba.

❼ Eating

Restaurant life on St Croix includes charcoal-broiled steaks and lobsters, West Indian Creole dishes and Danish and French specialities. Don't miss the open-air Crucian picnics. Local dishes include stewed or roast goat, red pea soup (a sweet soup of kidney beans and pork), callalou (dasheen soup); snacks, Johnny cakes (unleavened fried bread) and *pate* (pastry filled with spiced beef, chicken or salt fish); drinks, ginger beer, *mavi* (from the bark of a tree).

Christiansted *p490, map p495*

♚♚♚ Bacchus, Upstairs, 52 King Street, T692-9922, www.restaurantbacchus.com. 1800-2200. Fusion Italian, US and Caribbean dishes with veal, duck, lamb and fish on the menu. Extensive wine list, delicious desserts, coffee can be taken in the billiard room.

♚♚♚ Harbour Master Beach BBQ, Hotel on the Cay, Protestant Cay, T7732035. Tue 1900. Weekly beach barbecue with all you can eat ribs, fish and chicken, broken bottle dancers, fire eater and steel band.

♚♚♚ Truffles, 52 Company St, T7788783. Open Tue-Sat 1800-2130. Gourmet menu, good for vegetarians, try the organic beets, drizzled with a parmesan vinaigrette, or vegetable fettucini alfredo. Meat eaters may prefer the pesto chicken with grape tomatoes and a parmesan cream, or grilled salmon, spicy shrimp stir fry, grilled yellow tuna, seared duck breast, pan-roasted pork loin, braised lamb shank or filet mignon.

♚♚ Rumrunners, on the waterfront at Hotel Caravelle, T7736585. Breakfast, lunch and dinner. Sun brunch 1000-1400. Steak and seafood, burgers, pick your own lobster, on the boardwalk, tarpon feeding at sunset, happy hour cocktails and sushi.

♚ Stixx on the Waterfront, Pan Am Pavilion, 37 Strand St, T7735157. 1130-2200, bar open until 0200, happy hour 1700-1900. Informal, pasta, pizza, seafood, lobster, try the crab legs with garlic, daily specials, popular bar. Crab races Fri 1700.

♚ Café Misto, Company St, T7736911. Salads, soup and sandwich bistro at lunchtime, 1100-1600, great variety, good quality.

♚ Harvey's Bar and Restaurant, Company St, T7733433. Open for lunch and dinner. Local cuisine, conch, callaloo, goat stew.

♚ Lunchería, on Company St, in the courtyard of Apothecary Hall, T7734247. Mon-Sat lunch and dinner. Mexican food, cheap margaritas, live music.

♚ Morning Glory Coffee and Tea, Gallows Bay Market Place, T7236620. Mon-Sat 0700-1500. 26 blended coffees, also tea, New Orleans-style beignets, salads and wraps.

♚ Tommy T's Paradise Café, 53B Company St, T7732985. 0730-2200. Breakfast, lunch and dinner. Small local bar/restaurant, steak, sandwiches, veggie burgers and daily specials, claustrophobic, no credit cards.

Frederiksted *p491*

🍴 **The Blue Moon**, 17 Strand St, T7722222. Dinner Tue-Sat, Sun brunch. Seafood and native dishes plus music, daily specials, great Sun brunch with jazz.

🍴 **Coyote Café**, Princess Passage, Strand St, T7725400. Tue-Sat. Tapas bar and Sun brunch 1000-1400.

🍴 **Motown Bar and Restaurant**, Strand St, T7729882. Breakfast, lunch and dinner daily. Goat stew, conch, shrimp, cheap.

Around the island *p491, map p492*

🍴 **The Waves at Cane Bay**, T7781805. Tue-Sat dinner only. Expensive, good food, great atmosphere on the beach.

🍴 **Columbus Cove**, Salt River National Park, near Columbus Landing. Open daily for breakfast, lunch and dinner. Meat, fish and chicken, large portions, most under US$15.

🍴 **Cheeseburgers in Paradise**, on East End Rd, T7731119. Lunch and dinner, Very popular, always crowded, inexpensive.

🍴 **Golden Rail at St Croix Marina**, Gallows Bay. Tue-Sun all day. Cheap daily specials, American food and barbecue, no credit cards.

🍸 Bars and clubs

St Croix *p490, map p492*

Most hotels provide evening entertainment on a rotating basis, so it may be best to stay put and let the fun come to you. Some restaurants also provide entertainment, eg **Tivoli Gardens** (Queen Cross and Strand streets) and **The Galleon** (Green Cay Marina, piano bar).

🏔 Activities and tours

St Croix *p490, map p492*

Kayak

Virgin Kayak Co, in Cane Bay, T7780071. Explores the north shore from Annaly Bay to Salt River.

Sailing

There are several companies offering day sails on crewed yachts. **Jones Maritime** has a dock with a few moorings, teaches sailing and may rent boats for day sailing to qualified individuals.

Tennis

Most of the large hotels have tennis courts

US Virgin Islands St Croix Listings

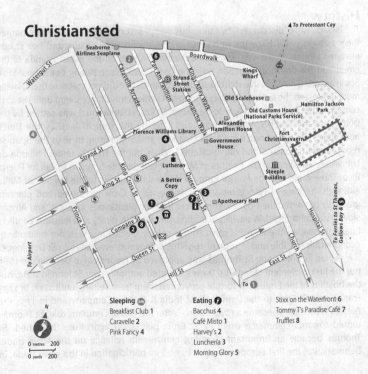

Christiansted

To Protestant Cay

Seaborne Airlines Seaplane

Boardwalk

Kings Wharf

Strand Street Station

Old Scalehouse

Old Customs House (National Parks Service)

Hamilton Jackson Park

Florence Williams Library

Alexander Hamilton House

Government House

Fort Christiansvaern

Lutheran

A Better Copy

Steeple Building

Apothecary Hall

To Ferries to St Thomas, Gallows Bay &

To Airport

To

N

0 metres 200
0 yards 200

Sleeping
Breakfast Club **1**
Caravelle **2**
Pink Fancy **4**

Eating
Bacchus **4**
Café Misto **1**
Harvey's **2**
Lunchería **3**
Morning Glory **5**

Stixx on the Waterfront **6**
Tommy T's Paradise Café **7**
Truffles **8**

for residents, but you can also play at the **Buccaneer Hotel**, the **Carambola**, Chenay Bay, **Club St Croix**, **The Reef Club**, the **Tamarind Reef Hotel** and others. There are 4 public courts at Canegata Park in Christiansted and 2 public courts near the fort in Frederiksted (free).

● Transport

St Croix *p490, map p492*
Boat
See Getting around, page 471.

Bus
The bus service runs between Christiansted and Frederiksted, 0530-2130, every 30 mins (every hr on Sun), US$2.

Taxi
From Christiansted taxis for 1-2 people cost US$12 to Morning Star, US$22 to Salt River, US$24 to Cane Bay or Frederiksted, US$30 to Carambola; from the airport it is US$12 to Frederiksted, US$15 to Cane Garden, US$20 to Carambola. A 3-hr taxi tour costs US$100 for up to 4 passengers, US$20 each for 5 or more. Contact **St Croix Taxi and Tours Association**, Henry E Rohlsen Airport, T7781088, F7786887; **Combined Tours**, T7722888. Taxi vans run between Christiansted and Frederiksted, US$2. For a limo service, try **Evans Limo Service**, T7734845, or **Mom's Limousine Service**, T7723669.

● Directory

Internet A Better Copy, Company St between King Cross St and Queen Cross St, Mon-Fri 0900-1700, also fax and photocopying. Florence Williams Library, Strand Street Station, in the Pan Am Pavilion, Christiansted, internet café, mail boxes, photocopies, faxes, pay phones, film processing, 0900-1900. **Medical services** St Croix has a 130-bed hospital, T7786311, and a 24-hr emergency service.

Background

History

The islands were 'discovered' by Columbus on his second voyage in 1493. He named them *Las Once Mil Vírgenes* in honour of the legend of St Ursula and her 11,000 martyred virgins. There were indigenous settlements on all the major islands of the group and the first hostile action with the Caribs took place during Columbus' visit. Spain asserted its exclusive right to settle the islands but did not colonize them, being more interested the Greater Antilles. European settlement did not begin until the 17th century, when few Indians were to be found. St Croix (Santa Cruz) was settled by the Dutch and the English around 1625, and later by the French. In 1645 the Dutch abandoned the island and went to St Eustatius and St Maarten. In 1650 the Spanish repossessed the island and drove off the English, but the French, under Philippe de Loinvilliers de Poincy of the Knights of Malta, persuaded the Spanish to sail for Puerto Rico. Three years later de Poincy formally deeded his islands to the Knights of Malta although the King of France retained sovereignty. St Croix prospered and planters gradually converted their coffee, ginger and tobacco plantations to sugar, and African slavery was introduced. Wars, illegal trading, privateering, piracy and religious conflicts finally persuaded the French Crown that a colony on St Croix was not militarily or economically feasible and in 1695 or 1696 the colony was evacuated to St Domingue.

A plan for colonizing St Thomas was approved by Frederik III of Denmark in 1665 but the first settlement failed. The Danes asserted authority over St John in 1684, but the hostility of the English in Tortola prevented them from settling until 1717. In 1733 France sold St Croix to the **Danish West India & Guinea Company** and in 1754 the Danish West Indies became a royal colony. After the end of Company rule, St Thomas turned towards commerce while in St Croix plantation agriculture flourished. St Thomas became an important shipping centre with reliance on the slave trade. Denmark was the first European nation to end its participation in the slave trade, in the early 1800s prevented enforcement of the ban.

The Danish Virgin Islands reached a peak population of 43,178 in 1835. Sailing ships were replaced by steamships which found it less necessary to transship in St Thomas. Prosperity declined with a fall in sugar prices, a heavy debt burden, soil exhaustion, development of sugar beet in Europe, hurricanes and droughts and the abolition of slavery. In 1847 a Royal decree provided that all slaves would be free after 1859 but the impatient slaves rebelled in July 1848. By the late 19th century economic decline became pronounced. The sugar factory on St Croix was inefficient and in the 20th century the First World War meant less shipping for St Thomas, more inflation, unemployment and labour unrest. The Virgin Islands became a liability for Denmark and the economic benefits of colonialism no longer existed. Negotiations with the USA had taken place intermittently ever since the 1860s for cession of the Virgin Islands to the USA. The USA wanted a Caribbean naval base and, after the 1914 opening of the Panama Canal, was particularly concerned to guard against German acquisition of Caribbean territory. In 1917, the islands were sold for US$25 million but no progress was made for several years. The islands were under naval rule during and after the war and it was not until 1932 that US citizenship was granted to all natives of the Virgin Islands.

A devastating hurricane in 1928, followed by the stock market crash of 1929, brought US awareness of the need for economic and political modernization. Several years of drought, the financial collapse of the sugar refineries, high unemployment and low wages characterized these years. In 1931 naval rule was replaced by a civil government. In 1934, the **Virgin Islands Company (VICO)** was set up as a 'partnership programme'. The sugar and rum industry benefited from demand in the Second World War. VICO improved housing, land and social conditions, but the end of the wartime construction boom, wartime demand for rum, and the closing of the submarine base brought further economic recession. However, the end of diplomatic relations between the USA and Cuba shifted tourism towards the islands. Construction boomed and there was even a labour shortage. VICO was disbanded in 1966, along with the production of sugar cane. Various tax incentives promoted the arrival of heavy industry, and during the 1960s the **Harvey Alumina Company** and the **Hess Oil Company** began operating on St Croix. By 1970, the economy was dominated by mainland investment and marked by managed enterprises based on imported labour from other Caribbean islands.

In September 1989, St Croix was hit by **Hurricane Hugo**, which tore through 90% of buildings and left 22,500 people homeless. The disaster was followed by civil unrest, with rioting, and US army troops were sent in to restore order. The territorial government, located on St Thomas, was slow to react to the disaster on St Croix and criticized. St Croix's feeling of neglect led to attempts to balance the division of power between the islands, but calls for greater autonomy grew. After some delay, a referendum was held in October 1993, which presented voters with seven options on the island's status, grouped into three choices: continued or enhanced status, integration into the USA, or Independence. However, the vote was inconclusive, with only 27% of the registered voters turning out; 50% were needed for a binding decision. Of those who did vote, 90% preferred the first option, leaving the process of constitutional change in some disarray.

Government

In 1936 the Organic Act of the Virgin Islands of the United States provided for two municipal councils and a Legislative Assembly in the islands. Discrimination on the grounds of race, colour, sex or religious belief was forbidden. In 1946, the first black governor was appointed to the Virgin Islands and in 1950 the first native governor was appointed. In 1968 the Elective Governor Act was passed, to become effective in 1970 when, for the first time, Virgin Islanders would elect their own Governor and

Lieutenant Governor. The USVI is an unincorporated territory under the US Department of Interior with a Delegate in the House of Representatives. The Governor is elected every four years. All persons born in the USVI are US citizens, but do not vote in presidential elections while on the islands.

Economy

USVI residents enjoy a comparatively high standard of living. Unemployment is low, but the working population is young and there is constant pressure for new jobs. Tourism is the primary economic activity, accounting for 80% of GDP and employment. The islands normally host 2 million visitors a year. Investment is continuing in the sector and will be boosted over the next few years by a US$100 mn project on St Croix to build a hotel, casino, conference centre and cultural theme park on 500 acres of Virgin Islands Port Authority (VIPA) land in Betty's Hope, near the airport. The manufacturing sector consists of petroleum refining, textiles, electronics, pharmaceuticals and watch assembly. The agricultural sector is small, with most food being imported. International business and financial services are a small but growing component of the economy. One of the world's largest petroleum refineries is at Saint Croix. In 1998 **Hess Oil Co** and **Petróleos de Venezuela** signed an agreement to create a company called Hovensa to operate the refinery. Industrial incentives and tax concessions equivalent to those enjoyed by Puerto Rico attract new investors with US markets to the islands. Many US corporations have manufacturing operations in the USVI. The islands' lack of natural resources makes them heavily dependent on imports.

Geography and people

The US Virgin Islands, in which the legacies of Danish ownership remain very apparent, comprise four main islands: St Thomas, St John, St Croix and Water Island. There are 68 islands in all, lying about 40 miles east of Puerto Rico. They have long been developed as holiday centres for US citizens. The population has always been English-speaking, despite the long period of Danish control. Some Spanish is used on St Croix. The West Indian dialect is mostly English, with inflections from Dutch, Danish, French, Spanish, African languages and Creole.

Flora and fauna

The Virgin Islands' national bird is the yellow breast (*Coereba flaveola*); the national flower is the yellow cedar (*Tecoma stans*). The mongoose was brought to the islands during the plantation days to kill rats that ate the crops. Unfortunately rats are nocturnal and mongooses are not and they succeeded only in eliminating most of the parrots and snakes. Now you see them all over the islands, especially near the rubbish dumps. There are many small lizards and some iguanas of up to 4 ft long. The iguanas sleep in the trees and you can see them and feed them (their favourite food is hibiscus flowers) at the Limetree Beach, at **Bluebeards Beach Club and Villas**, at Coral World and Frenchmans Reef. St John has a large population of wild donkeys on the upper hills.

Most of St John is a national park. Hassel Island, off Charlotte Amalie, is also a park. The headquarters of the **National Parks Service** ① *T7166201*, is on St John, with lots of information, reference books and interpretative programmes. On St Croix, the National Parks Service office is in the Old Customs Building on the waterfront. Buck Island is listed as an underwater monument. At the Arawak Suite 3 Gallows Bay, once a month the **Environmental Association** ① *T7731989, office in Apothecary Hall Courtyard, Company St*, runs hikes and walks, and in March to May, in conjunction with **Earthwatch** and the US **Fish and Wildlife Department**, you can see the leatherback turtles at **Sandy Point** ① *T7737545*, one of 13 significant nesting sites worldwide. The association has made Salt River a park for wildlife, reef and mangroves. *Virgin Islands Birdlife*, published by the USVI Co-operative Extension Service, with the US National Park Service, is available for birdwatchers.

British Virgin Islands

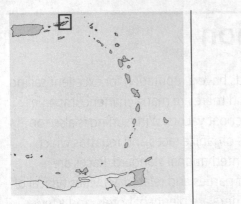

Footprint features

Introduction

The British Virgin Islands have a reputation for excellent sailing between the islands and there are many charter companies offering crewed or bareboat yachts. Windsurfing is also top quality and both sports organize races and regattas which attract competitors of international standard. Races are accompanied by lots of parties and related activities typical of the yachtie fraternity. There are plenty of hotels, and a few really special places in isolated spots – popular with newly weds or the seriously rich. While there are some luxury, sizable resorts in the BVI, there are no high-rise hotels or casinos, and very few nightclubs. In fact, there is very little to do at all on land and nearly everything happens in the beautiful water which surrounds the islands. If you are keen on watersports and sailing and have adequate finances (the Virgin Islands are not cheap), you will enjoy island hopping around Sir Francis Drake Channel. Tortola is the main island where most people live. Road Town is the capital, a small town around a busy harbour with marinas, jetties and inter-island transport, while there are also communities with docks and ferries at East End and West End which attract restaurants and a lively nightlife. The best beaches run around the north shore, where there are bays and inlets for mooring yachts. The other island with a sizable population is Virgin Gorda, site of the huge boulders known as the Baths and home to a number of luxury hotels and yacht havens. Some of the other islands are so small that they are occupied by a single resort or a single villa, the height of exclusivity, bolt holes for the celebrity rich.

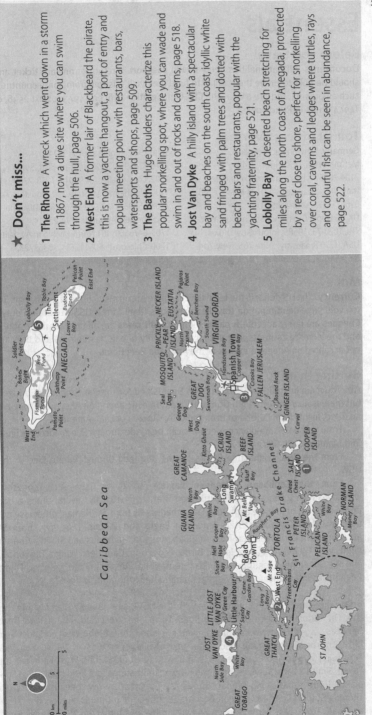

British Virgin Islands

★ **Don't miss...**

1 **The Rhone** A wreck which went down in a storm in 1867, now a dive site where you can swim through the hull, page 506.

2 **West End** A former lair of Blackbeard the pirate, this is now a yachtie hangout, a port of entry and popular meeting point with restaurants, bars, watersports and shops, page 509.

3 **The Baths** Huge boulders characterize this popular snorkelling spot, where you can wade and swim in and out of rocks and caverns, page 518.

4 **Jost Van Dyke** A hilly island with a spectacular bay and beaches on the south coast, idyllic white sand fringed with palm trees and dotted with beach bars and restaurants, popular with the yachting fraternity, page 521.

5 **Loblolly Bay** A deserted beach stretching for miles along the north coast of Anegada, protected by a reef close to shore, perfect for snorkelling over coral, caverns and ledges where turtles, rays and colourful fish can be seen in abundance, page 522.

Essentials

Before you travel

Documents All nationalities need a valid **passport**, a return or **onward ticket** and should be able to prove their ability to fund their visit. Visitors from some countries, such as Guyana, require a visa. The **Chief Immigration Officer**, T4943701 ext 2538, or T4944371, is in Road Town.

Tourist offices overseas

Germany, Schwarzbachstrasse 32, D-40822 Mettmann Bei, Dusseldorf, T(49) 2104-286671, bvi@travelmarketing.de.

Italy, Piazza Caiazzo 3, 20124 Milan, T(39) 0266714374, staff@aigo.it.

UK, 15 Upper Grosvenor St, London, W1K 7PJ, T020-73559585, infouk@bvi.org.uk.

USA, 1270 Broadway, Suite 705, New York, NY 10001, T212-6960400; 1275 Shiloh Rd, Suite 2930, Kennesaw, GA 30144, T770-8745951; 3450 Wilshire Blvd, Suite 1202, Los Angeles, CA 90010, T213-7368931; 5100 Westheimer St, Suite 200, Houston, TX 77056-5593, T713-9689256; 1800 Diagonal Rd, Suite 600, Alexandria, VA 22314, T703-6476560; 401 North Michigan Av, Suite 1200, Chicago, IL 60611, T312-8363723. info@bvitourism.com.

Money

Currency The US dollar is the legal tender. There are no restrictions on exchange. Try to avoid large-denomination traveller's cheques (they carry a US$0.10 stamp duty). Cheques are rarely accepted; cash is king. **Credit cards** are all right for most hotels and the larger restaurants, but not for the majority of bars/restaurants and they are not accepted on Anegada except at the **Anegada Reef Hotel**.

Getting there

Air The main international airport is on Beef Island for Tortola (connecting bridge), but there is also one on Virgin Gorda, with a domestic airport on Anegada. There are no direct flights from Europe or from the USA, Canada or Latin America.

From Europe: Same-day connections can be made through Puerto Rico, Antigua, Sint Maarten or St Kitts.

From the USA: Connecting flights can be arranged through Puerto Rico or the USVI.

From the Caribbean: American Eagle, T4952559, **Cape Air**, T4952100, www.flycapeair .com, and **LIAT/Caribbean Star**, T4951187, fly several times a day from San Juan, or arrange a charter. Only charters fly from St Thomas, otherwise get the ferry. **LIAT/Caribbean Star, American Eagle** and **Winair**, T4952577, from St Maarten. **LIAT/Caribbean Star** from Anguilla, Antigua, Barbados and St Kitts. Charter flights with **Fly BVI**, T4951747, **Island Birds**, T4952002, **Caribbean Wings**, T4956000, and **Air Sunshine**, T4958900, **Bohlke International Airways**, T340-7789177, **Flight Adventures International Ltd**, T4952311, **Island Helicopter Int**, T4992663.

Boat There are frequent connections with the USVI, see page 470, and within the BVI. On Tortola, ferries depart from Road Town and West End. **Inter-Island Boat Services**, T4954166, www.bviports.org/inter_island.htm (St John-West End, Jost Van Dyke and/or Virgin Gorda); also water taxi available, T7766501. **Native Son Inc**, T4954617, www.bviports.org/native_son.htm (Red Hook-St John-West End or Road Town), **Smith's Ferry Services**, T4944495, www.smithsferry.com (Red Hook-West End or Road Town and Virgin Gorda), **Speedy's**, T4955240, www.speedysbvi.com (St Thomas-St John-Road Town-Virgin Gorda), Caribbean Maritime Excursion, operating as **Road Town Fast Ferry**, T4942323, www.tortolafastferry.com (St Thomas-Road

Town), **Nubian Princess**, T4954999 (Red Hook-St John-West End). Fares are usually US$45 round trip St Thomas-Tortola, US$60 St Thomas-Virgin Gorda, with discounts for children.

Ports of entry: (British flag) Ports of entry are located in Road Town and West End on Tortola, Great Harbour on Jost Van Dyke and St Thomas Bay (Virgin Gorda Yacht Club) in Virgin Gorda, where there are Customs and Immigration officers. All vessels entering the territory must clear in with BVI Customs and Immigration immediately upon arrival into the territory.

Boat documents: The captain may clear the crew, taking passports and boat documentation ashore. Do not proceed to a marina until you have cleared your yacht. If you arrive after hours, raise your yellow flag and do not go ashore. You may seek permission in advance from Customs and Immigration for a late arrival by calling one of the ports of entry. Customs Mon-Fri 0830-1630, Sat 0830-1230, all other times incur overtime charges. A cruising permit (and a national parks mooring permit, see below) are required by everyone cruising in the BVI: 1 December-30 April, all BVI-based charter boats US$2 per person per day, all non-BVI-based charter boats US$4 per person per day; 1 May-30 November, US$0.75 and US$4 respectively. All privately owned yachts cruising in the BVI are charged nominal cruising fees. For further information see www.bvimarineguide.com

Anchorages: The **BVI National Parks Trust** ⓘ *57 Main St, Road Town, T4943904, www.bvinationalparkstrust.org*, has placed moorings at many dive sites, available on a first come, first served basis, with a 90-min time limit. Overnight use is not allowed. Purchase mooring use sticker from customs, fee US$2 per person per day or US$25 per week. Buoys are colour coded: yellow for commercial dive boats, orange for snorkelling, and blue for dinghy dock lines. Moorings have been placed and are maintained by Moor Seacure at West End (register at Soper's Hole Marina), Cane Garden Bay (Rhymer's Beach Bar), Fat Hogs Bay, East End (Penn's Landing), Trellis Bay, Beef Island (De Loose Mongoose), Marina Cay (Pusser's), White Bay, Jost Van Dyke (Ivan's Campground), Diamond Cay, Jost Van Dyke (Foxy's), Little Harbour, Jost Van Dyke (Abe's and Harris' Place), Norman Island (The Bight, Soldier's, Benures and Privateer's Bay), Great Harbour, Peter Island (Callaloo on the Beach), Manchioneel Bay, Cooper Island (Cooper Island Beach Club), North Sound, Virgin Gorda (Bitter End Yacht Club and Leverick Bay), Saba Rock, Spanish Town and Anegada (Anegada Reef Hotel and Neptune's Treasure), at US$20 per night. In winter months, northerly swells and high surf can make northern anchorages (and landing at the Baths) untenable. Listen to ZBVI 780AM for weather reports. There are 13 marinas on Tortola, 3 on Virgin Gorda, one on Peter Island, one on Marina Cay and a new one on Scrub Island to come in 2007-08.

> ‼ *Jet skis must be declared on entry to the BVI, private use is illegal.*

Touching down

Tourist information Local tourist office ⓘ *BVI Tourist Board, 2nd floor, AKARA Building, DeCastro Street, Wickhams Cay 1, Road Town, T4943134, www.bvitourism.com; also an office at Virgin Gorda Yacht Harbour, T4955181, F4956517*; some offices overseas can help with reservations. The *BVI Welcome* is a bimonthly colour tourist guide (www.bviwelcome.com). To find out what's on, weekly, monthly or annually, get the *Limin' Times*, updated every Thursday (T4942413, www.limin-times.com). The *Tourism Directory* is published annually and is a detailed listing of services. The tourist board has these and many other brochures.

Getting around

Air Clair Aero flies from Tortola to Anegada Monday, Wednesday, Friday and Sunday, T4952271. There are several charter airlines based at Beef Island for inter-island or sightseeing trips: **Island Birds**, T4952002, **Caribbean Wings**, T4956000, **Island**

Touching down

Departure tax US$10, if you leave by air, and US$5 departure tax by sea. There is a cruise ship passenger tax of US$7.
Emergency Police, Fire or Ambulance, T999. The Virgin Islands Search and Rescue (VISAR) is a voluntary 24-hour marine service, T999 or Ch 16.
Hours of business Banks: Mon-Fri 0900-1400 (FirstCaribbean 0900-1500; Chase Manhattan Mon-Fri 0900- 1600, Sat 0900-1200.
Government offices: Mon-Fri 0830-1630. **Shops**: Mon-Fri 0900-1700.
Country code +284.
Official time Atlantic Standard Time, 4 hours behind GMT, 1 hour ahead of EST.
Voltage 110 volts, 60 cycles.

Helicopters International, T4992663. **Fly BVI**, T4951747, www.fly-bvi.com, is another small charter airline with trips to Anegada US$155-600 one-way, depending on the size of the aircraft, also to Virgin Gorda. Pack light, there is limited luggage space on the small aircraft. Or take a day trip to Anegada, US$125 per person from Tortola, US$175 from Virgin Gorda (minimum two people), including taxi, air fare, lobster lunch at the **Big Bamboo**, contact **Fly BVI**. If you can fill the aircraft, charters often work out cheaper.

Boat The ferry fares between Tortola and Virgin Gorda are about US$25 return, US$15 one way, from Tortola to Jost Van Dyke US$20, US$12 one way and from Tortola to Anegada US$50 round trip, US$35 one way. Always check availability and departure times in advance. The **North Sound Express**, T4952138, has six daily crossings Beef Island-Virgin Gorda, calling at either The Valley, Leverick Bay (for Mosquito Island) or Bitter End, 30 minutes, reservations essential. Bus service (not included in fare) to and from Road Town waterfront (Pussers) and Beef Island ferry dock. **Speedy's**, T4955240, has six crossings Monday-Saturday, three crossings Sunday, between Virgin Gorda and Road Town. **Smith's Ferry Services**, T4954495, cross frequently from Virgin Gorda to Road Town then some boats continue to West End on their way to St John and St Thomas. They also have a service from Road Town to Anegada, Mon, Wed, Fri at 0700 and 1530, returning 0830 and 1700. They will pick up in Virgin Gorda with prior reservation. **Peter Island Ferry**, T4952000, has 10 daily crossings from the Peter Island Ferry Dock, Road Town, to Peter Island, US$15 round trip. **New Horizon**, T4954495, www.jostvandykeferry.com, five crossings a day between West End and Jost Van Dyke. **Marina Cay Ferry**, T4942174, runs between Beef Island and **Pusser's Marina Cay** eight times a day, with later runs for restaurant guests only, free. **Bitter End Ferry**, T4942746, between Gun Creek and Bitter End Yacht Club hourly. **Saba Rock Ferry**, T4957711, North Sound between Gun Creek and Saba Rock.

Road Car: There are only about 50 miles of roads suitable for cars. Drive on the left. Maximum speed limit 40 mph, in residential areas 20 mph. Jeeps may be more useful than cars for exploring secluded beach areas. They can be hired on Tortola, Virgin Gorda and Anegada. Car rental offices (or the **Traffic and Licensing Department**) provide the necessary temporary BVI driving licence (US$10) but you must also have a valid licence from your home country.
   Car hire: It is advisable to book in advance in the peak season. Rates range from US$40-45 per day for a small car, US$45-70 per day for jeeps. Credit card needed with US$500 deposit. A 5% tax is charged on all rentals.
   Taxi: There are several taxi firms on Tortola and Virgin Gorda, island tours arranged. Maximum taxi fares are set by the government but open air taxis tend to

charge less than private cabs. Tours of 2½ hrs maximum for 1-3 people are US$50, or US$15 per person for over three passengers, children under 10 half price. ▶ *See also Transport, pages 517 and 526.*

Maps The tourist office distributes a road map, updated annually with some tourist information on resorts, restaurants and what to do.

Sleeping

Hotels There is a 7% hotel tax and a 10% service charge in the BVI. Rates apply to double rooms, EP, winter-summer. Hotels are mostly small, intimate and low-rise but few are cheap. **Villas** There are some truly luxurious houses for rent, with the most famous, or infamous, being Richard Branson's house on Necker Island. A wide choice of stylish properties is on offer. **Camping** Allowed only on authorized sites.

Eating

Most things are imported and will cost at least the same as in Florida. Try local produce which is cheaper, yams and sweet potatoes rather than potatoes, for example. Fish dishes are often excellent, try snapper, dolphin (*mahi mahi*, fish, not the mammal), grouper, tuna and swordfish, and don't miss the lobster.

Once a rum producer for the Royal Navy, when sailors were issued a daily tot of rum by the ship's Purser, 'Pussers' (Pursers); rum is available from *Pusser's* or supermarkets. The custom was stopped in 1970, but in 1979, Charles Tobias gained the rights and blending information from the Admiralty and set up Pussers on Tortola, bottling and selling *Pussers Rum* to the public for the first time. It is a blend of five West Indian rums and is mostly pot-stilled for better flavour and has led to several awards, www.pussers.com. Local rums of varying quality are also sold by hotels and restaurants.

> ❣ Smoking is banned in all public places including all restaurants and bars.

Shopping

There are gift shops and boutiques in Road Town, Tortola and in Spanish Town, Virgin Gorda. The BVI Philatelic Bureau or Post Offices sell stamps for collectors. You can also buy BVI coins, but they are not used as a currency. **Samarkand** ① *Main St, Tortola, samarkand@caribwave.com*, sells gold and silver jewellery created by the local Bibby family with nautical themes; you can buy earrings of yachts, pelicans, etc and they will make anything to order, also a branch at Soper's Hole Wharf, West End: **Caribbean Jewellers**.

> ❣ The BVI are not duty-free, but there is no sales tax.

Sunny Caribbee Herb and Spice Co, is on Main St with **Sunny Caribbee Gallery** next door, also at **Skyworld Restaurant** and **Long Bay Hotel**, selling spices, herbs, preserves and handicrafts, mail order and shipping services available. **Pusser's Co Store** in Road Town and West End, Tortola, and Leverick Bay, Virgin Gorda, sells nautical clothing, luggage and accessories as well as Pusser's Rum. **Turtle Dove Boutique**, in Road Town, has a good selection of gifts and home furnishings and a limited selection of books. **Caribbean Handprints**, Main Street, has a silkscreen studio and shop with local designs and clothing made on site. **Crafts Alive**, Road Town, is a government funded crafts village where local artisans sell their work in a replica of a traditional village of wooden houses. Aragorn Dick-Read has a working studio in Trellis Bay as part of his Caribbean arts and crafts shop, giving lessons in pottery, woodcarving and basketry, T4951849, www.aragornstudio.com. His metal sculptures are featured in the Fireball Full Moon Party in Trellis Bay, see Bars and clubs, page 516. **Bamboushay** is a pottery studio in Nanny Cay where you can buy the work of Val Anderson, who specializes in blue and green glazes, the colour of the sea. **Pat's Pottery** is a roadside shop and studio run by Pat Faulkner on Anegada. She has a

> ❣ Don't buy turtleshell products or dishes containing turtle meat.

second outlet at Soper's Hole, West End, Tortola, where you can buy her bowls and domestic ware decorated with designs influenced by the sea.

Sport and activities

There are lovely sandy beaches on all the islands and many of them are remote, accessible only from the sea. The clean, crystal-clear waters around the islands provide excellent snorkelling, diving, cruising and fishing. Most of the hotels offer a wide variety of watersports, including windsurfing, sunfish, scuba, snorkelling and small boats.

Diving Considerable work is being done to establish marine parks and conserve the reefs. The Department of Conservation and Fisheries is in charge of the BVI's natural resources and fisheries management plan. The 11-mile **Horseshoe Reef** off the south shore of Anegada is one of the largest reefs in the world and is now a Protected Area. There are 80 visible wrecks around Anegada and many more covered by coral; about 300 ships are believed to have foundered on the reef.

Humpback whales migrate to the islands every year and the **Department of Conservation and Fisheries** is trying to estimate their numbers with the aim of designating the BVI waters as a marine mammal sanctuary. If you see any (mostly north of Tortola), let them know. Similarly, turtles are being counted with the help of volunteers in order to draw up protective legislation. Leatherback turtles travel to north shore beaches to nest, but their numbers have been declining fast. Hawksbill and green turtles are more common but still endangered. For several months of the year the killing of turtles or taking their eggs is prohibited and the export of turtle products is illegal. Despite the government's conservation policies, approval was granted for a captive dolphin programme, which started in 2001. Dolphins caught in the wild are now in the lagoon at Prospect Reef and tourists can swim with them.

> ❖ Jet skis are banned; the only licensed operator is at the Sand Box on Prickly Pear Island.

There are over 60 charted dive sites, many of which are in underwater national parks. They include walls, pinnacles, coral reefs, caverns and wrecks. The most-visited wreck is that of the *Rhone*, sunk in 1867 in a storm and broken in two. The bow section is in about 80 ft of water and you can swim through the hull. The stern is shallower and you can see the prop shaft and the propeller (and an octopus). Another wreck is the 246-ft *Chikuzen* sunk in 1981 about 6 miles north of Tortola, where you will see bigger fish such as barracuda and rays. Most Caribbean and Atlantic species of tropical fish and marine invertebrates can be found in BVI waters, with hard and soft corals, gorgonians and sea fans. Visibility ranges from 60-200 ft and the water temperature varies from 76°F in winter to 86°F in summer.

> ❖ Watch out for fire coral, sea urchins and the occasional bristle worm.

All users of moorings must have a national parks permit. These are available through dive operators, charter companies, government offices and the **National Parks Trust** ① *T4943904*. National Parks Trust moorings are located at The Caves, The Indians, The Baths, Pelican Island, Carrot Shoal, dive sites at Peter Island, Cooper Island, Ginger Island and Norman Island, the *Rhone's* anchor, the wreck of the *Rhone*, the wreck of the *Fearless*, Deadchest Island, Blonde Rock, Guana Island, The Dogs and other popular diving and recreational sites.

There are several dive shops around the islands which offer individual tours, package deals with hotels or rendezvous with charter boats. A 2-tank dive with equipment hire is US$80-90, a resort course US$95. ▸▸ *See individual islands for dive centres.*

Fishing Sport fishing day trips are popular. A local permit is required for fishing, call the **Fisheries Division** for information, T4945682; spearfishing is not allowed. There are areas known to house *ciguatera* (fish poisoning) around the reefs, so contact the Fisheries Division before fishing.

Sailing 'Bareboating' (self-crew yacht chartering) is extremely popular and the way most visitors see the islands. The BVI are one of the most popular destinations in the world for bareboaters. If you do not feel confident in handling a yacht, there are various options from fully crewed luxury yachts to hiring a skipper to take you and your bareboat out for as long as you need. You can also rent a cabin on a private charter yacht, several charter companies find this a useful way of filling a boat. Most of the islands have at least one beautiful bay and it is possible even at the height of the season to find deserted beaches and calm anchorages. Bareboaters are warned not to sail to Anegada because of the hazardous, unmarked route through the reef. The exception is the **Moorings** fleet, which organizes a special flotilla once a week from the **Bitter End Resort & Yacht Club** for its clients. If you are sailing independently, check the charts, ensure you approach in clear daylight when the sun is high, or call the **Anegada Reef Hotel** at Setting Point when you are within sight and they will direct you over the radio.

Navigation is not difficult, the water and weather are generally clear and there are many excellent cruising guides and charts for reference.

Regattas **Jan** sees the annual schedule kick off with the **Governor's Cup,** hosted by the Royal BVI Yacht Club, followed in **Feb** by the **Sweethearts Regatta** at West End Yacht Club. **Mar** is a busy month with the annual **Spring Regatta** (Royal BVI Yacht Club) is held in Sir Francis Drake's Channel, considered one of the best sailing venues in the world. It is one third of the Caribbean Ocean Racing Triangle (CORT) series of regattas, www.bvispringregatta.org. Contact the *Royal BVI Yacht Club,* T4943286, bviyc@surfbvi.com. Ask for regatta discounts on rooms or slips. The annual **Dark and Stormy Race** in the same month is from West End Yacht Club, Tortola to Anegada. Fireworks, dancing, food, drink and entertainment greet sailors on arrival in Anegada, where they take a day off before racing back to the **West End Yacht Club** (sponsored by the *Royal BVI Yacht Club,* T4943286 for information). The **BVI Sailing Festival** is also held in Mar at the Bitter End Yacht Club. In **Apr** Virgin Gorda holds the **Fisherman's Jamboree** and the **Virgin Gorda Festival. Foxy's Wooden Boat Regatta** is in **May**, while the **Highland Spring HIHO Windsurfing** race is in **Jun**. The **Annual Anegada Yacht Race** is in **Jul**, with a route from Road Town to Anegada, together with a youth regatta, the **KATS Chief Minister's Cup** and **Firecracker 500** hosted by the West End Yacht Club. In **Nov** things pick up again when *Pusser's* sponsor a **Round-Tortola** race and the **Pro-Am Regatta** is held at the Bitter End Yacht Club. There are races of one sort or another going on all year round; check The BVI Welcome, or www.bviwelcome.com, for what is coming up, or contact the Royal BVI Yacht Club.

Day sails Lots of yachts offer day-sails to all the little islands at around US$70-90 with snorkelling, beverages and sometimes lunch. When the cruise ships are in town they are often full. All day sail boats should carry the Daycharter Association of the British Virgin Islands symbol to prove they are licensed and have had safety checks.

There are many charter companies on Tortola and several more on Virgin Gorda. Contact the tourist office for a list of bareboats with prices.

Festivals and events

Jan New Year's Day.
1st Mon in Mar H Lavity Stoutt's birthday.
2nd Mon in Mar Commonwealth Day.
Mar/Apr Good Fri and Easter Mon.
May Whit Mon.
Last week May Annual BVI Music festival, Cane Garden Bay, started 2001.
2nd Mon Jun Queen's Birthday.
1 Jul Territory Day.

Aug Emancipation Festival, Mon-Wed beginning of Aug, celebrating the abolition of slavery. Entertainment every night with steel bands, fungi and calypso music, a Prince and Princess show and a calypso show.
21 Oct St Ursula's Day.
Dec Christmas Day and Boxing Day.

Communication Post There is a post office in Road Town, branches in Tortola and Virgin Gorda and sub-branches in other islands. Postal rates for postcards are US$0.30 to the USA, US$0.35 to Europe and US$0,45 to the rest of the world; for aerogrammes US$0.35; for letters to the USA US$0.45, to Europe US$0.50, to the rest of the world US$0.75.

Telephone: All telecommunications are operated by **Cable & Wireless**. Phone cards are available, US$5, US$10, US$15 and US$20, discount rates in evenings at weekends. To make a credit card call, dial 111 and quote your card number. Dial 119 for the operator or 110 for the international operator. **Cable & Wireless** is at the centre of Road Town at Wickhams Cay I, open 0700-1900 Mon-Fri, 0700-1600 Sat, 0900-1400 Sun and public holidays, T4944444, also in The Valley, Virgin Gorda, T4955444. They operate Tortola Marine Radio, call on VHF Ch 16, talk on 27 or 84. The **CCT Boatphone** company in Road Town offers cellular telephone services throughout the Virgin Islands for yachts, US$5 per day for service, US$4 per min; also a prepaid cellular service, **CCT Flexphone**, T4943825. To call VHF stations from a land phone, call Tortola Radio, T116. **Caribbean Connections** at **Village Cay Marina**, T4943623, has phone, fax, email, courier service. **Moorings** allows use of phone for collecting email. **Village Cay Marina** has a computer room. **Jolly Roger** has fax and email services.

Media Newspapers: *Virgin Islands Daily News* covers Tortola as well as the USVI and is available online, www.virginislandsdailynews.com. *The Island Sun*, www.islandsun.com, is published on Fri, while the *BVI Beacon* comes out on Thu. *The Limin' Times*, printed weekly, is a free magazine giving entertainment news: nightlife, sports, music etc. *Standpoint* on Tue, is popular with young islanders, with lots of advertising. *All At Sea* is a local monthly lively tabloid for yachties, T4951090, editor@allatsea.net.

Radio *Radio ZBVI* broadcasts on 780AM. Weather reports for sailors are broadcast hourly from 0730 to 1830 every day. There are 4 FM stations: *Reggae* at 97.3, *Country* at 94.3, *Z Gold* at 91.7and *ZROD* at 103.7.

Television: VITV, Channel 5, is a locally owned station showing news, sports and entertainment programmes. Cable TV is widely available.

Tortola → *Phone code: 284. Colour map 2, B6. Population: 16,000.*

Tortola, the main island, is where 81% of the total population live. Mount Sage, the highest point in the archipelago, rises to 1,780 ft, and traces of a primeval rainforest can still be found on its slopes. Walking trails have been marked through Mount Sage National Park. The south part of the island is mountainous and rocky, covered with scrub, frangipani and ginger thomas. The north has groves of bananas, mangoes and palm trees, and long sandy beaches. ▸ *For Sleeping, Eating and other listings, see pages 511-518.*

Road Town

On the south shore, is the capital and business centre of the territory, dominated by marinas and financial companies which line the harbour. There are many gift shops, hotels and restaurants catering for the tourist market. Main Street, the most picturesque street, houses some of the oldest buildings and churches and the colonial prison (replaced by a modern prison in 1997 for 120 inmates). Until the 1960s, Main Street was the waterfront road, but land infill has allowed a dual carriageway, Waterfront Drive and Wickhams Cay, to be built between it and the sea. Wickhams Cay has very grand and imposing government offices on the waterfront overlooking the harbour entrance. Also in this area are banks, offices, Cable & Wireless, a small craft village and the tourist office. Small cruise ships call frequently. **Old Government House** ① *Mon-Fri 0900-1400*, above Waterfront Drive overlooking the harbour has been restored and is now a public museum. There is a fine display of flamboyant trees. The 4-acre **Joseph Reynold O'Neal Botanic Gardens** ① *www.bvinationalparks trust.org/toparks_2.html, free admission, donations welcome*, near the police station in Road Town has a good selection of tropical and subtropical plants such as palm trees, succulents, ferns and orchids. There is a good booklet which gives a suggested route round the garden, pond, orchid house, fern house and medicinal herb garden. It is peaceful, luxuriant, with magnificent pergolas, recommended. The small **BVI Folk Museum** ①*Main St, opened on request*, in a lovely old wooden building, contains some Amerindian pottery and salvaged artefacts from the *Rhone*.

Around Tortola

There are also communities at East End and West End. **West End** has more facilities for visitors. **Soper's Hole** is a busy port of entry (ferries to St Thomas, St John and Jost Van Dyke leave from here) and popular meeting place for people on yachts, with bars, restaurants, boutiques and a dive shop. All the buildings are painted in bright pinks and blues. It is relaxing to sip cocktails on the dock and watch the yachts come and go. The **Jolly Roger**, on the opposite side of the bay, is a popular yachtie hangout. The area is famous for being the former home of Edward Teach (Blackbeard the pirate).

Watch out for strong rip currents at some of the north shore beaches, and seek local advice before swimming, especially if the surfers are out.

The best beaches are along the northwest and north coasts. **Smugglers Cove**, **Long Bay** and **Apple Bay**, West End, have fine sandy beaches. If you have no transport, Smugglers Cove is an hour's walk on a dirt road over a steep hill from West End. The beach is usually deserted, although there are plans to build a villa hotel here. Apple Bay is popular with surfers from November for a few months, as is the east end of Cane Garden Bay and Josiah's Bay. **Carrot Bay** is stony, there is no sand, but there are lots of pelicans and the village is pleasant, having a very Caribbean feel with several bars, palm trees and banana plants. **Cane Garden Bay** is the best beach and yachts can anchor there. There are two reefs with a marked gap in between. The **Callwood Rum Distillery** at Cane Garden Bay still produces rum with copper boiling vats and an old still and cane crusher in much the same way as it did in the 18th century. **Brewers Bay** is long and curving with plenty of shade and a small campsite in the trees by the beach. **Shark Bay** is a mixture of sand and rock, while on the hillside, in the Gaby Nitkin Nature Reserve, there are large volcanic boulders forming a 'Bat Cave' where wild orchids grow. Park on the main road and hike along the private road. **Elizabeth Bay** and **Long Bay**, East End, are also nice beaches.

Tortola is superb, but the full flavour of the BVI can only be discovered by cruising round the other islands. You can also take day trips on the regular ferry to Virgin Gorda, with lunch and a visit to The Baths included if you wish.

Beef Island

The main airport for the BVI is here. For many years the island was linked to Tortola by the **Queen Elizabeth bridge**, opened in 1966, but in 2003 it was dismantled and a new bridge was built (taxi to Road Town, US$15). **Long Bay beach** is on the north shore, as is **Trellis Bay** which has an excellent harbour and bars.

During the buccaneering days this land was famed as a hunting ground for beef cattle.

Marina Cay

This tiny private island of 6 acres just north of Beef Island was where Robb White wrote his book *Our Virgin Isle*, later made into a film starring Sidney Poitier and John

British Virgin Islands Tortola

Cassavetes. A reef encircles the island offering some of the best snorkelling in the BVI. If sailing, enter from the north.

Scrub Island

A 5-minute ferry ride from Beef Island, Scrub Island is one of those places no one ever writes about, a private island amounting to 230 acres of wilderness. Now, however, all that is changing, with the construction on 55 acres of a new resort and marina at the west end of the island facing Great Camanoe. Mainsail Hotels sold suites and villas before they were built, with the lure of a 65-slip full-service marina (Mainsail Scrub Marina) with an emphasis on sport fishing, luxury spa and health club, three beaches, eight pools, tennis courts, watersports, restaurants, shops, bars, observatory, amphitheatre and not one, but two helipads, with accompanying roads and infrastructure, all opening gradually in the winter season 2007-08, www.mainsailbvi.com.

Guana Island

North of Tortola, Guana Island is an 850-acre private island and wildlife sanctuary as well as having a very expensive hotel. The owners discourage visitors apart from hotel guests, in order to keep the island a sanctuary for wildlife. A few flamingos have been introduced to the island. They live in a small pond where the salinity fluctuates widely so their diets are supplemented with food and water if they need it. The birds used to live in a zoo, so they are fairly tame.

Tortola

Sleeping 🛏️
Beef Island Guest House & De Loose Mongoose Bar **17**
Brewer's Bay Campground **6**
Fort Recovery Beachfront Villas **2**

Frenchman's Cay **3**
Guana Island **15**
Jolly Roger Inn **9**
Josiah's Bay Cottages **12**
Josiah's Bay Inn **4**
Lambert Beach Resort **13**
Long Bay Beach Resort **5**

Nanny Cay Resort & Marina **14**
Pusser's Marina Cay **16**
Quito's Ole Works Inn **11**
Rhymer's Beach **1**
Rudy's Mariner Inn **7**
Sandcastle **8**

British Virgin Islands Tortola

Northeast of Tortola are The Dogs, a group of small, uninhabited islands. **West Dog** is a national park. On **Great Dog** you can see frigate birds nesting. The islands are often used as a stopping-off point when sailing from North Sound to Jost Van Dyke, and are popular with divers coming from North Sound for the interesting rock formations, with canyons and bridges underwater. The best anchorages are on **George Dog** to the west of Kitchen Point and on the south side of Great Dog.

Sleeping

There is lots of self-catering accommodation in what are variously known as houses, villas, apartments, guesthouses, 'efficiencies' or 'housekeeping units'. Prices are usually set on a weekly basis according to size and standard of luxury, and there is often a 30-40% discount in the summer. Contact the tourist office for a full list and individual brochures. Many are also listed on www.bviwelcome.com.

Road Town *p508, map p512*
LL-L Village Cay Resort and Marina,

directly opposite on the other side of the harbour, T4942771, www.Villagecay.com. 21 clean, bright rooms, well-furnished, TV, phone, cheaper rooms face inland, restaurant and bar overlooking yachts, good food, buffet with entertainment Fri 1800-2300, also showers, toilets and launderette for sailors.
LL-AL Fort Burt, on hillside opposite Marina, T4942587, http://bviguide.com/fortburt. On remains of Dutch fort, first hotel on island built 1953, now part of the **Pussers** chain, 17 rooms and suites, 2 of which have plunge

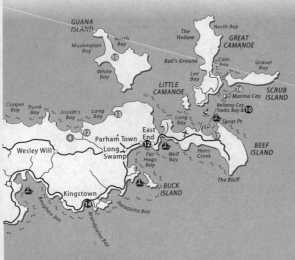

Sebastian's on the Beach **10**	Mrs Scatliffe's **7**	Sugar Mill **2**
	North Shore Shell	Struggling Man **15**
Eating	Museum **3**	
Brandywine Bay **14**	Peg Leg Landing **13**	
Clem's by the Sea **4**	Pusser's Landing **5**	
De Cal **12**	Quito's Gazebo **8**	
Last Resort **10**	Skyworld **1**	

pool, all have phone, fax and PC data ports, restaurant and bar, convenient location, good views but in need of some repairs and redecoration in 2007.
LL-AL Maria's By The Sea, T4942595, www.mariasbythesea.com. By new government buildings, overlooks sea but no beach, older part is simple, all have fridge, a/c, TV, phone, double beds; newer wing has bigger rooms, balconies, conference room, friendly, Maria's cooking recommended, specials include lobster, conch, steak, light and airy entrance with bar, pool.
LL-AL Moorings/Mariner Inn, at the dockside for bareboat charters, T4942332. 36 rooms with kitchenette, 4 suites, fan, tennis, small pool by bar, briefing room for those setting out on yachts. Convenient but

Road Town

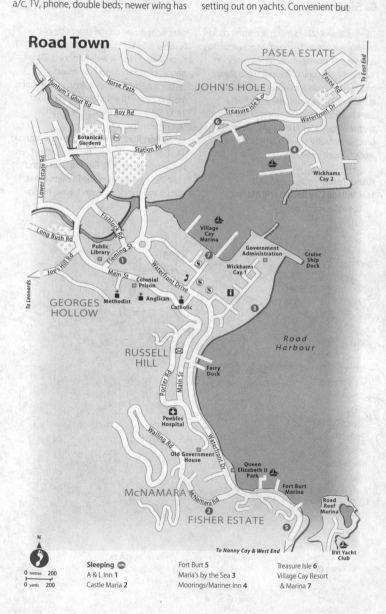

Sleeping
A & L Inn **1**
Castle Maria **2**

Fort Burt **5**
Maria's by the Sea **3**
Moorings/Mariner Inn **4**

Treasure Isle **6**
Village Cay Resort & Marina **7**

nothing special, most people only stay one night before boarding.

LL-AL Treasure Isle, on hillside overlooking the marina and Sir Francis Drake Channel, T4942501, www.treasureislehotel.net. 65 rooms, renovated 2006-07, pool, tennis, restaurant, a/c, TV, internet access, convenient for business travellers, used by people on crewed yacht charters for first and last night, helpful staff at front desk.

AL-A Hotel Castle Maria, up the hill overlooking Road Town, T4942553, hotelcastlemaria@surfbvi.com. 30 rooms, some triple and quads, kitchenette, a/c, cable TV, pool, restaurant, bar, car rentals, popular with local business travellers. Not luxury, some repairs needed, be prepared for cockerels crowing and dogs barking.

A A & L Inn, 3 Fleming St, T4946343, alguesthouse@hotmail.com. 14 rooms with 2 double beds, some are noisy, good a/c, fridge, TV, phone.

B-C Wayside Inn Guest House, Road Town, near library, T4943606. About the cheapest on the island. 20 rooms, with fan, adequate but basic, shared bathrooms but unclean.

Around Tortola *p509, map p510*
South coast

LL Frenchman's Cay Hotel, West End, T4954844, www.frenchmans.com. Beautiful hillside location on the cay overlooking the south coast of Tortola, small sandy beach with reef for snorkelling, tennis, pool, short trail out to point. Closed for renovations under new ownership in 2007.

LL-L Fort Recovery Beachfront Villas, T4954467, www.fortrecovery.com. 17 spacious and nicely furnished a/c villas of different sizes on small beach, built around 17th-century Dutch fort, commissary, restaurant for breakfast and dinner, 24-hr notice required for in-villa dining, yoga, massage, good snorkelling offshore, pool, Wi-Fi internet access, car essential.

LL-AL Nanny Cay Resort and Marina, T4944895, www.nannycay.com. 42 studios and suites, a/c, TV, VCRs, kitchenette, phone, deluxe rooms have 2 queen-size beds, standard rooms are darker, smaller, used by short stay people going out on bareboat charters, the marina hosts the **Spring Regatta** with a **Regatta Village** and lots of yacht facilities.

A Jolly Roger Inn, T4954559, www.jollyrogerbvi.com. A small inn and bar (for sale in 2007) on waterfront at Soper's Hole. Live music at weekends so do not stay here if you want peace and quiet, convenient for ferries (see above), 6 brightly decorated, clean rooms, some with shared bathroom, fans, screens, singles, doubles, triples available, good breakfasts, busy restaurant and bar, meeting place, email and ice services.

West coast

Heading northeast along this stretch of coast there are lots of rental villas, many of which are advertised simply with a notice outside, usually about US$120 per day.

LL Long Bay Beach Resort, T4954252, www.longbay.com. 80 rooms, studios and villas spread along the beach and up the hillside, a/c, TV, phone, fridge, 130-ft pool, the biggest in the BVI, tennis, pitch and put, spa and gym, car rental, 2 restaurants with vegetarian options, bars, surfboards, snorkelling equipment, nice beach, sandy with some rocks, level of sand can shift depending on season.

LL The Sugar Mill, Apple Bay, in an old mill, T4954355, www.sugarmillhotel.com. Run by Californians, Jinx and Jefferson Morgan, award-winning and the epitome of a 'boutique' hotel. Across the road from the beach, 23 rooms and suites, the height of luxury, set in lush gardens with a circular pool. Romantic, upmarket restaurant in the sugar mill.

LL-AL Quito's Ole Works Inn, Cane Garden Bay, T4954837, www.quitorymer.com. Built around 300-year-old sugar factory, on beach, 18 a/c rooms and suites, fridge, some with kitchenette, honeymoon tower with view of sunset and beach, bar, restaurant, gift shop, pool.

LL-A Sebastian's On The Beach, Apple Bay, T4954212, www.sebastiansbvi.com. Located either side of road, informal and popular surfers' hangout, the beachfront building was upgraded and expanded in 2002, now quite luxurious with large balconies, glass block showers, new tiled floors, also **Seaside Villas**, 9 luxury 2-bedroomed suites with huge balconies and views to Jost Van Dyke, fully equipped and every comfort, grocery 0800-2200, restaurant/bar overlooking sandy

beach, happy hour 1600-1800, blend own rum, surfboards and boogieboards for rent.
A Rhymer's Beach Hotel, Cane Garden Bay, T4954639, www.bviguide.com/rhymers.html. Excellent location, local feel, probably the best budget option, 27 basic but clean rooms, most with double and single bed, small bathroom, right on sandy beach, beach towels provided, free sunbeds on beach, store and shop, laundromat, restaurant/bar on beach which has good food and drinks at good prices, watersports companies on either side of hotel.

North coast

LL-L Lambert Beach Resort, East End, T4952877. On a beautiful cove, quite remote, 38 rooms and suites in villas which can sleep 8, beach-front dining, very large pool, lit tennis court, watersports, boat trips, diving and other excursions can be arranged, library, videos, Italian-owned, Italian decor.
LL-AL Josiah's Bay Cottages, Road Town, T4946186, www.bviwelcome.com/ads/josiahsbay. 9 1-bedroom cottages in garden, 5-min walk to beach, pool.
A Josiah's Bay Inn, Josiah's Bay, T/F4952818, www.bviwelcome.com/josiahsbayinn. Short walk to 4 beaches, 1-4 bedroom apartments, kitchens, TV, balconies with sea view, weekly rates, maid service twice a week, popular with surfers, take insect repellent.

Camping

Brewer's Bay Campground on north coast, T4943463. Quiet and isolated, separated from the sea by a line of seagrape trees, the only noise comes from the waves. 22 prepared sites fully equipped tents on platforms with mattresses, pillows (have seen better days) and linen, tables, chairs, propane lamp and stove, cooking utensils, ice chest, water container. Bare site US$15, tent hire US$40 for 2 people. Cold water in men's and women's bathhouse, babysitters available, beach bar and simple restaurant.

Beef Island *p509*

AL Beef Island Guest House, T4952303, www.beefislandguesthouse.com. The closest place to stay by the airport, 4 rooms with shared living room, breakfast included, on the beach, food available next door at its **De Loose Mongoose Bar**, VHF Ch 16, 0800-1600, 1800-2100, mostly burgers and sandwiches.

Marina Cay *p509*

LL-A Pusser's Marina Cay, comprises most of the island, T4942174, www.pussers.com/outposts/marinacay, or VHF Ch 16. Marina facilities (boats use mooring buoys and a dinghy dock), laundry, showers, diving, kayaking, sailing, snorkelling, etc, 4 rooms and 2 villas available, meal plans. Bar, restaurant, beach barbecue on Fri, **Pussers Co Store** sells clothes and travel accessories. Ferry service from Trellis Bay jetty, 8 daily, ferries after 1900 on request for restaurant guests only.

Guana Island *p510*

LL Guana Island, T4942354, www.guana.com. 15 rooms in stone cottages, 1 secluded beach house, tennis, restaurant, watersports, US$35 for airport transfers, no credit cards. The island is available for rent for up to 30 guests.

● Eating

Road Town *p508, map p512*

♥♥♥-♥♥ The Captain's Table, on the waterfront at Inner Harbour, T4943885. Lunch Mon-Fri, dinner daily from 1800, closed Sun out of season. A French restaurant serving escargots, lobster, fish.
♥♥♥-♥♥ Spaghetti Junction, T4944880, www.spaghettijunction.net. Italian restaurant run by John and April, long established and popular with locals, yachties and ex-pats, appetizers US$4-10, main courses US$10-24, bar and nightclub alongside, see below.
♥♥-♥ Café Sito, in Romasco building, T4947412. 1100-2300. West Indian and international food, coconut shrimp, lobster from Anegada, pasta, daily specials, alfresco dining.
♥♥-♥ Beach Club Terrace, at Baughers Bay, T4942272. 0800-2200. West Indian specialities, also Mexican and Mediterranean, fish, mutton, conch, etc, candlelit dinners, live jazz.
♥♥-♥ Capriccio di Mare, Waterfront Drive by ferry dock, overlooking water, T4945369. Mon-Sat 0800-2100. Italian café serving excellent coffee and delicious, if overpriced, snacks and continental lunches.

¶¶-¶ C & F Restaurant, Purcell Estate, T4944941. Dinner 1830-2300. Popular with visitors and locals, West Indian specialities, excellent local food, slow but friendly service.

¶¶-¶ Mac's, in the Clarence M Christian Building, Baugher's Bay, T4946364. 0700-2000. Local dishes, salads, pizza and pastries.

¶¶-¶ Midtown Restaurant, Main St, T4942764. Mon-Sat 0700-2300. Curried conch, baked chicken, beef, whelk, saltfish.

¶¶-¶ New Happy Lion, next to Botanic Gardens, T4942574. Mon-Sat from 0700, breakfast, lunch and dinner. Noted for fresh fish and local dishes, West Indian specialities, also apartments to rent.

¶¶-¶ Pusser's Co Store & Pub on Main St, Road Town, T4943897. 1100-2200. Yachties' meeting place, good atmosphere, on ground floor bar, store and restaurant for simple dishes such as English pies and New York deli sandwiches, nickel beer on Thu, really is US$0.05 but not recommended, Tue is Ladies' Night', 'Pain Killer' cocktails recommended, strongest is 'Brain Killer', Pusser's also at Soper's Hole, Marina Cay and Leverick Bay.

¶ Crandall's Pastry Plus, T4945156. 0800-1700. West Indian bakery across from Road Reef Marina, also rotis and main meals.

¶ Roti Palace, Russel Hill, T4944196. Huge rotis (curry in a wrap).

Around Tortola *p509, map p510*

¶¶¶ Brandywine Bay Restaurant, East End, T4952301, brandywn@surfbvi.com. Cocktails 1730, dinner 1830-2100, closed Sun. 10 mins' drive from Road Town, very exclusive restaurant, indoor and outdoor area, grills and Florentine food, full meal without wine about US$35-40 per person, reservations, Channel 16, anchorage 15-ft draft. Run by Cele and Davide Pugliese.

¶¶¶ The Sugar Mill, Apple Bay, in an old mill, T4954355, www.sugarmillhotel.com. 4-course dinner 1900. Run by Californians, Jinx and Jeff Morgan. Gourmet and elegant, reservations, on-line cookbook, with 250 recipes, hotel attached (no children in season), breakfast and lunch at beach bar.

¶¶¶-¶ Rhymers, Cane Garden Bay, T4954639. Breakfast, lunch and dinner. Lobster special Thu night. You can 'Jump Up' (Caribbean music), almost every night here.

¶¶¶-¶ Skyworld Restaurant, 10 mins' drive from Road Town or Cane Garden Bay T4943567. Open from 1000, lunch 1130-1430, dinner 1700-1945. With a panoramic view of all the Virgin Islands, food and prices reasonable, recommended for view.

¶¶¶-¶ Struggling Man's Place, Sea Cows Bay, between Road Town and Nanny Cay, T4944163. Breakfast, lunch and dinner. West Indian, lunch of curried mutton, rotis, fish and chips or chicken, dinner includes fish and lobster.

¶¶ Clem's By The Sea, Carrot Bay, T4954350. Mon, Sat 0900 until late. West Indian specialities, goat stew, boiled fish and fungi, steel band.

¶¶ Mario's Mountain View, at the foot of Sage Mountain National Park, T4959536. Lunch 1100-1500, dinner 1830-2200. Continental and local dishes.

¶¶ Mrs Scatliffe's, Carrot Bay, T4954556. Lunch Mon-Fri 1200-1400, dinner daily 1900-2100. Upstairs in a yellow and white building opposite the Primary School, local cuisine, home-grown fruit and vegetables, family fungi performance some evenings after dinner, reservations essential.

¶¶ North Shore Shell Museum, Carrot Bay, T4954714. Breakfast, lunch and dinner. Cracked conch, lobster, West Indian cooking, happy hour 1600-1800.

¶¶ Pusser's Landing, West End, T4954554. Lunch and dinner. Snacks and pizza all day. Lobster, seafood, steaks. Tue all you can eat shrimp.

¶ Sebastian's On The Beach, Apple Bay, T4954212. Breakfast, lunch and dinner. International, happy hour 1600-1800.

¶¶-¶ De Cal, East End, T4951429. Breakfast, lunch, dinner, 0700-2200. On Blackburn Highway at Fat Hog's Bay. Local style, rotis, pizza. Home-cooked dinners, excellent conch fritters, also after hrs dance spot.

¶¶-¶ Jolly Roger, West End, T4954559. 0700-2300. Fun, yachtie hangout, good pizza and burgers, good cheap breakfast, dinner US$7-15.

¶¶-¶ Peg Leg Landing, T4944895, water's edge at Nanny Cay. From 1600. Happy hour 1630-1830, bar meals from 1630, dinners from 1900.

¶¶-¶ Quito's Gazebo, Cane Garden Bay, T4954837. Lunch 1130-1500, dinner 1830-2130, closed Mon. Restaurant and beach bar at north end of Cane Garden Bay, rotis and burgers, fish fry Wed, local art work for sale. Folk music and reggae every night.

If you are self-catering, you can get reasonably priced food from **K Mart's** and other supermarkets at Port Purcell or at the **Rite Way** supermarkets a little closer to town. At the entrance to the Moorings, Wickhams Cay II, is the **Bon Appetit Deli**, T4945199. Cheese and wine as well as regular provisions; they also do sandwiches and lunch specials and party services. In Road Town is **Fort Wines Gourmet Shop**, T4942388, a wine shop with a high-class image but reasonable prices; you can also eat there, excellent light snacks (eg quiche) and wine by the glass.

Beef Island *p509*
¶¶ **The Last Resort**, a bar run by Englishman Tony Snell and based on Bellamy Cay, provides a buffet menu plus one-man show cabaret, US$26, bar open all day, happy hour 1700-1900, dinner 1930, cabaret 2130, ferry service available, reservations required, T4952520 or channel 16.

☉ Bars and clubs

See *The Limin' Times* for what's on. The full moon is an excuse for a party and there are several places where you can celebrate on a monthly basis: Bomba Shack is the traditional venue, but if you're not in that area, try the Mineshaft in Virgin Gorda or the Fireball Full Moon Party, Trellis Bay on Beef Island, which is good for families. The party starts around 1900 with a barbeque, followed by live fungi music, mocko jumbies, fire juggling and lighting of artist Aragorn Dick-Read's famous fireball sculptures at 2100. Hotels have live bands and movie nights. Concerts by visiting artistes and chamber orchestras are often held at the **H Lavity Stoutt Community College**, T4944994.

Road Town *p508, map p512*
Bat Cave, attached to **Spaghetti Junction**. Bar and nightclub, DJ music, happy hour 1700-1900 with wings for US$0.25, stay inside, a/c, or go outside on the 'Bat Decks'. **The Pub**, at Fort Burt Marina, T4942608. Dancing Fri-Sat, lunches and dinners, happy

hour 1700-1900 daily and all day Fri with free hot wings 1700-1900 and music 1800-2200. **Stone's Nest** is a weekend disco in Road Town, T4945182.

Around Tortola *p509, map p510*
Bing's Drop Inn Bar, East End, T4952627. After hours dance spot with late-night food at the bar.
Bomba Shack, on the beach in Apple Bay, T4954148. Music Wed and Sun, full-moon all-night party every month. The event to go to, try Bomba's infamous mushroom tea or Bomba Punch.
Calamaya, Maya Cove, on the dock side at Hodge's Creek Marina, T4952126. Breakfast, lunch, dinner. Fri live music, happy hour with tapas 1600-1800, bar menu.
Jolly Roger, West End, T4954559. Has live music and barbecue Tue, Fri, Sat in season, and often has bands.
Pusser's Landing, Frenchman's Cay, T4954554. Bands on Fri and Sat.
Quito's Gazebo, Cane Garden Bay, T4954837. Live music nightly and the beat is quickened at weekends and holidays.
Romeo's, Apple Bay, T4954307. Thu barbecue and music, Sat fish fry and music.

▲ Activities and sports

Tortola *p508, map p510*
Diving
Blue Water Divers, at Nanny Cay, T4942847 and at Sopers Hole, T4951200, www.bluewaterdiversbvi.com.
Cuan Law, T4942490, www.cuanlaw.com. Another trimaran, 105 ft, the world's largest, with 10 state rooms, 7 crew including dive instructors, kayaks, waterskis, hobie cats and underwater photography.
Promenade Sail, Village Cay Marina, T4992756, www.yachtpromenade.com. For diving and watersports cruises. They take 10-12 guests on a 65-ft trimaran with 5 crew including 2 dive instructors, with windsurfers, waterskiing and tubing for when you are not underwater.
Rainbow Visions Photo Center, Prospect Reef, T4942749, rainbow@caribsurf.com. Underwater photography, camera rental, and film processing available. They often join dive boats and take video film of you underwater.

Sail Caribbean Divers, a PADI 5-star facility, is at **Sunsail**, Hodges Creek Marina (T4941675, www.sailcaribbeandivers.com), and on Cooper Island which is also used as a surface interval between dives in the area, for example the **Rhone**.
Underwater Boat Services (UBS Dive Centre), T4940024, VHF 16, www.scubabvi .com. If you want your own dive boat for the day with instructor, US$175 pp for 2 divers, US$110pp for 4 divers, US$65 for snorkellers for a full day trip.

Fishing
Pelican Charters, Road Town, T4967386. Has a 46-ft Chris craft sportfisherman, US$600-950 for sportfishing, US$1,200 for marlin, full facilities.
Persistence Charters, West End, T4954122, ezrin@surfbvi.com. US$350 half day, US$650 full day on a 31-ft Tiara, everything included.

Sailing
Sunsail, www.sunsail.com. The largest charter in the Caribbean, is at Hodges Creek, Maya Cove, halfway between Road Town and Beef Island Airport, where it has some 150 yachts, restaurants, shops and provisioning.
For crewed yachts, try **The Moorings**, T4942332, www.moorings.com; **Yacht Connections**, T4948009, www.yacht-connections.com; **Sail Vacations** (operates the 72-ft luxury ketch *Endless Summer II*), T4943656, www.EndlessSummer.com; **Regency Yacht Vacations**, at the Inner Harbour Marina, Wickham's Cay I, T4951970, www.regencyvacations.com (luxury 45-200 ft yachts for 2-20 people, gourmet cuisine, watersports); **BVI Yacht Charters**, T4944289; **Catamaran Charters**, T4946661; **Wanderlust Yacht Vacations**, T/F4942405, www.wanderlustcharters.com, and several others, will match your needs with the many charter yachts available. Marinas are plentiful with yard services, haul out, fuel docks, water, showers.
Offshore Sailing School Ltd, www.offshore-sailing.com. Has courses on live-aboard cruising as well as learn-to-sail on dinghies.
Full Sail Sailing School, West End, T4940512, www.fullsailbvi.com. Offers day sail and liveaboard courses with ASA certification.

Windsurfing
Windsurfing is popular in the islands and there is an annual **Highland Spring Hi-Ho** (hook in and hold on) race which attracts windsurfers from all over the world, www.go-hiho.com.
Boardsailing BVI, Trellis Bay, Beef Island, T4952447, and Nanny Cay (a BiC Centre), T4940422, www.windsurfing.vi. With schools and shops. As well as windsurfing they offer kayaks, surf boards and sail dinghies.
Last Stop Sports, Wickham's Cay II, T4940564, www.laststopsports.com. Open 0800-1700. On the Moorings dock, has rental windsurfers, single and double kayaks, surfboards and bodyboards, specialises in renting to yachties, all gear for charter yachts, lessons available.

Other activities
There is a **tennis** club on Tortola and many hotels have their own courts. **Horse riding** can be arranged through the hotels, or T4942262, **Shadow's Stables**, or T4940704, Ellis Thomas, for riding through Mount Sage National Park or down to Cane Garden Bay, Tortola. **Walking** and **birdwatching** are quite popular and trails have been laid out in some places. Sage Mountain on Tortola is a popular hike. Spectator sports include **cricket** and soft ball. **Gyms** include Bodyworks, T4942705, and Cutting Edge, T4959570. **Prospect Reef** has a healthclub where you can do aerobics, yoga, also tennis and 9-hole pitch and putt, T4943311 ext 245.

❸ Transport

Tortola *p508, map p510*
See also Getting around, page 503.

Bus
There is a private local bus service with cheap fares (US$2-4) but erratic timetable. Call **Scatos Bus Service** for information, T4945873. They go to few tourist destinations.

Car
Alphonso Car Rentals, Fish Bay, T4948746, F4948735. Cars US$40-45 per day, jeeps US$50-70, 20% less in summer.
Avis Rent-a-Car, opposite Botanic Gardens, Road Town, T4942193, or West End,

T4954973. US$35-50 per day winter, US$25-40 summer, cheaper weekly rates. **Denzil Clyne Car Rentals**, West End, T4954900. Jeeps US$45-85 in winter, US$40-60 in summer.
International Car Rentals, Road Town, T4942516, intercar@candwbvi.net. US$40-70.
National Car Rental, Duff's Bottom and Long Bay, T4943197, www.nationalcarrentalsbvi .com. US$45-75.

Cycle

All bicycles must be registered at the Traffic Licensing Office in Road Town and the licence plate must be fixed to the bicycle, cost US$5. **Last Stop Sports**, T4940564, www.laststopsports.com, at Port Purcell, Road Town, T4941120, open Mon-Fri 0900-1700, Sat 0900-1500. Rents and repairs bikes. Mountain bikes US$30 per day, dual suspension or road bikes US$40 per day, cheaper for longer terms. All bikes come with a helmet (which is mandatory), lock, pump, water bottle and a seat pack (with tube, levers, patch kit). Mountain bikes are the best bet for touring the island, with a wide gear selection and powerful brakes for getting up and down the hills on rough terrain.

Taxi

Road Town, T4942322; on Beef Island,

T4952378. Taxis are easy to come by and fares are fixed, ask for a list or get one from the tourist office. The fare from Beef Island Airport to Road Town is US$15 or US$8 if shared.

● Directory

Tortola *p508, map p510*
Banks Bank of Nova Scotia, Road Town, T4942526. FirstCaribbean International Bank, Road Town, T4942173, F4944315, with agency at East End, Tortola. Development Bank of the Virgin Islands, T4943737. **Banco Popular de Puerto Rico**, Road Town, T4942117, F4945294. **VP Bank (BVI) Ltd**, 65 Main St, Road Town, T4941100, F4941199. ATM machines at all banks, at Beef Island Airport, *Rite Way Supermarket* (Pasea), Soper's Hole, HL Stoutt Community College (Paraquita Bay) and *K-Mark's Supermarket* (Purcell Estate). **Medical services** Peebles Hospital, Road Town, T4943497, is a public hospital with X-ray and surgical facilities. Private X-ray and laboratory facilities are offered by B&F Medical Complex and Medicure Ltd. There are 12 doctors on Tortola. The closest Decompression Chamber is in nearby St Thomas, about 45 mins away. Island Helicopters International, T4992663, www.helicoptersbvi.com, offers helicopter transfers for emergencies.

Virgin Gorda → *Country code: 284. Colour map 2, B6. Population: 5,000.*

Over a century ago, Virgin Gorda was the centre of population and commerce. It is now better known as the site of the geological curiosity called The Baths, where enormous smooth boulders form a natural swimming pool and underwater caves. The island is 7 miles long and the north half is mountainous, with a peak 1,370 ft high, while the south half is relatively flat. ►► *For Sleeping, Eating and other listings, see pages 522-526.*

Around Virgin Gorda

There is a 3,000-ft airstrip near the main settlement, **Spanish Town**. The Virgin Gorda Yacht Harbour is here and besides the marina facilities with full yachting chandlery, there is a good supermarket, dive centre, bar/restaurant, a craft shop selling stamps, souvenir and clothes shops and phones, post box and taxis. There are some 20 secluded beaches, the most frequented being **Devil's Bay**, **Spring Bay**, and **Trunk Bay** on the west coast. Between Devil's Bay and Spring Bay in the southwest are **The Baths**. The snorkelling here is good, especially going left from the beach. Unfortunately the popularity of The Baths with tour companies and cruise ships can lead to overcrowding. There are many day trips from Tortola and when a cruise ship is in port you cannot move on the beach. Just off the southwest tip of the island is **Fallen**

Jerusalem National Park, an islet named for its spectacular tumble-down rock formation. On the southeast tip is **Copper Mine Point**, where the Spaniards allegedly mined copper, gold and silver some 400 years ago; the remains of a mine begun by Cornish miners in 1838 can be seen with the typical Engine House and other ruins, and you can find stones such as malachite and crystals embedded in quartz.

North of the island is **North Sound**, formed to the south and east by Virgin Gorda, to the north by Prickly Pear Island, and to the west by Mosquito Island. **Bitter End** and **Biras Creek** are good anchorages and both have a hotel and restaurant. **Biras Creek** charges US$15 for moorings; yachtsmen may use Deep Bay beach but others are reserved for hotel guests. **Bitter End** charges US$20 including water taxi to shore in the evenings. There is no road to either resort, you have to get a hotel launch from Gun Creek or the North Sound Express from Beef Island to **Bitter End Resort & Yacht Club**. Saba Rock is just off **Bitter End**; with food at the **Saba Rock Resort**.

> 🛈 All land on Virgin Gorda over 1,000 ft is now a national park, with walking trails.

Prickly Pear Island
Prickly Pear Island forms the northeast edge of North Sound. It has a lovely beach at Vixen Point with a small beach bar and a watersports centre. This is a great spot for volley ball, with a net permanently on the beach. Moorings near the **Sand Box** beach bar (T4959122, VHF 16), with showers and ice. The only legal jet-ski rental operation in the BVI is here. The island gets crowded when cruise ships come in.

Necker Island
This 74-acre, private island (www.necker.com) northeast of Virgin Gorda is owned by Sir Richard Branson, who wanted a Virgin island to add to his Virgin enterprise. It is available for rent, either in its entirety or, during certain weeks, you can rent just a

British Virgin Islands Virgin Gorda

Virgin Gorda

0 km   1
0 miles   1
N

Sleeping 🛏
Biras Creek **1**
Bitter End Yacht Club
  & Resort **2**
Fischer's Cove **4**
Guavaberry Spring Bay **5**

Katitche Point
Greathouse **13**
Leverick Bay
  & Vacation Villas **6**
Little Dix Bay **7**
Mango Bay **8**

Nail Bay Estate Villas **9**
Ocean View/
  The Wheelhouse **10**
Olde Yard Village **11**
Toad Hall **14**

room and share with others. The house and two cottages, all in Balinese style, sleep 26, fully staffed and cost an arm and a leg. The **Bali Cliff** open-sided bedroom and bathroom was made in Indonesia and re-assembled on the island. There is also a Balinese beach pool and dining pavilion. Lovely beaches, protected by a coral reef, tennis and watersports provided, private. Powerboats take 40 minutes from Beef Island, expect to get soaked, or go by helicopter or boat from Virgin Gorda.

Mosquito Island

Mosquito Island is privately owned and enjoys beautiful views over North Sound to Virgin Gorda and Prickly Pear Island. This 125-acre island is just northwest of Leverick Bay and a mile from Necker Island. There is a lovely beach at South Bay, sandy with boulders, and there are other quiet, sandy coves. There used to be an exclusive small resort called Drake's Anchorage here, but in 2007 it was reported that Sir Richard Branson had purchased a second Virgin Island and Mosquito Island was to join the Virgin Group. He plans to convert it into a luxury, eco-friendly, carbon-neutral resort powered by wind, wave and solar energy.

Cooper Island

In the chain of islands running southwest from Virgin Gorda is Cooper Island, which has a beach and harbour at Manchioneel Bay with palm trees and coral reefs. The island is only 1½ miles long and ½ mile wide, there are no roads, cars, TVs or nightlife. It is a place to relax and escape the rest of the world. The supply boat leaves Road Town Monday, Wednesday and Saturday. There is a dive shop on the island and the beach club is used for surface intervals or to pick up divers from yachts anchored in the bay.

Salt Island

Very few people visit this lovely island, there are no ferries and access is only by private boat. There are two salt ponds from which salt was gathered and a bag sent to the British monarch every year as rent for the island, the remainder sold to visitors and local restaurants. The last remaining inhabitant and salt worker died in 2003. There is a reef-protected lagoon on the east shore. The main reason people come here is for a rest stop between dives. The British mail ship *Rhone*, a 310-ft steamer, sank off Salt Island in a hurricane in 1867 and the site was used in the film *The Deep*. Those who perished were buried on Salt Island. The wreck is still almost intact in 20-80 ft of water and is very impressive. The dive is usually divided between the bow section and the stern section; in the former you can swim through the hull at a depth of about 70 ft, be prepared for darkness. In calm weather it is possible to snorkel part of it.

Dead Chest

A tiny island in Salt Island Passage, between Salt Island and Peter Island, this is reputedly where the pirate Blackbeard abandoned sailors: "15 men on a Dead Man's Chest – Yo Ho Ho and a bottle of rum!".

Peter Island

This 1,000-acre island has a tiny population and offers isolated, palm-fringed beaches, good anchorage and picnic spots. There are 10 daily ferry departures from Tortola, a private guest launch from Tortola or St Thomas, and helicopter from St Thomas or San Juan. The marina by the dive shop has a commissary selling basic foods, snacks and ice creams, and there are shower facilities for visiting sailors.

Norman Island

The island is reputed to be the 'Treasure Island' of Robert Louis Stevenson fame. The floating bar/restaurant **William Thornton II** (T4968603, VHF Ch 16 or 74, www.williamthornton.com), is anchored in the Bight of Norman to the north of the island. The first *William Thornton*, a converted 1910 Baltic trader sank in 1995. There is also the **Billy Bones** beach bar, open for lunch and dinner, but otherwise the island is uninhabited. A launch service, the *Wet Willy*, operates from Nanny Cay Marina (daily at 1700, returning 2200 or later, free, T4966416 for reservations on Wet Willy).

On its rocky west coast are caves where treasure is said to have been discovered many years ago. These can be reached by small boats and there are several day trips on offer. There is excellent snorkelling around the caves and the reef in front slopes downward to a depth of 40 ft. **The Indians** off the northwest of Norman Island are pinnacles of rock sticking out of the sea with their neighbour, the gently rounded **Pelican Island**. Together they offer the diver and snorkeller a labyrinth of underwater reefs and caves. There are moorings, US$20, and tie-up for dinghies.

> ❖ *Be careful with the wild cattle: their tempers are unpredictable.*

Jost Van Dyke → *Population: 300.*

Lying to the west of Tortola, the island was named after a Dutch pirate. Dr William Thornton, who designed the US Capitol in Washington DC, was born here. It is mountainous, with beaches at White Bay and Great Harbour Bay on the south coast. Great Harbour looks like the fantasy tropical island, a long horseshoe-shaped, white sandy beach, fringed with palm trees and dotted with beach bar/restaurants. Jost Van Dyke is a point of entry and has a Customs House at the end of the dock at Great Harbour. Electricity and a paved road arrived in 1991. There are moorings in Little Harbour where a marina is being built and anchorages at Great Harbour, Sandy Cay and Green Cay. It is surrounded by smaller islands, one of which is **Little Jost Van Dyke**, the birthplace in 1744 of Dr John Coakley Lettsom, the founder of the British Medical Society.

Sandy Cay, a small uninhabited islet just east of Jost Van Dyke, is owned by Laurance Rockefeller. It is covered with scrub but there is a pleasant trail set out around the whole island, which makes a good walk. Bright white beaches surround the island and provide excellent swimming. Offshore is a coral reef.

Anegada → *Phone code: 284. Colour map 2, B6. Population: 153.*

Unique among this group of islands because of its coral and limestone formation, the highest point is only 28 ft above sea level. There are still a few large iguanas, which are indigenous to the island. The Anegada rock iguana is part of a national parks' trust breeding programme after numbers declined to only 100, largely because juveniles fell prey to wild cats. Contact Rondel Smith, the national parks trust warden on

British Virgin Islands Virgin Gorda

Anegada

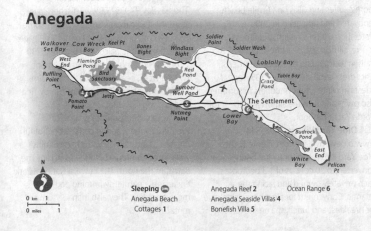

N

0 km 1
0 miles 1

Sleeping 🛏
Anegada Beach
Cottages **1**

Anegada Reef **2**
Anegada Seaside Villas **4**
Bonefish Villa **5**

Ocean Range **6**

Anegada (also a taxi driver), who can take you to see their burrows in the wild and the hatchlings in pens outside the Administration Building in the Settlement. Young adult rock iguanas will be released into the wild when they are big enough, but there are about 50 youngsters in captivity. Flamingos also used to be numerous on the island but were decimated by hunters. Twenty flamingos were released in 1992 in the ponds and four wild ones joined them two years later. In 1995 they bred five chicks, something of a record with flamingos reintroduced into the wild and now there are over 40 birds. They are best seen from the little bridge over The Creek on the road from the **Anegada Reef Hotel** to the airport turn-off. Hawksbill and green turtles nest all along the north shore; the Government has drawn up a conservation policy and the waters around the island are protected. The waters abound with fish and lobster, and the extensive reefs are popular with snorkellers and scuba divers who also explore wrecks of ships which foundered in years past. Some were said to hold treasure, but to date only a few doubloons have been discovered. Anegada has excellent fishing and is one of the top bone-fishing spots in the world. From the wharf on the south shore, all the way round to the west end, across the entire north shore (about 11 miles) is perfect, uninterrupted, white sandy beach. Any fences on the beach are to keep out cattle, not people. **Loblolly Bay** is popular with day trippers, partly because it has a beach bar at either end **The Big Bamboo** at the west end is busier and more accessible than **Flash of Beauty** at the east end, the only places where there is shade, partly because of the reef just offshore where snorkellers can explore caverns and ledges and see coral, nurse sharks, rays, turtles, barracuda and shoals of colourful fish. The beach is generally deserted. Bring water and sun screen.

> ❖ The island is very quiet and relaxed.

The Settlement is a collection of wooden homes and some newer houses, a smart new government building, a few bars, little shops, a bakery, jeep hire and church.

⊜ Sleeping

Virgin Gorda *p518, map p519*
There are several **villas** to rent around The Valley and Spring Bay and a few agencies, eg **Virgin Gorda Villa Rentals**, T4957421, leverick@surfbvi.com.

South of the island
LL Little Dix Bay, T4955555, www.littledixbay.com. Luxury hotel, with rooms, suites and villas on ½-mile beach, renovated and upgraded in 2006, watersports, tennis, health and fitness centre, clifftop spa, beachfront pool, hiking trails in surrounding hills, lovely gardens, strict dress code after sunset, 70% repeat guests in winter, honeymooners in summer, also owns and runs the airport and the Virgin Gorda Yacht Harbour.
LL-L Olde Yard Village, T4955544, www.oldeyardvillage.com. Formerly the Olde Yard Inn, the property has been converted to 20 condos of 1-3 bedrooms, each privately owned and facing the Atlantic. Convenient for airport, poolside café for breakfast and lunch, spa on site for massage and beauty treatments, yoga can be arranged.
LL-L Toad Hall, contact Stephen Green, T4955397, www.toadhallvg.com. Luxury rental home, sleeps 7, 3 bedrooms with garden showers, private access to The Baths beach, pool among the boulders, caves, great for children, US$4,000-6,000 per week.
LL-AL Fischer's Cove Beach Hotel, St Thomas Bay, T4955252, www.fischerscove.com. 12 studio rooms, some with fan, some a/c, or 8 cottages with kitchenette, less space, some beachfront, balcony restaurant (0730-2200) overlooking sea, live entertainment twice a week, beach barbecue when calm.
LL-AL Guavaberry Spring Bay, run by Tina and Ludwig Goschler, T4955227, www.guavaberryspringbay.com. Well-equipped wooden cottages, beautiful location, sandy beach with shade 5 mins' walk through grounds, to the south are The Baths, to the north The Crawl, a National Park enclosing a natural swimming pool and more boulders. They also manage some rental villas.

A **Ocean View/The Wheelhouse**, T4686284, butu@surfbvi.com. 12 rooms upstairs, close to ferry and harbour, pink building, small rooms but adequately furnished, TV, fan, a/c, restaurant downstairs, bar.

North of the island

LL Biras Creek, T4943555, www.biras.com. Reached by launch from Gun Creek, or on the North Sound Express from Beef Island, on a spit of land overlooking both North Sound and Berchers Bay, helipad for transfers and daytrips. Perhaps the most exclusive resort on the island, under new management and upgraded in 2006. Luxury cottages and suites spread along the Atlantic coast, restrictions on children, no phones or a/c, 2 tennis courts with pro, spa, sailing trips, free watersports instruction, small pool overlooking ocean, nice little beach in sheltered bay with mangroves, very private, beach barbecues, good menu and view from the split level restaurant, popular with honeymooners.

LL The Bitter End Yacht Club and Resort, North Sound, T4942746, www.beyc.com. Reached by launch from Gun Creek or the North Sound Express from Beef Island or by yacht. Good for water lovers with a marina, sailing in all sizes of boats for all ages, yacht charters, facilities for visiting yachts, fishing (reef and bone), windsurfing, diving, plus instruction, stay on your boat, charter one of the 8 liveaboard yachts, or stay on land in beachfront villa or North Sound suite, can be a long walk from your room to the clubhouse but taxi service available, 2 restaurants and pub for snacks and lunches, shops and food stores.

LL Katitche Point Greathouse, www.katitchepoint.com. Contact David Straker, Property Manager, T4956168. High up on a point looking over the bay to other islands in the distance, with its own horizon swimming pool, sunken bath made out of Virgin Gorda boulders in the master bedroom and hammocks in the Crow's Nest for great views, narrow sandy beach, 4 suites and master suite sleep up to 13.

LL-L Nail Bay Estate Villas, Nail Bay, T4948000, www.nailbay.com. A new 146-acre development of villas, apartments and hotel. They manage Diamond Beach Villas, Flame Trees, Sunset Watch and Turtle

Bay Villa, summer packages include car hire and you can also book dive packages.

LL-AL Mango Bay, T4955672, www.mangobayresort.com. 5 villas which can make 1-bedroomed units or the apartments can be connected to provide 2 or 3 bedrooms, plus 2 villas with 4 and 5 bedrooms, very clean, light and airy, a/c, phone, restaurant.

L-AL Leverick Bay Hotel and Vacation Villas, T4957421, www.leverickbay.com. Wide variety of spacious accommodation from hotel rooms to villas and condominiums built up a hillside with a great view of the jetty and the bay, Wi-Fi internet access in all rooms, **Pussers** is on site and all the buildings are painted the bright multi-colours which are **Pussers'** emblem, restaurant, tennis, pool, watersports, food store, laundry, shops, beauty therapy and massage at **The Spa**, T4957375.

Cooper Island *p520*

LL-L Cooper Island Hideaways, www.cooperisland.com. 2 beach-front 1-bedroom cottages, simple, peaceful, solar powered, use rainwater, contact Ginny Evans, 1920 Barg Lane, Cincinnati, OH 45230-1702, T513-2324126, ginnyevans@aol.com.

LL-AL Cooper Island Beach Club, T4943721, www.cooper-island.com. British owned and managed, there are 11 guest rooms with kitchen and bathroom, breakfast on request, lunch 1130-1430, dinner from 1830, reservations preferred, bar all day from 1000, do your grocery shopping on Tortola, shuttle service 3 times a week, electricity generator evenings only.

Peter Island *p520*

LL Peter Island Resort and Yacht Harbour, built on reclaimed land jutting out into Sir Francis Drake Channel, forming a sheltered harbour with marine facilities, T4952000, www.peterisland.com. Built by Norwegians, there are chalet-type cottages, harbour rooms, or beach rooms at this exclusive, luxury resort, a pool, tennis, horse riding, watersports, fitness centre, massage room, dress formally in evening.

Jost Van Dyke *p521*

LL Sandy Ground Estates, T4943391, www.sandyground.com. 7 luxury villas of differing sizes, provisioning, free water taxi from/to Tortola.

LL White Bay Villas, T410-5716692, www.jostvandyke.com. 1-, 2- and 3-bedroomed villas, luxury, cheaper in summer, great views, whales can sometimes be seen from the balcony.

LL-L Sandcastle, at White Bay, T4959888, www.sandcastle-bvi.com. Owned by Debby Pearse and Bruce Donath, 2 wooden beachfront cottages, 2 garden view cottages and 2 a/c rooms, basic amenities but great for total relaxation, hammocks between palm trees on the beach, snorkelling, windsurfing. **The Soggy Dollar Bar** is popular at weekends, most arrive by boat and swim or wade ashore, aspires to be the birthplace of the infamous 'Pain killer'.

Camping

C-D White Bay Campground, T4959312. Lovely site, popular, run by Ivan, right on beautiful, sandy, White Bay, rustic cabins behind the beach are hot and stuffy with lots of insects, better to have a tent/bare site on the beach, but beware the sand fleas. Very clean outdoor bathrooms, showers use brackish water, kitchen, honour bar, common areas, book swap.

Anegada   *p521, map p521*

Credit cards are not accepted on Anegada except at the **Anegada Reef Hotel**.

LL-L Anegada Reef Hotel, T4958002, www.anegadareef.com, or by VHF Ch16. 20 rooms, room only or all meals, there is an anchorage, fishing packages, dive equipment, beach bar, restaurant, great service, famous lobster barbecue and infamous Nubian goat, Charlie, if arriving by yacht radio in advance for directions through the reef, car, minibus and bicycle hire, taxi service, beach shuttle, boutique, closed Sep-Oct. Also Setting Point Villa along the beach at Setting Point, 4 bedrooms, and The Gatehouse, a 1-bedroom cottage in 2.5 acres with lawns leading down to the beach, both in walking distance of hotel.

LL-L Anegada Seaside Villas, West End, T4954966, www.anegadavillas.com. 1-bedroom villas on the beach, sofa bed in living room, fans, CD player, well-equipped kitchen, large porch, barbecue.

L Bonefish Villa, Nutmeg Point on waterfront mangrove flats, T4958045, bonefishvilla@hotmail.com. 2 bedrooms, sleeps 6, close to restaurant. Includes service and taxes.

L-AL Anegada Beach Cottages, Pomato Point, T4959234, www.anegadabeachcottages .com. Suites in cottages, 1 or 2 bedrooms, close to water right on the sand, well-spaced out from each other, simple accommodation with full amenities, snorkelling, fishing.

A Ocean Range, in the Settlement, T4959023/866-4686284, d_cuffy@ hotmail.com. 6 rooms, some adjoining, kitchenettes, sea view, a/c, TV, ceiling fans.

Camping

Mac's Place campsite, Loblolly Bay, T4958020. 8 ft by 10 ft tent or prepared sites US$25-45, showers, toilets, grills, eating area. Great location spread along the beach under the seagrape trees.

🍴 Eating

Virgin Gorda   *p518, map p519*

¶¶¶-¶¶ Giorgio's Table, Mahoe Bay, T4955684. 0900-2200. Next to **Mango Bay** resort at the foot of the point on which **Katitche Point** is built, authentic Italian food, 80% of ingredients imported from Italy.

¶¶¶-¶ Pusser's Leverick Bay, T4957369. Breakfast and lunch 0800-1800 at beach bar, dinner 1800-2200. Steaks, seafood.

¶¶¶-¶ Top of the Baths, T4955497. Breakfast, lunch and dinner. Indoor and outdoor dining, varied menu including steak and lobster.

¶¶ Anything Goes, The Valley, T4955062, VHF Ch16. 1100-2200. Curries and seafood, West Indian recipes, takeaway, local delivery.

¶¶ The Bath and Turtle, Virgin Gorda Yacht Harbour, T4955239. Daily 0730-2200. Standard pub fare, live entertainment Wed, good place to wait for the ferry.

¶¶ Mine Shaft Café & Pub, Coppermine Rd, T4955260, www.bviwelcome.com /mineshaft.html. Bar open from 1000, restaurant from 1100. Decorated as a mine shaft, evening entertainment, full moon parties, miniature golf, adults US$5, kids US$3, West Indian barbecue Tue 1700-2200, try their drink, 'cave-in'.

¶¶ Rock Café & Sports Bar, T4945482. Daily. Mix of Italian and Caribbean dishes, moonlight parties and sports.

Ψ Saba Rock Resort, opposite Bitter End, Yacht Club, T4957711. Bar with deck over the water, pub grub at lunchtime, buffet carvery and salad bar for dinner, also 5 rooms, water taxi service around North Sound.

ΨΨ-Ψ Crab Hole, South Valley, T4955307. Locals eat here, cheap West Indian food, curries, roti, conch, entertainment on Fri 0930-2400.

Ψ Mad Dog, next to the parking lot at The Baths, T4955830. 1000-1900. Drinks, sandwiches, T-shirts and friendly conversation.

Ψ Poor Man's Bar, on the beach at The Baths. 0930-1800. Also selling T-shirts, bring a bottle of water, toilets round the back.

Jost Van Dyke *p521*
Little Harbour

ΨΨΨ-Ψ Harris' Place, T4959302. Daily. Bar, restaurant, grocery, water taxi, live music, Harris calls his place the friendliest spot in the BVIs, breakfast, lunch and dinner, happy hour 1100-1500, live music, all-you-can-eat lobster night on Mon, ferries from Tortola and St Thomas/St John arranged for these feasts.

ΨΨΨ-Ψ Sidney's Peace and Love, T4959271 or VHF Ch 16. Open from 0900. Happy hour 1700-1830, pig roast Mon and Sat 1900, or all-you-can-eat pig and ribs, barbecue rib and chicken Sun, Tue and Thu, otherwise lunch and dinner usual steak, fish, shrimp or lobster.

ΨΨ-Ψ Abe's By The Sea, T4959329, abes@bvimail.com. Breakfast, lunch and dinner. Grocery store, happy hour 1700-1800, pig roast on Wed, US$18, call VHF Ch 16 for reservations, also has 3 rooms overlooking harbour, can be 1 apartment (**A**), friendly family.

Great Harbour

Restaurants take turns in sponsoring a pig roast nightly in season.

ΨΨΨ-ΨΨ Club Paradise, T4959267 or VHF Ch 16. Open daily, lunch 1030-1600, dinner 1800-2100. Mon lobster special, Wed pig roast, live entertainment regularly.

ΨΨΨ-ΨΨ Rudy's Mariner's Rendezvous, reservations T4959282 or VHF Ch 16. Open for dinner until 0100. Rooms for long term rental and weekly rental apartment up the hill by Rudy's house. No email so phone for details and rates.

ΨΨΨ-Ψ Sandcastle (see above), White Bay. For breakfast, lunch and gourmet, candle-lit dinner (must reserve dinner and order in advance to your specifications).

ΨΨ-Ψ Ali Baba's, T4959280. Breakfast, lunch and dinner. Run by Baba Hatchett, west of the Customs House. Happy hour 1600-1800, dinner reservations required.

ΨΨ-Ψ Foxy's Bar, T4959258. Daily. Friendly and cheap, lunch Mon-Fri rotis and burgers, dinner daily, reservations by 1700, spontaneous calypso by Foxy, master story-teller and musician, in afternoon until end of happy hour, big parties on **New Year's Eve** and other holidays, hundreds of yachts arrive, wooden boat regatta on **Labour Day** draws boats from all over the Caribbean for a 3-day beach party, very easy to get invited on board to watch or race, special ferry service to USVI and Tortola.

Anegada *p521*

Make dinner reservations before 1600. Ask around in The Settlement for restaurants serving native dishes.

ΨΨΨ-Ψ Anegada Reef Hotel, T4958002. Breakfast, lunch and dinner. Reserve by 1600 for dinner.

ΨΨΨ-Ψ The Big Bamboo, T4952019 (see above). Aubrey and his wife serve great lobster and conch on the beach at Loblolly Bay, VHF Ch 16.

ΨΨΨ-Ψ Cow Wreck Bar and Grill, Lower Cow Wreck Baech, T4959461, on the beach. Lunch and dinner. Lobster, conch and ribs.

ΨΨΨ-Ψ Flash of Beauty, at east end of Loblolly Bay, T4958104, VHF 16. 1000-2100. Drinks, snacks and seafood, including lobster.

ΨΨΨ-Ψ Lobster Trap, T4958466, VHF 16. Breakfast, lunch and dinner. Garden setting, on waterfront, open alternately with **Pomato Point**, reserve for dinner, barbecue lobster.

ΨΨ Neptune's Treasure, T4959439. Breakfast, lunch, dinner. Fine breads and chutneys, make sure you take some home.

ΨΨ Pomato Point Beach Restaurant, T4959466, VHF Ch 16. Barbecue dinners, reserve by 1600, **ABC Car Rentals** is here, T4959466.

ΨΨ-Ψ Dotsy's Bakery and Sandwich Shop, in The Settlement, T4959667. 0900-1900 for breakfast, lunch and dinner. Fish and chips, burgers, pizza as well as breads and desserts.

☺ Bars and clubs

Virgin Gorda *p518, map p519*
Live music at **The Bath and Turtle** and **Little Dix Bay**, live music and/or DJ at **Pirate's Pub**, **Pussers**, **Bitter End**, **Chez Bamboo** and **Copper Mine**. Mine Shaft (also a fun place to eat, see above), has sunset copper hour daily 1600-1800, monthly full-moon parties, live band on Fri, Ladies' Night. Check the bulletin board at the Virgin Gorda Yacht Harbour for special events and concerts.

▲ Activities and tours

Virgin Gorda *p518, map p519*
Diving
Dive BVI, a PADI 5-star operation (also NAUI courses) is at Virgin Gorda Yacht Harbour, Leverick Bay and Marina Cay, T4955513, www.divebvi.com.
Kilbride's Sunchaser Scuba, at the Bitter End Yacht Club, North Sound, Virgin Gorda, T4959638, www.sunchaserscuba.com.

Sailing
Sailing and boardsailing schools offer 3-hr to 1-week courses.
Bitter End Sailing School at Bitter End Resort & Yacht Club, North Sound, T4942746, www.beyc.com. Has sailing and windsurfing courses for all ages with a wide variety of craft, very popular, services principally for guests because of its isolated location.

Anegada *p521, map p521*
Fishing
Anegada Reef Hotel, Anegada, US$500-900, T4958002, www.anegadareef.com. Offers sport fishing on a 46-ft Hatteras, inshore and bonefishing and has a tackle shop.

⊖ Transport

Virgin Gorda *p518, map p519*
Car hire
Andy's Taxi and Jeep Rental, The Valley, T4955511, fischers@candwbvi.net, VHF16. US$50-55, guided tours US$30.
L & S JeepRentals, South Valley, T4955297, F4955342. Small or large jeeps, US$45-70, US$280-455 per week, free pick-up in Spanish Town.

Speedy's Car Rentals, The Valley, T4955235 and Leverick Bay, T4955240. Discount with return ferry ticket, US$40-80 per day.

Taxi
Mahogany Taxi Service, The Valley, T4955469, F4955072. Offers tours and day trips, as well as car and jeep rental.

Anegada *p521, map p521*
A short stretch of concrete road leads from The Settlement to the airport turn-off; all other roads on the island are sand. There is no public transport except taxis and the best way to get around is to hire a jeep, bicycle or walk (take an umbrella for the sun or walk in the early evening). There is an airstrip which can handle light aircraft. Day trips by boat from Tortola are available. There is now a regular ferry service, Mon, Wed, Fri, with Smith's Ferry, see page 504.

Car, minibus and bicycle rentals
ABC Car Rentals is at Pomato Point, T4959466.
Anegada Reef Hotel, T4958002.
DW Jeep Rentals, The Settlement, T4959677. 2-door jeeps and Subaru vans, US$40-55, US$240-300 per week, free drop-off and pick-up at airport.

☺ Directory

Virgin Gorda *p518, map p519*
Banks FirstCaribbean International Bank, The Valley, Virgin Gorda, T4955217, F4955163. ATM machines at bank and Virgin Gorda Yacht Harbour.

Background

History
Although discovered by the Spanish in 1493, the islands were first settled by Dutch buccaneers before being driven out by British buccaneers in 1666. In 1672 Britain formally claimed the islands when Tortola was annexed to the Leeward Islands, and in 1680 planters from Anguilla moved into Anegada and Virgin Gorda. Civil government was introduced in 1773 with an elected House of Assembly (white planters only) and a part-elected and part-nominated Legislative Council. Between 1872 and 1956 the islands were part of the Leeward Islands Federation (a British Colony), but then became a separately administered entity, in preference to joining the West Indies Federation of British territories. In 1960 direct responsibility was assumed by an appointed Administrator, later to become Governor. The Constitution became effective in 1967 with a ministerial system of government, but was later amended in 1977 to allow the islands greater autonomy in domestic affairs. In 1994, the British Government accepted a proposal from a constitutional review commission for the Legislative Council to be enlarged from nine to 13 seats. The four new members represent the territory as a single constituency. This plan created the first mixed electoral system in British parliamentary history, with voters having one vote for their constituency member as usual, plus four votes for the new territory-wide representatives. The British government pushed it into effect before 6 December 1994, the last date for the dissolution of the legislature. There was considerable disquiet in the BVI and in the UK at the way in which it was rushed through without prior consultation and without the support of Chief Minister Lavity Stoutt's government.

Mr H Lavity Stoutt, of the Virgin Islands Party (VIP), became Chief Minister in 1967 to 1971 and again in 1979 to 1983 and in 1986. At the elections in February 1995 the Virgin Islands Party, still led by Mr Lavity Stoutt, won a third consecutive term in office. However, Mr Stoutt died in May 1995 and the Deputy Chief Minister Ralph O'Neal took over as Chief Minister. The VIP won the by-election after Mr Stoutt's death.

In the May 1999 elections the VIP retained power, winning seven seats, but it faced a less divided opposition. The newly formed National Democratic Party (NDP), led by Orlando Smith, attracted support from young professionals, winning five seats, while the Concerned Citizens' Movement (CCM) won one and the United Party (UP) failed to win any. In June 2003 the VIP was swept aside after 17 years in power when the NDP captured eight of the 13 seats in the general elections. The new Chief Minister was Orlando Smith, who campaigned with promises to spend more on social services and less on large construction projects. Demand for change was evident in the large voter turnout, which exceeded 72%, compared with 65% in 1999. New elections were due in 2007 with no change in the parties' leadership.

Government
The islands are a British Overseas Territory with a Governor appointed by London, although to a large extent they are internally self-governing. The Governor presides over the Executive Council, made up of the Chief Minister, the Attorney-General and three other ministers. A Legislative Council comprises 13 members elected by universal adult suffrage (of which nine represent district constituencies and four represent the whole territory), one member appointed by the Governor, a Speaker elected from outside by members of the Council, and the Attorney-General as an ex-officio member.

Economy
The economy is based predominantly on up-market tourism and earnings are around US$150 mn a year. There are approximately 1,300 hotel rooms, half of which are on

Tortola and a third on Virgin Gorda, the rest being scattered around the other islands. Crewed yachts have been pushed rather than increasing bare boat charters. The **British Virgin Islands Film Commission** encourages film production in the islands and film crews bring considerable economic benefit through their use of local services and labour. A 550-ft cruise ship pier at Road Town, Tortola, can accommodate two medium-size cruise liners. The Government aims to attract the upper end of the cruise market and not to encourage the large ships.

A growth industry is the offshore company business, shipping, captive insurance and reinsurance, with little currency risk as the US dollar is the national currency; currently over one third of government revenue comes from this sector.

Industry on the islands is limited to small-scale operations such as rum, sand or gravel. Farming is limited to fruit, vegetables and some livestock, some of which are shipped to the USVI. Fishing is expanding both for export, sport and domestic consumption. However, nearly all the islands' needs are imported.

Geography

The British Virgin Islands (BVI), grouped around Sir Francis Drake Channel, are less developed than the US group, and number some 60 islands, islets, rocks, and cays, of which only 16 or so are inhabited. They are all of volcanic origin except one, Anegada, which is coral and limestone.

People

The two major islands, Tortola and Virgin Gorda, along with the groups of Anegada and Jost Van Dyke, contain most of the total population of about 20,000, mainly of African descent. The resident population was only 10,985 in 1980 and most of the increase has come from inward migration of workers from the English-speaking Eastern Caribbean for the construction and tourist industries. About half the present population is of non-BVI origin. There has recently been a return flow of people from the Dominican Republic, whose parents and grandparents were originally from Tortola, seeking a higher standard of living. Everyone speaks English.

Flora and fauna

There are 20 national parks, on land and underwater, protecting a variety of species of plant and wildlife. The BVI is home to the smallest lizard in the world, the cotton ginner, or dwarf gecko, while Anegada supports the last remaining population of the endangered indigenous *Cyclua pingui*, or Anegada rock iguana, which can grow up to 5 ft long (see page 521). Most of the land was cleared years ago for its timber or to grow crops, and it is now largely covered by secondary forest and scrub. In the areas with greatest rainfall there are mangoes and palm trees, while mangrove and sea grape can be found in some areas along the shore. There are a number of trees found only in the BVI. There are few large animals, but over 150 species of birds are found and there are lots of butterflies and other insects.

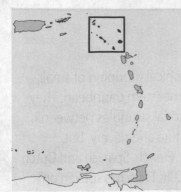

Leeward Islands

Introduction

The Leeward Islands are a geographical grouping of small, mostly volcanic islands in the northeastern Caribbean. They share a chequered history of territorial struggles between colonial powers, plantation agriculture and slavery, but, despite swinging between English, French, Spanish and Dutch control, they have diverged nationally. French is spoken on St-Barthélemy and St-Martin, Dutch on Sint Maarten, Saba and Sint Eustatius, and English everywhere.

St-Barthélemy is unmistakably French, from the aroma of croissants and coffee to the Parisian traffic and parking problems. Saba's neat and tidy villages are typically Dutch, though the landscape is far from flat. Nevis is the quintessential tropical British colony, despite its independence, with elegant plantation houses, verandas and manicured gardens. In colonial times they were nearly all sugar producers, but today their economies rely on tourism. Huge cruise ships block out the light when they dock at Philipsburg, Sint Maarten, and shopkeepers look forward to a bonanza, while English harbour in Antigua hums with the rigging of hundreds of yachts when a regatta is in full swing and the bars are filled with music and noisy revelry at night.

Antigua, Sint Maarten and St Kitts all receive long-haul flights, with smaller planes fanning out from these hubs to connect with the other islands. This makes it easy to island hop and plan a two- or three-centre holiday. From Antigua it is easy to visit Barbuda and Montserrat, from Sint Maarten it is a short hop to Anguilla, Saba, Statia and St-Barth, while St Kitts is paired with Nevis.

★ Leeward Islands

1 **Rendezvous Bay** Anguilla has many pristine white-sand beaches, but Rendezvous stretches for 1.5 miles along the south coast, a broad sweep with a view of St-Martin, page 535.

2 **Mount Scenery** The most spectacular hike in the Leeward Islands is up the 1064 irregular steps through forest to the summit, from where you can overlook the whole of Saba and several neighbouring islands, page 565.

3 **English Harbour** A relic of colonial times, Nelson's Dockyard in Antigua is the only existing Georgian naval dockyard in the world and as busy with sailing craft now as it ever was in Admiral Nelson's day, page 593.

4 **Frigate Bird Sanctuary** Barbuda has the largest frigate bird breeding colony in the world in the mangroves in Codrington Lagoon, where some 10,000 frigates raise their young, page 598.

5 **Brimstone Hill Fortress** This UNESCO World Heritage Site on St Kitts dates from 1690 when the British first mounted cannon on the hill to dislodge the French and it was not abandoned until 1852, page 617.

6 **Montserrat** The volcano, which started erupting in 1995 and is still active, is now a tourist attraction and visitors can view the activity, past and present, from the Montserrat Volcano Observatory, page 640.

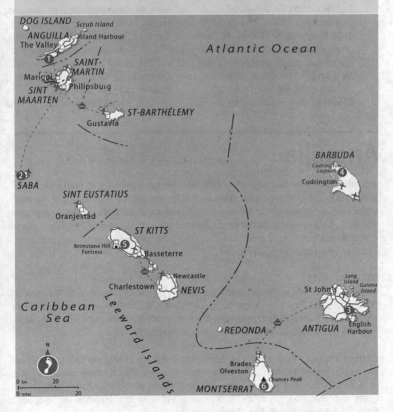

⁞ Touching down

Boat information (own flag) In Road Bay get a cruising permit for other anchorages. Customs and Immigration at Blowing Point ferry port and Road Bay at Sandy Ground (at police station next to Johnno's on north side, near small pier). Free **anchorage** in Road Bay and Blowing Point. Fees are based on official tonnage. Charter boats pay additional anchoring fees. Bring your crew lists. Little Bay, Sandy Island and Prickly Pear have permanent moorings, other places have designated anchoring sites. Boats may not anchor in Rendezvous Bay or Little Bay. Every boat visiting a marine park must get a permit to tie up or anchor, US$15 for private vessels, US$23 for charter boats. If you want to scuba dive the fee is US$4 per tank.

Business hours Banks: Mon-Thu 0800-1500, Fri 0800-1700. **Government offices**: Mon-Fri 0800-1600; **Shops**: 0800-1700 or 1800, some grocery stores are open until 2100, a few on Sun; gas stations in The Valley, Mon-Sat 0700-2100, Sun 0900-1300; at Blowing Point, Mon-Sun 0700-2400.

Clothing Bathing costumes are not worn in public places. Nude bathing and nude sunbathing are not allowed.

Currency The East Caribbean dollar, EC$. US dollars accepted. EC$2.67-US$1.

Departure tax US$20 by air; US$3 by sea.

Documents All visitors need an onward ticket and a valid passport. Visas are not required by citizens of the UK and other EU countries, USA, Canada, Australia and New Zealand. Proof of adequate funds may be required.

Emergency numbers T911/999.

Media Newspapers *Chronicle*, *The Daily Herald*. *The Light*, www.thelight-anguilla.com, and *The Anguillian*, www.anguillian.com, are both local weekly newspapers. *What We Do In Anguilla* is an annual tourist magazine with a monthly update edition, www.anguillatourguide.com. *Anguilla Life* is a magazine which comes out in Apr, Aug, Dec. **Radio** Radio **Anguilla** (T2218) is on medium wave 1505 kHz and **ZJF** on FM 105 Mhz.

Official time GMT -4 hrs; EST +1 hr.

Public holidays New Year's Day, Good Fri, Easter Mon, Labour Day, Whit

Anguilla → *Country code: 264. Colour map 3, A1. Population: 8,960 (1992 census).*

Anguilla is known for its luxury hotels and extensive sandy beaches. Its high standard of living makes it one of the safest islands and consequently one of the most relaxing. Visitors amuse themselves in the water during the day and eat at excellent restaurants and bars at night, taking in a weekend beach party with live music. There's not much else to do on this low-lying coral island, but that's why people come here. ▶▶ *For Sleeping, Eating and other listings, see pages 536-543.*

Ins and outs

Getting there International access points for Anguilla are Antigua, St Maarten or San Juan, Puerto Rico. From there you get a plane to **Wallblake Airport**, or a boat from St-Martin to **Blowing Point** ferry terminal. Hotel transfers are not allowed, so you have to take a taxi on arrival. ▶▶ *See Transport, page 542, for further details.*

Getting around There is no bus service but there are several **car hire** companies. Hired cars cannot be picked up from the airport because of local regulations, they have to be delivered to your hotel, but they can be dropped off at the airport. Watch out for goats and sheep on the roads. It is also possible to hire **bicycles** and **mopeds**. **Note** Driving is on the left. Speed limit 30 mph.

Mon, end of May (Anguilla Day, commemorates Anguilla Revolution which began 30 May 1967), the Queen's official birthday in Jun, the first Mon (Aug Mon) and the first Thu (Aug Thu) and Fri (Constitution Day) in Aug, 19 Dec (Separation Day), Christmas Day, Boxing Day.

Tourist information Anguilla **Department of Tourism**, Coronation Av, The Valley, T4972759, www.anguilla-vacation.com. Mon-Fri 0800-1700. The office at the airport is closed at lunchtime, but the customs officers will often phone for a hotel reservation for you. The **Anguilla National Trust** welcomes members, office in the Museum Building, The Valley, T4975297, axanat@anguilla net.com. They have a map of archaeological and historical sites of Anguilla, worth getting if you want to explore caves, Amerindian sites or sugar mill rounds. Contact them or the **Anguilla Archaeological and Historical Society** for further information.

Tourist offices overseas Canada, William & Sari Marshall, Xybermedia, 33 Hazelton Av, Suite 400, Toronto, Ontario, M5R 2E3, T416 9239813, Toll Free: T1-877-GO ANGUILLA, www.go-anguilla.com. **France**, Gerard Germin, c/o Sergat SARLI, 745 Av Du General Leclerc, 92100 Boulogne, T33 1 4608 5984, anguillaparis@wanadoo.fr. **Germany**, Gerlinde Hofbauer, GH Marketing, c/o Ersteetage, Orleansstrasse 34, 81667 Munich, T49(0)89 5439397, anguilla@exclusiveanddifferent.com. **Italy**, De Paoli Associati Communications, Via del Mare 47, 20142 Milano, T39 02 89 53 41 08, anguilla@depaoliassociati.com. **Monaco/Spain**, Maurizio Spinetta, Jet Travel Monaco, Le Coronado, 20 Av de Fontvieille, MC 98000 Monaco, T377 97 98 41 22, anguilla@jet-travel.com. **UK**, Carolyn Brown, CSB Communications, 7A Crealock St, London SW18 2BS, T44-(0)20 88710012, anguilla@tiscali. co.uk. **USA**, Mrs. Marie Walker, Anguilla Tourist Board, 246 Central Av, White Plains, NY 10606, T914 2872400, Toll Free: 1-877-4-ANGUILLA, mwturnstyle@aol.com.

Voltage 110 volts AC, 60 cycles. **Weights and measures** Metric, but some imperial still used.

Sights

Anguilla is a small island, about 35 miles square, and the most northerly of the Leeward Islands. It is arid, covered with low scrub and has few natural resources. The island's name comes from the Spanish word for 'eel', a reference to its long, narrow shape, 16 miles long but only an average of three miles wide. Its Carib name was *Malliouhana*, the sea serpent. The people of Anguilla, predominantly of African descent but with some traces of Irish blood, are friendly and helpful. It is one of the Caribbean's safest islands.

> ‡ *The island is low lying and, unlike its neighbours, it is not volcanic but of coral formation.*

Near **The Valley**, the island's administrative centre, with a population of 500, **Wallblake House** ① *T4972759, Mon, Wed, Fri 1000-1400, US$5 tour*, is a restored plantation house dating from 1787, the oldest and only surviving plantation house on the island, with intact kitchen, stables and workers' quarters, next to **St Gerard's Roman Catholic Church**. The church itself is worth a visit to see the unusual ventilation. Several resident artists exhibit their work on Saturday mornings during the winter season in the grounds of Wallblake House. Some of the oldest buildings can be found in Old Valley, on the road to Crocus Hill, including the **Methodist church**, the oldest church, dating from 1830, a pretty stone and timber building.

Road Bay/Sandy Ground Village is known for its nightlife and restaurants and is the starting point for most day trips, dive tours and a popular anchorage for visiting yachts, with races usually starting from here. You can see the salt pond, around Great

Leeward Islands Anguilla

Road Pond, although it is not currently in operation. There is a mini museum at the **Pump House bar** ① *T4972711, Sir Emile Gumbs, for tour Thu 1000*, Sandy Ground. The building was once part of the salt factory and equipment used in the salt-making process is on display. The tour explains the salt-making process and takes you around the pond. The Manse Building in Sandy Ground is a three-gabled house from the beginning of the 20th century, built for a local planter. In 1910 it was sold to the Methodist church and was the residence of the minister until 1962. Now restored, it houses two art galleries, a shop and offices.

A local historian, Mr Colville Petty OBE, collects traditional household artefacts and nostalgic old photos, displayed in what is known as the **Heritage Collection Museum** ① *Pond Site, East End, T2357440, Mon-Sat 1000-1700, US$5, children under 12 US$3.* Boat building, fishing, salt raking and house building are all documented as a vivid reminder of how hard life used to be. The 1967 Anguilla Revolution and its leaders are also preserved for posterity with newspaper cuttings and photos.

Northeast of The Valley, by Shoal Village, is **The Fountain** national park, closed at present. Its focus is a cave which has constant fresh water and Amerindian petroglyphs. Artefacts have been found and it is hoped they will be housed in a museum at the site. Anguilla awaits detailed archaeological investigation, but it is thought that the island had several settlements and a social structure of some importance, judging by the ceremonial items which have been found. **Big Spring Cave** is an old Amerindian ceremonial centre where you can see petroglyphs. It is near **Island Harbour**, a fishing village with Irish ancestry.

Islands offshore

Day trips can be arranged to some of the neighbouring islands or to the offshore islands and cays. **Sandy Island** is only 15 minutes from Sandy Ground Harbour and is a pleasant desert island for swimming or snorkelling. Lunch or drinks are available

Anguilla

Sleeping
Allamanda Beach Club 3
Altamer & Restaurant 2
Anguilla Great House 1
Cap Juluca 4
Carimar Beach Club 5

CuisinArt Resort & Spa 7
Frangipani Beach Club 9
Kú 6
La Palma 17
Lloyd's Guesthouse 11
Madeariman Beach Club 18

Malliouhana 12
Paradise Cove 14
Rendezvous Bay 15
Sea View 17
Serenity 13
Syd Ans Apartments 17

from a **beach bar** (T4976395) under coconut palms. Motorboats or sailboats cross over hourly (1000-1500, US$8 per person). There are worthwhile trips to **Prickly Pear**, six miles from Road Bay, where you can snorkel if you are not a scuba diver, or to some of the other cays where you can fish or just have a picnic. **Scrub Island**, two miles long and one mile wide, off the northeast tip of Anguilla, is an interesting mix of coral, scrub and other vegetation. It is uninhabited, except by goats. There is a lovely sandy beach on the west side and ruins of an abandoned tourist resort and airstrip. There can be quite a swell in the anchorage, so anchor well. Boats go from Road Bay, Shoal Bay or Island Harbour. Chartered yachts and motorboats leave from Road Bay or from Island Harbour for **Scilly Cay**, privately owned by Eudoxie and Sandra Wallace and also named **Gorgeous Scilly Cay** ① *bar and restaurant 1100-1700, Tue-Sun, Nov-May, Wed, Fri, Sun Jun-Aug, closed Sep-Oct, live music Wed, Sun*. They have their own boat with a free ferry service. The bar is on a palm-fringed beach where walls are made from conch shells. Good snorkelling.

Beaches and activities

There are 12 miles, 35 **beaches**, of fine white coral sand and crystal-clear water. Most of them are protected by a ring of coral reefs and offshore islands. Beautiful **Shoal Bay** is the most popular beach and very busy at weekends; island bands play here on Sundays until the evening. There are villas, guesthouses, casual restaurants and beach bars (**Uncle Ernie's** has the cheapest drinks) for lunch and dinner. The snorkelling is good, with the closer of two reefs only 10 yards from the shore, and you can rent snorkelling and other watersports equipment. You can also rent lockers, beach umbrellas, loungers, rafts and towels. There may even be someone to sell you live lobster. **Mead's Bay** is also popular, with a couple of small bars, top-class hotels and watersports. A controversial dolphin lagoon has been built here, stocked with dolphins allegedly caught in the wild by Cuba, which have been trained and are giving performances. Conservationists have protested against keeping the dolphins in captivity for the amusement of tourists. For further information, contact the **Whale and Dolphin Conservation Society**, see page 37. **Smitty's Bar**, at **Island Harbour**, is unsophisticated, tables made from old cable barrels, TV, pool room, popular with the locals. Seafood comes straight off the boats. Beach chairs and umbrellas are complimentary and snorkelling is good just off the beach. **Captain's Bay** is rougher but the scenery is dramatic and not many people go there. The dirt road is full of potholes and goats, and may be impassable with a low car. **Rendezvous Bay** stretches for 1½ miles along the south coast, a broad sweep of fine white sand popular with walkers and joggers and with very little development. At the end of **Limestone Bay** is a small beach with excellent snorkelling, but be careful, the sea can be rough here. **Little Bay**, with crystal-clear water and dramatic cliffs, is very difficult to reach but eagle rays, turtles and lots of fish can be seen, and as well as excellent snorkelling it is a birdwatcher's and photographer's dream; turn right in front of the old cottage hospital in The Valley, after about half a mile there are some trails leading down the cliff to the water, fishermen have put up a rope for the last bit down the rock face. Glass-bottom boats and cruise boats also come here or you can get a boat ride from Crocus Bay.

Diving and marine life The Government is introducing a marine parks system, installing permanent moorings in certain areas to eliminate anchor damage. Designated marine parks include Dog Island, Island Harbour, Little Bay, Prickly Pear, Sandy Island, Seal Island and Shoal Bay. Mooring permits are required. Do not remove any marine life such as coral or shells from underwater. Spear fishing is prohibited. **Stoney Bay Marine Park Underwater Archaeological Preserve** was opened in March 1999. The park is protecting the wreck of a Spanish ship, *El Buen Consejo*, which ran aground on 8 July 1772 off the northern tip of Anguilla while on its way to Mexico with 50 Franciscan missionaries bound for the Philippines. It now lies about 100 yd offshore at a depth of 30 ft, with cannon, anchors and historical artefacts. Dives are fully guided and can only be done with **Shoal Bay Scuba and Watersports**. You are shown a video and given an overview of the ship's history.

There are good **dives** just off the coast, particularly for novices or for night dives, while the others are generally in a line due west of Sandy Island, northwest of Sandy Ground, and along the reef formed by **Prickly Pear Cays** and Sail Island. Off **Sandy Island**, there are lots of soft corals and sea-fans, while at Sandy Deep there is a wall which falls from 15-60 ft. There are also several wrecks, nine of which have been deliberately sunk as dive sites around the island, the most recent in 1993.

Further west, **Paintcan Reef** at a depth of 80 ft contains several acres of coral and you can sometimes find large turtles there. Nearby, **Authors Deep**, at 110 ft, has black coral, turtles and a host of small fish, but this is more for the experienced diver. On the north side of the Prickly Pear Cays you can find a beautiful underwater canyon with ledges and caves where nurse sharks often go to rest. Most of the reefs around Anguilla have some red coral; be careful not to touch it as it burns.⟫ *For dive operators, see page 541.*

● Sleeping

Anguilla *p532, map p534*
A 10% tax and 10-15% service charge will be added to the bill. Anguilla caters for upmarket, independent travellers. This is reflected in the number of relatively small, chic and expensive hotels and beach clubs. Bargains can be found in the summer months, with discounts of over 50%, or you can try the guesthouses. The Anguilla Department of Tourism has a list of all types of accommodation, including rental houses and apartments.
LL Altamer, Shoal Bay West, T4984000, www.altamer.com. The height of luxury where you can be pampered in total privacy. 3, 4-storey, 5-6 bedroom villas with pools beside the **Altamer** gourmet restaurant. Futuristic style with lots of white concrete and glass, very open and light, equipped with every high-tech feature imaginable including elevator, home theatre, fitness centre and office. Impeccable service with staff of 10: chefs, butlers, housekeepers and gardeners. Conference centre alongside.
LL Cap Juluca, Maundays Bay, T4976666, www.capjuluca.com. Moorish design, a bright white, luxury resort facing possible change in ownership in 2007. 98 rooms, suites and 3-5 bedroom villas, every facility here, massage, scrubs in your room. 2 beaches, chilled towels twice daily and sorbet brought to your sunbed in the afternoon. Pool, watersports, tennis, croquet, full children's activity programmes, 3 restaurants or 24-hr room service, 179-acre estate, nature trail. Closed Sep-Oct.
LL CuisinArt Resort & Spa, Rendezvous Bay, T4982000, www.cuisinartresort.com. Spa

resort with lots of health treatments and 'wellness' programme. Also cooking classes, food is very important here, they grow fruit and vegetables using hydroponic technology. An imposing resort with blocks of rooms and suites on the beach and set back in the garden, all with huge marble bathrooms, blue and yellow colour scheme, walk-in wardrobes, patio with sun beds, doors sturdy enough to withstand 200 mph winds, children's playground. Closed Sep-Oct.
LL Frangipani Beach Club, Mead's Bay, T4976442, www.frangipaniresort.com. An attractive Spanish-style apartment hotel with red tiled roofs and white walls comprising 15 multi-level deluxe units of 1-3 bedrooms with tiled floors and fans, all cool and comfortable. Large pool. Meal plans available, very good restaurant on site. Substantial discounts in low season. Closed Sep-Oct.
LL Malliouhana Hotel & Spa, Mead's Bay, T4976111, www.malliouhana.com. A well-established hotel offering every luxury, very posh, attentive service, vastly expensive but no credit cards. 55 large, opulent rooms in cream and white, huge marble bathrooms with separate tub and shower , lots of cupboards, fridge and mini bar. Award-winning restaurant (lots of steps) and a more casual bistro on the beach. Spa, watersports (most complimentary), tennis, 2 pools, children welcome, playground and pool by the beach. Closed Sep-Oct.
LL-L Carimar Beach Club, Mead's Bay, T4976881, www.carimar.com. Colourful bougainvillea climbs over the arches of the patios and verandas and pretty gardens lead

to the beach. 24 comfortable 1-3-bedroom apartments on 2 floors in 2 Spanish-style blocks at right angles to the sand, each privately owned so decor and reading matter varies. Full kitchens, balcony or patio, fans, tennis, no pool, no restaurant but several within walking distance, also grocery store nearby. Closed Sep to mid-Oct.

LL-L Madeariman Beach Club, Shoal Bay East, T4983833, www.madeariman.com. A small, unprepossessing property by the beach and close to beach bars and watersports, suites, studios and villas, well furnished with Mexican wooden beds. Fridge and microwave in the studios, full kitchens in the suites, all with a/c, fan, TV, good bathrooms, daily maid service, lots of wardrobe space, futon for kids at extra charge. The bar/restaurant on the beach is open for breakfast, lunch and dinner and there are sunbeds on the sand for guests.

LL-L Paradise Cove, Lower South Hill, T4976603, http://paradise.ai. 5-min walk to the beach at Cove Bay, but right by the new golf course. Huge, comfortable studios, suites and penthouses in 3, 3-storey blocks, all tastefully decorated, large kitchen, patio, a/c, TV, fan, in-room internet access, with connecting doors to make family apartments. Laundry facilities in each block, meeting rooms, fitness centre, pool, jacuzzi, kids' pool and pool bar, beach shuttle. Café for breakfast and lunch, dinner can be ordered from outside, packages available with car hire.

LL-AL Anguilla Great House, Rendezvous Bay, T4976061, www.anguillagreathouse.com. Low-rise, low-key, family-run small hotel on the beach, great location looking across to St-Martin. 27 simple but spacious interconnecting rooms, all at ground level in a semi circle. Some are in need of renovation, but all have a/c, TV, fan, phone. Open-air restaurant and bar by the pool and beach, often with live music in the evenings.

LL-AL Kú, Shoal Bay East, T4972011, www.ku-anguilla.com. Designed by the Cap Juluca team to attract a younger crowd and compete with St-Barths, 27 suites in 5 renovated buildings, full kitchens, sofa beds in the living area, a/c, fans, TV, radio, DVD, CD players, bright and white with splashes of colour in cushions etc. Beachfront restaurant, bar, delicatessen, pool, gym, spa, boutique and dive shop on site.

LL-AL Rendezvous Bay Hotel, Rendezvous Bay, T4976549, www.rendezvousbay.com. 60-acre property, owned by the Gumbs family since it opened in 1962. Pleasant, unpretentious, relaxing and friendly. Garden rooms with verandas and a sea view or villa rooms on 2 floors (some with kitchens) on the sand along the lovely 2-mile empty beach, great for walking or jogging. Lots of tennis, art gallery, games room, TV, piano, library, pool, in-room internet access, good open-air restaurant, fleet of own cars and jeeps for hire. Closed mid-Sep to mid-Oct.

LL-AL Serenity, Shoal Bay East, T4973328, www.serenity.ai. A new and attractive modern Caribbean-style development set back from the beach. 4, 2-bedroom units which can be split as 4, 1-bedroom suites with kitchens and 4 studios with fridge and microwave. Very comfortable, light and airy and good value, particularly in summer. The living/dining area has sofa bed, large marble bathroom with walk in shower and picture window, closets and wardrobes, patio with path to beach, room service, maid service. Restaurant on site, open daily 0800-2100.

L-A Allamanda Beach Club, Shoal Bay East, T4975217, www.allamanda.ai. An older style block with a variety of studios, suites and apartments, all with full kitchen squeezed in somehow and small bathroom, TV, a/c, fan, phone, patio overlooking pool. You can get some good package deals in summer. **Gwen's Reggae Bar** is close by for casual lunch and dinner, while **Zara's**, T4973229, is on site for smarter dinner. A starter snack pack can be provided before you arrive. Short walk to the beach through the bush, sea view from top floor rooms only.

L-A Syd Ans Apartments, Sandy Ground, T4973180, www.inns.ai/sydans. Anne Edwards runs this family business of 10 studios or 1-bedroom apartments around a courtyard, just across the street from the beach. Some open onto the salt pond to the rear and some on to the courtyard. Convenient for nightlife as well as the yacht anchorage in the harbour.

AL-A Sea View, Sandy Ground, Road Bay, T4972427, www.inns.ai/seaview. Has the appearance of a large house, smartly painted pink and white with a white picket fence outside. The apartments have balconies, 1-2 bedrooms, ceiling fans, kitchen/dining room and are clean and comfortable in island style.

The beach is just across the road, the salt ponds are behind and there is always lots going on in this area.

A La Palma, Sandy Ground, Road Bay, T4973260, www.inns.ai/lapalma. You can't get any closer to the sea than this white colonial-style house with its fretwork balcony upstairs. There are 3 small studios with ceiling fans and fridge or kitchenette upstairs, or there is a 3-bedroom villa next door which can be rented as a whole house or divided into 2.

A Lloyd's Guesthouse, Crocus Hill, The Valley, T4972351, www.lloyds.ai. On the highest point at 213 ft, good view over The Valley, 5 mins' walk to Crocus Bay. Smartly painted in yellow and white, this is the oldest guesthouse, opened in 1959. Family-run, 14 small rooms, all with small bathroom but gradually being upgraded with good fittings, TV, fan, old-fashioned charm, breakfast included, other meals on request, family-style dining with other guests, local dishes, drinks served but no bar, pleasant sitting room with selection of books.

🍴 Eating

Anguilla *p532, map p534*

There are many excellent places to eat on the island for all palates and all budgets, from the elegant to beach barbecues. Many places offer early-bird specials, so you can eat cheaper if you eat early. Beach bars and casual waterfront places provide a good lunch, for example **Uncle Ernie's**, Shoal Bay. The tourist guide *What We Do In Anguilla* has a listing. Most restaurants are small and reservations are needed, particularly in high season.

'Relish' is the local word for meat, not the accompaniment to it. Fresh fish is brought to the fish market (**The Fishery**) on George Hill Mon-Sat between 1730-1900; call T4973170 to check what time the boats are coming in. Sometimes you might be approached on the beach by men selling live lobsters, which are on practically every menu on the island.

There is a smooth Anguillian rum, a blend from other islands matured in oak barrels, designed to be drunk on the rocks rather than in a punch. Visit the rum-tasting room at **PYRAT Rums'** factory on Sandy Ground Rd, T4975003, Mon-Fri 0800-1700.

♥ Altamer, Shoal Bay West, T4984040, www.altamer.com/restaurant. Breakfast, lunch and dinner, closed Wed. On the beach,

presided over by executive chef Maurice Leduc, stainless steel kitchen behind glass so you can see what is going on. Probably the best restaurant on the island, with fabulous food, special sampler menu. Expect to pay around US$100 per person with wine. Nightly entertainment in season. Closed Aug-Oct.

♥ Blanchard's, Mead's Bay, T4976100, blanchards@anguillanet.com. Dinner only, closed Sun. Run by Bob and Melinda Blanchard, in a delightful situation on the beach, blue shutters usually open to the elements. Elegant wine list and fine dining with Oriental influences. Vegetarian dinners on request, seafood and lobster, in interesting sauces using local ingredients, and a Caribbean sampler of baked *mahi mahi* with coconut lime and ginger, roast lobster and jerk chicken with grilled cinnamon-rum bananas for US$52. Closed Sep to mid-Oct.

♥♥-♥♥ Deon's Overlook, Back St, South Hill, T4974488. Lunch, dinner and cocktails. Tremendous view over Sandy Ground from top of cliff, great food island-style served up by Chef Deon Thomas. His trademark is the garlic-crusted snapper, but there is usually pasta, steaks and Caribbean dishes such as braised goat, Jamaican jerk chicken or crayfish with coconut run-down. Special prices for happy hour, 1700-1900. Very homely, with hand-hewn tables and chairs and artwork on the walls. In the summer, Deon moves to his other restaurant in Martha's Vineyard.

♥♥-♥♥ Flavours, Back St, South Hill, T4970629. Mon-Sat, lunch and dinner (1830-2200). Upstairs with view over Road Bay, run by chef Shayne Hughes. Caribbean cuisine, try the pumpkin soup and the parrot fish with fungi, washed down with an excellent rum punch.

♥♥-♥♥ Hibernia, Island Harbour, T4974290, www.hiberniarestaurant.com. Lunch and dinner, closed Mon and Sun lunch. Run by a French/Irish couple, international menu with influences from their travelling experiences gathered. 11 tables, in open-air West Indian house on the beach. Large wine cellar with wines imported directly from France. Closed Jul to mid-Oct.

♥♥-♥♥ Jacquie's Ripples, Sandy Ground, T4973380. Daily 1200-2400. Award-winning chef, try his lobster fritters, varied menu including vegetarian, anything from shepherd's pie to coconut soup using coconuts from the back garden. Early-bird specials on Sat 1700-1900 and happy hour every night 1700-1900. Friendly and fun, the bar stays full after eating is done.

Le Beach Bar & Restaurant, Shoal Bay East near Shoal Bay Villas, T4975598. Daily for breakfast, lunch and dinner, happy hour 1700-1830. One of several beach bars on Shoal Bay, offering the usual lunch fare of sandwiches, burgers, pizza and salads, and dinner of steak, surf'n'turf, chicken and fish. West Indian buffet on Wed at 1830 with live music.

Tasty's, South Hill, T4972737, chefcarty@ anguillanet.com. Fri-Wed, 0800-2200. One of the best independent restaurants on the island, owned by Dale Carty, chef, aided by his cousin, Patrick, sous chef. Mainly seafood but also chicken, meat and vegetarian options, main dishes around US$15-25 for dinner, cheaper for lunch, try fried fish and johnny cakes for breakfast, great salads for lunch, varied menu, includes local goat curry. Closed Sep-Oct.

Trattoria Tramonto & Oasis Beach Bar, West Pond Rd, Shoal Bay West, next to Blue Waters, T4978819. Tue-Sun lunch casual 1200-1500, sunset champagne cocktails 1700-1800, dinner 1900-2130. Northern Italian chef, serious Italian cuisine, only 10 tables so reservations essential for dinner. A modern white building with blue shutters raised to allow open-air feel. Beach chairs are provided for guests and the bar is open all afternoon, a great place to spend the day. Closed Sep-Oct.

Zen, South Hill Plaza, T4976502. Mon-Sat 1600 until late, dine in or take away. Anguilla's first Japanese restaurant, offering cooked food as well as raw. Extensive menu of sushi, sashimi, California roll, tempura, teriyaki, lots of seafood and other local ingredients.

E's Oven, South Hill, T4988258. 1200-2400, Wed-Mon. Look for the brightly painted red and yellow building on the main road. 'E' was the owner's late mother, who used to bake in the stone oven which used to stand where the bar now is. Mostly local flavours with eclectic menu ranging from blue fish in basil cream sauce to sandwiches, owned by award-winning chef, Vernon Hughes. Closed mid-Sep to mid-Oct.

Pepperpot, Albert Lake Drive, opposite high school, The Valley, T4972328. Mon-Sat 0700-2200, Sun 1200-1500. Local food prepared by Cora Richardson, local customers, especially after work, rotis, salt fish, curried goat, patties, takeaway available.

Roy's Place, beachfront, Crocus Bay, T4972470. 1200-1400, 1800-2100, happy hour 1700-1900, closed Sat lunch. Draught beer, fresh seafood, popular fish and chips, Sun brunch of roast beef and Yorkshire pudding. Roy and Mandy are English and run their bar pub style with the restaurant on the beach. 1 of the 2 bars is a/c. Happy hour on Fri is an institution, with entrées going cheap as well as drinks, tables fill up by 1800. Free internet, take your own laptop with wireless internet card, or use their desk top. Roy also has apartments to let.

Bars and clubs

Anguilla *p532, map p534*
In high season the resort hotels have live music, steel bands, etc, check in the tourist *What We Do in Anguilla* monthly magazine. Look for shows with **North Sound**, **Mussington Brothers** and **Happy Hits**, the most popular bands. **Dumpa and the Anvibes** is led by Pan Man Michael (Dumpa) Martin. **Xtreme Band**, formed in 2001 by several musicians who had been involved with the Mussington Brothers, plays a blend of Caribbean, French and Latin rhythms. Out of season there is not much to do during the week. On Fri the whole island changes, several bars have live music; check the local papers.

Dune Preserve, at Rendezvous Bay on the beach next to CuisinArt, www.dune preserve.com. Reggae and folk music from the Caribbean, run by the legendary Bankie Banx. The bar is the funkiest on the island, built out of bits of boats and driftwood with a boat in the middle, great location on the sand dunes. Full-moon parties are not to be missed. Also home to the annual **Moonsplash** festival.

Gorgeous Scilly Cay, T4975123. 1100-1700 Tue-Sun Nov-May, Wed, Fri, Sun Jun-Aug, closed Sep-Oct, see page 535. Live daytime music on Wed and Sun. **Sprocka** plays and sings on Wed with his guitar. An Anguillian band, **Happy Hits**, sings and plays on Sun with their ethnic instruments. The place to come for a rum punch and lobster lunch. You can have a massage at the same time. Africa will take you over to the cay by boat from Island Harbour. There is nothing else on the cay, just the one building, no electricity so the lobsters are stored in natural tidal pools.

Johnno's Place, Sandy Ground, T4972728, www.johnnos.com. Tue-Sun 1100-2200 for food, later for drinks and music. Good on Fri and then on Sun around 1500 for a beach party. A casual place on the sand where barefoot is acceptable and it's quite a local institution, having been in business since 1983. Lots of jazz. Bands play at weekends from 2100 to around 0230. When the music dies at **Johnno's** people go to the neighbouring bar, **Ship's Galley**, for the night shift. **Madeariman Reef**, Shoal Bay East, T4983833, www.madeariman.com. 0830-1900 for food, later for drinks and entertainment. Part of the **Madeariman Beach Club** hotel, but a beach bar open to all. Soca, calypso, reggae on Fri, Sat, Caribbean night Wed. Live music Sun afternoons with a party on the sand.
Mirrors Night Club and Bar, Swing High, above Vista Food Market, T4975522. 1900-0400 or later. Juke box with music from 1960s to now, happy hour nightly at 1900-2000, live entertainment at weekends, dancefloor, big screen, karaoke, billiards and darts. Come here after **Johnno's** and the **Pump House** close.
The Pump House, Sandy Ground, T4975154. Mon-Sat 1900-0200. In the historic Anguilla Rd Salt Co Factory. Eat, drink, dance or relax, great reggae on Sat, also soca and calypso. One of the main night spots and usually busy.
Red Dragon Disco, South Hill, T4972687. 2400-late weekends only. Part of a complex with shops west of the Sandy Ground roundabout. Dance floor outside in a courtyard and bar and disco inside as well. On the last Fri of the month they host very popular over-30s nights, which start earlier at around 2130 and have live bands.

⏺ Entertainment

Anguilla *p532, map p534*
Ruthwill Auditorium for drama and concerts.
Anguilla National Creative Arts Association (ANCAA) has a performing arts section, the **National Theatre Group**, which has training workshops and performs at hotels during high season. Visitors with theatre expertise are welcome to participate. Contact the theatre co-ordinator, Ray Tabor, T4976685, rbtabor@anguillanet.com.
Mayoumba Folkloric Theatre, T4976827, puts on a song, dance and drama show at La Sirena, Mead's Bay, Anguilla, on Thu nights.

⏺ Festivals and events

Anguilla *p532, map p534*
Mar The annual **Moonsplash Music Festival** is a 3-day event held during the full moon weekend at the end of the month at Dune Preserve on Rendezvous Bay, organized principally by Bankie Banx, www.dunepreserve.com.
Apr **Easter Mon Boat Racing** is a fun day with lots of activities and picnics.
May **Anguilla Yacht Regatta**, 3 days with international yacht crews and traditional Anguilla boat racing; then they swap over: locals man the yachts, professionals man the traditional boats; www.anguillaregatta.com.
30 May **Anguilla Day** commemorates the start of the Anguillian Revolution in 1967, with parades, boat races and sporting competitions. Events through the month with live concerts.
Aug (first week) **Carnival/Anguilla Summer Festival**, the island comes to life with street dancing, Calypso competitions, the Carnival Queen Coronation, the Prince and Princess Show, nightly entertainment in The Valley and beach barbecues, www.festival.ai. **J'ouvert Morning** is on the Mon at crack of dawn, when people from all over the island dance in the streets of The Valley until noon. There are also the **Heineken Cup Boat Race**, the **August Monday Boat Race** and the **August Thursday Boat Race** at Sandy Ground. Handmade boats compete every day for the grand prize.
Nov **Tranquillity Jazz Festival** has lots of bands playing on the beach, www.anguillajazz.org.

⏺ Shopping

Anguilla *p532, map p534*
Art galleries
Cheddie's Carving Studio, opposite Devonish Art Gallery, West End Road, The Cove, Anguilla, T4976027, www.cheddie online.com. Open Mon-Sat 1000-1800. Cheddie Richardson is a wood sculptor who uses the driftwood roseberry roots found among the rocks on the shore. He highlights a feature of the wood to carve and polish animals, birds, fish and people, leaving the rest of the wood untouched. He also works in coral and stone and limited edition bronzes.
Devonish Art Gallery, West End Rd, The Cove, Anguilla, T4972949, www.devonish gallery.com. Open 0930-1900 in high season. Local deposits of clay have been found and

pottery is now made on the island. The work of Barbadian potter and sculptor in wood, stone and clay, **Courtney Devonish**, his students and other artists, is on display. Courtney is the founder of the Anguilla International Arts Festival and a mover and shaker on Anguilla's art scene.

L'Atelier, North Hill, Anguilla, T4975668. Daily 1000-1730. Michèle Lavalette, a French artist and photographer who specializes in flowers, in oil, acrylic and pastels, has her studio here. She has designed postage stamps.

Loblolly Gallery, in Rose Cottage on the road from The Valley to Crocus Hill, Anguilla, T4976006, www.loblollygallery.com. Mon-Sat 1000-1700. Features a cooperative of local artists working in oil and acrylic, metal sculptures, pottery and crafts.

Mother Weme (Weme Caster), Sea Rocks, near Island Harbour, Anguilla, T4974504 for an appointment. Mother Weme sells originals and limited edition prints of her paintings of local scenes from her home. Prints start from US$75; acrylic and oil paintings from US$300.

Bookshop
National Bookstore, in the Social Security Complex next to Cable and Wireless, The Valley. Mon-Sat 0800-1700, wide choice of novels, non-fiction, magazines, children's books, tourist guides, Caribbean history and literature, managed by Mrs Kelly. A *Dictionary of Anguillian Language* is a 34-page booklet, published by the Adult and Continuing Education Unit.

Music
Ellie's Record Shop, Fairplay Commercial Complex, T4975073, F4975317. Open 1000-1800. Caribbean and international music.

▲ Activities and tours

Anguilla *p532, map p534*
Boat racing
The national sport, the boats being a wooden sloop made in Anguilla. There are frequent races, but the most important are on **Anguilla Day** (30 May) and during **Carnival Week** in Aug.

Cricket
First-class cricket is played at the Ronald Webster Park including international matches. Call the Sports Officer, T4972317, for information on fixtures, as well as other

spectator sports, such as **basketball, soccer, volleyball, softball, cycling** and **track and field**. Anguilla produced its first international cricketer in 2003 when 20-year-old Omari Banks played for the West Indies against Australia at the Kensington Oval, Barbados.

Diving
Anguillian Divers, based at La Sirena, Mead's Bay and Island Harbour, T4974750, www.anguilliandivers.com. Dive the east end of the island and offer PADI courses, in English, French, German or Spanish. **Shoal Bay Scuba & Watersports**, T4974371, www.shoalbayscuba.com. Spacious boat with plenty of shade and ladder for getting out of the water. Full service, towels, drinks and fruit provided. Single dive US$50, PADI Open Water course US$375.

Fishing
Gotcha, T4972956; **Johnno's**, T4972728; **Keg 2**, T4974487; **Miss Daisy**, T4973170; **No Mercy**, T4976383; **Sandy Island Enterprises**, T7720787.

Golf
Temenos Golf Club, Merrywing, West End, T4987000, www.troongolf.com. A Greg Norman, 18-hole championship course managed by Troon Golf opened in 2006 with a great view over the sea to St Maarten.

Horse riding
Seaside Riding Stables, T2353667. Beach and trail rides, 0930, 90 mins, US$50, 1100 and 1415, 1 hr, US$40, 1630, sunset ride US$50, private rides for experienced riders (English or Western saddles), US$60.

Tennis
The **Anguilla Tennis Academy** is expected to be completed end-2007, with state-of-the-art courts and a world class facility to train young Anguillians for international competition. There are public courts at **Ronald Webster Park**. Several hotels have tennis courts but some are for guests only; **Cinnamon Reef** has 2 at a cost of US$25 per hr for non-residents; **Carimar Beach Club**, US$20 per hr; **Masara Resort**, US$10 per hr; **Rendezvous Bay**, US$5 per hr; **Spindrift Apartments**, US$5-10 per hr.

Anguilla National Trust, T4975297, axanat@
anguillanet.com. Guided tours from the office
in The Valley to East End with stops at Fort Hill,
East End Pond Conservation Area for birdwatching and Big Spring Heritage site, pointing
out the island's flora, fauna and culture, US$15
adults, US$10 children, 24 hrs notice required.
Anguilla Travel Services, T4973613,
www.anguillatravel.ai.
Bennie's Travel and Tours, Caribbean
Commercial Centre, transfers, car rental, island
tours, T4972788, bennies@anguillanet.com.
Malliouhana Travel and Tours, The Quarter,
T4972431, mtt@anguillanet.com.

Watersports

Windsurfing and **sailing** are readily
available and some hotels offer waterskiing,
paddle boats, snorkelling, fishing and sunfish
sailing. **Parasailing** can be arranged at Shoal
Bay. **Anguilla Watersports** offer waterskiing,
T4975821. Jet skiing is prohibited. There are
glass-bottom boats which can be hired for 1
or 2 people to operate themselves or crewed
for groups. Yacht or motorboat charters are
offered with beach and snorkelling cruises
around the island or trips to Philipsburg, St
Maarten, charters to Saba, Statia, St-Barts
on request. Operators change frequently.

⊖ Transport

Anguilla *p532, map p534*
Air
Wallblake Airport is just outside The Valley,
T4972514. In 2004 the runway was extended
and the terminal renovated, a/c, with internet
café. **American Eagle**, T4973500, has a daily
air link with Puerto Rico which connects with
their other US flights. They also fly from St
Thomas. **LIAT/Caribbean Star**, T4978690,
have daily flights from Antigua and St Kitts
with connections from other islands. **Winair**,
T4972748, runs several daily flights from St
Maarten (7 mins) and St Thomas. In St Maarten,
you can get bookings for Anguilla on the spot.
Transanguilla, T4978690, www.transanguilla
.com and **Island Charters**, T4974064, are air
taxi services, offering the flight for US$40 single,
or US$360 for a 9-seater plane. **Carib Aviation**,
T268-4623147, charter flights will meet any
incoming flight in Antigua and fly to Anguilla
without having to clear Antiguan customs.

Boat
The principal port is **Sandy Ground**, T4976403.
The service for the 20-min ferry between
Blowing Point and **Marigot** starts at 0730 from
Anguilla and 0800 from Marigot, and continues
every 30-40 mins until 1900. 1-way fare US$12,
children under 12 US$6, US$15 on the last
ferries from Anguilla at 1815 and from
St-Martin at 1900 (check times), pay on board.
Put your name and passport number on the
manifest before boarding (at booth at head of
pier in Marigot or in the terminal at Blowing
Point) and pay departure tax of US$3 leaving
Anguilla, US$2.75/€2 leaving Marigot. You
must take your passport as you are entering a
French territory. **Link Ferries**, T4972231
www.link/ai, also do charters.

Car and bike
A local driving permit is issued on
presentation of a valid driver's licence
from your home country and can be bought
at car rental offices; US$20 per month.

There are several **car hire** companies,
including: **Apex (Avis)**, The Quarter, T4972642,
F4975032; **Thrifty**, The Valley, T4972656;
Island Car Rentals, T4972723, islandcar@
anguillanet.com; **Summer Set Car Rental**,
T4975278, summerset@anguillanet.com;
Highway Rent-a-Car, George Hill, by the
traffic lights, T4972183, www.rentalcars.ai;
Rodco, T4972773, www.mrat.com/rodco.
Rates are from US$25 per day off season, US$40
per day high season, plus insurance, jeeps
from US$45. You can bargain for a good rate if
you rent for more than 3 days, 7th day is usually
free, some offer discounts on internet bookings.

Anguilla is flat so cycling is popular. **Bikes**
are available from about US$10 per day, from
hotels or about 6 rental companies.

Taxi
Taxis are expensive and the driver usually
quotes in US dollars, not EC dollars; rates
are set by the government. The island is
divided up into 10 zones running west to
east, see www.anguillaguide.com. Between
1800-2400 you pay US$2 extra, from
2400-0600 you pay US$5 extra. To hire a taxi
for a 2-hr tour of the island is US$50 for
2 people, US$10 for additional passengers.
Dispatchers are at the airport (T4975054) and
ferry (T4976089); there is no central office.

⊙ Directory

Anguilla *p532, map p534*
Banks In The Valley, FirstCaribbean International Bank, T4972301, F4972980, Box 140; National Bank of Anguilla, T4972101, www.nba.ai; Scotiabank, Fairplay Commercial Centre, The Valley, T4973333, F4973344, ATM linked to Plus, Visa and Mastercard, maximum withdrawal US$600. ATMs are dotted around the island, at National Bank of Anguilla (NBA), Scotia Bank, Caribbean Commercial Bank, Wallblake Airport, Island Gases Co Ltd, Ashley & Sons Grocery, Sydan's, Romcan Grocery and Palma Plaza. **Embassies and consulates** As a British dependent territory, all are in the UK. **Internet** Most hotels offer internet access to their guests and there is an internet café at the airport. Internet Café Voyage, Caribbean Commercial Centre, The Valley, T4985551,

benjc@hotmail.com, Mon-Sat 0900-1800, Sun 1400-1800, US$2 for 15 mins, US$7 for 1 hr, printing US$1 per page. Bits & Bites, Sandy Ground, next to Johnno's, is a breakfast and internet café, also rooms to rent. **Medical services** The Princess Alexandra Hospital, T4972551/2. Emergency: T911/999. Pharmacy: T4972366/4973836. Most people drink bottled water, but there is also rainwater or desalinated water for household use. **Post** The main post office is in The Valley, T4972528, F4975455. Mon- Fri 0800-1530. Commemorative stamps and other collections sold. **Telephone** Cable and Wireless, T4973100, Mon-Fri 0800-1700, Sat, Sun, holidays 0900-1300. Caribbean phone cards are available throughout the islands. There are 2 AT&T USA direct telephones by Cable and Wireless office in The Valley and by the airport. For credit card calls overseas T1800-8778000.

Background

History

The earliest known Amerindian site on Anguilla is at the northeast tip of the island, where tools and artefacts made from conch shells have been recovered and dated at around 1300 BC. Saladoid Amerindians settled on the island in the fourth century AD and brought their knowledge of agriculture, ceramics and their religious culture based on the god of cassava. By the sixth century large villages had been built at Rendezvous Bay and Sandy Ground, with smaller ones at Shoal Bay and Island Harbour. Post Saladoid Amerindians from the Greater Antilles arrived in the tenth century, building villages and setting up a chiefdom with a religious hierarchy. Several ceremonial items have been found and debris related to the manufacture of the three-pointed zemis, or spirit stones, associated with fertility rites. By the 17th century, Amerindians had disappeared from Anguilla; wiped out by enslavement and European diseases.

Anguilla was mentioned in 1564 when a French expedition passed en route from Dominica to Florida, but it was not until 1650 that it was colonized by the British. Despite several attempted invasions, by Caribs in 1656 and by the French in 1745 and 1796, it remained a British colony. From 1825 it became more closely associated with St Kitts for administrative purposes and was incorporated in the colony. In 1967 St Kitts-Nevis-Anguilla became a State in Association with the UK and gained internal Independence. However, Anguilla opposed this development and almost immediately repudiated government from St Kitts. A breakaway movement was led by Ronald Webster of the People's Progressive Party (PPP). In 1969 British forces invaded the island to install a British Commissioner after negotiations broke down. The episode is remembered locally for the unusual presence of the London Metropolitan Police, who remained on the island until 1972 when the Anguilla Police Force was established.

The post of Chief Minister alternated for two decades between the rival politicians, Ronald Webster and Emile Gumbs, leader of the Anguilla National Alliance (ANA), the latter holding office in 1977-1980 and 1984-1994. Mr Gumbs (now Sir Emile) retired from politics at the general elections held in March 1994. The main political parties are the ANA, the Anguilla United Party (AUP) and the Anguilla Democratic Party (ADP).

The March 1999 general elections were won by the governing coalition: the AUP and the ADP won two seats each while the ANA won three. Hubert Hughes (AUP) was sworn in as Chief Minister. His period of office was short-lived, however. The House of Assembly was paralysed after Mr Hughes lost a legal case against the Speaker and the ruling coalition fell apart when the ADP leader, Victor Banks, resigned from the administration and allied his party with the ANA. New elections were held in March 2000. The ANA again won three seats, the AUP two, ADP one and an independent one. Osbourne Fleming, leader of the ANA, became Chief Minister. The ANA and the ADP later merged to become the Anguilla United Front (AUF), which won the elections in February 2005 and Osbourne Fleming was again sworn in as Chief Minister.

Government

Anguilla is a British Overseas Territory and Anguillians are British citizens with the right of abode in the UK. A Governor represents the Crown and has responsibility for international financial affairs. An Executive Council comprises four elected Ministers and two ex-officio members, and an 11-member legislative House of Assembly is presided over by a Speaker.

Economy

The main economic activities used to be livestock raising, lobster fishing, salt production and boat building, but tourism is now the major generator of foreign exchange and employment. There are some 1000 rooms available in guesthouses, villas, apartments and hotels. Growth has been led by tourism, construction, communications and financial services. There is offshore banking and the Government aims to establish a reputable offshore financial services industry. The British Government still provides aid for the development programme, along with donors such as the EU and the Caribbean Development Bank. There is no income tax and the Government gets its revenues from customs duties, bank licences, property and stamps.

Flora and fauna

Although you will see colourful gardens, the island appears mostly covered with scrub. Nevertheless, there are 523 recorded species of flora, of which around 60% is native and the rest naturalized but introduced. The **north coast** has the most unspoilt open areas which have not been cultivated or built on. There are steep cliffs of over 100 ft high, with caves and sink holes, and inland are areas of dense vegetation. The most common plants are the white cedar, pigeonwood, manchineel, frangipani, five-finger trees, bromeliads and cacti. In this area you can find lizards, iguanas, snakes, bats and birds. The tiny ground lizard (*Ameiva pleei*) is endemic to Anguilla and you can often see their ribbon-like trails in the sand on the dunes and along the pond shores. **Katouche Valley** has a beach, a mangrove pond and a forest where you can find orchids and bromeliads and some patches of bamboo among the pepper cinnamon, mawby, sherry and turpentine trees. The valley ends at Cavannagh Cave, which was mined for phosphorous in the 19th century, but now is home to bats, birds, crabs and lizards. **Birdwatching** is good at **Little Bay**, Crocus Bay's north point and at the many ponds and coves. The salt ponds at Sandy Ground, East End, West End and Little Harbour are good places to see sea birds, falcons and herons. Anguilla has 136 recorded species of bird, including the white-cheeked pintail, black neck stilts, blue-faced booby, kingfisher and the great blue heron. The national bird is the turtle dove. Bird identification cards (US$5) and *A Field Guide To Anguilla's Wetlands* (US$10) are available from the Anguilla National Trust in The Valley. **Turtle watching** can be done from April to November, best on the beaches at Maundays Bay, Meads Bay, Captains Bay and Limestone Bay. Peak season for leatherback turtles is May to July, while green and hawksbill turtles are seen occasionally in August and September.

Saint-Martin/Sint Maarten

→ *Country code: St-Martin 590; Sint Maarten 599-5. Colour map 3, B1. Population: St-Martin 36,000; Sint Maarten 41,000.*
Shared amicably between Holland and France, this island is the smallest in the world to
be divided by two nations and offers you two cultures within easy reach of each other.
Good international air links have encouraged the construction of large resort hotels with
casinos and duty-free shopping in the Dutch part. The French part, although
increasingly Americanized, is considered more 'chic' and packed with restaurants,
dedicated to the serious business of eating well. There are no border formalities, only a
modest monument erected in 1948, which commemorates the division of the island
three centuries earlier. Both sides have good harbours and marinas and are popular
with the sailing crowd. Heavily populated, there are not many places on the island
where houses have not been built, this is not somewhere to come to get away from it all,
but it is ideal for a fun beach holiday perhaps in combination with a quieter island
nearby. Island hopping is easy. ▸▸ *For Sleeping, Eating and other listings, see pages 550-560.*

Ins and outs

Getting there International flights arrive at the **Juliana Airport** on the Dutch side.
Sint Maarten has good long-distance air connections, with charter and scheduled
flights from Europe, the USA and the Caribbean. It is used as a jumping-off point for
many of the smaller islands in the area which do not have the capacity to receive large
aircraft, such as Saba or Anguilla. A taxi to Marigot will cost about US$15. On the
French side is the **Espérance Airport** which can only take 20-seater light planes for
short hops to neighbouring islands. There are good **ferry** connections with both
Anguilla and St-Barthélemy most days. It can be an unpleasant trip to the latter. If
rough, take the plane.

Getting around There are **buses** between Philipsburg on the Dutch side and
Marigot on the French side as well as to the main towns on the French side. There is no
regular bus service between Philipsburg and the airport. However, occasional buses
run from Philipsburg to Mullet Bay, past the airport, US$1.50. **Taxis** are available for
short journeys and island tours. There can be a shortage of **cars** or jeeps for hire in
high season. It is advisable to request one from your hotel when you book the room.
Out of season car rental is inexpensive. Traffic is very heavy, not just at rush hour, and
there are frequently traffic jams, so allow plenty of time for a journey.

Philipsburg

Philipsburg, the capital of Dutch Sint Maarten, is built on a narrow strip of sandy land
between the sea and a shallow lake which was once a salt pond. It has two main
streets, Front and Back, and a ringroad built on land reclaimed from the salt pond,
which all run parallel to beautiful **Great Bay Beach**, perhaps the safest and cleanest
20-m wide city beach anywhere, with a new boardwalk running along it. Front Street is
full of shops offering duty-free goods and has been enhanced with palm trees and
pretty street lighting as well as strategically placed benches. Back Street contains
low-cost clothes shops and low-budget Chinese restaurants. The historic **Courthouse**
dating from 1793, on De Ruyterplein, better known as Wathey Square, faces the pier.
In the past it has been used as a Council Hall, a weigh station, jail and until 1992, a
post office. Now renovated, it is used exclusively as a courthouse. The **harbour** is
frequented by cruise ships and a host of smaller craft. Captain Hodge's Wharf can
handle 1800 passengers per hour and has a tourist information desk, telephones,
toilets, taxis and live entertainment, but in 2001 another cruise ship harbour was
opened outside Philipsburg.

The **St Maarten Museum** ① *Museum Arcade, 7 Front St, T5424917, www.speet jens.com/museum, Mon-Fri 1000-1600, Sat 0900-1400, free, donations welcome*, is upstairs in a restored 19th-century house, exhibiting the history and culture of the island. There is a museum shop.

Fort Amsterdam was the first Dutch fort in the Caribbean, built in 1631 but captured by the Spanish in 1633 and partly pulled down before they left the island in 1648. It was still used for military purposes until the 19th century and as a signalling and communications station until the 1950s. Fort Amsterdam can be reached through the grounds of a private timeshare development. The guard allows visitors to park outside and walk to the fort. **Fort Willem**, started by the British at the beginning of the 19th century, has a television transmitting tower and there is a good view from the top.

A large part of the island is occupied by **Simpson Bay Lagoon** which straddles the international boundary and is fringed by a narrow strip of land round its southern, western and northern shores. There are two bridges allowing an outlet to the sea. The main one, just east of Juliana Airport, on Simpson Bay, opens for a maximum of 20 minutes at 0900, 1130 and 1730, to allow large boats to enter the lagoon. Just inside the lagoon by the bridge is a new harbour for mega yachts, an amazing sight. Allow extra time to get to the airport if coming from the east of the island at these times. The other bridge is a much smaller affair on the north side at Sandy Ground, just west of Marigot, used by fishing vessels and small craft.

Sint Maarten Park ① *Arch Rd in Madam Estate, T5432030, www.stmaarten park.com, daily 0900-1700, US$10, children 3-12 years US$5*, close to New Amsterdam shopping centre, has a small exhibition of the fauna and flora from the islands. All the animals were born in captivity and the emphasis is on conservation of endangered species.

Saint-Martin/Sint Maarten

Sleeping
Chez Martine 3
Club Orient 4
Delfina 5
Grand Case Beach
   Club 8

Hévèa 3
Horny Toad 10
La Samanna 12
Le Pavillon Beach 19
L'Espérance 11
Marcus 1

Mary's Boon Beach
Plantation 14
Tamarind 23
White Sands Beach
   Club 24

Marigot

The capital of French Saint-Martin lies between Simpson Bay Lagoon and the Caribbean Sea. (*Marigot* is a French West Indian word meaning a spot from which rain water does not drain off, and forms marshy pools.) Despite lots of new building works, Marigot still has charm and the modern architecture is in keeping with the traditional style. Rue de la République has 19th-century Creole houses with gingerbread fretwork and rue du Général-de-Gaulle is in the same style, though it dates only from the 1980s. Recent development includes the new, upscale Marina Fort-Louis in the bay in the shadow of the 18th-century fort on the hill, and the West Indies Shopping Mall overlooking the marina and the ferry.

Shopping is good. Boutiques offer French prêt-à-porter fashions and St-Barts batiks, and gift shops sell liqueurs, perfumes, and cosmetics at better duty-free prices than the Dutch side. At the **Marina Port La Royale** complex there are chic shops, cafés and bistros where you can sit and watch the boats. Rue de la République and rue de la Liberté also have good shopping with fashion names at prices below those of Europe or the USA. The market on the waterfront is a colourful affair with clothing and souvenirs available daily as well as fruit and vegetables. On the right-hand side of the market (as you face the sea) is the taxi stand and the ferry departures to Anguilla and St-Barts. It is a 10-minute climb to **Fort-Louis** (built 1767-1789) overlooking Marigot Bay and Marigot. It was built in 1767-1789 by Chavalier de Durat, who also oversaw the construction of a prison (now the fire station) and a bridge, known as the **Pont de Durat**, which opened up the village of Marigot to the north of the island. The fort was used to defend the settlement and its cotton, indigo and tobacco from pirates but fell into disuse after 1820.

Beside the **tourist office**, on the Route de Sandy-Ground, the historical and archaeological **On the trail of the Arawaks** ① *Mon-Fri 0900-1600, T0590-292284. US$5 (US$2 children)*, has an exhibition from the first settlers of Saint-Martin around 3500 BC to 1960. There are sections on pre-Columbian, colonial and 20th-century history and geology, with lots of information on the salt industry, photos and a gift shop. Most of the archaeological exhibits came from the Hope Estate Plantation, which grew sugar cane and cotton in 1750-1850. Christophe Henocq, curator and president, leads tours to **Hope Estate archaeological dig** ① *3 hrs, US$30*.

Grand Case (locally pronounced *grand cars* in English), 13 km east of Marigot, is a quaint town by an old salt pond (which has been partially filled in to provide the Espérance airstrip) with a long sandy beach, partly eroded at the north end by hurricane damage. At the far northeast end is another beach, **Petite Plage**, delightfully *petite* in a calm bay. **Pic Paradise** (424 m) is a good lookout point from where, on a fine day, you can see Anguilla, Saba, St Eustatius, St Kitts, Nevis and St-Barts. By 4WD you can reach the top on the track used for access to the radio-television transmitting tower at the top; take a turn-off at Rambaud on the Marigot-Grand Case road. There are also footpaths from **Colombier** (1½ km) and **Orléans** (1 km). Colombier is a small, sleepy village with some wonderful gardens, well worth a visit. In Orléans you can visit the home of **Roland Richardson** ① *Thu 1000-1800, T0590-873224*, the only well-known native artist on St-Martin. **Loterie Farm** ① *T0590-878616, loteriefarm@powerantilles.com, daily sunrise-sunset, US$5, children under 5 free, see page 554*, is a 150-acre farm at the foot of Pic Paradise, now a private nature reserve of humid forest. It is being restored by BJ Welch, who discovered it after damage caused by Hurricane Luis revealed a farmhouse (believed haunted by ghosts originating from a dispute and murder between the Gumbs and Fleming families) and stone walls. Trails once used by slaves have been marked in the forest up the mountain and in the fields for serious hiking or a gentle stroll. This is one of the few places left on the island where mature forest remains and it is a delight. You can also swing through the trees on a zip line and brave a tree top adventure park, the 'Fly Zone' if you are over 4 ft, or try 'Ti Tarzan' if you are shorter.

There's a fruit market every morning in market place next to Marigot harbour, best on Wednesday and Saturday.

Leeward Islands Saint-Martin/Sint Maarten

Touching Down

Boat information (Dutch/French flag) **Ports of entry**: Philipsburg and Marigot. Yacht clearance is done at the port, both in and out. Off-season hours Mon-Fri 0900-1200, 1300-1600, Sat 0900-1200, longer hours in season, page Port Authority for Sun clearance. **Anchorages and marinas: St Maarten** Great Bay Marina, Bobby's Marina, in Simpson Bay Lagoon: Simpson Bay Yacht Club, Island Water World, Port de Plaisance Marina, Palapa Marina. No fee yet for Simpson Bay Lagoon bridge. Dutch bridge openings 0900, 1130, and 1730, outbound boats first. This changes during the low season. The French side opens Mon-Sat 0900, 1400, 1730, Sun 0900, 1730. Groceries and laundry in Lagoon. Radio net VHF 78 at 0730. Duty-free Caribbean headquarters for boat parts, outboard motors. **St-Martin** Captain Oliver's Marina, Oyster Pond, T0590-873347; Marina Port La Royale, Marigot, T0590-872043; Marina Fort-Louis, Marigot Waterfront, T0590-511 111, marina fortlouis@wanadoo.fr; Port de Lonvilliers, Anse Marcel, T0590-873 194; Régie du Port de Marigot, T0590-875906. **Business hours** Banks: 0900-1530; **Offices**: 0900-1600; **Shops**: 0900-1800. **Currency** On St Maarten the currency

is the florin or Antillean guilder, while on St-Martin the official currency is the euro, but US dollars are accepted everywhere. Traveller's cheques and credit cards are widely accepted. ATMs on the French side issue euros, but a few also dispense US dollars.

Departure tax Departure tax from Juliana airport is US$10 to the Netherlands Antilles, and US$30 to international destinations. Espérance airport taxes are included in the airfare. Ferry departure tax to Anguilla is US$2. Passengers staying less than 24 hours are exempt with proof of travel, as are French visitors returning to Guadeloupe or France from Juliana airport.

Documents See page 950. All visitors to French Saint-Martin need a passport and visa, as do visitors to Dutch St Maarten, even if not visiting the French side. Therefore, many nationalities now have to obtain a French visa before embarking on a shopping trip to Philipsburg.

Emergency numbers Police: T542212, 0590-875010, **Fire**: T5426001, 0590-875008, **Ambulance**: T911 (Dutch side), T0590-292934 (French side).

Media St Maarten Newspapers: *The Daily Herald* and *Today* come out six

At Baie L'Embouchure, there is a **butterfly farm** ① *Le Galion Beach Rd, T0590-873121, www.thebutterflyfarm.com, daily 0900-1530, last tour at 1500, US$12 adults, US$6 children, 3 and under free, reusable ticket during your stay on the island*, just before you get to the riding centre and animal rescue. It was opened in 1994 but has been rebuilt five times because of hurricanes. It's best in the morning and in full sun when the butterflies are most active although afternoons are better for photography. Wear bright colours to attract them; they also like citrus-based perfume.

Beaches and activities

The bays on the south and west shores are excellent for swimming, diving and fishing, and the beaches are of fine white sand. **Great Bay** is home to Philipsburg and visiting cruise ships with a lovely clean beach lined with restaurants and bars. The peninsula of Fort Amsterdam protects **Little Bay**, the next bay west, which has the only shore dive site. **Cay Bay** is isolated and generally visited only by horse riders and mountain bikers because of its inaccessibility. **Simpson Bay** beach is a large sweep of sand with very few hotels on it, partly because of its proximity to the airport, sandwiched between the sea and the lagoon. **Maho Beach**, at the end of the runway, has regular Sunday beach parties with live music competitions; don't times a week. After 1500 in the shops on Front Street or at the airport you can find US newspapers. **Radio**: PJD2 Radio is on medium wave 1300 kHz and FM 102.7 mHz. **St-Martin Newspapers**: French newspapers are available 1-3 days after publication; *France Antilles*, same day. A few German and Italian magazines are sold at **Maison de la Presse** (opposite post office) and other locations.

Official time Atlantic Standard Time, 4 hrs behind GMT, 1 hr ahead of EST.

Public holidays St Maarten: New Year's Day, Carnival Mon (Apr), Good Fri, Easter Mon, Queen's Day 30 Apr, Labour Day (1 May), Ascension Day, St Maarten Day (11 Nov), Christmas Day, Boxing Day. **St-Martin**: see p657 for French holidays.

Safety Street crime and petty theft is increasing and there have been several reports of foreigners being attacked. Much of the crime is drugs-related and the Dutch islands are being used as a transshipment point between South America and Europe. Take precautions with your possessions and do not wander off the main roads at night.

Tourist information Local tourist office: Route de Sandy Ground, 97150 St-Martin, T875721, www.st-martin.org.

Mon-Fri 0830-1300, 1430-1730. Vineyard Office Park, 33 WG Buncamper Rd, Philipsburg, T5422337, www.st-maarten.com. Well supplied with brochures and guides. Also information desks on Front St.

Tourist offices overseas St Maarten Netherlands: Minister Plenipotentiary of the Netherlands Antilles, Antillenhuis, Badhuisweg 175, 2597 JP Den Haag, T31-70- 3066111, F31-70-3066110; **Argentina** Calle Florida 890, 2nd Floor G, 1107 Buenos Aires, T54 11- 43431100. **Brazil** Av Ipiranga 318 bl A - 5 Andar, Sao Paulo CEP 01046- 010, T55 11-32145588. **Canada** 2810 Matheson Blvd East, Suite 200, Toronto, Ontario L4W 4X7, T416- 6224300. **USA** St Maarten Tourist Bureau, 675 Third Av, Suite 1806, New York, NY 10017, T1-212-9532084, F1-212-9532145. **St-Martin France**: Office du Tourisme de St-Martin, 30 rue St Marc, 75002 Paris, T/FT53-299999, bureauparis@ st-martin.org; **USA**: St-Martin Tourist Board, 675 3rd Av Suite 1807, New York, NY 10017, T646-2279440, nyoffice@st-martin.org.

Voltage 220 volts 60 cycles on the French side. 110 volts AC,

forget to duck when planes arrive and hang on to your towel before it is blown into the sea. The most popular beach is **Mullet Bay**, where you can rent umbrellas, beach chairs, etc. It can get crowded in season and at weekends. It is good for surfing when the swell comes from the north. The most westerly beach on the Dutch side of the island is **Cupecoy**, where rugged sandstone cliffs lead down to a narrow sandy beach, providing morning shade and a natural windbreak. This beach changes according to the seasons and is the only beach on the Dutch side where nudity is more or less tolerated. **Baie Longue** lives up to its name as the longest beach on the island, stretching away from the luxury hotel, **La Samanna** (see page 551), on the cliff at the east end to **Pointe du Canonnier**, the most westerly point on the island. Round the point is **Plum Beach**, popular with surfers but also good for snorkelling around the points at each end. **Baie Rouge** is popular with cliffs at the eastern end to add interest. **Baie Nettlé** is a long strip of sand within easy reach of Marigot, but a number of hotels have made access to the whole length of it difficult. North of Marigot is **Friar's Bay**, a sheltered bay with a couple of restaurants, from where you can walk along a path to **Happy Bay**. **Grand Case** beach has been eroded by storms but the sand is gradually coming back with each new swell. It is difficult to walk the length of it because the sea now reaches the foot of the buildings lining the shore in places.

Little Beach, at the end of Grand Case beach has no shortage of sand but is dominated by the **Grand Case Beach Club** hotel. **Anse Marcel**, north of Grand Case, is a shallow beach, ideal for small children, but packed with guests from **Le Meridien** hotel. On the extreme north of the island is **Petites Cayes**, a narrow strip of sand fringed by reefs, a 25-minute walk along the coast from Cul de Sac.

On the east side, **Grandes Cayes** is popular for family picnics. **Cul-de-Sac** is a traditional village, and departure point for boats to the **Île de Tintamarre** (take all food and water with you) and **Pinel Island** (US$6 per person return) just offshore. The sea is calm and fishing boats come in here. **Baie Orientale** (Orient Bay) is beautiful but rough (beware of its undertow). There are several new developments along the beach and the area is often overrun with day visitors. At the southern end is a clothes-optional resort. Windsurfers and kitesurfers can be hired, with both a good protected area for beginners and more open waters. From here you can find boats to **Caye Verte**, just offshore. Round the point is **Le Galion**, good for families with protected water, and then **Baie de l'Embouchure**, a long strip of sand separating the Étang aux Poissons from the sea, great for windsurfing and kitesurfing. The next bay, **Baie Lucas** is good for snorkelling. **Oyster Pond** is a land-locked harbour which is difficult to enter because of the outlying reefs, but which is now home to a yacht club and bare boat charter. **Dawn Beach** nearby is popular with body surfers and snorkelling is good because of the reefs just offshore. However, the beach is now dominated by the 317-room Westin St Maarten Dawn Beach Resort and Spa, opened in 2006 with the biggest pool on the island, a casino and night club. **Guana Bay**, next to Dawn Beach, is the bodysurfers' best beach.

Diving and marine life Water visibility is usually 23-38 m and the water temperature averages over 21° C, which makes good snorkelling and scuba diving. Reefs surround the island providing habitats for a variety of fish while marine turtles nest on the beaches. **Wreck Alley** on Proselyte Reef, has several wrecks which can be explored on one dive. *HMS Proselyte* is a 200-year-old British frigate (mostly broken up and covered in coral, although cannon and anchors are visible), while *The Minnow* and *SS Lucy* are modern ships deliberately sunk as dive sites. Diving the east side is recommended in good weather, either from the shore or drift diving from a boat. The coral barrier reef is undamaged by silt run off and there are lots of fish, fed by Atlantic currents.

Day sails There are boat charter companies with sailing boats and motor boats, with or without a crew. You find most of them around Bobby's Marina, Philipsburg, from US$200 a day for bare boat, or around **Marina Port La Royale**, about US$360 per day for four people on a yacht with crew, or US$200-1500 for a motor boat. There are some 40 boats offering different trips around the islands, some just going out for snorkelling on the reefs or taking cruise ship passengers around. Sailing trips with lunch and snorkelling to beaches around the island or smaller islands such as Tintamarre, Sandy Island or Prickly Pear (see Anguilla), cost about US$70 each.

On certain days there are sailings from Pelican Marina at Simpson Bay, or from Marigot. The trip to St-Barts is normally quite rough and unpleasant on the way there but better on the return journey. Check the weather, the swell and the waves can be up to 3.5 m even on a nice day. Most boats offer some snacks, sodas and rum punch. Trips cost from US$50-75, plus departure tax. Check what is available from Marigot too. ▶▶ *For Tour operators, see page558.*

● Sleeping

On the Dutch side there is a 5-8% government tax on all hotel bills and a 10-15% service charge; the French side has a 5% tax. There are several large resort hotels, not listed here, offering lots of services and activities with all-inclusive packages available, most are on the Dutch side but a few are on the French side. Hotel prices are high but summer package deals can be good value if you shop around. For low-budget accommodation the Dutch half is better than the French. For long-stay visitors, the best way of finding an apartment is to look in the newspaper. A studio will cost about US$500 per month in a good residential location.

Saint-Martin/Sint Maarten *p545, maps p546 and p552*

LL La Samanna, Baie Longue, T590-(0)590-876400, www.lasamanna.com. One of the most exclusive resorts in the Caribbean, run by Orient Express, this white, Mediterranean- style hotel overlooks spectacular beaches and is set in 55 acres with lush gardens. 81 rooms, suites and villas with huge bathrooms (2 shower heads), all modern conveniences including data ports. On the beach guests are served fruit brochettes, towels and water. The dining and wine list are excellent with a lovely sea view from the restaurant. Fitness centre, luxury spa, pool, all watersports and tennis. Closed Sep-Oct.

LL-L Club Orient (naturist), Baie Orientale, T590-(0)590-873385, www.cluborient.com. Built at the end of the beach and away from the crowds. 136 beach or garden suites or chalets with kitchens for 3-4, in extensive grounds, being upgraded to dispel former camping atmosphere. Mature, relaxed clientele, mostly US, younger families in low season. Tennis, volleyball, watersports, massage, restaurant, internet, grocery and shop. Fairly quiet with not much entertainment. Facilities for the disabled include beach wheelchairs with fat tyres for going on the sand.

LL-AL Holland House Beach Hotel, 43 Front St, Philipsburg, T599-5422572, www.hhbh.com. 54 pleasant rooms in a tall block downtown but on the beach, making it convenient for shopping, the casino, the beach and public transport. Most rooms have kitchenettes, good-sized bathrooms and are in good order, painted white. In the lobby there is free internet access beside the open-air bar and restaurant.

LL-AL The Horny Toad, 2 Viaun Drive, Simpson Bay, T599-5454323, www.thtgh.com. The well-cared-for guesthouse run by Betty Vaughan is between the beach and the airport in a residential area, not seriously troubled by aircraft noise, lots of repeat guests. 8 different apartments in 2 blocks with full kitchens, some with a/c, beachfront apartments have fans, barbecue area. No children under 7.

LL-AL Le Pavillon Beach, Plage de Grand Case, T590-(0)590-879646, pavillon.beach@wanadoo.fr. Modern, elegant hotel on the beach by the lagoon, within walking distance of Grand Case and all the restaurants. 6 studios, 17 suites and 1 honeymoon suite on 2 floors, breakfast included, kitchenettes, balconies, phones, wheelchair accessible. Watersports and land sports can be arranged.

LL-AL Pasanggrahan Royal Inn, Philipsburg, T599-5423588, www.pasanhotel.com. Formerly the Governor's home, the oldest inn on the island and where the Dutch royal family would stay when visiting Sint Maarten. The name comes from the Indonesian word for guesthouse. Quaint old building surrounded by large trees with a white veranda, nice, casual atmosphere, the royal suite is now a bar, but the 30 rooms in the main house and annex are traditional, with 4-poster beds and tiny bathrooms. No children under 12.

LL-A Mary's Boon Beach Plantation, 117 Simpson Bay Rd, T599-5454235, www.marysboon.com. A plantation-style hotel with 24 rooms and studios with kitchenettes, right on the beach between the airport and the sea. Traditional-style decor, steps up to heavy wooden beds, good bathrooms, but avoid the lower lobby rooms which have no view and are dark. Restaurant open for breakfast, lunch and dinner (single sitting), US$30-40 for 3-course set menu with second helpings, excellent food, honour bar.

LL-C White Sands Beach Club, White Sands Drive 10, Beacon Hill, T599-5814630, tzotzo@bu.edu. A small, unpretentious, private hotel painted pink, 11 rooms on 2 floors, with balconies or terrace, kitchenette and sitting area, couples only. Discounts for cash but you have to pay US$100 deposit on arrival for breakages and loss of keys. All rooms have an ocean view, although the club is parallel to the airport runway so you can expect aircraft noise.

L-AL Grand Case Beach Club, T590-(0)590-875187, www.gcbc.com. On a headland at the north end of Grand Case beach with Petite Plage on the other side. 75 studios and suites in several blocks with kitchenettes, a/c, TV, large, comfortable rooms, light and airy, very casual. Lots going on, with tennis, non-motorized watersports, dive shop on site, video security which appeals to American guests, room service, car rental.

Leeward Islands Saint-Martin/Sint Maarten Listings

L-AL L'Espérance, 4 Tiger Rd, Cay Hill, T599-5425355, www.lesperancehotel.com. A pleasant hotel in a residential area popular with shoppers and local business travellers. 5-min walk to the main street and buses. 22 good value suites with glass doors opening onto a courtyard garden and pool. The 1-bedroom suites have a sitting room, TV, kitchenette, bedroom and bathroom, the 2-bedroom suites have a full kitchen but only 1 bathroom. Internet access in the lobby.

L-A Delfina, 14-16 Tigris Rd, Dutch Lowlands/Cupecoy, T/F599-5453300, www.delfinahotel.com. German run by Boris and Michael, gay friendly. 12 rooms, each named after a gay icon Hollywood star, in 3 traditional-style wooden painted buildings a/c, fan, fridge. An extended continental breakfast is included and served upstairs in the reception building where there is a bar, busy at happy hour. There are cats and a dog and a pool in the gardens, the beach is within walking distance. Cell phones are available with prepaid cards for national and international calls, no fee.

AL Chez Martine, 140 Blvd de Grand Case, T590-(0)590-875159. Small beach hotel right on the sea with a very Créole style. 5 simple rooms and 1 suite, each has a large bed, cane and wicker furniture, a/c and a fridge, mixed reviews following management change. The restaurant is an open-air veranda built out over the sand of Grand Case Bay with the waves lapping at the shore beneath. The food is excellent, bringing many repeat visitors.

AL-A Hévèa, 163 Blvd de Grand Case, T590-(0)590-875685, hevea@outremer.com. Small colonial-style hotel in the heart of the restaurant district. Very prettily painted in the gingerbread style with mosquito nets over the beds, old-fashioned Caribbean wash basins and antique furnishings, 8 rooms, suites and studios sleeping 2-4 people, with kitchenettes and high ceilings to the roof, a/c or fans. Gourmet restaurant on site and beach across the street.

AL-A Tamarind, Goldfinch Rd, Pointe Blanche, near Philipsburg, T5424359, tamarind@sint maarten.net. 48 apartments with kitchenettes, semi-residential, swimming pool, public laundry service, good for business travellers.

B-D Marcus, 132 Front St, T599-5422419. Right in the centre of town and convenient for the shops and casinos as well as the beach and restaurants. 7 rooms, always full. Mostly Caribbean visitors coming for the shopping. As they leave, they book the next trip.

● Eating

Saint-Martin *p545, map p546*
On the French side, check the dollar/euro exchange rate as not all restaurants use the same rate; ask for your bill to be made out in whichever currency is the stronger to avoid

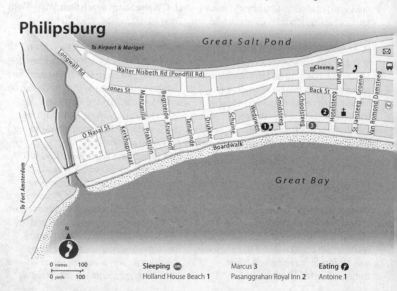

Philipsburg

To Airport & Marigot

Great Salt Pond

Longwall Rd

Walter Nisbeth Rd (Pondfill Rd)

Jones St

Manzanilla
Begoeide Kruythof
Kerkhopstraat
Prakit'zijn
Tamarinde
Druker
Schuine
Wedgwen
Smidsteeg
Schoolsteeg
Hotelsteeg
Cinema
Back St
CM Vlaun
Groene
St Jansteeg
Van Romond Damsteeg

O Nasal St

To Fort Amsterdam

Boardwalk

Great Bay

N

0 metres 100
0 yards 100

Sleeping
Holland House Beach **1**

Marcus **3**
Pasanggrahan Royal Inn **2**

Eating ●
Antoine **1**

overcharging. For travellers on a small budget try the snackbars and cafés on **rue de Hollande**, Marigot. Many bars on the waterfront serve barbecue lunch and dinner. **Grand Case** has a reputation of having more restaurants than inhabitants. Most are open only for dinner and are on the street next to the beach, but these are generally more expensive than those on the other side of the blvd and not recommended on a windy night. From the small snackbars, *lolos*, near the little **pier** come savoury smells of barbecue fish, chicken, ribs and lobster as well as other local snacks, good value, full meals for less than US$12, or just ribs for US$4, recommended. At weekends there is usually live music in one of the bars/restaurants along the beach.

♦♦♦ **The Bridge**, Sandy Ground, Marigot, T590-(0)590-296357. Wed-Mon 1800-2300, closed Sep. Grill, café and bar overlooking the lagoon; at night you can see huge fish feeding on shrimp and small fish, good local and Créole food, seafood, goat curry and delicious coconut tart. On Fri they put on a Grand Buffet Créole, with a live band.

♦♦♦ **Fish Pot**, 82 Blvd de Grand Case, Grand Case, T590-(0)590-875088, fish-pot@wanadoo.fr. 1130-1500, 1800-2230 in high season, dinner only in low season. Romantic location overlooking the sea, ask for a table away from the lobster tank if you don't want to see the chef arguing with the occupants.

Excellent sea food and formal service at a price, starters from €8, main courses from €22, desserts from €7 and wine from €25.

♦♦♦ **L'Alabama**, 93 Blvd de Grand Case, Grand Case, T590-(0)590-878166. Dinner only. In one of the top restaurants on the island, elegantly decorated with classic art work, welcoming owners Pascal and Kristin serve traditional French food with local touches in a garden away from any traffic noise; US$30-50 per person. An assortment of foie gras, served stuffed with mango, apricot or fig. Alternatively, try a starter of scallops with sesame on sweet potato mousse with honey, rum and a hint of curry.

♦♦♦ **L'Auberge Gourmande**, Blvd de Grand Case, Grand Case, T590-(0)590-877337, www.laubergegourmande.com. Dinner only, 1800-2230, in a 19th-century West Indian house, a good example of French Antillean architecture. The food is French and delicious, accompanied by an impressive wine list and the service is excellent. Lots of ingredients come from France but the fish is local. Wonderful desserts.

♦♦♦ **Le Cottage**, 97 Blvd de Grand Case, T590-(0)590-290330, www.restaurant lecottage.com. Dinner only, 1800-2300. Run by Bruno and Stephane this is a high-quality restaurant, somewhere to come for a special meal. A treat for lobster lovers, who can opt for the lobster 4-course dinner, the lobster ravioli is especially good. Also lots of foie gras and duck dishes. However, there are other excellent dishes with a more local flavour, such as shrimp with mashed sweet potato and spinach.

♦♦♦ ♦♦ **La Cigale**, by **Laguna Beach** hotel, Baie Nettlé, 590-(0)590-879023, www.restaurant-lacigale.com. Dinner, Mon-Sat, reservations essential. On the beach. A friendly, family-run restaurant where you feel more as though you are eating in someone's home than an upscale French restaurant. Very good food, try the Cigale appetizer plate to start and end the meal with their homemade rum-based digestif.

♦♦♦ ♦♦ **Rainbow**, 176 Blvd de Grand Case, Grand Case, T590-(0)590-875580. Traditional French cuisine but with oriental and Caribbean touches such as tuna sashimi or crispy roast duck with banana rum sauce, good service, seafront, with simple blue and white decor. Open-air terrace and bar on the 2nd floor overlooking the bay. One of the best on the island with an extensive wine list.

Harbour View **3**
L'Escargot **2**
Sint Rose Café **4**

Bikini Beach, Baie Orientale, T590-(0)590-874325, www.bikinibeach.net. Breakfast, lunch and early dinner. All sorts of cuisine here in a great location right on the beach, helped along with Brazilian music some nights. Spanish tapas, paella and sangria on Sun, as well as Angus beef and seafood. Garlic lovers should try the baked garlic mussels, while Thai noodles with shrimp are tasty and spicy. Generous portions but don't expect speedy service. Also fruit and veg smoothie bar.

Claude Mini-Club, Marigot, T590-(0)590-875069. Lunch and dinner, closed Sun evening. Closed Aug and Sep. Seafront restaurant with a bar and dining arbour. The cuisine is typically French and Créole, with lots of fish and seafood, great crab. Caribbean buffet including lobster Wed-Sat with all-you-can-eat food and drink for US$40, also a children's menu.

Le Ti Coin Créole, 2 rue Mezzanille, Blvd Grand Case, Grand Case, T590-(0)590- 879209. Daily for lunch and dinner. A traditional ginger-bread house is the setting for this reasonably priced restaurant serving French-island cuisine. Seafood is a speciality, with lobster bisque, tender conch, roasted or grilled snapper and shrimp, but you can also have curry goat.

Paradise View, Hope Hill, Baie Orientale, T590-(0)590-294537, paradiseview4@yahoo .com. Sun-Fri 0900-1800. Up on hill, fantastic panoramic view over Orient Bay and beyond, breezy, coach stop, gift stalls outside. Run by Claudette Davis, who has written a cookbook of local recipes. Burgers, sandwiches, soups and salads, all under US$10, main courses such as conch and dumplings US$15.

Hidden Forest Café , Loterie Farm, Pic Paradise. Bar open all day, restaurant Tue-Sat 1200-1500, 1830-2130, Sun 1200-1800. Local ingredients garnished with flowers from the farm, great menu all under US$17, kids' menu (US$5) includes 'cluck cluck on stick with peanut sauce' and 'moo cow burger'. Jazz bands during cocktail hour.

Zee Best, Marina Port Royale, rue de la Liberté, Marigot, T0590-(0)590-872751. 0800-1800. Café on the waterfront in the marina and a great place to start the day with breakfast of croissants and brioche. Wonderful pastries, melt-in-the-mouth chocolate almond, or cinnamon sugar. Also omelettes, quiche, crêpes and strong coffee. A real Parisian sidewalk feel if it weren't for the tropical heat, a good rest stop from shopping. There is another branch at the Simpson Bay Yacht Club, the Dutch one run by husband, Danny, and the French one run by wife, Tamela.

Sint Maarten *p545, maps p546 and p552*
On the Dutch side, there is a cluster of reasonable eating places around the **Maho Beach Resort and Casino** which are lively at night. If you pick one overlooking the street you will be entertained at times by dancers from the casino show, who come out onto the street and plaza to do a routine and drum up interest in the casino. **Simpson Bay** is another area for a wide variety of restaurants, all around the bridge and the yacht club. In Philipsburg, for the budget-minded try **Back Street**, where you mostly find Chinese and roti places. The traditional Sint Maarten liqueur is guavaberry. Unrelated to guavas (botanical name *Eugenia floribunda*), it is made from rum and the local berries. The berries, found on the hills, ripen just before Christmas and are used in cocktails.

Antoine, 119 Front St, Philipsburg, T599-5422964, www.antoinerestaurant.com. 1100-2200. Supposedly French and Italian cuisine, but more of an international mix using local fish and seafood, choice of US or Argentine steak, variety of pasta. Great for lunch of salads, sandwiches or burgers on the beach or dinner on the deck overlooking the sand.

L'Escargot, 96 Front St, Philipsburg, T599-5422483, www.lescargotrestaurant.com. Lunch and dinner. Prices around US$50 per person, 7 different recipes for snails, extensive menu based on cuisine from Provence with Caribbean touches, 50 bottles of hot sauce, owners Joel and Sonya do a cabaret Fri night, book 2 days in advance.

Temptation, at the back of the Atlantic Casino complex, Cupecoy. T599-5452254, dinojagtiani@aol.com. 1800-2200 Tue-Sun. A sophisticated restaurant run by an award-winning chef, Dino Jagtiani. His excellent food is accompanied by great wines and superb service. Traditional staples such as filet mignon or a surf'n'turf of grilled shrimp and tenderloin are beautifully presented and accompanied by a variety of vegetables. Leave room for the desserts, champagne and fig sorbet, or a deliciously light ricotta cheesecake. The entrance has water running in sheets down the windows and is cool and inviting. Piano music in the bar nightly except Sun.

¶¶-¶ **Mr Busby's/Daniel by the Sea**, Dawn Beach, near Oyster Bay Resort, T599- 5436828, www.dawnbeachsxm.com. Mr Busby's 0730-1800, Daniel's 1800-2200. Beach bar and restaurant, same location and owner, different menus and staff. In 2005 Daniel Jurczenko moved from the upmarket Italian restaurant Da Livio which he'd owned and operated for 10 years to start up this new venture, taking his staff with him. Huge breakfasts on the beach, lunches of salads, sandwiches, grills and burgers. Dinner mostly Italian with pasta, lots of veal, but also fresh local fish and live Saban lobster from the tank.

¶¶-¶ **PineApple Pete**, Airport Blvd opp Paradise Plaza Casino in Simpson Bay, T544 6030, www.pineapplepete.com. Daily lunch and dinner from 1100. Everything from lobster thermidor and steak to shrimp, burgers and wraps. Live music 3 nights a week. Games room with pool tables, darts board etc.

¶ **The Boathouse**, Simpson Bay, T599-5445409. Daily lunch and dinner, closed Sun in low season. A great place for fresh fish with excellent catch of the day, also lunch specials, very good wraps and burgers. The main menu offers coconut shrimp, filet mignon, scallops and there is also a children's menu. The dining terrace is on the lagoon, with a bright nautical atmosphere and there is a bar with wide-screen TV. Service is fast and efficient.

¶ **Top Carrot**, Plaza del Lago, Simpson Bay Yacht Club, Simpson Bay, T599-5443381. Mon-Sat from 0730 until late. Great-tasting health food, juice bar, vegetarian and gourmet café, makes you feel good about eating well.

¶¶-¶ **Harbour View**, Front St 89, Philipsburg, T599-5425200. Mon-Sat 0800-2200. Very popular, right by the sea with some tables on the sand, European and local food for breakfast, lunch or dinner. Choose from salads, sandwiches, burgers, fresh fish, very tender conch, ribs and local dishes such as goat curry with potato salad and macaroni cheese as traditional side dishes.

¶¶-¶ **Hot Tomatoes**, 46 Airport Rd, Simpson Bay, T599-5452223. Daily from 1500. Facing the lagoon and marina, yachtsmen can tie up their dinghies here. It is a good happy-hour spot with tapas and a pizza menu. The main menu has tuna ceviche, Aruban-Créole calamari, Anguillian lobster thermidor and pizza from the island's only wood-burning oven. Live music every night.

¶¶-¶ **Pride of India**, Simpson Bay Village, T5444917. Open daily lunch and dinner. Tandoori and North Indian dishes.

¶ **Carl's Bakery**, in the airport, at Cole Bay, T599-5442812, and Philipsburg, T599-543 1059. 0700-2000. Wonderful pastries, snacks, bread and cakes. Their main outlet is at the hotel, **Carl's Unique Inn**, www.carlsinn.com.0

¶ **Sint Rose Café**, Sint Rose Arcade, Front St, Philipsburg, T599-5541579, info@ sintrose.com. Daily 0800-1800, closed Sun in low season. An outdoor bar with tables on the plaza outside the Sint Rose Arcade, a perfect place to stop before, during or after shopping for breakfast, light lunches, salads and paninis as well as drinks and ice creams.

🔾 Bars and clubs

Saint-Martin/Sint Maarten *p545, map p546*

St Martin's Week lists what's on where and when for the coming week. *K-Pasa* lists new movies and parties and comes out on Wed, also distributing flyers with what's on. **Casinos** are a major attraction, most opening from noon to 0300. There are currently 12, all on the Dutch side and half of them in Philipsburg. The **Maho** area is very busy at night with a selection of restaurants, bars, a strip club and a casino around the plaza. **Grand Case** normally has live music and a big market Tue, Fri-Sun in high season with beach-party-style entertainment in one of the many bars. Every full moon there is a beach party at **Friar's Bay** starting around 2100-2200, and there are barbecues on the beach every Fri and Sat. Fri evenings and Sun afternoons (popular with all the family) locals like **Boo Boo Jam**, are at Baie Orientale, where there is lots of merengue, salsa and zouk.

Bliss, Caravanserai Resort, next to the **Sunset Beach Bar** (Beacon Hill), T5453996. Restaurant and nightclub, open-air dining and dancing attracts a young crowd. People start to arrive at 1230 and by 0100 it is packed, particularly popular Thu, Sat, Sun because of the DJs and music. There is also a martini bar and a pool.

Bamboo Bernie's, also at the **Caravanserai**, 2 Beacon Hill Rd, T5453622, www.bamboo bernies.net, is a hot place on Wed (ladies drink free), with DJs and international bands and artistes in high season. Almost surrounded by the sea, happy hour at the tiki bar, great cocktails for sunset watching, daily specials, a

sushi bar, restaurant, beach club, Kuta beach outdoor lounge and beach cinema Sun, Mon.
Bodeguita del Medio, Marina Port La Royale, T590-(0)590-879841. 1800-late. Modelled on the famous bar of the same name in Havana which revels in the atmosphere of the 1950s with screen stars and mob gangsters. Try the Cuban cocktails, they make a great *mojito*. Lively from around 2300, with Cuban music.
Calmos Café, 40 Blvd de Grand Case, Grand Case, T590-(0)590-290185, www.calmos cafe.com. 1000-2200. A colourful wooden bar on the beach playing classical music during the day and jazz at night. Live music from time to time. Lots of cocktails to choose from or soft drinks, but there is also a range of home-made flavoured rums, such as banana rum.
Casino Royale, Sonesta Maho Beach Hotel, T599-5452590, www.sonesta.com/stmaarten. Daily 1300-0400. Largest casino on the island.
Cliffhanger Beach Bar, Cupecoy, www.cliff hangerbar.com. 1130-late. Precariously perched on a sandstone cliff with wooden decking around the outside and a walkway to the sea, this is a great place for a sunset frozen cocktail waiting for the green flash. Often live entertainment and music in the evenings.
Greenhouse Bar and Restaurant, next to Bobby's Marina, Philipsburg, T599-5422941, www.thegreenhouserestaurant.com. 1100-2400, happy hour 1630-1900. A large open-sided bar and restaurant overlooking the bay. Great cocktails. **Margarita Mondays** offers half price margaritas all day and night with Tex Mex food, DJ on Tue with dancing from 2130 with 2 for 1 drinks, lobster and party or bingo night on Fri. Good for sunset watching.
Lady C, Simpson Bay, T599-5444710. 1600-late. Happy hour 1600-1800. Floating bar which can get wild at night and is very popular with a young crowd. DJ Marco keeps everyone hopping on Tue, Wed and Fri. The vessel is occasionally taken to other locations or cruises the lagoon, but is usually just east of the bridge. At the same dock you can get freshly cooked pizza at the Pizza Galley and good wines to take away.
The Pub, Blvd de Grand Case, Grand Case. A cocktail bar which holds a champagne party on Sun with a free glass to women after 2200. Great bands and music. Private members' club at the back, but no trouble getting in if you ask. The other side of the road from the *lolos*. Good for late nights with pizza to fill a hole.

Q Club, mezzanine level club at the **Casino**. Daily 2200-late. The latest music from Europe, the USA, Latin America and the Caribbean. Very busy at weekends and on Wed for ladies' night, popular with locals and tourists.
Showroom Royale, the theatre at the **Casino Royale**, T599-5452115. Nightly performances of Las Vegas-style casino shows with stunning costumes and excellent choreography. Stand-up comedians in season, with many from HBO or Carsons as well as local comedians or groups. Entry is in the Casino.
The Soprano's Bar, Maho, T599-5227088, open daily with live piano music 6 days a week, a real night club, dark and expensive.
Sunset Beach Bar, 2 Beacon Hill Rd, Maho Beach, T599-5453998, www.sunset beachbar.com. 1100-2200. Popular bar day and night with a very lively crowd; as the name suggests, this is a great place for sunset watching. You're right at the end of the runway and can see planes at very close range. Take your own laptop and you can hook up to their free wi-fi at the bar or on the deck. Live music or DJ every night.

☻ Entertainment

Saint-Martin/Sint Maarten *p545, map p546*
Bowling
FX Bowling, opposite the New Amsterdam Shopping Centre, T5428963. A cyberpub, restaurants and play areas for the kids.

Cinemas
Le Cinéma MJC, Sandy Ground, T590-(0)590-871844. New films shown, tickets US$5.
Megaplex, next to **Paradise Casino**, Cole Bay, T5444777, www.caribbeancinemas.com.
The Sunset Theatre, Simpson Bay, T599-5443630. Recent film releases, tickets US$6.

❀ Festivals and events

Saint-Martin/Sint Maarten *p545, map p546*
Feb In Saint-Martin **Carnival** is held pre-Lent in and most of the events are at the Carnival Village in Marigot. It is not as big and grandiose as on the Dutch side, but it is growing and there are calypso and beauty contests and a Grand Parade.
Mar Heineken Regatta, www.heineken

regatta.com, the largest annual regatta, takes place the first weekend in Mar and lasts for 3 days with a round-the-island race on the Fri. It is well attended with nearly 250 boats in 18 classes. It is a big party on both sides of the island with lots of events organized.

Mar-Apr In Grand Case **Easter parades** are held with costumes and music.

Apr Carnival in Sint Maarten lasts for 3 weeks, culminating in the burning of King Mo-Mo. It is one of the biggest in the area, with up to 100,000 people involved. Most events are held at the Carnival Village, next to the university.

14-21 Jul Bastille Day has live music, jump-ups and boat races; the celebrations move to Grand Case the weekend after (more fun) for **Schoelcher Day** on 21 Jul.

11 Nov Both sides of the island celebrate Discovery Day of St-Martin/St Maarten, the **Armistice** and there are celebrations in French Quarter.

Dec-Jan Christmas and New Year parades with costumes and music at Grand Case.

○ Shopping

Saint-Martin/Sint Maarten *p545, map p546*

Art galleries

Roland Richardson, 6 rue de la République, Marigot, T590-(0)590-873221, www.roland richardson.com, Mon-Sat. Lovely old 1840s home with courtyard garden where the family still take their lunch. In Orléans you can visit the home of Roland Richardson, the only well-known native artist on St-Martin, Thu 1000-1800, T590-(0)590-873224. Marigot has a large crop of art galleries. **Camaïeu**, rue Kennedy, T590-(0)590-872578, **Galerie Valentin**, 112 Les Amandiers, T590-(0)590-870894, **Galeries Gingerbread**, Arrière Port de Galisbay, T590-(0)590-877321, and **Graffiti's** at Les Amandiers, T590-(0)590-879533.

Duty-free

Shopping in Philipsburg is a tourist attraction, but it helps if you have an idea of prices at home to compare, and shop around as prices vary. In the electronics and camera shops many outdated models are on display. European visitors planning to take home hi-fi or domestic appliances should make sure that they can be switched to 220 volts. Most of the shops are along Front St, open 0900-1800. **Barrel Liquor**, 114 Old St (a mini mall), sells the cheapest in town. Many liquor stores will deliver to your hotel or boat.

Liquor Guavaberry Emporium, 8-10 Front St, is the best place to taste and buy the local liqueur, neat or in cocktail mixes.

▲▲ Activities and tours

Saint-Martin/Sint Maarten *p545, map p546*

Cycling

Authentic French Tours, Marigot, St-Martin, T590-(0)590-870511, frog.legs@wanadoo.fr. Mountain bike tours or just rental.

L2R (Location 2 roues), Galerie Commerciale Baie Nettlé, St-Martin, T590-(0)590- 872059, www.L2R-rentascoot.com. Mountain bikes from US$10 a day and scooters from US$20.

Tri-Sport, Simpson Bay, Sint Maarten, T599-5454384, www.trisportsxm.com. Bike rental and tours, also kayaks.

Diving

There are a dozen dive operators on the island offering a full range of courses. Boats are often small with no shade.

Blue Ocean, Baie Nettlé, St-Martin, T590-(0)590-878973, www.blueocean.ws. They have a fast boat for no more than 12 divers. As well as local sites they also go to Anguilla, St-Barth and Tintamarre. A snorkelling trip costs €23, a single dive €42 and a PADI Open Water course, €375.

Dive Safaris, in Philipsburg and in Simpson Bay, T599-5452501, Philipsburg, T5429001,www.divestmaarten.com. Platform boat for completing confined dives during courses. Single tank dive US$44 without gear, PADI Open Water certification US$360.

Ocean Explorers Dive Centre, Simpson Bay Beach, Sint Maarten, T599-5445252, www.stmaartendiving.com. LeRoy French runs this friendly outfit, offering PADI and NAUI courses for all levels, 2 dives daily except Sun, US$45 per dive, no more than 8 divers on the boat or 6 for resort courses, English, French, Spanish and German spoken.

Fishing

For fishing there are numerous boats available for a whole (US$750-950) or half (US$350-500) day from **Bobby's Marina**,

Pelican Marina, Dock Maarten (Great Bay Marina), the **Marina Port Royale**, **Marina Anse Marcel** or **Marina Oyster Pond**. Arrangements can be made through the hotels or ask the tourist offices for a list of operators. Marlin, barracuda, dolphin fish and tuna are the best catches. Game fishing tournaments are held all year round. The **St-Martin Billfish Tournament** is in Jun, attracting competitors from other islands and a lot of activity around Marigot waterfront. **Taylor Made**, Simpson Bay, Sint Maarten, T599-5527539, www.stmartinstmaarten .com/taylormade. The captain, Dougie, has been fishing since he was 9 and is expert at finding mahi mahi, wahoo, or tuna. Also trips for non-fisherfolk.

Golf
Mullet Bay Resort, Sint Maarten, www.stmaartengolf.com. For tee times call the golf shop, T599-5452850 ext 1850. There is an 18-hole par 70 championship golf course at Mullet Bay Resort, which stretches along the shores of Mullet Pond and Simpson Bay Lagoon. The resort is still closed after hurricane damage several years ago (although there are plans to redevelop the area following resolution of a long-running court case) and maintenance to the course has been lacking. Green fees are high for what you get, at US$93 for 18 holes for a non-resident, but it is busy at weekends.

Hiking
There are 40 km of trails for hiking, most of which are old paths used by settlers and slaves. They vary in length from 1 km to 6.5 km through inland or coastal scenery. For information contact **Association Action Nature**, T590-(0)590-879787, http://sxm.rando.free.fr, which has an information booth at the top of Pic Paradise, or the **Dutch Hiking Club**, T599-5424917.

Horse riding
Bayside Riding Club, route du Galion, Orient Bay, St-Martin, T590-(0)590-873664 (Dutch side T599-5576822), www.baysideridingclub.com. Beach rides (US$50 for 1 hr, US$70 for 2 hrs), pony rides and riding lessons. Catering for all levels, horse vacation leasing, western and English tack, variety of horses, many rescued,

including rehabilitated race horses. No more than 12 in a group, 6 horses/riders per guide. **Lucky Stables**, 2 Tray Bay Drive, in Cape Bay, Sint Maarten, T599-5445255, www.luckystable.com. Takes groups on a 2-hr trail and beach ride, 3 rides a day at 0930, 1500 and 2030, US$50 per person, children under 12 US$30.

Running
Road Runners Club, Sint Maarten (contact Rose), T599-5567815. A fun run of 5-10 km every Wed at 1730 and Sun at 1830, starting from the **Pelican Resort & Casino** car park. On Sun at 0700 there are 2, 20-km runs. There are monthly races with prizes and an annual relay race around the island to relive the legendary race between the Dutch and the French when they divided the island.

Sailing
Bobby's Marina, Philipsburg, Sint Maarten, T599-5422366, www.bobbysmarina.com. A popular excursion is match racing on *Canada II*, *True North*, *True North IV* or *Stars and Stripes*, boats from the Americas Cup, US$70, races daily, 3 hours.
St Maarten Yacht Club, Simpson Bay, Sint Maarten, T599-5442079, www.smyc.com. Other regattas held are for catamarans, match racing with charter boats, windsurfing, etc. For information contact Mirian Ebbers, or ask Robbie Ferron at Budget Marine in Cole Bay, T599-5443134, www.budgetmarine.com.

Day sails The *Swaliga II*, a motor catamaran (www.swaliga2.com, US$55 per adult, US$30 per child under 12, plus US$9 port charge, optional US$35 for lunch and island tour) sails Wed, Fri to **St-Barts** from Dock Maarten (formerly Great Bay Marina), Philipsburg, in front of Chesterfields Restaurant. Snorkelling stop at Ile Fourche on return journey. On Tue, Thu, they sail to **Anguilla** (US$80 adults, US$40 children, plus Anguilla port fee, including lunch, bar drinks, snacks and snorkelling gear) Take passports. Also the 70-ft motor catamaran, *Quicksilver*, and others which can be booked through Dockside Management (T599-5423436-7, www.docksidemanagement.net) or hotels. The *Golden Eagle*, a new wing mast 76-ft catamaran, sails to **Tintamarre** from Dock Maarten (Great Bay Marina), 4 hrs, US$50 pp, breakfast on board, snorkelling gear, T599-

5430068, www.sailingsxm.com. On Fri they do a round island trip, going from Philipsburg to Tintamarre, lunch in Grand Case, then to Marigot and back to Philipsburg, US$99.

Watersports
Club Nathalie Simon, Orient Beach, St-Martin, T590-(0)590-294157, www.gokitesurfing.com. Windsurfing, kitesurfing and hobie cats on the east coast. **Kontiki Watersport**, Orient Bay, St-Martin, T590-(0)590-874689, www.sxm-game.com. Wave runners, jet ski, parasailing, snorkelling equipment, banana boat and water taxi service to offshore islands.

● Transport

Saint-Martin/Sint Maarten *p545, map p546*
Air
The international airport is **Princess Juliana**, at Simpson Bay. A new terminal opened in Nov 2006 with duty-free shops, restaurants, bar and spa. Flight information T599-5455757. A **taxi** into Philipsburg costs US$10-15 and to Marigot US$15.

   From Europe KLM and **Air Holland** from Amsterdam, **Air France** and **Corsair** from Paris.

   From North America American Airlines from New York and Miami (and San Juan), **US Airways** from Philadelphia and Charlotte, **United Airlines** from Chicago, **Continental**) from Newark, **Delta** from Atlanta, **GWV** from Boston. **Air Transat** from Toronto, Montreal, Vancouver, Calgary, Halifax, **Air Canada**, **Conquest** and **Signature Vacations** also from Toronto.

   From the Caribbean There are many from Anguilla, Antigua, Barbados, Curaçao, Dominica, Fort-de-France, Jamaica, Nevis, Pointe-à-Pitre, Port of Spain, Saba, St-Barthélemy, USVI (St Croix and St Thomas), St Eustatius, St Kitts, Puerto Rico, Santo Domingo and the British Virgin Islands (Tortola), with a variety of regional and international carriers. If you have arrived at Juliana airport and have a **Winair** connection for another island, the check-in desk is now in the new baggage hall, so you don't have to exit after collecting your bags. Simply check in and proceed to the departure lounge, but stay alert as they don't always announce the flight and Winair can leave 30 mins early or late.

Espérance Airport information, T590-(0)590-875303. **Air Caraïbes** from Fort-de-France and Pointe-à-Pitre. **St Barth Commuter** from St-Barts. **Héliocéan**, for helicopter links and tours, Daniel Hazard, T590-(0)590-871192.

   Airline offices Most offices are on the Dutch side at Juliana Airport, **American Airlines**, T599-5452040. **Air France**, T599-545 4212, 590-(0)590-510202. **Caribbean Airlines**, T599-5454646. **Continental**, T599-5453444. **KLM**, T599-5454747. **Caribbean Star/LIAT**, T599-5454203. **US Airways**, T599-5454344. **Winair**, reservations, T599-5454230, flight information, T599-5454210, 800-6344907.

Boat
There are no long-distance sea communications except cruise ships which usually stay 5-9 hrs. Boats to **Anguilla**, **Saba** and **St-Barts**, leave from the French side. **Voyager**, T590-(0)590-871068, www.voyager-st-barths.com, daily high-speed ferries leave from Marigot (75 mins, 2 daily Mon-Sat) and Captain Oliver's marina, Oyster Pond (40 mins, 2-4 daily) to **St-Barts**. Credit cards accepted. Look out for special deals. See Saba, page 570 for details of ferries to **Saba**. Ferries from Marigot Waterfront to Anguilla leave at least every 30 mins.

Bus
There is a fairly regular bus service from 0700 until 2400 between **Philipsburg** and **Marigot** (US$1.50), **French Quarters** and **St Peters**, and from Marigot to **Grand Case** on the French side. After 2000 there are few buses. The best place to catch a bus is on Back St. Buses run along Back St and Pondfill and in towns only stop at bus stops. Outside towns, however, just wave to stop a bus. Fare is usually US$1 in town, US$1.50 for short trips, US$3 for long trips. There is no regular bus service between Philipsburg and the airport although the route to **Mullet Bay Resort** passes the airport. Buses on this route run mostly at the beginning and the end of the working day (although there are a few during the day) and drivers may refuse to take you, or charge extra, if you have a lot of luggage.

Car and bike
Foreign and international driving licences are accepted. Drive on the right. The speed limit is 40 kph in urban areas, 60 kph outside town, unless there are other signs.

Car hire Many car hire companies have offices at the airport or in the hotels; free pick-up and delivery are standard and you can leave the car at the airport on departure. Prices range from US$35-55 per day. Companies include all the international names and several local firms: **Cannegie Car Rental**, T599-542 2397; **Empress Rent-a-Car** T599- 5443637; **Safari Rentals**, T599-5453185, safari@sint maarten.net; **Alamo**, T599- 5455546; **Paradise**, T599-5453737. Both tourist offices have full lists.

Scooter/motorbike hire **Super Honda**, Bush Rd Cul-de-Sac, T5425712; **Moped Cruising**, Front St, T5422330; **OK Scooter Rental**, at Maho Beach Hotel and Cupecoy Resort, T5442115, 5444334; **Concordia**, T871424, from US$20 per day including helmets and insurance. If you have a heavyweight motorcycle licence, you can rent a Harley Davidson for US$112 a day at **Super Bikes**, 71 Union Rd, Cole Bay.

Taxi

There are plenty of taxis, which are not metered so first check the fare, which is fixed according to your destination (the island is divided into zones) and number of people. Tip 10-15%. Trips to beaches or tours of the island can be arranged with taxi drivers. From Philipsburg (or Marigot) to **Juliana Airport** US$12, to **Dawn Beach** US$18, **Mullet Bay** US$16, Marigot to **Grand Case** US$10, Marigot to **Oyster Pond**, US$25, all for 2 passengers, additional passengers US$4, luggage extra, children under 12 half price. Night tariffs are an extra 25% 2200-2400, an extra 50% 2400-0600. Pick up taxi at the square next to the Courthouse in **Philipsburg**, T599-5422359, **Juliana Airport**, T599-5454317, or **dispatch office**, T147, in **Marigot**, T590-(0)590-875654, in **Grand Case**, T590-(0)590-877579.

❶ Directory

Saint-Martin/Sint Maarten *p545, map p546*

Banks Banks on St-Martin include **Banque des Antilles Françaises (BDAF)** and **Banque Française Commerciale (BFC)**. There are exchange houses for changing from euros to dollars in rue du Kennedy, Marigot, and in the Marina Royale complex. In Philipsburg on Sint Maarten, **Scotiabank**, **Windward Islands Bank**, **FirstCaribbean International Bank**, **RBTT Bank**, **Antilles Banking Corporation**. There are lots of ATMs, including one at the airport taxi rank dispensing guilders, US dollars or euro. **Internet** **Tel Net**, Front St, Philipsburg, 0730-1200, internet US$3 per hr, also phones and phone cards. **Cyberzone**, Emmaplein, Philipsburg, opposite Jump Up casino, internet café upstairs, lots of computers, good comfy seats, US$2.50 per hr. **Notions**, **The Mailbox** on the airport road near Simpson Bay. **St Maarten Yacht Club Marina Business Centre** and **Simpson Bay Marina Business Centre** have computers and email service. **Starbucks** coffee shop in the Maho area has a cybercafé. **Medical services** **Concordia Hospital**, Saint-Martin T590-(0)590-295757/ 522525. **Ambulance**, T590-(0)590-292934/ 771391. **Cay Hill**, Sint Maarten, T140, or T599-5431111. 60 beds, a haemodialysis department and 24-hr emergency services. A helicopter airlift to Puerto Rico is available for extreme medical emergencies. **Post** The **French post office**, 25 rue de la Liberté, will hold mail, but only for 2 weeks. Letters sent c/o **Capitainerie Marina Port La Royale**, Marigot, will be kept 4-6 weeks. 2 safe places for holding mail are **Bobby's Marina**, PO Box 383, **Philipsburg and Island Water World**, PO Box 234, Cole Bay. It is not possible to send a parcel by sea, only airmail which is expensive. **Telephone** To call the Dutch side from the French use the international code 00599 followed by the 7-digit number. To call the French side from the Dutch use the international code 00590- 590 followed by a 6-digit number. Calls from one side of the island to the other are expensive. When calling within the Netherlands Antilles, dial 0 before the 7-digit number. There are several telephone booths on the **French side** but they only take telephone cards. 120 units for €13.7, sold at the post office and at the bookshop opposite. There are 8 telephones on the square in Marigot and 2 in Grand Case in front of the little pier. Telephone cards for the **Dutch side** of the island can be bought at **Landsradio** (Tel em) telecommunications office in Cannegieter St, open 0700-2400, or at Landsradio's offices at Simpson Bay, Cole Bay and St Peter's. Note that card phones at Juliana Airport, although marked as 'téléphone' and displaying instructions in French, do not work with French phone cards. The GSM network covers both the Dutch and French sides.

Background

History

The Amerindians who originally settled on the island named it Sualiga, meaning land of salt. The belief that Columbus discovered the island on his second voyage in 1493 is disputed, with historians now claiming it was Nevis he named St Martin of Tours, and that later Spanish explorers misinterpreted his maps. The Spanish were not interested in settling the island and it wasn't until 1629 that French colonists finally arrived in the north, and 1631 that the Dutch were attracted to the salt ponds of

❦ *See also backgrounds to the Netherlands Antilles, the ABC Islands and the French Antilles.*

the south. In the absence of the departed Caribs, the two nationalities lived amicably together. Spain then reconsidered and occupied Sint Maarten from 1633-1648, fending off an attack by Peter Stuyvesant in 1644 which cost him his leg.

When the Spanish left, the Dutch and French settlers returned and after a few territorial skirmishes, they divided the island between them with the signing of the 23 March 1648 Treaty of Mount Concordia. Popular legend has it that the division of the island was settled with a race starting from Oyster Pond: The Frenchman went north and the Dutchman went south, but the Frenchman walked faster because he drank only wine while the Dutchman's penchant for genever (a drink similar to gin) slowed him down. Since 1648, however, Sint Maarten has changed hands 16 times, including brief occupations by the British, but the Dutch-French accord has been peaceably honoured at least since it was last revised in 1839.

At the height of its colonial period, sugar cane and livestock were the main agricultural activities, although the poor soil and lack of rain meant they were not very profitable. The abolition of slavery in 1863 broke up the plantation system and the population began to decline as ex-slaves left to look for work elsewhere. Most of the salt produced from the Great Salt Pond behind Philipsburg was exported to the USA and neighbouring islands, but by 1949 this industry had also ended and a further exodus to other islands took place. The remaining population survived on subsistence farming, fishing and remittances from relatives abroad.

However, in 50 years the island has become unrecognizable. Hotels, resorts, villas and guesthouses now line the shore and there is no bay untouched by tourism. Cruise ship passengers, day trippers and stayover visitors are attracted by the duty-free shopping, casinos and a wide range of accommodation, as well as the beaches and watersports. Little of historical interest remains, but this has not hindered the tourist industry, which is among the most successful in the region. For those who want more than sun, sand and sea, the island's well-developed transport links make it an excellent jumping-off place for visiting other islands.

In 1994 the electorate on the Dutch side were asked whether they wished to remain part of the Netherlands Antilles, have separate status within the kingdom (like Aruba), have complete integration with the Netherlands, or be independent. At the referendum, 59.8% voted for the status quo, while about 30% wanted separate status. This was the lowest vote in favour of remaining in the Federation, compared with 90.6% in St Eustatius, 86.3% in Saba, 88% in Bonaire and 73.6% (in 1993) in Curaçao. In April 2000 the

❦ *France and the Netherlands jointly monitor air and sea traffic around the island.*

electorate once again was asked whether they wished to remain part of the once Netherlands Antilles or become independent. A majority of around 60% voted for 'status aparte'. Changes are gradually being implemented throughout the Netherlands Antilles, an entity which will cease to exist, see ABC islands, page 983.

Geography

The island is shared amicably by the Dutch, who have the southern 37 sq km of the island, and the French, calling their half Saint-Martin, who own the northern 52 sq km, an arrangement settled by the 1648 Treaty of Mount Concordia. The salt ponds in the south of the island attracted the Dutch and during the early 19th century the island enjoyed modest prosperity. The Dutch side of the island has the main airport and seaport and the majority of tourists. The west part of the island is low-lying and mostly taken up by the Simpson Bay Lagoon, with a safe anchorage for small craft. The lagoon is parted from the sea by a thin strip of land on which the airport has been built. The rest of the Dutch part is hilly and dry and covered with scrub but it can soon turn green after rain.

People

The population of at least 77,000 (41,000 in Sint Maarten and 36,000 in Saint-Martin) has mushroomed with the tourist boom: the 1950 Sint Maarten census gave the total population as 1484. While many of the residents were formerly ex-patriates who returned to their island, there is a large proportion who have come from other Caribbean islands to work. Few people speak Dutch, the official language of Sint Maarten, although Papiamento has increased with the migration of people from the ABC Dutch islands. Nearly everybody speaks English and there is a large Spanish-speaking contingent of workers from the Dominican Republic. The French side is noticeably Gallic and fewer speak English.

Flora and fauna

In 1997 the **Nature Foundation Sint Maarten** ① *T599-5420267, www.naturefoundation sxm.org*, was set up, with assistance from the WWF, to protect and manage natural parks and provide education on their significance. Two parks form the initial programme, a marine park covering all the coastal waters of the Dutch side from Oyster Bay to Cupecoy Beach and some adjacent coastline, and a hillside park in the Cul de Sac area. A **Nature Reserve** ① *T590-(0)590-290272*, was set up in the French part in 1998, with over 2900 ha underwater and 170 ha on land in a strip along the coast in the northeast. Three large ecosystems included in the reserve are mangrove swamp, sea grass beds and coral cliffs, with the aim of maintaining biodiversity, flora and fauna and water quality.

Saba → *Country code: 599. Colour map 3, B1. Population: 1,500.*

This tiny Dutch island Saba, pronounced 'Say-bah', rises out of the sea, green and lush. It is the smallest of the three Netherlands Antilles in the Leewards group, and despite some development it is still deserving of its official title, the 'Unspoiled Queen'. An extinct volcano, its peak is aptly named Mount Scenery. Underwater, the landscape is equally spectacular and divers treasure the marine park, noted for its 'virginity'. When not under water, visitors find walking rewarding. Ancient trails weave their way around the island, the most stunning being the 1,064 irregular steps up Mount Scenery through different types of tropical vegetation according to altitude. Lodging is expensive, in small, friendly hotels, guesthouses and cottages, where you won't need a key – there is no crime. ⏩ *For Sleeping, Eating and other listings, see pages 566-570.*

Ins and outs

Getting there From Sint Maarten, Saba is 20 minutes by air or 1½ hours by sea. Saba claims to have the world's shortest commercial airport runway (400 m). Large aircraft cannot be accommodated. Planes do not land in bad weather in case they skid off the end. Sit up front behind the pilots for an excellent view of Saba when landing. On windy days the boat crossing can be very rough.

Getting around There are no buses on the island but you can hire a jeep or car. It is about 1½ hour's hike from the airport up to Windwardside, through different scenery, vegetation and climate. There are taxis at the airport and a few others around the island. They can be hired for tours (US$40) and the drivers are knowledgeable guides.

Sights

There are four picture-book villages on Saba, connected by a single spectacular 10.5-km road which begins at the airport and ends at the pier. The road itself is a feat of engineering, designed and built in the 1940s by Josephus Lambert Hassell (1906-1983), who studied road construction by correspondence course after Dutch engineers said it was impossible to build a road on Saba. From the airport, the road rises to **Hell's Gate** and then on through banana plantations to **Windwardside**, where most of the hotels and shops are situated. There is a small museum, a bank and post office. **Lambee's Place**, originally the home of Josephus Lambert Hassell, has been redeveloped into a little shopping precinct and now houses **Sea Saba Dive Shop**, **Peanut Art Gallery**, **El Momo Folk Art** and **Y2K Café** (bakery, bar and grill). The **Harry L Johnson Museum** ① *Mon-Fri 1000-1200, 1300-1600, US$2*, was once a sea captain's house, built in 1840 and a typical, tiny, four-room Saban house on one floor. It is now filled with antique furniture and family memorabilia. The kitchen is in its original state. Croquet is played on Sunday afternoon in the museum grounds.

The road goes on past Kate's Hill, Peter Simon's Hill and Big Rendezvous to **St John's**, where the schools are, and which has a wonderful view of St Eustatius, then climbs over the mountain and drops down to **The Bottom**, the island's seat of government, with a population of 350 which doubles when the students are in residence at the Medical University. The Bottom is on a plateau, 245 m above the sea. It can be hot, as there is little breeze. The 1935 Sacred Heart Roman Catholic Church has a magnificent mural around the altar by Heleen Cornet incorporating local plants, architecture and children. The pretty 1919 Wesleyan Holiness Church is being restored

Saba

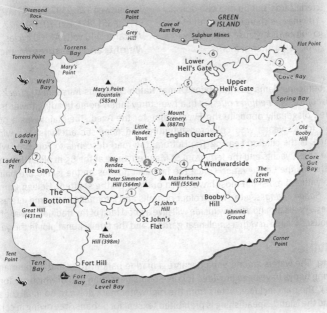

Sleeping 🛏	Nature trails ○	Mount Scenery Stairwell **4**
Ecolodge Rendez-Vous **2**	Crispeen Track **1**	Sandy Cruz Track **5**
Gate House **3**	Flat Point **2**	Sulphur Mine Track **6**
Queen's Garden Resort **5**	Maskehorne Hill Trail **3**	The Ladder **7**

⁞ Touching down

Boat information (Dutch flag) Go ashore to clear immigration with the Harbourmaster at Fort Bay or with the Police in The Bottom. Fort Bay has three free moorings but it is rolly with southeast winds. The Ladder and Well's Bay moorings (yellow buoys) are available for use by yachts for US$2 per person for anchoring and snorkelling, and US$3 per person for each dive you take on your own. Use a strong line and plenty of scope. Marine patrol will collect fees and explain the rules and regulations. The marine park has a leaflet with map of anchorages and dive sites.

Business hours Banks: 0900-1530; **Offices**: 0900-1200, 1400-1800; **Shops** 0900-1700.

Currency The florin or Antillean guilder is the local currency, but US dollars are accepted. Hotels and dive shops accept (Visa and Mastercard) credit cards, but no one else does. You may be charged extra for using credit cards because of the slow processing arrangements.

Departure tax Airport departure tax is US$5 to Netherlands Antilles, US$20 elsewhere.

Documents Saba is a free port so there are no customs formalities.

Emergency numbers Hospital: T4163288.

Official time Atlantic Standard Time, 4 hrs behind GMT, 1 hr ahead of EST.

Public holidays New Year's Day, Good Fri, Easter Sun and Mon, Queen's Day (30 Apr), Labour Day (1 May), Ascension Day (Thu), Saba Day (Dec 7), Christmas Day, Boxing Day.

Tourist office Saba Tourist Board (Glenn Holm), Windwardside, PO Box 15, T599-4162231-2, www.saba tourism.com. Mon-Fri 0800-1200, 1300-1700. Plenty of leaflets and maps, and friendly and helpful staff.

Tourist office overseas Netherlands: Antillenhuis, Badhuisweg 175, 2597JP Den Haag, T31-70-3512811, F31-70-3512722.

Voltage 110 volts AC, 60 cycles.

Weights and measures Metric.

after hurricane damage. The **Major Osmar Ralph Simmons Museum** ① *check with tourist office for opening hours*, is in a two-storey family home heading towards The Ladder, diagonally opposite the Every Home for the Aged. The Major was a police officer for 40 years, who collected furniture and domestic artefacts. His widow, Carmen, is the curator. Leaving The Bottom, the road descends to **Fort Bay**, where cruise ships, yachts and the ferry from St Maarten arrive at the 85-m pier. Dive shops and the Marine Conservation Office are here. All houses on the island are painted white with red roofs and most have green outlines on the shutters. Heleen Cornet's book, *Saban Cottages*, gives watercolour portraits and information on some interesting houses. A walk around Windwardside will give a good idea of the traditional way of life, the houses walled in with a small neat garden, and the family burial plot in the yard.

Activities

Diving The waters around Saba became a marine park in 1987 and 30 permanent mooring buoys have been provided for dive boats (less than half of which are for big boats). The park includes waters from the highwater mark down to 60 m all the way around the island. Spearfishing is prohibited (except for Sabans, free diving in certain areas), as is the removal of coral or shells (Sabans are limited to 20 conches per person a year without the use of scuba). Saba has no permanent beaches so diving and snorkelling are from boats, mostly along the calmer south and west coasts.

The west coast from **Tent Bay** to **Ladder Bay**, together with **Man of War shoals**, **Diamond Rock** and the sea offshore comprise the main dive sites, where anchoring and fishing are prohibited. From Ladder Bay to Torrens Point is an all-purpose recreational zone which includes Saba's only beach at **Well's Bay**, a pebbly stretch of coast with shallow water for swimming and areas for diving, fishing and boat anchorage. The beach comes and goes with the seasons and ocean currents but when it is there it is scenic and good for snorkelling. The concrete road ends here but there are no facilities, so take your own refreshments and arrange for a taxi to pick you up later. Another anchorage is west of Fort Bay. East of Fort Bay along the south, east and north coast all the way to Torrens Point is a multiple-use zone where fishing and diving are permitted. Torrens Point is a snorkeller's favourite with an alley through the rocks and a tunnel for divers. Some of the most-visited dive sites are **Third Encounter**, **Outer Limits**, Diamond Rock and Man of War. **Tent Reef** is also a favourite. **Ladder Labyrinth** is a dive site which is good for snorkelling.

> **❖** *There is a picnic place overlooking Ladder Bay.*

Dive operators collect the mandatory visitor fees to help maintain the park which is now self-financing. The **Marine Park Office** ① *T/F599-4163295, www.sabapark.org, is at Fort Bay.* The *Guide to the Saba Marine Park*, by Tom Van't Hof, published by the Saba Conservation Foundation, is highly recommended, available at dive shops, the museum and souvenir shops, US$15. There are many dive sites of 27-30 m; if you are doing three dives a day you must follow your dive tables and stay within your limit. It is recommended that you take every fourth day off and rest or go hiking. Summer visibility is 23-30 m with water temperatures of about 30°C, while winter visibility increases to 38 m and water temperatures fall to 24°C.

Not much fishing is done in these waters, so there is a wide range of sizes and varieties of fish to be seen. Tarpon and barracuda of up to 2.5 m are common, as are giant sea turtles. From January to April humpback whales pass by on their migration south and can be encountered by divers, while in the winter dive boats are often accompanied by schools of porpoises. Smaller, tropical fish are not in short supply, and, together with bright red, orange, yellow and purple giant tube

> **❖** *Saba has a four-person recompression chamber at Fort Bay, operated by medical school people.*

sponges and different coloured coral, are a photographer's delight. Divers are not allowed to feed the fish as it has been proved to alter fish behaviour and encourage the aggressive species.

Hiking Before the road was built people got about Saba by donkey or on foot, and there are still numerous steep trails and stone steps linking villages which make strenuous, yet satisfying, walking. The **Saba Conservation Foundation** (see Flora and fauna page 571) preserves and marks trails for those who like a challenge and for those who prefer a gentle stroll. All of them are accessible from the road and many can be done without a guide. However, they are all on private land and you are requested not to stray off the tracks. Named trails include: **The Ladder**, **Crispeen Track**, **Maskerhorne Hill Trail**, **Mount Scenery Stairwell**, **Sandy Cruz Track**, **Sulphur Mine Track** and **Flat Point**. Before you set off, register at the **Saba Trail Shop** ① *Windwardside, T4162630, Tue-Fri 0930-1530, Sat-Sun 1000-1400*, where you pay the US$3 fee for park maintenance and receive a disk entitling you to hike on any trail. US$1 for hire of walking stick recommended.

The most spectacular hike is probably the one from Windwardside up 1064 steps of varying sizes and intervals to the crest of **Mount Scenery**, best done on a clear day otherwise you end up in the clouds. It is a hard slog, 1½ hours each way, but a road goes part of the way up if you want to avoid the steps from Windwardside to Rendezvous. The summit has now been cleared (**Cable & Wireless** have built a telecommunications tower there by helicopter drops) and there is a spectacular view

● Saba's rugged, volcanic terrain is replicated underwater where there are mountains, swim
● throughs, lava flows, overhangs, reefs, walls, pinnacles and elkhorn coral forests.

Leeward Islands Saba

down to Windwardside and the surrounding isles if it is not cloudy. Take a sweater and waterproof jacket, it can be very rough and slippery after rain. There are lots of birds, lizards, snakes and land crabs, and the botanical changes are noticeable as you climb. There is also a five-hour walk through a variety of ecosystems circling Mount Scenery. Starting from Windwardside, walk up the road to Upper Hell's Gate, then take the Sandy Cruz trail to the banana plantation. Proceed on the Sandy Cruz trail extension to Troy Hill, where you meet the road which takes you to The Bottom. A short walk up the road out of The Bottom towards Windwardside brings you to the start of the Crispeen Track, which is followed back to Windwardside.

A very nice lookout point is from **Booby Hill**, up the 66 terraced steps to the Booby Hill Peak. **The Ladder** is a long path of stone steps from the shore up to The Bottom, up which all provisions used to be hauled from boats before the road was built. For the **Sulphur Mine** take the **Sandy Cruz Trail**. Walk for about 20 minutes until you get to a sign for a turning to the right on the **All Too Far Trail** leading down to the remains of the old mines and the cliffs of the north coast, with splendid scenery. There is a shorter route starting in Lower Hell's Gate following part of the **North Coast Trail**. Mining was discontinued in 1915 and the Sulphur Mining Company donated the land to the SCF for a national park, which now covers 43 ha (100 acres). It is possible to carry on along the north coast to **Mary's Point** and Wells Bay. However, the SCF does not recommend you go far along this old path as several people have got lost. You are advised to take a guide. There are magnificent views of the northern coastal cliffs, but there is a danger of rock falls set off by feral goats which may be above you.

The tourist office has leaflets on the nature trails and hiking on Saba, but in many places a guide is recommended. Interpretative and directional signs are variable because of weather damage. *Saban Trails... A Walking & Hiking Guide* published by the Saba Conservation Foundation, gives information on 11 trails and the flora, fauna and historical remains. However, it was published in 1998 before Hurricane Lenny.

Sleeping

Saba *p562, maps p563 and p567*

Hotels do not usually give you a room key; there is no crime. The 4 policemen on the island boast that the cells are only used as overspill when the hotels are full!

There are no resort hotels yet on Saba and even the most expensive are small and friendly. Dec-Apr is the busiest and most expensive season, although divers come throughout the year. Jul is also busy because of Carnival and students return from foreign universities. All the hotels offer dive packages. There is a 5% room tax, sometimes a 3% turnover tax (TOT) and usually a 10-15% service charge. The **tourist office** has a list of 1- to 3-bed cottages and apartments for rent from US$50 a night, which can be let on a weekly or monthly basis.

LL Queen's Garden Resort, Troy Hill, The Bottom, T599-4163494, www.queensaba.com. Spectacular view overlooking The Bottom through the mountains to the sea below. 12, 1- or 2-bedroom very expensive luxury suites, fully equipped, beautiful bedrooms with antique furniture from Europe. 9 have a jacuzzi with a view. In the garden there is a horizon pool. Discounts for weekly rates, lots of packages available. **King's Crown** gourmet restaurant is slightly down the hill, sit inside or outside under the mango tree and the jasmine. French cuisine with Caribbean flair using local fresh ingredients and interesting wines. Poolside barbecues, dinner and dance, Sun brunch in season.

L-AL Juliana's, Windwardside, T599-4162269, www.julianas-hotel.com. Run by Johanna van't Hof and Wim Schutten, the hotel is scattered in several buildings. 9 rooms, the smaller ones with a garden view are a bit dark, but have a/c, the larger ones with a sea view have a balcony with hammocks, fridge, some kitchenettes, cable TV. 1-bedroom apartment and 2 renovated 2-bedroom Saban cottages. A Common Room has 2 computers for internet access (or there are wi-fi hotspots), while yoga and dive classes are held here, and there is a book exchange. The pool and **Tropics** café and bar are across the road. Fri is movie and burger night, US$10,

with a screen hung between 2 flagpoles.
AL The Cottage Club, Windwardside,
T599-4162486, www.cottage-club.com.
Owned by the Johnson family who also own
the supermarket. 10 white cottages with red
roofs in local style, on a hill with wonderful
views of Mount Scenery, English Quarter and
the sea. All rooms are the same, open to the
roof, with 1 or 2 beds, full kitchen for self-
catering, good-sized bathroom, TV, phone.
The swimming pool is in a lovely private area
with rainforest trees all around and a view
down to the end of the runway. No
restaurant but several in walking distance.
AL-A El Momo Cottages, T/F599-4162265,
www.elmomo.com. For sale in 2007 but still
operating. Halfway up Jimmy's Hill, 5 mins
from Windwardside. 60 steps up to the pool
area, many more up to the wooden cottages
built in rough Saban style and 130 to the top
one with the best view and the most privacy,
so be prepared. Superb view, beautiful
garden. The rooms vary, private or shared
bathrooms, with or without kitchenette,
simple but clean, friendly. Great breakfast for

US$7.50 with home-made bread and yoghurt,
snacks and drinks available, family-style
dinners once a week, reservations essential.
AL-A Scout's Place, Windwardside,
T599-4162205, www.sabadivers.com Run by
Barbara and Wolfgang, of Germany. Price
includes breakfast, tax and service, lots of
packages available. 4 rooms in the former
government guesthouse, 10 rooms in a newer
wing, all with cable TV, in-room internet
access for your own laptop, fan and fridge.
Also 2-bedroom Scout's Pirate Cottage, sleeps
4-6, fully self-contained with use of hotel's
facilities. Scout's Place is simple and relaxed,
with beautiful views, a pool, restaurant with
daily specials, 10% discount for hotel guests
on all meals, bar (happy hour 1700-1800), Fri
night karaoke, and boutique. Dive packages
available (dive shop in Fort Bay).
A Ecolodge Rendez-Vous, T599-4163348,
www.ecolodge-saba.com. 5-min hike from
the nearest road or a 20-min climb up steps
from Windwardside on the way to Mount
Scenery, but a quad bike will carry your bags
(Eco the donkey became too stubborn). Out in

Windwardside

To Hell's Gate

Roman Catholic
Church of St Paul's
Conversion

Lambee's Place
El Momo Folk Art

Sea Saba Dive Shop   Peanut Gallery   First Caribbean
Lambee's Place

To St John's

Holy Trinity Anglican

Harry L Johnson Museum

RBTT

Library

The Level

Booby Hill

N

0 metres   50
0 yards   50

Sleeping
Cottage Club **1**
El Momo Cottages **2**
Juliana's & Tropics Café **3**

Scout's Place & Saba
Divers **4**

Eating
Brigadoon **1**
Saba's Treasure **4**
Y2K Café **3**

the middle of nowhere, very rural, 11 Saba-style simple cabins sleeping 2-4 (2 downstairs, 2 in the loft), all individually decorated, solar shower bags, solar lighting, composting toilets, balcony and hammock. There is a sweat lodge (sauna), like a leather patchwork turtle, cold tub and hot tub and a hand-dug 8ft x 12ft pool. Excellent restaurant using home-grown organic fruit, vegetables and herbs. Indonesia rijstafel Tue night. Family-run by artist Heleen Cornet, conservationist Tom van't Hof, their son, Bernt, who is a chef.

● Eating

Saba *p562, maps p563 and p567*
Many restaurants close by 2130, so eat early. Cuisine is fairly international with local fruit and vegetables. Pizzas and burgers are as readily available as catch of the day. If you are self-catering remember that the supply boat only comes in once a week, so check when that is so you can get things fresh. Supermarkets are small and carry a limited stock of a wide variety of items. **Saba Spice** is the local rum, very strong (150° proof) and mixed with spices, particularly cloves, and sugar.

♜♜♜ Gate House, Hell's Gate, T599-4162416. Breakfast, lunch and dinner. Food is taken very seriously here. The French hosts have lived in the USA, so the menu is a fusion of French and international with Saban touches, using lobster, lamb, pork and seafood. Excellent wine list, assistance given in choosing something to accompany your meal. Dining is in an old Saban house on a hillside and accommodation is available. Rooms in the main house, a villa and a cottage available (**AL**) including breakfast with fruit and home-made jam.

♜♜ Brigadoon, Windwardside, T599-4162380. Daily 1800-2100. In an old Saban house close to the centre of the village enjoying a good reputation with the locals. Dinner costs from US$10, lunch for groups by reservation only. International, Créole and Caribbean food, fresh seafood, lobster tank.

♜♜ Lollipop, St John's, T599-4163330. Breakfast, lunch or dinner. A small restaurant on the mountainside overlooking The Bottom on the way to St John's. Free taxi pick-up (waiter is also the driver), excellent 3-course meal, lobster, conch melts in the mouth, local cuisine including goat and land crab. A good place for lunch, you can walk it off on the trails.

♜♜ Rainforest Restaurant, at Ecolodge Rendez Vous, Windwardside, T599-4163888, www.ecolodge-saba.com. Breakfast, lunch and dinner. Situated along the Crispeen Trail just past the junction and rest halt for the Mt Scenery Trail. Either work up an appetite climbing the steps from the Trail Shop in Windwardside, or drive along to the end of the Mountain Road and walk 5 mins down from there. Wonderful fresh juices, guava from the garden, salads, sandwiches, fish, shrimp in red curry/coconut for lunch. The dinner menu has more entrées with barbeque ribs and steak. Lots of organic home grown fruit, vegetables and herbs, fresh and very tasty, plenty of vitamins. Accommodation available, see page 567.

♜♜ Saba's Treasure, Windwardside, T4162819. Mon-Sat 1000-2200. Pub atmosphere with historical theme, maps and old pictures on the walls, high pews, dark wood tables bound with fishing ropes. Popular thick crust pizzas baked in stone oven, US$7-11 depending on the size with extra toppings. Medical students come here to be filled up. Short menu of steak, shrimp, chicken and catch of the day, served with rice, fries or baked potato, followed by Saba lime pie or Saba spice walnut cake. 3 rooms available upstairs, sharing a living and dining room, kitchen and bathroom, or you can rent the whole place, separate entrance.

♜♜ Y2K Café, Lambee's Place, Windwardside, T4162538. Mon-Sat, 1100-1430, 1830-2030. Excellent casual restaurant, eat on the patio or under cover, a few steps away from the foot of the Mt Scenery trail. Extensive menu with salads, sandwiches and burgers, try the *Divers-up/Hikers-down* with mushrooms, onions, peppers, bacon, Swiss cheese and blue-cheese dressing. Main course prices range from US$11-15 and pasta from US$7.50-15.50. Fri is a special burger-and-salad day when you can choose your own toppings, burger platters from 1500-2030 with Heineken at US$1.

● Bars and clubs

Saba *p562, maps p563 and p567*
Most of the nightlife takes place at the restaurants. At **Scout's Place** on Fri night 2000-2330 there is karaoke. At **Tropics Café** at

Juliana's there is a movie on Fri night and steel pan on Sat. On Fri and Sat nights, La Bella Vita restaurant makes way for a disco, popular with all sections of the community, playing soca, reggae, rap and disco, loud. It's the only really late-night activity on the island. At weekends there are sometimes barbecues, steel bands and dances. Generally, though, the island is quiet at night.

Swinging Doors, Windwardside, T4162506. 0900-late. A bar with a split personality, part English pub, part Wild West saloon with its swinging doors. Food is available, with an eclectic menu, but the best meals are the barbeques on Tue and Fri nights, with ribs or chicken or a combo. Owner Eddie Hassell is a fount of information about life on Saba.

⊛ Festivals and events

Saba p562, maps p563 and p567
30 Apr Queen's Birthday, with ceremonies commemorating the coronation of Queen Beatrix and the Queen Mother's birthday.
Jul Carnival (Saba Summer Festival) is a week near the end of the month and is celebrated with jump-ups, music and costumed dancing, shows, food, games and contests including the Saba Hill Climb. There are parades on the last weekend and Carnival Mon at the end is a public holiday.
Dec Saba Days are a mini-carnival on the first weekend, with donkey races, dancing, steel bands, barbecues and other festivities.

○ Shopping

Saba p562, maps p563 and p567
Art galleries
There are several art galleries in Windwardside where local artists have their studios and sell their watercolours, oil paintings, prints and sculptures. Ask the tourist office for a leaflet.
Peanut Gallery, Lambee's Place, Windwardside, Saba, T599-4162509, judysaba@hotmail.com. Tue-Fri 1000-1700, Sat 1000-1600, Sun 1100-1500. Local and regional art and a few crafts.

Crafts
Jobean's Hot Glass Studio, Windwardside, Saba, T599-4162490, www.jobeanglass.com. Handmade coloured glass skilfully crafted into beads, mermaids, tiny frogs and lizards. Watch

the artists at work or sign up for a tutorial and have a go. Jewellery and glassware for sale.
The Saba Artisan Foundation, The Bottom, Saba. Local crafts have been developed by the foundation and include dolls, books and silk-screened textiles and clothing. The typical local drawn-thread work 'Saba lace' (also known as 'Spanish work' because it was learned by a Saban woman in a Spanish convent in Venezuela at the end of the last century) is sold at several shops on the island. Taxi drivers may make unofficial stops at the houses where Saba lace, dolls, pillows, etc, are made.

▲ Activities and tours

Saba p562, maps p563 and p567
Diving
The marine park fee/hyperbaric chamber fee is US$4 per person per dive, payable to dive shops.
Saba Deep, Fort Bay, T599-4163347, www.sabadeep.com. NAUI, PADI, SSI, TDI and IANTD instructors and a full-service dive centre with Nitrox and Drager Rebreathers. 3 dives daily and return to the harbour between dives for the surface interval. All your gear is washed and taken care of during your stay and loaded on the boat for you, or there is well-maintained rental equipment. Dive rates are US$60 single dive, US$110 double, US$150 triple, US$75 night, including all equipment, plus 6% tax and 4-6% fee for credit cards. Dive packages, accommodation and transfers, are available.
Saba Divers, Fort Bay, T599-4163840, www.sabadivers.com. Award-winning dive centre run by Wolfgang and Barbara Tooten, of Germany. PADI, SSI, DAN, CMAS courses offered in several languages, diving and accommodation packages available. An NRC facility with a Nitrox compressor offering Nitrox at no extra charge. 3 dives a day at 0930, 1130, 1330 and night dives on request, US$47 per dive with tank and weights unless you are a guest at Scout's Place or book a package. Other equipment US$10 a day. Special prices for yachties, who can be picked up from their boat, contact the office or the boats, Big Blue and Big Star, on VHF Ch 16.
Sea Saba Dive Centre (office and extensive retail shop), Lambee's Place, Windwardside, T599-4162246, www.seasaba.com (Fort Bay harbour depot for all rental equipment and compressors as well as a fabrication shop). PADI and NAUI courses from beginner to

divemaster and also Nitrox diving at US$59 a week, unlimited. **Sea Saba** has 2 large, 40-ft boats, but limits groups to 10 divers. 2 dives between 0930 and 1330 with the surface interval spent at Well's Bay for sunbathing, snorkelling or ocean kayaking. Drinks are available on board, some people take snacks. US$90 for 2 dives, including tax and equipment. Night dives on request.

Hiking

James Johnson, T599-4162630, the trails manager, does guided tours after 1500 weekdays and all day at weekends, US$40-50 per group, maximum 8. He knows the island intimately and local plant and animal names.

⊖ Transport

Saba *p562, maps p563 and p567*
Air

Winair, the only scheduled airline, has 5-6 daily 15-min 19-seater flights from St Maarten, some of which come via St Eustatius. You must reconfirm your return flight. Buy on-line at www.fly-winair.com.

Boat

A deep-water pier at Fort Bay allows cruise ships to call. Two ferries cross from Sint Maarten: *The Edge* is good for day trips or if you have overnighted in Sint Maarten; *Dawn II* leaves later, meaning that if you land at Juliana airport early afternoon you can get to Saba the same day by boat. **Dawn II**, T599-4163671, www.sabac transport.com. Ferry crossings Tue, Thu, Sat leaving Saba at 0630, returning from Dock Maarten, Philipsburg at 1700, one-way ticket

US$35, round trip US$60. A/c cabin with 22 seats. Get there 30 mins before departure. **The Edge**, T599-5442640, www.stmaarten-activities.com, sails Wed, Thu, Fri, Sat and Sun at 0900, check in 0815, from **Simpson Bay/Pelican Marina**, St Maarten, returns 1530, arrives St Maarten 1700, US$45 one way, US$65 return, children half price.

Car

Driving is on the right. **Car hire** at Caja's Car Rental, The Bottom, T499-4162318, takijah77@hotmail.com. Rates approximately US$50 per day. **Taxi** at the airport.

❶ Directory

Saba *p562, maps p563 and p567*
Banks There are no ATMs on the island. FirstCaribbean, Windwardside, T599-4162216. Mon-Fri 0830-1530, exchange, advances, transfers, TCs. RBTT, Windwardside, T599-4162454. Mon-Fri 0830-1530. **Internet** Island Communication Services Business Centre, next to RBTT, Windwardside, opposite Scout's Place and post office, Mon-Fri 1000- 1900, Sat 1000-1700, US$5 per 30 mins, also video rental. **Medical services** Hospital, T599-4163288. Doctor, Ms Anita Radix, T599-4163289. Saba Marine Park Hyperbaric Facility, T599-416 3295, serving the Eastern Caribbean. **Post** Airmail takes about 2 weeks to the USA or Europe. The post office in Windwardside is open 0800-1200, 1300-1700, T599-4162221, in The Bottom, T599-4163217. **Telephone** Most hotels have direct dialling worldwide, otherwise calls can be made from Landsradio phone booths in Windwardside or The Bottom.

Background

History

Saba was first discovered by Columbus on his second voyage in 1493 but was not colonized. Sir Francis Drake sighted it in 1595, as did the Dutchmen Pieter Schouten in 1624 and Piet Heyn in 1626. Some shipwrecked Englishmen landed in 1632, finding it uninhabited. In 1635 the French claimed it but in the 1640s the Dutch settled it, building communities at Tent Bay and The Bottom. However, it was not until 1816 that the island became definitively Dutch, the interregnum being marked by 12 changes in sovereignty, with the English, Dutch, French and Spanish all claiming possession.
➤➤ *See also background to the Netherlands Antilles, page 982.*

Geography

The island is an extinct volcano which shoots out of the sea, green with lush vegetation but without beaches. In fact there is only one inlet amidst the sheer cliffs where boats can come in to dock. The highest peak of this rugged island, Mount Scenery (887 m), also known as 'the Mountain', is also the highest point in all the Netherlands. Because of the difficult terrain there were no roads on Saba until 1943, only hand-carved steps in the volcanic rock. The main road has concrete barriers, partly to prevent cars driving over the edge and partly because of landslides, which can be frequent after rain. Only 13 sq km, Saba lies 45 km south of St Maarten and 27 km northwest of Sint Eustatius.

People
Although the island was once inhabited by Caribs, relics of whom have been found, there is no trace of their ancestry in the local inhabitants. The population is half white (descendants of Dutch, English and Scots settlers) and half black. Their physical isolation and the difficult terrain has enabled them to develop their ingenuity for self sufficiency and to live in harmony with their environment. Originally farmers and seafarers, the construction in 1963 of the Juancho E Yrausquin Airport on the only flat part of the island, and the serpentine road which connects it tenuously to the rest of the island, brought a new and more lucrative source of income: tourism.

The island's geographical limitations have meant that tourism has evolved in a small, intimate way. About 24,000 tourists visit each year, most of whom are day trippers. There are only 100 beds available in the hotels and guesthouses, as well as a few cottages to rent. Those who stay are few enough to get to know the friendliness and hospitality of their hosts, who all speak English, even though Dutch is the official language. Currently, the major source of income is the US Medical School, opened in 1993, which attracts over 250 (mainly US) students from overseas, who spend about US$1,000 a month. Development is small scale; the island still merits its unofficial title, 'the Unspoiled Queen'. There is no unemployment among the workforce of 600. The island is spotlessly clean; the streets are swept by hand every day.

Flora and fauna
In September 1998, **Hurricane Georges** passed just a few kilometres south of Saba, with wind speeds of 290 kmph high up in the hills. Many of the bigger trees were blown down, but the island quickly recovered and the lower mountain slopes became green and lush after the rain. However, in 1999 **Hurricane Lenny** attacked from the west, the Caribbean side of the island, and almost totally destroyed the rainforest. Most of the trees were blown down or snapped off so that the mosses and rainforest undergrowth did not grow. Since the hurricane local people have worked very hard to restore the forest and it is getting back to its old shape.

Vegetation on Saba changes according to altitude, and a walk up Mount Scenery is a sightseeing highlight for the many different types of tropical vegetation. At an altitude of 490-610 m there is secondary rainforest with trees of between 5 and 10 m tall. Further up there are tree ferns of 4-5 m, then palm trees, then at 825 m the cloud forest begins (known as Elfin forest); this is where you find the mountain mahogany tree (*Freziera undulata*). Since Hurricane Lenny, however, the forest remains only in protected pockets. Wildlife on the island is limited to the endemic and widespread anole lizard (*Aanolis sabanus*), iguanas (the green iguana, *Iguana iguana*, the island's largest, can be seen sunbathing on Old Booby Hill in the afternoon), a harmless red-bellied racer snake (*Alsophis rufiventris*, which can be seen on the Sandy Cruz and Mary's Point trails if you are quiet), and over 60 species of bird have been recorded, with many migratory birds coming to nest here. The trembler and the purple-throated hummingbird can be seen in the Elfin forest and the Sandy Cruz rainforest, where you can also find the wood hen.

The **Saba Conservation Foundation (SCF)** ① *PO Box 501, Windwardside, Saba, T/F4162709*, preserves the environment on land and underwater, developing protected areas, maintaining trails and promoting nature conservation. The foundation can be contacted through the tourist office. Janine le Sueur, executive director of the SCF, can be contacted for information on hiking and rates. The trail manager and hiking guide of the SCF is James Johnson, appointments are made through the **Saba Trail Shop** ① *T599-4162630*.

Sint Eustatius → *Country code: 599-3. Colour map 3, B1. Population: 2,100.*

Very few tourists make the effort to visit this Dutch outpost, but Sint Eustatius has a rich colonial history and a prosperous past. Having made its fortune in the 18th century out of the slave trade and commerce in plantation crops, it lost it in the 19th century with the abolition of slavery and has never really recovered. The main town, Oranjestad, still has the fortifications and remains of warehouses from its heyday, parts of which are being restored as hotels and restaurants. Renovation is already well under way, tourism is picking up and this off-the-beaten-track destination is worthy of investigation, particularly by divers. There are walking trails up into the rainforest of the extinct volcano, The Quill, and diving is good in the marine park. The name 'Statia' comes from St Anastasia, as it was named by Columbus, but the Dutch later changed it to Sint Eustatius. Unofficially it is known as 'the historic gem'. ▸▸ For Sleeping, Eating and other listings, see pages 576-579.

Ins and outs

Getting there It is possible to get to Statia in a day from many US cities, but you will have to change planes in Sint Maarten. All flights are in small planes, although the airport has been extended to 1600 m to allow larger jets to land. There are now no ferries.

Getting around There is no public transport on the island but cars and taxis can be hired. Driving is on the right, but some roads are so narrow you have to pass where you can. Watch out for cows, donkeys, goats and sheep roaming around freely. They are a traffic hazard. Taxi drivers are well-informed guides and can arrange excursions, although most places are within walking distance if you are energetic (less than 30 minutes' walk from the airport to town). ▸▸ *See Transport, page 579, for further details.*

Oranjestad

Oranjestad is the capital, divided between Upper Town set on a cliff overlooking Lower Town on the long beach below. They are connected by an old slave road, a mixture of cobblestones and concrete for pedestrian use only as well as a modern, longer road for vehicles. The Historic Core Development Plan involves restoring and modernizing many of the old houses in the centre, but the outskirts of town are littered and scruffy. The town used to be defended by **Fort Oranje** (pronounced Orahn'ya) perched on a rocky bluff. Built in 1636 on the site of a 1629 French fortification, the preserved ruins of the fort have now been restored following a fire in 1990, and large black cannon still point out to sea. Some administrative buildings of the island's Government and the tourist office are here. Other places of historical interest include the ruins of the **Honen Dalim Synagogue** built in 1739 and the nearby cemetery. Statia once had a flourishing Jewish community and was a refuge for Sephardic and Ashkenazic Jews, but with the economic decline after the sacking of Oranjestad by Admiral Rodney, most of the Jewish congregation left. The **Dutch Reformed Church**, consecrated in 1755, suffered a similar fate when its congregation fled. The square tower has been restored but the

It's possible to walk round the village and see the sights in a morning. The museum or tourist office will provide you with a Walking Tour brochure listing the historical sites.

walls are open to the elements. Legend has it that Admiral Rodney found most of his booty here after noticing that there were a surprising number of funerals for such a small population. A coffin, which he ordered to be opened, was found to be full of valuables and further digging revealed much more.

On Wilhelminaweg in the centre, the 18th-century Doncker/De Graaff House, once a private merchant's house and also where Admiral Rodney lived, has been restored and is now the **St Eustatius Historical Foundation Simon Doncker Museum** ① *T599-3182693, info@steustatiushistory.org. Mon-Fri 0900-1700, Sat, Sun and holidays 0900-1200, US$2, children US$1.* There is a pre-Columbian section which includes an Amerindian skeleton and a reconstruction of 18th-century rooms at the height of Statia's prosperity. It is worth a visit for the graphic descriptions of the slave trade. Archaeological excavations at Golden Rock near the airport have uncovered a large Amerindian village with the only complete floor plan of Indian houses found in the Caribbean. All the houses are round or slightly oval, vary in size and accommodate up

Sint Eustatius

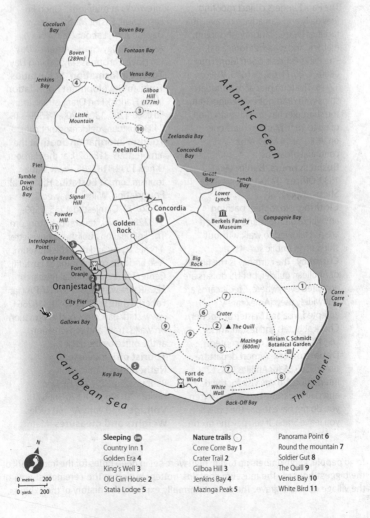

Sleeping 🛏	Nature trails ◯	Panorama Point **6**
Country Inn **1**	Corre Corre Bay **1**	Round the mountain **7**
Golden Era **4**	Crater Trail **2**	Soldier Gut **8**
King's Well **3**	Gilboa Hill **3**	The Quill **9**
Old Gin House **2**	Jenkins Bay **4**	Venus Bay **10**
Statia Lodge **5**	Mazinga Peak **5**	White Bird **11**

0 metres 200
0 yards 200

⁞ Touching down

Boat information For Customs and Immigration, the Harbour Office is open Mon-Fri 0800-1600, Sat, Sun 0800-1100, after hours sailors should see guard at the gate who will give directions to the local police station. If not leaving before 0800 clear customs in the morning, T599-318 2888, F599-3182205, VHF Channel 14. Fly an Antillean flag. Oranje Baai is the only anchorage. The Marine Park maintains 12 yacht moorings in the bay (yellow buoys). There is a yacht fee of US$10/night or US$30/week. The Park Rangers collect mooring fees daily and can advise on available facilities (water, laundry, shopping, fuel, ice, and weather forecasts). The Parks Office is open Mon-Thu 0800- 1700, Fri 0800-1600, VHF 17/16. The long pier accommodates ships with draft not exceeding 14 ft, the short pier has vessels with draft of up to 10 ft. Marine weather is on VHF 1 or 162.550 Mhz continual broadcast.

Business hours Banks: 0900-1530; **Offices**: 0900-1600; **Shops**: 0900-1700.

Clothing No topless bathing anywhere on the island and men are not allowed to walk without shirts on in public streets.

Currency The currency is the florin or Antillean guilder, but US dollars are accepted everywhere. Credit cards are not widely used (Amex rarely accepted, Visa and Mastercard better). Check at hotels and restaurants. US$100 bills often not accepted.

Departure tax Airport departure tax is US$5.65 for Antilles, US$12 international. If you visit for the day and pay departure tax on St Maarten, you do not have to pay the tax when you leave Statia. If you pay the tax on Statia and are in-transit on St Maarten you do not have to pay tax on St Maarten. You will need to show your tickets and boarding pass for your next flight at the tax window.

Documents A valid passport is required of all visitors. Most nationalities do not need a visa for stays of up to 3 months. There are no customs regulations as Statia is a free port.

Official time Atlantic Standard Time, 4 hrs behind GMT, 1 hr ahead of EST, all year.

Public holidays New Year's Day (fireworks at midnight), Good Fri, Easter Sun, Easter Mon, Queen's Day (30 Apr), Labour Day (1 May), Ascension Day, Statia/America Day (16 Nov), Christmas Day, Boxing Day.

Tourist information St Eustatius **Tourism Development Foundation** (Alida Francis), Fort Oranjestraat, Mon-Fri 0800-1200, 1300-1700, T/F599-318 2433, euxtour@goldenrocknet.com.

Tourism Information booth at the airport, T599-3182620; at the Harbour Office, T599-3182205, www.statia tourism.com. **St Eustatius Historical Foundation**, Wilhelminaweg 3, PO Box 71, Oranjestad A255, T599-3182288, www.steustatiushistory.org. The Foundation publishes a newsletter 4 times a year and runs the museum. Also under its control is the St Eustatius Center for Archaeological Research, SECAR, www.secar.org. **STENAPA** (Jan Faber), White Wall Rd, T599-3182661, www.statiapark.org. Good information on walks, trails and conservation at the office by the dock.

Tourist office overseas Netherlands, Antillenhuis, Badhuisweg 175 , 2597JP Den Haag, T70-3066111, F70-3066110.

Voltage 110 volts A/C 60 cycles.

Weights and measures Metric.

to 30 people. Large timbers up to 8 m high were set in deep holes for the framework of the biggest houses. The museum contains pottery buried in the ceremonial area of the village next to a grave. The curator normally explains the history of the exhibits.

In its heyday **Lower Town** stretched for 3 km along the bay, with warehouses, taverns and slave markets attracting commercial traffic. The ruins are visible along the shore line, where they collapsed into the sea. Parts are now being restored as hotels or restaurants.

Berkels family museum ① *T599-318 2338*, with a collection of household utensils, photos and antiques, is on the Lynch Plantation, on the northeast side of the island. It is housed in two wooden replica buildings. One is the size of a garden shed but it is referred to as the plantation house, and the other is a replica of the three-room house in town, recently restored.

Beaches and activities

Oranje Beach stretches for 1.5 km along the coast away from Lower Town. The length and width of the beach varies according to the season and the weather, but being on the Leeward side it is safe for swimming and other watersports. On the Windward side are two fine beaches, but there is a strong undertow and they are not considered safe for swimming. **Zeelandia Beach** is 3 km of off-white sand with heavy surf and interesting beachcombing, particularly after a storm. It is safe to wade and splash about in the surf but not to swim. There is a short dirt road down to the beach; do not drive too close to the beach or you will get stuck in the sand. Avoid the rocks at the end of the beach as they are very dangerous. **Lynch Beach**, also on the Atlantic side, is small and safer for children in parts, but ask local advice.

Diving Statia's waters offer a wonderful combination of coral reefs, marine life and historic shipwrecks. Diving is excellent, with plenty of corals, sea fans, hydroids and big fish such as groupers and barracudas, as well as rays, turtles and the occasional dolphin. There are even daily sightings of flying gurnards, not commonly found in the Caribbean, but unlike some other Caribbean diving destinations, you will not bump into any other divers underwater. **St Eustatius Marine Park** was established in 1996 and became operational in 1998. **STENAPA** has identified four protected areas: the southern part from Crooks Castle to White Wall is a restricted fishing zone; the wreck sites in Oranje Bay, STENAPA Reef (a modern wreck site) and the northern marine park are open for fishing and diving. Marine park fees are US$3 per dive, US$3 per snorkelling trip when using the park buoys; US$15 for an annual pass. You may not anchor anywhere in the park, spear guns and spear fishing are prohibited in all waters around Statia, nothing may be removed, whether animals, plants or historical artefacts, you may not touch or feed marine life. Report any turtle and cetacean sightings. The turtle conservation programme was started in 2002, with nightly patrols of beaches during the nesting season (Apr-Oct) so that all turtles can be measured and tagged. A new National Park Visitor Centre opened in 2006 at Lower Town, close to the harbour. It has offices for staff, meeting room, internet facilities for visitors, souvenirs for sale, information centre, picnic tables, toilets, showers and a maintenance facility for the marine park boat.

> *Water visibility can be over 30 m and diving and snorkelling are very good.*

Hiking There are seven linked trails around the **Quill National Park** ① *www.statiapark.org*. Get a trail tag, US$3, from the parks office in Gallows Bay, or the Tourist Office, which supports maintenance of the trails, together with a leaflet about the trails with a map of the routes. Guided hikes can be arranged by the park. A clearly marked trail from Rosemary Lane has been built to the rainforest crater at the top of The Quill, which is remarkable for its contrast with the dry scrub of the rest of the island. The Quill Trail leads to the crater rim. The walk up to the lip of the **crater** is easy if you are moderately fit. You will see butterflies, all sizes of lizard, hundreds of land crabs and, if you go quietly, the red-bellied racer snake. The plant life includes mahogany and bread fruit trees, arums, bromeliads, lianas and orchids. Although it is still quite a hike (about 45-50 minutes), the new path is in much better shape than the old one. At the top you have three options: in one direction is the trail to Panorama Point (30 minutes), from where you can see Saba, Sint Maarten and St-Barths. The other direction leads to the highest point on the island, called **Mazinga Peak** (one hour), which affords a magnificent view of Statia, St Kitts, Nevis and Montserrat. The first 10 minutes of the walk to the Mazinga is easy, then there is a turn to the left marked where it becomes a scramble because of hurricane damage. The last 20 m up to the summit is only for the very experienced and you should go in the company of a park ranger. From the rim, hikers can take the third option down the Crater Trail (1½ hours) scrambling down a poor path to the centre of the crater. The vegetation in the crater is dense, forming the breeding ground for land crabs, which Statians catch at night. There are massive silk cotton trees and other rainforest vegetation luxuriating in the fertile volcanic soil. A local guide is recommended as once you are in the crater it is difficult to get your bearings.

An alternative route is to walk the Round the Mountain Trail (five hours), which has spurs to the **Miriam C Schmidt Botanical Garden** ① *open sunrise to sunset, tours Mon-Fri mornings or by prior appointment, US$5, donations welcome, see page 580,* with a further bird observation trail (20 minutes). The southern route to the botanical gardens is in better condition than the northern path, which is overgrown in parts as it is less used. It starts with a road, and then a track, which leads round the lower slopes of The Quill to the **White Wall**, a massive slab of limestone which was once pushed out of the sea by volcanic forces and is now clearly visible from miles away across the sea. You can also see it from **Fort de Windt**, built in 1753, the ruins of which are open to the public, at the end of the road south from Lower Town. St Kitts can also be seen clearly from here. About 14 forts or batteries were built around the island by the end of the 18th century, but the ruins of few of them are accessible or even visible nowadays. STENAPA has also made a new trail to the **Boven**, the highest peak on the north side of the island. This is a strenuous, steep, four-hour hike (round trip) but well worth it for the view.

● Sleeping

Sint Eustatius *p572, maps p573 and p577*
Expect a 7% government tax, a 15% service charge and sometimes a 5% surcharge on top of quoted rates. The tourist office has a list of home rentals. Some of these are recently renovated traditional cottages with a/c and lots of other modern conveniences.
LL-AL Old Gin House, Lower Town, T599-3182319, www.oldginhouse.com. Built with the old bricks of an 18th-century cotton gin house, this is the most attractive of the hotels with an olde worlde atmosphere, but take precautions against mosquitoes. There are 2 fancy suites on the waterfront with a sea view and balcony, 14 dark rooms on the other side of the road behind the **Gin House** overlooking the pool. Large beds and bathrooms, a/c, TV, phones, internet access in the lobby. Gourmet restaurant in the old house, breakfast and lunch are served on the waterfront across the road.
AL Golden Era Hotel, Lower Town, T599-3182345, goldenerahotel@gmail.com. On the waterfront, a modern 20-room block at right angles to the sea so only the end rooms have a sea view. Gradually being

remodelled and upgraded but they have tiny bathrooms. All have a/c, fridge, TV, phone and a desk. Restaurant and bar on the waterfront with waves crashing underneath, food average, car or scooter hire arranged.
AL King's Well, between Upper and Lower Town in King's Well, north end of beach by Smoke Alley, T/F599-3182538, http://kingswellstatia.com. Run by Win and Laura, the rooms are past their decorative best but are large and comfortable with ceiling fans, fridge and TV, some with a/c. Breakfast, tax and service included in rate. Some rooms overlook the bar, while the more expensive have a spectacular sea view, the best on the island. One has a water bed. The hotel is very casual and popular with divers and sailors. Sandy beach across the road. Easy walk to the other hotels, restaurants and dive shops.
AL Statia Lodge, White Wall, T599-3181900, www.statialodge.com. The newest hotel on the island. 10 wooden bungalows with 1 or 2 bedrooms, fully-equipped kitchen, tiled floors, bathroom, fan, terrace with sea view. Good pool overlooking the ocean. Car or

scooter hire arranged, dive packages available. Credit card surcharge of 3.5%.
B Country Inn, Concordia, T599-3182484, country-inn@statiatourism.com. A bit remote but excellent value. A family home with guest rooms attached. Some rooms are larger than others but all have a cosy bedroom and a living area with fridge, table and chairs, good-sized bathroom, a/c, TV, tiled throughout. Some have 2 double beds and sleep 4, with US$10 charged for extra persons. Breakfast US$5, other meals on request. The owner, Mrs Iris Pompier (wife of a policeman), is an excellent cook and does catering for government functions, specializing in local delicacies. Price includes tax, but no credit cards accepted.

Eating

Sint Eustatius *p572, maps p573 and p577*
There are very few restaurants to choose from but there are places to eat in the hotels and bars as well as those listed here. Options are limited if you are self-catering too. For fresh fish, go to the fish processing plant (**Statia Fish Handling**) at Lower Town opposite short pier, Mon-Fri, usually 0800-1300, depending on the catch; they will clean the fish for you. If it is not available at the fish plant, approach the local fishermen at the harbour. Grocers sell frozen fish. Lobster is available fresh Nov-Mar. Fresh bread is baked daily and best bought at 'fresh bread time', which varies according to who makes it. Bake sales are announced by

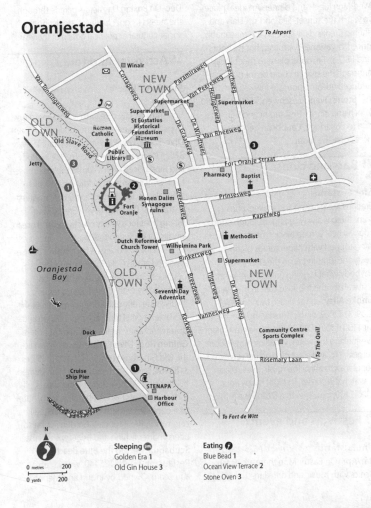

Oranjestad

Leeward Islands Sint Eustatius *Listings*

Sleeping
Golden Era 1
Old Gin House 3

Eating
Blue Bead 1
Ocean View Terrace 2
Stone Oven 3

the town crier: open-air takeaway meals of
local dishes some Fri and Sat, from 1100,
usually at **Charlie's Place**, just below Mazinga
Gift Shop and Africa Crossroads Park opposite
museum. Hotels serve purified water. Tap
water is usually rainwater and not for drinking.
†¶-¶ **Blue Bead Bar and Restaurant**, by the
dock, T599-3182873. 1000-2200, bar until
2300. Closed Mon and Tue in May. Swiss-
owned. Very good menu based on fish and
seafood with interesting twists, also meat
and pizzas. Daily specials on a board.
Outdoor dining and very pretty at night
looking out to the lights of boats in the
harbour, friendly service, one of the nicest
places to eat and understandably popular.
†¶-¶ **Ocean View Terrace**, just by tourist
office and Governor's House, T599-3182934.
Wed-Mon lunch and dinner. An ideal place
to watch the sunset. Seafood specials and
shrimp Créole, daily specials are reasonably
priced, occasional live music, happy hour
and BBQ on Fri, good place to meet locals,
although the service could be friendlier.
Reduced opening hours in low season.
†¶-¶ **Stone Oven**, Faeschweg, T599-3182480.
Lunch and dinner. Restaurant and bar, local
and regional food, Caribbean décor,
occasional live music.

❶ Bars and clubs

Sint Eustatius *p572, maps p573 and p577*
Statians like partying and at weekends
something is always going on. Quite often
you will hear a 'road block' from far away:
cars stopped with huge stereos blaring and
everyone jumping up in the street. Ask
anybody what is going on next weekend, or
just wait for the music to start in the evening.
Smoke Alley, on the beach by King's Well.
T599-3182002, titanic@goldenrock.net. Mon-
Sat 1130-1400, 1800-2200. Open-air restaurant
overlooking the water, varied menu, Mexican,
burgers, etc, and a fun place to be, very
popular, occasional live music, lovely place
to watch the sunset. Fri night happy hour
1800-2100, usually with a DJ and live music.

❀ Festivals and events

Sint Eustatius *p572, maps p573 and p577*
Mar/Apr On Easter Mon there are beach
picnics with music and drinking.

30 Apr Queen Mother Juliana's birthday
is celebrated with cultural events, sports,
food and music.
1 Jul Emancipation Day celebrates the
abolition of slavery.
2nd week of Jul The Antillian Games, with
sporting competitions between all the
islands of the Netherlands Antilles.
Jul/Aug Carnival, the main event of the year
is held over 10 days and is celebrated with
steel bands, sports and contests and includes
a **Grand Parade** on the last Sun of the month.
21 Oct Antillian Day, with flag ceremonies,
games and fetes.
16 Nov Statia/America Day, with lots of
cultural festivities and activities commemorating the First Salute to the American Flag
by a foreign government in 1776.
Dec On Boxing Day actors parade through
the streets (Nigger business) depicting the
social, cultural or political gossip of the year.

▲ Activities and tours

Sint Eustatius *p572, maps p573 and p577*
Diving
You must by law dive with a local company.
Hyperbaric chamber at the medical school.
Dive Statia, Lower Town, Oranjestad, T599-
3182435, www.divestatia.com. Run by Rudy
and Rinda Hees, with a comfortable, purpose-
built, 26-ft catamaran for diving, on which
they take up to 10 divers and 2 dive masters/
instructors. They also have a 36-ft diving/
fishing boat for a variety of activities and ocean
kayaks for exploring the coast and underwater
scooters for lazy divers. A full range of courses
is offered at this Gold Palm 5-star PADI
operation, including Nitrox certification.
3 dives a day with night dives on request,
all dives are fully guided. Equipment rental is
available, snorkel trips , accommodation and
diving packages available with most hotels.
Golden Rock Dive Centre, Lower Town at
the Old Gin House Hotel, Oranjestad, T599-
3182964, www.goldenrockdive.com. Owned
by Glen and Michele Faires, 2 dive boats, all
surface intervals taken at the dive shop, hotel/
dive packages, groups of up to 18 specially
catered for, PADI courses. **Golden Rock** also
offers charter fishing and boat trips to Saba.
Scubaqua, next to the **Blue Bead
Restaurant**, T599-3185440, www.scub
aqua.com. Owned by Ingrid and Menno

Walther, of Switzerland (PADI, CMAS), 1 boat, taking 15 divers. Groups of no more than 6 per instructor and the captain stays on board the boat. Multilingual instructors and dive masters. Drift diving for whale watching is organized between end-Jan and Apr.

Tour operators
For a 2-hr historical tour by minibus around the island, ask for Mr Danial at the tourist office in Fort Oranje, US$40.

● Transport

Sint Eustatius *p572, maps p573 and p577*
Air
Winair has several daily 20-min flights from St Maarten connecting with flights from the USA, Europe and other islands. There are other connecting Winair flights from Saba (10 mins). Reservations T5454230, flight information T545 4210, online booking at www.fly-winair.com.

Car
To hire a car you need a driving licence from your own country or an international driver's licence. The speed limit is 50 kph and 30 kph in residential areas. Car hire companies include **Brown's**, T/F599-3182266, US$45 per day including tax and insurance, weekend deals; **Rainbow**, T599-3182811, F3182586, US$35 plus US$5 collision damage waiver; **ARC**, T599-3182595, F599-3182594, US$35 plus tax and insurance, near airport.

● Directory

Sint Eustatius *p572, maps p573 and p577*
Banks FirstCaribbean, Emmaweg, T599-3182392, F3182734. Mon-Fri 0830-1530. **Centrale Hypotheek Bank**, W Flemming, Princess Garden, T599-3182107. The **Windward Islands Bank**, by Mazinga Gift Shop, Mon-Fri 0830-1200, 1330-1530, T599-3182846, F599-3182850. **Internet** Computers & More Internet Club, Fort Oranjestraat 20, T599-3182596, Mon, Tue, Thu, Fri 1000-1800 or 1900, Wed, Sat 1000-2100, small building, 3 computers, US$5 per hr. The Public Library also has access. **Post** The post office is at Cottage Rd, T599-318 2207, F599-3182457. Mon-Fri 0730-1600. Express mail is available. There are special stamp issues and First Day Covers for collectors. UPS agent is Arlene Cuvalay, Golden Rock, T599-3182595, F599-3182594. **Lady Ama's Services** is agent for **Federal Express**, Fort Oranjestraat, T599-3182712, F599-3182572. **Telephone** Telephone cards of US$10 and US$17 can be used at phone booths near the police station and at the corner of Korthalsweg, at the airport, at the harbour and the road to the airport, for local or international calls. When calling within the Netherlands Antilles, dial 0 before the 7-digit number. **Medical services** The Queen Beatrix Medical Centre, Prinsesweg, T599- 3182371 (for Nurses Station or an ambulance), or T599-318 2211 (for a doctor). Doctors are on 24-hr call.

Background

History
Sint Eustatius, or Statia, was originally settled by Caribs. The island was sighted by Columbus on his second voyage but never settled by the Spanish. The Dutch first colonized it in 1636 and built Fort Oranje. The island reached a peak of prosperity in the 18th century, when the development of commerce brought about 8000 people to the tiny island, over half of whom were slaves, and the number of ships visiting the port was around 3500 a year. Trading in sugar, tobacco and cotton proved more profitable than trying to grow them and the slave trade was particularly lucrative, gaining the island the nickname of 'The Golden Rock'.

The island still celebrates 16 November 1776 when the cannon of Fort Oranje unknowingly fired the first official salute by a foreign nation to the American colours. At that time, Statia was a major trans-shipment point for arms and supplies to George Washington's troops. The arms were stored in the yellow ballast brick warehouses built all along the Bay and then taken by blockade runners to Boston, New York and Charleston. However, the salute brought retaliatory action from the English, and in 1781 the port was taken without a shot being fired by troops under Admiral George

Brydges Rodney, who captured 150 merchant ships and £5 million of booty before being expelled by the French the following year.

With continuing transfers of power, the economy never recovered, many merchants were banished and the population began to decline. The emancipation of slaves in 1863 brought an end to any surviving plantation agriculture and the remaining inhabitants were reduced to subsistence farming and dependency upon remittances from relatives abroad. Limited prosperity has returned recently with the advent of small-scale tourism but the island is still relatively underdeveloped. ▸▸ *See also background to the Netherlands Antilles, the ABC chapter, page 982.*

Economy
The traditional economic activities of fishing, farming and trading have been augmented by an oil storage and refuelling facility, but tourism has had a slow start. The island is popular with divers looking for something a bit different and off the beaten track. It is the sort of place where you will be greeted by passers by and there is no crime.

Geography
The island of Sint Eustatius, 56 km south of St Maarten and 27 km southeast of Saba, is dominated by the long-extinct volcano called 'The Quill' at the south end, inside which is a lush rainforest. The north part of the island is hilly and uninhabited except for Statia Terminals, a fuel depot; most people live in the central plain where the airport is.

People
Statia is quiet and friendly and the poorest of the three Dutch islands, with only 2,100 people living on the 30.6 sq km island. A variety of nationalities are represented, the island having changed hands 22 times, but most are of black African descent. Everybody speaks English, although Dutch is the official language and is taught in schools.

Flora and fauna
Despite the small size of the island, in the 17th and 18th centuries there were more than 70 plantations, worked intensively by slaves. As a result, most of the original forest has disappeared except on the most inhospitable parts of the volcano. Nevertheless there are 17 different kinds of orchid and 58 species of bird, of which 25 are resident and breeding, 21 migrants from North America and 12 seabirds. There are iguanas, land crabs, tree frogs and lots of butterflies. Unfortunately there are lots of goats too, which eat everything in sight. The Antilles iguana (*Iguana delicatissima*) is rare and threatened and has now been protected by law. The young and females vary from bright green to dull grey, while the large males can be nearly black. The population is stronger on St Eustatius than on neighbouring islands because the mongoose was never introduced here. Neither was the green iguana, with which it has interbred on some islands. The red-bellied racer (*Alsophis rufiventris*) is a small snake found only on Statia and Saba. It is brown with black markings on its back and a pink belly. It is not poisonous and kills its prey (small reptiles and baby rats) by strangulation.

STENAPA ① *T599-3182884*, the St Eustatius National Parks Foundation, was founded in 1996. This organization is responsible for the marine park, The Quill, Boven, Gilboa Hill, Signal Hill and Little Mountain. In 1998 **The Quill** was declared a national park, consisting of the volcano and the limestone **White Wall** to its south. The Quill is protected above 250 m, but the White Wall is protected down to the high water line. At the crater of The Quill there are many species usually found in tropical rainforest: huge tree ferns, mahogany, giant elephant ears, begonias, figs, plantains, bromeliads, the balsam tree and many more. The southern slope of the mountain has not been fully explored by botanists. STENAPA is developing the 5.6-ha **Miriam C Schmidt Botanical Garden** on the southeast side of The Quill in the area called 'Behind the Mountain'. The aim is to make the gardens educational and to include an ecolodge. ▸▸ *See also page 576.*

Saint-Barthélemy

→ *Country code: 590. Colour map 3, B1. Population: 10,000.*

Saint-Barthélemy (also known as St-Barth or St-Barts), a piece of France picked up and put down in the tropics, has a well-deserved reputation as a holiday heaven for the rich and famous. Pop stars and film stars have been seen here, but mostly they hide away in their luxury villas or exclusive hotels where management understands the meaning of privacy. Gourmet French restaurants, Créole bistros and chic designer boutiques all enhance the image of expensive indulgence, but in fact prices are no higher than in France, and that includes the wine. It is a beautiful island of only 24 sq km, with rugged volcanic hills and 22 splendid white sandy beaches, most of which are protected by both cliff and reef. ▸▸ *For Sleeping, Eating and other listings, see pages 584-590.*

Ins and outs

Getting there St-Barts is only a short hop from St Maarten/St-Martin and there are dozens of daily flights from both the French and Dutch sides from 0700-1700 in small planes. There are also good links with other neighbouring islands. It is difficult to get there in a day from Europe, although it is possible from Paris via Sint Maarten. From the USA, the best connections are via San Juan. You can also get there by boat from St-Martin.

Getting around Taxi tours are available for a quick tour of the island, but if you are renting a villa you will need car or mini moke hire for visiting different beaches or for shopping. ▸▸ *See page 589 for further details.*

Saint-Barthélemy

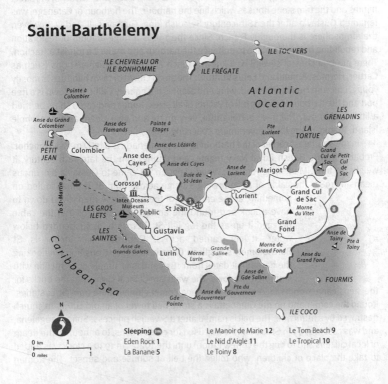

Leeward Islands Saint-Barthélemy

Sleeping
Eden Rock **1**
La Banane **5**
Le Manoir de Marie **12**
Le Nid d'Aigle **11**
Le Toiny **8**
Le Tom Beach **9**
Le Tropical **10**

Touching down

Boat information (French flag). Outside the inner harbour of Gustavia, daily anchorage fee of US$2.50-5, depending on location. Inside the main harbour, stern to or on double moorings, fees are based on length of boat. Water, waste disposal, showers and toilets are available at the dock. Other anchorages around the island are free. Provisions and some marine supplies. For the Réserve Naturelle, contact the harbour office in Gustavia, T0590-278818, www.reserve-naturelle-stbarthelemy.com.

Business hours 0800-1200, 1430-1700, Wed-Sat am only.

Currency The euro, but dollars are widely accepted.

Embassies and consulates None (other than a Swedish Consulate) as it is a French département.

Emergency numbers Gendarmerie T0590-276012, **Police** T0590-276666, **Fire** T0590-276231.

Official time GMT minus four hours.

Public holidays See Guadeloupe, page 657.

Tourist information Quai de Gaulle, Gustavia, T0590-278727, odtsb@wanadoo.fr. Mon-Thu 0830-1230, 1400-1730, Fri 0830-1230, 1400-1700. Very helpful; lots of leaflets.

Voltage 220 volts AC, 50 cycles.

Weights and measures Metric.

Gustavia

For most of its colonial history, St-Barts was French, but in 1784-1878 it belonged to Sweden, traded by France in return for shipping rights in Göteburg. The Swedish influence is still evidenced in the city hall, the belfries, the forts (Karl, Oscar and Gustave), the street names and the trim stone houses which line the harbour. The harbour, or Carénage, was renamed Gustavia after the 18th-century Swedish king, Gustavus III. Today, however, the atmosphere is thoroughly French. Since the 1980s a huge amount of restoration and rebuilding has taken place to enhance the harbour and make it a tourist attraction. There are branches of several well-known French and other designer shops (such as **Cartier, Hermès, Armani** and **Louis Vuitton**). The small crowd of town habitués is mostly young, chic and French. The food, wine and aromas are equally Gallic. The town is a free port and the harbour is always full of yachts of all sizes; ferries and cargo ships berthed a little further out. The town is delightful, very pretty and very clean, as is the whole island, thanks to the local government collecting rubbish daily.

In the southeast corner of the harbour by the promenade is a truly massive **anchor**. Probably from a British Royal Navy frigate, and dating from the late 18th century, it weighs 10 tons. Marked "Liverpool...Wood...London", it came to Gustavia by curious means in 1981. The cable of a tug towing a barge across from St Thomas fouled on something at the entrance of the harbour. A man dived down to have a look and found the anchor. It is thought that the cable dragged it up as the tug left St Thomas and, suspended below water, it got carried across. Opposite the anchor is **St Bartholomew's Anglican Church**, in a prime position overlooking the harbour. It dates from 1855 and is of simple construction with shuttered windows. The walls are of local stone, but the bricks for the steps came from France and the dark lava corner stones came from St Eustatius. Round the corner and up rue Gambetta is a stone **bell tower** of an old Lutheran church destroyed by a hurricane. The bell is named after a Swedish princess, Sofia Magdalena, and was cast in 1799 in Stockholm. It was used for celebrations, to announce the death of local citizens and to ring the curfew (2000) until the 1920s. In 1930 a clock was added to take the place of children, who tolled the bell at sunrise and sunset. The Roman

The Caribs called the island Ouanalao, but it was renamed in honour of Christopher Columbus' brother after he spotted the island in November 1496.

Catholic Church, **Notre Dame de L'Assomption**, was built in 1822 but was destroyed in 1837. Rebuilt in 1842, it is of Hispanic design rather than French or Swedish, which is unusual in the French islands. Its bell tower is higher up the hill to allow the sound to carry further and prevent damage if the bells should fall during a hurricane.

Anse de Grands Galets, in Gustavia, three or four minutes' walk from the harbour front, is also known as **Shell Beach**. It is a small bay, with cliffs and rocks at either end and patches of pink shells. There is a beach bar here, **Dõ Brazil**, and boulders among which you can settle yourself for the day, but no shade.

St-Barts Municipal Museum① *La Pointe, T0590-297155, Mon 1430-1800, Tue- Fri 0830-1230, 1430-1800, Sat 0900-1300, €2*, has a fair cross section of historical material including clothing, household items, fishing tools and Amerindian archaeological finds, as well as old photos and models of traditional houses on the ground floor of the Wall House which is believed to date from the end of the 18th century.

Around St-Barts

The main resort area is **Baie de Saint-Jean**. There are several small and medium-sized hotels here, many restaurants, bars, shopping plazas and other entertainment, strung along the coast. It is also very close to the airport runway and if you walk along the beach you may feel you need to duck when the small planes come over. The large bay is divided by **Eden Rock**, upon which is a luxury hotel (under renovation 2005). The sand extends quite a way out but the beach is protected by a shallow reef and swimming is safe, ideal for families. It is breezy, making it good for windsurfing. Motorized watersports are only allowed 300 m off the beach.

Lorient is another large and popular bay, although quieter than St-Jean. There are a couple of paths down to the beach in between the villas along the shoreline. The village is pleasant, with a couple of good supermarkets stocked with French cheeses and other delicacies. The name Lorient has nothing to do with the orient. It is a corruption of Quartiers d'Orléans, stemming from the old administrative name for the area.

Corossol is a typical fishing village and maintains an air of days gone past. There are many old wooden houses here, mostly neatly kept and brightly painted. The **Inter Oceans Museum** ① *T0590-276297, Tue-Sun 0900-1230, 1500-1700, €3*, is an absorbing, private collection of 9,000 seashells, corals and stuffed fish from all around the world. The owner, M Ingenu Magras, is enthusiastic about his collection and will introduce you to the 100,000 species distributed around the oceans of the world, of which some 1,600 species are found in the Caribbean.

Colombier beach is one of the most unspoilt beaches on the island. It cannot be reached by car but is well worth the 20 or 30 minutes' walk for the majestic views of the island. There are two trails going down to the beach. One is a steep one down from Colombier on top of the hill, but a nicer one with spectacular views of all the little islands offshore starts from La Petite Anse just beyond Anse des Flamands. There is no shade and no facilities. There are also several day tours by boat from Gustavia. **Anse des Flamands** beach is of very clean white sand with three hotels and numerous villas. The bay is not in the marine reserve, so watersports are available. From April to August, female sea turtles come to Colombier, Flamands and Corossol to lay their eggs.

Beaches and activities

Marigot is a small bay with crystal clear water of many colours, rocky beach with small patches of sand and outcrops of rocks, this is a good beach for snorkelling. It is in the high protection area of the marine reserve, so no fishing, motorized watersports or scuba diving are allowed and it is very quiet. For details on the **Réserve Naturelle** ① *T0590-278818, www.reserve-naturelle-stbarthelemy.com*, contact the office in Gustavia on the harbour front. The **tourist office**① *T0590-278727*, distributes leaflets with a map. **Grand Cul de Sac** bay is so protected from the sea by the peninsula and reef that it is almost like a lagoon, with very tranquil, shallow water in a variety of blues and greens with patches of rocks and weed as well as sand. Windsurfing, kitesurfing and other non-motorized watersports are available at the **St Barth Beach Hotel** and there is a dive shop on the road leading to the beach.

Anse de Toiny and **Anse du Grand Fond** are on the Atlantic side of the island and unprotected from the currents. Swimming is not advised here, although surfing is popular. **Anse du Grand Saline** is a wide expanse of beach with beautiful white sand. Backed by sand dunes and protected by cliffs and rocks at either end, this is one of the most beautiful beaches in St-Barts, if not the Caribbean. Behind the beach is the salt pond, from which the area gets its name, and here there are three restaurants where you can get lunch and/or dinner.

To get to **Gouverneur** from Gustavia take the road to **Lurin**, a high point on the island marked by a satellite mast. A sign will direct you to the very steep road leading down to the beach, with parking at the end of the road. The bay is very quiet and undeveloped. A legend says that the 17th-century pirate, Montbars the Exterminator, hid his treasures in a cove at Gouverneur and they have never been found.

Diving There is excellent diving all round St-Barts, especially out round the offshore rocks, like the Groupers, and islands like Île Fourche. Sometimes in May the migrating sperm whales pass close by. Marine life has improved since the marine park was introduced and turtles now nest in greater numbers at Colombier, Fourchue and other beaches around the island. Divers are asked to contribute €1 per dive or €15 for an annual pass towards the running of the reserve. ➤➤ *See also Activities and tours, page 589.*

⊖ Sleeping

Saint-Barthélemy *p581, maps p581 and p585*
Some of the Caribbean's most luxurious and expensive hotels can be found on this island, while cheap guesthouses are few and far between, but there are no large resorts and no all-inclusive hotels to dominate the beaches. There are also very many stylish and comfortable villas, on the beach or up in the hills with glorious views and sea breezes, and many people choose to take advantage of the well-stocked supermarkets with their French delicacies and cheap wine and cater for themselves. With that in mind, quite a few hotel rooms now have kitchenettes, so that you can make the best of both worlds. There is no occupancy tax added to the bill.
LL Eden Rock, Baie de St-Jean, T0590-297999, www.edenrockhotel.com. Amazing location on a rock jutting out into the sea. Completely rebuilt to the highest standards, beautiful, colourful suites and cottages on the rock or on the beach, all with lovely sea views. Huge breakfast buffet, mouth-watering menu for lunch and dinner. Watersports, fitness centre with yoga and pilates, shop with all the latest designer wear, Jane's Gallery exhibits and sells art with a studio where you can have a go at painting too.

LL La Banane, Lorient, a few hundred metres from Lorient Beach, T0590-520300, www.la banane.com. Pastel-painted bungalows, with square modern lines, 9 rooms all named after tropical fruits, a/c, fan, phone, TV, DVD, 2 pools, lots of bananas, fine dining, breakfast, library, boat and car available. Airport transfers and service included in rate.
LL Le Toiny, Anse de Toiny, T0590-278888, www.hotelletoiny.com. Out of the way but one of the most high-class hotels on the island with tremendous attention to detail. 15 modern villa suites, huge 4-poster beds, rooms decorated in white with blue, red or green trimmings, a/c, TV, mostly with plasma screens and other high-tech entertainment. Spacious bathrooms with walk-in shower, kitchenette with fridge and enormous minibar selection, 24-hr room service, large plunge pools with ocean view and very private. The hotel has the best restaurant on the island, Le Gaïac, world-renowned for refined and elegant dining with a huge menu and wine list overlooking the rugged Atlantic coast. The set menu for dinner is €110, while entrées cost €30-40. Also a great place to come for Sun brunch. Closed Sep-Oct.
LL Le Tom Beach Hotel, St-Jean,

T0590-275313, www.tombeach.com. 12 rooms in a small property between the road and the beach but only the most expensive and largest 2 have a sea view, the rest face in to the patio garden. Luxury 4-poster beds, a/c, fans, TV, DVD, video, private terraces, hammocks, multilingual staff. The colour scheme can be considered bright and cheerful or an assault on the senses, depending on your state of mind, with scarlet, blue, green and yellow in the hotel and violet and purple added in the restaurant, part of which is on the sand. The rooms are more muted, which is a relief. Moroccan design around the L-shaped pool with huge cushioned areas for lounging.

LL-AL Le Manoir de Marie, Route de Salines, Lorient, T0590-277927, www.lemanoirst barth.com. Delightfully romantic yet family friendly just 50 m from the beach with well-stocked supermarkets 2 mins away. The main house dates from 1610 and started its life in Normandy before being dismantled and shipped to St-Barts in 1984. Cottages in the garden have been built in the same style. Owner Marie-Dominique Delemazure has put her stamp on the interior design, with French antique furniture, pretty drapes and cushions, daybeds and flowers. Each room is different in size and design, some for couples, some sleep up to 5, some have kitchenettes and dining areas, some have outdoor bathrooms. Good-value packages available with car hire. Breakfast available but no restaurant.

LL-AL Le Tropical, St-Jean, T0590-276487, www.tropicalhotel.net. Créole gingerbread style with romantic lacy bedspreads and flowing mosquito nets, set in a lush garden with lots of flowering plants and palm trees. 20 seaview and garden-view rooms, a/c, fan, TV, phone, terrace. Have breakfast on the veranda overlooking the beach or in your room. The pool has a sea view. No restaurant but a short walk to the beach and restaurants. Excursions arranged. Closed 1 Jun-15 Jul.

AL-A Sunset, Gustavia, T0590-277721, www.st-barths.com/sunset-hotel. 10, 2-star rooms upstairs, on the waterfront overlooking the ferries. Painted a cheerful yellow and white on the balcony. Newly decorated rooms, a/c, TV, mini-bar, a good option for a town centre hotel.

A Le Nid d'Aigle, Anse des Cayes, T0590-277520, www.saint-barths.com/niddaigle. Up on the hill with a view over the town and the sea. 3 rooms in Gigi's villa with a/c, phone, airport transfers, pets allowed, pool with a view.

B La Presqu'île, Gustavia, T0590-276460, estflorvillegreaux@wanadoo.fr. On the waterfront, 10 rooms overlooking the harbour and the boats, all upstairs with a balcony, not large, not fancy, but comfortable, clean and adequate, light and airy. Large lounge and bar area with a view.

Gustavia

Quai Jeanne d'Arc

Fort Gustav

To Airport

Caribbean Sea

Fort Oscar

Municipal Museum

Pharmacy

To Saint Jean

Rue Duquesne

Rue Chanzy

Rue Avatel

Supermarket

Town Hall

R du Port

Rue Jean Bart

Rue Schoelcher

To St-Martin

R de la France

Rue du Roi Oscar II

Rue du Général de Gaulle

Rue Jeanne d'Arc

Rue Dugomier

Anchor

Rue Irénée de Bruyn

Rue du Centennaire

Rue Courbet

Rue de l'Eglise

Rue Victor Hugo

Fort Karl

Anse de Grands Galets (Shell Beach)

N

| 0 metres | 100 |
| 0 yards | 100 |

Sleeping
La Presqu'île **1**
Sunset **2**

Eating
Dô Brazil **3**
Eddy's **4**
Wall House **6**

Bars & clubs
Baz/Bête à Z'Ailes **1**
Le Repaire **5**
Le Select **2**

⚫ Eating

Saint-Barthélemy *p581, maps p581 and p585*

St-Barts is a gourmet delight. Nearly everything is imported from France or from the French Antilles. Expect to pay an absolute minimum of US$25 for dinner; more likely you'll end up paying US$75-100 with drinks and 3 courses. There are around 70 restaurants on this small island, many of them excellent, mostly French but some Créole and Italian, even Indonesian, a few vegetarian options and lots of seafood.

Some of the best restaurants are in the top hotels. See *Ti Gourmet Saint-Barth*, a free pocket booklet, for a listing, the *Ti Creux* section lists snacks and takeaways.

If self-catering, there are fine supermarkets in Gustavia, the airport, St-Jean and Lorient, with a wide range of French foods at French prices. This is a duty free island, so wine and spirits are very cheap. Many supermarkets close at lunchtime and Sun afternoons.

⫪⫪ Eddy's, opposite the Anglican Church, Gustavia, T0590-275417. Dinner only. Tucked down a side street in the town centre, a combination of colonial French and Southeast Asia after Eddie's travels to Thailand. Recommended are the green papaya salad, grouper in ginger sauce, beef and shrimp on noodles, rhubarb tart, everything on the menu. Good for vegetarians too with a vegetable platter and veg with noodles. Eddy is very welcoming and the restaurant is always crowded. No reservations.

⫪⫪ K'fe Massai, Centre l'Oasis, Lorient, T0590-297678, kfmassai@hotmail.com. Thu-Tue, dinner only from 1900. African-inspired funky decor but the food is mostly French, incorporating exotic touches, with a excellent value 3-course *prix fixe* dinners for €29, €39 and €49. The manager used to be a wine merchant and has added a tapas and wine bar.

⫪⫪ La Mandala, Gustavia, T0590-279696. Dinner only. Up on top of a steep hill overlooking Gustavia this Far Eastern restaurant and cocktail bar has the same owners and same chef, Kiki Barjettas, as **Dô Brazil**. The decor is designed to take you away from your everyday life to a higher place, watched over by a Buddha and other statues. Delicious Thai cooking with French

Caribbean ingredients make this one of *the* places to eat and be seen.

⫪⫪⫪-⫪⫪ Le Gommier, opposite salt pond, La Grande Saline, T0590-275057. Lunch and dinner. Can be a bit smelly at the edge of the pond, but the restaurant is in a delightful spot, housed in a wooden, airy building in local style, all open sided with the shutters propped up to catch the breeze. Stylish, excellent food, a mix of local and European dishes, with curry goat, coconut chicken, stuffed crab, lobster and salads at lunch, more elegant options for dinner with a *prix fixe* menu and live music.

⫪⫪⫪-⫪⫪ L'Esprit Salines, opposite salt pond, La Grande Saline, T0590-524610, lesprit3@wanadoo.fr. Lunch and dinner, closed Tue. Started by chefs formerly at **Maya's** in Public, it has attracted an enthusiastic clientele. Quite casual with a garden dining room and bar, a good place for a leisurely lunch after a morning on the beach nearby. Finish with a home-made digestif of lemon grass rum, the lemon grass is grown on the property.

⫪⫪⫪-⫪⫪ Maya's, Public, T0590-277573, mayasrestaurant@wanadoo.fr. Mon-Sat dinner only, sunset drinks from 1600. Almost an institution, **Maya's** has been serving regular visitors for years at this colourful spot right on the water. Maya is from Martinique (then Guadeloupe) and you can expect the real deal with her French Créole cuisine. The menu changes daily depending on the local ingredients available. The downside is the popularity, it can get crowded and noisy if a party comes in. **Maya's to go**, opposite the airport, Les Galeries du Commerce, St-Jean, T0590-298370, mayastogo@wanadoo.fr. Great if you are in a villa and want a special ready-meal without having to cook, or a picnic, snacks, pastries, whatever you fancy. There are stools outside under an arbour if you want to eat there.

⫪⫪⫪-⫪⫪ Zanzibarth, Route de Saline, St Jean, T0590-275300. Dinner daily until 2300, bar 1800-0100, brunch Sat, Sun. Minimalist design, all white in the lounge and restaurant with modern art canvasses on the walls. The food is a mixture of French, Belgian and Italian and is very good. Opt for the French menu rather than the English version, translations are unintelligible.

⫪⫪⫪-⫪ Dô Brazil, Shell Beach, Gustavia,

T0590-290666, www.dobrazil.com. Lunch and dinner. Created by Boubou and Yannick Noah, the tennis player, this is a lively restaurant and snack bar on the beach. Upstairs there is a Brazilian-themed dining room for evening meals (although the chef is keen on Thai food) while downstairs the beach bar serves sandwiches, fresh fruit cocktails and snacks. Try the *caipirinhas*.

♥♥ **Chez Andy**, The Hideaway, Villa Créole shopping plaza, St-Jean, T0590-276362, www.hideaway.tv. Tue-Sat 1200-1400, 1900-2030, Sun 1900-2030. Andy (British) doesn't take himself too seriously and his menu offers 'corked wine, warm beer, lousy food, view of the car park'. However he serves up some of the best food at good prices and the restaurant is always full and cheerful. Interesting salads, lots of choice of entrées and huge, really thin-crust pizzas. The vanilla rum digestif is a winner.

♥♥ **Cocoloba Beach Bar**, Grand Cul de Sac. T0590-277567. Tue-Sun 1000-2230. Open-air seating under the shade of sea grape (*cocoloba*) trees on rustic, brightly painted wooden tables and stools or benches. Tasty panini, burgers and salads, standard desserts, cocktails with or without alcohol. Waitresses are rushed off their feet at lunchtime.

♥♥ **Wall House**, on the waterfront near the museum, Gustavia, T0590-277183, www.wall-house-stbarth.com. 1200-1400, 1900-2100. French cuisine offering light lunches and gourmet dinners on the waterfront with a harbour view, *plat du jour* at lunch €9, dinner good 5-course menu €25, wines to suit all tastes.

♪ Bars and clubs

Saint-Barthélemy *p581, maps p581 and p585*

St-Barth is known for its gourmet restaurants rather than its discos and many of the bars are attached to restaurants. Baie de St-Jean is busy at night, but there is plenty going on in Gustavia as well, which is where the yachtsmen are based. You can find a good selection of French wines at no more than you would pay in France, as well as good Martiniquan rums. Many places make their own digestifs, flavoured rums which are delicious with coffee after a meal. There are no casinos, no cinema, but check the weekly flyers for what's on where. Most places close at midnight, at least during the week.

Bar Le Select, rue de la France with rue Gal de Gaulle, Gustavia, T0590-278687. Mon-Sat 1100-2400. Also known as **Cheeseburgers in Paradise**, this bar and burger place is famous for being the subject of the Jimmy Buffet song of the same name. Open for burgers and snacks during the day and good for lunch, it is best visited at night, when live music is often performed. Jimmy Buffet has been known to play here.

Baz Bar/Bete a Z'Ailes, rue Samuel Fahlberg, Gustavia, T0590-297409. Mon-Sat 1100-2400. Lovely position on the waterfront with a boardwalk for outdoor seating, a great place to watch the boats. Lively at night with a variety of music including zouk, live bands.

Le Petit Club, Gustavia, T0590-276633, lepetitclub@saint-barths.com. From 2200. Popular with the yachting crowd, this disco close to the harbour doesn't get going until after midnight and is often still thumping at 0300. Dress smartly, no jeans.

Le Repaire des Rebelles et des Emigrés, rue de la République, Gustavia, opposite where the Voyager docks, T0590-277248. Bar open all day until 2400, lunch, dinner and takeaway. Known simply as **Le Repaire**, the bar/restaurant overlooks the ferry and the harbour and is a pleasant spot to watch boats during the day or for an after dinner drink at night. There is a billiards room. Well-prepared Créole food, salads, fish and lobster, the daily special costs €19.

Le Ti St-Barth, Pointe Milou, T0590-279771. 1930-late daily in high season, closed Sun Apr-Nov. A bistro and bar with a party atmosphere and entertainment which changes nightly. Mon live acoustic music, Tue Italian specialities, Wed plastic boots party, Thu sexy fashion show, Fri theme party, Sat Ti St-Barth Saturday night, Sun Gourmet Delights. Barbecue food, lots of music and often dancing on the tables.

Wine and Dinner Club, Colombier, T0590-298022. 1700-2400. An elegant dining room and cocktail bar, decorated with liberal use of leather, the main attraction here is the wine list. You can choose from a list of 40 wines served by the glass, or 360 by the bottle, including several *grand cru* wines. Tapas are available to accompany your drink if you don't want to eat a full meal.

⊛ Festivals and events

Saint-Barthélemy *p581, maps p581 and p585*

Jan Festival of Calssical Music, folk, jazz music and ballet performed by both school children and guest artists from abroad.

Feb/Mar Carnival is held before Lent. Children's parades, a Grand Parade through Gustavia for Mardi Gras, a black-and-white parade to Shell Beach on Ash Wed when Vaval, Carnival King, is burned.

Apr Caribbean Film Festival. Films by Caribbean film makers, with subtitles.

May Transat AG2R Race. Arrives every other year (2006, 2008) from Lorient in Brittany, France, after a stopover in Madeira. All boats are 33-ft, single hull, Figaro Beneteau, with same sails, safety equipment and 2 sailors.

Jul St Barth Open Fishing Tournament. Organized by Océan Must.

End-Jul Fête des Quartiers du Nord. Music, volley ball, dancing and fireworks at Flamands.

Aug Fête du Vent. Held in Lorient with a regatta, music and fireworks. Festival of Gustavia. Dragnet fishing contests and parties.

24 Aug Feast of St Barthélemy, the island's patron saint, when the church bells ring, boats are blessed and there are regattas, fireworks and a public ball.

25 Aug Feast of St Louis is celebrated in the village of Corossol, with a fishing festival, *pétanque, belote,* dancing and fireworks.

1-2 Nov All Saints' Day on 1 Nov is a public and religious holiday. At dusk thousands of candles are lit in the cemeteries. All Souls' Day on 2 Nov is also a public holiday.

24 Nov Swedish Marathon Race/Gustavialoppet, with distances of 3 and 12 km for children, women and men.

Dec Mondial Billes, a marbles competition; the winner qualifies to play in the next regional heat before joining the international players.

○ Shopping

Saint-Barthélemy *p581, maps p581 and p585*

In addition to its gourmet food, St-Barts is famous for its chic designer shops where you can find all the top labels for clothes, shoes, watches and jewellery. It is the place to find designer labels such as **Armani**, **Cartier**, **Hermès** and **Ralph Lauren**, most of which are in shops in Gustavia. There are 6 small shopping centres in Saint-Jean: **La Savane**, **Les Galeries du Commerce, La Villa Créole, Le Pélican, Vaval** and **Centre Commercial de Neptune**, with boutiques, food shops and restaurants.

Art and crafts

Made in St-Barth I, Villa Créole Shopping Centre, St-Jean, T590-(0)590-275657, madeinstbarth@wanadoo.fr, and **Made in St-Barth II**, rue Gal de Gaulle, Gustavia, T590-(0)590-275745. Local art and crafts in 2 outlets. There are several other art galleries in Gustavia and St-Jean.

▲▲ Activities and tours

Saint-Barthélemy *p581, maps p581 and p585*

Diving

Plongée Caraïbes, T0590-275594, www.plongee-caraibes.com. A single dive is €60, or there are packages of 5 or 10 dives for €286 or €540. PADI open-water certification costs €500. Several other dive companies in Gustavia.

Yellow Submarine, Gustavia, T0590-524051, www.yellow-submarine.fr. A semi-submersible, taking up to 47 passengers from Gustavia on a 1-hr tour every hour from 0900, through the marine park to Gros Ilets towards Les Petits Saintes, passing 3 wrecks where you can see lots of fish. Night departure once a week. €40 adults, €25 children under 12.

Fishing

Marine Service at Quai du Yacht Club, Gustavia, T0590-277034, www.st-barths.com/marine.service VHF 74. Deep-sea fishing trips, watersports and boat rentals including motorboats, catamarans, jet ski, scuba diving. The price for fishing depends on the type of boat (4-8 people) and ranges

from €350-470 for a half day to €575-810 for a full day with open bar and picnic.
Océan Must Marina at La Pointe, Gustavia, T0590-276225, VHF 10. Deep-sea fishing, charter boats for cruising, diving and waterskiing.

Horse riding
St-Barth Equitation, Ranch des Flamands, T0690-629930, www.st-barth-equitation.com. Contact Coralie Fournier for lessons or beach and countryside rides.

Sailing
Sailing and snorkelling cruises are offered by several catamarans. They go to Colombier Beach, Fourche Island, Tintamarre, Anguilla or St-Martin. Half-day cruises cost €40-45 pp, whole day with lunch €65-70, sunset cruises €34.
Marine Service, Gustavia, T0590-277034. A range of craft for hire, motorboats, catamarans, jet ski, scuba diving.
Sailing Yannis Marine, Gustavia, T0590-298912, www.yannismarine.com. Motor boat rentals, island tours from €600, sunset cruises, jet ski €100 per hr, diving, water-skiing, bareboat charters and sailing trips.

Tennis
ASCCO, Colombier, T0590-276107. 2 lit courts.
AJOE, Lorient, T0590-276763. 2 courts, 1 lit court. Also at several hotels, priority to guests.

Watersports
Carib Water Play, Baie de Saint-Jean, T0590-277122. Is a BiC Centre, offering windsurfing lessons and equipment rental.
Wind Wave Power, Grand Cul de Sac, T0590-278257. Has Mistral gear at their windsurf school.

⊖ Transport

Saint-Barthélemy *p581, maps p581 and p585*
Air
Scheduled flights from Anguilla (**Coastal Air Transport**), Pointe-à-Pitre (**Air Caraïbes**), St Croix (**Coastal Air Transport**), Sint Maarten (**Winair**, **Air Caraïbes**, **Saint Barth Commuter**), St-Martin (**Saint Barth Commuter**), St Thomas (**Air St Thomas**), San Juan (**Air St Thomas**). Charters available locally with **St Barth**

Commuter, T0590-275454 and **Air Caraïbes**, T0590-276190, **Winair** T0590-276101, **Air St Thomas** T0590-277176.

Boat
Several catamarans go to St-Barts from Sint Maarten, leaving in the morning, returning in the afternoon so you can do a day trip.
Voyager, www.voyager-st-barths.com, have scheduled services between St Maarten/St Martin and St-Barts, leaving from both Marigot (Mon-Sat) and Captain Oliver's Marina, Oyster Pond (daily), one way €44, day trip €52, open return €71. Contact **St-Barth Ship Service** for details, Quai de la République, T0590-275410, 871068.
The Edge, Pelican Marina, Simpson Bay, Sint Maarten, T599-5442640, www.stmaarten-activities.com, offers day trips for €40, one way €30, open round trip €59. Port fee €9, luggage €3.5 per item.

Car and scooter
There are 2 gas stations, 1 near the airport terminal (Mon-Sat 0730-1700), the other in Lorient (Mon-Wed, Fri 0730-1700, Sat morning).
It is not easy to hire a car for only 1 day, except out of season, mini mokes from €25 per day; ask your hotel to get a car if required. There are many local and international agencies at the airport: **Gumbs Rental** T0590-277532; **Island Car Rental** T0590-277001; **Questel** T0590-277322; **Soleil Caraïbes** T0590-276718; **Turbe** T0590-277142. **Scooters** can be rented from **Rent Some Fun** T0590-277059; **Chez Beranger** T0590-278900; **Saint Barth Moto Bike** T0590-276789; **Denis Dufau**, Saint-Jean, T0590-275483, a Harley Davidson shop.

Taxi
There is a taxi stand at the airport T0590-277581, and in Gustavia T0590-276631.

❶ Directory

Saint-Barthélemy *p581, maps p581 and p585*
Banks Banque Nationale de Paris (BNP), Banque Française Commerciale (BFC), Crédit Agricole. The BFC ATM at Galeries du Commerce, St-Jean, dispenses both US$ and euros. The bank here is open on Sat morning.

Internet Many hotels have internet facilities for their guests but there are also a couple of places in Gustavia near the harbour. **Medical services** Hospital, T0590-276035. Doctor on call: T0590- 277304. **Post** In Gustavia there are 3 post offices: Mon, Tue, Thu, Fri 0730-1500, Wed, Sat 0730- 1200, T0590-276200; in **Saint-Jean**: Mon, Tue, Thu, Fri 0800-1400, Wed, Sat 0730-1100, T0590-276402. In **Lorient**: Mon-Fri 0700-1100, Sat 0800-1000, T0590-276135. **Telephone** There are phone booths on the **Quai de Gaulle**, at the airport, **Galeries du Commerce** and **Flamands**, among other places. There are some phones which take coins but most take phone cards. **USA Direct** phone at the airport.

Background

History

Although called Ouanalao by the Caribs, the island was renamed after Christopher Columbus' brother, when discovered in November 1496. It was first settled by French colonists from Dieppe in 1645. After a brief possession by the Order of the Knights of Malta, and ravaging by the Caribs, it was bought by the **Compagnie des Îles** and added to the French royal domain in 1672. In 1784, France ceded the island to Sweden in exchange for trading rights in the port of Göteborg. In 1801, St-Barts was attacked by the British, but for most of this period it was peaceful and commercially successful. The island was handed back to France after a referendum in 1878.

Government

St-Barts is attached administratively to the Département de Guadeloupe and is administered by the sub-prefect in Saint-Martin who resides here two or three days a week. However, in 2007, the French government voted to allow St-Barts to split from Guadeloupe and become a COM (overseas collectivity), reporting directly to France. The change will take some time to implement and the new territorial council members will have to make decisions about local taxes, building permits, paving of the roads, and other issues of importance to the islanders. The island has its own mayor, who is elected for a six-year term of office.

People

St-Barts is inhabited mostly by people of Breton, Norman and Poitevin descent. Norman dialect is still widely spoken, while many islanders also speak English, but French is dominant. A few elderly women still wear traditional costumes (with their characteristic starched white bonnets called *kichnottes*); they cultivate sweet potato patches despite the dry, rocky soil, also weaving palm fronds into hats and bags which they sell in the village of Corossol. The men traditionally smuggled rum among neighbouring islands and now import liqueurs and perfumes, raise cattle and fish for lobsters offshore. Immigrants from France have taken most of the best jobs in hotels and restaurants, though, and relations are sometimes strained. St-Barts has become a 'chic' and expensive destination; the Rockefellers and Rothschilds own property on the island, while the rich, royal and famous stay in the luxury villas dotted around the island. However, its popularity is not confined to the wealthy few and nowadays the island hosts some 200,000 tourists a year, most of whom arrive in the high season, putting huge pressure on the infrastructure and causing a traffic gridlock. The traffic is a frequent topic of conversation among residents, along with the number of houses being built to cater for the growing resident population as well as the visitors. In November 2006 there were 4400 homes on the island, a 25% increase over 1999 when they were last counted. The 2007 population census is expected to reveal 10,000 people living on the island, compared with 6852 in 1999.

Antigua → *Country code: 268. Colour map 3, B/C3. Population: 75,741.*

Direct, non-stop flights from Europe and North America together with great beaches, watersports and safe swimming make this island ideal for introducing children to the Caribbean. English Harbour is particularly picturesque, with yachts filling a historic bay that has been a popular staging post for centuries. Nelson's Dockyard and ruined forts are overlooked by the old battery on Shirley Heights, now better known for Sunday jump-ups, reggae and steel bands. Antigua, with about 108 sq miles, is the largest of the Leewards, and also one of the most popular. Its dependencies are nearby Barbuda and Redonda. The island is low-lying and composed of volcanic rock, coral and limestone. There is nothing spectacular about its landscape, although the rolling hills and flowering trees are pretty. The coastline however, curving into coves and graceful harbours with 365 soft white-sand beaches fringed with palm trees, is among the most attractive in the West Indies. Some 30 miles to the north of Antigua, the coral island of Barbuda is attractive for hikers, nature lovers, cyclists and beachcombers. ▸▸ *For Sleeping, Eating and other listings, see pages 599-610.*

Ins and outs

Getting there Antigua has excellent comunications by air with Europe and North America as well as with neighbouring islands, making Antigua ideal for a two-centre holiday or the starting point for more protracted island hopping. It is not so easy to get there by sea, other than on a cruise ship or cargo boat, as there are no formal ferry links except to the sister island of Barbuda. ▸▸ *See Transport, page 608, for further information.*

Getting around Renting a **car** is probably the best way to see the islands' sights, as the bus service is inadequate, but be aware that roads are very bumpy and narrow and speed bumps are poorly marked. Finding your way around is not easy, there are no road signs and street names are rarely in evidence. **Cycling** is not very interesting. There are car hire companies in St John's and some at the airport, most will pick you up. Be careful with one-way streets in St John's. At night people do not always dim their headlights and watch out for pedestrians. **Minivans** (shared taxis) go to some parts of the island (for example Old Road) from the West End bus terminal by the market in St John's. **Buses** serve the southern part of the island but not the north, so there are no buses to the airport.

‼ Drive on the left, watch out for pot holes, narrow streets and animals straying across the street in the dark.

Leeward Islands Antigua

St John's → *Population: 30,000.*

Built around the largest of the natural harbours is St John's, the capital, formerly guarded by Fort Barrington and Fort James either side of the entrance to the harbour. The town is a mixture of the old and the new, with a few historical sites. Some of the old buildings in St John's, including the **Anglican cathedral** ① *Newgate St and Long St, donations requested,* have been damaged several times by earthquakes, the last one in 1974. A cathedral in St John's was first built in 1683, but replaced in 1745 and then again in 1843 after an earthquake, at which time it was built of stone. Its twin towers can be seen from all over St John's. It has a wonderfully cool interior lined with pitch pine timber. The **Antigua Recreation Ground** alongside the cathedral contains what was the main cricket pitch, used for Test matches, but this was replaced by a new ground for the 2007 Cricket World Cup. There are still some run-down parts but the cruise ship docks area has been developed for tourism: boutiques, duty-free shops and restaurants compete for custom. Most activity now takes place around the two quay developments: **Redcliff Quay** is a picturesque area of restored historical buildings now full of souvenir shops; **Heritage Quay** is a duty-free shopping complex with a casino, strategically placed to catch cruise ship visitors. When a cruise ship is in dock many passengers come ashore and it becomes very crowded. There is a vendors' mall next to Heritage Quay, selling souvenirs.

The **Museum of Antigua and Barbuda** ① *Long St, T/F4624930/1469, www.antigua museums.org, Mon-Fri 0830-1600, Sat 1000-1400, free (donations requested)*, at the former courthouse is worth a visit, both to see the exhibition of pre-Columbian and colonial archaeology and anthropology of Antigua, and for the courthouse building itself, first erected in 1750, damaged by earthquakes in 1843 and 1974, but now restored. There is also Viv Richards' cricket bat, with which he scored the fastest century. The **Historical and Archaeological Society (HAS)** based at the museum publishes an interesting newsletter. They also organize field trips. The **Environment Awareness Group** is also here and there's an interesting gift shop with locally made items.

West of St John's are the ruins of **Fort Barrington**, on a promontory at Goat Hill overlooking Deep Bay and the entrance to St John's Harbour. It was erected by Governor Burt, who gave up active duty in 1780 suffering from psychiatric disorders; a stone he placed in one of the walls at the fort describes him grandly as 'Imperator and Gubernator' of the Carib Islands. The previous fortifications saw the most action in Antigua's history, with the French and English battling for possession in the 17th century. At the other side of the harbour are the ruins of **Fort James**, from where you can get a good view of St John's. There was originally a fort on this site dating from 1675, but most now dates from 1749. To get there, head north out of St John's, turn west by **Barrymore Hotel** to the sea, then follow the road parallel to the beach to the end.

The southwest

Fig Tree Drive between Old Road and the Catholic church on the road going north from Liberta, is a steep, winding road, through mountainous rainforest. It is greener and more

Antigua

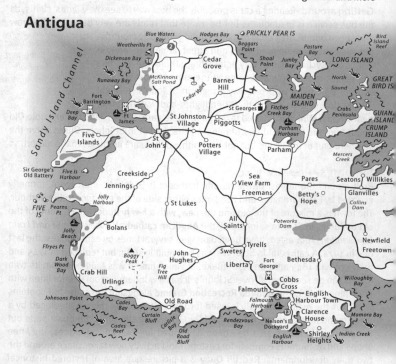

scenic than most of the island, but the rainforest is scanty and incomparable with
islands like Dominica. If travelling by bicycle make sure you go *down* Fig Tree Drive from
the All Saints to Liberta road, heading towards Old Road; the hill is very steep.

Boggy Peak, in the southwest, is the highest point on the island and from the top
you can get wonderful views over to Guadeloupe, St Kitts, Nevis and Montserrat. It is a
good walk up, or you can take a car. From Urlings walk (or take minibus) just over half
a mile in the direction of Old Town. There is a clear track on the left (ask the bus driver
to drop you off there) which is very straight then ascends quite steeply. When you get
to the top, walk round the fence surrounding the Cable & Wireless buildings to get a
good view in all directions. It takes over an hour to walk up (signs say it is a private
road) and you are advised not to wander around alone.

English Harbour and Nelson's Dockyard
ⓘ *US$5 entrance to the Dockyard (guided tour), the Interpretation Centre (guided
tour), the Block House and Shirley Heights, children under 12 free. Souvenirs and
T-shirts are on sale at the entrance. Parks Commissioner, T4601379.*

On the other side of the island from St John's is **English Harbour**, which has become
one of the world's most attractive yachting centres and is now a 'hot spot' at night for
tourists. Here Nelson's Dockyard, the hub of English maritime power in the region, has
been restored and is one of the most interesting historical monuments in the West
Indies. It is the only existing Georgian naval dockyard in the world and was designated
a national park in 1985. Nelson served in Antigua as a young man for almost three
years, and visited it again in 1805, during his long chase of Villeneuve which was to end
with the Battle of Trafalgar. The TV film *Longitude*, starring Jeremy Irons, was filmed
here, standing in for Jamaica and Barbados. The **Nelson's Dockyard Museum** has been
renovated to give the complete history of this famous Georgian Naval Yard and the story
of famous English Harbour. See **Admiral's Inn**, with its boat and mast yard, slipway and
pillars still standing, but which suffered earthquake damage in the 19th century. The
Copper and Lumber Store is now a hotel, bar and restaurant. On the quay are three large
capstans, showing signs of wear and tear. Boat charters can be arranged from here;
also a 20- to 30-minute cruise round the historic dock-yard for US$6 on *Horatio*, from
outside the **Copper and Lumber Store**, depending on seasonal demand. A footpath
leads round the bay to **Fort Berkeley** at the harbour mouth, well grazed by goats, and
wonderful views. Near the dockyard, **Clarence House** still stands where the future
King of England, William IV, stayed when he served as a midshipman.

On the left of the road from English Harbour to Shirley Heights are the remains of
the British Navy's magazines and a small branch road to the Dow Hill Interpretation
Centre, which offers an interesting 15-minute multimedia show every 15 minutes on the
history of the island. There is a gift shop, restaurant and small museum with shell
display. Local guides are also available.

Sleeping
Blue Waters 2
Carlisle Bay 1
Catamaran 3
Coco's Antigua 4
Country Inn 5
Murphy's Apartments 6
Palm Bay Beach Resort 9
Siboney Beach Club 10
Sleep Inn 13
Tree Tops Cottage 11

⁝ Touching down

Boat information (Own flag). All yachts must clear in and obtain a cruising permit in Antigua but may clear out of either Antigua or at the C & I office in Barbuda. Customs and Immigration offices are at English Harbour (no overtime charges), Crabbs Marina, St John's and Jolly Harbour (boats must be brought inside the marina for exit clearance). Entry fees and monthly cruising permits are on a sliding scale depending on the size of boat. There are additional fees for anchoring or stern to dockage in English Harbour and Falmouth, an US$1.85 per person charge plus electricity and water used. Dinghies must show lights at night and barbecues are prohibited in the harbour. The Antigua and Barbuda Marine Guide is distributed free by the Department of Tourism and contains lots of information on anchorages and marine supplies, www.antiguamarine guide.com. There are marinas at English Harbour, Falmouth Harbour (Antigua Slipway, Falmouth Harbour Marina, Catamaran Marina, Antigua Yacht Club), Parham Harbour (Crabbs Slipway), Jolly Harbour, St James's Club, and anchorages at Cades Reef, Carlisle Bay, Morris Bay (Curtain Bluff), Ffryes Bay, Crab Hill Bay, Five Islands Bay, Deep Bay, Morris Bay (Jolly Beach), Dickenson Bay, Parham Harbour and at several of the small islands if you can negotiate the reefs, for example Long Island, Guiana Bay, Green Island and Nonsuch Bay.

Business hours Banks: Mon-Thu 0800-1400; Fri 0800-1200, 1400-1600. Bank of Antigua opens Sat 0800-1200. **Shops:** Mon-Wed and Fri 0800-1200, 1300-1600. Thu and Sat are early closing days for most non-tourist shops. On Sun most places close, though the supermarkets at Woods Centre, English Harbour and Jolly Harbour open all day. **Currency** Eastern Caribbean dollars are used, at a rate of EC$2.70=US$1. **Exchange** US dollars are accepted in most places, but no one will know the exchange rate of other currencies. The conventional rate of exchange if you want to pay in US dollars is EC$2.50= US$1, so it is worth changing money in a bank. Credit cards are accepted, especially Visa and American Express, but small restaurants will take only cash or TCs. Always verify whether hotels, taxis, etc are quoting you US or EC dollars, you can be cheated. Take care not to get left with excess EC$ on departure. The airport bank is open Mon-Thu 0900-1500, 0900-1330 Fri, so closed when most long-haul flights come in.

Departure tax Airport departure charges amount to US$30 per person. Children under 12 pay half. Cash only. **Documents** A valid passport and onward ticket only are required by UK, US and Canadian citizens, nationals of Commonwealth countries, British Dependent Territories, and many other countries if their stay does not exceed 6 months. Citizens of EU countries and most of Latin America and the

At **Shirley Heights**, overlooking English Harbour, are the ruins of fortifications built in the 18th century, with a wonderful view. Some buildings, like officers' quarters, are still standing, restored but roofless, which give an idea of their former grandeur. At the lookout point, or **Battery**, at the south end is a bar and restaurant. On Sunday a steel band plays 1600-1900, followed by reggae 1900-2200, very loud and popular. There are barbecued burgers, chicken, ribs and salad available. It is usually full of tourists, often packed, and later on the crowd can be drunk and rowdy. **Great George Fort**, on Monk's Hill, above Falmouth Harbour (a 30-minute walk from the village of Liberta, and from Cobb's Cross near English Harbour) is less well preserved.

Caribbean do not need visas. Those in transit for less than 24 hours don't need visas. Visitors must also prove that they have enough money for their stay, and provide an address (even a temporary one).

Emergency numbers Police: T4620125, **Hospital:** T4620251.

Health Tiny sandflies, known locally as 'noseeums' often appear on the beaches in the late afternoon and can give nasty stings. Keep a good supply of repellent and make sure you wash off all sand to avoid taking them with you from the beach. Do not eat the little green apples of the manchineel tree, as they are poisonous, and don't sit under the tree in the rain as the dripping oil from the leaves causes blisters. Some beaches, particularly those on the west coast, get jellyfish at certain times of the year, for example Jul/Aug.

Official time Atlantic standard time, 4 hrs behind GMT, 1 hr ahead of EST.

Public holidays New Year's Day, Good Fri, Easter Mon, Labour Day (first Mon in May), Whit Mon (end May), Queen's Birthday (second Sat in Jun), Caricom Day (beginning of Jul; whole island closes down), Carnival (first Mon and Tue in Aug), Independence Day (1 Nov), Christmas Day and Boxing Day.

Safety Travel in Antigua is generally hassle free, but normal precautions against theft should be taken. There have been some serious incidents on isolated beaches, so caution should be taken in these areas.

Tourist information Antigua Tourist Office, Nevis St/Friendly Alley, T4620480, www.antigua-barbuda.org. Mon-Fri 0830-1600, Sat 0830-1200. Gives list of official taxi charges and hotel information. **Barbuda** has a Tourism Department here, too. The Antigua Tourist Office at the airport helps book accommodation mainly at the more expensive resorts. **Antigua Hotels and Tourist Association**, Lower Newgate St, St John's, T4620374, www.antiguahotels.org.

Tourist offices overseas

Canada: 60 St Clair Av East, Suite 304, Toronto, Ontario, M4T IN5, T416-9613085, info@antigua-barbuda-ca.com. **France**: 43 Av de Friedland, 75008 Paris, T33-1-53751571, ot.antigua-barbuda@wanadoo.fr. **Germany**: Thomas Str 11, D-61348, Bad Homburg, T49-617221504, antigua-barbuda@karibik.org. **Italy**: Via Santa Maria alla Porta 9, I-20123 Milan, T/F39-2877983, infoantigua@antigua-barbuda.it. **UK**: 2nd Floor, 45 Crawford Place, London W1H 4LD, T020-7258 0070, enquiries@antigua-barbuda.com. USA: 3 Dag Hammarskjold Plaza, 305 E 47 Street, Suite 6A, New York, NY 10017, T212-5414118, info@antigua-barbuda.org; 25 SE 2nd Av, Suite 300, Miami, FL 33131, T305-3816762.

Voltage 110 or 220 volts; check before using your own appliances. Many hotels have transformers.

The northeast

If you have a car, try taking the road out to the airport from St John's, now called the Sir George H Walter Highway. Do not enter the airport, but take the right fork which runs alongside it. After about 1½ miles take a right turn down a small road to **St George's Church**, on Fitches Creek Bay, built in 1687 in a beautiful location, and with interesting gravestones. From there, it may be possible to follow the rough road (only by 4WD) round the coast to **Parham**, which was the first British settlement on the island and has an attractive and unusual octagonal church, **St Peter's**, which dates from the 1840s, surrounded by flamboyant trees. From Parham go due south and then east at the petrol station through Pares to Willikies. On this road, just past Pares village, is a sign to

Betty's Hope ① *visitor centre Mon and Wed-Sat 0830-1600, for a guided tour contact the Antigua Museum, T4624930,* tells the story of life on a sugar plantation, a ruined sugar estate built in 1650 and owned by the Codrington family 1674-1944. Restoration was carried out by the Antigua Museum in St John's, it was officially opened in 1995 and is well worth a visit. One of the twin windmills can sometimes be seen working.

After Willikies the road is signed to the **Pineapple Beach Club** at Long Bay, but before you get there, take a right turn down a small road, which deteriorates to a bumpy track, to **Devil's Bridge** at Indian Town Point (look for signs for the Verandah). The area on the Atlantic coast is a national park where rough waves have carved out the bridge and made blowholes, not easily visible at first, but quite impressive when the spray breaks through. There's a good view of Long Bay and the headland.

Beaches and activities

The government is to implement plans to protect and develop facilities on 14 beaches with restrooms and shops. The nearest beach to St John's is **Fort James** which can be pleasant, with its palm trees and a popular bar-restaurant. However, it gets crowded at weekends, and at times it becomes rough and so has a milky appearance, lots of weed and is not good for swimming. Further north, but better, are **Dickenson Bay/Runaway Bay**, adjacent long stretches of white sand, separated by a small promontory. Dickenson Bay is wall-to-wall, low-rise hotels, with watersports outlets, bars and restaurants on the beach. The sea is calm and perfect for children, with roped off areas to ensure safety from motor craft. Much of the southern beach has been eroded by storms and there are some ruined beach houses at that end. **Soldier's Bay**, next to the **Blue Waters Hotel**; is shallow and picturesque. Instead of following the sign, park your car in the hotel car park, which has shade, walk left across the property, climb through the hole in the fence and in about three minutes you are there. Also good is **Deep Bay** which, like most beaches, can only be reached by taxi or car. There are several nice beaches on the peninsula west of St John's. On **Trafalgar Beach** condominiums have been built on the rocks overlooking the small, sheltered bay. If you go through Five Islands village you come to **Galley Bay**, a secluded and unspoilt hotel beach which is popular with locals and joggers at sunset. The four **Hawksbill** beaches at the end of the peninsula are crescent shaped, very scenic and unspoilt. Hotel guests tend to use the second beach, leaving the other three empty. Take drinks to the furthest one (clothes optional, secluded and pleasant) as there are no facilities and you may have the place to yourself. Heading south from St John's, you pass the marina at Jolly Harbour, where there is a beach and large hotel development, before reaching **Dark Wood Beach** and **Cades Bay** on the road to Old Road round the southwest coast. Both have a bar and restaurant. Near English Harbour is **Galleon Beach**, which is splendid, water taxi from English Harbour, US$1.10. It has an excellent hotel and restaurant. There is a cave on **Windward Beach**, near English Harbour, which is good for a moonlight bonfire (go in a group, not just as a couple). Follow the road past the Antigua Yacht Club leading to Pigeon Beach and turn left to Windward Beach on a bumpy track, best with a 4WD. At **Half Moon Bay**, in the east there is plenty of room on a lovely long, white-sand beach; the waves can be rough in the centre of the bay, but the water is calm at the north end. **Harry's Bar** serves very local food and cold drinks, but does not open regular hours.

> ⚑ *Tourist brochures will never tire of telling you that there are 365 beaches on Antigua, one for every day of the year, some of which are deserted.*

Diving Diving is mostly shallow, up to 60 ft, except below **Shirley Heights**, where dives are up to 110 ft, or **Sunken Rock**, with a depth of 120 ft and where the cleft rock formation gives the impression of a cave dive. Popular sites are **Cades Reef**, which runs for 2½ miles along the leeward side of the island and is an underwater park; **Sandy Island Reef**, covered with several types of coral and only 30 ft to 50 ft deep;

Frigate birds

Fregata magnificens are indeed magnificent when seen soaring high in the air, using the thermals to suspend themselves on their huge wings for days at a time. Frigates are one of the oldest known birds, with a history spanning 50 million years, and during that time they've picked up a trick or two. One of them, piracy, has earned them the nickname of Man-O'-War bird. Their fishing technique relies on finding fish or squid close to the surface which they can just skim off. Failing that they have developed a method of hassling other seabirds and encouraging them to regurgitate whatever they have just caught. In an amazing display of aerobatics, the frigates catch the food before it hits the water and get a free meal.

The breeding colony on Barbuda is believed to be the largest in the world, larger even than that of the Galápagos. Locals will tell you that there are some 10,000 birds, having recovered from the effects of Hurricane Luis in 1995, but numbers are anyone's guess. The breeding season is roughly September-January, although even later you can still see males displaying their bright red pouches, blowing them up like balloons to attract a mate. It is the male who chooses a nest site, and when he is sure he has found a long-term partner, he builds a precarious nest of twigs in the mangroves alongside all the other males. The female lays a single egg, which the male incubates and initially cares for once it is hatched. The chick is born white and fluffy and sits on the twiggy nest, suspended above the water, for 8-10 months until it is fully fledged. It takes a lot longer to be fully proficient at flying and feeding itself.

Horseshoe Reef, Barracuda Alley and Little Bird Island. There are also some wrecks to explore, including the *Andes*, in 20 ft of water in Deep Bay, but others have disappeared in hurricanes. At **Pasture Bay**, on Long Island, the hawksbill turtle lays its eggs from late May to December. The **Environmental Awareness Group (EAG)** ① *T4626236*, organizes turtle watches.

Barbuda → *Country code: 268. Colour map 3, B3. Population: 1,500.*

Some 30 miles to the north of Antigua is Barbuda, a flat coral island 68 miles square, one of the two island dependencies of Antigua. A visit here is like going back in time: there are few paved roads, no crime and the people are friendly – life is slow and simple.

Most residents live in the only village on the island, **Codrington**, which stands on the edge of a large lagoon. Barbuda has a fascinating history, having been privately owned in colonial times by the Codrington family, who used it to supply their sugar estates on Antigua with food and slaves. This caused problems after emancipation as all property belonged to the Codringtons and the freed slaves were trapped with no jobs, no land and no laws. After many years and court cases, Antiguan law was applied to the island, but while Barbudans may own their own houses, all other land is generally held by the Government. In places you can see the remains of the stone wall used to demarcate the limit of the village within which everybody had to live until 1976, when the creation of a local government inspired people to move further afield. You can also see the village well which was used to draw water until the 1980s.

This is one of the few islands in the area where there is still abundant wildlife, although much of it has been introduced by man (duck, guinea fowl, plover, pigeon, wild deer, pigs, goats, sheep, horses and donkeys), left over from the Codrington era.

There is an impressive **Frigate Bird Sanctuary** (the largest colony in the world) in the mangroves in Codrington Lagoon, particularly on Man of War Island where thousands of birds mate and breed between August and February. The sanctuary is worth a visit and the sight of 10,000 frigates raising their young is stunning (see box, page 597). Visitors are taken to only one or two spots to view the birds, and ropes keep the boats from getting too close. The rest of the birds are left entirely at peace. There are also brown boobies nesting alongside the frigates, and pelicans can be seen in the lagoon. An endemic warbler (*Dendroica subita*) lives on Barbuda and although DNA studies have been carried out, numbers and habitat requirements are so far unknown.

The **Gunchup Caves** near Two Foot Bay are interesting to explore. Men have used them for shelter since the days of the Amerindians. **Dark Cave** is home to a blind shrimp (*Typhlatya monae*) found only in these pools and in the Mona Island off Puerto Rico, but access is difficult. A road is planned. The island has a **Martello tower and fort**, the most complete historical site on the island. The tower is 56 ft high and once had nine guns to defend the southwest approach. From Codrington, River Road runs three miles to **Palmetto Point**, past Cocoa Point and on to Spanish Point, a half-mile finger of land that divides the Atlantic from the Caribbean Sea. There is a small ruin of a lookout post here and the most important Arawak settlements found in Barbuda. Horse racing takes place on a dirt track south of Codrington. You can sometimes see the horses being exercised around the island and taken for a swim behind a boat in the lagoon.

Detailed **maps** are available locally from the Codrington post office, otherwise from the map shop in Jardine Court, St Mary's, St John's, or the Barbuda Board of Tourism in Antigua see page 594.

Beaches and activities

The beaches are an outstanding feature of Barbuda and are arguably the most magnificent in the whole Caribbean. The longest beach is a swathe of white sand stretching for 17 miles down the west side, while the most spectacular is the pink-sand beach at Palmetto Point, made up of zillions of tiny pink shells. There are no beach bars or vendors, you will probably be the only person for miles. There is no shade except around Palm Beach where a few palm trees survived past hurricane damage.

Palaster Reef is a marine reserve to protect the reef and the shipwrecks (there are around 60 ships documented and the Codringtons made a healthy income from wrecking). The seas are rich with impressive formations of elkhorn and staghorn coral, all types of crustacean and tropical fish. Lobster is plentiful and a mainstay of nearly every meal. Diving, for certified divers only, is extremely rewarding, particularly if you like exploring wrecks, but you will need to take a guide. Snorkelling is also enjoyable.

❧ *Barbuda has one of the most spectacular beaches in the West Indies, a 17-mile stretch of uninterrupted sand, and the world's largest frigate bird colony.*

Redonda → *Colour map 3, C2.*

Antigua's second dependency, 35 miles to the southwest and half a mile square, is little more than a rocky volcanic islet and is uninhabited. Columbus sighted the island on 12 November 1493 and named it after a church in Cadiz called Santa María la Redonda. He did not land, however, and thus did not formally claim the island. Neither did anyone else until 1865 when Matthew Dowdy Shiell, an Irish sea-trader from Montserrat, celebrated the birth of a long-awaited son by leading an expedition of friends to Redonda and claiming it as his kingdom. In 1872, the island was annexed by Britain and came under the jurisdiction of the colony of Antigua, despite protests from the Shiells. The title of King was not disputed, however, and has survived to this day. The island was never inhabited, although for some years guano was extracted by the **Redonda Phosphate Company** until the works were blown away by a hurricane.

In 1880 MD Shiell abdicated in favour of his son, Matthew Phipps Shiell, who became King Felipe of Redonda, but emigrated to the UK where he was educated and became a prolific and popular novelist. His best known novel, *The Purple Cloud* (1901), was later made into a film, *The World, the Flesh and the Devil*, starring Harry Belafonte. On his death in 1947, he appointed as his literary executor and successor to the throne his friend John Gawsworth, the poet, who became Juan, the third King of Redonda, but continued to live in London. His reign was notable for his idea of an 'intellectual aristocracy' of the realm of Redonda and he conferred titles on his literary friends, including Victor Gollancz, the publisher, JB Priestley, Dorothy L Sayers and Lawrence Durrell. This eccentric pastime hit a crisis when declining fortunes and increasing time spent in the pub sparked a rash of new titles to all and sundry, and a number of abdications in different pubs. The succession was, and still is, disputed.

The **Redondan Cultural Foundation** is an independent association of people interested in Redonda, its history and its monarchs, which tries to steer through the minefield of Redondan politics. It was established in 1988 by the late Reverend Paul de Fortis and exists to promote the writings of MP Shiell, John Gawsworth and other authors of the realm's 'intellectual aristocracy'. It celebrates Redonda as 'the last outpost of Bohemia'. The foundation published *The Kingdom of Redonda 1865-1990* in association with the Aylesford Press (1991), and also publishes a regular newsletter.

Meanwhile, on Redonda, all is much the same for the goats, lizards and seabirds, who live an undisturbed life apart from the occasional birdwatcher who might come to find the burrowing owl, now extinct on Antigua.

Sleeping

Antigua *p591, maps p592, p600 and p601*
There is a 10% service charge and 10.5% sales tax at all hotels. The greatest concentration of developments is in the area around St John's, along the coast to the west and also to the north in a clockwise direction to the airport, taking advantage of some of the best beaches. You would only really want to stay in St John's if you were there on business or visiting for a cricket match. A second cluster of hotels is around English Harbour and Falmouth Harbour in the southeast of the island. These are very pleasant with lovely views of the harbours and yachts at anchor. Many may be closed Sep-Oct. There are several all-inclusives, most of which are not included here. There are lots of self-catering apartments, but a common complaint is that sufficient provisions are not available locally and you have to go into St John's for shopping, requiring a taxi or car hire. Camping is illegal.

LL Blue Waters, on the north coast, T4620290, www.bluewaters.net. One of the most upmarket on the island, with lush tropical gardens and huge mature trees on a very pretty bay. 77 large colonial-style rooms, suites and villas with patios or balconies, solid furniture and chintz fabrics. Rates include breakfast and afternoon tea or you can opt for half board or all inclusive. There is a pool and watersports, a gym and tennis.

LL Carlisle Bay, Old Road, T4840002, www.carlisle-bay.com. The sister hotel of One Aldwych in London and the newest luxury hotel to hit the Antigua scene with great fanfare. Huge suites have been designed with dark wooden furniture, cream, white and grey furnishings and clean minimalist lines. Every luxury including offices in the rooms with wireless internet access, well-stocked mini bars, 2 restaurants, a separate cinema and a library with computers. Peter Burwash tennis centre with 9 courts, pool, spa, gym and non-motorized watersports. The beach is lovely and calm in a very protected pretty bay with a view of Montserrat.

LL Palm Bay Beach Resort, Browns Bay, just past Harmony Hall, T4604173, www.palm bayantigua.com. 4 cottages in pretty gardens with lots of bougainvillea on the beach, 2 bedrooms, 2 bathrooms, terrace, pool, watersports with diving and sailing craft. Complimentary boat shuttle to Green Island for snorkelling. Italian owned, with a restaurant, Tamarind, open for lunch and dinner (breakfast for villa guests only), serving Italian dishes. Lively crowd around the bar.

LL-L Siboney Beach Club, Dickenson Bay, T4620806, www.siboneybeachclub.com. Proprietor Tony Johnson has made this one of the nicest small, independent places to stay. 12 comfortable suites in a 3-storey block on the beach. Decor and view vary but each has a bedroom, separate sitting/dining room with sofa bed, tiny kitchenette tucked away in a cupboard for making snacks, balcony, a/c, fan, CD player, phone. Pool, good restaurant under separate management, watersports nearby.

LL-L Tree Tops Cottage, Half Moon Bay, T4604423, www.caribbeanavenue.com/tree tops/index.html. Charming 2-bedroom, 2-bathroom West Indian-style villa with ginger-bread fretwork on the veranda, perched on a hillside in open countryside 5 mins from Half Moon Beach. Daily maid service. Comfortable, breezy, with a lovely deck, where humming-birds come to be fed, for relaxing and trying to spot dolphins and whales offshore, quiet, only the sounds of birds and goats, car needed.

LL-AL Admiral's Inn, English Harbour, T4601027, www.admiralsantigua.com. This handsome Georgian brick building dating from 1788 was once a store room for pitch, turpentine and lead, while upstairs were the offices for the engineers for the Royal Naval Dockyard; the hand-hewn beams, wrought-iron chandeliers and a bar which is an old work bench scarred by the names of ships that once docked there. 13 rooms, very

pleasant, excellent location, good food in the restaurant overlooking the water, live music Sat night. Transport to the beach, compli-mentary sunfish and snorkelling equipment.

LL-AL Catamaran Hotel and Marina, Falmouth Harbour, T4601036, www.cata maran-antigua.com. On a narrow man-made beach by the yachts, on a bus route or a 30-min walk to Nelson's Dockyard. 14 rooms and suites in a block on 2 floors, a/c, fans, some with TV, single or double beds, cribs for kids.

LL-AL Coco's Antigua, Jolly Harbour, T4602626, www.cocoshotel.com. Price per person, all-inclusive. 19 rooms in chattel-style wooden cottages with gingerbread fretwork, fan, fridge and a view of Jolly Beach and Five Islands. Lovely location built on a bluff with gorgeous balconies and pleasant breeze, very romantic, restaurant, pool.

LL-AL Galleon Beach, English Harbour, T4601024, www.galleonbeach.com. On the beach at Freemans Bay, 1-, 2- or 3-bedroom comfortable, fully equipped and tasteful cottages and villas in different styles with an additional sofa bed and veranda. Spacious grounds, glorious views of the old dockyard at English Harbour and the many yachts at anchor, tennis, sunfish, windsurfing, beach bar and restaurant, ferry to Nelson's Dockyard.

L-AL Murphy's Apartments, All Saints Rd, St John's, T5625358, ccck2901@hotmail.com. 15 rooms and apartments, a/c, TV, internet access,

English Harbour & Shirley Heights

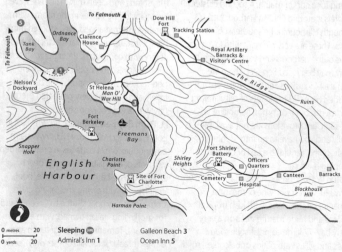

To Falmouth
Dow Hill Fort
Tracking Station
Ordnance Bay
Clarence House
Tank Bay
Royal Artillery Barracks & Visitor's Centre
To Falmouth
The Ridge
Nelson's Dockyard
St Helena Man O' War Hill
Ruins
Fort Berkeley
Freemans Bay
Snapper Hole
Fort Shirley Battery
English Harbour
Charlotte Point
Shirley Heights
Officers' Quarters
Canteen
Barracks
Site of Fort Charlotte
Cemetery
Hospital
Blockhouse Hill
Harman Point

N

0 metres 20
0 yards 20

Sleeping
Admiral's Inn 1

Galleon Beach 3
Ocean Inn 5

with every amenity and a lovely garden. Breakfast included. Longer-term possible.

L-A Ocean Inn, English Harbour, T4601263, www.theoceaninn.com. On a hillside overlooking English Harbour, with a spectacular and breezy view of the yachts and old buildings and a small pool. A rather haphazard appearance of rooms having been built below the main house when the owner felt like it. Rooms and bathrooms are small and basic, but they have a TV, a/c, fridge, carpet or tiles, some of the cheaper rooms in the main house share a bathroom. Breakfast is included, other meals on request.

AL Country Inn, Monk's Hill Rd, Cobb's Cross, T4601469, www.countryinncottages.com. Self-catering cottages in traditional ginger-bread style on the hillside overlooking Falmouth Harbour, breezy, balconies, hammocks, open-plan, and very colourful. Small pool on the hill top and you have to be good at climbing to stay here. Access is up a poor road and steep hill, 4WD essential.

B Cappuccino Lounge, Nelson's Alley between Church St and Newgate St, St John's, T5626808, www.caplounge.com. New in 2004, with bar/restaurant downstairs and renovated rooms upstairs. Simple, small a/c rooms with minmalist furniture, all with double bed and small bathroom, clean and nicely painted, convenient for town, transport and cricket. Good for single travellers especially women travelling alone. Breakfast available. TV in bar. Try a speciality coffee, West Indian style.

C Joe Mike's Hotel, in Corn Alley and Nevis St, St John's, T4621142, joemikes@candw.ag. Special rates can be negotiated but not by phone. Rooms OK but there are no balconies, and weak a/c. Downstairs are a fast food restaurant and bar, casino, ice cream parlour, cocktail lounge, beauty salon and mini-mart.

C-D The Sleep Inn, just outside the gates of Nelson's Dockyard, T5623082. 14 rooms, very simple but tidy inn, good value, private bath, ceiling fans, shared kitchen, meals on request, very local.

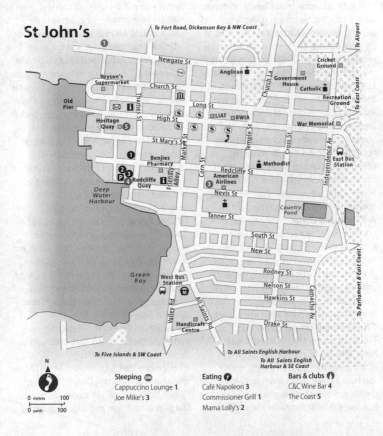

St John's

To Fort Road, Dickenson Bay & NW Coast
To Airport
Newgate St
Cricket Ground
Anglican
Government House
Catholic
Church St
Church La
Bryson's Supermarket
Old Pier
Heritage Quay
Thames St
High St
Long St
St Mary's St
LIAT
BWIA
Temple St
Cross St
War Memorial
Recreation Ground
To East Coast
Benjies Pharmacy
Mark St
Corn St
Redcliffe St
Methodist
East Bus Station
Independence Av
Deep Water Harbour
Redcliffe Quay
Friendly Alley
American Airlines
Nevis St
Tanner St
Country Pond
Green Bay
West Bus Station
All Saints Rd
Valley Rd
South St
New St
Rodney St
Nelson St
Hawkins St
Camacho Av
Drake St
To Parliament & East Coast
Handicraft Centre
To Five Islands & SW Coast
To All Saints English Harbour
To All Saints English Harbour & SE Coast

N
0 metres 100
0 yards 100

Sleeping
Cappuccino Lounge 1
Joe Mike's 3

Eating
Café Napoleon 3
Commissioner Grill 1
Mama Lolly's 2

Bars & clubs
C&C Wine Bar 4
The Coast 5

Accommodation is either expensive and exclusive or basic, with little in between. Take mosquito repellent and earplugs if you are in the centre of Codrington at weekends. Several private homes offer accommodation, although these change if a long-term rental is taken. See www.barbudaful.net for further options.

LL The Beach House, Palmetto Point, T7254042, www.thebeachhouse barbuda.com. Newly renovated and redesigned, very light and white, this is the ultimate in luxury on a pink-sand beach, where each of the 21 suites is assigned 2 personal butlers who can organize anything for you. Prices include air fare to and from Antigua and breakfast. All meals can be taken anywhere, any time, on the beach, in the restaurant, in your room, wherever you want. Bicycles, horse riding and massages can be arranged.

LL Coco Point Lodge, in the far south, T462 3816, www.cocopoint.com. A hideaway since the 1960s and the ultimate in exclusivity, you have to be 'someone' to stay here, non-guests are not admitted. Set on a stunning white-sand beach it occupies 164 acres of the peninsula at the tip of Barbuda. There are rooms with shady verandas or cottages of different sizes with high ceilings, living room, bar and beach-front patio.

LL K-Club, in the south, T4600300, www.kclub barbuda.com. Just north of Coco Point and also on a fabulous beach of white, powdery sand stretching for miles, untouched and unspoilt. Italian owned and designed in an open plantation-house style. 45 rooms, painted turquoise and white. 9-hole golf course, watersports and a pool. Islanders and non-residents are welcomed, excellent food, open mid-Nov to end-Aug, no under 12s.

A-B The Island Chalet, in the heart of Codrington, T7730066, Miss Myra Askie. 4 rooms on the 1st floor with a small double bed and a rollaway, so they can sleep 3 at a pinch, but it gets a bit hot. Shared kitchen and living room facilities of a good standard, grocery across the square, price comes down at weekends when noise levels rise at night.

C Nedd's Guest House, Codrington, T4600059. Run by Mcarthur and Natalie Nedd, who can offer excursions and tours with fishing. They also run a supermarket and have a collection of 100 tortoises. 4 double rooms with shower room and balcony, shared sitting room and kitchen.

● Eating

Antigua *p591, maps p592, p600 and p601*
Food There are some local specialities, found in smaller restaurants in St John's, should never be missed: **saltfish** (traditionally eaten at breakfast in a tomato and onion sauce), **pepper-pot** with fungi or *foungee* (a kind of cornmeal dumpling), **goat water** (hot goat stew), **shellfish** (the local name for trunk fish), **conch stew** and the local staple, **chicken and rice**. Johnny cake is rather like a savoury doughnut, but you will find variations on the theme in other islands. **Ducana** is made from grated sweet potato and coconut, mixed with pumpkin, sugar and spices and boiled in a banana leaf. **Tropical fruits and vegetables** found on other Caribbean islands are also found here: bread fruit, cristophine, dasheen, eddo, mango, guava and pawpaw (papaya). Oranges are green, while the native pineapple is called the Antigua black and is very sweet. Locally made Sunshine ice cream, American-style, is available in most supermarkets.

Be aware that there is **ciguatera** in the waters around Antigua and across to Florida.

Drink Imported wines and spirits are reasonably priced but **local drinks** (fruit and sugar cane juice, coconut milk, and Antiguan rum punches and swizzles, ice cold) must be experienced. The local Cavalier rum is a light golden colour, usually used for mixes. Beer can be bought at good prices from most supermarkets and the Wadadli Brewery on Crabbs peninsula. There are no licensing restrictions. Tap water is safe only in hotels and resorts; bottled water is available if you are unsure or prefer it. VAT is 15%. 10% service is usually added to your bill.

♥♥♥ Chez Pascal, Galley Bay Hill, Galley Bay, T4623232, www.chezpascalantigua.com. Tue-Sat 1130-1500, 1830-late. Daily lunch and dinner. Wonderful view overlooking Galley Bay, eat indoors in the cool or on the patio by the pool. Gourmet, authentic French food from chef Pascal Milliat, with extensive French wine list. Considered one of the best restaurants on the island; the place to come for a special meal or for a celebration. Accommodation also available.

♥♥♥ Harmony Hall, Brown's Bay, T4604120, www.harmonyhall.com. Daily 1200-1530, dinner 1930-2200 Fri-Sat, closed summer. Old plantation house and sugar mill dating back to 1843, now a restaurant and art gallery with accommodation, reached via several miles of unmetalled road. Bar in the mill, restaurant on the patio overlooking Nonsuch Bay and Green Island. Bought in 2006 by Antigua Yacht Club Marina as a sister property, service initially declined. Pool, beach, complimentary boat trips to Green Island for guests, dock for visiting yachts.

TTT Le Bistro, Hodges Bay, T4623881, www.lebistro-antigua.com. Tue-Sun 1830-2230. Excellent French food prepared by head chef, Patrick Gauducheau. One of the best restaurants on the island and featured in international magazines and TV programmes. Varied menu includes vegetarian options, delicious pâté and melt-in-the-mouth pastries. Reservations required.

TTT Pavilion, 7 Pavilion Drive at the entrance to the airport, T4806800, www.thepavilion antigua.com. Mon-Sat 1800-2130. French food with Cajun touches created by a New Orleans chef is divine, pink linen table cloths, pink roses in the centre of each table, sterling silver cutlery and silver water goblets. 5-star dining, jacket and tie required for men, very expensive at about US$100 per person. Cold a/c, but you can warm up after the meal on the wrap around veranda overlooking the cricket ground, which is nice for coffee. Reservations required.

TTT-TT The Beach, Antigua Village, Dickenson Bay, T4806940, www.bigbanana-antigua.com/beach.htm. Daily breakfast, lunch and dinner. East meets West theme, with smoked sushi, Middle Eastern dishes and salads, pastas and seafoods, ribs and burgers, something for everyone, lively and busy atmosphere overlooking the sea, credit cards accepted, reservations suggested.

TTT-T Commissioner Grill, Redcliffe St, St John's, T4621883. Daily 1000-2300. A casual restaurant on the street corner in the heart of town, high ceilings and ceiling fans cool things down while staff sweat over their pans at the back. Owned by Conroy White, a local chef who prepares West Indian dishes with a breakfast of saltfish and plenty of seafood, lobster, steak, chicken, burgers, ribs and salads and sandwiches. Excellent vegetable plate with mixed vegetables, plantain, black beans and *foungee* or rice and peas, but if you are vegetarian ask them not to fry the plantain in the same oil they use for fish. Draught beer.

TTT-T The Sticky Wicket, 20 Pavilion Drive, at the airport, T4817000, www.thesticky wicket.com. Lunch and dinner daily. Restaurant and bar, overlooks the cricket ground and has TVs for watching sporting events, convenient if you have a long wait for your plane, much more comfortable than the airport but expensive. Wide-ranging menu, with international dishes such as steaks and fish or you can get burgers or nachos if you just want a snack to pass the time.

TT Café Napoleon, Redcliffe Quay, T5621802, cafenapoleon@hotmail.com. 0800-1600. In the heart of St John's, a great spot for casual breakfast and lunch, popular with islanders and business people as well as visitors.

TT Cloggy's Café, next to Abracadabra in English Harbour, T4638083, cloggyscafe@yahoo.com. Mon-Sat, food 1000-1530, drinks and tea until 1700. Some of the best baguettes sandwiches and salads on the island. Lunch served on a patio with a tropical flavour.

TT HQ, upstairs in the historic Headquarters Building inside English Harbour, T5622562. Daily, breakfast, lunch and dinner. Dining tables are inside and outside on the veranda overlooking Nelson's Dockyard, popular with a lively yachting crowd and there is live music some nights. Their speciality is fish and there is a live lobster tank. Dinner reservations suggested.

TT-T Catherine's Café at the Antigua Slipway in Nelson's Dockyard, English Harbour, T4605050. Wed-Mon for lunch, drinks and dinner. French chef, divine crêpes, quiches, assorted salads. Lovely setting right on the water with a boardwalk where you can sit and watch the yachts and the harbour.

TT-T Mama Lolly's, in Redcliffe Quay, St John's, T5621552, mamalol@candw.ag. Mon-Sat 0830-1700. In the heart of the shopping area, best vegetarian lunch, with lasagne, bean stew, tofu, salad bar, choice of 2, 3, or 4 cooked dishes plus a salad for a set price, great mixed fruit and vegetable juices, freshly extracted. Limited seating, locals often get a takeaway.

TT-T Papa Zouk, Hilda Davis Drive, Gambles, St John's, T4646044. Mon-Sat 1800-2300 in season, otherwise Wed-Sat. Unprepossessing and casual place known for its specialities of bouillabaisse, a meal in itself, paella Créole, fresh fish and seafood, although chicken and meat is also available and vegetarian food on request. Congenial host, Bert Kirchner, goes through the daily specials with you and chats at the table while zouk music is played in the background. Very popular, always full.

♦♦–♦ Turner's Beach Bar, Johnson's Point, Jolly Harbour, T4629133. Daily 1000 until everyone goes home. Beach bar at the end of a long stretch of sand with a covered terrace or umbrellas on the beach. You can get breakfast, lunch, snacks, drinks or dinner. Local food, good selection, salads, huge roti, fish and chips, tender conch.

♦ OJ's Beach Bar & Restaurant, Crab Hill, Jolly Harbour, T4600184. Daily 1000-2200. Excellent setting, on the beach, simple menu but good food and service, fresh seafood, delicious snapper, great lobster salad as well as burgers and sandwiches, economical prices, no credit cards. On Sun there is live jazz from 1600.

♦ Zanzibar, on the water in Falmouth Harbour, T4637838, info@zanzibarantigua.com. Hotel and restaurant for those on a tight budget, casual meals, fish, soups and salads with a special fish and chips night on Sat.

Barbuda *p597*

There are not many restaurants on Barbuda and they tend to close in the evening, so check beforehand. Food is cooked at lunchtime and is available until about 1700, or when it runs out. You have to talk to the owner if you want an evening meal. For home cooking try the **Block Boys**, T4600012, at weekends. They are a group of young men who cook to raise money for sports and charitable events.

♦♦ Palm Tree, at the edge of Codrington, T4600517. Advance bookings required. Cerene Deazle runs this restaurant as well as a guesthouse, serving local food on request such as lobster, conch, fish and venison. The local deer is a speciality on Barbuda. She will also cook chicken or burgers and fries.

♦♦–♦ Waomoni's, Codrington, T5611933, waomonisbest@hotmail.com, Mon-Sat 1900-2200. Waomoni is the Amerindian name for Barbuda. The restaurant is owned by Jackie Joseph, who offers dine in or takeaway meals, even picnics with advanced booking. Prices range from US$5.55-26 for seafood specials, grilled or stuffed lobster, fish, sandwiches, salads, chicken, with daily Barbudian specials like bullfoot soup.

🅞 Bars and clubs

Antigua *p591, maps p592, p600 and p601*

The largest hotels around the island provide dancing, calypso, steel bands, limbo dancers and moonlight barbecues so that their guests need never leave the property. Entertainment comes to them, with live music and other acts rotating between the various hotels. English Harbour area has become the hot spot for tourists, particularly for the yachting fraternity who come ashore for a good time. Most nightlife happens in bars, or restaurants with bars which can host live music, see Eating, above. There are a couple of clubs frequented by Antiguans in their 20s, where you can dance into the wee small hours. Try the popular and hugely erotic bump and grind dance style. A free newspaper, *It's Happening, You're Welcome*, contains lots of information on events.

Abracadabra, at the car park at the entrance to Nelson's Dockyard, English Harbour. T4602701. Bar 1800-late. A restaurant and video bar with a deck under the palm trees which is nearly always lively with dancing late into the night. Casual, no strict dress code.

C&C Wine Bar, Redcliff Quay, T4607025. Mon-Sat 1130-late. Next to the **Pottery Shop**, a wine bar serving South African wines and cheese platters, very popular with the local professional crowd as well as tourists.

Club Havana, English Harbour, T7252308. Mexican cantina and bar, house favourites are mojitos, caipirinhas, margaritas, coladas, while José Cuervo tequilas start at only US$1.85.

The Coast, Heritage Quay, St John's, T5626278. Dock side venue with 3 bars, a restaurant serving Italian-Caribbean food, and a night club with 2 dance floors, free entry, open Wed-Mon.

Last Lemming, Yacht Club Road, Falmouth, T4606910. Mon-Sat 1100-1500, Sun 1030-1500 for brunch, daily 1900-2200. A restaurant and bar right by the mega yachts at the Yacht Club Marina with a great view of how the rich go on holiday. Live reggae and dancing on Fri from 2100, guitarist sings pop and calypso on Sat nights.

Life, a floating bar at the entrance to the Dockyard, T5624057. Mon-Sat until late. Owned by a former London DJ, all types of music, dancing, casual dining, very lively bar.

Mad Mongoose, Falmouth Harbour, T4637900. Nov-May Tue-Sun 1500-2300.

Restaurant and bar in a large wooden shack overlooking the harbour. Loud music attracts the younger yachting crowd. Deck with outside seating.

Mainbrace Pub, Copper and Lumber Store Hotel, in Nelson's Dockyard, English Harbour, T4601058. Daily 0700-2300. A traditional English pub with beer on tap, the old stone walls and exposed beams of the dockyard buildings. Wed night jazz, Thu karaoke, Fri night 2 drinks for the price of 1. Go for the beer or mixed drinks at US$3.

Miller's by the Sea, at Runaway Bay, Fort James, T4629414. Daily 0800-2300. Serves lunch, dinner or just drinks, often has live music: jazz, calypso or reggae bands, especially on Sun after Shirley Heights, owned by a local jazz hero. Beach barbecues on Sun with dancing on the sand.

Putters Bar and Grill, Dickenson Bay, T4634653. Daily 1600-late. Nightly specials vary from hot dogs to T-bone steaks. Activities for families, crazy golf US$5.55 adult, US$3.70 children (under 4s free), Jungle Gym with swings, slides, climbing frames, ropes and ladders, air hockey, pinball and pool tables.

Rush Night Club, Runaway Bay, T5627874, hadeedej@candw.ag. Daily 1600-late. Night club right on the coast, deck overlooking the sea. Very modern decor, fusion music played with something for everyone. Also on site is **Conor's Sports Bar**, with TVs, pool tables, darts, dominoes.

Shirley Heights Lookout. T4601785, VHF 68. Thu, Sun 1600-1900 steel pan followed on Sun by reggae 1900-2200. A very touristy but fun party, with barbecued burgers, chicken, ribs and salad at stalls on the hill overlooking English Harbour. Bus loads of revellers are brought from hotels all round the island and while the steel band is good family entertainment, it can get rowdy by the time the reggae band comes on if people have been drinking all afternoon.

Barbuda *p597*

Green Door, in the centre of Codrington, T5623134. Daily 0700-2400 or later. The island's first bar, run by Byron Askie and a pivot for social life on Barbuda. Open in the day for bingo, pool, TV, entertainment in the evenings and a weekend disco, food on request, usually spicy chicken wings.

Jackie's Seafood Bar, Codrington, T4600408. 1200 until the last customer goes home. Lunch spot with evening food cooked to order, also a bar, with TV, dominoes and cards. **The Lyme**, by the lagoon, Codrington, T4600619. Bar and restaurant, open daily throughout the day and evening. At weekends it becomes a night club, with a band and disco for the younger crown. Varied menu, including lobster, food any time. **Madison's Bar**, Madison Sq, Codrington, T4600465. Wed-Thu 1400-2400, Fri-Sat 0900-0200, Sun 1700-0100. A bar with a wide range of drinks as well as burgers, chicken, spare ribs and fries to eat in or take away.

⦿ Entertainment

Antigua *p591, maps p592, p600 and p601* **Deluxe Cinema**, High St and Cross St, St John's, T4623664. A duplex showing all the latest releases. Tickets cost US$5.55.

⦿ Festivals and events

Antigua *p591, maps p592, p600 and p601* **Apr** The Classic Yacht Regatta, www.antigua classics.com. Spectacular, with yawls, ketches, schooners and square-masted vessels, contact the Antigua Yacht Club, T4601799.
Apr-May Antigua Sailing Week, T4628872, www.sailingweek.com. A huge regatta with participants from over 30 countries, fun events, live music, Nelson's Dockyard.
Jul-Aug Carnival is at the end of Jul and lasts until the 1st Tue in Aug. The main event is 'J'ouvert', or 'Juvé' morning when from 0400 people come into town dancing behind steel and brass bands. There are competitions for the Calypso Monarch with sections for women and children as well as beauty pageants. Hotels and airlines tend to be booked up well in advance. Contact the Carnival Committee, High St, St John's, T4624707.
Oct 2 weeks of preparations build up to Heritage Day on 21 Oct. Schools and offices prepare decorations for judging and various events lead up to National Dress Day on 31 Oct with a Food Fair and Exhibition followed by a ceremonial parade on 1 Nov.

Barbuda *p597*

May Barbuda has a small carnival known as **Caribana**.

☉ Shopping

Antigua *p591, maps p592, p600 and p601*
Art and crafts
Harmony Hall, Brown's Bay Mill, near
Freetown, Antigua, T268-4604120. Daily
1000-1800, Nov-Apr. An art gallery and gift
shop, exhibiting and selling paintings, sculpture
and crafts from leading Caribbean artists,
popular for a lunch stop at the restaurant (see
Eating above) while touring by car or yacht.
The Pottery Shop, Redcliffe Quay, St John's,
Antigua, T268-5621264, fullerj@candw.ag.
Mon-Fri. Lovely pottery and interesting designs
by Sarah Fuller, hand crafted using local clay.
You can visit the studio on the beach, 2 miles
north of the airport, well signposted, where
they will make anything to order.
Woods Gallery, Woods Mall opposite the
post office, T4622332. Mon-Sat 1000-1730.
Opened in 2005 as a cooperative of over 20
Antiguan artists selling arts and crafts with
10 shows or exhibitions a year.

Bookshops
The Best of Books, Lower Long St, St John's,
Antigua, T5623198, bestofbooks@yahoo.com.
It really does have the best selection of
Caribbean and international books, newspapers
and magazines in all the Leeward Islands. Also
stocks a selection of things made in Antigua.

Markets
Market day in St John's, Antigua, is Sat but the
main market is open Mon-Sat. The market
building is at the south end of Market St but
there are goods on sale all around. In season,
there is a good supply of fruit and vegetables.

Shopping centres
Heritage Quay and Redcliffe Quay, St John's,
Antigua. Shopping complexes with expensive
duty-free shops (and public toilets) in the
former, and boutiques. The latter has bars and
restaurants and a parking lot, free if you go are
shopping there. Some tourist shops offer 10%
reductions to locals and compensate by overcharging tourists. Duty-free shops at the airport
are more expensive than those in town.
Woods Center is a modern shopping mall
with a wide variety of shops including **The
Epicurean Supermarket**, the most modern,
well-stocked supermarket on the island, a

drugstore, post office and dental clinic.
Jolly Harbour is a good place for day-to-
day shopping, and also has a large
Epicurean Supermarket.

▲ Activities and tours

Antigua *p591, maps p592, p600 and p601*
Cricket
Cricket is the national sport and Antigua has
produced many famous cricketers, including
captains of the West Indies team Sir Viv
Richards and Richie Richardson; fast bowlers
Andy Roberts and Curtly Ambrose, Kenneth
Benjamin, Eldine Baptiste and Winston
Benjamin. In 2007 the brand new **Sir Vivian
Richards Cricket Stadium** was inaugurated in
time for the Cricket World Cup. Located
between St John's and the airport on Factory
Road, renamed the Sydney Walling Highway
for the occasion, it was built with the help of
the Chinese, who also paid for most of its
construction. It has a permanent capacity of
10,000, but temporary stands boosted that to
20,000 for the World Cup. Although it is a
multi-purpose stadium, it will be used
principally for cricket and has all the
technology required of a world class facility,
with a practice pitch, training infrastructure
and a media centre as well as underground
tunnels for the players to use. Test matches
are also played at the **Antigua Recreation
Ground** (**ARG** to locals). Matches are helped
along by DJ Chickie's Hi Fi and characters like
Gravy, the cross-dressing cheerleader, now
retired but who occasionally puts in a cameo
performance, entertaining during intervals.
Brian Lara scored his world record 375 here in
1994 and again in 2004 with 400 not out,
both times against England. There are also
good cricket pitches at the **Sticky Wicket** by
the airport and at the **Jolly Beach Hotel**
(where the teams usually stay), which are used
as practice grounds during an international
match, team training for the West Indies and
for touring teams. There are matches between
Antiguan teams and against teams from other
islands, and local matches can be seen in St
John's near the market and all over the island in
the evenings and at weekends. The **West
Indies Cricket Board**, T4605462, has
information on Test Matches. The cricket
season runs from Jan to Jul.

Cycling

Bikes Plus, Independence Drive, St John's, T4622453. Mountain bikes rental, Mon-Sat.
Paradise Boat Sales Rentals and Charters, T4607125. Daily. Rent mountain bikes and scooters as well as boats.

Diving

Dive shops, many of which are based at hotels, are located all round the island.
Aquanaut Divers, English Harbour, T7287688, aquanaut@candw.ag. Leaving from the Antigua Slipway dock, they dive the south coast and Atlantic side of the island, double dives in the morning, single in the afternoon.
Deep Bay Divers, Redcliff Quay, St John's, T4638000, www.deepbaydivers.com. Catching the cruise ship market and surrounding hotels, they cater for beginners as well as advanced divers, taking up to 14 divers on the boat and going to Sandy Island, Cades Reef and Ariadne Shoal.
Dive Antigua, next to the Halcyon Beach Hotel, T4623483, www.diveantigua.com. The oldest dive operation on the island, 'Big John' also gives a mini marine biology class.
Jolly Dive, Jolly Beach Hotel, T4628305, www.jollydive.com. Near Cades Reef.

Fishing

Nightwing, Falmouth Harbour, T4644665, www.fishantigua.com. A 31-ft Bertrum, US$680 for 6 hrs, US$800 for 8 hrs, plus tip, maximum 6 people, split charters, good for beginners or experienced fishermen.
Overdraft, English Harbour, T4644954, www.antiguafishing.com. A 40-ft fishing boat leaves from Nelson's Dockyard, US$495 for 4 hrs, US$650 for 6 hrs, or US$790 for 8 hrs.

Golf

Cedar Valley, near St John's, T4620161, www.cedarvalleygolf.ag. An 18-hole, par-70 championship course which sometimes gets dried out but has pleasant coastal views. Green fees are US$35 for 18 holes. The Antigua Open is played here in Nov.
Jolly Harbour, T4623085, golf@jollyharbour antigua.com. A par-71 championship course in a parkland setting with 7 lakes, designed by Karl Litton. Clubhouse, pro-shop, rental, tuition, restaurant.

Hiking

In the Nelson's Dockyard National Park there are 5 trails up to 1½ miles long in the hills, past fortifications and with fantastic views. Pick up a copy of *A Guide to the Hiking Trails in the National Park* at the museum or entrance to the dockyard. Hikes are arranged to historical and natural attractions and can be a good way of seeing the island. The **Historical and Archaeological Society** organize monthly hikes free of charge. **Hash House Harriers** arrange hikes off the beaten track every other Sat at 1600, free of charge, contact Bunnie Butler T4610643 or David Crump T4610686. The **Environmental Awareness Group** offers monthly excursions, T4626236.
Tropical Trails, St John's, T7232322. Mon-Fri 0800 and 1500. Tours for US$70 per person include drinks, lunch, water and walking sticks, hotel pick-up, 5-6 hrs to Body Pond, Monk's Hill, the government pineapple farm, Fig Tree Drive, Boggy Peak and silk cotton tree at Cades Bay, where 10 people can stand inside the trunk.

Sailing

For cruisers or bareboat charters Antigua offers good provisioning and marine supplies, with facilities to haul out boats at Antigua Slipway or Jolly Harbour. There are several marinas. Charter fleets include **Sun Yacht Charter Services**, T5622893, www.salty seas.com, and **Nicholson's Yacht Charters**, T4601093, www.nicholsonyachts.com.
Adventure Antigua, T7273261, www.adventureantigua.com. Eco tour by boat around the North Sound islands, exploring those less visited, snorkelling, lunch and drinks for US$100. Also complete tour of the island, US$170. Book either tour online for 10% discount.
Antigua Yacht Club, English Harbour, Antigua, www.antiguayachtclub.com. Holds races every Thu and those wishing to crew should listen to English Harbour Radio at 0900 on VHF 68/06 that morning.
Jolly Harbour Yacht Club, Jolly Harbour Marina, just south of Ffryes Point, Antigua, T4626042, www.jollyharbourantigua.com/ marina. Holds Sat races as well as the **Red Stripe Regatta** in Feb and **Jolly Harbour Regatta** in Sep. There are 150 slips (103 fully serviced) for yachts of up to 260 ft and 12 ft draft, with a mega yacht facility.

Wadadli Cats, T4624792, www.wadadli cats.com. Trips round the island with stops at smaller islands such as Bird Island, Prickly Pear Island, US$80-90 on these catamarans.

Tennis
Many of the large hotels have courts. **Temo Sports**, English Harbour, Antigua, T4601781, VHF 68. Mon-Sat 0700-2200. A tennis/squash club open to the public with floodlit tennis courts, glass-backed squash courts, bistro, equipment rental, no credit cards. **BBR Sportive**, Jolly Harbour, Antigua, T4626260, VHF Channel 68. 0800-2100. Lit tennis and squash courts (US$20 per 30 mins) and a 25 m swimming pool, food and drink.

Watersports
A wide range of watersports is available, with waterskiing, windsurfing, parasailing, snorkelling, kayaking, kite surfing and swimming with stingrays. Dickenson Bay is the only beach with public hire of watersports equipment, but some hotels will hire to the public, especially out of season. The **Sandals** all-inclusive resort on Dickenson Bay will admit outsiders, at US$150 per couple 1000-1800 or US$130 for the evening, giving you the use of all sports facilities, meals, bar, etc. Most watersports operators offer hotel transfers. **Kayak Antigua**, T4801225, tropad@candw.ag. Kayaking through mangroves in the northeast. **Kite Antigua**, Jabberwock Beach, T7273983, 0900-1700, T/F 4603414 after 1800, www.kite antigua.com. Kitesurfing lessons, rentals and sales are offered by an IKO-approved school. 30-min orientation classes on land for US$30. **Paddles**, T4631944, www.antigua paddles.com. Offers an excellent half-day eco tour of the mangroves and islands off the northeast shore with snorkelling and hiking. **Patrick's Windsurfing School**, Dutchman's Bay north of the airport, T4619463, wind surfingantigua@hotmail.com. Instruction to beginners (guarantee to achieve in 2 hrs or no charge), intermediate and advanced windsurfers. Patrick will travel to any hotel. **Sting Ray City**, Seatons, T5627297, www.sting raycityantigua.com. Snorkellers can interact with stingrays, wading or swimming with them and feeding them. The rays are confined in a spacious pen on a sand bank in the sea.

Barbuda *p597*
Cycling
Jonathan Pierra, T7739599. Bicycle tours. He is on the island 4 months of the year.

Tour operators
Day tours include the Bird Sanctuary, Highland House, the caves and the Martello tower, anything can be arranged, eg bicycles, horse riding, hiking, contact **Red Fox**, T4600065, **George Burton**, T4600103, **Linton Thomas**, T7279957, **Barbuda Vacations**, Kenroy Walcott, T7737660. The **Barbuda Taxi Association** will do tours, T7279957. Before booking, ask whether the boat has lifejackets, communication equipment and insurance in the event of an accident. The **Excellence** catamaran departs Dickenson Bay for Barbuda 0930, 1 hr 15 mins, US$135, including a tour of the frigate bird colony, lunch and a cruise along the coast with stops for swimming and snorkelling, contact **Tropical Adventures**, T4801225, www.tropicalad. com/excellence.

⊖ Transport

Antigua *p591, maps p592, p600 and p601*
Air
V C Bird Airport, some 4½ miles from St John's, is the centre for air traffic in the area. **British Airways** (T4620876, from London Gatwick, connections with Barbados, Port of Spain and St Lucia), **Caribbean Airlines** (from London Heathrow) and **Virgin Atlantic** (from Gatwick). **BMI** (www.flybmi.com) have a weekly service from London Heathrow and Manchester. **American Airlines** (from Miami, Baltimore, Boston, Philadelphia and Washington via San Juan, New York via St Maarten, Raleigh/Durham direct), **Continental** (from Newark, NJ), **Delta** (from Atlanta), **US Airways** (from Charlotte and Philadelphia), **Air Canada**, T4621147 (from Toronto). There are frequent air services to neighbouring islands (Anguilla, Barbados, Barbuda, Dominica, Grenada, Guyana, Jamaica, Nevis, Guadeloupe, Trinidad, St Croix, St Kitts, St Lucia, St Maarten, St Thomas, St Vincent, Puerto Rico, Tortola) operated by **LIAT/ Caribbean Star** (T4620700), **Caribbean Airlines** (T4620260), **Winair** , **Continental**, **American Eagle**. **Carib**

Aviation (flights to Montserrat) arranges charters, T4623147, 0700-1800, after office hours T4611650, www.carib-aviation.com. They will meet incoming flights if you are transferring to another island, and make sure you make your return connection. Also day tours. See Montserrat, page 647 for details of flights from Antigua.

Helicopter Caribbean Helicopters, T4605900, www.caribbeanhelicopters.com. Helitours, custom charters and day trips, daily, half-island tour, US$85 per person, full-island tour US$150, Montserrat Volcano tour, US$220.

Boat
Daily (except Tue) ferry to Barbuda, T5607989, www.antiguaferries.com. Take your passport.

Bus
Buses are banned from north of the line from the airport to St John's, but run frequently between **St John's** and **English Harbour**, US$1. There are also buses from the east terminal by the war memorial to Willikies, whence a 20-min walk to **Long Bay Beach** and to **Parham**. There are no buses to the airport and very few to beaches though 2 good swimming beaches on the way to Old Road can be reached by bus. Bus frequency can be variable, and there are very few after dark or on Sun. Buses usually go when they are full, ask the driver where he is going. They are numbered and destinations are on display boards at the West Bus Station. Buses to **Old Road** are half hourly on average, though more frequent around 0800 and 1600.

Car
A local driving licence, US$20, valid for 3 months, must be purchased on presentation of a foreign (not international) licence. There is a 24-hr petrol station on Old Parham Rd outside St John's. Petrol costs US$2.25 per gallon everywhere.

Car hire A complete list of hire companies is available on the Board of Tourism website. Hertz, T4814440; Dollar Rent a Car, T4620362 (Sydney Walling Highway); National, T4622113; at Oakland Rent-A-Car, T4623021. Rates are from US$45 per day, US$225 a week (no mileage charge), including insurance charges, in summer, more in winter.

Taxi
Taxis have TX registration plates. In St John's there is a taxi rank on St Mary St, or outside the supermarket. They are not metered and frequently try to overcharge, or else have no change, so agree a price first, they should have a EC$ price list so ask to see it. There is a list of government-approved taxi rates posted in EC$ and US$ at the airport just after customs. The following prices were expected to rise in 2007. From St John's to Runaway Bay, 10 mins, is US$12. From the airport to **Admiral's Inn**, **St James's Club**, **Falmouth Beach Apartments**, **Curtain Bluff**, **Harmony Hall**, **Darkwood Beach**, etc, is US$31; to **Sandals**, **Antigua Village** and **Dickenson Bay** area US$16; to **Blue Waters** US$13; **Hawksbill** and **Five Islands** US$20. From the airport to town US$11. If going to the airport early in the morning, book a taxi the night before as there are not many around. A day tour normally costs about US$72-120 for 1-4 people, or an hourly rate of US$24 for up to 4 passengers. Taxi excursions advertised in the hotels are generally overpriced. Tips for taxi drivers are usually 10%.

Barbuda *p597*
Air
There are 2 airports; the main one is just south of Codrington. Flights take 10 mins from St John's. **Carib Aviation** will arrange charters and day trips. Return ticket costs US$74. The 2nd airport only serves **Coco Point**.

Boat
Daily service from Antigua, the **Barbuda Express**. Catamaran ferry Wed-Mon from St John's to Barbuda, 1½ hrs, US$30 one-way, US$52 return. Best days for a day trip from Antigua are Wed, Fri, Sat, Sun. Contact **Barbuda Express**, T5607989, or in Barbuda, Nathalie Nedd, T4600059, timetable on www.antiguaferries.com. See also Tours, above.

Car
It is possible to hire **jeeps**: Linton Thomas, T4600081, has a pick-up truck for US$50 per day or US$65 overnight; **Byron Askie** rents jeeps for US$60 a day or negotiate longer rental rate, T5623134, 7736082; **Junie Walker**, T4600619. **Horses** can be hired in Codrington.

⊕ Directory

Antigua *p591, maps p592, p600 and p601*
Banks Aside from those in the centre of St
John's, there's a bank outside the airport and
a branch of FirstCaribbean on old Parnham
Rd. Most take Mastercard and Visa. A tax of
1% is levied on all foreign exchange
transactions but there may be additional
charges on TCs. Also note that long queues
are common. Casinos will change TCs
without a fee. **American Express** is at
Antours near Heritage Quay, staff helpful
and friendly. **Embassies and consulates**
The British High Commission is at the Price
Waterhouse Centre (PO Box 483), 11 Old
Parham Rd, St John's, T4620008/9, F4622806.
Internet You can set up internet access for
your own computer before arriving through
www.cwantigua.com, with charges billed to
a credit card. Cable & Wireless Cybercafé at
Antigua Yacht Club (bring your own
computer, or use theirs). Also email,
messages, etc, at International Connections
at AYC dock. Internet Café, Upper Church St,
St John's. Kangaroo Express Internet Café, St
Mary's St, St John's, T5623895. Cyber Stop II,
Falmouth Harbour, T4603575, Mon-Fri
1000-1800, Sat 1000-1400, US$7.50 for 35
mins, US$11 for 1 hr, US$3.70 each
subsequent 30 mins. **Comnett Ltd**, upstairs
above Fedex in Redcliffe Quay, St John's,
T4621040, www.comnett-online.com good
machines, US$3 for 15 mins. **Medical
services** Holborton Public Hospital,
T4620251, in poor state of repair. A new
Mount St John's Hospital is being built but
lacks financing for completion. **Adelin
Medical Centre** is a private practice,
T4620866. **Post** Post office at the end of
Long St, St John's, opposite the supermarket.
Mon-Thu, 0815-1200, 1300-1600, until 1700
on Fri; also a post office at the Woods
Shopping Centre, the airport and at English
Harbour. A postcard to the USA costs
US$0.25. **Federal Express** is on Church St.
DHL is in the Vernon Edwards building on
Thames St. **Telephone** Cable and Wireless
Ltd, Long St, St John's, the Woods Mall and
at English Harbour. Prepaid cards are
available for overseas calls and for cell
phones. GSM tri-band handsets can be used
by purchase of a SIM card from Apua
T7272782, www.apua.ag.

Background

History

Antigua (pronounced Anteega) was first inhabited by the Siboney (stone people),
whose settlements date back to at least 2400 BC. The Arawaks lived on the island
between about AD 35 and 1100. Columbus landed on his second voyage in 1493 and
named the island Santa María de la Antigua. Spanish and French colonists attempted
to settle there, but were discouraged by the absence of freshwater springs and attacks
by the Caribs. In 1632 the English successfully colonized the island and, apart from a
brief interlude in 1666 when held by the French, the island and its dependencies,
Barbuda and uninhabited Redonda, remained British. Sir Christopher Codrington
established the first large sugar estate in Antigua in 1674, and leased Barbuda to raise
provisions for his plantations. Barbuda's only village is named after him. Forests were
cleared for sugarcane production and African slave labour was imported. Today, many
Antiguans blame frequent droughts on the island's lack of trees to attract rainfall, and
ruined towers of sugar plantations stand as testament to the destruction and consequent
barrenness of the landscape. In the 17th and 18th centuries, Antigua was important for its
natural harbours, where British ships could be refitted safe from hurricanes and from
attack. The Dockyard and the many fortifications date from this period.

The slaves were emancipated in 1834 but economic opportunities for the freed
labourers were limited by a lack of surplus farming land, no access to credit, and an
economy built on agriculture rather than manufacturing. Conditions for black people
were little better than under slavery and in many cases the planters treated them worse.
Poor labour conditions persisted and violence erupted in the first part of the 20th century
as workers protested against low wages, food shortages and poor living conditions. In

1939, to alleviate the seething discontent, the first labour movement was formed: the Antigua Trades and Labour Union. Vere Cornwall Bird became the union's president in 1943 and with other trade unionists formed the Antigua Labour Party (ALP). In 1946 the ALP won the first of a long series of electoral victories, being voted out of office only in 1971-1976 when the Progressive Labour Movement won the general election.

Antigua was administered as part of the Leeward Islands until 1959 and attained associated status, with full internal self-government in 1967. Antigua and Barbuda, as a single territory, became independent in November 1981, despite a strong campaign for separate Independence by Barbuda. Vere C Bird became the first Prime Minister and in 1989, at the age of 79, he took office for the fourth consecutive time. The general elections were marked by some irregularities and allegations of bribery, but the ALP won 15 of the 16 seats for Antigua in the 17-seat House of Representatives, the remaining seats being taken by the United National Democratic Party and the Barbuda People's Movement, for Barbuda. Mr Bird appointed a largely unchanged cabinet which included several members of his family.

In 1990 the Government was rocked by an arms smuggling scandal, which exposed corruption at an international level when allegations were made that Antigua had been used as a transit point for shipments of arms from Israel to the Medellín cocaine cartel in Colombia. Communications and Works Minister, Vere Bird Jr, the Prime Minister's son, became the subject of a judicial inquiry, following a complaint from the Colombian Government, for having signed authorization documents. His Cabinet appointment was revoked but he remained an MP. The Blom-Cooper report recommended no prosecutions, although it undermined the credibility of the Government and highlighted the rivalry between the two sons, Vere Jr and Lester Bird. The report also recommended that Vere Bird Jr be banned from holding public office.

Repeated calls for the resignation of Prime Minister Vere Bird were ignored although several ministers resigned from his Government. Demonstrations were organized in 1992 by the newly formed three-party United Opposition Front, seeking the resignation of the Prime Minister amid allegations of his theft and corruption. Fresh allegations of corruption were published in 1993 by the weekly opposition newspaper, *Outlet*, concerning property development contracts and misuse of public funds, resulting in a libel action issued by Lester Bird. *Outlet*, for many years edited by Tim Hector, who died in 2002, was the most outspoken critic of the Bird administration, frequently exposing corruption and fraud.

Vere Bird finally retired as Prime Minister in February 1994 at the age of 84. He was succeeded by his son, Lester, who led the ALP into the general elections held in March, winning its ninth out of 10 elections held since 1951 but with a reduced majority. The United Progressive Party (formerly the United Opposition Front), led by Baldwin Spencer, won five seats, the largest number for any opposition party in the country's history.

The new government was not free of allegations of corruption scandals (Ivor Bird, a younger Bird brother and general manager of the ZDK radio station was arrested and fined for taking possession of 12kg of cocaine at the airport) although Prime Minister Bird made efforts to portray a more professional administration. Economic adjustment was given priority and new tax policies sparked protest demonstrations and strikes. Efforts were made to clean up Antigua's poor reputation with the appointment in 1996 of a special advisor on control of illicit drugs and money laundering. Eleven offshore banks were closed by the end of 1997 and new legislation was approved in 1998 to close loopholes taken advantage of by international criminal organizations. However, this did not go far enough to satisfy US and UK regulators, who believed money laundering was still taking place. The Government bowed to the criticism and set up a committee in 1999 to study the areas of concern in its offshore financial services legislation.

In March 1999 the ALP won its sixth successive general election, increasing its representation in parliament to 12 seats, while the UPP won four and the BPM retained the Barbuda seat. The new cabinet was notable for the appointment of Vere

Bird Jr as Minister of Agriculture, Lands and Fisheries. Corruption was still endemic, with a scandal in 2002-2003 surrounding fraud in the state health insurance fund, where over US$230 million was unaccounted for.

The year 2004 was a momentous one for Antigua, when decades of rule by the Bird family were swept aside at the ballot box. The ALP was beaten into second place with only four seats, while the UPP won 12 and Lester Bird lost his seat. The new government of Baldwin Spencer faced an uphill struggle, given the scale of its financial and social problems, but it enjoyed overwhelming support of the people during its first year in office, with many celebrations of the new order and a general feeling of optimism. By 2005, however, the shine had lost its lustre with a general outcry over the introduction of income tax, even though it was to be paid by only 25% of the population. Lester Bird was re-elected as head of the ALP and forecast his comeback, promising to rescind any income tax legislation.

Government

Antigua and Barbuda is a constitutional monarchy within the Commonwealth, and the British Crown is represented by a Governor General. The head of government is the Prime Minister. There are two legislative houses: a directly elected 17-member House of Representatives and a 17-member Upper House, or Senate, appointed by the Governor General, mainly on the advice of the Prime Minister and the Leader of the Opposition. Antigua is divided into six parishes: St George, St John's, St Mary, St Paul, St Peter and St Phillip. Community councils on Antigua and the local government council on Barbuda are the organs of local government. The Barbuda Council has nine seats, with partial elections held every two years.

Economy

The economy was long dominated by the cultivation of sugar, the major export earner until 1960 when prices fell dramatically and crippled the industry. By 1972 sugar had largely disappeared and farming had shifted towards fruit, vegetables, cotton and livestock. The economy is now based on services, principally tourism. Hotels and restaurants contribute about 25% of gross domestic product and employ about one-third of the work force. Tourism receipts make up about 60% of total foreign exchange earnings and there are about 5,000 hotel rooms. Tourist numbers are highly susceptible to disasters such as hurricanes, the 11 September terrorist attacks in the USA, and the vagaries of the airline industry.

There is some light industry which has been encouraged by tax and other incentives, but manufacturing for export is hampered by high wages and energy costs. A major expansion of tourist infrastructure has taken place, with development of harbour, airport, road and hotel facilities. This investment has not yet touched the bulk of the population, and in rural areas small wooden shacks still constitute the most common form of dwelling, often alongside resorts and villa developments.

Flora and fauna

Around 150 different birds have been observed in Antigua and Barbuda, of which a third are year-round residents and the rest seasonal or migrants. Good spots for birdwatching include **Potworks Dam**, noted for the great blue heron in spring and many water fowl. **Great Bird Island** is home to the red-billed tropic bird and on **Man of War Island**, Barbuda, frigate birds breed. The Antiguan Racer Conservation Project was set up in 1995 to save the harmless Antiguan racer snake (*Alsophis antiguae*) which had been devastated by mongooses and black rats. The 60 remaining snakes were all on Great Bird Island and a campaign to eliminate the rats here and on other offshore islands helped their numbers to increase, together with other rare wildlife. Racers have now been reintroduced to other islands.

St Kitts and Nevis → Country code: 869. Colour map 3, B2.

The islands of St Kitts (officially named St Christopher) and Nevis are in the north part of the Leeward Islands in the Eastern Caribbean. Slightly off the beaten track, neither island is overrun with tourists; St Kitts is developing its southern peninsula where there are sandy beaches, but most of the island is untouched. Rugged volcanic peaks, forests and old fortresses produce spectacular views, and hiking is very rewarding. Two miles away, the conical island of Nevis is smaller, quieter and very desirable. Plantation houses on both islands have been converted into some of the most romantic hotels in the Caribbean, very popular with honeymooners. While one federation, the sister islands are quite different. St Kitts, the larger, is more cosmopolitan and livelier, while Nevis is quieter and more sedate. Wherever you go on these two small islands there are breathtaking, panoramic views of the sea, mountains, cultivated fields and small villages. ▸▸ *For Sleeping, Eating and other listings, see pages 625-637.*

Ins and outs

Getting there There are direct flights from London Gatwick, Miami, Charlotte and Philadelphia in the USA and winter services from Toronto to St Kitts, but otherwise you have to fly to a neighbouring island such as Puerto Rico and change planes. Cruise ships call at St Kitts, but links by boat with other islands are few and informal.

Getting around **Buses** on both islands are cheap and speedy. Drivers are generally very obliging and, if asked, may even divert their route to accommodate you. They run from very early in the morning until 2300 on St Kitts, but on Nevis there is a reduced service after 1600 and very few after 1800. Buses are identified by their green H registration plate, flag them down with a wave. **Cars**, jeeps and mini mokes can be hired from a variety of agencies on both islands. Driving is on the left. The main road on St Kitts is, for the most part, very good and motorists, especially bus drivers, can drive very fast. On Nevis the paved road round the island is good except in the northeast, but storm ditches frequently cross it, so drive slowly and carefully. Parking in both Basseterre and Charlestown is difficult. **Ferries** transporting passengers between St Kitts and Nevis are *Carib Breeze* and *Carib Surf* owned and operated by **M & M Transportation**; *Sea Hustler* and *Mark Twain* owned and operated by **Wesk Agency Limited**; *Carib Queen* owned and operated by **Francis & Francis Ltd**; and *Geronimo* and *Geronimo Express* owned by **St Kitts Fast Ferries**.

St Kitts → Phone code: 869. Colour map 3, B2. Population: 35,340.

St Kitts is made up of three groups of rugged volcano peaks split by deep ravines and a low-lying peninsula in the southeast where there are salt ponds and fine beaches. The dormant volcano, Mount Liamuiga (1156 m, 3792 ft, pronounced Lie-a-mee-ga) occupies the central part of the island. The mountain was previously named Mount Misery by the British, but has now reverted to its Carib name, meaning 'fertile land'. The foothills of the mountains, particularly in the north, are covered with sugar cane plantations and grassland, while the uncultivated lowland slopes are covered with forest and fruit trees. St Kitts was the last 'sugar island' in the Leewards group, but the industry operated at a loss and finally closed in 2005. A clockwise route around the island will enable you to see most of the historical sites. A cheap way of touring the island is to take a minibus from Basseterre (Bay Road) to Dieppe Bay Town, then walk to Saddlers (there might be a minibus if you are lucky, but it is only half a mile up the road) where you can get another minibus back to Basseterre along the Atlantic coast

Evidence of sugar cane is everywhere on the comparatively flat, fertile coastal plain. You will drive through large fields of cane and glimpse the narrow-gauge railway that was used to transport it from the fields. Disused sugar mills are also often seen. Around the island are the Great Houses: Fairview, Romney Manor (destroyed by fire in 1995), the White House, Golden Lemon, Rawlins and Ottley's. The last three are now luxury hotels and have excellent restaurants. ►► *For Sleeping, Eating and other listings, see pages 625-637.*

Basseterre → *Population: 15,000.*

The port of Basseterre is the capital and largest town, founded in 1727. Earthquakes, hurricanes and finally a disastrous fire destroyed the town in 1867 and consequently its buildings are comparatively modern. There is a complete mishmash of architectural styles from elegant Georgian buildings with arcades, verandas and jalousies, mostly in good condition, to hideous 20th-century concrete block houses. **The Circus**, styled after London's Piccadilly Circus (but looking nothing like it), is the centre of the town. It is busiest on Friday afternoon and comes alive with locals 'liming' (relaxing). The clock tower is a memorial to Thomas Berkely, former president of the General Legislative Council. In recent years, the development of tourism has meant a certain amount of redevelopment in the centre. An old warehouse on the waterfront has been converted into the **Pelican Mall**, a duty-free shopping and recreational complex. It also houses the Ministry of Tourism and a lounge for guests

St Kitts

N
0 km 2
0 miles 2

Sleeping 🛏
Frigate Bay Resort **3**
Gateway Inn **4**
Golden Lemon **5**
Inner Circle Guest House **6**
Mule House **1**

Ocean Terrace Inn **8**
Ottley's Plantation Inn **9**
Rawlins Plantation **10**
Rock Haven B&B **7**
Timothy Beach Resort **12**

of the **Four Seasons Resort** in Nevis awaiting transport. A new cruise ship berth has been built on the waterfront between Bramble Street and College Street in the heart of Basseterre, capable of accommodating the largest ships afloat, together with a sailing and power boat marina, and berthing facilities for the inter-island ferries.

At the south end of Fort Street on Bay Road is the imposing façade of the **Old Treasury Building**, with a dome covering an arched gateway. It has been converted into a museum of national culture and arts, and also houses the **St Christopher Heritage Society** ① *T4655584, Mon and Tue, Thu and Fri 0830-1300, 1400-1600, Wed and Sat, 0830-1300*, which has a small, interesting display of old photographs and artefacts. They work on conservation projects and are grateful for donations. Head north up Fort Street, turn left at the main thoroughfare (Cayon Street) and you will come to **St George's** church, set in its own large garden, with a massive, square buttressed tower. The site was originally a Jesuit church, Notre Dame, which was razed to the ground by the English in 1706. Rebuilt four years later and renamed St George's, it suffered damage from hurricanes and earthquakes on several occasions. It, too, was a victim of the 1867 fire. It was rebuilt in 1869 and contains some nice stained-glass windows. There is a fine view of the town from the tower.

Independence Square was built in 1790 and is surrounded now by a low white fence; eight gates let paths converge on a fountain in the middle of the square (it looks like the Union Jack when seen from the air). There are gaily painted muses on top of the fountain. Originally designed for slave auctions and council meetings, it now contains many plants, spacious lawns and lovely old trees. It is surrounded by 18th-century houses and, at its east end, the **Roman Catholic Cathedral** with its twin towers. Built in 1927, the Immaculate Conception is surprisingly plain inside. At 10 North Square Street you can visit the very attractive building housing the **Spencer Cameron Art Gallery** ① *T/F4651617*. See Rosey Cameron-Smith's paintings and prints of local views and customs, as well as an impressive selection of work by other artists. On West Independence Square, the **Courthouse** reflects the old one which burnt down in 1867. It is an impressive building in the colonial style. The **Bank of Nova Scotia** houses some interesting paintings of Brimstone Hill by Lt Lees of the Royal Engineers, circa 1783.

The **International House Museum** ① *Central St, T4650542, Mon-Fri 1000-1700, Sat 1000-1300, Sun 1300-1700. US$5 for visitors, US$1.85 for locals*, was designed by Winston Zack Nisbett, a cultural preservationist and friend of the previous owner of the property, Edgar Challenger, a well-known trade unionist and historian, who died in 2001. Challenger's residence was a gold mine of traditional utensils and equipment used between 1920 and 1940, as well as books on the history of the Federation.

The west coast

The west coast is guarded by no less than nine **forts** and the magnificent Brimstone Hill Fortress. Taking the road out of Basseterre, you will pass the sites of seven of them: Fort Thomas, Palmetto Point Fort, Stone Fort, Fort Charles, Charles Fort, Sandy Point Fort and Fig Tree Fort. The remaining two are to the south of Basseterre: Fort Smith and Fort Tyson. Little remains of any of them.

The first point of interest is situated just before Old Road Town. Sir Thomas Warner landed at Old Road Bay in 1623 and was joined in 1625 by the crew of a French ship badly mauled by the Spanish. They were initially befriended by the local chief Tegreman, but the Caribs became alarmed at the rapid colonization of the island. 3,000 Caribs tried to mount an attack in 1626. Two thousand of them were massacred by the combined French and English forces in the deep ravine at **Bloody Point** (the site of Stone Fort). An amicable settlement meant that the English held the central portion of the island roughly in line from Sandy Point to Saddlers in the north to Bloody Point across to Cayon in the south. French names can be traced in both of their areas of influence (Dieppe Bay Town in the north, the parishes are called Capisterre and Basseterre in the south). The southeast peninsula was neutral. This

Touching down

Boat information (Own flag). List all anchorage stops on cruising permit at the Port Authority in Basseterre and clear with immigration in Nevis. Port dues start at US$2.20 based on size. There is no additional charge in Nevis once you have cleared in St Kitts.

Anchorages Port Zante Marina in Basseterre, White House and Ballast Bay are the best on St Kitts, Oualie Beach on Nevis is beautiful. Groceries, alcohol, laundry, propane. Can have fuel delivered to dock and buy water by the cubic ton. Marina charges including water: under 40 ft, US$0.40 per ft; 40-70 ft, US$0.60; over 70 ft, US$1.20. For information, Port Authority, T4658121, Port Zante, T4665021.

Business hours Offices: 0900-1600; **Shops**: Mon-Sat 0800-1600, some open on Sun if a cruise ship is in port. Early closing Thu and also Sat for some shops.

Currency East Caribbean dollar, EC$. US dollars accepted. EC$2.70=US$1. When prices are quoted in both currencies, for example for departure tax, a notional rate of EC$2.50=US$1 is used. There are no restrictions on the amount of foreign currency that can be imported or exported, but the amount of local currency exported is limited to the amount you imported and declared. Visa and Mastercard are the most widely used credit cards.

Departure tax There is an airport departure tax of US$22 per person from St Kitts, US$20.50 from Nevis, not payable for stays of less than 24 hrs (or when you leave on the same flight number as you arrived the previous day, that is slightly more than 24 hrs).

Documents OECS nationals need a driver's licence or birth certificate. Other nationalities need passports and a return ticket, but for up to six months visas are not required for Commonwealth and EU countries and nationals of member countries of the OAS, with the exception of the Dominican Republic and Haiti. Visas can be extended for US$20 per month for the first three months and then US$30 for the following three months up to a maximum of six months.

Embassies and consulates None.

Emergency numbers T911.

Media Newspapers *The Observer*, *The Democrat*, *The Leeward Times* (weekly) or *The Labour Spokesman* (twice weekly). **Radio and TV** AM/FM

rapprochement did not last long as, following the colonization of Martinique and Guadeloupe, the French wished to increase their sphere of influence. St Kitts became a target and in 1664 they squeezed the English from the island. For 200 years the coast was defended by troops from one nation or another.

At Old Road Town you turn right to visit **Wingfield Estate** ⓘ *Mon-Fri, 0830-1600. T4656253*, home to *Caribelle Batik*. You drive through a sugar mill and the edge of rainforest. Unfortunately, Romney Manor was destroyed by fire in 1995, but the gardens remain with views over the coast and a 350-year old saman tree. Apart from a well-stocked shop you can watch the artists producing the colourful and highly attractive material. A guide will explain the process. Also near here the remains of the island's Amerindian civilization can be seen on large stones with drawings and petroglyphs. If you keep driving to the left of Romney Manor and *Caribelle Batik*, you will find one of the highest paved roads on the island. It is a tough climb so be sure to have a sturdy car. A large flat rock at the top is perfect to admire the view. To the right is a smaller path that leads to an incredible overview of Bat Hole Ghaut. The views of tropical rainforest in myriad greens are magnificent. You can reach the attractive, but secluded, **Dos d'Ane Pond** near **Mount Verchilds** from the Wingfield Estate, a guide is recommended.

At the village of **Middle Island**, you will see, on your right and slightly up the hill, the church of St Thomas at the head of an avenue of dead or dying royal palms. Here

ZIZ Radio medium wave 555 kHz and 96 FM; Choice 105.3 FM; Sugar City Rock 90.3 FM; Goodwill Radio 104.5 FM; WINN 98.9 FM; Big Wave 96.7 FM. VON Radio in Nevis 895 kHz medium wave and Radio Paradise 825 kHz. Two TV stations: the state run ZIZ and Nevis-based Christian station Trinity Broadcasting.

Official time Atlantic Standard Time, 4 hrs behind GMT, 1 hr ahead of EST.

Public holidays New Year's Day (1 Jan), Carnival Day/Las' Lap (2 Jan), Good Fri, Easter Mon, May Day (1st Mon in May), Whit Mon (end May), the Queen's birthday (Jun), Aug Mon/Emancipation Day (beginning of Aug), National Heroes Day (16 Sep), Independence Day (19 Sep), Christmas Day (25 Dec), Boxing Day (26 Dec).

Safety Note that the penalties for possession of narcotics are very severe and no mercy is shown towards tourists. Theft has increased, do not leave your things unattended in a car or on the beach.

Health Mains water is chlorinated, but bottled water is available if preferred for drinking, particularly outside the main towns. A yellow fever or cholera vaccination certificate is required if you are arriving from an infected area.

Tourist information St Kitts Tourism Authority, Pelican Mall, Basseterre, T4652620, www.stkitts-tourism.com, Mon-Fri 0800-1600. **Nevis Tourism Authority**, Old Treasury Building, Main St, Charlestown, T4697550, www.nevisisland.com, Mon-Fri 0800-1700, Sat 0830-1200. Both are extremely helpful, with plenty of information available.

Tourist offices overseas
Canada: 133 Richmond St West, Suite 311, Toronto, T416-3686707, Canada.office@st.kittstourism.kn.
UK: 10 Kensington Court, London W8 5DL, T020-73760881, uk-europe.office@stkittstourism.kn.
USA: 414 East 75th St, New York NY 10021, T212-5351234, info@stkittstourism.kn; 3216 New Mexico Av NW, Washington DC 20016-2745, T202-3648123, Abdullah.skerritt@stkittstourism.kn.
Voltage 230 volts AC/60 cycles (some hotels have 110 volts).
Weights and measures Imperial.

is buried Sir Thomas Warner who died on 10 March 1648. The raised tomb under a canopy is inscribed 'General of y Caribee'. There is also a bronze plaque with a copy of the inscription inside the church. Other early tombs are of Captain John Pogson (1656) and Sir Charles Payne, 'Major General of Leeward Carribee Islands', who was buried in 1744. The tower, built in 1880, fell during earth tremors in 1974.

Brimstone Hill

① *T4652609, www.brimstonehillfortress.org, daily 0930-1730, entry US$8 for foreigners, US$0.75 for nationals, children half price; allow up to 2 hrs.*

The **Brimstone Hill Fortress National Park**, one of the 'Gibraltars of the West Indies' (a title it shares with Les Saintes, off Guadeloupe), sprawls over 38 acres on the slopes of a hill 800 ft above the sea. It commands an incredible view of St Kitts and Nevis and on clear days you can see Anguilla (67 miles), Montserrat (40 miles), Saba (20 miles), St Eustatius (five miles), St-Barts (40 miles) and St-Martin (45 miles). The English mounted the first cannon on Brimstone Hill in 1690 in an attempt to force the French from Fort Charles below and the fortress was not abandoned until 1852. It has been constructed mainly out of local volcanic stones and was designed along classic defensive lines. The five bastions overlook each other and also guard the only road as it zig zags up to the parade ground. The entrance is at the Barrier Redan where payment is made. Pass the Magazine Bastion but stop at the Orillon Bastion which contains the massive ordnance store (165 ft long with walls at least 6 ft thick). The hospital was located here and under the south wall is a small cemetery. You then arrive at the Prince of Wales Bastion (note the graffitied name of J Sutherland, 93rd Highlanders 24 October 1822 on the wall next to one of the cannon) from where there are good views over to the parade ground. Park at the parade ground, there is a small snack bar and good gift shop near the warrant officer's quarters with barrels of pork outside it. Stop for a good video introduction at the DL Matheson Visitor Centre. A narrow and quite steep path leads to Fort George, the Citadel and the highest defensive position. Restoration is continuing and several areas have been converted to form a most interesting museum. Barrack rooms now hold well presented and informative displays (pre-Columbian, American, English, French and Garrison). Guides are on hand to give more detailed explanations of the fortifications. To get there, turn right off the coastal road just before J's Place (drink and local food, open from 1100, T4656264; the caged green vervet monkeys are very aggressive). The local minibus to Brimstone Hill is US$2, then walk up to the fortress (less than 30 minutes but extremely steep; for fit climbers only).

Brimstone Hill Fortress was inaugurated as a national park by the Queen in October 1985 and made a UNESCO World Heritage Site in October 2000.

Mount Liamuiga

The island is dominated by the southeast range of mountains (1159 ft) and the higher northwest range which contains **Mount Verchilds** (2931 ft) and the crater of Mount Liamuiga (3792 ft). To climb Mount Liamuiga independently, get a bus to St Paul's. Just after the village entrance sign there is a track leading through farm buildings which you follow through the fields. After 20 minutes take a left fork. At the edge of the forest, the track becomes a path, which is easy to follow and leads through wonderful trees. At 2600 ft is the crater into which you can climb, holding on to vines and roots; on the steady climb from the end of the road note the wild orchids in the forest. A full day is required for this climb which is really only for experienced hikers. To get beyond the crater to the summit you need a guide.

The north coast

Rawlins Plantation, reached up a long drive through canefields, has magnificent gardens full of tropical plants and flowers and is an excellent place to stop for lunch on a tour of the island. Alternatively, there is a black sand beach at **Dieppe Bay** with the excellent **Golden Lemon Inn**. The beach has been moved around by hurricanes but it is still a good place to stroll, with lots of sandpipers and herons and a view of The Quill on Sint Eustatius in the distance. Pass through Saddlers to the **Black Rocks**. Here lava has flowed into the sea, providing interesting rock formations. The main road continues south through Cayon (turn right uphill to Spooners for a look at the abandoned Cotton Ginnery) back to Basseterre via the RL Bradshaw Airport.

The southeast peninsula

To visit the southeast peninsula, turn off the roundabout at the end of Wellington Road (opposite turning to the airport) and at the end of this new road turn left. This leads to the narrow spit of land sandwiched between North and South Frigate Bays. This area is being heavily developed with large hotels and condominiums, the natural lagoons providing an additional attraction. **Frigate Bay** is now dominated by the huge **Marriott Hotel** on the north (Atlantic) side and adjacent golf course. Breakers have been built so that guests can get into the water. South Frigate Bay is on the Caribbean Sea and is popular with locals as it is the closest beach to the capital. There are several beach bars here and watersports. The six-mile Dr Kennedy A Simmonds Highway runs from Frigate Bay to Major's Bay along the backbone of the peninsula. From the top there is a lookout with a great view of North Friars Bay Beach on the

The Sugar Train

The sugar industry was revolutionized in St Kitts when first the estates moved from wind to steam power in 1870 and then a central sugar factory was built in Basseterre in 1912. A narrow-gauge railway was built in 1912 to 1926 to deliver cane from the fields to the central sugar mill and it was the beginning of the end for all the small estate-based sugar mills dotted around the island. Many sail-less windmills still stand as relics of the old ways. Although the track initially ran as two spurs either side of the island, planters soon saw the sense of abandoning other delivery systems and it was extended to be a circular route all round the coast. With the decline in the sugar industry at the end of the 20th century, the track fell into disrepair but has now been renovated with new rails and bridges by the company running the tourist train. The St Kitts Scenic Railway, which opened in 2003, is the perfect way to see the whole island, far better than touring by car as you get a much better view. The railway is mostly uphill from the road, although in many places it runs along the coast, and with the double-decker carriages you are above the sugar cane which blocks your view from a car.

The locomotive originated in Romania but was sold to Poland for sugar beet transport before coming to St Kitts for sugar cane. The power car was built in Colorado, USA, while the 'island series' carriages, the first of their kind, were built in Seattle, Washington, USA. The rails were brought from the UK, Belgium, the USA and abandoned sugar track in Cuba, the sleepers are hard wood from Guyana. An Alaskan engineer is always on board to answer questions and a Kittitian choir will serenade you.

St Kitts Scenic Railway departs 0820 and 1310 from Needsmust station near the airport, 3 hours 10 minutes. It is expensive, at US$89 per adult, US$44.50 per child, or break your journey with a tour of Brimstone Hill Fortress for US$123, returning to the starting point by bus. A maximum of 28 guests per carriage have a seat on both levels, the upper open-air deck and the lower, enclosed, a/c carriage. Reservations essential, T4657263, www.stkittsscenicrailway.com.

Atlantic and South Friars Bay Beach on the Caribbean Sea, with Nevis at the end. You may see green vervet monkeys before descending to White House Bay. Skirt the Great Salt Pond. Halfway round turn left to reach Sand Bank Bay, a lovely secluded bay (unmarked left turn down dirt road). Continue on the main highway and turn left for Cockleshell Bay and Turtle Beach (good for watersports and stunning views across to Nevis). The main road leads to Major's Bay.

Beaches and activities

Most of the beaches are of black, volcanic sand, but several of those fringing the southeast peninsula have lighter coloured or white sand. Swimming is not safe on the Atlantic side of the island because of strong currents, but is very good in the Frigate Bay area where all watersports are available. **North Friars Bay** is a broad sweep of sand, but it is on the Atlantic and not protected. **South Friars Bay** on the Caribbean coast is lovely and the most popular beach for cruise ship passengers, with lots of beach bars, and it can get very busy at weekends. **White House Bay** is on the Caribbean and popular as an anchorage for yachts, as well as a great dive site for wrecks. **Sand Bank** is a lovely curved bay with good sand, and protected despite being

If you hear something in the upper branches, look up before the monkeys disappear.

Leeward Islands St Kitts & Nevis

on the Atlantic. Kite flying is good but you can also potter about in the shallow water, but don't swim; there is an undertow and drownings have occurred. **Banana Bay, Cockleshell Bay** (Hyatt has bought land for hotel development here) and **Mosquito Bay**, also known as Turtle Beach, all have sandy beaches, calm water and picturesque views of Nevis just across the straits. There has been little development here so far, but there is the **Turtle Beach Bar and Grill** at Mosquito Bay with watersports on offer. The beach is cleaned regularly because lots of weed comes in if the wind is in the wrong direction. On Cockleshell Beach there is a bar at weekends with local food. The calm and shallow water here is great for families. **Major's Bay** has been messed up by hurricanes and storms and a wrecked barge lies offshore. It is also rather smelly and there are cows and goats everywhere. In the north, the black sand beach at **Dieppe Bay** has lots of birds and fishermen, also cows, donkeys, goats and dogs, with good snorkelling on the reef.

Diving There is very good snorkelling and scuba diving. Most dive sites are on the Caribbean side of the islands, where the reef starts in shallow water and falls off to 100 ft or more. Between the two islands there is a shelf in only 25 ft of water which attracts lots of fish, including angelfish, to the corals, sea fans and sponges. There is black coral off the southeast peninsula, coral caves, reefs and wrecks with abundant fish and other sea creatures of all sizes and colours. Off St Kitts good reefs to dive include **Turtle Reef** (off Shitten Bay) which is good for beginners and snorkelling, **Coconut Reef** in Basseterre Bay and **Pump Bay** by Sandy Point. Much of the diving is suitable for novices and few of the major sites are deeper than 70 ft.

The waters around St Kitts are the resting place of several ship wrecks. The Anglo-Danish Maritime Archaeological Team (ADMAT) set up a field school in 2003, the largest of this sort ever carried out in the Caribbean. The aim is to record two pre-1760s ship wrecks uncovered by recent hurricanes in White House Bay, Diving around St Kitts can be an exciting adventure as you are taken back in history to a time when the Caribbean was a battleground and a burial ground. Several wrecks and some other sites are actually shallow enough for very rewarding snorkelling although the very best snorkelling around St Kitts is only accessible by boat.

Hiking St Kitts has comparatively clear trails including Old Road to Philips, the old British military road, which connected the British settlements on the northeast and southwest coasts without going through French territory when the island was partitioned. There are also trails from Belmont to the crater of Mount Liamuiga, from Saddlers to the Peak, from Lamberts or the top of Wingfield Heights to Dos d'Ane pond. There are excellent hiking tours to the volcano and through the rainforest.

Nevis → *Phone code: 869. Colour map 3, B2. Population: 9,000.*

Across the two-mile Narrows Channel from St Kitts is the beautiful little island of Nevis. The circular island covers an area of 36 sq miles and the central peak, 3,232 ft, is usually shrouded in white clouds and mist. It reminded Columbus of Spanish snow-capped mountains and so he called the island 'Las Nieves'. For the Caribs, it was Oualie, the land of beautiful water. Smaller than St Kitts, it is also quieter. The atmosphere is low-key and easy-going; all the same, it is an expensive island. The delightful plantation inns have long been a favourite with the well-heeled British but the construction of the Four Seasons Hotel now attracts golfing Americans.

Charlestown

The main town is Charlestown, one of the best-preserved old towns in the Caribbean, with several interesting buildings dating from the 18th century. It is small and compact, on Gallows Bay, guarded by Fort Charles to the south and the long sweep of

Pinney's Beach to the north. Nevis had the only court in the West Indies to try and hang pirates. Prisoners were taken from the courthouse across the swamp to where the gallows were set up, hence the name, Gallows Bay. There are plans for a national park to protect the swamp, which is a habitat for many birds, animals and plants.

D R Walwyn's Plaza is dominated by the balconied **Old Customs/Treasury House**, built in 1837 and restored in 2002. The **tourist office** is here. **Memorial Square**, to the south, is larger and more impressive; the War Memorial is in a small garden. The **Courthouse and Library** ① *Mon-Fri 0900-1800, Sat 0900-1700 (the courthouse is closed to the public, except when a case is in progress)* were built here in 1825 and used as the Nevis Government Headquarters, but were largely destroyed by fire in 1873 and subsequently rebuilt. The building still houses the library upstairs and the Nevis High Court and Registrar below. The little square tower was erected in 1909 to 1910. It contains a clock which keeps accurate time with an elaborate pulley and chain system. In the library you can see it, together with the weights, among the roof trusses.

Along Government Road is the well-preserved **Jewish Cemetery**. The earliest evidence of a Jewish community on the island dates from 1677 to 1678, when there

Nevis

Sleeping		
Banyan Tree B&B 1	Old Manor 8	Double Deuce 3
Golden Rock Plantation	Oualie Beach 9	Gallipot 4
Inn 2	Philsha's 10	Jade Garden 5
Hermitage Plantation Inn 3	Sea Spawn Guesthouse 12	Martha's Tea House 6
Montpelier Plantation Inn 5		Miss June's 7
Nisbet Plantation Beach	**Eating**	Natural Livity 8
Club 7	Bananas 1	Seafood Madness 9
	Cla Cha Del 2	

N

0 km 1
0 miles 1

were four families. By the end of the century there were 17 households, a thriving synagogue and part of the main street was known as Jew Street, but invasion by the French in 1706 and 1783, hurricanes and the decline of the sugar industry in the 18th century led to an economic downturn and emigration. By the end of the 18th century only three Jewish households remained, and now there is no evidence of their presence except for the cemetery where 19 stones date from 1679-1730.

Charlestown **market** ① *Mon-Sat 0730-1500*, has a wide range of island produce and crafts. Market Street to the right houses the **Philatelic Bureau** ① *Mon-Fri 0800-1600*. The **Cotton Ginnery** was, until 1994, in use during the cotton-picking season (February to July). In 1995 it was moved out to the New River Estate, Gingerland, where it is in a renovated building next to the sugar mill ruins there. As part of the Nevis Port upgrade, another Cotton Ginnery building now houses 10 gift shops and a restaurant. On Chapel Street the **Wesleyan Holiness Manse**, built in 1812, is one of the oldest stone buildings surviving on the island, while the **Methodist Manse** (next to the prominent church) has the oldest wooden structure, the second floor was built in 1802.

The **Museum of Nevis History** ① *between Main St and the sea, T4695786. Mon-Fri 0900-1600, Sat 0900-1200, US$5*, at the Birthplace of Alexander Hamilton, is next to the sea and set in an attractive garden. The original house was built around 1680 but destroyed in the 1840s, probably by an earthquake. This house was rebuilt in 1983 and dedicated during the islands' Independence celebration in September of that year. The Nevis House of Assembly meets in the rooms upstairs, while the rather cramped museum occupies the ground floor. Alexander Hamilton, Nevis' most famous son, was born in Charlestown on 11 January 1757. He lived on Nevis for only five years before leaving for St Croix with his family. About half of the display is given over to memorabilia and pictures of his life. The rest contains examples of Amerindian pottery, African culture imported by the slaves, cooking implements and recipes, a rum still, a model of a Nevis lighter, the ceremonial clothes of the Warden which were worn on the Queen's birthday and Remembrance Day and a section on nature conservation. A small shop sells local produce and some interesting books. All proceeds go to the upkeep of the museum.

Around the island

Taking the road south out of Charlestown, you can visit the rather unkempt **Fort Charles**. Fork right at the Shell station and again at the mini roundabout, keep right along the sea shore (rough track), past the wine company and through gates at the end of the track. The fort was built before 1690 and altered many times before being completed 1783-1790. Not much remains apart from the circular well and a small building (possibly the magazine). The gun emplacements looking across to St Kitts are being badly eroded by the sea, some cannon have been moved to hotels. The Nevis Council surrendered to the French here in 1782 during the siege of Brimstone Hill on St Kitts.

Back on the main road and only about half a mile outside Charlestown lies the largely ruined **Bath Hotel** and **Spring House**. Built by the Huggins family in 1778, it is reputed to be one of the oldest hotels in the Caribbean. It has been under restoration recently and there are plans to develop the entire Bath Spring area as a massage/therapeutic centre. Work is in progress on two thermal dipping pools. The Spring House lies over a fault which supplies constant hot water at 108°F. Most locals bathe further down stream, often stark naked. The **Horatio Nelson Museum** ① *Mon-Fri 0900-1600, Sat 0900-1200, US$5*, commemorates the 205th anniversary in 1992 of the wedding of Admiral Nelson to Fanny Nisbett. Based on a collection donated by Mr Robert Abrahams, an American, the museum contains memorabilia including letters, china, pictures, furniture and books (request to see the excellent collection of historical documents and display of 17th-century clay pipes). A replica of Nelson's military uniform was unveiled at the museum and presented to the local government by the British High Commissioner in January 2001. Nelson was not always popular, having come to the island to enforce the Navigation Acts which forbade the newly independent American states trading with British colonies. In his ship *HMS Boreas,* he impounded four American ships and their cargoes. The Nevis merchants immediately claimed £40,000 losses against Nelson, who had to remain on board his ship for eight weeks to escape being put into gaol. It was only after Prince William, captain of *HMS Pegasus,* arrived in Antigua that Nelson gained social acceptability and married the widow, Fanny Woodward Nisbett (reputedly for her uncle's money; this proved a disappointment as her uncle left the island and spent his wealth in London). The museum also contains some pre-Columbian artefacts and displays on local history, including sugar and slavery. Outside, behind the museum rests the *Pioneer,* a Nevis lighter and the last sugar boat sailing to St Kitts. There are plans to renovate it, but to get a better idea of what it looked like, there is a model in the museum. There is also a gift shop.

More evidence of the Nelson connection is found at the **St John's Fig Tree Anglican Church** about two miles on from the Bath House. Originally built in 1680, the church was rebuilt in 1838 and again in 1895. The marriage certificate of Nelson and Fanny Nisbett is displayed here. There are interesting memorials to Fanny's father William Woodward and also to her first husband Dr Josiah Nisbett. Many died of the fever during this period and if you lift the red carpet in the central aisles you can see old tombstones, many connected with the then leading family, the Herberts. The graveyard has many examples of tombstones in family groups dating from the 1780s.

Slightly off the main road to the south lies **Montpelier Great House** where the marriage of Nelson and Mrs Nisbett actually took place; a plaque is set in the gatepost. The plantation is now a hotel with pleasant gardens; a great place for lunch or a drink. Enormous toads live in the lily ponds formed out of old sugar pans. Beyond the house lies **Saddle Hill** (1,250 ft). It has the remains of a small fort, **Saddle Hill Battery**, and it is reputedly where Nelson would look out for illegal shipping. Nevisians had a grandstand view from here of the siege of Brimstone Hill by the French in 1782. You can follow several goat/nature trails on the hill, giant aloes abound, a track starts at Clay Ghaut, but most trails beyond the fort are dense and overgrown. Near Montpelier are the **Botanical Gardens** ① *T4693509, gardens Nov-Mar Mon-Sat 1000-1630, other months phone ahead, US$10, children half price,* 7 acres of nicely laid out plants from around the world: cactus, bamboo, orchids, flowering trees and shrubs, heliconias and rose gardens, a mermaid fountain, a greenhouse with bridges, ponds, waterfall and tea house (T4693399, 1000-1700) with English high tea and gift shop. The landscaping is beautiful and it is the perfect spot for relaxation, picnics, small gatherings, weddings, but it's not wheelchair friendly.

The small parish of **Gingerland** is reached after about three miles. Its rich soils made it the centre of the island's ginger root production (also cinnamon and nutmeg), but it is noteworthy for the very unusual octagonal Methodist church built in 1830. You turn right here along Hanleys Road to reach **White Bay Beach**. Go all the way down to the bottom and turn left at the Indian Castle experimental farm, past the race course (on Black Bay) and Red Cliff. There is a small shelter but no general shade. Beware, this is the Atlantic coast, the sea can be very rough and dangerous. On quieter days, the surf is fun and there are good views across to Montserrat. On the way back beware of the deep storm drain crossing the road near the church.

After Gingerland the land becomes more barren and this side of the island is much drier. Several sugar mills were built here because of the wind, notably **Coconut Walk Estate, New River Estate** (fairly intact) and the **Eden Brown Estate,** built around 1740. A duel took place between the groom and the bride's brother at the wedding of Julia Huggins. The brother was killed and the fiancé fled the island to escape trial and execution. Julia became a recluse and the great house was abandoned. It has the reputation of being haunted. Although government owned and open to the public, the ruins are in poor condition and care should be taken.

The island road continues north through Butlers and Brick Kiln (known locally as Brick Lyn), past St James' Church (Hick's village), Long Haul and Newcastle Bays (with the **Nisbet Plantation Inn**) to the small fishing community of **Newcastle** and the airport. You can visit the **Newcastle Pottery** where distinctive red clay is used to make, among other things, the traditional Nevis cooking pot.

The road continues through an increasingly fertile landscape, and there are fine views across the Narrows to the southeast peninsula of St Kitts, with **Booby Island** in the middle of the channel, the latter being mostly inhabited by pelicans (all birds are referred to as boobies by the local population). It offers good diving. The small hill on your left is **Round Hill** (1014 ft). It can be reached on the road between Cades Bay and Camps Village. Turn off the road at Fountain village by the Methodist church. There are good views from the radio station at the top over Charlestown, across to St Kitts and beyond to Antigua. There is a small beach at **Mosquito Bay** and some good snorkelling under the cliffs of Hurricane Hill. The **Oualie Beach Hotel** offers watersport facilities including scuba diving and snorkelling equipment. On Sunday afternoons there is often live music and a barbecue at Mosquito Bay. Sailing trips can be negotiated with locals.

Under Round Hill lies **Cottle Chapel** (1824). It was the first Anglican place on Nevis where slaves could be taught and could worship with their masters. Under restoration, its beautiful little font can be seen in the Museum of Nevis History. Nearby, just off the island road, lies **Fort Ashby**, which is on long-term lease from the government to a private owner who has rebuilt it in its original form with four cannon remaining in their original positions. It is occasionally used as a restaurant/beach bar and is open to the public. It protected Jamestown, the original settlement and former capital, which was supposedly destroyed by an earthquake and tidal wave in 1690, and was originally called St James's Fort. Drive past the **Nelson Springs** (where the barrels from HMS Boreas were filled) and **St Thomas's Church** (built in 1643, one of the oldest surviving in the Caribbean) to **Pinney's Beach**. There are many tracks leading down to the beach, often with a small hut or beach bar at the end of them. The **Four Seasons Hotel** lies in the middle of the beach. Behind the resort is the **Robert Trent Jones II** golf course which straddles the island road. The manicured fairways and greens are in marked contrast with the quiet beauty of the rest of the island but the hotel's considerable efforts at landscaping have lessened its impact.

Beaches and activities

The beautiful four mile **Pinney's Beach** is only a few minutes' walk from Charlestown and is never crowded. The entire middle stretch the beach has been given over to a 218-room **Four Seasons Hotel**. The sun loungers are for guests only, but the public has access to the beach and there are watersports available. Huge amounts of sand were imported after Hurricane Lenny and breakwaters were built to protect the beach by the hotel, but much of it has remained stony. **Tamarind Bay** is now popular, with plenty of sand. On the Atlantic side of Nevis, the beaches tend to be rocky and the swimming treacherous; there is, though, an excellent beach at **White Bay** in the southwest.

Diving Snorkelling is excellent off **Oualie Beach** and is also good at **Nisbett Beach** and **Tamarind Bay**. Good dive sites include **Monkey Shoal**, where you can find angel fish, black durgons, octopus, flying gurnard and maybe nurse sharks in the overhangs, crevices and grottos of this densely covered reef. **Devil's Caves** are another series of grottos, where you can see lobster and squirrelfish and often turtles riding the surge. **Nag's Head**, just off Oualie Beach, is a schooling ground for big fish such as king mackerel, barracuda, jacks and yellowtail snappers. Some dive operators will take you as far as Redonda, where diving is superb and untouched.

 On Sunday church bells start ringing from 0600, calling the faithful to services lasting three hours or more, and it is a quiet day everywhere.

St Kitts

p613, maps p614 and p625

There is a 9% occupancy tax and 10% service charge. A wide variety of lodgings from first-class plantation inns and beach hotels to rented cottages, but it is advisable to book in advance. Reductions are available in summer. **St Kitts/Nevis Hotel Association**, PO Box 438, Basseterre, St Kitts, T4655304.

Breaking with tradition and out of character with the rest of the hotels, a monstrous new 5-star **St Kitts Marriott Royal Beach Resort and Casino** has been built on Frigate Bay, with 640 rooms, the largest casino in the Caribbean, a golf course, amphitheatre, state-of-the-art gym and spa, restaurants, etc. **LL Golden Lemon**, Dieppe Bay, T4657260, www.goldenlemon.com. On the beach about 15 miles from Basseterre with a view of Saba and Statia. Opened in 1963 and still run by the distinguished elderly gentlemen, owner Arthur Leaman and manager Martin Kreiner. 34 rooms in a charming old plantation house dating from 1610, with wooden floors, high beds reached by step ladder, or in 1- to 2-bedroom new, spacious cottages with pools, antique furniture and modern elegance. No cottage overlooks another, each is shaded by gardens. Excellent restaurant, breakfast included, lovely atmosphere. No children.

LL Ottley's Plantation Inn, Cayon, T4657234, www.ottleys.com. 520 ft above sea level in 35 acres with view to the Atlantic. Rooms in the 1832 great house or in luxury modern cottages in the beautiful tropical gardens with its sweeping lawns and palm trees, spacious, elegantly furnished, with large bathrooms, a/c, fans, plunge pools. The full-size pool is in the ruins of a sugar estate. Run by a US family

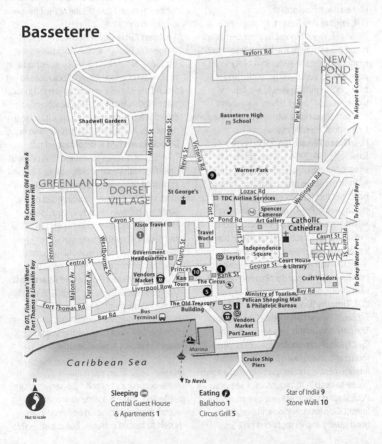

Basseterre

Taylors Rd

NEW POND SITE

To Airport & Conaree

Park Range

Shadwell Gardens

Basseterre High School

Market St

College St

Nevis St

Victoria Rd

Warner Park

9

To Cemetery, Old Rd Town & Brimstone Hill

GREENLANDS

DORSET VILLAGE

St George's ✝

Lozac Rd

TDC Airline Services

Spencer Cameron Art Gallery

Catholic Cathedral ✝

Wellington Rd

To Frigate Bay

Cayon St

Kisco Travel **1**

Fiennes Av

Westbourne St

Central St

Malone Av

Durant Av

Fort Thomas Rd

Bay Rd

To OTI, Fisherman's Wharf, Fort Thomas & Limekiln Bay

Government Headquarters

Vendors Market

Liverpool Row

Church St

Travel World

@ Leyton

Princes St

10

Kan Tours

The Circus **1**

S

Fort St

Pond Rd

Hart St

Independence Square

George St

Bank St

5

Court House & Library

Caunt St

NEW TOWN

Pitcairn St

To Deep Water Port

Craft Vendors

Bay Rd

Ministry of Tourism
Pelican Shopping Mall
& Philatelic Bureau

The Old Treasury Building

Bus Terminal 🚌

Vendors Market

Port Zante

Marina ⚓

To Nevis

Cruise Ship Piers

Caribbean Sea

N

Not to scale

Sleeping 🛏
Central Guest House
& Apartments **1**

Eating 🍴
Ballahoo **1**
Circus Grill **5**

Star of India **9**
Stone Walls **10**

who are very hospitable and knowledgeable. There are nice walks in the area or you can take the beach shuttle. Popular spa for massages in a little chattel house in the trees. The excellent **Royal Palm** restaurant caters for all diets and provides elegant dining in a cool, natural environment built into the side of old sugar mill buildings.

LL Rawlins Plantation, 16 miles from Basseterre in the northwest, T4656221, www.rawlinsplantation.com. 350 ft above sea level, British colonial style, offers grass court tennis, swimming pool, croquet, great walking opportunities. 10 rooms in cottages in the garden of the main house built on the remains of the boiling house, and a honeymoon suite in the sugar mill, decorated with bright cotton fabrics and wooden floors. Breakfast and dinner included. Mid-morning coffee or afternoon tea on the terrace. Excellent food under the control of Claire Rawson, a Kittitian chef, who sources the ingredients from the kitchen garden or locally.

LL-L Frigate Bay Resort, Frigate Bay, T4658935, www.frigatebay.com. 5-min walk round the hillside to the beach from the 64 rooms, studios and suites in 4 blocks, all painted a colourful yellow, white and blue, pool or hillside views, a/c, fan, TV, fridge, studios have kitchen. A pleasant medium-sized hotel, with a casual restaurant by the pool, friendly management.

LL-L Ocean Terrace Inn (OTI), Wigley Av, Basseterre, T4652754, www.oceanterrace inn.net. Nondescript modern architecture, apartments, suites and rooms, a/c, TV, fan, 3 pools, hot tub, fitness centre, business centre, beach shuttle. **Pro-Divers** and **Fisherman's Wharf** across the road on the water front, extending out so you feel you are on top of the water. Fairly expensive but pleasant restaurant with views over Basseterre harbour, popular locally for special occasions as well as with guests, good service throughout.

LL-L Timothy Beach Resort, Frigate Bay, T4658597, www.timothybeachresort.com. The only hotel in this area actually on the Caribbean. 3-star, good value, connecting rooms and studios with kitchens, versatile arrangements to make apartments or a town house to sleep 2-10, mountain or sea view. Pool, steps down to sea, internet access, **Sunset Café** for local food and burgers, good quality and value, priced in EC$.

AL-A Mule House, Brighton Plantation, T4668086, www.holiday-rentals.co.uk/ mulehouse. Brighton is the oldest plantation on the island and the **Mule House** has been built on the site of the former mule barn in the plantation yard. 4 self-catering apartments, each with their own entrance, kitchen, lounge/diner, CD player, huge shower room and 2 bedrooms with mosquito nets, books and a balcony with sea view. Fruit and flowers from the beautiful garden, together with rum, are offered as a welcome pack and they meet you at the airport and help with excursions.

A Gateway Inn, Frigate Bay, T4657155, gateway@caribsurf.com. On the Frigate Bay Road opposite the Sugars complex where there are 2 restaurants and evening entertainment. Built in a horseshoe shape and surrounded by lawns, 10 self-catering apartments all on the ground floor with their own entrance, comfortable but not luxurious, with a/c, phone, TV and laundry. 10 mins from the beach or golf course, one of the cheaper options in this area.

A-B Inner Circle Guest House, in the village of St Paul's, 14 miles from Basseterre T4665857. Newly built 2-storey guesthouse in the middle of village life, on a bus route to get around the island. If you are interested in local culture rather than non-stop beach activities, then this is a perfect place to stay. It is also a popular night spot so expect action and noise.

B Rock Haven Bed & Breakfast, Frigate Bay, T/F4655503. 2 suites available at this bed and breakfast, with views of both coasts; 1 is an attractively decorated, roomy bed-sitting room with its own patio surrounded by the garden. It has twin beds, fully equipped kitchen, spacious bathroom, ceiling fan, TV and phone. The other suite upstairs is spacious and airy with mahogany louvred windows looking on to the garden.

B-D Central Guest House and Apartments, Market Street, Basseterre, T4652278. Ideally located in the heart of town in a 2-storey building. Rooms with or without kitchenette, nothing fancy but ideal for those who just want the basics at an affordable rate.

Nevis *p620, maps p621 and p627*

A 9% occupancy tax and 10% service charge are levied. There is a wide variety of accommodation ranging from first-class hotels to rented cottages, but it is advisable to book in advance. Reductions are available in summer. The **St Kitts/Nevis Hotel Association** can be reached at PO Box 438, Basseterre, St Kitts, T4655304, F4657746. Accommodation on Nevis tends to be upmarket, in reconstructions of old plantation Great Houses, tastefully decorated in an English style (collectively called **The Inns of Nevis**). They are small and intimate in contrast to the 218-room **Four Seasons Resort Nevis** which dominates Pinney's Beach with its luxury spa (15 masseurs) and golf course.

LL Hermitage Plantation Inn, St John's Parish, T4693477, www.hermitagenevis.com. Run by Richard and Maureen Lupinacci, beautiful wooden cottages, all different, some rather small, 4-poster beds. The **Planter's House** dates from 1680-1740 and is believed to be the oldest wooden house in the Lesser Antilles, old furniture and prints on the walls, chintz furnishings, tennis, pool, stunning rural setting with view down to sea, equestrian/adventure/diving packages offered, stables on site. Lunch on the terrace, dinner indoors, lamb and pork home grown, as are the fruit and vegetables. Maggie Lupinacci runs **Mangoes**, just north of the of the **Four Seasons Hotel** on Pinney's Beach, offering light lunches and more substantial dinners. Beach chairs on the sand, sunset cocktails and happy hours on Fri, occasional live music.

LL Montpelier Plantation Inn and Beach Club, T4693462, www.montpeliernevis.com. The Hoffman family run this beautiful old property on 30 acres, 750 ft above sea level, a favourite with British tourists. Luxury touches include a welcome with cold towels and rum punch, being taken straight to your room, registering later. Delightful, friendly and helpful, long-serving staff, pool, tennis, lovely gardens, beach shuttle, child reductions, 17 rooms painted white with cool green or blue flourishes, fresh fruit daily. The **Terrace Restaurant** offers fine dining using home-grown fruit, vegetables and herbs. You can see the lights of St Kitts. The menu has a limited choice, but is varied. In **The Mill**, no more than 12 guests dine by candlelight with a gourmet *prixe fixe* dinner.

LL Nisbet Plantation Beach Club, St James, on ½-mile beach close to airport, T4699325, www.nisbetplantation.com. The only plantation inn on the beach, 38 comfortable rooms in hexagonal cottages/suites in the gardens of the 1776 Great House, spread out down the hill to the sea, a/c, fans, tennis, pool, croquet, beach bar for lunch, restaurant, bar and TV lounge in the traditional plantation-style Great House, huge breakfasts, delicious afternoon tea and great dinner included.

LL The Old Manor, T4693445, www.oldmanornevis.com. In restored 1690 sugar plantation has 12 spacious rooms and suites which incorporate the stone walls of the old mill buildings, with wooden walls, shutters and louvred windows, 800 ft above sea level, delightfully breezy and cool, no a/c needed, old furnishings, and prints of old maps and pictures on the walls, good restaurant with view to Montserrat, tropical gardens, beach shuttle, pool.

LL Oualie Beach Hotel, T4699735, www.oualiebeach.com. Comfortable, 32 well-equipped rooms/studios, in cottages with view of bay, deluxe rooms on beach, a/c, fans, TV, non-smoking, massage room, email for guests, meal plans available. Relaxed bar and restaurant on the sand under tamarind trees: Caribbean buffet Sat with live music and masquerade dance, surf-and-turf beach barbecue on Tue with rhythm and blues, steel

Charlestown

Sleeping 🛏
JP's 1

Eating 🍴
Café des Arts 1

Eddy's **3**
Jamakie's **6**
Le Bistro **2**
Nature's Way **5**
Patio **7**

N
Not to scale

pan Sun. Mountain bikes, diving, kayaking and other watersports.

LL-AL Golden Rock Plantation Inn, St George's Parish, T4693346, www.golden-rock.com. 7 cottages, 14 simple but comfortable rooms around 18th-century plantation house, 2-storey suite in old windmill for honeymooners/families, antique furniture, 4-poster beds, plenty of breeze up on the hill, no a/c needed, ocean view all the way to Montserrat, family plan available, pool (formerly the sugar mill cistern), tennis, beach shuttle, specialist interest tours, principally of ecological content, excellent hiking excursions, enjoy afternoon tea and watch the monkeys.

L Banyan Tree Bed & Breakfast, T800-639 6109, www.banyantreebandb.com. 2 rooms in the guesthouse and 1-bedroom suite with kitchenette in Bamboo House, 700 ft above sea level near Morning Star village on 6-acre farm growing flowers, spices and raising Barbados black-belly sheep, lots of fruit trees and a 300-year-old banyan tree.

A JP's, in town near pier and market, T4690287, jpwalters@caribsurf.com. Popular with yachties wanting terra firma, simple rooms, a/c, fans, fridge, lounge with TV, restaurant.

A Philsha's, Pinney's Rd, a few mins from Charlestown, T4695253, www.geocities.com/philshas. Family-run, close to beach, single and double rooms in modern building, white with turquoise trimmings, a/c, some self-catering, TV, laundry, phone, large rooms, tiled floors, Nevisian-style decor, clean and new.

A Sea Spawn Guesthouse, outskirts of Charlestown, T4695239. 18 newly renovated rooms with TV and phones in modern cream and blue building with balconies, ideal for beach and town.

● Eating

St Kitts *p613, maps p614 and p625*
There is a wide variety of fresh seafood (red snapper, lobster, kingfish, blue parrot), and local vegetables as well as imported produce. Try some of the local dishes: conkey (usually available during Easter), ital which the local rastas make (food seasoned with all natural spices, no salt but very delicious), also black pudding, goat water, saltfish and johnny cakes and souse. They are all foods which Kittitians love to eat, especially on Sat when no one wants to cook at home. Most of the

Plantation Inns offer Sun brunch, usually a 3-course meal and excellent value at around US\$30 per person. Most restaurants close on Sun in Basseterre. There are many places offering snacks, light meals, ice cream and drinks in Basseterre and in the Frigate Bay area. Look out for excellent local patties and fruit juices. Local bakeries have a variety of savoury and sweet baked goods at affordable prices and many have dining sections too.

The excellent local spirit is CSR – **Cane Spirit Rothschild** – produced in St Kitts by Baron de Rothschild (in a joint venture with Demerara Distillers Ltd of Guyana). It is drunk neat, with ice or water, or with 'Ting', the local grapefruit soft drink (highly recommended). Tours of the CSR factory are possible.

††††-†† Marshall's, at Horizons Villa Resort, Frigate Bay, T4668245. Romantic poolside dining with an ocean view, exquisite food, not to be missed. Visitors come here for fine dining and locals use it for special occasions.

††††-†† Serendipity Restaurant and Lounge Bar, T4659999. Lunch from 1130, dinner from 1830, reservations essential. Premier fine dining experience overlooking the Basseterre coastline, luxurious comfort and meals with Caribbean and European dishes including an excellent steak and onion sandwich.

††††-†† Waterfalls, Fortlands, T4652754. 0700-2200. Romantic, open-air restaurant overlooking Basseterre and the coast, surrounded by lush tropical plants with the sound of running water in the pond. For more seclusion, book the a/c private dining room. Trade mark dishes include ginger-scented duck breast or medallion of beef with blue cheese, croutons and roasted garlic.

††††-† Turtle Beach Bar and Grill, at the end of the peninsula, T4699086, www.turtle beach1.com. Daily 0945-2300, later at weekends, reduced evening opening out of season. Wooden beach bar with seating under cover or on the deck. Good food, vegetarian options, friendly, but expensive, check your bill. Dancing is usually from sunset until midnight. Steel band on Sun in season.

†† Rock Lobster, Frigate Bay, T4661092. Thu-Tue from 1500. The name speaks for itself, the lobster rocks! Also tapas, steak, nachos, à la carte, full bar. There is inside and outside seating. Located close to the sea shore in the resort area. Great weekend spot, closes when the action stops.

Star of India, Victoria Rd, Basseterre, T4661537. Mon-Sat 0900-2200. Chef from Bombay, authentic Indian food with good tandoori and curries. Many locals only get takeaway, but there is seating if you prefer, although there isn't much privacy.

Ballahoo, corner of Bank St and Fort St, Basseterre, T4654197, www.ballahoo.com. Mon-Sat 0800-2200. Great central meeting place with a fun, laid-back atmosphere, lovely view of The Circus, excellent local food at reasonable prices. A favourite with visitors who like to sit overlooking the bustle of the town centre from the terrace on the first floor.

Circus Grill, The Circus, Basseterre, T4650143. Mon-Sat 1130-2200. Good well-presented food and friendly staff. More expensive and formal than **Ballahoo** but popular with the office trade as well as visitors.

Island Spice, underneath **Bobsy's** at the Sugar's Complex, Frigate Bay Rd, T4650569. Mon-Fri 1100-2300, Sat-Sun 1800-2300, closed holiday Mon. Award-winning chef Lynn Williams' speciality is the National Dish of the Federation, comprising spicy plantains, coconut dumplings, stewed saltfish and seasoned breadfruit, but you can opt for the lesser menu items of sandwiches and burgers from US$8, omelettes, salads or catch of the day. Daily specials such as curry mutton, US$12.

Sprat Net, Old Road Town, by the sea, T4656314. Thu-Sun. Run by the Spencer family, this is one of the places to be at weekends, when it gets busy. People come from all over the island for their fresh fish and goat water. Highly recommended for a good atmosphere and reasonably priced food.

Stone Walls, Princes St, Basseterre, T4655248. Mon-Sat 1700-2300. Excellent food, special theme nights, in a pleasant garden surrounded by a stone wall. Lovely atmosphere, very secluded and private.

Buddies Beach Hut, T6683926. Mon-Fri from 1700, Sat, Sun from 1100. Johnny will welcome you and stays open at weekends until the last guest leaves. Good value cook-up, spare ribs, fries, garlic bread, on the beach, no need to pack a picnic basket.

Lamby's Weekends, just outside Basseterre heading east at entrance to Keys village. T4656830. Fri-Sun 1700-2300. Delicious traditional local food not found anywhere during the week, specializes in black pudding and souse. Family atmosphere around 4

tables in the plain white inside and on a narrow terrace with a great view of the sea. Come with time on your hands, the food will be worth waiting for.

Rank's Eat Rite Specialities, corner Johnston Av and Union St, Basseterre, T4658190. Very local and gaily painted, mainly takeaway light meals rather than the family dinner. Good for vegetarians and Rastafarians. Fresh, low-fat meals, veggie/fish burgers, tuna melt, fish meals, local drinks.

Razba's Veggie Pizza Parlour, Johnston Av, Basseterre, T4656738. 1830 until the last customer leaves. For a very local experience, most of the clientele are Rastafarian vegetarians who come for a good 'lime' and are friendly to new faces. Decorated in the Rastafarian red, green and gold, with a mural in red painted by the Guinness company.

Nevis *p620, maps p621 and p627*
In restaurants a 10-15% tip is expected. The best, upmarket ones are in the hotels and it is usually necessary to reserve a table; they offer exceptional cuisine as well as barbecues and entertainment on certain nights of the week. There are very few eating places in Charlestown and none of them is expensive. In the off season most restaurants only open in the evenings, and some shut completely.

Miss June's, Jones Bay, T4695330, www.missjunes.com Open on request when there is enough demand. Miss June, originally from Trinidad, serves a Caribbean 5-course dinner party in an old West Indian plantation house setting with lush foliage and open-air terraces. Cocktails and hors d'oeuvres on the veranda at 1930. Wine, coffee and liqueurs with limitless refills are included in the price of US$65 including tax but not service. Credit cards accepted, reservations essential. Acclaimed by many food critics, and even Oprah Winfrey.

Bananas, Cliffdwellers at Hamilton, T4691891. Dinner only Mon-Sat 1800-2200. Perched up on the cliff top with spectacular views of St Kitts, you take a cable car up to the bistro. Lounge with comfy sofas, Turkish style, where you can wait for your table with a drink or retire after dinner. Good food, different menu nightly, mix of Thai, European and Caribbean dishes, salads, ribs, seafood, chicken, etc. Live music Sat from 2100 until about 0200 depending on demand.

¶¶-¶ **Double Deuce Restaurant and Bar**, Pinney's Beach, T4692222. Tue-Sun 0900-until the last customer leaves. Specializes in local sea foods such as *mahi mahi*, lobster, snapper , conch. **The Bar** is also open on Thu for karaoke from 2100 until late.

¶¶ **Gabriella's Restaurant and Bar**, Beach Road, St Johns, T4696783. Serves Caribbean and international cuisine in the family hill estate, tucked away in private grounds, idyllic comfortable surroundings, perfect eating out. Green vervet monkeys drop in hoping you will share.

¶¶-¶ **Eddy's**, on Main St opposite Memorial Sq and the handicraft cooperative, Charlestown, T4695958. A tourist favourite for local food, drinks and music with string bands, bush bands or steel bands Sat 2000-2300, happy hour Wed 1700-2000 with free snacks. Karaoke, dancing till early morning.

¶¶-¶ **Gallipot**, Tamarind Bay, on the beach north of Oualie, T4698230. Thu-Sat 1200-2200 (kitchen open 1200-1500, 1800-2100), Sun 1200-1730. Lovely location on a little bay, perfect for yachts, providing showers, laundry and cottages as well as food. Family-run, you can spend all day here, with towels, soap and shampoo if you ask. Great fresh fish any day but they are known for their Sun special roast beef lunch, very popular, reservations essential.

¶¶-¶ **Jade Garden**, Newcastle, T4699762. Tue-Sat 1000-2200. A casual café and bar set in extensive grounds with an organic vegetable garden producing for the kitchen. Healthy cuisine with an extensive menu catering for everyone, salads, pizza (Veggie Volcano), seafood (Shanghai Shrimp), deli. You can use the pool or the games room.

¶¶-¶ **Jamakie's**, Prince William St, Charlestown, T4698748. Daily from 1000. The best in West Indian food but specializes in Jamaican cuisine including jerk chicken.

¶¶-¶ **Le Bistro**, Chapel St, Basseterre, T4695110. Mon-Fri lunch and dinner. Owned by chef Matt Lloyd, who used to work at the Montpelier Inn, this tiny restaurant in a 1930s, typically West Indian chattel house offers a variety of food, from quiche to curry or coconut chicken. Fresh fish is usually caught by Matt himself. Fri happy hour 1700-1900 is buzzing with the after-work crowd, very popular.

¶¶-¶ **Mingles Restaurant and Bar**, Cades Bay, T4691841. Lunch and dinner, closed Thu and Sun lunch. For excellent local food and large portions, lots of seafood and fish, but try West Indian vegetables such as cristophene and sample Pas' great cocktails such as mango colada. Completely out of the way with a good atmosphere at weekends when there are sometimes parties and music. The restaurant opens out onto the beach.

¶¶-¶ **Natural Livity**, Cotton Ground, T4694825. Home-made vegetarian fare Nevis style.

¶¶-¶ **Nature's Way**, Cotton Ginnery Mall, T4690688. Mon-Fri 1130-1530, dinner by reservation only. Another fine vegetarian restaurant, tasty, healthy and cheap meals.

¶¶-¶ **Patio**, Parkville Complex, Charlestown. Daily. A cool, breezy and sparkling clean establishment away from the hustle and bustle of city life. Local dishes and drinks including in season mauby, ginger beer, passion fruit, etc. Fast buffet lunch, à la carte dinner.

¶¶-¶ **Seafood Madness**, Pinney's Rd, Charlestown, T4690558. 0730-2100. Great for takeaways, all sorts of seafood, chicken and ribs. Reservations preferred for dinner, when the place is transformed with fairy lights and candles. Very tasty blackened or Créole fish, also conch or steak. Rum cocktails a speciality.

¶ **Café des Arts**, between the museum and Unella's, on the waterfront, Charlestown, T4697098. Mon-Fri 0800-1600, Sat 1000-1500. Open for breakfast and lunch, for salads, sandwiches, quiche, tables outside under the trees and parasols. Upstairs and at the back of the house is an art gallery exhibiting and selling work by local artists.

¶ **Martha's Tea House**, Botanical Gardens, T4693680. 1000-1700. For breakfast, lunch, tea or drinks, serves sandwiches, salads, a ploughman's lunch with cheese and pickled onions, scones with Devonshire cream and tapas. The tea house is inside the Botanical Gardens with panoramic views from the veranda over the island.

♦ Bars and clubs

St Kitts *p613, maps p614 and p625*
The club scene has no set hours; doors open around 2200 with people arriving at around 2300-2400 and leaving at 0500 when the sun comes up. Most dance floors provide a wide variety of music and entrance costs US$3.50-18.50, depending on the occasion, with overseas performers commanding the

upper limit. Nightclubs have a great mix of calypso, soca, salsa, hip-hop, reggae, dance hall, R&B, house, techno and other types of music. For the real local experience, visit dance spots out in the country area: **BCA**, T4657606/7, at Saddlers; **Manhattan Gardens**, T4659121, and **Sprat Net**, in Old Road, **Off Limit**, in Cayon, T4669821, and the **Inner Circle Club**, at St Paul's, where action takes place by announcement. These venues are frequented by some of the region's top DJs as well as local bands playing local music. **Bobsy's**, Sugar's Complex, Frigate Bay Rd, T4666138. 1200-late. A breezy roof-top bar and restaurant on a hill above Frigate Bay with a panoramic view over the island to the sea and Nevis in the distance. Tables outside in the sunshine or under cover. In the evening the clientèle ranges from the happy hour crew to the intimate dinner romantics to the nightlife enthusiasts, up for salsa classes, karaoke and dancing at weekends.
Dolce Cabana, Frigate Bay Beach, T4651569. Club Fri 2200-0400. Restaurant Wed-Mon 1600-2200. Bar Wed-Mon 1600-0200. Currently the most popular club, Fri only and getting going around 0030, with a good mix of locals and visitors. There are tables under cover and picnic benches outside if you want to eat there. Steps lead down to the beach, where lots of people end up, dancing under the stars. On other nights there is karaoke (Thu, Sun) or theme nights such as salsa (Sat).
Moon Dance, at the **Angelus Hotel**, Frigate Bay, T4666224. It's a fair walk from the hotel next to the Marriott down to the beach, but worth it. Snorkelling reef with lots of fish where visitors have caught their own lobsters to cook on the grill, so bring your snorkelling gear for a daytime visit. Fri night beach bonfire and grill, with local reggae and steel pan, weekend beach volley ball, with 4 courts set up for players, Sun Beach Lime for relaxing, listening to local music, eating and drinking.
OTI, Basseterre, T4652754, www.ocean terraceinn.com. Daily 1900-2300. Fri night is Caribbean night, when a Caribbean buffet is served in the **Waterfalls** restaurant, calypso music is played and you can dance. There are fountains, tropical plants and beautiful landscaping in the gardens and there is a view down to the sea and Basseterre.
The Pumpkin, Newton Ground. Looks like an orange pumpkin but very small so expect to be very 'intimate' with other guests. Visitors should go with a local if interested, its not a place for softies, nor for lovers of R&B, hip hop, jazz and the like. Expect wild Caribbean music which calls for a knowledge of hip gyration or a passion to learn. Lots of fun and dancing with the local crowd, hot on Fri and Sat, DJs and occasionally local bands perform.

Nevis *p620, maps p621 and p627*
Nevis is quiet and most visitors content themselves with a good meal in the evening and maybe an after-dinner drink. However, there is entertainment for visitors and locals, particularly at the weekends. Hotels organize activities on different nights in high season. The **Nisbet Plantation** (see page 627), T4699325, has live music on Thu, **Four Seasons Resort** on Pinney's Beach, T4691111, has live music on Fri and Sat nights, **The Old Manor** at Gingerland, T4693445 (page 627), hosts steel pan on Fri nights, **Oualie Beach Hotel** (page 627), T4699735, has a Sat buffet with live string band, and the **Golden Rock** (page 628), T4693346, also has a string band on Sat nights. Look for posters, radio announcements or ask what's on at the tourist office.
Rumours Bar, Newcastle Village near the airport, T4698412. Daily lunch and dinner. A new, very local bar, casual with live music occasionally. The restaurant serves local dishes.
The Spotlight, Bath Village. Weekends 2200-late in season. A trendy club featuring live local entertainment as well as popular artists from the Caribbean. Full bar and local food served and a popular location for private functions and parties. Dress code smart casual.
Tequila Sheilas, Cades Bay, T4698633. Thu-Sun lunch and dinner. A beach bar and circular restaurant with a disco on Sat night for romantic dancing on the sand late into the night. Sun jazz brunch is also popular. Themed evenings throughout the year with a popular steak night.

⊕ Festivals and events

St Kitts *p613, maps p614 and p625*
May The St Kitts Triathlon, an ITU international race, www.stkittstriathlon.com, is held on the 2nd Sun in May. The grandstand is at the **Timothy Beach Hotel**.
Jun St Kitts holds a **music festival** at the end of Jun; 4 nights of calypso, reggae, R&B, jazz,

street-style, gospel, country and western and rap, with local and famous overseas artists.
Dec The liveliest time to visit is for the Carnival held over Christmas and the New Year, with parades, calypso competitions and street dancing. It is a favourite time of year for many Kittitians and Nevisians with never a dull moment. For details, contact the Ministry of Culture, www.stkittscarnival.com.

Nevis *p620, maps p621 and p627*
Jul-Aug The annual equivalent of carnival is Culturama, held end-Jul and Aug, finishing on the first Mon in Aug. There is a Queen show, calypso competition, local bands and guest bands and 'street jams'. The Nevis Tourist Office has full details or contact the Department of Culture, T4695521, Mon-Fri 0800-1600.

O Shopping

St Kitts *p613, maps p614 and p625*
Art galleries
The Plantation Picture House, at Rawlins Plantation, 1100-1700, T4657740, is Kate Spencer's studio and gallery of portraits, still life and landscapes in oils and watercolours, her designs are also on silk. She also has a shop in Basseterre, on Bank St, just off The Circus, called **Kate**, with paintings, prints, silk sarongs, hats by Dale Isaac.

Bookshops
Mini-Walls, Princess St, Mon-Thu 0800-1700, Fri 0800-1800, Sat 0800-1630. Has a good selection of music and Caribbean books.

Clothes
Brown Sugar clothing line, The Bay Rd, T4664664, www.mybrownsugar.com. Is owned by Judith Rawlins, a young local designer. Her clothing is very attractive, Caribbean style without the bright colours, all designed and sewn by Judith herself.
The Island Hopper Boutique at The Circus, under **Ballahoo** restaurant, T4652905, Mon-Fri 0800-1600, Sat 0800-1300. Stocks **Caribelle Batik** range of cotton fashions and clothes from Trinidad, St Lucia, Barbados and Haiti.
Island Fever, Palms Arcade, The Circus, T4652599, www.islandfever.biz, Mon-Fri 0830-1630, Sat 0830-1500. Another shop specializing in souvenirs and island-style clothing, bags and watches.

Crafts
Local Sea Island cotton wear and cane and basketwork are attractive and reasonable. There are vendors' markets at the Craft House on the Bay Rd and on Lower College St Ghaut and Liverpool Row.
The Stonewall Boutique, Princes St. Sells quality local crafts and imports.
Glass Island, 4 Princes St, T/F4666771, www.glassisland.com. Is a working glass shop which produces glass tiles, platters, jewellery and gifts.

Food
The public market in Basseterre is busiest Sat morning, good for fruit and vegetables, also fish stalls and butchers. Supermarkets in Basseterre include **B & K Superfood** on the south side of Independence Sq and George St, **Horsfords Valumart** on Wellington Rd, and **Rams** on Bay Rd and at Bird Rock.

Stamps
The St Kitts' philatelic bureau is in **Pelican Shopping Mall**, Mon-Wed, Fri-Sat 0800-1200, 1300-1500, Thu 0800-1100.

Nevis *p620, maps p621 and p627*
Art galleries
Eva Wilkin Gallery, Clay Ghaut, Gingerland, T4692673. Mon-Fri 1000-1500, or by appointment. Started by Howard and Marlene Paine, it has an exhibition in an 18th-century windmill of paintings and drawings by Nevisian Eva Wilkin MBE (whose studio it was until her death in 1989), prints of which are available, also antique maps and contemporary pieces by local and international artists.

Clothes
The Island Hopper Boutique, The Arcade, Charlestown, T4691491. Stocks the **Caribelle Batik** range of cotton fashions and clothes from Trinidad, St Lucia, Barbados and Haiti.
Island Fever, Henville's Plaza, Charlestown, T4690867, www.islandfever.biz, Mon-Sat 0900-1700. Souvenirs and island-style clothing, bags and watches.

Crafts
Nevis Handicraft Co-operative, Main St, Charlestown, next to the tourist office, T469 1746. A good collection of local artisans' work.
Newcastle Pottery, Newcastle. Mon-Fri

0900-1600. The pottery makes red clay artefacts including bowls and candleholders. You can watch potters at work. The kilns are fired by burning coconut husks.

Food
The Gourmet Shop, Farms Estate, T4697475, gourmetshop@caribsurf.com. Mon-Fri 0900-1700, Sat 0900-1300. Specializes in quintessential gourmet foods and fine wines.
Supermarkets Nisbets in Newcastle and **Superfood**, Parkville Plaza, Charlestown.

Market
The public market in Charlestown is busiest Sat morning, good for fruit and vegetables, also fish stalls and butchers.

Stamps
Nevis Philatelic Bureau, Charlestown, Mon-Fri 0800-1600. Nevis is famous for its first-day covers of the island's fauna and flora, undersea life, history and carnival.

▲ Activities and tours

St Kitts *p613, maps p614 and p625*
Cricket
St Kitts and Nevis are cricket-mad and have produced 4 players, all from Nevis, to play in the West Indies team in Test matches. In Jul 2004 the sister islands were delighted to be picked to host matches in the 2007 Cricket World Cup. Warner Park outside Basseterre was the venue for Australia's opening matches in the group stages against South Africa, The Netherlands and Scotland. The stadium is new, with a permanent capacity of 8000, although this was temporarily increased for the World Cup. It is small but scenic and well-designed, with the comfort in mind of players, media, officials and spectators. The new ground hosted its first One Day International and first Test Match between the West Indies and India in 2006. There is also an adjoining football field and netball and tennis courts.

Cycling
Blue Water Safaris, T4664933, waterfun@caribsurf.com. Mountain biking tours (US$15), island biking tours and beach outings.
St Kitts on Wheels, Cayon St, Basseterre, T4663912. They hire 21-speed mountain bikes, with helmet, lock, touring information.

Diving
Kenneth's Dive Centre, Bay Rd, Basseterre, T4652670. Kenneth Samuel, a PADI-certified Dive Master (friendly and helpful), offers courses, dive packages (single-tank dive US$50, US$75 2-tank dive, 4-day package US$245) and all equipment. There are facilities for people with disabilities.
Pro-Divers at Ocean Terrace Inn, Basseterre, T4663483, prodiver@caribsurf.com. Large boat takes large parties diving, PADI instruction. Dive gear available for rent, dive packages available, single-tank dive US$45, 2-tank dive US$70, 3-hr snorkelling US$35. Ocean kayaks for hire.

Fishing
Oliver Spencer, Old Rd, St Kitts, T4656314. A fisherman who is happy to take visitors deep-sea fishing.

Golf
Royal St Kitts Golf Club, Frigate Bay, T4662700, www.royalstkittsgolfclub.com. An 18-hole international championship golf course. Completed in 2004, built on 125 acres, with 2 holes on the Caribbean and 3 holes on the Atlantic. Brackish water is used to irrigate the special grass which can tolerate salt. Green fees are US$150 for 18 holes, US$100 for 9 holes, reduced rate for juniors and discounts in summer.
Golden Rock, T4658103. 9-hole course; a fun day is held on the last Sun of the month.

Hiking
Greg's Safaris, T4654121, www.skbee.com/safaris. Pleasant and informative, US$40-80.
Kriss Tours, T4654042. US$50 per full day, overnight camping US$90.
Periwinkle Tours, T4656314. Guided walks, US$30-35.

Horse racing
The **Beaumont Horse Racing Track and Pavilion** is being built in the north of the island, to be opened winter 2005-06.

Sailing
Blue Water Safaris, St Kitts, T869-4664933, www.bluewatersafaris.com. Has 1 boat, *Caretaker* (38 ft) and 2 catamarans, *Falcon* (55 ft) and *Irie Lime* (65 ft), offering fishing (US$60 per person), moonlight cruises

(US$25), party cruises (US$25), Nevis day tours (US$60), sunset cruises (US$35) and snorkelling trips (US$35), private snorkelling, sailing and fishing charters (US$360 half day). **Leeward Island Charters**, next Ballahoo restaurant above the Circus, Basseterre, St Kitts, T869-4657474. *Caona II*, a 47-ft catamaran, 67-ft *Eagle*, or *Spirit of St Kitts*, a 70-ft catamaran for a sail, snorkel and barbecue. **St Kitts-Nevis Boating Club**, T869-4658766, organizes sunfish races, check the bulletin board for details at **PJ's Pizza Bar** (T869-4658373), Frigate Bay, the **Ballahoo** (T869-4654197) in Basseterre, or Dougie Brookes who manages the boatyard **Caribee Yachts** (T869-4658411).

Tour operators

Caribbean Journey Master Tours, below Frigate Bay Police Outpost, T4668110, www.caribbeanjourneymasters.com. 0800-2100. Party bus, pub crawls and charters. For those who like riotous entertainment, Spuddy, the friendly tour guide takes you on a crazy tour bus with lots of music – unforgettable.

Watersports

Fantasy Parasailing, T4668930, bentels@caribsurf.com. Takes up to 6 up in the air with optional dips in the sea.
Mr X Watersports, next to **Monkey Bar** in Frigate Bay, T4654995. Rents windsurfing and snorkelling equipment, and offers fishing trips and weekly all-inclusive packages. Also jet skis, waterskiing, windsurfing.

Nevis *p620, maps p621 and p627*
Cycling

Windsurf'n'Mountainbike and Wheel World cycling shop, at the Oualie Beach Club, T4699682, www.mountainbike nevis.com. Winston Crooke organizes races, triathlons, tours, bike hire (US$20-35 a day, US$120-195 a week) and a cycle club, **The Trailblazers**; often competitions going on.

Diving

Scuba Safaris, Oualie Beach, T4699518, scubanev@caribsurf.com. A 5-star operation run by Ellis Chaderton. Diving costs US$45 for a single-tank dive, US$80 for 2 tanks, PADI and NAUI instruction and equipment rental. Also trips to see dolphins and humpback whales.

Fishing

Nevis Water Sports, Oualie Beach, T4699060, www.fishnevis.com. The *Sea Brat* and *Sea Troll* can be chartered for fishing or leisure tours. Oct-Dec is peak wahoo season, Feb-Apr is best for tuna and wahoo, Jun-Aug for billfish, all of which are released.

Golf

The Four Seasons, T4691111. An excellent 18-hole, par 71 championship course designed by Robert Trent Jones Jr. People fly in from other islands just to play golf here. It is beautifully maintained and offers fabulous views, but green fees are US$175. For something completely different, the **Nevis Golf Course** costs only US$15 and has 2 holes with different approaches, while the **Cat Ghaut Course** opposite the entrance to the **Mount Nevis Hotel**, T4699826, US$10.

Hiking

Eco-Tours, T4692091, droll@caribsurf.com. David Rollinson is very knowledgeable; he offers 'eco rambles' over the 18th-century Coconut Walk and New River Estates, a 'Sugar trail' Mountravers hike over the old Pinney Estate (US$25 per person) as well as Sun morning strolls around historic Charlestown (US$10 per person).
Heb's Nature Tours run by Michael Herbert, Rawlins Village, Gingerland, T4692501. Offers Mount Nevis hike (5 hrs, US$35-40), rainforest hike (4 hrs, US$25-30), Saddle Hill hike (3 hrs, US$20-25), medicinal plants (2 hrs, US$15) and Camp Spring (2½ hrs, US$15-20), price depends on numbers.
Sunrise Tours, T4692758. Trips to Nevis Peak (4 hrs round trip, US$35), Saddle Hill (1½ hrs, US£30) or the Water Source (3 hrs, US$40).
Top to Bottom, T4699080, run by biologists Jim and Nikki Johnson. Organize walks to suit you, including a night-time star-gazing walk, 2-3 hrs, US$25, children half price, snacks of fruit and coconut.

Horse riding

Nevis horses are thoroughbred/Créole crosses, mostly retired from racing on Nevis, where it is the 2nd most popular sport after cricket.
Hermitage Plantation, T4693477. Horse-drawn carriage tours, US$50 per 30 mins, and horse riding US$45 for 1½ hrs.
Nevis Equestrian Centre, Main Rd, Clifton

Estate, Cotton Ground, T4698118, guilbert@ caribsurf.com. Run by John and Ali Jordan Guilbert and Erika Guilbert-Walters. 10 different rides from US$50 with a combination of trail and beach, English or Western saddles, for novice or experienced riders, and have an arena for lessons, US$20-30. They even have a 6-hr cross island ride, but don't try that if you're not used to sitting in a saddle.

Nevis is known for its large number of donkeys. A donkey ride is an unusual and exciting way to see the sights. Make sure you're wearing jeans. Some donkey rides are organized through hotels and tour agents.

Horse racing
The **Nevis Turf and Jockey Club** meets at least 6 times a year to race island thorough-breds: New Year's Day, Tourism Week (Feb), Easter, May Day, Aug during *Culturama*, Independence Day and Boxing Day. Facilities past Market Shop and down Hanley's Rd include a grandstand seating 200, washrooms, a pari-mutuel booth, good food and dancing well into the night; this is part folk festival, part carnival, with no social barriers. There is a minimum of 5 races on the seaside track, where you can see Redonda, Montserrat and Antigua in the distance and often whales breaching. Races start mid-afternoon and end at dusk. An average of 4 horses in each race run clockwise over a distance of 5.5 to 8 furlongs (1 mile), with a hill up to the home stretch. Contact Richard Lupinacci, who resurrected racing in the 1980s, at the **Hermitage Inn** for details, T4693477. Look out for the more amusing **donkey races**.

Watersports
Under the Sea, Oualie Beach, T4691291, www.undertheseanevis.com. A small aquarium run by Barbara Whitman as an excellent educational venture for all ages. She takes groups snorkelling after a hands-on talk about the contents of her aquarium and you learn to look out for the smaller creatures underwater. Highly recommended **Touch and Go** snorkelling US$50 (US$35 children 5-11), snorkel gear included but if you want to hire it separately it is US$10 per day. Snorkelling lessons US$25, or US$15 for trip participants. **Windsurf'n'Mountainbike Nevis**, Oualie Beach, T4699682, www.sindsurfing nevis.com. Windsurfing, rentals and lessons: beginners

US$50 for 2 hrs, intermediate and advanced US$30 for 1 hr, rentals US$65-95 a day, US$20-30 an hr. Sea kayaks can be rented for US$15 per hr single, US$20 for a double, hobie cats are US$45-95 per hr, no credit cards.

⊖ Transport

St Kitts *p613, maps p614 and p625*
Air
In season there are weekly charter flights from North America and Europe, but these change frequently. **Excel** flies weekly from London Gatwick to St Kitts. **American Airlines** have 3 flights a week from Miami. **US Airways** has a direct flight from Charlotte and Philadelphia. **Sky Service** offers a weekly winter flight directly into St Kitts from Toronto. Connections with the USA and Europe can be made through San Juan (**American Eagle**), St Maarten (**LIAT/Caribbean Star** and **Winair**), Barbados (**LIAT/Caribbean Star**) and Antigua (**LIAT/Caribbean Star**). There are good connections with other Caribbean Islands with **LIAT/Caribbean Star** and **Winair**.

Airports RL Bradshaw International Airport is 2 miles from Basseterre. There are taxis, which charge fixed rates for 1-4 passengers. Alternatively, when returning you can get a bus from the bus stop at the roundabout northeast of Independence Sq, US$1, to the airport and walk the last 5 mins from the main road; some buses might go up to the terminal. If you don't have much luggage, it is easy to walk from Basseterre to the airport. There are duty-free and gift shops and a café, but they tend to open for long-haul flights only. Even the bar in the departure lounge is often shut.

Airlines USAir, Kisco Travel, Central St, Basseterre, T4654167. **TDC Airline Services**, Basseterre, T465-2511/2286, general sales agent for **American Airlines** and **British Airways**; **Caribbean Airlines**, T4652286; **American Eagle**, T4658490; **Winair**, Sprott St, Basseterre, T4652186; **Carib Aviation**, T4653055 (The Circus, Basseterre and R L Bradshaw Airport). **Nevis Express**, T4699755/6, F4699751, www.nevisexpress .com. **Air St Kitts Nevis**, Basseterre, T4658571, F4699018, is a charter company specializing in day excursions and other services to neighbouring islands. Also air ambulance with medical staff.

Boat
Port Zante can accommodate 2 of the largest
cruise ships. For ferry information to Nevis,
see page 613 and page 636.

Bus

Minibuses do not run on a scheduled basis, but
follow a set route (more or less), US$2 on most
routes, US$2 from Basseterre to the north of the
island, frequent service from the bus terminal
close to the market area on the Bay Rd from
where buses go west to Sandy Point.
Passengers pay upon entrance to the bus. To
catch a bus east, wait off Bakers Corner at the
east end of Cayon St. There are no minibuses to
Frigate Bay and the southeast peninsula.

Car

Car hire If visiting at carnival time you
should book car hire a long time in advance.
Companies insist on you having collision
damage waiver, which adds another US$5-10
to quoted rates. There is also a 5% tax on car
rentals. Most rental companies will help you
obtain the obligatory temporary driving
licence, US$20, valid for a year, from the Traffic
Department. If you rent for 3-day minimum
you can arrange for a car on the sister island if
you do a day trip to St Kitts or Nevis. Hire
companies include: **Avis Car Rental**, South
Independence Square St, T4651043, F4666846
(Suzuki jeeps, Nissan automatics, efficient);
Thrifty/TDC Rentals, West Independence
Square St, Basseterre, T4652991, F4668855, or
Bay Rd, Charlestown, T4695690, also at Four
Seasons, T4691111, tdcrent@caribsurf.com;
Caines Rent-A-Car, Princes St, Basseterre,
T4652366, F4656172; **Sunshine Car Rental**,
Cayon St, Basseterre, T4652193, Hondas and
Korando jeeps. Others include **A & T Car**,
T4654030; **Delisle Walwyn**, T4658449;
Huggins, T4658080; **Courtesy Car Rentals**,
Wigley Av, Basseterre, T4657804; **G & L**, CAP
Southwell Industrial Site, T4668040/1,
www.gandlcarrentals.com.

Taxi

Taxis have a yellow T registration plate.
Maximum taxi fares are set, for example from
airport to Basseterre US$7, to Frigate Bay,
US$11, to Sandy Point US$15. Round trip from
Basseterre to Romney Manor US$26, to
Brimstone Hill US$40. Taxis within Basseterre
cost US$3.70, with additional charges for

waiting or for more than 2 pieces of luggage.
A southeast peninsula tour is US$40, an island
tour US$60. A 50% extra charge is made on
both islands between 2200 and 0600.

Nevis *p620, maps p621 and p627*
Air

In season there are weekly charter flights
from North America and Europe, but these
change frequently.

 From Europe, British Airways, Condor or
Virgin Atlantic to **Antigua** then
LIAT/Caribbean Star or Carib Aviation from
there to Nevis. Other connections are via **Sint
Maarten** (Air France, KLM). From the USA the
best route is via San Juan, from where
American Eagle have direct flights, or via Sint
Maarten then **Winair** to Nevis. Flights to Nevis
from **Anguilla** (Coastal Air Transport),
Antigua (Winair), **St-Barts** (Coastal Air
Transport), **St Croix** (Coastal Air Transport),
St Eustatius (Winair), **St Kitts** (Winair) and **St
Maarten** (LIAT/Caribbean Star and Winair),
San Juan (American Eagle). The grander
hotels on Nevis arrange chartered air transfers
from Antigua/St Kitts for their guests, highly
recommended to avoid the crush.

 Airports Vance Amory Airport is at
Newcastle, 7 miles from Charlestown (on the
main road, bus to Charlestown US$1.65). The
terminal is new and smart and there is a Visa
ATM. Expect to have your baggage searched
on your way in.

 Airlines Evelyn's Travel, on Main St,
Charlestown, general sales agent for
American Airlines and **British Airways**,
Charlestown, T469-5302/5238; **Winair**,
T4695583 on Nevis; **Carib Aviation**, T4699295
(Newcastle Airport, Nevis).

Boat

The crossing between St Kitts and Nevis takes
45-60 mins and costs US$10 one way plus
US$0.35 tax (*Caribe Queen, Sea Hustler, Caribe
Breeze, Caribe Surf, Mark Twain, Geronimo*).
Several daily departures from 0700, depending
on the boat. Confirm sailing times with
Ministry of Communications, T4652521,
Mon-Fri 0800-1600. Tickets can only be
purchased from the quay just prior to
departure, so turn up about 1 hr in advance.
Island tours operate from St Kitts and there is
also a **water taxi** service between the 2
islands: US$25 return, minimum 4 passengers,

20 mins, operated by **Kenneth's Dive Centre**, T4652670 in advance, or **Pro-Divers**, US$20, 10 mins, T4653223. The **Four Seasons Hotel** has ferry boats running exclusively for guests' flights, US$57 round trip. **Oualie Beach** also arranges transfers for guests from St Kitts Airport via Turtle Beach (day) or Port Zante (night) with a water taxi.

Bus

Minibuses start outside **Foodworld Cash & Carry** and go to all points, but are not very regular, US$0.75-1.65; an island tour is possible, if time consuming.

Car

Car hire Hire companies include: **Thrifty/ TDC Rentals**, Bay Rd, Charlestown, T4695690, F4691329, also at Four Seasons, T4691111, tdcrent@caribsurf.com; **Nisbett Rentals Ltd**, 100 yds from Newcastle Airport, mini moke US$40 per day, collision damage waiver US$8 per day, recommended, particularly if you are flying in/out of Nevis, T4699211, open 0700-1900; **Striker's**, Hermitage, T4692654, **Nevis Car Rental**, Newcastle, T4699837, **Avis**, Stoney Grove, T4691241, and others.

Taxi

Taxis have a yellow T registration plate. Maximum taxi fares are set, for example: a taxi from the airport to Charlestown costs US$14, to **Oualie Beach**, US$9. A 50% extra charge is made between 2200 and 0600. Tours of Nevis cost US$20 per hr and a whole-island tour costs US$50. Recommended is **TC Taxis**, T4692911, T0783-6628301, tctaxi@carib surf.com, TC is fun, knowledgeable of the island and works with other good drivers.

⊙ Directory

St Kitts *p613, maps p614 and p625*
Banks If you are in a hurry, choose a foreign bank as their queues are often shorter. ATMs are available at all banks but dispense local currency only. **Eastern Caribbean Central Bank (ECCB)** is based in Basseterre, and is responsible for the issue of currency in Antigua and Barbuda, Dominica, Grenada, Montserrat, St Kitts and Nevis, St Lucia and St Vince/ Grenadines. **St Kitts-Nevis-Anguilla National Bank**, 5 branches: on the corner of Central St and West Independence Square St; Pelican Mall; Sandy Point, T4652204, Mon-Wed 0830-1500 except Thu 0830-1200, Sat 0830-1100; a branch at Saddlers village, T4657362, Mon-Wed and Fri 0830-1300, Thu 0830-1200, Sat 0830-1100. **FirstCaribbean International Bank**, on The Circus, Basseterre, T4652519, Mon-Thu 0800-1500, Fri 0800- 1700, and at Frigate Bay, T4652264, Mon-Thu 0800-1300, Fri 0800-1300, 1500-1700. **Royal Bank of Canada**, on The Circus, Basseterre, T4652519, Mon-Thu 0800-1500, Fri 0800- 1700. **Scotia Bank**, Fort St, T4654141, Mon- Thu 0800-1500, Fri 0800-1700. **Hospital** Joseph N France General Hospital, T652551. **Internet** At the Pelican Mall on the Bay Rd in Basseterre, where Cable & Wireless has a public internet machine. **Leyton's Internet Café**, at the Amory Mall, T4667873, US$0.10 per min or US$10 per hr. **Dot Com** internet café on The Circus, Basseterre, Mon-Fri 0900- 1630, Sat 0900-1300. **Post** Post office in Basseterre is on Bay Rd, Mon-Wed and Fri 0800-1500, Thu 0800-1100, Sat 0800-1200. Courier services including **DHL** and **Fed Ex**. **Telephone** Liberalization of telecommu- nications has opened up the market to **Cable & Wireless**, **Digicel** and **UTS Cariglobe**, while more providers are expected and rates are falling. **Cable & Wireless** main office is on Cayon St, Basseterre. Credit card calls T1-800- 8778000. USA direct public phones available at C & W office. Phone cards are sold in denominations of EC$10, 20 and 40. Coin boxes take EC quarters minimum and EC dollars. Call charges are from US$5 for 3 mins to the USA, Canada or the UK. **The Boat Phone Company** on the Victoria Rd, T/F4663003, F4653033, offers cellular phone service for yachts.

Nevis *p620, maps p621 and p627*
Banks All banks are in Charlestown: the Bank of Nevis, Main St, T4695564; **First Caribbean**, Main St, T4691988; Bank of Nova Scotia, Main St, T4695411. Open 0800-1400 Mon-Fri, except last Fri in month 0800-1600. Avoid lunchtimes (1200-1300) as banks are busy with local workers. Visa and MasterCard accepted. **Internet** Connextions Internet Café on Main St, T4699675, EC$0.50 per min, or EC$50 a day, 0900-2100 Mon-Sat, also Sun if cruise ship in port. **Post** Post office in Charlestown on Main St, Mon-Wed and Fri 0800-1500, Thu 0800-1100, Sat 0800-1130. Courier services including DHL and Fed Ex.

Background

History

Before Columbus's arrival in 1493, there were Amerindians living on both islands, and their relics can still be seen. As in most of the other islands, they were slaughtered by European immigrants, although the Caribs fought off the British and the French for many years and their battles are celebrated locally. St Kitts became the first British settlement in the West Indies in 1623 and was important for its sugar industry, with the importation of large numbers of African slaves. In April 1690 a severe earthquake caused heavy damage to St Kitts, Nevis and Redonda. It was followed by a tidal wave which compounded the damage and, it is believed, destroyed Nevis' first capital, Jamestown.

For a time St Kitts was shared by France and England; partition was ended by the Peace of Utrecht in 1713 and it finally became a British colony in 1783. From 1816, St Christopher, Nevis, Anguilla and the British Virgin Islands were administered as a single colony until the Leeward Islands Federation was formed in 1871.

From 1958, St Kitts-Nevis and Anguilla belonged to the West Indies Federation until its dissolution in 1962. In 1967 their constitutional status was changed from Crown Colony to a state in voluntary association with Britain, in a step towards Independence. Robert L Bradshaw was the first Premier of the Associated State. Local councils were set up in Anguilla and Nevis to give those islands more authority over local affairs. Anguilla broke away from the group and was re-established as a Crown Colony in 1971. During the 1970s Independence was a burning issue but Nevis' local council was keen to follow Anguilla's lead rather than become independent with St Kitts. Negotiations were stalled because of British opposition to Nevis becoming a Crown Colony. Eventually, on 19 September 1983, St Kitts and Nevis became independent as a single nation.

The main political parties are the People's Action Movement (PAM), the St Kitts and Nevis Labour Party (SKNLP), the Nevis Reformation Party (NRP) and the Concerned Citizens Movement (CCM). Dr Kennedy Simmonds (PAM) was elected Prime Minister in 1980 and held office until July 1995. Elections in November 1993 were highly controversial when PAM and the SKNLP each won four seats, the CCM two and the NRP one. The CCM declined to join a coalition government or to form a majority with either party. The Governor then asked Dr Kennedy Simmonds to form a minority government with the support of the NRP, PAM's previous coalition partner. This was extremely unpopular, given that the Labour Party had won 54.4% of votes cast in St Kitts compared with 41.7% for PAM. A state of emergency was declared for 10 days in December because of rioting. More clashes greeted the budget presentation in February 1994 with the SKNLP boycotting parliament (except to take the oath of allegiance in May) in support of fresh elections.

Also during 1994, St Kitts was rocked by a corruption scandal linked to senior political officials involving drugs trafficking, murder and prison riots. It was alleged that traffickers were exploiting St Kitts and Nevis and avoiding better monitored routes. The crisis pushed the Government to call a forum for national unity, at which it was decided that a general election should be held, three years ahead of schedule. In the meantime, all parties in the National Assembly participated in decisions on matters such as foreign investment and a code of conduct to regulate political activity. A Commonwealth observer team monitored the elections to prevent a recurrence of the 1993 disturbances.

In the months leading up to the 3 July elections, British police officers were brought in to assist the local police. The campaign was marred by political party rivalry which was often violent, but the result was an overwhelming victory for the SKNLP, which won seven seats. PAM was reduced to one, while the CCM and the NRP continued to hold two seats and one seat respectively. Dr Denzil Douglas became Prime Minister.

The Premier of Nevis is Mr Joseph Parry (NRP). He became Premier in 2006, defeating Mr Vance Amory (CCM), who had been in power for over 20 years. Although Mr Amory had been in favour of the secession of Nevis from the federal state, Mr Parry

The SKNLP returned to power in 2000, winning all eight seats in St Kitts. There was no change in Nevis, the CCM winning two seats and the NRP one. PAM had claimed massive fraud in the elections, in which it won 35.5% of the vote in St Kitts but no seats. In October 2004, the SKNLP won again, with seven of the eight seats, while in Nevis the CCM won two seats and the NRP one. The Hon Dr Denzil Douglas remains Prime Minister, while the leader of the opposition in Parliament is the Hon Sean Richards (PAM).

Government

St Christopher and Nevis is a constitutional monarchy within the Commonwealth. The British monarch is Head of State and is represented locally by a Governor General. The National Assembly has 11 seats, of which three are from Nevis constituencies and eight from St Kitts. There are also four nominated Senators. Under the Federal system, Nevis also has a separate legislature and its own premier. Under the constitution it may secede from the Government of the Federation.

Economy

Sugar was for centuries the traditional base of economic production. Low prices for sugar in the world markets, hurricane damage, droughts, cane fires and the falling value of the euro, meant the industry was running at a loss and was finally closed in 2005. More vegetables, sweet potatoes and yams are now being grown, while on Nevis, Sea Island cotton and coconuts are more common on smallholdings. Livestock farming and manufacturing are developing industries. There are enclave industries, such as electronic assembly, data processing and garment manufacturing (now over a quarter of total exports), which export to the USA and Caricom trading partners, while sales of sugar-based products such as pure cane spirit go mainly outside the region.

Tourism has become an important foreign exchange earner, and contributes about 10% of GDP. The construction industry has benefited from the expansion of tourist infrastructure. The Government is increasing cruise ship arrivals with port improvement projects enabling several cruise liners to berth at once. Stopovers will be encouraged by resort development projects on the southeast peninsula of St Kitts.

Flora and fauna

Both islands are home to the green vervet monkey, introduced by the French 300 years ago. They can be seen in many areas including Brimstone Hill but can be a pest to farmers. To keep down numbers, many have been exported for medical research. The monkey is the same animal as on Barbados but the Kittitians used to eat them. Another animal, the mongoose, imported to kill rats and snakes, never achieved its original purpose (rats being nocturnal whereas the mongoose is active by day). It has, however, contributed to the extinction of many species of lizard, ground-nesting birds, green iguanas, brown snakes and red-legged tortoises. There are some wild deer on the southeast peninsula, imported in the 1930s from Puerto Rico. In common with other West Indian islands, there are highly vocal frogs, lizards (the anole is the most common), fruit bats, insect bats and butterflies. Birds typical of the region include brown pelicans, frigate birds and three species of hummingbird.

St Kitts and Nevis have the earliest documented evidence of honeybees in the Caribbean.

St Kitts and Nevis are small islands, yet have a wide variety of habitats, with rainforest, dry woodland, wetland, grassland and salt ponds. The forests on the sister islands are restricted in scale, but St Kitts is one of the few areas of the world where the forest is expanding. It provides a habitat for wild orchids, candlewoods and exotic vines. Fruits and flowers, both wild and cultivated, are in abundance, particularly in the gorgeous gardens of Nevis. Trees include several varieties of the stately royal palm, the spiny-trunked sandbox tree, silk-cotton tree, and the turpentine or gum tree.

Montserrat → Phone code: 664. Colour map 3, C2. Population 4,500.

Montserrat is like nowhere else. The Irish-influenced 'Emerald Isle' is totally unspoiled by tourism but its volcano has put it on the map, having wiped out the southern part of the island. Here you can enjoy views of a glowing volcano, volcanic moonscapes, deserted black-sand beaches, a network of challenging mountain trails, historic sites, waters teeming with fish, coral and sponges, and perhaps the friendliest people in the region. Only the northern third of the island is populated because of the volcano and the inhabitants are developing the area in style. ▸▸ *For Sleeping, Eating and other listings, see pages 643-648.*

Ins and outs

Getting there A new airport has been built to replace the one on the east coast which was hit by volcanic activity. **Geralds Airport** received its first scheduled flight in July 2005. **Winair** provides several daily flights from Antigua with connecting flights from other islands. **Air Montserrat** offers charter flights from neighbouring islands using 9-seater Islander aircraft. ▸▸ *See Transport, page 647, for further details.*

Getting around Driving is on the left. Roads are paved and fairly good, but narrow and twisty. There are many pebbles on the roads and you must be careful, especially when walking on inclines. Drivers travel fast, passing on blind corners with much use of their horns. There are several car hire companies. Hitching is safe and easy. The standard fare in minibuses is EC$3. Outside the fixed times and routes they operate as taxis and journeys can be arranged with drivers for an extra fee. Taxis are usually small buses, which can be shared. Fares are set and listed by the Tourist Board.

Sights

The volcano is now a tourist attraction and can best be viewed from the **Montserrat Volcano Observatory** ① *T4915647, www.mvo.ms, Thu 1530-1600. US$4 adults, US$2 children.* If the volcano is dangerously active visitors are excluded. Video shows of volcanic activity and a tour of the monitoring rooms and equipment are available, and an expert guide from the scientific community will be available to show you around. Spectacular views of the volcano and its damage can also be viewed in safety from the Jack Boy Hill picnic spot in the east, close to the start of the Exclusion Zone. Do not enter the Exclusion Zone as it is very dangerous and hefty fines are levied on anyone caught in there. From here you can see the grey, ash-covered flanks of what was Chances Peak, in stark contrast with the Centre Hills, which are still green, forested and fertile. This viewing spot is popular at night time as you get excellent views of the glowing dome. Another vantage spot is from the top of Garibaldi Hill near to the communications tower; a long drive up a twisting, winding road (a 4WD vehicle is recommended). However, this entails crossing the Belham Valley which should not be attempted during heavy rains and was in the new Exclusion Zone imposed early-2007.

Plymouth, the former capital, is now covered by mud flows and only the tops of a very few buildings can be seen above the mud and ash. A great vantage point for looking out over Plymouth is the site of the old museum on Richmond Hill as well as the abandoned Montserrat Springs Hotel, but there is no access to Plymouth as the site is quite dangerous and further mudflows have occurred as recently as October 2006. Administrative offices have now moved to the new Government Headquarters at **Brades** in the north of the island. **Little Bay** is being developed as a future capital. The port is here and a state-of-the-art cultural performance/convention centre is now open. A public market and a sports ground are under construction.

Beaches and activities

Watersports Montserrat's beaches are volcanic 'black' sand, which in reality means the sand may be a silvery grey or dark golden brown colour. The single white coral beach is at **Rendezvous Bay** in the north of the island. It is a stiff hike from Little Bay along a very steep mountainous trail (not suitable for small children). Take food and water, it is a long hot walk until you reach your refreshing swim. There is no shade on the beach, avoid the poisonous manchineel trees and the spiny sea urchins among the rocks at the north end. You can also take a boat, and it is quite a good idea to walk there and arrange for a boat to come and pick you up at an agreed time. The best of the rest of the beaches, all on the west of the island and black sand, are **Little Bay** and **Carr's Bay**

Montserrat

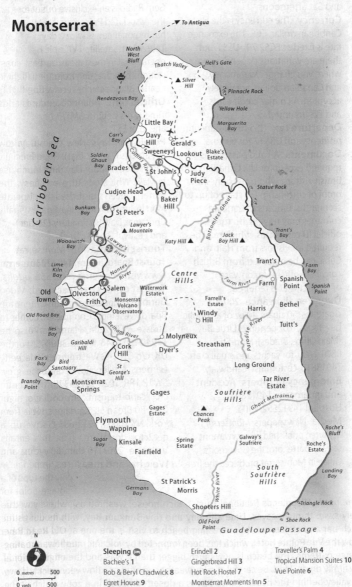

Sleeping		
Bachee's **1**	Erindell **2**	Traveller's Palm **4**
Bob & Beryl Chadwick **8**	Gingerbread Hill **3**	Tropical Mansion Suites **10**
Egret House **9**	Hot Rock Hostel **7**	Vue Pointe **6**
	Montserrat Moments Inn **5**	

⁝ Touching down

Boat information Little Bay, 55-m jetty with a depth of 1.7 m-4.6 m. Contact the Montserrat Port Authority, channel 16, for mooring details.

Business hours Government offices: Mon-Fri 0800-1600; **Shops:** 0800-1600, but early closing Wed and Sat afternoons.

Currency The currency is the East Caribbean dollar, EC$. The exchange rate is fixed at EC$2.70=US$1, but there are variations depending on where you change your money. US and Canadian dollars are widely accepted. All major credit cards and TCs accepted.

Departure tax US$10 for Caricom residents and US$17 for visitors.

Documents A valid passport is required except for US, Canadian and British visitors, who must only show proof of citizenship for stays of up to six months. Citizens of Caricom countries may travel with their official ID card. Visas, which may be required for visitors from Haiti and Cuba, can be obtained from British consulate offices. An onward or return ticket is required.

Duty-free allowance 200 cigarettes, 50 cigars, 40 oz of alcoholic beverages, 6 oz perfume. Little Bay (Main Office, Brades), Mon-Fri 0800-1600, for yachts and small craft, T4913816, customms@candw.ag.

Emergency numbers Accident and emergency T4912802, **Hospital** T4912552/7404.

Media Newspapers: *Montserrat Reporter*, published Fri, www.mont serratreporter.org; the Governor's Office in Montserrat produces the free monthly *The Montserrat Newsletter*, www.montserrat-newsletter.com.

Radio: Radio Montserrat ZJB relays the BBC World Service news at 0700 daily. ZJB posts a daily, local, 10-min news broadcast at www.mratgov.Com/newsradio.htm. Gem Radio is an exclusive outlet for the Associated Press. Family FM has regional news twice a day.

Television: Satellite TV/Cable is operational in most areas, and stations broadcasting from nearby islands can be received.

Official time Atlantic Standard Time, 4 hrs behind GMT, 1 hr ahead of EST.

Public holidays New Year's Day, St Patrick's Day (17 Mar), Good Fri, Easter Mon, Labour Day (first Mon in May), Whit Mon (7th Mon after Easter), Queen's birthday (middle Mon in Jun) first Mon in Aug, Christmas Day, Boxing Day (26 Dec) and Festival Day (31 Dec).

Tourist Information Montserrat Tourist Board, Salem, T4912230, www.visitmontserrat.com.

Tourist offices overseas
Germany, Montserrat Tourist Board/West India Committee, Lomer Strasse 28, D-22047 Hamburg 70, T4940-6958846, F4940-3800051. **UK**, c/o CTO, 42 Westminster Palace Gardens, Artillery Row, London SW1P 1RR, T020-72224325, cto@carib-tourism.com. **USA**, c/o CTO, 80 Broad St, 32nd floor, New York, NY 10004, T212-6359530, get2cto@dorsai.org.

Voltage 220/110 volts, 60 cycles.
Weights and measures Imperial.

in the north, **Woodlands** (National Trust, beach house, washrooms), where you can safely swim through caves, **Lime Kiln Bay** and tiny **Bunkum Bay,** with its delightful beach bar and restaurant. An interesting beach to visit is the one at **Old Road Bay**, below the **Vue Pointe Hotel**, which has been impacted by volcanic mudflows, creating strange patterns. The beach is now much bigger than it was and the original pier is now firmly on dry land. Be careful in rainy weather as mud can flow very quickly down the valley behind the beach. **Foxes Bay** is a deserted beach in a zone which at the height of the volcanic crisis was a no-go area. The area has now reopened and the beach is a delight. From the northern end of **Barton Bay**, below the abandoned Montserrat Springs Hotel in Richmond Hill, you can walk round to **Foxes Bay** at low tide. Take the road down to the old hotel beach bar.

Diving The volcano has had an unexpected benefit for Montserrat's underwater life, as the three 4-km exclusion zones have created a marine reserve, with no one going in to the area for some years. The waters are teeming with fish, coral and sponges and their larvae have drifted with the currents to the reefs of the north where the best dive sites are. Shore diving is good from **Lime Kiln Bay**, where there are ledges with coral, sponges and lots of fish; **Woodlands Bay**, where there is a shallow reef at 25 to 30 ft; at **Carr's Bay** where there are some excellent coral and interesting fish about 400 yd from the shore; and at **Little Bay**. There are some shallow dives from boats, suitable for novices or a second dive, but also deep dives for experienced divers. **Pinnacle** is a deep dive, dropping from 65 to 300 ft, where you can see brain coral, sponges and lots of fish.

● Sleeping

Montserrat *p640, map p641*
Hotel tax is 10% and service is usually 10% too. There are a couple of hotels but most accommodation is in guesthouses or with people who rent out rooms and apartments in their houses. Villa rentals are also available from around US$1000 a week through agencies: **Tradewinds**, T4912004, **Montserrat Enterprises**, T4912431, **West Indies Real Estate**, T4921067, **Neville Bradshaw Agencies**, T4915235.

AL Tropical Mansion Suites, Sweeneys, T4918767, www.tropicalmansion.com. Opened in 1999, 2-storey 20-room hotel in the north of the island, views over Little Bay, small pool, some rooms with a/c and four poster beds. Bar and restaurant with good food. Friendly staff and service much improved under personal management of Merle Galloway, daughter of the owners. Popular with holiday makers as well as government and business visitors.

AL Vue Pointe, Old Towne, T4915210, www.vuepointe.com. Traditionally the premier hotel on the island. Closed for many years because it was within the exclusion zone, reopened by the persevering Osborne family, but closed again Jan 2007 because of volcanic activity threatening the Belham Valley, so check it is open. Fantastic views of the volcano in the distance and close to a black-sand beach. Self-catering cottages in the garden.

AL-C Gingerbread Hill, St Peter's, T4915812, www.volcano-island.com. David and Clover Lea run a delightful guesthouse with incredible views and lovely 3-acre gardens.

Several options for accommodation: rooms in a separate house, including a backpacker's special in a basic room, or you can rent the whole house, or take the charming room adjoining their own house, bathroom, deck, fridge, TV, phone, email, meals on request. A tent and camping equipment is available, also bikes and a rental car. Family atmosphere, the Leas have 3 sons to enliven your stay.

A Erindell, Gros Michel Drive, Woodlands, T4913655, erindell@candw.ag. 2 pleasant rooms alongside the family home, twin beds, private bathroom, TV, phone, fans, microwave oven and toaster. Breakfast and lunch for anyone but dinner for guests only. Welcome pack of snacks, fruit and drinks. Pool outside the rooms, free laundry, discounts for Caricom residents, internet access, no credit cards. 1-min walk to a bus route, 15-min walk to Woodlands beach. Snorkelling equipment is available and hiking and diving packages are offered.

A-B Bachee's, Olveston, T4917509. Round the corner from **The Attic** and convenient for other restaurants too. Bachee built this as a home and guesthouse. 2 rooms, 1 en suite, quiet, comfortable, very good value and in lovely gardens.

A-B Montserrat Moments Inn, Manjack Heights, T4917707, flogriff@candw.ag. A family home with children of school age, renting 3 downstairs rooms of different sizes with TV, fridge, a/c or fan, shared or private bathroom. Breakfast is included, other meals by reservation, or you can use the shared kitchenette. Email and laundry facilities available. Credit cards accepted. Florence is a very welcoming and helpful hostess and will find you somewhere else to stay if she is full.

A-B Traveller's Palm, Olveston, T/F4914816, www.travellerspalmmontserrat.com. Guest house in modern home overlooking the sea, nice gardens, sundeck and pool, TV, phones, Wi-Fi internet access, fans, 3 rooms. Roy and Lottie McDonald from the UK ensure you have a great English breakfast to start your day. Lottie is a BSAC dive leader and there is lots of space for dive gear.

B Bob and Beryl Chadwick, Woodlands, T4919251. 1-bedroom apartment attached to the family home in pleasant gardens. Bob and Beryl will cook you a good breakfast. This is a nice residential area, not far to the beach at Woodlands Bay.

E Hot Rock Hostel, Salem, T4919877, www.hotrockhostel.com. Hilary Alexander runs this B&B within walking distance of the MVO for students and backpackers, groups welcome, opened 2006, all new furniture and fittings, kitchen, living room, bunk beds.

● Eating

Montserrat *p640, map p641*

Several places do takeaway meals and there are lots of 'snackettes' where you can pick up a decent local lunch on the side of the road. Bakeries are also good places to get a snack. Some places only open if you make a reservation in advance, so it is best to check. Restaurant opening times are from 0730-1000, 1130-1400 and 1900-2200, although not all are open for breakfast and several only open in the evenings if there is demand.

A large frog called **mountain chicken**, indigenous here and in Dominica, is the local delicacy. **Goat water stew** is another local dish commonly found on the menu. Most other foods, like steak, are imported.

♥♥♥ Ziggy's Restaurant, Mahogany Loop, Woodlands, T4918282. Dinner only, by reservation. Right on top of the hill over-looking Salem, the 2nd turning on the right from the main road. Dine under canvas in cool gardens; the area is like parkland. Ziggy has been serving great food since the early 1990s: lobster quadrille, jerk pork, chocolate sludge. A full dinner with wine costs around EC$100. She has an excellent wine list with Chilean and Australian reds. Good wine store next door.

♥♥♥ Gourmet Gardens, Olveston, T4917859. Thu-Tue 1100-1400, 1800-2000. Approached up an alley way just below the Salem Police Station and set in lovely gardens, the restaurant is in a plantation-style outhouse with thick stone walls and a veranda. Dinner is by appointment only, so call ahead. Good food and good wines. Dutch run, so more European dishes than Caribbean.

♥♥♥ JJ's Cuisine, Main Rd, St John's, T4919024. Breakfast, lunch and dinner. A roadside restaurant and just round the corner from **Tropical Mansions**, so guests come here to eat in preference to the hotel. The food is excellent and popular with locals for lunch, international cuisine, call ahead for evening reservations. In a small, modern, purpose-built timber building with a veranda.

♥♥♥ Tina's Restaurant, Brades Main Road, T4913538. Lunch and dinner. Like many restaurants, this is a new wooden building in plantation style with a veranda. Very popular with locals, it is a good meeting place. Local food, chicken and fish and local vegetables, prices from US$16.50-24 for a meal. Its wine list is improving, which helps bring in the ex-pat market. Set back off the main road it has the best car park on Montserrat.

♥♥♥ The Windsor Restaurant, Cudjoe Head, T4912900. Daily, breakfast from 0800, lunch from 1200, tea 1600, dinner 1930 by reservation only. A new building on 3 floors, with rental apartments downstairs, the restaurant on the middle floor and boutiques to come on the top floor. Quite smart, a/c, with good views, this establishment serves Caribbean and international cuisine. Lunch costs EC$25-30, expect to pay double that at dinner. Small stage for occasional music.

♥ Bitter End Beach Bar, Little Bay, T4913146. 0600-late. Seafood and snacks on the beach, lunch from US$5.50-9.50, dinner from US$7.50. Moose always seems to be open. Look out for his lobster special nights. Occasionally presents live bands from Antigua and the wider Caribbean.

♥ Dawn's, Flemings, T4919730. A simple bar during the week but turned into a thriving restaurant on Fri nights, popular with everybody, both locals and tourists. Try the spare ribs if on the menu.

♥ Jumping Jack's Bar, Olveston, T4915645. Lunch and dinner Wed-Sat. Danny and Margaret serve from their home when the

Hurricanes and volcanoes

In 1989, Montserrat was devastated by Hurricane Hugo, the first hurricane to strike the island for 61 years. No part of the island was untouched by the 150 mph winds as 400-year-old trees were uprooted, 95% of the housing stock was damaged or destroyed, agriculture was reduced to below subsistence level and even the 180-ft jetty at Plymouth harbour completely disappeared, causing problems for relief supplies. However, within a few months, all public utilities were restored and the remaining standing or injured trees were in leaf again.

In 1995 the lives of Montserratians were again disrupted, this time by volcanic activity, the first in recorded history. The residents of Corkhill, Plymouth and villages in the south and east were evacuated to the north as pyroclastic and mud flows from the Soufrière Hills poured down southern areas of the island. Activity increased in 1997; during March and April pyroclastic flows reached two miles down the south side of the volcano, the former tourist attractions of the Great Alps Waterfall and Galways Soufrière were covered, there was a partial collapse of Galways Wall and lava flowed down the Tar River Valley. In May the volcanic dome was growing at 3.7 cubic metres per second, and in June a huge explosion occurred when a sudden pyroclastic flow of hot rock, gas and ash raced down the volcano at 200 mph. It engulfed 19 people, destroyed seven villages and some 200 homes, including Farms and Trant's to the north of the volcano. The flow, which resulted from a partial collapse of the lava dome, reached to the sea north of the airport runway, which subsequently closed and never reopened. In August another bout of activity destroyed Plymouth, which caught fire under a shower of red hot lava. It now looks like a lunar landscape, completely covered by grey ash and mud. In December 1997 there was a huge dome collapse which created a 600-yd amphitheatre around Galways Soufrière. The lava flows destroyed the deserted communities of St Patrick's, Gingoes and Morris and severely damaged Trials, Fairfield and Kinsale, south of Plymouth. The White River delta was increased to about 1 mile and the water level rose by about 3 ft. During 1998 and 1999 dome collapses continued, with ash clouds at times up to eight miles high, but scientists reported that the dome, while still hot, was gradually cooling and entering a quieter phase. In 2000 there was further activity and in July 2003 and again in May 2006 the dome of the volcano collapsed and a thick cloud of ash and rocks spread across the island. Since the May 2006 collapse the dome has grown back quickly and further collapses are expected. Some former areas making up the Day Time Entry Zone (DTEZ) have reopened for 24-hr access, including Richmond Hill, which allows excellent views of the destroyed Plymouth from a distance. The St Georges Hill area has now been made an Exclusion Zone due to its close proximity to the growing dome. Plymouth is also out of bounds, is extremely dangerous and should on no account be visited. Ash from the volcano can be carried by prevailing winds and can cause disruptions to air traffic. The northern, safe zone of Montserrat is totally protected from the volcanic flows by the Centre Hills range of mountains. For daily scientific updates about the volcanic activity: www.mvo.ms. Weekly updates are also given every Friday afternoon on Radio Montserrat (ZJB).

volcano prevents them using their building on the beach, as happened at the beginning of 2007. The cheapest place to get a meal, simple but adequate. The fish is recommended here, all caught by Danny and very fresh.

¶**La Colage Bar & Restaurant**, Sweeney's, T4914136. Créole cuisine, lunch and dinner. Very good value, people come here after work for something quick and a couple of drinks. Veranda and a pagoda in the garden. Local fishermen supply the restaurant and sell the surplus in a fish shop alongside.

¶**Morgan's Spotlight Bar & Restaurant**, Sweeney's, T4915419. Lunch. Adjacent to the hospital, long established in an old rum shop type building, with the restaurant at the back of the bar. Local food, large portions, it is traditional to come here for Fri lunchtime to eat goat water and people travel miles for it.

❶ Bars and clubs

Montserrat *p640, map p641*
There are 3 night clubs, all only open at weekends, normally 2100-0200, but there are over 70 bars, ranging from the simple to the sophisticated, some with pool tables and darts. Bars occasionally present live music featuring calypsonians and other musicians over from Antigua or other islands; these are advertised on the radio. The veteran **Arrow** (Alphonsus Cassell) is now an international superstar but can still be found on the island, having moved his operation north out of the volcano evacuation zone.

Club Illusions, St Peter's, T4912100. Cunningly situated underneath the Tower Hill petrol station. Caters for a sophisticated clientele and operates a strict dress code.

Club VIP, Baker Hill, no phone. Great ocean views. Popular with the younger market.

Gary's Wide-awake Bar, Salem, T4917156. One of the most popular late-night bars, often open after all the others close and remaining open as long as there are customers. An island institution and not to be missed.

Good Life Night Club, Little Bay, T4914576. Newly built on a hillside overlooking the beach, which is only 20m away, plantation style with decking receiving a lovely sea breeze. Great disco for weekend dancing with a mixed clientele. Open for lunch 3-4 times a week, with a Caribbean-style buffet. The food is OK but it is a better bar than restaurant.

❀ Festivals and events

Montserrat *p640*

17 Mar St Patrick's Day (a national holiday) is celebrated on the 'Emerald Isle' with concerts, masquerades and other festivities lasting for nearly a week.

2nd Sat in Jun The Queen's Birthday is celebrated with parades, salutes and the raising of flags.

1st Mon in Aug Emancipation Day commemorating the abolition of slavery in 1834. It is a public holiday and there are beach barbecues and picnics all weekend. **Cudjoe Head Day** on the Sat before starts with a big breakfast and carries on late into the night, while **St Peter's Anglican Fete** is held in the village rectory grounds on the Mon.

Dec The island's main festival is the Christmas season, which starts around the first weekend and continues through New Year's Day. There are shows, concerts, calypso competitions, jump-ups and masquerades and of course lots of festivities and parties on **New Year's Eve**, helped down with lots of goat water.

❂ Shopping

Montserrat *p640, map p641*
Arts and crafts
Arts & Crafts Association, Brades. Mon-Fri 0900-1400. The association is very active and their outlet should not be missed for great hand made local souvenirs.

Clothes
Arrow's Manshop, Salem, T4913852, or Sweeneys, T4916355. Mon, Tue, Thu 0800-1630, Wed 0800-1400, Fri, Sat 0800-1800. The Manshop is owned by Arrow and stocks clothes for men and boys, as well as shoes, hats, luggage, hair products, CD players, mobile phones and music, mainly gospel, reggae and calypso. Don't forget your volcano T-shirt.

Stamps
Montserrat Philatelic Bureau, Salem, T4912996. Montserrat's postage stamps have traditionally been collectors' items. The island has issued its own stamps since 1876 and there are 6 issues a year and a definitive issue every 4-5 years. The volcanic eruption

is featured, as is the eclipse of the sun. The bureau can be combined with a visit to the National Trust as it shares the same building.

▲ Activities and tours

Montserrat *p640, map p641*
Cricket
First class cricket is played at the **Salem Cricket Ground**, and each weekend in Jan-Jun you can see local and regional cricketers playing.

Diving
Sea Wolf Diving School, Little Bay beach, T4917807, www.seawolfdivingschool.com. A morning 2-tank boat dive costs US$88, a single-tank afternoon boat dive US$55, a shore dive US$35, night dive in Carr's Bay from boat US$70, from shore US$60, scuba, snorkel and photographic equipment hire, PADI courses (price depends on the number signed up) with Open Water from US$400. Full-day dive trips to Redonda if 8 people sign up. They also offer kayaks, US$50/day, fishing charters and boat trips including snorkelling.
Green Monkey Inn and Dive Shop, Little Bay beach, T4912960, www.dive montserrat.com. Run by Troy and Melodie Deppermann. Custom designed dive programmes depending on experience. Full range of courses including PADI Open Water US$350, two-tank morning boat dive US$80, two-tank afternoon shore dive US$70, night dive from shore US$50, from boat US$70. Snorkelling trip to Rendezvous Bay US$35pp, sunset cruise along west coast US$45pp, boat ride round whole island US$50pp. Also land-based tours, hiking and deep-sea fishing. Accommodation available.

Fishing
Bruce Farara, Olveston, T4918802. Can take you fishing in a power boat.
Danny Sweeney, Olveston, T4915645, mwilson@candw.ag. Long-time fisherman Danny Sweeney can take you fishing or organize any number of watersports. Both the dive shops also offer fishing charters.

Football
There is a brand new football stadium at **Blakes**, in the north and football is played at weekends Jul-Dec.

Hiking
There are some excellent mountain walks in the north of the island. Contact **Montserrat National Trust**, T4913086, as they maintain the trails and can advise you on guides. Hiking with a ranger is usually US$20 per person depending on the size of the group.

Tour operators
Sightseeing can be arranged with **Double X Tours**, Olveston, T4915470, meader@candw.ag; **Grant Enterprises & Trading**, Olveston, T4919654, casselj@candw.ag; **Jenny's Tours**, St John's, Antigua, T268-4619361, burkeb@candw.ag; **Runaway Travel**, Sweeneys, T4912776, runaway@candw.ag; **Slim's Tours**, T4914479.

⊖ Transport

Montserrat *p640, map p641*
Air
Winair from Antigua several daily, from US$50 one way, small planes, 19 seats. **Air Montserrat** charter services from Antigua, Anguilla, Nevis and St Kitts using even smaller planes, T664-4916728 or T612-2843672 www.airmontserrat.com. Charter helicopter service is offered by **Caribbean Helicopters**, with a 45-min aerial Montserrat Volcano Tour from Jolly Harbour, Antigua, see page 609 for details.

Car
With a valid driving licence, you can obtain a local 3-month licence (EC$50/US$20) at the police station in Salem, or at Police HQ in Brades. **Be-Peep's Car Rentals**, Olveston, T4913787, for cars and jeeps; **Equipment & Supplies Ltd**, Olveston, T4912402, for cars and vans; **Ethelyne's Car Rental**, Olveston, T4912855; **Grant Enterprises & Trading**, Olveston, T4919654; **KC's Car Rentals**, Olveston, T4915756; **Montserrat Company Ltd**, Old Towne, T4912431; **Neville Bradshaw Agencies**, Olveston, T4915270; **Joe Oliver**, Barzey's, T4914276, for jeeps; **MS Osborne Ltd**, Brades, T4912494; **Pickett Van Rentals**, Salem, T4915470, for vans; **Zeekies Rentals**, Baker Hill, T4914515.

Taxi
Joe Phillip, T4913432, phillipj@candw.ag. Is recommended for tours and taxi service.

● Directory

Montserrat *p640, map p641*

Banks Bank of Montserrat, Brades, T4913843, F4913163, Mon, Tue, Thu 0800-1400, Wed 0800-1300, Fri 0800-1500. **Royal Bank of Canada**, Brades, T4912426-8, F4913391, Mon-Thu 0800-1400, Fri 0800-1500. The **American Express** agent is Trans World International Travel, at Davy Hill, T4917940. **Internet** CompuGET cybercafé in Brades, T4919654, granten@ candw.ag; Jim Lee's Computer Services, St Peter's, T4918499, leej@candw.ag. **Medical services**

The hospital is in St John's, for most routine and surgical emergencies, T4912802. Private doctors and a dentist are also available. Serious medical cases are taken by helicopter to Antigua or Guadeloupe. **Post** Post office in Government HQ in Brades, open Mon-Fri 0815-1555, T4912457. **Telephone** Cable & Wireless (West Indies) Ltd, at Sweeneys, T4912112, F4913599, Mon-Fri 0800-1600, with a digital telephone system, international dialling, telegraph, fax and data facilities. Phone cards are available, as are credit card service, toll free 800 service and cell phones.

Background

History

Columbus sighted Montserrat on 11 November 1493, naming it after an abbey of the same name in Spain, where the founder of the Jesuits, Ignacio de Loyola, experienced the vision which led to his forming that famous order of monks. At that time, a few Carib Indians lived on the island but by the middle of the 17th century they had disappeared. The Caribs named the island Alliouagana, which means 'land of the prickly bush'. Montserrat was eventually settled by the British Thomas Warner, who brought English and Irish Catholics from their uneasy base in the Protestant island of St Kitts. Once established as an Irish-Catholic colony, the only one in the Caribbean, Catholic refugees fled there from persecution in Virginia and, following his victory at Drogheda in 1649, Cromwell sent some of his Irish political prisoners to Montserrat. By 1648 there were 1,000 Irish families on the island. It was an Irishman who brought some of the first slaves over in 1651 and the economy became based on sugar. Slaves quickly outnumbered the original British indentured servants. A slave rebellion in 1768, appropriately enough on St Patrick's Day, led to all the rebels being executed, and today they are celebrated as freedom fighters. Montserrat was invaded several times by the French during the 17th and 18th centuries, sometimes with assistance from the resident Irish, but the island returned to British control under the Treaty of Versailles (1783) and has remained a colony.

Political parties include the New People's Liberation Movement (NPLM), the Montserrat Democratic Party (MDP) and the Movement for Change and Prosperity (MCAP). In General Elections in May 2006, the MCAP won four seats, the NPLM three seats, the MDP one seat and an independent candidate one seat. A coalition government was formed by the NPLM, the MDP and the independent. Dr Lowell Lewis (MDP) became Chief Minister.

The main concern of the government since the eruption of the volcano began has been to replace the destroyed infrastructure of the south. British and EU funding has contributed to the building of new schools, housing, hospital, fuel terminal, power station, factory shells, offices, roads, water systems, port and airport. In all, over £300 million has been spent by the British Government and the EU to rebuild Montserrat. A few Montserratians are beginning to return home from overseas and there has been an influx of workers from other Caricom countries to help the rebuilding process.

Geography

Montserrat, known as 'the Emerald Isle', is dominated by three mountain ranges. Mount Chance, in the Soufrière Hills, rises to 3000 ft above sea level. This active

volcano has been erupting since 1995, destroying some villages and the capital,
Plymouth. As a result, the south, which like the rest of the island used to be all lush green, is now grey with ash. Montserrat was off-limits for tourism for a few years, but the still-active volcano is now attracting visitors and facilities are quickly being restored. The island is about 11 miles long and seven miles wide, although the volcano's eruptions have increased the land surface in the south.

Government

A British Overseas Territory, Montserrat has a representative government with a ministerial system. Queen Elizabeth II is Head of State and is represented by a resident Governor. The Government consists of a Legislative and an Executive Council, with elections being held every five years for membership in the former. The head of Government is called the Chief Minister; a Speaker presides over the eleven-member Legislative Council (nine elected and two ex-officio members). As executive authority and head of the civil service, the Governor is responsible for defence, internal security, financial services and external affairs.

Economy

Gross domestic product grew rapidly at the end of the 1980s, expanding by 12.8% in 1988, although a slower rate was recorded in 1989 because of the devastation wreaked by Hurricane Hugo. 95% of the housing stock was totally or partially destroyed; production and exports were disrupted, infrastructure was severely damaged; public sector finances were hit by reduced income and greater expenditure demands; tourism slumped. Similar economic disruption occurred as a result of the volcanic eruption in 1995-1997 (see box) when the south had to be evacuated to the north. Most ex-pats left the island and tourists stayed away. The island now depends on aid from the UK but is beginning to recover, with new construction and hotels opening up again. A new airport has been built with British and EU monies and daily flights began in 2005.

People

The vast majority of the people are of African descent. Before the volcano erupted there was an influx of white Americans, Canadians and Britons who purchased retirement homes on the island. Montserratians are notable for their easy friendliness to visitors, speaking English flavoured by dialect and the odd Irish expression. There is virtually no crime and everyone leaves their doors unlocked. The population used to hover around 11,000, but emigration since the volcano started erupting in 1995 has reduced numbers to 4,800. Montserratians are British citizens with the right of abode in the UK. Around 30% of the current population are nationals of other Caribbean countries who have come to work in the rebuilding industry.

Culture

The Irish influence can still be seen in national emblems. On arrival your passport is stamped with a green shamrock. The island's flag and crest show a woman, Erin, of Irish legend, complete with her harp; there are many Irish names, of both people and places, and the national dish, goat water stew, is supposedly based on a traditional Irish recipe, although some historians claim it is of African origin. A popular local folk dance, the Bam-chick-a-lay resembles Irish step dances and musical bands may include a fife and a drum similar to the Irish bodhran. The new Government House at Woodlands has a shamrock fixed to its roof.

The African heritage dominates, however, whether it be in Caribbean musical forms like calypso (the veteran Arrow is now an international superstar and can still be found on the island, having moved his operation north out of the volcano evacuation zone), steel bands or the costumed masqueraders who parade during the Christmas season. Another element in the African cultural heritage are the Jumbie Dancers, who combine dancing and healing. Only those who are intimate with the island and its inhabitants will be able to witness their ceremonies, though. Local choirs, like the long-established Emerald Community Singers, who can often be seen performing at the Vue Pointe Hotel, mix calypso with traditional folk songs and spirituals in their repertoire, and the String Bands of the island play the African *shak-shak*, made from a calabash gourd, as well as the imported Hawaiian ukelele.

Sir George Martin's famed recording studios, the **Air Studios**, on the edge of Belham Valley, used to attract rock megastars such as Elton John, the Rolling Stones and Sting to the island, but the studios were closed after Hurricane Hugo. You can stroll around the gardens associated with the studios. Sir George recently built a Performing Arts/Cultural Centre at Little Bay with funds raised in 1997 at a gala fundraising concert for Montserrat at the Royal Albert Hall in London. Participating stars included Paul McCartney, Elton John, Eric Clapton, Sting, Mark Knopfler, Jimmy Buffet and Arrow, all of whom had used Air Studios in the past. At the same time a show was put on at Gerald's Bottom on Montserrat by other musicians who had used the recording studios. The Climax Blues Band reformed for the occasion and Bankie Banks appeared, along with 18 local acts in what was optimistically called 'Many Happy Returns'. Lately, some of the touring calypso artists such as Shadow and Sparrow, that have played Antigua, have taken the opportunity to come over to Montserrat and put on memorable shows at the **Bitter End Beach Bar** in Little Bay.

> *On Montserrat a 'maroon' is not a runaway slave but the local equivalent of 'barn-raising', when everyone helps to build a house, lay a garden, etc.*

Flora and fauna

Natural vegetation is confined mostly to the summits of hills, where elfin woodlands occur. At lower levels, fern groves are plentiful and lower still are cacti, sage bush and acacias. Flowers and fruit are typical of the Caribbean with many bay trees, from which bay oil (or rum) is distilled, the national tree, the mango and the national flower, *Heliconia caribaea* (a wild banana known locally as 'lobster claw'). There are 34 species of bird resident on the island and many more migrants. Unique to Montserrat is the Montserrat oriole, *Icterus oberi*, a black and gold oriole named the national bird. The British FCO is funding a project to study the effect of the volcano on the oriole. There are also the rare forest thrush, the bridled quail dove, mangrove cuckoo, trembler and purple-throated carib. Many of these can be seen along the Centre Hills trail in the middle of the island between the ash-covered Soufrière Hills and the Silver Hills. The vegetation here is biologically diverse and supports a variety of wildlife. The Centre Hills area is the subject of a major environmental project which will see it developed as a national park. Montserrat cannot boast many wild animals, although it shares the terrestrial frog, known as the mountain chicken, only with Dominica. Agoutis, bats and lizards, including iguanas which can grow to over 4 ft in length (they used to take the balls on the golf course, mistaking them for eggs), can all be found and tree frogs contribute to the island's 'night-music'.

The **Montserrat National Trust** ① T4913086, *www.montserratnationaltrust.com, Mon-Fri 0830-1630, Sat 0900-1300*, is in Olveston, on the North Main Road, with a Natural History Centre and a botanical garden.

French Antilles

☗ Footprint features

Introduction

The French Caribbean Islands form two Départements d'Outremer: one comprises Martinique, and the other Guadeloupe with its offshore group, Marie-Galante, Les Saintes and la Désirade. Two more distant islands, Saint-Martin and Saint-Barthélemy, which are administratively part of Guadeloupe, are included in the Leeward Islands chapter (see pages 545 and 581). Geographically, Guadeloupe and Martinique form the northern group of the Windward Islands, with the former British island of Dominica in between them; there are good ferry links for island hopping. The two main islands are large and both have mountains, volcanoes and forests where you can find rushing streams, waterfalls and pools for bathing in. The best beaches, however, are in the more arid parts, which are flatter, and these have become holiday resorts, popular principally with the French. The smaller islands are fairly hilly but dry, particularly those in the Leewards. Some beautiful French colonial architecture remains, sometimes with iron balconies and intricate fretwork, but many modern buildings are concrete blocks and lack charm.

Visitors are often surprised by how French the islands are. The inhabitants are French citizens, the currency is the euro and the people eat croissants and baguettes. However, the African connection is strong too, dating back to slavery on the plantations. Most people speak Créole as well as French, there are African rhythms and instruments in the music and African influences in art and literature. Créole cuisine uses West Indian ingredients, many of which were introduced to feed the African slaves, but with a French flair which distinguishes it from its neighbours. Even the rum is different, made from the juice of the sugar cane instead of the molasses as elsewhere in the Caribbean, but it packs the same punch.

★ Don't miss ...

1 **Fort Louis Delgrès** Protecting Basse-Terre, the fort was renamed many times as battles changed its ownership, page 662.
2 **Parc Naturel** Much of Basse-Terre is protected national park, the seventh largest in France, page 665.
3 **Trace des Crêtes** An easy trail on Terre-de-Haut, Les Saintes, which leads from the village to the lovely golden beach of Pont Pierre, page 676.
4 **Marie-Galante** A traditional, rural, way of life, deserted beaches and small, intimate hotels and guesthouses, page 677.
5 **St-Pierre** The atmospheric ruins of the 'Petit Paris' of the West Indies, which was destroyed by molten ash in 1902, page 686.
6 **Le Domaine de la Pagerie** Empress Josephine was born here in 1763; a hurricane blew away the graceful plantation house in 1766. The ruins and some renovated buildings can be visited, page 689.

French Antilles

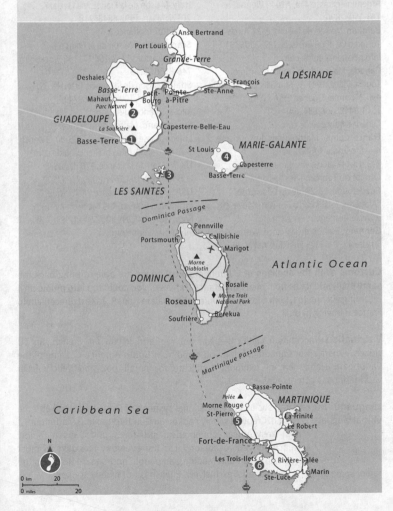

Essentials

Before you travel

Documents The regulations are the same as for France. In most cases the only document required for entry is a **passport**, the exceptions being citizens of Australia, South Africa, Bolivia, Dominica, Barbados, Jamaica, Trinidad and Tobago, Haiti, Honduras, El Salvador, Dominican Republic, Turkey, when a **visa** is required. St Lucians are allowed to enter without visas for visits of up to 15 days. Any non-EU citizen staying longer than three months needs an extended visa. An onward ticket is necessary but not always asked for. EU citizens need not fill in a landing card. They are entitled to use local medical services on production of a European Health Insurance Card (EHIC), obtainable in their home country (eg UK Post Office).

Tourist offices overseas

Austria, Maison de la France, Argentinierstrasse 41a, A1040 Vienna, T43-15032890.

Belgium, Maison de la France, 21 Av de la Toison d'Or, 1060 Brussels, T32-25053819, info.be@franceguide.com.

Canada, Maison de la France/Martinique Tourist Office, 1981 Av MacGill College, Suite 490, Montréal, Quebec, H3A 2W9, T514-8448566/2884264, Canada@franceguide.com.

France, Comité Martiniquais du Tourisme, 2 rue des Moulins 75001, Paris T33-01-44778600, www.martinique.org. Comité du Tourisme des Iles de Guadeloupe, 23-25 rue du Champ de l'Alouette, 75013 Paris, T33-(0)1-40629907, www.lesilesdeguadeloupe.fr.

Germany, Maison de la France, Westend Strasse 47, D-60325 Frankfurt AM Main,

T49-699 7580131, franceprofi@mdlf.de.

Italy, Maison de la France, Via Larga, 7, 20122 Milan, T392-58486218, info@turismofrance.it.

Scandinavia, Maison de la France, Nanrnalmstorg 1A 5tr, SE 111146 Stockholm, T46-856612216.

Spain, Maison de la France, Gran Vía 59, 28013 Madrid, T0034-915489740, info.es@franceguide.com.

Switzerland, Maison de la France, Lowenstrasse 59, Postfach 7226, 8023 Zurich, T41-12174600, info.ch@franceguide.com.

UK, Maison de la France, 178 Piccadilly, London W1V 0AL, T44-(0)20 73993500.

USA, Maison de la France/Martinique Promotion Bureau, 444 Madison Av, 16th floor, New York, NY 10022, T212-8387800, info@martinique.org.

Customs With the abolition of EU frontiers, Europeans are able to bring back the same entitlements as from mainland France. However you could run into problems if returning via Antigua, with a long, uncomfortable wait in transit. Take a direct flight to France if buying in bulk.

Vaccination Vaccination certificates are not required if you are French, an EU citizen, American or Canadian, but if you come from South America or some of the Caribbean Islands an international certificate for small pox and yellow fever vaccinations is compulsory.

Language The cultural, social and educational systems of France are used and the official language is French. Créole is widely spoken on Guadeloupe and Martinique; it has West African grammatical structures and uses a mainly French-derived vocabulary. It is the everyday language of most Guadeloupean and Martiniquan people and can be heard on the radio; some stations use it almost exclusively. English is not widely spoken.

❖ *A knowledge of French is a great advantage.*

Festivals and events

Jan New Year's Day.
Mar/Apr Easter Sun and Easter Mon.
May/Jun Ascension Day and Whit Mon.
1 May Labour Day.
8 May VE Day.
27 May Slavery Abolition Day.

14 Jul National/Bastille Day.
Aug Assumption Day.
21 Aug Schoelcher Day.
1-2 Nov All Saints' Day and All Souls' Day.
11 Nov Armistice Day.
25 Dec Christmas Day.

Money

There are money-changing offices in the big hotels and at airports. The euro is the legal tender although US$ are accepted except in post offices and on buses. There is no limit to travellers' cheques and letters of credit being imported, but a declaration of foreign bank notes in excess of €533.60 must be made.

Eating

Restaurants divide fairly neatly into French cuisine or more moderate Créole. There is often a *plat du jour* as there would be in France and very reasonable two- or three-course *menu touristique* meals. Children may find Créole food rather spicy.

Local cuisine A delightful blend of French, African, and Indian influences is found in Créole dishes, the cuisine is quite distinctive. Basic traditional French and African recipes using local ingredients; seafood, tropical fruits and vegetables are combined with exotic seasonings to give rich colour and flavour. These local specialities are not to be missed: *Ti-boudin*, a well seasoned sausage; *blaff* is red snapper or other fish, possibly sea urchins (*chadrons*) cooked with local spices and onions, somewhere between a soup and a stew; *ragout*, a spicy stew often made with squid (*chatrous*), or conch (*lambis*), or with meat; *colombo*, a recipe introduced by Hindu immigrants in the 19th century, is a thick curry; *poulet au coco*, chicken prepared with coconut; chunks of steakfish seasoned and grilled; *morue* (salt cod) made into sauces and *accras* (hot fishy fritters from Africa) or *chiquetaille* (grilled), or used in *feroce d'avocat*, a pulp of avocados, peppers and manioc flour; *langouste* (lobster), *crabe* (crab), *écrevisses*, *ouassous*, *z'habitants* (crayfish), *gambas* (prawns) and *vivaneau* (snapper) are often fricasseed, grilled or barbecued with hot pepper sauce. A good starter is *crabe farci* (stuffed land crab). Main dishes are usually accompanied by white rice, breadfruit, yams or *patate douce* (sweet potatoes) with plantains and red beans or lentils. *Christophine* (Créole: chayotte) *au gratin*; a large knobbly vegetable grilled with grated cheese and breadcrumbs, or fresh *crudités* are delicious, lighter side dishes. Fresh fruit often ends the meal; pineapples, papayas, soursops and bananas can be found all year round and mangoes, guavas and sugar apples in season. Ice cream (*glace*) is also a favourite dessert, particularly guava or soursop (*corossol*).

Drink Tap water is drinkable. As in other Caribbean islands the main alcoholic drink is rum. It is nearly all made from the juice of the cane, *rhum agricole*, unlike elsewhere in the Caribbean where it is made from molasses. *Ti punch* is rum mixed with a little cane syrup or sugar syrup and a slice of lime and is a popular drink at any time of the day. *Shrub* is a delicious Christmas liqueur made from macerated rum and orange peel. **Planteur** is a rum and fruit juice punch. Martiniquan rum has a distinctive flavour and is famous for its strength, but rum from Guadeloupe and Marie Galante has been equally praised. There is a huge choice of Martiniquan rum, recommended brands being Trois Rivières, Mauny, St James and St Clément. On Guadeloupe try Damoiseau and especially on Marie Galante, Père Labat. French wines are everywhere and are not expensive in supermarkets or even small village shops. A good local beer is *Lorraine*, a clean-tasting beer which claims to be 'brewed for the tropics'. Locally-brewed Guinness, at 7% alcohol by volume, stronger than its Irish counterpart, is thick and rich. *Malta*, a non-alcoholic beverage similar to malt beer, is produced by most breweries and said to be full of minerals and vitamins. Thirst quenching non-alcoholic drinks to look out for are the fresh fruit juices served in most snack bars and cafés. Guava, soursop, passion fruit and sugar cane juice are commonly seen.

Festivals and events

Pre-Lenten Carnival is a feature in both Guadeloupe and Martinique. It's less touristy than most, and ends with impressive Ash Wednesday ceremonies (especially in Martinique), when the population dresses in black and white, and processions take place that combine the seriousness of the first day of the Christian Lent with the funeral of the Carnival King (Vaval).

Sport and activities

The spectacles of cockfighting and mongoose versus snake are popular throughout the French Islands. Betting shops are full of atmosphere (they are usually attached to a bar). Horse racing is held on Martinique, but not Guadeloupe, but on both islands gambling on all types of mainland France track events is very keen.

Guadeloupe

➔ *Country code: 0590 (local code is also 590). Colour map 4, A4. Population: 397,000.*

Guadeloupe is really two islands: the western Basse-Terre, which is mountainous and forested, 'green Guadeloupe', with a huge national park on and offshore; and Grande-Terre, to the east, which is smaller, flatter and more densely populated. The comparatively low-lying Grande-Terre is mainly given over to sugar cane, livestock raising and fruit trees (mango, coconut, papaya, guava, etc'. Mostly a limestone plateau, it does have a hilly region, Les Grands-Fonds, and a marshy, mangrove coast extending as far north as Port-Louis. The vegetation of Basse-Terre ranges from tropical forest (40% of the land is forested: trees such as the mahogany and gommier, climbing plants, wild orchids) to the cultivated coasts: sugar cane on the windward side, bananas in the south and coffee and vanilla on the leeward. On both parts the flowers are a delight, especially the anthuriums and hibiscus.The best beaches are of golden sand from the coral limestone of Grande-Terre. Tourists come mostly from France. The outer islands of Les Saintes, La Désirade and Marie Galante are easily reached from Guadeloupe but are quiet and untouched by mass tourism,with no large hotels, although Les Saintes are a popular day trip. ➤➤ *For Eating, Sleeping and other listings, see pages 667-675.*

Ins and outs

Getting there All European connections are with Paris and there are daily flights with **Air France, Air Corsair** and **Air Caraïbes**. There are also charter flights. Apart from **Air Canada**, which flies from Montréal, and **Air Transat** and **Air Transat**, which fly once a week in high season, the only other scheduled services from North America are **Air France**'s daily flights from Miami, **Delta** and **American Airlines**. Connections are good with neighbouring islands if you want to island hop. This is also possible by sea, as there are high-speed ferries between Guadeloupe, Les Saintes, Martinique, St Lucia and Dominica. Cruise ships call frequently and are increasingly using Guadeloupe as a useful repositioning stopover on their way to the Mediterranean for summer cruising. ➤➤ *See also Transport, page 673, for further details.*

Getting around There are three main **bus** terminals in Pointe-à-Pitre. It is possible to cover the whole island by bus in a day – cheap, interesting and easy, but

Touching down

Anchorages Pointe-à-Pitre has good groceries, marine supplies, fuel, water, free 220 electricity, bus to town from marina. Free dinghy dock in marina. Duty free fuel when you clear out of the country. Charter companies include Moorings, Jet Sea, Stardust.

Departure tax Included in fares.

Emergency numbers
Gendarmerie: T0590-820059, **Police**: T0590-821317 in Pointe-à-Pitre, 0590811155 in Basse-Terre; **Nautical assistance**: T0590-829108.

Exchange Rates vary so shop around. Post offices change dollars but not all. Exchange facility at the airport. There is a 24-hour ATM at Bas-du-Fort marina which accepts euros, sterling, US, EC and Canadian dollars and yen. It can be difficult to change EC dollars.

Hours of business **Shops**: 0800-1200, 1430-1700 weekdays, morning only on Sat; **Government offices**: open 0730-1300, 1500-1630 Mon and Fri, 0730-1300 Tue-Thu. **Banks**: 0800-1200, 1400-1600 Mon to Fri.

Ports of entry (French flag) Deshaies, Basse-Terre and Pointe-à-Pitre are ports of entry but Îles des Saintes is not. No charge for EU or US citizens. French forms to fill in.

Tourist information Tourist offices in Guadeloupe, www.lesilesdeguadeloupe.com: 5 Square de la Banque, BP 422-97163, Pointe-à-Pitre, T0590- 820930, F0590- 838922 (the *Gîtes* office next door is helpful); Maison du Port, Cours Nolivos, Basse-Terre, T0590- 812483; Av de l'Europe, Saint-François, T0590- 884874, and at airport.

Maps The *Serie Bleu* maps (1:25,000, 7 maps of Guadeloupe, No 4601G-4607G) issued by the Institut Géographique National, Paris, which include all hiking trails, are available at the bigger book stores in the rue Frébault in Pointe-à-Pitre, and at **Le Joyeux** hotel in Trois Rivières/Le Faubourg. Also available from MapLink in the USA, T805-6926777.

Official time GMT minus 4 hours.

Voltage 220 volts AC, 50 cycles.

exhausting. You can just stop the bus at the side of the road or wait at the bus stations in the villages. Buses are crowded at peak times; have your money ready when you get off. **Car hire** is available mainly at the airport, but can also be arranged through the major hotels. A small, old Peugeot will cost about €36 per day. International and local agencies are represented. Pointe-à-Pitre has a dual carriage ring road which runs from Gosier across the Rivière Salée to the industrial centre at Baie-Mahault and south towards Petit-Bourg. The metred taxis are expensive and some now accept credit cards. Fares increase at night. They are mainly found at the airports and outside the main hotels, although you can also phone for one. From the airport to Place de la Victoire, €8-10, more at weekends. **Bicycles** can be rented.

> Buses play zouk music at top volume – exhilarating or deafening, depending on your mood.

Grande-Terre

Pointe-à-Pitre → *Population: 141,000. Colour map 4, A4.*

On Grande-Terre at the south end of the Rivière Salée, Pointe-à-Pitre is the chief commercial centre of Guadeloupe. The ports for inter-island ferries, commercial and cruise shipping are at its heart while the airport, Pole Caraïbes, is nearby. The inhabitants call themselves 'Les Pointus'. The city lies to the south of the Route National N1 to Basse-Terre and any of the intercepts will take you to the old city centre.

Its early colonial buildings were largely destroyed by an earthquake in 1843; nowadays it is an odd mixture of parts which could have been transplanted from provincial France and parts which are Caribbean, surrounded by low-cost housing blocks.

The central **Place de la Victoire** is where the French Revolutionary troops defeated the British invaders in 1794. Robespierre sent Victor Hugues from Paris with two aims:

Guadeloupe & outer islands

throw out the British and bring the Terror to the island. He brought a portable 659 guillotine in his luggage, set it up here, and guillotined or shot over 700 whites, and even a few men of colour, for bearing arms on the British side. Most were from the plantocracy. Their estates were confiscated, and all slaves freed. The streets adjacent to the square contain the oldest buildings, mostly from the 19th and early 20th

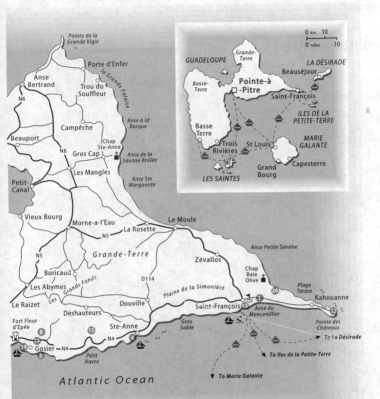

Sleeping
Anse des Rochers **1**
Auberge de la Distillerie **2**
Auberge le Grand Large **4**
Chez Honoré **26**
Chez M Eric Bernier **6**
Corossol **8**
Domaine de
  Malendure **9**
Grand' Anse **11**

Iguana Bay Villas **12**
Kaye' la **13**
La Cocoteraie **13**
La Créole Beach **14**
La Marie-Gaillarde **15**
La Toubana **4**
La Vigie **16**
Le Jardin Malanga **17**
Le Joyeux **18**
Les Flamboyants **19**

Mini Beach **4**
Pointe Batterie Villas **22**
Sofitel Auberge de la
  Vieille Tour **3**
St-Georges **25**

centuries, including the Sous-Préfecture, once a barracks. There are some flame trees at the north end and pleasant gardens. In the middle is a bust of Félix Eboue (1884-1944), the only black governor in colonial times, 1936-1938. At the southwest corner is a war memorial dedicated to *La Guadeloupe et ses enfants, morts pour La France 1914-18*, flanked by two First World War guns. Behind it is the **tourist office**. On the east side of the square is the art deco Renaissance Cinema. At its south end is **La Darse**, where fishing boats come in. To the west is the new Port Authority development for inter-island ferries and cruise ships.

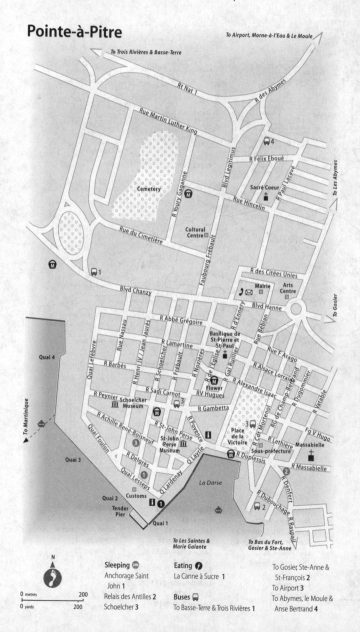

Pointe-à-Pitre

Sleeping 🛏
Anchorage Saint John **1**
Relais des Antilles **2**
Schoelcher **3**

Eating 🍴
La Canne à Sucre **1**

Buses 🚌
To Basse-Terre & Trois Rivières **1**

To Gosier, Ste-Anne & St-François **2**
To Airport **3**
To Abymes, le Moule & Anse Bertrand **4**

0 metres   200
0 yards   200

The **Place de l'Église** lies northwest of the Place de la Victoire behind the **Hôtel Normandie**. The 1840s ochre-coloured Basilique de St Pierre et St Paul is held up by unusual metal columns supporting a gallery around the top of the church with some elaborate gingerbread-style metal work. Outside there is a bubbling fountain and a bust of Admiral Gourbeyre, the governor who helped the people of Pointe-à-Pitre after the huge 1843 earthquake in which 5,000 lost their lives and most buildings were partially or completely destroyed (see also Fort Louis Delgrès, Basse-Terre). The square is flanked by the 1930s art deco Palais de Justice and flower stalls.

The red-roofed central **market** place (between rues Peynier, Fréboult, St-John Perse and Schoelcher) is the nearest thing to local hustling. Women (some wearing the traditional Madras cotton headties) try to sell you spices, fruit, vegetables or hats. There are other markets on the dockside in Place de la Victoire, between Blvd Chanzy and the docks and between Blvd Légitimus and the cemetery. Local handicrafts, and Madras cotton are good buys.

Musée Schoelcher ① *24 rue Peynier, T0590-820804, Mon-Fri 0900-1700, €2, children half price*, celebrates a key figure in the liberation of the slaves. He gave some of his personal art collection in 1883 to Guadeloupe, which survives in its original, elaborately decorated, specially built, 'Belle Epoque' home. Other exhibits on his life and on the slave trade. **Musée Saint-John Perse** ① *9 rue Nozières et A R Boisneuf, T0590-900192, www.sjperse.org/museesjp.htm, Mon-Fri 0900-1700, Sat 0830-1230, €2, children half price*, in a lovely colonial-style house, is dedicated to the poet and diplomat born in Guadeloupe of planter stock. His real name was Alexis Saint-Léger. The collection gives a picture of the lifestyle of island whites, the *békés*.

Bas du Fort

Just outside Pointe-à-Pitre on the N4 towards Gosier is **Bas du Fort**, the site of a large marina, one of the biggest in the Caribbean. The **Aquarium** ① *T0590-909238, daily 0900-1900, €5.35, children under 12 €3*, is here, at Place Créole. It has about 30 ponds with species only from the Caribbean Sea, including fish, turtles and nurse sharks. At the next turning off the main road to Gosier (follow the signs to the CORA hypermarket) are the ruins of the 18th-century fortress, **Fort Fleur d'Épée** ① *daily 0800-1800, free*, which once guarded the east approaches to Pointe-à-Pitre. There are now pleasant, shady gardens within the ramparts. Art exhibitions are regularly held either in the officers' quarters or in the underground rooms. Also note the graffiti with pictures of old sailing ships. The views of Pointe-à-Pitre and across Petit Cul-de-Sac Marin towards the mountains of Basse-Terre are excellent.

Gosier

The corridor leading to Gosier from Pointe-à-Pitre is built up, extending up into the hills above the coast road. Nevertheless, Gosier is a pleasant place with plenty of atmosphere. There is a marvellous picnic spot overlooking a small beach (**Plage de l'Anse Canot**). Don't miss the little island about 100 m offshore (**Ilet du Gosier**) and lighthouse. You could swim to it, there is a channel marked by buoys, but watch out for speed boats. Fishermen provide a regular ferry service and locals picnic here at weekends. Old Gosier has one of the finest hotels in the island, the **Auberge de la Vieille Tour**, built around an 18th-century windmill tower, and has a great selection of restaurants, ranging from high cuisine at the **Auberge** and **La Mandarine** to takeaways on the main street, Blvd Charles- de-Gaulle. The modern part of the resort with three-star beach hotels is at the western side, between Pointe de la Verdure and under Fort Fleur de l'Épée. Built on reclaimed mangrove marshes, the beaches are quite acceptable with the usual watersports facilities.

‼ *Gosier is the original holiday centre of Guadeloupe, with hotels, restaurants, nightclubs.*

The south coast between Gosier and **Sainte-Anne** is hilly with cliffs, and on most headlands there are huge condominium developments looking across the sea to Marie-Galante as well as to the south tip of Basse-Terre. Sainte-Anne is a small, pleasant town and has a small church with a slightly crooked spire overlooking the square. Here you will find the **Plage de la Caravelle**, rated by some as the best on the island. The land gradually subsides towards St-François, originally a fishing village but now home to luxury hotels. There is a light aircraft landing strip and a golf course. You can catch the ferry to La Désirade from here.

The rugged **Pointe des Châteaux** at the easternmost tip of the island is part of the national park. From the car park, there is a small, self-guided walk to the cross (**Pointe des Colibris**) erected in 1951, on the point where there are two 'compass' tables showing distances to landmarks. The limestone outcrop is steep in places. The view over the island of **La Roche** (housing a colony of sooty terns, *Sterna fuscata*) to La Désirade is spectacular, especially on a windy day when the sea whips over the rocks. Take the longer return path around the headland as you get good views of the flat Petite Terre with its lighthouse and on clear days Marie-Galante (30 km), Les Saintes (60 km) and Dominica (75 km). Note the **Grandes Salines** (salt lagoons) where flamingoes were once common. There are stalls selling handicrafts, spices and a local aphrodisiac, *bois bandé*. A tree bark, this is also available as a liqueur ('gives strength to men, pleasure to women') and as an infusion in rum. The beach between the two points is dangerous.

Le Moule was the original capital of Guadeloupe and there are still some cannon from the fortifications against English attack. A pre-Columbian Arawak village, called

> ‼ *Take a good map - it is easy to get lost on roads in the sugar cane fields.*

Morel, has recently been uncovered on the beautiful sandy beaches north of the town. The **Musée de Prehistoire Amerindienne Edgar Clerc** ① *T0590-235757, 0850-1650 in winter, 0950-1750 in summer, free*, is at La Rosette. It houses the collection of the researcher, Edgar Clerc, of artefacts found on Guadeloupe and also puts on temporary exhibitions. On the Abymes road (D101) from Le Moule is the **Distillerie Bellevue** ① *Mon-Fri 0700-1500, Mon-Sat, Jan-Aug, La Cabane shop open 0800-1800 Mon-Sat all year*, makers of *Rhum Damoiseau*.

Leeward coast

Grande-Terre's leeward coast has beaches at Port-Louis and Petit-Canal which are the usual concrete towns with restaurant and filling station. North of Anse Bertrand there is a fine clean, sandy beach, **Anse Laborde**, which has plenty of shade, a restaurant, and a reef close to the beach, good for snorkelling. Inland, at **Morne-à-l'Eau**, there is a remarkable terraced cemetery built around a natural amphitheatre, very atmospheric on All Saints' Day when lit by thousands of candles.

Basse-Terre

Basse-Terre town

On the other wing of the island, the town of Basse-Terre is the administrative capital of Guadeloupe and the entire Départment. It is a charming port town of narrow streets, pretty colonial buildings and well laid-out squares with palm and tamarind trees in a lovely setting between the sea and the great volcano La Soufrière. Market day is Saturday.

There is a 17th-century cathedral and the well-preserved ruins of **Fort Louis Delgrès** ① *T0590-813748, daily 0700-1700, free*. The British occupied the fort from 1759 to 1763 and again from 1810 to 1816. It was fought over and renamed many times, being given its present name in 1989 in memory of the black commander who died resisting the re-imposition of slavery. The **Grande Caverne** is a museum, with an exhibition of clothes and photographs of the area. In the cemetery is a monument to Admiral Gourbeyre. The date is not that of his death (he disappeared at sea in 1845) but of 8 February 1843 when there was a huge earthquake; the Admiral worked tirelessly to help its victims.

Saint-Claude, a wealthy suburb and summer resort 6 km into the hills, is surrounded by coffee trees and tropical gardens. **La Bonifièrie**, an old coffee plantation still has its old wooden waterwheel, while **Mangofil** has a *canopée* (a wooden walkway through the tree tops). **Matouba**, above Saint-Claude, is an East Indian village in lovely surroundings (waterfall and springs, the mineral water is bottled here) with a good restaurant. On the outskirts of the village is a monument to Louis Delgrès on the spot where he and his companions were caught and killed by Napoléon's troops. There are hot springs a good walk above the village (1,281 m).

La Soufrière

On Basse-Terre island one of the main sights is the volcano **La Soufrière**, reached through a primeval rainforest. A **Maison du Volcan** ① *0900-1300, 1400-1600*, at Saint-Claude gives information on the volcano. A narrow, twisty road leads up from

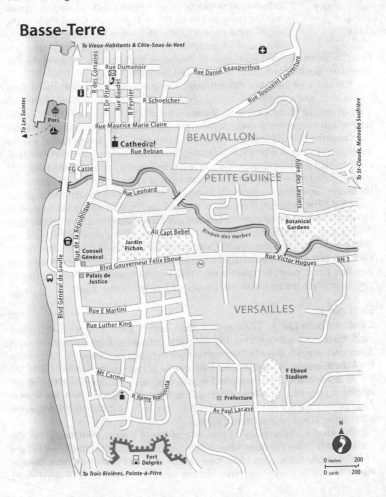

Basse-Terre town to a car park at **Savane à Mulets** (1,142 m) from where the crater, 300 m higher, is a 1½-hour climb up the Chemin des Dames, a fascinating trail with changing flora, but becoming eroded through overuse. Buses go to Saint-Claude from where it is a 6-km walk to Savane à Mulets. From the top there is a spectacular view; observe the mountain for a few days beforehand to see whether early morning or midday is clearest. The summit is quite flat; the main vent is to the south and there are discs in the ground to help you find it in the fog. You can come down along a forest path, the **Trace Carmichael**, to the **Chutes de Carbet** waterfalls.

> ‼ Don't wear too much clothing for the climb, but take a sweater as it can get quite chilly.

There are three waterfalls 20 m, 110 m and 125 m. You can swim in the warm, sulphuric pools, but beware of flash floods after rain higher up. The path is rough and often muddy. There is a picnic place, **Aire d'Arrivée**, after 15 minutes, where there are barbecue stalls (good chicken). The D4 road starts here and descends to St-Sauveur.

La Citerne, a neighbouring volcano, has a completely round crater. There is a trail but part requires climbing ladders straight up the wall. Also on this side are **Grand Étang** and **Étang Zombi**. You can drive, hitchhike or walk down the D4 road from the Chutes de Carbet to the edge of Grand Étang and walk around it, about one hour through lush vegetation. Do not swim in the lake because of bilharzia. There are also marked trails to **Étang de l'As de Pique**, high above Grand Étang to the south on the slope of La Madeleine (two hours) and the Trace de Moscou which leads southwest to the Plateau du Palmiste (2½ hours), from where a road leads down to Gourbeyre. Walk down to St-Sauveur for fine views over banana plantations, the coast and Les Saintes.

> ‼ Allow at least five hours to walk from Capesterre to St-Sauveur via the waterfalls and Grand Étang and wear good hiking shoes.

You can walk the **Trace Victor Hugues**, along the main ridge of Basse-Terre (a 29-km hike), and a number of other *traces*. A parallel route follows the River Moreau from Goyave up to the **Chutes du Moreau**. Turn off the N1 opposite the turning to Goyave and signposted to the falls. The made up road turns to gravel and then ends. From here the trail will take you about two hours with five river crossings, so take appropriate footwear. After the fifth crossing the trail rises steeply and there are steel ropes to help you up the slope. From here it is another 10 minutes to the falls. Also recommended is the **River Quiock trail**, three or four hours depending on conditions, but take the Serie Bleu map; despite being well marked originally, storm damage has made it difficult to find all the markers. It can be very muddy, wear good boots. You can start from the car park at the **Cascade aux Écrevisses** (see above) on the D23. Walk 300 m along the road and take a path to the right (follow the sign to the Pathfinders camp) to Piolet, near the entrance to the Bras-David-Tropical-Parc on the other side of the road. The trail leads down to where the River Quiock meets the larger river Bras-David, carefully cross the river, then the trail heads west along the Quiock until returning to the D23. ▸▸ *For hiking guides, see Activities and tours, page 671.*

East coast

Capesterre-Belle-Eau is Guadeloupe's third largest town and is an important agricultural centre with a market. The Allée de Flamboyants, a spectacular avenue of flame trees which flower May-September lines the coast road heading north, while the **Allée Dumanoir**, is a magnificent 1-km avenue of royal palms heading south.

At **Sainte-Marie**, a statue erected in 1916 commemorates the site of Columbus' landing in 1493. It has now been defaced by nationalists. South of Sainte-Marie, near Carangaise, there is a Hindu temple, built in 1974 by René Komla, richly decorated with statues of Vishnu and Ganesh outside.

The most northern town on this side of Basse-Terre is **Petit-Bourg**, on the opposite side of the bay from Pointe-à-Pitre and overlooking the little islands in the Petit Cul-de-Sac Marin. Inland from here, at Cabout, is **Le Domaine de Valombreuse, Parc Floral** ① *To590-955050, www.valombreuse.com, 0900-1700, guided tours* *available for groups*, where over 1,000 species of flowers can be found and masses of birds enjoying the plant life. Flowers are for sale and can be packed for export and collected at the airport. There's a restaurant by a river in the forest open for lunch, and for dinner for groups of 10 or more by reservation.

Southern Basse-Terre

The **Centre de Broderie** ① *Fort l'Olive, Vieux-Fort, T0590-920114, daily 0830-1800*, showcases the work of some 40 lacemakers and embroiderers in the ruins of the fort. There are attractive gardens surrounding the lighthouse at **Vieux-Fort**, with good views.

Amerindian rock carvings dating from around AD 300-400, are at the **Parc Archéologique des Roches Gravées** ① *T0590-929188, 0830-1700, €1 entry, children free*, near Trois Rivières; the most important is a drawing of the head of a Carib chief inside a cave. The archipelago of Guadeloupe has a large concentration of inscribed stones. The site is now in a garden setting, with wardens (it's a good idea to consult the leaflet because some of the engravings on the stones are hard to decipher; many are badly eroded; the pamphlet also explains the garden's trees). The park is a 10-minute walk down from the church in Trois Rivières where the buses stop. Five minutes further down the hill is the boat dock for Les Saintes (paying car park).

West coast

Between Basse-Terre town and the Route de la Traversée on the west (Leeward) coast (Côte-Sous-le-Vent, or the Golden Corniche), are **Vieux-Habitants**, with a restored 17th-century church, the largest coffee museum on the island and the **Underwater Reserve** developed by Jacques Cousteau.

Contact the **Syndicat d'Initiative de Bouillante** ① *T0590-987348*, for information on the Bouillante area, which considers itself the capital of diving.

North of the Traversée, on the N2, is **Pointe Noire**, a small fishing town. Just south of the town is the **Maison du Bois** ① *T0590-981690, Tue-Sun, 0930-1700, €1, closed Sep-mid-Oct*, at Bourg, a cabinet-making and woodworking centre with a permanent exhibition of furniture and other things made of wood. Also near here at Grand Plaine is the **Maison du Cacao** ① *Mon-Sat 0900- 1700, T0590-982523, maisoncacao@wanadoo.com*, with displays on the origin of cocoa, its cultivation and processing and you can taste it. There are several coffee museums and plantations you can visit. The **Maison du Café** ① *T0590-985496, daily 0900-1700, closed Sep, €6.10 adults, children half price, guided tours of about 1½ hrs*, is the largest museum at **L'habitation La Grivelière**, Vallée de Grande Rivière, devoted to the celebrated Bonifieur coffee. The tour shows you the entire growing, picking, drying and roasting process, as well as giving information on all the many fruit trees on the plantation. At **Le Domaine de Vanibel** ① *near Vieux-Habitants, T0590-984079, www.vanibel.com, Mon-Sat 0900-1600, guided tours at 1400, 1500, 1600 Jan-Apr, at 1500 May-Dec, closed Sep-Oct*, another coffee plantation also growing vanilla and bananas, offers tours and accommodation, part of the **Gîtes de France**. At **Acomat** is **La Caféière Beauséjour** ① *T0590-981009, www.cafeierebeausejour.com, Tue-Sun 1000-1700, closed Sep-Oct*, in a 17th-century house with coffee museum, restaurant and good cottage accommodation (AL). On the Côte-Sous-Le-Vent are the calm, clean beaches at Ferry and Grand-Anse and the rougher ones at Deshaies.

> ✦ *A good three-hour hike is the Trace des Contrebandiers, from the Maison du Bois (when you leave the trail on the other side you will need to hitchhike).*

Parc Naturel

① *Habitation Beausoleil, BP 13 Montéran, 97120 Saint-Claude, T0590-802425, F0590-800546.*
The island's national park, the seventh largest in France, includes 30,000 ha of forest land in the centre of Basse-Terre, which is by far the more scenic part. As the island is

volcanic there are a number of related places to visit. Do not pick flowers, fish, hunt, drop litter, play music or wash anything in the rivers. Dogs are banned. Trails have been marked out all over the park. The national park includes three protected land and sea reserves, open to the public: **Les Réserves Naturelles des Pitons du Nord et de Beaugendre, La Réserve Naturelle du Grand Cul-de-Sac Marin** and **La Réserve Naturelle de Pigeon,** or **Réserve Cousteau.** The waters after which the Caribs named the island come hot (as at the Ravine Chaude springs on the Rivière à Goyaves), tumbling (the waterfalls of the Carbet River and the Cascade aux Écrevisses on the Corossol) and tranquil (the lakes of Grand Étang, As de Pique and Étang Zombi).

‡ *The park has no gates, no opening hours and no admission fee.*

A **Maison de la Fôret** ① *1000-1700, closed Mon*, on the Route de la Traversée gives information on the surrounding forest. From the Maison de la Forêt there are 20- and 60-minute forest walks which will take you deep among the towering trees. The **Cascade aux Écrevisses**, a waterfall and small pool, is about 2 km from the Maison (clearly marked) and is a popular place to swim and spend the day. A picnic site has been established at the edge of the Bras David river, where you can fish for ouassous (fresh water shrimp). Enjoy it while you can, a dam is planned. The **Parc Zoologique et Botanique** ① *T0590-988352, 0900-1700, €3.80, children, €2.30.* above Mahaut, houses many of the species which exist in the Natural Park, such as mongoose, racoon, iguana and land turtle, unfortunately in very small cages. A hanging bridge, the *Canopée*, links the tree tops. Fine panoramic views from the café (free drink included in entrance ticket) and the simple but excellent **Ti-Racoon** restaurant serves lunch daily except Monday.

The national park's emblem is the *raton laveur* (racoon) which, although protected, is very rare. You are much more likely to see birds and insects in the park.

Northern Basse-Terre

Round the north of Basse-Terre is the town of **Sainte-Rose** where you can visit the rum museum, **Musée du Rhum**, at the **Distillerie Reimonenq**, Bellevue Sainte-Rose ① *T0590-287004, Mon-Sat 0900-1700, €6 adults, €4 children.* In addition, there is a display of 5,000 butterflies and other insects in the **Galerie des Plus Beaux Insectes du Monde**, and 30 model sailing ships from the earliest to the present day. The road continues south to Lamentin and the hot springs at **Ravine Chaude** ① *Thermal Station T0590-257829.* Near Lamentin you can visit the **Domaine de Séverin** ① *T0590-289196, Mon-Sat 0830-1300, Mon-Fri 1430-1700, tours in the morning*, distillery at La Boucan, still using a paddle wheel. Guided tours on a miniature train at 0930, 1045, 1530. You can taste and buy rums and fruit punches as well as the freshwater shrimp and pepper sauce grown on the property. The restaurant is open for lunch Tuesday to Sun, and dinner on Thursday, Friday and Saturday (local specialities, accommodation available, LL, T0590-235066, www.habitation-severin.com).

Beaches

Petit Havre is popular with its small coves and reefs offshore. Here are mostly fishermen and locals and a small shed selling fish meals and beer. The best is at **Sainte-Anne** where the fine white sand and crystal clear water of a constant depth of 1.5 m far from shore make idyllic bathing; the **Plage du Bourg** in town is ideal for young children, the **Plage de la Caravelle** west of town, is excellent; part is public and part with access only through the **Club Med.** About 2 km from the town is the **Plage de Bois Jolan**, reached down a track, where the water is shallow enough to walk to the protecting reef. Further east are good beaches at **St-François** and the 11-km road to Pointe des Colibris skirts the **Anse Kahouanne** with lots of tracks going down to the sea; sand is limited but there are snorkelling possibilities.

On the north coast of the peninsula is **Plage Tarare,** where there is a good restaurant by the car park. This is the only official nudist beach in Guadeloupe. **Plage de l'Anse à la Gourde** has good sand and is popular with campers at weekends.

On the leeward coast of Basse-Terre are some good beaches. South of Pointe Noire on the west coast is **Plage Caraïbe,** which is clean, calm and beautiful, with restaurant **Le Reflet** (helpful owners), picnic facilities, toilets and a shower. In the northwest, **La Grande Anse,** 30 minutes' walk north of Deshaies, is superb and undeveloped with no hotels, golden sand but no snorkelling except round a large rock where the current is quite strong. Body surfing is good when the waves are big. Beach restaurant at the south end with charcoal-grilled chicken. On Sunday people sell hot Créole food quite cheaply. The beaches on the north coast of Basse-Terre can be dangerous and at **Plage de Clugny** there are warning signs as there have been drownings.

> *Guadeloupe has excellent beaches for swimming, mostly between Gosier and St-François on Grande-Terre. More deserted beaches can be found on the northeast of Grande-Terre.*

Sleeping

Guadeloupe *p656, map p658*
The tourist board has current hotel price lists; there's an information desk at the airport but no reservations.

Gîtes
Throughout the island there are a large number of *gîtes* for rent on a daily, weekly or monthly basis. Weekly rates range from €72 to €325, but most are in the €100-160 bracket. The tourist offices in both Pointe-à-Pitre and Basse-Terre have lists of the properties available and should be consulted in the first instance, or you can contact the Association Guadeloupéenne des Gîtes Ruraux et du Tourisme Vert (Relais Guadeloupe des Gîtes de France), at the Centre d'Échanges Ruddy Nuthila, T0590-916433, F0590-914540. *Gîtes* are arranged by the local Syndicat d'Initiative, who charge a 5% rental fee.

Camping
Camping is not well organized and the tourist office does not therefore have much information. Ask mayors if you may camp on municipal land, or owners on private property. Camper vans can be arranged through **Découverts et Loisirs Créoles** in Abymes, T0590-205565.

Pointe-à-Pitre *p657, map p660*
A Anchorage Saint John Perse, rue Quai Ferdinand Lesseps, T0590-825157, F0590-825261. A/c, TV, balcony, comfortable, very good, breakfast included. View of cruise ships and statue of Saint John Perse.

B-C Pension Mme Rilsy, 34 Bis rue Peynier, T0590-918171. Breakfast included, very friendly. Reported to take students only.
B-C Relais des Antilles, 38 rue Denfert, corner of rue Massabielle and rue Vatable, just off the Place de la Victoire, T0590-834362. Basic, noisy but friendly, 5 rooms, a/c, fridge, TV.

Gosier *p661*
LL-AL La Créole Beach, Pointe de la Verdure, T0590-904646, www.deshotelsetdesiles.com/us/hotel-creole -beach.html. 218 good-sized rooms and suites, breakfast included, pool, bar and restaurant, watersports arranged, tennis, volley ball and putting green available. Also under same management are **Les Résidences Yucca,** 100 studios which share facilities of La Créole Beach.
LL-AL Sofitel Auberge de la Vieille Tour, Montauban, 97190 Gosier, T0590-842323, h1345-SB@accor-hotels.com. Named after an 18th-century sugar tower incorporated into the main building. On a bluff over the sea, beach, pool, tennis, 182 rooms, 3 2-room bungalows and 8 rooms in French colonial style, good deals booking on internet, gourmet restaurant, with the only Maître Cuisinier in the French Antilles.
A-B Les Flamboyants, Chemin des Phares et Balises, T0590-841411, F0590-845356. Pool, seaview, some kitchenettes, friendly, clean, a/c.
D-E Hotel Corossol, Mathurin, T0590-843989. 8 rooms, friendly, good meals, 20 mins' walk to Gosier. Many places advertise rooms to let.

LL Iguana Bay Villas, Pointe des Châteaux, T0590-884880, www.iguanabay.org. 17, 3-bedroom villas, sleep 6, good value off-season for a group, private pools, overlooking La Désirade, pretty beach, private.

LL La Cocoteraie, Av de l'Europe, St-François, T0590 887981, www.lacocoteraie.com. Beautiful hotel, 52 deluxe suites overlooking the marina, lagoon, pool or private beach, octagonal baths and separate showers, tennis courts and fitness room, golf close by.

LL-AL La Toubana, Ste-Anne, T0590-882578, www.deshotelsetdesiles.com /us/toubana.html. Reopened 2007 after 6 months' renovation. 32 cottages, the ones near the sea are more elegant, a/c, kitchenettes, phones, modem, terraces, pool with waterfall, small private beach, tennis, **Toubana** is Arawak for 'little house', restaurant serves French and Créole cuisine.

LL-A Anse des Rochers, St-François, T0590-939031, www.anse-des-rochers.com. 228 spacious rooms in 6 buildings plus 24 villas with 4 rooms each, a/c, kitchenettes, beautiful seaside resort, Créole architecture, in 25 acres of gardens, fine restaurants, huge pool, tennis, volleyball, excursions, watersports, golf nearby.

LL-A Chez Honoré, Plage de l'Anse à La Gourde, 5 km from St-François, T0590-850393, www.chezhonore.com. 8 studios, 8 suites, 4 villas on long, unspoilt beach, restaurant, lobster specialities, pool.

L-AL Hôtel Kaye'la, St-François, T0590-887777, F0590-887467, on the marina. Built 1990, 75 rooms for up to 4 people on 3 floors with elevator, marina or sea view, terrace or balcony, a/c, pool, bar, restaurant, walking distance to restaurants, convenient for boat trips from marina.

AL Mini Beach, Ste-Anne, T0590-882113, F0590-882113. 1 km from town, on the beach, relaxed, good location, many restaurants nearby, can fall to half price in summer, good restaurant.

A-B Auberge le Grand Large, Ste-Anne, T0590-854828, www.aubergelegrandlarge .com. Neither grand nor large, simple rooms and bungalows, some with kitchenettes, friendly and with good restaurant on the beach, reef-protected and good for kids.

A-B La Marie-Gaillarde, between Gosier and Ste-Anne, at La Marie-Gaillarde,

T0590-858429, overlooking Les Grands Fonds, 2 km from Petit Havre beach. 7 rooms, 2 studios with kitchenette can fit 3-4 people, with restaurant and bar.

Basse-Terre town *p662, map p663*
Accommodation is neither plentiful nor high class in Basse-Terre city.

AL-A St-Georges, rue Gratien Parize, Saint-Claude T0590-801010, www.hotelstgeorges.com . 40 rooms including 2 suites, a/c, TV, view over Basse-Terre to the sea, fitness room, squash, pool, billiards, meeting rooms, bar, restaurant *Le Lamasure*, snack bar.

Southern Basse-Terre *p665, map p663*
LL Le Jardin Malanga, Trois Rivières, T0590-926757, www.deshotelsetdesiles.com/ us/jardin-malanga.html. Beautifully renovated 1927 Créole house, rooms and bungalows, verdant hillside setting in banana plantation, lovely views, terraces, mini-bar, bath tubs, huge beds, pool, car rental in advance recommended.

AL Grand'Anse, Trois Rivières, T0590-929047, F0590-929369. 20 bungalows, sleep 3, a/c, fan, fridge, TV, pool, Créole restaurant and bar.

B Le Joyeux, Trois Rivières, a €0.35 bus ride from the centre of the town (bus stop right outside) or short walk, in Le Faubourg, 100 m above the sea, T0590-927478, F0590-928984. Simple rooms, kitchenettes, Créole restaurant, bar, disco, closed Mon except for reservations, good views to Les Saintes, very friendly, transfers to the boat dock.

West coast *p665*
LL-A Pointe Batterie Villas, Deshaies, T0590-285703, www.pointe-batterie.com. 24, 1- to 2-bedroom villas scattered among lush gardens and trees, a/c, decks, pool, on the water, charming, some have private pools, excellent restaurant, plus the only spa at a hotel in Guadeloupe.

L-AL Domaine de Malendure, Morne Tarare Pigeon, Bouillante, T0590-989212, malendure@leaderhotels.gp. 50 loft suites with views of Ilet Pigeon, on very steep hillside, 400 m from sea, good location for diving or walking, pool, restaurant, car rental, shuttle to Malendure beach or Grand Anse beach, car rental in advance recommended.

AL Créol'Inn, Bel'Air Desrozières, T0590-942256, www.hotel-creolin-guadeloupe.com. Designed by the owner of **Auberge de la Distillerie**, 20 cabins in wooded area, sleep 4, a/c, fan, TV, kitchenette, hammocks, pool, barbecue, snack bar/restaurant.

AL-A Auberge de la Distillerie, Route de Versailles, Tabanon, T0590-942591, F0590-941191. 18 rooms, pool, jacuzzi, pocket billiards, country inn at entrance to Parc Naturel surrounded by pineapple fields, Créole restaurant, **Le Bitaco** and small pizza café.

A La Vigie, overlooking Deshaies bay, T0590-284252. Small studios with kitchenette, bathroom, terrace, fan, cleaned daily.

D Gîtes Manu Reva, T0590-284004 or 0590-284270. Chez M Eric Bernier, Résidence Gros Morne, rooms, studios and apartments on waterfront, opposite **Le Mouillage** restaurant more rooms are available, sea view or mountain view.

🍴 Eating

Look in the excellent free guides *Ti Gourmet Guadeloupe* or *Délices de la Guadeloupe* for recipes, restaurants, cafés and pâtisseries. Many are closed in the evening. For a description of local cuisine, see page 655. Menus (3-course lunch) start at €10.

Pointe-à-Pitre *p657, map p660*

♦♦-♦ La Canne à Sucre, Quai No 1, Port Autonome, T0590-892101. Faces the sea, wharfside café, mixes Créole and French, set menus, Créole buffet Sat 1200, also does teas, ice creams.

Bas du Fort *p661*

♦♦♦-♦♦ Asia, La Digue, Résidence Bas du Fort, T0590-908654. Lovely setting, built out over the water and open view of Basse-Terre and passing craft. Mix of Asian cuisine, good but not cheap, pleasant service.

♦♦♦-♦♦ Le Planteur, Bas du Fort. T0590-908874. 1200-1400, 1900-2215, closed Sun and Mon lunch. Renowned for its ouassous (écrevisses), excellent service, you get a warm welcome and the food is good too. Menus from €15-25 or à la carte.

Gosier *p661*

Lots of small restaurants in Gosier: pizzas,

Vietnamese, Chinese and of course French. The local pizza house is near the park, good for takeaways. The *pâtisserie* is good for an early morning coffee while collecting the *baguettes*.

♦♦♦-♦♦ La Mandarine, 4 rue Simon-Radegonde, T0590-843028. French and Créole cuisine, highly rated, good service and food, vegetarians can also enjoy a gourmet meal but best to give advance notice.

♦♦♦-♦♦ Lola Palooza, 122 Av de Montauban, T0590-845618. Cuban café and bar, lots of Cuban music, salsa and *mojito*, lobster on the grill, good food and service, great atmosphere, surrounded by tropical vegetation.

♦♦ Au P'tit Paris, 6 Impasse a Clara, T0590-845665. In a pretty Créole house, make a reservation for their special evenings as very popular, jazz, concerts, café theatre, good food, excellent pizzas, a pleasant night out which won't break the bank.

♦♦ Bobisto, Chemin de la Plage, T0590-846988. Simple but excellent local food, tasty grilled fish, good-sized portions, nice setting and pleasant atmosphere.

♦♦ Le Palmier, 7 Route de la Verdure, T0590-846381. Close to Créole Beach, small, intimate restaurant, serving Créole food and Mediterranean dishes, service friendly and quick.

Sainte-Anne and the east *p662*

♦♦♦ Chez Man Michel, Tarare, Saint-François, T0590-887279. Open for lunch in the week and also for dinner Fri, Sat. Local food, typical restaurant, great seafood, try the lobster or the fricassee de ouassous, by the beach, friendly service, reservations recommended.

♦♦♦ Iguane Café, Route de la Pointe des Châteaux, Saint-François, T0590-850309. On the way to Pointe Tarare, large restaurant but popular, so soon fills up. Service sometimes slow; ratio of waiters to guests too low, but courteous and professional. Food excellent, wonderful beef, heavenly desserts.

♦♦♦ La Porte des Indes, on the road to la Moule heading out of St-François, T0590-213087. Closed Sun. Reservations essential for this excellent southern Indian gourmet restaurant, where the service is impeccable.

♦♦♦ La Terrasse, Route du Lagon, Saint-François, T0590-850202. Tables on the terrace overlooking the marina, great location for lunch or dinner, Créole and seafood, delicious ouassous, lots of fresh fish.

Le Colombo, Section La Coulée, Saint-François. T0590-884129. Lobster from the tank cooked on wood-fired grill, also traditional cuisine, all the food is very fresh, friendly service, well thought of, reservations advised, essential at weekends.

Le Bambou,18 rue de la Petite Saline, T0590-886902. Vietnamese and Chinese, tasty food, good service, welcoming staff, indoor or outdoor dining.

Du Lagon, Plage du Lagon, Saint-François, T0590-887544. Lovely location on the beach, with sun loungers (*transat*) to rent, shade, great place for drinks, snacks, lunch or dinner on the beach brought to your bed or move into the restaurant.

Le Navy, La Marina, Saint-François, T0590-880722. Great place to go to eat *moules frites*, nothing special in decor, but convivial service, wash the food down with a good punch and follow with tasty desserts.

Quai 17, La Marina, Saint-François, T0590-885236. Lunch and dinner. Good pizza and pasta, large portions, good service, bar.

Resto des Artistes, 9 Av de l'Europe, Saint-François, T0590-887544. Italian, overlooking the marina, can get busy so go early for the best tables, good pizza and pasta, service quick and friendly.

Basse-Terre town *p662, map p663*
Le Tamarinier, Place de la Mairie, Saint-Claude, T0590-800667. Good home cooking, authentic Créole, choice of 3 dishes which change daily, family-run.

East coast *p664*
Domaine de Valombreuse, Cabout, Petit Bourg, T0590-955050. In the heart of the forest. Watch the many-coloured birds while you eat, crayfish special.

West coast *p665*
Karacoli, beside Grand Anse Beach, Deshaies, T0590-285340. Authentic Créole cooking at its best, the local Salcede brother and sister who run it have won many awards, fish and shellfish superb, reservations recommended on Sun when it is very popular with locals, dancing spot at weekends.

Le Madras, Le Bourg, Deshaies, T0590-284988. Créole cuisine, tables on the deck overlooking the sea.

Chez Loulouze, Plage de Malendure, Bouillante, T0590-987034. Beach restaurant, Créole fare, seafood specialities.

Chez Olga, Fromager, Bouillante, T0590-987576. Good value, food cooked to your liking, pleasant atmosphere and friendly service.

Bars and clubs

Guadeloupe *p656, map p658*
There is no shortage of nightlife, most of it in the hotels and at the marinas. Around the Marina Bas-du-Fort there are several bars with live music, such as piano or jazz and a choice of waterfront nightclubs, usually packed. Several are listed below, but others include Le Wallis, Pharaon, Vol du Nuit, La Cascade, and New Land, outside Gosier and one of the longer-established clubs. At Le Moule, there is the attractive Shiva; in Goubeyre, Basse-Terre, the chic Plantation is the most exclusive disco; in Bouillante the disco Espace Vaneau offers dancing until dawn at weekends; in Abymes there is Palace and in Jarry, L'Extase, while in Deshaies at La Note Bleue you can listen to live piano music on Sat.

To check what's on and where to find live music, go to www.annouay.com. Hotels often organize folk dancing displays or dinner dancing, particularly in high season. The most popular music is zouk, played everywhere, but you will also hear Cuban rhythms, merengue from the Dominican Republic, reggae and other Caribbean styles, often played live. Discos usually charge €11-22, which can include the first drink, but subsequent cocktails are overpriced at up to €11. They start at around 2300 or later and carry on until dawn.

Barrio Caliente, Bas-du-Fort. Bar and dancing to Latin rhythms, merengue, bachata, salsa, etc.

Caraïbes II, Carrefour de Blanchard, Bas-du-Fort, T0590-909716. The place to go for Brazilian music.

Cheyenne, Gosier. A well-known night club. Admission varies, €15-20, but if you go really late, say around 0300, it is free.

Fanzy Bar, Mathurin Poucette, T0590-844134. A variety of music played here, from Edith Piaf and French songs of the 1940s and 1950s, to Bob Marley or French disco.

Le Spy Bar, Route des Hôtels, Bas-du-Fort. Come here to see the rich and famous of the young and fashionable French in-crowd holidaying in Guadeloupe. Bar, dancing, associated with the stylish **Hôtel Le Coste** in Paris.

Les Tortues, off the N2 near Bouillante, Basse-Terre, T0590-988283. Popular bar with divers and locals, good place to down a Corsaire beer or a Ti-ponch and catch up on the day's activities. Also good food, a variety of fresh fish make up the catch of the day and lobster is on offer in season.

Lola Palooza,122 Av de Montauban, T0590-845858. Lively Cuban café and bar, see Eating, lots of Cuban music, salsa and mojito, dancing on the tables, cocktails from around €6.

Zenith, Route de la Riviera, Gosier, T0590-907204. Nightclub and disco, can be fashionably packed or completely empty.

Zoo Rock Café, La Marina, Gosier, T0590-907777, zoorock@ais.gp. Timber everywhere, wood panelling but open to the breeze, themed nights including Brazilian music, New Orleans jazz.

Casinos

Mon-Thu 2100-0300, Fri-Sat and the day before holidays 2100-0400, admission €10. Legal age is 18. Passport or driving licence is required as proof of identity before entering the gaming room. Slot machines are outside the gaming room. **Casino in Gosier**, 43 Pointe de la Verdure, T0590-847968, closed Sun, local and international artistes at the cabaret. **Casino de la Marina**, Av de l'Europe, St-François, T0590-884131, closed Mon.

Cinemas

Cinéma L'Image, in Gosier.
D'Arbaud, in Basse-Terre, T0590-811835. 2 screens.
Rex, in Pointe-à-Pitre, T0590-822020. 4 screens.

Theatre

The **Centre des Arts**, Pointe-a-Pitre. Stages concerts, ballets and plays with both local and international stars.

✸ Festivals and events

Guadeloupe *p656, map p658*
Feb Carnival warm-up starts on Epiphany with different events each Sun, until the climax on the last weekend, with the frenetic parading of *les jours gras* Sun, Mon, and **Mardi Gras**. On **Ash Wed** (*Mercredi des Cendres*) devils and she-devils dance and sing to tam-tams as the effigy of **Valval**, the spirit of Carnival, is taken off to be burned and thrown into the sea.
Mid-Apr The Fish and Sea Festival has beach parties, boat races, crab races, etc.
Jul The Fête du Gwo Ka, or Festival of the Big Drums is a celebration of local ethnic music.
Aug La Fête des Cuisinières (Cooks' Festival) in the middle of the month is a lot of fun with parades in Créole costumes and music as well as food and cooking. It is held on the feast of St Lawrence, the patron saint of women cooks, and the event starts with a Mass. Some 250 cordon bleu cooks from the **Women's Cooking Association** wear their typical colourful dresses with Madras scarves and lots of jewellery for the parade through Pointe-à-Pitre.
Oct Old Créole Songs Festival.
Nov St Cecilia's Day, the patron saint of music.

✪ Shopping

Guadeloupe *p656, map p658*
There are lots of hypermarkets just like in France, stocked with excellent cheese counters and massive wine departments. Generally Mon-Sat 0800-2030. Most things are imported from France. In Gosier there is a supermarket on the road to Plage de l'Anse Canot, open on Sun, otherwise hypermarkets are better value and cleaner. Small minimarts, local corner shops, can also be found.

▲▲ Activities and tourss

Guadeloupe *p656, map p658*
Bullock cart racing
Popular on the west coast of Grande-Terre, drawing large crowds. They race along the flat, then turn sharply and charge up a steep hill. The wheels are then chocked and they have to see how far they can get, zig-zag

fashion, with about 10 mins of very hard work. Much shouting, plenty of beer, food tents and an overloud PA system.

Cockfighting

Very popular and there are pits all over the place. The season runs from Nov-Jul and involves serious gambling. The only pit open all year is Bélair, Morne-à-l'Eau, Tue, Thu, Fri and Sun, T0590-242370.

Cycling

In Aug a cycling race takes place over 10 days, going to all parts of the island. Le Tour Cycliste de la Guadeloupe draws local and international competitors and is an excuse for festivities and parties. The Association Guadeloupéenne de VTT (mountain biking association) can be contacted at Pointe-à-Pitre, T0590-828267. For cycling tours of Guadeloupe, Karucyclo, T0590-822139, 0590-284659.

Diving

Lots of dive companies along the Leeward coast, Basse-Terre and on Grande-Terre, with no shortage of dive sites. Diving trips can be arranged at Les Heures Saines, T0590-988663, www.heures-saines.gp, at Rocher de Malendure, or Chez Guy et Christian, Plaisir Plongée Caraïbe, T0590-988243, F0590-988284, friendly, recommended for beginners' confidence, well equipped, packages with accommodation provided, at Pigeon, Bouillante. Nautilus, T0590-988908, www.lesnautilus.com. A glass-bottom boat, takes you round the marine park, departing from Malendure beach, south of Mahaut 1030, 1200, 1430 and 1600. €20 adults, €12 children 5-12 years. The boat anchors for about 15 mins off Ilet Pigeon for snorkelling, but it is rather deep to see much. In wet weather the water becomes too murky to see anything. The boat is often booked solid by cruise ship visitors.

Fishing

Deep-sea fishing is best off the Côte-sous-le-vent, where the fishing area is 20 mins from Ilet Pigeon. Blue marlin, kingfish, barracuda and bonita can be fished all year round, but there are seasons for other species. There are lots of fishing contests organized throughout the year. Well-equipped boats go out for full- or half-day excursions from Bouillante: Fishing Club Antilles, T0590-987010, Francis Ricard, T0590-987377; and from Le Rocher de Malendure: Franck Nouy, T0590-987084, who also offers 5- and 8-day trips. Fishing boats also go out from Marina Bas du Fort and Gosier.

Golf

There is an 18-hole, international golf course on the edge of the lagoon at Saint-François, T0590-884187, www.guadeloupe-fr.com /golfsaintfrancois, designed by Robert Trent Jones, €40 green fee for 18 holes.

Hiking

In the Parc Naturel, contact the Organisation des Guides de Montagne de la Caraïbe (OGMC), Maison Forestière, 97120 Matouba, T0590-800579, or in St-Claude, T0590-802425, or the Bureau des Guides, Basse-Terre, T0590-991873. Guides certified by the French government are available for hikes of 1-5 days. A guided hike to La Soufrière will cost around €32, make sure the guide speaks a language you understand. Approximate hiking times, mileage and description of terrain and flora are included in the booklet *Promenades et Randonnées*.

Horse riding

Riding at Gosier, T0590-840486, La Martingale, La Jaille, T0590-262839 and Ranch Caraïbes, T0590-821154. Also Horse Farm, St-Claude, T0590-815221, F0590-819073, for groups of 6-12 people riding in the forest.

Sailing

Sailing boats can be chartered for any duration. There are 2 marinas between Pointe-à-Pitre and Gosier, and good, shallow-draught anchorage at Gosier. The Route du Rhum race is held every 4 years, with multi-hull boats racing between St-Malo, France, and Pointe-à-Pitre. The record is 14 days, 10 hrs and 8 mins.

There are several excursions offered, ranging from the booze cruise or sunset cruise variety to more scientific and educational trips.
Awak, Centre Comercial Marina Golf, T0590-885353, F0590-886043. A 46-ft

glass-bottomed vedette, also goes to Petite-Terre.

La Compagnie des Bateaux Verts, Marina Bas-du-Fort, T0590-907717, F0590-907920. Starts with the Aquarium and then takes you to the marine park on the 48-passenger glass-bottomed *Kio*, with scientists on board to explain the ecosystems.

From **Pigeon Bouillante** there are several glass-bottomed boat excursions:
Aquarius, T0590-988730, F0590-901185. Has 2-hr trips at 1000, 1230 and 1500.
Nautilus, has 2 glass-bottomed boats and a submarine.

Surfing

Surfing is popular at Le Moule, Port-Louis, La Pointe des Châteaux, Ste-Anne and St-François; Anse Bertrand in winter; on Basse-Terre, Deshaies, Pointe Noire, Bananier at Capesterre Belle Eau.
Arawak Surf Club, T0590-236068, www.arawak-surf.gp. Dedicated surfers, competitions, instruction.
Karukera Surf Club, Le Moule, T0590-236615, www.karukerasurfclub.com. Tuition, competitions, club activities.
LookaSurf, Chemin du Rotabas (Plage de la Caravelle), T0590-881517, www.lookasurf.com. Rental and purchase of funboards, windsurfing and kitesurfing equipment. Tuition available.
Tropical Fun, Pointe de la Verdure, Plage du Salako, Gosier, T0590-913262, tropical.fun @wanadoo.fr. Rental of surf boards, sailing boats, motor boats and jet skis.

Tour operators

Emeraude Guadeloupe, St-Claude, T0590-819828, http://emeraudeguadeloupe .ifrance.com. Offers hiking in forests and mountains, with cultural visits and contact with local families, also lodging in small hotels, mountain bike excursions and other activities.
Vert Intense, T0590-993473, www.vert-intense.com. Canyoning, mountain biking, hiking.

Windsurfing

Most beach hotels offer windsurfing for guests and visitors, and some arrange waterskiing and diving courses. Windsurfers gather at the **UCPA Hotel Club** in St-François. The tradewinds are best Dec-May and the best places are St-François, Sainte-Anne and Gosier. Courses and board rental are available at **Sport Away Ecole Nathalie Simon**, St-François, T/F0590-887204, *LCS*, Ste-Anne, T0590-881517, F0590-881521, and **UCPA**, St-François, T0590-886480, F0590-884350.
Action Kite Caraïbes, St Francois, T0690-868135, www.akc.fr. The first kitesurfing school on the island, lots of activities.

☉ Transport

Guadeloupe *p656, map p658*
Air
From Europe Like Martinique, Guadeloupe is on **Air France**'s daily direct route from Paris (about 8 hrs) from both Orly and Charles de Gaulle airports. **Air Corsair** and **Air Caraïbes** also fly daily from Orly, Paris.
From North America Air Canada has direct flights from Montréal. **Air France** flies from Miami. **American Eagle** has flights from San Juan, with connections from the USA.
From the Caribbean LIAT/Caribbean Star offers inter-Caribbean connections via Antigua and Dominica. **Air Caraïbes** connects Pointe-à-Pitre with Fort-de-France (lots of flights every day), La Désirade, Marie- Galante, St Barts, St Lucia, Sint Maarten, St-Martin, Santo Domingo and Terre-de-Haut. **Air Antilles Express** flies to Fort-de-France and St-Martin. Other services include **Air France** from Cayenne, Fort-de-France and Port-au-Prince; **Cubana** from Havana.
Airport Le Raizet Airport is used for regional flights while the new, modern **Pole Caraïbes Airport** is for international ones. Information, T089689755. They are quite far apart, a taxi ride, and if you have a rental car (kept on the old airport side of the airfield) you will have to get the shuttle to the new terminal. There is no bus service to the new airport, but take the shuttle bus to Le Raizet and then bus into town from the other side of the car park, over roundabout and outside **Cora (Mamouth)** supermarket, €0.60 to Place de la Victoire. No buses Sat afternoon or Sun. Taxi fares (T0590-207474) from the airport are approximately €14.50 to Gosier, €29 to Ste-Anne, €43.50 to Saint-François and €1150 to Bas-du-Fort. Prices go up by 40% 2100-0700, all day Sun and on holidays.

Airlines Air France, Blvd Légitimus, Pointe-à-Pitre, T0590-825000; **Air Canada,** T0590-836249; **LIAT/Caribbean Star,** T0590-211393; **Air Antilles Express,** T0590-648648, www.airantilles.com; **American Eagle,** T0590-211180.

Boat

Numerous cruise lines sail from US and French ports. Pointe-à-Pitre has berths for 4 cruise ships and marinas for yachts. There are fast, scheduled **ferry** services from Pointe-à-Pitre to Marie-Galante, Les Saintes, Dominica, St Lucia and Martinique. L'Express des Îles has a car ferry daily from Pointe-à-Pitre to Fort-de-France at Mon-Sat 0800, Sun 1400 and an additional service at 1200 on Fri, 3 hrs 45 mins. See St Lucia and Dominica chapters for details of services to those islands.
ATE/Trans Antilles Express (L'Express des Îles) offers excursions with accommodation, day trips with lunch, or transport only, T0590-831245, F0590-911105, La Darse, Pointe-à-Pitre. Agents include **T-Maritimes Brudey Frères,** Gare Maritime de Bergerin, 97110 Pointe-à-Pitre, T0590-916087, with offices in Trois Rivières, T0590-926974, St-François, T0590-886667 and **Quai Débarcadère,** Grand Bourg, Marie Galante, T0590-977782, www.brudey-freres.fr. You can get a small motor-sail vessel to Dominica from Pointe-à-Pitre for not much less than the flight, leaving at 1300, 3 days a week, 2 hrs.

Bus

There are 3 main bus terminals in Pointe-à-Pitre: from **rue Dubouchage,** La Darse (by Place de la Victoire), buses run to **Gosier, Ste-Anne, Saint-François** (€3.85); for north Grande-Terre destinations, buses leave from the **Morne Ferret and Mortenol** station, off Blvd Légitimus. From Rue Pernier to the airport, €0.80. From **Bergevin** station, Blvd Chanzy (near the cemetery) they go to **Trois Rivières** and **Basse-Terre** (€6.15, 2 hrs). Pointe-à-Pitre to **La Grande Anse,** 1¾ hrs. Buses from Pointe-à-Pitre to **Deshaies** leave from **Gare Routière,** 1¼ hrs. **Basse-Terre** to **Trois Rivières,** 20 mins. The terminal in Basse-Terre is on **Blvd Général-de- Gaulle,** between the market and the sea. Buses run between 0530 and 1900, leaving for the main destinations every 15 mins or when full. After 1800 and after

1300 on Sat and Sun it is often impossible to get anywhere.

Car and scooter
There can be major traffic holdups in the rush hour in and around Pointe-à-Pitre; expect to find slow moving traffic on the major routes for up to 20 km out of the capital. Bottlenecks include the roundabout at the university at Bas-du-Fort, the turning to Le Raizet and beyond to Abymes and the turnoff to Baie-Mahault. In the city, parking is bad in the daytime. There are no car parks, just meters. There are 2 zones, green (about €0.70 for maximum 8 hrs) and orange (cheaper). The system doesn't operate 1230-1400. Most traffic is one way.
  Car hire Avis, T0590-211354, F0590-211355; **Budget,** T0590-827250, F0590-917208; **Europcar,** T0590-266064, F0590-268373; **Hertz,** T0590-938945, F0590-916959, and there are offices at the airport. At Trois Rivières, Rosan Martin, **Location de Voitures,** is close to the dock, T0590-929424. **Tropic-Car,** 25 rue Schoelcher, T0590-918437, F0590-913194, evenings and weekends T0590-840725, has a variety of models for hire. Fully equipped camper vans can be hired from several agencies: **Antilles Local Soleil,** Gosier, T0590-957200. **Vert'Bleu Location,** T0590-285125, F0590-285295. There are also mopeds for hire in Pointe-à-Pitre, Gosier, Saint-François, or through hotels. Motorbikes from **Equateur Motos,** T0590-845994, F0590-845977. **Dom Location,** rue Saint-Aude Ferly, Saint-François, T/F0590-888481, hires scooters, motorbikes and cars half day to 1 week, scooters €18 per day. Mokes and scooters can be rented at Ste- Anne. If you don't have a credit card you normally have to deposit up to €500 for a car; €310 for a scooter; and €105 for moped or bicycle.

Cycle
Bicycle rental from **Rent- a-Bike,** *Kalenda Raut Hotel,* Saint-François, T0590-845100, or **Atlantic,** Saint-François, around €7 per day.

● Directory

Guadeloupe *p656, maps p658*
Banks Banque Nationale de Paris (good for Visa cash advances). Banque Populaire, Banque des Antilles Françaises, Crédit

Maritime, **Crédit Agricole** and **Société Générale de Banque aux Antilles**, all have branches throughout the island. Banks charge 1% commission and 4% *dessier* (filing fee). No commission charged on French traveller's cheques. Exchange is handled up to midday so go early to avoid the late morning pandemonium. **American Express** is at Petreluzzi Travel, 2 rue Henri IV, English spoken, helpful. Credit cards are widely accepted, including at the hypermarkets.
Consulates (All embassies are in France.) Germany, T0590-503839. Holland, T0590-733161. Sweden, T0590-735494. Switzerland, T0590-503650. US, T0590-631303. **Internet** Hotels often have internet access for guests' use. There are several cybercafés in the tourist strip. **Cybart**, Rond Point Blanchard, Gosier, T0590-887377. **Le Caméléon**, Marie Gaillard, Gosier, T0590-858320. **@robas Café**, Marina, St-François, T0590-887377. **Medical services** Hospital, T0590-891010/ 891120, in Pointe-à-Pitre. There are 9 hospitals and 15 clinics. **Post** Post office and telephone building in Pointe-à-Pitre is on Blvd Hanne, crowded, sweltering. Post and phones in Basse-Terre is on rue Dr Pitat, between Dumanoir and Ciceron, smaller but a bit more comfortable than the Pointe-à-Pitre office. Parcel post is a problem and you can usually send parcels of up to 2 kg only. In Pointe-à-Pitre there is an office near the stadium where you can mail parcels of up to 7 kg by air but it is unreliable. Unlike in France, stamps are not sold in bars and tobacconists (although if you buy a postcard or envelope they will probably have a stamp).
Telephone The phone system on Guadeloupe is modern and cellular and internet services are available. **France Télécom** (T1014) provides telecommunications services for Guadeloupe. For local calls you must buy phone cards (*télécartes*, available at post offices and other local agents for use in Télécom phone booths;. There are no coin phones. Many phones will now accept VISA, MasterCard or other credit cards for long distance calls. Operator-assisted calls are higher in cost. AT&T Calling Cards, AT&T Corporate Cards, American Express, Diners Club, Discover/NOVUS, MasterCard and Visa, T0800 990 011 + area code + local number and follow the voice prompts. For BT, T0800 990244, input your account number and PIN, then dial the number you require. For **Canada Direct**, service is available for country-to-country calls with calling cards from **Bell**, MTS, **Aliant**, **SaskTel** and **Telus**, T0800 990016 to reach a Canadian operator directly. For MCI MinutePass, T0800 990019, for **Sprint**, T0800 990087, and follow the voice prompts. **Orange Caraïbes** (T0590- 381300) and **Digicel** (T5965-96420900, French Guiana) provide cellular roaming services.

The Outer Islands

→ *Phone code: 590. Colour map 4, A4. Population: 2,036.*
On Les Saintes, a string of small islands named 'Los Santos' by Columbus, only Terre-de-Haut and Terre-de-Bas are inhabited. The people are mostly descendants of poor Breton colonists who until recently intermarried little with other West Indian races. Sugar cane was never introduced here as a plantation crop and so large numbers of black slaves never came either. The population is predominantly light-skinned and many people have blue eyes. Some still wear the round bamboo and linen hat, the salako, *which the locals call a* chapeau annamite. *A Saintois sailor brought one back from Indo-China (Annan) over a century ago, and everybody took to it. Fishing is still the main occupation, but tourism is increasingly important. The islands are a popular excursion from Guadeloupe and with a good, natural harbour, many small cruise ships spend the day here. Nevertheless, an overnight stay is recommended so that you can appreciate the islanders' traditional way of life, once the day trippers leave at 1600. Public holidays are particularly heavy days with hundreds of day trippers.*

Marie Galante and La Désirade are much quieter, with few visitors. Their traditional way of life is preserved and they have an old-fashioned feel, with glorious, empty beaches and delicious home-made food. ▸▸ *For Sleeping, Eating and other listings see pages 679-682.*

Terre-de-Haut

Terre-de-Haut is the main island visited by tourists (**tourist office** ① *39 rue de la Grande Anse, T0590-995860, www.omtlessaintes.fr/omt*). Irregularly shaped and surprisingly barren, it is about 6 km long and 2 km wide at its widest point. Most of the 1,500 inhabitants live around the Anse Mire, looking across to Ilet à Cabrit where there are the ruins of Fort Joséphine. There are some excellent beaches including **Pont Pierre**, or Pompierre, where snorkelling is good and camping is possible, **Marigot**, **L'Anse du Figuier** (good diving, no shade), **L'Anse Crawen** and **Grand'Anse** (white sand, rougher waters, swimming not allowed). The UCPA sailing school at **Petit Anse** offers sailing or windsurfing courses. Walking on the islands is good, either to the beaches, or to the top of **Le Chameau** (TV mast on top) on Terre-de-Haut's west end (spectacular views of Les Saintes, Marie-Galante, Guadeloupe and Dominica). It's a killer climb, though; it may be only 350 m or so, but it is steep.

An easy trail, **Trace des Crêtes**, starts at Terre-de-Haut (goats can be a nuisance if you decide to picnic). Turn right at the pier, follow the main street about 100 m, turn left at the chapel and follow the road up to Le Marigot (look out for the *sentier du morne morel* sign behind the restaurant on the south side of the bay) and on to the

Terre-de-Haut & Les Saintes

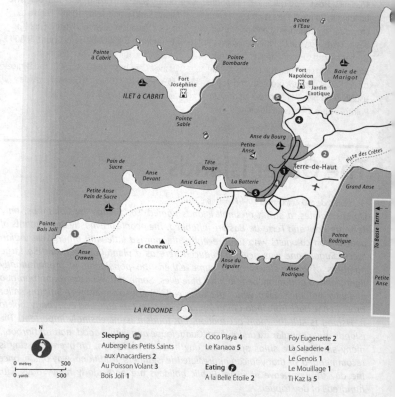

N

| 0 metres | 500 |
| 0 yards | 500 |

Sleeping 🛏
Auberge Les Petits Saints
  aux Anacardiers **2**
Au Poisson Volant **3**
Bois Joli **1**

Coco Playa **4**
Le Kanaoa **5**

Eating 🍴
A la Belle Étoile **2**

Foy Eugenette **2**
La Saladerie **4**
Le Genois **1**
Le Mouillage **1**
Ti Kaz la **5**

beach of Pont Pierre, a lovely golden beach with rocks, **Roches Percées**, in the bay. 677
Boats and diving equipment can be rented at the landing stage. At the end of the
beach the trail leads up the hill where you have a good view of the islands, if you keep
left, one branch of the trail leads to Grand'Anse beach. The pretty 'white' cemetery, La
Cimétière Rose, with paths bordered by shells, is worth visiting is close to the beach
and from here you can walk back to Terre-de-Haut, about 1½ hours in total.
Alternatively, you can walk along Grand'Anse and on to **Pointe Rodriguez** and the
small cove Anse Rodriguez below it.

Fort Napoléon ① *0900-1230 (except 1 Jan, 1 May, 15-16 Aug and 25 Dec), E2.15,
students with identity cards and children 6-12 E2.10*, is high up on Pointe à l'Eau, and
the museum in the fort gives the French view of the decisive sea battle of Les Saintes
(1782 – the English Admiral Rodney defeated and scattered the fleet of France's
commander the Comte de Grasse, who was sailing to attack Jamaica). The fort itself
dates only from the 1840s. The exhibitions are good with interesting models of the
ships and battles. A guide will give you a 30-minute tour (in French) of the main
building. There are exhibits also of local fishing (including a *saintois*, a boat, originally
with a sail, but now diesel-powered) and crafts, a bookshop and drinks on sale.
Around the ramparts is the **Jardin Exotique** which specializes in growing succulents
and includes a wild area where plants native to Les Saintes are grown.

Terre-de-Bas

Terre-de-Bas is home to about 1,500 people, mostly fishermen, but many have left for work in France. Boats land at **Grande Baie** which is a small inlet guarded by a fort and two small statues. You get good views of **La Coche** and **Grand Ilet** (two of the uninhabited islands) on the way across. There is a good little information centre at the dock. Buses will meet the ferry and you can go to the main settlement at **Petite Anse** where there is a fishing port, secondary school for the islands and a pretty little church with a red roof. The beach at Grand Anse is very pleasant and there are a few bars and restaurants nearby (**A La Belle Étoile** – see Eating, below – is actually on the beach). There is a track from Petite Anse to Grand Anse which is a good walk. It is very quiet compared with Terre-de-Haut. Salakos and wood carvings are made locally.

Marie-Galante → *Phone code: 590.*
Colour map 4, A5. Population: 13,463.

Marie-Galante, a small pancake-round, mostly flat island of 158 sq km, 22 km south of Grande-Terre, is simple and old-fashioned but surprisingly sophisticated when it comes to food and drink. It was named by Christopher Columbus after his own ship, the *Santa María La Galante*, and has three settlements. The largest is **Grand-Bourg** in the southwest with a population of around 8,000; **Capesterre**

French Antilles The Outer Islands

is in the southeast and **Saint-Louis** (sugar factory) in the northwest. By Grand-Bourg plage try the *batterie de sirop*, selling a treacle-like sugar cane syrup mixed with rum and lime or with water.

If you want an authentic (and proud of it) island, friendly, but determined to preserve its own way of life, this is it. Information is available from **Office de Tourisme de Marie Galante** ⓘ *T0590-975651, www.ot-mariegalante.com*. There is only one medium-sized hotel. The islanders are resisting further hotel developments preferring *gîtes* and guesthouses. It's a traditional rural way of life, based on sugar cane. Peasant proprietors still take canes to the mill by ox-cart. This makes a good photo, which they don't mind a bit. The beaches, so far almost completely untouched by the tourist flood, are superb. By Capesterre, the **Plage de la Feuillère** has fine sand beaches and is protected by the coral reef offshore. Follow the path north to **Les Galeries**, which are large cliffs eroded by the sea to make a covered walkway over 15 m above sea level. There is a pleasant beach at **Anse de Vieux Fort**, the site of the first settlement on the island in 1648 and of a series of fierce skirmishes between the French and the Amerindians.

The **Trou à Diable** (off the D202) is a massive cave which runs deep into the earth. To visit it, it is essential to have strong shoes, a torch, and a guide. The descent requires ropes and should not be unassisted. The D202 road meets the D201 at La Grande Barre, from where there are views of the north end of the island and to Guadeloupe. On the coast there are limestone cliffs which have been eroded in places to form arches. One is at Gueule Grand Gouffre and another is further east at Caye Plate.

Marie Galante

In the 19th century the island boasted over 100 sugar mills; a few have been restored and may be visited: **Basses, Grand-Pierre, Agapy** and **Murat**. Only at **Bézard**, (around 7 km due north of Capesterre), can you appreciate the glory of a great windmill in full sail. The former plantation houses of **Château Murat** and **Brîlle** ⓘ *museum Mon-Thu 0900-1300, 1500-1800, Sat and Sun 0900-1200, free*, are interesting. Murat gives a good impression of the great 18th-century plantations; below the sweeping lawn lies the old sugar mill with cane-crushing machinery still intact. Behind the house is a walled herb garden. The **Bellevue** rum distillery on the D202 is a cottage industry. The rum (*agricole*, made from sugar cane) is very powerful and you will be invited to taste and buy. You may also be offered bags of brown sugar and dessicated coconut, a surprisingly nice combination. At the **Distillerie Bielle** ⓘ *T0590-979362, Mon-Sat 1000-1200*, you can taste and buy rum as well as ceramic rum flasks made at the pottery *atelier*. The **Distillerie Poisson** ⓘ *T0590-970379, Mon-Sat 0700-1100, free*, in the west on the N9 makes the *Père Labat* rum and is open for visits (also small museum) with tastings of rum and liqueurs. Fascinating old 19th-century machinery, still in use. On the road to Duclos, going north, is the *mare au Punch* (the 'sea of Punch'). The story is that when the revolution came, the slaves, to celebrate, gathered together all the rum they could find and, in this pond, made the biggest bowl of punch the Caribbean had ever seen. Alas, as the display boards indicate, this attractive tale is unlikely, but it's a good story, with underlying truth of the fight against oppression.

La Désirade → *Colour map 4, A5. Population: 1,700.*

La Désirade is an attractive but rather arid island – 10 km east of the Pointe du Chateau on Grande-Terre – whose inhabitants make their living in fishing, sheep- rearing and in cultivating cotton and maize. A 10-km road runs from the airport along the south coast to the east end of the island, where there's a giant cactus plantation. At the northeast end of the island is **Pointe du Mombin** where there is an outstanding view of the coastline. There are excellent beaches, such as at **Grande Anse** and **Souffleur**. Perhaps the nicest is in the east at a village called **Baie-Mahault**, enhanced by a good restaurant/bar (**Chez Céce**) where you can sample dozens of different rum punches. The northern part of the island is rugged, with cliffs against which the Atlantic waves crash, and ravines, savagely beautiful but inhospitable; no one lives here.

Columbus named the island as it was the first land he saw on his second voyage in 1493. Archaeological research has shown evidence of Amerindian settlement but it was uninhabited when Columbus passed by. La Désirade was occupied by the French for the first time in 1725, when all the lepers on Guadeloupe were sent there during an epidemic. In 1930 a leper hospital was built, but was closed in 1954.

Rainfall is very low here and the dry season lasts from January to August. The lack of fresh water has always hampered economic activity. In 1991, however, La Désirade was linked to Grande-Terre underwater with a fresh water supply. A plaque at l'Anse des Galets commemorates this. The dryness and few people have helped wildlife to survive: rare birds, the agouti (a very edible rodent, the size of a small rabbit), and the iguana (also edible).

⊜ Sleeping

On both Terre-de-Haut and Terre-de-Bas there are rooms and houses to rent; tourist office has list of phone numbers, see website Reservations are recommended in peak season, especially Christmas and New Year.

Terre-de-Haut *p676, map p676*
L-A Auberge Les Petits Saints aux

Anacardiers, La Savane, T0590- 995099, www.petitssaints.com. Former mayor's house overlooking town and bay, furnished with French antiques, attractive, intimate, 3 rooms, 3 bungalows, 2 studios/4 suites a/c, clean, pool, sauna, art gallery, good restaurant.

L-A Bois Joli, reached by 10-min boat ride or

5-min scooter ride from town, at the west end of the island on hillside and beach, T0590-995038, www.hotelboisjoli.fr. Gorgeous setting, hotel van transport to town or airport, 23 rooms, 6 bungalows, meal plans, pool, bar, restaurant serving very good food including excellent fish crêpes, 2 beaches, watersports, good snorkelling, Wi-Fi internet access.

AL Coco Playa, Fond de Curé, T0590-924000, www.cocoplaya.com. 10 rooms, 1 suite, breakfast included, pool, restaurant, on the beach

AL Le Kanaoa, Anse Mire, T0590-995136, F0590-995194, kanaoa@wanadoo.fr. 23 rooms and suites, some with kitchenettes and 2 bedrooms, a/c, but rather basic, fair restaurant used by tour groups with sea view, evening entertainment in season, English spoken, beautiful waterfront setting 10 mins' walk from landing jetty, very quiet.

Terre-de-Bas *p677, map p676*

A-B Au Poisson Volant, Le Bourg, T/F0590-998047. 9 rooms, the only hotel, also restaurant.

Marie-Galante *p677, map p678*

There is no shortage of accommodation but most of the properties are small and only have a couple of rooms or apartments. 24-hour advance booking is necessary. The tourist office has a list of places to stay, see website.

L-AL Cap Reva, Plage de la Feuillère, Capesterre, T0590-975000, www.cap-reva .com. On white-sand beach lined with coconut palms, 16 studios sleep 2-3 people, 12 duplex sleep 4-5 with loft room, kitchenettes, pool, ping pong, diving, restaurant, piano bar, excursions by bus, on mountain bikes, quad bikes or horses, baby sitting, packages available.

L-AL Cohoba, at Plage de Folle Anse, 3 km from St Louis, T0590-975050. cohoba@ leaderhotels.gp. 100 rather small rooms, 30 with kitchenettes, some have sitting room with sofa bed sleeping 1, a/c, TV, breakfast included, 2 restaurants, pool, tennis, large conference room, bar, white-sand beach, windsurfing, bicycles for hire.

AL-B Au Village de Ménard, north of St-Louis, 2 km from Vieux-Fort beach on a cliff, T0590-970945, magtour@ outremer.com. 7 bungalows in country

setting with sea view, pool, mountain bikes, English spoken.

AL-B Le Soleil Levant, 42 rue de la Marine, overlooking Capesterre and sea, T0590-973155, www.im-caraibes.com /soleil-levant. On 2 sites, Hauteurs de Capesterre on the hillside overlooking the village, 200 m from the beach, with 8 rooms, 2 apartments and 2 bungalows, pool, or on the waterfront in 2 buildings, 6 rooms in Hotel Bourg de Capesterre and 3 apartments in Résidence Marine. All share same hotel services and facilities.

A-B Etoile de Mer – Chez Séna, Section Les Caps, Capesterre, T0590-974314, www.im-caraibes.com/etoile-de-mer. 4 studio apartments with balcony and sea view to Dominica, kitchenette, 4 guest rooms facing banana plants to the rear, a/c, TV, fridge, communal kitchen and dining area, barbecue.

B Hotel Hajo, Section Bernard, Beaurenom, Capesterre, T0590-973276. 4 rooms, sleep 3, fan, pretty, quiet, restaurant and bar, reservations essential because they only cook if they know you are coming.

C L'Auberge de l'Arbre à Pain, rue Jeanne d'Arc, Grand-Bourg, T0590-977369. 7 rooms, breakfast included, a/c, restaurant and bar.

B Le Belvedère, Brumant, 4 km from Capesterre, 5 km from Grand-Bourg, 2 mins from the beach, T/F0590-973295. 8 rooms, sleep 3, restaurant open for lunch and dinner, Créole seafood, crayfish, bouillabaisse, evening entertainment, welcome cocktail.

B Le Salut, St-Louis, rue La Cimitière, in the town centre south of the pier, T0590-970267. 15 rooms, a/c, restaurant and bar.

B Le Touloulou, T0590-973263, www.letouloulou.com. On the Grand Bourg road, 2 km from Capesterre. Clean, well-equipped bungalows with or without kitchenette, backing directly on to the sea, disco (salsa lessons on Fri) and restaurant attached, menu with local specialities.

La Désirade *p679*

A-B Gîtes Désirada, 150 m from Petite-Rivière beach, T0590-200048, www.desirada-gites.com. Studio apartments for 2-4 people and villa for up to 7, pool, meals and takeaway meals available.

B Le Mirage, Le Désert, T0590-200108, F0590-200745. 7 rooms, restaurant.

B **Les Gîtes de la Grande Source**, rue du Souffleur, T0590-200964, www.antilles-info-tourisme.com/guadeloupe/source.htm. 1-bedroom bungalows with sofabed sleep up to 4, or can be doubled up for larger groups, walking tours arranged, meals available in your bungalow or table d'hôte, sea view.
B **L'Oasis du Désert**, Quartier Désert Saline, T0590-200212. 6 rooms, restaurant, reservations advisable.

🍽 Eating

Terre-de-Haut *p676, map p676*
There is a shortage of water on the island. Home-made ice cream in various tropical fruit flavours is the local speciality, sold on the street as well as in cafés. Home-made coconut rum punches are recommended too, particularly in the little bar on the right-hand side of the *gendarmerie* in front of the jetty. Check beer prices before ordering.
🍴🍴 **Le Mouillage**, waterfront, T0590-995057. Beautiful location with a terrace overlooking the harbour, food a bit expensive.
🍴 **La Saladerie**, at top of steps on road to Fort Napoléon, T0590-995343. Consistently praised for food and service, popular, not always open out of season.
🍴 **Le Gênois**, Le Mouillage, T0590-995945. Popular and convivial with large tables for a family dining experience, food simple but tasty, on water's edge by harbour square.
🍴 **Ti kaz la**, Fonds de Curé, T0590-995763. On the beach, fabulous location dipping your feet in the water, good food, large portions, friendly service.
The *boulangerie* next to the Mairie is open from 0530. The supermarkets are expensive, double French prices. There are a couple of markets every morning on the road towards the post office, good for fresh produce.

Terre-de-Bas *p677, map p676*
🍴🍴🍴 🍴 **A La Belle Étoile**, Grand Anse, T0590-998369. You hardly need to get out of the water to enjoy the food here, from sandwiches to full meals, excellent service and fast.
🍴 **Foy Eugenette**, Grand Anse, T0590-998183. Delicious food, great value for money, lobster, fresh fish and local specialities such as cristophene and accras, have a siesta on the beach afterwards.

🍴 **La Payotte**, Plage de Fifi, Beauséjour, T0590-200129. Small blue and yellow house with lovely view of boats, wonderful fish and seafood and plenty of it, typical cuisine, beach outside for siesta afterwards under the coconut palms.
🍴 **Le Providence**, Baie Mahault, T0590-200359. Créole food cooked by cordon bleu chef, delicious and good value.

🚍 Transport

Terre-de-Haut *p676, map p676*
No public transport after dark.

Air
Daily flights from Pointe-à-Pitre, although only those at weekends are guaranteed to depart as they will only take off if full, 15 mins, Air Caraïbes, T0590-824700, €145 return including taxes, €85 one way. 9-seater planes are used, the 9th seat is up beside the pilot for a great view.

Boat
There are daily ferries from Pointe-à-Pitre (€39 round trip, children €27, plus €0.74 tax) and Trois-Rivières (€22 round trip, children €17). Competition is tough between the ferry companies and you may be approached by the crew to persuade you to take their boat. Some ferries stop at Terre-de-Bas before reaching Terre-de-Haut. Ask where you are. Terre-de-Haut has a new pier, built 2006, for passenger ships, while the pier at Fond de Curé is a freight pier. Many day charters take you to Les Saintes from the marina at Bas du Fort (Gosier), from Saint-François and from Sainte-Anne, about €50 per person.
Ferry companies include: **Deher CTM**, T0590-995068 in Les Saintes, T0590-216951, F0590-822580 in Trois Rivières; **Express des Îles**, T0825-359000, www.express-des-iles.com, from Gare Maritime de Bergevin, **Pointe-à-Pitre**; Transport Maritimes Brudey Frères, T0590-900448, www.brudey-freres.fr, from **Trois Rivières** and **Pointe-à-Pitre**; SMIS (Ouyva & Wapayou), T0590-983008, from Trois Rivières; Comatrile, T0590-222631 (Iguana Beach and Iguana Sun), from St-François and Ste-Anne also runs 2 round trips a week between Les Saintes and Marie-Galante. Les

Saintes is also a port of call on the route to and from Martinique. The ferry between Terre-de-Haut and Terre-de-Bas, **Navette L'Inter**, runs about 5 times a day passing the Pain de Sucre.

Bus
Mini-buses take day trippers all over Terre-de-Haut; tour of the island €10, including to Fort Napoléon.

Cycle and scooter
Several central locations rent bikes and scooters. It is not necessary to hire a scooter, as you can walk to most places. Scooters are banned from the town 0900-1200, 1400-1600 and have to be pushed. At the Mairie (town hall) you can get basic information.

Marie-Galante *p677, map p678*
Air
To get to the island there are regular flights (20 mins) from Pointe-à-Pitre, which is only 43 km away (**Air Caraïbes**, as above). Marie-Galante Aviation, T0590-977702, offers charters and air taxi service.

Boat
Transport Maritimes Brudey Frères, T0590-900448, www.brudey-freres.fr, from **Pointe-à-Pitre** to Grand Bourg (€39 round trip, children €27) usually 3 a day, some via St-Louis, 1½ hrs. **Express des Îles**, T0590-831245, Quai Gatine Gare Maritime, Pointe-à-

Pitre, to Grand-Bourg, also 3 a day, to Saint-Louis Mon-Sat 1245. *Amanda Galante*, a car ferry, T0590-831989, crosses from Pointe-à-Pitre to Saint-Louis. **Express des Îles** offer day tours to Marie-Galante from Pointe-à-Pitre, includes boat trip, visits to beaches, the towns, sugar factories, rum distillery (plus tasting) and other sites (€81 adults, €59 children under 12). You are better off hiring a car or scooter and doing it independently.

Bus
On the island there are buses and taxis.

Car
Self-drive cars can be hired from the airport or in the towns.

La Désirade *p679*
Air
There are daily 10-min air services from Guadeloupe depending on demand (**Air Caraïbes**).

Boat
Services from St-François, Guadeloupe, by *Le Colibri*, T0590-850086, otladesirade@wanadoo.fr, takes 45 mins. Some companies offer day trips with tours and meals.

Road
Taxis/minibuses normally meet incoming flights and boats. There are bicycles and scooters for hire.

Martinique → *Country code: 596. Colour map 4, B5. Population: 392,000.*

Martinique at first glance is a piece of France transported to the tropics, where language and customs have adapted to the climate. There is something for everybody here: a variety of hotels, good beaches, watersports, historical attractions, beautiful scenery, hiking, birdwatching and countless other activities. Tourism is well developed in the south, but a large part of the more mountainous north is taken up by protected rainforest. The scenery is dramatic and very beautiful, with lush rainforest coating the slopes of the mountains and swathes of sugar cane grown on the plain. The volcano, Pelée, last erupted in 1902, when it destroyed the former capital, St-Pierre, killing all but one of its 26,000 inhabitants. ▸▸ *For Sleeping, Eating and other listings, see pages 690-700.*

Ins and outs
Getting there There are several daily flights from Paris, but no direct flights from any other European or North American cities. There are connections using American Eagle from San Juan, Puerto Rico, but a better hub is being developed in St Lucia, using Take

Air Lines, which has a franchise with Air Caraïbes and operates daily flights from St Lucia allowing connections from several US cities and Toronto. Links with neighbouring islands are good, both by air and by sea, so island hopping is easy.
▶ *See Transport, page 698 for further details.*

Getting around There are no buses to the airport (though the Sainte-Anne buses go

Martinique

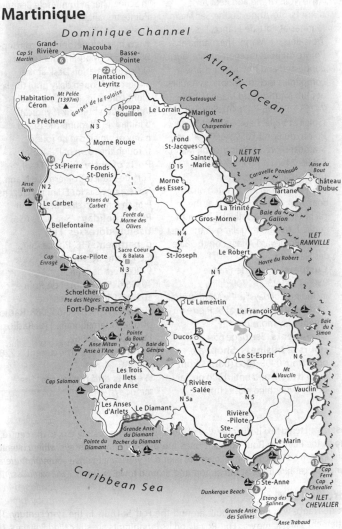

Anse Caritan **2**
Auberge de l'Anse Mitan **3**
Aux Délices de la Mer **4**
Batelière **10**
Calypso **5**
Chanteur Vacances **6**
Chez Julot **7**
Diamant les Bains **8**

Domaine de Belleford **9**
Habitation Lagrange **11**
Karibea Resort Ste-Luce **1**
La Bonne Auberge **12**
La Frégate Bleu **13**
La Nouvelle Vague **14**
Le Cristophe Colomb **15**
Le Nid Tropical **16**

Les Brisants **17**
Le Village de Tartane **18**
Le Village du Diamant **19**
Madras **20**
Marouba Club **21**
Plantation de Leyritz **22**
Primerêve **23**
St Aubin **24**

0 km ⊢——⊣ 2
0 miles ⊢——⊣ 2

Sleeping ⬤
Airport **25**

⁛ Touching down

Anchorages The facilities are among the best in the Caribbean. Anchorages at St-Pierre, Fort-de-France, Anse Mitan, Les Trois-Ilets, Anse Noir, Grand and Petit Anse d'Arlets, Ste-Anne, Cul-de-Sac Marin. Marinas at Fort-de-France, Les Trois-Ilets, Le Marin. The marina at Pointe du Bout is reported safe, but congested and hot. Major charter companies include Moorings Antilles at Club Nautique du Marin (T0596-747539, F0596-747644), Sun Sail (Soleil et Voile, Capitainerie Marina Pointo du Bout, T0596-660914), and Stardust (Port de Plaisance du Marin, T0596-749817, F0596-749812). Many other smaller companies.

For those looking to hitch on a boat, look at noticeboards at the Yacht Clubs, especially the bar at the Public Jetty and refuelling at the west end of Boulevard Alfassa on the Baie des Flamands.

Customs In Fort-de-France 0800-1100, 1300-1700 daily, including holidays; at Le Marin from 0730 until lunchtime, at St Pierre on Wednesday morning.

Documents See page 654.

Hours of business Shops are open from 0900-1800 (**banks** from around 0730) and until 1300 on Sat. Nearly everything closes from 1200-1500 and on Sun.

Tourist information
Martinique Tourist Office CMT (Comité Martiniquais du Tourisme) is in Schoelcher at Immeuble Beaupré Pointe de Jaham 97233, T0596-616177, www.martiniquetourisme.com, open 0800-1630, Mon-Fri. The Tourist Office Information Desk at the airport stays open daily until the last flight comes in. There are local information bureaux (Syndicat d'Initiative) all round the island, many of which can be found through the town hall (Mairie).

Ports of entry (French Flag) Fort-de-France, St-Pierre, Le Marin. No fees or visas for EU or US citizens. French forms to clear in and out.

Public holidays See page 656.

Useful addresses Fire department: T18. **Police**: T17. **Gendarmerie**, rue Victor Sévère, 97200 Fort-de-France, T0596-635151. **Hôtel de Police**: T0596-553000. **Sea rescue**: T0596-639205, 0596-632088. **Radio phone** (international), T10. **Radio taxi**: T0596-636362.

Voltage The electric current is 220 volts AC.

Weights and measures The metric system.

close), a metered taxi is the only way of getting into town, costing €15 to the centre, or €39 to the Point du Bout hotels. Buses are best for short journeys while collective taxis, known as **Taxicos,** run all over the island. If you want to drive yourself, there are numerous car hire firms at the airport and around town. ▶▶ See page 698 for details.

Fort-de-France

Fort-de-France was originally built around the Fort St-Louis in the 17th century. The settlement's first name was Fort-Royal and its inhabitants are still called Foyalais. The city of today consists of a crowded centre bordered by the waterfront and sprawling suburbs extending into the surrounding hills and plateaux. The bars, restaurants, and shops give a French atmosphere quite unlike that of other Caribbean cities. Traffic is very dense. Most people live in the suburbs and even the discos are out of the old town centre, which is deserted at weekends after Saturday midday. However, a new commercial centre is underway downtown, and improvements to the waterfront are almost complete.The port is to the east of the town centre, where the **Baie du**

Carenage houses the naval base, yacht club, cargo ships and luxury cruise liners.

The impressive **Fort St-Louis** still functions as a military base. Built in Vauban style, it dominates the waterfront. It is still an active military base and has been closed to the public after the 9/11 terrorist attack in New York. Adjacent to the fort is **La Savane**, the old parade ground, a 5-ha park planted with palms, tamarinds, and other tropical trees and shrubs, is having an elegant makeover. The park contains statues of two famous figures: **Pierre Belain d'Esnambuc**, the leader of the first French settlers on Martinique, and **Empress Josephine** (now beheaded by *Independentistes*), first wife of Napoléon Bonaparte, who was born on the island.

The **Bibliothèque Schoelcher** ① *T0596-702667, Mon-Thu 0830-1730, Fri-Sat 0830-1200*, is situated on the corner of rue Victor Sévère and rue de la Liberté, across the road from the Savane. Schoelcher (1804-1893), who devoted his life to the abolition of slavery, gave much of his library to Martinique, but most was burned in the fire of the town centre in 1890. The building to house the collection was commissioned, but not built, before the fire. It was designed by Henry Picq, a French architect married to a woman from Martinique. The Eiffel engineering company constructed it in iron, shipped it to the island and it opened in 1893. On the exterior you can see the names of freedom campaigners, including John Brown, of the USA, William Wilberforce, of the UK and Toussaint

Fort-de-France

Sleeping	Impératrice 1
Balisier 5	La Malmaison 2
Carib 4	Un Coin de Paris 3

0 metres 100
0 yards 100

Louverture, of Haiti. Today it still functions as a library and regularly holds exhibitions.

Just along the rue de la Liberté towards the seafront is the **Musée Départemental d'Archéologie Précolombienne** ⓘ *To596-715705, Mon-Fri 0900-1300, 1430-1700, Sat 0900-1200, €1.50.* It contains relics of the Arawak and Carib Indians: pottery, statuettes, bones, reconstructions of villages, maps, etc. Worth a visit. In the centre of town, in the Square of Seigneur Romero, rue Schoelcher, there is a second chance to see the architecture of Henri Picq with the **Cathedral of St-Louis** which towers above the Fort-de-France skyline. This, too, is mainly of iron, in a romanesque-byzantine style. The arms of past bishops, in stained glass, give colour to the choir. In a beautiful Créole villa dating back to 1887, is the **Musée Régional d'Histoire et d'Ethnographie de la Martinique** ⓘ *10 Blvd Générale de Gaulle, opposite Atrium Theatre, To596-728187, Mon, Wed-Fri 0800-1700, Tue 1400-1700, Sat 0800-1230, €6 for adults, €1 for children and students.* It is a modern museum, opened in 1999, and strong on the origins, customs and traditions of the people of Martinique.

The **Parc Floral et Culturel** (which includes the **Galerie de Géologie et de Botanie** and the **Exotarium**) ⓘ *Mon-Fri 0900-1230, 1430-1730, €1.75 adults, €0.50 children, To596-706841,* is a shady park containing two galleries, one of which concentrates on the geology of the island, the other on the flora, and mid-19th-century wooden barracks now housing 11 workshops for local artisans. Almost 2,800 species of plants have been identified in Martinique and the Parc Floral has a very good selection. Next to the Parc Floral are a feature of Fort-de-France not to be missed, the **markets**. The fishmarket is by the Madame River, facing the Place José Martí, where fishermen unload from their small boats or *gommiers.* Close by is one of several markets selling fruit, vegetables and flowers as well as exotic spices. The markets hum with activity from 0500 to sunset, but are best on Friday and Saturday.

The northwest coast

The coastal road heading north through Schoelcher from Fort-de-France hugs the coast, zigzagging north through **Case-Pilote** (named after a friendly Carib chief), where there is a 17th-century church. It then passes through several fishing villages and is flanked by beaches that gradually become blacker with volcanic sand. **Le Carbet** is where Columbus is presumed to have landed (monument). A *carbet* was the great meeting house of the Caribs. There are several good restaurants, mostly fish, on the beach. **Habitation Anse Latouche** ⓘ *To596-781919, Mon-Sat 1000-1600, €2, children 7-12 €1.50, or €5.80 and €2 for joint entry to Balata Gardens,* is at the end of Carbet village on the coast. The ruins of a 17th-century sugar plantation are surrounded by a beautiful garden focusing on local flowers and shrubs and an exhibition of butterflies. There is not much left of the main house, having been destroyed by the 1902 volcanic eruption (see below), but there is a beautiful viaduct from a dam to a big waterwheel which used to drive the sugar mill. At the popular beach of **Anse Turin** just north of Le Carbet, is the small **Gauguin Museum** ⓘ *To596-782266, daily 0900-1730, €3.* The artist stayed at Anse Turin during 1887 before he went to Tahiti. The museum has copies (mostly photographic) of letters, sketches and some reproductions of his work. Nothing is original. Local artists' paintings and ceramics are sometimes on sale. There is an interesting section on the local traditional women's costume and its elements, *la grande robe, le madras,* and *le foulard,* the head-tie which was knotted to indicate how engaged the wearer's affections were.

St-Pierre

To the north of Carbet is the famous **St-Pierre**. The town is well worth a visit and is an eerie reminder of destructive natural forces in the Caribbean. The modern village is built on the ruins of the former capital of Martinique, which was destroyed by a cloud of molten volcanic ash when **La Montagne Pelée** erupted on 8 May 1902. As the cultural and economic capital, the town was known as the 'Petit Paris' of the West Indies. Out of (also known as Sylbaris), a casual labourer who had been thrown drunk into a cell for the night. Today his small cell is one of the ruins that visitors can still see. The prison is beside the remains of the once splendid and celebrated theatre of St-Pierre on rue Victor Hugo. You can see the broad sweep of steps up to the entrance, the huge stage area, the first floor boxes and the rusting remains of the electric stage lighting. In the **Musée Volcanologique Franck-Perret** ① *To596-781516, daily 0900-1700, €1.50*, is an interesting collection of objects (mostly by Perret, an American) and documents evoking life before 1902 and remains from the disaster: household metal and glass objects charred and deformed by the extreme heat, photographs and volcanology displays. The bridge over the Rivière Roxelane, built in 1766, leads to the oldest part of the town, the Quartier du Fort. The ruins of the church are most moving.

> *On 6 March 1806, the first ice creams ever eaten in the tropics were enjoyed at St-Pierre. A Boston entrepreneur, Frederic Tudor, whose mother was French, had the ice cut in huge blocks from frozen Massachusetts rivers, packing 130 tons in sawdust and straw. Enough survived to lead to a world-wide export trade which made him rich.*

A new attraction on the road north out of St-Pierre is **Le Centre de Découverte des Sciences de la Terre** ① *To596-528242, www.cdst.org, Wed-Sun 0900-1700, or 1000-1800 in July-Aug and school holidays, adults over 26 €5, 13-25 €3.50, children 6-10 €2.50, discounts for family tickets, groups, schools, pensioners and the disabled*, part scientific, part educational, part tourist site. Permanent and temporary exhibitions include information on volcanoes, earthquakes and hurricanes.

The next village on the coastal road is the picturesque fishing village of **Le Prêcheur**. Madame de Maintenon, who married Louis XIV lived here. The three bells outside the church date from that time. The road then continues towards the spectacular beach of **Anse Céron** where the sand seems to be at its blackest. A rock called the Pearl juts out from the sea which is roughish but swimming is possible. It is a wild and beautiful beach, a pleasant change from the calm, white-sand tourist beaches in the south. The coast road peters out here, only a trail continues into the mountains to the north. Turn inland to **Habitation Céron** ① *To596-529453, daily 0930-1700, see Eating, below*, a plantation where the early sugar buildings are largely intact and there is an attractive botanic walk taking you to a huge 300-year-old Zamana tree covering more than half a hectare. There are huge ponds where succulent crayfish are raised. These, with homegrown fruit and vegetables make an excellent three-course lunch for €25 including a rum punch.

It is possible to follow a track 18 km through the rainforest around the northern coast, but a guide is essential. The first 20 minutes on a concrete road are discouraging, but once in the forest the path is cooler and the views beautiful. At the extreme

> *Watch out for fer-de-lance snakes and bilharzia in the streams.*

north of the island is another small fishing village, **Grande Rivière** set in breathtaking scenery characteristic of this part of the island; plunging cliffs covered with the lush vegetation of the rainforest. The island of Dominica faces the village from across the sea. Winding roads lead through the mountains to the next village, **Macouba**, perched on top of a cliff.

The tropical rainforest and La Montagne Pelée

La Route de la Trace winds through the tropical rainforest on the slopes of the Pitons du Carbet from Fort-de-France to **Morne Rouge** on the southern slope of Montagne Pelée. The town was hit by a second eruption of Pelée on 20 August 1902. At **Le Jardin de la Pelée** ① *To596-524201*, on the hill above the town, there is a fine display of local flora, well labelled, and information on the volcano. The Parc Naturel forest itself is

● *It was on Martinique at the end of the 17th century that the Dominican friar, Père Labat, perfected the process of making rum.*

French Antilles Martinique

truly magnificent, covering the sides of the steep, inland mountains (Les Pitons de Carbet and Pelée) with a bewildering array of lush, green vegetation that stretches for miles. Giant bamboo, mountain palms, chestnut and mahogany trees, over a thousand species of fern and many climbing and hanging parasitic plants and orchids are examples of rainforest vegetation.

At **Balata,** not far from the capital along the Route de la Trace is the bizarre sight of the **Sacré Coeur,** a smaller version of Paris's votive Sacré-Coeur de Montmartre, perched high up in the forest. A little further along the road is the **Le Jardin de Balata** ① *To596-644873, Fo596-647340, daily 0900-1700, €5.80, children aged 7-12 €2, includes entry to Habitation Anse Latouche, signs are in French*, with superb views across the Baie de Fort-de-France to Trois-Ilets. The gardens feature a collection of 3,000 species with magnificent anthuriums, numerous hummingbirds and brilliant green lizards.

La Montagne Pelée is reached via a track branching off the Route de la Trace, between Morne Rouge and Ajoupa-Bouillon, where there is a delightful garden-park, **Les Ombrages Botaniques** ① *0900-1700, E2.10, children E1.10*. From the car park at the foot of the volcano there is a view of the Atlantic Coast, Morne Rouge and the bay of St-Pierre. The mountain air is deliciously fresh and cool even at the foot of the volcano. Not far away are **Les Gorges de la Falaise,** a series of small gorges along 3 km of the Falaise River, wonderful for swimming in, accessible only by following the course of the river on foot. Much of the walk is actually wading in the water and you clamber over waterfalls. The local **Syndicat d'Initiative** ① *Ajoupa-Bouillon, To596-533287*, organizes guided tours up the river (€6.50 including waterproof pack and fruit juice).

North coast

The area of **Basse-Pointe** is the pineapple cultivation area of the island, where huge fields of spikey pineapple tops can be seen. Basse-Pointe is an old settlement with a late 17th-century church and a good view of the cliffs from the cemetery. Inland from here is **Plantation Leyritz** ① *To596-785392, daily 1000-1700, €2.50, children under 12 free*, a former plantation, complete with slave houses and machinery. The 18th-century owner's house is now an elegant hotel where the French government has entertained foreign presidents. You can walk round the gardens and eat in what was once the sugar boiling house. There is also the Musée de Poupées Végétales, an exhibition of tiny tableaux featuring dolls made from plants and vegetables, exploiting the colours and textures of tropical leaves.

From the N1 road along the northeast coast tempting beaches with crashing waves are visible, but the Atlantic Coast is too dangerous for swimming, except at **Anse Azérot,** just south of **Sainte-Marie**. To the north is **Fond St-Jacques** ① *To596-691012, Mon-Fri 0800-1700, Sat 0900-1200, €2.50 adults, €1 children*, a cultural centre also known as the Musée de Père Labat, which used to be a Dominican monastery and sugar plantation. Buildings date from 1689 and at its height the Dominicans utilized 1,000 slaves. It was here that Père Labat perfected the distilling of rum. His memoirs are a prime source of information on plantation life. Modern art exhibitions are also held at the centre. Nearby, **Musée du Rhum Saint-James** ① *St James Distillery, To596-693002, Mon-Fri 0900-1800, Sat-Sun 0900-1300, free*, explains the process and history of rum production, and rum tasting. Northeast, above Sainte-Marie, is the **Musée de la Banane**① *Mon-Sat 0900-1700, Sun in winter 0900-1700, Sun in summer 0900-1300, €4.60 adults, €2.50 children*, a new museum on a working estate, Habitation Limbé. You can visit the former plantation house which contains the exhibition telling you all you ever wanted to know about bananas, the working banana packaging plant from where the fruit are exported, shops in former workers' huts and walk through gardens of tropical flowers and a variety of banana plants.

Caravelle peninsula

The seafront at **La Trinité** is a grand promenade with modern and 19th-century

buildings and monuments, which looks out onto the **Presqu'île de la Caravelle**, where
the vegetation is scrubby but the scenery is gently interesting. The peninsula has
beaches at **Tartane** (the only village on the Caravelle), Anse l'Étang (the best, surfing
possible) and **Anse du Bout**. It is an area protected by the **Parc Naturel of Martinique**;
several well-marked paths criss-cross the peninsula so that visitors can enjoy the
varied flora and fauna. It is also possible to visit the historic ruins of the **Château
Dubuc** ① *To596-474548, daily 0830-1700, €2.50, children €1*, and various buildings
that belonged to the Dubuc family, including slave smugglers and privateers.

Southeast coast

From the Caravelle peninsula the Atlantic coast is characterized by deep, protected,
shallow, sandy bays, good for swimming, surfing and sailing and innumerable islets
offshore. The road runs southeast through Le Robert and Le François to the more
mountainous area around **Le Vauclin** where the main activity is fishing. There are
some interesting art-deco buildings from the 1920s on its steep streets. The
Baignoire de Josephine has sand-banks and is featured on local boat trips. **Pointe
Faula** is a very safe beach, with dazzling white sand and shallow water. To the south
of Vauclin a road leads to Anse Macabou, a group of impressive white-sand beaches.
A trip inland from Vauclin takes you to Le St-Esprit, worth visiting for the **Musée des
Arts et Traditions Populaires** ① *Mon-Sat 0900-1230, 1400-1700, €4.60 adults,
€1.50 children under 16*, near the local marketplace which exhibits furniture,
glassware, pottery and crafts indigenous to the area.

South Martinique

The small village of **Les Trois-Ilets**, across the bay from Fort-de-France, has a charming
main square and is surrounded by tourist attractions. Empress Josephine, born Marie
Joseph Rose Tascher de la Pagerie, was baptized in the church on the square. Her
mother is buried here and the church, restored by Napoléon III, is a shrine to the
Napoleonic legend. Even more so is **Le Domaine de la Pagerie**
① *To596-683834, Fo596-683841 Tue-Fri 0900-1730, Sat-Sun
0900-1300, 1430-1730, €3, €1 children*, the family's sugar
plantation, about 4 km from the village. Josephine was probably
born here in 1763, and lived here until she was 16. In 1766 a
hurricane blew away the graceful plantation house and the family
lived above the sugar boiling house. The ruins can be seen and, in
the renovated kitchen, a stone building, there is an excellent collection of furniture,
documents and portraits. At Pointe Vatable, 2 km east of Trois-Ilets, is the sugar cane
museum, **La Maison de la Canne** ① *To596-683204, Tue-Sun 0900-1730, €3, children
€1*, which uses documents, machinery and superb models to illustrate the history of
the Martiniquan sugar industry. Recommended; guided tours are available.

Ferries – vedettes – every 15 minutes Fort-de-France to Pointe du Bout, three companies, tickets valid on all ferries, bicycles at no extra charge.

A short bus ride from Trois-Ilets is the tourist complex of **Pointe du Bout**, directly
opposite Fort-de-France. There is a marina, a Créole village, where some of the shops,
cafés, bars, restaurants and souvenir stands can be found, discos, sports and a
conglomeration of luxury hotels. The first beach after stepping off the ferry is a crowded
strip of sand in front of the **Hotel Meridien**, almost completely covered with deckchairs
for hire. Perhaps preferable is the beach at **Anse Mitan** (ferry from Fort-de-France), a
five-minute walk away, where there are numerous reasonably priced restaurants and
bars. **Anse à l'Ane**, a little way along the coast to the west is quieter and has a pleasant
atmosphere. **Grande Anse** is a magnificent beach, although it does get crowded at
weekends. Just south of the nearby pretty village **Anse d'Arlets** (ferry from
Fort-de-France) and around the **Pointe du Diamant** is **Le Diamant**. This is an idyllic
golden-sand beach stretching for 4 km along the south coast and dominated by the
famous **Rocher du Diamant** (Diamond Rock). This huge 176-m rock, of volcanic origin, is
about 4 km out to sea and was occupied by the English during the Napoleonic Wars.

Island of three queens

Martinique was historically the aristocrat of the French Antilles, looking down on the more bourgeois Guadeloupais. Josephine, the first wife of Napoléon I was born at Trois-Ilets. Her cousin, Aimée Dubuc de Rivery, was kidnapped on the high seas, and sold to the Sultan of Turkey, becoming one of his favourite wives, and mother of his successor. Madame de Maintenon spent much of her youth in the island: later she secretly married Louis XIV. Thus, to some, Martinique was known as 'the island of three queens'.

They stationed four cannon and about 20 sailors there in 1804 before the French reconquered it 1½ years later. Negotiate with a fisherman if you want to visit.

Inland and to the east of Diamant is the town of **Rivière-Pilote**, the largest settlement in the south of the island, with the **Mauny Rum Distillery** ① *T0596-626208, Mon-Fri 0930-1730, Sat 0900-1300, free guided tours*. The famous **Cléry cock-fighting pit** ① *T0596-626169, Sun afternoon*, stages regular mongoose-snake fights. The largest marina on the island is at **Le Marin**, which boasts a very fine 18th-century Jesuit church. Southwards are long white-sand beaches lined with palm groves, and calm clear sea.

At **Sainte-Anne** there is a long public beach backed by a pleasant promenade park. The water is calm, ideal for toddlers and there is shade from trees overhanging the sea in places. A former **Club Med Resort** is closed for renovation until late 2005. There is a wide selection of lively bars and restaurants and all types of watersports equipment. Ferries sail from Fort-de-France, 2½ to 3½ hours. There is a Jesuit church of 1766 opposite the jetty.

The road heading east from Marin leads to the beach at **Cap Chevalier**, a popular family beach at weekends. Among others along the barrier reef, the **Ilet Chevalier**, a bird sanctuary, is visible from here. At the southernmost tip of the island is the famous **Grande Anse des Salines** and the beaches of **Dunkerque, Baham** and **Anse Trabaud**, all of which are remarkably attractive. Inland from Anse Trabaud lies the salt marsh and the forest petrified by former lava flow. Birdwatching is good at the **Étang des Salines** and in the sandy marshes around the Baie des Anglais.

Sleeping

The following are useful websites: www.handicaptourisme.net, and www.martiniquetourisme.com, website of the Martinique Tourism Committee.

Information and reservations for around 100 small and medium-sized hotels, grouped under the name **Relais Créoles** can be made through the main **Centrale de Réservation**, Immeuble le Beaupré, Point de Jaham, 97233 Schoelcher, T 0596-616177, centrale@martiniquetourisme.com.

The tourist office at the airport is helpful and will help you get a room for your first night if you have not booked beforehand. Alternatively, for *gîtes* and country guesthouses, contact the **Fédération** Martiniquaise des Offices de Tourisme et Syndicat d'Initiative, Maison du Tourisme Vert, 9 Blvd du Général de Gaulle, BP 1122, 97248 Fort-de-France Cédex, T0596-631854, F0596-701716, or *Gîtes de France*, T0596-737474. Logis Vacances Antilles also offers rooms in private homes, as well as holiday studios and houses, T0596-631291.

Generally, prices are high, but there are some bargains at the best resort hotels, especially out of season, which can work out cheaper than other inferior hotels nearer Fort-de-France. The Sofitel/Accor hotels often offer up to 40% off; book online at www.accorhotels.com.

Some hotels add 10% service charge

and/or 5% government tax to the bill. The big resort hotels are clustered around the Pointe de Bout, a short trip of a few mins across the bay of Fort-de-France.

Fort-de-France *p684, map p685*

LL-L Batelière, 20 rue des Alizés, Schoelcher, on the outskirts of Fort-de-France, T0596-614949, reservationbateliere@fram.fr. Pool, tennis courts, gym, disco, conference facilities, restaurant, bars, casino, very fine hotel.

L-AL Karibea Squash Hotel, 3 Blvd de la Marne, T0596-728080, www.karibea.com. 108 modern rooms, pool, 3 squash courts, gym, dancing room, saunas, jacuzzi, billards, conference facilities, impersonal, concrete ambience, but friendly staff.

AL Impératrice, 15 rue de la Liberté, T0596-630682, F0596-726630. Decor and architecture, apparently unchanged since it was built in 1957.

A La Malmaison, rue de la Liberté, opposite the Savane, T0596-639085. Good and clean, spacious. Lively bar and restaurants frequented by a young crowd.

A Le Gommier, 3 rue Jacques Cazotte, T0596-718855, F0596-730696. One of the oldest buildings in town. Clean spacious rooms and good continental breakfasts, friendly management.

B Airport, Ducos, T0596-560183. 6 rooms if you have to stop over at the airport, basic a/c, hot water, no restaurant.

B Balisier, 21 rue Victor Hugo, T/F0596-714654. Very centrally located with view over the port, good value.

B Carib, 9 rue du Matouba, T0596-601985. A/c, wrought-iron beds, hardwood floors, very clean and appealing, good location.

B Un Coin de Paris, rue Lazare Carnot, T0596-700852, F0596-630951. Small, friendly and cheap.

Youth hostels

Fédération des Oeuvres Laiques (FOL), head office at 31 rue Perrinon, Fort de France, T0596-635022, F0596-638367, has a hostel (B-C) along the Route de Didier, rue de Prof Raymond Garcia, T0596-640410. It is several kilometres from the town centre and difficult to find. No public transport in evenings, taxis can make staying here expensive. Rooms sleep 2 or 4 with shower and toilet, basic.

LL-AL Marouba Club, Carbet, T0596-780021, F0596-780565. Apartments and bungalows, pool, disco, meal plans.

B La Nouvelle Vague, within easy reach of the ruined town of St-Pierre, T0596-781434. 5 rooms over bar, overlooks beach.

B Le Cristophe Colomb, Carbet, T0596-780538, F0596-780642. On beach, good value.

North coast *p688, map p683*

LL Habitation Lagrange, Le Marigot, T0596-536060, www.habitationlagrange.com. 16 rooms, 1 suite, 4-poster beds, terraces, luxury, in tropical gardens, 18th-century buildings, decorated in colonial style, private, romantic, beautiful pool, tennis, superb restaurant, in the rainforest, 20 mins from beach. Under the same management is L'Ilets Oscar, a villa on a little private island just offshore from the François marina, for unbeatable privacy and luxury.

AL-A Plantation de Leyritz, Basse-Pointe, T0596-785392, www.karibea.com. Former plantation house in beautiful grounds with lots of insects because of all the fruit trees and water, glamorous accommodation, excellent restaurant serving local specialities, efficient and friendly service, pool, tennis courts, health spa, disco.

C Chanteur Vacances, Grand-Rivière, T0596-557373. Simple, clean hotel, 7 rooms, shared facilities, restaurant.

Caravelle peninsula *p688, map p683*

AL Le Village de Tartane, near Tartane, T0596-580633, F0596-635332. Bungalows with kitchenette around pool.

AL-A Hôtel Primerêve, Anse Azérot, just south of Ste Marie, T0596-694040, F0596-690937. 20 rooms, 80 suites, new hotel on hillside, elegant, 5-min walk to superb beach, secluded cove, pool, good restaurant, tennis, snorkelling, easy access to rainforest.

AL-A St Aubin, on the old NI, near Trinité, within easy reach of the Caravelle peninsula, T0596-693477, F0596-694114. A magnificent colonial-style hotel, once a plantation house, splendid location, views and exterior, but interior badly damaged by 1960s refurbishment, 15 a/c rooms.

A Madras, Tartane, T0596-583395, F0596-583363. On the beach, spotless rooms, seaview or road view, restaurant.

LL-A La Frégate Bleue, Cap Ferré,
T0596-545466, www.fregatebleue.com. 7
spacious, elegant seaview rooms decorated
with antiques, Persian rugs, 4-poster beds,
kitchenettes, terraces, charming hilltop site,
gingerbread trimmings, helpful,
English-speaking staff.

AL-A Les Brisants, T0596-543257,
F0596-546913, at François, provides good
Créole cuisine.

A-B Chez Julot, rue Gabriel Perí, Vauclin,
T0596-744093. Modest but pleasant hotel,
one street back from foreshore road, a/c,
restaurant, bar.

South Martinique *p689, map p683*

LL-AL Hôtel Anse Caritan, just south of
Ste-Anne on sandy beach, T0596-767412,
caritan.direction@wanadoo.fr. 96 rooms with
views across to Diamond Rock, a/c, terraces,
kitchenettes, phone, pool, restaurant,
watersports and excursions arranged.

L-AL Domaine de Belleford, 97227
Ste-Anne, T0596-769232, F0596-769140. 186
rooms and suites in 5 sections, 500 m from
beach, popular with Europeans, terraces,
kitchenettes, 4 pools, 2 restaurants, bar,
boutiques, car rental.

L-AL Karibea Resort Ste-Luce, formerly 3
hotels, Amyris, Amandiers and Caribia, on
two beaches, Ste-Luce, T0596-621200,
F0596-621210, www.karibea.com. 3-star, a
total of 300 rooms, suites and apartments,
a/c, fridge, TV, phone, of which some are
wheelchair accessible, all amenities, very
nice.

AL Calypso, Les Hauts du Diamant,
T0596-764081, hotel.calypso@wanadoo.fr,
500 m from beach, walking distance to
village. 60 rooms and suites in 11 buildings,
superb views of Diamant Rock, pool, bar,
restaurant, car rental.

AL Le Village du Diamant, T0596-764189,
le-village-du-diamant@wanadoo.fr. Basic,
beachside bungalows, rooms or apartments
for rent.

AL-A Diamant les Bains, T0596-764014,
diamantlesbains@wanadoo.fr. Fine views
over swimming pool and sea.

AL-A Auberge de l'Anse Mitan,
T0596-660112, F0596-660105. A friendly,
family-run hotel with apartments and rooms.

A Aux Délices de la Mer, Ste-Luce,

T0596-625012. Offers fishing amongst other
activities, only 5 rooms, Créole restaurant.

A La Bonne Auberge, Les Trois llets,
T0596-660155, F0596-660450. Basic but
clean, offering underwater fishing and
watersports.

A-B Le Nid Tropical, Anse à l'Ane,
T0596-683130, F0596-684743. Rents studios
and has a lively beach bar and restaurant,
Also camping, see below.

Camping

Camping can be done almost everywhere in
Martinique. Campsites are available in the
mountains, forests and on many beaches
(although indiscriminate camping is not
permitted).

Tropicamp at Gros Raisins Plage, Ste Luce,
T0596-624966. One of several companies
with full camping services, including hot
showers.

Nid Tropical at Anse a l'Ane near Trois llets,
T0596-683130. Another comfortable camp
with showers and toilets.

There is also a campsite at Vauclin on the
southeast Atlantic coast, T0596-744040, and
one at Pointe Marin near the public beach of
Ste Anne, T0596-767279. A nominal fee is
charged for facilities.

For details, call the **Office National des
Forets**, Fort-de-France, T0596-713450. You
can rent tents from **Chanteur Vacances**, 65
rue Perrinon, Fort-de-France, T0596-716619.

● Eating

The small booklet, *Ti Gourmet Martinique*,
gives many restaurants, with details and
prices. Sampling the French and Créole
cuisine is one of the great pleasures of
visiting Martinique. A meal at a decent
restaurant without wine would be €5-11,
depending on the venue and the menu. For
a description of local food, see page 655.

Fort-de-France *p684, map p685*
Good snackbars and cafés serve various
substantial sandwiches and *menus du jour*.
The area around **Place Clemenceau** has lots
of scope. In the **market** at Fort-de-France are
small kiosks selling Créole *menu du jour* for
€5 including dessert and drink, other meals
also served, with tablecloths and flowers on
table. As in France, there are *traiteurs* opening

up, offering stylish takeaway meals which you select at the shop, helpful to vegetarians. Ask for the latest list at the tourist office. The place to head for in the evening when these eateries close, is the **Blvd Chevalier de Ste-Marthe** next to the Savane. Here, every evening until late, vans and caravans serve delicious meals to take away, or to eat at tables under canvas awnings accompanied by loud zouk music. The scene is bustling and lively, in contrast to the rest of the city at night-time and the air is filled with wonderful aromas. Try *lambis* (conch) in a sandwich (€1.50) or on a *brochette* (like a kebab) with rice and salad (€3). Paella and *Colombo* are good buys (€4.50) and the crêpes whether sweet or savoury are delicious.

††-† **Au Traiteur Gourmet**, 185 Blvd de la Pointe des Nègres, T0596-615411. A high quality restaurant with service described as '*formidable*'.

††-† **La Crêperie**, 4 rue Garnier Pagès, T0596-606209. Closed Sat midday, Sun. For crêpes and salads. Simple, nothing special.

††-† **Le Vieux Milan**, 60 Av des Caraïbes, T0596-603531. Closed Sat, Sun. Italian atmosphere, excellent pizza €5-8.

† **Kowossol**, behind the Parc Floral on rue de Royan, T0596-631237. A tiny vegetarian café which serves a cheap and healthy *menu du jour*. The pizzas and the fruit juice especially delicious – try *gingembre* (ginger) or *ananas* (pineapple).

† **Le Chinatown**, 20 rue Victor Hugo, T0596-718262. Mon-Fri lunch. One of several serving Vietnamese and Chinese food.

† **Le Lem**, 124 Blvd Général-de-Gaulle, T0596-637249. Open until 2100. Superior fast food at low prices and a young crowd. It also stays open later than many restaurants that close in the evenings and on Sun.

† **Le Xuandre**, rue Vincent Placoly, T0596-615470. Evenings only, closed Mon. Vietnamese food.

Northwest coast *p686, map p683*

†††† **Le Trou Crabe**, Le Coin, at beginning of village, Le Carbet, T0596-780434, F0596-780514. Open daily except Sun evenings. Beach restaurant, rather smart, French and Créole cuisine, offers Lyonnais specialities as well as lobster and seafood, quality of food and service varies.

†††-†† **Au Tan Lontan**, Place Bertin, St-Pierre, T0596-783959. Traditional Créole cuisine of a high standard, specialities include lobster, conch, prawns, served with great christophene. Reservations advised.

†††-†† **Habitation Céron**, see page 687, T0596-529453. 0930-1700 all year except Christmas Day. The restaurant specializes in fresh crayfish, raised in huge ponds on the plantation. Eat under cover or in open air. Pleasant lunch stop after a tour of the area.

†† **Chez Ginette**, Les Abymes, on the coast, north of St-Pierre, T0596-529028. Fri-Wed. Simple menu but everything beautifully cooked and served with the personal touch of Ginette. Not cheap, but people come all the way from the south to eat here.

†† **La Cabane des Pêcheurs**, Le Carbet, on the beach, T0596-780702. Tasty seafood and exotic atmosphere, reservations advised as it is very popular, friendly staff.

††-† **Grain d'Or**, Le Carbet, T0596-780691. Open daily. Spacious, airy restaurant, good spot to sample Martinique's seafood.

††-† **L'Imprévu**, Le Carbet, on the beach, T0596-780102, F0596-780866. Daily except Sun and Mon evenings. Créole musical entertainment Fri evening except during Lent, very local, excellent dinner of Créole specialities including shark, lobster, 3 courses and house wine from €16.

† **Antonio Beach**, on the Mouillage Beach, rue Gabriel Perry, St-Pierre, T0596-781736. 1000-1500, 1830-2230. Fresh, local crayfish.

† **Kout Flanm**, Courtes Flammes, rue Bouillé, St-Pierre, T0596-781927. 1200-2200, closed Thu, Sun evening, all Oct. English spoken, homely Créole atmosphere. Shark columbo (curry), grilled lobster, crayfish in coconut milk.

North coast *p688, map p683*

†††-†† **Chez Tante Arlette**, rue Louis de Lucy de Fossarieu, Grand' Rivière, T0596-557575. Excellent Créole food in cool, pleasant surroundings, finished off with fabulous desserts and home made liqueurs. Reservations essential Sun when there is live music.

†† **Plantation Leyritz**, near Basse-Pointe, T0596-785392. Open daily. In restored plantation house, waterfalls trickling down the walls giving a cool, peaceful feel to the place, elegant dining, good food and service.

There are many restaurants a few minutes' by vedette (ferry) across the Bay of Fort-de-France, around the Pointe du Bout peninsula to Anse Mitan.

🍴🍴 **Le Balaou**, Le Manoir de Beauregard, Route des Salines, Ste-Anne, T0596-767575. Definitely worth stopping at this restaurant/auberge if you are going to the beach, lots of delicious tropical fruit used in the cuisine.

🍴🍴-🍴🍴 **Les Tamariniers**, Place de l'Eglise, Ste-Anne, T0596-767562. 1200-1330, 1900-2130, closed Tue evenings, Wed. French and Créole food, lots of seafood, fruits de mer, live lobster. Chef decorates expensive dishes with flowers.

🍴🍴 **La Case Créole**, Place de l'Église, Diamant, T0596-761014. Daily 1100-1600, 1900-2330. French and Créole, seafood and other specialities, welcoming hosts.

🍴🍴-🍴 **Bambou**, Anse Mitan. On the beach, specializes in fresh fish and offers an excellent *menu du jour*.

🍴🍴-🍴 **Chez Gracieuse**, Cap Chevalier, T0596-767243. Daily. Good, moderate-price Créole restaurant, choose the terrace and order the catch of the day, lobster a speciality.

🍴🍴-🍴 **Chez Jojo**, on the beach at Anse à l'Ane, Trois-Ilets, T0596- 684772. A varied seafood menu. Best on Fri nights when there is live music, compas, biguine, mazurka, reserve a table beside the beach for a lovely view across the bay.

🍴🍴-🍴 **Les Filets Bleus**, on the beach, Ste-Anne, T0596-413151. 1000-1600, 1800-2300, closed Mon. Choose from Créole, French or Oriental dishes.

🍴🍴-🍴 **Poi et Virginie**, Bourg Place de l'Eglise, Ste-Anne, T0596-767686. Tue-Sun. Overlooks bay with good seafood.

🍸 Bars and clubs

Martinique *p682, map p683*

Check the local newspaper, France-Antilles, for what's on. Nightclubs abound and tend to be expensive (€7.25 to get in and the same price for a drink, whether orange juice or a large whisky). There are several bars (*piano bar* or *café théâtre*) where you can listen to various types of music, some have karaoke or cabaret some nights. Discos are plentiful and you can hear a wide range of music. In Fort-de-France, the best place to find nightlife is the Blvd

Allègre on the bank of the Madame river, where there are lots of places to choose for late-night music and dancing.

Cotton Club, Anse Mitan, Trois-Ilets. Popular for local music, zouk, beguine and also jazz, bar, small dance floor, mostly Martiniquans.

'H' Club, Quartier Ducos, Beauville. Late night disco with live or taped local music.

Latin'Club, 11 rue Lamartine, Fort-de-France, T0596-631860. Piano bar.

Le Calebasse Café, Marin, not far from the beach, T0596-746927, www.calebasse.com. Very lively at night with high-quality performances by local musicians and artists, excellent café ambiance, internet access. If you want a table at weekends make a reservation for dinner.

Le Cheyenne, 8 rue Joseph Compère, Fort-de-France, T0596-703119. Piano bar with live music.

Le Coco Loco, rue Ernest Deproge in Fort-de-France, T0596-636377. Bar and restaurant with dinner shows, regular jazz sessions.

Le Crazy Night, ZAC Les Côteaux, Ste-Luce, T0596-685668. Lively dance venue, occasional live music, crowded and popular.

l'Embarquerie, Pointe du Bout. Snack bar by ferry dock has happy hour 3 times a day, 1030-1130, 1430-1530, 1700-1800, buy a local Corsaire beer, get one free.

Le Mayflower, 28 rue Ernest Deproge, T0596-705445. Bar and restaurant, pub style with karaoke.

Le Terminal, 104 rue Ernest Deproge, T0596-630348. A bar/nightclub.

Le Tribal, 12-14 François Arago, Fort-de-France, T0596-630578. Bar, food and disco.

Le Zenith, Blvd Allègre, Fort-de-France. Live music and dancing till late.

Top 50, at Trinité in the northeast at Zone Artisanale Bac, T0596-586143. Disco draws large crowds for late-night dancing, particularly at weekends.

Waïkiki, rue du Commerce, Pointe Simon, Fort-de-France, T0596-732318. A bar with entertainment.

🎭 Entertainment

Martinique *p682, map p683*
Casinos
Casinos charge €10 entrance fee, take passport or identification card.

Casino Batelière Plaza, Schoelcher, T0596-617323. 1000-0300. The main casino with tables for roulette and black jack and 140 slot machines.

Dance

Ballet Martiniquais, T0596-634388. One of the world's most prestigious folk ballet companies. Representing everyday scenes in their dance, they wear colourful local costume and are accompanied by traditional rhythms. The tourist office has information about performances and venues.

Cinemas

There are several comfortable, a/c cinemas in Fort-de-France and the *communes* (local councils). No film is in English; tickets cost €3. A state-of-the-art multiscreen complex is in the **Palais de Congres de Madiana**, T0596-721515, at Schoelcher. Turn off the main highway just before Anse Madame, taking the road right, leading to the university. The road to the Palais is the first on the right.

Theatre

Centre Martiniquais d'Action Culturelle (CMAC), Av Franz Fanon, Fort-de-France, T0596-617676. Organizes plays, concerts, film and documentary screening all year round and an annual festival in Dec. The main theatres are the **Théâtre Municipal** in the fine old Hôtel de Ville building and **Théâtre de la Soif Nouvelle**, Place Clemenceau. The **Théâtre Atrium**, on the corner of rue de la Redoute du Marouba, opened in 1998, state of the art hall, shows every evening, operas, plays, concerts, dance, etc, T0596-607878, F0596-608820, atrium-info@cgste.mq.

⊛ Festivals and events

Martinique *p682, map p683*
Every village celebrates its **Saint's Day** with games, shows and folk dancing, usually over the nearest weekend.
Feb/Mar The main pre-lenten **carnival** attracts the whole of Martinique to take to the streets in fantastic costume. Sun is the day of disguises and masked revellers, Mon sees burlesque marriages of improbable couples, Tue **Mardi Gras** is the day of the horned red devils and themed floats. On Ash

Wed, black and white clad 'devils' parade the streets of Fort-de-France lamenting loudly over the death of Vaval, a gigantic *bwabwa* (the figures carried in *Carnaval*), both the symbol and the presiding 'god' of carnival, his guise differs from year to year. It is chosen secretly by the carnival committee and only revealed at the first parade on Tue.
Mar/Apr At **Easter**, children fly coloured kites which once had razors attached to their tails for kite fights in the wind.
Apr Martinique Food Show, a culinary fair with lots of competitions.
May The **May of St-Pierre** which commemorates the eruption of the volcano La Montagne Pelée.
Jul SERMAC (Parc Floral et Culturel and at the Théâtre Municipal) organizes a 2-week **arts festival** in Fort-de-France with local and foreign artistes performing plays and dance, T0596-716625. The town of Saint-Marie holds a **cultural festival** and Ajoupa-Bouillon has a **festival of the crayfish**.
Aug The town of Marin holds its **cultural festival**.
Nov At **Toussaint** the towns are lit by candlelight processions making their way to the cemeteries to sit with the dead.
Dec The biennial International **Jazz Festival**, or **World Crossroads of the Guitar**.

○ Shopping

Martinique *p682, map p683*
Fort-de-France has an abundance of boutiques selling the latest Paris fashions, as well as items by local designers, and numerous street markets where local handicrafts are on sale. Rue Victor Hugo and its 2 *galleries* (malls) have clothing and perfume. Jewellery shops are mostly in rue Isambert and rue Lamartine, selling crystal, china and silverware, and gold jewellery. At markets in the Savane and near the cathedral bamboo goods, wickerwork, shells, leather goods, T-shirts, silk scarves and the like are sold. Wines and spirits imported from France and local liqueurs made from exotic fruits are readily available, and Martiniquan rum is an excellent buy. There are large shopping centres at Cluny, Dillon, and Bellevue and the big La Galléria on the airport road. **Annette** supermarket at Le Marin has a free shuttle service from the Marina. St Anne has several

small groceries open daily, catering to the tourist trade. US and Canadian dollars are accepted nearly everywhere and many tourist shops offer a 20% discount on goods bought with a credit card or TC's.

▲ Activities and tours

Martinique *p682, map p683*
Adventure Parks
Mangofil, Trois-Ilets, T0596-680808, www.mangofil.net. Daily 0900-1700, €15 for Mangokid, €20 for Big Mango and €15 for Mangokaid. Canopy walkways, ropes and ladders and other obstacles in the trees, swing through the forest like Tarzan with 3 levels of difficulty from kids to superheroes.
Caraïbes Aventures, Domaine de Sigy, Parcours d'Aventure, Vauclin, T0596-662911, Mohawk.aventure@wanadoo.fr. Daily 0900-1700, €10 children, €18 adults. Same idea as **Mangofil**, 3 routes taking you over rivers and among the trees with footbridges and lianas, culminating in an 18-m jump to a safety net below.
Aqualand Martinique, Carbet, on the road to St-Pierre, T0596-784000, www.aqualand-martinique.fr. Daily 0900-1700, closed Sep-mid Dec, €16 adults. €13 for 3-12 year olds. An aqua park with water slides, slaloms, wave pool and other attractions suitable for children and adults.

Cycling
Touring the island by bike is one of the activities offered by the **Parc Naturel Régional**, 9 Blvd Général de Gaulle, Fort de France 97206, T0596-644259. They have designed several itineraries in cooperation with local bike clubs. **VT Tilt**, Anse Mitan, Trois-Ilets, offers excursions by bike and cycle groups, T0596-660101, F0596-511400.

Diving
Diving is especially good along the coral reef between St-Pierre and Le Prêcheur, over the wrecks off St-Pierre and along the south coast. There are lots of dive operators, most of which are based at the large hotels. For those who do not dive, there are the **Kelennea**, T0596-660550, F0596-660552, glass-bottomed boat at Marina Pointe du Bout, Trois Ilets, and the **Aquabulle** at Marin, T0596-746969, which has a glass hull. To get even further under the water, there are two

semi-submersibles: **Aquascope Seadom Explorer**, Marina Pointe du Bout, T0596-683609, and **Zemis Aquascope**, rue de Caritan, Ponton de la Mairie, T0596-748741.

Fishing
Many hotels organize fishing trips for their guests. Deep-sea fishing can be arranged with **Yves Pélisson**, Le Diamant, T0596-762420, on his boats, Little Queeny and Maverick Too.The **Association Coup de Senne**, Bellefontaine, T0596-551388, can arrange for you to fish with local fishermen using local techniques and equipment.

Golf
Golf Country Club de la Martinique, 97229 Trois-Ilets, T0596-683281, www.golf martinique.com. A magnificent, 18-hole championship golf course, *Golf de l'Impératrice Joséphine*, designed by Robert Trent Jones, with various facilities including 2 tennis courts, shops, snackbar, lessons and equipment hire. Green fees are €46 and an electric cart for 2 people is €46, or you can book for a week or a month. Equipment is available for rent.
    There are mini-golf courses are at **Madiana Plage à Schoelcher** and **Anse l'Étang à Tartane**.

Hiking
One of the best organized and most popular sports is hiking, whether in the rain forest, up the volcano, the pitons, mornes or beaches. 3 outdoor organizations (the Parc Naturel Régional, T0596-644259/731930, the **Office National des Forêts**, T0596-713450 and a hiking club, **Le Club des Randonneurs**) have developed a network of more than 30 trails, all well marked and maintained, designed for hikers to use on their own. The trails are described in two guidebooks published in French: *31 Sentiers Balisés*, available at local bookstores for about €10, and *Belles Balades de la Martinique*, €28. Hikes costing about €15 per person are conducted for local citizens year round by **Parc Naturel** guides, but visitors also are welcome to participate. Commentary is in French. Among serious hiking tours is a two-hour climb, with guide, up Mont Pelée Volcano through thick foliage and overgrown trails. Less difficult, but still requiring skill, is the trek through a dense coastal rain forest between Grand Rivière

and Le Prêcheur. Fairly easy are hikes at Les Ombrages, a nature trail at Ajoupa-Bouillon, or along the Gorges de la Falaise, a ravine leading to a waterfall where guided canyoning is the local sport. Presqu'île de la Caravelle, near the town of Trinité, has safe beaches and well-marked paths to historic Château Dubuc's ruins.

Riding
Black Horse, La Pagerie, Trois-Ilets, T0596-683780.
Ranch Jack, Morne Habitue-Quartier Espérance, T0596-683769.

Sailing
Trips can be taken on boats rented at hotels by the hour or aboard yachts, bareboat or crewed, chartered by the day, week or month at the marinas of Le Marin, Le François, Pointe du Bout, Le Robert or Ste-Anne.
Base de Plein Air et de Loisirs, Anse Spoutourne, Tartane, T0596-582432. There are motor boats and sailing boats for hire.
Club de la Voile de Fort-de-France, Pointe de la Vièrge, T0596-422029, and Pointe des Carrières, T0596-633137.
Club Nautique de Marin, Bassin la Tortue, Pointe du Marin, T0596-749248.
Club Nautique du François, Route de la Jetée, T0596-645141.
Club Nautique du Vauclin, Pointe Faula, T0596-745083.
Yacht Club de la Martinique, Fort de France, T0596-632696.
Yole (yawl) races (large sailing boats with coloured sails and teams of oarsmen) are an amazing sight at festivals all over the island from Jul to Jan. In Fort-de-France races take place in Nov and Dec from the little beach next to Desnambuc quay. Other major sailing occasions include the **Schoelcher International Nautical Week** in Feb, with sailing and windsurfing competitions; **International Sailing Week** in Mar (Yacht Club of Fort-de-France); the **Aqua Festival**, the **Great Nautical Celebration** at Robert in Apr; the **Yawl Regatta Tour of Martinique** in Jul or Aug, when about 20 yawls race over 8 days.

Spectator sports
Mongoose and **snake** fights and **cockfights** are widespread from Dec-Aug at Pitt Quartier Bac, Ducos, T0596-560560; Pitt

Marceny (the most popular), Le Lamentin, T0596-512847; **Pitt Cléry**, Rivière-Pilote, T0596-626169; and many others. **Horse racing** is at the **Carrière** racetrack at Lamentin, T0596-512509.

Tennis
Tennis courts are at many large hotels where visitors can play day or night. There are about 40 clubs on the island where you can obtain temporary membership. For more information contact **La Ligue Régionale de Tennis**, Petit Manoir, Lamentin, T0596-510800.

Tour operators
Guided bus tours of the island, trips on sailing boats and cruise ships around Martinique and to neighbouring islands, and excursions on glass-bottom boats are organized.
AVS Angle des rues F Arago et E Deproge, Fort-de-France, T0596-635555.
Biguine Voyages, 51 rue Victor Hugo, Fort-de-France, T0596-718787, F0596-605596. Ms Mylene Richard.
Caribbean Spirit, 23 rue Simón Bolívar, 97200 Fort-de-France, T0596-274651, F0596-724651. Arranges tours and accommodation for the physically disadvantaged.
Carib Jet, Lamentin Airport, T0596-519000.
Caribtours, Marina Pointe du Bout, 97229 Trois-Ilets, T0596-660448, F0596-660706.
Colibri Tours, Immeuble Laouchez-ZI, Cocotte 97224, Ducos, T0596-771300, F0596-771289.
Madinina Tours, 89 rue Blénac, 97200 Fort-de-France, T0596-706525, F0596-730953.
M Vacances, 97290 Marin, T0596-748561, F0596-747107.
STT Voyages, 23 rue Blénac, Fort-de-France, T0596-716812.

Watersports
Windsurfing is available at most of the places where Sailing is listed, above, and on hotel beaches where there are board rentals.
Jet skiing, **sea scooters** and **waterskiing** at Pointe du Bout hotel beaches, **Marouba Club** (Carbet) and Pointe Marin beach in Ste-Anne.
Kayaking tours are offered by **Caraïbe Coast Kayak**, T0596-767602, with full or half day trips around the islets of Sainte-Anne; **Les Kayaks du Robert**, T0596-653389, with trips around the islets of Robert; **Fun Kayak**, in Ducos,

T0596-560060, in the coastal mangroves.

Canyoning is done in the north of the island near Grand-Rivière, contact **Aventures Tropicales Antilles**, T0596-645849, or **Basalt**, T0596-525782.

Transport

Martinique *p682, map p683*
Air
Scheduled direct flights:

From Europe (Paris only) are with **Air France**, **Air Corsair** and **Air Caraïbes**, www.aircaraibes.com.

From North America, the most convenient connection is through St Lucia, **Take Air Lines**, www.takeairlines.com, under franchise from **Air Caraïbes**, has daily flights connecting with **American Airlines** from Miami, **US Airways** from Philadelphia and Charlotte, **Delta** from Atlanta and **Air Canada** from Toronto.

From the Caribbean, Air Caraïbes and/or **Take Air Lines** fly from Antigua, Barbados, Bequia, Canouan, Caracas, Dominica (Canefield and Melville Hall), St-Martin/Sint Maarten (Grand Case and Juliana), Grenada, Saint Lucia (Hewanorra and Vigie), Santo Domingo, Marie Galante, Montego Bay, Pointe-à-Pitre, Port-au-Prince, St Vincent, Tobago and Union Island. **Cubana** from Havana.

Airport **Lamentin Airport**, T0596-421600. There is a tourist office for hotel reservations and information, T0596-421805, **Crédit Agricole** and **Change Caraïbes** for foreign currency exchange (see below), car rental offices and ground tour operators. To get to the airport at Lamentin, either take a taxi, or take a bus marked 'Ducos' and ask to be set down on the highway near the airport. The fare is €0.90 and the buses take reasonable-sized luggage. Do not attempt to cycle to or from the airport, and Fort-de-France or Trois-Ilets, as the highway is 4 lanes each way, traffic is heavy and fast, and the shoulder is almost non-existent.

Airline offices Air France, T0596-553300; Air Corsair, T0596-705970; LIAT, T0596-421602, 0596-512111; **Take Air Lines**, T0596-421608. Charter companies include **Air Foyal**, T0596-511154; **Air Caraïbes**, T0596-511727; **Air St-Martin**, T0596-515703; **Jet Aviation Service**, T0596-515703; **Antilles Aero Service**, T0596-516688; **Envol**, T0596-684549 (sight seeing trips round the island).

Boat
L'Express des Îles hydrofoil ferry service to St Lucia, Dominica and Pointe-à-Pitre, Guadeloupe. Fares and schedules appear in the daily paper, *France-Antilles* or contact **Terminal InterÎles**, 97200 Fort-de-France, T0596-631211, F0596-633447. Overnight packages available with several hotels, also car hire. Agents are **Brudey Frères**, 108 rue Victor Hugo, 97200 Fort-de-France, T0596-700850 for timetable information.

Martinique is on the route of most Caribbean cruises. Information on travelling by cargo boat can be obtained from the travel agency next door to the CGM office at the harbour, but if going to South America it is cheaper to fly.

There are ferries (navettes or vadettes) running between Quai d'Esnambuc on the seafront and Pointe du Bout, Anse Mitan and Anse à l'Ane. These run until about midnight to Pointe du Bout and 1830 to Anse Mitan and Anse à l'Ane and apart from a few taxis are about the only form of transport on a Sun or after 2000. Make sure you get on the right one. The 20-min ferry from Fort-de-France to Trois-Ilets costs €5 return (half price for children 2-11), is punctual, pleasurable and saves a 45-min drive by road. There are also irregular ferries from Fort-de-France to Ste-Anne, 2½ -3½ hrs. For information about ferry timetables call T0596-730553 for **Somatour** (Fort-de-France to Trois-Ilets, Anse Mitan beach and Anse à l'Ane), T0596-630646 for **Madinina** (Fort-de-France to Trois-Ilets) and T0596- 767345 for **Matinik Cruise Line** (Fort-de-France to down town Trois-Ilets, Sainte-Anne via Anse d'Arlet).

Bus
There are plenty of buses running between Fort-de-France and the suburbs which can be caught at Blvd Général-de-Gaulle. The buses are all managed by **Mozaik**, and leave when they're full. Short journeys cost around €0.95 if paid for in advance at a company kiosk, €1.14 if paid on the bus, children €0.55; buses run from 0500-2000 approximately. To request a stop shout *Arrête!* To go further afield, eg to Balata, costs €1.68. The *taxi*

collectif or *taxico* (8-seater estate cars or minibuses) run all over the island until about 1800. From Fort-de-France to Ste-Anne €6.14, Diamant €3.16, St-Pierre €3.49. The main terminal is at Pointe Simon.

Car

A valid driver's licence is needed to rent a car. Minimum age is 21. Most car rental companies in Fort-de-France are open 0800-1730 Mon-Fri with a 2-hr lunch break and 0800-1200 Sat. At the airport, hours depend on international flight schedules. Rates can begin as low as €35 a day or €215 a week, including taxes, insurance and unlimited mileage. Major credit cards are accepted everywhere. You can get a discount if you book your car from abroad at least 48 hrs in advance. One look at Fort-de-France's congested streets will tell you it's well worth avoiding driving in the city centre. What is more, parking in central Fort-de-France is only legal with a season ticket and the capital's traffic wardens are very efficient; cars may be towed away. Park near the **Savane** (€0.30 per hr).
Europcar interent, Aéroport Lamentin, T0596-421688, F0596-518115, Fort-de-France T0596-733313 and several hotels; **Hertz**, kiosk at the airport, T0596-421690, F0596-514626; **Avis** at the airport, T421692. Prices start from €21.50 a day for a Citroën AX or Renault 5.

Cycle

A bicycle can be hired for €5 per day, €26 per week, €36 per fortnight, from **Funny**, T0596-633305, Fort-de-France; **Discount**, T0596-665437, Pointe du Bout; **TS Autos**, Fort-de-France, T634282.

Motorcycle

Mopeds can be hired at **Funny**, in Fort-de-France, T0596-633305; **Discount**, Trois-Ilets, T0596-660534; and **Grabin's Car Rental**, Morne Calebasse, T0596-715161. Motorcycles of 125cc and over need a licence, those of 50cc do not. Rental for all is about €45 per day.

Taxi

There is a 40% surcharge on taxi fares between 2000 and 0600. Taxi stands are at the **Savane**, along **Blvd Général-de-Gaulle** and **Place Clemenceau**. For a radio taxi, T0596-636362 or 0596-631010.

Martinique *p682, map p683*
Banks Change Caraïbes, airport, Mon-Sat 0730-2130, Sun 0800-1200, 1400-2100, T0596-421711; rue Ernest Deproge, 97200, Fort-de-France, Mon-Fri 0730-1800, Sat 0800-1300, T0596-602840. **Crédit Agricole** also has an office at the airport for currency exchange, Tue-Fri 0730-1230, 1430-1800, Sat 0800-1130, T0596-512599; also at rue Ernest Deproge, T0596-731706, Tue-Fri and Sat morning. **Banque Française Commerciale**, 6/10 rue Ernest Deproge, T0596-638257. **Banque des Antilles Françaises**, 34 rue Lamartine, T0596-607272. **Société Générale de Banque aux Antilles**, 19 rue de la Liberté, T0596-597070. **Crédit Martiniquais**, 17 rue de la Liberté, T0596-599300. **BRED**, Place Monseigneur Romero, T0596-632267. **Martinique Change**, 137 rue Victor Hugo, T0596-638033 and in Trois-Ilets T0596-660444. **Banque National de Paris**, 72 Av des Caraïbes, T0596-594600 (the best for cash advances on Visa, no commission). Banks and exchange houses charge 5% commission on TCs. Not all banks accept US dollar TCs. Some banks charge €1.50-3 for any size transaction, so change as much as you think you're going to need. Always go to the bank early; by mid-morning they are very crowded. Do not change US dollars at the Post Office in Fort-de-France, nor at restaurants, supermarkets and shops because you lose about 30% because of the poor exchange rate and commission. Check the rate when you pay for things with US dollars cash, credit card purchases are better. **American Express** at Roger Albert Voyages, 10 rue Victor Hugo, upstairs, efficient.
Consulates (see also Guadeloupe directory). **Belgium**, Dillon Valmenière, T0596-595052. **Denmark**, 13 rue Victor Sévère, Fort-de-France, T0596-713786, gdj@aquaform.net. **Germany**, Acajou, Lamentin, T0596-505097. **Italy**, 28 Blvd Allègre, Fort-de-France, T0596-705475. **Netherlands**, 44 Av Maurice Bishop, T0596-733161. **Spain**, Lot Haute Frégate, François, T0596-542779. **Switzerland**, La Trompeuse, Le Lamentin, T0596-501243. **UK**, Le Petit Pavois, 96 Route du Phare, T0596-615630. **Internet** Le Web, 4 rue Blénac, T0596-735397, high-speed

connection, scanner, web cam, printer, English, French and German spoken, €3 per 15 mins, €6 per 30 mins, half price for students, soldiers and unemployed, Mon-Sat 0900-2400. **Medical services** There are 18 hospitals and clinics which are well equipped and well staffed. EU citizens have reciprocal state health rights and hospitals are up to metropolitan France standards. In an emergency: SAMU, Pierre Zobda Quitman Hospital, 97232 Le Lamentin, T0596-751515. Ambulance service, T0596-715948.

Post Post offices are open from 0700-1800 and Sat mornings. The main post office is on rue de la Liberté and always has long queues. Post card to USA €0.35.

Telephone Nearly all public telephones are cardphones except a few in bars and hotels which take coins. At the PTT office in rue Antoine Siger, just off the Savane, there are numerous card and coin phones and *Télécartes* (phone cards) are sold. These can also be bought in most newsagents, cafés, and some shops. A 50-unit card lasts nearly 4 mins when phoning North America. Don't get caught out on arrival at the airport where there are only cardphones. Try the tourist office where they are very helpful and will phone round endless hotels to find the unprepared new arrival a room. You cannot have a call returned to a payphone. See Guadeloupe, page 675 for dialling abroad with credit cards.

Background

History
Both Guadeloupe and Martinique were sighted by Columbus on his second voyage in 1493, but no colonies were established by the Spanish because the islands were inhabited by the Caribs; it was not until 1635 that French settlers arrived. Because of their wealth from sugar, the islands became a bone of contention between Britain and France, but were not lost like some other islands. The important dates in the later history of the islands are 1848, when the slaves were freed (Victor Schoelcher guiding the legislation through parliament); 1946, when the islands ceased to be colonies and became Départments (Départements d'Outre Mer - DOM); and 1974, when they each also became economic Régions.

Guadeloupe Christopher Columbus named Guadeloupe after the Virgin of Guadalupe, of Extremadura, Spain, in 1493. The Caribs, who had inhabited the island, called it **Karukera**, meaning 'island of beautiful waters'. As in most of the Lesser Antilles, the Spanish never settled, and Guadeloupe's history closely resembles that of Martinique, beginning with French colonization in 1635. The first slaves had been brought to the island by 1650. In the first half of the 17th century, Guadeloupe did not enjoy the same levels of prosperity, defence or peace as Martinique. After four years of English occupation, in 1763 Louis XV handed over Canada to Britain to regain his hold on the islands with the Treaty of Paris. The French Revolution brought a period of uncertainty, including a reign of terror under Victor Hugues. Those landowners who were not guillotined fled; slavery was abolished, only to be restored in 1802 by Napoléon. The slaves were finally freed in 1848, largely because of work by Victor Schoelcher. After 1848, the sugar plantations suffered from a lack of manpower, although indentured labour was brought in from East India.

Despite having equal status with Martinique, first as a Département then as a Région, Guadeloupe's image as the less sophisticated, poor relation persists. In common with Martinique, though, its main political voice is radical (unlike the more conservative Saint-Barthélemy and Saint-Martin), often in the past marked by a more violent pro-Independence movement.

Martinique When Christopher Columbus first sighted Martinique, it was inhabited by the Carib Indians who had killed or absorbed the Arawaks, the previous settlers of the Lesser Antilles some 200-300 years previously. He did not land until 15 June 1502, when he put in at Le Carbet. Columbus named the island Martinica in honour of St Martin; the Caribs called it **Madinina**, or island of flowers. The Spanish never settled. In 1635 Martinique was colonized by the French under the leadership of Pierre Belain d'Esnambuc. His nephew, Jacques du Parquet, governed in 1637-1658 and started to develop the island; when he died, his widow took over. The cultivation of sugar cane and the importation of slaves from West Africa commenced. Fierce battles took place between the Caribs and the French until 1660 when a treaty was signed under which the Caribs agreed to occupy only the Atlantic side of the island. Peace was shortlived, however, and the Indians were soon completely exterminated. Louis XIV bought many of the du Parquet land rights and appointed an administrating company, making Martinique the capital of France's Caribbean possessions. In 1762 England occupied Martinique for nine months, only to return it with Guadeloupe to the French in exchange for Canada, Senegal, the Grenadines, St Vincent and Tobago. France was content to retain Martinique and Guadeloupe because of the importance of the sugar trade at the time.

More unrest followed when in 1789 the French Revolution inspired slaves to fight for their emancipation. White artisans, soldiers, small merchants and free people of mixed race also embraced its principles. In 1792 a royalist governor re-established control but he was expelled by a revolutionary force sent from France. The capital, Fort-Royal became République-Ville and Paris abolished slavery. Martinique was occupied by the English again from 1794 to 1815 (with one interruption), at the request of the plantation owners of the island who wanted to preserve slavery. Slavery was finally abolished in 1848 in the French colonies and in the following years 25,000 immigrant workers from India and a few from Indo-China came to Martinique to supplement the remaining workforce on the plantations.

In 1946 Martinique became an overseas Département (DOM), with all the rights of any department in metropolitan France. The bill was steered through the National Assembly by Martinique's Deputy at the time, Aimé Césaire (1913-), poet, mayor of Fort-de-France and a pioneer of *négritude* (see page 703). In 1974 Martinique also became a Région, giving it more economic advantages.

Geography

Guadeloupe Guadeloupe is really two islands, **Basse-Terre** and **Grande-Terre**, separated by the narrow bridged strait of the Rivière Salée. Together they have an area of 1,709 sq km and a population of 397,000. To the west is mountainous Basse-Terre, with the volcano Grande Soufrière (1,484 m) at its centre. The administrative capital of the same name is on its southwest coast. The commercial capital is Pointe-à-Pitre, situated in the flat half of the island, Grande-Terre. On the cliff-edged Caribbean coast, there was only one low-lying and hospitable shore. This was settled first, substantially from the 1640s, and became the capital. At that time, only the mountainous western island was called Guadeloupe. On its east coast was another settlement, Capesterre (which means that part of an island first sighted on the voyage from Europe). Grande-Terre came into its own around two or three decades later, when sugar cane cultivation took off. As it assumed the greater commercial importance the name 'Guadeloupe' came to refer to both islands.

Martinique The island is 80 km from north to south and 32 km at its widest, with an area of 1,102 sq km. There are mountains in the north and south and a low-lying 'waist' where most people live (population 385,000). The coastline is irregular in the southern half, with peninsulas and promontories protecting islets and sandy bays. Martinique's neighbouring islands are Dominica to the north and St Lucia to the south. Martinique is volcanic in origin and one active volcano still exists, La Montagne Pelée (1,397 m), situated to the northwest, which had its last major eruption in 1902. The rest of the island is also very mountainous; the Pitons de Carbet (maximum 1,196 m) are in the centre of the island and La Montagne du Vauclin (504 m) is in the south. Small hills or *mornes* link these mountains and there is a central plain, Le Lamentin, where sugar cane is planted. An extensive tropical rainforest covers parts of the north of the island, as well as pineapple and banana plantations. The coastline is varied: steep cliffs and volcanic, black and grey sand coves in the north and on the rugged Atlantic coast, and calmer seas with large white or gold sand beaches in the south and on the Caribbean coast.

Economy

Guadeloupe Agriculture and tourism are the principal activities. Bananas have displaced sugar as the single most important export earner accounting for 25% of all exports. Sugar and its by-products generate about 15% of exports. Melons and tropical flowers have been promoted for sale abroad, while many other fruits, vegetables and coffee are grown mainly for the domestic market. Wages and conditions similar to those in metropolitan France force the price of local products to levels viable only on the parent market; 66% of all exports go to France and 11% to Martinique (most exports are agricultural products). Unemployment is high. Infrastructural projects are funded by the French government and the EU's regional aid programmes.

Martinique Martinique is dependent upon France for government spending equivalent to about 70% of GNP, without which there would be no public services or social welfare. Fishing contributes to the local food supply but much of the domestic market is met by imports. Most manufactured goods are imported, adding to the cost of living. There is some light industry and the major industrial plants are an oil refinery, rum distilleries and a cement works, while there is also fruit canning, soft drinks manufacturing and polyethylene and fertilizer plants.

Tourism is the greatest area of economic expansion. Of total stopover visitors, 80% come from France and 3% from the USA, while of total cruise ship visitors, 72% come from the USA, 14% from the whole of Europe and 9% from Canada. Tourism income is now around €220 mn a year.

Government

The people of Martinique and Guadeloupe are French citizens, and both Départements are officially and administratively part of France. The President of the French Republic is Head of State. Local government is run by a Prefect (appointed by the French Minister for the Interior), the General Council (directly elected) and the Regional Council (elected, proportional representation). There are two different legislative bodies: the General Council and the Regional Council. Each Département is represented by four directly elected Deputies to the National Assembly in Paris, by two indirectly elected Senators in the Senate and by one representative on the Economic and Social Council. The General Council votes on matters of interest to the Département, administers and manages local services and allocates funds to the local councils, or *communes*. The Regional Council concentrates on economic development.

Culture

Music and dance African dances: the *calinda, laghia, bel-air, haut-taille, gragé* and others are still performed in remote villages. The famous biguine is a more sophisticated dance, and the mazurka can also be heard. French Antillean music is, like most other Caribbean styles, hybrid, a mixture of African (particularly percussion), European, Latin and, latterly, US and other Caribbean musical forms. Currently very popular, on the islands and in mainland France, is zouk, a hi-tech music which overlays electronics on more traditional rhythms. Guadeloupe has a more overt African culture than Martinique, and here, the *gros-ka*, now written as spoken in Créole, *gwo-ka* (big drum), has seven distinct rhythms, some, like the *Mendé*, directly attributable to African origins. Musicians such as Robert Oumaou in Guadeloupe work within this framework, outreaching via such styles as jazz to create new and vibrant music.

Customs Traditional costume is commonly seen in the form of brightly coloured, chequered Madras cotton garments. The mixture of French and Créole language and culture gives Martinique and Guadeloupe an ambience quite different from that of the rest of the Caribbean. An extra dimension is added by the Hindu traditions and festivals celebrated by the descendants of the 19th-century indentured labourers.

Literature The dominance of French educational and social regimes on its colonial possessions led, in the 1930s and 1940s, to a literary movement which had a profound influence on black writing the world over. This was *négritude*, which grew up in Paris among black students from the Caribbean and Africa. Drawing particularly on Haitian nationalism (1915-1930), the *négritude* writers sought to restore black pride which had been completely denied by French education. The leaders in the field were Aimé Césaire (1913-) of Martinique, Léopold Senghor of Senegal and Léon Damas of Guyane. Césaire's first affirmation of this ideology to become well-known was *Cahier d'un retour au pays natal* (1939); in subsequent works and in political life (he was mayor of Fort-de-France and a deputy in the National Assemby in Paris for half a century) he maintained his attack on the "white man's superiority complex" and worked, in common with another Martiniquan writer, Frantz Fanon, towards "the creation of a new system of essentially humane values" (Mazisi Kunene in his introduction to the Penguin edition of *Return to My Native Land*, 1969). The town hall still maintains an office for him to use, where, at 93, he met the French Prime Minister and his wife who were visiting at Christmas 2006.

Windward Islands

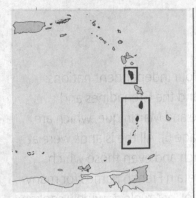

⁝ Footprint features

Introduction

The Windward Islands include four independent nations: Dominica, St Lucia, St Vincent and the Grenadines and Grenada, as well as Guadeloupe and Martinique, which are Départements of France (see page 6). All the islands were at one time colonized by the French and even those which eventually became British still retain French names for many of the towns and villages. Kwéyòl, or Créole, is widely spoken, while there are French influences in the old colonial buildings, with gingerbread fretwork and jalousie shutters. The islands are a series of volcanic peaks jutting out of the sea and forming a barrier between the Atlantic Ocean and the Caribbean Sea. Sulphur fumaroles and hot springs can be found on the biggest islands where the volcanoes are dormant but not dead and even under the sea. There are large areas of lush rainforest with national parks protecting places of biodiversity or natural beauty on land or underwater. The islands are a haven for birds with lots of endemic species although several of the parrots are endangered, while the sea is teeming with fish and other marine life including whales and dolphins. Hikers and birdwatchers are spoilt for choice in the larger islands of the Windwards, and yachtsmen are similarly blessed when navigating among the smaller Grenadines, one of the world's most popular sailing destinations. Tourism is now the leading economic activity with visitors appreciating the beaches as well as the rainforest. Bananas, the traditional crop grown by small farmers and their families are still an important source of income on the Windward Islands, but agriculture is diversifying with other tropical fruits and flowers being exported.

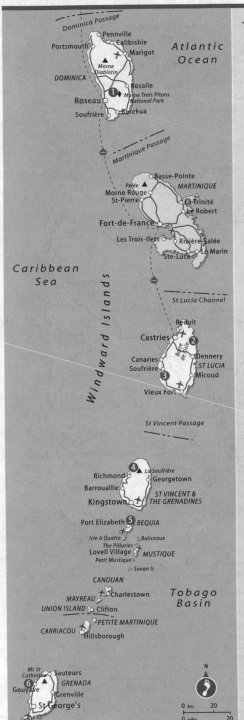

★ Don't miss ...

1 **Morne Trois Pitons National Park** Hot springs and a boiling lake in the rainforest, trails leading to freshwater lakes and cool waterfalls, page 711.

2 **Soufrière** Old wooden houses hug the bay in this most spectacular part of St Lucia, where conical Pitons shoot up out of the sea, page 738.

3 **Grande Anse Turtle Watching** March-July is the season for leatherback turtles to haul themselves on to the coast of St Lucia to lay their eggs, page 740.

4 **Baleine Falls** A boat trip, then a short walk upstream through the crevasse to a pretty pool with waterfall for a refreshing dip, page 769.

5 **Bequia** The largest of the Grenadines, hilly and forested, Admiralty Bay is a natural harbour, popular with yachts, page 781.

6 **Gouyave** 'Spice island', one of the world's leading producers of nutmeg; see where it is dried, graded and separated from the mace, page 808.

Dominica

Guadeloupe Channel

Cape Melville
Clifton
Carib Point
Pennville
Toucari Bay
Savane Paille
Morne dux Diables
Vieille Case
Autrou Bay
Anse de Mai
Grand Baptiste Estate
Turtle Beach
Douglas Bay
Tanetane
Thibaud
Hampstead 22
17
Cabrits National Park
Calibishie
23 2
Larieu 24
Crompton Point
Fort Shirley (Ruins)
4 Portsmouth
Dos D'Âne
Woodford Hill
10
Picard Beach
Glanvillia
Indian River
Wesley
Londonderry Bay
Prince Rupert Bay
Melville Hall
Mango Hole Bay
Pte Augustine
Anse Mulâtre
Marigot
Pagua Bay
Northern Forest Reserve
Hatton Garden
12
15
Dublanc
Syndicate Estate
Crayfish River
Colihaut
Morne Diablotin
Carib Territory
Horse Back Ridge
Sineku
Jenny Point
L'Escalier Tête-Chien
Coulibistrie
Central Forest Reserve
26
1
27
13 Salisbury
Penrice Falls
Jacko Flats
Bells
Castle Bruce
4 5
Mero
Layou River
Mourne Couronne
Emerald Pool
Grand Marigot Bay
26
St Joseph
Transinsular Rd
Petite Soufrière
Layou
Layou Valley
Pont Cassé
Rosalie
Rosalie Bay
Tarou Pt or Rodney's Rock
Mahaut
8
Morne Trois Pitons
Middleham Falls
Boeri Lake
Massacre
Sylvania
Freshwater Lake
Morne Trois Pitons National Park
Canefield
Cochrane
19
Morne Macaque
16
Laudat
Titou Gorge
La Plaine
14
9
Trafalgar
6
Trafalgar Waterfalls
Boiling Lake
Sari Sari Falls
Goodwill
Woodbridge Bay
Roseau
18
Giraudel
11
Wotten Waven
Valley of Desolation
Victoria Falls
Pointe Daniel
1
Castle Comfort
Morne Anglais
Délices
Savane Mahaut
Pointe Mulâtre Bay
3
Loubiere
Bellevue Chopin
Pointe Michel
Anse Bateaux
Sulphur Spring
Geneva Estate
Petite Savane
Pointe Guignard
Tête Morne
Berekua 15
Soufrière Bay
Grand Bay
Scotts Head
Soufrière
5
Morne Rouge Estate
Petit Coulibri Estate
Pointe des Fous
Scotts Head
Martinique Channel

Caribbean Sea

0 km 2
0 miles 2

Dominica → *Country code: 767. Colour map 4, A5. Population: 74,400.*

Known as the 'Nature Island' of the Caribbean, Dominica (pronounced Domineeca) is the place to come for dense forests, volcanic hills, rivers, waterfalls and the Boiling Lake. Dominica was the first country to be Green Globe benchmarked. It is also a highly regarded diving destination, with a good marine park system, and for much of the year you can see whales and dolphins offshore. Hotels around the island are small, intimate and low-key, greater development being deterred by the lack of beaches. It is the only island where Caribs have survived and they still retain many of their traditions such as canoe carving. The island's culture and language are an amalgam of the native and immigrant peoples: Carib, French, English and African.
▶▶ *For Sleeping, Eating and other listings, see pages 717-727.*

Ins and outs

Getting there There are no direct flights from Europe or North America to Dominica. Connections must be made in Puerto Rico, St Maarten, Antigua, Barbados or the French Antilles. There are ferry services from St Lucia and the French Antilles, but it can be rough in the channel. ▶▶ *See Transport, page 725, for further details.*

Getting around It is a good idea to rent a car or jeep as buses take a lot of planning. There are few road signs, but with a good map finding your way is not difficult. Dominicans drive fast so you may want to take a taxi to enjoy the views. Main roads are fairly good, but in towns and south of Roseau, roads are narrow and in poor condition. Apart from the Massacre to Soufrière/Scotts Head route, it is difficult to get anywhere on the island by public transport and return to Roseau in one day; it is just possible to get to Portsmouth and return in one day, the first bus is at 1000, returning at 1600.

Roseau

Roseau, the main town, is small, ramshackle and friendly, with a surprising number of pretty old buildings still intact. The houses look a bit tatty with rusting tin roofs and a general lack of paint, but there is still some attractive gingerbread fretwork in the traditional style on Castle Street and others. A typical house, called a Ti Caz, has a stone base, the walls are boarded with timber and the windows have hurricane shutters for protection or jalousie shutters for privacy. The roofs are steeply pitched, with the ends hipped, giving additional bracing against hurricanes, while verandas give shelter from the sun and rain. Quite a lot of redevelopment has taken place over the last few years, improving access and making the

> ⁑ *Streets have been given signs but it is still tricky to find your way around Roseau; you may need to ask for directions.*

waterfront more attractive. The Old Market Plaza is a pedestrian area, with shops in the middle. The old, red market cross has been retained, with 'keep the pavement dry' picked out in white paint. Between the Plaza and the sea is the old post office, now housing the **Dominican Museum** ① *T4482401, Mon-Fri 0900-1600, Sat 0900-1200, EC$2*, which is well worth a visit. The **market**, at the north end of Bay Street, is a fascinating sight on Saturday mornings from about 0600-1000; it is also lively on Friday morning, closed Sunday. The sea wall was completed in late 1993, which has greatly improved the waterfront area of town, known as the **Bay Front** or **Dame Eugenia Charles Blvd**, after the Prime Minister who promoted the development. A promenade with trees and benches, a road from the Old Jetty to Victoria Street, and parking bays take up most of the space. The current cruise ship jetty is T-shaped and for a several weeks in the winter season ships tower above the town pouring forth tourists.

The 40-acre **Botanical Gardens**, founded as an offshoot for Kew Gardens in London and dating from 1891 are principally an arboretum; they have a collection of plant species, including an orchid house. Storms and hurricanes over the last century have taken their toll on the gardens and wiped out the ornamental garden area. You can still see the old bus crushed by a baobab tree during hurricane David in 1979. Several Jacquot and Sisserou parrots can be seen in the bird sanctuary in the park, thanks in part to the Jersey Wildlife Preservation Trust. Breeding programmes are underway; some of the offspring will be released to the wild. The gardens are now the main open space and recreational area for Roseau. Parades, cultural events and cricket matches are all held here. The Forestry Department is based here, forestry@cwdom.dm.

> ‡ Entrance to 'ecological' sites in Dominica is US$2; day-pass US$5; week-pass US$10, ticket should be bought in advance from agencies or at the sites.

Trafalgar falls

The Trafalgar waterfalls in the Roseau Valley, 8 km from the capital, have been the most popular tourist site for many years. Hot and cold water used to flow in two spectacular cascades in the forest, but unfortunately the volume of the hot fall was sharply diminished by a hydroelectric scheme higher up and a landslide after the September 1995 hurricanes covered both the hot and cold water pools. The path from the visitor centre to the viewing platform at the falls is easy to follow, but if you want to

Roseau

Sleeping 🛏	Eating 🍴	Pearl's Cuisine 6
Cherry Lodge 1	Cornerhouse 1	Ti-Caz (Coco Rico) Café 7
Fort Young 2	Garden Chinese 10	
Garraway 3	Guiyave 2	Buses 🚌
Ma Bass Central	La Robe Créole 3	Northbound Buses 1
Guest House 7	Mousehole Café 3	Southbound Buses 2
Sutton Place 6	O'Byrne's Pub & Grub 4	Buses to Trafalgar &
	Paiho 5	Laudat 3

0 metres 100
0 yards 100

go further than the viewing point, take a guide because there is a lot of scrambling over rocks and it can be difficult at times. Trying to cross over the falls at the top is very hazardous. Bathing is possible in pools in the river beneath the falls. There are always lots of guides. Some guides can be abusive if you insist on going alone. Agree the price before setting out (around EC$10 for two or more people in a group). The Trafalgar Falls are crowded because they are close to the road (bus from outside the Astaphan supermarket in Roseau or walk). A natural sulphur pool has been set up at Papillote restaurant by the falls, in lovely gardens. There is also a road from the sulphur springs of the settlement of Wotten Waven through forest and banana plantations across the Trois Pitons River up to the Trafalgar Falls.

Morne Trois Pitons National Park

Much of the south part of the island (17,000 acres) has since 1975 been designated the Morne Trois Pitons National Park and in 1998 it became a UNESCO World Heritage Site. Evidence of volcanic activity is manifested in hot springs, sulphur emissions and the occasional small eruption. Its attractions include the Boiling Lake (92°C), which may be the largest of its kind in the world (the other contender is in New Zealand) and reached after a 6-mile, 3-hour climb from Laudat, returning on the same path. An experienced guide is recommended as, although easy to follow, the trail can be treacherous, particularly when mist descends. Possible guides are Lambert Charles, T4483365; Kenrich Johnson; Edison and Loftus Joseph, Wotten Waven, T4489192 (at a telephone box). Expect to pay EC$150 for two people. Make sure you wear clothes you don't mind getting wet and muddy and wear good hiking boots or trainers. For a description of the hike, see www.avirtualdominica.com/thelake.cfm.

In 1999 a guide fell in the lake. He was burned up to his waist and spent three months in hospital.

Below the Boiling Lake is a spectacular region known as the Valley of Desolation, where the forest has been destroyed by sulphuric emissions. At the beginning of the trail to the Boiling Lake is the Titou Gorge, now considerably damaged by rock fall from the hydroelectric development in the area, where a hot and a cold stream mingle. However, there is nothing more refreshing or soothing after hiking to and from the Boiling Lake than swimming through the Titou Gorge. The Kent Gilbert Trail starts in La Plaine and is about 4½ miles long. It affords views of the Sari Sari and Bolive Falls, but avoids the Valley of Desolation. While this makes it a less strenuous route, it is also less impressive.

Also in the park is the Freshwater Lake, east of Morne Macaque at 2,500 ft above sea level, and two miles from Laudat. A road leads to both the Freshwater Lake and on to the start of the 45-minute trail to the island's highest lake, Boeri, between Morne Macaque and Morne Trois Pitons.

Do not swim here as it is the drinking water reservoir for Roseau.

The National Park Service has built a series of paths, the Middleham Trails, through the rainforest on the northwest border of the park. The trails are accessible from Sylvania on the Transinsular Road, or Cochrane, although the signs from Sylvania are not clear. The road to Cochrane is by the Old Mill Cultural Centre in Canefield; once through the village the trail is marked. About 1½ to two hours' walk from Cochrane are the Middleham Falls (about 250-ft high) cascading into a beautiful blue pool in the middle of the forest. Once past the Middleham Falls the trail emerges on the Laudat road. Turn inland at Sisserou Hotel and then immediately right behind the Texaco garage (30 minutes' walk from Roseau) a steep road leads 2½ miles up to Giraudel (50 minutes' walk). From behind the school here a trail goes up through a succession of smallholdings to Morne Anglais (3,683 ft; a two-hour walk from Giraudel). This is the easiest of the high mountains to climb. The trail is fairly easy to follow but someone will need to show you the first part through the smallholdings. Ask in the village or go with a guide.

⁝ Touching down

Boat information (own flag) Roseau, Portsmouth and Anse de Mai in the east are ports of entry. Obtain coast-wide permit. EC$1 to clear in. Customs main office (T4484462) is at the deep water harbour at Woodbridge Bay where all the large ships come in. You can also clear at the Bayfront. Other offices are at Roseau, Anse de Mai, Portsmouth and at both airports. **Anchor** at Salisbury, Castaways Beach Hotel, Layou River, ALDive in Loubiere, Sukie's Marina in Newtown. A marina at the Coconut Beach Hotel near Portsmouth, has slips for 40 boats, full service. Do not anchor in Scotts Head/Soufrière Bay (marine reserve) or Douglas Bay or where fishing activities are underway. Waste disposal at the commercial docks in Portsmouth and Roseau.

Business hours Banks: Mon-Thu 0800-1400, Fri 0800-1700. **Government offices**: Mon-Fri 0800-1300, 1400-1600. **Shops**: Mon-Fri 0800-1300, 1400-1600, Sat 0800-1300. Many supermarkets in Roseau now stay open at lunch and some until 2000.

Clothing Informal, though swimsuits are not worn on the streets. A sweater is recommended for the evenings. When hiking, take good walking shoes as well as a raincoat or poncho; a dry T-shirt is also a good idea.

Currency East Caribbean dollar, EC$. EC$2.67=US$1.

Departure tax EC$55/US$20; day trippers pay EC$5; under 12s are free.

Documents All visitors entering Dominica must be in possession of an outward ticket and a valid **passport**. Proof of citizenship with photo is acceptable for Canadian citizens, but if they are returning home via the USA they will need a passport. A Carte d'Identité allows French nationals to visit for up to two weeks. Immigration normally grants stays of 21 days on arrival; extensions can be applied for and require an outward ticket.

Emergency numbers T999 for Police, Fire and Ambulance.

Language English is the official language but **Kwéyòl** is spoken widely. It is very similar to that spoken on St Lucia and to the Créole of Martinique and Haiti but people tend to speak more slowly (see page 728).

Media DBS (State radio) broadcasts on AM 595 kHz and FM 88.1, 88.6. 89.5, 103.2 and 103.6 MHz. Kairi Fm has a more lively presentation style, on FM 93.1, 107.9 MHz. Q95 (95.1 FM) is

South coast

In the far south are the villages of **Soufrière** and **Scotts Head**. Both are worth visiting for their stunning setting on the sea with the mountain backdrop and brightly painted fishing boats on the shore. There are plenty of buses to Scott's Head, over the mountain with excellent views all the way to Martinique. Ask around the fishing huts if you are hungry, and you will be directed to various buildings without signs where you can eat chicken pilau for EC$6 and watch dominoes being played.

On the south coast is **Grand Bay**, where there is a large beach (dangerous for swimming), the 10 ft-high **Belle Croix** and the **Geneva Estate**, founded in the 18th century by the Martinican Jesuit, Father Antoine La Valette, and at one time the home of the novelist Jean Rhys. It is being upgraded to a heritage park. From Grand Bay, it is a two-hour walk over the hill, past Sulphur Spring to Soufrière. The area has a reputation for violence related to the growing of marijuana, see Safety, page 712.

Leeward coast

The Leeward coastal road, north from Roseau, comes first to **Canefield**, passing the turning for the twisting Imperial Road to the centre of the island, and then the small popular. Vol is on AM 1060 KHz, FM 102.1, 90.6 MHz. There are two religious radio stations (one Protestant and one Catholic) as well as a repeater for St Lucian Radio Caribbean International on FM 98.1 Mhz.

Official time Atlantic Standard Time, four hours behind GMT, one ahead of EST.

Public holidays 1 Jan; Carnival; Good Fri and Easter Mon; first Mon in May; Whit Mon; first Mon in Aug; 3-4 Nov (Independence); Christmas Day and Boxing Day. A merchant's holiday takes place on 2 Jan, when all shops and restaurants and most government offices are closed, although banks and hotels stay open.

Safety Crime is rising and there have been muggings on beaches at Castle Bruce and L'Escalier Tete Chien in the east and Hampstead on the northeast coast. There have been robberies around Calibishie and you must never leave valuables unattended on the beaches in that area, even if you can see them. At Carnival time avoid the Grand Bay area, where celebrations are 'enthusiastic', and include guns and machetes. Theft is normally non-violent and is of cash and easily saleable items (for example jewellery) rather than credit cards. Always report theft to the police, they generally have a shrewd idea of where to look for stolen goods and sometimes recover them.

Tourist information The Dominica Division of Tourism has its headquarters in the National Development Corporation, in Valley Rd, Roseau, T4482045, www.discoverdominica.com. A useful brochure is *100+ Things to Do* available from the tourist offices in the Old Market Square (Mon-Fri 0800-1600, Sat 0900-1300) and at both airports (Canefield Airport, daily 0615-1115, 1415-1730 or last flight; the Melville Hall one is only open at flight arrival times). Other useful guides and booklets are produced by the **Forestry Division** and are available from their offices in the Botanical Gardens, priced from EC$0.25-EC$15.

Tourist offices overseas UK: Saltmarsh Public Relations, London, T020 79281600, dominica@saltmarshpr.co.uk. **USA**: New York, T718 2619615, toll free 1888 6455637, dominicany@discoverdominica.com.

Voltage 220/240 volts AC, 50 cycles.

Weights and measures Imperial.

airport. The coast road passes through **Massacre**, reputed to be the settlement where 80 Caribs were killed by British troops in 1674. Among those who died was Indian Warner, Deputy Governor of Dominica, illegitimate son of Sir Thomas Warner (Governor of St Kitts) and half-brother of the commander of the British troops, Colonel Philip Warner. From the church perched above the village there are good views of the coast. The next village is **Mahaut** and just north of here near DCP a newly paved road, called Warner Road, climbs steeply up towards Morne Couroune. It then levels out and joins the main Layou Valley road at the Layou Valley Plaza, a few miles west of the Pont Cassé roundabout. The views are stunning and are best when coming downhill.

North of the Transinsular road are the **Central Forest Reserve** and **Northern Forest Reserve**. In the latter is **Morne Diablotin**. From Dublanc, walk 1½ hours on a minor road and you will see a sign. The trail to the summit is very rough, about three hours' steep walking and climbing up and 2½ hours down, not for the faint hearted, take a guide.

The coastal road continues to **Portsmouth**, the second town. Nearby are the ruins of the 18th-century **Fort Shirley** on the Cabrits, which has a **museum** ① *site pass required, US$2 at the gate*, in one of the restored buildings. It has recently been renovated and there is an excellent plan of how the fort once was. Clearly marked paths lead to the Commander's Quarters, Douglas Battery and other outlying areas. The cruise ship Jetty (small ships only) has a visitors' centre. Prince Rupert Bay has been much visited: Columbus landed here in 1504, and in 1535 the Spanish Council of the Indies declared the bay a station for its treasure ships. Sir Francis Drake, Prince Rupert and John Hawkins all traded with the Caribs. Construction of Fort Shirley began in 1774. It was abandoned in 1854 and initial restoration began in 1982.

From the bridge just south of Portsmouth, boats make regular trips up **Indian River** ① *US$15 per person, 40 mins*, through a tunnel of vegetation, a peaceful trip as long as you are not accompanied by boatloads of other tourists. There is a bar open at the final landing place on this lovely river which accommodates large numbers of cruise ship passengers and serves them the very potent spiced rum, aptly named *Dynamite*. You can then walk through fields and forest to the edge of a marsh where migrating birds come in the winter.

❖ Insist the boatmen use oars rather than a motor.

The north

From Portsmouth, a road carries on to the **Cabrits National Park** and the island's north tip at **Cape Melville**. A new road leads off this at Savanne Paille; it is a beautiful journey over the mountain, through a valley with sulphur springs, to Penville on the north coast, where you can pick up the road heading south.

Another road from Portsmouth heads east, following the Indian River for much of the way, winding up and down to the bays and extensive coconut palm plantations of the northwest coast, Calibishie, Melville Hall Airport and Marigot. There are some beautiful sandy beaches at Hampstead and Larieu. **Calibishie** is a charming fishing village looking across to Guadeloupe. There are hiking trails to the forest and wide, sandy beaches nearby; local guides are available. Transport to most areas in the north is good, as is accommodation. There are some grocery stores, restaurants, post office, petrol station and a health clinic.

Transinsular road

The shortest route from Roseau to Marigot and Melville Hall is via the Transinsular Road. It climbs steeply with many bends from Canefield. You will see coconut and cocoa groves, banana plants all along the gorge, together with dasheen, tannia, oranges and grapefruit. At Pont Cassé, the road divides three ways at one of the island's few roundabouts.

Heading west from Pont Cassé the road affords some spectacular views. Layou River has some good spots for bathing, one of which is particularly good. Just over five miles from the roundabout there is a narrow footpath on the right, immediately before a sizeable road bridge. It passes through a banana field to the riverside. On the opposite bank a concrete bath has been built around a hot spring to create an open-air hot tub (Glo Cho) with room for four or five good friends.

❖ Watch for land crabs' holes; orange juveniles come out by day, white adults by night.

Heading north from Pont Cassé, a 20-minute walk from **Spanny's Bar** on the main road leads you to **Penrice Falls**, two small waterfalls. There is great, but cold, swimming in both pools. At Bells there is a fascinating and beautiful walk to **Jacko Flats**. Here a group of maroons (escaped slaves) led by Jacko had their encampment in the late 17th and early 18th centuries. Carved into the cliffs of the Layou River gorge, a flight of giant steps rises 300 ft up to a plateau where the maroons camped. Ask in Bells village for a guide and dress for river walking since much of the trail is in the river itself.

Heading east from Pont Cassé, the path up the Trois Pitons is signed on the right just after the roundabout, three hours to the summit. The **Emerald Pool** is a small, but pretty waterfall in a grotto in the forest, 15 minutes by path from the Pont Cassé-Castle Bruce road. Don't go when cruise ships have docked. There is a reception area, with snack bar, interpretation centre, stalls and toilet facilities. There are no buses from Roseau. Catch a minibus to Canefield and wait at the junction for a bus going to Castle Bruce.

The Atlantic coast

This coast is much more rugged than the Caribbean, with smaller trees, sandy or pebbly bays, palms and dramatic cliffs. **Castle Bruce** is a lovely bay and there are good views all around. After Castle Bruce the road enters the **Carib Territory**, although there is only a very small sign to indicate this; to appreciate it fully, a guide is essential. **Horseback Ridge** affords views of the sea, mountains, the Concord Valley and Bataka village. At **Crayfish River**, a waterfall tumbles directly into the sea by a beach of large stones. Nearby is the **Carib Cultural Village**, or Kalinago Barana Autê, ① *T4457979, www.kalinagobaranaaute.com, US$8 site pass; tours, drinks, meals and performances cost extra.* The Kalinago (Carib) people have a reception centre, snack bar and gift shop with an easy trail round the huts (ajoupas) in the village. A Karbet (the biggest hut) is used for cultural and theatrical performances. Traditional activities include canoe building, cassava processing, calabash decorating, basket weaving and cooking. You can buy pottery, woven goods, coconut products and other crafts.

The **Save the Children Fund** assisted the Waitikubuli Karifuna Development Committee to construct two traditional buildings near **Salybia**: a large oval *karbet* (the nucleus of the extended Carib family group), and an A-frame *mouina*. The former is a community centre, the latter a library and office of the elected chief. The Carib chief is elected for five years and his main tasks are to organize the distribution of land and the preservation of Carib culture. The Church of the Immaculate Conception at Salybia is based on the traditional *mouina* and has a canoe for its altar, murals about Carib history both inside and out. Outside is a cemetery and a three-stone monument to the first three Carib chiefs after colonization: Jolly John, Auguiste and Corriett.

> ❧ *In May 1997 11 Caribs paddled a traditional 35-ft canoe, carved from a gommier tree, to Guyana, reversing the migratory journey of their ancestors.*

L'Escalier Tête-Chien, at Jenny Point in Sineku is a line of rock climbing out of the sea and up the headland. It is most obvious in the sea and shore, but on the point each rock bears the imprint of a scale, circle or line, like the markings on a snake. It is said that the Caribs used to follow the snake staircase (which was made by the Master Tête-Chien) up to its head in the mountains, thus gaining special powers. Do not go without a guide as there have been a number of incidents of mugging.

In the southeast at La Plaine a fairly easy trail can be followed to the **Sari Sari Falls** (about 150 ft high). At Délices, you can see the **Victoria Falls** from the road. Take an experienced guide if you want to attempt the steep hike to either of these falls and avoid them in the rainy season. The White River falls in to the Atlantic at **Pointe Mulattre**, reached by a steep road from Delices down to the sea. There are great places to picnic, rest or swim in the river. At the weekend local families picnic and wash their cars here. Be wary of flash floods and do not cross the river after heavy rainfall.

The road between **Petite Savanne** and the **White River** links the south and east coasts. It is extremely steep but offers spectacular views of both the Victoria Falls and the steam rising from the Boiling Lake. A new eco-friendly 50-cottage resort and spa has been built close to the White River (www.junglebaydominica.com).

Beaches and activities

The Caribbean side of Dominica gains or loses sand according to swells and storms but the black coral sandy areas are few and far between. A small one exists just off Scott's Head (favoured as a teaching ground for divers, snorkellers and canoeists, so sometimes crowded), but further north you must travel to Mero beach or **Castaways Beach Hotel**. **Macoucheri Bay** and **Coconut Beach** near Portsmouth are probably the best areas for Caribbean bathing. Don't be tempted to swim anywhere near Roseau or the larger villages because of effluent. For some really beautiful, unspoilt, white sandy beaches, hire a 4WD and investigate the bays of the northeast coast. **Turtle Beach**, **Pointe Baptiste** (impressive

> ❧ *Several beaches, coves and rivers were used as locations for the filming of Pirates of the Caribbean 2 and 3; tours are available to some sites.*

red cliffs), **Hampstead** and **Woodford Hill** are all beautiful but the Atlantic coast is dangerous. Look at the sea and swim in the rivers is the safest advice. Very strong swimmers may be exhilarated by **Titou Gorge**, near Laudat, where the water flows powerfully through a narrow canyon and emerges by a hot mineral cascade.

Diving Dominica is highly regarded as a diving destination and has been featured in most diving magazines as 'undiscovered'. Features include wall dives, drop-offs, reefs, hot, freshwater springs under the sea, sponges, black coral, pinnacles and wrecks, all in unpolluted water. Due to steep drops the sediment falls away and visibility is excellent, at up to 30 m depending on the weather. Many drop-offs are close to the beaches but access is poor and boats are essential. There is a marine park conservation area in **Toucari Bay** and part of **Douglas Bay**, north of the Cabrits, but the most popular scuba sites are south of Roseau, at **Pointe Guignard**, **Soufrière Bay** and **Scott's Head**. An unusual site is **Champagne**, with underwater hot springs where you swim through bubbles, good for snorkelling. This area in the southeast, **Soufrière-Scott's Head**, is now a marine park without moorings so that all diving is drift diving and boats pick up divers where they surface. Along the south and southeast coast there are more dive sites but because of the Atlantic currents, these are for experienced, adventurous divers only. Note that the taking of conch, coral, lobster, sponge, turtle eggs, etc, is forbidden and you may not put down anchor in coral and on reefs; use the designated moorings. Snorkelling is good in the same general areas as diving, including Douglas Bay and the Scott's Head/Soufrière Bay Marine Reserve.

Whale and dolphin watching Whale watching is extremely popular, and the success rate is the best in the eastern Caribbean. The female whales and their calves are in the Caribbean waters for much of the year, with only the mature males leaving

to feed for any length of time. If your trip is successful, you could be treated to the sight of mothers and their young swimming close to the boat, or young males making enormous jumps before diving below the waves. Dolphin are abundant too, particularly in the Soufrière Bay area and even if you miss the whales your boat is often accompanied by a school of playful dolphin. Several different types of whales have been spotted not far from the west shore where the deep, calm waters are ideal for these mammals. Sperm whales are regularly seen, especially during the winter months, as are large numbers of spinner and spotted dolphins. You can also sometimes see pilot whales, pseudorcas, pygmy sperm whales, bottlenose dolphins, Risso's dolphins and melon-headed whales.

● Sleeping

Roseau *p709, map p710*

There are some small, informal hotels and guesthouses not listed here. Do verify whether VAT (10%) is included in the quoted rate. Apartments are available to rent in and around Roseau; check at the tourist office, look in the weekly *Chronicle* or ask a taxi driver.

LL-A Fort Young Hotel, within the old fort, T4485000, www.fortyounghotel.com. Ocean front rooms and suites of fine standard and full conference facilities for the business traveller, lots of facilities, service brusque, food adequate, pool, exercise room, jetty, waterfront restaurant, relaxed atmosphere at weekends, special events like concerts and barbecues, Happy Hour every Fri, 1800-1900.

AL-A Garraway, Place Heritage, 1 Bay Front, T4498800, www.garrawayhotel.com. 31 rooms and suites, again of a good standard, conference facilities, restaurant, cocktail bar, senior citizen discounts and weekend deals available.

AL-A Sutton Place Hotel, 25 Old St, T4498700, www.suttonplacehotel dominica.com. 8 rooms, beautiful decor, excellent service, self-catering suites available.

D Cherry Lodge, 20 Kennedy Av, T4482366. Historic but basic, some rooms with bath, rooms can be noisy and mosquitoes abundant, coils provided but no fans, good-value meals available to order.

D Ma Bass Central Guest House, 44 Fields Lane, T4482999. 11 rooms, fans, food available.

Trafalgar Falls *p710*

AL Papillote Wilderness Retreat, T4482287, www.papillote.dm. 10 suites or cottage in beautiful botanical gardens landscaped by owner Anne Jean Baptiste, with hot mineral pool and geese, birdwatching house, food good but slightly limited for long stay; restaurant for non- residents near road, lunch and dinner, food well prepared and nicely presented, closed Sun (avoid days when cruise ship passengers invade, reservations required), arts and crafts boutique, take torch and umbrella, good road from the nearby village of Trafalgar all the way to the falls car park, spectacular setting.

AL-B Roxy's Mountain Lodge in Laudat, T/F4484845, www.avirtualdominica .com/eiroxys. 2,000 ft above sea level, established 1960, good breakfast and hearty supper, friendly owners, 17 rooms, VAT included, good beds, hot showers, also apartment, 4-6 people, Boiling Lake, Boeri Lake, Middleham Falls, Trafalgar Falls and Freshwater Lake, all within walking distance, guides arranged if required, transport into Roseau 0700 except Sun, returning 1615, EC$3.50.

B D'Auchamps, on the road to Trafalgar and Papillote, T4483346, www.avirtualdominica .com/dauchamps. The Honychurch family rents 2 self-contained cottages on their lovely estate, where guests can enjoy the lush botanical gardens. The small cottage has one bedroom and twin beds in the living room, the large cottage two bedrooms, both have kitchens, bathroom, hot water.

South coast *p712*

L-AL Exotica, close to Giraudel, T4488839, www.exotica-cottages.com. Nestled under the peaks of Morne Anglais, ecotourism centre, run by Athie Martin, president of the Dominica Conservation Society, 7 wooden cottages with bedroom, bathroom, kitchen and living room with veranda overlooking the sea and lovely gardens, sympathetic design, good base for hiking, meal plans available or with advance notice Athie's wife, Fae, will prepare organic meals at the Sugar Apple Café.

L-A Reigate Hall, outside Roseau, up a steep and windy hill (King's Hill), T4484031, Reigate@cwdom.dm. A splendid location but laid-back management, recommended for sunset rum punch to watch the Green Flash. 15 rooms and suites, a/c, service in restaurant sloppy and slow, bar, swimming pool, dive packages with Dive Dominica.

AL Castle Comfort Lodge, on seafront, Castle Comfort, T4482188, www.castlecomfort divelodge.com. Breakfast and dinner included in price. Very friendly, professional, 15 rooms, excellent local food, good service. Dive packages available including transfers, tax and service. Closed Sep.

AL Cocoa Cottage, in the Trafalgar Valley, T4480412, www.cocoacottages.com. A neat, clean and homely guest house. 6 different rooms each with bathroom and individually furnished with local materials, including a bed made out of a wooden telephone wire spool. Very rustic and you feel part of the forest. Some rooms sleep 4 in two double beds. Meals available. Tours arranged, including canyoning with Extreme Dominica. Short walk to Middleham Falls.

AL-A Anchorage, on seafront, Castle Comfort, T4482638, www.anchoragehotel.dm. Waterfront restaurant, tatty rooms, bar, friendly but slow service, food nothing special but Thu barbeque buffet good and popular with locals, swimming pool and diving facilities, dive packages available.

A-E Chez Ophelia Cottage Apartments, further up the Roseau Valley, close to Trafalgar Falls, T4483438, www.cwdo.dm/chezophelia. Your host is the famous singer Ophelia, Dominica's 'First Lady of Song'. 5 cottages, in traditional style, each with two connecting apartments sleeping 4 in bedroom, bathroom, kitchen and living room with twin beds, cell phones for rent, Wi-Fi internet access, restaurant serves dinner by reservation only, souvenir shop stocks Ophelia's and other Dominican music.

Leeward Coast *p712*

LL-AL Sunset Bay Club, Batalie Beach in the middle of the west coast, T4466522, www.sunsetbayclub.com. Run by French-speaking Belgian family, all-inclusive or bed and breakfast, rooms, bungalows, suites, pool, beach, discounts for children.

L Crescent Moon Cabins, high above Mahaut but reached from the main Transinsular Rd, about 30 mins from Roseau, T/F4493449, www.crescentmooncabins .com. Well-furnished wooden cabins in a delightful, secluded setting, double and single bed, run by Americans Ron (former chef) and Jean Viveralli, good home cooking, local style, fresh organic fruit and vegetables from on-site greenhouse and gardens, own roasted coffee and cocoa, fresh spring water, cold water in cabins but hot shower by main house, water from Riviere La Croix, drinking water from a spring, breakfast included, dinner US$35, car hire recommended, **Island Car Rentals** will give a discount for guests.

AL Castaways, Mero, T4496245, www.castaways-dominica.com, just north of St Joseph. Convenient with hired car for visiting all parts of the island, on black sand beach, restaurant, beach barbecue on Sun, popular, watch out for beach cricket balls, staff slow but friendly, rooms all with balcony and seaview but hotel is run down and in need of redecoration, ask for fan and mosquito net, tennis court, sailing sometimes available, German spoken.

AL-A Tamarind Tree Hotel & Restaurant, near Salisbury, T/F4497395, www.tamarind treedominica.com. On cliff between Macoucherie and Salisbury beaches, 9 rooms, wheelchair accessible, adjoining rooms/suites for families, fan, fridge, pool, food recommended, Sun brunch all-you-can-eat buffet 1000-1300, included for stays of at least 2 nights, Kubuli beer on draught.

AL-B The Hummingbird Inn, Morne Daniel, Roseau, T/F4491042, www.find-us.net /hummingbird. Rooms (small, luggage is a problem) or a suite, run by Mrs Finucane who is knowledgeable on Dominica, peaceful, simple, comfortable, good food, slow service, stunning views down the hill over the sea, 5 mins north of Roseau, on bus route.

B-C Chez La Doudou Pension, Salisbury, T4996575, http://eastcaribdive.free .fr/doudou. Pleasant guesthouse, run by Beatrice (French) and Harald (German), the owners of **East Carib Dive Centre** (see p724), rooms and apartments 5-10 mins from dive centre.

Portsmouth *p713*

AL-A Coconut Beach, Picard Beach,

T4455393, www.coconutbeachdominica
.com. Beachfront bungalows, apartments,
snorkelling, diving, windsurfing, volleyball,
excursions, restaurant, marina.
AL-A Picard Beach Cottage Resort,
T4455131, pbh@cwdom.dm. An attractive
open-sided restaurant and bar, self-catering
cottages which can sleep 3, good sea
bathing with coral reef, 7-night, 10-dive,
package available.
B Sister Sea Lodge, Prince Rupert's Bay.
T/F4455211, www.sistersealodge.com.
Beach bar, fresh fish and 6 apartments set in
lovely gardens, spacious, self-contained,
insect nets, 2 double beds, bathroom, run by
Harta (German) Sango, yachts can moor in
the bay, sandy outside beach bar.
D Casa Ropa, on Bay St, T4455492,
F4455277. Rooms or apartments with bath,
single downstairs, friendly, clean.

The north p714
LL-L Pointe Baptiste estate, Calibishie,
T4458900, www.pointebaptiste.com. The
Main House sleeps 8, includes cook and
maid, weekly rates available, spectacular
view from the airy veranda, cool breezes,
house built in 1932, wooden, perfect for
children, cot, also smaller house sleeping 2
(**B**), self-catering, book locally through the
manager Carol Ann Watson.
L Eden Estate House, 3 miles from Melville
Hall Airport, T4482638, F4485680. 3
bedrooms, in middle of coconut and fruit
plantation, maid service can be provided.
AL Wind Blow Estate, Calibishie,
www.windblowestate.com. 3 apartments, 1
or 2 bedrooms, fans, sun deck, great views
across to Guadeloupe, parking, security
guard, sisserou parrot nests on the estate.
AL-A Sea Cliff Cottages, 15 mins' walk from
Calibishie, T/F4458998 Dec-May,
T/F6137563116 Jun-Nov, www.dominica-
cottages.com. 3 cottages above Hodges Bay,
1-3 bedrooms, kitchens, veranda, fruit trees
in the garden for seasonal use, path to
beach, snorkelling good, river good for
children to play in, small island within
swimming distance.
AL-A Sunrise Garden Apartments,
Calibishie Ridge Rd, Calibishie, T4458462,
www.calibishiesunrise.com. New 1 or 2
bedroom suites, 2 km from centre of
Calibishie, 3 km from beaches.

A-C Veranda View, Calibishie, T4458900,
www.lodgingdominica.com. Run by Mrs
Teddy Lawrence, facing beach, beautiful
view of Guadeloupe, clean, light cooking
facilities, rooms sleep 2 or 3, hot showers,
Wi-Fi internet access, breakfast available.
B Windswept Guest House, between
Calibishie and airport, T4458982. Quiet,
secluded, clean, close to excellent beach.

The Atlantic coast p715
L Beau Rive, between the Carib Territory and
Castle Bruce, T4458992, www.beaurive.com,
closed Sep. Quiet, elegant, 6 bright and airy
rooms with shower room and balcony, pool,
internet access, buffet breakfast on the terrace
included, dinner is a 3-course set menu for
about US$28 at 1900. Set in 3 acres of gardens
and forest looking down to Anse Francais and
Wakaman Point, you can walk down the
Richmond River to get to the beach, where
there is a rock pool you can sometimes bathe
in. Local artwork on the walls by Marie
Frederick, www.indigo.wetpaint.com.
L Zandoli Inn, Roche Cassee near fishing
village of Stowe in the south, T4463161,
www.zandoli.com. Secluded, superb seaviews
across the bay and to Martinique, 5 rooms
with balconies, meal plans available, plunge
pool, 6 acres of seaside tropical forest.
A Floral Gardens, Concord Village, at the edge
of the Carib Territory, T/F4457636. Comfortable
rooms, with breakfast, apartments, excellent
food but expensive and service very slow,
lovely gardens by the Pagua River where you
can swim, 15 mins away from beaches of
Woodford Hill, electrics basic, ask for a
mosquito coil for your room, many minibuses
in the morning, easy to get a pick-up, bus to
Roseau 1 hr, bus to airport and Woodford Hill
Beach, lovely walks in the area, either into the
Carib territory or around Atkinson further north.
B Carib Territory Guest House, Crayfish
River, on the main road, T4457256,
www.avirtualdominica.com/ctgh.htm. Charles
Williams (the current Carib chief) and his wife,
Margaret, run this guesthouse. She cooks if
meals are ordered in advance but there are no
restaurants nearby, water intermittent, good
base, he also does island-wide tours but is
better on his own patch.
B Domcan's Guest House, north of Castle
Bruce, T4457794, www.domcansguesthouse
.com. 3 new apartments, each with

kitchenette, living room, bathroom and bedroom, with one balcony looking inland to the forest and mountains and another looking through the coconut palms to the sea. Domcan's Restaurant attached, where guests get 10% off all meals.

D Olive's Guest House at Atkinson, T4457521, http://web.ai/olive. Slightly set back off the road, 5 bamboo huts, shared bathroom, comfortable, friendly, meals extra, home grown and roasted coffee, lots of fruits.

Camping

Camping in the national parks is forbidden but some places cater for campers.
A-E 3 Rivers Resort, T4461886, www.3riversdominica.com. On the Rosalie River, variety of accommodation, offering cottages, dormitories, tent sites, jungle cabins, hammock space and guided camping tours, award-winning for its green credentials.

● Eating

Fried chicken, *bakes* (a fried dough patty filled with tuna, codfish or corned beef) and *rotis* (pancake-like parcel of curried chicken and veg) are the most popular snacks available in most bakeries. There is plenty of local fruit and vegetables, fish and *mountain chicken* (crapaud, or frog) in season. Try the seedless golden grapefruit, US$1 for 6 in the market. The term *provisions* on a menu refers to root vegetables: dasheen, yams, sweet potatoes, tannia, pumpkins, etc. Try the sea-moss drink, rather like a vanilla milk shake (with a reputation as an aphrodisiac), also drunk on Grenada, see page 820.

Dominicans eat their main meal at lunch. On weekdays in the capital the lunch hour begins at 1300 and places fill up quickly. There are lots of 'snackettes' in Roseau and Portsmouth.

In restaurants, 15% VAT is added to meal charges and service charge may also be added.

Roseau *p709, map p710*
Cornerhouse, 15 King George V St, T4499000. Mon-Tue 0800-1600, Wed-Fri 0800-2100. Soups, salads, sandwiches, bagels, and burgers, but full meals are pricey, especially when VAT is added. Music, books, magazines, newspapers, internet access.

La Maison, 4 Fort Lane, T4405287. Mon-Sat 1900-2300. French and Creole cuisine, expensive but excellent service and pleasant setting.

La Robe Créole, 3 Victoria St, T4482896. Mon-Sat 1100-1500, 1830-2130. Creole and European, vegetarian available, good but expensive, service frequently inattentive.

Marquis de Bouille, Fort Young Hotel, T4485000. Lunch and dinner. The more formal of the 2 restaurants in this hotel. Serves international and Creole food with themed buffet lunches.

Ti-Caz (Coco-Rico) Café, Bayfront. Mon-Fri 0800-1600. French restaurant, bar, wine store and grocery, excellent range, good service, pleasant environment, sidewalk café.

The Waterfront, Fort Young Hotel, T4485000. Tue-Sun 0700-2200. Has a charming, wooden-balconied seafront location with a romantic and elegant style.

Garden Chinese Restaurant, 80 King George V St, opposite Astaphan's store, T4483389. Mon-Sat 1000-2200. Behind a slightly run-down exterior is a good restaurant with a wide range of well-priced Chinese dishes, with a/c.

Guiyave, 15 Cork St. Mon-Fri 0900-1600, Sat 0900-1400. For midday snacks and juices, patisserie and salad bar, popular, plant-lined balcony, crowded after 1300.

O'Byrne's Pub & Grub, Castle St, behind La Robe Creole, T4404337. Open from 1700 Mon-Sat. Irish-themed pub and restaurant. Lively, with draft Kubuli and bangers and mash.

Pearl's Cuisine, 50 King George V St. Mon-Sat 0900-1900. Good range of inexpensive local food, with pleasant balcony.

Restaurant Paiho, 10 Church St, T4488999. Mon-Sat 1100-1500, 1730-2230, Sun 1800-2200. Good Chinese food, delicious fruit punch, uncrowded, balcony, slightly pricey.

Mousehole Café, underneath La Robe Creole, T4482896, same ownership. Mon-Fri 0800-1600, Sat 0800-1300. Excellent for pies and local pasties.

Trafalgar Falls *p710*
Papillote (see page 717), T4482287. Daily 0700-2200. Book before 1600 for an evening meal, take swimming costume and towel to bathe in sulphur pool under the stars.

South coast *p712*

¶¶ Taiwanese Delicacies, between Newtown and Castle Comfort. Open daily from 2000. Chinese restaurant with a good atmosphere, good food and friendly hosts, see Nightlife, below for karaoke.

¶ Chez Wen, Scott's Head, T4486668. Daily 1200-late. Overlooking the bay, serving shellfish and drinks, popular with divers, good prices.

Leeward coast *p713*

On Portsmouth's Bay Rd there are several snackettes selling roti and bakes at lunchtime.

¶¶ Mango's Bar & Restaurant, Bay St, Portsmouth, T4453099. Daily 0800-2300. Yellow and white house with tin roof, mural inside of island life, varied menu, credit cards accepted.

¶¶ Purple Turtle, Lagon, Portsmouth, T4455296. Mon-Fri 1000-2300, Sat-Sun 1000-0200. On beach, snacks and full meals, good roti, local and international food, karaoke at weekends.

¶ The Shacks, next to Ross Medical School on the Portsmouth-Roseau road in Portsmouth are food stalls serving cheap and good snack food, pizza, hot roti and fried chicken, bakes, pastries, fruit, fresh juices.

The Atlantic coast *p715*

¶¶ DomCan's Café, north of Castle Bruce on the main road, T4457754. Open 0900-2200. Good service, lunch of sandwiches and burgers, dinner fish, chicken, mountain chicken.

Bars and clubs

Dominica *p709, maps p710 and p708*

Fri is *the* night out, with people (locals and tourists alike) moving from **Fort Young**'s Happy Hour across to **La Robe**'s Happy Hour or to **Garraway**'s, into town and on to **Cellar's Bar** or **O'Byrnes Irish Pub**. If you've still got energy, it's on to one of the discos such as **Warehouse** (see below), which never get going until after midnight. However, there are a growing number of places to eat and hang out south of Roseau, in the 2-mile stretch from the city centre to the village of Loubiere. They represent a good cross section of bars, places to eat and nightspots, ranging from down-to-earth to upmarket. For lovers of zouk music, look out for live performances by WCK, Midnight Groovers or First Serenade.

Cellars Bar, downstairs at Sutton Place Hotel, Old St, Roseau. Daily 1600-2200, later on Wed and Fri. Big screen TV, karaoke, jazz, a/c.

Fort Young Hotel, Roseau. Nightclub open Fri and Sat, Fri night happy hour 1800-1900. Live music, popular.

Green Flash Grille, Loubiere, T4482145. Wed-Sun 1700-2200. A nice casual spot with tables by the sea and a good range of food and drinks. Great place to watch the sun go down.

Palm Grove, Louisville in the Roseau Valley, about 2 miles from Roseau, T4485434. Mon-Sat 1000-2300. A popular nightspot, particularly good around Carnival when it hosts Calypso shows, 'tents', EC$25, major shows EC$45. Food served.

Rivers International Nightclub and Bar, opposite Ross University, Portsmouth, T4454777. Fri-Sun from 2200. Local and international music, a/c.

Spiders, Loubiere, no phone. Daily 2230-late. Guaranteed to be open when everywhere else has closed, it is a hole in the wall with great Caribbean music, some of the cheapest beers, fried chicken and the famous *spider pies* (they are actually fish and cost EC$1.25).

Symes-Zee, King George V St, Roseau, T4482494. Mon-Sat 2200-late. The spot to be on Thu night with live jazz, nice atmosphere.

Yacht Inn, between Newtown and Castle Comfort, T4483497. Mon-Sat 1200-2300. Start your evening with brazed shrimp or sweet and sour. If it's happening, join in the karaoke.

Warehouse, Canefield, no phone. Sat from 2200. Disco in converted sugar mill by the airport, gets going after 2400. Recommended.

Entertainment

Dominica *p709, maps p710 and p708*
Theatre

The Arawak House of Culture, Hillsborough St in Roseau, next to Government HQ, T4491804. Can seat 540 for plays, concerts, dance shows and recitals.

Old Mill Cultural Centre in Canefield, T4491804. Performances are also held here.

❂ Festivals and events

Dominica *p709, maps p710 and p708*
For information about any festivals contact the Dominica Festivals Commission, T4482045, dfc@cwdom.dm.
Feb/Mar Carnival is on the Mon and Tue before Ash Wed; it lacks the sponsorship of a carnival like Trinidad's, but it is one of the most spontaneous and friendly. Sensay costume has returned to the streets: layer upon layer of banana or cloth is used for the costume, a scary mask is worn over the face, usually with horns, and big platform clog boots finish the effect. Large quantities of beer are required for anyone who can wear this costume and dance the streets for several hours in the midday sun. During Carnival, laws of libel and slander are suspended.
Jun-Jul Fête Marin (St Peter's) in Portsmouth as well as in Soufrière/Scott's Head, Colihaut/Dublanc and Anse de Mai.
Jul Divefest, with lots of activities, races, underwater treasure hunts, cruises, etc. Contact the Watersports Association, T4482188, dive@cwdom.dm.
Oct Dominica hosts the World Creole Music Festival, with Cadence, Zouk, Compas, Bouyou and Soukous. Artists come from other islands such as Haiti, Martinique and Cuba, or further afield from Africa, the UK and Louisiana, as well as from Dominica. A season ticket costs US$70, or US$38 on the gate. **Last Fri in Oct** Creole Day, when the vast majority of girls and women wear the national dress, 'la wobe douillete', to work and school and most shop assistants, bank clerks, etc, speak only Creole to the public.
3-4 Nov Independence Day celebrations feature local folk dances, competitions, storytelling, music and crafts.

◐ Shopping

Roseau *p709, map p710*
Art galleries
The Art Asylum, Massacre. Is the gallery of Earle Etienne.
Coco Rico Art Craft, Bayfront, Roseau, T4498686. Has a crafts shop and houses the art gallery of Ellingsworth Moses.
Indigo, Bourne, and at Beau Rive Hotel, www.indigo.wetpaint.com. Is the gallery of Marie (Bouvet) Frederick.

Books
Front Line Co-operative Services Ltd, 78 Queen Mary St, T4488664. Books, CDs, cassettes, stationery, photography, etc.
New Paperbacks, Great George St, T4485998. Caribbean and other English books and magazines.

Crafts and gifts
Straw goods are among the best and cheapest in the Caribbean; they can be bought in the Carib Territory and Roseau.
Other good buys are local Bay Rum (aftershave and body rub), coconut soap, tea, coffee, marmalade, hand cream, shampoo, spices, chocolate and candles. Bello 'Special' or 'Classic' pepper sauce is a good souvenir.
Craft Market, at the Old Market, Roseau. A good place to start and get an idea of what is available.
Tropicrafts, Queen Mary St, Roseau. You can see the women making the famous vetiver-grass mats. It takes 4 weeks to complete a 10 ft mat. Note 4% extra charged on VISA.

Food
If you are in a self-catering cottage anywhere on the island, local farmers may visit with their fresh produce for sale. To buy fresh fish listen for the fishermen blowing their conch shells in the street; there is no fish shop in Roseau but fish can be bought at the Fisheries Complex or in the market on Fri and Sat, get there early, usually EC$7 per pound. Fishing villages such as Calibishie (north coast) or Fond St Jean (south coast) are good sources of fresh fish; go down to the bay side around 1630 when the boats come in and get some kingfish or snapper for your evening meal.
Brizee's Mart, 5 mins from Roseau centre, T4482087, Canefield. Mon-Thu 0900-2000, Fri-Sat 0900-2100. One of the largest supermarkets.
Whitchurch Supermarket, Old St, Roseau. Mon-Thu 0800-1900, Fri-Sat 0800-2000. Has good range at reasonable prices.

Portsmouth *p713*
Crafts and gifts
Portsmouth has a sizeable craft shop at the Cruise Ship Berth on the Cabrits but prices are much higher than in Roseau.
Dominica Pottery has a showroom on

corner of Bayfront and Kennedy Av with plenty of original pieces made by inmates of the prison.

Batiks are made locally and available from **Cotton House Batik**, 8 Kings Lane. Many local crafts available at the **NDFD Small Business Complex**, 9 Great Marlborough St.

Food

James Supermarket, opposite Ross Medical School. Good selection of staples and imported foodstuffs, frozen meats, ham, etc, also prepaid phone cards.

Markets

At Portsmouth there is an excellent market twice a week where you can find fresh fruit, vegetables and spices locally grown.

▲ Activities and tours

Dominica p709, maps p710 and p708

Adventure parks

Rainforest Aerial Tram, T4488775, www.rfat.com. Ride through the rainforest canopy or walk a trail which crosses an exciting suspension bridge. Open only when there is cruise ship in port.

Wacky Rollers, T2356264, www.wackyrollers.com. Runs the Adventure Park on the Layou River in the forest with suspended walkways and platforms connected by cables, zip lines and a Tarzan jump. Varied levels for different abilities, a children's park and picnic area. Opening times restricted if it is a non-cruise ship day.

Canyoning

Extreme Tours, Roseau Valley, T4480412, www.cocoacottages.com. Rock climbing, abseiling and rappelling. Plenty of waterfalls, gorges, rivers and pools to keep anyone occupied, including Ti Tou Gorge, Middleham Falls and up the White River to the Boiling Lake. Small group of local guides certified by Ti Mountaineering. Maximum 10 people. Safety helmets, harnesses and all necessary equipment for rappelling and climbing, life jackets and waterproof bag all provided. Wet suits are essential and can be rented.

Climbing

Mountain climbing can be organized

through the **Forestry Division**, T4482401. Guides are necessary for any forays into the mountains or forests, some areas of which are still uncharted.

Cricket

Cricket is among the most popular national sports; watch it in the beautiful setting of the **Botanical Gardens** or at the dramatic pitch at **Petite Savanne** where 2 sides of the boundary line run along a cliff overlooking the Atlantic. The new national stadium in Roseau will be completed in 2007 and seat 12,000. The next best pitch is at **Macoucherie**, close to the rum distillery.

Cycling

Cycling is growing in popularity and the island's roads, although twisty, are good. traffic is generally light with the exception of the stretch from Roseau to Layou. Between Canefield and Pont Cassé it is very steep, twisty and challenging. Mountain bikes can be hired from **Nature Island Dive** at Soufrière, T4498181, natureidive@ cwdom.dm, where there are marked off-road trails. Mountain bike rental, US$11 per hr, US$21 half day, US$32 per day. Biking trips also arranged, US$84 per person with guide.

Diving

Snorkelling trips, around US$26, are particularly recommended for the Champagne area. Scuba diving is permitted only through one of the island's registered dive operators or with written permission from the **Fisheries Division**. Single-tank dives are from US$42 and 2-tank dives are from US$63. There is a US$2 per dive user fee in the marine reserves. A hyperbaric chamber was installed in 2006.

ALDive, Loubiere, T4403483, www.aldive .com. Diving, including courses, whale and dolphin watching US$50, surfing, kayaks. Run by Billy and Samantha Lawrence. A single dive is US$55, a two-tank dive US$80, Open Water Diver certification is US$400.

Anchorage Dive Centre, T4482638, anchorage@cwdom.dm, is based at the **Anchorage Hotel**, Castle Comfort, with a sister operation at the **Portsmouth Beach Hotel**. This is another long-established operation with a good reputation, owned by Andrew Armour.

Cabrits Dive Centre, operate from Picard Estate, Portsmouth, T4453010, www.cabritsdive.com. Diving and snorkelling in the less-visited north of the island.

Dive Dominica Ltd, at **Castle Comfort Lodge**, T4482188, www.castlecomfortdivelodge .com. Offers full diving and accommodation packages, courses, single or multiple day dives, night dives and equipment rental. Owned by Derek Perryman, this is one of the most friendly and experienced operations, recommended for its professional service.

East Carib Dive Centre, Salisbury, T4996575, www.eastcaribdive.dm.

Nature Island Dive at Soufrière, T4498181, www.natureislanddive.com. Also snorkelling, kayaking and mountain biking, is run by a team of divers from around the world. Ask about accommodation and dive packages; they have a bayside wooden cottage on stilts with porch for up to 4 divers, **Gallette**.

Fishing
Dive Dominica, see above, with charters at US$460 half day or US$920 full day.

Hiking
Hiking in the mountains is excellent, and hotels and tour companies arrange this type of excursion.
Lambert Charles, strong on conservation and hiking, no office but T4483365.

Horse riding
High Ride Stables, Bellevie Chopin on the road to Grand Bay, T4486296, highridestables@yahoo.com. Contact Dave Winston. US$25 per hr. Dave also offers **ATV** tours through the rainforest.

Kayaking and windsurfing
Freshwater Lake, T2255332, warmmaeletang@gmail.com. Contact Warmmae Letang for kayaking on the Freshwater Lake or take a guided boat tour, US$10 per hr per 2-person kayak.
Nature Island Dive (see above). Rents out sea kayaks for US$11 per hr, US$26 per half day and US$42 per full day, lifejackets and instruction in Soufrière Bay provided. Guided tours are available.
Wacky Rollers, T2356264, www.wackyrollers.com, and **Dominica Adventure Vacations**, T440RIDE, both offer guided river tubing and kayaking down the Layou River, Dominica's largest. Price for 3-hr trip starts at US$40. Tours are geared to cruise ship visitors so check for availability beforehand.
Wave Dancer at Portsmouth, T4454580. Offers kayaks, tubing and windsurfing.

Sailing
Gusty winds coming down from the hills make sailing difficult and unreliable; conditions are rarely suitable for beginners. The best harbour for yachts is Portsmouth (Prince Rupert Bay), but you should guard your possessions. Stealing from yachts is quite common. The jetty in Roseau is designed for small craft, such as yachts, clearing for port entry. Some hotels have moorings: **Fort Young** charges US$5 per day, US$30 per week, US$100 per month; **Reigate Waterfront** and **Anchorage** have moorings and a pier, and yachtsmen and women are invited to use the hotels' facilities.

Tour operators
Island tours can be arranged through many of the hotels.
Alfred Rolle's Unique Tour Services, Trafalgar Village, T4487198, or through **Papillote**. Alfred is recommended.
Ken's Hinterland Adventure Tours and Taxi Service (Khatts Ltd), Fort Young Hotel, Roseau, T4484850, www.kenshinterlandtours .com. The most knowledgeable operators. Ken and Clem recommended, lots of languages spoken.
Nature Island Destinations, PO Box 1639, Rosseau, T4496233, www.natureisland.com. Arrange everything from accommodation to car hire, scuba diving and whalewatching, for all budgets and tastes.
Whitchurch Travel Agency, Old St, Roseau, T4482181, www.whitchurch.com. Handles local tours as well as foreign travel and represents American Express Travel Related Services, several airlines and L'Express des Îles.

Whale watching
Whale watching trips can be arranged with the *Anchorage Hotel* (Thursday, Sunday 1400-1800), *Dive Dominica* (Wednesday, Sunday 1400), or *ALDive*, see above. Trips cost US$40-50 per person.

☉ Transport

Dominica *p709, maps p710 and p708*

Air

Airport Dominica has 2 airports, **Melville Hall** (DOM) in the northeast, which handles most planes (including **LIAT/Caribbean Star**), and **Canefield** (DCF) near Roseau, which takes only very small aircraft. Check which your flight will be using. Melville Hall has no currency exchange facilities, so if you are arriving from Europe it is best to have US dollars to hand. Melville Hall is 36 miles from Roseau; shuttle taxis cost US$18 per person, whichever route the driver takes. From Melville Hall to Portsmouth by taxi is EC$30. These rates are per seat; find someone to share with, or it will be assumed you want the vehicle to yourself, which is much more expensive. Canefield is only a 10 mins drive from Roseau; taxi fare to town is US$8 per person for up to 4 passengers. Minibus (public transport) fare from Canefield to Roseau is EC$2. (You must flag one down on the highway passing the airport, frequent service weekdays, fewer on Sun.)

Variable winds and short landing strips mean that planes do not land before 0600 or after 1800 in the dark, although night landing is planned.

From Anguilla, Antigua, Barbados, Fort-de-France, Grenada, Pointe-à-Pitre, Port of Spain, St Kitts, St Lucia, Sint Maarten, St Vincent and Tortola/Beef Island (BVI) **LIAT/Caribbean Star** or **Winair**; from San Juan, **American Eagle**.

Airline offices LIAT/Caribbean Star, King George V St, Roseau, T4482421/2; Canefield Airport, T4491421; Melville Hall, T4457242. **American Eagle/AA**, Melville Hall, T4457204. **Whitchurch Travel** are recommended for any enquiries, T4482181, www.whitchurch.com.

Boat

L'Express des Îles ferries operate from Roseau bayfront to **Fort-de-France** (1½ hrs), **Pointe-à-Pitre** (1¾ hrs) and **Castries** (3-3¾ hrs). The fare is the same to whichever island you are going to, EC$195 one way, EC$218 with a stopover, EC$275 return. Port taxes must be paid on departure from each port. Day trips are usually only possible to Fort-de-France and Pointe-à-Pitre Mon and Wed, all other routes require an overnight stay. Check timetables before planning a trip. They vary week to week and month by month. There is no service for 3 weeks in Jun and for 3 weeks end-Sep-beginning of Oct. The **L'Express des Îles** agency office is upstairs in the Whitchurch Centre, T4482181, www.whitchurch.com or www.express-des-iles.com.

Bus

Minibuses run from point to point. Those from Roseau to the northwest and northeast leave from between the east and west bridges near the modern market; to **Trafalgar** and Laudat from Valley Rd, near the Police HQ; for the south and **Petite Savane** from Old Market Place. They are difficult to get on early morning unless you can get on a 0630 bus out to the villages to pick up schoolchildren. Many buses pass the hotels south of Roseau. Fares are fixed by the Government. Roseau to **Salisbury** is EC$4, to **Portsmouth** EC$8, to **Woodford Hill** EC$9.95, to **Marigot** EC$9.50, to **Castle Bruce** EC$7.50, **Canefield** EC$2, **Laudat** EC$3.50, **Trafalgar** EC$2.75, **Soufrière/ScottsHead** EC$4.

Car

Driving is on the left. The steering wheel may be on either side. The speed limit is 10 mph near schools, 20 mph in Roseau and villages. No limit elsewhere.

If you are aged between 25 and 65, with two year's driving experience, you may purchase a local driving permit, valid for 1 month, for US$12, for which a valid international or home driving licence is required. The permit may be bought from the police at airports, rental agencies, or at the Traffic Dept, High St, Roseau or Bay St, Portsmouth (Mon to Fri).

Car hire Rates are about US$60 per day for a car, including collision damage waiver and 5% tax, and US$70 for a jeep; unlimited mileage for hiring for 3 days or more. A car rental phone can be found at the airport and several of the companies will pick you up from there and help to arrange the licence. It is extremely difficult to hire a vehicle between Christmas and New Year, or at Carnival and Independence without prior reservation.

Anselm's, 3 Great Marlborough St, T4482730.
Best Deal, T4499204, www.bestdealrentacar

.com. Popular and reliable.

Budget, Canefield Industrial Estate, opposite airport, T4492080. Recommended as cheaper, more reliable and informative than some other companies, courteous and efficient, cars in good condition. Recommended for service is Courtesy Car Rental, 10 Winston Lane, Goodwill, Roseau, T4487763, www.avirtualdominica.com/courtesycarrental. Cars from US$39 per day, and jeeps up to US$66 per day, cheaper for longer, plus tax and collision damage waiver, free pick up and drop off from Canefield, ferry and hotels within 5 miles of office, but not from Melville Hall, which incurs extra charges.
Garraway Rent-a-Car, 17 Old St, Roseau, T4482891, www.avrtualdominica.com /garrawaycarrental. A/c car US$50 per day.
Island Car Rentals, Goodwill Rd, Roseau, T448-2886/3425, www.islandcar.dm. From US$45 daily including VAT, 24-hr emergency service.
STL, Goodwill Rd, T4482340. US$387 per 10 days including EC$20 licence and insurance, free deliveries as for Valley, but only in Roseau area.
Valley, on Goodwill Rd, next to Dominican Banana Marketing Corporation, T4483233, or in Portsmouth, T4455252, www.valleydominica.com. Free delivery to Canefield and within 5 miles of Roseau or Portsmouth offices, cars in need of maintenance but in the cheaper category.
Wide Range Car Rentals, 79 Bath Rd, T4483181. Rents out old Lada cars for US$30 per day, not recommended for smaller roads, also Suzuki jeeps, US$60 per day including 80 miles and free collision damage waiver.

Taxi
Taxis and minivans have HA or H on the licence plate. A sightseeing tour by taxi will cost US$18 per hr per car (4 people), but it is wise to use experienced local tour operators for sightseeing, particularly if hiking is involved. Fares on set routes are fixed by the Government. Ask at your hotel for a taxi and if you want one after 1800 you should arrange it in advance.
In Roseau, Mally's Tour & Taxi Service, 64 Cork St, T4483360/3114, F4483689 (if planning a day trip out of town on public transport, you can sometimes arrange to be picked up and returned to Roseau by their airport taxi service); Eddie, 8 Hillsborough St, T4486003; and others.

❶ Directory

Dominica *p709, maps p710 and p708*
Banks Royal Bank of Canada, Bay St, Roseau, T4482771. FirstCaribbean International Bank Plc, 2 Old St, T4482571 (branch in Portsmouth, T4455271). National Commercial Bank of Dominica, 64 Hillsborough St, T4484401. Opens lunchtime, branch at Portsmouth, T4455430, and at Canefield near the airport. Scotia Bank, 28 Hillsborough St, T4485800. Visa and MasterCard accepted with cash advances from all banks. **Embassies and consulates** Belgium, T4482168. France, T4482033. Netherlands, T4483841. Spain, T4482063. Sweden, T4482181. UK, T4481000. **Internet** Cornerhouse, 15 King George St, T4499000, 3 computers for internet access, cornerhoused@hotmail.com, with food. Cable & Wireless, Kennedy Av, Roseau, T4481000, www.cwdom.dm, has cellular service, credit card calling and a cybercafé. **Medical services** There are three public hospitals on the island: the Marigot Hospital, T4457091, the Portsmouth Hospital, T4455237, and the Princess Margaret Hospital, T4482231. Casualty and intensive care units are available at the Portsmouth Hospital and the Princess Margaret Hospital (PMH). The PMH also has a hyperbaric chamber. Several specialists and general practitioners operate private clinics. Hillborough St Clinic is quite large with pharmacy attached. Note that you have to pay in advance for everything (for example EC$80 for consultation, EC$160 for X-ray). **Post** Post office at Hillsborough St and Bay St, Roseau, Mon-Fri 0800-1600. A mural depicts the development of the postal service in Dominica. It has a philately counter and list of other stamp sellers around the island. A postcard to the USA or Europe costs EC$0.55, letters EC$0.90. Post your mail at the main post office if possible, post boxes around the country are not all in operation and there is no indication of which ones are out of service. DHL is near the Whitchurch Centre, represented by Whitchurch Travel Agency, T4482181, F4485787.

Telephone Telephone and fax services at
Cable & Wireless (Dominica), Mercury
House, Hanover St, Roseau. Mon-Sat
0700-2000. **Phone cards** are available for
EC$10, 20 and 40. **Cable & Wireless**, **Digicel**
and **Orange** all offer cellular service.

727

Background

History

The Caribs, who supplanted the Arawaks on Dominica, called the island Waitikubuli, ('tall is her body'). Columbus sighted it on 3 November 1493, a Sunday (hence the current name), but the Spanish took no interest in the island. It was fought over by the French, British and Caribs. In 1660, the two European powers agreed to leave Dominica to the Caribs, but the arrangement lasted very few years; in 1686, the island was declared neutral, again with little success. As France and England renewed hostilities, the Caribs were divided between the opposed forces and suffered the heaviest losses in consequence. In 1763, Dominica was ceded to Britain, and in 1805, possession was finally settled. Nevertheless, its position between the French colonies of Guadeloupe and Martinique, and the strong French presence over the years, ensured that despite English institutions and language the French influence was never eliminated.

During the 19th century, Dominica was largely neglected and underdevelopment provoked social unrest. Henry Hesketh Bell, the colonial administrator from 1899 to 1905, made great improvements to infrastructure and the economy, but by the late 1930s the British Government's Moyne Commission discovered a return to a high level of poverty on the island. Assistance to the island was increased with some emphasis put on road building to open up the interior. This, together with agricultural expansion, house building and use of the abundant hydro resources for power, contributed to development in the 1950s and 1960s.

In 1939, Dominica was transferred from the Leeward to the Windward Islands Federation; it gained separate status and a new constitution in 1960, and full internal autonomy in 1967. The Commonwealth of Dominica became an independent republic within the Commonwealth in 1978. The Dominica Labour Party dominated island politics after 1961, ushering in all the constitutional changes. Following Independence, however, internal divisions and public dissatisfaction with the administration led to its defeat by the Dominica Freedom Party in the 1980 elections. The DFP Prime Minister, Miss (now Dame) Mary Eugenia Charles, adopted a pro-business, pro-United States line to lessen the island's dependence on limited crops and markets. She was re-elected in 1985 and again in 1990, having survived an earlier attempted invasion by supporters of former DLP premier, Patrick John.

In 1995 Dame Eugenia retired at the age of 76, having led her party since 1968. The general elections won by the United Workers Party (UWP) and Mr Edison James was sworn in as Prime Minister. The general elections in 2000 gave the Dominica Labour Party (DLP) 42.9%, the UWP 43.4% and the DFP 13.6% of the vote. The DLP and DFP formed a coalition and on 3 February Mr Rosie Douglas was sworn in as Prime Minister. However, the country was stunned by his death, aged 58, in 2000. He was replaced by his deputy, Pierre Charles, who also died suddenly in January 2004. Charles was replaced by Roosevelt Skerrit, who became the world's youngest Prime Minister at age 31. He contested and won a close General Election on 5 May 2005.

Government

Dominica is a fully independent member of the British Commonwealth. The single chamber House of Assembly has 31 members: 21 elected by the constituencies, nine Senators appointed by the President on the advice of the Prime Minister and Leader of the Opposition, and the Attorney-General. The Prime Minister and Leader of the Opposition also nominate the President, who holds office for five years.

Owing to the difficulty of the terrain, only about a quarter of the island is cultivated. Nevertheless, it is self-sufficient in fruit and vegetables and agriculture contributes about 20% to gross domestic product. The main products are bananas (the principal export), coconuts (most of which are used in soap and cooking oil production), grapefruit, limes and other citrus fruits. The opening up of the European market in 1992 affected Dominica's banana industry. Together with the other Windward Islands producers it has to compete with the large exporters from the US dollar areas, mainly in Latin America. Other crops are under development: coffee, cocoa, mango, citrus and root crops such as dasheen, to diversify away from bananas.

Manufacturing industry is small but takes advantage of locally generated hydroelectricity. **Dominica Coconut Products (DCP)** is Dominica's largest business. Labour intensive electronic assembly plants, data processing and clothing manufacturing are being encouraged for their foreign exchange earnings potential. Tourism is being promoted with the emphasis officially on nature tourism. Total stayover visitor arrivals are around 79,000 a year. The aim is for the development of sustainable long-term niche tourism projects.

Geography

Dominica is one of the largest and most mountainous of the anglophone Windward Islands. It is 29 miles long and 16 miles wide, with an area of 290 sq miles. The highest peak, **Morne Diablotin**, rises to 4,747 ft and is often shrouded in mist. It is known as the Nature Island of the Caribbean with parks and reserves protecting vast areas of forest that cover most of the interior. The rainy season is from July to November though showers occur all through the year. Note that the mountains are much wetter and cooler than the coast. Roseau receives about 85 ins of rain a year, while the mountains get over 340 ins. In addition, the frequent rainfall and many rivers have led to some very dramatic seascapes with beautiful hard and soft coral.

People

The island's mountainous terrain discourages the creation of large estates and so there are many small farmers. In Dominica, over 2,000 descendants of the original inhabitants of the Caribbean, the once warlike Caribs, live in the Carib Territory, a 3,700-acre 'reservation' established in 1903 in the northeast. There are no surviving speakers of the Carib language on the island. The total population is otherwise almost entirely of African descent, of whom about 29% live in the parish of St George, around Roseau. Other parishes are more sparsely populated. The parish of St John, in which Portsmouth (the second largest town) is situated contains only about 5,000 people, or 7% of the population.

Like St Lucia, Dominica was once a French possession and although English is the official tongue, most of the inhabitants also speak Kwéyòl (French-based patois). In the Marigot/Wesley area a type of English called *kokoy* is used; the original settlers of the area, freed slaves, came from Antigua and are mostly Methodists. Catholicism predominates, though there are some Protestant denominations and an increasing number of fundamentalist sects, imported from the USA.

Culture

❖ *The World Creole Music Festival in October is a great insight into regional music trends, whether it's Cadence, Soukous, Compas, Zouk or Bouyou.*

Popular culture reflects the mixture of native and immigrant peoples. While most places on Dominica have a Carib, a French or an English name, the indigenous Carib traditions and way of life have been localized in the northeast, giving way to a dominant amalgam of Creole (French and African) tradition. Dominicans are proud of their local language, which is increasingly being used in print. A dictionary was published in

You can get hold of this at the **FrontLine Bookshop**, Independence St, Roseau.

There is a thriving music scene, helped by the WICE recording studio in Dominica. Popular local bands include **WCK**, **First Serenade** and **Midnight Groovers**, who you can often catch at discos and nightclubs. **Midnight Groovers** is led by Phillip 'Chubby' Mark, known as the 'King of Cadence-Lypso'. Anthony Gussie leads his band **Black Affairs Plus**, and sings in French, English, Kwéyòl and Kokoy.

Flora and fauna

There are several national parks, including the **Morne Trois Pitons** (17,000 acres and a UNESCO World Heritage Site) in the south, the **Central Forest Reserve** and the **Northern Forest Reserve**, which together protect rainforest covering much of the island's mountainous interior. At the highest levels on the island is elfin woodland, characterized by dense vegetation and low-growing plants. Elfin woodland and high montane thicket give way to rainforest at altitudes between 1,000 and 2,500 ft, extending over about 60% of the island. The Morne Trois Pitons Reserve has the richest biodiversity in the Lesser Antilles. It contains five volcanoes, on the slopes of which there are 50 fumaroles and hot springs, freshwater lakes and a 'boiling lake'.

❦ Dominica is a botanist's and a birdwatcher's paradise.

The **Cabrits Peninsula** in the northwest was declared a national park in 1986. Covering 1,313 acres, its twin hills covered by dry forest, it is separated from the island by marshland (a pier and cruise ship reception centre have been built) which is a nesting place for herons and doves and hosts a variety of migrant bird species. A walk through the woods and around the buildings of **Fort Shirley** (abandoned in 1854) will reveal much flora and wildlife. The scuttling hermit (or soldier) and black crabs, ground lizard (*abòlò*) and tree lizard are most visible.

In addition to the huge variety of trees, many of which flower in March and April, there are orchids and wild gardens in the valleys. Bwa Kwaib or Carib wood (*Sabinea carinalis*) is the national flower; found mostly growing along parts of the west coast. Indigenous birds to the island are the imperial parrot, or sisserou (*Amazona imperialis*), which is critically endangered, and its marginally less threatened relative, the red-necked parrot, or Jacquot (*Amazona araúsiaça*). The sisserou is the national bird. They can be seen in the **Syndicate** area in the northwest, which is now a protected reserve (accessible by 4WD only). There is a nature trail but signs are difficult to spot. The parrots are most evident during their courting season, in April and early May. To get the best from a parrot-watching trip, it is worth taking a guide (Bertrand Jno Baptiste, of the Forestry Division, T4482401, and Homid Laurent, T4497147, have been recommended). While there are other rare species, such as the forest thrush and the blue-headed hummingbird, there are a great many others which are easily spotted (the purple-throated carib and Antillean-crested hummingbirds, for instance), or heard (the *siffleur montagne*). Waterfowl can be seen on the lakes, waders on the coastal wetlands (many are migrants).

There are fewer species of mammal (agouti, manicou-opossum, wild pig and bats in caves, most particularly at Thiband on the northeast coast), but there is a wealth of insect life (for example, over 55 species of butterfly) and reptiles. There is the rare iguana, the *crapaud* (a large frog, eaten under the name of 'mountain chicken') and five snakes, none poisonous (includes the boa constrictor, or *tête-chien*). Certain parts of the coast are used as nesting grounds by sea turtles (hawksbill, leatherback and green). As a result of over-hunting, the Forestry Division has extended the close season for hunting wildlife like *crapaud*. **The Forestry Division** ① *Botanical Gardens, Roseau, T4482401, F4487999*, has a wide range of publications, trail maps, park guides, posters and leaflets (some free) on Dominica's wildlife and national parks.

The best known of Dominica's writers are the novelists **Jean Rhys** and **Phyllis Shand Allfrey**. Rhys (1894-1979), who spent much of her life in Europe and wrote mainly about that continent; only flashback scenes in *Voyage in the Dark* (1934), her superb last novel, *Wide Sargasso Sea* (1966, which was made into a film in 1991), her uncompleted autobiography, *Smile Please*, and resonances in some of her short stories draw on her West Indian experiences. Allfrey published only one novel, *The Orchid House* (1953); *In the Cabinet* was left unfinished at her death in 1986. Allfrey was one of the founder members of the Dominica Labour Party, became a cabinet minister in the short-lived West Indian Federation, and was later editor of the *Dominica Herald* and *Dominica Star* newspapers. *The Orchid House* was filmed by Channel 4 (UK) in 1990 for international transmission as a four-part series.

For a history of the island, see *The Dominica Story*, by Lennox Honychurch (ISBN 0-333-62776-8).

St Lucia → *Country code: 758. Colour map 4, B5.*

Very popular as both a family holiday destination and a romantic paradise for honeymooners, St Lucia (pronounced 'Loosha') offers something for everyone. Its beaches are golden or black sand, some with the spectacular setting of the Pitons as a backdrop, and many are favoured by turtles as a nesting site. Offshore there is good diving and snorkelling, with a marine park along part of the west coast. Rodney Bay is one of the best marinas in the West Indies and windsurfing and other watersports are available. The mountainous interior is outstandingly beautiful and there are several forest reserves to protect the St Lucian parrot and other wildlife. Sightseeing opportunities include sulphur springs, colonial fortifications and plantation tours. St Lucia has a rich cultural heritage, having alternated between the French and English colonial powers, both of whom used African slaves, and has produced some of the finest writers and artists in the region. The island has the distinction of having produced two Nobel prize winners, the highest per capita number of Nobel Laureates ever, anywhere. ▶▶ For Sleeping, Eating and other listings, see pages 742-760.

Ins and outs

Getting there St Lucia is well served with scheduled and charter flights from Europe and North America and you can often pick up quite cheap deals on package holidays. Connections with other islands are good and it is easy to arrange a multi-centre trip. Some flights come via Antigua, and some via Barbados. You can also get to St Lucia by sea from the French Antilles. ▶▶ *See Transport, page 757, for more details.*

Getting around **Bus** is the cheapest means of getting around the island. St Lucia's buses are usually privately owned minibuses and have no fixed timetable, so they may not run when you want them to. The north is better served than the south and buses around Castries and Gros Islet run until 2200, or later for the Fri night jump-up at Gros Islet. There are several **car hire** companies on the island, some of which are open to negotiation, but it is cheaper and more reliable to hire in advance. Castries roads are very congested and there are lots of one-way streets. The West Coast Road is full of mountain curves but has less traffic than the East Coast. Together they present a very scenic drive round the island. If you're **cycling**, the best way to get round the island is anti-clockwise, thus ensuring long but gradual uphills and steep, fast downhills.

St Lucia

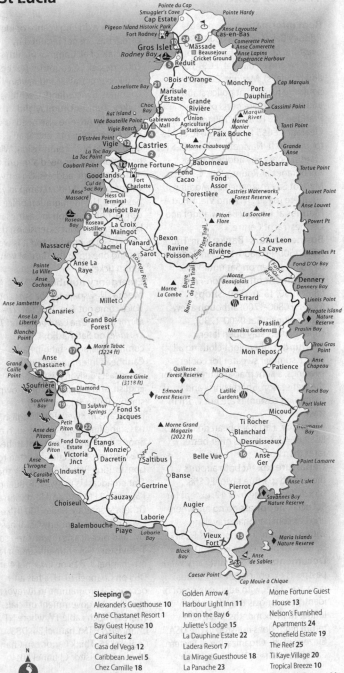

Sleeping

Alexander's Guesthouse **10**	Golden Arrow **4**	Morne Fortune Guest
Anse Chastanet Resort **1**	Harbour Light Inn **11**	House **13**
Bay Guest House **10**	Inn on the Bay **6**	Nelson's Furnished
Cara Suites **2**	Juliette's Lodge **15**	Apartments **24**
Casa del Vega **12**	La Dauphine Estate **22**	Stonefield Estate **19**
Caribbean Jewel **5**	Ladera Resort **7**	The Reef **25**
Chez Camille **18**	La Mirage Guesthouse **18**	Ti Kaye Village **20**
Crystals **17**	La Panache **23**	Tropical Breeze **10**
Foxgrove Inn **3**	Mago Estate **8**	Villa Beach Cottages **14**
Friendship Inn **4**	Manje Domi **16**	Windjammer Landing **21**
	Marigot Beach Club **9**	

Touching down

Boat information (own flag) Rodney Bay (Customs 0800-1800 but overtime charges of EC$10 from 1630 Mon-Fri and all day Sat, EC$15 on Sun and holidays), Marigot, Castries, Soufrière (clear in at police station) and Vieux Fort are ports of entry. Pratique EC$10 up to 100 tons. Clearance EC$5 for under 40 ft, EC$15 for over 40 ft. Navigational aids EC$15. Charter boats pay additional fees. Anchorages at Rodney Bay, Castries, Marigot Bay (managed by Moorings), Soufrière (page 741) and Vieux Fort. **Marinas** at Rodney Bay, Marigot and Castries Yacht Centre.

Business hours Banks: Mon-Thu 0800-1500, Fri 0800-1700, in Rodney Bay banks open on Sat until 1200. **Government offices**: Mon-Fri 0830-1230, 1330-1600. **Shops**: Mon-Fri 0800-1700, although a few shut for lunch, Sat 0800-1230), supermarkets stay open later.

Clothing Lightweight clothing all year; a summer sweater for cooler evenings, a light mac and umbrella for the wet season. Short shorts and swimming costumes are not worn in town.

Currency East Caribbean dollar, EC$. EC$2.67=US$1. Banks offer better rates than hotels.

Departure tax At both airports there is a departure tax of EC$68, US$25, for anyone over 12, except for St Lucian **nationals** going anywhere and Caricom nationals travelling within Caricom, for whom it is EC$45. By ferry, departure tax is EC$30.

Documents Visitors must carry valid passports except citizens of Canada, who may enter with adequate proof of identity, as long as they do not stay longer than six months and their return flight does not stop in the USA. Citizens of the Organization of Eastern Caribbean States (OECS) may enter with only a driving licence or identity card. Visas are not required by nationals of all Commonwealth countries, all EC countries (except Eire and Portugal), all Scandinavian countries, Switzerland, Liechtenstein, Turkey, Tunisia, Uruguay and Venezuela. Anyone else needs a visa, check requirements, etc, at an embassy or high commission. Without exception, visitors need a return ticket and an onward address. On arrival you will be given a 42-day stamp in your passport. The immigration office at the central police station in Castries is bureaucratic about extensions; they cost EC$40 per period and it is worth getting one up to the date of your return ticket.

Emergency numbers T911.

Media Newspapers: *The Star* and *The Voice* come out Tue, Thu, Sat, *The Mirror* on Fri, *One Caribbean* and *The Crusader* on Sat. **Radio**: The commercial radio station, Radio Caribbean International (RCI), broadcasts daily in Kweyol and English, and the government-owned station, Radio St Lucia (RSL), broadcasts in Kweyol and English. It has some fine programmes such as Sports Zone and if you want to hear the concerns of St Lucians listen to Constitution Park at 1400 (only the Thu broadcast is in Kweyol). RCI and RSL have 2 FM and an AM station each. Other stations are Radio 100 (Helen FM); the Wave (formerly GEM) has 2 FM, and broadcasts rhythm and soul. **Television**: Government station NTV on Channel 3, HTS on Channel 4 and DBS on Channel 10. HTS has an occasional programme in Kweyol and speeches by government officials. There is much cable TV, where NTV is Channel 2, HTS Channel 34, DBS Channel 35, Think Caribbean Channel 45 and The Visitor Channel 50.

Official time Atlantic Standard Time, four hours behind GMT, one ahead of EST. In 'summer time', five hours behind GMT, on a par with EST.

Public holidays New Year's Day (1 and 2 Jan), Independence Day on 22 Feb, Good Fri, Easter Mon, Labour Day on 1 May, Whit Mon, Corpus Christi, Carnival, Emancipation Day (1 Aug), Thanksgiving Day (1st Mon in Oct), National Day on 13 Dec, Christmas Day and Boxing Day.

Safety When visiting the waterfalls and sulphur springs on Soufrière be prepared to say no firmly; 'guides' are sometimes persistent and bothersome. Visiting with a hired car (H reg) can be a hassle. The signs to Sulphur Springs are sometimes removed so you have to ask the way and are expected to give a tip. Unemployment and poverty have increased with the world economic downturn. Harassment and hostility towards tourists, drug abuse and crime is a problem, but not of a violent nature. People using organized tours generally have no problem. Be careful taking photographs, although everybody seems to be accustomed to cameras in the market. The use and sale of narcotics is illegal and penalties are severe. Most readily available is marijuana, which is frequently offered to tourists, but hard drugs can also be a problem. Never sleep at night on the beach; you will lose your belongings. Avoid going alone off the beaten track, do not wear expensive jewellery when shopping and stay in well-populated parts of the beach. In Castries stay in the central part of town as the US Advisory Service has listed Grass St, Wilton's Yard (The Graveyard) and Marchand (southeast of our map) as no-go areas.

Tourist information St Lucia Tourist Board, Sure Line Building, on main Castries-Gros Islet highway just north of the Vigie roundabout, Castries, St Lucia, T4524094, www.stlucia.org. Information centres at the Pointe Seraphine Duty-Free Complex;Place Carenage; George F Charles Airport (most helpful but closed for lunch 1300-1500), T4522596; Hewanorra Airport (very helpful, particularly with hotel reservations, only open when flights are due or leave), T4546644 and Soufrière (very helpful, local phone calls free), T4597419. *The Tropical Traveller* is distributed free to hotels, shops, restaurants, etc every month and contains some extremely useful information, www.tropicaltravellers.com. The **St Lucia Hotel and Tourism Association** publishes a tourist guide, *Visions of St Lucia*, T4525978, www.stluciatravel.com.lc, also of a high standard and widely available. *Paradise St Lucia*, is a free booklet published twice a year and includes a hotel directory.

Tourist offices overseas France: ANI, 53 rue François Ler, 7th floor, Paris 75008, T47-203966, F47-230965. **UK:** 421a Finchley Rd, London NW3 6HJ, T0870-9007697, stlucia@axissm.com. **USA:** 9th Floor, 800 2nd Av, New York, NY 10017, T800-4563984, stluciatourism@aol.com. **Canada**: 8 King St East, Suite 700, Toronto, Ontario M5 1B5, T416-3624242, sltbcanada@aol.com.

Voltage 220 v, 50 cycles. A few hotels are 110 v, 60 cycles. Most sockets take three-pin square plugs (UK standard), but some take two-pin round plugs or flat US plugs. Adaptors generally available in hotels.

Weights and measures Imperial, though metric measurements are being introduced.

The capital, Castries, is splendidly set on a natural harbour against a mountainous background. Largely rebuilt after being destroyed by four major fires, the last in 1948, the commercial centre and government offices are built of concrete. Only the buildings to the south of Derek Walcott Square and behind Brazil Street were saved. Here you will see late 19th- and early 20th-century French-style wooden buildings with three storeys, their gingerbread fretwork balconies overhanging the pavement. The other area which survived was the1894 iron **market** on the north side of Jeremie Street. A new market has been built next door to house the many fruit sellers on the ground floor, while on the first floor and in an arcade opposite are vendors of T-shirts, crafts, spices, basket work, leeches and hot pepper sauce. On the eastern side of the old market there is a little arcade with small booths where vendors provide good vegetarian food, Creole meals and local juices. There are duty-free shopping centres for cruise ship passengers at La Place Carenage by the main dock and at Pointe Seraphine to the north (see page 754). The tallest building in the city is the seven-storey Financial Centre at the corner of Jeremie and Bridge Streets, with a joyous sculpture by local artist, Ricky George.

Derek Walcott Square was the site of the Place D'Armes in 1768 when the town transferred from Vigie. Renamed Promenade Square, it then became Columbus Square in 1893. In 1993 it was renamed in honour of poet Derek Walcott (see page 762) and contains busts of both Nobel Laureates. It was the original site of the courthouse and the market and is now used for ceremonial occasions and entertainment, including concerts during the Jazz Festival. The library, built by US millionaire Andrew Carnegie, is on its west side. The giant Saman tree in the middle is about 400 years old. On its east side lies the **Roman Catholic Cathedral of the Immaculate Conception** which bursts into colour inside. Suffused with yellow light, the side altars are often covered with flowers while votive candles placed in red, green and yellow jars give a fairy tale effect. The ceiling, supported by iron arches and braces is decorated with panelled portraits of the apostles. Above the central altar with its four carved screens, the apse ceiling has paintings of five female saints with St Lucy in the centre. The walls have murals by Dunstan St Omer, one of St Lucia's better known artists (see page 763). They are of the stations of the cross and are unusual in that the people in the paintings are black. The twelve stained glass windows were created by his son, Giovanni.

The ridge of **Morne Fortune** just south of the city centre enjoys wonderful views over Castries and the harbour and receives pleasant breezes to temper the tropical sunshine. For this reason the British built their grand houses up here as well as their military buildings. **Government House** with its curious metalwork crown, is at the top of Morne Fortune and dates from 1895. The house is not open to the public but there is a small museum with a collection of photos artefacts and documents, called **Le Pavillon Royal Museum** ① *T4522481, www.stluciagovernmenthouse.com, Tue and Thu 1000-1200, 1400-1600, donations welcome*. There are six historical military sites on Morne Fortune under the control of the **National Trust of St Lucia** ① *www.slunatrust.org*, who run tours of the area. **Fort Charlotte**, the old Morne Fortune fortress, is now the Sir Arthur Lewis Community College. The Apostles' battery (1888) and Provost's redoubt (1782) have spectacular views, but the best is from the Inniskilling Monument at the far side of the college (just beyond the old Combermere barracks) where you get a fine view of the town, coast, mountains and Martinique. Sir Arthur Lewis, Nobel Laureate in Economics, is buried in front of the monument.

North of Castries

The part of the island to the north of Castries is the principal resort area, it contains the best beaches and the hotels are largely self contained. It is the driest part of the island. The John Compton highway leaves Castries past Vigie Airport and follows the curves of Vigie Beach and Choc Bay. Where the road leaves the bay and just before it crosses the Choc River, a right turn to Babonneau will take you past the **Union Agricultural station** (about one mile), the site of the **Forestry Department Headquarters** ⓘ *T4502231 Ext 316, www.geocities.com/sluforestrails*. There is a visitor centre, nature trail and a small, well-run zoo, where you can see indigenous species such as the agouti and the endemic St Lucia parrot as well as iguanas. The Forestry Department organizes hiking across the island (see page 742).

At Babonneau is the **Rain Forest Sky Rides** ⓘ *T4585151, reservations.slu@rfat.com, open daily, US$72 adults, US$62 children, US$98 including transfers, cheaper for residents, birdwatching tours with Forestry Tue, Thu, US$65 including transfers, reservations recommended*, a new attraction where you are taken up the side of La Sorciere in a gondola seating eight. You ascend at one level and descend at a higher level through the forest canopy, so you see two layers of rainforest, all of which is explained by

Castries

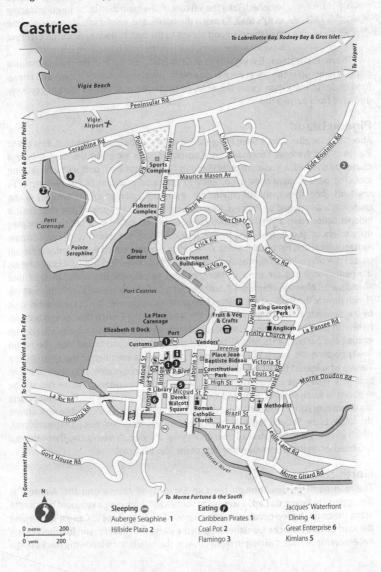

Sleeping 🛏
Auberge Seraphine **1**
Hillside Plaza **2**

Eating 🍴
Caribbean Pirates **1**
Coal Pot **2**
Flamingo **3**

Jacques' Waterfront
Dining **4**
Great Enterprise **6**
Kimlans **5**

the guides. Great views of both sides of the island and to Martinique in the distance. There are also 10 zip lines to speed you down the hill and sky walks will come on stream in 2008, allowing family groups all to do their own thing.

Rodney Bay

This whole area supports a mass of tourist facilities – hotels, restaurants, shops and clubs – between the lovely beach at Reduit and the first-class Rodney Bay Marina, but it was formerly the site of the **US Naval Air Station of Reduit**. Built in 1941, the Americans made an attempt to reclaim the swamps and the bay was dredged. It was the first of a chain of bases established to protect the Panama Canal and supported a squadron of sea planes. Closed in 1947, it was not until the 1970s when a causeway to Pigeon Island and a marina were built that the wetlands vanished. Take the left turn off the main road at the junction leading to **JQ's Mall**, to reach the hotels and restaurants. At the end of the road there is good access to the beach. Rodney Bay is an excellent base for watersports, both on the beach and from the marina.

> ❧ *At the World Travel Awards in 2006 St Lucia was voted the number one wedding and honeymoon destination in the world. Some hotels do several weddings a day, so pick your spot carefully to avoid the production line.*

The normally sleepy fishing village of **Gros Islet**, just north of the marina, holds a popular jump-up in the street each Friday night, with music, dancing, bars and cheap food (more tourists than locals but enjoyed by night owls). Things start to get lively and loud from 2200-2300.

Pigeon Island

About ¾ mile after Elliot's Shell filling station on the outskirts of Gros Islet, turn left to Pigeon Island National Landmark, once an island, now joined to the mainland by a causeway on which a 300-room hotel (**Sandals Grande**) has been built with a bright blue roof. The **park** ① *daily 0900-1700, entry to park and museum EC$10 visitors, EC$5 residents (free after 1700 but only to the restaurants, see p750)*, at the end of the causeway was opened by Princess Alexandra on 23 February 1979 as part of St Lucia's Independence celebrations. It has two peaks which are joined by a saddle. The higher rises to about 360 ft. Managed by the National Trust, the island is of considerable archaeological and historical interest. Amerindian remains have been found, the French pirate François Leclerc (known as Jamb de Bois for his wooden leg) used the large cave on the north shore and the Duke of Montagu tried to colonize the island in 1722 (but abandoned it after one afternoon). From here, Admiral Rodney set sail in 1782 to meet the French navy at the Battle of Les Saintes (see under Guadeloupe). It was captured in 1795 by the Brigands (French slaves freed by the leaders of the French Revolution) but was retaken in 1798 by the English. Used as a quarantine centre from 1842 it was abandoned in 1904 but became a US observation post during the Second World War. The island finally became the home of Josset Agnes Huchinson, a member of the D'Oyly Carte Theatre who leased the island from 1937 to 1976. The bay became a busy yacht haven and 'Joss' held large parties to entertain the crews. Her abandoned house can still be seen on the south shore of the island. On the lower of the two peaks lies **Fort Rodney**. The small **museum** is in the Officers' Mess and rebuilt to the original design, while upstairs are the offices of the St Lucia National Trust. There are two small beaches on Pigeon Island, which you can get to by water taxi from Rodney Bay if you don't have a car. There are also two beaches on the causeway either side of the Sandals hotel.

North coast

The road north passes through the Cap Estate (golf course and the **Almond at Smugglers**) to **Pointe du Cap**, a viewpoint some 470 ft high with a splendid panorama along the coast. A good circular walk from Gros Islet can be done to **Cas-en-Bas** taking the road past **La Panache Guesthouse** (ask the owner, Henry Augustin for directions if necessary, he is always willing to help) down to the beach, then following tracks north until you reach the golf course, from where you return along the west coast to Gros Islet. Cas-en-Bas beach now has the Cotton Bay resort behind it and the tracks north pass through an area being developed by Cap Estate as a continuation of the golf club, but you will see cacti, wild scenery and Martinique. The sea is too rough to swim.

▶▶ *For more details see Beaches and watersports, page 740.*

East coast to Vieux Fort

The transinsular road goes through extensive banana plantations before climbing steeply over the **Barre de l'Isle**, the mountain barrier that divides the island. There is a short, self-guided trail at the high point on the road between Castries and Dennery, which takes about 10 minutes and affords good views of the rainforest and down the Roseau Valley. There is a small picnic shelter. It can be slippery after rain. The experience is rather spoilt by the noise of traffic. A longer walk to **Mount La Combe** ① *guides available Mon-Fri 0830-1500, pay on site, US$10*, can also be undertaken from this point, returning on the same trail. Park by a snack bar on the main road where the Forestry Department guides wait. Be careful in this area as it is known as the drug-growing region. Cyclists and hikers have reported that the locals are not particularly friendly and their stares can make you feel uncomfortable.

The road descends through Grande Rivière to **Dennery** where the vegetation is mostly xerophytic scrub. Dennery is set in a sheltered bay with Dennery Island guarding its entrance and dominated by the Roman Catholic church. Here you can see the distinctive St Lucia fishing boats pulled up on the beach. Carved out of single tree trunks, the bows are straight and pointed rather than curved and are all named with phrases such as *God help me*. At the weekend the town invites visitors to a **fish fest**, when from 1600-0200 you can join in a street party, eat freshly caught and cooked seafood and enjoy music and dancing.

Inland from Dennery along the Dennery River, is the **Rainforest Canopy Adventure** ① *Palm Services, T4580908, open daily 1000-1600, booking through Palm Services US$85 including transfers (available Mon, Thu, Sat), through a hotel tour desk US$100, or US$75 if you drive direct to the estate*, with seven zip lines where you are strapped into a harness and slide down a cable from one platform to another through the forest canopy. Plenty of instruction, excellent guides, and time to look around you on the platforms up in the trees above the river.

Just after Dennery you will see a sign for the **Eastern Nature Trail** ① *closed in 2007 because of development at le Paradis*, which winds its way along the coast between the road and the sea for 3½ miles from Mandele to Praslin Bay. **Praslin Island** in the bay is one of only two islands where St Lucian whiptails live. They used to live only on Maria Major Island until being successfully introduced here to prevent extinction.

Fregate Islands Nature Reserve ① *National Trust, T4525005, natrust@candw.lc, also closed in 2007 because of development*, on the north side of Praslin Bay has two small islands, nesting sites for the frigate bird and the north promontory of Praslin Bay gives a good vantage point. Birds nest on the offshore rocks and a trail runs down to the shore and back up by another route. The dry forest also harbours the trembler, the St Lucian oriole and the ramier. The reserve includes a section of mangrove and is the natural habitat of the boa constrictor.

Despite the whiptails and the birds, this area is being transformed into a major tourist resort, to open in 2008. 554 acres have been absorbed by the construction of the Westin Le Paradis Golf & Beach Resort, which will encompass 300 Westin four-star condo-hotel units, 76 villas, a Greg Norman signature golf course, a 100-slip private marina for yachts up to 150 ft, five star boutique hotel, a spa, shopping and conference facilities.

The village of Praslin is a fishing community known for its traditional boat building. Between Praslin and Mon Repos are the **Mamiku Gardens** ① *T4528236, www.mamiku.com, daily 0900-1700, EC$15 for foreigners, EC$10 for locals*. The botanical gardens and woodland walks on an estate once owned by Baron de Micoud when he was Governor of the island for France in the 18th century but later a British military post. There is an ongoing excavation at Mamiku which is producing interesting finds from the ruins of the house where the British soldiers were surprised and massacred by the Brigands. The gardens are lovely; you can take a guided tour or wander around among the frangipani and ginger lilies with a map and plant guide. There are several different sections, including a bush medicine garden, but every plant is numbered for easy identification. There is also a snack bar and souvenir shop.

Vieux Fort → *Population: 14,000.*

Vieux Fort is the island's industrial centre, with a Free Zone and the Hewanorra International Airport. It is an active town with a good Saturday market and a lot of traditional housing. The town boasts two new supermarkets in malls, *JQs* and *Julian's*. The latter has a cinema. The police station and post office, on Theodore Street, are right in the middle of the town. The bus terminal is at the end of Clarke Street near the airport.

The perimeter road skirts Anse de Sables beach (excellent kitesurfing and windsurfing, see page 741), and looks across to the **Maria Islands** ⓘ *T4525005, natrust@candw.lc, entry on Sun only by prior reservation, US$40 per person minimum 4 people, for boat and guide; package of transport, tour, lunch for min 4 people is US$80 per person; able swimmers only*. Just offshore, these National Trust islands are home to two endemic reptiles, a colourful lizard and small, rare, harmless snake, the Kouwes snake. The lizard, **Cnemidophorus vanzoi**, is known as **zandoli te** in Creole. The males, about 18 cm long, sport the colours of the national flag. Interpretive facilities are at Anse de Sables, but are not always open. There's a pleasant, small beach on Maria Major, and excellent snorkelling, which makes a good full-day trip. Unauthorized access (including windsurfers from Anse de Sables) to the islands is not allowed. From April to September public access is restricted while seabirds are nesting in their hundreds on the cliffs and on the ground.

Cap Moule à Chique is the most southerly point on the island, with a lighthouse, from where you can see the Pitons, Morne Gomier (1,028 ft) with Morne Grand Magazin (2,022 ft) behind it. Unfortunately Morne Gimie (3,118 ft) is largely obscured. Further to the east is Piton St Esprit (1,919 ft) and Morne Durocher (1,055 ft) near Praslin.

West coast to Soufrière and the Pitons

The West Coast Road is in excellent condition with good signposting. It is a curvy, but spectacular, drive down to Soufrière. On reaching the **Roseau Valley**, one of the main banana growing areas, take the signposted road to **Marigot Bay**, a beautiful inlet and natural harbour which provided the setting for the 1967 film, *Dr Doolittle*. It supports a large marina and, not surprisingly, a large number of yachts in transit berth here to restock with supplies. There is a police station and immigration post here, bars, disco, restaurants and accommodation.

The main road continues to Soufrière and passes through the fishing villages of **Anse La Raye** and Canaries (no facilities), where you can see old wooden cottages, many of them with attractive decorative details and verandas. Anse La Raye has become very popular for its fish fry on the seafront road on Fridays, which attracts hundreds of people to eat lobster in season and fish and seafood at any time of year, freshly caught and cooked at stalls along the street. During the day the street is lined with souvenir stalls.

Soufrière → *Population: 9,000.*

ⓘ *Organized tours are available from the hotels further north, by sea or road, from around US$65-80 including lunch, drinks, transfers and a trip to Soufrière and the Sulphur Springs (see below). There are no buses back to Castries after midday unless you make a roundabout journey via Vieux Fort. If you arrive by boat head for the north end of the bay, you will find plenty of help to tie up your yacht (EC$5) and taxis will* *appear from nowhere. It is a much cheaper alternative to tying up at the jetty.*

After Canaries the road goes inland and skirts Mount Tabac (2,224 ft) before descending into Soufrière. This is the most picturesque and interesting part of the island, with marvellous old wooden buildings at the foot of the spectacular Pitons, now a UNESCO World Heritage Site.

Soufrière dates back to 1713 when Louis XIV of France granted the lands around Soufrière to the Devaux family. The estate subsequently produced cotton, tobacco, coffee and cocoa. During the French Revolution, the guillotine was raised in the square by the Brigands but the Devaux family were protected by loyal slaves and escaped. There are lots of French colonial houses with shutters and overhanging balconies with gingerbread fretwork, creating shady walkways around the square. A market lies to the north of the harbour but the waterfront is the centre of action. The water here is extremely deep and reaches 200 ft only a few yards from the shore, which is why boats moor close in.

To reach **Anse Chastanet** and its marine park from here take the rough track at the north end of the beach (past the yacht club) about one mile. This is an absolute must if you enjoy snorkelling (the south end near the jetty is superb but keep within the roped-off area; the north end is also good with some rocks to explore, but avoid the middle where boats come in). The hotel has a good and inexpensive restaurant (although if you are on a budget you may prefer to take a picnic) and the dive shop is extremely helpful, they will hire out equipment by the hour.

From the square take Sir Arthur Lewis Street east past the church and look for a right hand turning to reach the **Diamond Gardens**① *T4524759, Mon-Sat 1000-1700, Sun and holidays 1000-1500, EC$7, children EC$3, EC$7 to use the outdoor hot baths, EC$10 for private bath; only official guides are allowed in, do not accept offers from those at the gates; all the car parks are free, no matter what some people may tell you.* The gardens were developed in 1784 after Baron de Laborie sent samples taken from sulphur springs near the Diamond River to Paris for analysis. They found minerals present which were equivalent to those found in the spa town of Aix-la-Chapelle and were said to be effective against rheumatism and other complaints. The French King ordered baths to be built. Despite being destroyed in the French Revolution, they were eventually rebuilt and can be used by the public. The gardens are better than ever; well maintained and many native plants can be seen.

Take the Vieux Fort road between wooden houses about halfway along the south side of Soufrière square. Follow the road for about two miles and you will see a sign on the left for the **Sulphur Springs**① *daily 0900-1700, EC$3, compulsory tour with guide takes about 30 mins.* You will be able to smell the springs before you reach them. Originally a huge volcano about 3 miles in diameter, it collapsed some 40,000 years ago leaving the west part of the rim empty (where you drive in). The sign welcomes you to the world's only drive-in volcano, although actually you have to stop at a car park. The sulphur spring is the only one still active, although there are seven cones within the old crater as well as the pitons which are thought to be volcanic plugs. Tradition has it that the Arawak deity **Yokahu** slept here and it was therefore the site of human sacrifices. The Caribs were less superstitious but still named it

> It is very dangerous to stray onto the fenced-off grey area; the most famous 'crater' was formed a few years ago when a local person fell into a mud pocket. He received third-degree burns.

Qualibou, the place of death. Water is heated to 180°F and in some springs to 275°F. It quickly cools to about 87°F below the bridge at the entrance. From the main viewing platform, you can see over a moonscape of bubbling, mineral rich, grey mud.

South of Soufrière

Petit Piton (743 m/2,437 ft) is a volcanic plug rising sheer out of the sea and since June 2004 a UNESCO World Heritage Site, along with its sister, **Gros Piton** (770 m/2,526 ft). It is a focal point of all views around Soufrière. It is possible to climb

Petit Piton, an extremely steep ascent, but it is not encouraged. Local guides will take you up for about US$50, but it is dangerous and you will be damaging the mountain. In the valley between Petit Piton and Gros Piton, a luxury all-inclusive resort, **Jalousie Plantation Resort and Spa**, has been built despite complaints from ecological groups and evidence from archaeologists that it is located on a major Amerindian site. An important burial ground is believed to be under the tennis courts and there have been many finds of petroglyphs and pottery. A rather fine petroglyph is at the back of the beach in front of Lord Glenconner's **Bang Between the Pitons**. Lord Glenconner used to own much of the land here. Take the turning opposite the Morne Coubaril Estate (closed) on the unsigned concrete road. Halfway along the drive to Jalousie you will see a little sign to a small, warm waterfall on your left. Someone will collect about US$2 for access. Relax in the warm waters.

South of Soufrière, near Union Vale estate, is the **Gros Piton Trail**. The village of **Fond Gens Libre** is at the base of the mountain, accessible by jeep or high-clearance car although you will have to ford a couple of streams. The trip up and back is about four hours through the different ecosystems of the mountain, with stops to look at brigand caves and tunnels. It is strenuous, so you must be in good physical condition. It should not be attempted in wet weather even though the trail has been improved. Contact the **Gros Piton Tour Guide Association** ① *T4599748*, who are assisted by the **Forestry Department** ① *T4502231 ext 316*, or the **Fond Gens Libre Tour Guides Association** ① *T4593833*. A guide costs about EC$20.

Beaches and activities

The Atlantic east coast has heavy surf, is dangerous and difficult to get to without local knowledge or the Ordnance Survey map and 4WD. However, it is very spectacular and isolated beaches make a pleasant change from the west coast. Much of it provides an important habitat and nesting sites for the island's wildlife. **Cas en Bas Beach** can be reached from Gros Islet (45 minutes' walk, or arrange a taxi); it is sheltered, shady but challenging for experienced windsurfers. **Marjorie's Beach Bar**, T4508637, can organize hikes and horse riding finishing with a meal at the restaurant. A residential development, Cotton Bay, opened in 2006 which should eventually lead to road improvements. **Donkey Beach** can be reached from there by taking a track to the north (20 minutes' walk), the scenery is wild and open and it is windy. To the south of Cas en Bas Beach are **Anse Lavoutte**, **Anse Comerette** and **Anse Lapins**; follow the rocks, it is a 30-minute walk to the first and an hour to the last. They are deserted, windswept beaches and headlands. There are Indian stone carvings on **Dauphin Beach**, which can be reached from Monchy (reasonable with a jeep). Once on the beach, wade across the river and walk back in the flat, clear area below the bush land. After about 50 yd you'll find stone lines with regular depressions. Another 20 yd and you'll find a stone pillar about which Robert Devaux wrote: "The carving appears to be a family of three – male, female and child. It is finely executed and must have taken some prehistoric 'Michelangelo' a considerable time to complete the carving" (*St Lucia Historic Sites*, St Lucia National Trust, 1975, highly recommended, available in the library at the Folk Research Centre). It is now used as the St Lucia National Trust's logo. Unfortunately the stone pillar has been badly tampered with. **Grande Anse**, further south, is a long windy beach where turtle watching is organized, March-July by the Desbarra community, contact **Heritage Tours** (see page 757) or the **Turtle Watch hotline** ① *T4523224, for information and reservations*. The package of EC$120 includes hotel transfers, evening meal and breakfast; you set off at 1600 and return around 0700, take snacks, drink, torch, insect repellent, good walking shoes and warm clothing; tents are supplied. There is a new road from Desbarra to **Anse Louvet**, a sheltered beach in a stunning setting. La Sorcière mountain forms a long wall which seems to separate Louvet from the rest of

❗ Swimming is not safe on the Atlantic (east) side as there's a strong undertow.

and there is a blow hole. The road continues to Aux Leon and then to the main Castries-Dennery road.

The beaches on the west coast, north of Castries can be reached by bus with a short walk down to the sea. **Vigie** (1½ miles from Castries) is a lovely strip of sand with plenty of shade, popular and cleaned regularly. Its only drawback is that it runs parallel to the airport runway, but that is compensated by the lack of hotels (except **Rendezvous** at one end) and low levels of pollution. **Choc Bay** has good sand, shade and chairs provided by the restaurant, **Wharf** (get off the bus after **Sandals Halcyon**). Used mainly by cruise ship passengers and locals, there are kayaks, sea cycles and sunfish for hire (daily 0900-1800). **Trouya** is a small, usually deserted bay (except on public holidays), best reached on foot or 4WD. **Rodney Bay** has another excellent beach at **Reduit**, dominated by three large hotels. The northern part of the bay and Gros Ilet is cut off by the entrance to the marina and is now a 45-minute walk or five- to 10-minute bus ride to Gros Islet. The whole of the western side of the causeway to **Pigeon Island** is beach, interrupted by Landings and Sandals, while there are two small beaches on Pigeon Island itself. Further north by **Almond at Smugglers** (formerly Club St Lucia) is **Smugglers' Cove**, another good snorkelling spot.

> **:** *All the west coast beaches have good swimming but many are dominated by resort hotels.*

Heading south from Castries, beaches at small towns are not generally used by tourists; lack of proper sanitation means they are often polluted. Beaches away from habitation are always a better bet. **Marigot Bay** is a popular tourist spot. **Anse Cochon** is also popular, visited by boats doing day trips, and guests at the **Ti Kaye Village**. The smell of motor boats can be unpleasant. **Anse Chastanet** is well used with great snorkelling and diving. The trade winds blow in to the south shore and the long, sandy beach of **Anse de Sables**, near Vieux Fort on the Atlantic side, offers ideal **windsurfing** and **kiteboarding**. The sea here is wild and invigorating and comes straight across the Atlantic. You can walk for miles along the sand without seeing anyone.

Diving and marine life There is some very good diving off the west coast, although this is somewhat dependent on the weather, as heavy rain tends to create high sediment loads in the rivers and sea. Diving off the east coast is not so good and can be risky unless you are a competent diver. One of the best beach entry dives in the Caribbean is directly off **Anse Chastanet**, where an underwater shelf drops off from about 10 ft down to 60 ft and there is a good dive over **Turtle Reef** in the bay, where there are over 25 different types of coral. Below the **Petit Piton** are impressive sponge and coral communities on a drop to 200 ft of spectacular wall. There are gorgonians, black coral trees, huge barrel sponges and plenty of other beautiful reef life. The area in front of the **Anse Chastanet Hotel** is a buoyed-off Marine Reserve, stretching from the west point at **Grand Caille North** to **Chamin Cove**. Only the hotel boats and local fishermen's canoes are allowed in. By the jetty, a roped-off area is used by snorkellers and beginner divers. Other popular dive sites include **Anse L'Ivrogne, Anse La Raye Point** (good snorkelling also at **Anse La Raye**) and the **Pinnacles** (an impressive site where four pinnacles rise to within 10 ft of the surface), not forgetting the **wrecks**, such as the *Volga* (in 20 ft of water north of Castries harbour, well broken up, subject to swell, requires caution), the *Waiwinette* (several miles south of Vieux Fort, strong currents, competent divers only), and the 165-ft *Lesleen M* (deliberately sunk in 1986 off Anse Cochon Bay in 60 ft of water).

Visitors must dive with a local company. It is illegal to take any coral or undersized shellfish. Corals and sponges should not even be touched. It is also illegal to buy or sell coral products on St Lucia. The **Soufrière Marine Management Association** preserves the environment between Anse Chastanet and Anse L'Ivrogne to the south. They have placed moorings in the reserve, which yachts are required to take, charges

> **:** *The Fisheries Department is pursuing an active marine protection programme.*

are on a sliding scale depending on the size of the boat. Collection of marine mammals (dead or alive) is prohibited, spearguns are illegal and anchoring is prohibited. Rangers come by at night to collect the fee and explain the programme. Dive moorings have been installed and are being financed with **Marine Reserve Fees** ⓘ *US$4 daily, US$12 a year.*

Hiking and birdwatching St Lucia has an extensive network of trails maintained by the Forestry Department, for which you need a permit (usually US$10, half price for children), payable at the entrance or in advance. Guides are available at the start of most trails (Monday to Friday 0830-1500), or you can reserve one for a different time or at weekends for an extra charge; they are particularly useful if you want to set off early to sight birds at dawn, but they are not mandatory. In the north of the island is the **Forestière Rainforest Trail**, a 3-mile, two-hour walk along part of an old road from Castries to Gros Islet. **La Sorcière** and **Piton Flore** are densely forested mountains in the north with excellent rainforest vegetation. Piton Flore can be walked up in 40 minutes although it is a strenuous climb and you will need to ask how to get to the top, from where there are spectacular views. It is the last recorded location of Semper's warbler. There is a good chance of seeing the St Lucian parrot on the **Barre de l'Isle Rainforest Walk**. The **Des Cartiers Rainforest Trail** starts 6 miles south of Mahaut on the east coast and is a loop of about 2½ miles taking around two hours through thick rainforest perfect for birdwatching, with many of the endemics found here. You can stay overnight by prior arrangement at a very basic lodge called **La Porte**, if you want to see parrots at dawn. On the west coast is access to the **Millet Bird Sanctuary Trail**, which meanders around the lake and the catchment area of the Roseau Dam through secondary rainforest, and is particularly good for birdwatching. The Forestry Department tour is US$30. In the **Edmond Forest Reserve** is the **Enbas Saut Trail** (below the falls), moderate to strenuous, at the foot of Mount Gimie, with a combination of rainforest, cloud forest and elfin woodlands. The 2½-mile trail with 2,112 steps has been cut down to the Troumassée river, where there are a couple of waterfalls and a pool where you can bathe. The **Edmond Rainforest Trail** runs through the forested heart of the island and, with prior arrangement, you can hike all the way across, joining up with the Des Cartiers Rainforest trail in the east.

Sailing At Marigot Bay and Rodney Bay you can hire any size of craft, the larger ones coming complete with crew if you want. Many of these yachts sail down to the Grenadines. Rodney Bay has been developed to accommodate 1,000 yachts (with 232 berths in a full-service boatyard and additional moorings in the lagoon, T4520324, www.rodneybaymarina.com) and hosts the annual Atlantic Rally for Cruisers race, with about 250 yachts arriving there in December. There is an annual regatta to coincide with the boats leaving the Canary Islands (26 Nov 2006). Charters can be arranged to sail to neighbouring islands. Soufrière has a good anchorage, but as the water is deep it is necessary to anchor close in. There is a pier for short term tie-ups.

As some of the best views are from the sea, it is recommended to take at least one boat trip. There are several boats which sail down the west coast to Soufrière, where you stop to visit the volcano and some local sights, followed by lunch and return sail with a stop somewhere for swimming and snorkelling. The price usually includes all transport, lunch, drinks and snorkelling gear.

● Sleeping

St Lucia has a wide and varied selection of hotels, guesthouses, apartments and villas. There is a 10-15% service charge and 8% tax on all hotel bills. The majority of hotels are small, friendly and offer flexible service depending on your wants and needs. They cater for all budgets, from the height of luxury at **Ladera Resort** or **Anse Chastanet**, to simple guesthouses in Gros Islet where you fall into bed after the Fri night jump-up. The all-inclusive resorts are large but avoidable.

Castries *p734, map p735*

AL Auberge Seraphine, Vigie Marina, T4532073, www.aubergeseraphine.com. A gleaming white, modern hotel on the edge of the harbour close to Vigie airport. 22 rooms on 2 levels, a/c and TV, terrace and pool with good views of the boats. Attractive and well-run, very pleasantly located. Flocks of egrets fly in to roost here. The restaurant serves a great 3-course lunch for US$10-12, good fish, lots of local veg.

A Cara Suites, La Pansée, overlooking Castries, T4524767, www.carahotels.com. 54 comfortable but rather dull rooms, with a/c, TV, VCR, video library, minibar, but worth it for the magnificent view and excellent value for business or pleasure. The higher your room, the better the view, if you don't mind stairs.

A-B Casa del Vega, south side of Vigie peninsula, T4590780, www.casadelvega.net. 12 a/c rooms or 1-3 bedroom suites, on the waterfront overlooking the harbour, watersports, internet access, cooking facilities, restaurant, about a mile to Vigie beach and the airport. Also fishing charters, cruises and whale and dolphin watching.

B Hillside Plaza, la Clery, a few mins walk from Vigie beach, T4524371. Run by Miss Hunte, 30 rooms, of which 23 have a/c. Very convenient for buses, only 2-3 mins' walk from Vigie beach.

B-C Harbour Light Inn, City Gate, T4523506, F4519455. A 3-minute walk to Vigie Beach, at the end of Vigie airport runway, parking, 16 rooms, a/c or fan, private bath, hot water, cable TV, balcony all round building, panoramic view of the west coast and the airplanes, restaurant, bar.

D Morne Fortune Guest House, Top of the Morne, across the road from the Sir Arthur Lewis Community College campus, T4521742. Single rooms are big enough for 2, shared bathrooms, spacious, well-equipped kitchen, very clean. Restaurants and bakery close by. Run by Mrs Regina Willie, helpful, informative, monthly rates available, good access to public transport.

LL-L Windjammer Landing, Labrellotte Bay, T4520913, www.wlv-resort.com. A beautiful luxury resort in a lovely hillside setting, but isolated, 30-min walk to a bus route or EC$20 taxi to Rodney Bay. The best villa complex with hotel facilities, 1-bedroom suites, 2- to 4-bedroom villas spread out with own plunge pool, all white and multilevel in the style of a southern Spanish development. Tennis and watersports, on a much-improved beach, honeymoon, family, diving packages. The food is good, international and aimed at pleasing everybody, families well catered for.

L Villa Beach Cottages, Choc Beach, T4502884, www.villabeachcottages.com. Under same ownership as **La Dauphine Estate**. Beachfront cottages sandwiched between the main road and the sea next to **The Wharf** restaurant, with gingerbread fretwork, wooden shutters and jalousies, 1 or 2 bedrooms with 4-poster beds, a/c, fans, TV, phone, data ports, kitchen, living room, balcony with hammocks, Derek Walcott used to spend his holidays in what is now called the 'Nobel Cottage', lovely honeymoon villa, 9 new villa suites, **Coconuts** restaurant with bar and grill, car rental, tours desk.

A-B Friendship Inn, Sunny Acres, Gablewoods Mall, T4524201, F4532635. Opposite **Sandals** near the Mall, convenient if you come in to Vigie airport after dark. 10, 1-bedroom apartments overlooking the main road with kitchenette and small pool. The restaurant offers local dishes for breakfast and dinner at moderate prices. Daily happy hour, barbecue specials beside the pool on Sat nights, babysitting services.

C-D The Golden Arrow, Gablewoods Mall, on highway to Gros Islet, T4501832, F4502329. 15 clean, pleasant rooms, private bathroom, modern house with balcony and veranda, view down to the bay. Within walking distance of beach and bus, friendly host, breakfast and dinner available.

Rodney Bay *p736, map p745*

LL-AL Coco Resorts (Coco Palm and Coco Kreole), Rodney Bay Blvd, T4562800, www.coco-resorts.com. Two boutique hotels close to restaurants. The larger **Coco Palm** is behind **Coco Kreole** so that guests at the smaller, cheaper property can walk through the gardens to use the more elaborate restaurant and bar at **Coco Palm**. Rooms and suites at **Coco Palm** are elegant and traditional, with French style dark wooden furniture but with all the modern conveniences, pool, spa treatments in your room or wherever you choose, **Ti Bananne** restaurant. Rooms at **Coco Kreole** are not large but are adequately equipped. Both hotels offer TV, a/c, fridge, coffee maker, Wi-Fiand good lighting although at **Coco Kreole** there is only limited wardrobe space and no chair. Rooms there are designed in pairs so that they can connect to make a family suite. Bar overlooks the pool, buffet breakfast included.

LL-AL Harmony Suites, southern end of Rodney Bay marina with waterfront docking, T4528756, www.harmonysuites.com. Small, pleasant hotel, locally owned and managed by the owners' daughter. 30 suites, classic, premium and luxury waterfront, with kitchenettes. **Edge** restaurant on site, see below, also shop, massage, car rental, internet access, pool.

LL-AL Marlin Quay, Gros Islet, T4520393, www.marlin-quay.com. On the waterfront in Rodney Bay, a Mediterranean-style villa resort offering a variety of rooms, studios and 1-2 bedroomed terraced villas, very comfortable and spacious, well equipped, views over lagoon, some with jacuzzi on roof, decks, verandas. Highly recommended for families or couples, restaurants attached, 2 pools, 1 is small, 1 is 40 ft long for exercise swimming.

LL-AL The Village Inn and Spa at Rodney Bay (formerly Rainbow), T4583300, www.villageinnstlucia.com. Further down same road as **Rex** and **Royal**, across the road from the beach. 76 a/c rooms and suites, breakfast included, tennis, spa, pool, beach towels, snack bar, restaurant, pleasant, internet access, linked with Cap Estate Golf Course, golf packages offered.

L-AL Ginger Lily, T4580300, www.theginger lilyhotel.com. 11 apartments of which 4 are superior deluxe (the cheapest), 4 seaview and 3 executive apartments (the most expensive), each of which have a fridge, TV, phone, Wi-Fi internet access and fan and are conveniently located right opposite **Spinnakers**, the Yacht Club and the beach.

L-AL Tuxedo Villas, T4528553, www.nbi.net/tuxedo. 1 min from Reduit Beach next to the **Ginger Lily Hotel** opposite the entrance to **Spinnakers**. A stylish pink modern building built around a pool. Four 1-bedroom and 6 2-bedroom self-catering apartments with a/c, TV, phone, maid service, kitchenette.

AL Caribbean Jewel, T4529199, www.caribbeanjewelresort.com. On hillside at south end of the bay with glorious view to Pigeon Island and to Martinique on a clear day. Rooms and suites are a good size, a/c and TV. Some have kitchens, some jacuzzis in the bath. Executive suites have 2 bedrooms, living/dining room and 2 bathrooms. Several pools on the property at different levels, including a children's pool.

A Villa Zandoli, just down the road from **Rumours** restaurant, T4528898, www.saintelucie.com. 5-bedroom guesthouse, clean and colourful rooms, doubles, twins, triple, private or shared bathroom, mosquito nets, cable TV, fans, a/c. Excursions and activities can be arranged. The family speaks English, French, Spanish and Kwéyòl. Kitchen available, also living room with TV, CD player, books. Continental breakfast included, internet access, laundry services, airport transfers.

A-B Mango Sands, T4529800, www.razmatazstlucia.com. 2 attractive twin-bed rooms behind **Razmataz** restaurant, each with veranda, fridge, tea and coffee-making facilities. Short walk to beach across the road. Rate includes fruit and pastries for breakfast, tax and service. No smoking.

North coast *p736, map p731*

A-B Tropical Breeze, 38 Massie St, Massade, Gros Islet, T/F4500589, www.stluonestop /tropical. Guesthouse with bedrooms only or 1-4 bedroomed apartments, fully equipped, TV, phone, kitchens, group rates on request. Bed & Breakfast is available. Modern white building overlooking Rodney Bay, backs on to police station and is within easy reach of the cricket ground or the venues for the Jazz Festival. Excellent value for groups.

B La Panache, Cas-en-Bas Rd, Gros Islet, T4500765, www.lapanache.com. Run by Henry Augustin, helpful and friendly, and Roger Graveson, who is working with the Forestry Department to complete a listing of the plants of St Lucia (www.ecotourismstlucia.info/), information on Atlantic beaches and coastal walking, birdwatching tours. 2 studio apartments and a 2-bedroom apartment, all with balcony, bathroom, fridge, cooking facilities, insect screens, fans, gardens with plants labelled, breakfast packs US$4, self-service bar, library, computer.

B-C Bay Guest House, Bay St, Gros Islet, T4508956, www.bay-guesthouse.com. Minimum stay 2 nights, spacious rooms, fan, bathroom, 2 studios with kitchenettes, painted bright orange, on beach, run by Will and Stephanie, an English/French couple.

B-D Alexander's Guesthouse, Mary Thérèse St, Gros Islet, T4508610, F4508014. A new building 1 min from beach. Clean, safe, friendly, helpful, kitchen, credit cards accepted.

C Nelson's Furnished Apartments, Cas-en-Bas Rd, Gros Islet, T4508275. 300 m uphill from main road to Castries. Run by Marilyn and Davy, hot water, fan, TV, mosquito net, balcony with nice view over Rodney Bay, towels and toilet paper supplied, free but slow internet access.

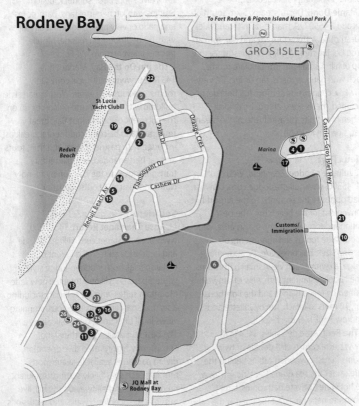

Rodney Bay

To Fort Rodney & Pigeon Island National Park

GROS ISLET

St Lucia Yacht Club

Reduit Beach

Palm Dr

Orange Cres

Flamboyant Dr

Cashew Dr

Reduit Beach Av

Marina

Castries–Gros Islet Hwy

Customs/ Immigration

JQ Mall at Rodney Bay

To Bois d'Orange

N

Not to scale

Sleeping
Coco Kreole 1
Coco Palm & Ti Banane
  Restaurant 2
Ginger Lily 3
Harmony Suites &
  The Edge Restaurant 4
Mango Sands 5
Marlin Quay 6
Tuxedo Villas 7
Villa Zandoli 8
Village Inn & Spa at
  Rodney Bay 9

Eating
Breadbasket 1
Buzz 2
Café Claude 3
Café Olé 4
Café Rio 5
Cat's Whiskers 6
Charthouse 7
Elena's Ice Cream Parlour 9
Key Largo 10
Ku De Ta 11
La Roulotte 12
Lime & Upper Level
  Nite Club 13
Memories of Hong Kong 14
Razmataz 15
Red Snapper 16
Scuttlebutts 17
Shores & Bar 18
Spinnakers 19
Tilly's 2x4 21
Waterfront Seafood
  (Eagles Inn) 22

Bars & clubs
Iguana Wanna 23
Mango's 24
Rumours 25
Triangle Pub 26

A **Foxgrove Inn**, Mon Repos, T4553271, www.foxgroveinn.com. On hillside with wonderful view of Praslin Bay and Fregate Islands, this Swiss/St Lucian-owned hotel is just by Mamiku Gardens. It has 12 bedrooms, a 1-bedroom and a 2-bedroom apartment, TV, fan, balcony, ask for view to front, nothing fancy but comfortable, large pool, nature trails, riding stables, good food, breakfast included, meal plans available, discounts for long stay, German and French spoken, a good base for exploring the east coast.

A **Manje Domi**, Desruisseaux, 5 km south of Micoud, T4550729, manje-domi@candw.lc. Guesthouse with restaurant and bar, turn at Anse Ger junction, 1½ km to guesthouse on top of hill. 4 small but immaculate rooms, each with patio, screens, fan or a/c, TV, very low-key, countryside setting, full breakfast included, meals are seafood, fresh local vegetables, fruits, pleasant (the name means 'eat, sleep' in Kwéyòl).

Vieux Fort *p738, map p731*

AL **Juliette's Lodge**, Beanfield, Vieux Fort, T4545300, www.julietteslodge.com. Down a road opposite the entrance to the airport but convenient for the beach too. The best option for accommodation in this area, with good-value rooms and apartments of varying sizes, balconies, a/c, TV, some have fridge, all with ocean view, small bathrooms, small pool, restaurant with view of runway framed by Maria Islands and the lighthouse, bar, 10 mins to beach, run by Juliette and Andrew Paul, friendly, helpful.

B **The Reef**, Anse de Sables, T4543418, www.slucia.com/reef. 4 double or twin rooms in rustic wooden cabins behind the café under the sea grape trees, no sea view, no hot water, private bathrooms, fans, mosquito nets, breakfast included at the café on the beach.

West Coast to Soufrière *p738, map p731*

LL-L **Ti Kaye Village**, just south of Anse La Raye, T4568101, www.tikaye.com. Romantic and popular for weddings and honeymoons. White wooden cottages with decorative fretwork, large verandas with rocking chairs and double hammocks. Outside showers, large bedroom with louvred windows but also a/c and fan. Some rooms have own plunge pool. Main pool by bar and restaurant, good food and extensive cocktail list (Piton Snow recommended: white rum, triple sec, coconut cream, frozen). 169 steps down the cliff to pretty Anse Cochon beach.

LL-AL **Marigot Beach Club**, on the north shore of Marigot bay, T4514974, www.marigotdiveresort.com. Waterfront restaurants and bar, **Big Bamboo** and **Doolittle's**, live entertainment most nights, steel bands, casino. Lots of activities including sailing, kayaking, **Dive Fair Helen** PADI dive shop, pool, sundeck, beach. Studios with kitchenette, fans, bathrooms and patio or very pretty, light and airy villas with 1-3 bedrooms on hillside. Mobile phones in every room, Wi-Fi.

L **The Inn On the Bay**, Marigot Bay, T4514260, www.saint-lucia.com. Only 5 rooms, spacious, in a white West Indian style building with wrap-around balconies up on the hill overlooking Marigot Bay, great view from pool and balcony, continental breakfast included with pastries, cereal and fruit, tours and car hire arranged, complimentary transport down to the bay, run by friendly Normand Viau and Louise Boucher.

Soufrière *p738, map p731*

LL **Anse Chastanet Resort**, T4597000, www.ansechastanet.com. Hilltop, hillside and beachside suites, all different but all really special, from wooden-lodge style to white-Spanish style and then the new Jade Mountain suites with every facility including a second spa, romantic, luxurious, stunning views in all directions, open balconies, airy. The best scuba diving on the island, consistently highly rated dive operation, diving packages available, watersports, tennis, beach spa, lovely setting, restaurants on the beach and halfway up the hill, live music in the evenings, walks and excursions available, isolated.

LL **Ladera Resort**, T4597323, www.ladera .com. Spectacular setting between Gros Piton and Petit Piton, 1,000 ft up, 24 rooms, each lacking a west wall over a drop that only Superman could climb, providing an uninterrupted view of the Pitons, 1-3 bedroomed villas and suites, every luxury, very cold plunge pools, 60s-style swimming pools, used to film *Superman II*, good restaurant, lots of birds and mosquitoes.

LL Stonefield Estate, T4597037, www.stonefieldvillas.com. Small hillside villa resort, romantic, with stunning views of Petit Piton and overlooking Malgretoute beach. Villas sleep 2-8 with outdoor showers, kitchens, hammocks on the veranda and many have plunge pools. The older ones are nicer than the new villas. A 26-acre former cocoa estate, the grounds are forested, with many fruit trees and birds and a nature trail to some petroglyphs, which are the resort's logo. Good restaurant, but a shuttle will take you to Soufrière if you want to shop for food. Fruit from the estate is complementary.

LL-L Crystals, Colombette, overlooking Soufriere, T3848995, www.stluciacrystals .com. 5 cottages in lush hillside gardens with exceptional view of sea and Pitons, rustic outside but every luxury inside, 1 or 2 a/c bedrooms, full kitchen, each has a sun deck and a plunge pool, swimming pool or Jacuzzi.

LL-L Mago Estate Hotel, T4595880, www.magohotel.com. Originally a private home, built by an architect into the cliff and incorporating all the natural and geological features, now a small, luxury hotel with 10 beautiful rooms and suites framed by bougainvillea overlooking the bay, Pitons and mountains, 4-poster beds, huge louvred windows fold out to give uninterrupted view, open bathrooms, suites are spacious and have plunge pools, breakfast included, MAP available, pool bar in the roots of a huge mango tree, tree house above, lounge bar built into rock formation and mango trees, **Yin & Yang** health spa if you need a detox.

LL-AL La Dauphine Estate (see **Villa Beach Cottage**, page 743, for contact details) a 4-bedroom Great House and 2-bedroom Chateau Laffitte on a 200-acre plantation 5 miles from Soufrière. Built in 1890 in gingerbread style, surrounded by lush gardens and hills, recently refurbished to modern standards, housekeeper/cook provided, good hiking along nature trails and through fruit plantation.

L Fond Doux Estate, Soufriere, T4597545, info@fonddouxestate.com. Traditional old chattel houses which were about to be demolished in Castries were bought and reassembled on the estate, modernised and furnished with comfortable beds, TV, phone, mini bar, polished wooden floors and bathrooms. They have a villa at US$350, two cottages at US$200 and a suite t US$150. Gorgeous setting in a tranquil and beautiful landscape.

A Chez Camille, 7 Bridge St, T4595379, www.cavip.com/en/hotels/chezcamille.html. Older-style house with wrap-around balcony and St Lucian decor and furnishings. Clean and friendly, 5 rooms, family room available. Kitchen for guests' use or the maid can cook for you, good restaurant attached where guests get 10% discount (does takeaways).

C La Mirage Guesthouse, T4597010. English owner of Jamaican descent, Gilroy Lamontaigne, 4 rooms sleep 3, bathroom, fan and fridge, lounge with cable TV, restaurant.

Eating

The local style of cooking is known as Creole and is a mixture of all the cultural influences of the island's immigrants over the centuries, from starchy vegetables to sustain African slaves to gourmet sauces and garnishes dating from the days when the French governed the island. The movement of people along the chain of Caribbean islands means that you can also find rotis from Trinidad and jerk meats from Jamaica, although these have been adapted from what you can expect on those islands. Fish and seafood are fresh and delicious, but make sure you only eat lobster and conch in season (Sep-Apr) to avoid overfishing. A local speciality is *accra*, a deep fried fish cake made of salted cod, an ingredient also used in saltfish and green fig, where the fig is actually green banana. There is a range of tropical fruit and vegetables on offer and it is worth strolling round the market to see what they look like before ending up on your plate. Breadfruit, called *bwapen* in Kwéyòl, is usually eaten fried or boiled and has been a staple for centuries.

The standard of cooking in restaurants is high, but for really authentic Creole food you should try local cafeterias and street vendors.

The best places for freshly caught seafood, cooked to your specification, are the street parties at **Anse La Raye**, **Dennery** and **Vieux Fort**, where local fishermen sell their catch to be cooked on huge oil drum barbecues.

Like most islands, St Lucia has its own rum used in cocktails and liqueurs. The local beer is

Piton, brewed in Vieux Fort and drunk very cold for maximum refreshment. A shandy on St Lucia is a mixture of beer and ginger ale; if it's a Piton shandy it can be with lemon or sorrel.

Castries p734, map p735

There are about 10 good-value local eateries in the street adjoining the central market, tables outside, offering heaped plates of local food, at lunchtime only. A standard meal of meat, plantains, potatoes, macaroni, rice and lettuce washed down with a glass of passion fruit juice costs around EC$10. Vendors outside Julian's at Gablewoods Mall sometimes sell home made cassava bread and a local delicacy called permi made of cornmeal and coconut wrapped up in a banana leaf. For other foods such as bakes, floats, fish, chicken, dal rotis (split pea), be sure that they are freshly cooked for the best flavour.

♥♥Caribbean Pirates, Place Carenage, T4522543. Mon-Thu 0800-1800, Fri 0800-2200, Sat 1000-1600, closed Sun unless a cruise ship is in port. Good food, modest prices, you can get bwigi (whelks) and lambi (conch) here as well as local fish. There is another branch opposite the main Post Office on Bridge St, upstairs with a small balcony overlooking the street.

♥♥The Green Parrot, Top of the Morne, T4523399. Lunch and dinner. 4-course dinner US$37, serves excellent lunches daily, lots of Caribbean specialities and good selection of tropical vegetables, have a cocktail in the lounge before dinner, the chairs are worth it alone, shows Wed, Sat, Ladies' Night on Mon when you get 2 dinners for the price of 1 (dress smartly, the waiters are in tuxedos).

♥♥Oceana, on the main La Toc road next to the entrance to Sandals Regency, T4560300. Tue 1130-1500, Wed-Sat 1130-2100, Sun brunch 1100-1500. In what was once a military building, tables inside or on the balcony with a superb view of Castries, the harbour and the northwest coast. Good food at moderate prices.

♥♥-♥Great Enterprise, on Mongiraud, next to the S&S building, T4530893. Mon-Sat 1100-2130, Sun and holidays 1730-2130. Chinese fast food, popular at lunchtimes with several stir fry dishes at the counter or à la carte menu with an extensive selection of over 100 seafood, meat and vegetable dishes. Eat in or takeaway, friendly service.

♥Flamingo, William Peter Blvd. Open until about 1600, closes about 1200 on Sat. Favourite local place for a cheeseburger (EC$6.50) or roti, for a chicken roti specify you want it without skin and bones.

♥Hardest Hard, on the main La Toc road just past the roundabout a the entrance to the Millennium Highway, T4524047. Mon-Sat from 0700 until late. Good local food, fresh juices, 'everything made from scratch daily'. Very lively if a bit noisy. Popular local hangout.

♥Kimlans, Derek Walcott Square, T4521136. Mon-Sat 0700-2300. Upstairs café and bar with veranda, cheap, serves local food. A chicken and potato roti washed down with a local juice overlooking the square will renew your energy for sightseeing. Good place for people watching.

North of Castries p734

♥♥♥-♥♥Coal Pot, at Vigie Marina, T4525566. Mon-Fri lunch and dinner, Sat dinner only, closed Sun. The place to eat, outstanding, reservations essential. A very romantic, candlelit interior with beautiful artwork or terrace dining overlooking the marina. Sophisticated international cuisine, delicious fresh food with all the trimmings, accompanied by a good wine list.

♥♥♥-♥♥Jacques Waterfront Dining, Vigie Cove, T4581900, www.froggiejacques.com. Mon-Sat 1200-1430, 1900-2130. Waterfront bistro, open- air dining in a garden with French and Caribbean cuisine, all beautifully presented. Try their home-smoked local fish, or the salsa with breadfruit chips. Run by French chef, Jacques Rioux. St Lucia Perfumes is in the garden behind the restaurant.

♥♥-♥Miss Saigon, Gablewoods Mall, T4517309. Breakfast, lunch and dinner. Serves full English breakfast, EC$18, Chinese and Oriental food for other meals. St Lucians who work in the area come here for lunch.

♥BJ's Pepper Pot, along the main road in Marisule, near Gablewoods Mall, T4501030. Tue-Sat from 1100. Jamaican cooking with jerk food to get you sweating and pepper pot, prices up to EC$18.

♥Friends at Casa Vigie, 1st floor, just below the Venezuelan embassy, T4581335. Mon-Thu 0730-1900, Fri, Sat 0900-2100. Patisserie and café, very good sandwiches, good midday meal but you have to get there early to make sure of getting it, attractive, lovely walk from here to the Vigie lighthouse.

♟ **Sub-Station**, Gablewoods Mall, T4517300. Mon-Sat 0800-1600. Popular for lunchtime with office crowd, tables in the courtyard, lots of fast food takeaway business.

♟ **Tiggy's**, Gablewoods Mall, T4536926. Mon-Sat 1100-1800. Brisk trade at lunch time, a substantial Creole meal for EC$10-15, indoor area with bar and banquettes. Also takeaway.

♟ **The Wharf**, Choc Bay, short distance past Gablewoods Mall, T4504844. Daily 0900-2400, happy hour 1800-1900. Beach setting, sandwiched between the road and the sea, waiter service to your sunbed, varied menu, reasonable prices, beer EC$5-6, house wine EC$6, BLT EC$12, hamburger EC$15. Lively in the evenings, restaurant, bar and dancing, karaoke Wed and Fri nights, soul, salsa and smooch Thu with ladies' night after 2100, live music Sat, brunch on Sun.

Rodney Bay *p736, map p745*

♟♟♟ **The Edge**, Harmony Suites, T4503343. Daily 0700-1100, 1200-1500, 1900-2300. Waterfront deck area with raised main dining room and central square bar, fine dining with fusion European dishes, artistically presented and created by chef Bobo Bergström. There is also a ♟ **Sushi Bar**, open for dinner and takeaway, closed Tue.

♟♟♟-♟♟ **Buzz**, opposite **Royal St Lucia**, T4580450, www.buzzstlucia.com. 1700-late, closed Mon in summer, Sun brunch in season. Seafood and grill, local and international dishes, lobster, lamb, pepperpot and vegetarian. *The* place to be, reservations recommended unless you are prepared to wait an hour or more. Indoor or outdoor seating, even indoors is very open and airy with shutters raised, blue and lemon yellow decor in West Indian-style building, smart but comfortable.

♟♟♟-♟♟ **Charthouse**, overlooking the lagoon, by Reduit Beach, T4528115. Mon-Sat 1800-2230. Open-air restaurant, a room without walls overlooking the yachts. Known for its prime US beef, particularly the roast rib, as well as steak, lobster, seafood and spare ribs, excellent rib steak, Cuban cigars. Accompaniments often of lower quality and generally considered overpriced.

♟♟ **Café Claude**, next to **Coco Kreole**, T4580847. Mon-Tue 0800-1800, Wed-Sat 0800-2300. Convenient location at the centre of everything. Pleasant café/bar, baguettes, pastries and good salads. Book your Rainforest Skyride, wander next door into Bambu for gifts and clothes, then out again to sit on the balcony, order a cold drink and place your lunch order.

♟♟ **Café Rio**, Rodney Bay Drive, between Memories of Hong Kong and Razmataz, T4580008. Tue-Sun 0800-late, breakfast, lunch and dinner. Good food at reasonable prices, ranges from imported strip loin, local fresh fish or beefburger with trimmings.

♟♟ **The Cat's Whiskers**, just by **Spinnakers**, T4528880. Tue-Sun 0800-2300. Also known as the **English Pub**. Traditional English pub food, Sun roast beef and Yorkshire pudding, steak and kidney pie, Cornish pasties, etc.

♟♟ **Key Largo**, on highway, past the supermarket, T4520282. Wood oven baked pizzas, pasta dishes, salads, outside tables and small trampolines for children.

♟♟ **Ku De Ta**, between **Café Claude** and **Coco Kreole**, T4584968. A/c and open air Thai restaurant. Extensive cocktail list.

♟♟ **La Roulotte**, on the main street opposite **Mango's Bar**, T4878611. Roadside hut (a truck parked sideways in the hedge) with a couple of tables on the pavement, serving kebabs, burgers, pizzas, paninis, coffee and juices, great for a late night snack.

♟♟ **The Lime**, T4520761. Wed-Mon 1100 till late. Friendly, casual, open air, serves good meals such as steak cooked over a charcoal grill, fish, shrimp, lobster and rotis and snacks at moderate prices. Jerk pit for spicy chicken, fish or pork. Good portions, nothing fancy.

♟♟ **Memories of Hong Kong**, opposite **Royal St Lucian Hotel**, T/F4528218. Mon-Sat 1700-2230. A breezy location with fairy lights and lanterns around the veranda and tables. Chinese chef from Hong Kong, good food, plenty of it.

♟♟ **Red Snapper**, upstairs above **Pizza Pizza**, by **Elena's**, T4668377. Dinner only Wed-Mon. Great seafood place, offering lobster, conch, scallops and mussels, freshly caught local fish

● *Buy a cocoa stick (10 for US$5). To make hot chocolate, put 2 tablespoons of grated cocoa in a pan with half a pint of water and boil for 15 minutes, strain, then add dry milk, sugar, cinnamon and nutmeg to taste.*

such as mahi mahi, tuna and kingfish. Other options include burgers, pizzas, pasta and vegetarian dishes for quick and easy meals.

Scuttlebutts, at the marina, T4520351, VHS Channel 68. 0730-2400 or later. Right on the water, decorated with a nautical theme and offering an extensive menu of salads, pasta, ribs, chicken, steak, chilli and an all-day breakfast menu. On-board catering and provisioning packs for yachties as well as a dinghy dock and takeaway service. Lively atmosphere and stays open as long as there are clients, TV screens for sport, complimentary internet access, pool and pool bar, barbecue, lawn area with 5-a-side games.

The Shores, on the road going down to Reduit beach, T4520284. Daily 0700-2300. Right in the centre of the strip and convenient for going to a club or bar in the evening. Seafood a speciality. Tables indoors and outdoors under a tent in what was once the garden. Inside there is a night club, see below.

Spinnakers, directly on the beach at Reduit, T4528491. Breakfast, lunch and dinner daily, happy hour 1800-1900. Full English breakfast EC$26, excellent location, though food and service suffer when it is busy, good too for coffee and desserts, they also hire out loungers for EC$5 per day.

Ti Bananne, Coco Palm Resort, T4520712. See the murals painted by Dunstan St Omer and other regional artists, giving a true Caribbean feel to go with the food, which includes local favourites such as plantain and saltfish. Trinidadian chef who has worked in Martinique, introduces créole touches. International dishes also served and there is a create-your-own sandwich selection.

Tilly's 2x4, on the highway, just past Key Largo, T4584440. Daily 1000-2400. Like an old chattel house and rum shop, serving good Creole food, lots of fish, grilled, baked or Creole, with side dishes of Caribbean vegetables. Happy hour 1700-1900 with a great rum punch. Entrance from the road on foot but around the back by car.

Waterfront Seafood Restaurant (Eagles Inn), at the entrance to Rodney Bay Marina, T4520650. 1000-0200. You can sit on the terrace for a drink or lunch and watch the boats go by and enjoy good and not too expensive cuisine. Great fish, freshly caught and prepared, worth waiting for.

Razmataz, opposite **Royal St Lucian**,

T/F4529800. Fri-Wed from 1600, happy hour 1700-1900. Indian, chefs from Nepal, good, wide range of dishes, particularly good for vegetarians, very popular with British clientele, friendly, on Sat a belly dancer weaves her way around the diners.

Breadbasket, at the marina, T4520647. Mon-Sat 0700-1700, Sun 0600-1300. A favourite for breakfast and for fantastic home-made bread, great rotis, sandwiches and pastries. Very good value.

Café Olé, Rodney Bay Marina, T4528726. Open daily. Freshly made baguettes, salads, light meals, a complete range of Elena's ice cream, the tiramisu, when they have it, is fantastic.

Elena's ice cream parlour, Rodney Bay village, T4580576. Mon, Wed-Fri 0900-2300, Sat-Sun 0900-2400. Tables under umbrellas outside in a small courtyard, home-made ice cream and local fruit sorbets, good cappuccino and snacks.

Pigeon Island p736

Jambe de Bois, T4580728/4520321. From breakfast until 2130 except Mon when it closes at 1700. Rustic, wooden furniture with seating outside or inside. The stone walls are in the style of the military buildings and the roof is thatched. Serves reasonably priced meals, offering baguettes, fish, soup, cakes, salads, art gallery, book swap, post cards, internet access at EC$20 per hr. On Sun evening there is a jazz group, around 1830-2130, very pleasant to sit at the tables on the deck at the water's edge.

Captain's Cellar Pub and Oscar's Restaurant, T4500918, thecaptainscellarpub@ hotmail.com. Wed-Sun 1000-2300 or later, Tue 1000-1700, Mon closed. Underneath the Interpretation Centre, with tables outside with good view over the channel and Burgot Rocks, or in the original Captain's cellar where provisions were stored under low arches, where there may be a ghost. Open for breakfast, snacks and lunch in the pub daily, then dinner in Oscar's alongside 6 nights. Simple dishes such as burgers, roti, sandwiches, chilli, curries, vegetarian dishes, salads and fish. Bottled and draught Piton and other beers.

North Coast p736

Milo's, Gros Islet Highway, Massade, T4500098. Mon-Sat 0900-2200. New, clean and very good restaurant in colonial house, Milo is a super host and prices are medium for the area. Creole food to order.

The Wall, corner of Marie Thérèse and Dauphin streets, T4500338. Mon-Sat 0700-2300, much later on Fri. Excellent value, US$4.50 for huge plateful, rooms available (D) behind the restaurant on the beach.

East coast to Vieux Fort *p737*

Whispering Palm, Foxgrove Inn, Mon Repos, T4553800, www.foxgroveinn.com. Breakfast, lunch and dinner. Spectacular view from balcony of restaurant over Praslin Bay and the Atlantic Ocean. Very good food, try the smoked fish or smoked duck salad for a delicious lunch, washed down with a local juice such as guava or passion fruit. Main dishes include fish, steak or pasta. Good place to stop during a tour of the east coast.

Manje Domi, Desruisseaux, T4550729, manje-domi@candw.lc. Guesthouse (see p746) and restaurant run by Kenny G deep in the countryside, offering local food with Creole, curry or ginger sauces, all freshly prepared, vegetarian meals on request.

Vieux Fort *p738*

Pointe Sable Beach Resort (formerly Sandy Beach), Anse de Sables, T4546002. Open all day until the last guest leaves. On the beach and on the highway. Excellent location, delightful beach bar stopping place if you're touring the island, good food, a bit overpriced, have a swim and lunch.

The Annex, close to Hewanorra Airport, T4546200. Mon-Fri 0900-1200, Sat and Sun 1000-0200. Good local food. One of the best places within walking distance of the airport for drinks, meal or a swim if you are passing time before a flight.

The Reef Beach Café, at Anse de Sables beach, T4543418, www.slucia.com/reef. Breakfast, lunch and dinner. Owned by Cecile Wiltshire, pleasant bar, local drinks and delicacies, milk shakes and cocktails, seafood, fish and chips, burgers and baguettes, reasonable prices, tables out by the beach under sea grape trees as well as inside the building. Wi-Fi internet access.

West coast to Soufrière *p738*

Rainforest Hideaway, Marigot Bay, T2860581. Beautiful décor and setting, part

of the Discovery development. Take the ferry across from the jetty by the police/customs building and fare is deducted from your meal. Good food, fusion Caribbean

Chateau Mygo, Marigot Bay, T4514772, www.chateaumygo.com. Daily 0700-2300. Waterfront bar and grill. Serves traditional hot bakes and cocoa tea for breakfast, Tue night steak, US$12, with music and dancing on the beach, thin crust pizzas from US$8, credit cards accepted, reservations advised, gift shop, car rental, phone cards.

JJ's Restaurant and Bar, Marigot Bay, T4514076. 1000 till late. Several hotels at Marigot Bay have restaurants, but JJ's on the bay is a cheaper alternative. Specializes in fresh local dishes, reasonably priced crayfish, crab and lobster, Wed night crabs and a live band, Fri salsa, Sat live band.

Shack Bar & Grill, Marigot Bay, T4514145. Mon-Fri from 1500, Sat-Sun from 1200, happy hour 1700-1900, dinner 1830-2200. Built over the water, tie up for dinghies, burgers, steaks, seafood, reservations advised for dinner.

Soufrière *p738*

Dasheene, at Ladera Resort, T4597323. Breakfast for hotel guests only, lunch 1130-1430, and dinner 1830-2130. Up on a hillside, 1,000 ft above sea level, wonderful views of the Pitons, worth coming here even if only for a drink just for the views. Good food, light and modern Caribbean Creole, mostly produce from local farmers and fishermen used as well as some international delicacies.

The Humming Bird, on the beach, north end of Soufrière, T4597232. Open from 0700. A nice place to eat and take a swim. French, Creole and seafood, daily specials, varied menu, fish, steak, surf'n'turf, vegetarian meals, lunchtime salads and sandwiches, good but expensive, barman is a great fund of information on horoscopes, good views of the town and Petit Piton. Also a hotel.

Mango Tree, Stonefield Estate Villa Resort, T4597037, www.stonefieldvillas.com. Daily 0730-2200. Gorgeous setting overlooking Petit Piton and Malgretoute beach and great for sunset watching. Serving breakfast, lunch and dinner, the menu is varied and wide ranging, with some vegetarian dishes as well as the usual seafood, meat and pasta. A barbeque on Thu

with live music is usually heavily booked, so even guests have to make reservations.
Pirates Cove, 2 Bay St, by the jetty, Soufrière, T4521800, www.piratescovestlucia.com. Waterfront dining in a building dating from 1898, lovely setting and good view but can be noisy, music and other entertainment for catamaran visitors and others, credit cards.
La Haut Plantation, on the west coast road 1½ miles north of Soufrière, T4597008, www.lahaut.com. 0800-1100, 1200-1600, 1700-2100. Huge TV in sports bar, excellent lunch with some unusual items such as pumpkin chips, crêpes and rotis, dinner also delicious with good wine list, stunning views of Pitons and Sulphur Springs, also 7 rooms.
Jalam's, Market St. A pleasant rasta eating place run by Jalam, in a wooden house up a couple of steps from street level, small, clean, cheap, EC$10 for a dal, a roti and 2 fresh juices.

● Bars and clubs

Most of St Lucia's nightlife revolves around the hotels, while some restaurants host live bands. Bars and clubs are concentrated around Rodney Bay, all within easy walking distance of each other. Some have strict entry restrictions on age and dress, so check beforehand. They offer a mix of live bands and DJs playing regional and international music. For more informal entertainment there are street parties. Fri nights are big for going out and St Lucians enjoy eating fresh local food while socializing in the open air, known as 'liming', followed by music and dancing, known as a 'jump up'. The highlight of the week is currently **Seafood Friday**, at Anse La Raye, just south of Castries, where you can get the cheapest and freshest lobster on the island in season and fish at any time of year. The entire street running parallel to the bay has chairs and tables under awnings, serving seafood of your choice. However it is so popular that food tends to run out by 2100, so get there early. Everyone is very friendly and there is no hassling. Music is at a bearable pitch and sometimes you can hear a local *quadrille* band. If you are on the east coast, you can try Dennery for fish-on-the-beach at weekends, 1600-0200, while Sware, Vieux Fort, is a lively Fri street party where you can eat unlimited fish accompanied by the beat of local music.

The jump up In Gros Islet starts from 2200. Food includes barbecued chicken legs, lambi/conch, accra (fish cakes) and floats from the street stalls.

Castries *p734, map p735*
Nashville Palace, upstairs, above the market. Sat night country and western music and dance, very popular, taken very seriously but great fun. Also Fri nights sometimes.

Rodney Bay *p736, map p745*
Iguana Wanna, between **The Charthouse** and **Pizza Pizza**. Daily 1200-0200. Upstairs lounge and terrace restaurant, ground floor sports bar with pool table and night club (age restrictions). Classy Creole food, chef was previously in New Orleans.
The Lime, see Eating, above, T4520761. Music and dancing every night until everyone goes home.
Mango's, beside **Coco Kreole**. Lively bar on the main street, convenient place between dinner and dancing.
Rumours, opposite Scotia Bank, T4529249. Open from 1730. Bar, restaurant (also open for lunch Mon-Fri 1130-1430), pool tables, dance floor. Wed night is Latin night when the Cuban medical staff from the polyclinic come out to salsa. Great fun and very energetic. Tue is karaoke and Thu-Sat Marcus and DJ Play provide club music. Entry fee of EC$10 after 2300 unless you have a VIP card.
The Shores, T4520284. Daily for food 0700-2300, night club 2100 until late. Good food, seafood a speciality. Age restriction of 21 and over at the night club and dress code.
Triangle Pub, across from **The Lime**, T4520334. Daily 1100-late. Local food and barbecue, eat in or take out, karaoke some nights.
Upper Level Nite Club (upstairs at **The Lime**). Tue, Fri, Sat until late. Popular place for those who just want to hang out. Live music, karaoke and food. Sometimes has special events with a cover charge.

North coast *p736*
Panache, Cas-en-Bas Rd, T4500765, augustinh@candw.lc. Bar attached to the guesthouse run by Henry Augustin. Recently improved bar area, pleasant place to stop in for a drink, great rum punches.

West coast to Soufrière and the Pitons *p738*

JJ's Paradise, Marigot, T4514076. Open until very late. Casual, good mixture of locals and tourists, live, loud Caribbean music at weekends in simple disco, Fri can be very busy, Sat pleasantly so, happy hour all night. Wed is **Seafood Night**, which is so popular that reservations are required. Frequent shows, karaoke, taxi service can be arranged.

⊗ Festivals and events

St Lucia *p730, map p731*

22 Feb Independence Day is celebrated extensively. There is a large exhibition lasting several days from the various ministries, business and industry, and NGOs, such as the National Trust, and various sporting events, serious discussions and musical programmes.
May The annual **St Lucia Jazz Festival** is now an internationally recognized event, drawing large crowds every year. Most concerts are open-air and take place in the evening, although fringe events are held anywhere, anytime, with local bands playing in Castries at lunchtime. As well as jazz, played by international stars, you can hear Latin, salsa, soca and zouk, steel drums or reggae. For more details T4518566, www.stluciajazz.org. Tickets from US$35 or a season pass US$230. Tickets available at the Department of Culture and **Sunshine Bookstore** (Gablewoods Mall).
29 Jun St Peter's Day is celebrated as the Fisherman's Feast, in which all the fishing boats are decorated.
Jul Carnival is a high point, when colourful bands and costumed revellers make up processions through the streets. There is lots of music, dancing and drinking. Everything goes on for hours, great stamina is required to keep going. On the Sat are the calypso finals, on Sun the King and Queen of the band followed by J'ouvert at 0400 until 0800 or 0900. On Mon and Tue the official parades of the bands take place. Most official activities take place at Marchand Ground but warming-up parties and concerts are held all over the place. Tue night there is another street party.
30 Aug Feast of the Rose of Lima (*Fét La Wòz*). Members of the societies gather in various public places around the island to dance and sing in costume.

Oct The first Mon is **Thanksgiving**, held either to give thanks for no hurricane or for survival of a hurricane. **17 Oct La Marguerite**, a festival to rival the Rose with a church service, parade with participants dressed as kings and queens, officers and members of the court, then lots of music, food and drink. Both festivals have their origins in the secret societies formed by slaves under French and British colonial rule. **Jounen Kwéyòl** (Creole Day), on the last Sun, although activities are held throughout the month. 4 or 5 rural communities are selected for the celebration. There is local food, craft, music and different cultural shows. Expect traffic jams everywhere as people visit venues across the island. A lot is in Kwéyòl/patois, but you will still have a good time and a chance to sample mouth-watering local food.
Nov Food and Rum Festival, held in Rodney Bay (1-4 Nov 2007), with lots of tastings, cooking demonstrations from chefs around the Caribbean and concerts.
Dec Kalalu World Music Festival, a new annual event at the beginning of the month with musicians from Africa and the Caribbean playing traditional and contemporary styles, great concerts held in Samaans Park, tickets US$25-30. **13 Dec St Lucy's Day** used to be called **Discovery Day**, but as Columbus' log shows he was not in the area at that time, it was renamed. It is now known as **National** Day. St Lucy, the patron saint of light, is honoured during National Day by a procession of lanterns called the **Festival of Lights and Renewal**. For details contact **Castries City Council**, T4522611 ext 7071.

○ Shopping

St Lucia *p730, maps p731*
Art and crafts
Artsibit, corner of Brazil and Mongiraud streets, T4527865. Mon-Fri 0900-1230, 1330-1700, Sat 1000-1200. High-quality local crafts, pottery, sculpture, prints and paintings. Also outlet on first floor of La Place Carenage.
Bagshaw's, La Toc, T4522139, also shops at La Place Carenage, Marigot and Windjammer Landing. Silk screening studio, Mon-Fri 0830-1630, Sat 0830-1200. Take return air ticket for discount. Close to Bagshaw's is the military fort, La Toc Battery; call Alice

Bagshaw, T4526039, for a tour, or enquire at the shop. Very popular.

Caribbean Art Gallery, Rodney Bay Marina, T4528071, www.caribbeanartandantiques .com. Mon-Fri 0900-1700, Sat 0900-1300. **Llewellyn Xavier**'s gallery, with cheap framed prints and antique maps and jewellery as well as his own work and that of local artists: water colours, oils, pen and ink, pencil drawings, limited edition prints, hand-painted silk, collages, woodcuts, mixed media, art cards. Credit cards accepted, worldwide shipping with Fedex. Llewellyn Xavier has a second gallery, **Arts & Antiques** at Pointe Seraphine, T4514150, same opening hours. You can visit his studio, T4509155 for an appointment.

Eudovics Art Studio, in Goodlands, coming down from the Morne heading south, T4522747. Local handicrafts and beautiful large wood carvings.

Inner Gallery, Rodney Bay opposite Capone's, T4528728, www.theinnergallery .com. Exhibits the work of local artists including Arnold Toulon, Cedric George, Chris Cox, Nancy Cole, Sophie Barnard, Alcina Nolley, Jonathon Gladding.

Books

Sunshine Bookshop, Gablewoods Mall (Mon-Fri 0900-1745, Sat 0900-1630), JQ Mall (Mon-Sat 0900-1800, Sun 1000-1300), and Point Seraphine (Mon-Fri 0830-1630, Sat half day). Books, foreign newspapers and magazines.

Flowers

Garden Gate Flowers, at Bois D'Orange, T4529176, at Hewanorra, T4547651, F4529023. Takeaway boxes (cargo transport) and bouquets (hand luggage) of ginger, heliconia, anthuriums, 48 hrs notice required for export, US$12-30.

Markets

Market day in **Castries** is Sat, very picturesque (much quieter on other days, speakers of Patois pay less than those who do not). A new public market has been built on the Castries waterfront, with the old market building renovated and turned into a craft market. **Wire World**, booth 3, charming figures by the award-winning Paulinus Clifford, T4538727, also at Pointe Seraphine, he and the next artisan, **Augustus Simon**, a

potter, T4521507, will craft to order. Buy a coal-pot (native barbecue) for EC$12 and bring it home on your lap. **Soufrière** has a market on the waterfront, as does **Anse La Raye** along the seafront road, with tourist stalls selling clothing and souvenirs and a fish market.

Fisherman's Co-operative Market on the John Compton Highway at the entrance to Pointe Seraphine. Fish is also sold by a Martiniquan woman inside the public market, good variety, hygienically displayed, and at an outlet outside the supermarket at JQ's Mall, Rodney Bay. Fishermen still sell their catch wherever they can. Fish is cheap and fresh.

Music

Vibes Music Store, Rodney Bay Shopping Centre, T4580056, www.vibesmusicstore .com. The latest releases in a variety of styles. **Vintage Music**, 83 Brazil St, Castries, T4525079.

Shopping malls

Gablewoods Shopping Mall, between Rodney Bay and Castries, has a selection of boutiques, gift shops, book shop, post office, pharmacy, deli, open-air eating places and Super J. Next door is a delicatessen. A few doors away is the **Sea Island Cotton Shop**, the main outlet for Caribelle Batik clothes. **JQ Mall at Rodney Bay**. Also a duty-free facility. On the top floor there is a local arts and crafts outlet guaranteed 100% St Lucian. **La Place Carenage**, Jeremie St, Castries, T4527318. Duty-free shopping mall right by the cruise ships with jewellers, arts and crafts, clothing, places to eat, internet café, tour desk, taxi service, tourist information, car rental. The Desmond Skeete Animation Center, 3rd floor, T4532451, is a small historical museum with a 20-min light and sound show dramatizing St Lucia's history. **Pointe Seraphine**, next to the main port in Castries. Mon-Fri 0900-1600, Sat 0900-1400. Ferry from La Place Carenage every 10 mins, US$1. Duty-free shopping centre, so take your airline ticket and passport, with many tourist-oriented outlets, restaurants, entertainment and tour operators. Goods bought here can be delivered directly to the airport. Cruise ships can tie up at the complex's own berths.

▲▲ Activities and tours

St Lucia *p730, maps p731*

Cricket

Beausejour Cricket Ground, T4578834. St Lucia hosted its first Test Match in 2003 between the West Indies and Sri Lanka at the Beausejour Cricket Ground, built in 2002, and other Test and international matches have been held here since including the World Cup. Benefiting from state-of-the-art technology, the stadium has hospitality suites, a media centre and players' pavilion, and was the first ground in the West Indies to install floodlighting, allowing it to host a day/night match against Zimbabwe in 2006. The four stands are sponsored by local businesses. For the cricket World Cup in 2007 new stands were erected, increasing capacity from 15,000 to 20,000. St Lucia hosted the first round matches of the group anchored by England and one semi-final game. Women's cricket is strong in St Lucia and several St Lucian women play in the West Indies team. In 2004 left-hander Nadine George became the first West Indies woman to hit a century in a Test Match, scoring 118 against Pakistan in Karachi. Nicknamed 'The Lion', she was awarded an MBE in 2005.

Cycling

Bike St Lucia, T4597755, www.bikestlucia .com. On a beach just north of Anse Chastenet (linked to Scuba St Lucia), they offer off-road riding on trails through 400 acres of forest (jungle biking). The fleet of Cannondale F800 CAAD-3 bikes are not for use away from their trails. Accessible only by boat, they organize transfers from your hotel, lunch, snorkelling, etc, US$89.
Carib Travel, T4522151. They have 15 Rockhoppers and offer a trip starting at Paix Bouche through mountain villages down to Gros Islet. Cycling has become popular, mostly in groups with a guide.
Island Bike Hikes, T4580908, www.cyclestlucia .com. Vehicle-supported and tailor-made bike tours from US$58, a great way to explore the beaches of the northeast coast.

Diving

A single-tank dive costs around US$35-55, introductory resort courses are about US$65-90, a 6-dive package US$175-200 and open-water certification courses US$380-495, plus 10% service charge.
Aquabulle, operated by Water Sport World at Rodney Bay Marina, T4584292, watersports@candw.lc. You can see the underwater world without getting wet by taking a ride on this semi-submersible. Departures are at 0900 and 1500, 1½ hrs, US$30 adults, US$15 under 16, 1 child under 10 free if accompanied by 2 adults.
Buddies Scuba, Rodney Bay Marina, T/F4529086. PADI, BSAC, 2-tank day dives, 1-tank night dives, camera rental, open water certification or resort course, dive packages available.
Dive Fair Helen, Castries, T4517716, www.divefairhelen.com. 1 dive US$60, 2 dive package US$84, PADI Open Water Course US$489, 2 dive boats with wash room and shower and shade as well as platform and easy access to the water. Snorkelling and kayaking also offered.
Island Divers, Anse Cochon at Ti Kaye Hotel. Run by Terroll and his team. A beginner's resort course costs US$75, a 2-tank dive is US$70 including tank, weights, mask, fins and snorkel, other equipment for rent.
Scuba St Lucia, Anse Chastanet, Soufrière, www.scubastlucia.com, or contact them through the hotel. PADI 5-star, SSI and DAN, the first and only dive centre to be accredited as a National Geographic Dive Center in the Windward Islands. 3 dive boats with oxygen on each, photographic hire and film processing, video filming and courses, day and night dives, resort courses and full PADI certification, multilingual staff, pick-up service Mon-Sat from hotels north of Castries, day packages for divers, snorkellers, beginners and others include lunch and equipment.
Scuba Steve's Diving, Rodney Bay Marina near the Fisheries Complex, T4509433, www.scubastevesdiving.com. New boat, takes up to 12 divers, offers PADI courses, night dives and wreck dives.

Fishing

Fishing trips for barracuda, mackerel, king fish and other varieties can be arranged. Several sport fishing boats sail from Rodney Bay Marina. There is an annual billfish tournament, at which a 940-lb blue marlin was recently landed, putting the earlier record of 705 lbs in the shade. For more information, check www.worldwidefishing.com/stlucia.

Golf

St Lucia Golf & Country Club, Cap Estate, T4508523, www.stluciagolf.com. A 6,829-yd, par 71, 18-hole golf course and driving range, green fee US$70-90 for 9 holes, US$95-125 for 18 holes, depending on the time of year, golf carts mandatory. Club rental, Pro Shop, restaurant and group packages.

Greg Norman's Le Paradis Championship Golf Course will open at Praslin Bay in 2008, to be managed by Troon Golf.

Hiking and birdwatching

You need a permit from the **Forestry Department** for walking in the national parks, US$10 (US$5 for children). Tours are franchized to tour operators and a guide is certainly useful but organized tours are often noisy. Get your own permit from the Forestry Department if you feel confident about finding your own way.

Forestry Department organizes hiking across the island. Contact Adams Toussaint, T4502231 ext 306 or 4502078, who is in charge of all Forestry Department tours. **Donald Anthony**,T4521799, a senior Forestry Officer, is also available as a private guide for hikers and birdwatchers.

Sky Rides, has a guided 0600 birdwatching hike on Tue and Sat, US$65 including transport from hotels in the north, a guide for each party of 8 and breakfast at the restaurant on the Sky Rides site. The hike up and back takes about 3 hrs.

St Lucia National Trust, T4525005, has fairly regular field trips, usually the last Sun of the month, popular with locals and tourists of all ages. The cost varies according to transport costs, membership US$10 a year.

Horse riding

Belle Cheval, Cas en Bas, T5191280. US$40 1 hr, US$55 2 hrs, US$75 half-day trip with beach barbecue. They will arrange champagne breakfasts, barbecues and picnics. Prices usually include transfers and service is very good.

International Pony Club, Beausejour, Gros Ilet, T4528139, www.stluciatravel.com.lc /internat.htm. Trail rides and caters for all levels, choice of English or Western style, US$35 1 hr, US$50 2hrs, US$70 half-day barbeque trip, drinks or barbeque lunch at Marjorie's on Cas-en-Bas beach.

North Point Riding Stables, Cap Estate, T4508853. Takes groups to Cas-en-Bas Beach, Donkey Beach, Pigeon Point or Gros Islet, US$35 1½ hrs, minimum age 12.

Trim's Stables, Cas-en-Bas, T4508273. Riding for beginners or advanced; also offers lessons, 1-hr rides US$40, 2hrs US$50 and picnic trips to the Atlantic, US$75.

Sailing

Destination St Lucia (DSL), Rodney Bay Marina, T4528531. Yachts from 38-52 ft, bareboat charters, multilingual staff.

The Moorings, Marigot Bay, T4514357. Bareboat fleet of 38-50 ft Beneteaus and crewed fleet of 50-60 ft yachts, 45-room hotel, watersports, diving, windsurfing.

The Unicorn, T4528644 (ask for Monica), is a 140-ft replica of a 19th-century brig which started life in 1947 as a Baltic trader (used in the filming of *Roots* and *Pirates of the Caribbean*). Sailings are Mon-Fri 0930 in high season, recommended, US$90 per person, children under 12 US$45, including lunch. Champagne and sunset cruises available on Mon, Wed, Fri 1700-1900, adults, US$45, children US$23. You can also book through hotel tour desks. Other vessels in their fleet include **The Lion**, a similar sailing ship, and three catamarans, **Mango Tango I and II** and **Tango**. Other excursions on catamarans (*Endless Summer I, Endless Summer II*, T4508651, www.stluciaboattours.com) and private yachts can be booked with tour operators in Castries or through the hotels. The catamarans can be overcrowded and devoid of character but cost the same as the *Unicorn*. **Freespirit**, T5196860, www.freespirit-charters.com, is a 43-ft twin engine boat which does half or full-day tours down the coast with stops, or cruises at sunset to Marigot and the Rainforest Hideaway restaurant for dinner.

Squash and tennis

Many hotels have tennis courts, some of them lit for night play. There is a squash court near **Cap Estate Golf Club House** and at the **St Lucia Yacht Club**, T4528350. The **St Lucian Hotel** has 2 tennis courts for public bookings and lessons, T4528351.

The St Lucia Racquet Club, Cap Estate, T4500551. 9 floodlit tennis courts and squash court with instruction. They host an annual competition open to all amateur tennis and squash players.

Tour operators

Heritage Tours, T4516058 at Pointe Seraphine, T4581726, at La Place Carenage, info@heritagetoursstlucia.com. Heritage Tours were developed to give greater community involvement in tourism, with environmental sustainability and economic viability. If you book a tour you can visit a number of different places including **Latille Falls** (20-ft waterfall and pools where you can swim), **Fond d'Or Nature and Historical Park** (hiking trails to plantation house ruins, Amerindian remains and the beach), **Fond Latisab Créole Park** (demonstrations of traditional methods of making cassava bread, etc), **Fond Doux** (19th-century plantation house and nature trails through fruit gardens, where the Battle of Rabot was fought against the British army) and the **Folk Research Centre** (19th-century building on Mount Pleasant documenting Kwéyòl culture and history). They also run a **Castries Heritage Walk** telling you about the architectural history of the city and an east coast hike with lunch. Costs vary from US$12 for the Castries Heritage Walk to US$69 for a full-day tour to Soufrière, Toraille Falls, the volcano and lunch at Fond Doux Estate.

Travel agents Barefoot Holidays, T4500507, www.travelfile.com/get/baredays.html. **Barnards Travel Agency**, Bridge St, Castries, T4522214. **Carib Travel Agency**, Micoud St, Castries, T4522151. **Hibiscus Travel Agency**, Bourbon St, Castries, T4531527. **International Travel Consultants**, Bourbon St, Castries, T4523131. **L'Express Des Isles**, Cox & Co, William Peter Blvd, Castries, T4522211. **Pitons Travel Agency**, Richard Fanis Building, Marisule, Gros Islet, T4501486. **Solar Tours & Travel**, Castries, T4525898. **Spice Travel**, T4520866, www.casalucia.com. **St Lucia Reps/Sunlink Tours**, T4528232, www.stluciareps.com. **Travel World**, American Drywall Building, Vide Bouteille Highway, Castries, T4517443, travelworld@candw.lc.

Whale watching

Whale and dolphin watching is good, Nov-Jun is best, when sperm whales and humpbacks are seen.

Captain Mike's (Mike Hackshaw), T4527044, www.captmikes.com. Whalewatching as well as sport fishing and pleasure cruises. They use a 55-ft boat, *Free Willy*, which has an upper and lower deck for viewing, and the trip lasts 3 hrs.
Hackshaw's Boat Charters (Chris), T4530553. US$50 plus transfers.
Mystic Man, Soufriere, T4597783. Whalewatching trips with a 42-ft power boat.

Windsurfing and kiteboarding

The winds off Anse de Sables in the southeast of the island are very good for both windsurfing and kiteboarding, with the latter taking place off a cove slightly to the north. Jan, Feb, May and Jun are the best months with lots of wind blowing unobstructed cross-onshore from the left. The sickle shaped beach is bordered leeward by Moule à Chique peninsula, so you are safe from drifting off into the Atlantic. In the summer the wind is unreliable and the operators close until end-Oct. See www.slucia.com/windsurf and www.slucia.com/kitesurf.

The Reef Kite and Surf, next to **The Reef Beach Café**, Anse de Sables, T4543418. The windsurfing centre uses Mistral windsurfing boards and North rigs, while the kitesurfing centre has North kites and boards. Free Wi-Fi internet access. Surf boards are hired out at US$45 for 4 hrs. For kitesurfing US$75 for a 2-hr introductiory session, US$11 for two sharing.

Transport

St Lucia *p730, maps p731*
Air

Check in is 3 hrs before a flight, kill time on the beach at Vigie or at Anse des Sables.

From Europe Direct scheduled services with **Caribbean Airlines**, **Virgin Atlantic**, **British Airways** and **Excel** from London and **Virgin Atlantic** and **BMI** from Manchester, while **Condor** comes in from Frankfurt. There are many charter flights in season.

From North America Caribbean Airlines, Air Jamaica, US Airways, Delta from a range of cities. Many flights connect in Antigua or Barbados and some come via Montego Bay. **American Airlines** connects with **American Eagle** in San Juan. **Air Canada** flies from Toronto.

From the Caribbean Lots of flights from Anguilla, Antigua, Barbados, Dominica, Fort-de-France, Grenada, Montego Bay, Pointe-à-Pitre, Port of Spain, St Kitts, St Vincent, San Juan and Tortola with **American Eagle**, **LIAT/Caribbean Star**, **Caribbean Airlines** and **Air Jamaica**.

Airports St Lucia has 2 airports: **George F Charles Airport** (formerly Vigie), T4521156, mainly for short-hop inter-island flights only (2 miles from Castries, taxi for US$7.50), and **Hewanorra International Airport**, T4546355, in the Vieux Fort district; there is an air shuttle to Vigie by helicopter, 12 mins, US$90. Alternatively a taxi to Castries costs US$60 (though, out of season, you can negotiate a cheaper rate) and it will take you 1½-2 hrs to reach the resorts north of Castries. A cheaper service is the **St Lucia Air Shuttle**, run by **Paradise Tourist Services**, Rodney Bay, behind Julian's Supermarket, by reservation only, US$17.50 one way, US$33 round trip, per person, credit cards accepted, T4529329. You can also negotiate a ride with 1 of the transfer buses from hotels for EC$40, enquire at **St Lucia Reps**, T4569100, www.sunlinktours.com. If you are travelling light you can walk to the main road and catch the minibus or route taxi to Castries, or if you are staying in Vieux Fort you can walk there, but be careful of the fast traffic. No baggage storage yet available at Hewanorra. Try to arrange it with one of the Vieux Fort hotels.

Airlines Air Canada, Bridge St, Castries, T4523051, Hewanorra T4546249, toll free 1-800-7442472. Air Caraïbes, George FL Charles Airport, T4530357. Air Jamaica, Hewanorra Airport, T4548870, Reservations, T1-800-5235585. American Eagle, George FL Charles Airport, T4521820/1840. British Airways, 15-17 Brazil St, Clico Building, Castries, T4527444/3951, Hewanorra Airport, T4546172. Caribbean Airlines, Micoud St, Castries, T1-800-5382942, Hewanorra Airport, T4545075. LIAT/Caribbean Star, George FL Charles Airport, T188-8445428. St Lucia Helicopters, Island Flyers Hangar, George FL Charles Airport, T4536950, www.stluciahelicopters.com. Virgin Atlantic, Hewanorra Airport, T4543610, toll free T1-800-7447477.

Boat
Look out for schools of dolphins on the crossing to Martinique; the view is good from the upper deck.

Express des Îles, links St Lucia with the **French Antilles** and **Dominica**, reservations T4565000, www.express-des-isles.com, or **Cox & Co Ltd**, William Peter Blvd, T4522211. You cannot buy a ticket at the dock, so remember to buy weekend tickets in advance as the office is shut then. Tickets ordered in advance and collected at the dock cannot be paid for by credit card. The fare is the same to whichever island you are going to, EC$195 one way, EC$218 with a stopover, EC$275 return. Port taxes must be paid on departure from each port. Check timetables before planning a trip. They vary week to week and month by month. There is no service for 3 weeks in Jun and for 3 weeks end-Sep-beginning of Oct. Sat is usually the best day for a day trip, you get there in time for coffee and a croissant, with plenty of time for sightseeing and eating well but sometimes the boat doesn't leave until 1600. Customs clearance can be tedious with several hundred passengers. Sailing times to **Fort-de-France** 1 hr 20 mins, **Roseau** 3½-4 hrs and **Pointe-à-Pitre** 5¾-6¼ hrs.

Ferries around the island include: **Rodney Bay Ferry** shuttles between the marina shops, Marlin Quay, **St Lucian Hotel**, **Mortar and Pestle** and Pigeon Island, fares within the marina US$8 return, children under 12 half price, T4520087, also half-day trips to Pigeon Island including lunch, US$40, bookings at the yellow hut by the entrance to the **Lime Restaurant's** car park. The **Gingerbread Express** in Marigot Bay costs EC$5 return, but is refunded by **Doolittle's Restaurant** if you eat or drink there and present your tickets. Water taxis and speedboats can be rented. **Water taxis** ply between Soufrière waterfront and Anse Chastenet; it's easier than driving the awful road.

Bus
Bus stands in Castries are at the bottom of Darling Rd on the west side of the gardens and extending back to the multi-storey car park on Peynier St. **Route 1** is Castries to Gros Islet, **Route 2** Castries to Vieux Fort, **Route 3** Castries to Soufrière, **Route 4** Vieux Fort environs, **Route 5** Castries central zone. Each route then has sub-routes, eg

Route 1A is Castries-Gros Islet, Route 1B is Castries-Union- Babonneau, etc.

Short journeys are only EC$1.25, rising to EC$2.25 Castries to Gros Islet, or to Soufrière, EC$10; from Gros Islet to Rodney Bay EC$1.25; from Castries to Vieux Fort EC$6; children half price. With oil prices rising in 2005, fares are expected to go up. Ask the driver to tell you when your stop comes up.

Car

Driving is on the left. Filling stations are open Mon-Sat 0630-2000, selected garages open Sun and holidays 1400-1800. They only sell unleaded fuel, at EC$9.50 per US gallon.
Car hire It is often cheaper to organize car hire from abroad. You can only hire a car if aged 25 or over. The cost is about US$50-100 per day, with discounts for weekly rates. Some car hire companies are open to negotiation. Optional collision damage waiver is another US$10-22 per day. A 5% tax is added to everything. A 1-day licence costs US$12, or US$21 for up to 3 months. If arriving at George FL Charles (formerly Vigie) Airport, get your international licence endorsed at the immigration desk (closed 1300-1500) after going through customs. Car hire companies can usually arrange a licence. Check for charges for pick-up and delivery. If dropping off a car at George FL Charles Airport you can sometimes leave the keys with the tourist desk if there is no office for your car hire company. **Alto Rent-A-Car**, Castries, T4520233, Hewanorra, T4545311. **Avis**, Hewanorra, T4546325, George FL Charles Airport, T4522046, Pointe Seraphine, T4522700, and lots of other locations, reservations T4516976. **Budget**, T4529887, Hewanorra, T4547470, www.budget stlucia.net. **Candida**, Rodney Bay, T4527076. **Cool Breeze Jeep Rentals**, Soufrière, T4597729, Castries, T4582031. **Courtesy**, Bay Gardens Inn, T4528140. **Hertz** headquarters at Rodney Bay, T4520680, Hewanorra, T4549636, George FL Charles, T4517351. **National**, Massade, Gros Islet Highway, T4508721, also at Lobster Pot, Beanfield, Vieux Fort, T4546699, and at Pointe Seraphine, T4530085, carrental@candw.lc. **TJ's**, Rodney Bay, T4520116.

Motorcycle
Wayne's Motorcycle Centre, Vide Bouteille,

T4520680. Rents motorbikes; make sure you wear a helmet and have adequate insurance.

Taxi

Registered taxis have red number plates with the TX prefix. Minibuses have the T prefix. Fares are set by the Government, but the US$60 Castries-Soufrière fare doubles as unlucky tourists discover that there are no buses for the return journey. Sample fares are: Castries-Gros Ilet US$25, Rodney Bay-Gros Ilet US$10, Rodney Bay-Pigeon Island US$10, Castries-Soufriere US$70, Castries-Vieux Fort US$60, Castries-Anse La Raye US$30. If in doubt about the amount charged, check with the tourist office or hotel reception. You can see a copy of the fixed fares at the airport. At rush hour it is almost impossible to get a taxi so allow plenty of time, the traffic jams are amazing for such a small place. A trip round the island by taxi is about US$25 per hr for 1-4 people, with an additional US$5 per hr for a/c.

⊙ Directory

St Lucia *p730, maps p731*
Banks **Scotiabank**, William Peter Blvd, Castries, T4562100, Corner High St and Chaussee Rd, T4523797, Rodney Bay, T4528805, Vieux Fort, T4546314. **FirstCaribbean International Bank**, William Peter Blvd, Castries, T4523751, Bridge St, T4561000, Rodney Bay Marina, T4529384, Vieux Fort T4546255, Soufrière, T4597255. **RBTT Bank**, Micoud St, Castries, T4517469, Gablewoods Mall, T4522265. **Royal Bank of Canada**, William Peter Blvd, T4569200, Rodney Bay, T4529921. Nearly all banks have ATMs. **Embassies and consulates** **Cuba**, Rodney Heights, T4584665, embacubasantalucia@candw.lc. Mon-Fri 0930-1400. **France**, Vigie Rd, T4556060, F4556056, Mon, Tue, Thu, Fri 0800-1500, Wed 0830-1300. **Germany**, Gros Islet, T45080500, karencave@candw.lc. **Netherlands**, M & C Building, Bridge St, Castries, T4523592, peterd.mc@candw.lc, Mon-Fri 0800-1630. **Norway**, Ward & Company Building, Bridge St, Castries, T4522216, Mon-Fri 0800-1630. **UK**, **British High Commission**, NIS Building, Waterfront, Castries, T4522484, F4531543, Mon-Thu 0800-1600, Fri 0800-1300. **Medical**

services As on most Caribbean islands, there periodic outbreaks of dengue fever so take mosquito repellent. **Hospitals**: for emergency T911 or go to the **Gros Islet PolyClinic**, T4509661, Mon-Fri 0800-1630. **Aerojet Ambulance** for air evacuation, T4521600, F4532229. **Victoria Hospital**, Castries, T4522421/4537059. **St Jude's**, Vieux Fort, T4546041. **Soufrière Casualty**, T4597258. **Dennery**, T4533310. **Tapion**, T4592000, 24-hr emergency service, pay first, treatment later, expensive, pharmacy, X-ray, CAT scan, laboratory services, specialist doctors. The **Rodney Bay Medical Centre**, T4528621, is a collection of private doctors and dentists on the left just inside the turning to JQ's Mall. Larger hotels have resident doctors or doctors 'on call', visits cost about EC$70-100. If given a prescription, ask at the pharmacy whether the medication is available 'over the counter', as this may be cheaper. **Pharmacies**: in Castries, on the Gros Islet Highway, in Gablewoods Mall and in JQ Charles Mall, Rodney Bay.

Internet/email Services at the Gablewoods Mall office of **Cable & Wireless**, EC$5 for 30 mins, at Jambe de Bois on Pigeon Island, EC$10 per hr, and also in the University Centre. **Inspirations**, Noble House, 6 Brazil St, in the old Kentry Edmunds Building, T4530139, books, gifts, comfy chairs, internet access and café serving baguettes, sandwiches, patties and cakes, pleasant meeting place. **ClickCom**, Shop 9, La Place Carenage, T4524444, clickcom@candw.lc, has broadband at US$12 per hr, phones and prepaid cards, bank CDs and floppy disks and cameras. Many hotels offer internet services to guests.

Post offices Main post office is on Bridge St, Castries, Mon-Fri 0830-1630, poste restante at the rear. Other branches in Gablewoods and JQ's Malls (open on Sat 0830-1230). Postcards to Europe EC$0.75, to the USA, UK and Canada EC$0.65, unsealed cards EC$0.50; letters to Europe EC$1.10, to the USA, Canada and UK EC$0.95. **DHL Worldwide Express**, 20 Bridge St, Castries, T4531538. **Federal Express**, Castries, T4521320. **LIAT Quick Pak**, 20 Bridge St, Castries, T4560455. **Parcels Express**, Vide Bouteille, T4527211. **UPS**, Castries, T4525898. **Erands Courier Services**, Cadet St, Castries, T4526709, erands911@hotmail.com.

Telephone Cable & Wireless, Digicel and AT&T, www.attwireless.com/caribbean, all with offices on Bridge St, Castries. Charges vary, depending on time of day and day of week. Pay phones use EC$0.25 and EC$1 coins or cards. Cable & Wireless phone cards are sold for EC$10, EC$20, EC$40 or EC$50 plus tax (a EC$10 card costs EC$11); with these you can phone abroad. There is a credit card phone at Vigie Airport operated via the boat phone network, daily 0800-2200. Call USA, T1-800-6747000; Sprint Express, T1-800-2777468; BT Direct, T1-800-3425284; Canada Direct, T1-800-7442580; USA Direct phone at Rodney Bay Marina, or T1-800-8722881. If you want to dial a toll-free US number, replace the 800 with 400. You will be charged a local call.

Background

History

Even though some St Lucians have claimed that their island was discovered by Columbus on St Lucy's day (13 December, the national holiday) in 1502, neither the date of discovery nor the discoverer are in fact known, for according to the evidence of Columbus' log, he appears to have missed the island and was not even in the area on St Lucy's Day. A Vatican globe of 1520 marks the island as Santa Lucía, suggesting that it was at least claimed by Spain. In 1605, 67 Englishmen en route to Guiana made an unsuccessful effort to settle, though a Dutch expedition may have discovered the island first. At this time the island was inhabited by Caribs. There are Amerindian sites and artefacts on the island, some of which are of Arawak origin, suggesting that the Caribs had already driven them out or absorbed them by the time the Europeans arrived, as no trace of the Arawaks was found by them. The Indians called their island *Iouanalao*, which may have meant 'Where the iguana is found'. The name was later changed to *Hiwanarau* and then evolved to Hewanorra. In 1638 the first recorded settlement was made by English from Bermuda and St Kitts, but the colonists were killed by the Caribs about three years later.

In 1642 the King of France, claiming sovereignty over the island, ceded it to the **French West India Company**, who in 1650 sold it to MM Houel and Du Parquet. There were repeated attempts by the Caribs to expel the French and several governors were murdered. From 1660, the British began to renew their claim to the island and fighting for possession began in earnest. The settlers, who were mostly French, developed a plantation economy based on slave labour. In 1782 Admiral George Rodney led the English fleet from Pigeon Island in an epic assault on the French navy, on its way to attack Jamaica. During the French Revolution, Victor Hugues used his base in St Lucia to support insurrections in nearby islands. The guillotine was erected in Castries and the island became known by the French as St Lucie La Fidèle. Britain invaded again and fought a protracted campaign against a guerrilla force of white and black republicans until it was finally pacified by General John Moore. In all, St Lucia changed hands 14 times before it became a British Crown Colony in 1814 by the Treaty of Paris. In 1834 Britain abolished slavery.

From 1838, the island was included in a Windward Islands Government, with a Governor resident first in Barbados and then Grenada. In 1885 St Lucia was chosen as one of Britain's two main coaling stations, selling Welsh coal to passing steam ships. By the end of the 19th century Castries was the 14th most important port in the world in terms of tonnage handled. In the 20th century, however, the rise of oil brought decline. In 1935 coal workers went on strike and a warship was brought in to quell violence. In 1937 sugar workers also went on strike and gained a small increase in wages. St Lucia's first trade union was formed in 1939, a movement which grew into the St Lucia Labour Party (SLP), led by George FL Charles (1916-2004). Universal adult suffrage was introduced in 1951. The SLP won the elections in that year and retained power until 1964. George Charles was the first Chief Minister and pushed through several constitutional reforms, enhancing labour legislation for the benefit of workers. The sugar industry declined and bananas were promoted as suitable for smallholder production, eventually dominating the economy. The United Workers' Party (UWP) then governed from 1964 to 1979 and from 1982 onwards. In 1958 St Lucia joined the West Indies Federation, but it was short-lived following the withdrawal of Jamaica in 1961 to 1962 (see page). In 1967, St Lucia gained full internal self-government, becoming a State in voluntary association with Britain, and in 1979 it gained full Independence.

From 1964 until 1996 the UWP was led by Mr John Compton, who held power from 1964 to 1979 and subsequently won elections in 1982, 1987 and 1992. In 1996 Mr Compton retired as leader of the UWP and was replaced as Prime Minister and leader of the party by Dr Vaughan Lewis, former Director General of the Organization of Eastern Caribbean States (OECS), who led the party into the 1997 elections. The May 1997 elections were a triumph for the SLP, who had been in opposition for 25 years apart from a brief period from 1979 to 1982. Led by Dr Kenny Anthony, they won 16 of the 17 seats, with the UWP gaining the single remaining seat, a result which took even the SLP by surprise. In the December 2001 election the Labour government was returned with a smaller majority (14 seats). Its popularity had slipped in areas hit by the banana crisis and the world economic downturn with its knock-on effects on the tourism industry. By the 2006 elections, the tide had turned firmly against the government and after a hard fought campaign, the UWP was returned to power. The elderly John Compton came out of retirement to lead the UWP, which won 11 seats against the SLP's six, and at the age of 82 was sworn in as Prime Minister.

Government

St Lucia is an independent member of the Commonwealth and the British monarch is the Head of State, represented by a Governor General (Dame Pearlette Louisy, the first woman to hold the post). The 17-member House of Assembly is elected every five years, while the 11 members of the Senate are appointed by the Governor General, six on the advice of the Prime Minister, three on the advice of the Leader of the Opposition and two of her own choice.

Economy

St Lucia has the largest banana crop in the Windward Islands, but production has slumped and the industry is in turmoil. Farmers have suffered because of low prices, storm damage and labour disputes. Greater competition in the European banana market, particularly after EC unification in 1992, is leading to diversification away from bananas; cocoa, coconuts, dairy farming, flowers and fisheries are being encouraged.

There is some light industry, but tourism is the major employer and foreign exchange earner. Some 250,000 visitors stay on the island each year, and numbers are increasing. New hotels are being built and existing hotels enlarged, boosted partly by the 2007 ICC Cricket World Cup. Efforts are being made to attract more yachting visitors. Rodney Bay Marina was sold in 2006 and the new owners are planning to put in more and better berths for larger craft. Marigot Bay has had a facelift and another marina, Landings, is soon to come on stream.

Geography

St Lucia is the second largest of the Windwards, lying between St Vincent and Martinique with an area of 238 sq miles. The scenery is outstandingly beautiful, and in the neighbourhood of the Pitons, it has an element of grandeur. The highest peak is Morne Gimie, 3,118 ft, but the most spectacular are Gros Piton, 2,619 ft, and Petit Piton, 2,461 ft, which are old volcanic forest-clad plugs rising sheer out of the sea near the town of Soufrière on the west coast. A few miles away is one of the world's most accessible volcanoes with *soufrières* (vents in the volcano which exude hydrogen sulphide, steam and other gases and deposit sulphur and other compounds in pools of boiling water). The mountains are intersected by numerous short rivers which in places debouch into broad, fertile and well-cultivated valleys.

Culture

There is a good deal of French cultural influence. Most of the islanders, who are predominantly of African descent (though a few people of Carib descent are still to be found in certain areas, noticeably around Choiseul), speak Creole/Kwéyòl, a similar language to French, and in rural areas many people, particularly the older generation, have great difficulty with English. There is a French provincial style of architecture; most place names are French and about 70% of the population is Roman Catholic. The French Caribbean also has an influence on music, you can hear zouk and cadance played as much as calypso and reggae. The **Folk Research Centre** has recorded local music. *Musical Traditions of St Lucia* has 32 selections representing all the musical genres, with information on the background of the various styles. *Lucian Kaiso* is an annual publication giving pictures and information on each season of St Lucian calypso. In the pre-Christmas period, small drum groups play in rural bars. Traditionally, singers improvise a few lines about people and events in the community and the public joins in. The singing is exclusively in Kwéyòl, wicked and full of sexual allusions.

One of the Caribbean's most renowned poets and playwrights in the English language, **Derek Walcott**, was born in St Lucia in 1930. He has published many collections of poems, an autobiography in verse, *Another Life*, critical works, and plays such as *Dream on Monkey Mountain*. Walcott uses English poetic traditions, with a close understanding of the inner magic of the language (Robert Graves), to expose the historical and cultural facets of the Caribbean. His books are highly recommended, including his narrative poem *Omeros*, which contributed to his

⁞ Kwéyòl for beginners

The main language in St Lucia is English but 75% of the population also speak a patois, Lesser Antillean Creole French, called Kwéyòl. This is a language which evolved so that African slaves could communicate with their French masters and it has survived even though St Lucia has been British since 1814. It is similar to the Creole spoken in Haiti, Guadeloupe, Martinique and other former French colonies, but it is closest to the Kwéyòl of Dominica, another French island which became British. It is said that Dominicans and St Lucians understand each other 98% of the time. Standard French, however, is understood by no more than one in 10 St Lucians. Kwéyòl is a formal language, with grammar and syntax, but it has only recently been written down and many Kwéyòl speakers can not in fact read it. It is spoken by St Lucians in all walks of life, including politicians, doctors, bankers, ministers and the Governor General, Dame Pearlette Louisy, who has done a great deal to promote it as a written language.

For people interested in learning a few phrases of Kwéyòl, there is a handwritten booklet by Mary Toynbee, A Visitor's Guide to St Lucia Patois, EC$20, and the Kwéyòl Dictionary, EC$10, published by the Ministry of Education, available in local bookshops.

For the more ambitious reader there are traditional story booklets written in a simple style with an English translation at the back. Contact the Summer Institute of Linguistics, Box 321, Vieux Fort, price around EC$5 each. For the serious student Jones Mondesir's Dictionary of St Lucian Creole (1992) would be the definitive work but it costs over EC$300. The **Folk Research Centre** (PO Box 514, Mount Pleasant, Castries, T4522279, F4517444, Monday-Friday 0830-1630), preserves and documents the local culture and folklore and has published several books, a cassette (EC$30) and CD (EC$60): Musical Traditions of St Lucia. A Handbook for Writing Creole gives the main points and features, while a Dictionary of St Lucian Creole and Annou Di-Y an Kwéyòl, a collection of folk tales and expressions in Creole and English, accompany it well.

A visit to the market in Castries is one of the easiest ways to listen to Kwéyòl being spoken in the street or there are Kwéyòl programmes on the government information service, GIS.

winning the 1992 Nobel Prize for Literature. Other St Lucian writers worth reading are the novelists **Garth St Omer** (The Lights on the Hill) and Earl Long (an MD in the USA), and the poets Jane King-Hippolyte, Kendal Hippolyte, John Robert Lee (Artefacts) and Jacintha Lee, who has a book of local legends. New authors to emerge in the 21st century include Anderson Reynolds, with his novel Death By Fire, and Michael Aubertin (head of the Dept of Culture) with his period romance Neg Maron.

St Lucia has also produced painters of international renown. **Dunstan St Omer** was born in St Lucia in 1927 into a Catholic family and is best known for his religious paintings. He created the altarpiece for the Jacmel church near Marigot Bay, where he painted his first black Christ, and reworked Castries Cathedral in 11 weeks in 1985 prior to the Pope's visit. St Omer and his four sons, Alwyn, Luigi, Giovanni and Julio, have also painted other countryside churches (Monchy and Fond St Jacques) and a quarter of a mile of sea wall in Anse La Raye, while Giovanni and Julio installed the new windows in Castries cathedral. **Llewellyn Xavier** was born in Choiseul in 1945 but moved to Barbados in 1961, where he discovered painting. Galleries in North America and Europe have exhibited his work and his paintings are in many permanent collections. Xavier returned to St Lucia in 1987, where he was shocked by the environmental damage. He has since campaigned vigorously for the environment through his art. *Environment Fragile* is a recent work created from recycled materials embedded with shards of pure gold and can not be bought. It is given to those whose 'voice can be heard above the din of global commerce'. You can visit the artist's studio, T4509155 for an appointment, but he also has a gallery at the Rodney Bay Marina.

Other outstanding artists include **Ron Savory** (Ron's Atelier and Framing Co, Vide Bouteille Industrial Park, just past the roundabout at the end of the airport runway – called La Clery junction – T4524412), whose rich rainforest scenes and dancing figures are impressive; he sells collectables, souvenir art, paintings from originals to limited prints to prints. **Sean Bonnett St Remy** paints wonderful local scenes, village scenes with nostalgic charm and accuracy, he can be contacted at **Photographic Images**, 42 Brazil Street. **Winston Branch** is splashy, modern abstract, and shows internationally from London to Brazil. He is currently teaching in the USA. **Chris Cox** paints St Lucian birds, such as the parrot and the nightjar. He won an award at the Arts Award ceremony in January 2000 and is now head of Planning in the Ministry of Agriculture. Other contemporary artists such as Arnold Toulon, Cedric George, Chris Cox, Nancy Cole, Sophie Barnard, Alcina Nolley and Jonathon Gladding exhibit their works at the **Inner Gallery**. Daniel Jean-Baptiste makes hand-painted, limited edition, silk artwork (T4508000 for a private studio visit). **Alcina Nolley**, an artist and teacher of art, can refer you to many artists and artisans, particularly of the **Arts and Crafts Association** ① T4532338, nolleym@candw.lc.

The last week in January is **Nobel Laureate Week**, with lectures celebrating the two Nobel prize winners produced by the island (Sir Arthur Lewis and Derek Walcott). They were both born on 23 January. Other events include the annual Arts Awards, during which the Cultural Centre is packed, www.stlucia-arts.com.

Flora and fauna

The fauna and flora of St Lucia are very similar to that of Dominica, the Windwards chain of islands having been colonized by plants and animals originally from South and Central America, with some endemic species. For instance, all the parrots of the islands are of the genus *Amazona* but most islands have a unique species such as the *versicolor* in St Lucia and the *sisserou* and *imperialis* in Dominica. Saint Lucia, like the other islands in the Windwards, would have at one time been covered by dense forest, but during colonization much of this was lost to agriculture. Today, what is left is protected to safeguard the island's water supply and its wildlife. Driving over the Barre de l'Isle or along the west coast road magnificent tree ferns, relics of prehistoric times, can be seen while on the roadside banks of wild ginger perfume the air. On the mountainsides the orange-red blossoms of the Imortelle light up the landscape. Many of the more exotic **flowering plants**, like the hibiscus, the bougainvillea, the African tulip tree and the flamboyant were introduced during the establishment of the plantation system. Recent surveys have listed more than 1,600 species of plants, including nine endemics. There are several endemic **reptile** species including St Lucia tree lizard, pygmy gecko, Maria Islands ground lizard and Maria Islands grass snake. The only snake which is dangerous is the *fer de lance* which is restricted to dry scrub woodland on the east coast near Grande Anse and Louvet and also near Anse La Raye and Canaries in the west. Attacks are rare. The bite is not fatal but requires hospitalization. Avoid walking through the bush, especially at night, and wear shoes or boots and long trousers. The largest group of **mammals** is made up of six or more species of bat. These include fruit eating, insect eating and even fishing bats. The cave on the northern side of the bay approaching Soufriere is home to thousands. They emerge at dusk. The forest dwelling agouti is rarely seen, but the manicou is present throughout the island, and is frequently seen on the road, a victim of the night the cane fields, is also present.

The national **bird** is the colourful St Lucian parrot (*Amazona versicolor*), seen in the dense rainforest around Quillesse and Barre de l'Isle. Other endemic birds are the St Lucia oriole (endangered), Semper's warbler (believed extinct), the St Lucia warbler (formerly the Adelaide's warbler) and the St Lucia black finch (endangered). In the north of the island birdwatching is good at Bois d'Orange swamp, Piton Flor Reserve and Grande Anse; in the west at Edmond Forest Reserve and in the south Eau Piquant Pond, also called Boriel's Pond.

The isolated east coast beaches are rarely visited and have exceptional wildlife. Leatherbacks and other **turtles** nest at Grande Anse and Anse Louvet. Turtle watching is organized from March to July when green, hawksbill and leatherback turtles come ashore on Grande Anse to lay eggs. This area is also the main stronghold of the white-breasted thrasher and St Lucia wren; there are also iguanas (although you will be lucky to see one).

St Vincent → *Country code: 784. Colour map 4, C5.*

St Vincent is green and fertile with a lush rainforest and mountainous interior, beautiful volcanic beaches and fishing villages, coconut groves and banana plantations. It is widely known for the superb sailing conditions provided by its 32 sister islands and cays and most visitors spend some time on a yacht, even if only for a day. Bareboat and crewed yachts are available for wherever you want to go. There are also very competitive regattas and yacht races held throughout the year, accompanied by a lot of parties and social events. ►► *For Sleeping, Eating and other listings, see pages 774-760.*

St Vincent & the Grenadines

Ins and outs

Getting there There are no direct flights from Europe or North America but same day connecting flights are available through Antigua, Barbados, Puerto Rico and Trinidad. **Grenadine Airways** offer daily shared charter services from Barbados to St Vincent, Bequia, Mustique, Canouan and Union Island. Many people arrive on yachts, having sailed across the Atlantic or through the Caribbean. There is an informal international ferry on a wooden fishing boat between Union Island and Carriacou (Grenada). ►► *See Transport, page 778, for further details.*

♪ *Air taxi services connect the islands with short hop flights lasting only a few minutes.*

Flights within the Grenadines are cheap and reliable. **Grenadine Airways,** an alliance of **SVG Air, Trans Island Air** and **Mustique Airways,** fly daily scheduled services from St Vincent to Bequia, Mustique, Canouan and Union Island. There are several ferries between St Vincent and Bequia, while the mail boat, the *Barracouda*, links St Vincent with Bequia, Canouan, Mayreau and Union Island with a twice weekly service. Most, but not all, of the islands have a cheap bus service, which can be a minibus or a pick-up truck with seats in the back. Car hire is available on St Vincent and Bequia.

Kingstown → *Phone code: 784. Colour map 4, C5.*

The capital, Kingstown, stands on a sheltered bay and is surrounded on all sides by steep, green hills, with houses perched all the way up. However, it is a generally

St Vincent

Sleeping
Beachcombers **1**
Bella Vista Inn **5**
Ferdie's Footsteps **2**
Grand View Beach **1**
Grenadines House **5**

Harmony Hotel
Apartments **3**
Mariners **1**
New Montrose **6**
Petit Byahaut **7**
Sea Breeze Guest House **8**

Tranquility Beach **9**
Tropic Breeze **10**
Umbrella Beach **1**
Villa Lodge **1**
Young Island Resort **11**

unattractive port city with the waterfront dominated by the container port, cruise ship terminal, fish market and bus station. There is no promenade along the seafront and buildings along the reclaimed land look inland rather than out to sea. Nevertheless, an active beautification association is making huge strides in cleaning up the city, with overgrown bridges repaired or rebuilt, buildings painted and re-roofed and plants maintained. Some buildings have been demolished. The most attractive and historical buildings are inland along the three main parallel streets, **Bay Street**, **Long Lane** and **Grenville/Halifax Street**, also known as Front Street, Middle Street and Back Street.

Kingstown is known as the 'city of arcades' and it is possible to walk around most of the centre under cover. There are even building regulations to encourage the practice in new construction. The shopping and business area is no more than two blocks wide, running between Bay Street and Halifax Street/Grenville Street. The **New Kingstown Fish Market**, built with Japanese aid, was opened in 1990 near the Police Headquarters. This complex, known as Little Tokyo, has car parking and is the point of departure for minibuses to all parts of the island. On Halifax Street at the junction with South River Road is the **Old Public Library**, an old stone building with a pillared portico.

The **Market Square** in front of the Court House is the hub of activity. A new covered market with cream and brown horizontal stripes has been built from Upper Bay to Halifax Street. Fruit and vegetables are downstairs and clothing is upstairs. In the middle of the market building is a circular area where farmers sell their produce on Fridays.

Kingstown has two **cathedrals**, St George's (Anglican) and St Mary's (Roman Catholic). **St George's**, consecrated in 1820, has an airy nave and a pale blue gallery running around the north, west and south sides. It became a cathedral in 1877 when the Diocese of the Windward Islands was constituted and the chancel and transepts date from 1880 to 1887. The cupula was blown down by a hurricane in 1898 and after that battlements were added to the tower. There is an interesting floor plaque in the nave, now covered by carpet, commemorating a general who died fighting the Caribs. Other interesting features include a memorial to Sir Charles Brisbane (1772-1829) who captured Curaçao. A lovely stained-glass window in the south transept was reputedly commissioned by Queen Victoria on the death of her grandson. She took exception to angels in red rather than the traditional white and it was put into storage in St Paul's Cathedral. It was brought to St Vincent in the 1930s. **St Mary's** is of far less sober construction, with different styles, Flemish, Moorish, Byzantine and Romanesque, all in dark grey stone, crowded together on the church, presbytery and school. Building went on throughout the 19th century, with renovation in the 1940s. The exterior of the church is highly decorated but dark and grim, while the interior is dull in comparison but quite light and pretty. The **Methodist church**, dating from 1841, also has a fine interior, with a circular balcony. Its construction was financed largely through the efforts of freed slaves. There is a little bell tower at the south end, erected in 1907.

> ❢ The town is always busy as there are few shops in the rest of the island, but Friday is the busiest day.

The **Botanical Gardens** just below Government House and the Prime Minister's residence are well worth a visit and are the oldest in the Western Hemisphere (see Flora and fauna, page 799). The **Nicholas Wildlife Complex** ① *daily 0600-1800*, has parrots, agouti, Barbados green monkey and St Vincent parrot, but they aren't very well housed. The gardens are about a 20-minute walk from the market square: go along Grenville St, past the cathedrals, turn right into Bentinck Square, right again and continue uphill to the gate. Or take a bus, EC$1 from the terminal.

Fort Charlotte (completed 1805) is on the promontory on the north side of Kingstown Bay, 636 ft above sea level, 15 minutes drive out of town (EC$1.50 from bus terminal to village below, if you ask the driver he might take you into the fort for EC$1-2, worth it if it is hot). Although the fort was designed to fend off attacks from the sea, the main threat was the Black Caribs and many of its 34 guns (some of which are still in place) therefore faced inland. The gatehouse, 1806, was where Major Champion of the Royal Scots Fusiliers was killed on 13 October 1824 (see plaque in St George's Cathedral) by Private Ballasty. The murderer was executed at the scene of the crime. In the old barrack rooms, a series of paintings shows the early history of St Vincent. Painted by William Linzest Prescott in 1972, they suffer from poor lighting and their condition is deteriorating. There is also a coastguard lookout which controls the comings and goings of ships entering the port. Below, the ruins of a military hospital can be seen, as well as a bathing pool at sea level on the end of the point, used when the fort housed people suffering from yaws. The **National Trust of St Vincent and the Grenadines** ① *PO Box 752, T4562591*, has further information.

> ⚑ The views of Kingstown and surroundings are spectacular; on a clear day the Grenadines and even Grenada are visible.

Kingstown

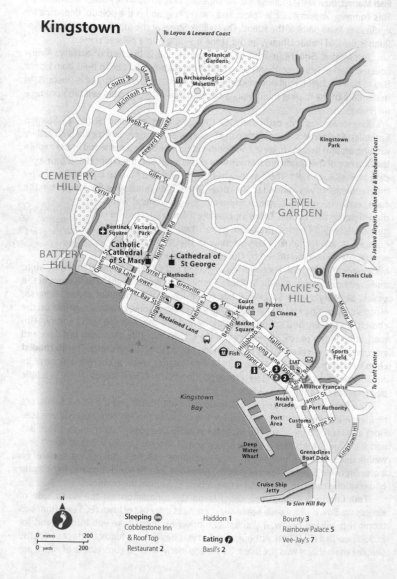

Sleeping 🛏
Cobblestone Inn & Roof Top Restaurant **2**

Haddon **1**

Eating 🍴
Basil's **2**

Bounty **3**
Rainbow Palace **5**
Vee-Jay's **7**

Leeward coast

The Leeward Highway is a dramatic drive along the west coast towards La Soufrière; there are lush valleys and magnificent seaviews. It is a very crumpled landscape and the road is steep and twisty. The road leaves Kingstown and initially heads inland. There are views down into Campden Park Bay, to a deep water port complex and flour mill. The road passes through the small village of Questelles (good party at **Philo's Disco**, listen for them on the radio) before rejoining the coast briefly at Buccament Bay and down into Layou where there are a few excellent examples of gingerbread houses.

About a mile after Questelles look for the **Vermont Nature Trail** sign, then turn right up the Buccament Valley to Peniston and Vermont. The car park at 975 ft is close to the Vermont Nature Centre. Buses from Kingston go to Peniston from where it is a long walk. Get a trail map from the information hut on the right. A guide is not necessary unless you want scientific information as you walk along this marvellous trail. There is a rest stop at 1,350 ft, and a Parrot Lookout Platform at 1,450 ft, probably the best place to see the St Vincent parrot. Be prepared for rain, mosquitoes and chiggars, use insect repellent.

There are some interesting **petroglyphs** and **rock carvings** dating back to the Siboney, Arawak and Carib eras. The best known are just north of Layou, carved on a huge boulder next to a stream. They can only be visited on payment of US$2 for the owner, Mr Victor Hendrickson to open the gate to the fenced off area. Ask the local children to show you his house and the petroglyphs (for a tip), well worth a visit.

Passing Mount Wynne and Peter's Hope, **Barrouallie** is the next village of any size. It is a fishing village and on the beach are fishing boats, nets, pigs and chickens scratching about. The local speciality catch is 'black fish', in reality a short-finned pilot whale, which grows to about 18 ft. Here, in the playground of the Anglican secondary school, there is a petroglyph dated at 800 BC, known as the **Ogham Stone**. One theory claims that it is in Celtic script. If the children are not in class they will highlight the picture in white chalk for you. The road also passes through the remains of a sugar mill (the furnace chimney is still standing) and then heads inland from the popular anchorage and restaurant at Wallilabou Bay. A stone gateway marks the entrance to the **Wallilabou Falls** (Wally-la-boo). You can swim here but the falls are not much more than a spurt (6 ft at the most). There are no changing rooms. On the opposite side of the road is a nutmeg plantation.

> ⁞ *The drive from Kingstown to the end of the road at Richmond takes about two hours; minibuses race along at great speed and some passengers complain of queasiness.*

Wallilabou Bay was one of the settings for the movie, *Pirates of the Caribbean*, with copies of 18th-century piers and storage houses being built here to replicate Port Royal in Jamaica. Many of the Grenadine islands were also used for location shooting, including Union Island, the Tobago Cays and Petit Tabac, where Captain Sparrow and Elizabeth were marooned by Barbossa at the end of the film. Stephen Russell, the owner of the land on which the reconstruction of Port Royal stands, wants to turn the shooting location into a theme park.

The road goes inland along the **Wallilabou Valley** before quickly rising over the ridge into the North Leeward district. Another pretty beach is reached at **Cumberland** and the road climbs quickly to **Coulls Hill** with perhaps the best view on the coast. The road is most attractive through **Chateaubelair** (restaurant, use their facilities to change for a swim and have a snack), skirting Petit Bordel (drugs-financed speed boats on the beach) with small islands offshore, to **Richmond** and **Wallibou beach**. There are some beach facilities at Wallibou.

A boat trip to the **Baleine Falls** (on the northwest coast) is recommended. A few minutes up a river which originates on Soufrière, you come to the falls. At the base is a natural swimming pool. You can climb up the side behind the falls and then jump off into the pool. It is possible to reach the falls on foot, but it is easier to take an excursion by motor boat, which includes a stop for snorkelling, and a picnic lunch, for US$35-40.

⁝ Touching down

Boat information Ports of entry (own flag) are Wallilabou, on the northwest coast, Kingstown, Bequia (police station), Mustique and Union Island (airport, EC$10 weekdays during working hours, EC$25 overtime, holidays and weekends). Yachtsmen often anchor at Blue Lagoon or Young island and bus/taxi to Kingstown to complete customs and immigration formalities. Fees are EC$10/US$4 per person (EC$25 on Sat on Union Island) and charter yachts are charged US$2 per foot per month. For an **exit stamp**, go to the airport customs and immigration one day before departure. On Bequia local businesses deliver water, fuel, laundry, beer and groceries. Men and boys meet yachts in the northern St Vincent anchorages and ask to assist in tying stern line to a tree or offer other services. EC$10 is the current fee for tying up; other services negotiable. Others meet boats in Bequia, Union and the Tobago Cays, offering to supply seafood and groceries as well as selling T-shirts and jewellery. **Anchorages** at Wallilabou, Young Island, Petit Byahaut, Blue Lagoon, Bequia, Palm (Prune) Island, Mustique, Canouan, Mayreau (Salt Whistle Bay and two others), Tobago Cays, Union Island (Clifton, Frigate Island, Chatham Bay), Petit St Vincent. **Marinas** at Caribbean Charter Yacht Yard, Lagoon Marina, Ottley Hall Marina & Shipyard, Bequia Slipway, Anchorage Yacht Club on Union Island. **Moorings** at Young Island, Blue Lagoon, Friendship Bay, Union Island, Palm Island, Petit Byahaut (US$10 fee is deducted if you have dinner), Mustique. For possibilities of crewing on yachts, see the noticeboard at the Frangipani Yacht Services, Bequia.

Business hours Banks: Mon-Fri 0800-1200 or 1300, plus 1400 or 1500-1700 on Thu or Fri. The bank at the airport Mon-Fri 0830-1230, 1530-1730; **Government offices**: Mon-Fri 0800-1200, 1300-1615; **Shops**: Mon-Fri 0800-1200, 1300-1600, Sat 0800-1200.

Clothing Wear light, informal clothes, but do not wear bathing costumes or short shorts in shops or on Kingstown's streets.

Currency The East Caribbean dollar, EC$. EC$2.67=US$1.

Departure tax There is a departure tax of EC$40.

Documents All visitors must have a passport and an onward, or return, ticket. Visas are required from nationals of the Dominican Republic, Jordan, Syria, Lebanon, the People's Republic of China, Iraq, Iran and Nigeria. You will be asked where you will be staying on the island and will need a reservation, which can be done through the tourist office at the airport, before going through immigration (or you can make one up). You will usually be given entry until

Windward coast

The Queens Drive takes you into the hills south of Kingstown and gives splendid views all around. The Marriaqua Valley with its numerous streams is particularly beautiful. In the valley, beyond Mesopotamia (commonly known as Mespo), the lush, tropical gardens of **Montreal** ① *T4581198, montrealgard@vincysurf.com, open Mon-Fri, Dec-Aug 0900-1600, closed holidays, EC$5*, are worth a visit; anthuriums are grown commercially for the domestic market. The owner, Timothy Vaughn, is a well-known landscape gardener in Europe and this is his first tropical garden, full of organic flowers and colourful foliage, with glorious views of Argyll and Mesopotamia Valley. It is designed in three sections, one of which includes a wild garden leading down to a river and a pool where you can swim.

The road meets the **Windward Highway** at Peruvian Vale. It gets progressively the day of departure on your ticket. If you are only given entry of a few days and want to stay longer, extensions are easily obtained for EC$20.

Duty-free allowance 200 cigarettes, or 50 cigars, or 250 grams of tobacco, and 40 fl oz of alcoholic beverage may be imported duty free.

Emergency numbers T999 or 911.

Media Newspapers: *The Herald* is daily and contains news from wire services, including pages in French, Italian, Spanish, etc. Three newspapers, *The Vincentian*, *Searchlight* and *The News*, are published weekly. *The News* is editorially independent and by far the best. **Radio**: four radio stations: AM 705kHz, Nice FM 96.3, Hitz FM 107.3, WE FM 99.9. Weather can be heard on SSB weather net 4001 at 0800, 8104 at 0830. **TV**: two TV stations and Karib cable (26 channels).

Official time Atlantic Standard Time, four hours behind GMT, 1 hour ahead of EST.

Public holidays 1 Jan, Discovery and National Heroes Day (22 Jan), Good Fri and Easter Mon, Labour Day in May, Whit Mon, Caricom Day and Carnival Tue (in Jul), Aug Bank Holiday first Mon in Aug, Independence Day (27 Oct), Christmas Day and Boxing Day.

Tourist information St Vincent and the Grenadines Ministry of Tourism and Culture, Cruise Ship Terminal, Kingstown, T4571502, www.svgtourism.com, Mon-Fri 0800-1200, 1300-1615; helpful desk at ET Joshua Airport, T4584379, hotel reservation EC$1; on Bequia (by the jetty), Bequia Tourism Association, T4583286, www.bequiatourism.com, Sun-Fri 0900-1230, 1330-1600, Sat morning only; on Union Island, between the dock and the Clifton Beach Hotel, T4588350, daily 0800-1200, 1300-1600. The **Tourist Office** and the **Hotel Association** publish *Ins and Outs of St Vincent and the Grenadines* in association with Miller Publishing, an informative magazine on the islands. Bequia publishes its own brochure, *Holiday Bequia*, and **Grenadine Airways** also has a magazine, *The Grenadine Air Alliance*.

Tourist offices overseas Canada: 333 Wilson Av, Suite 601, Toronto M3H 1T2, T416 3984277, svgtourismtoronto@rogers.com. **UK** 10 Kensington Court, London W8 5DL, T020-79376570, svgtourismeurope@aol.com. **USA**: 801 2nd Av, 21st floor, New York, NY 10017, T212-6874981, svgtony@aol.com, and 6505 Cove Creek Place, Dallas, Texas, 75240, T214-2396451, scubasvg@aol.com.

Voltage 220/240 volts, 50 cycles, except Petit St Vincent and Palm Island, which have 110 volts, 60 cycles.

Weights and measures Imperial.

drier as the road goes north hugging yellow sandstone cliffs which contrast with the white waves surging in towards the black volcanic beaches. A number of banana packaging stations are passed especially around Colonarie. There is a particularly impressive view of the coast just after the **Black Point tunnel**. The tunnel is 350 ft long and was constructed by Colonel Thomas Browne using Carib and African slaves in 1815. It was blasted through volcanic rock from one bay to the other and the drill holes are still visible, as are storage rooms and recesses for candles. It is very atmospheric and there are a few bats as well as people washing in the water which pours out of the rock. It provided an important link with the sugar estates in the north and sugar was hauled through the tunnel to be loaded on to boats in Byera Bay. Black sand Byera Beach is the longest in St Vincent and the sea is rough, but in the days of the sugar plantations the coast curved round more giving protection to shipping and there was a jetty. You cannot see the tunnel from the road, which goes over the top. Turn towards the sea between the gas station and the river down a dirt road which leads to Black Point Recreation Site where cricket is played and people gather for Easter Monday celebrations.

Georgetown is almost like a ghost town, an economically depressed area since the loss of sea cotton and arrowroot and now there are problems with bananas. The **St Vincent Rum Distiller**, a restaurant and guesthouse, does good business from visitors to the volcano, see above. North of here is parrot territory with cooling rivers and deep pools.

The road to **Sandy Bay** (beyond Georgetown), where St Vincent's remaining Black Caribs live, is now good, however, you have to cross the Dry River, a jumble of rocks, grit, rubbish and dead wood swept down from the mountains above, which sometimes is not dry and therefore not passable. Rocks and sand are extracted for the building industry. Sandy Bay is poor but beyond it is an even poorer village along a rough dirt road, **Owia**. Here is **Salt Pond**, a natural area of tidal pools filled with small marine life. The rough Atlantic crashes around the huge boulders and lava formations and it is very picturesque. The villagers have planted flowers and made steps down to the Salt Pond area. There is also an arrowroot processing factory which can be visited. Past Owia is **Fancy**, the poorest village on the island, also Black Carib and very isolated, reached by a rough jeep track which makes a nice walk. Baleine Falls (see above) are a two-mile hike from here around the tip of the island, rugged and not for the unadventurous. Fishing boats can be hired in Fancy to collect you (do not pay in advance).

The south

The airport is just southeast of Kingstown at **Arnos Vale**, a residential area where there is also a sports complex. The road runs round the runway and down towards the coast at Indian Bay. There are several hotels in this area, stretching along the seafront to Calliaqua Bay. It is very pleasant, with light sand beaches, Young Island just offshore, Bequia in the distance and dozens of moored yachts. Many people stay here rather than in the capital, as it is an easy commute into Kingstown if you need to go in, while there are marinas, dive shops, the best restaurants and watersports facilities here. The southeast of the island is drier and has different vegetation and birdlife.

Beaches and activities

St Vincent has splendid, safe beaches on the leeward side, most of which have volcanic black sand. The lightest coloured sand can be found on the south coast in the Villa area, where there are several hotels, watersports and marinas. At **Sunsail Lagoon** in Calliaqua there is a lovely long, crescent-shaped beach, **Canash**, which is perfect for young children. Further round the rocks, there are two more beaches becoming progressively more golden the closer to the point you get. Just offshore is **Young Island** (see Sleeping, below), which has a small, golden sand, 'improved' beach. The windward coast is rockier with rolling surf and strong currents, making it dangerous for swimming. **Brighton Salt Pond** beach has lovely swimming conditions most days and magically clear water. Cruise ships sometimes bring their guests here. All beaches are public. Some are difficult to reach by road, but boat trips can be arranged to the less accessible beauty spots such as **Breakers Beach**, Prospect.

‼ *Sea urchins are a hazard, as in many other islands, especially among rocks on the less frequented beaches.*

Diving The underwater wildlife around St Vincent and the Grenadines is varied and beautiful. There are many types and colours of coral, including black coral at a depth of only 30 ft in places. On the New Guinea Reef (Petit Byahaut) you can find three types of black coral in six different colours. The coral is protected so do not remove any. There are 10 marine protected areas including the northeast coast of St Vincent (and the Devil's Table in Bequia, Isle à Quatre, all Mustique, the east coast of Canouan, all of Mayreau, the Tobago Cays, the whole of Palm Island, Petit St Vincent and the surrounding reefs). However, the protected areas are very poorly policed and there are no marine park fees. Spearfishing is strictly forbidden to visitors and no one is allowed to spear a lobster. Buying lobster out of season (1 May-30 September) is illegal as is buying a female lobster with eggs. Fishing for your own consumption is allowed outside the protected areas. Contact the **Fisheries Department**① *T4562738*, for more information on rules and regulations.

There is reef diving, wall diving, drift diving and wrecks to explore. The St Vincent reefs are fairly deep, at 55-90 ft, so scuba diving is more rewarding than snorkelling. Dive sites include **Bottle Reef**, **the Forest**, **the Garden**, **New Guinea Reef** and **the Wall**. In Kingstown Harbour there are three wrecks at one site, the *Semistrand*, another cargo freighter and an ancient wreck stirred up by Hurricane Hugo, as well as two cannons, a large anchor and several bathtubs.

Hiking The highest peak on the island, **La Soufrière** volcano, rises to about 4,000 ft. In 1970 an island reared up out of the lake in the crater; it smokes and the water round it is very warm. Hiking to the volcano is very popular, but you must leave very early in the morning and allow a full day for the trip. Take water and insect repellent. About two miles north of Georgetown (van from Kingstown to Georgetown EC$4, you can ask the driver to make a detour to the start of the trail for an extra charge) on the Windward side you cross the Dry River, then take a left fork and walk/drive through banana plantations to where the trail begins. It takes about three hours to reach the crater edge and it is a strenuous hike along a marked trail, the first three miles are through the Rabacca plantation, then up, along Bamboo Ridge and all the way to the crater's magnificent edge; the top can be cloudy, windy, cold and rainy, take adequate clothing and footwear. There is an alternative, unmarked and even more challenging four-hour route from the leeward side starting from the end of the road after Richmond, but you will need a guide. There are guided tours which start on the windward side and end on the leeward side, about six or seven hours, around US$30 if there are about 10 of you, with the advantage that you are met at your destination by the driver and do not have to worry about scarce public transport. Leave an extra set of clothes in the van in case you get wet through.

An easier climb is up **Mount St Andrew**, near Kingstown. A tarmac track runs up to the radio mast on the summit of the peak, at 2,413 ft, passing first through banana and vegetable gardens and then through forest. There are no parrots but it is particularly good for the Antillean crested hummingbird and black hawks. The view from the summit covers the Grenadines and the Vermont and Mesopotamia valleys. To reach the track either take a van running along the Leeward Highway and ask to be put down at the junction with the Mount St Andrew road, or walk from Kingstown.

Sailing Sailing is excellent, indeed it was yachtsmen who first popularized the Grenadines and it is one of the best ways to see the islands. You can take day charter boats, easily arranged through hotels, or charter your own boat. There is a variety of boats for skippered day charters. Talk to the operators about size and predicted wind conditions if you are inclined towards seasickness. The large catamarans are usually quite stable so that you will hardly know you are on a boat, but they take quite large groups. If you hire a local yacht or motor boat for a day, make sure that the captain has life jackets and other safety equipment (eg a radio) on board and that he is properly insured. This may seem obvious, but do not take anything for granted and be prepared to ask lots of questions. A tourist and his son taking a short hop boat ride between islands recently found themselves drifting hopelessly off course when the boat's engine failed. The captain had no radio and they were eventually found several days later at death's door off the Venezuelan coast.

The main regattas are Bequia Easter Regatta, Union Island Easterval, SVG Game Fishing Tournament (May) and Fisherman's Day (May).

⊖ Sleeping

Kingstown *p766, map p768*

Government VAT tax of 10% on hotel rooms; most add a 10% service charge. Camping is not encouraged and there are no organized campsites. The tourist office has a list of homestays around the island: www.svgtourism.com/ channels/1.asp?id=25.

L-AL Haddon, McKies Hill, T4561897, www.newhaddonhotel.com. The best place to stay in town, good for business travellers, within walking distance of the centre but away from the bustle, large rooms and suites, business centre and conference facilities, good restaurant and bar, friendly and efficient service.

L Grenadines House, Kingstown Park, T4581800. Originally the governor's residence and the oldest guesthouse on the island (formerly **Roy's Inn**), but completely modernized as a 20-room boutique hotel, reopened in 2007. Comfortable, with views of the garden or mountains, quite a walk into town through a run-down area. Pool, bar, restaurant, indoor or outdoor dining with a view to the sea.

L-A Harmony Hotel Apartments, Harmony Hall, T4569113, www.harmonyhotel apartments.com. Set in a beautiful, lush, hillside location overlooking the south coast, this peaceful **Aparthotel** offers a variety of accommodation options from studios to 3-bedroom apartments. Dive packages available, all needs catered for, dietary and otherwise, even long-term rental apartments for retirement homes.

AL-A New Montrose Hotel, New Montrose, T4570172, www.newmontrosehotel.com. 25 modern rooms, studios and apartments, 1-2 bedrooms, balcony, some kitchenettes, a/c, TV, phone, business centre, view of Kingstown and Grenadines, close to Botanical Gardens.

AL-A Tropic Breeze, Queen's Drive, 3 miles from Kingstown, 1 mile from airport, T4584618, www.tropicbreezesvg.com. 12 rooms with balconies, 9 a/c, some with kitchenettes, good views, restaurant, bar, pool, Wi-Fi internet access, room service.

A Cobblestone Inn, Upper Bay St, T4561937. Upstairs in a charming building dating from 1814 which used to be a sugar and arrowroot warehouse. Violet and white decor, rooms good, with a/c, TV, rooftop restaurant and bar for breakfast, lunch and dinner.

C Bella Vista Inn, behind Roy's Inn, Kingstown Park, T/F4572757, bellavista@caribsurf.com. 7 rooms, 3 with private bath, fans, run by Nzinga Miguel and her daughter Cleopatra, friendly, homely atmosphere, breakfast, dinner on request.

Leeward coast *p712, map p766*

LL Petit Byahaut, T/F4577008, VHF68, www.petitbyahaut.com. Set in a 50-acre valley in a lovely secluded bay with a nice beach, very pretty hideaway retreat. No road, TV or phones, 4 wooden cabins, queen-sized bed, open air shower, toilet, sink, fans, screens, wooden deck, sitting area and hammock, includes all meals, great snorkelling, sail and row boats, kayaks, hiking, excellent scuba diving, US$10 per tank for certified divers with own equipment, excursions, ecological and conservation emphasis, solar powered.

Windward coast *p770, map p766*

C Ferdie's Footsteps, on the main street in Georgetown, red pillars and blue walls, shop downstairs, entrance at the side on Cambridge St, T4586433. Food and accommodation, also 3-bedroom house for monthly rental.

The south *p772, map p766*

LL Young Island, T4584826, www.youngisland.com. A tiny, privately owned islet, 200 yd off the coast at Villa, with the only resort hotel on St Vincent. **Fort Duvernette**, on a 195-ft high rock just off Young Island, was built at the beginning of the 19th century to defend Calliaqua Bay. The 100 steps up to the fort have been partially washed away by hurricanes and rock falls have left it unsafe so you can no longer visit the fort. 28 cottages, some plunge pools, spa treatments, meal packages available, part sailing, diving, wedding and honeymoon packages offered. You can even hire the whole resort for your wedding and 56 guests. There is a lovely lagoon swimming pool, surrounded by tropical flowers and a golden-sand beach overlooking Indian Bay.

LL-AL Grand View Beach, Villa Point, 3 miles from town, close to airport, T4584811, www.grandviewhotel.com. A former cotton plantation house, 19 rooms, pool, tennis, squash, fully equipped gym, sauna, excursions arranged, 2 restaurants, room service.

L-AL Mariners Hotel, Villa Bay, T4574000, www.marinershotel.com. 20 rooms on the beach, a/c, room service, TV, comfortable, jetty overlooks Young Island, French Verandah restaurant for lunch and dinner, Fri night barbecues, business centre, free internet café.

L-AL Villa Lodge Hotel, Villa Point, T4584641, www.villalodge.com. 11 rooms and 8, 1- or 2-bedroom fully equipped apartments overlooking Indian Bay, discounts for longer stay, a/c, fans, TV, internet access, pool with lovely view, restaurant, bar, meal plans available.

A Beachcombers Hotel, Villa Beach, T4584283, beachcombers@cariaccess.com. Small, family-run, breakfast included, laundry service, restaurant and bar, food 0700-2200, bar open later, happy hour 1700-1830, also sauna and steam room, business centre and internet café.

B Tranquillity Beach, Indian Bay, T4584021, www.tranquillityhotel.com. Excellent view, 1-, 2-, 3-bedroom apartments, some a/c, kitchen facilities, fans, TV, laundry service, restaurant, clean, friendly, very helpful owners, Mr and Mrs Providence.

B Umbrella Beach Apartments, T4584651, pressie@caribsurf.com. 9 double rooms with kitchen, bath, balcony, internet access, restaurant, pool, tennis, nice, simple, opposite Young Island.

C Sea Breeze Guest House, Arnos Vale, near airport, T4584969, seabreezetours@ vincysurf.com. Run by the Daize family, Hal Daize operates Sea Breeze Nature Tours. 6 rooms with bath share 2 kitchenettes and sitting room with TV, noisy, friendly, helpful, bus to town or airport from the door.

ⓔ Eating

Kingstown *p766, map p768*

Kingstown has several restaurants in the centre serving local food or fast food, but the better restaurants are in the Villa beach area

several miles east. At the bus station (Little Tokyo) you can buy freshly grilled chicken and corn cobs, good value and tasty. Cafés on the jetty by ferry boats serve excellent, cheap, local food, eg salt cod rolls with hot pepper sauce. On market days fruit is plentiful and cheap, great bananas.

ᵞᵞ ᵞ Basil's Bar and Restaurant (see below) has a branch underneath the **Cobblestone Inn**, in Upper Bay St, T4572713. 0800-2200. Buffet Mon-Fri 1200-1400 for hungry people, acceptable but not startling, also à la carte lunch and dinner, pleasant for an evening drink and a chat.

ᵞᵞ ᵞ Bounty Restaurant and Art Gallery, Egmont St, upstairs, T4561776. Mon-Fri 0730-1700, Sat 0730-1330. The oldest restaurant in town, windows open to catch the breeze, breakfast and lunch, patties, rotis, cakes and pastries, iced coffee/tea.

ᵞᵞ ᵞ Cobblestone Roof Top Restaurant, belonging to the Cobblestone Inn, T4561937. Mon-Sat 0700-1500. West Indian lunches and hamburgers, good place for breakfast.

ᵞᵞ ᵞ Rainbow Palace, West Indian fast food, Grenville St, T4561763. Mon-Fri 0800-1630, Sat 0800-1400. Genuine West Indian food and local company.

ᵞᵞ ᵞ Vee-Jay's, Lower Bay St. Mon-Sat 1000-1900, Fri until late. Friendly and offers good local food. also **Vee-Jay's Rooftop Diner & Pub** on Upper Bay St, above Roger's Photo Studios, T4572845. Mon-Sat 0900-2200. Sandwiches, rotis, etc, for lunch, good local juices, cocktail bar, entrées EC$12-45, great steel band, karaoke at weekends.

ᵞ Pizza Party, in Arnos Vale by the airport, T4564932. Until 2300. Delivery and takeaway of pizza, chicken, ice cream, snacks, no credit cards.

ᵞ Stop-Light Restaurant and Bar, Frenches Gate, opposite Karib Cable, T4562859. Extremely tasty rotis and other snacks and meals, good value.

ᵞ Sweetie Pie Bakery and Café, between the Grenadines dock and the shops, T4512168. Snacks, pastries and drinks.

Leeward coast *p712, map p766*

ᵞᵞᵞ ᵞᵞ Buccama, on Buccament beach, T4567855. Lunch and dinner. Fabulous location, luxuriously designed, very spacious bar, restaurant and lounge, excellent food, not cheap but worth it, great *pina coladas* and fruit punch. Parties and special events often hosted.

♔Beach Front Restaurant & Bar, Chateaubelair, T4582853. Lunch and dinner. Eat inside or outdoors, roof terrace with shade, good view of bay, rotis and fish meals for lunch, happy hour Fri, there can be a swell here so if you are on a yacht it is sometimes better to stop at Wallilabou.

♔Wallilabou Anchorage, T4587270, www.wallilabou.com. Lunch and dinner. Caters mainly for yachties, mooring facilities, West Indian specialities, chicken, fish or veg lunch, juices, internet access, also 12-room hotel overlooking bay. Site of much of the filming for the 3 Pirates of the Caribbean movies, see the poster of Johnny Depp in the ladies restroom.

The south *p772, map p766*
The best restaurants are usually in the hotels, eg the upscale **French Verandah** at **Mariner's Hotel**, or **Wilkie's** at **Grand View Beach Hotel**.

♔♔-♔♔Ocean Allegro, T4584972, VHF Channel 68. Mon-Sat 0900-2130, Sun 1700-2130 (in high season). Canadian management, one of the best places for both service and food, fine wines, Cuban cigars, try a 'Black Pearl' special martini, lobster pond, lovely beach view, gardens with beach bar, limbo games and good occasional salsa nights.

♔♔-♔♔Sunset Shores, 32-room hotel and restaurant overlooking Young Island, T4584411 for reservations, www.sunsetshores .com. 0700-2130. International, steak, fish, lobster, chicken, daily chef's special, full English, West Indian or continental breakfast, buffet with live entertainment Wed, barbecue Sat, Sun brunch 1200-1500, credit cards.

♔Barefoot Bistro, Blue Lagoon, T4569880. 0800-2300. International, waterfront pub-style restaurant with yachtsmen's specials and light meals available on the veranda, dinghy dock.

♔Surfside Beachbar/Restaurant, T4575362. Tue-Sun 1000-2200. Informal Continental/West Indian, pizza and seafood.

♔♔-♔Ron Jon's Rum Shop/Triangle Pub, Villa Flat, Calliaqua, T4574270. 1100-late. A rum shop with food. Callaloo soup, curried conch, conch souse and other fishy features,

barbeque and live music Fri night. Great place to be at weekends.

♔♔-♔Spin City on the Callaquia playing field, T4574942. Lunch only. The adventurous should try for inexpensive local lunches, beef, chicken, turkey, fish, all natural food served in calabash bowls.

♥ Bars and clubs

St Vincent *p765, map p766*
The local rum is *Sunset*, at around US$4-5, except for the very strong rum which will set you back about US$5-6 a bottle and blow your head off.

Many hotels and restaurants have live music in the evenings. **Young Island** is particularly good, with live bands, steel bands on Sat and local musicians on other nights. Check for happy hours at bars for lower-priced drinks, snacks and often entertainment.
Attic, Pauls Av. 1100 till late. Nightly live entertainment, jazz, karaoke, dancing, large screen video, music bar. Very popular with locals, food, buffet lunch Wed.
Basils Too, Villa Beach, T4584205. Offers lunch, dinner and dancing on the beach. Dress smartly.
Calliaqua Culture Pot, Calliaqua. Fri from 2000. A form of street party in the beach area, where you can find music and food, singing and dancing, arts and crafts.
Emotions, Grenville St, Kingstown. A small but well-known night club.
Iguana, opposite **Mariners Hotel**. Good on a Fri evening, start with a quiet drink but after midnight the party really gets going. A popular spot on the local night scene.
Marcomay, Villa, T4575044, clubmarcomay@ hotmail.com. A/c dancehall, quiet lounge area, cable TV, bar, restaurant. Happy hour Tue, Thu 1700-1800, 2100-2200, Wed karaoke, Fri barbecue and DJ, Sat live jazz from 2000 and DJ.
Touch Entertainment Centre, Kingstown, T4571825. Dance hall run by the Vincentian band, **Touch**.

◉ Entertainment

St Vincent *p765, map p766*
Casinos
Emerald Valley Casino, Peniston Valley, T4567824. Wed-Mon 2100-0300. Call for

transport, low key casino with bar, Ladies' Night Wed.

Cinemas
Cinemas Caribbean Ltd, Georgetown, T4586669.
Cinerama, Kingstown, T4856364. 3 screens, every night.
Russell's Cinema, Montrose, T4579308.

⊛ Festivals and events

St Vincent *p765, map p766*
Feb St Vincent Blues Festival, followed by St Vincent Yacht Club Regatta.
Mar National Heroes and Heritage Month, with tributes and celebration of the national heroes, taking in National Heroes Day on 14 Mar, a public holiday.s
Jun-Jul St Vincent's Carnival, called **Vincy Mas**, is held in the last week of Jun and the 1st week of Jul for 10 days. Mas is short for masquerade, and the 3 main elements of the carnival are the costume bands, the steel bands and the calypso. During the day there is *J'Ouverte, ole mas*, children's carnival and steel bands through Kingstown's streets. At night calypsonians perform in 'tents', there is the **King and Queen** of the bands show, the steel bands competition and **Miss Carnival**, a beauty competition with contestants from other Caribbean countries (a talent contest, a beauty contest and local historical dress). Thousands of visitors come to take part, many from Trinidad.
Oct Independence Celebrations.
16-24 Dec Carolling Competition and Nine Mornings Festival, during which, for 9 mornings, people parade through Kingstown and dances are held from 0100. There is also an art and craft exhibition.

◯ Shopping

St Vincent *p765, map p766*
Arts and crafts
The Artisans Art & Craft Centre, Bay St, upstairs in the Bonadie Building, T4562306. Mon-Fri 0830-1600, Sat 0830-1200. Handicrafts from about 70 artisans around the country.
Noah's Arkade, Blue Caribbean Building, Bay St, Kingstown, T4571513, lmg@caribsurf.com. For handicrafts, resort wear and books.

Nzimbu Arts & Craft, McKies Hill, T4571677, www.gligli.com. Goat skin drums, batik and banana leaf artwork, Nzimbu is often found on Bay St on Fri, selling his crafts on the roadside.

Food
Basil's, T4562602. Good wine.
Gourmet Food, Calliaqua, T4562983, and **Stanley's Deli**, Kingstown, T4858585. Gourmet provisions.
Kingstown market (do not take photos of the vendors) for excellent fresh fruit and vegetables.

▲ Activities and tours

St Vincent *p765, map p766*
Cricket
Test Match cricket ground at the Arnos Vale Sports Complex, near the airport. St Vincent was not chosen as one of the venues for the 2007 Cricket World Cup, but 4 warm-up matches were played there. It is one of the most picturesque grounds in the world with a view of the Grenadines and was extensively refurbished in 2006-7 to give it a capacity of 15,000, with an operations centre, a large players' pavilion and media centre. Alongside there are netball and tennis courts.

Diving
Dive St Vincent (Bill Tewes) at Young Island Dock, T4574714, www.divestvincent.com. Set up in 1977, benefits from a wealth of local knowledge and experience. NAUI, PADI certification courses, equipment and camera rental, trips to Bequia and the Falls of Baleine. Specializes in small groups.
Indigo Dive, Barefoot Marine Centre, Blue Lagoon, Ratho Mill, T4939494, www.indigodive.com. Single tank dive US$60, 2-tank dive US$110, night dive surcharge US$20, PADI Open Water course US$499. The newest dive shop, they cater for small groups and tailor-made packages.

Sailing
Barefoot Yacht Charters, Blue Lagoon, T4569526, www.barefootyachts.com. An American Sailing Association (ASA) sailing school and the longest-established charter company, offering bareboat or crewed yachts and catamarans, internet café,

restaurant and bar, in-house travel agency and charter airline.

Horizon Yacht Charters, T1-866-4637245, toll free, 1-473-4391000 in Grenada, www.horizonyachtcharters.com. Allow a one-way charter so you start your charter in Blue Lagoon, St Vincent and sail down to True Blue Bay in Grenada, or vice versa, for an extra fee of US$700.

Sunsail, at Blue Lagoon, Ratho Mill, T4584308, www.lagoonmarina.com. Bareboat and crewed yachts are available through the largest sailing company in the world, full service marina with hotel, restaurant, bar, pool and watersports.

TMM Bareboat Vacations, Blue Lagoon, T4569608, www.sailtmm.com. Bareboat or crewed yachts and catamarans of 38-51 ft, also offer one-way charter to Grenada.

Spectator sports

Soccer, rugby (international – Amazonia Guildingii – and junior team practices, Wed, Sat, 1630, club secretary Jackie De Freitas, T4561590), netball, volleyball and basketball. Pick up games of basketball are played on St Vincent after 1700, or after the heat has subsided, at the Sports Complex behind the airport and Calliaqua (same times, right on the street). Everyone is welcome, although it can get very crowded, so arrive early. Players beware, fouls are rarely called, although travelling violations are. No one is deliberately rough but overall the game is unpolished, unschooled but spirited.

Squash

Cecil Cyrus Squash Complex, St James Place, Kingstown, reservations T4561805. Grand View Beach Hotel and the Prospect Racquet Club.

Tennis

Many of the more expensive hotels have tennis courts but there are others at the Kingstown Tennis Club and the Prospect Racquet Club. A club house and floodlit courts have been built in Calliaqua, T4574090, Peter Lanten for reservations. Take the road opposite Howards Marine before the bridge.

Tour operators

Fantasea Tours, at Villa Beach, T4575555, www.fantaseatours.com. Large catamaran for cruises and speed boats for excursions as well as deep sea fishing, snorkelling, dolphin and whale watching and land tours, cycling, bird watching and jeep safaris.

HazECO Tours, T4578634, www.hazecotours.com. Similar tours, also with emphasis on nature. Land tours, scenic tours (jeep safari tours) and boat tours.

Sea Breeze Nature Tours, T4584969, www.vincy.com/seabreeze. Hal Daize runs coastal boat tours of St Vincent visiting the Falls of Baleine as well as whale and dolphin watching, snorkelling and fishing charters.

Surfing

Surfing is good on the reef off Lagoon Bay (Canash) and at Shipping Bay and Argyll on the Windward coast for strong surfers.

⊖ Transport

St Vincent *p765, map p766*

Air

Not only do they weigh your luggage, but small planes also need to know the weight of their passengers, so be prepared to divulge this information.

There are no direct flights from the USA or Europe; you have to change in Barbados, Grenada, Martinique, St Lucia, Puerto Rico or Trinidad, which have daily connections to St Vincent, Union Island, Canouan, Mustique or Bequia with LIAT/Caribbean Star, American Eagle, Air Martinique and Grenadine Airways, a merger of SVGAir, TIA and Mustique Airways.

Airport ET Joshua Airport, small and rather chaotic, is 2 miles from Kingstown. The taxi fare to town is EC$20 (with other fares ranging from EC$15-40 for nearer or more distant hotels set by government); minibus to Kingstown EC$1.50, 10 mins. Frequent and easy minibuses also run east if you need to get to Young Island or Calliaqua. The airport currency exchange desk is open Mon-Fri 0830-1230, 1530-1730, and is more convenient and quicker than a bank, Visa/MasterCard accepted.

Airlines LIAT/Caribbean Star, Halifax St, Kingstown, T4571821/4565800 for reservations, airport office T4584841, on Union Island T4588230. American Eagle, T4565555. Grenadine Airways (a merger of Mustique Airways, SVGAir (T4575124, www.svgair.com) and Trans Island Air), at the airport: inter Grenadine flights, T4566793, shuttles@grenadineairways.com, and in Barbados: shared charter flights, T246-4181654, res@grenadineairways.com.

Boat

MV *Barracuda*, the 'mail boat', sails south on Mon and Thu from Kingstown at around 1030 to (Bequia sometimes) Canouan, Mayreau and Union Island, arriving at around 1530-1600; on Tue and Fri she returns, leaving Union Island at 0630, arriving St Vincent 1200. On Sat she sails Kingstown-Union-Kingstown with no intermediate stops. All times are approximate, depending on the amount of goods to be loaded and schedules change frequently. Cargo takes priority and passengers are allowed on board once all the goods are stowed. On holidays day trips are often arranged, eg from Kingstown to the beach on Canouan. There are 3-4 cabins, 2 of which are used by the crew but you can negotiate for one quite cheaply if you need it. Fares: Kingstown to Bequia EC$15, to Canouan EC$20, to Mayreau EC$25, to Union EC$30.

MV *Gem Star*, departs Kingstown 1100 Tue, Fri for Canouan and Union Island, returning Wed, Sat 0730 from Union Island for Canouan and Kingstown. See also Transport, page 795.

Bus

Minibuses from Kingstown leave from the **Little Tokyo Fish Market** terminal to all parts of St Vincent island, including a frequent service to **Villa** and **Indian Bay**, the main hotel area; they stop on demand rather than at bus stops. At the terminal they crowd round the entrance competing for customers rather than park in the bays provided. They are a popular means of transport because they are inexpensive and give an opportunity to see local life. No service on Sun or holidays. Fares start at EC$1, rising to EC$2 (Layou), EC$4 (Georgetown on the Windward coast), to EC$5 to the Black Carib settlement at **Sandy Bay** in the northeast (this is a difficult route, though, because buses leave Sandy Bay early in the morning for Kingstown, and return in the afternoon). The number of vans starting in Kingstown and running to **Owia** or **Fancy** in the north is limited. The best way is to take the early bus to Georgetown and try to catch 1 of the 2 vans running between Georgetown and Fancy (EC$10). To get to **Richmond** in the northwest take a bus to Barroualie and seek transport from there. A day trip to **Mesopotamia** (EC$2.50) is worthwhile.

Car

Driving is on the left. There are limited road signs. A local driving licence, costing EC$75, must be purchased at the police station in Bay St, or the Licensing Authority on Halifax St, on presentation of your home licence. **Car hire** Only jeeps may be used to go beyond Georgetown on the east coast. **Avis**, at the airport, T4564389; **David's**, T/F4564026; **Rent and Drive**, T4575601, rentanddrive@vincysurf.com.

Cycling

Cycling is rewarding. The ride between Layou and Richmond is a strenuous 4 hrs one way, but absolutely spectacular. Expect long, steep hills and lots of them. Be careful in the north, which is a drug producing area. Contact **Sailors Cycle Centre**, Middle St, T4571712, www.sailortours.com, owned by Trevor 'Sailor' Bailey, who also operates **Sailor's Wilderness Tours** for escorted hiking and biking.

Taxi

Taxi fares are fixed by the Government but you must check with the driver first to avoid overcharging. Late at night and early morning fares are raised. Tip about 10%. Kingstown to airport EC$20, Indian Bay EC$25, Mesopotamia EC$40, Layou EC$40, Orange Hill EC$80, Blue Lagoon EC$35, airport to Young Island EC$20, airport to Blue Lagoon EC$25. Hourly hire EC$40-50 per hr for up to 4 passengers.

Vibie Taxi, T4565288, and **Clinton McCloud**, T4584573, both recommended, helpful. **Young Island Taxi Association** can be reached through Young Island on VHF 68.

❶ Directory

St Vincent *p765, map p766*
Banks FirstCaribbean International Bank, T4561706, exchange, Visa and MasterCard, ATM. **Scotia Bank**, T4571601, Visa and MasterCard, exchange, ATM. **National Commercial Bank of St Vincent**, T4571844, all

on Halifax St. **NCB** has branches at ET Joshua Airport, Georgetown, Barrouallie and agencies at Layou and Chateaubeleair. Some banks have 24-hr ATMs, but they will not necessarily accept your card. **Embassies and consulates** France, Middle St, Box 364, Kingstown, T4561615. Italy, Queen's Drive, T4564774. **Netherlands Consulate**, in the East Caribbean Group of Companies building in Campden Park, T4571918. UK, British High Commission, Grenville St, Kingstown, T4571701 (after hrs T4584381), F4562750. **Venezuela**, Granby St, T4561374. **Internet** Some hotels offer email and internet service for guests, while marinas (eg **The Lagoon** and **Mariners Hotel**) and other places frequented by yachties are good places to try. **Medical services** Milton Cato Memorial Hospital, Kingstown, T4561185. **Emergency**: T999 or 911. **Pharmacy**: The People's Pharmacy,

Greenville St, Kingstown, T4561170, Mon-Sat 0800-2000. **Post** Halifax St, Mon-Fri 0830-1500, Sat 0830-1130. **St Vincent Philatelic Services Ltd**, General Post Office, T4571911, F4562383. For old and new issues, **World of Stamps**, Bay 43 Building, Lower Bay St, Kingstown. **St Vincent Philatelic Society**, Bay St, between Higginson St and River Rd, sells stamps for collectors. **Telephone** The international code is 784, followed by a 7-digit local number. **Cable & Wireless** is on Halifax St; there is a 5% tax on international phone calls. Phone cards and fax available. From many cardphones you can reach USA Direct by dialling 1-800-8722881. **Digicel**, AT&T and **Cable & Wireless** b-mobile offer digital and GSM mobile phone network. Portable phones can be rented through **Boatphone** or you can register your own cellular phone with them upon arrival, T4562800.

The Grenadines

The Grenadines, divided politically between St Vincent and Grenada, are a string of 100 tiny, rocky islands and cays stretching across some 35 miles of sea between the two. They are still very much off the beaten track as far as tourists are concerned, but are popular with yachtsmen. The southern Grenadines are particularly beautiful, a cluster of picturesque, hilly islands with glorious white-sand beaches and rocky coves, excellent harbours and lots of opportunities for snorkelling, diving and other watersports. The Grenadines have a certain exclusivity, some of the smaller islands are privately owned and Mustique is known for its villas owned by the rich, royal and famous. There are some fabulously expensive and luxurious places to stay, but there are also more moderate hotels, guesthouses and rental homes for those who don't want to spend all their time afloat. ▶▶ *For Touching down information, see box page 770.*

Ins and outs

Getting there Grenadine Airways, www.grenadineairways.com, a merger of **Mustique Airways**, **Trans Island Air** and **SVG Air**, operates daily shared charter services from Barbados to St Vincent, Mustique, Bequia, Union Island and Canouan and inter Grenadine scheduled flights from St Vincent to the same islands.

All the ferries are cheap and cheerful and an excellent way of getting around if the sea is not too rough. The *Barracuda* is the islands' main regular transport and carries everything, families and their goods, goats and generators; she rolls through the sea and the trip can be highly entertaining (see page 779). For other services, check at the Grenadines dock in Kingstown. There are often excursions from Kingstown to Bequia and Mustique on Sunday. From Bequia you can take a boat trip to Mustique for US$40 per person by speedboat from Friendship Bay or by catamaran from Port Elizabeth, ask at Sunsports at *Gingerbread*. Throughout the Grenadines power boats can be hired to take small groups of passengers almost any distance. Try to ensure that the

Island hopping by boat is easy and cheap, but be flexible in your schedule. Be prepared to get wet from the spray as the crossings are often rough.

are flexible.

To travel further south to Carriacou (Grenada), you can catch a fishing boat ferry, the *Jasper*, from Ashton, Union Island to Carriacou, 0700, one hour, Monday and Thursday, although days vary according to demand and weather, returning Carriacou-Union Island from Hillsborough Pier, 1500, EC$15. You will probably have to sit on deck and hang on to whatever you can, as the hold is usually full of luggage and crates of soft drinks for sale in Carriacou. Check out with immigration at the airport in Clifton the day before you travel. The boat captain will take you through Grenadian formalities on arrival at Hillsborough. In high season more frequent boat trips are organized, ask at hotels, take your passport and expect thorough searches of your luggage at Customs and Immigration. ▸▸ *For further information, see Transport, page 795. See also map, page 813.*

Bequia → *Population: 6,000.*

Named the island of the clouds by the Caribs (pronounced Bek-*way*), this is the largest of the St Vincent dependencies. Nine miles south of St Vincent and about seven miles square, Bequia attracts quite a number of tourists, chiefly yachtsmen but also the smaller cruise ships and, increasingly, land-based tourists. The island is quite hilly and well forested with a great variety of fruit and nut trees. Its main village is **Port Elizabeth** and here Admiralty Bay offers a safe anchorage. Boat building and repair work are the main industry. Experienced sailors can sometimes get a job crewing on boats sailing on from here to Panama and other destinations. When you get off the ferry you will find to your left the fruit and veg market, with some clothes stalls and souvenirs. Straight in front of you is the green-roofed **Tourist information** ① *T4583286, www.bequiatourism.com, Mon-Fri 0830-1800, Sat 0830-1400, Sun*

Bequia

N

0 km   1
0 miles   1

Sleeping 🛏
Bequia **11**
Bequia Beachfront Villas **13**
Blue Tropic **2**
Creole Garden **1**

De Reef Apartments **3**
Frangipani **4**
Friendship Bay **5**
Gingerbread **6**
Julie's Guest House **7**

Keegan's Guesthouse **12**
KingsVille Apartments **8**
Old Fort Country Inn **9**
Plantation House **10**

0830-1200, run by the **Bequia Tourism Association**. (They publish *Bequia This Week*, which has daily listings of what's on.) Across the road is the administration and finance building, and next to it is the Bayshore Mall, a new blue and white building which contains a bank, a few shops and airline offices. The Anglican **St Mary's Church** was built of local limestone and ballast bricks in 1829, replacing an earlier church which was destroyed by a hurricane in 1798. It is open and airy and has some interesting memorial stones. The southern part of the bay is known as **Belmont**, where a waterfront walkway runs past hotels, restaurants, bars and dive shops on the narrow strip of sand. Above Port Elizabeth a paved road runs to the **Hamilton Battery**, which used to guard the bay.

The nearest beach to Port Elizabeth is the pleasant **Princess Margaret beach** which shelves quickly into the clear sea. It was named after the princess in 1958 when she swam there while visiting the island by yacht. However, access is deliberately made difficult and there are no beach bars to spoil this stretch. At its south end there is a small headland, around which you can snorkel from **Lower Bay**, where swimming is excellent and the beach is one of the best on the island. Hurricane Lenny washed up extra sand in 1999 and the shore now shelves quite steeply into the sea. Damaged trees are further evidence of the swell but there are still trees for shade. Avoid the manchineel trees when it rains or you will get blisters. Local boys race their homemade, finely finished sailing yachts round the bay. In the village there are several places to stay as well as good restaurants and bars on the beach and up the hillside. Lower Bay gets very busy at holiday times.

Away from the west side of the island the beaches are empty. Take a taxi over the hills to the east coast and the wild beaches on that side of the island. There are bigger trees on the Windward side, including hard woods such as white cedar, used for making boats. Drive through coconut groves to **Spring Bay**, where there is a hotel and a beach bar (may be closed) and a pottery in a partially renovated sugar mill. The **Spring Pottery and studios** ① *The Old Sugar Mill, Spring, T4573757, magspottery@vincysurf.com, daily 0730-1630*, produces domestic pottery and gardenware as well as local paintings. **Industry Bay** is another nice beach surrounded by palms with a brilliant view across to Bullet Island, Battowia and Balliceaux where the Black Caribs were held before being deported to Roatán. Food and drink available at the **Industry Beach Bar**. Both beaches are narrow with shallow bays and a lot of weed, making them less good for swimming and snorkelling. In the wet season there can also be a lot of runoff from the hills. In the northeast corner of the island, at Park Beach, is **Old Hegg Turtle Sanctuary** ① *T4583245, oldhegg@vincysurf.com, EC$10/US$5 entrance fee, but donations warmly welcomed*. It's an extremely worthwhile conservation project to save the hawksbill turtle (*Eretmochelys imbricata*), founded and maintained by a Bequian, a former fisherman, Orton 'Brother' King. Local people contact him if they see turtles hatching and he goes to the beaches to collect them, releasing them into the wild when they are about 2½ years old. There is only about a 50% success rate and a lot of injuries from the turtles biting each other, but it is still better than the natural survival rate. A few green (*Chelonia mydas*) and leatherback (*Dermochelys coriacea*) turtles can also be seen in the tanks. Larger tanks are needed if the enterprise is to improve its success rate.

The walk up **Mount Pleasant** from Port Elizabeth is worthwhile (go by taxi if it is too hot), the shady road is overhung with fruit trees and the view of Admiralty Bay is ever more spectacular. There is a settlement of airy homes at the top, from where you can see most of the Grenadines. By following the road downhill and south of the viewpoint you can get to **Hope Bay**, an isolated and usually deserted sweep of white sand and one of the best beaches. At the last house (where you can arrange for a taxi to meet you afterwards), the road becomes a rough track, after half a mile turn off right down an ill-defined path through cedar trees to an open field, cross the fence on the left, go through a coconut grove and you reach the beach. The sea is usually gentle but sometimes there is powerful surf, a strong undertow and offshore current, so take care.

Friendship Bay on the south coast is particularly pleasant, with a long sandy beach; there is some coral but also quite a lot of weed. It takes about 30 minutes to walk from Port Elizabeth to the **Friendship Bay Hotel**, at the east end of the bay, or a taxi costs EC$15. Alternatively, take a dollar bus (infrequent) in the direction of Paget Farm, get out at the junction (EC$1.50) and walk down to the west end of the bay.

At **Paget Farm**, whale harpooning is still practised from February to May (the breeding season) by a few fishermen who use three 26-ft long cedar boats, powered by oars and sails. If you can arrange a trip to **Petit Nevis**, to the south, you can see the whaling station and find out more about Bequia's whaling tradition. Despite pleas from conservationists, a humpback mother and calf have been harpooned off Bequia each year for the last few years. Bequia has an annual quota of two whales and with traditional technology and power it is easier to kill a calf and then its mother than an adult male. There is a whaling museum on the way to Paget Farm, **Athneal's petite museum** ① *US$2*, which has whale bones, old photos and tools of the trade.

The tourist office can help you visit the cliffside dwellings of **Moon Hole**, at the southwest, where a rocky arch frames the stone dwelling and the water comes up the front yard. People live here without any electricity or running water.

Activities

Bequia is great for **diving**, with a leeward wall and 30 dive sites around the island, reached by boat in 15 minutes. The **Devil's Table** is good for snorkelling and diving. Other sites are *M/S Lirero*, the Wall off West Cay, the Bullet, the Boulders and Manhole.

St Vincent is a **whaling** nation and each year two humpback whales are killed off Bequia. In addition, short-finned pilot whales, known as 'black fish' are caught in Vincentian waters for the local market. For those who would rather watch than eat these mammals, whale-watching tours are available.

❗ *Jet skis and spear guns are banned.*

Yacht races include the **Bequia Easter Regatta**, an official Mount Gay Red Cap event. There are races for all sizes and types of craft, even coconut boats chased by their swimming child owners or model sailing yachts chased by rowing boats. Everyone is welcome and there are crewing opportunities. There are other contests on shore (sandcastle building) and the nights are filled with events such as dancing, beauty shows and fashion shows. The centre of activities is the **Frangipani Hotel**, which fronts directly on to Admiralty Bay.

Mustique

Lying 18 miles south of St Vincent, Mustique is 3 miles long and less than 2 miles wide. In the 1960s, Mustique was acquired by a single proprietor who developed the island as his private resort where he could entertain the rich and famous. It is a beautiful island, with fertile valleys, steep hills and 12 miles of white sandy beach, but described by some as 'manicured'. The whole of the island, its beaches and surrounding waters are a conservation area. It is no longer owned by one person and is more accessible to tourists, although privacy and quiet is prized by those who can afford to live there. Most visitors are day-trippers from Bequia or other neighbouring islands on private or chartered yachts, who stay on the beach and eat at **Basil's**. There is no intention to commercialize the island; it has only one petrol pump for the few cars.

You can walk, ride a horse or hire a moped to tour the island. The main anchorage is Britannia Bay, where there are 18 moorings for medium-sized yachts with waste disposal and phones. Take a picnic lunch to **Macaroni Beach** on the Atlantic side. This white-sand beach is lined with small palm-thatched pavilions and a well-kept park/picnic area. Swimming and snorkelling is also good at **Lagoon Bay**, **Gallicaux Bay**, **Britannia Bay** and **Endeavour Bay**, all on the leeward side. **L'Ansecoy Bay** in the north is a wide beach, notable for the wreck of the French liner the *Antilles*, which went aground offshore in 1971.

Basil's Bar and Restaurant is *the* congregating spot for yachtsmen and the jet set. Snorkelling is good here too. From it there is a well beaten path to the **Cotton House Hotel,** which is the other congregating point. There is an honour system to pay for moorings at **Basil's Bar,** EC$50 a night, EC$20 second night.

Mustique

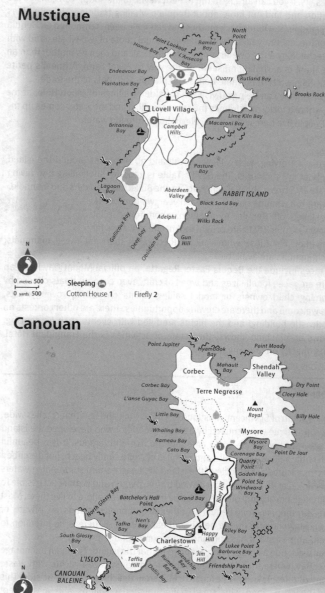

N

0 metres 500
0 yards 500

Sleeping
Cotton House 1   Firefly 2

Canouan

N

0 metres 500
0 yards 500

Sleeping
Ocean View 3

Raffles Resort
Canouan Island 1

Tamarind Beach 2

Canouan

A quiet, peaceful, crescent-shaped island, Canouan lies 25 miles south of St Vincent, with excellent reef-protected beaches. Evidence of human occupation dates back to 200BC, pendants and pottery shards having been found during construction work on the airport and hotels. The island was valuable for plantation crops during the colonial period, namely sugar then cotton, which was grown until 1924. The Snagg family who owned the land were unable to keep the plantation going and the north reverted to acacia scrub and thicket. The estate was sold to the government in 1946. Other local families include the Comptons and the Mitchells, shipwrights who arrived in the 19th century. At that time there was plenty of cedar (for the hull), mahogany (for planking) and bamboo (for masts) for ship building. In 1939 Reginald Mitchell built the largest schooner ever in the Lesser Antilles. The three-masted *Gloria Colita* was 165 ft long, 39 ft wide and weighed 178 tons. Unfortunately only two years later it was found abandoned and awash in the Gulf of Mexico and no one knows what happened to Captain Mitchell and his crew.

The Canouan Yacht Race is in August.

The village, on the leeward side in Grand Bay, is **Charlestown**, founded after a devastating hurricane destroyed the settlement at Carenage Bay in 1921. It is architecturally uninteresting, untidy and scruffy but the white-sand beach is superb, running the length of the bay and broken only by the jetty. On holidays, day trips are organized from St Vincent on the *Barracuda*, and then the beach is full of people. Cricket matches are held on the sand, ranging from little boys to family groups to serious young men who carefully measure their wicket and dispute calls. Balls constantly go in the water and stumps are made of any sticks found on the beach. The beach at the **Canouan Beach Hotel** in the southwest is splendid with white sand and views of numerous islands to the south. Mahault Bay on the north coast is beautiful, isolated, with steep hills all around, and great for a picnic. Turtles come here to nest.

Much of the north of the island, 800 of the island's 1,866 acres, is now taken up by the **Raffles Resort Canouan Island**. There are two nice beaches, but being on the windward side the sea is often choppy and has a fair amount of weed. The beaches are open to the public, up to the high water mark, but access has to be from the sea, making a visit problematic unless you are a hotel guest or have your own boat. The centre of the bay is taken up with a golf course running up and over the hill.

Dive trips can be arranged through **Blueway Diving** at the **Tamarind Beach Hotel**. The hotels organize boat trips to the Tobago Cays and non-hotel guests are permitted to make up numbers if the boat is not fully booked. The **Trump International Golf Club** is an 18-hole, par 72 course designed by Jim Fazio at the **Raffles Resort**. It covers 60 acres along the bay and up the hillside, giving lovely views of the sea. Rental equipment and buggies are available.

Mayreau

Mayreau is small privately owned island with deserted beaches, one hotel and one guesthouse. It is only 1½ square miles and 254 people live there, mostly descendants of slaves imported by the Saint-Hilaire family who acquired the island after fleeing France in the Napoleonic Wars. The Eustace family inherited it through marriage on the death of Miss Jane-Rose de Saint-Hilaire in 1919 and their descendants still own all but 22 acres purchased by an Canadian family and 21 acres belonging to the government of St Vincent, on which the village is built. The village, with no name, is tightly packed on the hillside above the harbour. You can reach it only by boat and the *Barracuda* calls on its way from St Vincent to Union. There is no deep water dock, though, so goods and passengers are offloaded into little boats and dinghies which then struggle to the jetty in great danger of being swamped by a wave. The beaches are glorious and Mayreau is a popular stop-off point for yachties, particularly in **Salt Whistle Bay**, a perfect horseshoe-shaped bay in the northwest, on a spit of land with a long, wild beach on the other side, which is to windward. Many day charters include the bay as a useful lunch stop when visiting the Tobago Cays. The only disadvantage to its popularity is that it can be noisy at night in season with revellers enjoying entertainment at the restaurant and on board their yachts.

Mayreau & the Tobago Cays

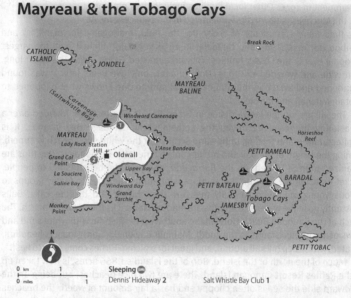

Sleeping
Dennis' Hideaway **2**   Salt Whistle Bay Club **1**

Union Island

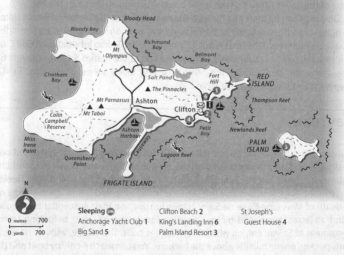

Sleeping   Clifton Beach **2**   St Joseph's
Anchorage Yacht Club **1**   King's Landing Inn **6**   Guest House **4**
Big Sand **5**   Palm Island Resort **3**

Tobago Cays

The Tobago Cays are a small collection of islets just off Mayreau, protected by a horseshoe reef and surrounded by beautifully clear water. The beaches are some of the most beautiful in the Caribbean and there is diving and snorkelling on Horseshoe reef and wall. Anchor damage, together with over-fishing and removal of black coral has killed some of the reef; hard coral lies broken on the bottom, but overall it is in remarkably good condition considering the volume of visitors it receives. Do not touch anything underwater, coral dies if you do. The Tobago Cays are crowded with unlimited charter boats, liveaboard boats or day charter catamarans out of St Vincent, Bequia, Canouan and Union Island which can number over 150 in high season. Mooring buoys have been put in to prevent anchoring on the reef, but there are not enough. Although the yachts anchor on sand, their dinghies do not and they are damaging the coral by putting down anchor wherever they want to snorkel. The flat, calm water within the reef has become popular as a place to kitesurf. Although exhilarating, it is extremely dangerous with so many snorkellers on the surface of the water. There are also anchorages in the cut between Petit Rameau and Petit Bateau, or to the south of Baradel. You can shop at your boat or on the beach: ice, butter, fresh fish, lambi, lobster, T-shirts, even French designer clothes are brought to you by boat men. Don't give them your garbage though, or you'll be sunbathing next to it on the beach later.

> ‡ Arrival by air is spectacular as the planes fly over the hills and descend steeply to the landing strip.

The Tobago Cays were used for the filming of *Pirates of the Caribbean*, and the *Scaramouche*, a two-master boat used for taking tourists to the cays, was converted into an impressive Portuguese merchant ship.

Union Island

The most southerly of the islands belonging to St Vincent, Union Island is 40 miles from St Vincent and only three miles long by one mile wide. It has two settlements, **Clifton** and **Ashton**. The **tourist office** ① *T4588350, daily 0900-1600*, is on your left as you come off the ferry. Seventy-five per cent of the population live in Ashton, but 95% of the action takes place in Clifton. Union is distinguished by some dramatic peaks. **Mount Olympus** (637 ft) is in the northwest, while **Mount Parnassus** (920 ft) and **Mount Taboi** (1,002 ft) stand side by side in the centre-west and in the centre-east are the jagged **Pinnacles** (925 ft). The landscape around Ashton is more rugged and mountainous than around Clifton. **Parnassus**, or 'Big Hill', is a good hike. Take the upper level road in Ashton. In front of a clearing are some steps leading to a path. After two or three

> ‡ The cays are a marine reserve, although nothing is done to police it. The best snorkelling is found in the Tobago Cays and Palm Island.

minutes, fork to the left. The path winds round the hill to the top, from where the views are as fine as you would imagine. North of the airport is Fort Hill (450 ft), where the site of a 17th-century French fort gives a panoramic view of dozens of islands. A walk around the interior of the island (about two hours Clifton-Ashton-Richmond Bay-Clifton) is worth the effort, with fine views of the sea, half a dozen neighbouring islands, pelicans and Union itself.

The beach at **Chatham Bay** is beautiful and deserted, but not particularly good for swimming as there is a coral ledge along most of it just off the beach. Snorkelling and diving are good, though. It is one of the last undeveloped anchorages in the Grenadines. There is no road and you have to walk 30 minutes along a footpath through the bush from the end of the road just above Ashton down to the bay. Women should not go there alone, there have been reports of attacks. **Bloody Bay** has a long, sandy beach, best reached from the sea, although there is some surf. **Richmond Bay** is also pleasant, good for swimming and easily reached as the road runs alongside it. However, it is dirty and there is broken glass on the sand, so take care. Round the point, **Belmont Bay**, or Big Sands, is another sandy beach, with villas for rent.

Clifton serves as the south point of entry clearance for yachts. The immigration office and customs are at the airport, so if you arrive by boat you check in at the **Yacht Club** and the airport. Similarly on departure, check out at the airport, even if you are leaving by ferry from Ashton to Carriacou. For visiting yachts there are anchorages at Clifton, Frigate Island and Chatham Bay, while the **Anchorage Yacht Club** marina has some moorings. There is also a 20-berth marina at **Bougainvilla** ① *T4588678, bougainvilla@caribsurf.com*, a smart new complex of businesses next to the **Anchorage**, offering apartment accommodation, a restaurant, a boutique, a wine shop, internet access and laundry at **Erika's Marine Services** (see below), the offices of **Moorings, VPM Dufour Yachting, Bamboo Yachting, Oversea Sailing, Star Voyage, Wind and Sea Ltd** (cruise ship agent and charter), and **Unitech Marine** supply and repair.

Activities

Sailing A good reason to visit Union Island is to arrange day trips to other islands or to find a ride on a yacht to Venezuela towards the end of the season (May-June). Day trip boats to other islands leave from Clifton around 1000 and are all about the same price (EC$120 including lunch). **Yannis Tours** ① *T4588513*, moored at the **Clifton Beach Hotel** arranges tours to the nearby Tobago Cays (see below), Palm Island, Petit St Vincent and other small islands. They have a comfortable catamaran, which is recommended if the sea is a bit rough, and provide breakfast, lunch, rum punch and soft drinks. Alternatively, you can hire a local skipper to take you in a smaller boat wherever you want to go. This is recommended if the sea is calm so that you can spend the maximum time snorkelling at the Tobago Cays. The **SVG Water Taxi Association** sets prices, so don't be fooled into a 'good rate'. Check at the tourist booth, a water taxi to the Tobago Cays for three or four people is US$80 one way.

Petit St Vincent

Locally referred to as PSV, this is a beautiful, privately owned, 113-acre island with one of the Caribbean's best resorts. At the **Petit St Vincent** you will find laid-back luxury, casual and stylish, with an excellent standard of service. If relaxation is what you want, you can get it here in spades. There are lots of trees and flowers providing a peaceful atmosphere and you can see most of the southern Grenadines from one view or another, even Mustique on a really clear day. The island is owned and managed by Haze Richardson, with help from his wife, Lynn, a staff of 80 (for 44 guests) and seven rather elderly labradors. Accommodation is in 22 secluded cottages mostly on the northeast side of the island, which have the most glorious views of the reef and the changing colours of the sea, encompassing all the blues and turquoises imaginable. Steps lead down the cliffs to the beach, where you can snorkel. The beaches benefited from Hurricane Ivan in 2004, which brought lots of fresh sand. There is a tennis court, fitness track and water toys: sunfish, hobie cats, windsurfers, glass-bottom kayaks. You can have room service (especially nice for breakfast) or eat in the central building. Picnics can be arranged on the south-facing beach (hammocks and shade thoughtfully provided) or on the tiny islet Petit St Richardson. You can snorkel and dive off the **Mopion** and **Punaise** sandbar islands to the northwest and Ivan created a new one, known as **Petit St Ivan**. The island can be reached by charter flight from Barbados to Union Island and the resort's launch picks you up

❖ Communication is achieved with coloured flags hoisted outside your cottage; staff come round in golf carts to pick up your requests.

there. The anchorage and jetty are on the south side opposite Petite Martinique, protected by a reef. Beaches are public, so don't be surprised to see local children from Petite Martinique swimming or playing cricket near the anchorage.

Palm Island

Also known as **Prune Island**, this is another privately owned, luxury resort, about a mile from Union Island, with coral reefs on three sides. The island was developed by John and Mary Caldwell, after they had made several ocean voyages. John is the author of *Desperate Voyage*, a book describing his first ocean crossing; with virtually no previous experience, he sailed from the USA to Australia to meet Mary. The boat was demasted, wrecked on a reef and John was stranded on an island and had to eat slime from his boat until he was rescued. The Caldwells later leased this low-lying, swampy island from the St Vincent government and the family built the resort.

There are four beaches, of which the one on the west coast, **Casuarina**, is the most beautiful, helped along with copious amounts of sand washed up by Hurricane Lenny in 1999. A casual bar and restaurant facing Union Island is open to yachties and passengers of small cruise ships, but the rest of the island is reserved for guests. Even access to the beach from the jetty is prevented by ropes and notices. Water purchase is possible for yachts, moorings available. Sailing, windsurfing, scuba diving, snorkelling, fishing, tennis and health club are all available, snorkelling and diving is usually on the Mopion and Punaise sandbar islands. Shared charter flights can be arranged from Barbados to Union Island, where you will be met and brought over by the resort's launch, 10 minutes.

Windward Islands The Grenadines

● Sleeping

Bequia *p781, map p781*
Many villas are available for rent. For a list letting agencies, www.bequiatourism.com.

Port Elizabeth
LL Plantation House Hotel, Admiralty Bay, T4583425, www.hotel-plantation.net. On beach at Admiralty Bay at the far end of the Belmont walkway. Rebuilt after a 1988 fire, Italian-owned, 27 rooms in pink and turquoise cottages with verandas, gingerbread style, meal plans, honeymoon packages, etc, Italian restaurant in replica plantation house, tennis, swimming pool, watersports, jetty, **Dive Bequia** dive shop alongside, entertainment at weekends.
LL-AL Gingerbread, Admiralty Bay, on Belmont walkway by the beach, T4583800, www.gingerbreadhotel.com. New luxury suites with kitchens overlooking Admiralty Bay, old apartments at lower rates. Restaurant and bar upstairs, café downstairs, both open daily, with **Gingerbread BBQ** outdoors on bayside 1200-1500, live music 3 nights a week, dive shop, tennis, **Surf'n'Send** internet/email access on site, friendly.

L-B Frangipani, Admiralty Bay, T4583255, www.frangipanibequia.com. Cheaper rooms share cold water bathroom, garden units and deluxe suites have fridge, good facilities and sea view, on beach or hillside along Belmont walkway, pleasant, bar, mosquito net provided, restaurant serving seafood and gourmet West Indian cuisine, snacks all day, jump-up and live music Thu, with steel band and barbecue buffet.
B-C Julie's Guest House, T4583304. 19 rooms with bath and shower, close to ferry dock, mosquito nets in rooms, good local food, good cocktails in noisy bar downstairs, meeting place for travellers to form boat charter groups.

Mount Pleasant
LL The Old Fort Country Inn, T4583440, www.theoldfort.com. A rental villa in a 17th-century French-built fortified farmhouse, probably oldest building on Bequia, magnificent views with a good breeze on top of the hill, quiet and peaceful, pool with view of 25 islands, beach within walking distance.

LL-L Harmony Retreat, T4569113, www.bequiabeachvillas.com. Set in beautiful, lush, hillside location on to Friendship Bay, this peaceful aparthotel has studios and 2-bedroom apartments.

LL-L Friendship Bay, T4583222, www.friendshipbayhotel.com. Lovely location, lush tropical gardens, 27 ocean front or ocean view rooms and 1 suite, boat excursions, dive shop, water and other sports facilities, friendly, Moskito beach bar and more formal **Touch of Class** restaurant in the main building, food good but expensive, lobster barbecue Wed night, happy hour Sat, Sun 1700-1800, live music after that.

A-B Blue Tropic, T4583573, www.bluetropic .de. Popular with Germans, renovated 2006, 10 simple rooms with balconies, fan, mosquito nets, double and single beds, view of bay, restaurant, bar, breakfast included, 100 m to the beach, dive packages.

Spring Bay

LL Bequia Hotel, T4583414, www.hotelbequia .com. Formerly Spring on Bequia, recently bought by the owners of Firefly Hotel on Mustique and being transformed into the Firefly Hotel Bequia. Part of a 200-year-old working plantation, set among coconut palms on a hillside to catch the breeze, 6 rooms, pool, tennis, bar, restaurant, beach bar on unspoiled beach, quiet, rustic and relaxing.

Lower Bay

AL-A KingsVille Apartments, Lower Bay, T4583404, www.kingsvilleapartments.net. Run by Bert and Kay King, 1- or 2-bedroom apartments in cottages, right by the beach, a/c, modern, convenient for restaurants.

A-B Creole Garden Hotel, above Corner Bay and Lower Bay beach, T4583154, www.creolegarden.com. 7 rooms, 2 of which have kitchenettes, meal plans, porch with sea view, kettle and tea. **Dawn's Creole Beach Café** just below.

A Keegan's Guesthouse, T4583530, keegansbequia@yahoo.com. Lovely position on the beach, 11 rooms, fan, mosquito nets, includes breakfast and evening meal, will cater for vegetarians, also 1-2 bedroom apartments US$400-490 per week, table tennis, volley ball, no credit cards.

A-C De Reef Apartments, Lower Bay,

T4583484. 5 apartments of 1-2 bedrooms in gardens by the beach, fans, kitchens, terrace or balcony.

Mustique *p783, map p784*

LL Cotton House, T4564777, www.cottonhouseresort.com. A 20-room refurbished (by Oliver Messel) 18th-century cotton plantation house, very expensive, spa and fitness centre, pool, tennis, windsurfers, sailfish, snorkelling, all complimentary, horse riding and scuba diving available, sailing packages tailor made.

LL Firefly, T4563414, www.mustiquefirefly .com. Smaller, slightly less expensive. All 5 rooms with view overlooking the bay, breakfast included, 2-tiered pool with a view, bar.

LL The Mustique Company Ltd, T4888000, www.mustique-island.com. 50 of the 82 private residences are available for rent, with staff, from US$4,000 per week in summer for a 2-bedroomed villa to US$48,000 per week in winter for a 9-bedroom villa.

Canouan *p785, map p784*

LL Raffles Resort Canouan Island, T4588000, www.lhw.com. The largest and most luxurious resort in the Grenadines, with 89 rooms, 67 suites, built to the highest specifications on 300 acres of a 1,200-acre private estate. Several gourmet restaurants offering everything from caviar to pasta in pretentious surroundings. **Amrita Spa** with treatment rooms dotted around the resort and even built out over the coral reef. The fitness centre has private trainers, yoga and aerobics. Tennis centre with 4 all-weather, flood-lit courts and pro-shop, lots of water-sports and water toys, day trips by boat. Donald Trump golf club, villas and casino add to the general upmarket and expensive nature of the resort.

LL Tamarind Beach Hotel and Yacht Club, T4588044, www.tamarind.us. Part of the Raffles empire but less exclusive. Set in lovely mature gardens, green and lush, 45 comfortable rooms and suites, all with sea view and right on beach, everything wood and wicker, popular restaurant, humming with yachties at night, watersports, PADI dive shop on site. Grenadines base for **Moorings** yacht charter business, long dock for dinghies, moorings rather rolly, more comfortable sleeping to anchor in north corner of bay. They also provide water, ice, bread, showers, to yachties.

A-B Ocean View Inn, Grand Bay, T4820477, VHF Ch 68, www.oceanview-can.com. Recently built by the **Moorings** in plantation style with balconies and verandas all round. A good budget option, beachfront, 5 rooms, fans, TV, iron, a/c available, internet, dinner on request.

Mayreau *p785, map p786*
LL Salt Whistle Bay Club, T4588444, VHF16, www.saltwhistlebay.com. 10 rooms in rather dark cottages built of local stone and hardwood, breakfast and dinner included, yacht charters and picnics on nearby islands. Hammocks strung between palm trees, flaming torches line the beach in the evening to guide you to the bar, boutique and restaurant. Restaurant open to non-guests, entrées around EC$50-70, seafood and imported meat. Closed Sep-Oct.
A Dennis' Hideaway, T4588594, www.dennis-hideaway.com. Renovated 2006, 5 twin rooms with a/c, balcony over looking the sea for a sunset view, bar, restaurant, breakfast included, good food and drinks at reasonable prices, pool with spectacular view, yacht charter US$75-100pp per day, fishing trips.

Union Island *p787, map p786*
L-AL Big Sand Hotel, Richmond Bay, 1 mile from Clifton, T4858477, www.bigsandhotel .com. 20 rooms, studios and suites right on the sand, each with balcony, a/c, fan, 2 with kitchen. Isolated and peaceful. Open-air beach restaurant with French, Belgian and local cuisine, some home-grown fruit and veg from the garden. Bar open all day, stocks Belgian beer. French, Dutch, English and some German spoken.
L-A Anchorage Yacht Club, Clifton, T4588221. Bought by Palm Island in 2006, changes likely. Beside the runway, marina service, French restaurant, terrace bar, steel band or piano music, rooms and bungalows for families, small beach, boutique, very sad shark pool with very bored nurse sharks in very little water.
L-A King's Landing Inn, Clifton, T4588327, www.kingslandinginnhotel.com. Recently renovated, 17-room hotel in gardens on the

harbour. Balcony, a/c, TV, wireless internet, fridge, large new pool in the garden. Bungalows have kitchen and dining facilities. Breakfast included.

A St Joseph's Guest House, Clifton, T4858335 at Erika's Marine Services, www.unionisland.com. Guesthouse built just above the new RC church, run by Father Andrew Roach, stupendous views of Palm Is, PSV, Petit Martinique and Carriacou, delightfully breezy and peaceful on the spacious balconies, 2 rooms share kitchen on balcony, meeting facilities with computer room, access to beach at the bottom of the hill, good snorkelling, jeep rental. Father Andrew organizes classes for local youngsters and volunteer labour from guests is welcome. You don't have to be religious to stay, all are made to feel at home.
A-C Clifton Beach Hotel and Guest House, T/F4588235, clifbeach@caribsurf.com. The oldest hotel on the island, Adams family now in third generation of innkeepers, open since 1952, now with a wide range of accommodation over 4 locations. Main guest house rooms on the waterfront, TV, kitchenettes, a/c available, fans, jacuzzi. Old but comfortable, clean and friendly, meal plans available, restaurant overlooking water, laundry, friendly service, water and ice for boats, bike, car and jeep rental.

Petit St Vincent *p788*
LL Petit St Vincent Resort, PO Box 841338, Pembroke Pines, Florida 33084, T954-9637401, 800-6549326, www.psvresort.com. One of the Leading Small Hotels of the World. All meals, room service and all facilities, closed Sep-Oct. Activities include hobie cats, sunfish, windsurfers, glass bottom kayaks, snorkelling, lit tennis court, speed boat and sailing boat for tours to Tobago Cays or elsewhere, massage and facials, yoga and meditation.

Palm Island *p789*
LL Palm Island Resort, T4588824, www.eliteislandresorts.com. Suites and beachfront bungalows, meals included.

🍴 Eating

Bequia *p781, map p781*
There is a wide range of restaurants, from

gourmet French to local West Indian, with pizzas, burgers and sandwiches also on offer. Reservations are recommended in high season, particularly during the Easter Regatta, when things get very busy.

Port Elizabeth

₸₸₸-₸₸ L'Auberge de Grenadines, Belmont walkway, T4583201, www.caribrestaurant.com. Lunch and dinner, happy hour 1730-1830. French with emphasis on lobster in season, large tank of live specimens, lobster lunch, filling lobster burgers. Serve river lobster from St Vincent when out of lobster season. A la carte or 3-course set dinner for EC$80-100. Live band weekly, reservations advised, rooms available.

₸₸₸-₸₸ Le Petit Jardin, Back St, T4583318, VHF 16 and 68, doris_freshfood@yahoo.com. Daily 1130-1400, 1830-2130. French and international gourmet cuisine, reservations preferred, EC$30-85 for entrées.

₸₸₸-₸ Mac's Pizzeria & Bakeshop, Belmont walkway, T4583474, beqvilla@caribsurf.com. Daily 1100-2200. Very popular, get there early or reserve in advance, also takeaways, try the lobster pizza, pricey at EC$60 for a small one, but covered with lobster, don't add other ingredients. Extensive menu also includes sandwiches and snacks such as samosas and conch fritters and an assortment of freshly baked goods.

₸₸₸-₸ Whaleboner, Belmont walkway, T4583233. Mon-Sat 0800-2200, Sun 1400-2200. Food fresh from their own farm, EC$5-65, pizza and roti EC$8.

₸₸ Tantie Pearl's Café & Restaurant, T4573160, VHF 68, http://tanties.bequia.net. 1130-1400, 1830-late. West Indian cooking, lobster and conch sandwiches, up on Cemetery Hill 2 mins by taxi above Port Elizabeth, nice breeze. Owned by Pearl and Garfield McIntosh, try Garfield's cocktails, excellent sundowners.

₸₸-₸ Porthole, at the start of the Belmont walkway, T4583458. Mon-Sat 0730-2100. Local Creole dishes, rotis, Mexican, fish, pickled conch, sandwiches. Noelina and Lennox Taylor run this low-key restaurant with a small grocery store alongside. Live music in season.

₸₸-₸ Rainbow's End, T4573688. 0900 until late. Local and international snack menu, bar, disco, karaoke Tue, Band night Fri.

Lower Bay

₸₸₸-₸₸ Coco's Place, T4583463, VHF 68. Lunch and dinner daily. Fabulous view over harbour, up on hill at end of bay, lovely balcony, friendly pub and local kitchen, Tue and Fri lobster special and live music.

₸₸₸-₸ Dawn's Créole Garden, at the far end, T4583154, www.creolegarden.com. Beach café from 1130 for lunch, drinks and light meals. Evening meals in restaurant, bar opens 1730, dinner from 1930. Good home-cooked food, Creole stews, lobster and shrimp, fairly expensive, must book for dinner. Sunday beach party.

₸₸ Fernando's Hideaway, T4583758. Dinner only Mon-Sat. Local-style fresh food, fish caught by 'Nando, candlelit dinner, special goat water soup on Sat.

₸₸-₸ De Reef, T4583958. Lovely position on the beach, popular with yachties and locals, informal bar and restaurant, curried conch or conch souse, fish, salads and sandwiches, 3-course meals, bar snacks, Sun lunch with music jam sessions in the afternoon, Sat seafood buffet dinner with live music.

₸₸-₸ Keegan's, T4583530, keegansbequia@yahoo.com. Breakfast, lunch and dinner. Right on the beach. Local meals, inexpensive 3-course meals and bar snacks all day, reservations advised in high season for dinner.

Mustique *p783, map p784*

₸₸-₸ Basil's Bar, T4888350 for reservations, www.basilsmustique.com. Kitchen open 0800-2200, bar open later. For seafood and nightlife, entrées EC$10-75. Locals' night on Mon with buffet for EC$35, Wed is good with barbeque and jump-up. On Sat go to the Cotton House. Reservations required at the Cotton House and Firefly.

Canouan *p785, map p784*

The hotel restaurants serve international food with local specialities. A few local restaurants have opened in the village and are much cheaper than the hotels. There is a bar by the ferry dock but it does not always serve food.

₸₸₸-₸ Hill Top also known as **R&C Restaurant and Bar**, up the hill opposite the entrance to the **Tamarind Beach Hotel**, T4588264, VHF 16. Breakfast, lunch and dinner. Run by Catherine and Roland Williams, Cornell and Johanna, open from 0730, seafood and local dishes such as roti, nice and breezy with good view over the harbour. Local restaurant offering Caribbean dishes and range of cocktails as well as imported wines. Takeaway, delivery to yachts, vegetarian meals all available. Captain's meal free for groups of more than 4 people.

Mayreau *p785, map p786*
Ⅲ-Ⅰ Combination Café, T4588561, VHF 16/68. Breakfast, lunch and dinner. Bar and restaurant with internet service. Dining on roof deck, good sunset views, West Indian and international dishes.
Ⅲ-Ⅰ Island Paradise, T4588941. Up the hill, everything fresh, good lobster, fish and curried conch, half price happy hour 1800-1900, barbecue Fri with local band, free ride up, skipper's meal free with more than 3 for dinner.
Ⅲ-Ⅰ J & C Bar and Restaurant, T4588558. Just beyond **Dennis'** up the hill, best view of the harbour with soft music, boutique, room for a large group, good lobster, fish and lambi, for parties of 4 and over the captain's dinner is free.

Union Island *p787, map p786*
Most places have a happy hour 1800-1900.
Ⅲ-Ⅰ Seaquarium, at the **Bougainvilla** complex, Clifton, overlooking the sea, T4588311, VHF16. Lunch and dinner. Probably the best restaurant, choose your own lobster from the aquarium, French and Creole cuisine, but mostly seafood and fresh fish, sashimi, open air, pleasant, tropical fish tank with more than just fish. Also bar and pizzeria by the sea with games tables and pool table, happy hour 1730-1830. Free water taxi to boats.
Ⅲ-Ⅰ West Indies, Clifton, T4588311, VHF 16. Mon-Sat 1100 until late. French and Creole food, on the waterfront with a jetty for dinghies and a boat. Fish caught daily, lobster with advance notice, imported steak.
Ⅲ-Ⅰ Janti's, Ashton, T4588343, VHF16. A small restaurant and bar on the left as you go into Ashton from Clifton. Snacks are available but dinner reservations required, good food, specializes in local fish, lobster in season, vegetarian meals, fruit juices and punches, free taxi if there are enough of you.
Ⅲ-Ⅰ Lambi's Restaurant, next to the **Clifton Beach Hotel**, T4588549, VHF 16. Breakfast, lunch and dinner. Reached by alley from main street or from the sea, barn-like dining room with long tables for parties, all meals are buffet in season, dinner from around 1900, à la carte the rest of the year. Steel band at night, get there by 1800 for the happy hour, free water taxi service or free moorings if you eat there, also rooms to rent but noisy.
Ⅰ Sydney's Bar & Restaurant, T/F4588320, VHF 16, Clifton, towards the airport. Owned by Sydney, who handpaints T-shirts for sale in Tobago Cays, and run by Marin from Munich, local meals, snacks, seafood crêpes, happy hour 1800-1900, also guesthouse.

❶ Bars and clubs

Bequia *p781, map p781*
Jump-ups and live music can be heard on different nights in the hotels and restaurants, including **Plantation House**, **Frangipani**, **Friendship Bay**, and **Gingerbread**. Check bars for happy hours. There is something going on most nights either at Admiralty Bay, Lower Bay or Friendship Bay. Look in *Bequia This Week* which has daily listings. Bands play reggae music in the gardens of several hotels.

Mustique *p783, map p784*
Basil's Bar, see Eating. The centre of social life, Wed barbeque and jump-up, karaoke most Sun nights, always lots of parties, music, DJ or house band to get you dancing, blues festival, see below.
Piccadilly, up the hill from **Basil's**. The local pub, rotis and beer, and pool table; foreigners are welcome, but it is best to go in a group and girls should not go on their own.

Union Island *p787, map p786*
Twilight Bar, near the main wharf in Clifton. Good drinks, the owner, Bert, sings and plays guitar most evenings.

✷ Festivals and events

Mustique *p783, map p784*
Jan/Feb Mustique Blues Festival at **Basil's Bar**, 23 Jan-6 Feb 2008.

Union Island *p787, map p786*
Mar/Apr At **Easter** there are sports, cultural shows and a calypso competition.
May Big Drum Festival, an event which marks the end of the dry season, culminating

in the **Big Drum Dance**, derived from African and French traditions. It is also performed on other occasions, for weddings or launching boats and even in times of disaster.

◎ Shopping

Bequia *p781, map p781*
There are several marine stores and fishing tackle shops here.

Books
Bequia Bookshop, Port Elizabeth, T4583905. Run by Iain Gale, who keeps an excellent stock of books, particularly of Caribbean literature, maps and charts.

Clothing
Crab Hole, overlooking Admiralty Bay on Belmont walkway, T4583290. Mon-Sat 0800-1700 in season, closing earlier out of season. A boutique where silk-screened fabrics are made downstairs and sewn into clothes upstairs.

Crafts
Mauvin's and **Sargeant Brothers**' model boat shops (the latter up the hill going out of town), where craftsmen turn out replicas of traditional craft and visiting yachts. Many shops stock *Scrimshaw* knives, intricately designed and engraved by Sam McDowell, whose studio is at the **Banana Patch**, Paget Farm.
Noah's Arcade, at the **Frangipani** on Belmont walkway, T4583424, noahs@hairoun.com. Mon-Fri 0900-1700, Sat-Sun 0900-1300. Is a branch of the enterprise on St Vincent, stocking gifts, books, handicrafts and the artwork of resident artists, whatever their origin.

Food
There is a market for fruit and veg by the jetty and there are small supermarkets in Port Elizabeth with improving selection of groceries and beverages but at higher prices than in St Vincent; for cash and carry purchases of items like soft drinks or beer (good for yacht provisioning), go to **Euro Shopper** up the hill in Belmont on the road to Paget, Mon-Sat 0800-1800, T4573932, VHF 68; fish is sometimes on sale in the centre by the jetty.

Union Island *p787, map p786*
Food
Fruit and veg stalls line the road by the ferry dock, with the best of what's in season. There are a few supermarkets in Clifton, **Lambi's**, next to the **Clifton Beach Hotel**, T4588022, VHF68, and **Grand Union** (also a guesthouse), to your right as you come off the main dock, T4588178, will deliver to the dock, and 4-5 smaller groceries sell fresh produce and hardware.

▲ Activities and tours

Bequia *p781, map p781*
Diving
Diving is good around Pigeon Island, afternoon and night dives are usually on the leeward side of the southwest peninsula, there are a few sites around Isle à Quatre and shallow dives for training can be done around Petit Nevis.
Bequia Dive Adventures, Belmont walkway, next to **Mac's Pizzeria**, T4583826, VHF68 and 16, www.BequiaDiveAdventures.com. Full-service PADI dive centre. Diving and accommodation packages from US$645pp a week.
Dive Bequia, Belmont, T4583504, VHF16 or 68, www.dive-bequia.com. Run by Bob and Cathy Sachs. In operation since 1984, this company has the biggest boats, with shade and more room to move around and manoeuvre tanks and gear. US$90 for 2-tank dive including all gear, US$495 for PADI Open Water certification course.

Sailing
For a list of charter yachts for day trips or longer, see www.bequia.net/sailing.
Friendship Rose is an 80-ft auxiliary schooner, T4583373, www.friendshiprose .com. US$110pp for day-long cruise 0700 or 0800-1730 to Tobago Cays, Mustique or St Vincent with meals, hammocks on board, deck cushions, snorkelling gear, launch for island exploring.
Quest is a 44-ft centre cockpit yacht based at Paget, T4583917. Owned by Johnny Ollivierre, who also has **Petrel**, a 47-ft Swan for day trips to Mustique.
Meteor, a 51-ft yacht, and **SY Pelangi**, a 44-ft cutter, are based at the **Frangipani Hotel**, T4583255, frangi@caribsurf.com.

Tennis

Tennis can be played at the **Gingerbread**, **Friendship Bay**, **Plantation House** and **Spring** hotels.

Tour operators

Most tours of Bequia are little more than taxi tours taking around 3 hrs and cost about US$60. For travel arrangements try **CITS**, in the Bayshore Mall, T4583062, cits@caribsurf.com, or **Grenadine Travel** at the Gingerbread, Belmont, T4583795. **Sam's Taxi Tours** is based on St Vincent and in Bequia, T4583688, sam-taxi-tours@caribsurf.net.

Union Island *p787, map p786*
Diving

Grenadines Dive, T4588138, www.grenadinesdive.com. Run by the very experienced Glenroy Adams, diving, mostly around the Tobago Cays.

Sailing

At Clifton, **Captain Yannis** has catamaran day tours starting in Union Island (early morning flights from other islands), visiting the Tobago Cays, Palm Island, etc, T4588513. Glenroy Adams of **Grenadines Dive** arranges customs clearance for yachtsmen in the southern Grenadines.

Travel agents

Eagle's Travel Agency, opposite NCB just past **Grand Union** supermarket, T4588179, eagtrav@caribsurf.com. For reservations and ticketing for local airlines.
James Travel, on the main street, T4858306. Offers similar services.

Transport

Bequia *p781, map p781*
Air

JF Mitchell Airport has been built on reclaimed land with a 3,200-ft runway, a terminal and night landing facilities, at the island's southwest tip.

Bus

Buses (minivans and open pick-up trucks called dollar vans) leave from the jetty at Port Elizabeth and will stop anywhere to pick you up but do not cover the whole island; a cheap and reliable service.

Car

Car hire is available at around EC$140/day, cheaper if you rent for a week, try **Phil's Car Rental**, T4583304; **Lubin's Car Rental**, T4583349; **Handy Andy Rentals**, T4583722; or **B & G Jeep Rentals**, T4583760. **Ryan & Gus's Rentals** have mokes, T4573238, short and long term rental, price negotiable. If staying in an apartment, your landlord may already have an agreement with a supplier and can offer you a good deal.

Taxi

Taxis on Bequia, when not operating as buses, are pick-up trucks with benches in the back, brightly coloured with names like 'Messenjah'.

Boat

Admiralty Transport Co Ltd, T4583348, admiraltrans@vincysurf.com, and **Bequia Express**,T4583472, bequiaexpress@ vincysurf.com, run 4 ferries between them from **Kingstown** to Bequia (1 hr, EC$20 one way, EC$35 return with the same company). They start in Bequia, leaving Mon-Fri 0630, 0730, 0930, 1300, 1400, 1630 and 1700; departing Kingstown at 0800, 0900, 1100, 1300, 1600, 1630, 1800 and 1900. On Sat the ferry departs Bequia 0630, 0930, 1015, 1630 and 1700, departing Kingstown 0800, 0900, 1200, 1230, 1800 and 1900. On Sun and holidays it leaves Bequia at 0700, 0730, 1630 and 1700, departs Kingstown at 0830, 0900, 1800 and 1900.
Water taxis scoot about in Admiralty Bay, Princess Margaret Beach and Lower Bay for the benefit of the many yachts and people on the beach, whistle or wave to attract their attention, fare EC$15 per trip. For those arriving on yachts, there are anchorages all round either side of the channel in Admiralty Bay, Princess Margaret Beach, Lower Bay, Friendship Bay and off Petit Nevis by the old whaling station. Bequia Slipway has dockage, some moorings are available.

Mustique *p783, map p784*
Air

International connections are best through Barbados, a 50-min flight with **Mustique Airways**, although other connections are possible via Grenada and the neighbouring islands of St Vincent, Bequia, Canouan and

Union with one of the companies making up **Grenadine Airways**. The airstrip, being in the centre of the island is clearly visible, so check-in time is 5 mins before take off (that is after you've seen your plane land).

Boat
Fresh water is shipped in on Mustique boats *Robert Junior*, T4571918, and the *Geronimo*. Both take passengers and excursions on Sun (EC$20, 2-hr trip). Many people arrive on private or chartered yachts.

Canouan *p785, map p784*
There is no public transport.
Air
There is a good runway and terminal building. **American Eagle** flies in from San Juan via St Lucia, allowing connections from the USA and Europe. **Air Caraïbe** flies in from Fort-de-France and Union Island. There is a good service from Barbados (55 mins) or Grenada (20 mins) with **Grenadine Airways**. These small planes also link Canouan with other islands nearby, Martinique (1 hr), St Lucia (40 mins), St Vincent (15 mins).

Boat
The main anchorage for yachts is **Grand Bay**. Others are at **Canouan Beach Hotel** and **Rameau Bay**, **South Glossy** and **Friendship** bays in settled weather. The *Barracuda* calls here on its way from St Vincent to Union Island and back twice a week, with occasional day trips at holiday times.

Union Island *p787, map p786*
Air
There are 5 main gateways for air services: St Lucia, Grenada, Barbados, St Vincent and Martinique, while there are also 5-min flights from Canouan and Carriacou. **Grenadine Airways** has 3 flights a day from St Vincent, US$77 return, and 2 flights from Barbados, US$165 one way. **SVG Air** and **Mustique Airways** offer charters.

Boat
There is an international ferry service between Ashton and Hillsborough on Carriacou. The *Jasper* is a wooden fishing boat which makes the 1-hr trip to Hillsborough at 0730, Mon and Thu, US$10, returning same day around 1500. The captain takes you through immigration procedures, but you should check out at Immigration at Clifton Airport the night before. Expect to have your bags thoroughly searched on arrival at Customs and Immigration at Hillsborough. If coming from Carriacou to Union Island, get on the bus at Ashton and go to the airport for Immigration formalities. For ferry services with other islands in the St Vincent Grenadines, see above. The **SVG Water Taxi Association** sets rates for water taxis. From a yacht in harbour to land is US$2 per person during the day and US$3 per person at night. Clifton to Ashton or Palm Island is US$30 for 3-4 people one way, Chatham Bay, Mayreau, PSV or Petite Martinique US$60.

Land
Minibuses run between Clifton and Ashton, EC$3. They convert to a **taxi** on request. **Bicycles** can be hired from **Erika's Marine Services**, T4858335, US$18/day, US$64/week.

⊙ Directory

Bequia *p781, map p781*
Banks National Commercial Bank, T4583700, has an ATM for Visa and MasterCard. **Customs and immigration** On the main road by the dock, Mon-Fri 0830-1600, Sat 0830-1200, Sun 0900-1200, 1500-1800. Overtime fee may be charged outside office hrs and on holidays. **Internet** Plenty of places due to the number of yachties. **Surf'n Send**, T4583577, downstairs at the Gingerbread complex, email, photocopying, computer accessories, Mon-Fri 0800-1730, Sat 0800-1430. **Sam Taxi & Tours Ltd**, T4583686, behind the new Revenue Building, internet access EC$20 per hr, also printing, scanning, yacht clearance, brokerage and numerous other services for yachties. **Icon**, in Port Elizabeth, T4573727. **RMS**, Port Elizabeth, T4583556. **Sailor Cyber Café**, Ocar Reform, T4573105. **Cyber City Internet Café** is upstairs in the Bequia Bookshop, Port Elizabeth, T4573161, F4856480. Non-member rates EC$5 per ¼ hr, EC$16.50 per hr. **Medical services** Bequia Casualty Hospital, Port Elizabeth, T4583294. **Police** Turn up the road by the banks, past the hospital and the police station is on your

right before you get to the Clive Tannis Playing Field, T4583350, VHF16. **Post** The post office is on Back St behind CBC, Mon-Fri 0830-1500, Sat 0830-1200.

Canouan *p785, map p784*
Banks National Commercial Bank, in centre of village at the road junction, T4588595, Mon-Fri 0800-1300, Thu 0800-1300, 1500-1700, always busy with queues, not enough motivated staff, no ATM. **Internet** Tamarind Beach Hotel, US$7/hr. **Medical services** Canouan Clinic. **Post** On the main street on the left heading south, no sign outside, the building used to be a bar and still looks like one.

Mayreau *p785, map p786*
Telephone There is a payphone in the village.

Union Island *p787, map p786*
Banks The NCB is to your right as you come off the dock, Mon-Thu 0800-1300, Fri 0800-1300, 1500-1700, T4588347. There is a 24-hr ATM, but if it is broken try Erika's. **Customs** Airport, T4588360; Seaport, T4588294, Mon-Fri 0830-1800. **Emergency** Fire, T999. **Police**, T4588229. **Internet** Erika's Marine Services at the Bougainvilla complex, run by Heather Grant (Canadian), T4858335, VHF68, www.erikamarine.com, fast machines, EC$10/15 mins, Mon-Sat 0900-1730, also Sun 0900-1400 in season. Additional services include bicycle hire, laundry, book exchange,

telephone, fax, computer rental, DHL, cash advances on Visa, MasterCard and Eurocard with 10% commission, currency exchange. Internet access at **Western Union**, upstairs on main street, Clifton, 4 terminals, some keyboards work better than others, EC$5/15 mins, Mon-Fri 0800-1630, Sun 0800-1200, or later if you are already on the machine, also phone calls, EC$7/min to Europe, EC$5 to North and South America, EC$3 to the Caribbean and EC$10 elsewhere. **Union Island Communications Centre (Unicom)**, is opposite the main gates to the Anchorage by the airport, T4588660, EC$0.50/min or EC$25/hr. Phone calls can be made via cardphone at **Anchorage Hotel**, the airport or in town. USA direct operator can also be reached by dialling 1-800-8722881 and credit card calls or operator assisted calls can be made. **Internet Café/Seaside Internet**, Clifton, T4858082, internetcafe@ vincysurf.com, Mon-Fri 0800-1700, Sun 0800-1200. ADSL connection, laptop hoop up, photocopying, local and international calls, cell phone rental, currency exchange and advances on credit cards. **Medical services** Hospital, T4588339; Harvey's Pharmacy, T4588596; Doctor, T4588547/4588339. **Post** The post office is on the main street in Clifton, on the right as you walk to Ashton. Stamps for postcards/letters to the Caribbean EC$0.60/0.70, Australia EC$0.75/1.40, to Canada/USA EC$0.65/0.90, to Europe EC$0.70/1.10. **Federal Express**, T4588843; DHL, T4858335.

Background

History
By the time Columbus discovered St Vincent on his third voyage in 1498, the Caribs were occupying the island, which they called Hairoun. They had overpowered the Arawaks, killing the men but interbreeding with the women. The Caribs aggressively prevented European settlement until the 18th century but were more welcoming to Africans. In 1675 a passing Dutch ship laden with settlers and their slaves was shipwrecked between St Vincent and Bequia. Only the slaves survived and these settled and mixed with the native population and their descendants still live in Sandy Bay and a few places in the northwest. Escaped slaves from St Lucia and Grenada later also sought refuge on St Vincent and interbred with the Caribs. As they multiplied they became known as 'Black Caribs'. There was tension between the Caribs and the Black Caribs and in 1700 there was civil war.

In 1722 the British attempted to colonize St Vincent but French settlers had already arrived and were living peaceably with the Caribs growing tobacco, indigo, cotton and sugar. Possession was hotly disputed until 1763 when it was ceded to Britain. It was lost to the French again in 1778 but regained under the Treaty of Versailles in 1783. However, this did not bring peace with the Black Caribs, who repeatedly tried to oust the British in what became known as the Carib Wars. A treaty with them in 1773 was soon violated by both sides. Peace came only at the end of the century when in 1796 General Abercrombie crushed a revolt fomented the previous year by the French radical Victor Hugues. In 1797, over 5,000 Black Caribs were deported to Roatán, an island at that time in British hands off the coast of Honduras. The violence ceased although racial tension took much longer to eradicate. In the late 19th century, a St Vincentian poet, Horatio Nelson Huggins wrote an epic poem about the 1795 Carib revolt and deportation to Roatán, called *Hiroona*, which was published in the 1930s.

In the 19th century labour shortages on the plantations brought Portuguese immigrants in the 1840s and East Indians in the 1860s, and the population today is largely a mixture of these and the African slaves. Slavery was abolished in 1832 but social and economic conditions remained harsh for the majority non-white population. In 1902, La Soufrière erupted, killing 2,000 people, just two days before Mont Pelée erupted on Martinique, killing 30,000. Much of the farming land was seriously damaged and economic conditions deteriorated further. In 1925 a Legislative Council was inaugurated but universal adult suffrage was not introduced until 1951.

St Vincent and the Grenadines belonged to the Windward Islands Federation until 1959 and the West Indies Federation between 1958 and 1962. In 1969 the country became a British Associated State with complete internal self-government. Government during the 1970s was mostly coalition government between the St Vincent Labour Party (SVLP) and the People's Political Party. In 1979 St Vincent and the Grenadines gained full Independence, but the year was also remembered for the eruption of La Soufrière on Good Friday, 13 April. Fortunately no one was killed as thousands were evacuated, but there was considerable agricultural damage. In 1980 Hurricane Allen caused further devastation to the plantations and it took years for production of crops such as coconuts and bananas to recover. Hurricane Emily destroyed an estimated 70% of the banana crop in 1987.

The National Democratic party (NDP), held power under Prime Minister James Mitchell (Sir James after receiving a knighthood in 1995) from 1984 until 2001. In the 1998 elections, the NDP won eight of the 15 seats in the House of Assembly, and its share of the vote fell. The United Labour Party (ULP) called for new elections because the ULP won 54.6% of the vote compared with only 45.3% for the winning NDP. The Government was often criticized for its handling of the economy and for failing to deal with drug trafficking and health and education issues. US officials believed that offshore banks in St Vincent were being used to launder drugs money and that the southern Grenadines were a transshipment point for cocaine. Marijuana is grown in the hills of St Vincent and the USA regularly carries out eradication exercises. Farmers complain they have no other crop to grow, particularly since the collapse in banana exports.

Political tensions in 2000 were defused by the mediation of the Caribbean Community (Caricom). Conflict arose when the government increased pension and gratuities for members of parliament. The ULP, trade unions and others organized strikes and called for the government's resignation. The Caricom agreement called for general elections to be brought forward by two years and held no later than end-March 2001. Sir James Mitchell (69) resigned the leadership of the NDP in August 2000. The 2001 elections resulted in a landslide victory for the ULP and Ralph Gonsalves became Prime Minister. Elections in December 2005 were described as the 'mother of all political battles' as the NDP campaigned vigorously to unseat the ULP, but they were unsuccessful and Prime Minister Gonsalves and the ULP retained a 12-3 majority over the NDP.

Government

St Vincent and the Grenadines is a constitutional monarchy within the Commonwealth. The Queen is represented by a Governor General. There is a House of Assembly with 15 elected representatives and six senators.

Economy

The St Vincent economy is largely based on agriculture and tourism, with a small manufacturing industry which is mostly for export. The main export is bananas, the fortunes of which used to fluctuate according to the severity of the hurricane season, but the fall in prices brought about by the new European banana policy has hit hard. Bananas account for over 60% of the labour force and 50% of exports. The **Banana Growers Association** is in debt and has been attempting to cut costs, but is also investing in improving land, irrigation and packing sheds. Quality, prices, planting and production have all

‡ *Over half of all exports are sold to the UK.*

recovered strongly. Nevertheless, the Government is encouraging farmers to diversify and reduce dependence on bananas with incentives and land reform. Arrowroot starch is the second largest export crop, St Vincent is the world's largest producer. Arrowroot is now used as a fine dressing for computer paper as well as the traditional use as a thickening agent in cooking. Other exports include coconuts, copra, anthurium lilies, orchids, sweet potatoes, tannias and eddoes. Fishing has received aid from Japan. In return, St Vincent supports Japan on whaling issues.

Tourism in St Vincent and the Grenadines is a major employer and source of foreign exchange. The Government has encouraged upmarket, often yacht-based tourism, mainly in the Grenadines. Expansion is limited by the size of the airport and the willingness of international airlines to fly into the islands. Stopover tourist arrivals are around 60,000 a year. Visitor expenditure is about US$50 mn a year.

Geography

St Vincent, and its 32 sister islands and cays which make up the Grenadines were, until fairly recently, almost unknown to tourists except yachtsmen and divers. They remain uncrowded. St Vincent is a green and fertile volcanic island, with lush valleys, rugged cliffs on the leeward and windward coasts and beaches of dark volcanic sand. The highest peak on the island is La Soufrière, an active volcano in the north rising to about 4,000 ft. It last erupted in 1979 but careful monitoring enabled successful evacuation before it blew. The mountain range of Morne Garu rises to 3,500 ft and runs southward with spurs to the east and west coasts. Most of the central mountain range and the steep hills are forested. St Vincent is roughly 18 miles long and 11 miles wide and has an area of 133 sq miles, while the Grenadines contribute another 17 sq miles all together. Temperatures the year round average between 77°F and 81°F, moderated by the trade winds; average rainfall is 60 ins on the coast, 150 ins in the interior, with the wettest months May to November. Best months to visit are therefore December to May. You can expect a shower most days in the hills of St Vincent, but the Grenadines are less forested and therefore drier.

People

About 25% live in the capital, Kingstown and its suburbs, 8% live on the Grenadines; 66% of the population are black and 19% as mixed, while 2% are Amerindian/black, 6% East Indian, 4% white and the remainder are 'others'. In the north of the island there are people of Carib descent, see History above. Nelcia Robinson, above Cyrus Tailor Shop on Grenville Street, is of Garifuna descent and is Co-ordinator of the **Caribbean Organization of Indigenous Peoples**.

Flora and fauna

St Vincent has a wide variety of tropical plants, most of which can be seen in the

Botanical Gardens, where conservation of rare species has been practised since they were founded in 1765. There you can see the mangosteen fruit tree and one of the few examples of *Spachea perforata*, a tree once thought to be found only in St Vincent but now found in other parts of the world, as well as the famous third generation sucker of the original breadfruit tree brought by Captain Bligh of the *Bounty* in 1793 from Tahiti. Other conservation work taking place in the gardens involves the endangered St Vincent parrot, *Amazona guildingii*, which is the national bird. An aviary, originally containing birds confiscated from illegal captors, now holds 12 parrots. The main colonies are around Buccament, Cumberland-Wallilabou, Linley-Richmond and Locust Valley-Colonarie Valley. A parrot reserve is being established in the upper Buccament Valley.

> ✷ The Wildlife Protection Act covers most of the island's birds, animals and reptiles and carries penalties for infringements.

Another protected bird unique to St Vincent is the whistling warbler, and this, as well as the black hawk, the cocoa thrush, the crested hummingbird, the red-capped green tanager, green heron and other species can be seen, or at least heard, in the Buccament Valley. There are nature trails starting near the top of the valley, passing through tropical forest, and it is possible to picnic. The Forestry Department have prepared official trail plans. A pamphlet details the **Vermont Nature Trails, Wallilabou Falls, Richmond Beach, Trinity Falls, Falls of Baleine, Owia Salt Pond** and La **Soufrière Volcano Trails.**

Grenada → *Country code: 473. Colour map 4, C4.*

Known as the spice island because of the nutmeg, mace and other spices it produces, Grenada (pronounced 'Grenayda'), the most southerly of the Windward Islands, has a beautiful mountainous interior and is well endowed with lush forests and cascading rivers. Hikers and nature lovers enjoy the trails in the national parks, where many different ecosystems are found, from dry tropical forest and mangroves on the coast, through lush rainforest on the hillsides, to elfin woodland on the peaks. St George's, the capital, is widely acknowledged as the prettiest harbour city in the West Indies, blending the architectural styles of the French and English with a picturesque setting on steep hills overlooking the bay. The southern coast, with its sandy beaches, bays and rocky promontories, is being developed for tourism. In 2004 Grenada was blown away by Hurricane Ivan, which killed dozens and destroyed or seriously damaged nearly every building on the island when the 'eye' of the storm passed directly over. Now, however, business is back to normal as Grenadians have bounced back, although you can still see hurricane damage in the forests and some homes and churches have not yet been rebuilt. ▶▶ *For Sleeping, Eating and other listings, see pages 815-829.*

Ins and outs

Getting there Air links with Europe and North America usually involve a change of plane in San Juan, Trinidad or Barbados, although there are some direct flights from London, Frankfurt and Philadelphia. There are charter services but these are seasonal. Unless you are on a yacht or a cruise ship it is not easy to get to Grenada by sea either, although there is a ferry between Union Island (St Vincent) and Carriacou, allowing island hopping from the north.

Getting around There is a good and colourful bus service connecting St George's with most parts of the island. It is cheap, but driving is fast and roads are twisty, so if you have a tendency to car sickness this may not be for you. One alternative is car hire, if you are good at finding your way around and are not intimidated by local drivers. **Maps** are often not accurate, so navigation becomes particularly difficult. Also be careful of the deep storm drains along the edges of the narrow roads. Cycling is good around Grenada, with accommodation conveniently spaced. The ride between Sauteurs and Victoria is peaceful with spectacular views. From Gouyave to St George's via Grand Étang is difficult but rewarding with some steep hills in the beautiful forest reserve and small, friendly communities. Allow five to six hours. There are many tours offered if you want someone else to do the driving, usually by minibus and reasonably priced and informative. ▶▶ *See Transport, page 827, for further details.*

Grenada

Sleeping 🛏

Allamanda Beach
 Resort & Spa 1
Almost Paradise 24
Bel Air Plantation 5
Blue Horizons Cottage 2
Calabash 3
Coral Cove Cottages 4
Fox Inn 20
Flamboyant 6
Gem Holiday Beach 23
Grenada Rainbow Inn 8
Jenny's Place 14
Laluna 9
Lance aux Epines
 Cottages 16
La Sagesse 10
Maca Bana Villas 7
Monmot 17
Morne Fendue
 Plantation House 13
Petit Bacaye Cottage 15
Sam's Inn 18
Siesta 19
Spice Island Beach
 Resort 21
The Lodge 12
True Blue Bay Resort
 & Marina 22
Wave Crest Holiday
 Apartments 11

St George's is one of the Caribbean's most beautiful harbour cities. The town stands on an almost landlocked sparkling blue harbour against a background of green and hazy blue hills, with its terraces of pale, colour-washed houses and cheerful red roofs. The capital was established in 1705 by French settlers, and much of its charm comes from the blend of two colonial cultures: typical 18th-century French provincial houses intermingle with fine examples of English Georgian architecture. Unlike many Caribbean ports, which are built around bays on coastal plains, St George's straddles a promontory. It has steep hills with long flights of steps and sharp bends, with police on point duty to prevent chaos at the blind junctions. At every turn is a different view or angle of the town, the harbour or the coast.

The Carenage runs around the inner harbour, connected with the Esplanade on the seaward side of Fort George Point by the **Sendall Tunnel**, built in 1895. There is always plenty of dockside activity on the Carenage, with goods being unloaded from wooden schooners. Cruise ships now come in to a new deep water cruise ship port on the Esplanade on the western side of the city, while the ferries and hovercraft from Carriacou and Petite Martinique still dock in the middle of the Carenage. Restaurants, bars and shops line the Carenage. The harbour is the crater of an old volcano. In 1867 the water in the lagoon started to boil and the air stank of sulphur. The water level in the harbour has risen about 5 ft above sea level on three occasions, causing flood damage on the Carenage.

> ❢ *You can walk through the Sendall Tunnel but there is no sidewalk and it is narrow, so watch out for the traffic.*

The small **National Museum** ① *T4403725, Mon-Fri 0900-1630, Sat 1030-1300, US$2*, in the centre of town (corner of Young and Monckton Streets) is worth a visit. It used to be the **Antilles Hotel**, part of the former French barracks built in 1704. From 1767-1880, the British used parts as a prison, then the ground floor became a warehouse and upstairs a hotel. Note the cast iron balcony, not many of which are left in St George's. Displays are rather dusty and old-fashioned, but cover a wide range of historical topics, pre-Columbian, natural history, colonial, military, Independence, the Cuban crisis, some items from West Africa, exhibits from the sugar and spice industries and of local shells and fauna. The **Public Library** is in a renovated old government building on the Carenage. In this part of the city are many brick and stone warehouses, roofed with red, fishtail tiles brought from Europe as ballast. A fire on 27 April 1990 damaged six government buildings on the Carenage, all now restored. Also on the Carenage is a monument to the Christi Degli Abbissi, or Christ of the Deep, moved from the entrance to the harbour, which commemorates 'the hospitality extended to the crew and passengers of the ill-fated liner', *Bianca C*. It stands on the walkway beside Wharf Road.

Fort George (1706) on the headland is now the police headquarters, but public viewpoints have been erected from which to see the coast and harbour. Photographs are not allowed everywhere. Some old cannons are still in their positions and the views all round are tremendous. The French called it Fort Royale but the British named it Fort George. After the overthrow of Eric Gairy's government in 1979 it was briefly renamed Fort Rupert, but reverted to George after the return of democratic rule in 1983. Just down from the Fort is St Andrew's Presbyterian Kirk (1830) also known as Scot's Kirk. On Church Street are a number of important buildings: **St George's Anglican Church** (1825), the **Roman Catholic Cathedral of the Immaculate Conception** (tower 1818, church 1884) and the **Supreme Court** and **Parliament** buildings (late 18th, early 19th century). St George's oldest religious building is the **Methodist Church** (1820) on Green Street. Many of these buildings lost their roofs and

Johnson Beharry, a Grenada-born private in the British Army was presented with the Victoria Cross in 2005; it was the first time the highest award for bravery had been awarded to a living soldier since 1965.

sustained other damage from wind and rain during Hurricane Ivan in September 2004 803
and were still not repaired by 2007. There are proposals to reconstruct the Cathedral,
keeping the tower and the sanctuary, which are structurally sound, but demolishing
the rest and replacing it with a steel structure and new roof costing EC$3 mn and
counting. The Anglican Church needs EC$2 mn as the roof fell in and the interior is
nearly all destroyed, as are the parish buildings alongside.

The **Esplanade** has recently been developed to take pressure off the Carenage.
The cruise ship pier and terminal is here, the entry point for thousands of tourists.
Further north is the main bus terminal and a car park, then the new fish market, all
built on reclaimed land on the seaward side of the road. The **Market Square**, off

St George's

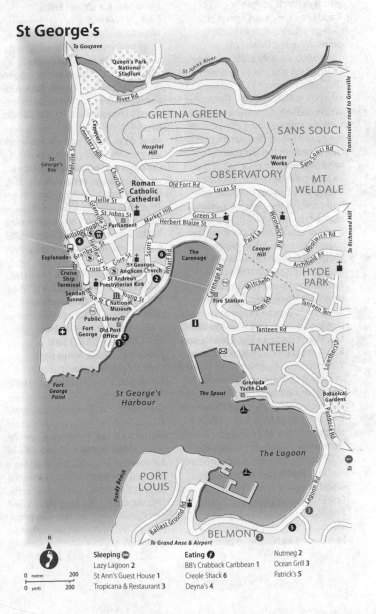

Sleeping
Lazy Lagoon 2
St Ann's Guest House 1
Tropicana & Restaurant 3

Eating
BB's Crabback Caribbean 1
Creole Shack 6
Deyna's 4

Nutmeg 2
Ocean Grill 3
Patrick's 5

Touching down

Boat information Ports of entry: (own flag) are Hillsborough on Carriacou, the site of the former Grenada Yacht Services at St George's, Grenada Marine, St David's Harbour, The Moorings at Lance aux Épines and Spice Island Marina at Prickly Bay. No port fees for clearing in or out of Prickly Bay, Lance aux Épines or St George's during normal working hours, Mon-Thu 0800-1145, 1300-1600, Fri until 1700, overtime charges will apply outside those hours. On Carriacou, moor in Tyrrel Bay and take bus to Hillsborough. Three crew and/or passenger lists, immigration cards for anyone going ashore, ships stores and health declaration, port clearance from the last country and valid passports. To clear out of the country take the boat to Prickly Bay (where they can see the boat), and four copies of the crew list. Firearms must be declared. Seal in a locker on board or take to an official locker on shore to be returned on departure. **Yachting fees** on Grenada are: less than 50 ft US$10, 50-100 ft US$12. **Anchorages** are at Halifax Harbour (may have smoke from garbage burning), St George's Lagoon (security problems noted), True Blue Bay, Prickly Bay, Mount Hartman Bay, Clark's Court Bay, Port Egmont, Calivigny Harbour, Westerhall Bay. Hog Island can be used as a day anchorage; government and coast guard uncertain about overnight use; occasionally clear out all boats but then don't come back for a while. Can dinghy to Lower Woburn from Mount Hartman or Hog Island to catch bus to St George's, otherwise taxi from Secret Harbour. **Prohibited anchorages**: Grand Anse Bay, Prickly Bay (Lance aux Épines), Pingouin (Pink Gin) Beach, Point Salines, Tyrrel Bay (Carriacou), Mangrove Lagoon, the entire inner Lagoon and within 200 yd of any beach. The outer Lagoon is prohibited to yachts and other liveaboard vessels. The Mangrove Lagoon may only be entered to shelter from a hurricane. Marine weather for Grenada and the Windward Islands on VHF Ch 6 at 1000. **Spice Island Marine Services** in Prickly Bay (Lance aux Épines), T444-4257/4342, www.spiceislandmarine.com, has a small boatyard with bar, restaurant, ship's store, laundry and market, where boats can be stored or repaired on land as well as stern-to-dock, fuel and water. Grenada Marine at St David's harbour, east of Little Bacolet Bay, T4431667, www.grenadamarine.com has haulout facility with 70-ton, 30-ft wide lift, **Customs and Immigration**, repair services, storage, restaurant and bar, beach, internet, laundry, showers. **True Blue Bay Marina**, T4438783, www.true bluebay.com. **Carriacou Yacht Services** in Tyrrel Bay provide mail, phone, fax and message service to yachts.

Business hours Banks: Mon-Thu 0800-1300 or 1400; Fri 0800-1200 or 1300, 1430-1700. **Government offices**: Mon-Fri 0800-1145, 1300-1600. **Shops**: Mon-Fri 0800-1600, Sat 0800-1300.

Clothing Casual, lightweight summer clothes suitable all year. Bathing costumes not accepted off the beach.

Currency East Caribbean dollar, EC$. EC$2.67=US$1.

Departure tax For stays of over 24 hours, departure tax is EC$50, (EC$25 for children 2-12). EC$10 airport tax is charged on departure from Lauriston Airport, Carriacou.

Documents Citizens of the UK, USA and Canada need only provide proof of identity (with photograph) and an onward ticket (but note that if you go to Grenada via Trinidad, a passport has to be presented in Trinidad and returning US citizens need a passport to re-enter the USA). For all others a passport and onward ticket are essential. Departure by boat is not accepted by the immigration authorities. Citizens of certain other countries (not the Commonwealth, Caribbean – except Cuba –, South Korea, Japan and most European countries) must obtain a visa to visit Grenada. Check before leaving home. When you arrive in Grenada expect to have your luggage examined very thoroughly. It may take you at least 45 minutes to get through passport control and customs. You must be able to give an accommodation address when you arrive.

Emergency numbers Ambulance T434 in St George's, T724 in St Andrew's and T774 on Carriacou.

Media Newspapers: there are no daily papers, only weeklies, including *Grenadian Voice*, *Indies Times*, *Grenada Guardian*, *The National*, and *The Informer*. **Radio**: there are four radio stations, on AM 535, AM 1400, FM 90, 96.3, 101.7, 105.5 kHz. **Television**: there are three television stations but many hotels have satellite or cable reception.

Official time Atlantic Standard Time, 4 hours behind GMT, 1 hour ahead of EST.

Public holidays New Year's Day (1 Jan), Independence Day (7 Feb), Good Fri and Easter Mon, Labour Day (1 May), Whit Mon (in May/Jun), Corpus Christi (Jun), Aug holidays (first Mon and Tue in Aug) and Carnival (second weekend in Aug), Thanksgiving (25 Oct), 25 and 26 Dec.

Safety On the Carenage in St George's, you may be pestered for money, particularly after dark, but it is no more than a nuisance.

Unemployment and drug abuse are problems; over 75% of the prison population have been sentenced for drug-related crimes. Night police patrols operate in hotels and beach areas. In the countryside people are extremely helpful and friendly and there is no need anywhere for anything other than normal precautions against theft. If visiting St George's it is best to pick a day when there are no cruise ships in port, to avoid hassle from vendors and touts. Carriacou is generally safe, despite smuggling, but avoid deserted beaches as serious incidents involving tourists have occurred in the past.

Tourist information Grenada Board of Tourism, Box 293, Burn's Point, St George's, T4402279, www.grenadagrenadines.com. 0800-1600, very helpful, lots of leaflets. There is also a cruise ship office, T4402872, and tourist office at the airport, helpful, hotel reservation service, T4444140. On Carriacou, Main St, Hillsborough, beside the Osprey office, T4437948, carrgbt@spiceisle.com. The **Grenada Hotel Association** is at Ross Point Inn, Lagoon Rd, T4441353, www.grenadahotelsinfo.com.

Tourist offices overseas Canada: 439 University Av, Suite 920, Toronto, Ontario M5G 1Y8, T416-5951339, tourism@grenadaconsulate.com. **Germany**: Schenkendorfstrasse 1, 65187 Wiesbaden, T0611-267 6720, grenada@discover-fra.com. **UK**: 11 Blades Court, 121 Deodar Road, London, T020-8877 4516, grenada@representationplus.co.uk. **USA**: PO Box 1668, Lake Worth, FL 33460, T561-5888176, cnoel@grenadagrenadines.com.

Voltage 220/240 volts, 50 cycles AC.

Weights and measures Imperial.

Halifax Street (one of the main streets, one steep block from the Esplanade), is always busy although the weekly market is on Saturday. There is a wide variety of local produce, herbs, spices and local crafts including luxuries such as nutmeg oil, nutmeg soap, rich cocoa balls, sold under cover. The trades people are keen to sell, but are polite, good-humoured and not pushy.

Just north of the city is **Queen's Park National Stadium**, rebuilt after Ivan with the help of the Chinese, which is used for all the main sporting activities, cricket, carnival shows and political events. From **Richmond Hill** there are good views (and photo opportunities) of both St George's and the mountains of the interior. On the hill are Forts Matthew (built by the French, 1779), Frederick (1791) and Adolphus (built in a higher position than Fort George to house new batteries of more powerful, longer range cannon), and the prison in which were held those convicted of murdering Maurice Bishop before Hurricane Ivan blew the roof off in 2004.

East of St George's

The Eastern Main Road heads east from Richmond Hill through numerous villages, twisting and turning, and there are a few places of interest for short excursions from St George's. To see a good selection of Grenada's flowers and trees, visit the **Bay Gardens** ① *EC\$5*, at Morne Delice (turn off the Eastern Main Road at St Paul's police station, the gardens are on your left as you go down). It's a pleasant place with a friendly owner; the paths are made of nutmeg shells. They will show you around if you want and explain the uses of all the fruits, herbs and spices. If you take the next turning off the Eastern Main Road, just before the Texaco station, you reach the **Morne Gazo Nature Trails** ① *Mon-Sat 0900-1600, Sun 1000-1500, closed public holidays, EC\$5, car park*, on your right. Morne Gazo (or Delice Hill) rises to 1,140 ft and the Forestry Department has created trails covered with nutmeg shells in the forest. At the summit a lookout platform gives a panoramic view of the island, down to the airport in the south, across to La Sagesse and up to the hills around Grand Étang. Information leaflets are available in several languages. Further along the Eastern Main Road near Perdmontemps, is the turning for **Laura Spice and Herb Gardens** ① *closed Sat, EC\$5*, where you can see nutmeg, cloves and all the other spices and herbs grown on the island.

Southwest Grenada

From the Carenage, you can take a road which goes round the Lagoon, another sunken volcanic crater, now a yacht anchorage. This area is the site of a massive development, Port Louis, which will transform Lagoon Rd. A mixed use resort and maritime community development is being built with a world class marina for yachts up to 90 m, houses, apartments, a 120-room 5-star hotel and a 120-room mid-range hotel, reclamation and renovation of the seafront and upgrading of Pandy Beach with provision of watersports and more sand. Carrying on to the southwest tip you come to **Grand Anse**, Grenada's most famous beach. Along its length are many hotels, but none dominates the scene since, by law, no development may be taller than a coconut palm. Rather surprisingly, the St George's University School of Arts and Sciences has a campus here, right on the beach. Access to the beach and parking is at Camerhogue Park at the north end by the **Spiceland** shopping mall. From Grand Anse the road crosses the peninsula to a roundabout, from where roads lead off to the Point Salines Airport or the Lance aux Épines headland. The road to Portici and **Parc à Boeuf** beaches leads to the right, off the airport road. **Portici** beach is virtually deserted, with good swimming despite a steeply shelving beach and excellent snorkelling around Petit Cabrits point at its northeast end. The next road to the right leads to **Magazine Beach**, then comes **Pink Gin Beach** and, practically as far as you can go, is the all-inclusive **La Source** (closed 2005 for renovation after Ivan), all very close to the airport. On the south side of the peninsula, at **Prickly Bay** (the west side of Lance aux Épines) are hotels, the Spice Island Marina and other yachting and watersports facilities. Luxury homes take up much of **Lance aux Épines** down to Prickly Point. There is a glorious stretch of fine white sand, the lawns of the **Calabash Hotel** run down to the beach, very nice bar and restaurant open to non-residents, steel bands often play there. The next bay west, **True Blue Bay**, is smaller and quieter, with no real beach, but also has a hotel and yachting facilities as well as the university's School of Medicine.

From the Point Salines/Lance aux Épines roundabout you can head east along a road which snakes around the south coast. At **Lower Woburn**, a small fishing community (bus from St George's), you can see vast piles of conch shells in the sea, forming jetties and islets where they have been discarded by generations of lambi divers. Stop at **Island View Restaurant** or a local establishment, **Nimrod and Sons Rum Shop**. Yachtsmen visit this spot to sign the infamous guest register and to be initiated with a shot of Jack Iron rum (beware, it is potent!). Past Lower Woburn is the **Clarks Court Rum Distillery** (tours available with rum sales, tip the guide). It is a steam-driven operation, unlike the river Antoine water-wheel system. Any number of tracks and paths go inland to join the Eastern Main Road, or run along the rias and headlands, such as Calivigny, Fort Jeudy, Westerhall Point or La Sagesse with its nature reserve (see below). Many of Grenada's most interesting and isolated bays are in the southeast, accessible only by jeep or on foot; taxis can drop you off at the start of a path and pick you up later.

West coast Grenada

Heading north out of St George's, past Queen's Park stadium and Grand Mal Bay, you can turn inland to see petroglyphs, or rock carvings, near **Hermitage** (look for a sign on the road). Beauséjour Estate, once the island's largest, is now in ruins (except for the estate Great House). It is private, but from the road you can see the remains of the sugar mill and distillery on the opposite side of the road from the sports ground. Beyond Beauséjour is Halifax Bay, a beautiful, sheltered harbour, and the second most protected harbour in Grenada, but onland it is marred by a rubbish dump with smoke rising from it. Looking back over Halifax harbour is an old plantation house, Woodford Estate, a wooden building with pretty tiles but unfortunately falling apart.

The beautiful west coast road from St George's hugs the shore all the way to Duquesne Bay in the north with lovely views.

At Concord, a road runs up the valley through nutmeg, cocoa, cashew, guava and clove trees to the First **Concord Falls** (45-minute hot walk from the main road or go by car, driving slowly, children and vendors everywhere). It is very busy at the end of the road with tour buses and spice stalls. There are toilets and changing facilities (small fee) if you want to bathe in the small cascade, but there is not much water in the dry season. The Second Concord Falls are a 30-40 minute walk (each way), with a river to cross seven times; there is no need for a guide but it is advisable. Three hours further uphill is **Fedon's Camp**, at 2,509 ft, where Julian Fedon (see page 830) fortified a hilltop in 1795 to await reinforcements from Martinique to assist his rebellion against the British. After fighting, the camp was captured; today it is a historical landmark. It is possible to hike from Concord to Grand Étang in five hours; it's a hard walk, but rewarding. The trail is hard to spot where it leaves the path to the upper falls about two-thirds of the way up on the left across the river.

North of Concord, just before Gouyave (pronounced *Gwarve*), is a turn-off to **Dougaldston Estate**. Before the revolution 200 people were employed here, cultivating spices and other crops. Now there are only a handful, the place is run down, the buildings in disrepair, the vehicles wrecked, but you can walk round and see the old machinery and imagine how it used to be. Hurricane Ivan destroyed 80% of the nutmeg trees and 60-70% of cocoa bushes on the island, while many are still covered in vines. At Dougaldston they still dry spices in the traditional way on racks which are wheeled under the building if it rains and someone will explain all the spices to you. However, there is no fermentation here now and the family has turned to tourism rather than agriculture. Samples cost EC$5 for a bag of cinammon, cloves or nutmeg, or there are mixed bags.

Gouyave, 'the town that never sleeps', is a fishing port, nutmeg collecting point and capital of St John's parish. There are a few interesting old buildings; the post office, just past the shiny red fire engine, has an iron balcony. At the **Nutmeg Processing Station** ① *a tour for US$1 is highly recommended*, you can see all the stages of drying, grading, separating the nutmeg and mace and packing (give a tip). On the top floor **mace** is dried for four months in Canadian pine boxes before being graded. There are three grades, used for culinary spice, corned beef or cosmetics, and only Grenada produces grade one mace for cooking. On the first floor, **nutmeg** is dried on racks for two months, turned occasionally with a rake. The lighter ones are then used in medicine and the heavier ones for culinary spices. The husks are used for fuel or mulch and the fruit is made into nutmeg jelly (a good alternative to breakfast marmalade), syrup or liquor. The station is a great wooden building by the sea, with a very powerful smell. No photos are allowed. A little shop sells nutmeg products. There are two other processing plants, at Victoria and Grenville, but this is the largest. There is also a nutmeg oil distillery at Sauteurs. All are open to the public. Gouyave is the principal place to go to for the **Fisherman's Birthday** festival. On Fridays, Gouyave is open to tourists on a grand scale, in the evening the main street is closed to traffic, there is seafood, drink and music and dancing.

Northern Grenada

The road continues around the northwest coast, turning inland at Duquesne (pronounced *Duquaine*) where there is a beautiful grey sand and petroglyphs on the beach (not particularly clean because of fishing), before returning to the sea at **Sauteurs**, the capital of St Patrick's parish, on the north coast. There is a lovely, wild beach with leaning palm trees as you approach along the coast road. The town is renowned as the site of the mass suicide of Grenada's last 40 Caribs, who jumped off a cliff rather than surrender to the French (see page 830). Leapers Hill is appropriately in the cemetery by the church, behind the school. Recently redeveloped, there is an interpretation centre with a model of a Carib village, washrooms and shops, while a board shows all the islands you can see looking out to the north. In March Sauteurs celebrates St Patrick's Day with a week of events, exhibits of arts and crafts and a mini street festival. **Helvellyn House** is perched on a hill in lovely gardens often used as a lunch stop for tour parties with a view of the Grenadines and the mountains inland. At the side of the drive up to the house is an artisanal pottery being developed with the help of a Moroccan potter, who has been teaching local children in schools. The first designs were all Moroccan, but they are developing local themes and experimenting with local clay. **Morne Fendue** plantation house is just south of Sauteurs and a popular place for tour groups to stop for lunch. The house was built in 1912 and still has all the old mouldings, cornices and light fittings of that time. The buffet lunch features local specialities and is served in an open air dining room in front of the old colonial house with a view of Mt St Catherine. Reservations essential.

East coast Grenada

From Sauteurs a road approaches **Levera Bay** (see above) from its west side. Turn left at **Chez Norah's** bar, a two-storey, green, corrugated-iron building (snacks available); the track rapidly becomes quite rough and the final descent to Levera is very steep, suitable only for 4WD. A better way to Levera approaches from the south. The road forks left about two miles south of Morne Fendue, passes through river Sallee and past Bathway Beach. The river Sallee Boiling Springs are an area of spiritual importance; visitors are inspired to throw coins into the fountain while they make a wish. **Bathway Beach** is a popular weekend spot when it can get busy. It is a huge dark golden stretch of sand,

The word Bathway comes from a fish called the batwey.

with cliffs at either end, trees for shade, a beach bar, picnic tables, and the **Levera National Park** visitors' centre. There is a ridge of rocks just offshore, parallel with the beach, which provides protection for swimming, almost like a swimming pool, but you must not swim beyond the rocks or you will be drowned. From here a dirt road leads past Levera Pond, which has not yet recovered from Hurricane Ivan and both the road and the mangroves are in a sorry state. Birds are best seen early morning or late evening. Swimming is good at the beautiful and wild Levera Beach where leatherback turtles come to nest in April-June, and there is surf in certain conditions. It is not as busy as Bathway because not many people want to subject their vehicles to the dusty/muddy, potholed, dirt road. Do not swim far out as there is a current in the narrows between the beach and the privately owned Sugar Loaf Island.

A huge resort development is planned for Levera Beach, which will include an 18-hole championship golf course (nine holes already complete), a 600-room hotel and 200 villas, casino, medical centre and shops. The population explosion will completely change the character of the area.

On the east side of the island, the coastal road runs south past the circular crater lake, **Lake Antoine** where, like St George's and Grand Étang, the water has risen at times of volcanic activity, notably in 1902. Nearby is the **River Antoine Rum Distillery**, driven by a water mill, the oldest in the Caribbean (guided tours, T4427109). Grinding of the sugar cane is done in the mornings and the basic distillation process results in the Rivers Royale Grenadian Rum, which at 75% alcohol is breathtaking firewater. At the distillery there is also the Rivers Restaurant and Bar. The **Dunfermline Rum Distillery** can also be visited. There are no actual tours but the staff will show you around.

Inland from here is the old **Belmont Estate** ① *T4429524, www.belmontestate.net, still closed end-2006 because of hurricane damage, expected to reopen 2007, check opening times, normally Sun-Fri, tours from 0800 US$5, lunch 1200-1430 US$15,* which dates from the 17th century. When open, you can tour the 400-acre estate and follow the beans from bush to export. A heritage museum is complemented by shows of traditional activities such as stick fighting, nation drumming, bele and pique dancing and games practised by the slaves. A lavish buffet is offered for lunch, with indoor or outdoor dining, reservations required by 0900. To get there turn towards Sauteurs when you reach the Tivoli/La Poterie junction near Tivoli RC church; at the next junction turn left and Belmont is on your right after a minute or so. Do not miss a visit to the **Grenada Chocolate Factory** ① *a mile away at Hermitage, T4420050. www.grenadachocolate.com.* Using certified organic cocoa beans from the Belmont Estate and organic sugar from a cooperative in Paraguay, this tiny factory roasts and grinds all its own beans and produces some of the world's finest chocolate. The whole operation is solar powered and the shells and dust are recycled as fertilizer around the cocoa bushes. Staff will explain and show you the manufacturing process, and you can buy their delicious organic chocolate (61% or 70% cocoa) or cocoa powder/drinking chocolate. It will not melt in the car on the way home and survives island hopping or transatlantic flights perfectly!

Amerindian remains can be seen at an archaeological dig near the old **Pearls Airport**. Apparently it's so unprotected that lots of artefacts have been stolen. The airport is worth a quick visit to see the two old Cuban and Russian planes and the duty-free shop, a ghost town, although the runway is well used for driving lessons, cricket, biking, go-karting and social encounter in general.

Grenville is the main town on the east coast and capital of St Andrew's Parish, the largest parish in Grenada with a population of about 25,000. It is a collection point for bananas, nutmeg and cocoa, and also a fishing port. There are some well-preserved old buildings, including the Court House, Anglican Church, police station and post office. Funds are being raised to restore and convert the old Roman Catholic church into a library, museum, art gallery and cultural centre.

Saturday is market day, worth seeing. Weavers turn palm fronds into hats, baskets and place mats.

Windward Islands Grenada

Construction of the church began in 1841 and it was used as a church until 1915, when mosquitoes finally triumphed over worshippers. From 1923 to 1972 it was used as a school, but then abandoned. Good local food can be found here along the main street, try Ebony's for curry mutton, stewfish, Creole fish and rice and peas, or **Rins**, right by the buses to town, which is the best place for roti. The **Rainbow City Festival** is held here at the start of August, with arts and crafts displays, street fairs, cultural shows and a 10-km road race.

Two miles south of Grenville are the **Marquis Falls**, also called Mount Carmel Falls, the highest in Grenada. Trails are being improved, with signposts and picnic areas. Marquis village was the capital of St Andrew's in the 17th and 18th centuries. Nowadays it is the centre of the wild pine handicraft industry.

The interior

There are several routes up **Mount St Catherine**, perhaps easiest from Grenville. Take a minibus to the Mount Hope road, this is a 4WD track which becomes the path up the mountain. It takes about two hours from leaving the minibus. A guide is not necessary. Do not go alone, however, and do not go at all if you suffer from vertigo. Don't take chances with daylight either. For information on this and anything else, contact Mr and Mrs Benjamin at **Benjamin's Variety Store** ① *Victoria Street, Grenville, T4426200*. Mrs Benjamin is on the Tourist Board. Telfer Bedeau, from Soubise, is the hiking expert.

The transinsular, or hill road, from Grenville to St George's used to be the route from the Pearls Airport to the capital, which all new arrivals had to take. It is well surfaced, but twisty and narrow. The minibus drivers on it are generally regarded as 'maniacs', one bend is called 'Hit Me Easy'. The road rises up to the rainforest, often entering the clouds. If driving yourself, allow up to 1½ hours from Levera to St George's. Shortly before reaching the **Grand Étang** (see page), there is a side road to the St Margaret, or **Seven Sisters Falls**. They are only a 30-minute walk from the main road, but a guide is essential, or else get very good directions. A guide will show you a circular route, which is steep but more interesting than returning on the same path and takes two hours. The trail runs over private land, so a small fee is payable to the owners who keep the paths clear, at their place by the main road. After Grand Étang, there is a viewpoint at 1,910 ft overlooking St George's. A bit further down the hill is a detour to the **Annandale Falls** which plunge about 40 ft into a pool where the locals dive and swim. Tourists are pestered for money here, for diving, singing, information, whether requested or not. If coming from St George's on Grenville Road, fork left at the Methodist Church about half way to Grand Étang.

> ❗ *Avoid the mountain roads around Grand Étang in the dark, although the night-time sounds of the dense jungle are fascinating.*

The peaks in the southeast part of the Grand Étang Forest Reserve can be walked as day trips from St George's. For **Mount Maitland** (1,712 ft), take a bus from the Market Place to Mardigras, or if there is none, get off at the junction at St Paul's and walk up. At the Pentecostal (IPA) church, turn left and immediately right. The paths are reasonably clear and not too muddy. The walk takes less than one hour each way. There are good views from the top over both sides, with some hummingbirds.

Mount Sinai (2,306 ft) is not as spectacular as Mount St Catherine, nor as beautiful as Mount Qua Qua, but is not as muddy either. Take a bus to Providence, then walk up (two hours) the particularly lovely road to Petit Étang and beyond, where the road turns into a track in the banana fields. The path up the mountain begins behind a banana storage shed and must be closely watched. The terrain is a bit tricky near the top. There is a path down the other side to Grand Étang. Local opinions vary as to how badly you would get lost without a guide as the paths are no longer maintained.

⦂ Cricket Grenadine style

Cricket is played throughout the Grenadines on any scrap of ground or on the beach. In Bequia, instead of the usual three stumps at the crease, there are four, and furthermore, bowlers are permitted to bend their elbows and hurl fearsome deliveries at the batsmen. This clearly favours the fielding side but batsmen are brought up to face this pace attack from an early age and cope with the bowling with complete nonchalance. Matches are held regularly, usually on Sundays, and sometimes internationals are staged. In Lower Bay v England, which Lower Bay usually wins, the visitors' team is recruited from cricket lovers staying in the area. Ask at De Reef; it is best to bat at number 10 or 11.

Beaches and activities

There are 45 beaches on Grenada. The best are in the southwest, particularly **Grand Anse**, a lovely stretch of white sand which looks north to St George's. It can get crowded with cruise passengers, but there's usually plenty of room for everyone. Beach vendors have a proper market with 78 booths, washroom facilities, a tourist desk and a jetty for water taxis, to prevent hassling on the beach. **Morne Rouge**, the next beach going southwest, is more private, has good snorkelling and no vendors. There are other nice, smaller beaches around **Lance aux Épines**. The beaches at **Levera** and **Bathway** in the northeast are also good, wild and unimproved.

Diving The reefs around Grenada provide excellent sites for diving. A popular dive is to the wreck of the Italian cruise liner, *Bianca C*. Other dive sites include **Boss Reef**, **The Hole**, **Valley of Whales**, **Forests of Dean**, **Grand Mal Point** (wall dive), **Dragon Bay** (wall dive) ends at Molinière, **Happy Valley** (drift with current to Dragon Bay). Three wrecks from cargo ships off Quarantine Point, St George's, are in strong currents. **Molinière** reef for beginners to advanced has a sunken sailboat, the *Buccaneer*; **Whibble** reef is a slopey sand wall (advanced drift dive); **Channel** reef is a shallow reef at the entrance to St George's with many rusted ships' anchors; **Spice Island** reef is for resort dives and beginners as well as the wrecks *Red Buoy*, *Veronica L* and *Quarter Wreck*. Dive sites around Carriacou include **Kick Em Jenny** (a submarine volcano), **Isle de Rhonde**, **Sandy Island**, **Sister Rocks** (to 100 ft, strong currents), **Twin Sisters** (walls to 180 ft and strong currents), **Mabouya Island**, **Saline Island** (drift dive). Local dive shops and agencies are working towards setting up a marine park to preserve the underwater world of Carriacou. The reefs are unspoilt, with forests of soft corals growing up to ten feet tall with a wide range of creatures living among them. Dive sites are reached with a 10-15 minute boat ride and the reefs are about 20-30 feet down. There is no shore diving. In 2005 a 1960s tugboat, *Westsider*, was sunk as a wreck dive site in the planned marine park and has already been colonised by marine life.

The best **snorkelling** is around Molinière Point and up to Dragon Bay and Flamingo Bay. Flamingo Bay is named after a snail, not a bird. Snorkelling trips by boat will usually bring you to this area, often in the afternoons so that divers on board can do a shallow dive as well. You can see a wide variety of fish and invertebrates on the rocks and coral, even moray eels in holes if you look carefully.

Whale watching Humpback whales can be seen off Grenada and Carriacou during their migrations in December-April. Pilot whales, dolphins and several other whales are also found in Grenadian waters (see Whale and dolphin watching, page 37). Contact Mosden Cumberbatch (see Tour operators, below) for whale-watching tours, he has a boat especially designed for whale watching, taking up to 35 people on a four-hour trip.

Carriacou → *Colour map 4, C4. Population: 6,800.*

Carriacou (pronounced Carrycoo) is an attractive island of green hills descending to sandy beaches. It is less mountainous than Grenada, which means that any cloudy or rainy weather clears much quicker. Efforts are being made by the Government to curb contraband and drug smuggling in Carriacou, but a lot comes in around Anse la Roche, where there are picturesque smugglers' coves. Hurricane Ivan caused far less damage in 2004 than it did in Grenada and all hotels remained open.

Ins and outs

Getting there There are flights from Barbados and Grenada in small planes, or you can get here by sea on a hovercraft, large ferries for cargo and passengers or yacht. It is a lovely route, following the length of Grenada's western coastline before crossing the channel to Carriacou and seeing the Grenadines coming into view. On the crossing look out for dolphins which follow the boats. The *Osprey* hovercraft is recommended as being the most reliable service and the boat is in good condition. In heavy seas you may get seasick on any boat, said to be worse going to Carriacou than coming back. ▸▸ *See Transport, page 828, for further details.*

Getting around Minibuses run to most parts of the island and will convert to a taxi to take you off route. Car hire is available, which is useful if you are staying in self-catering accommodation and need to shop. Cycling is recommended, the traffic is very light. Many of the roads are in very poor repair, giving the semblance of off-road cycling, although some of the main roads have recently been repaved. Potential for lots of flat tyres in the dry season as there is an abundance of cacti. Walking is equally rewarding, the heat being the main problem. There is good walking on the back roads and the woods are teeming with wildlife such as iguanas. Some beaches can only be reached on foot or by boat. Water taxis are on hand to take you to beaches in remote parts of the island, or to the islets offshore for picnics and snorkelling.

Sights

Carriacou's capital, **Hillsborough**, has a population of about 1,000. It dates from a colonial settlement towards the end of the 18th century and was used by Admiral Ralph Abercrombie who came with 150 ships to launch an attack on the Spanish in 1796 and capture Trinidad. Main Street runs parallel to the sea and the hub of activity is the dock area where you find Customs, Immigration, Police, taxis, buses and fruit and vegetable stalls. Also along Main Street there are guesthouses, a few restaurants, bars, a supermarket, shops, internet access, banks and a dive shop. The town is also blessed with a lovely beach, a huge curve of white sand with good swimming, despite the presence of the jetty and large cargo ships. Along Paterson Street are the telephone office, the tourist office and the small museum. The **Carriacou Historical Society Museum** ① *Mon-Fri 0930-1600, Sat 1000-1600*, has exhibits from Amerindian settlements in the island and from later periods in its history (there's a small shop for gifts, cards, books and local music). The people maintain a strong adherence to their African origins and the annual **Big Drum Dances**, which take place around Easter, as well as those performed at weddings, wakes, tombstone feasts, boat launches and community gatherings, are almost purely West African. French traditions are still evident at L'Esterre and there is a vigorous Scottish heritage, especially at **Windward**, where the people are much lighter skinned than elsewhere on the island. Windward used to be the centre for the craft of hand-built schooners but in recent years the boat builders have expanded to Tyrel Bay. Begun by a shipbuilder from Glasgow, the techniques are unchanged, but the white cedar used for the vessels is now imported from Grenada or elsewhere. The sturdy vessels are built and repaired without the use of power tools in the shade of the mangroves at the edge of the sea. To show the qualities of these local boats, the **Carriacou Regatta** was initiated in 1965, see page 824.

Just north of Hillsborough, the Anglican Rectory is in what remains of the **Beausejour Great House**, on a slight hill so that the master could watch his slaves in the sugar and cotton fields below. The house is now single storey, having lost the second floor in Hurricane Janet in 1955. At **Belair Park** by a nature centre and a forest reserve, you can see the ruins of the old government house. The house was stripped bare during the US invasion of Grenada but the park is now used to hold the annual Maroon Festival. On Hospital Hill, Belair, northeast of Hillsborough, there is an old sugar mill with stunning views. The tower is well preserved, but not much else is left. The slaves had to carry the sugar cane all the way up the hill. The best views, however, are from the **Princess Royal Hospital** itself, built on top of the hill in 1907-1909 because of an outbreak of malaria. The wind up on the hill is too strong for mosquitoes and it was also considered a nice, quiet spot for patients to recuperate. From here you get a fabulous view of Hillsborough, and most of the southern part of the island. A few old cannons were put here in 1948. Under the flamboyant tree in the courtyard there are some large, bored tortoises (*morrocoy*).

South of Hillsborough the road runs along the coast through Coconut Grove (Hurricane Lenny washed the palms away in 1999) and across the airport runway to Paradise Beach and L'Esterre. **Paradise Beach** is one of the nicest beaches on the island. The local painter, Canute Calliste (1914-2005), had his studio at **L'Esterre**. His naive style captured the scenes of Carriacou. The road then cuts across the peninsula to **Harvey Vale**, at Tyrrel Bay. Visitors should see the oyster beds at **Tyrrel Bay** where 'tree-oysters' grow on mangrove roots. Tyrrel Bay is an anchorage for yachts and the mangroves are a hurricane hole.

Carriacou

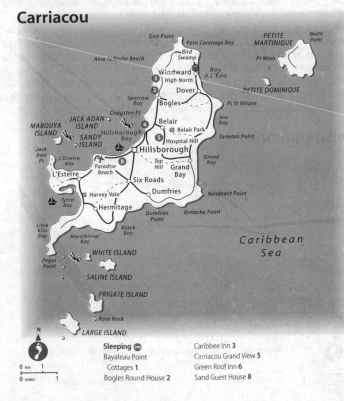

Sleeping
Bayaleau Point Cottages 1
Bogles Round House 2
Caribbee Inn 3
Carriacou Grand View 5
Green Roof Inn 6
Sand Guest House 8

Sandy Island is a tiny, low-lying atoll in Hillsborough Bay off Lauriston Point, a sand spit with a few palm trees for shade and a bit of scrub. Excellent swimming and snorkelling, take food and drink (boat from Paradise Beach, five minutes, or from Hillsborough EC$60, 30 minutes each way); pick a day when the islet is not swamped with cruise ship visitors. These small cruise ships offload 200 tourists to trample all round the islet and their anchor chains do untold damage to the coral. Yachts anchor here too and there are no mooring buoys in place yet. Alternatively, try **White Island**, a similar islet in Manchineel Bay off the south coast, ask for boats at **Cassada Bay Hotel**.

North of Hillsborough, **Bogles** is the most northerly village on the west side of the island and the end of the concrete road. From here 4WD or at least high clearance is necessary in the wet season. The Bogles emporium is an old building at the junction of the road to Windward, built in the mid-19th century by a merchant. Although desperately in need of renovation, the top floor overhang still has the original iron supports, denoting prosperity at the time of construction. A beautiful beach is **Anse La Roche**, which faces west and has a spectacular view across the strait to the mountains of rugged Union Island. Snorkelling is good, particularly among the rocks at the side. Take food and drink and no valuables of any sort; there are no facilities and few people. It is very easy to get lost walking to Anse La Roche beach and it is easier to take a water taxi there. It's very peaceful, watch the yachts rounding the headland on their way to anchorage; at night turtles swim ashore to lay their eggs.

This end of the island has the highest elevation, High North Peak, which rises to 955 ft and is part of a protected area. The **Kido Ecological Research Station** ① T/F4437936, kido-ywf@caribsurf.com, is near Anse La Roche and High North Park, where you can go birdwatching, hiking, cycling, whale watching and even volunteering for one of the conservation projects. However, you should contact them in advance as their pack of dogs deters uninvited visitors. There has been local opposition to their plans to convert the whole of the north of the island into a national reserve.

You can walk all round the north of the island. The British placed a cannon here in the 1780s. A path leads down (opposite a mauve-painted house) to the beach at Petit Carenage Bay, which has coarse, coral sand, good swimming and modest surf in some conditions. Returning to the road, Windward is a few minutes walk further on, a few shops and local bars. The Caribbean coast is spectacular in places and a walk from Windward to Dover, then following the coast road until it becomes a dirt road leading to Dumfries, is very pleasant and secluded.

Hillsborough

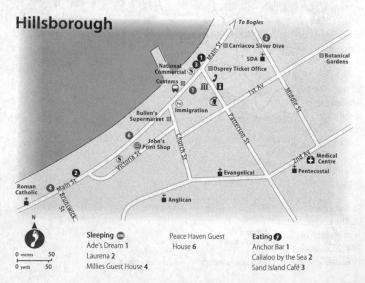

To Bogles

Carriacou Silver Dive
SDA
Botanical Gardens
National Commercial
Osprey Ticket Office
Customs
1st Av
Middle St
Immigration
Bullen's Supermarket
Patterson St
John's Print Shop
Church St
2nd Av
Medical Centre
Victoria St
Evangelical
Pentecostal
Roman Catholic
Main St
1st Brunswick St
Anglican

N

0 metres 50
0 yards 50

Sleeping 🛏
Ade's Dream **1**
Laurena **2**
Millies Guest House **4**

Peace Haven Guest House **6**

Eating 🍴
Anchor Bar **1**
Callaloo by the Sea **2**
Sand Island Café **3**

Petite Martinique → *Colour map 4, C4. Population: 1,000.*

Petite Martinique is the only offshore island from Carriacou on which people live, descended from French fishermen, Glaswegian shipwrights, pirates and slaves. Its area is 486 acres, rising to a small, volcanic peak, and only a very small channel separates it from Petit St Vincent, where many people work at the resort. The principal legal occupations are boatbuilding and fishing, but for generations the islanders have been involved in smuggling and they are noticeably more prosperous than their neighbours. There was excitement in 1997 when the government proposed to build a house for 12 Coast Guard personnel in the campaign against drug smuggling. Half the population turned out to demonstrate against the arrival of government surveyors and clashed with armed police and the Special Services Unit. There is a dock with fuel, water, ice and other yachting supplies. Water taxis are available from Windward on Carriacou. The *Osprey Express*, the other ferries and the mailboat call here after Hillsborough coming from St George's.

● Sleeping

Hotel rooms are subject to a 10% service charge and 8% tax on accommodation, food and beverages. Grenada is particularly well served with good, mid-range, small hotels and guesthouses. Most of the hotels are still small enough to be comfortable and friendly, catering for individual travellers, package tours and luxury getaways. The majority are in the Grand Anse area. In St George's there are more guesthouses than hotels. Hurricane damage in 2004 meant that many hotels had to close for several months for repairs. Some of these took the opportunity to upgrade and improve their facilities, reopening after this book went to press. Only a couple of hotels were expected to remain shut until 2006.

Homestays are another option
Homestays Grenada, T4445845, www.homestaysgrenada.com, organize all sorts of accommodation, living with families around the island in their homes or in self-catering apartments or villas, many hosts are retired, returned from living abroad. Prices from US$30 single, plus 5% tax, including cleaning and linen change and may include breakfast and one other meal, airport transfers if staying 4 nights or more.

St George's *p802, map p803*
LL The Lodge, on the Morne Jaloux ridge ½ mile south of Forts Matthew and Frederick, T4402330, www.thelodgegrenada.com. House dates from 1920s, built on site of older place, lots of character, high ceilings, old style plantation house windows, wooden furniture made of blue mahoe. Damage from hurricane Ivan gradually being repaired along with ongoing restoration of entire building. Strictly vegan full-board accommodation, Intimate, with only 2 rooms, luxuriously furnished, 25-m chemical-free lane pool, panoramic views of sunrise, sunset and mountains from garden terrace and veranda looking through spectacular passion fruit vine. Great food using organic produce from hillside garden, chocolate puddings using Grenada Chocolate Factory delights. The house was once the Venezuelan embassy and when the Americans invaded they didn't recognize the flag and thought it was Cuban; gunshot holes are still visible on the veranda.
A Tropicana, Lagoon Rd, T4401586, www.tropicanainn.com. Double and triple rooms, pleasant, fridge, TV, a/c, balcony, small but adequate bathroom, high ceilings, view over water (except for triple room overlooking rear), some interconnect, nicest rooms on top floor, room service, restaurant and bar at street level, convenient for buses.
B Lazy Lagoon, Lagoon Rd, T4435209, www.grenadaexplorer.com/lazylagoon. 6 basic wooden cabins with kitchenettes, fridge and shower, opening onto balcony with view of Lagoon and St George's, very close to Port Louis development. Bar on site, see below. A good budget option.
D St Ann's Guest House, Paddock, beyond

Botanic Gardens (some distance from centre), T4402717, info@stannsguesthouse.com. Single or double rooms, shared or private bathroom, basin in room, fan, very thin walls, no more than partitions, a bit difficult to sleep because of dogs and roosters, take ear plugs.

Southwest Grenada p806, map p801

LL Calabash, Lance aux Épines, T4444334, www.calabashhotel.com. Winner of a prestigious Golden Fork award for quality of food and hospitality and now notable for having a **Rhodes Restaurant**, Gary Rhodes' only restaurant outside the UK, see below. Suites and villas around an elegant central lawn with palm trees and flowering bushes leading down to the sea. This is one of the oldest hotels on the island with one of the loveliest settings and good beach. Very comfortable, spacious, breakfast served on suites' large balconies, complimentary afternoon tea, canapés in your room at 1800. Pleasant and unpretentious, excellent service. Watersports, tennis, fitness room, computer/TV room.

LL Laluna, Morne Rouge, T4390001, www.laluna.com. The most expensive on the island when it opened in 2000, 16, 1- or 2-bedroom colour-washed cottages on 10 acres of hillside and beach at the end of the bay, private, height of luxury, open Italian/Indonesian minimalist style with Italian linens, drapes, furniture from Bali, shower with sea view, bath goodies from monastery in Italian Alps, Wi-Fi internet connection, private plunge pools on veranda. The main buildings on the beach are wooden and cement with thatched roofs around the main pool, dining room serving Italian and Thai food. Yoga, pilates, tai chi, meditation and massage on your veranda, complimentary mountain bikes, snorkelling, hobie cats and kayaks. children under 10 not welcome in high season.

LL Maca Bana Villas, Point Salines, T4395355, www.macabana.com. Perched on top of hill looking all along coastline to St George's, charming 1-2 bedroom villas, spacious and comfortable with state-of-the-art kitchen and open plan living/dining area leading onto expansive veranda with hot tub and sunbeds, all well-designed and welcoming. Pretty

gardens attract birds and butterflies while lizards clean up any unwanted insects. Walking distance from airport, where you can catch a bus. Activities organized including cookery class with chef from Aquarium restaurant below, painting class with owner/artist Rebecca on river bank, beach or waterfall, massages, reiki and spa treatments with visiting masseur. Short walk downhill to beach and restaurant, see Eating.

LL Spice Island Beach Resort, Grand Anse, T4444423, www.spiceislandbeachresort.com. Reopened end-2005 after a complete renovation and upgrade into a luxury 5-star all-inclusive resort for couples and families. Cool white buildings with white roofs, warm colours for interior furnishings and bed covers. 64 very private and romantic suites of varying sizes, amazing bathrooms, on the beach with view to St George's and cruise ships, or in the garden with a sea view, all with flat screen TV, DVD player, double whirlpool bath, Italian linen and armfuls of bathroom goodies. Jamissa's spa and fitness centre for a range of treatments, bright, white and sterile. Also an activity centre for children, the **Nutmeg Pod**, although children under 5 are not accepted in winter. Good food, own kitchen garden, self-sufficient in some organic veg.

LL-AL Allamanda Beach Resort, Grand Anse, T4440095, www.allamandaresort.com. 50 spacious rooms on 3 floors in blocks on narrow plot with beach access, rather dated style but good location, TV, fridge, small bathroom, bar with TV and sofas, restaurant by pool.

LL-AL Blue Horizons, Grand Anse, T4444316, www.grenadabluehorizons.com. Set back from beach, short walk, use of facilities at Spice Island, the sister hotel on beach. 32 tastefully decorated rooms in muted colours, 6 studios and 26 suites with kitchenettes, some of which interconnect, lounge with TV and books, Wi-Fi internet access, business centre, parking, pool, pleasant grounds with intact mature, tall trees and palms, **La Belle Créole** restaurant is good.

LL-AL The Flamboyant, Grand Anse, T4444247, www.flamboyant.com. 60 units in standard or superior rooms, suites and cottages, at the south end of Grand Anse on hillside, lovely views, steep walk down to beach from upper rooms with best views, but transport for people with mobility problems to restaurant and beach, quite a walk to bus stop. The road goes through the property with gym, pool, restaurant and late-night sports bar at sea level and rooms above the road. Dive Grenada on site.

LL-AL True Blue Bay Resort and Marina, True Blue Bay, T4438783, www.truebluebay.com. Small, intimate, helpful and friendly, British-Mexican owners, large rooms, suites, cottages and apartments, all colourfully painted, kitchenettes, a/c, fan, wireless internet access, sea view, balconies with hammocks, child friendly, high chairs and play equipment, infinity pool with sandy shore and delightful fence of colourful pretend chattel houses around it, gym, spa/beauty treatments, car hire, dock facilities, boat charter available, dive shop on site, kayaks, hobie cats, restaurant over water, good food, Mexican specialities and separate bar, **Dodgy Dock**, see below.

LL-A Coral Cove Cottages, Lance aux Épines, T4444422, www.coralcovecottages.com. Opened 6 weeks before the Revolution, still under same ownership. Several, lovely, breezy, well-equipped cottages, 1 or 2 bedrooms, also apartments, beautiful view of Atlantic coast, at the end of the road, 15 mins' walk to restaurants and minimarket, own beach and jetty with gazebo at the end, good snorkelling, shallow water, pool, tennis, very private, great for kids, attracts lots of repeat visitors.

L-AL Lance aux Epines Cottages, Lance aux Épines, T4444565, www.laecottages.com. 7 cottages and 4 apartments set apart from each other in 3 acres of gardens right on the beach in walking distance of several restaurants and minimart, next to Calabash. Full kitchen, staff will cook if you shop, spacious rooms, quarry tiled floors, slightly old-fashioned wooden furniture, built in 1970s and still under same family ownership. Great for families, beach toys for kids, kayaks, hobie cats, cots and highchairs, babysitting.

L-A Jenny's Place, Silver Sands, Grand Anse, T4395186, www.jennysplacegrenada.com. At the northern, uncrowded end of the beach with restaurant on waterfront, 6 studios and suites, sleep 2-4, huge rooms, kitchenettes, high ceilings, big bathrooms with bathtub and shower over, balcony, TV,

a/c, fans, breakfast 0830-1000 included, no charge for room service, excellent value for location, comfortable, laid-back and interesting fellow guests. Friendly hosts, gracious Grenadian Jenny (former Miss World) and British Shaun are happy to arrange water taxis, watersports, tours and other activities. Get the bus into town, walk along the beach for other restaurants, everything is handy and convenient.

L-A Monmot, Saaman Drive, Lance aux Épines, T4393408, www.monmothotel.com. Under new management in 2006, locally-run, upgraded and improved. Rooms around central small pool, studios with kitchen, little patio area at the back overlooking the bush with picnic tables. Interconnecting rooms for families, rather dark, a/c essential, TV, safety box, short walk to beach, beside Calabash.

L-B Siesta, Grand Anse, T4444646, www.siestahotel.com. Refurbished after Ivan, all new in 2006, bright and white, functional, comfortable, convenient, friendly service. Variety of rooms, efficiencies, studios and 1-2 bedroom apartments, all with TV, phone, a/c, safe box, iron, Wi-Fi internet access. No restaurant but breakfast is provided, not on beach but only short walk, close to shops.

AL-A Gem Holiday Beach, Morne Rouge Bay, T4444224, www.gembeachresort.com. Rooms, suites with kitchen, a/c, TV, iron, balcony, good but not luxurious, comfortable living room with dining table, 2-bedroom apartment has double and single bed in each room, old but adequate kitchen units. Beach bar and restaurant 'Sur la Mer' on beach, reasonable food, internet room, pool room, roof terrace for quiz nights and other activities, popular with guests, medical students and locals on Thu nights, also Fantazia 2001 night club attached.

AL-A Wave Crest Holiday Apartments, Grand Anse, T4444116, www.grenadawavecrest.com. On the main road from the airport, just before the shops and supermarket at Grand Anse, 10-min walk to beach, no 1 bus into St George's stops outside. 1-2 bedroom apartments with reasonably well-equipped kitchens, choice of bed sizes, all renovated after Ivan, ocean view worth the few dollars extra. Dabs Car Rentals, www.dabscarrentals.com, run by general manager of hotel.

A Fox Inn, on main road to airport, T4444123, www.foxinn-grenada.com. Modern concrete block painted orange, 300m to beach, no sea view, 22 rooms, newly painted, light and bright, TV, a/c, phone, table and chairs, wardrobe, small but good bathroom, hairdryer, iron and board, all better than it looks from the outside. Conference room for weddings and functions, hotel used for shows, concerts and parties, including a daybreak party once a month lasting until 0900.

Northern Grenada *p808, map p801*
AL-A Almost Paradise, Sauteurs, T4420608, www.almost-paradise-grenada.com. Simple, wooden rooms and cottages of varying sizes in delightful hillside garden setting with an amazing view to the Grenadines and the nicest place to stay this end of the island. Outdoor shower, balconies with hammocks, kitchen corner in living room, colourful bedrooms, high ceilings, fans, solar power, small dark sand beach at bottom of hill, links with local boatmen for tours to Sandy Island, massages. Restaurant, see below, breakfast and dinner for guests US$35pp.
B-C Morne Fendue Plantation House, T4429330, caribbean@spiceisle.com, see page 808. Good base for exploring the north, including Bathway beach and the Carib jump at Sauteurs. 8 rooms in new block with wonderful views. Evening meals on request.

East coast Grenada *p808, map p801*
LL Bel Air Plantation Villas, St David's harbour, T4446305, www.belairplantation.com. Luxury villas and cottages built in traditional style and painted pretty pastel colours, set along the cliffside in gardens with lovely sea views. Very comfortable, excellent furnishings, good kitchens and bathrooms, veranda and pretty private garden. Shuttle to La Sagesse beach, kayaks for exploring coastline, grocery store 0800-1600. Octagonal **Water's Edge** restaurant and bar has seating on the veranda or on waterfront patio, breezy, shady, lovely view, fresh fish, home grown produce, happy hour 1600-1900 bar menu of substantial snacks, upstairs lounge has 360° views, great for sunset watching. Quiet and peaceful, very remote.
LL-AL Petit Bacaye Cottage Hotel, on bay

of same name, Westerhall, T/F4432902, www.petitbacaye.com. Very desirable place to stay, romantic hideaway on beach. 5 thatched cottages of different sizes, 1-2 bedrooms, 40 m from the water with lovely sea views, no TV or radio, rates include tax and service. Also **Plantation House Suite** with vast bedroom and veranda, and the **Spice House**, 2 bedrooms, great deck but not suitable for small children, both looking through the palms to the sea. Colourful restaurant on the lawn by the beach for breakfast, lunch and dinner, mostly seafood, fisherman call daily with fish and lobster, reef and own bird sanctuary islet (egret roost) 200 m offshore in shallow water, jeep and guide hire arranged, another sandy beach round the bluff.
L-AL La Sagesse, T4446458, www.lasagesse.com (see page 833). Former residence of the late Lord Brownlow, a cousin of the Queen,marvellous location, although design leaves something to be desired. 12 rooms, some of which are in the 'manor house' and others built alongside beside the water although not all can see the sea. Beautiful setting on a sandy bay lined with coconut palms and cliffs at one end. Open-air restaurant and beach bar, children friendly. Hiking trails over headland to neighbouring beaches for snorkelling. Buses to St George's pass the end of the road.
B-C Grenada Rainbow Inn, Grenville, St Andrew's, T4427714, http://spiceisle.com/rainbowinn. Run by Neitha Williams (Aunty Nits) and her daughter Yvonne Williams, 15 rooms or apartments (sleep 4), with or without a/c, rooms vary, old wooden furniture, some 4-poster beds, no door on bathroom in alcove, no smoking in rooms, some have small balcony, tired appearance, buses stop outside, organic food, fresh juices, credit cards accepted.
B-C Sam's Inn, Dunfermline, T/F4427853, samsinn@caribsurf.com. 10 rooms with double and single bed, a/c or fans, and 3 2-bedroom apartments in modern block, some with TV, good-sized bathrooms have wardrobe in them, large balcony overlooking road, no smoking, restaurant and bar, country setting, view of Pearl's Airport, small store close by, Mrs Ellen Sam is very friendly owner.

Camping

Camping is not encouraged as there are no facilities, but it is permitted in the **Grand Étang National Park** and in schools and church grounds on **Carriacou**.

Carriacou *p812, map p813*

Out of season the island is quiet and not all the hotels are open.

LL-L Caribbeen Inn, Prospect, T4437380, macaws@spiceisle.com. Lovely but isolated setting on promontory above the sea, north of Bogles, renovated 2005, spacious and romantic rooms, all different, 4-poster beds with mosquito nets, hammocks on balcony or veranda, fans, thick gardens all around, home to imported macaws, lizards and biting insects, take repellent, path down to rocky bay for swimming and snorkelling. Candlelit dinners at restaurant which serves French Creole food.

L-AL Laurena, Middle St, Hillsborough, T4438759, www.hotellaurena.com. New, central location, a/c rooms and apartments with 2 rooms for the handicapped, breakfast included, TV, phone, fitness centre, computer facilities, conference rooms.

AL-A Bayaleau Point Cottages, Windward, T/F4437984, www.carriacoucottages.com. 4 lovely, well-equipped and colourful cottages, clean, own little beach, good snorkelling, owners Ulla and Dave Goldhill are helpful, friendly, dinner available several nights a week, good for children, lots of Labrador dogs, Wi-Fi internet access.

AL-A Carriacou Grand View, Belair Rd, overlooking Hillsborough, T4436348, www.carriacougrandview.com. 14-room new apartment hotel high up on the hill, breezy, fans, TV, restaurant, bar, pool, good views.

AL-A Green Roof Inn, on hillside overlooking sea, 10 mins north of Hillsborough, just past the desalination plant, T/F4436399, www.greenroofinn.com. Swedish owned, 4 double rooms with private bathroom, 1 single room which can be added to one of the doubles to make a suite, also cottage in the garden with kitchenette, extra beds available, mosquito nets, fans, airport/jetty transfers, sandy area in front of hotel for swimming, day trips arranged. Tue-Sun for dinner, lunch on request. Restaurant has spectacular views,

roof, but no walls, mainly seafood, lobster, barracuda, swordfish, Caribbean ingredients, European preparation.

AL-C Millies Guest House, Main St, Hillsborough, T4437310, millies@ spiceisle.com. Room or 1-, 2- or 3-bedroomed apartments with kitchen, bathroom/shower, fans, a/c, ocean view. Also **Millie's Yacht Charter** for exploring other islands.

A Bogles Round House, Bogles, T/F4437841, www.boglesroundhouse.com. 3 cottages, self-contained, sleep 2-3, comfortable, located away from the main tourist areas, path down to sea. Now run by Roxanne and Phil, a British couple. Restaurant and bar serving local and European food and drinks. Reservations needed for large groups.

B-D Ade's Dream, T4437317, adesdea@ spiceisle.com, Main St, Hillsborough. 23 rooms or apartments, close to dock, well equipped, own kitchenette or share large kitchen, clean and popular, supermarket downstairs open daily, restaurant across the road with sea frontage.

C Peace Haven Guest House, south of pier on seafront, Main St, Hillsborough, T4437475. Rooms on 1st floor large, each with kitchenette, fridge, fan, contact Lucille Atkins.

C-D Sand Guest House, T4437100, between Hillsborough and the airport. Quiet, basic but clean, nice beach across road, 11 rooms, with or without shared kitchen and bathroom, or apartment.

Petite Martinique *p815*

B-C Melodie's Guest House, T4439052, www.spiceisle.com/melodies. 10 rooms, some with balconies, ceiling fans, shared kitchen, restaurant downstairs, on the beach, tours and watersports offered.

● Eating

Tax of 8% and service of 10% is usually added to the bill

Grenada's cooking is generally very good. *Lambi* (conch) is very popular, as is *callaloo* soup (made with dasheen leaves), *souse* (a sauce made from pig's feet), pepper pot and pumpkin pie. The national dish is 'oildown', a stew of salt meat, breadfruit, onion, carrot, celery, dasheen and dumplings, cooked slowly in coconut milk. There is a wide choice of seafood, and of vegetables. Goat and wild meat (armadillo, iguana, manicou) can be sampled. Nutmeg features in many local dishes, try nutmeg jelly for breakfast, ground nutmeg comes on top of rum punches. Of the many fruits and fruit dishes, try stewed golden apple, or soursop ice cream.

Rum punches are excellent. Be sure to try the local sea-moss drink (a mixture of vanilla, algae and milk). There are 3 makes of rum, whose superiority is disputed by the islanders, *Clark's Court*, *River Antoine* and *Westerhall Plantation Rum*, made by Westerhall Distilleries. All 3 can be visited for a tour and sampling of rum and products for sale. Several readers have endorsed *Westerhall Plantation Rum* for its distinct flavour and aroma. The term 'grog', for rum, is supposed to originate in Grenada: taking the first letters of 'Georgius Rex Old Grenada', which was stamped on the casks of rum sent back to England. Grenada Breweries brew *Carib Lager*, *Guinness* and non-alcoholic malt beers.

St George's *p802, map p803*

₮₮₮-₮₮ BB's Crabback Caribbean Restaurant, Progress House, at the end of the Carenage, T4357058, www.bbscrabback.com. Open for lunch until 1600 Mon-Fri and Sat in season. Local seafood dishes and curry mutton. Owned by Brian Benjamin, who has a restaurant of the same name in west London.

₮₮₮-₮₮ Ocean Grill, on the Carenage near the Library, next to BB's, T4409747, jrshereen@hotmail.com. 1100-2200. Excellent location, upstairs and over the water, good view of all the boats in harbour, lunch specials US$13-20, soups, burgers of many varieties, seafood and meat dishes.

₮₮₮-₮ Patrick's, Lagoon Rd, T4400364. 1100-1400, 1700-2200 or until last guest leaves. Fixed price dinner of 20 different dishes and dessert. A huge variety and interesting combinations of local foods, breadfruit salad and green papaya salad are outstanding while you can also be offered stir fry rabbit, green papaya in cheese sauce, cou-cou, tannia cakes with shrimps, oildown with coconut cream, many dishes you may

never have tried before. Patrick is very entertaining, high camp. Very popular, friendly and sociable atmosphere, popular with groups.

₮₮ Nutmeg, on the Carenage above the **Sea Change Book Store**, T4402539. Mon-Sat 0800-2300, Sun 1600-2300. Delicious local dishes and its own famous rum punch, very popular, breakfast, snacks, lunch, sandwiches, rotis, soups, salads, get a table by the wide open windows overlooking the Carenage and the boats in the harbour.

₮₮-₮ Creole Shack, on the Carenage, T4357422. Mon-Thu 1100-2000, Fri, Sat 1100-after 2400 for karaoke nights. Local food and popular at lunchtime with long queues, specials such as curry lambie, stew oxtail and salt fish souse, oildown and fresh juices.

₮₮-₮ Tropicana, on the Lagoon, T4401586, tropicana@caribsurf.com. 0730-2400. Popular, Chinese and local food, good, entrées from EC$10-45, excellent egg rolls and rotis, vast portions. Seating inside or out on covered patio, barbecues, reservations recommended in high season, also takeaway. Accommodation, see above.

₮ Deyna's, Melville St, opposite waterfront bus station, T4406795. Mon-Sat 0800-2100, Sun 1000-1600. New, modern, good local food at local prices, and lots of it, rotis, crowded at lunch, separate queue for takeaway meals. Also good place to stop for a drink as a break from shopping or sightseeing, try sorrel, mauby or passionfruit.

₮ Pitch Pine Bar, Esplanade, T4401976. Fun place on the waterfront for a drink or meal, curry mutton, fish broth.

Southwest Grenada *p806, map p801*

₮₮₮ Rhodes Restaurant, Calabash Hotel, T4444334. 0700-2230. Gary Rhodes' only restaurant outside the UK but always supervised by one of his top chefs to ensure consistent quality, using Rhodes' recipes and local ingredients. Open-air dining, entertainment most nights, complimentary transport available.

₮₮₮-₮ Aquarium Restaurant, Point Salines Beach, T4441410, www.aquarium-grenada.com. Tue-Sun 1000-late, dinner reservations requested. Wed specials, Sun barbeque, showers, toilets, snorkelling offshore, great location, good food, lobster, fish, steak, sandwiches, live music and buffet from 1900 first Sat in month. Very popular, particularly at weekends with families on the beach, same ownership as Maca Bana Villas.

♉♉-♉ **Beach House**, close to Rex, T4444455, beachhouse@caribsurf.com. Mon-Sat 1100-2230, reservations preferred, can get water taxi from Carenage. Very pretty, open air, in gardens on the beach, white cotton tablecloths and pillow cases for chairs. Good food, lots of oriental influences with sushi and satay, fish, steak and other meats, also good kids menu and yummy desserts. Ask for the daily specials, staff sometimes forget to tell you.

♉♉♉-♉ **Coconut Beach**, Grand Anse, T4444644, coconutbeach@spiceisle.com. 1230-2200, closed Tue. North of vendor's market, easy walk along the beach from the hotels. French Creole restaurant, jalousie windows opened to let in the breeze, colourful, painted purple, green, orange, picnic tables on beach or more formal seating indoors. Lots of fish and seafood, plenty of lobster, also steak, chicken and vegetarian dishes. Lunch time options of sandwiches, crêpes, omelettes, salads, local desserts such as coconut pie or opt for crêpes au chocolat.

♉♉♉-♉ **Red Crab**, Lance aux Épines, T4444424, crab@spiceisle.com. 1100-1400, 1800-2300. Closed Sun. Scottish-run, indoor and outdoor dining. Excellent local seafood and, fabulous steak dinner, also soups, salads, sandwiches, burgers and catch of the day for lunch, live music Mon, Fri in season, darts Wed nights.

♉♉♉-♉ **Turning Point Diner**, Silver Sands, Grand Anse, T4395186, www.jennysplace grenada.com. 1100-2200, closed Wed. At very northern point of beach, seafront bistro right on the water gets its name because people walk or jog along the beach and then turn round to go back at this point. Austrian chef, variety of food, menu changes frequently, soups, pasta, salad, burgers, sandwiches for lunch or chicken curry, steak au poivre, catch of the day, pork tenderloin, sushi, Caribbean brunch on Sun, all you can eat. Owners Jenny (former Miss World) and Shaun are friendly and enthusiastic hosts. See the photos of Jenny's glory days on the wall. Accommodation, see above.

♉♉-♉ **Boots Cuisine**, Grand Anse Valley Rd, Woodlands, T4442151. Mon-Sat 1100-1400, 1830-2200. Reservations required or you will have to wait a long time. Ruby and Roland (Boots) McSween run this small, delightful family restaurant serving excellent local food, melt-in-the-mouth lambi, delicious callaloo, lamb roti, curried chicken, stew rabbit, grill fish, lobster, baked provisions and stew peas, must leave room for carambola pie and banana ice cream. Coming from Grand Anse Valley on Woodlands Rd, it is just before Clarkes Court on the right, small sign, rustic, open air dining under a roof, surrounded by plants.

♉♉-♉ **Fish 'n' Chick**, at Sugar Mill roundabout, T4444132. Barbecue, fried and grilled fish and chicken, very local, fast food and takeaway, soaks up alcohol at night.

♉♉-♉ **La Boulangerie**, Le Marquis Mall complex above Grand Anse Beach, T4441131. Mon-Sat 0830-2130, Sun 0900-2130. Good for breakfast with croissants, Danish pastries or full American, coffee and freshly squeezed juice, lunch and dinner of pizza and pasta, salads, sandwiches, Italian ice cream.

♉♉-♉ **Roger's**, Island View building, next to Rumours, Woburn, T4435962. Mon-Sat, open from 0800, lunch 1130 onwards, kitchen closes 2230, bar 2300. Large building over the water looking towards Calivigny island, sit outside on terrace or indoors at bench seating, like a diner, or at tables in centre of room. Bar serves good local juices, restaurant offers soups, crab backs, lambie, salads, pasta, sandwiches, burgers, seafood with catch of the day, roti, steak, chicken, lobster and kids meals.

♉♉-♉ **Rumours**, Woburn, T4435650, rumoursgrenada@yahoo.com. 1800-2300, closed Jun. Down by the water looking across to Calivigny island, 2 dining rooms, one a little more formal and quieter than the other. Vegetarian dishes and seafood, all cooked to order, no menu, veg lasagne, pasta, soya dishes, squashes, cantaloupes, home grown produce from own farm, very popular with students.

♉ **University Kitchen**, Grand Anse. Right on the beach, cheap meals open to all, great for lunch. Choose your meat or fish and it comes with typical accompaniments: rice and peas, macaroni, provisions, salada, potato salad. Try the local juices, lime, sorrel, passion fruit etc. Eat at benches with sea view or takeaway. Due to be moved to build a resort, so make the most of it now.

♦♦-♦ Almost Paradise, Sauteurs, T4420608, www.almost-paradise-grenada.com. Tue-Sun 1200-1700, dinner by reservation only. Lovely location on hillside overlooking the Grenadines, run by Kate (Canadian) and Uwe (German) Baumann, who use all the local produce and make their own rum liqueurs as *digestifs*. Great place for a lunch stop in an island tour, fish, shrimp, soup, salads, home made bread and cocktails.

East coast Grenada *p808, map p801*
♦♦♦-♦♦ La Sagesse (see page 833), T4446458 for reservations which are recommended, especially for dinner. Breakfast, lunch and dinner. Fresh lobster, grilled tuna, outdoor restaurant, beautiful location, walk it off afterwards, good hiking over the mountain, US$30 for return transport, lunch, guided nature walk with exotic fruit tasting, dinner packages available, entrées EC$15-50.

Carriacou *p812, map p813*
The market near the pier in Hillsborough comes alive on Mon when the produce is brought in. 'Jack Iron' rum (180° proof) is a local hazard, it is so strong that ice sinks in it. It is distilled in Barbados but bottled in Carriacou; it costs around EC$10 per bottle and is liberally dispensed on all high days and holidays (fairly liberally on other days too). Some basic local bar/restaurants often run out of food quite early or close in the evenings, check if they will be open for dinner. Finding cheap meals can be difficult at weekends. Several small bars and restaurants in Tyrrel Bay do takeaways and other services such as emails and faxes for visiting yachts. For hotel restaurants, see Sleeping, above.

♦♦-♦ Callaloo by the Sea, Main St, Hillsborough, on the beach, T4438004. Daily, lunch and dinner. Probably the best restaurant in town, good drinks, nice veranda overlooking sea with view of dock, breezy, good for a swim before lunch, popular, entrées EC$16-50, plenty of choice, good value despite upmarket appearance.
♦♦-♦ Hardwood Bar, Paradise/L'Esterre Beach, http://hardwood.carriacou.biz. Open for lunch and dinner, snacks, drinks, good beach bar, menu includes catch of the day and other seafood such as lobster, also

chicken and roti. Snorkelling gear for rent, water taxi service to Sandy Island or other places.

♦♦-♦ Poivre et Sel, above **Alexis Supermarket**, Tyrrel Bay, difficult to find, T4438390, VHF 16. Lunch and dinner. Excellent French food, French chef, try the lobster crêpe, a nice change from West Indian, casual but lively meeting place for the local French community.
♦♦-♦ Turtle Dove, Tyrrel Bay, T4438322, VHF16. Lunch 1200-1400, dinner from 1900 by reservation. Pizzeria, bar, internet, Italian food, run by Luciana, Daniela and Scarlett.
♦ Anchor Bar, Main St, Hillsborough. Lunch and dinner. Owned by Bill Paterson, at the junction with Patterson St, rum shop facing the street but if you go round the side passage you find a café on a balcony overlooking the sea, cheap and cheerful, chicken, conch and fish meals, chicken wings and a cold beer make a good lunch/snack.
♦ E & A's, very close to the pier, Hillsborough. Lunch and dinner. Good local cooking, ask for a large plate of vegetables.
♦ Sand Island Café, Hillsborough, T4436189. Mon-Sat lunch and dinner. Set over the water, Grenadian chef, Jenson, seafood and pizzas.
♦ Scraper's, Tyrrel Bay, T4437403, scrapers@caribsurf.com. Lunch and dinner. Very good lunch but not much atmosphere, Mr Scraper and his family are very hospitable. Also 6 rooms in cottages (**C**) with or without a/c.

The ice cream parlour just round Tyrrel Bay after **Scraper's** is recommended.

Petite Martinique *p815*
♦♦-♦ Palm Beach Restaurant and Bar, T4439103, VHF 16. Mon-Sat 1000-2200, Sun 1400-2200. Seafood, free water taxi service for those anchored in Petit St Vincent.

❶ Bars and clubs

Grenada *p800, map p801*
Hotels provide evening entertainment, including dancing, steel band and calypso music, limbo, etc. There are few discos and nightclubs outside the hotels and low season can be very quiet.
Bananas, True Blue Rd, T4444662, www.bananasgrenada.com. Mon-Fri 1200-late, Sat, Sun 1600-late, happy hour

1730-1900, 2400-0100, kitchen closes 2230. Bar and restaurant with party nights, usually EC$30 entrance including all drinks, so its a drunken night. Gets going after midnight but open for a quiet drink before then. Daily lunch specials and special students' menu with buffalo wings and burgers. EC$5 cover charge for bar Fri, Sat, free other nights. Events have different entries. Student night Wed, Latin night Thu with instructors.

Dodgy Dock, at True Blue Bay, T4391377, moorings available. Daily 1500-2300, happy hour 1700-1800. Built from debris picked up after Ivan, good cocktails and bar snacks or move on to the restaurant at the **True Blue Bay**. Lounge chairs under tent roof, some more comfortable than others, or plastic tables and chairs in the open air. Pleasant for sundowner or after dinner drink.

Fantazia 2001 Cultural Centre, Gem Holiday Beach Resort, Morne Rouge Beach, T4442288. 2400-dawn. Doesn't get going until after midnight, even midweek. Circular dance floor with seating along the sides, mixed clientele depending on the night, funky, soca, fast calypso, reggae, hot and steamy, best night is Wed when they have old soul and reggae – 'blast from the past', Fri ladies free before midnight, gents US$4, Sat cabaret night.

Gouave Fish Fry Gouave. Fri night. Lots of stalls selling different seafood with a variety of recipes, shrimp kebabs, baked fish in garlic sauce, stir fry lobster with noodles, fried snapper, jack etc, grilled lobster. Walk around and look at everything before you make your choice. Popular, busy and crowded. Live entertainment at one end of the street, including drum music and folk dancing. Goes on quite late but the best food runs out so best to get there before 2130.

Grenada Yacht Club, St George's, T4403050, www.grenadayachtclub.com. Sun, Mon 1000-2200, Tue-Thu, Sat 1000-2300, Fri 1000-0100. Yachtsmen and others welcome, great place to sit and watch the boats entering the lagoon (and see if they are paying attention to the channel markers or run aground).

Horny Baboon/Lazy Lagoon, Lagoon Rd next to Foodland and close to Patrick's. Happy hour 1700-1800. Rustic bar, small but enough room for dancing on party nights,

popular with locals and ex-pats. A few basic rooms, see above.

Kudos Bar & Grill, L'Anse aux Épines, just before Red Crab, T4441250, kudos@spiceisle.com. Mon-Sat 1300-0200, Sun 1800-late. Fri karaoke, nightclub party nights, big screen, popular with medical students and others at weekends, live music in season.

🎭 Entertainment

Grenada *p800, map p801*
Cinemas
Deluxe Cinema, Grenville, T4426200.
Reno Cinema, off Lagoon Rd, next to Tropicana, T4405368. Movies nightly at 2030, EC$5 for double feature.

Theatres
Marryshow Folk Theatre in the University of the West Indies building on Tyrrel St. Has concerts, plays and special events.

⚜ Festivals and events

Grenada *p800, map p801*
Late Jan Grenada Sailing Festival is held over 5 days, T4404809, www.grenadasailingfestival.com.
7 Feb Independence Day.
Mar/Apr Easter is a time for lots of events, both religious and otherwise. There is a **kite flying competition** at the old Pearls Airport, with music, food and drink, and other activities. At Easter there are **yacht races** and a **power boat regatta** off Grand Anse as well as the Petite Martinique 2-day **regatta**.
May or Jun Grenada's **Spice Jazz Festival** with lots of music, cooking, sports. Concerts are mostly held in the big hotels, such as the **Rex Grenadian**, or at the stadium, and tickets are quite expensive although a season ticket is better value. It doesn't yet have the reputation and popularity of St Lucia's jazz festival, but it is growing.
Late Jun Throughout the island, but especially at Gouyave, the **Fisherman's Birthday** is celebrated (the feast of saints Peter and Paul); it involves the blessing of nets and boats, followed by dancing, feasting and boat races.
Jul Grenada Summer Regatta is a 4-day affair, with beach parties and other activities.

Early Aug The Rainbow City Cultural Festival takes place in Grenville over the first weekend of Aug, and goes on for about a week. **Mid-Aug** Carnival, second weekend in Aug, although some preliminary events and competitions are held from the last week in Jul, with calypsos, steel bands, dancing, competitions, shows and plenty of drink. The Sun night celebrations, **Dimanche Gras**, continue into Mon, J'Ouvert; Djab Djab Molassi, who represent devils, smear themselves and anyone else (especially the smartly dressed) with black grease. On Mon a carnival pageant is held on the stage at Queen's Park and on Tue the bands parade through the streets of St George's to the Market Square and a giant party ensues. For information on playing Mas with a band contact Derrick Clouden, T4402551, or Wilbur Thomas, T4403545, of the **Grenada Band Leaders Association**. During Carnival it is difficult to find anywhere to stay and impossible to hire a car unless booked well in advance.

Nov Every month the **Grenada Yacht Club** (T4406826, www.grenadayachtclub.com) holds races off Grand Anse and there is usually an end-of-hurricane season yacht race at the end of Nov.

Carriacou *p812, map p813*
Feb Carriacou celebrates its **carnival** at the traditional Lenten time, unlike Grenada. It is not spectacular but it is fun and there is a good atmosphere. An interesting feature is the **Shakespeare Mas**, when participants, or 'pierrots' (*paywos*) dress up and recite from Shakespeare's plays. If they forget their lines or get something wrong, they are thumped by the others with a bull whip, so their costumes require a lot of padding and they wear a special cape which covers the back of the head. It is very competitive and carnival has traditionally been very violent, with battles between villages or between north and south of the island, led by their carnival 'kings'. The police have in the past frequently had to restore peace.

End-Apr 3-day **Maroon Music Festival**, a recent revival of traditional customs held in the historic Belair Park. You can see a display of the **Big Drum Nation Dance**, string band music and quadrille dancing, as well as more modern entertainment such as reggae.

There are also stalls selling local food, cultural and art exhibitions, www.grenadines.net/carriacou/maroon musicfestival.html.

Aug **Carriacou Regatta** on the first weekend, with races for work boats, yachts, model boats, donkeys and rowing boats, as well as the greasy pole, tug-o-war and cultural shows, contact the **Carriacou Regatta Committee**, T4437930, www.grenadaexplorer.com/events/carriacou _regatta.htm.

Mid-Dec The **Parang** runs over 3 evenings (Fri-Sun) from about 2100-0200 at the Tennis Club in Hillsborough (entrance EC$20 per night). It is a musical celebration: local groups perform on Fri, Sat is the most lively night with visiting Calypsonians and performers from Grenada and other islands judged by visiting dignitaries, and Sun is comedy day.

O Shopping

Grenada *p800, map p801*
Arts and crafts
Art Fabrik, 9 Young St, T/F4400568, batikart@caribsurf.com. Mon-Fri 0830-1630, Sat 0900-1300. Batik clothing and gift shop, expensive, artisan demonstrating batik at table by door. Art gallery upstairs exhibiting regional artists.
Art in Grenada, 2nd floor Grand Anse Shopping Complex, T4442317, designco@caribsurf.com. Mon-Sat 1000-1700. Fine art gallery, showcasing the work of Richard Buchanan, Susan Mains and others.
Grenada Craft Centre on Lagoon Rd, next to the **Tropicana Inn**. Houses Grenadian craftspersons selling jewellery, pottery, batik, wood, basketry and T-shirts.
White Cane Industries on the Carenage adjacent to the Ministry of Health. Features a wide variety of arts and crafts.
The Yellow Poui Art Gallery, above **Gifts Remembered** souvenir shop on Cross St, T4403001. Mon-Fri 0900-1600, Sat 0915-1215. Sells Grenadian paintings, sculpture, photography, antique prints and engravings.

Books
Fedon Books, side entrance on Herbert

Blaize St. Mon-Fri 0900-1700, Sat 0900-1300. Caribbean novels, geography, cooking and children's books.

Sea Change, is on the Carenage, beneath the **Nutmeg** bar, T4403402. It has **USA Today** when cruise ships come in.

St George's Bookshop, Halifax St, T4402309. Reasonable selection of Caribbean and international literature as well as school texts.

Market

On the first Thu of every month except Sep, a **Farmers' Night Market** is held at Grenada Rainbow Inn, Grenville, T442 62777, featuring farm produce, crafts, wine, food music and farm animals; a social event, good shopping and fun for children.

Shopping malls

Esplanade Mall, on the Esplanade by the cruise ship terminal. Duty free shops, gift shops, juice bars, pizza and US fast food, internet café, tourist bureau, toilets, phones. Outside there are craft stalls but only a short walk away is the market for a more authentic experience.

Spice products

Grenada prides itself on its spices, which are ideal souvenirs and are cheaper in the supermarket than on the street or in the market.

Arawak Islands Ltd, Frequente Industrial Park, T/F4443577, www.arawak-islands.com. Factory and retail outlet, Mon-Fri 0830-1630. They make a range of spices, sauces, herbal teas, candied nutmeg pods, perfumes, soap, bath goodies and massage oils, scented candles and incense sticks; mail order available.

De la Grenade Industries, T4354819, www.delagrenade.com. Makes nutmeg jams, jellies, syrups, sauces and drinks, available in supermarkets and groceries. Their nutmeg syrup is an essential ingredient for a Grenadian rum punch, also delicious on pancakes.

The Grenada Co-operative Nutmeg Association, T4402117, gcnanutmeg@ caribsurf.com. Purchases nutmeg from its membership of 7,000 farmers and markets it worldwide. It sells nutmeg oil in 15 ml and 30 ml bottles.

Spice Island Perfumes, on the Carenage. Sells perfumes and pots pourris made from the island's spices, as well as batiks, T-shirts, etc.

▲ Activities and tours

Grenada *p800, map p801*
Cricket

The island's main land sport, is played from Jan-Jun. The locals play on any piece of flat ground or on the beaches, but international test matches are played at the **Queen's Park National Stadium**, north of St George's. Built in 1998, it became the 84th Test venue when the West Indies played New Zealand there in 2002, but it was destroyed by Hurricane Ivan in 2004. It was refurbished for the 2007 Cricket World Cup (6 Super-8 matches were played there) with the help of the Chinese, to give it a capacity of 13,000 seats. The stadium hosts cricket, football, athletics, cycling, cultural events and exhibitions. There are also training and practice grounds around the island. St George's University, home of the **Shell West Indies Cricketing Academy**, has cricket practice facilities. Touring school, college or university teams are welcomed.

Diving

There is usually a dive company at any of the larger resorts but they change frequently. The nearest recompression chamber is in Barbados or Trinidad, both 30 mins by air ambulance. Members of the **Grenada Scuba Diving Association** all carry oxygen on board their boats.

Aquanauts Grenada, T4441126, www.aquanautsgrenada.com. A PADI 5-star and BSAC operation, has 2 locations: at the **True Blue Bay Marina** and **Spice Island Beach Resort**, offering easy access to a variety of dive sites. A 2-tank dive is US$91, and a day trip with diving to Isle de Rhonde is US$130, tax included.

Dive Grenada is at the **Flamboyant Hotel**, T4441092, www.divegrenada.com. PADI courses (Open Water US$450), wreck dives for experienced divers, night dives (US$65), snorkelling (US$30). A 2-tank dive is US$85, while a package of 5 dives is US$200, plus 5% tax.

Fishing

Deep-sea fishing can be arranged through **True Blue Sportfishing**, T4442048, www.yesaye.com, with Captain Gary Clifford, and **Wayward Wind Fishing Charters**,

T5389821, www.grenadafishing.com, with Captain Stewart. At the end of Jan each year, Grenada hosts **The Spice Island Billfish Tournament**, T4402198 for information.

Golf
Grenada Golf and Country Club, Woodlands, above Grand Anse, T4444128. Open daily 0800 to sunset, but only till 1200 on Sun. A 9-hole golf course.

Sailing
Sailing in the waters around Grenada and through the Grenadines, via Carriacou, is very good. There are lots of other companies offering day sails, no shortage of choice, see www.grenadagrenadines.com/sail.
Carib Cats, T4443222, caribcats@caribsurf .com. Full-day snorkelling or sunset cruises.
First Impressions, T4403678 (Mosden Cumberbatch), www.catamaranchartering .com. Catamarans for all types of charters, day, sunset, 14 different tours offered.

Tennis
Hotels have courts and public courts are found at Grand Anse and Tanteen, St George's.

Tour operators
There is a 5% tax on all tours. Lots of companies offer day tours of the island, stopping to visit waterfalls, nutmeg processing plants, and have lunch in the north or a picnic on Bathway beach. These are usually in minibuses or small buses and are primarily designed to give cruise ship passengers a taste of the island, so they can seem rushed.
Ecotrek (part of **Ecodive** at the Coyaba Beach Resort), T4447777, www.ecodiveandtrek.com. They offer something a bit different including coastal, rainforest and mountain walks and island safaris, tailor-made tours for small groups or even a single person.
Henry's Safari Tours, T4445313, VHF channel 68, www.henrysafari.com. Dennis Henry conducts tours of the island and is very well informed on all aspects of Grenada. Henry's also services yachts, dealing with laundry, gas, shopping, etc.
Let's Tour Grenada, T4492652, gpeters@spiceisle.com. Small operation run by Gail Peters, English/Spanish spoken,

private jeep tours of southern part of island for groups of max 4 people, personal service, half-day US$60 or full day US$90-100pp, including lunch and soft drinks, reductions for children. Different itinerary from other tour operators, mix of historical, local interest, nature, beach activities and good lunch stops.
Mandoo Tours, T4401428, www.grenadatours.com. Island tours and trekking, Concord Falls, Mt Qua Qua, Seven Sisters Falls, lots of options.
Telfor Hiking Tours, Telfer Bedeau in the village of Soubise on the east coast offers guided hikes; you must ask around for him (or T4426200 or see if the Tourism Department can put you in touch). Hikes to the Seven Falls, Mt Qua Qua, Claboney, Hot Springs, Concord Falls, US$23 for 1 person, US$15pp for 2, US$12pp for 3, US$10pp for 4 people.

Watersports
Windsurfing, waterskiing and parasailing all take place off Grand Anse beach. Inshore sailing on sunfish, sailfish and hobiecats is offered by Grand Anse and Lance aux Épines hotels and operators.
Fun Sun, T4393925, funsun@spiceisle.com. Offer a River Rush River Tubing tour on the Balthazar river, a mild, 3-hr adventure suitable for ages 6yrs and up.

Carriacou *p812, map p813*
Diving
Carriacou Silver Diving at Main St, Hillsborough, T/F4437882, www.scubamax.com. Run by Max and Claudia Nagel, an enthusiastic German couple who have been on the island since 1993, 2 boats, very professional.

Tour operators
Taxi drivers will offer to take you on a tour of the island, the tourist office will give you a recommendation or else contact the **Carriacou Owners and Drivers Association**, T4437386, VHF16. A full tour of the island is set at EC$150 for 2½ hrs, and a half tour for EC$75. Several captains offer tours of nearby islands by boat. Be sure to check safety equipment, they are not licensed. If the engine fails has he got oars or sails as an alternative? Is there a radio? Life jackets? A

motor boat on its way to White Island for a picnic broke down and drifted for 3 days, eventually being found off the Venezuelan coast.

First Impressions, T4437277, www.catamaranchartering.com (see Grenada), has a 40-ft Morgan sloop. *Cinderella*, for tours of the Grenadines. Reggie Haemer or Captain Bubb, T4438468, has a 41-ft Morgan ketch, *Chaika*. Captain Carl McLawrence, T4437505, has a West Indies sloop, *Good Expectation III*.
Water taxis will also take you on trips to the little islands offshore or to other Grenadines close by: Snaggs water taxi, T4438293, VHF16; Scooby water taxi, T4336622.

⊙ Transport

Grenada *p800, map p801*
Air
From Europe British Airways, Virgin Atlantic and Excel direct from London, Caribbean Airlines via Trinidad. Condor flies weekly in Nov-Apr from Frankfurt.

From North America Air Jamaica from New York. American Eagle from San Juan connects with American Airlines services from the USA. Air Canada Vacations has a direct flight from Toronto in the winter. All other flights connect in Trinidad or Barbados with LIAT/Caribbean Star.

From the Caribbean LIAT/Caribbean Star fly everywhere in the Eastern Caribbean with lots of flights from Barbados and Trinidad and Tobago, with connecting flights from other islands. Charter or air taxi services such as SVGAir connect Grenada with Carriacou and neighbouring islands in the Grenadines under the umbrella company of Grenadine Airways.

Airport The Point Salines Airport is 5 miles from St George's: taxis only, fixed rates to St George's, EC$30 (US$14), 15 mins; EC$25 (US$10) to Grand Anse and Lance aux Épines. Journeys within 1 mile of the airport EC$7 (US$2.75). Add EC$10 (US$3.75) between 1800 and 0600. However, if you start walking down the road towards St George's, the taxi changes into a bus and will pick you up for much less (only feasible with light luggage). If you are energetic, it takes an hour to walk to Grand Anse, longer to St George's. On departure, pay your tax after

check in and before going through to the departure lounge. There is a snack bar in the departure lounge but a better restaurant is Liftoff upstairs, before going through Immigration, T4442896, 0500-2200. The duty free gift shops are not cheap, no bargains.
Airlines American Eagle, T4442222, at airport T4445151. British Airways, T4441664, 0900-1700 at the airport. Condor, Carin Travel Services, Grand Anse, T4444363. LIAT/Caribbean Star, T4405428 (T4444121/2 Point Salines, T4437362 Carriacou). SVGAir, at the airport, T4443549.

Boat
Apart from cruise ships there are no international services. Grenada and Carriacou are linked by ferries, of which the best and quickest is a hovercraft, the *Osprey*.

Bus
Buses or minivans (look for the letter H on the number plate) run to all parts of the island from the new bus station on the Esplanade in St George's. Fares are EC$2 for any journey starting and finishing within the same parish and for any journey of 3 miles or less. Other fixed fares are EC$3.50 from St George's to Grand Étang, and EC$5.50 to Grenville. There is also a regular bus service between Grenville and Sauteurs. It can be difficult to get a bus away from Grand Étang in either direction as most of them are full. The last buses tend to be in mid-afternoon and there are very few on Sun.

Car
Cars can be rented from a number of companies for about US$65-75 a day (cheaper for longer), plus US$2,500 excess liability and 5% tax (payable by credit card). You must purchase a local permit, on presentation of your national driving licence, for EC$30/US$12; a local permit is not required if you hold an international driving licence. Daily rates quoted over the phone are not always honoured when you pick up the car; check that the company does not operate a 3-day minimum hire if you want a rate for 1 day only, this often applies in high season. Companies in St George's include: David's, at the airport and several hotels, T4443399; Dollar Rent-a-Car, airport, T4444786; Maitland's (also rent

motorcycles), Market Hill, T4444022, office at the airport which is often open for late arrivals when others are closed; **McIntyre Bros**, cars and jeeps, T4443944, macford@caribsurf.com; **Spice Island Rentals** (Avis), Paddock and Lagoon Rd, T4403936; **Y&R Car Rentals**, airport and L'Anse aux Epines, T4444448, www.y-r.com, 0730-2100.

Hitchhiking is quite easy though the roads are not very good.

Cycle

Bike rentals can be arranged with **Trailblazers**, at True Blue Bay Resort, T4445337, open 0800-1100, 1500-1800, US$15 per day, US$90 per week, including mandatory helmet. Bike parts, but no repairs, at **Ace Hardware**, Lagoon Rd, south end.

Taxi

Fares are set by the tourist board on a per mile basis. From the Airport to St George's is usually EC$30, to Grand Anse hotels EC$25-35, from St George's to La Sagesse EC$80, to Grenville or Sauteurs, EC$90 (EC$10 charge extra 1800-0600). Waiting is EC$15 per hr, and a tour of the island is EC$40 per hr. Large speakers blast out steel bands or reggae music; taxi drivers will adjust the volume on request.

A **water taxi** service runs from in front of the **Nutmeg** restaurant, St George's to the Grand Anse beach.

Carriacou p812, map p813

Air

Carriacou's airport is **Lauriston**, a EC$15 taxi ride from Hillsborough. Disconcertingly, the main road goes straight across the runway, traffic is halted when aircraft are due. Every day **TIA** fly from Barbados and **SVG Air** from Grenada, also 3 times a week from Barbados via Union Island, linking with North American and European flights. **LIAT/Caribbean Star** flies from Mustique and Union Island.
Airline offices See under Grenada, page 827.

Boat

Osprey Lines, T4408126 (Grenada), T4438126 (Carriacou), www.ospreylines.com. A punctual and efficient hovercraft service, the *Osprey Shuttle* from **Grenada** to Carriacou in 70 mins and the *Osprey Express* in 90 mins, continuing to Petite Martinique. Office in Hillsborough on the corner of Main St and Paterson St, get ticket in advance if you want to catch the early morning boat, then you can just walk straight on with your luggage. On Mon-Fri the twice daily service starts in Petite Martinique 0530 and 1500, leaving Carriacou 0600 and 1530, arriving in St George's harbour opposite the fire station 1¼ hrs later. It returns from Grenada at 0900 and 1730, leaving Carriacou for Petite Martinique at 1030 and 1900. On Sat the 2 services to Grenada are the same but there is only one crossing back from Grenada, at 0900, then on Sun it starts in Grenada at 0800 and 1730, leaving Carriacou for Petite Martinique at 0930 and 1900. Fares from Grenada to Carriacou or Petite Martinique are EC$70 one way, EC$140 return, from Carriacou to Petite Martinique EC$20 one way, EC$40 return. There are also day tours to either Carriacou or Petite Martinique for US$100 including lunch.

A second hovercraft service is the **Lexiana Jet Express**, T4436930, F4437179. It leaves Carriacou Mon-Sun at 0615 and 1515, returning from **Grenada** at 0915 and 1730 Mon-Sat and 0800 and 1730 on Sun.

A **ferry** (*Alexia II, Alexia III, Adelaide B*) also sails from the Carenage, St George's to Hillsborough, Carriacou, Tue 0930, Wed 1000, Fri 1100, Sat 0800, Sun 0700, returning Mon 1000, Wed 0930, Thu 1000, Sat 0900, Sun 1200, 3-4 hrs. Cargo boats leave from the other side of the Carenage from the *Osprey Express*, usually daily but enquire for times. There are also services between these islands; ask around. Carriacou is 1 hr by boat from **Union Island**; fishing boats leave irregularly between Hillsborough and Ashton. The ferry, *Jaspar*, runs twice a week (see above, Union Island).

Water taxis to beaches cost EC$60-100 depending on the length of the journey. Fishing and sailing trips from Hillsborough pier or ask at hotels.

Bus

Buses go from Hillsborough to **Bogles**, **Windward** (EC$3) and to **Tyrrel Bay**. To get from Tyrrel Bay to Windward you would have to change buses in Hillsborough. Buses cost EC$2 for 1 mile, EC$3 for more than that.

The same van may be a taxi and cost US$12, ask for 'bus' and be prepared to wait. There are also plenty of taxis, which cost EC$15 from the airport to Hillsborough, up to a maximum fare of EC$30 to Petit Carenage.

Car
You can hire a car or jeep. **Desmond's**, T4437271; **Quality Jeep Rental**, T/F4438307; **Sunkey's Auto Rentals**, T4438382.

ⓘ Directory

Grenada *p800, map p801*
Banks FirstCaribbean International Bank (branches in St George's-Halifax St, Grand Anse, Grenville and Carriacou), T4403232. National Commercial Bank of Grenada (Halifax St and Hillsborough St, St George's, Grand Anse, Grenville, Gouyave, St David's, Carriacou), T4403566. **Scotiabank** (Halifax St, St George's), T4403274. **Grenada Bank of Commerce** (Halifax and Cross St, St George's, and Grand Anse), T4404919. **Grenada Co-operative Bank** (Church St, St George's, Grenville and Sauteurs), T4402111.
Embassies and consulates Cuba, Lance aux Épines, T4441884, granadaembacuba@caribsurf.com. France, 5 Lucas St, T4406349. Germany, T4432156. **Netherlands**, T4403459. **Spain**, Jonas Browne & Hubbard Ltd, Carenage, T4402087. **Sweden**, Today's Wonders, Grenville Street, T4402765. UK, British High Commission, Netherlands Building, Grand Anse Shopping Centre (on the main road in a new building by FirstCaribbean International Bank), open Mon-Fri 0800-1300, T440-3222/3536, bhcgrenada@caribsurf.com. USA, Lance aux Épines Stretch, St George's, T4441173, usemb_gd@caribsurf.com. Venezuela, Archibald Av, St George's, T4401721, embavengda@caribsurf.com.
Internet Most hotels offer internet access and Wi-Fi access is widespread. **Carenage Café**, in the Otway building on the Carenage. 0800-1500 for breakfast, snacks and lunch, 2 computers for internet access, very popular, long queues, sofas, book swap. **James Computer Service**, T4401600, Scott St at top of alley going up from Daihatsu on Carenage, side entrance to 1st floor for computers and internet access, pay downstairs at main entrance, a/c, functional,

good and fast machines, no queues.
Medical services St George's General Hospital, Fort George's Point, T4402050. There is also the private **St Augustine Medical Centre**, T4406173. **Black Rock Medical Clinic**, Grand Anse Shopping Centre, has 24-hr emergency service. **Ambulance**: T434 in St George's, T724 in St Andrew's and T774 on Carriacou. **Post** General Post Office in St George's is at Burns Point near the pier, south of the Carenage, Mon-Fri 0800-1600, only postage stamps are sold during the lunch hr, 1200-1300. Villages have sub-post offices. **Telephone** Cable & Wireless Grenada Ltd, T4401000, gndinfo@caribsurf.com, with offices on the Carenage, St George's, operates telephone services, including USA Direct and calls to USA on Visa card, etc, fax and cellular phones. Payphones take coins or phone cards, available at outlets near payphones. **Home Direct Service** can be made from any phone, if you have a credit or telephone charge card, and is available to the UK through **BT Direct** and to Canada through **Teleglobe**. Credit card holders and Visaphone card holders' access number is 1-800-8778000 for domestic and international calls. If you dial 1-800-8722881 at any public phone (no coin required), you get through to AT&T. A call to the UK costs approximately EC$37.50 for 5 mins. **Grentel Boatphone** provides mobile cellular phone service.

Carriacou *p812, map p813*
Banks FirstCaribbean International Bank is on Main St on the left as you head south. The **National Commercial Bank** is on Main St on the left as you head north, both Mon-Thu 0800-1400, Fri 0800-1730. **Currency exchange** is quicker at FirstCaribbean International. **Internet** John's Print Shop, on the main street in Hillsborough, next to FirstCaribbean International Bank, T4438207, www.grenadines.net, also sells inter-island air tickets. The Studio, next to Alexis Supermarket on Tyrrel Bay, T/F4438625, VHF 16, has email and internet access, mail drop, bookswap, bar, coffee shop, music, closed Sun, small and pleasant. **Medical services** Princess Royal Hospital, Belair, T4437400. Hillsborough Health Centre, T4437280. Charles Pharmacy, T4437933. Ambulance: T774. **Police and Immigration** Hillsborough, T4437482.

Background

History

When Columbus discovered the island on his third voyage in 1498, it was inhabited by Caribs, who had migrated from the South American mainland, killing or enslaving the peaceful Arawaks who were already living there. The Amerindians called their island Camerhogue, but Columbus renamed it Concepción, a name which was not to last long, for shortly afterwards it was referred to as Mayo on maps and later Spaniards called it Granada, after the Spanish city. The French then called it La Grenade and by the 18th century it was known as Grenada. Aggressive defence of the island by the Caribs prevented settlement by Europeans until the 17th century. In 1609 some Englishmen tried and failed, followed by a group of Frenchmen in 1638, but it was not until 1650 that a French expedition from Martinique landed and made initial friendly contact with the inhabitants. When relations soured, the French brought reinforcements and exterminated the Amerindian population. Sauteurs, or Morne des Sauteurs, on the north coast, is named after this episode when numerous Caribs jumped to their death in the sea rather than surrender to the French.

The island remained French for about 100 years, although possession was disputed by Britain, and it was a period of economic expansion and population growth, as colonists and slaves arrived to grow tobacco and sugar at first, followed by cotton, cocoa and coffee. It was during the Seven Years' War in the 18th century that Grenada fell into British hands and was ceded by France to Britain as part of a land settlement in the 1763 Treaty of Paris. Although the French regained control in 1779, their occupation was brief and the island was returned to Britain in 1783 under the Treaty of Versailles. The British introduced nutmeg in the 1780s, after natural disasters wiped out the sugar industry. Nutmeg and cocoa became the main crops and encouraged the development of smaller land holdings. A major slave revolt took place in 1795, led by a free coloured Grenadian called Julian Fedon (see page 807), but slavery was not abolished until 1834, as in the rest of the British Empire.

In 1833, Grenada was incorporated into the Windward Islands Administration which survived until 1958 when it was dissolved and Grenada joined the Federation of the West Indies. The Federation collapsed in 1962 and in 1967 Grenada became an associated state, with full autonomy over internal affairs, but with Britain retaining responsibility for defence and foreign relations. Grenada was the first of the associated states to seek full Independence, which was granted in 1974.

Political leadership since the 1950s alternated between Eric (later Sir Eric) Gairy's Grenada United Labour Party (GULP) and Herbert Blaize's Grenada National Party. At the time of Independence, Sir Eric Gairy was Prime Minister, but his style of government was widely viewed as authoritarian and corrupt, becoming increasingly resented by a large proportion of the population. In 1979 he was ousted in a bloodless coup by the Marxist-Leninist New Jewel (Joint Endeavour for Welfare, Education and Liberation) Movement, which formed a government headed by Prime Minister Maurice Bishop. Reforms were introduced and the country moved closer to Cuba and other Communist countries, who provided aid and technical assistance. In 1983, a power struggle within the government led to Bishop being deposed and he and many of his followers were murdered by a rival faction shortly afterwards. In the chaos that followed a joint US-Caribbean force invaded the island to restore order. They imprisoned Bishop's murderers and expelled Cubans and other socialist nationalities engaged in building an airport and other development projects. Elections were held in 1984. They were won by the coalition New National Party (NNP), headed by Herbert Blaize, with 14 seats to GULP's one in the legislature. After the intervention, Grenada moved closer to the USA which maintains an embassy near the airport, but on 1 December 1999 diplomatic relations with Cuba were restored and embassies were opened in St George's and Havana.

sentences on 14 people convicted of murdering Maurice Bishop. Amnesty International and other organizations appealed for the release of Mrs Phyllis Coard, one of the 14 convicted, on grounds of ill-health following years of solitary confinement. She was allowed to go to Jamaica for cancer treatment in 2000, but was not pardoned. In 2006 the Truth and Reconciliation Commission released its long-awaited report about the events of October 1983, but it still left some questions unanswered.

Factionalism was rife in the 1980s and 1990s and political parties frequently divided until there were nine by 1999. Herbert Blaize died in 1989 and Sir Eric Gairy in 1997. The January 1999 general elections were a victory for the New National Party (NNP), which won all 15 seats. The opposition parties were too numerous and weak to provide a challenge, although the National Democratic Congress (NDC) received 24% of the vote. Keith Mitchell was sworn in for a second term as Prime Minister. The latest elections, in November 2003, gave him a third term in office and in December 2004 he celebrated 20 years in parliament, becoming the only member to have been re-elected in five consecutive general elections.

September 2004 was the month no Grenadian will forget, when Hurricane Ivan passed directly over the island, killing 37 people, damaging or destroying practically every building and leaving 50,000 homeless. Water, electricity and phone services were cut off, looting was rife and a dawn to dusk curfew was imposed with the help of regional security services, who were also drafted to help guard prisoners after the prison had its roof blown off. It took several weeks for power to be restored, but shortages of food and building supplies continued for months, with many homes unrepaired for lack of materials. Most hotels were soon open for business, even if some rooms were still out of action, although some took the opportunity for an extended closure to carry out improvements and upgrading. By the winter season, cruise ships were calling again and the airport was back to normal. Today there is still some evidence of the hurricane's passing. Apart from the church roofs still missing and the tree stumps in the forest, houses are more visible without the trees which used to obscure them and residents feel that their neighbours are closer than they thought.

Government

Grenada is an independent state within the Commonwealth, with the British monarch as Head of State represented by a Governor General. There are two legislative houses, the House of Representatives with 15 members, and the Senate with 13 members.

Economy

In the last decade, Grenada has seen a huge expansion of its tourism industry and the economy has been driven by the construction sector meeting demand for new hotels, villas and infrastructure projects. Stopover visitors and cruise ship passengers have risen steadily and the yacht charter business has also expanded considerably. Agriculture accounts for about 12% of GDP but is falling. The number of farmers has fallen by 25% since 1961, with the area of prime farming land decreasing by 50% to about 30,000 acres in the same period. The major export crops are nutmeg, bananas and cocoa, but all three were badly damaged by Hurricane Ivan and many of the nutmeg and cocoa bushes are overgrown with creepers and unproductive; nutmeg and mace traditionally account for about 14% of all exports and Grenada is a leading world producer of this spice. There is also a nutmeg oil distillation plant.

Geography

Grenada, the most southerly of the Windwards, has two dependencies in the Grenadines chain, Carriacou and Petit (often spelt Petite) Martinique. They, and a number of smaller islets, lie north of the main island. The group's total area is 133 sq miles. Grenada itself is 21 miles long and 12 miles wide. The highest point is Mount St Catherine, at 2,757 ft. The island seems to tilt on a northeast-southwest axis: if a line is drawn through ancient craters of Lake Antoine in the Northeast, the Grand Étang in the central mountains and the Lagoon at St George's, it will be straight. Northwest of that line, the land rises and the coast is high; southeast it descends to a low coastline of rias (drowned valleys). The island is green, well forested and cultivated and is blessed with plenty of rain in the wet season. Grenada is described as a spice island, for it produces large quantities of cloves and mace and about a third of the world's nutmeg. It also grows cacao, sugar, bananas and a wide variety of other fruit and vegetables. Some of its beaches, especially Grand Anse, a dazzling two-mile stretch of white sand, are very fine. The majority of the tourist facilities are on the island's dry southwest tip, but the rest of the island is beautiful. With an area of 13 sq miles, Carriacou is the largest of the Grenadines. It lies 23 miles northeast of Grenada; 2½ miles further northeast is Petit Martinique, which is separated by a narrow channel from Petit St Vincent.

People

The population of some 98,400 (of which 7,000 live on Carriacou and Petit Martinique) is largely of African (85%) or mixed (11%) descent. In contrast to other Windward Islands which have had a similar history of disputed ownership between the French and English, the French cultural influence in Grenada has died out. Nevertheless, it is a predominantly Catholic island, though there are Protestant churches of various denominations. Many people who emigrated from Grenada to the UK are returning to the island and are building smart houses for their retirement which are in stark contrast to the tiny shacks which are home to many of their countrymen. The population is young; 38% are under 15 years old and nearly 26% are in the 15-29 years' age bracket.

Flora and fauna

Hurricane Ivan stripped bare the lush rainforests, dry tropical forest and fruit trees of the fertile plantations of Grenada. Parts of the island looked as though they had been through a nuclear holocaust as all leaves vanished, trees lost their bark and branches were broken or whole trees were uprooted. However, a natural recovery is taking place, new shoots and leaves have sprouted and a replanting programme is helping to fill in gaps. It is to be hoped that within a few years the passage of Ivan will be unnoticeable.

A system of national parks and protected areas is being developed. Information is available from the Forestry Department, Ministry of Agriculture, Archibald Avenue, St George's. The focal point of Grenada's nature tourism is the **Grand Étang National Park** ① *Sun-Fri 0800-1600, US$2*, 8 miles from the capital in the central mountain range. It is on the transinsular road from St George's to Grenville. The Grand Étang is a crater lake surrounded by lush tropical forest. A series of trails has been blazed which are well worth the effort for the beautiful forest and views, but can be muddy and slippery after rain. The **Morne Labaye** nature trail is only 15 minutes long, the return is along the same route; the shoreline trail around the lake takes 1½ hours and is moderately easy; much further, 1½ hours' walk, is **Mount Qua Qua**. The trail then continues for an arduous three hours to **Concord Falls**, with an extra 30-minute spur to **Fedon's Camp** (see page 807). From Concord Falls it is 25 minutes' walk to the road to get a bus to St George's. Mount Qua Qua, Fedon's Camp and Concord are hard walks; wet, muddy, it rains a lot and you will get dirty. Take food and water. A guide is not essential, but useful. There are two other trails in the Grand Étang area and one at Annandale. All hikes are graded for difficulty. An **interpretation centre** ① overlooking the lake has videos, exhibitions and explanations of the medicinal plants in the forest. Leaflets about the trails can be bought here for EC$2-3 each. There is a bar, a shop and some amusing monkeys and parrots. Accommodation is available at **Lake House**, T4427425, or enquire at forest centre, also for camping.

The high forest receives over 160 ins of rain a year. Epiphytes and mosses cling to the tree trunks and many species of fern and grasses provide a thick undergrowth. The trees include the gommier, bois canot, Caribbean pine and blue mahoe. At the summit, the vegetation is an example of elfin woodland, the trees stunted by the wind, the leaves adapted with drip tips to cope with the excess moisture. Apart from the highest areas, the island is heavily cultivated. On tours around the country look for nutmeg trees, cloves, cinnamon, allspice, bay, turmeric and ginger. In addition there are calabash gourds, cocoa, coffee, breadfruit, mango, paw paw (papaya), avocado, sugar cane, bananas and coconuts.

In the northeast, 450 acres around **Levera Pond** was opened as a National Park in 1994. As well as having a bird sanctuary and sites of historic interest, Levera is one of the island's largest mangrove swamps; the coastal region has coconut palms, cactus and scrub, providing habitat for iguana and land crabs. There are white beaches where turtles lay their eggs and, offshore, coral reefs and the Sugar Loaf, Green and Sandy islands. You can swim at Bathway but currents are strong at other beaches. The coast between Levera Beach and Bedford Point is eroding rapidly, at a rate of several feet a year. South of Levera is **Lake Antoine**, another crater lake, but sunken to only about 20 ft above sea level; it has been designated a Natural Landmark.

⁝ Leatherback turtles come ashore here in April, May and June.

On the south coast is **La Sagesse Protected Seascape**, a peaceful refuge which includes beaches, a mangrove estuary, a salt pond and coral reefs. In the coastal woodland are remains of sugar milling and rum distilleries. To get there turn south off the main road opposite an old sugar mill, then take the left fork of a dirt road through a banana plantation. Close to the pink plantation house (see Sleeping), a few feet from a superb sandy beach, is **La Sagesse** bar and restaurant, good food, nutmeg shells on the ground outside. Walk to the other end of the beach to where a path leads around a mangrove pond to another palm-fringed beach, usually deserted. The snorkelling and swimming is good and there is a reef just offshore.

Marquis Island, off the east coast, can be visited; at one time it was part of the mainland and now has eel grass marine environments and coral reefs. Nearby is **La Baye Rock**, which is a nesting ground for brown boobies, habitat for large iguanas and has dry thorn scrub forest. It too is surrounded by coral reefs.

The only endemic bird is the Grenada dove, which inhabits scrubby woodland in some west areas. In the rainforest you can see the emerald-throated hummingbird, yellow-billed cuckoo, red-necked pigeon, ruddy quail-dove, cocoa thrush and other species. Wading and shore birds can be spotted at Levera and in the south and southwest. The endangered hook-billed kite (a large hawk) is found in the Levera National Park; the only place in the world. It uses its beak to pluck tree snails (its only food) out of their shells. A pile of shells with holes is evidence that a kite ate there.

There is little remarkable animal life: frogs and lizards, of course, and iguana, armadillo (tatoo) and manicou (possum), all of which are hunted for the pot. The tree boa (*Corallus enydris*) is known locally as a *sarpint* and eats rodents. It grows to about 6 ft and sleeps during the day 50-70 ft above the ground in the trees. The higher they live the darker colour they become. They are quite common, but, being nocturnal, are rarely seen. A troop of Mona monkeys, imported from Africa over 300 years ago, lives around the Grand Étang. Once hunted for the pot (a male can weigh 50 lbs), they are now endangered. Another import is the mongoose.

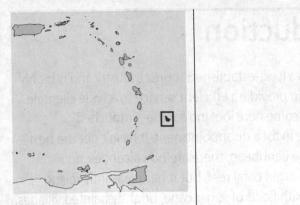

Barbados

Footprint features

Introduction

Barbados has a long-established tourist industry and is highly experienced in providing efficient service to a wide clientele. Tourists who come here looking for the 'untouched' Caribbean are in for a disappointment. It hasn't got the best beaches in the Caribbean, there are no volcanoes, no rainforest, no virgin coral reef, but it has pleasantly rolling countryside with fields of sugar cane, brightly painted villages, flowering trees and open pastures and visitors come back time and time again. You can pay hundreds or thousands of dollars for a hotel room and be truly cosseted or rent a moderate apartment and look after yourself. You can play golf (the courses are very highly rated), tennis, squash and any number of other sports, or you can watch cricket, horseracing or polo. There is lovely walking along the rugged north and east coasts on the Atlantic side, while watersports are offered along the more protected west and south coasts on the Caribbean. For sightseeing, there are fortifications, plantation houses, museums, rum distilleries and gardens. Barbados' history as a British colony is evident in its political system and place names, but times are changing. You can still stand in Trafalgar Square and look at Nelson's statue; but the Lord High Admiral has lost his pre-eminence and the square now honours National Heroes.

★ Don't miss ...

1 **Bathsheba** On the east coast and windswept, this is an excellent surfing beach with the Atlantic rollers trailing white surf. International championships are held here. Rock pools offer a safe and quiet alternative for bathers, page 841.

2 **The Garrison** 19th-century military buildings are grouped around the old parade ground, which is now a horse race track. Built in British colonial style with bricks brought over as ballast on ships from England, the Barbados Museum is housed in the old military prison, page 847.

3 **Orchid World** 20,000 blooms grow in this hillside garden, a fantastic display of colours and shapes in a lovely location, page 854.

4 **Sunbury Plantation** An elegant Georgian plantation house with antique furniture, carriages and domestic items on display, page 854.

5 **Oistins** The historical town is now chiefly known for its fish market, where you can see flying fish being filleted at tremendous speed, page 854.

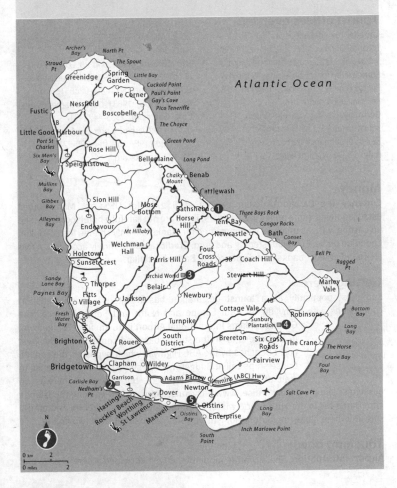

Essentials

Before you travel

Documents Visitors from North America, Western Europe, Commonwealth African countries, Argentina, Venezuela, Colombia, and Brazil need a **passport** but no **visa**.

❢ *Work permits are very difficult to obtain; regulations are strictly enforced.*

Visitors from most other countries are usually granted a short stay on arrival, and tourist visas are not necessary. You must have a ticket back to your country of origin as well as an **onward ticket** to be allowed in. Immigration officers do check. You will also need an accommodation address on arrival, they do not check your reservation but if you say you do not know where you will be staying, you will be sent to the back of the queue. State the maximum period you intend to stay on arrival. Overstaying is not recommended if you wish to re-enter Barbados at a later date. Extending your stay is possible by applying to the **Chief Immigration Officer** ① *Immigration Department, Careenage House on the Wharf in Bridgetown (T4261011, 0830-1630 Mon-Fri), US$12.50*; take your passport and return ticket; it's a time consuming procedure.

Tourist offices overseas

Canada, 105 Adelaide St W, Suite 1010, Toronto, Ontario, M5H 1P9, T416-2149880, 1-800-268 9122, canada@barbados.org.
France, c/o Tropic Consulting, 48 rue des Petites Écuries, 75010 Paris, T33-1 47 70 82 84, france@barbados.org.
Germany, c/o The Mangum Group, Sonnenstrasse 9, D-80331 Munich, T49 89 23 66 21 70, germany@barbados.org.
Italy, c/o G & A Martinengo, Via F.lli Ruffini 9,

20123 Milano, T02 4802 2768, Barbados@martinengo.it.
UK, 263 Tottenham Court Rd, London W1P 0LA, T020-76369448/9, btauk@barbados.org.
USA New York, NY, T212-9866516/8 or toll-free 800-2219831, btany@barbados.org; Coral Gables, FL, T305-4427471, btamiami@barbados.org; Los Angeles, CA, T213-380 2198/9, toll free 800-2219831, btala@barbados.org.

Money

Currency The Barbados dollar, pegged at B$2.00 for US$1.00. Many tourist establishments quote prices in US dollars; if you are not careful a hotel room may end up costing twice as much as you bargained for. Banks will only change the US dollar, Canadian dollar, EC dollar, sterling and euro. **Credit cards** are widely accepted. **ATMs** are found at most banks and dispense the Barbados dollar.

Getting there

Barbados' popularity as a tourist destination has resulted in good transport connections with many flights from Europe and North and South America. The

❢ *Flights to Barbados are heavily booked at Christmas and for Crop Over (July-early August).*

Grantley Adams International Airport is 16 km from Bridgetown, near the resorts on the south coast and connected to the west coast beaches by the ABC Highway which bypasses the capital. Cruise ships call at Bridgetown and some passengers choose to start or break their journey here, but otherwise there is no passenger shipping. Easy Cruise, www.easycruise.com, started cruising the islands from Barbados in the 2005/2006 winter season, allowing you to get on and off the ship anywhere along the route as long as you stay on board at least two nights.

Touching down

Airport information The airport is modern and well equipped. There is a helpful

Touching down

Departure tax US$27.50, included in the cost of your flight or holiday, not payable for stays of less than 24 hours.
IDD code +246.
Official time Atlantic Standard Time, 4 hours behind GMT, 1 hour ahead of EST.

Voltage 120 volts and 50 cycles per second. Some houses and hotels also have 240-volt sockets for use with British equipment.
Weights and measures Imperial.

Tourism Authority office, **Barbados National Bank** (bureau de change in the Arrivals and Departure areas is open from 0800-2400), a post office, car hire agencies and quite a wide range of shops including an Inbound Duty-Free Shop (very useful, saves carrying heavy bottles on the plane).

Across the car park there are two lively rum shops; the shop in the gas station is open when terminal shops are closed, selling food, papers, etc. Taxis stop just outside customs. Check the notice board on the left as you come out of arrivals, as it gives the official taxi fares. Talk to the dispatcher if necessary. Drivers may attempt to charge more if you haven't checked. There is a bus stop just across the car park, with buses running along the south coast to Bridgetown, or (over the road) to the **Crane** and **Sam Lord's Castle**.

Tourist information **Barbados Tourism Authority** ① *main office Harbour Rd, Bridgetown, T4272623, www.barbados.org; also offices at the deepwater harbour, T4261718, and the airport, T4280937*. Two good sources of information are *Visitor* and the *Sun Seeker*, published fortnightly and distributed free. *Sun Seeker* has an amazing listing of every possible club and society. Also lists where to worship, entertainment and daily events. *Signature* is a free magazine with articles on culture, profiles, environment, business, etc. *Sporting Barbados*, www.sportingbarbados.com, is another free glossy, with useful information. *Ins and Outs of Barbados*, www.insandouts-barbados.com, is published annually, a free glossy with lots of historical articles and useful year-round calendar, distributed by the **Barbados Hotel & Tourism Association** ① *4th Av Belleville, St Michael, T4265041, bhta@lnuccs.com hb*.

Safety Take normal precautions against theft, which has risen in recent years. Do not leave your things unattended on the beach, shut windows and lock patio doors at night. There are some areas of Bridgetown, such as Nelson Street, you would not want to walk round late at night. Baxters Road is generally quite safe although it attracts cocaine addicts (*paros*). Take care along deserted beaches (avoid at night; there have been machete attacks); watch out for pickpockets and bag snatchers in tourist areas and people who wash cars unasked and then demand US$5. Police have patrols on beaches and plain clothes officers around some rural tourist attractions.

Getting around

The island is fairly small but it can take a surprisingly long time to travel as the rural roads are narrow and winding. The Adams Barrow Cummins highway runs from the airport to a point between Brighton and Prospect, north of Bridgetown. This road skirts the east edge of the capital, giving access by various roads into the city. Minibuses and route taxis run around the capital, cheaply and efficiently, but are terribly slow in rush hour. You can get a bus or taxi from the airport to Bridgetown. The highway and roads into Bridgetown get jammed morning and afternoon; the city centre is worst in the middle of the day. ▸▸ *See also Transport, page 867.*

Taxis are expensive. There are plenty at the airport, main hotels, and in Bridgetown. There are standard fares, displayed just outside 'arrivals' at the airport, and are also listed in the *Visitor* and the *Sunseeker*. You may have to bargain hard for tours by taxi but always agree a fare in advance. They will sometimes try to exceed the official rate per hour of US$16.

Buses Flat fare of B$1.50 (B$1 for schoolchildren in uniform) per journey anywhere on the island, so if you change buses you pay again. Almost all the routes radiate in and out of Bridgetown, so cross-country journeys are time-consuming if you are staying outside the city centre. However, travelling by bus can be fun. There are some circuits which work quite well; for example: **1)** any south coast bus to Oistins, then cross country College Savannah bus to the east coast, then direct bus back to Bridgetown; **2)** any west coast bus to Speightstown, then bus back to Bathsheba on the east coast, then direct bus back to Bridgetown. Out of town bus stops are marked simply 'To City' or 'Out of City'. For the south coast ask for **Silver Sands** route.

❧ *Buses are cheap, frequent and crowded.*

Maps *GeoCenter* publish a Holiday Map, 1:60,000 scale Bridgetown inset, 1:7,500, the Garrison, the west coast and the south coast with sites of tourist interest marked. **Insight** do the same map in a laminated edition. **Esso** distributes a road map with the free *Barbados in a Nutshell* booklet (advertising), with Bridgetown, west and south coast insets with hotels marked.

Eating

Food Fresh fish is excellent. The main fish season is December-May, when there is less risk of stormy weather at sea. Flying fish are the national emblem and a speciality with two or three to a plate. Dolphin fish (*dorado*, not the mammal, and now usually called *mahi mahi* on restaurant menus as in the USA) and kingfish are larger steak-fish. Snapper is excellent. *Sea eggs* are the roe of the white sea urchin, and are delicious but not often available. Fresh fish is sold at the fish markets in Oistins, Bridgetown and elsewhere in the late afternoon and evening, when the fishermen come in with their catch. **Oistins** lively Friday evening fish fry on the south coast is *the* place to eat the freshest of fish, or for something quieter, try **Half Moon Fort** in the north. *Cou-cou* is a filling starchy dish made from breadfruit or corn meal. *Jug-jug* is a Christmas speciality made from guinea corn and supposedly descended from the haggis of the poor white settlers. Pudding and *souse* is a huge dish of pickled breadfruit, black pudding and pork.

Drink Barbados rum is probably the best in the English-speaking Caribbean, unless of course you come from Jamaica, or Guyana or... It is worth paying a bit extra for a good brand such as VSOP or Old Gold, or for Sugar Cane Brandy, unless you are going to drink it with Coca Cola. A rum and cream liqueur, *Crisma*, is popular in cocktails or on the rocks. *Falernum* is sweet, sometimes slightly alcoholic, with a hint of vanilla. *Corn and oil* is rum and falernum. Often refreshing *Mauby* is bitter, and made from tree bark. *Sorrel* is a bright-red Christmas drink made with hibiscus sepals and spices; very good with white rum. Banks beer has Bajan Light and other beers. Water quality is excellent, coming mostly from deep coral limestone wells.

❧ *Malibu, the rum and coconut drink, now also in a lime flavour, comes from Barbados. For rum tours, see page 865.*

Festivals and events

Many villages hold street fairs from time to time. For a diary of events and festivals see http://barbados.org/eventcd.htm.
1 Jan New Year's Day.

2nd week Jan Jazz Festival, contact Gilbert Rowe, T4374537, www.barbadosjazzfestival.com.
21 Jan Errol Barrow Day.

Feb The Holetown Festival (contact Alfred Pragnell, T4356264), commemorating the first settlers' landing in Feb 1627.

Mar The Holders Season is a popular festival started in 1992 with a season of opera, Shakespeare, cabaret with international performers and sporting events such as cricket, golf and polo. Performances are beautifully staged outdoors at Holders, an old plantation house overlooking the polo field. Take a picnic and an umbrella, tickets US$15-90. T4326385, www.holders.net.

Mar/Apr Good Fri and Easter Mon. The Oistins Fish Festival, held around Easter, celebrates the signing of the Charter of Barbados and the history of this fishing town with three days of competitions, parades and demonstrations of fishing and cooking skills. A big street party goes on late into the night and lots of fried fish and fish cakes are consumed.

28 Apr National Heroes Day.

Late Apr Congaline Street Festival finishing with a Mayday jump-up in the streets from Garrison Savanna to Spring Garden. Bajan and other Caribbean music. Contact the National Cultural Foundation, T4240909.

May Gospel Fest (contact Adrian Agard, T4307300) and the Celtic Festival, music, dance and sports.

1 May Labour Day

May/Jun Whit Mon, 7 weeks after Easter.

Jul-Aug Crop Over, parades and calypso competitions over the weekend leading up to Kadooment Day (the first Mon in Aug), and calypso 'tents' (mostly indoors though) for several weeks beforehand. The celebrations begin with the ceremonial delivery of the last canes on a brightly coloured dray cart pulled by mules, which are blessed. There is a toast to the sugar workers and the crowning of the King and Queen of the crop (the champion cutterpilers). The bands and costumes have improved but are a pale imitation of what Trinidad has to offer. However, even Trinidadians now take Barbadian soca and calypso seriously and talk of the Bajan invasion. The big crowd is on the Spring Garden Highway outside Bridgetown Mon afternoon, which has roadside music and places selling drinks for 2 weeks before Kadooment. Next to the highway there is Festival village, an area for open-air parties with live music, small entry fee. Baxters Rd Mall runs for a couple of weekends beforehand; the road is closed off for fried fish, music and beer. For information contact the National Cultural Foundation, T4240909, http://barbados.org/cropover.htm.

1 Aug Emancipation Day.

First Mon in Aug Kadooment Day.

Oct Blowin' in de Windies, a youth jazz festival with school bands from the UK, North and South America participating in performances and workshops.

Nov NIFCA, the National Independence Festival of Creative Arts is a more serious affair, with plays, concerts and exhibitions in the 4 weeks before Independence Day.

30 Nov Independence Day. Several events are held throughout the month commemorating Barbados' independence from Britain in 1966.

Dec Christmas Day and Boxing Day.

Beaches and activities

There are beaches along most of the south and west coasts. Although some hotels make it hard to cross their property to reach the sand, there are no private beaches in Barbados. For example, just north of Speightstown there is a narrow road between **Almond Beach** and the **Port St Charles Marina**, which ends in a small car park giving access to the good beaches which front these properties. The west coast beaches are very calm, and quite narrow, beach erosion is a serious worry and the Government's Coastal Conservation Unit is trying to sort it out. A swell can wash up lots of broken coral making it unpleasant underfoot. The south coast can be quite choppy, but there is more sand. The southeast, between the airport and East Point, has steep limestone cliffs with a series of small sandy coves with coconut trees, and waves which are big enough for surfing. **Bottom Bay** is currently *the* place to go. Be careful on the east side of the island, currents and undertow are strong in places. Don't swim where there are warning signs, or where there are no other bathers, even on a calm day. **Bathsheba**, on the east coast, is quite spectacular, with wonderful views. Some hotels sell day

Barbados

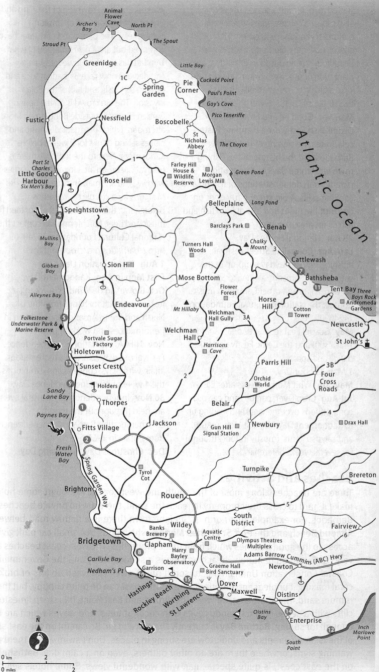

passes for the use of their facilities: pool, showers, deck chairs, etc. Work on the new **Sandals Resort** at **Paradise Beach** has been shelved and the beach is beautifully deserted. Go to north end of Spring Gardens Highway, then up west coast road Highway 1 for about half a mile, then turn sharp left. Drive down to Batts Rock Beach, walk south to get to Paradise Beach. You can keep going along the shoreline as far as Deepwater Harbour, a nice walk, mostly beach. Near the south end of this stretch at **Brandon's Beach** and accessible also from Spring Gardens Highway, is **Weiser's Beach Bar** ① **T4256450**, which has beach volleyball and an afternoon happy hour (Friday happy hours 1700-1900, 2200-2300), but it can be crowded if there's a cruise ship in. Just south of Bridgetown is **Bayshore** ① *in the old police station site on Bay St*, T4352909, set up as a beach facility for cruise passengers, beach chairs US\$5, lockers US\$5, beach volleyball, small pool, internet café, **Joe's** bar and restaurant, dinner main course US\$20 and up.

> ⚓ A 2-km stretch of marine reserve from Coral Reef to Sandy Lane Hotel includes Dottin's Reef and Vauxhall Reef.

Diving The **Barbados Sub Aqua Club**, a branch of the British Sub Aqua Club (BSAC) meets at 0800 on Sunday at the **Boatyard Pub**① *on the waterfront on Bay St, Bridgetown*. They don't hire out equipment but if you have your own they are welcoming to members from other branches, T4216020, Rob Bates. There is a recompression chamber at St Anne's Fort, T4278819, inform the operator of an emergency.

There is an extensive roped-off area for snorkelling at the **Folkestone Underwater Park** and equipment can be hired here, US\$10, Monday-Saturday 0900-1700. Life jackets, diving flags, lockers and children's equipment can also be hired.

Several **turtle-watching** tours are on offer as part of a day-sail to the area around Alleynes Bay and Gibbs Beach, where groups of them can be found. Individual turtles can also be found at

Barbados Essentials

snorkelling spots on the south coast. The hawksbill frequently nests on local beaches July to October, the leatherback occasionally in February to June. Green turtles are occasionally found in Bajan waters. ►► *For listings of Dive operators, see page 863.*

Windsurfing, kitesurfing and surfing The south coast is good for windsurfing and kitesurfing. The centre of the action for windsurfers is Silver Rock. There is a two-mile stretch of reef providing excellent waves for wave sailors and a lagoon for those who are less confident. The best place to learn to windsurf is in the Sandy Beach area inside the lagoon, while outside the reef you can sometimes get good wave sailing. On the north coast the waves can be very big at Cow Pens and Red Backs. Access is not easy as there is only a very small each from which to launch yourself. The International Funboard Challenge is held in March. The Barbados Windsurfing World Cup is in January. The Waterman Festival, in late January and early February, is a professional international event where you can see lots of acrobatics. Contact the **Barbados Windsurfing Association** ① *Silver Sands, T4287277*. Kitesurfing is best done further east near the airport, at Long Beach, where the wind is side on shore. The wind is best from November to July. When the wind is light and windsurfers can't go out, then the area between Silver Sands Resort and Silver Rock Resort is good for beginners. The Casuarina Beach is also good as the wind is a bit stronger here and funnels down the coast. The best surfing is on the east coast at the Soup Bowl, Bathsheba, which has the most consistent break. The best time is August to November when you get perfect barrelling waves. Experienced surfers also like Duppies on the north coast, where you have a long paddle out and there is a lot of current, but the waves are really big. The south coast is good for beginners and for boogie boarding. There is a good break at Brandons, while the west coast has some good spots with good access, often best when there are no waves on the east coast. Sandy Lane, Tropicana, Gibbs and Maycocks are all worth trying. The Barbados International Surfing Championship is held at the Soup Bowl, Bathsheba, in late November. Contact the **Barbados Surfing Association** ① *Roger Miller, T4265837*.

Keeping in touch

Communications Telephone Calls from a pay phone cost 25 cents for 3 mins. Otherwise local calls are free. Many business places will allow you to use their telephone for local calls. International calls can be made from most hotels or (more cheaply) from **Cable & Wireless** (Wildey). Faxes can also be sent from and received at Cable & Wireless's office by members of the public. Cable & Wireless has a public office on the Wharf in Bridgetown for international calls and fax. Phone cards are available for Bds$10, 20 and 40 from airport arrivals duty-free shop, cruise terminal, phone company offices, and long list of other outlets; a cheaper way of making overseas calls than using hotel services, and can be used in most of the English-speaking Caribbean except Trinidad, Jamaica, Guyana, Bahamas. There are several cellphone rental companies. Roaming is possible with 800 Mhz analogue or digital TDMA phones, but is costly.

Media Newspapers *The Advocate*, also publishes *The Sunday Advocate* and *Sun Seeker*. *The Nation* (also publishes *Sunday on Saturday*, *Sunday Sun*, *The Visitor* and *Barbados Business Authority* Mon, US$0.50). *Broad Street Journal* is a free business weekly. **Radio CBC Radio**, medium wave 900 kHz; **Starcom Gospel**, medium wave 790 kHz; BBS, FM 90.7 MHz; Love FM, FM 104.1 MHz; **Radio Liberty**, FM 98.1 MHz, FAITH 102 FM. **Television** One terrestrial channel, **CBC**, mostly US imports. Also multi-choice TV with 30 channels and satellite-based **DirecTV** with 70 channels in several languages.

Around Barbados → *IDD code:246. Colour map 4, C6.*

Being the most easterly island and extremely difficult to attack, there are few defensive forts on Barbados. Instead the great houses of the sugar-growing plantocracy give the island its historic perspective and most of its tourist attractions. Many parish churches are also impressive buildings. The island is divided into 11 parishes named after 10 saints, Christ Church being the 11th. Barbados is not large but it is easy to get lost when driving. There seem to be far too many narrow, winding roads threading their way through sugar cane fields. Deep gullies cut in the coral limestone which is the surface rock over most of the island. These are often full of wildlife and plants but make travelling around very confusing. A good map is essential. The bus service is cheap and efficient and recommended even for families with small children. ►► *For Transport details, see page 839 and page 867. For Eating, Sleeping and other listings, see page 855-869.*

Bridgetown

The capital, Bridgetown, is on the southwest corner of the island. The city itself covers a fairly small area. It is busy and full of life. There are two interesting areas, downtown Bridgetown with National Heroes Square on the north side of the Careenage and the historic area at Garrison. There are no really large buildings except Tom Adams Financial Centre, which houses the central bank. Swan Street is now a lively pedestrian street where Barbadians do their shopping and street music is sometimes performed. On Broad Street you will find a whole range of sophisticated shops for tourists, with large shopping malls and department stores. More developments are planned along the Careenage where old warehouses are being converted for other uses. The suburbs sprawl most of the way along the south and west coasts, and quite a long way inland. Many of the suburban areas are very pleasant, full of flowering trees and 19th-century coral stone gingerbread villas.

National Heroes Square was until 1999 called Trafalgar Square, with a statue of Lord Nelson, sculpted by Sir Richard Westmacott and predating its London equivalent by 36 years. It has recently been the subject of some controversy as it was thought to link Barbados too closely with its colonial past. First Nelson was turned 180° so that he no longer looked down Broad Street, the main shopping area, but now he may be removed, if a suitable home can be found. The square is now celebrating 10 official national heroes, including Sir Grantley Adams. There is a memorial to the Barbadian war dead and the fountain commemorates the piping of water to Bridgetown in 1861. To the north is the Parliament Building. Built in 1872, the legislature is an imposing grey building with red roof and green shutters. Built in gothic style, the clock tower is more reminiscent of a church. You can walk between the buildings (providing you are correctly dressed).

> ♥ *The Tourism Authority does a useful free leaflet with map for a self-guided walking tour.*

Take the northeast exit out of National Heroes Square along St Michael's Row to reach the 18th-century **St Michael's Cathedral**. It has a fine set of inscriptions and a single-hand clock. The first building was consecrated in 1665 but destroyed by a hurricane in 1780. The present cathedral is long and broad with a balcony. It has a fine vaulted ceiling and some tombs (1675) have been built into the porch. Completed in 1789, it suffered hurricane damage in 1831. If you continue east, you reach **Queen's Park**, a pleasant, restful park just outside the city centre. **Queen's Park House** is now a small theatre (Daphne Joseph Hackett Theatre) and art gallery. There is a small restaurant and bar, which does a good lunch and a buffet on Friday.

The **Nidhe Israel synagogue** ① *Mon-Fri 0900-1200, 1300-1600, T4277611*, is an early 19th-century building on the site of a 17th-century one, one of the two earliest in the Western hemisphere. The original synagogue, was built in the late 1660s by Jews fleeing Recife, Brazil, who heard that Oliver Cromwell had granted freedom of worship for Jews and gained permission to settle in Barbados. The tomb of Benjamin Massiah, the famous circumciser of 1782 lies on the left-hand side of the graveyard, just inside the entrance. The synagogue was out of religious use for 60 years, and in the 1950s was the office of the **Barbados Turf Club**. Recently painstakingly restored, it is now used for religious services again and is open to visitors.

> ‼ Jews in Barbados were granted the right to worship publicly even before Jews in London, and Barbados was the first British possession to grant Jews full political rights.

The **Harry Bayley Observatory** ⓘ *Clapham, T4245593, Fri 2030-2330, US$4 adults, US$2.50 children*, is not far from **Banks Brewery**. A chance for northern visitors to look at the Southern Hemisphere stars.

A short bus ride from town is **Tyrol Cot** ⓘ *T4242074, Mon-Fri 0900-1700, US$5.75, children US$2.90*, built in 1850, home of Sir Grantley Adams. There is a Heritage Village with craftwork on sale, plus chattel-house museum, gardens and restaurant in the old stables. It is run by the National Trust.

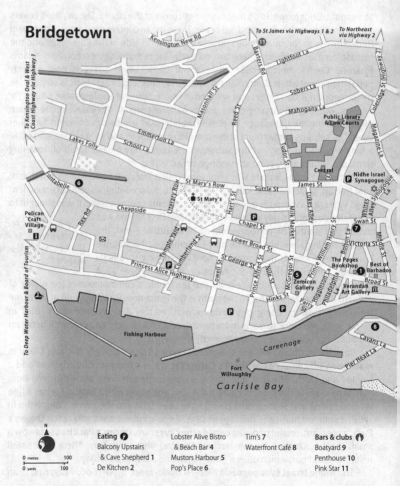

Bridgetown

Eating ⓻
Balcony Upstairs
 & Cave Shepherd **1**
De Kitchen **2**

Lobster Alive Bistro
 & Beach Bar **4**
Mustors Harbour **5**
Pop's Place **6**

Tim's **7**
Waterfront Café **8**

Bars & clubs ⓵
Boatyard **9**
Penthouse **10**
Pink Star **11**

Cross the Careenage by the Charles Duncan O'Neale Bridge (one of the bus terminals and market area are just to the west) and follow Bay Street around the curve of Carlisle Bay. You will pass St Patrick's Cathedral (Roman Catholic), the main government offices with St Michael's Hospital behind it before reaching the historic Garrison area. From here you can visit **Fort Charles** on Needham Point (turn right at the Pepsi plant). The fort was the largest of the many which guarded the south and west coasts, but is currently part of a building site because it forms part of the gardens of the **Hilton Hotel** which is being rebuilt. Only the ramparts remain but there are a number of 24 pounder cannons dating from 1824. There is a military cemetery here and the Mobil oil refinery was the site of the naval dockyard. Built in 1805, it was subsequently moved to English Harbour, Antigua. The buildings were then used as barracks before being destroyed in the 1831 hurricane.

Carry on up the hill to the **Garrison Historical Area,** which contains many interesting 19th-century military buildings, grouped around the Garrison Savannah parade ground, which is now a six furlong race course. The buildings that surround the racecourse were built out of brick brought as ballast on ships from England. They are built on traditional British colonial lines, the design can be seen throughout the Caribbean but also in India. Painted bright colours, some now contain government offices. There are several

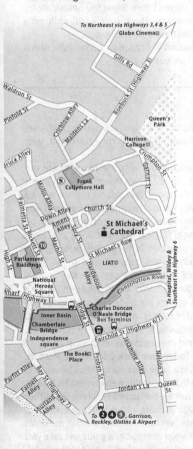

memorials around the oval race course, for instance in the southwest corner, the 'awful' hurricane which killed 14 men and one woman and caused the destruction of the barracks and hospital on 18 August 1831 and outside the Barbados Museum in the northeast corner to the men of the Royal York Rangers who fell in action against the French in Martinique, Les Saintes and Guadeloupe in the 1809 to 1810 campaign.

Across the road is **St Anne's Fort** which is still used by the Barbados defence force. You cannot enter but look for the crenellated signal tower with its flag pole on top. It formed the high command of a chain of signal posts, the most complete of which is at Gun Hill (see below). The long, thin building is the old drill hall. **The Main Guard**, overlooking the savannah, has a nice old clock tower and a fine wide veranda. It has been turned into an information centre and houses exhibits about the West Indian Regiment. The Garrison Secretary of the Regiment is here, (T4260982). Outside is the **National Cannon Collection** which he created, an impressive array of about 30 cannon, some are mounted on metal 'garrison' gun carriages. There are also a number of newer howitzers, dating from 1878.

The **Barbados Museum** ① T4270201, www.barbmuse.org.bb, Mon-Sat 0900-1700, Sun 1400-1800, US$5.75, children US$2.90, is housed in the old military prison on the northeast corner of the savannah. Based on a collection left by Rev N B Watson (late rector of St Lucy Parish), it is well set out through a series of 10 galleries. It displays natural history, local history, a fine map gallery including the earliest map of Barbados by Richard Ligon (1657), colonial furniture (Plantation House Rooms), military history (with a reconstruction of a prisoner's cell), prints and paintings which depict social life in the West Indies, decorative and domestic arts (17th- to 19th-century glass, china and silver), African artefacts, a children's gallery and one to house temporary exhibits. The **Museum Café** is under the trees in the museum courtyard. The **Shilstone Memorial Library** ① *Mon-Fri 0900-1300. US$10 for visitors, US$5 for locals, plus VAT*, is available for research purposes.

George Washington House is where he stayed in 1751 for a few months when, as a 19-year old, he accompanied his sick brother Lawrence (who later died). This was George Washington's only excursion outside his homeland and Bridgetown was the largest town he had seen. He contracted smallpox but acquired immunity to the virus which enabled him to survive an outbreak of the disease during the American War of Independence. The **Barbados National Trust** is raising funds for restoration.

Nearby there are stables for the race course. Races go clockwise. A good place to watch is from the Main Guard. At other times, it is used as a jogging course for people in the mornings, when you can see the horses being exercised, or on weekday evenings. There is also rugby, basketball, etc, played informally in the Savannah; go and see what is going on on Sunday afternoons. There is a small children's playground in one corner. However, at night prostitutes parade here.

Also near Garrison is **Mallalieu Motor Collection** ① *T4264640, US$5, daily*, with a Bentley, Vanden Plas Princess, Wolseley and Lanchester, etc.

West coast Barbados

Highway 1 north of Bridgetown is wall to wall hotels and villas, but nothing high-rise. Highway 2A runs parallel inland and goes through the sugar cane heartland, with small villages and pleasant views.

Holetown today is a thoroughly modern town but was the place where the earliest settlers landed on 17 February 1627. The Holetown monument commemorates Captain John Powell claiming the island for England. Initially named Jamestown, it was renamed Holetown because of a tidal hole near the beach. It was quite heavily defended until after the Napoleonic Wars. Little trace of the forts can be seen now. Well worth visiting is **St James Church**. Originally built of wood in 1628, it was replaced by a stone structure in 1680. This building was extended 20 ft west in 1874 when columns and arches were added and the nave roof raised. You can see the original baptismal font (1684) under the belfry and in the north porch is the original bell of 1696. Many of the original settlers are buried here (although the oldest tombstone of William Balston who died in 1659 is in the Barbados Museum). Church documents dating to 1693 have been removed to the Department of Archives. It was beautifully restored between 1983-86 and the organ was restored in 2005.

❢ For more information on west coast beaches, see page 841.

On the beach behind the church is the **Folkestone Park and Marine Reserve** ① *T4222314, open daily*. Here you can snorkel in a large area enclosed by buoys. The reef is not in very good condition but there are fish. Snorkelling equipment for hire as are glass-bottomed boats which will take you over the reef to two small wrecks further down the coast. A diving platform about 100 yds offshore allows you to snorkel over the wrecks. There are lockers, toilets and a shower here. There's a small **museum** ① *Mon-Fri 0900-1700; buy ticket B$1.15 in gift shop alongside*; a guide will take you upstairs to see some dusty exhibits, then show you a video of marine life along the US seaboard (not Barbados), then let you into the museum.

The **Sir Frank Hutson Sugar Machinery Museum** ① *T4320100, Mon-Sat 0900-1700, US$7.50 when factory is running Feb-May, US$4 the rest of the time, children half price*, inland beside the **Portvale Sugar Factory** off Highway 2a has an interesting exhibition on the story of sugar and its products, guided tour recommended. Jars of excellent molasses and sugar syrup for sale.

Speightstown

Follow the coast road and glimpse the sea at Gibbes and Mullins Bays to reach Speightstown where William Speight once owned the land. An important trading port in the early days, when it was known as Little Bristol. Speightstown is now the main shopping centre for the north of the island. There are several interesting old buildings and many two-storey shops with Georgian balconies and overhanging galleries (sadly many have been knocked down by passing lorries). **Arlington** is a 17th-century structure built on the lines of an English late medieval town house.

The National Trust runs the **Arbib Nature and Heritage Trail** ① *T4262421 (the National Trust), walks Wed, Thu and Sat 0930 and1430, US$7.50*, starting in Speightstown. There are routes of 3½ miles and 4½ miles, starting from St Peter's church (call the day before to reserve).

A US$60 mn marina for six mega-yachts and 140 yachts has been built at Heywoods Beach just north of Speightstown, known as **Port St Charles**, ww.portstcharles.com. There are 145 residential units, a restaurant, a yacht club, heliport and watersports.

Northern Barbados

North of Speightstown

The road north of Speightstown is mercifully free of buildings and there is a good sandy beach on **Six Men's Bay**. Go through Littlegood Harbour and notice the boat building on the beach. The jetty you can see is at Harrison Point. Almost any of the roads off Highway 1B will take you to the north coast, at first green and lush around Stroud Point but becoming more desolate as you approach North Point. The northwest coast, being slightly sheltered from the Atlantic swells, has many sandy coves (Archers Bay). The cliffs are quiet and easy to walk. You may spot turtles in the sea.

The **Animal Flower Cave** ① *daily 0900-1600, US$5, children US$2.50*, at North Point is a series of caverns at sea level which have been eroded by the sea. The animals are sea anemones but there are now so few of them the cave should be renamed. There are various 'shapes' in the rock which are pointed out to you and a pool at the mouth of the cave where you can swim looking out to sea. The view from **North Point** over the cliffs and ledges is worth the trip even if (or particularly when) the cave is shut because of high seas. Eight miles of caverns have been created along the coast by the erosion

⁝ *Pronounced Spitestown or Spikestong in broad dialect.*

of the waves. The main cave can be closed due to dangerous seas. The floor of the cave is very stoney and can be slippery. Bar, toilets, souvenir shops outside.

Good walks along the cliffs can be enjoyed, for instance from River Bay to Little Bay along the Antilles Flat, but beware as there is no shade and there are shooting parties during the season. If driving, several back roads go through the attractive communities of Spring Garden and St Clements. At Pie Corner you can rejoin the coast and visit **Little Bay**. This is particularly impressive during the winter months with the swell breaking over the coral outcrops and lots of blowholes. Note the completely circular hole on the north edge of the bay. If you climb through this natural archway in the cliff, there is a big, calm pool, just deep enough to swim between the cliffs and a line of rock on which the enormous waves break and send up a wall of spray. Wear shoes to stop your feet getting cut to pieces on the sharp rock.

At **Paul's Point** is a popular picnic area. If the ground looks wet park at the millwall by the Cove Stud Farm as it is easy to get bogged down. You will get a good view of **Gay's Cove** with its shingle beach (safe to swim in the pools at low tide) and beyond it the 240-ft high **Pico Teneriffe**, a large rock (named by sailors who thought it looked like the mountain on Teneriffe in the Canaries) on top of a steeply sloping cliff. The white cliffs are oceanic rocks consisting of myriad tiny white shells or microscopic sea creatures. The whole of the coast to Bathsheba is visible and it is easy to see the erosion taking place in Corben's Bay. Indeed you get an excellent impression of the Scotland District, where the coral limestone has been eroded. The whole coast between North and Ragged Points has been zoned, no further development will be allowed along the seafront.

Scotland District

Just to the northwest is **St Nicholas Abbey** ① US$13, which is approached down a long and impressive avenue of mahogany trees. Dating from around 1660 and recently restored by new owners, it is one of the oldest domestic buildings in the English-speaking Americas (**Drax Hall**, St George, open occasionally under the National Trust Open Houses programme, is probably even older). Three storied, it has a façade with three ogee-shaped gables. It was never an abbey, some have supposed that the 'Saint' and 'Abbey' were added to impress, there being lots of 'Halls' in the south of the island. Visitors are given an interesting tour (or follow the information leaflet for a self-guided tour) of the ground floor and a fascinating film show in the stables behind the 400-year-old sand box tree, showing life on a sugar plantation in the 1930s. You will see the millwall in action and the many skilled workers from wheel wrights to coopers who made the plantation work. The importance of wind is emphasized. If the windmill stopped, the whole harvest halted, as the cane which had been cut would quickly dry out if it was not crushed straight away. The waste was used to fuel the boilers, as it is today in sugar factories. From time to time the old machinery is used to grind sugar cane, a special event.

Going back down the steep Cherry Tree Hill you come to the National Trust-owned **Morgan Lewis Mill** ① T4227429, Mon-Sat 0900-1700, US$5, children US$2.50, a millwall with original machinery which the National Trust has restored. Note the 100-ft tail, this enabled the operators to position the mill to maximize the effect of the wind. It is on a working farm. On the flat savannah at the bottom of the hill, the cricket pitch is a pleasant place to watch the game at weekends.

⚑ Built around 1776, Morgan Lewis Mill is the largest, complete windmill in the Caribbean. You can

The **Barbados Wildlife Reserve** ① T4228826, http://barbadosmonkey.dhc-ltd.com, daily 1000-1700, US$11.50, children half price, established with Canadian help in 1985, is set in four acres of mature mahogany off Highway 2. They have a huge collection of the large red-footed Barbados tortoise, apparently the largest in the world, which roam slowly around all over the paths, while deer and agouti lounge about. There is an architecturally interesting bird house with snakes upstairs and you look down through the floor to the aviary. The population of the rabbit pen is seriously out of control and the lone wallaby kept with the rabbits and guinea pigs looks stunned. It is an excellent place to see lots of Barbados green monkeys close up if they haven't taken off to the forest next door. The primate research centre helps to provide farmers with advice on how to control the green monkeys who are regarded as a pest. The animals are fed near it at about 1400. The centre has also developed a nature trail in the neighbouring **Grenade Hall Forest**, with over a mile of coral pathways and interpretative signs. They can be rough, steep and slippery and are not wheelchair friendly. An early 19th- century **signal station** next to Grenade Hall Forest which closed in 1884, rendered obsolete by the telephone, has been restored. The panoramic view conveys its original role in the communications

⚑ Most of the animals are not caged, you are warned to be careful as you wander around the shady paths.

network and an audio tape gives the history. There's a Café and shop. You can get there by bus from Bridgetown, Holetown, Speightstown or Bathsheba.

Farley Hill House ① T4223555, daily 0830-1800, US$1.75 per vehicle, St Peter, is a 19th-century fire-damaged plantation house; a spectacular ruin on the other side of the road from the Wildlife Reserve, set in a pleasant park with spectacular views over the Scotland District. There is a large number of imported and native tree species, some labelled, planted over 30 acres of woodland. There are picnic benches under the trees and it is popular with Bajan families on Sunday.

Atlantic Parishes

The five-mile East Coast Road, opened by Queen Elizabeth on 15 February 1966 affords fine views. From Belleplaine, where the railway ended, it skirts Walker's Savannah to the coast at Long Pond and heads southeast to **Benab**, where there is **Barclays Park**, a good place to stop for a picnic under the shady casuarina trees. Walk up **Chalky Mount** for magnificent views of the east coast, easily reached at the end of the bus line from Bridgetown. If you ask locally for the exact path you are likely to be given several different routes. Walk down through the meadows to Barclays Park for a drink. Ask staff in the café for bus times to either Bathsheba or Speightstown. The East Coast Road continues through **Cattlewash**, so named because Bajans brought their animals here to wash them in the sea, to Bathsheba.

The tiny hamlet of **Bathsheba** has an excellent surfing beach (see page 841). Guarded by two rows of giant boulders, the bay seems to be almost white as the surf trails out behind the Atlantic rollers. Surfing championships are often held here. Swimming here is not recommended due to the strong currents, only surfers usually venture out. Splashing around in the rock pools is a cooling alternative. A railway was built in 1883 (but closed in 1937) between Bridgetown and Bathsheba. Originally conceived as going to Speightstown, it actually went up the east coast to a terminus at Belleplaine, St Andrew. The cutting at My Lady's Hole, near Conset Bay in St John is spectacular, with a gradient of 1:31, which is supposed to have been the steepest in the world except for rack and pinion and other special types of line. The railway here suffered from landslides, wave erosion, mismanagment and underfunding so that the 37-mile track was in places in very bad condition. The crew would sprinkle sand on the track, the first class passengers remained seated, the second class walked and the third class pushed. There is good walking along the old railway track, through Bath to Conset Bay, although you have to scramble on some bits.

Above the bay at Hillcrest (excellent view) are the **Andromeda Gardens** ① T4339261, daily 0900-1700, US$6, children US$3. Owned by the Barbados National Trust, the gardens contain plants from all over Barbados as well as species from other parts of the world. There are many varieties of orchid, hibiscus and flowering trees. The **Hibiscus Café** has good juices (closes 1645).

From Bathsheba you can head inland to **Cotton Tower signal station** (National Trust owned. Not as interesting as Gun Hill). Then head south to Wilson Hill where you find Mount Tabor Church and **Villa Nova**, aprivately-owned plantation Great House (1834), which has furniture made of Barbadian mahogany and beautiful gardens. It was once owned by the former British Prime Minister, Sir Anthony Eden. You can continue from here via Malvern along the scenic **Hackleton's Cliff** (allegedly named after Hackleton who committed suicide by riding his horse over the cliff) or via Sherbourne to Pothouse, where **St John's Church** looks over the Scotland District. Built in 1660 it was a victim of the hurricane of 1835. There is a pulpit made from six different kinds of wood. You will also find the grave of Fernando Paleologus "descendant of ye imperial line of ye last Christian emperors of Greece". The full story is in Leigh Fermor's *The Traveller's Tree*.

⁞ The National Trust

The National Trust runs an Open House programme of visits to interesting private houses on Wednesday afternoons from January to April every year (B$18, children 5-12 half price, B$15 for members of foreign National Trusts. For anyone without transport, Boyces Garage do a tour plus entrance for B$40, T4251103, www.toursbarbados.com.). The houses are not necessarily old, in fact many of them are modern in the extreme, often occupied by diplomats. A **National Trust Heritage passport** is available for sites maintained by the Trust. A full passport costs US$35 and gives a 50% discount to 15 National Trust sites as well as invitations to the open house programme. A mini passport costs US$18 and allows half price entry to five sites. The **Duke of Edinburgh Award Scheme** (Bridge House, Cavans Lane, Bridgetown, T4369763) and **National Trust** joint scheme also arrange early Sunday morning walks to places of historical and natural interest. There is a reciprocal free entry to **National Trust Properties** for members of the National Trust in the UK, Australia, New Zealand, Fiji and Zimbabwe. The same arrangement applies to members of the **National Trust for Historic Preservation** in the USA and the **Heritage Canada Foundation**. The National Trust Headquarters is at Wildey House, Wildey, T4262421, natrust@sunbeach.net, open 0800-1600, which houses the Trust's collection of antique furniture and the Euchard Fitzpatrick and Edward Stoute photography collections.

Turn left after a few miles for the downhill road to **Bath**. Here you will find a safe beach, popular with Barbadians and a recreation park for children. It makes a good spot for a beach barbecue and a swim and a beach bar does a good lunch.

Codrington College ⓘ *US$2.50*, is one of the most famous landmarks on the island and can be seen from Highway 4B down an avenue of Cabbage (Royal) Palm trees. It is steeped in history as the first Codrington landed in Barbados in 1628. His son acted as Governor for three years but was dismissed for liberal views. Instead he stood for parliament and was elected speaker for nine years. He was involved in several wars against the French and became probably the wealthiest man in the West Indies. The third Codrington succeeded his father as Governor-General of the Leeward islands, attempted to stamp out the considerable corruption of the time and distinguished himself in campaigns (especially in taking St Kitts). He died in 1710, a bachelor aged 42, and left his Barbadian properties to the Society for the Propagation of the Gospel in Foreign Parts. It was not until 1830 that Codrington College, where candidates could study for the Anglican priesthood, was established. From 1875 to 1955 it was associated with Durham University, England. Apart from its beautiful grounds with huge lily pond (flowers close up in the middle of the day) and impressive façade, there is a chapel containing a plaque to Sir Christopher Codrington and a library. You can follow the track which drops down 360 ft to the sea at the beautiful Conset Bay. To get there, you can take the Sargeant St bus as far as Codrington College, then walk 7 miles back along the Atlantic Coast to Bathsheba.

At **Ragged Point** is the automatic **East Point lighthouse** standing among the ruined houses of the former lighthouse keepers. There are good views north towards Conset Point, the small Culpepper island, and the south coast. Note the erosion to the 80-ft cliffs caused by the Atlantic sweeping into the coves. An atmospheric station close to the shoreline measures air quality; this is the first landfall after blowing across the Atlantic from the coast of Africa.

Central Barbados

Northeast of Holetown and reached from St Simon's Church are **Turners Hall Woods**, a good vantage point. It is thought that the wood has changed little to that which covered the island before the English arrived. The 50-acre patch of tropical mesophytic forest has never been clear-felled (although individual trees were often taken out). You can cross the steep paths and see species ranging from the sandbox tree to Jack-in-the-box and the 100-ft locust trees supported by massive buttresses.

On Highway 2, take the Melvin Hill road just after the agricultural station and follow the signs to the **Flower Forest** ① *T4338152, ffl@sunbeach.net, daily 0900-1700, US$7, children 5-16 half price*, a 50-acre, landscaped plantation, opened in 1983 with beautifully laid out gardens. Dropping downhill, the well-maintained paths afford excellent views over the valley to the east coast. To the west you can see Mount Hillaby, at 1,116 ft the island's highest point. It contains species from Barbados and from all over the world, they are arranged with plenty of colour all year round. There is a **Best of Barbados** shop, cafeteria and toilets. Good information sheet. Nearby is **Springvale Eco-Heritage Museum** ① *T4387011, Mon-Sat 1000-1600, US$5, café*, a folk museum on an 80-ha former sugar plantation with a presentation of historical rural Barbadian life. The owner, Newlands Greenidge, can trace his ancestry back to 1631 and a ship which came from Greenwich. He will explain the day-to-day items in the museum showing how people used to live in colonial times, and will take you along a path outside pointing out the various plants and their uses.

Close by and to the south on Highway 2 is **Welchman Hall Gully** ① *T4386671, daily 0900-1700, US$6, children US$3*, a fascinating walk through one of the deep ravines so characteristic of this part of Barbados. You are at the edge of the limestone cap which covers most of the island to a depth of about 300 ft. There is a small car park opposite the entrance (despite the sign to the contrary). Maintained by the National Trust, a good path leads for about half a mile through six sections, each with a slightly different theme. The first section has a devil tree, a stand of bamboo and a judas tree. Next you will go through jungle, lots of creepers, the 'pop-a-gun' tree and bearded fig clinging to the cliff (note the stalactites and stalagmites); a section devoted to palms and ferns: golden, silver, macarthur and cohune palms, nutmegs and wild chestnuts; to open areas with tall leafy mahogany trees, rock balsam and mango trees. At the end of the walk are ponds with lots of frogs and toads. Best of all though is the wonderful view to the coast. On the left are some steps leading to a gazebo, at the same level as the tops of the cabbage palms.

Harrison's Cave ① *T4386640, daily 0830-1630, US$12.50, children US$5*, nearby has a centre with restaurant (fair), shop and a small display of local geology and Amerindian artefacts. You are taken into the cave on an electric 'train'. The visit takes about 20 minutes and you will see some superbly lit stalactites and stalagmites, waterfalls and large underground lakes. There is a guide to point out the interesting formations and two stops for photo-opportunities. It is all rather overdone, you have to wear hard hats (to prevent complaints of bumped heads) and serviettes on your head despite the fact that the caves are totally stable. The bus from Bridgetown to Chalky Mount stops near Harrison's Cave and the Flower Forest.

If you take Highway 2 heading to Bridgetown you will pass **Jack-in-the-Box gully**, part of the same complex of Welchman Hall Gully and Harrison's Cave. **Coles Cave** (an 'undeveloped' cave nearby, which can easily be explored with a waterproof torch or flashlight) lies at its north end.

At **Gun Hill** ① *T4291358, Mon-Sat 0900-1700, US$5 (children half price), guide book US$1*, is a fully restored signal tower. The approach is by Fusilier road and you will pass the Lion carved by British soldiers in 1868. The road was built by Royal Scot Fusiliers between September 1862 and February 1863 when they were stationed at

Gun Hill to avoid yellow fever. The signal station itself had its origins in the slave uprising of 1816. It was decided that a military presence would be maintained outside Bridgetown in case of further slave uprisings. It was also intended for advance warning of attack from the sea. The chain of six signal stations would give very rapid communications with the rest of the island. They quickly lost importance as military installations but provided useful information about shipping movements. The hexagonal tower had two small barrack rooms attached and would have been surrounded by a pallisade. The fusiliers' cookhouse has been converted to a snack bar.

Orchid World ① *Groves, St George, T4330306, 0900-1700, US$7, children half price, discount if you visit Flower Forest*, is a 6½-acre orchid garden, 20,000 of them, mind-blowing, beautifully designed, don't miss it. There's a gift shop and snack bar.

Southern Barbados

The southeast coast

The area around Six Roads was where the Easter Rebellion of 1816 took place. Turn north at Six Roads roundabout for **Sunbury Plantation** ① *T4236270, daily 0930-1630, US$7.50*. Some 300 years old, the house is elegantly furnished in

❧ *Six Roads was called Six Cross Roads until they installed a roundabout.*

Georgian style, much of it with mahogany furniture, and you can roam all over it as, unusually, there is access to the upstairs rooms. In the cellars, you can see the domestic quarters. There is a good collection of carriages. The house and museum were damaged by fire in 1995 but have been restored and opened again. There's a restaurant in the courtyard.

Sam Lord's Castle ① *hotel currently closed and in receivership*, on the southeast coast is high on the list of tourist attractions because of the reputation of Sam Lord who reputedly lured ships onto Cobbler's Reef where they were shipwrecked. There is supposed to be a tunnel from the beach to the castle's cellars to facilitate his operation. The proceeds made him a wealthy man although the castle was more likely to have been financed from his marriage to a wealthy heiress. The castle is not particularly old or castle-like, being in fact a regency building.

Crane Bay, southwest of Sam Lord's Castle, is worth a detour. It is a pleasant cove with lovely pink sand and body-surfing waves, overlooked by 80-ft cliffs. **Crane Hotel** at the top of the southern cliffs charges a fee for admission, but it is worth it for the spectacular view over the bay from the cliff top restaurant. Popular for Sunday

❧ *Loungers, umbrellas, body boards for hire.*

buffet lunch as an interlude from the beach. You can access the beach from the north end without paying admission, but parking is tricky at weekends. Turn down a narrow lane off a little roundabout by Crane House.

South coast

Oistins, the main town in the parish of Christ Church, was named after Edward Oistine, a plantation owner in the area. It was important in colonial times as the place where the 'Charter of Barbados' was signed in 1652, giving the island to the Commonwealth Parliament. It is now the main fishing port and has quite a large fish market where you can see and buy the recent catch. It is fascinating to watch the workers filleting flying fish at tremendous speed and efficiency and bagging them up for sale. Friday night 'fish fry' is the big event here (see Entertainment, page 861). Christ Church parish church overlooks the town and is notable for its cemetery containing the Chase Vault. When the vault was opened in 1812 for the burial of Colonel Thomas Chase, the lead coffins were found scattered around inside. It happened again in 1816, 1817, 1819 and 1820, whereupon the coffins were removed and buried separately in the churchyard.

Graeme Hall Bird Sanctuary, Worthing, near St Lawrence Gap, T4359727, www.graemehall.com, has 36 acres of wetland and mangroves around a lake. It is the **855** largest expanse of inland water in Barbados and a natural habitat for birds; there are 18 resident species and 150 migrants. A boardwalk is open to the public but the rest is to be a bird sanctuary for scientific research only. Three endangered Caribbean duck species are found here.

🛏 Sleeping

Most accommodation offered is very pleasant, if not particularly cheap. 15% VAT is levied on hotel services. Generally, the top hotels in the **super luxury** category costing well over US$300 a night are on the west coast, while **cheap and cheerful** places can be found on the south coast, and **'getaways'** on the east coast at Bathsheba. However, you can find an **apartment** to rent on the west coast for as little as US$25 a night if you are not too demanding. **Self-catering** is popular on Barbados, partly because restaurants are not cheap, and if there is a group of you, you can find good value places to stay. The **Barbados Tourist Authority**, www.barbados.org, has a range of brochures, including one on rates for hotels, guesthouses and apartments and a brochure on lodging with families and family apartments around the island.

West coast Barbados *p848, map p842*
LL Cobblers Cove, St Peter, T4222291, www.cobblerscove.com. 40 suites, small and exclusive, English country-house style, run by Hamish Watson, wins lots of awards, high proportion of repeat business.
LL Coral Reef Club, Holetown, St James, T4222372, www.coralreefbarbados.com. Lovely landscaped gardens, lawn running down to sea, cottage style, very highly regarded.
LL The House, Paynes Bay, T4325525, www.thehousebarbados.com. The height of luxury where your personal 'ambassador' brings cold towels and drinks to your sunbed and you get a jet lag revival massage on arrival. 32 suites around a courtyard, beautifully decorated and furnished with mahogany and rattan, minibar, fridge and espresso machine, Daphne's restaurant alongside, breakfast, tea and canapés included. Well-regarded for service and atmosphere, which is unpretentious. Use of facilities of **Tamarind Cove** next door.
LL Little Good Harbour, north of

Speightstown, T4393000, www.littlegoodharbourbarbados.com. Small wooden villas around pool, across the road from the sea, nicely laid out and furnished but a bit cramped, good restaurant.
LL Lone Star Motel, on the beach next to restaurant of same name, by **Royal Pavilion**, T4190599, www.thelonestar.com. 4 huge rooms, uncluttered, simple mahogany furniture building was originally a garage built in 1940s by Romy Reid, who ran a bus company and called himself the Lone Star of the west coast, then it was a nightclub and then a house, owned by Mrs Robertson, of the jam company, who waterskied offshore until her late 80s.
LL Sandy Lane, T4442000, www.sandylane.com. Most luxurious and pretentious hotel on the island and rates vary from US$1,200 to US$6,000 a night depending on season and category. Golf, tennis, state-of-the-art spa with everything from detox to pedicures. It is worth going to the **L'Acajou** French restaurant or **Bajan Blue** or for Sun brunch buffet, 1230-1500, just to see the place (good food and not all that expensive), but you have to book ahead to get past the gate, T4442030.
LL Tamarind Cove, Paynes Bay, T4321332, www.tamarindcovehotel.com. 110 large rooms and suites overlooking pleasant gardens leading on to the beach, where there are comfy sun loungers and watersports. Room only or meal plans available, good food, also Daphne's restaurant next door for a romantic dinner. Very comfortable hotel on 3 floors, spacious balconies, wheelchair access to ground floor rooms, internet access, water taxi to the sister properties in the Elegant Hotels group.
LL-A Sandridge, 1 mile from Speightstown, T4222361, www.sandridgehotel.com. Good-sized rooms or family apartments with cooking facilities, north-facing balconies overlook pool, friendly staff and management, watersports free for guests, barbecue evenings, excellent for families.

Barbados Around Barbados Listings

L-A Sunswept Beach Hotel, Holetown, T4322715, www.sunsweptbeach.com. On the beach in town, great value for money considering the location, particularly out of season, 23 comfortable rooms, a/c, fan, TV, kitchenettes and balcony, small pool with direct access to sea, very convenient, lots of restaurants close by, shopping centre across the road, bank alongside, right in the centre of things for Holetown Carnival. Friendly staff, relaxed with no frills.

Apartments

LL-A Calypso Rentals, Paynes Bay, T4226405, www.calypso-rentals.com. Specializes in simple budget apartments and villas on the west coast. Some are right on the beach, others are a 5-min walk away from the water, whether they are pretty chattel houses or 4-bedroom villas with staff.If you are travelling in a group, it is possible to rent a property for as little as US$20 per person per day in summer.

L-AL Angler Apartments, Clarke's Rd, Derricks, T/F4320817. Owners live on premises, priority given to service, friendly, informal, family orientated, rather tired furniture and linen, but clean and good budget option, 2-min walk to beach. Chandra is exceptionally helpful and will prepare your breakfast if you want.

AL-A Villa Marie, Fitts Village, St James, T4321745, www.barbados.org /villas/villamarie. 3 large rooms, 2 apartments with kitchen (sleep 4), huge kitchen and dining room shared by all, well equipped, huge showers, pleasant garden with loungers and mature trees, barbecue, 5 mins' walk from supermarket and beach, very quiet, up side road, lots of repeat guests, run by Peter (German) and friendly guard dog Booboo.

Atlantic parishes *p851, map p842*

LL-A Edgewater Inn, Bathsheba, T4339900, www.newedgewater.com. Imposing hotel overlooking sea from the top of the cliffs, 20 a/c rooms, pool. Style outdated, with dark reception area but new management is undertaking a major renovation and upgrading project, adding balconies to the rooms and making it much more attractive. A couple of rooms are particularly sought after for their size and view.

AL-A Atlantis, Bathsheba, T4339445, www.atlantisbarbados.com. Spectacular setting, opened 1884 alongside railway, now old and tired, feeling effects of Atlantic weather. New owners have given the rooms a face lift, but they remain simple, with basic bathrooms. Enid Maxwell, who ran it from 1945-2001, has now retired.

AL-A Round House Inn, Bathsheba, T4339678, www.roundhousebarbados.com. Building dates from 1832 and overlooks the sea from the hillside, 4 rooms in round part, all different, one considerably nicer than the others with roof terrace, others cramped but light and bright, good restaurant, best place to eat in the evenings in the area, run by Robert and Gail Manley.

AL-A Sea-U, Bathsheba, T4339450, www.seaubarbados.com. The nicest place to stay on this side of the island, colonial-style wooden house on top of cliffs, 5 spacious guesthouse rooms with kitchenettes opening on to veranda with sea view, 2 studio apartments in separate cottage can be rented separately or as a single unit (**L**), run by Uschi (German), family-style meal served 2-3 times a week or when 4 or more people want to eat in, US$27.50, huge breakfast US$8, honour bar, lots of hammocks, quiet, peaceful, popular with active types who go to bed early.

South coast *p854, map p842*

Most of the South coast is wall-to-wall hotels from Hastings to Dover popular with package holiday makers. It's close to the airport, with plenty of watersports and nightlife.

LL-L Coral Sands, Worthing Beach, T4356617, www.coralsandsresort.com. Attractive hotel, 31 large oceanfront studios, all with fully-equipped kitchens, large balconies and good bathrooms, clean, fresh and elegant but comfortable. 5-min walk to The Gap for nightlife, 2-min walk to good supermarket. No entertainment at this quiet hotel but **Carib Beach Bar** is only 100m away. Area popular at weekends and the beach can get dirty. Hotel has small pool overlooking the broad sandy beach; no beach chairs.

LL-L The Savannah, Hastings, between Garrison Savannah and beach, T4359473, savannah@gemsbarbados.com.100 rooms, 21 in recently renovated historic building, antique furniture, each room different, the rest in new blocks in similar design, very smart, high-quality facilities, earth-friendly bathroom goodies, gym, pool, short walk to beach at **Hilton**, recommended for business visitors.

LL-AL Southern Palms, Christ Church, T4287171, www.southernpalms.net. Short walk to all the restaurants and nightlife of The Gap. Comfortable and unpretentious beach hotel with rooms and spacious suites with kitchenettes. Popular with couples or families, mainly British guests, lovely stretch of beach.

C-D Beach House Cleverdale, 4th Av, Worthing, T4281035, www.barbados-rentals.com. Looks like a chattel house from the outside, 15 m from Sandy Beach. Rent rooms or whole house, 5 double rooms, 4 have washbasins, 2 bathrooms, mosquito screens, large living/dining room with TV, stereo, use of kitchen, veranda and barbeque, internet access arranged, help with finding alternative accommodation if full, German-run.

Apartments
L-B Chateau Blanc Apartments On Sea, 1st Av, Worthing, T4357518, www.barbados.org. Right on the beach, apartments range from seafront 1-2 bedrooms to seaview studios or rooms with kitchenettes. Good value, well-equipped, friendly management.

AL-A The Nook Apartments, Dayrells Rd in Rockley, T/F4276502, www.thenookbarbados.com. Apartments and studios, small rooms, renovated 2005, with pool, maid service, TV, phone, clean, secure, convenient for shops and restaurants, 2 mins from Accra/Rockley beach.

AL-C Venice Gardens & Bonanza Apartments, 4th Av, Dover, T4289097, bonanza@sunbeach.net. Studio, 1 or 2 bedrooms, helpful, quite convenient but not too clean.

A Melrose Beach Apartments, Worthing, T4357985, www.melrosebeach-apts.com. Good location, 2-min walk to beach, but on main road, parking, 14, 1-bedroom units in pink concrete block, a/c, kitchenette, living room, tiled floors, large bed, simple.

A-B Roman Beach Apartments, Enterprise, near Oistins, T4287635, www.romanbeach.com. Friendly, simple, comfortable studios with kitchenette, across the road from beautiful Miami beach.

857

B-C Just Home, Aquatic Gap, T4273265, justhome1@msn.com. 6 rooms from single sharing bath and kitchen to studio apartment with kitchenette, next to **Grand Barbados** and **Brown Sugar** restaurant, clean and nice, run by Caroline Phillips.

Southeast corner *p854, map p842*
LL-L Crane Beach, T4236220, www.thecrane.com. Fairly near the airport, but definitely a taxi ride away, spectacular clifftop setting, good beach, and good pool, tennis, luxury prices and usually fairly quiet with only 18 rooms, but an extra 250 timeshare units, have totally changed the character of the hotel.

LL-A Silver Sands Resort, Christ Church, T4286001, www.silversandsbarbados.com. A windsurfing resort with **Club Mistral** centre open Nov-Jun, 20 mins' drive from airport, on the sea at South Point, spacious and well equipped, good service, food dull, good beach but waves strong and high, good for surfing but children and weak swimmers should use the pools.

🍴 Eating

Barbados has a very wide range of places to eat, many of them in an interesting setting and an open-air waterfront or garden terrace. The price range in a restaurant for a main course is US$12-40, but in cheap places you can get a filling lunch for US$6. Eating out can be expensive, cheap local places are few and far between after lunchtime unless you want fried chicken every night. Fast food places include **Chefette**, **KFC**, **Pizza Man Doc** and **Chicken Barn**. The cheapest meals are in supermarkets, around US$5.

Bridgetown *p845, map p846*
♥♥♥-♥♥ **Brown Sugar**, Bay St, Aquatic Gap, T4267684. All-you-can-eat buffet lunch US$19-20 Sun to Fri 1200-1430, dinner daily from 1800. Main courses US$15-36, Bajan specialities, filling and hearty, attractive setting, lots of greenery and waterfall.
♥♥♥-♥♥ **Lobster Alive Bistro and Beach Bar**, Carlisle Bay on beach, next to **Boatyard** on Bay St, T4350305. Daily 1200-2100. Mostly lobster flown in from the Grenadines, but also other seafood and delivery.
♥♥♥-♥♥ **Waterfront Café** on the Careenage, T4270093. Food 1000-2200, drinks until

Barbados Around Barbados Listings

2400, closed Sun. Interesting food, plenty to look at and a good social centre in the evenings, live entertainment some nights, good Caribbean Buffet Tue, US$22.50. Live entertainment, mostly jazz.

♥ **Balcony Upstairs**, in Cave Shepherd on Broad St. Lunch Mon-Fri 1100-1500.

♥ **Christie's Canteen**, at Light and Power Company, on Bay St and at Spring Gardens. Open to the public, huge traditional lunch.

♥ **De Kitchen**, on Bay St, near **Boatyard**, T4272214. Does combo plate US$7.

♥ **Mustors Harbour**, McGregor St, T4265175. Mon-Fri 0900-1600. Third generation family business, snackette downstairs with Bajan fishcakes, etc, restaurant upstairs, tasty, filling Bajan food.

♥ **Pop's Place**, on Cheapside Rd, T4305979. Nice setting, very clean, only US$7 for good, filling lunch.

♥ **Port Hole**, Fontabelle, near Board of Tourism Office. Friendly bar, good solid lunch for US$6.

♥ **Tim's**, 43 Swan St. Local food, eat in or takeaway, on balcony or a/c, US$2-3 per portion, busy at lunchtime with office workers.

West coast *p848, map p842*

♥♥♥ **The Cliff**, Derricks, St James, T4321922. Dinner only, Mon-Sat, plus Sun in winter season. Worth the prices for a glimpse of the decor, stunning desserts, attractive and delightful meal, another recommended as the best food on the island.

♥♥♥ **Daphne's**, Payne's Bay, T4322731. 1200-1500, 1830-2130, cocktail bar open from 1200. Italian, chic and contemporary, try to get waterfront table when booking.

♥♥♥ **La Mer**, at Port St Charles Marina, T4192000. Tue-Fri lunch, Tue-Sat dinner, Sun brunch. Waterfront dining overlooking the lagoon and the yachts berthed outside luxury apartments.

♥♥♥ **Lone Star**, Mount Standfast, T4190599, www.thelonestar.com. 1130-2230. With caviar bar, 3 types from Iran, lunch US$20-3,000, depending on how much caviar you eat, sushi, oriental and Asian dishes as well as Caribbean, wonderful setting, beach level, plenty of space, not ruinous if you choose carefully.

♥♥♥ **Mango's by the Sea**, Speightstown, T4220704, www.mangosbythesea.com. Dinner only, 1800-2145. Nice waterfront setting in old wooden building, romantic, free shuttle from all points north of Holetown.

♥♥♥ **Mannie's Suga Suga**, Mullins Bay, just south of Speightstown, St Peter, T4223892. Daily 0900-2200, no dinner Thu, Sun. What was once a beach bar is now very posh with sun lounger service on the beach and a restaurant overlooking the sand. Meals and snacks served all day. Mon nights there is a cabaret show, US$3 cover charge. Japanese and Thai food.

♥♥♥ **Olives**, 2nd St, Holetown, T4322112. Dinner only, last orders 2230. Mediterranean/Caribbean, bistro atmosphere. Pizza and pasta or more elaborate main courses. Pudding lovers must try the bread and butter pudding with toffee brandy sauce.

♥♥♥ **The Tides**, Holdtown, T4328356, www.tidesbarbados.com. Mon-Fri lunch, Mon-Sat dinner, reservations required. Seafood, meat and vegetarian dishes, served on an ocean–front terrace, a/c lounge for drinks. Very highly thought of, one of the best restaurants on the island. Home to On the Wall art gallery.

♥♥♥ ♥♥ **Angry Annie's**, 1st St, Holetown, T4322119. Very colourful, informal, brightly painted, sociable host, dinner only, ribs, steak, lobster, rack of lamb, curries.

♥♥♥-♥♥ **The Fish Pot**, T4392604, at **Little Good Harbour Hotel**, north of Speightstown, in 18th-century Fort Rupert. Imaginative menu, nice setting, reservations advised.

♥♥♥-♥♥ **The Mews**, 2nd St, Holetown, T4321122. Daily from 1830. Quite expensive but superb food, mix of local and French dishes, very pretty house, tables on balcony or interior patio. Live jazz Fri.

♥♥ **Café Indigo**, Highway 1, Holetown, opposite Methodist Church, T4320968. Open for breakfast and lunch 0800-1700. Upstairs in old building, full English US$10, pub lunch, US$8-12.50 main course, well-stocked bar.

♥♥ **Cocomos**, Holetown, T4320134. On beach, varied and interesting menu, salads, seafood, steak, burgers and pasta, good solid food, spacious, airy, quick service, pleasant staff, nice atmosphere. Happy hour 1600-1800.

♥♥ **Jumbo's**, 1 Clarke's Gap, Derricks, T4328032. Closed Mon, Fri lunch only, Sat, Sun dinner only. Chattel conversion with added veranda, lunch buffet, good wine list, reasonable prices, adventurous food with Thai, Japanese and Bajan influences.

⍢ Sitar, 2nd St, Holetown, T4322248. Indian, just the place for a tandoori or a hot vindaloo, veg lunch buffet US$15.

⍢ The Tree House, Earthworks Pottery, Edgehill Heights No 2, St Thomas, T4252890, treehouse@sunbeach.net. Mon-Fri 0900-1700, Sat 1000-1430. Time your shopping trip to the pottery so you can have lunch with a wonderful view from the veranda over the coasts. Marguerite Moe runs one of the best cafés on the island, offering imaginative salads, sandwiches, panini, focaccia, pita bread, cakes, juices, smoothies, iced or hot teas and coffees, soups in winter, all delicious, beautifully presented on Earthworks' tableware.

⍢ Fisherman's Pub in Speightstown, T4222703. 1000-1600, happy time 1600-1800, dinner 1800-2130 except Sun 1800-2200. Good meal for US$7 and right on seafront, order and pay for food at bar, take ticket and hand in to kitchen, no frills, no table service, Wed night dinner from 1900 with steel band and floor show from 2000 on the deck over sea, diners US$17.50, non-diners US$2.50.

⍢ Patisserie Flindt, 1st St, Holetown, St James, T4322626, patisserieflindt@ caribsurf.com. Mon-Fri 0700-1700, Sat 0700-1400, Sun 0700-1200. Also smaller outlet at Quayside Centre, Rockley, T4352600, Mon-Wed 1000-1800, Thu-Sat 1000 2130. Two locations but the Holetown is the larger, with seating for breakfast, lunch or tea, or a snack at any time of day. The cakes, desserts and sweets in the patisserie are divine but pricey and the hand-made chocolates are out of this world. Sandwiches, salads and pasta are on offer at lunchtime and at weekends they do a full English breakfast. Picnics can be made to order. Ideal for an event such as the Holders Season.

South coast *p854, map p842*

⍢⍢⍢ Champers, Hastings, T4356644. Mon-Sat 1130-late. Waterfront bar and bistro, dining room upstairs on balcony, champagne from US$60.

⍢⍢⍢ Josef's, St Lawrence Gap, T4207638. Dinner only, 1830-2200. Small, delightful, is well used by Barbadians, you need to book well ahead, arrive early and have pre-dinner drinks on the lawn with the sea lapping the wall a few feet below you, candlelit elegance, delicious food.

⍢⍢⍢ Pisces, St Lawrence Gap, T4356564. From 1830. Perfect candlelit waterfront setting with waves lapping beneath you, good fish dishes, flying fish, lobster, excellent vegetarian platter, very popular, staff rushed off their feet, service suffers.

⍢⍢⍢-⍢⍢ 39 Steps, on the coast road near the Garrison, T4270715. Mon- Fri 1200-2400, Sat 1800-2400, closed Sun and holidays. Well run and lively, imaginative blackboard menu and choice of indoors or balcony, popular, so book at weekends.

⍢⍢⍢-⍢⍢ Bellini's Trattoria, Little Bay Hotel, St Lawrence Gap, T4357246. Daily 1800-2230. Italian menu, fresh pasta, but not just spaghetti and pizza, food average, come here for the view of te bay and boats.

⍢⍢⍢-⍢⍢ Zafran, El Sueño, Worthing Main Rd, Worthing, T4358995. Tue-Sun 3-course lunch US$19, Mon-Sat dinner. Indian, Persian and Thai, wine and tapas upstairs in bell tower or late-night lounge bar, afternoon tea on the croquet lawn.

⍢⍢ Café Sol, St Lawrence Gap, T4359531. 1800-2300, happy hours 1800-1900, 2200-2300. Grill and **Margarita** bar, 15 flavours of margaritas, very popular, Mexican American, 10% discount for takeaway on street corner, good for people watching.

⍢⍢ Carib Beach Bar, Worthing, T4358540. Open from 0900, happy hour Mon-Fri 1700-1800. Inexpensive meals (main course US$10-15) and drinks, barbecue and music twice a week, excellent rum punches, great fun even if you are not eating.

The Atlantic parishes *p851, map p842*

There are several decent beach bars on the east coast serving lunch, drinks and snacks: **Barclays Park Beach Bar**; **Sand Dunes**, Belleplaine, T4229427, open 0900-2100, Fri pm fish fry; **Beach Bar** at Bath; **Lighthouse Restaurant & Bar**, at Ragged Point and **Bonito Bar**, Bathsheba.

⍢⍢⍢-⍢⍢ Naniki, Suriname, St Joseph, T4331300, www.lushlife.bb. Tue-Sun 1000-sundown, lunch 1200-1500, tea 1600-1800. Difficult to get to but well worth the effort, car or strong legs required, take turning off Highway 3 just south of St Joseph's church, signs to **Lush Life Nature Resort** (Naniki), on hillside overlooking Atlantic coast, great view over fields and palm

trees, anthurium farm on property, cool and airy, eat on deck or inside, Sun buffet; full-moon dinners by arrangement, local ingredients, much of it organic, Bajan style, a special place, run by Tom Hinds.
₸₸₸-₸₸ Roundhouse Inn, Bathsheba (see Sleeping). 0800-1000, 1130-1500, 1830-2100. Good, lovely restored location, overlooks sea, the best place to eat at night in the area, tasty starters, unusual combinations of ingredients, jazz Wed nights, reggae Sat, guitarist Sun lunch, closed Sun night.

⊙ Bars and clubs

Barbados *p845, maps p842 and p846*
Look in *Visitor* and *Sun Seeker* or in *Weekend Nation* on Fri for information about what's on each night. There are quite a selection. Most charge US$12.50 or more for entry on 'free drinks' night, less when you are paying for the drinks. It's worth phoning in advance to find out what is on offer. There are live bands on certain nights in some clubs. Most do not get lively until almost midnight, and close around 0400. Some have a complicated set of dress codes or admission rules, which is another reason for phoning ahead.
Casbah, in Holetown, otherwise known as **Baku**, same building as **La Terra** and **Baku** restaurants. The best place on the west coast, billed as 'European style' and 'Moroccan themed', Thu free drinks, Wed Latin beat, excellent live music some nights with local bands, popular with those in their 20s and 30s, glorious setting beside the sea, get a table lit by fairy lights overlooking the water, very romantic.
After Dark, St Lawrence Gap. Huge selection at the bar, very lively, live music quite often, more Bajans than tourists.
The Boatyard, T4362622, is the sailor's pub in front of the anchorage at Carlisle Bay, Bay St, Happy hour 1700-1800 and 2000-2100 Wed, 1700-1900 and 2100-2300 Fri. Free drinks on Tue, US$17.50 with live band, sunset beach party on Wed, after work wind down Fri with entertainment, US$5, very lively all week, popular with land-lubbers too.
Bubba's Bar, Rockley. Has 10-ft video screen plus 10 other TVs for watching sports while you drink.
Chiller's, Worthing, north side of main road

opposite **Sandy Beach**. A lively pub with music and dancing, no entry charge.
Coach House, Paynes Bay, St James, T4321163. Lively pub.
Harbour Lights, Bay St, T4367225, www.harbourlightsbarbados.com. A younger crowd, lots of tourists and expats, open-air on the beach, local and disco music, crowded. Fri US$17.50 entry covers 'free' drinks, Sun and Thu 2130-0300 no cover charge, Mon and Wed beach party with dinner and show with fire eaters, limbo dancers, karaoke, all ages 1900-2230, drinking continues after then.
McBride's Irish Pub, St Lawrence Gap, T4207646. Has DJ or live music every night except Fri, which is karaoke. Aksi quiz nights, Latin dancing, back in time dancing, games room with pool tables.
Reggae Lounge, St Lawrence Gap, T4356462. A bit sleezy but can be fun, different happenings every night, events change with the season, check the weekly 'what's on' section in Friends magazine.
The Ship Inn, St Lawrence Gap, T4207447, has a big outdoor area and is often packed, especially at weekends, live music, major parties and Thu and Sat, happy hours 1600-1800 and 2200-2300.
Waterfront Café, the Careenage, Bridgetown, T4270093. Is really a bar/restaurant, not a dance place, but has live entertainment Mon-Sat, most nights are jazz or steel pan.

Dances and fêtes
Try one of the dances which are advertized in the *Nation* newspaper on Fri: ballroom dancing to slows and 'back in times'. People hire a dance hall, charge admission (usually US$5), provide a disco, and keep the profits. There are few foreigners, but the atmosphere is friendly, and the drinks cheaper than in the smarter nightclubs. There are also fêtes, younger crowd and Jamaican-style dub music, advertised by poster and sometimes on the radio. Venues include **Penthouse**, close to Parliament buildings in Bridgetown, **Cactus** in Silver Sands, **Liberty** in Black Rock, **De Base** on Bay St in Bridgetown, etc. Unfortunately, there have been a few fights at 'Dub' fêtes and they are no longer as relaxed as they were.

Rumshops

For Rum tours, see page 865. **Baxters Rd** in Bridgetown used to be the place to try but fewer people go there now. The one-roomed, ramshackle, rumshops are open all night, and there's a lot of street life after midnight. Some of the rumshops sell fried chicken (the **Pink Star** is recommended, it has a large indoor area and clean lavatories) and there are women in the street selling fish, seasoned and fried in coconut oil over an open fire. Especially recommended if you are hungry after midnight.

Nelson St rumshops are really houses of ill repute but have amazing larger-than-life naif paintings on the outside. Interior upstairs bar decor is a mix of girlie pix, fluorescent pointilliste and portraits of politicians.

Oistins on a Fri night is a major event for both Bajans and tourists. Lots of shops selling fish meals and other food, dub music one end and at the other a small club where they play oldies for ballroom dancing. It continues on Sat and Sun, though a bit quieter, some food places also stay open through the week. In the north of the island there is a smaller fish fry at Half Moon Fort, just north of Little Good Harbour, with tuna, barracuda, kingfish, next to the beach and under a breadfruit tree. US$7.50, Fri, Sat and Sun 1800 till very late. Also recommended is **Fisherman's Pub** on the waterfront in **Speightstown**, lots of music on Wed (see above).

If you drink in a rumshop, rum and other drinks are bought by the bottle. The smallest size is a mini, then a flask, then a full bottle. The shop will supply ice and glasses, you buy a mixer, and serve yourself. The same system operates in dances, though prices are higher; night clubs, of course, serve drinks by the glass like anywhere else. Wine, in a rumshop, usually means sweet sherry. If you are not careful, it is drunk with ice and beer.

Party cruises

The **Jolly Roger**, T4300900, www.tallshipcruises.com, run 4-hr daytime and evening cruises along the west coast to Holetown, near the Folkestone Underwater Park (where the fun and games take place) from the deepwater harbour. The drinks are unlimited (very). There is also a meal, music, dancing, etc, US$55 for the dinner cruise. On daytime cruises, there is swimming and snorkelling.

The **Harbour Master**, The Shallow Draught, Bridgetown, T4300900. www.tallshipcruises.com, Tue-Thu 1100-1600, 1800-2200. Unlike the other cruises it pulls up on the beach, a floating fun palace, 100 ft long, 40 ft wide with 4 decks like a Mississippi paddle steamer. During the day it rolls out the Malibu Splash water slide and is a semi-dubmersible, while at night there is limbo dancing and a floor show as well as live music and a DJ during the dinner cruise, see Sailing, page 865.

⊙ Entertainment

Barbados *p845, maps p842 and p846*
Cinemas
Globe, Upper Roebuck St, Bridgetown, T4264692. **Olympus Theatres Multiplex** at Sheraton Mall, T4371000, 6 screens. **Globe drive-in**, off ABC Highway, T4370479.

Shows
1627 And All That, The Barbados Museum, T4281627, Thu, 1830, US$62.50 including transport. Colourful show, bar, hors d'oeuvres, buffet dinner, tour of the museum, steel band.
Bajan Roots and Rhythms Tropical Spectacular Dinner Show at the **Plantation Restaurant**, St Lawrence, T4285048. US$75 with buffet dinner and transport from hotel (US$47.50 without transport), Wed and Fri, starts 1830.

Theatres
There are several good semi-professional theatre companies. Performances are advertised in the press. It is usually wise to buy tickets in advance. Most people dress quite formally for these performances. The **Daphne Joseph Hackett Theatre** in Queen's Park or the **Frank Collymore Hall** in the Central Bank are common venues.

⊙ Shopping

Barbados *p845, maps p842 and p846*
Prices are high, but the range of goods available is excellent. Travellers who are going on to other islands may find it useful to do some shopping here. If coming from another Caribbean island there are strict controls on bringing in fresh fruit and vegetables.

Duty-free shopping is well advertised.

Visitors who produce passport and air ticket can take most duty-free goods away from the store for use in the island before they leave, but not camera film or alcohol. Cameras and electrical goods may be cheaper in an ordinary discount store in the USA or Europe than duty free in Barbados. A duty-free shopping centre for cruise ship passengers is inside the deep water harbour, the **Bridgetown Cruise Terminal**.

Art galleries

Barbados Arts Council, Pelican Craft Village, Bridgetown, T4264385. Daily 0900-2130. Also at The Coach House, St James. A non-profit organization set up to foster Barbadian art and artists. Works exhibited at these galleries are drawn from its 300 members, both established artists with an international reputation and those just starting out.

Gallery of Caribbean Art, Queen St, Speightstown, T4190858. Mon-Fri 0930-1630, Sat 0930-1400. A range of contemporary regional art work.

The Kirby Gallery, The Courtyard, Hastings, T4303032, www.kirbyartgallery.com. Mon-Fri 0900-1700, Sat 0900-1300. Opposite Savannah Hotel, has a bit of everything, paintings, prints, ceramics, used to be the best but now there is more competition with about 12 galleries on the island.

Verandah Art Gallery, Old Spirit Wharf, Bridgetown, T4262605. Mon-Fri 0900-1630, Sat 0900-1300. A reasonable selection with some Haitian art and temporary exhibitions.

Zemicon Gallery, James Fort Building, Hincks St, Bridgetown, T4300054. Tue-Fri 1000-1600. Shows some of the best local artists, making a statement.

Bookshops

Bookshops are much better stocked than on other islands.

The Book Place on Probyn St. Specializes in Caribbean material and has a good second-hand section.

The Cloister on Hincks St, T4262662. Probably has the largest stock with a good range of Caribbean material.

The Pages Bookshop at Cave Shepherd (Broad St and West Coast Mall). Also has a reasonable selection.

Crafts

Best of Barbados, Mall 34, Broad St in Bridgetown, Chattel Village in Holetown, Southern Palms and Walkers' World in St Lawrence Gap, Quayside Centre in Hastings, Orchid World and the Bridgetown Cruise Terminal, www.best-of-barbados.com. The ultimate gift shop with every Barbados souvenir imaginable. The designes mostly stem from the work of Jill Walker, who has been living and painting in Barbados since 1955, and they have a network of cottage workers making things exclusively for the shop. Her prints of local scenes are on sale, mugs, candles and T-shirts. Walkers' World sells furniture and home accessories as well as gifts and has a café overlooking the beach.

Earthworks Pottery, Edgehill Heights No 2, St Thomas, T4250223, www.earthworks-pottery.com. Mon-Fri 0900-1700, Sat 0900-1300. Solid houseware and pots in blues and greens with several different designs, used in local cafés. VAT-free for visitors, also has restaurant/café, **The Tree House**, see above, and gift shops with crafts from several local artists.

Pelican Craft Centre, Princess Alice Highway near the harbour. Mon-Fri 0900-1800, Sat 0900-1400. Good displays of craft items, all made in Barbados, at over 25 shops in replica chattel houses where you can watch artisans at work.

Red Clay Pottery and **Fairfield Gallery**, Fairfield Cross Rd, just outside Bridgetown sells very good ceramics, T4243800. Family business using local clay to make ceramic art, crockery and garden pots in an old syrup boiling house. Demonstration and tour.

Food

The best stocked supermarket is **JB's Mastermart** in Wildey. **Big B** in Worthing and **Supercentre** in Oistins and Holetown are also good, and are easier to reach by public transport. **Supercentre** will take online orders and deliver (no delivery charge, minimum order B$50; payment by credit card; orders also by fax, F4369820). Supermarkets open on Sun 0900-1300.

Big B, Worthing. Mon-Tue 0800-1900, Wed-Sat 0800-2000, Sun 0900-1300. Photocopying available.

Gourmet Shop, Holetown in the Chattel Village, T4327711, thegourmetshop@

caribsurf.com. Mon-Sat 0900-1800, holidays and festivals 1000-1400. Lots of luxuries, excellent selection of food and wine.

Jewellery

Broad St is dominated by enormous jewellers: **Colombian Emeralds, Diamonds International, Diamonds in Paradise, Jewelers Warehouse** and **Little Switzerland**.

▲ Activities and tours

Barbados *p845, maps p842 and p846*
See also page 841. Contact the **National Sports Council**, Blenheim, St Michael, T4366127, for more information.

Athletics
Sir Garfield Sobers Sports Complex, Wildey, St Michael, T4376016. A multi-purpose gymnasium offering badminton, bodybuilding, boxing, basketball, gymnastics, handball, judo, karate, netball, table tennis, volleyball and weightlifting. There are plenty of changing rooms and showers, also sauna and massage rooms, a medical room and warm-up/practice area.

Cricket
Lots of village cricket all over the island at weekends. A match here is nothing if not a social occasion. Great Bajan cricketers become icons and 5 have been knighted for their services to the game and their country: Sir Garfield Sobers (the only living National Hero), Sir Conrad Hunte, Sir Everton Weekes, Sir Clyde Walcott and Sir Frank Worrell. In addition to Test Matches and inter-island competitions there are tournaments for the young and old: the Sir Garfield Sobers International Schools Tournament and the Sir Garfield Sobers Seniors Cricket Festival being two of the most important. Barbados is the premier cricket tour destination in the world and cricket lovers should try to arrange their visit to coincide with a Test Match or a One Day International at the new Kensington Oval. For the Cricket World Cup in 2007, Barbados hosted the Final at the Oval. This historic ground first hosted a Test Match in 1929-1930, but for the CWC had a major upgrade to add extra seats and improve facilities for the players, media and sponsors.

No sedate Sunday afternoon crowd this – the atmosphere is electric – with DJ music, constant whistling, horn-blowing, cheering and banter. For information about the bigger matches at Kensington Oval phone the **Barbados Cricket Association**, T4361397. If you and your local team want to tour Barbados, contact **Sporting Barbados**, T2289122, www.sportingbarbados.com, for help with discounts and keeping the costs down or to put you in touch with a specialist tour agency.

Cycling
Cycling is best on the east coast, but traffic is dangerously heavy everywhere and rush hr from 1600 makes cycling unpleasant almost anywhere on the island. Roads are narrow, potholed and twisty and lots of people lose their deposit because of damage.
Flex Bicycle Rentals, T2311518 (mob), T4240321, gmgriff@sunbeach.net. Run by Paul Griffith, bike hire US$15, tours Fri, Sat.
Mountain Bike Association, Wayne Robinson, T4310419, or Robert Quintyne, T4293367.
Odyssey Tours, T2280003. Ecological and historical excursions by bike.

Diving
Scuba diving to reefs or wrecks around the coast can be arranged with a number of companies on the south and west coasts, www.barbados.org/diveops/htm. They offer PADI courses, equipment rental and other facilities.
Carib Ocean Divers, Royal Pavilion, T4224414. Good, 32-ft boat with shower, dive platform and ladder, oxygen on board. 2-tank dive US$92, Open Water Certification US$432, PADI and NAUI staff, good with beginners.
Dive Blue Reef, Mount Standfast, St James, T4223133. Only 6 divers taken out on their 30-ft pirogue. Underwater camera rental.
Hightide Watersports, Coral Reef Club, St James, T/F 4320931, and at other locations such as Tamarind Cove, hightide@sunbeach.net. Small groups of no more than 8.
Roger's Scuba Shack, at the Boatyard, Bridgetown, T4363483, www.rogers-scubashack.com. 2-tank dive US$85 plus 15% VAT, while snorkelling trips are offered for US$15. Lots of courses available.
West Side Scuba Centre, Baku Beach,

Holetown, T4322558, www.westsidescuba
.com. 2 boats, small groups, certification and
speciality courses available, dive packages
and accommodation offered. In the summer
they dive the east coast where you can see
larger fish and different underwater terrain.
Atlantis Submarine is at Shallow Draft
Harbour, T4368929, www.atlantisadventures
.com. For those who want to see the
underwater world without getting wet. The
day and night dives at US$89, children aged
13-17 US$57, 4-12 US$44.50, discounts in low
season. The tour starts with a short video and
then you go by bus to the deep water port or
join the launch at the Careenage. The boat
takes about 10 mins to get to the submarine,
sit at the front to be first on the sub, an
advantage as then you can see out of the
driver's window as well as out of your own
porthole. 2 divers on underwater scooters join
the submarine for the last 15 mins, putting on
a dive show. The weekly 1700 dive is the best
as the submarine turns on its lights which
bring out pretty colours not seen by daylight.
Booking is necessary, check in 30 mins before
dive time; whole tour takes 1½ hrs. They also
offer power snorkel tours too, US$57 for age
15 and over in groups of 8-12, Mon-Sat 0900,
1100, 1300, 1500.

Fishing

Charter boats for game fishing are lined up
along the Careenage, Bridgetown.
Barbados Game Fishing Association, 230
Atlantic Shores, Christ Church, T4286668,
www.barbadosgamefishing.com (Dave
Marshall, Secretary). Runs an international
tournament in Feb-Apr. The targets are blue
marlin, yellow fin tuna, white marlin, sailfish,
wahoo and dolphin fish (mahi mahi).
Fishing Charters Barbados, T4292326,
www.bluemarlinbarbados.com. Can arrange
deep-sea fishing with *Blue Marlin, Idyll Time,
Blue Jay*.

Golf

The **Barbados Open Golf Championship** is
held in Nov; the Senior PGA European Golf
Tournament in Mar. The **Sir Garry Sobers
Festival of Golf in Apr** is played on 3 courses
with 240 players including former Test
cricketers, celebrities and professional golfers.
Almond Beach Village, T4224900. 9-hole
course built next to the **Heywoods** course in

the northwest.
Barbados Golf Club, T4288463.
www.barbadosgolfclub.com. Open to the
public, 18-hole course, at Durants, Christ
Church. Green fee US$120 in high season,
US$80 in low season, also tuition, 3- and
7-day passes, etc.
Ocean Park, Balls, Christ Church, T4207405.
18-hole mini course, fun for families, not
serious golfers. Attached to Ocean Park, a
new aquarium, included in the price.
**Royal Westmoreland Golf and Country
Club**, St James, T4224653. An 18-hole, par 72
course spread over 480 acres on a hilly site in
St James with views over the west coast. To
play here you must be staying in one of the
villas or at a hotel with an access agreement.
Members can use the hotel's beach club
facilities 5 mins' drive away. Construction of
350 villas around one of the 9-hole loops has
now started, 3 club houses, a swimming
pool and 5 tennis courts.
Sandy Lane, T4322946. Traditionally the
best and most prestigious of the 3
championship courses, now has 2, 18-hole
courses and a 9-hole course, all on 600 acres
of former sugar cane land next to the hotel.
Tiger Woods got married on the course here.

Hiking

The most beautiful part of the island is the
Scotland District on the east coast. There is
also some fine country along the St Lucy
coast in the north and on the southeast
coast. There is a particularly good route
along the old railway track, from Bath to
Bathsheba and on to Cattlewash. The
National Trust, together with the Duke of
Edinburgh Award Scheme, and the Future
Centre and Heart Foundation, organizes
walks at 0600 Sun and either 1530 or 1730
(depending on moon). Details are usually
printed in the *Visitor* and *Sunseeker*
magazines or T4369033. Their walk to Chalky
Mount in the Scotland District has been
recommended. 3 speeds: 'stop and stare',
5-6 miles, 'here and there', 8-10 miles, 'grin
and bear', 12-14 miles.

Riding

There are riding schools offering beach
and/or country rides. Some do not give
instruction and cater for pleasure riding only.
Barbados Equestrian Association, Jenny

Rum tours

Mount Gay Visitor Centre, Brandons, St Michael, T4258757, does a very good 45-min tour of the blending and bottling plant, with an exhibition of rum, rum tasting and shop near the deep-water port in Bridgetown on the Spring Garden Highway. Mon-Fri 0930-1530, a special luncheon tour Tue, Thu 1200, or cocktail tour Wed 1430.

Malibu Visitor Centre, T4259393, Brighton, St Michael, near the West India Rum Refinery. Mon-Fri 0900, video presentation and tour of the distillery, last tour at 1545.

Foursquare Rum Factory and Heritage Park, T4201977, in an old sugar factory, with sugar machinery, craft market, pottery, bottling plant, folk museum, pet farm, pony stables and Foundry Art Gallery. Mon-Thu, 0900-1700, Fri-Sat 1000-2100, Sun 1200-1800.

Banks Brewery T2286486, has a tour and also does a 'beer trail', whereby you get your card stamped in participating bars and restaurants (five stamps for a free brewery tour, 15 get you a T-shirt). Tours Mon-Fri 1000, 1200 and 1400.

Wilson, T2289144, jengi@sunbeach.net. Dressage events organized by the Association are all held at Congo Road, near Six Roads, St Phillip. For information, Jean Ray, T4326404.

Beau Geste Stables, St George, T4290139.

Big C Riding Stables, Christ Church, T4374056.

Brighton Stables, on west coast, T4259381.

Caribbean International Riding Centre, St Joseph, T4227433. US$60 for 1½ hrs, US$82.50 for 2½ hrs, good for trail riding.

Congo Road Riding Stables, T4238293. 1-hr ride Including lift to and from hotel is US$25, beginners or advanced.

Tony's Riding School, St Peter, T4221549.

Trevena Riding Stables, St James, T4326404.

Sailing

Barbados Yacht Club, Carlisle Bay, T4271125. Holds regattas and offers sailing courses. Sailing can be a bit choppy along the south coast to Oistins and most races head up the west coast where the waters are calmer. The 3-day Annual Mount Gay Rum Boatyard Regatta in May is the main event of the year. Carlisle Bay is the main anchorage and focal point for the sailing fraternity. There are lots of motor and sailing boats available for charter by the week, day or for shorter periods. Large boats make you wear life vests for safety when you snorkel, smaller ones don't.

Tall Ships Incorporated, T4300900, tallships@sunbeach.net, runs *Excellence I* and *II, Irish Mist, Tiami* and *Spirit of Barbados* catamarans, US$61.50, *Harbour Master* and *Jolly Roger* (the last 2 being boozy fun cruises).

Heatwave, T4299283, www.caribbean-connection.com/heatwave. Usually takes about 30 passengers but will go out with only 10, good lunch, friendly crew, but not eco- conscious, US$61.50, also runs **Wet'n'Wild Cruise**, a combination of cruise, snorkelling, jet skis, kayaks and banana boat rides.

Ocean Mist, T4367639, 60-ft power catamaran, run by Ian and Jennifer Banfield, offers 1-day charters of 5-6 hrs, maximum 16 passengers, US$75 including food, drink, snorkelling gear, or the boat can be chartered, bareboat, for 7 days to the Grenadines, maximum 8 people, US$750 per day plus US$1,250 for fuel, clearances and licences.

Rubaiyat, T4359913. For something less crowded, try lunch and dinner cruises, US$65, maximum 20 people.

Wayzäro, T4237196. A glass-bottomed boat used for party cruises and snorkelling trips, eg 4-hr Sun-lunch trip with steel pan, sunset cruises from 1600 including drinks.

Other operators are moored in the Careenage in Bridgetown, with phone numbers displayed. Most are equipped for fishing and snorkelling, and will serve a good meal on board. Rates and services offered vary widely. Catamarans like Small Cats, Super Cats or Wild Cats (turtle and shipwreck adventure, US$43.50, T4363687), also take small groups.

Spectator sports

Hockey Barbados Hockey Federation, T4233980, bhf@cariaccess.com. **Banks International Hockey Festival** is the largest event of its type in the Americas and is held in Aug with 37 local teams and 26 from overseas.

Horse racing Barbados Turf Club, T4263980, www.barbadosturfclub.com. Holds meetings at the Garrison on Sat during 3 seasons (Jan-Mar, May-Oct and Nov-Dec). The biggest one being the Sandy Lane Gold Cup held in Mar, which sometimes features horses from neighbouring islands. This is something of a social occasion.

Polo Polo has been played since cavalry officers introduced the game in the 19th century and the Polo Club was formed in 1884. There are now 4 polo fields on Barbados. **Barbados Polo Club**, T4276022. National and international matches are played at Holders Hill, St James, between Nov and May, Thu and Sat at 1400. **Clifton Equestrian Centre**, St Thomas, T2312444, set among cane fields with panoramic views, it hosted the inaugural Barbados Open and caters for visiting players as well as beginners. **Lion Castle Polo Estate**, St Thomas, part of a luxury new housing development on 64 acres with wonderful views to the south and east coasts. **Waterhall Polo Stables and Polo Field**, Apes Hill, St James, ponies for hire and training facilities for beginners, hosting many top visiting teams.

Road tennis Road tennis is an indigenous game dating from the 1930s, with defined rules, played with a low wooden 'net' on some minor (and some main) roads, car parks and school playgrounds. It is rather like a cross between tennis and table tennis, played with wooden bats and a skinned tennis ball, but scored like table tennis with most matches being the best of five games. Contact Dale Clarke, **Road Tennis Association**, T2338268, www.proroadtennis.com. The **Racquets of Fire Road Tennis Championship** is held in

Oct and the World Road Tennis Series at the end of Nov.

Tour operators

See also Rum tours, p865.
Adventureland, T4293687. Also 4WD and same price.
Bajan Tours, T/F4372389. Cheaper and better value than some, no pressure on tipping, US$32.50 per half day, US$50 full day including lunch.
Island Safari, T2925337, www.islandsafari.bb. Tour is with 4WD Landrovers so can get to some less accessible beaches, US$40 half day, US$57.50 full day with lunch, US$90 land and sea tour, kayaking also on offer.
L E Williams, T4271043. US$50-75 day tour (has a sign up in the bus: 'no 10 % service charge is paid with the tour price'), heavy pressure selling of tapes, limited drinks from bar.
Ultimate Outback Tours, T4205418, limbolady@sunbeach.net. Also 4WD charter with driver US$47 per hr, minimum 4 hrs, up to 6 passengers, children welcome, lunch at restaurant en route. Longer tours generally include lunch. A criticism of the tours with some companies is that it can take 1½ hrs to pick up everyone from hotels and those further north do not get the full tour through Bridgetown and Holetown.

Other activities

Chess, draughts and dominoes Chess, draughts (checkers) and dominoes are played to a high standard. Join a rum shop match at your peril. Barbados has a world champion draughts player, Suki King. The island's Sports Person of the Year 2001 was the first Barbadian chess player to reach the rank of International Master, 34-year-old Kevin Denny.

Swimming Aquatic Centre, adjacent to the Sir Garfield Sobers Sports Complex, T4297946, with a 10-lane Olympic-size swimming pool, tennis courts, hockey, football and cricket pitches outside. Water polo is played; visitors are welcome to join in practice sessions with the team. Training Mon, Wed 1830, while matches are played Sat 1400. Call Stephen Lewis, T4296767 (work), 4286042 (home).

Running Run Barbados Series is held in

early Dec and comprises a 10-km race, a marathon, a half marathon and a 4-km walk. Contact Morris Greenidge at the Barbados Tourism Authority, T4272623. Less ambitiously **Hash Harriers**, Sat, followed by barbecue and drinks, T4208113, www.barbadoshash.com.

Squash **Barbados Squash Club**, Hastings, 3 courts, T4277193. **Squash Racquets Association**, Chris Skinner, T2284926.

Tennis Nearly all the major hotels have tennis courts and many are lit for night play. There is a combination of public and private tennis facilities and some top class professional coaches providing tuition. The Sir Garfield Sobers Sports Complex is the official home of the National Tennis Centre, with other main centres at Club Rockley Resort and the West Side Tennis Centre at Sunset Crest behind the Chattel House Village, Holetown. A David and John Lloyd Tennis Village, www.sugarhillbarbados.com, is at Sugar Hill in a development of villas and condos as well as a central clubhouse, pool, fitness centre, restaurant and bar. The main court has lots of seating for spectators. Contact Barbados Lawn Tennis Association, Ellie Brown, T4302400.

⊖ Transport

Barbados *p845, maps p842 and p846*
Air
From North America Miami (American Airlines); New York (American Airlines, Air Jamaica, USAir); Philadelphia (USAir); Toronto and Halifax (Air Canada).

From Europe British Airways, Virgin Atlantic and Caribbean Airlines have several flights a week from London. Condor flies weekly from Frankfurt, Nov-Apr. There are also lots of charter flights which are usually cheaper and recommended if you are staying only on Barbados.

From South America LIAT/Caribbean Star from Georgetown, Guyana; flights from Caracas, with connections from other countries, involve a change in Port of Spain.

From Caribbean
Islands LIAT/Caribbean Star, Caribbean Airlines and Air Jamaica have good connections with all the islands. American Eagle, flies to San Juan, Puerto Rico and Canouan. Check different airlines for inter-island travel, the Trinidad route is particularly competitive, **British Airways** often has good offers between Barbados, Antigua and St Lucia and a comfortable plane. It is usually worth organizing ticketing at the start of your journey so that Barbados appears as a stopover rather than as the origin for any side trips you make.

Helicopter Bajan Helicopters do tours from US$75 per 20 mins, US$125 per 30 mins round the coastline. The heliport is near the deep water harbour at Bridgetown, T4310069, www.bajanhelicopters.com. Also **Barbados Light Aeroplane Club**, US$37.50 for 30-min flight. T4287102 ext 4676.

Airline offices Virgin allows you to check in at your hotel and turn up at the airport only 50 mins before departure, T4362110. The LIAT/Caribbean Star office is at St Michael's Plaza, St Michael's Row, T4345428. **Caribbean Airlines**, T4262111, **British Airways**, T4366413, are all on Fairchild St. **American Airlines**, T4284170, and **Air Canada**, T4285077, have offices at the airport. **Virgin Atlantic** is in Hastings, T1800-744747. **Aeropostal**, Lower Bay St, T4361858, **Air Jamaica**, Bayside Plaza, T2286625.

Boat
The cruise ship passenger tax is US$8.50. Barbados is not well served by small inter-island schooners. You may be able to get a passage to another island on a yacht, ask at the harbour or at the **Boatyard** on Carlisle Bay. Mooring facilities are available at the Shallow Draft next to the Deep Water Harbour, or there are calm anchorages in Carlisle Bay. Several companies run mini-cruises based on Barbados.

Bus
There are 2 routes from the **airport**: Yorkshire buses go straight to Bridgetown, others go along the south coast past the hotels to Bridgetown.

Around Bridgetown, there are plenty of small yellow privately owned minibuses and route taxis with ZR number plates; elsewhere, the big blue and white Mercedes buses (exact fare required or tokens sold at the bus terminal) belong to the Transport Board, T4366820. Private buses tend to stick to urban areas while the public buses run half empty in rural areas and in evening. There is a **City Circle** route, clockwise and anti-clockwise round the inner suburbs of

Bridgetown which starts in Lower Green. **Terminals for the south:** Fairchild St for public buses, clean, modern; Probyn St, or just across Constitution River from Fairchild St for minibuses; further east by Constitution River for ZR vans. **Terminals for the west:** Lower Green for public buses; west of post office for minibuses; Princess Alice Highway for ZR vans, but from 1800-2400 all leave from Lower Green. During the rush hour, all these terminals are chaotic, particularly during school term. On most routes, the last bus leaves at or soon after midnight and the first bus at 0500.

Car

The speed limit is 80, 60 or 40 kmph. Drive on the left. Mini-mokes are fun but not recommended in the rainy season.

Car hire Drivers need a visitor's driving permit (Visitor Registration Certificate) from Hastings, Worthing or Holetown police stations (cost US$5). You will need this even if you have an International Driving Licence. Car hire companies usually sort it out for you. A medium-sized car will cost on average US$105 per day, US$400 per week. **Sunny Isle Sixt Rent a Car**, Dayton, Worthing, T4357979, www.BarbadosTraveller.com; **Courtesy Rent a Car**, airport, T4314160, www.courtesyrentacar.com, are helpful, and will arrange to meet you at the airport if you telephone in advance, internet booking; **Regency Rent-a-Car**, 77 Regency Park, Christ Church, T4275663, F4297735, free pick up and delivery; **Eastmond's Car Rentals**, T4287749, a smaller operator, pick up and delivery wherever you want, 7 adequate cars, US$288 per week including VAT; discounts available (including free driver's permit) and tourist magazines frequently contain 10-15% vouchers.

Taxi

Between the airport and any point north of Speightstown, US$27.50, to Holetown, US$19, to Bridgetown Harbour US$15, to Garrison US$12, to Oistins US$8; between the city centre and **Sam Lord's Castle** US$19, to Oistins US$10, Dover US$9; between **Sandy Lane** and Oistins US$18. Fares are quoted also by mile (US$1.25) or kilometre (US$0.75) but there are no taxi meters. Vehicles which look like route taxis but with ZM numberplates, are taxis plying for individual hire, and will charge accordingly.

---

❶ Directory

Barbados *p845, maps p842 and p846*
Banks FirstCaribbean International Bank, the Royal Bank of Canada, CIBC Caribbean Ltd, Scotiabank, Caribbean Commercial Bank, Barbados Mutual Bank and Barbados National Bank all have offices in Bridgetown. The first 5 also have branches in the main south and west coast tourist centres. Opening hours for banks are Mon-Thu 0800-1500 and Fri 0800-1300, 1500-1700. **Caribbean Commercial Bank** in Hastings and Sunset Crest is also open Sat 0900-1200. All banks now have ATMs at most branches. Banking facilities in JB's and **Big B Supermarkets**, Mon-Thu 1000-1900, Fri 1000-2000, Sat 1000-1500. No banks on the east coast, but the supermarket at Belleplaine has a Royal Bank counter. **Embassies and consulates** Australia High Commission, Bishop's Court Hill, T4352843. Brazil Embassy, 3rd floor, Sunjet House, Fairchild St, T4271735. **Canada High Commission**, Bishop's Court Hill, St Michael, T4283550. **Costa Rica**, Dayrells Court, T4310250. **Cuba**, Collymore Rock, T4352769. **France**, Hastings, Christ Church, T4356847. **Germany**, Banyan Court, Bay St, St Michael, T4271876. **Sweden**, Branckers Complex, Fontabelle, St Michael, T4274358. **UK British High Commission**, Lower Collymore Rock, St Michael, T4366694, F4365398. **US Consular Section**, Alico Building, Cheapside, Bridgetown, T4364950. **Venezuela**, El Sueño, Hastings, Christ Church, T4357619. **Internet** Lots of hotels have internet access for guests. Business services and internet access on the west coast at **Global Business Centre**, West Coast Mall, Holetown, T4326508, Mon-Fri 0900-1700, Sat 0900-1300, B$5 per 10 mins, B$0.50 per min thereafter; also at Quayside Centre on south coast. **Web Café**, Sunset Crest, turn up by Royal Bank of Canada, parking outside, Mon-Fri 0800-2000, Sat, Sun 0900-1700, B$5 per 15 mins, internet phone calls B$1.50 per min to EU, USA, Caribbean, (B$4.50 for normal phone calls) drinks, friendly service. In Bridgetown, **Netcafé**, Sogo Plaza, 20 Broad St, T4354736. Also in Broad St Mall, Bridgetown, opposite CIBC, US$3 for 15 mins, US$10 for an

hr, Mon-Thu 0900-1700, Fri 0900-1800, Sat 0900-1400. **Connect**, just off Broad St, upstairs from **Windjammer** on Lancaster Lane opposite Cave Shepherd, US$1 for 7 mins, US$2 for 15 mins, US$7 for an hr, free coffee, student rates with ID, net2phone calls, send photos, Mon-Thu 0900-1700, Fri 0900-1800, Sat 0930-1430, T2288648, toilets next door. **Computer Internet Services**, in Broad St Mall, 8 terminals, no eating or drinking, US$1 for 10 mins, US$6 for an hr, Mon-Thu 0900-1700,
Fri 0900-1800, Sat 0900-1400. In St Lawrence Gap, **Bean 'n Bagel Café**, 'gourmet coffee', light meals under B$20, breakfast B$19.99, T420- 4604, 0700-1730 for the café, 0800-1730 for computers, B$3 for 5 mins,

B$10 for 30 mins, B$15 for an hr. **Happy Days**, Chattel Village, 0800-1500, burgers and sandwiches under B$15, B$4 for 15 mins, B$12 for an hr, B$20 for 2 hrs.

Post The **General Post Office Headquarters** is in Cheapside, Bridgetown and there are District Post Offices in every parish. Collections from red post boxes on roadsides. Local postal rates are B$0.45 for priority, B$0.40 non-priority. Airmail rates to North America B$1.15 or B$0.45, to Europe B$1.40 or B$0.70, to the Caribbean B$0.90 or B$0.45. There is an express delivery service of 48 hrs worldwide: to the Caribbean B$28 per 1kg plus B$3 per 500gm extra, USA B$45 + B$8, Europe B$55 + B$12. A Philatelic Bureau issues first-day covers 4 times a year.

Barbados Background Listings

Background

History

There were Amerindians on Barbados for a thousand years or more. The first Europeans to find the island were the Portuguese, who named it 'Os Barbados' after the bearded fig trees which grew on the beaches, and left behind some wild pigs. These bred successfully and provided meat for the first English settlers, who arrived in 1627 and found an island which was otherwise uninhabited. It is not clear why the Amerindians abandoned Barbados, although several theories exist. King Charles I gave the Earl of Carlisle permission to colonize the island and it was his appointed Governor, Henry Hawley, who in 1639 founded the House of Assembly. Within a few years, there were over 40,000 white settlers, mostly small farmers, and equivalent in number to about 1% of the total population of England at this period. After the 'sugar revolution' of the 1650s most of the white population left. For the rest of the colonial period sugar was king, and the island was dominated by a small group of whites who owned the estates, the 'plantocracy'. The majority of the population today is descended from African slaves who were brought in to work on the plantations; but there is a substantial mixed-race population, and there has always been a small number of poor whites, particularly in the east part of the island. Many of these are descended from 100 prisoners transported in 1686 after the failed Monmouth rebellion and Judge Jeffrey's 'Bloody Assizes'.

The two principal political parties are the Barbados Labour Party (BLP) and the Democratic Labour Party (DLP). The DLP held office from 1986 to 1994. Economic difficulties in the 1990s eroded support for the government. The Prime Minister Erskine Sandiford narrowly lost a vote of confidence in June 1994, and stood aside for his Finance Minister David Thompson, who led the party into a general election on 6 September. The BLP won the elections with 19 seats, compared with eight for the DLP and one for a third party, the NDP. Mr Owen Arthur, then 44, an economist, became Prime Minister and took on the portfolios of Finance and Economic Affairs. In the January 1999 general elections, the BLP was returned with an overwhelming vote of confidence. It won 26 of the 28 seats, while the DLP won the other two. In the latest elections, on 21 May 2003, the BLP won a further landslide with 23 seats over the DLP's seven in the newly-expanded Assembly.

Barbados has been an independent member of the Commonwealth since November 1966. The British Monarch is the Head of State, represented by a Governor General. There is a strong parliamentary and democratic tradition. The House of Assembly is the third oldest parliament in the Western Hemisphere dating from 1639, although voting was limited to property owners until 1950. There are 21 senators appointed by the Governor General, of whom 12 are on the advice of the Prime Minister, two on the advice of the Leader of the Opposition and seven at his own discretion to reflect religious, economic and social interests. Thirty single-member constituencies elect the House of Assembly.

A 1998 Commission on the constitution chaired by a former BLP leader and Attorney General, Sir Henry Forde QC, recommended abolition of the monarchy, with the Governor General replaced by a ceremonial president, changes in the composition of the Senate, and replacement of the London-based Privy Council as final appeal court by a Caribbean Court of Justice.

Economy

Natural resources are few. Sugar is still the main crop but many producers have abandoned the land, while trying to get planning permission for golf courses or housing developments. There is a well-established service sector and an expanding offshore financial sector with a good reputation. A range of light industries produce mainly for the local, regional, and North American markets. Manufacturing is the second largest foreign exchange earner. There is a small oil industry. Barbados National Oil Company's onshore field in St Philip produces enough for local requirements (although it is refined overseas). There is also enough natural gas for piped domestic supply to urban and suburban areas.

By far the main foreign exchange earner is now tourism, which accounts for 15% of GDP and employs 10,300 people. In 2004, 551,953 stopover tourists and 736,626 cruise ship passengers visited the island, an increase of 3.9% and 27.2% respectively over the previous year as the world economy picked up. In contrast with most Caribbean islands, the UK is the main tourist market, accounting for 39% of arrivals compared with 25% from the USA. Barbados has no hotels with more than 330 rooms. The emphasis on small scale tourism may be an advantage in the British market, but has held back sales in North America, where customers prefer branded hotel chains.

Geography

Barbados is 21 miles long and 14 miles wide, lying east of the main chain of the Leeward and Windward islands. Most of the island is covered by a cap of coral limestone, up to 600,000 years old. Several steep inland cliffs or ridges run parallel to the coast. These are the remains of old shorelines, which formed as the island gradually emerged from the sea. There are no rivers in this part of the island, although there are steep-sided gullies down which water runs in wet weather. Rainwater runs through caves in the limestone, one of which, Harrison's Cave, has been developed as a tourist attraction. The island's water supply is pumped up from the limestone. In the Scotland District in the northeast, the coral limestone has been eroded and older, softer rocks are exposed. There are rivers here, which have cut deep, steep-sided valleys. Landslides make agriculture and construction hazardous and often destroy roads.

People

Barbados has a population of 269,000. This is more than any of the Windwards or Leewards, and is considered enough to make the island one of the 'big four' in the Caribbean Community. With population density of 1,620 per square mile in 2002,

Barbados is one of the most crowded countries in the world.

Because Barbados lies upwind from the main island arc, it was hard to attack from the sea, so it never changed hands in the colonial wars of the 17th and 18th centuries. There is no French, Dutch, or Spanish influence to speak of in the language, cooking or culture. People from other islands have often referred to Barbados as Little England, and have not always intended a compliment. Today, the more obvious outside influences on the Barbadian way of life are North American. Most contemporary Barbadians stress their Afro-Caribbean heritage and aspects of the culture which are distinctively 'Bajan'. There are extremes of poverty and wealth, but these are not nearly so noticeable as elsewhere in the Caribbean. This makes the social atmosphere relatively relaxed. However, there is a history of deep racial division. Although there is a very substantial black middle class and the social situation has changed radically since the 1940s and 50s, there is still more racial intolerance on all sides than is apparent at first glance. Barbadians are a religious people and although the main church is Anglican, there are over 140 different faiths and sects, including Baptists, Christian Scientists, Jews, Methodists, Moravians and Roman Catholics.

Literature

Two Barbadian writers whose work has had great influence throughout the Caribbean are the novelist **George Lamming** and the poet **Edward Kamau Brathwaite**. Lamming's first novel, *In The Castle Of My Skin* (1953), a part-autobiographical story of growing up in colonial Barbados, deals with one of the major concerns of anglophone writers: how to define one's values within a system and ideology imposed by someone else. Lamming's treatment of the boy's changing awareness in a time of change in the West Indies is both poetic and highly imaginative. His other books include *Natives Of My Person*, *Season Of Adventure* and *The Pleasures Of Exile*.

Brathwaite is also sensitive to the colonial influence on black West Indian culture. Like Derek Walcott (see under St Lucia) and others he is also keenly aware of the African traditions at the heart of that culture. The questions addressed by all these writers are: who is Caribbean man, and what are his faiths, his language, his ancestors? The experience of teaching in Ghana for some time helped to clarify Brathwaite's response. African religions, motifs and songs mix with West Indian speech rhythms in a style which is often strident, frequently using very short verses. His collections include *Islands*, *Masks* and *Rights Of Passage*.

Books

A to Z of Barbadian Heritage (Heinemann Caribbean). Worth reading (new edition in preparation).

Barbados – Photos from Within (Miller Publications). A good photo book.

Cummins, Alissandra, et al *Art in Barbados*, (1999, Ian Randle Publishers and Barbados Museum and Historical Society). Examines the work of Barbadian artists over 6 decades.

Fraser, Harry S *Treasures of Barbados* (Macmillan). A guide to Barbadian architecture.

Machel, Hans *Geology of Barbados* (Barbados Museum publication).

O'Callaghan, Sean *To Hell or Barbados – Irish Slavery in Barbados* (2000, Brandon Book Publishers).

Watson Yates, Ann (editor) *Bygone Barbados. History of Barbados* (1848, Schomburgk). Reprint. Probably the best of several books of old photos; a natural history and geography of the island in early Victorian times.

Barbados Background

Trinidad and Tobago

Introduction

Trinidad and Tobago are only just off the coast of Venezuela, yet they share little of the culture of South America. The people are a cosmopolitan mix of African, East Indian, Chinese, European and Syrian and the music, cuisine, culture, society and politics of the islands reflect this. You can listen to calypso, parang or chutney soca, while eating East Indian, Chinese or West Indian dishes and the food and music are so good that Trinidad's influence has spread through the Caribbean and worldwide.

Trinidad's ebullient carnival is world famous too and attracts thousands of visitors ready and willing to spend days jumping up and parading in the hot sun, carried along by the crowd and fuelled by alcohol, dancing and singing to the latest calypsos. However, wealth comes from oil, gas and manufacturing rather than tourism and many of its beaches remain empty of foreign tourists and fairly unspoilt. Beach tourism has been developed on its smaller, sister island of Tobago, where hotels are spreading around the coastline, but there are still glorious bays and coves and resorts are low key.

Both islands have a huge array of flora and fauna, and birdwatching is a major attraction. The species found here are directly related to those found in South America as well as in the Caribbean islands. The forests and wetlands are denser and contain a greater diversity of animal and plant life than anywhere else in the Caribbean. There are several protected areas and wildlife sanctuaries where, in addition to the birds, you can find a number of mammals such as monkeys and manatee as well as reptiles like iguanas and cayman.

★ Don't miss...

1 **Asa Wright Nature Centre** An old plantation house overlooks a beautiful wooded valley set in a nature reserve of around 700 acres including streams, pools and trails. Guides are on hand for birdwatching tours or you can sit on the veranda and watch the hummingbirds, page 893.

2 **Grande Riviere** Remote and unspoiled, this long and lovely beach is a favourite with nesting turtles. Guesthouses can organize turtle watching in season, page 893.

3 **Caroni Bird Sanctuary** Take a boat through the mangroves at dusk to see the scarlet ibis returning to roost at sunset from their feeding grounds in Venezuela, a magnificent sight, page 894.

4 **Pitch Lake** Looking like an enormous parking lot, the lake is 116 acres of black tar. It is possible to walk on it but take a guide as air bubbles up from the pressure under the ooze, page 895.

5 **Little Tobago** A forested islet off Speyside and a sanctuary for birds including a huge breeding colony of the red-billed tropic bird. Snorkelling is excellent and glass-bottomed boats do tours of the coral gardens, page 913.

6 **Charlotteville** The village is on a lovely horseshoe bay with a good beach and excellent swimming, snorkelling and diving. This is the most remote part of Tobago and there are several beautiful walks to other, deserted beaches used only by fishermen, page 914.

Trinidad & Tobago

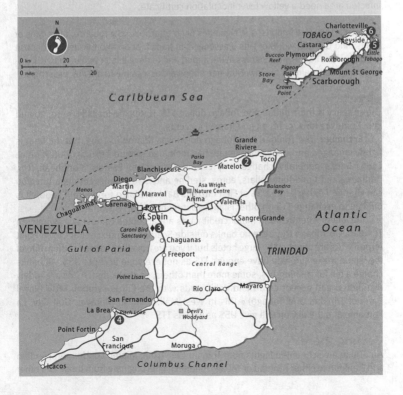

Essentials

Before you travel

Documents Passports are required by all visitors. Visas are not required for visits of under three months by nationals of Caricom (except Haiti), most Commonwealth countries, West European countries, USA, Argentina, Brazil, Colombia, Israel, Iceland and Turkey; holders of OAS passports; and by Venezuelans for stays of up to 14 days. Citizens of some Commonwealth countries do need visas, however; these include Australia, New Zealand, India, Sri Lanka, Nigeria, South Africa, Uganda, Tanzania and Papua New Guinea. A visa normally requires 48 hours' notice. A waiver for those with no visa from some countries can be obtained at the airport, but it costs TT$50. Entry permits for one to three months are given on arrival; a one-month permit can be extended at the **Immigration Office** ⓘ 67 Frederick St, Port of Spain, T6253571, 0600-1400; 131 Covvee St, San Fernando, T6536691, 0700-1430; Port Authority Building, Milford Road, Scarborough, T6392681. Your first visit is to make an appointment for a couple of days later; allow several hours for return visit, making sure you take all documents including ticket to home country. The fee varies according to nationality. Try and get a three-month entry permit if planning a long stay. Business visitors are allowed to work without a work permit for one month in any 12 consecutive months.

Even though you may not get asked for it, all travellers need a return ticket to their country of origin, dated, not open-ended, proof that they can support themselves during their stay and an address at which they will be staying in Trinidad (the tourist office at the airport can help). A ferry ticket to Venezuela has often satisfied immigration officials, but it is unwise to rely on this. Only those coming from an infected area need a yellow fever inoculation certificate.

Customs Duty-free imports: 200 cigarettes or 50 cigars or 250 g tobacco, 1 litre wine or spirits, and US$480 worth of gifts. Passengers in transit, or on short visits, can deposit goods such as liquor with customs at the airport and retrieve it later free of charge. Duty-free prices at the airport are low. Duty-free shops are accessible to arriving passengers.

Money

The currency is the Trinidad and Tobago dollar, TT$. Notes are for TT$1, 5, 10, 20 and 100. Coins are for 1, 5, 10, 25 and (rarely) 50 cents.

Exchange The Trinidad and Tobago dollar was floated in 1993, but the float is tightly managed and the exchange rate has remained around TT$6.25 = US$1 since 1996. Banks generally change only certain currencies: Eastern Caribbean, US, Barbados and Canadian dollars, euros, sterling and Swiss franc. On departure you can change TT$ back into US$ at **First Citizens Bank** at Piarco (open until 2200). It is difficult to exchange TT$ on other islands (but quite easy in Guyana).

Travellers' cheques and major credit cards are accepted almost everywhere on Trinidad. On Tobago there are no banks outside Scarborough (except at Crown Point Airport); TCs are changed by large hotels but if you are travelling to the northern end of the island make sure you have enough TT$ as not everyone accepts US$. All banks charge a fee for cashing TCs, some more than others, so check first. ATMs are widely distributed and accept credit and debit cards with the Cirrus symbol. RBTT (Royal Bank of Trinidad and Tobago) ATMs in West Mall, Park St, Maraval, Gulf City, La Romaine and the airport will give US$ as well as TT$.

Getting there

Air There are scheduled flights from Toronto, New York, Miami, London, Amsterdam and Frankfurt to either Trinidad or Tobago. Charter flights originate from those and other

⁞ Touching down

Business hours Banks: Mon-Thu 0800- 1400, Fri 0800-1200, 1500-1700. Some banks have extended hours until 1800. **Businesses and shops**: Mon-Fri 0800- 1600 or 1630 (shops 0800-1200 on Sat). Shopping malls usually stay open Mon-Sat until 2000. **Government offices**: Mon-Fri 0800-1600.

Clothing Beachwear is for the beach. In the evening people dress more smartly but are not formal.

Departure tax There is a TT$100 exit tax payable in local currency, or US$17. Passengers in transit do not have to pay, but are required to obtain an 'exempt' ticket from the departure tax window before being allowed through to the immigration officers on the way to the departure lounge. Visitors leaving by sea pay the departure tax to the shipping agent. Your immigration card must be presented on departure. See also page 877.

Country code +868.

Official time Atlantic Standard Time, 4 hrs behind GMT, 1 hr ahead of EST.

Tipping If no service charge on bill, 10% for hotel staff and restaurant waiters; taxi drivers, 10% of fare, minimum of TT$10 (but no tip in route taxis); dockside and airport porters, about TT$5 for each piece carried.

Voltage 110 or 220 volts, 60 cycles AC.

Weights and measures Metric. Road signs are given in kilometres, but people still refer to miles.

cities, many of them straight to Tobago. There are some connections with the north of South America, with flights to Caracas, Paramaribo and Georgetown. There are many flights to other Caribbean islands if you want to island hop.▶▶ *See Transport, page 908.*

Sea There is a regular ferry service between Güiria, Venezuela, and Pier One, at Chaguaramas, see Transport, page 908, but from the north, cruise ships are the only passenger service calling at Port of Spain. The ferry service between Trinidad and Tobago is cheap, comfortable, but heavily booked at weekends and holidays.

Yachts Chaguaramas, Trinidad, and Scarborough, Tobago are the ports of entry. In Chaguaramas, take the boat to the customs dock (T6344341, open 24 hours) to clear on arrival in Trinidad and fill in combined customs and immigration form. Overtime fee for after hours, 1600-0800, weekends and holidays, so it pays to arrive during normal working hours. A clearance out certificate from your last port is required. Immigration and Customs at Scarborough is open 0800-1600 weekdays, T6392415.

Departure by sea Clear out with customs and immigration. Pay port fees of US$8 for each month that the boat was in Trinidad and Tobago waters. To go from one island to the other clear out with Immigration and in on the new island. Clear customs only when making final departure. New arrivals must be signed aboard the vessel as crew by immigration in Chaguaramas.

Departure by air Boats can be left in storage; yacht yards will help with paperwork, present it to customs and clear with immigration within 24 hours of departure for exemption from departure tax. When returning to Trinidad by air, go to third party line at airport to get paperwork to take with baggage to Chaguaramas customs to clear. Arriving outside office hours leave boat parts for weekday review. Arriving guests should have return ticket and letter to Trinidad immigration stating vessel name and official number.

Information *The Boca* is a useful monthly 'yachtie' magazine available locally or at www.boatersenterprise.com. The annual *Boaters Directory* (produced December,

Trinidad & Tobago Essentials

T6342622) lists services for yachties: US$10 overseas, free to arriving yachties. The editor, Jack Dausend, T6342055, is prepared to offer advice to potential visitors. The **Yacht Services Association** ① *T6344938*, is also extremely helpful.

Marinas The Trinidad marinas are all west of Port of Spain along the coast to Chaguaramas. **Trinidad and Tobago Yacht Club (TTYC)** ① *Bayshore, T/F6374260*, a private club, leases members' slips to visiting yachts when available, 60 in-water berths, security, restaurant, bar, laundry. **Trinidad and Tobago Sailing Association (TTSA)** ① *Chaguaramas, T6344519*, a private members' association with moorings and anchorage available to visiting yachts, full service haul-out yard, 15-ton marine hoist, moorings, repair shed, bar, restaurant, laundry. **Power Boats Mutual Facilities** ① *Chaguaramas, T6344303, F6344327*, haul-out and storage, 50-ton marine hoist, 23 in-water berths, boat storage, marine supplies, fibreglass repairs, welding, woodworking, apartments, grocery, restaurant, laundry. **Peake Yacht Services** ① *Chaguaramas, T6344423, F6344387*, full service marina, 150-ton marine hoist, capable of beams to 31 ft, 21 in-water berths, boat storage, 10-room hotel, restaurant, wi-fi, laundry, skilled maintenance, recommended. **Industrial Marine Services (IMS)** ① *Chaguaramas, T6252104, F6344437*, full service haul-out and storage yard, 70-ton marine hoist, paint shop, chandlery, sailmaker, fibreglass repair, welding, woodworking, sandblasting, restaurant, laundry. **Crews Inn Yachting Centre** ① *Chaguaramas, T6344384*, is best equipped with on-shore facilities, including a 46-room hotel with pool and gym, **Lighthouse** restaurant, **Republic Bank** with ATM, **Econocar** car rental agency, T6342041, hair salon, duty-free liquor store. Tardieu Marine nearby will lift and dry storage. **Sweet Water Marina**, also nearby, T6344046, has a restaurant. All locations charge a fee to anchored boats for use of shoreside facilities.

Touching down

Airport information This is one of the few countries to charge departure tax to passengers arriving to change planes and leave same day; it's cheaper, therefore, to change planes in, say, Barbados.

Trinidad Piarco International Airport is 16 miles southeast of Port of Spain. The enormous terminal has plenty of space, if few comfortable places to sit. Downstairs departure area has ATMs, several fast food restaurants (quiet one upstairs) and a **First Citizens Bank** foreign exchange office open 0600-2200, shops selling snacks, crafts and souvenirs. There are a number of duty-free shops; upstairs for a fairly well-stocked bookshop, a bar and (very expensive) fast food. Try to avoid overnight connections here. Airline schedules ensure that it is possible to arrive at Piarco after the check-in counters have closed until next morning, so you cannot go through to the departure lounge. Sky cap has 24-hour left luggage service. If you are in transit always check that your bags have not been off-loaded at Piarco, some are not checked through despite assurances. Telephone (Companion) cards are for sale at the book stall close to Check-in (a long walk from Arrivals).

‡ *There is a 15% VAT on airline tickets purchased in Trinidad and Tobago.*

Tobago Crown Point Airport is within walking distance of the hotels in the southwest. It is also uncomfortable for a long wait, often with no food available after you have been through immigration control. There are a few shops, snack bars and a bank with an ATM outside the terminal building but only a small duty-free inside. If you are booked on a large aircraft, such as Virgin Atlantic's, expect long, slow queues from check-in, past the departure tax booth, all the way up the stairs to the X-ray machines, which can take an hour to clear.

Airlines

Caribbean Airlines replaced BWIA in January 2007, offering flights to Toronto, New York, Miami, London (direct using a codeshare arrangement with British Airways or via Barbados) and Caribbean destinations, Sunjet House, 30 Edward St, Port of Spain, T6272942, www.caribbean-airlines.com, with offices also at Piarco, San Fernando and Crown Point, Tobago. Tobago Express, also at 30 Edward St, T6252470, www.tobagoexpress.com, opens for reservations at 0800. American Airlines, 69 Independence Sq, T8216000, at Piarco, T6690261. Air Canada is at Piarco, T6694065. LIAT, 9-11 Edward St, T6276274, at Piarco,

T6694770, at Crown Point, T6390484. Martinair, T6312000, bookingoffice@beautifultobago.com, or in Amsterdam T312-06011767. Surinam Airways, T6274747. Caribbean Star, at Piarco Airport, T6698153. Aeropostal 110-112 Frederick St, T6236641, and at Piarco, T6698593. Continental Airlines, Furness Building, Independence Sq, T6242764. United Airlines and Avior, 13 Pembroke St, T6238201. Conviasa, 78 Wrightson Rd, T6274118. Virgin Atlantic, Crown Point, Tobago, T1-800 7447477. British Airways, Crown Point, Tobago, T1-800 7442997. Excel, Crown Point, Tobago, T6390484.

Safety

The people of both islands are, as a rule, very friendly but several areas are no longer safe, especially for women. Most locals are rightly concerned about the increase in violent crime; however, the vast majority of visitors have a safe and enjoyable stay. To the east of Charlotte Street, Port of Spain becomes increasingly unsafe. You should avoid Laventille, Morvant and East Dry River. Central Port of Spain is fairly safe, but is quiet at night, apart from around Independence Square, so exercise caution. Avoid the area around the port or bus terminal except when making a journey. Do not underestimate crime in **Tobago**. We have received reports of theft and muggings on the Pigeon Point road and parts of Scarborough are known to have crack houses. Do not walk in the Turtle Beach area after dark. There have also been attacks on tourists near waterfalls, on deserted beaches and in other beauty spots. Soft-top jeeps are at risk of theft. Leave nothing in them. Leave your valuables in your hotel safe if you can. Women alone report feeling 'uncomfortable', particularly if they look like a tourist. Violent crime and rape of foreigners has been reported in Tobago, although an increased police presence is helping. Male and female prostitution has become a problem in Store Bay and elsewhere. HIV infection rates are high on both islands. Do not be tempted to dabble in narcotics. Penalties are severe and foreigners and their vehicles may be searched. Tourists have occasionally been killed as a result of suspected drug deals and many more are behind bars after failed attempts to take home narcotics.

> ♥ Care must be taken everywhere at night and walking on the beach after dark is not safe; stick to main roads and look as if you know where you are going.

Tourist information The **Tourism Development Company (TDC)** ① *Level 1, Maritime Centre, 29 Tenth Av, Barataria, T6757034, tourism-info@tdc.co.tt, open 0800-1600*, gives you a nice little carrier bag with maps and this year's event calendar, etc. Very quiet, the pleasant staff have plenty of time to help. They have lists of hotels, restaurants, tour operators, monthly schedule of events, maps for sale, etc. The **office at the airport** ① *T6695196, daily 0900-2300*, is helpful with hotel or guesthouse reservations for your first night (maps of Trinidad and Port of Spain for sale). The **National Carnival Commission** ① *Queen's Park West, Port of Spain, T6271350, nccmac@tstt.net.tt*, **Division of Tourism and Transportation** ① *Doretta's Court, 197 Mt Marie, Scarborough, Tobago, T6392125, www.visittobago.gov.tt, or at Crown Point Airport, T6390509, or at the port.*

Maps Large-scale and island-wide maps of both islands can be bought from the **Lands and Survey Division** ① *118 Frederick St, T6279204*. Some areas are out of print.

Air Tobago Express, T6275160, flies the Trinidad to Tobago route offering lots of daily flights; **Caribbean Star** also flies once a day. The crossing takes 20 minutes and costs US$50 return (or TT$300 which works out slightly cheaper). Departures, however, are often heavily booked at weekends and holidays, particularly Christmas and afterwards, also pre- and post-Carnival and Easter weekend (at other times tickets can sometimes be bought the same day).

Boat Taking the ferry is time-consuming; it is easier to fly. Boats from Port of Spain to Tobago two or three times a day; times vary monthly. Fast ferry, *The Lynx* (800 passengers, 200 vehicles), or *The Cat*, do the crossing in under 2½ hours. *The Panorama* 5½ hours, and *The Warrior Spirit*, 7 hours are older and less comfortable. Tickets are sold at the **Port Authority** ① *T6392417 in Tobago or T6232901 ext 160 in Trinidad) on the docks. Tickets for the fast ferries are US$8 each way, slower ferries US$6 each way, cabin for 2 US$12.80 when available, children under 12 half price, under 3 free, office hours Mon-Fri 0700-2300, Sat 0700-1600, Sun 0700-1400*. Buy passage in advance, everyone will recommend you to queue at 0800, but 1000 is usually early enough. At peak times such as Christmas, Carnival and Easter it is best to book several weeks ahead. Weekends also get booked up quickly. You need a boarding pass and not just a ticket before you can board. Ferry also takes cars but it is easier to rent separately each end.

Road Driving is on the left and the roads are narrow and winding. On **Trinidad** there are dual carriageways from Port of Spain south to San Fernando, west to Diego Martin and east to Arima, but these and other roads are not of a high standard. Neither is the driving. No-entry signs are misleadingly placed; some have a little notice underneath saying they apply only to public transport (private cars can enter). The rush hour on Trinidad starts early and ends late. Traffic is very heavy. Allow at least an hour to leave Port of Spain in the late afternoon. There may be traffic jams at surprising times, eg returning from Chaguaramas small hours of weekends, or after beach on Sun pm; or whenever there is a police roadblock exercise. There are lots of pot-holes almost everywhere and traffic weaves about all over the place at high speed to avoid them. Taxis (licence plates beginning with H) tend to stop suddenly in the middle of the road to pick up/drop off passengers. Allow a full day if going from Port of Spain to Toco in the northeast or to the far southwest, if you want to have time to see anything or relax before returning. On rural roads there are prominent kilometre posts. The older mile posts are still often there too and are used in some postal addresses (eg 21 mile post, Toco Road). In some of the more chaotic suburbs, light poles have a similar role (eg M Smith, opposite Light Pole 12, Smith Trace, Morvant). On **Tobago** the roads are fairly good in the south but storms and landslides frequently disrupt passage in the north. Mountain bikes are fine if you can stand the hills and the heat.

Landslides are a risk on both islands during (or after) heavy rain, and can block roads, eg along the north coast of Trinidad. Flooding may also block roads particularly in the Caroni plains of central Trinidad.

International and most foreign driving licences are accepted for up to 90 days; after that you need to apply for a Trinidad and Tobago licence and take a written test. All drivers must always carry their licence and insurance with them. Documents are inspected at police road blocks, which are frequent on many main roads. Do not leave anything in your car, theft is frequent. Be careful where you park in Port of Spain, police 'wreckers' are diligent and will tow the car away. It costs US$17 to retrieve it and you need to show your driver's licence and insurance documents. There are a few car parks (eg Independence Square), mostly charging US$0.80 an hour.

Car hire Some companies only rent for a minimum of three days. Rental can be difficult on Trinidad, particularly at weekends and around Carnival, because of heavy demand. Best to make reservations in advance. Several companies do not accept credit cards, but require a considerable cash deposit. Small, older cars can be rented from US$30 a day upwards, unlimited mileage, check tyres before driving off. Deposit varies from company to company, as does method of payment, book in advance. Many companies have offices at the airport.

Bus On all routes, purchase your ticket at the kiosk before boarding the bus; you may have to tender the exact fare. In **Trinidad**, the word 'taxi' includes most forms of public transport. The word 'travelling' means going by bus or taxi rather than by private car. Buses are run by the **PTSC**. A/c buses, **Express Commuter Service** (ECS), with a/c lounge for waiting passengers, run on main routes from City Gate Terminal to Arima, Chaguanas, Five Rivers, Sangre Grande, Chaguaramas and San Fernando, also from Arima to Sangre Grande. Rural buses are extremely infrequent. The **PTSC** office (T6237872) is located at the remodelled South Quay railway station, called City Gate, and is the main terminal for both buses and maxi taxis. You can get information showing how to reach the various sights by bus. **Unified Maxi Taxi Association** is T6243505. On **Tobago** all buses originate in Scarborough (PTSC T6392293). Schedules are changed or cancelled frequently. The route taxi system is difficult for the foreigner, being based on everyone knowing every car and therefore where it is going, but official route taxis have an 'H' (for hire) at the start of the licence plate. Ask for directions for where to assemble for a particular route.

Taxi Look for cars with first letter 'H' on licence plates (no other markings). Taxis are expensive. **St Christopher's** taxis or airport taxis, T6251694, operate from the main hotels, **Ice House taxis**, T6276984, and **Independence Square Taxi Service**, T6253032, from Independence Square. Helpful drivers approach all stray white people on Independence Square, but this can be confusing if you are really looking for a route taxi (or a beer). There are fixed fares (eg US$20 to the airport during the day, US$30 after 2200), but agree on a price before the journey and determine whether the price is in TT$ or US$. Book ahead if you have a flight to catch. **Phone A Taxi**, T6288294, and **Kalloo's**, T6229073, slightly cheaper day or night. Take a taxi if you have a complicated journey, or you have heavy baggage, or it is raining. At night it can be a lot cheaper than getting robbed. **Route taxis** (similar to *colectivos*) are very cheap but not as comfortable. These cannot easily be distinguished from ordinary taxis, so ask the driver. They travel along fixed routes, like buses, but have no set stops, so you can hail them and be dropped anywhere along the route. During rush hour they often pass full, however, and in general it takes time to master the system. They are the only means of transport on some suburban routes, such as to St Ann's, and in rural areas away from main roads. Travelling to remote areas may involve three or more taxis, not really a problem, just ask where the next one stops. Major routes run all night and are amazingly frequent during the day, others become infrequent or stop late at night. There are also 'pirate' or 'PH' taxis with the P registration of a private car, which cost the same as the ordinary route taxis. Use these with caution; they are unlicensed and not insured for carrying paying passengers. Robberies have been reported. 'Ghost' taxis accept fares and drive off with your luggage as well – be warned. Maxi-taxis are minibuses; they are frequent and go as fast as the traffic will allow, often a bit faster (see Transport, page 924).

Hitchhiking Hitching is not common and is not advised anywhere – why take the risk when route taxis are cheap and frequent!

Sleeping

Hotels There are many hotels on the islands including some very good guesthouses and smaller hotels. Information about accommodation can be obtained from TDC, see Tourist information, above. VAT (15%) is charged by all hotels and in most a 10% service charge is added to the bill. Some, like the **Hilton**, add a 2% surcharge.
Camping is unsafe and is not recommended. ►► *See pages 898 and 916 for further details.*

Trinidad & Tobago Essentials

⁚ Carnival

Trinidad's carnival culminates each year on the two days before Ash Wednesday which marks the beginning of the Christian season of Lent (27-28 February 2006). In practice, the festivities start months ahead, with the Mas' camps abustle, the calypsonians performing most nights of the week and the impressive Panorama with competing steel bands at the Queen's Park Savannah stadium: preliminaries, semi-finals, then finals, which are held on Carnival Saturday before Mas' proper. Band launching parties, where band leaders show off their costumes, start long before Christmas. Calypso 'tents', where calypsoes are played, start in January. Try **SWWTU Hall** on Wrightson Road (Revue), also **Spektakula**, and various others with no permanent home – check newspaper ads, cost up to US$19, around 0800-0130. Panyards start practising every night even earlier. **BP Renegades** are at Charlotte, Port of Spain; **Exodus** is at St John's Road on Eastern Main Road, St Augustine; **Witco Desperadoes** are at Laventille Road, Port of Spain (hilltop, view, friendly but in an iffy crime area); **BWIA Invaders** are opposite the Oval in Tragarete Road. **Phase 2**, also **Starlift** off Audrey Jeffers Highway, west of Port of Spain, **Trinidad All Stars**, Duke Street, Port of Spain. There

are parties most of the time from then on. The biggest public fetes – on successive weekends from January, then also midweek, at the fire service, flour mill, licensing authority, water authority (WASA), army, customs, etc – draw huge crowds. There is lots of crowd participation and flag-waving, a bit like a big football match. The largest is usually the **PSA Caribbean Brass Festival** in a sports field near Long Circular Road. Getting a ticket in advance (slightly cheaper) from somewhere like **Rhyners Records** in Port of Spain or **Crosby's** in St James, or arriving early (eg 2130) saves a struggle at the gate; most go on until 0400-0500.

Night events and big pre-Carnival parties are fairly safe, but exercise caution; there is plenty of pick-pocketing and a small number of stabbings, policing has been tighter since the murder of an American after a street robbery in 2002.

Panorama steel band finals are held on Carnival Sat before Dimanche Gras. Parties on Sun start early. The Dimanche Gras show at the Savannah that night has a little bit of everything. There are two main carnival shows for children: the **Red Cross Kiddies Carnival** one week before Carnival proper, and the school-based **children's carnival** the following

Eating

Food Hotels and guesthouses serve a wide variety of European, American and traditional West Indian (or Creole) dishes, including pork souse, black pudding, roast suckling pig, *sancoche* and *callaloo* stews, and many others. There is also a strong East Indian influence and lots of Chinese restaurants too. Seafood, particularly crab and shrimp, is excellent. If you've a yen for the best pepper shrimps in the Caribbean, the Chinese restaurants in Trinidad are generally good, with chefs often direct from

⁚ *The variety of juices and ice creams made from local fruit is endless.*

China. However, the standard can drop abruptly when the chef gets his US visa. There is plenty of choice, and the menus are fairly 'authentic', even in some cheap places, although others can be greasy and nasty. There is a local fish called salmon, which is a white fish, no relation to the Scottish/Canadian variety. Smoked herring and salt cod are often eaten with a fried bake, especially for breakfast. The many tropical fruits and vegetables grown locally include the usual tropical fruits: large and juicy pineapples, pawpaws, very good sapodillas, and starchy eddoes and yam tanias. Varieties of bananas include the mini sweet siquier, the large plantain (eaten fried) and the savoury green fig salad. Citrus season is January to March. Fruit

Saturday. Their costumes are much more creative these days than the adults' and they are a treat to watch. On Carnival Monday, the festivities start with **J'Ouvert** at 0400, which involves dressing up in the cheapest and most outlandish disguises available ('old mas'), including 'mud', which will inevitably be transferred to the spectators and is murder to wash out of your clothes. Starting mid-morning the **Parade of Bands** at the Savannah, features very large and colourful bands. Though the Savannah is the main venue, on both Carnival Monday and Tuesday the bands march right around Port of Spain and are required to appear before the judges at other locations, including Independence Square and Victoria Square. Monday afternoon sees 'night mas' in St James, with few costumes but plenty of music; the same on Tuesday until midnight. **Ash Wednesday** has big beach parties sponsored by radio stations, usually at Maracas and Manzanilla, very heavy traffic. (Big beach parties also at Easter.)

Tickets for all **National Carnival Commission** shows (about US$10 for most events) are sold at the Queen's Park Savannah, where the shows are held. You can join one of the Mas' camps by looking in the newspaper for the times and locations of the camps (or use the internet, see below). If you are early enough you can get a costume, which will allow you to participate in one of the 'tramps' through town. The Tourist Office has a list of names and addresses of the bands you can contact in advance to organize a costume (US$160-300 and more). There is a lot of alcohol consumed during the road marches but no drunken brawls. Police are much in evidence on the streets. Note that it is illegal to sell tapes of carnival artists but 'bootleg' tapes and CDs are inevitably sold. If you have the strength, **Last Lap**, involves jumping up with a steel band around Port of Spain to squeeze the last ounce out of the festival, prior to its official end at midnight on Tue, but police may close it down earlier. Leave in time to beat the morning traffic ahead of the enormous beach parties at Manzanilla and Maracas on Ash Wednesday.

Useful contacts: National Carnival Commission, www.carnivalncc.com, T6271350; National Carnival Bands Association, T6271422; Pan Trinbago, www.pantrinbago.com, T6234486; Trinbago Unified Calypsonians Association, T6275912, truekaiso@hotmail.com.

and vegetables to seek out later in the year include mangoes (a huge variety: julie, graham, peter, starch, pineapple, long, doudou, etc) and large, creamy avocados (locally called *zaboca*). Coconut water from a fresh nut is refreshing, usually sold around the Savannah, Port of Spain and on Independence Square after dark, US$0.65 per nut. A distinctive local herb is *chadon beni*, tastes a bit like coriander.

The *roti*, a chapatti pancake which comes in various forms, filled with peppery stew, shrimp or vegetable curries, is very good, US$1.50 or so for vegetable, up to US$4 for shrimp. *Buss up shut* is a torn-up *paratha*, or Indian bread accompaniment to curries. Creole food (African-influenced, home-cooked food) is popular at lunchtime. *Pelau*, savoury peas and rice and meat cooked with coconut and pepper, is also good. Some other popular meat dishes are cow-heel soup and chicken-foot and pig-foot souse. Use the local pepper sauce in moderation unless you are accustomed to *chili* dishes. Non-meat-eaters are well catered for. Try *saheena*, deep-fried patties of spinach, dasheen, split peas and mango sauce. *Pholouri* are fritters made with split peas. *Buljol* is a salt fish with onions, tomatoes, avocado and pepper. Callaloo is a thick soup based on dasheen leaves. *Doubles* are curried chickpeas (*channa*) in two pieces of fried *barra* (mini pancakes), eaten for breakfast and bought from street stalls across the country. A *hops* is a crusty bread roll. If you go to Maracas Bay, have *shark-and-bake*, a spicy fried bread sandwich of fried shark with a variety of sauces such as tamarind, garlic, *chadon beni*; kingfish-and-bake, shrimp-and-bake are alternatives; also sugar cakes, made with grated coconut. *Pastelles*, eaten at Christmas, are maize flour parcels stuffed with minced meat, olives, capers and raisins, steamed in a banana leaf. Dumplings are a must on Tobago, particularly good with crab. A local sweet in Tobago is *benny balls*, made from sesame seeds. *Salt prunes* (Chinese) and *red mango* are on sale almost everywhere. There's a huge variety at the lookout before you get to Maracas. In rural areas you may come across wild meat festivals (coincide with the hunting season Oct-Dec), consisting of a rich stew of local meats, bones and all, such as agouti, quenck, lappe, tattoo (armadillo), manicou.

Drink A local non-alcoholic drink is *mauby*, slightly bitter and made from the bark of a tree. Sorrel is a bright red Christmas drink made from sepals of a plant from the hibiscus family. There is also ginger beer, and you can get sorrel and ginger beer shandy. Fresh lime juice is recommended; it is sometimes served with a dash of Angostura bitters. There are lots of rums to try, many of which are better without punch or Coke. Local beers are *Carib* and *Stag*, both owned by the same company, which also brews *Carlsberg*, *Mackeson*, *Royal Stout* and *Guinness*; *Samba* is a locally brewed independent.

Festivals and events

Trinidad

There is a festival or special event of some kind just about every week of the year in Trinidad. Make sure you use enough sunblock.
Jan New Year's Day.
Feb/Mar The Hindu festival of Phagwa, or Holi, the colour, or spring, festival on the day of the full moon in the month of Phagun (Feb/Mar). Usually celebrated at Tunapuna Hindu School and the Divali Nagar. Everyone gets squirted with brightly coloured dyes (*abeer*); strict Hindus have their doubts about some of the dancing styles.
Mar Carnival Mon and Tue before Ash Wed (not officially holidays).
30 Mar Spiritual Shouter Baptist Liberation Day.
Mar/Apr Good Fri, Easter Mon.
Late Apr/early May Point Fortin Borough Week, with steel bands and street parties.
May La Divina Pastora, in the southern town of Siparia, celebrated by Catholics and Hindus.
30 May Indian Arrival Day, celebrating the arrival of Indian labourers in 1845.
19 Jun Corpus Christi, Labour Day.
Jul St Peter's Day in Carenage and fishing villages along the north coast is the first weekend in Jul.
1 Aug Emancipation Day.
29 Aug Feast of St Rose of Lima is celebrated in Arima. Descendants of the original

Amerindians come from all over the island to walk in solemn procession round the church.
31 Aug Independence Day.
24 Sep Republic Day.
Oct/Nov Hindu festival Divali, usually Nov (depends on Hindu religious calendar), is a family affair and involves a lot of good food in Indian homes, with pretty oil lamps or *deyas* burning outside. The display at Felicity in central Trinidad is spectacular, but go early to avoid the traffic.
25-26 Dec Christmas Day, Boxing Day.
The Hosay, or Hosein Festival, commemorating the murder of Mohammed's sons-in-law, Hussein and Hassan, starts 10 days after the first appearance of the new moon in the Moharrun month of the Moslem calendar (10-11 days earlier each year – late Jan or early Feb (2006-07). These are Shia festivals, commemorating a defeat by the Sunni. Most Trinidad Muslims are Sunni and disapprove of the event; the drumming is increasingly late at night; in recent years this has sharply reduced the casual crowd. Although beer and rum are on sale nearby, try not to flaunt it immediately around the *tajjas*. Also celebrated is the Muslim festival of Eid ul-Fitr, marking the end of Ramadan (changes according to religious calendar, will be around 13 Oct 2007 and 1 Oct 2008).

Tobago

Mar Tobago's carnival is very quiet compared with Trinidad's.
Mar/Apr On Easter Mon and Tue, there are crab, goat and donkey races at Buccoo

Village.
Jul The **Tobago Heritage Festival** lasts for the second fortnight of the month, with historical re-enactments, variety shows and parades.

Keeping in touch

Telephone Country code: 868.
Media Newspapers: The main daily papers are the *Daily Express*, the *Trinidad Guardian* and *Newsday*. The *Mirror* on Friday and Sunday has interesting if unreliable investigative journalism. *Tobago News* is weekly. There are several racier weekly papers which appear on Friday or Saturday. *Punch*, *Bomb*, *Heat* and *Blast* are sensational tabloids. *Discover Trinidad and Tobago*, is published annually and distributed free to all visitors through hotels.

Radio: There are at least 20 FM stations, some niche-marketed, for example for an Indo-Trinidadian audience, or community based. These include ICN Radio (610 AM), Radio Trinidad (730 AM), Music Radio (97 FM), 98.9 Yes FM, WABC (103 FM), ICN Radio (100 FM), Radio 95 FM, Radio Tempo (105 FM), Radio 96.1 FM, Rhythm (Radio 95.1 FM), Radio 1CN (91.1 FM), Sangeet (106.1 FM), Love Radio (94.1 FM), Hot (93 FM), Central Radio (90.5 FM), Power 102 FM.

Television: Major local TV stations in **Trinidad** are CCN TV and the news channel CNC, independent, also smaller independents: Gayelle, IETV, National Carnival Commission TV, IBN (Islamic Broadcasting Network), and ACT (Christian channel). There are 66 cable channels, mostly US, but also the **BBC** and Indian channels. **Tobago** has its own 56 channels, including Deutsche Welle TV. DirecTV (satellite) has channels in Spanish, Portuguese, French, German and Italian as well as US basics and BBC.

Trinidad

Trinidad is one of the most diverse islands in the Caribbean, offering a vibrant metropolitan area and a range of natural features to explore. The lush northern coast, with its golden beaches, crescent bays and headlands is backed by forested mountains where there is good hiking and excellent birdwatching. Elsewhere there are swamps, mangroves and wetlands, home to innumerable birds and other creatures such as manatee or caymans. In the south are unusual geological features such as the Pitch Lake, a huge area of tar, and active mud volcanoes. ►► *For Sleeping, Eating and other listings, see pages 898-910.*

Port of Spain → *Phone code: 868 Colour map 5, C6. Population: 379,000 (including suburbs).*

Port of Spain lies on a gently sloping plain between the Gulf of Paria and the foothills of the Northern Range. It is a busy port city with constant coming and going of shipping as well as being an important financial centre and business hub. All the multicultural aspects of Trinidad can be found here, it is full of life and an exciting city. Restaurants abound for every conceivable cuisine, the capital is renowned for its delicious food, while at night the clubs and bars offer a variety of music going on into the early hours. A little of the fretwork wooden architecture remains among the modern concrete and office towers; many of the main buildings of interest are within easy reach of the port.

Ins and outs

The taxi fare from Piarco Airport to Arouca is US$17 and to the centre of Port of Spain is US$25, to Maraval US$30, Diego Martin US$35, San Fernando US$40 (50% more after 2200). Taxi despatchers find taxis for new arrivals, ask to see the notice board or rate card for taxi fares. Kalloo's has a branch at the airport and is slightly cheaper. Unlicensed taxis outside the main parking area charge less, depending on the volume of business, at your own risk. Public transport is at some distance. From the roundabout at the end of the airport terminal approach road you can catch a route taxi to highway or to Arouca (US$0.50), then take a route taxi or maxi-taxi from the junction into Port of Spain (US$0.80). People are very helpful if you need to ask. There are also a few buses, see Transport page 908. Tickets are not available at the airport. From City Gate terminal you will have to walk to Independence or Woodford Square for a route taxi. This is not advisable at night, especially if carrying luggage. Take a taxi.

You can see most of the sights of Port of Spain by walking around the town centre. For further afield, however, there are taxis, buses, route taxis and maxi-taxis.
▶ See also pages 880 and 908.

Sights

On the south side of **Woodford Square**, named after former Governor Sir Ralph

Trinidad

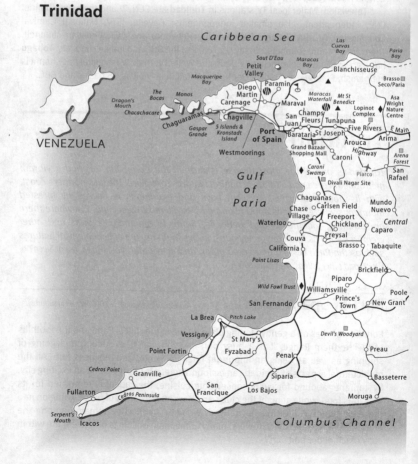

Woodford, is the fine **Anglican Cathedral Church of the Holy Trinity** (consecrated
1823), with an elaborate hammer-beam roof festooned with carvings. It was built
during Woodford's governorship (1813-1828) and contains a very fine monument to
him. The **Red House** (completed 1907) contains the House of
Representatives (usually meets Friday afternoon, can watch from
public gallery if there is room), the Senate and various
government departments. It was the scene of an attempted
overthrow of the Robinson Government by armed black Muslim
rebels in July 1990. The rebels held the Prime Minister and

> 🏴 The 'University of
> Woodford Square' is
> Trinidad's equivalent to
> Speaker's Corner in
> London's Hyde Park.

several of his Cabinet captive for five days before surrendering to the Army. On the
west side of the Red House, at the corner of St Vincent and Sackville streets, the
former **Police Headquarters**, which the rebels firebombed before launching their
assault on the Red House, has been rebuilt. The first Red House on this site was
destroyed by fire in 1903 during riots over an increase in water rates. On the opposite
side of the square to the cathedral are the modern **Hall of Justice** (it is sometimes
interesting to look in and listen to a trial) and the **City Hall**, with a fine relief sculpture
on the front. A new National Library is nearby.

On **Independence Square** (two blocks south of Woodford Square) is the **Roman
Catholic Cathedral of the Immaculate Conception**, built on the shore-line in 1832 but
since pushed back by land reclamation.
The central area of Independence Square,
from the cruise ship complex to the
cathedral, has been made into an
attractive pedestrian area, known as the
Brian Lara Promenade in honour of the
Trinidadian cricketer and West Indies
captain. This is lively in the evening with
people liming, drinking beer or playing
chess. Behind the cathedral is **Columbus
Square**, with a brightly painted statue of
the island's European discoverer. South
of Independence Square, between
Edward and St Vincent Streets, is the
financial complex, two tall towers and **Eric
Williams Plaza**, housing the Central Bank
and Ministry of Finance. A little to the
south of the square, the old neoclassical
railway station, now known as **City Gate**,
is a transport hub for taxis and buses
travelling between Port of Spain and
eastern Trinidad. Close to the waterfront is
the **San Andres fort**, built about 1785 to
protect the harbour, and a lighthouse
which has settled into the ground with a
rakish tilt.

To the north of the city is **Queen's
Park Savannah**, a large open space with
many playing fields and a favourite haunt
of joggers. It was the site of Trinidad's
main racecourse for decades, until racing
was centralized in Arima. In the middle of
the Savannah is the Peschier cemetery,
still owned and used by the family who
used to own the Savannah. Below the

level of the Savannah are the **Rock Gardens**, with lily ponds and flowers. Opposite are the **Botanic Gardens** ① *0600-1800*, founded in 1818 by Sir Ralph Woodford. There is an amazing variety of tropical and sub-tropical plants from Southeast Asia and South America, as well as indigenous trees and shrubs. Adjoining the gardens is the small **Emperor Valley Zoo** ① *0930-1800, no tickets after 1730, US$1.60, children 3-12 US$0.80*, dating from 1952, which specializes in animals living wild on the island. It has a number of reptiles, including iguanas, eight species of boas and the spectacled caiman. Also next to the gardens is the presidential residence, a colonial-style building in an 'L' shape in honour of Governor James Robert Longden (1870-1874). Just off the Savannah (on St Ann's Road) is **Queen's Hall**, where concerts and other entertainments are given.

There are several other Edwardian-colonial mansions along the west side of Queen's Park Savannah, built in 1904-1910 and known as the **Magnificent Seven**: from south to north, they are **Queen's Royal College**; **Hayes Court**, the residence of the Anglican Bishop; **Prada's House**, or Mille Fleurs; **Ambard's House**, or Roomor; the **Roman Catholic Archbishop's residence**; **White Hall**, which has regained its status as the Prime Minister's office after a no-expense-spared restoration; and **Killarney**, also known as Stollmeer's Castle (now owned by the Government). Apart from Hayes Court, which was built in 1910, all were built in 1904. A walk along the north and west sides of the Savannah is best in the early morning (before it gets too hot), arriving outside Queen's Royal College as the students are arriving and the coconut sellers are waking up outside. The **Anglican Church of All Saints** ① *13 Queen's Park West*, is also worth a visit; its stained-glass windows are recently restored. **Knowsley**, another 1904 building, and the new headquarters of the **BPtt Oil Company**, formerly the historic **Queen's Park Hotel** (1895), both on the south side of the Savannah, are interesting too.

Just off the Savannah, at the corner of Frederick and Keate streets, is the small **National Museum and Art Gallery** ① *T6235941, Tue-Sat 1000-1800, Sun 1400-1800, free*, in the former Royal Victoria Institute. It has sections on petroleum and other industries, Trinidad and Tobago's natural history, geology, archaeology and history, carnival costumes and photographs of kings and queens, and art exhibitions (including a permanent exhibition of the work of the 19th-century landscape artist, M J Cazabon, see also page 928).

Port of Spain suburbs

The suburbs around Port of Spain vary considerably, some are desirable places to live, others are to be avoided (see Safety, page 879). To the east is **Sea Lots**, a rough squatter area on the shoreline. **Beetham Estate** is even rougher public housing along the highway. **Laventille** is a working-class hillside suburb, breezy with good views and two big water tanks, **Our Lady of Laventille** and the **Desperadoes** panyard (see Carnival, page 884). For a pleasant drive in the hills with attractive views of city, sea and mountains, go up Lady Young Road, about two miles from Savannah, to a lookout 563 ft above sea level (not on a taxi route, but some cars take this route from the airport), or Lady Chancellor Road . In the northeast, **Belmont** is a run-down but charming area of older housing. **Cascade** is a pretty valley with houses stretching up the hillsides. **St Ann's** is another pretty valley with the Prime Minister's residence (**La Fantasie**) and the psychiatric hospital. To the northwest, **Newtown** is crowded, commercial and busy, while **St Clair** is spacious, expensive and quiet. **Maraval** is in the next valley with the road running through it to **Maracas** on the coast (heavy rush-hour traffic). Away from the city centre, to the west of Port of Spain, is the suburb of **Woodbrook**; **Ariapita Avenue**, is full of restaurants and pubs, while **St James** is known as the city that never sleeps. In Ethel Street there is a large Hindu temple, the **Port of Spain Mandir**, and on Nepaul Street is the childhood home of writer **VS Naipaul**. From **Fort George**, a former signal station at 1,100 ft, there are also excellent views. The fort was built around 1804 and formerly called **La Vigie**. Although it was

Port of Spain

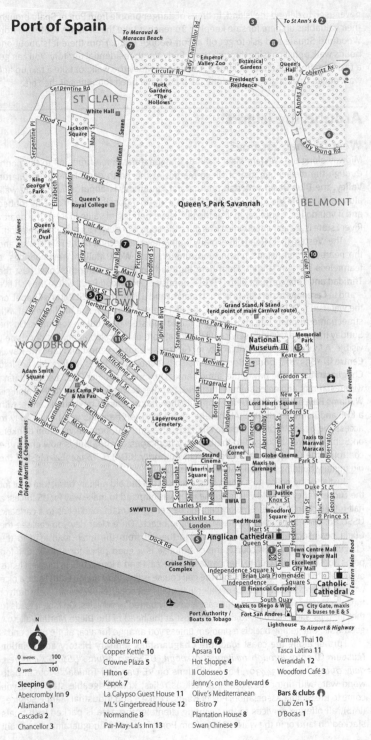

Trinidad & Tobago Trinidad

To Maraval & Maracas Beach
To St Ann's &

St Clair
White Hall
Jackson Square
King George V Park
Queen's Royal College
Serpentine Rd
Flood St
Serpentine Pl
Elizabeth St
Alexandra St
Hayes St
Mary St
Seven
Magnificent
St Clair Av
Queen's Park Oval
Sweetbriar Rd
Gray St
Maraval Rd
Picton St
Alcazar St
Marli St
Woodford St
Rust St
Herbert St
Warner St
New Town
Luis St
Alfredo St
Carlos St
Tagarete Rd
Cipriani Blvd
Stanmore Av
Woodbrook
Roberts St
Kitchener St
Baden Powell St
Buller St
Ariapita Av
Adam Smith Square
Murray St
Fitt St
Cornelio St
French St
Gatacre St
Methuen St
McDonald St
Conville St
Wrightson Rd
Mas Camp Pub & Ma Pau
Lapeyrouse Cemetery
Tranquility St
Albion St
Dere St
Melville L
Victoria Av
Borde St
Fitzgerald L
Dundonald St
Philip St
Flament St
Stone St
Scott-Bushe St
Shine St
Melbourne St
Richmond St
Edward St
Strand Cinema
Victoria Square
Charles St
Green Corner
Maxis to Carenage
St Vincent St
Abercromby St
Pembroke St
Frederick St
New St
Lord Harris Square
Oxford St
Gordon St
Keate St
Chancery La
National Museum
Memorial Park
Circular Rd
Belmont
Queens Park West
Grand Stand, N Stand (end point of main Carnival route)
Queen's Park Savannah
Rock Gardens "The Hollows"
Circular Rd
Emperor Valley Zoo
Botanical Gardens
President's Residence
Queen's Hall
Coblentz Av
St Annes Rd
Lady Young Rd
To St James
Globe Cinema
Taxis to Maraval Maracas
Park St
Observatory St
To Laventille
Hall of Justice
Knox St
Woodford Square
Duke St
Chacute St
Henry St
George St
Prince St
SWWTU
Sackville St
London St
Dock Rd
Anglican Cathedral
Red House
Hart St
Queen St
Frederick St
Chacon St
Town Centre Mall
Voyager Mall
Excellent City Mall
To Eastern Main Road
Cruise Ship Complex
Independence Square N
Brian Lara Promenade
Independence Square S
Financial Complex
South Quay
Maxis to Diego & W
Fort San Andres
Lighthouse
Catholic Cathedral
City Gate, maxis & buses to E & S
Port Authority / Boats to Tobago
To Airport & Highway
To Jean Pierre Stadium, Diego Martin & Chaguaramas

N

| 0 metres | 100 |
| 0 yards | 100 |

Sleeping
Abercromby Inn 9
Allamanda 1
Cascadia 2
Chancellor 3
Coblentz Inn 4
Copper Kettle 10
Crowne Plaza 5
Hilton 6
Kapok 7
La Calypso Guest House 11
ML's Gingerbread House 12
Normandie 8
Par-May-La's Inn 13

Eating
Apsara 10
Hot Shoppe 4
Il Colosseo 5
Jenny's on the Boulevard 6
Olive's Mediterranean Bistro 7
Plantation House 8
Swan Chinese 9
Tamnak Thai 10
Tasca Latina 11
Verandah 12
Woodford Café 3

Bars & clubs
Club Zen 15
D'Bocas 1

never used to defend the island, in times of danger people from Port of Spain brought their valuables up here for safe keeping. To reach it take the St James route taxi from Woodford Square and ask to get off at Fort George Road. From there it is about one hour's walk uphill passing through some fairly tough residential territory. You can get a taxi from Bournes Road, St James, if you don't fancy the walk, or take a taxi up and walk down. Go in a group, not alone, as there have been robberies at the Fort.

Around the island

West to Chaguaramas

Midway along the Western Main Road to Chaguaramas a road runs off to the north, through the residential area of Diego Martin. At the north end of the **Diego Martin Valley**, the **Blue Basin waterfall** and natural landmark, is about a five-minute walk along a path from the road. (Visit the falls in a group if possible to avoid being robbed and if you do leave your car to visit the fall, leave nothing of value in it.) At the nearby River Estate is a waterwheel which was once the source of power for a sugar plantation.

The Western Main Road offers many pretty views, especially of the Five Islands and the nearby Carrera island prison, and runs on past **West Mall** in Westmoorings, a featureless modern suburb. From here the road continues along the coast past the **Trinidad and Tobago Yacht Club (TTYC)** – opposite Goodwood Park, where the rich live – and to **Carenage**, where there is a fish market and a little church, **St Peter's Chapel**, on the waterside. **St Peter's Day festival**, the first weekend in July, is a mini-Carnival with street parties running late into the night, music and steel pan, but no costumes. On the Sunday there is a religious service, the original core of the celebration, but now barely visible. A former transhipment facility for Guyanese bauxite is next and then the **Kayak Centre** ① *T6337871, 0600-1800*, which also has mountain bikes, before you are into **Chaguaramas**, on the bay of the same name. On your left is Pier One, a small marina with restaurant and entertainment facilities, popular at weekends, and further along is **Williams Bay**, a dirty public beach opposite the **Chaguaramas Convention Centre**, with a KFC and some small bars. At the end of the road is **Chagville**; you have to pay to access the beach, facilities include changing area and bar, popular with rum drinkers on Sun. This area belonged to the US Navy from 1945 to 1964 but is now under the control of the **Chaguaramas Development Authority (CDA)** ① *T6344364*. Most of the old military buildings are still there, with new ones.

Just after the police post which marks the start of the old military base, turn right for the **Tucker Valley**. The old village on the right was emptied to make way for US forces; a half-ruined church and a cemetery can still be seen. The main road leads to a car park, US$0.80, with steps down to the Macqueripe beach. On a clear day you can see the Güiria peninsula of Venezuela. Turnings to the left from the main road lead to the Chaguaramas public golf course; the club house is a good place for a drink. Cliff-top paths from the car park run to the headland to the east and a longer one to the west leads eventually to the golf club. Also from the golf course is the short trail to **Edith Falls**, a nice walk, but there is barely a trickle of water in the falls except after heavy rain. Just south of the beach an asphalted road to the east is usually barred to vehicles. On foot, it leads to the cliff tops and eventually to the North Post at the head of the **Diego Martin Valley**. A good walk, but getting back is a problem unless you arrange for a car at the other end.

Further along the coast road, the **Chaguaramas Military History and Aviation Museum** ① *entry through military checkpoint, US$3.20 adults, US$1.60 children, daily 0900-1700. T6344391*, has exhibitions on VE Day and Trinidad's role in both world wars with intricate models as well as relics. knowledgeable staff. Next you come to the Sailing Association, Power Boats, Peake's and Industrial Marine Services (IMS), all offering services to the yachting clientele; the area is packed with boats stacked on land or in the water. Buses from Port of Spain to Chaguaramas run about

From **Island Property Owners Association** ① *T6344443*, the last boatyard west of Chaguaramas, you can get a launch (known locally as a *pirogue*) to the offshore islands which dot the Bocas, between Trinidad and Venezuela. Usual return fares for a boat with up to six people are US\$21 per boat to **Gaspar Grande** (**Gasparee Caves** ① *Mon-Fri US\$9.60 adults, US\$8 children, Sat, Sun and public holidays US\$16 adults, US\$13.60 children*), US\$21 to **Scotland Bay** beach (no road access), US\$96 to **Chacachacare** (a larger island with ruins of a former leper colony and several good beaches), or US\$40 per hour for just touring around. Use of their car park is US\$3.20 a day, or US\$1.60 per person for walking through the compound to board your pirogue. **Pier One**, T6344472, offers all-inclusive party tours to Chacachacare (good for large groups, you rent the boat with DJ, drinks, food, security etc). The Chaguaramas Development Authority, T6344364, also offers tours to the Gasparee Caves, US\$20 adults, US\$17.60 children under 17 at weekends and holidays, weekdays cheaper, including return transport and entrance fee to the caves. The Gasparee Caves are certainly worth a visit. It is about a 20-minute boat ride from the Crews Inn marina. The landing stage is at the west end of Gaspar Grande which has many weekend homes. The caves are about 15 minutes from the landing stage up a good path through woods, quite steep in places and hot. The caves are locked and it is necessary to have a guide from the house at the end of the path (water available). The complex of caves is large but you are only shown one, with good steps leading down and naturally lit from a blow hole. There is a beautiful lake (tidal) at the bottom with stalactites which the guide will light. Parts of the path around the cave are quite slippery. There is no swimming allowed in the cave on crowded days. Be prepared for a wait at the landing stage as, despite all assurances, a number of boatmen will not wait for you, preferring to return to the island and then come back to pick you up (which they usually do). There are excellent views of the other islands making up the Dragon's Mouth. This is much frequented by boats and yachts at the weekend but is virtually deserted during the week. **Monos Island**, at the west tip of Trinidad, has many deep caves and white sandy beaches, popular for weekend homes with more affluent Trinidadians.

> ‼ Try to get a pirogue with a canvas shade as these are used to dealing with tourists and are likely to be more reliable.

North coast

North of Port of Spain is **Maraval**, just beyond which is the 18-hole St Andrews golf course at **Moka** (there is also a swimming pool, US\$3 for non-members, T6294653). From Maraval village (church, police station) 4WD taxis run to the hilltop village of **Paramin**, where several families still speak French Creole, and there is an annual Parang music festival before Christmas (see Culture, page 929). The North Coast Road branches left off Saddle Road (which runs through Maraval back over the hills to meet the Eastern Main Road at San Juan), leading to Maracas Bay, Las Cuevas and Blanchisseuse. There is a lookout point on the road to Maracas Bay at the Hot Bamboo Hut, where a track goes steeply down to a secluded beach. The stall-holder can call the toucans in the forest; take binoculars to see them fly close and answer him. There is a hiking route across the Northern Range from the Santa Cruz Valley, well marked trail from Gasparillo village (not to be confused with Gasparillo near San Fernando, Gasparillo can be reached by route taxi from San Juan). The Northern Range locations for hiking are best reached from the coastal villages.

Las Cuevas is a lovely bay with a wide, sandy beach and calm waters, popular with families on Sundays. **Blanchisseuse** is divided between the Upper Village and Lower Village, with the Arima road as the dividing line. There is a post office, health centre, RC Church, government offices and police station in Lower Village, while Upper Village has the recreation field, school

> ‼ This town was named after the washerwomen who used to do their laundry in the Marianne River.

and several artisans working in wood and leather. All this part of the coast is very beautiful with the forest coming down to the sea. You can hike east all along the coast from here to Matelot and on to Grande Riviere, starting at the 100-year-old Silver Bridge just outside the village. It can be done in a day, or two if overnighting in Paria and a guide is useful; ask Fred (at Laguna Mar) to arrange it.

From Arima you can drive, taxi or hitchhike to Brasso Seco and Paria. From here the trail runs to **Paria Bay**, possibly the best beach on the island (can be littered after public holidays), about eight miles, ask directions, or see the **TIDCO Sites** (trail guide) book for the route. There is a primitive shelter on the beach but no other facilities so take provisions with you. At the beach, turn right to get to the bridge over the Paria River, from where it is a five-minute walk inland to the spectacular Paria waterfall. Another path from the beach leads west to Blanchisseuse (seven miles), where the track forks.

East of Port of Spain

The east-west corridor from Port of Spain is a line of industrial and residential suburbs linked by the Eastern Main Road and, more quickly, by a dual carriageway or priority bus/taxi route. Although the flat bits are mostly unattractive, you are never more than a mile or two from the hills and both high- and low-income neighbourhoods extend up the hillsides, with wonderful views of Central Trinidad and across to the Gulf of Paria. The older centres along the Eastern Main Road (San Juan, Curepe, Tunapuna, Arouca) are lively, with shops, small bars, Chinese restaurants and fruit and vegetable markets, the latter jamming up the traffic even on Sunday morning. Just east of Port of Spain on Eastern Main Road is the **Angostura rum distillery** ① *T6231841, tours Mon-Fri 0830 and 1300, US$5.50*, with small museum, rum, bitters, local history, also has a historic butterfly collection. An old warehouse to the east near Morvant Junction is now **CCA7** ① *T6240695, Wed-Fri 1200-1700, Tue, Thu 1200-2000, Sat 1000-1700*, artists' studio space, also with occasional exhibitions and Thursday evening films. At Champs Fleurs is the **Carib brewery**, then the Mount Hope teaching hospital. **St Joseph** was once the seat of government, as San José de Oruña. The imposing Jinnah Memorial Mosque stands here. North of St Joseph is the **Maracas Valley** (no road to Maracas Bay, although there is a footpath), which has a 300-ft waterfall.

Further east, high on a hill, is **Mount St Benedict** monastery (the oldest Benedictine complex in the Caribbean), reached through St Johns Road in St Augustine. Although the monastery was founded by a Belgian, the first Benedictine monks came from Bahia, Brazil, in 1912. It started with a tapia hut but construction of the main building on Mount Tabor began in 1918. The monastery has a retreat, lots of educational facilities, a drug rehabilitation centre, a farm and a guesthouse and is popular with birdwatchers and

❧ *It is possible to walk to Maracas from Maraval in about three hours; start with a maxi or route taxi from Port of Spain.*

walkers. There are marvellous views over the Caroni Plain to the sea. A priority maxi-taxi from Port of Spain to St Augustine takes 20 minutes, US$0.50, then a route taxi up St John's Road and then St Michael's Road will take you close to the monastery, but unless you pay to go off route it is still a stiff walk uphill. Otherwise take a private taxi all the way. From Caura Road, a little further east, a route taxi will take you up the valley of the Caura River, where the pools are popular spots for weekend picnics (river limes).

A little further along the Eastern Main Road at Arouca, the road branches south to Piarco International Airport, or north winding 10 km up into the forested mountains to the **Lopinot Complex**, an estate built by the Comte de Lopinot (see page 925) at the turn of the 19th century. Originally called La Reconnaissance, it is now a popular picnic spot and destination for school trips; there is a small museum. There is a bar across the road, open, like most others in Trinidad, 'anyday, anytime'. It hosts a Parang music festival before Christmas.

High on a ridge in the Maracas Valley are the only known Amerindian (probably Arawak) petroglyphs in Trinidad, known as the **Caurita drawings**. They show a series

of faces with curving lines indicating limbs. To get there it is a stiff climb of 1-1½ hours
in the valley, with access from the main crossroads between San Juan and Tunapuna.

Arima → *Population: 28,000.*

Arima is 25 km east of Port of Spain, reached by bus or route taxi. The landmark at the centre is the Dial, an old public clock. It has been repaired after an argument with a heavy truck, and plays the radio on Friday and Saturday nights. A few miles west of Arima is a small but interesting Amerindian museum at the Cleaver Woods Recreation Centre, housed in a reproduction Amerindian long house; entrance is free but donations are welcome. A group of people regard themselves as descendants of the original Amerindians of the area, although there are none left of pure blood. They have a figurehead Carib queen and call themselves the **Santa Rosa Carib Community**. West of the church in the centre of town is the Santa Rosa Carib Community Crafts Centre selling traditional crafts: cassava squeezers, serving trays, carvings, etc.

North of Arima

About eight miles north of Arima, off the Blanchisseuse Road, you can get to the **Asa Wright Nature Centre** ① *T6674655, wwww.asawright.org, 0800-1700, US$10 entrance and tour, give 48 hrs notice of your visit if possible*, an old plantation house overlooking a wooded valley and a must for bird-lovers (car or taxi from Arima, US$10, the driver should wait for you, or a warm 2½-hour walk uphill through lovely forests). The nature centre now owns nearly 1,500 acres of forest (not all of which are at the centre) and the annual Christmas bird count usually numbers 161 to 186 species. There is a beautiful man-made pool where you can swim, a network of trails and guided tours. Sit on the veranda and watch the hummingbirds. Take binoculars. The rangers are very knowledgeable and can tell you about the plants and insects (easier to see) as well as the birds. The rare oilbirds in **Dunstan Cave** (also called Diablotin Cave), can only be seen if you stay more than three nights. Field trips for guests are organized to the Caroni Swamp, Nariva Swamp, Aripo Savannah, Arena Forest and Blanchisseuse, while turtle-watching tours are also offered to the east and west coasts during leatherback nesting season (March to September).

This road carries on to Blanchisseuse, see page 891. A 9-mile walk from the road are the **Aripo Caves** (the longest system in Trinidad) with spectacular stalagmites and stalactites (in the wet season, June to December, a river runs through the caves). Oilbirds can be seen at the entrance. Only fully equipped spelunkers should venture beyond the entrance. To get there, turn at Aripo Road off the Eastern Main Road, turn right at the 4-mile post, over the bridge into Aripo village. Keep left, continuing uphill to a wide bend to the left where you may park off the road and begin the walk uphill. Turn left at the small house. After a further 10 minutes take the trail to the right of the junction and to the left at the next junction, continuing uphill along the river. At a shelf of rock there is a well cleared trail away from the river. Keep to this trail heading north until the top of the hill. Go downhill for five minutes to the stream leading into the cave.

❧ *Do not enter the caves without a flashlight, rope and other equipment; a knowledgeable guide is recommended.*

Northeast coast

The northeast coast is one of the most remote and unspoiled parts of the island, partly because the road does not extend along the whole of the north coast from Blanchisseuse. **Grande Riviere** lies in the middle of this area. It has a long and lovely beach, with accommodation and eco-tourism. Guesthouses can organize tours into the forest and along the path to Blanchisseuse, and in season you can watch the protected turtles laying their eggs in the sand. There is a wide river, also good for bathing, and hiking trails in the hills behind.

Grande Riviere is easy to reach by private car but not easy by public transport.

From Port of Spain take a bus (faster than a maxi) to Arima, US$0.65. From Arima to Sangre Grande there are buses and maxis (ask around) but a route taxi may be easiest; turn left just past **Scotia Bank** and the third lot of route taxis is for Sangre Grande. At Sangre Grande buses, maxis and route taxis all stop in the same place. It is relatively easy to get a maxi to Toco and possibly on to Sans Souci, but this still means a six-mile walk (very pleasant, no traffic) through the woods to Grande Riviere. There are some maxis and route taxis in the morning from Grande Riviere to Sangre Grande, returning at about 1600. As a last resort a route taxi in Sangre Grande would very soon become a private taxi. Guesthouses at Grande Riviere can also arrange to pick you up, price negotiable. Whichever way you go, the effort is worthwhile.

If you are driving yourself, from Arima the road runs either to **Toco** at Trinidad's northeast tip (which is well worth a visit with a few small beaches nearby for bathing) or, branching off at Valencia, to the east coast. Left fork at **Valencia**, then left again at **Honey Corner** (where there are bottles of locally made honey on sale), through small villages, woods and, after Salybia, beaches a short distance off the road to the right. The **Salybia Waterfall** is close to the 13-mile post; cross the bridge and turn left after the old 14¼-mile post into the Salybia/Matura Trace. Follow a 20-minute, rather rough drive and park in front of two houses. Walk 15 minutes along the trail, turn left at the junction, continue about 10 minutes to a second junction where the path narrows on the right going slightly uphill into Mora Forest. Keep on the trail, crossing first a small stream and then a larger river. 10 minutes later at another junction you may bear right over a small hill or walk upstream. Either route will get you to Salybia Waterfall and pool in 10 minutes. The pool is 6 m deep and recommended for good swimmers. There is also a picnic area.

At **Galera Point**, reached off the road which goes to Toco, over a rickety wooden bridge, there is a small, pretty lighthouse. If you arrive before 1530 it is often open and you can climb to the top for a breathtaking view from the ramp. You can continue by car (quite a long drive) to Grande Riviere and the small hotels on a wide, sandy beach (see page 893).

South of Port of Spain

Driving south from Port of Spain along the highway (turn right at the Grand Bazaar shopping mall) or the old Southern Main Road (turn right opposite the big *KFC/Pizza Hut*), you will see sugar, citrus and rice fields, and maybe a few buffalypso (buffaloes which have been selectively bred for meat), Hindu temples and mosques. There are boat trips to the **Caroni Bird Sanctuary** (signposted from the highway), the home of scarlet ibis, whose numbers are dwindling as the swamp in which they live is encroached upon and polluted. Boats leave around 1600 from near the Visitor's Centre to take people to see the ibis returning to their roost at sunset. There are two boat operators in the swamp (**Moodoo Tours**, T6630458, and **Winston Nanan**, T6451305, US$10, group rates available. Nanan rarely guides now and not all his boatmen are informative; enquire at the **Asa Wright Centre** for more detailed tours; if possible take a cold bag with drinks. Mosquito repellent is essential when you get off the boat at the end of your trip). To get there, take a bus or route taxi from Port of Spain or San Fernando to Bamboo Grove Settlement No 1, on the Uriah Butler Highway, from where the boats leave, US$0.32-65 or US$0.65-95 respectively. Maxi-taxi (green bands) leave from Independence Square; ask to be dropped off at the Caroni Bird Sanctuary.

On the left before you get to **Chaguanas**, a large blue statue of the Hindu god, Lord Shiva and a large white statue of Viveka Nanda, a Hindu philosopher, mark the site of the annual **Divali Nagar exhibition** in October/November. **Chaguanas** (pop: 62,000) is a busy place, not an architectural must, but full of bargains for the shopper. At the centre is the imaginatively named junction Busy Corner. The **Lion House** (on the main road to the east, close to the police station) is the original for VS Naipaul's *A House for Mr Biswas*. Continuing south on the Southern Main Road parallel to the highway, Carlsen Field has several small potteries, using open wood-fired kilns. Most of the pots are a bit unwieldy, but wind chimes, etc are easily portable, as are the tiny lamps, or *deyas*, which are made for Divali. Turn off the Main Road at Chase Village, and three miles to the west is **Waterloo**, where a small Hindu temple has been built in the sea. It is reached by a short causeway and it is the successor of a structure built by Siewdass Sadhu, a sugar worker who selected his site in the shallow waters of the Gulf of Paria after being unable to find land to build on. Close by is the Dattatreve Centre with an impressive Hanuman murti, the largest murti (statue) built outside India. Continuing south, the Southern Main Road leads to the Point Lisas industrial estate.

Alternatively, a left turn-off the highway at **Freeport**, or points south, takes you into the Central Range through sugar and citrus fields, then forests, with cocoa trees. There are cocoa houses with a sliding roof so that the beans can dry in the sun but go under cover when it rains. Pretty little villages with wooden houses and well-kept gardens overflow with hibiscus and bougainvillea. The roads are narrow and winding, so unless you are a map-reading wizard, you are bound to get lost. At **Chickland Village** near Freeport, the **Ajoupa Pottery** ① *T6730604, Mon-Fri 0800-1600, Sat 0900-1200* (see Shopping, page 906), with a wooden 19th-century estate house, is well worth a visit.

San Fernando → *Population: 49,000.*

San Fernando on the southwest coast is a busy, hot city, as yet unspoilt by tourism but spoilt by just about everything else. A highway connects Port of Spain with San Fernando, making it a 30-minute drive (90 minutes in the afternoon rush hour, US$1 by air conditioned express, route taxi US$2). The waterfront area is a mess, in spite of continual talk of restoration, although Harris Promenade is pleasant. City Hall, the Our Lady of Perpetual Help church and the old railway engine are worth a look. Library Corner has the old Carnegie public library and is the main centre for maxis and route taxis. Coffee Street is also lively. Above the city is San Fernando Hill, oddly shaped as a result of quarrying and easily picked out from Northern Range viewpoints or from Chaguaramas. It is now landscaped, and you can either walk or drive to the top for a spectacular view.

North of San Fernando are the principal industrial area of **Point Lisas** and the **Pointe-a-Pierre** oil refinery. Within the oil refinery is the 26-ha **Wild Fowl Trust** ① *T6584200 ext 2512, Mon-Fri 0800-1700, Sat, Sun 1000-1700, US$1.30 adults, US$0.80 teenagers (12-16), children US$0.50*, a conservation area with two lakes and breeding grounds for many endangered species, an interesting museum and interactive centre. Many birds bred in captivity are later released into the wild. Call 48 hours in advance to get permission to enter the compound (many entrances, it can be confusing).

A famous phenomenon to visit on the southwest coast just after La Brea is **Pitch Lake** ① *US$4.80, children under 12 US$1.90, route taxi from San Fernando to La Brea (US$1)*, about 116 acres of smooth surface of black tar; it is 135 ft deep. It is possible to walk on it, with care, watching out for air holes bubbling up from the pressure under the ooze. In the wet season, however, most of the area is covered with shallow fresh water. The legend is that long ago the gods interred an entire tribe of Chaima Indians for daring to eat sacred hummingbirds containing the souls of their ancestors. In the place where the entire village sank into the ground there erupted a sluggish flow of black pitch, which gradually became an ever-refilling large pool. Go to the TDC information office inside the car park where you will find an official guide. Locals who pose as guides outside the entrance harass tourists for large tips. Agree on a price in advance as there are no fixed rates. Sometimes there are crowds of guides who are difficult to avoid, but on the other hand it is difficult to understand the lake without explanation.

> ‡ The lake has been described by disappointed tourists, as looking like a parking lot, although others have pointed out that it is parking lots that look like the Pitch Lake.

Beyond La Brea the road continues to **Point Fortin**, a small but busy town with a liquefied natural gas plant and a small beach. The road carries on down the southwest peninsula, deteriorating as it goes, through **Cedros** (fishing village, beach) to Icacos, from which the mangroves of the Orinoco delta are clearly visible a few miles across the water. From the Point Fortin-Icacos road there are side roads leading to beaches such as **Erin** or **Columbus Bay**.

East of San Fernando

East of San Fernando the main road runs through rolling hills with sugar-cane fields, past the **Usine Sainte Madeleine** sugar mill to Princes Town, then continues to Rio Claro and Mayaro on the east coast. It runs parallel to the south coast, most of which is fairly inaccessible. Near Princes Town is the **Devil's Woodyard**, one of 18 mud volcanoes on Trinidad. This one is considered a holy site by some Hindus (it is also a natural landmark). It last erupted in 1852 and the bubbling mud is cool.

South coast

From St Julien, east of Princes Town, a road leads after 19 miles (slow driving) to the fishing village of **Moruga**. Every year around mid-July they have a celebration of Columbus' 1498 landing on the beach. Fishing boats are decked out as caravels, complete with the red Maltese cross. Columbus, a priest and soldiers are met by Amerindians (local boys, mostly of East Indian and African extraction); after the meeting everyone retires to the church compound where the revelry continues late into the night.

The **Karamat mud volcano** at Moruga, erupted in 1997. Thick mud spurted 150 ft into the air, killing one man, burying animals alive and engulfing houses, leaving 100 homeless. Seek local advice before visiting. To get there, from Penal Rock Road proceed west to the 8-mile post. On the right head down Haggard Trace driving south until the Moruga West oil field gate. Enter on the road and continue left for 1 mile. Pass a series of tank batteries, No 7, on the left, and continue to an oil pump on the right. Take the side road for 400 yds. Park near the oil pump at a well-head. Continue uphill. There is another mud volcano at **Piparo**, which erupted suddenly in 1994,

❈ Try shark-and-bake, shark meat in a heavy fried dough, a Maracas speciality, very tasty, sold all along the beach.

destroying a section of the village and cutting off the approach by road from the northeast. What remains is a big expanse of dry mud. Nearby is a large and tasteless house, with adjoining Hindu temple. Now a drug rehabilitation centre, it was once the home of the notorious drug dealer and murderer, Dole Chadee, who was hanged in 1999 along with his associates. The eruption of the volcano was seen by some villagers as divine retribution for Chadee's activities.

It is quite difficult to get beyond Arima and San Fernando by bus, but there are route taxis, and privately operated maxi-taxis, or you can hire a car. A full-day circuit of the island can be driven from Port of Spain south to San Fernando, east to Mayaro then north to Sangre Grande and Arima. An alternative route back from Mayaro runs through Biche and the eastern fringe of the Central Range to Sangre Grande.

Beaches and activities

Close to Port of Spain, **Chaguaramas** is dirty, but if you drive north through Tucker Valley, **Macqueripe** is a small beach in a pretty, wooded bay, with surprisingly good snorkelling (car park US$.80 at weekends). **Scotland Bay**, near the northwest tip of the island, is very pretty but can only be reached by boat. **Maracas Bay**, 10 miles from the capital, has a sheltered sandy beach fringed with coconut palms; despite small waves there can be a dangerous undertow here and at other beaches, and drownings have occurred; do not swim far out and watch the markers. Swim at the east end away from the river mouth. Very crowded on Sundays and holidays with loud

❈ Trinidad's best beaches are on the north coast and the views from the coastal road are spectacular as you drive through forest and look down on sandy bays and rocky promontories.

music and parties down the far end of the beach, but fairly quiet otherwise. Lifeguards are on duty until 1800; there are changing rooms, showers, etc, car parking and cabanas for beach vendors. There are route taxis from Park St, but all transport is irregular and infrequent. Easy at weekends but less so during the week. Difficulties in catching the bus have led travellers to recommend car hire or taxis: from Port of Spain a hotel or **Ice House** taxi costs US$25 one way.

Next to Maracas Bay is **Tyrico Bay** (surfing, lifeguard, another horseshoe-shaped beach with undertow). **Las Cuevas**, also on the north coast (changing rooms, showers, lifeguards, surfing at the far end occasionally, beware of the sandflies in the wet season), is a picturesque bay with fishing boats moored at the east end. The west end is very beautiful but can be isolated, so best to go in groups. It is busy on Sunday but quiet during the week. There are smaller beaches beyond **La Fillette** and at **Blanchisseuse** where one beach has a sweet water lagoon where the river runs into the sea (parking US$1.60). The place is kept clean by the owners of **Cocos Hut** restaurant/**Laguna Mar Beach Resort**, who are establishing a 28-acre nature reserve on the banks of the river. Eric Blackman has kayaks to rent (US$3.20 for 30 minutes, T6692963) which you can paddle up river. There are lots of birds but also mosquitoes and sandflies. Leatherback turtles come on to Blanchisseuse beach in the nesting season. The coast road ends at Blanchisseuse. At the northeast end of the island, near **Toco**, are a number of bays, including **Salybia** for good bathing, reached by a separate road via Sangre Grande and Toco.

The Atlantic coast from Matura to Mayaro is divided into three huge sweeping bays, with enormous palm trees in some places. Of these bays **Mayaro** and **Manzanilla** both have beautiful sandy beaches, but the Atlantic currents can make swimming dangerous. There are several beach houses to rent at Mayaro, heavily booked in peak holiday periods, some are poor, check beforehand. Manzanilla has public facilities and a hotel. From nearby **Brigand Hill Lighthouse**, a TSTT signal station, you can get a wonderful view of the east coast, the Nariva Swamp and much of Trinidad. Light patches of green are rice fields encroaching illegally on the swamp. In the southwest, near La Brea and the Pitch Lake, is the party beach resort of **Vessigny**. The southwest, or **Cedros**, peninsula is a three-hour car trip from Port of Spain to unspoilt beaches and miles of coconut palm plantations. There are plans to industrialize the area, enjoy it while you can. Generally, the beaches are difficult to get to except by taxi or car.

The **leatherback turtle** nests March to September on several beaches on Trinidad (Matura, Fishing Pond on east coast, Paria, Tacaribe and Grande Riviere on north coast) and Tobago (Great Courland Bay known as Turtle Beach, Stonehaven Bay, Bloody Bay and Parlatuvier), up to eight times a season, laying 75 to 120 eggs each time about 10 days apart. Incubation is 60 days.

Turtle-watching tours are organized by the Asa Wright Nature Centre.

Diving
The most varied marine wildlife off Trinidad is found in the channels called the Bocas, between the islands off the northwest peninsula (**The Dragon's Mouth**). However, the currents are cold, so protective gear is essential. At many north coast beaches, particularly **Macqueripe** on the west peninsula, a few miles north of the marinas, the diving and snorkelling are safer, if less spectacular. The waters flowing from the Orinoco around Trinidad reduce visibility, but the sea is full of nutrients. There is lots to see but you may not be able to see it, especially in the rainy season.

Sailing
Yachting has become big business in Trinidad and there are now several marinas attracting custom from other islands more at risk from hurricanes, with 2,000 visiting craft a year. Provisioning is excellent and there are boat repair and maintenance

facilities; local teak costs a fraction of US prices, workmen are highly skilled, services are tax-free and spare parts can be imported duty free. Marinas have both dry storage and stern-to docks. Facilities have also been built at Courland Bay, Tobago, to attract the yachting crowd.

⊜ Sleeping

VAT of 15% will be added to your bill. If you intend to stay in Trinidad for Carnival you must book a hotel well in advance. Most hotels raise their prices steeply and some insist you stay for the full period. If arriving without accommodation arranged at Carnival time, the tourist office at the airport may help to find you a room in a hotel, or with a local family, though both options will be expensive. Reservations are sometimes cancelled and hotels which have not sold their full package may make rooms available at the last min. For most of the year, hotels in Port of Spain cater almost exclusively for business visitors and rooms can be hard to find if your visit coincides with a conference. *Discover Trinidad and Tobago* has a full listing of the smaller bed and breakfast places, etc.

Port of Spain *p885, map p889*
LL-L Coblentz Inn, 44 Coblentz Av, T6210541, www.coblentzinn.com. Well-run boutique hotel, 16 rooms, Jacuzzi but no pool, good restaurant with creative international and Caribbean menu, **Battimamzelle** (name means dragonfly), T6210591, Mon-Fri 1100-2300, Sat 1800-2300, last order 2145. One of the best restaurants in town.
LL-L Crowne Plaza, Wrightson Rd, T6253366, www.cplazahotel.com. In the business centre, all facilities very nice, friendly, small pool, two restaurants: Olympia 0630-2300 and 360° revolving restaurant 1800-2300.
LL-L Hilton, corner of Lady Young and St Ann's Rds, northeast Queen's Park Savannah, T6243211, www.hiltontrinidad.com. Public areas and pool deck are on top and 380 rooms and 26 suites on lower levels, facilities for the disabled, restaurants, bars, lovely pool, non-residents can eat/swim there (monthly membership US$28), tennis, gym, conference centre, ballroom, executive suite, frequent entertainment. Major upgrade due for completion by 2008.
LL-L Kapok, 16-18 Cotton Hill, St Clair, northwest Queen's Park Savannah, T6225765, www.kapokhotel.com. 94 rooms, friendly, comfortable, light, big windows, some studios with kitchenette, excellent **Tiki Village** restaurant, T6225765, daily 0630-2215, with Chinese and Polynesian cuisine, Dim Sum buffet Sun, 1200-1430, also light meals at bar downstairs, small pool, shopping arcade.
LL-AL The Chancellor, 5a St Ann's Av, T6230883, www.thechancellorhotel.com. Small pool, **Waterfront Bistro**.
LL-AL Normandie, off St Ann's Rd, at the end of Nook Av (No 10), T6241181, www.normandiett.com. Renovated 2007, 54 standard, superior and loft rooms, a/c, reduced rates for businessmen, service criticised, swimming pool, in a complex with craft and fashion shops, good Italian restaurant daily 1800-2200, café 0700-1700 and outdoor theatre 'Under the Trees'.
L Cascadia, 67 Ariapita Rd, St Ann's, T6234208, www.cascadiahotel.com. 68 rooms up in the hills, children under 12 free, rooms and suites vary, nice pool, chutes and waterslide (US$4 for non-guests), sports and conference facilities, **Coconuts Club** disco open occasionally, restaurant, bar, busy at weekends.
A-B Par-May-La's Inn, 53 Picton St, T6282008, www.parmaylas.com. Convenient for Carnival and cricket, double or triple rooms with bathroom, a/c, TV, phone, facilities for the disabled, parking, local cuisine with roti, evening meals on request, credit cards accepted. Nearby the same owner has 15 apartments, **C Sun Deck Suites**, 42-44 Picton St, T6229560, www.sundecktrinidad.com. A/c, with cooking facilities, sleep 2/3.
B The Abercromby Inn, 101 Abercromby St, T6235259, aberinn@carib-link.net. 28 rooms, a/c, TV, phone, internet access, laundry facilities, some large and some very small economy rooms with thin walls, breakfast, tea and coffee available, 5 mins' walk to Queen's Park Savannah.

C **Copper Kettle Hotel**, 66-68 Edward St, T6254381. Central, rooms with shower, a/c, restaurant for breakfast and lunch.

Port of Spain suburbs *p888, map p889*
L **Courtyard Marriott**, Invaders Bay, Audrey Jeffers Highway, T6275555. 116 rooms and 3 suites, some with auxiliary aids for wheelchair users. Sandwiched between office building and busy highway, overlooks Jean Pierre Stadium. Close to **Movie Towne** complex. Designed for business travellers, desks in rooms, complimentary internet access, 2-line data port, TV, parking, pool, fitness centre. **Courtyard Café** for hot breakfast buffet and dinner, no lunch, no bar.
A **Alicia's Guest House**, 7 Coblentz Gardens, St Ann's, T6232802, www.aliciashouse trinidad.com. 27 rooms, some cheap, all a/c, fan, TV, phone, fridge, family rooms, suites, small pool, jacuzzi, meals available, excursions organized.
B-C **Allamanda**, 61 Carlos St, Woodbrook, T6227719. 9 rooms, friendly, Spanish and Portuguese spoken.
B-C **La Calypso Guest House**, 46 French St, Woodbrook, T6224077, F6286895. Cheaper rooms share bathroom. Kitchen, car hire available, pool at their other guesthouse.
C **ML's Gingerbread House**, 25 Stone St, Woodbrook, T6253663, mark@wow.net. 3 double rooms with bathrooms, breakfast included, other meals on request, varied cuisine, excursions arranged.

West to Chaguaramas *p890, map p886*
L **Crew's Inn**, Chaguaramas, T6344384, www.crewsinn.com. 46 rooms, clean and well-run, pool, gym, shops, bank, beauty salon and **Lighthouse** restaurant 0730-2300 daily on same marina site.
A-B **The Cove**, T6344319. Rather run-down, with or without a/c, maid and laundry, kitchenette, 1 3-bedroom apartment. Pool and restaurant under renovation in 2007.
B **The Bight**, Lot 5, Western Main Rd, T6344839, F6344387. 10 rooms, sports bar, marina, meals daily 0700-2300.

North coast *p891, map p886*
AL-A **Laguna Mar Nature Lodge**, Blanchisseuse, at milepost 65½ just before suspension bridge over Marianne River, T6692963, www.lagunamar.com. Owned by Fred Zollna, close to beach and lagoon, 10 rooms with 2 double beds, bathroom, jogging trail, **Cocos Hut** restaurant attached.
AL-A **Maracas Bay Hotel**, Maracas, west of beach, T6691914, www.maracasbay.com. Meals included, 28 a/c rooms with shower, each with porch overlooking bay, under renovation 2007.
A **Monique's Guest House**, 114-116 Saddle Rd, Maraval, T6283334, www.moniques trinidad.com, on way to golf course and north coast beaches. Easy access from city, 10 rooms in main house, 10 more over the hill, large rooms, different sizes sleeping 4/5, a/c, TV, phone, some kitchenettes, **Pink Anthurium** restaurant serves good local food, clean, attractive, facilities for the disabled, Monica and Michael Charbonné are helpful and hospitable.
B **Second Spring**, 13 Damier Village, at milepost 67¾, T6693909, F6234328. Cottage or 3 studios, breakfast US$8, rustic, comfortable, in gardens on clifftop with wooden walkway, spectacular views of coast, beaches within walking distance, restaurant 5 mins' walk, owned by Ginette Holder who is friendly and hospitable, excellent value.
B **Surf's Country Inn**, Lower Village, Blanchisseuse, T6692475. Good restaurant on hill above coast road, 3 rooms, with or without breakfast, nice furnishings, picturesque, small beach below.
C **Carnetta's House**, 28 Scotland Terr, Andalusia, Maraval, just off Saddle Rd, T6282732, www.carnettas.com. Children under 12 free, a/c, all 8 rooms different sizes, fridge, some kitchenettes, TV, phone, ironing board, carpets, family room, laundry, nice gardens, grow some produce, meals on request, parking, family atmosphere, videos for TV, lots of repeat business, maxi-taxi will drop you at gate for extra US$0.50, run by Carnetta and Winston Borrell.
C **Carnetta's Inn**, 99 Saddle Rd, Maraval, T6225165/2884. 6 rooms with mini-fridge, most with kitchenette, single, double, triple and connecting rooms, TV, a/c, phone, internet access, **Bamboo Terrace** restaurant serves local cooking, **Shipwreck Bar** for special cocktails. Run by Carnetta and Winston Borrell. An Italian-run restaurant, **Garibaldi**, is in the same building

A Airport Suites Ltd, 7 Factory Rd, Golden Grove, Piarco, T6690362, rrttra@tstt.net.tt. 7 rooms with a/c, TV, transport to/from airport included, breakfast US$8, lunch US$12, dinner US$14.

A Sadila House, run by Savitri and Dinesh Bhola, Waterpipe Rd, Five Rivers, Arouca, T6403659, F6401376, close to airport. Rooms sleep 1-4 people, credit cards accepted, weekly and group rates available, a/c, TV.

A Valsayn Villa, 34 Gilwell Rd, Valsayn North, T/F6451193. Very large, modern, private house with beautifully furnished rooms, lovely garden and pool, breakfast included, or fully furnished villas (**B** and up), in one of the safest residential areas, close to university, 15 mins from airport, 20 mins by bus from downtown Port of Spain, excellent home-cooked Indian meals available.

B Airport View Guesthouse, St Helena Junction, close to Piarco Airport, T6694186. Convenient, a/c, hot water, fridge, double rooms sleep 4, restaurant nearby serving American-style food.

B Pax Guesthouse, Mt St Benedict, Tunapuna, T/F6624084, www.paxguest house.com. Built 1932, original furniture made by monks, 18 rooms, popular with birdwatchers, 147 species of bird on estate, donkey trails into forest, rooms have high ceilings, no a/c necessary, 1 family room, most share showers, simple but wholesome food, lovely view of central Trinidad as well as of occasional monk.

C Chateau Guillaume, 3 Rawle Circular, Arima, T6676670, joanwilliam@yahoo.com. Run by Matthew and Joan William, 2 double and 2 triple rooms, bathroom, very clean, lower price for long stay, airport transfers, very helpful.

North of Arima *p893, map p886*

LL Asa Wright Nature Centre, 7½-mile mark, Blanchisseuse Rd, Arima, T6674655, www.asawright.org. Price includes all meals including afternoon tea, rum punch, tax and service, 2 main-house rooms in colonial style, high ceilings, wooden furniture and floors, fan, bathroom, 24 standard rooms and bungalow in gardens, all designed to be private and secluded, facilities for the disabled, verandas for birdwatching, 80% of guests in high season are birdwatching groups.

A Aripo Cottage, Hollier Trace, Aripo Estate, Heights of Aripo, 9 miles north of Arima, T/F6456736, www.aripocottage.com. Cottage in converted cocoa house, or cabana with 3 units, each sleep 3-5 people, mostly in bunk beds, full kitchens, restaurant, pool, birdwatching, pretty view of mountains, nature trails, river bathing.

B Alta Vista, up the road from **Asa Wright**, no phone on premises but T6298030 or T7715301 for reservations. 6 wooden cabins with bathroom and fan, meals can be provided for long stay guests, otherwise bring your own cooking things, attractive pool for swimming, veranda overlooking forest, nice waterfall along a trail.

Northeast coast *p893, map p886*

Beach houses in the Toco-Manzanilla area are advertised in the local newspapers. Standards vary, so check first or be prepared for basic standards. Often need to bring own linen, but kitchen utensils usually provided. Places get very booked up during school and public holidays.

L Salybia Nature Resort and Spa, Salybia, T6685959, info@salybiaresort.com. Good view up and down coast, pool, gym, bland restaurant, popular with tour groups, less intimate than other northeast coast places.

AL Acajou, Grande Riviere, T6703771, www.acajoutrinidad.com. Luxurious wooden cabanas designed and built by French architect, each with deck overlooking river mouth. The nicest place to stay in Trinidad, with delicious food and proper coffee served at a very laid-back pace.

AL-A Mount Plaisir Estate Hotel & Spa, Hosang St, Grand Riviere, T6702216, www.mtplaisir.com. 10 beachfront rooms right by the place where the leatherback turtles nest, nature trails, birdwatching, with excursions organized, overnight camping tours with local guide, breakfast included, restaurant 0800-2100.

A Le Grande Almandier, 2 Hosang St, Grand Riviere, T6701013, www.legrande almandier.com. Also on the beach, good standard of accommodation, a/c, breakfast included, very good restaurant daily 0700-2200, cater to individual tastes including vegetarian, ask for the corn soup, meal plans available, a few suites sleep 4-5, knowledgeable and accessible proprietor.

A-B McEachnie's Haven, T6701014, www.mchaventt.com. 6 basic but clean rooms, a/c, friendly staff, meals available, use of hotel kitchen. Higher rates for credit cards. On hill opposite the practising hut of local band, Roots and Branches, who often perform in the popular bar.

D-E Sea Sand Camp, Toco, turn right off the Toco Main Rd after the police station, T6708356. Run by local character Patsy Bravo, surfer's hangout, very basic bunk bed accommodation, good value, hearty meals provided.

San Fernando p895
LL Cara Suites Pointe-à-Pierre, Southern Main Rd, Claxton Bay, T6592230, www.carahotels.com. 52 comfortable rooms and suites in former **Farrell House Hotel**, pool, business centre with complimentary internet access, bar, view over muddy Gulf of Paria, this West Indian hotel chain is highly regarded. **Metropolitan** restaurant, T6595885. 0600-0930, 1130-1400, 1800-2200, good creative menu.

AL Tradewinds, 36-38 London St, St Joseph Village, San Fernando, T6529463, delia@tradewindshotel.net. 50 rooms, some with kitchenette, bar, restaurant daily 0500-0100, gym, pool, Jacuzzi, games room. Complimentary shuttle to airport at 0500.

A Royal Hotel, 46-54 Royal Rd, T6523924, www.royalhoteltt.com. A/c, kitchenette, lovely hilltop garden.

A-B Marion's Hotel and Restaurant, 15 Railway Av, Plaisance Village, Pointe-à-Pierre, T/F6592584. 13 rooms, a/c, private bath, meal plans, restaurant daily 0700-1700 but you can make reservations for dinner, TV, pool, pleasant, convenient for oil refinery and Wild Fowl Trust.

South coast p854
B Harry's, Grand Lagoon, south end of Mayaro, T6696310. Right on beach (plastic litter), nice grounds, rather peculiar building, apartments range in size from tiny room with double bunk bed, kitchenette, bathroom, a/c, TV, to larger units, some with verandas, watch out for US$8 service charge.

B Mrs Paria's, guesthouse, just beyond the BP/Amoco compound, T6308030. Self-contained room, TV, breakfast, beautiful modern home.

Eating

Opening hours are liable to change at short notice. Many places close on Sun, and some public holidays. They may close or reduce their hours over Carnival when most customers are too preoccupied to eat properly and staff are otherwise engaged. Most of the smarter restaurants do lunch for around US$20 but are much more expensive in the evening. A free magazine, *Cré Olé* prints menu extracts and prices for better-known places, useful for pre-dinner browsing. Good hotel restaurants are mentioned under Sleeping, above.

Port of Spain p885, map p889
Laughing Buddha, 86 Frederick St, T6270100. 1100-2300, Sat, Sun, all-you-can-eat buffet 1100-1500, US$30. Mostly Japanese. Small tatami room, sushi, some other Japanese dishes, combination platters, good presentation, much better than other Japanese restaurants. Convenient parking in spite of city center location. No windows, no view, but authentic Japanese feel.

Tasca Latina, 16 Phillip St, T6253497. Mon-Sat 1700-2300. Good Venezuelan-style food, Latin music sometimes and Sat Latin dance class.

Excellent City Mall upstairs, **Town Centre Mall** and **Voyager Mall** on Frederick St have indoor halls with a varied and good selection of stands selling cheap food of different nationalities during the day, seating in the middle. Some booths stay open until 1800 but supplies become limited after 1330. **The Bocas**, Chacon St is good for fish dishes, lunch-times. At night it becomes a bar, good on Fri.

Port of Spain suburbs p888, map p889
Plenty of choice west of city centre: **Ariapita Av** for full price range, from street snack to smart night out. **Maraval Rd** for cheap and cheerful. All along **Western Main Rd** in St James there are lots of cafés, snack bars and restaurants, all reasonably priced around US$5-10, lots of choice.

A La Bastille, Ariapita Av and Verteuil St, T6221789. Tue-Sat 0730-1100, Mon-Sat 1100-1500, 1800-2230. French-run brasserie, good breakfast with freshly-made croissants, creative menu, good wine, excellent fixed-price lunch.

Trinidad & Tobago Trinidad Listings

Solimar, 6 Nook Av, close to the *Normandie*, T6246267. Mon-Sat 1800-2230, Fri 1130-1430. International, very good service, outdoor dining, excellent food, reservations advisable and essential at weekends although not always honoured. Tapas from 1700, a good set lunch on Fri.

Verandah, 10 Rust St, St Clair, T6226287. Mon-Fri lunch 1130-1345, Thu-Sat dinner, 1900-2145. Caribbean ingredients but not just the standard dishes. Old house in a pretty location – with a veranda.

Apsara, 13 Queens Park East, T6237659. Mon-Sat 1130-1500, 1800-2300. Very good food, pleasant surroundings, North Indian and tandoori rather than Indo-Trini.

Il Colosseo, 16 Rust St, St Clair, T6281494. Mon Fri 1130-1430, Mon-Sat 1830-2230. Luxurious surroundings, food has mixed reviews, from ecstatic to diabolical.

Plantation House, Ariapita Av and Cornelio St, T6285551. Daily 1130-1430, 1830-2230. US-style Cajun food, nicely served and presented. Old suburban house, good fish dishes, pork and gumbo.

Tamnak Thai, 13 Queens Park East, T6250647. Mon-Sat 1800-2300, Mon-Fri, 1100-1500. Excellent Thai restaurant, beautiful setting with pretty outdoor area overlooking the Savannah. **Apsara** is upstairs.

Jenny's on the Boulevard, 6 Cipriani Blvd, T6251807. Restaurant Mon-Thu 1100-2200, Fri-Sat 1100-2300. Bar Mon-Thu until 2400, Fri-Sat until 0100. Wide variety of mainly Chinese dishes in elaborate setting, lively pub-style bar downstairs with light meals and snacks, also Chinese. Fri lime starts after work around 1700.

Kam Wah, 74 Maraval Rd, T6288888. Mon-Wed 1100-2200, Thu-Sat 1100-2230. Good Chinese, takeaway or eat in, smarter than most of its rivals, but the menu includes the standard list.

Olive's Mediterranean Bistro, 22 Sweetbriar Rd, St Clair, T6229688. Mon-Fri 1100-1430. Good food, mix of Mediterranean and Caribbean ideas. Breezy setting in pretty old house near the cricket oval.

Veni Mangé, 67A Ariapita Av, T6244597. Mon-Fri 1130-1500, dinner Wed, Fri only 1900-2200. Small, friendly, good food, imaginative menu includes vegetarian dishes.

Woodford Café, 62 Tragarete Rd, Newtown, T6222233. Mon-Tue 1100-1700, Wed-Sat 1100-2200. Newly refurbished, popular meeting point for lunch or after work lime on Fri. Good choice of local Creole food: callaloo, breadfruit oildown, etc.

Creole Kitchen, 22 Boissiere Village, Maraval, opposite Ellerslie Plaza, next to fuel station, T6220804. Daily 0800-1800. Excellent home-cooked Creole food, vafeteria-style, generous portions.

Hot Shoppe, in Maraval Rd and Mucurapo Rd, T6224073. Mon-Sat 1000-2130. Rotis, which are of a slightly heavier texture than some.

Irie Bites, 71A Ariapita Av, Woodbrook and 15A Mucurapo Rd, St James, T6227364. Mon-Thu 1100-2100, Fri, Sat 1100-2200. Specializes in Jamaican jerk meats, huge portions, relaxed atmosphere.

Paradis de la Crème, in the Movie Towne complex, Audrey Jeffers Highway, T6249984. Daily 0900-2300. Wonderful European pastries and desserts prepared by Spanish pastry chef. Also excellent soup at lunchtime.

Patraj, 159 Tragarete Rd, T6226219. Mon-Sat 1000-1630. The best place for roti. If you are watching cricket at the Oval this is a good place to buy food.

The Swan Chinese Restaurant, Maraval Rd, T6222611. Mon-Sat 1100-1430, 1700-2130, last orders at 2100. Very good food but unprepossessing interior.

West to Chaguaramas *p890, map p886*

Popular with yachties, live entertainment some nights.

Lighthouse at Crew's Inn, T6344384. Daily 0700-2200. Breezy, open on all sides, good view of yachts. You can see into the kitchen, always a good sign, fine selection of complicated cocktails, some interesting dishes on the menu, eclectic mix of Mediterranean, Caribbean and Indian.

The Bight, Peake's, T6344839. 0700-2300. Bar and restaurant overlooking the Chaguaramas anchorage. Small restaurant with outdoor terrace upstairs overlooking the boats. Unpretentious menu.

North coast *p891, map p886*

Joseph's, Rookery Nook, Maraval, T6225557. Mon-Fri 1130-1430, Mon-Sat 1830-2230. Arab and other dishes, excellent service, popular, run by a Lebanese, Joe.

Cocos Hut, also on coast road at Mile 65½ by Marianne River. Small, friendly, no menu, but usually a choice of fish or meat dishes, slow service but all food freshly cooked. Don't forget the shark-and-bake at Maracas, see Eating, page 884.

Lawrence of Arabia, in Shoppes of Maraval, T6282722. Mon-Sat 1100-2200. Good Arabic food at around US$5.

Surf's Country Inn, North Coast Rd, Blanchisseuse, T6692475. Daily 1000-1830. Good value, delicious meals, beautiful setting, changing rooms available.

East of Port of Spain *p892, map p886*

Botticelli's, City of Grand Bazaar, Valsayn, T6458733. Mon-Fri 1100-2300, Sat 1600-2300. Italian, pricey but good. Shopping plaza location, so no parking problems, but restaurant has a very indoors feel.

Rasam, also at the City of Grand Bazaar, Valsayn, T6450994. Mon-Sat 1100-1500, 1800-1100. South Indian, imported chefs.

Bootleggers, Trincity Mall, T6408448. 1100-2400. Unexciting menu ribs, steaks, etc but useful if you need somewhere in the east.

Valpark Chinese Restaurant, Valpark Shopping Plaza, Churchill Roosevelt Highway, Curepe, T6624540. 1000-2300. Fairly standard Chinese menu, but well cooked and well served, unspectacular but pleasant setting, unobtrusive live music some nights.

Chinese Wok, Trincity Mall, T6403512. Mon-Thu 1100-2100, Fri, Sat 1100-2200. Good and also has branches in Tunapuna, T6625296, Chaguanas, T6656637, and Arima, T6672250.

Pax Guesthouse on Mt St Benedict, above Tunapuna, T6624084. Book 24 hrs ahead, enquire about opening times when booking. Very different and slow-paced. Tea is a tradition and all the bread, cakes, jam, honey, etc are hand-made by the monks, wholesome and tasty, lovely views of Trinidad from patio. Lunches US$11 and dinners US$13, excellent value.

South of Port of Spain *p894, map p886*

Bougainvillea, 85 Rivulet Rd, Brechin Castle, Couva, T6364837. Mon-Sat 1100-2200. Chef claims to specialize in 'American, Italian, Spanish, Creole, Chinese and seafood delights'.

Buffet King, Centre Pointe Mall, Chaguanas, T6718795. Mon-Thu 1100-1500, 1830-2130, Fri-Sat 1100-1600, 1830-2230. Mix of Chinese and non-Chinese dishes, with salad bar and dessert bar.

Kam-Po, 53 Ramsaran Park, Chaguanas, opposite Centre Pointe Mall, T6654558. Mon-Thu 1030-2200, Fri and Sat 1100-2300. A good Chinese restaurant. Also has high-quality imported US steaks and seafood.

San Fernando *p895*

Soongs Great Wall, 97 Circular Rd, T6522583. Mon-Thu 1100-2200, Fri, Sat 1100-2230. For Chinese food, round the corner from the Royal Hotel. Very good reputation, but not as good as it used to be, the distinctive, Trinidadian version of Chinese food.

Spices, 13 Sutton St, 6577809. Mon-Fri 0600-2100, Sat 1000-2200. Indian, recommended.

🍸 Bars and clubs

Trinidad has plenty of evening entertainment. For those wishing to visit the places where the local, rather than tourist population goes, anyone in the street will give directions. The atmosphere will be natural and hospitality generous; it will not be luxurious but the local rum is likely to flow freely. Places run late, starting to get lively around 2300-midnight and closing 0400-ish (any opening hours listed are likely to vary at a moment's notice). Fri has a bigger crowd than Sat but no night is completely quiet. In central Port of Spain, clubs and bars tend to be fun but more rough and ready. Several lively bars on and close to Brian Lara Promenade, though some are very dirty. Some of the smarter places are in Chaguaramas. All-inclusives are 'free drinks' once you have paid the cover charge, or else free drinks up to a certain time. Less expensive are the 'cooler fetes', where you take a cooler with ice and your own drinks. Car parking can be a problem, and there are often traffic jams in and out on the road through Carenage; around Carnival, these can last for hours. Other hazards include drivers who have been over-enthusiastic with the free drinks. Closer to Port of Spain, St James is famously the 'city that never sleeps'. Further east, in **Tunapuna**, there are several small and lively bars. All along **Eastern Main Rd** there are bars and restaurants with a busy crowd, especially on Fri, take your pick.

The centre of **Arima** is full of life in the evenings, especially Fri after work. Lots of little bars, cheap Chinese restaurants, some of which open late. To the south of Port of Spain, the bars in **Chaguanas** are rougher than some but still lively, particularly at weekends to around 0300-0400. South of Chaguanas at **Edinburgh** and **Chase Village** are some fairly raunchy strip clubs which are frequently raided by the police. Risky and best avoided. **San Fernando** has several clubs worth trying, while **Coffee St** is lively, with plenty of bars.

Port of Spain *p885, map p889*
Club Zen, Keate St, close to Queen's Park Savannah, T6259936. Wed, Thu, Fri, Sat 2100-0400. Admission from US$8, more for special events, women free some nights. In converted Art Deco cinema, very glitzy, good security, massively floodlit streets around, wonderful views and breeze on roof terrace, but you pay extra for that and VIP area. Easy to run foul of complicated dress codes, rastas with baggy styles not encouraged. Massive queues.
D'Bocas, Chacon St, T6273474, www.dbocas.com. Open Mon-Thu 0930-2200, Fri 0930-0300. Creole food 0930-1700, DJs play music after 1700. Fri night lime, very popular after work. No cover charge. Much the liveliest place in Port of Spain, down to earth, mature crowd.
Higher Level, above Church's Chicken, corner of Independence Sq. No phone. Pulls a crowd. Music in the evenings, popular for after-work limes, quite small so gets very busy on Fri with a young crowd.

Port of Spain suburbs *p888, map p889*
51 Degrees, Maraval Rd, T6270051. Tue-Thu from 1700, Fri from 1600, Sat from 2100, closing 'late', admission some nights US$8. Live music Wed and weekends, karaoke Thu and comedy Tue, dress code.
Mas Camp Pub, Ariapita Av, Woodbrook. No phone. Nightly entertainment including calypso and steel band, best place to see live calypso out of season (cover charge usually US$5); however has managerial

ups and downs.
More Vino, 23 O'Connor St, Wodbrook, T6228466. Very popular wine bar, also sells spirits, fine selection of cheeses and hors d'oeuvres, hookah pipes, indoor and al fresco tables, after work lime most nights, occasional live DJs and functions, security guards walk you to your car. Accordingly expensive.
Smokey and Bunty, corner of Western Main Road and Dengue St, St James, no phone. A lively rum shop, usually open until dawn or after at weekends. Most expats and tourists go at least once. However, it can be irritatingly beset by crack addicts, prostitutes, etc.
Trotter's, Maraval Rd, T6278768. Sun-Thu 1130-2400, Fri and Sat1130-0200. Meals and drinks both hideously overpriced, but has interesting tabletops decorated with newsclippings of past corruption scandals. Reference to trotters is globe, not pigs'.

West to Chaguaramas *p890, map p886*
MOBS Two, Chaguaramas. No phone. Good for special events, lively most weekends, sometimes big fetes, live music, etc.
Pier One, Williams Bay, Chaguaramas, T6344472. Thu-Sat 1200-0400. Smart, hosts many carnival fetes, lively at weekends.

East of Port of Spain *p892, map p886*
Beer Garden, Grand Bazaar, T6621631. Mon-Thu 1200-2400, Fri and Sat 'a little later', Sun 1500-2400 Sun. Open-air and indoor sections, very busy.
Island Village, on Hollis St, Arima. Fri night until 0400. Lively bar, unpretentious, open-air with booths.
La Luna, Arouca Junction on Eastern Main Rd. Open 24 hrs. Lively, music, nearby places have snacks and fast food. Might be a possibility if stuck between flights as fairly near to the airport (leave your luggage somewhere safe, eg airport check-in).
Lair, Barataria. Open to around 0400 weekends. Younger crowd, not posh.
Parrot, Grand Bazaar, Uriah Butler Highway, Valsayn, T6625631. Mon-Thu 1000-2400, Fri and Sat 1000-0400, Sun 1600-2400. Meals around US$9.60, older and richer crowd and extremely crowded.
Trevor's Edge, 1 St John Rd, St Augustine, T6453131. 1000 till late. Lively bar close to the university. Lunches served Mon-Sat,

snacks available in the evening. Frequent entertainment includes vintage calypso and parang. Hosts Songshine, monthly open mic concert series, extremely popular, call T7604655 for details.

San Fernando *p895*
Club Celebs, Gulf City Mall, La Romaine, T6527641. Open until 0400 weekends. One of the presentable places in San Fernando, lively, young crowd.
HiRPM, same mall, T6523760. Open until 0400 weekends. More informal than **Club Celebs**, lively, youngish crowd, smoky, indoors, good mix of music.

● Entertainment

Trinidad *p885, maps p886 and p*
Casinos
There are several casinos, some of which run through the night. They are small and seedy by Bahamian or Aruban standards, but you can lose money just as effectively: slot machines, blackjack, roulette, etc, with 'free' sandwiches to keep you at it and 'free' drinks if you lose heavily. Best known are **Club De Vegas** on Frederick St, Port of Spain, cover charge, secure parking, **Ma Pau**, in Ariapita Av and **Island Club**, at Grand Bazaar shopping mall, all open pretty much round the clock. Alternatively you can lose money in smaller amounts in most bars and neigh-bourhood shops through government-run gambling: *Play Whe*, which is based on traditional Chinese gambling, and the weekly *Lotto* draw.

Theatres
See press for details of performances.
Queen's Hall, 1-3 St Ann's Rd, Port of Spain, T6241284. **Little Carib**, White and Roberts streets, Port of Spain, T6224644. **The Strand**, Park St, Port of Spain, T6235108. A former cinema converted to a theatre, also serves as a calypso tent during carnival.
Central Bank Auditorium, Eric Williams Plaza, Edward St, Port of Spain, T6230845.
Naparima Bowl, San Fernando, T6578770, has reopened after a lengthy period of renovation.

For information on the folk theatre of the **South National Institute of Performing Arts**, T6535355. See Culture, p929.

Cinemas
See listing in daily papers.
Movie Towne, on highway west of Port of Spain, T6278277 (US$5.60, or US$4 Tue). US-style multi-screens. The main venue for the Embassy-sponsored **European film festival** in Oct-Nov. Good place for Florida-style night out, with **Ruby Tuesday's**, T6246566, US-style restaurant upstairs, a few bars (**Shakers**, open to 0100) and eateries outside, and (rather expensive) fast food on sale in palatial lobby.
Caribbean Cinemas at Trincity Mall, near highway to Piarco, T6408788 (US$2.90). The other multiscreen.
Kay Donna, Valsayn, also on highway to the east. Drive-in.
Studio Film Club, at CCA7, studiofilm@ wow.net, screens a classic, foreign-language or independent film most Thu around 1930. Not easy to find, just west from Morvant junction, through the big gates and look for the parked cars, then up outside metal staircase 2 flights. No charge, beer, etc available for a donation.

There are 10 other cinemas, all very cheap, advertised in daily papers, occasionally showing something good, including **Globe**, on St Vincent St, Port of Spain.

○ Shopping

Trinidad *p885, map p886*
Bargains can be found in fabrics, carvings, leather and ceramics. Most shops take US dollars but at a poor exchange rate. The main **Port of Spain** shopping areas are **Frederick St**, **Queen St**, **Henry St** and **Charlotte St** (fruit and vegetables), less exciting but more pleasant are **Long Circular Mall** at the junction of Long Circular Rd and Patna St, St James; **West Mall**, **Cocorite**, Port of Spain; **City of Grand Bazaar** at **Valsayn**, east of Port of Spain. A local clothing company, **Radical**, do reasonably-priced linen shirts and trousers. There are also good but pricier local designers such as Meiling or Richard Young of **The Cloth**. Try shops in **Kapok** and **Normandie** hotels. Purchases can be made at in-bond shops in Port of Spain and at the airport. There is a huge selection of duty-free shops.

Handicrafts can be purchased at some markets. In Port of Spain there are street vendors on **Frederick St**, **Independence Sq** and elsewhere selling hand-painted T-shirts, etc. Crafts can be found at **East Mall** on Charlotte St and at the cruise ship complex. There are several kilns in the **Freeport** area, turn off the Uriah Butler Highway before the Hindu temple for Chase Village. Good-quality local pottery in a variety of designs is available from **Ajoupa Pottery**, owned by Rory and Bunty O'Connor. You can get it in Port of Spain but a wider selection can be viewed at their kiln at Freeport, central Trinidad; T6225597 at **Rainy Days**, at Ellerslie Plaza, Maraval, or T6730604 at kiln/factory. Batik can be bought at many places in most malls and at Rainy Days.

Bookshops

Metropolitan Books, 11-13 Frederick St and in Valsayn, has a good selection. **R I K Services Ltd**, 87 Queen St, Port of Spain, and 104 High St, San Fernando, stocks mostly school books. **Ishmael M Khan and Sons**, 20 Henry St, Port of Spain is another good bookshop. **Nigel R Khan**, booksellers are at Price Plaza Shopping Mall, Endeavour Rd, Chaguanas, T6728138, Ellerslie Plaza, Corner Rapsey St and Maraval Rd, Port of Spain, T6283618, The Falls at West Mall, Westmoorings, T6320350, and Gulf City, Gulf City View Link Rd, San Fernando, T6521800. Black literature at **Afrikan World Books** and **Kultural Items**, Park Plaza on Park St and St Vincent St, T/F6272128, good selection, history, contemporary issues. **Paper Based** is a small shop with a good selection in the **Normandie** hotel. **A Different View** on Warren and Gallus St, Woodbrook, T6223648, has a good selection of Caribbean and Trinidad material, novels, New Age, good secondhand section. **Lexicon**, Boundary Rd, San Juan, T6753395, are wholesalers, but have very good selection and also do retail. There are secondhand bookshops in Town Centre Mall and various side streets.

Food and drink

Watch expiry dates carefully when buying food. Expired food frequently remains on display. Scanner systems are inefficient, so shelf price is often different from price charged at checkout. Locally grown fruit and veg is often heavily sprayed, so wash well or peel. Markets offer a wide variety of fruit and veg. **San Juan** opens from about 0400, lively, good selection, also bars and eateries which make a last stop when everywhere else has closed as Fri night turns into Sat morning. The **Central Market** on the Beetham Highway is big, cheap fruit and veg, opens very early. Fresh fish by **Western Main Rd** in Carenage or on the highway near Valsayn. **T-Wee**, 24 Panka St, St James, Port of Spain, T6220877, is recommended shop for booze and has the best aged rums, eg Guyanese *El Dorado*. **More Vino**, 23 O'Connor St, and **Vintage Imports**, 42 Hunter St, both in Woodbrook, for wine.

Music

Crosby's Music Centre, 54 Western Main Rd, St James, or **Kam's**, Long Circular Mall, St James. Production costs are a problem so prices of local CDs are high, and despite being the main music outlets in this island of music they frequently have no stock. Bootlegged copies are, however, sold widely in downtown Port of Spain.

▲ Activities and tours

Trinidad *p885, map p886*
Cricket

Cricket is very popular. Test matches are played at **Queen's Park Oval**, T6222295, the oldest ground in the Caribbean, west of Queen's Park Savannah, Port of Spain, renovated for the 2007 Cricket World Cup; take a cushion, sunhat/umbrella, whistle (!) and drinks if sitting in the cheap seats. It is a private club but a friendly gate guard might let you in for a look around when matches are not being played. There are smaller grounds for club cricket throughout both islands.

Fishing

Charters can be arranged, for deep-sea fish or bonefish and tarpon in the mangroves and flats. Prices for deep-sea fishing are around US$350 for 4 hrs, US$600 for 8 hrs, maximum 6 people and for tarpon fishing US$350. The annual **Wahoo Tournament** is held in Mar, **The International Game Fishing Classic** in Apr, the **Kingfish Tournament** in Jun and a **Funfish Tournament** in Nov.

Contact the **Trinidad and Tobago Game Fishing Association**, T6245304, www.ttgfa.com for information.

Football

Hockey and soccer are played at the **Oval** (**Football Association**, T6245183) or at the **Jean Pierre stadium**, and rugby, basketball, cycling and marathon running are also popular. Many players from Trinidad and Tobago play for top football clubs in Europe and the USA. Dwight Yorke is one of the best known of Trinidadian footballers, playing for many years for Manchester United, where he became one of the top 10 highest goal scorers in the Premier League, before moving to Australia in 2005. He captained the Trinidad and Tobago team in the 2006 World Cup, the smallest country ever to qualify. Football fever has since gripped the nation and members of the 'Soca Warriors' team are national superstars.

Golf

St Andrews (Moka) Golf Club, T6294653. There are 5 other golf clubs on Trinidad, including a 9-hole public course at **Chaguaramas**, T6344349.

Horse racing

There is horse-racing at **Santa Rosa Park**, Arima, about 15 km outside Port of Spain.

Sailing

Every Jul/Aug, there is a power boat race from the **Trinidad and Tobago Yacht Club** (**TTYC**), Trinidad to Store Bay, Tobago. The **Trinidad and Tobago Sailing Association** (**TTSA**), T6344210, sponsors **Carnival Fun Race** and a weekly racing programme in winter and spring.

Squash

The **Cascadia Hotel**, Ariapita Rd, St Ann's T6233511, has 2 courts with seating for 100 spectators per court, tennis courts, sauna and gym with lots of equipment and facilities, open for non-members but difficult to get a booking, Mon-Fri 0600-2100, Sat 0900-1700.

Swimming

Hilton Hotel, US$5 (US$2.50 children), or monthly season ticket US$28; **Cascadia Hotel**, chutes and waterslides, very busy at weekends and holidays; **La Joya**, at St Joseph, check first for availability, T6626929.

Tennis

Trinidad Country Club Maraval, T6223470, temporary membership, advance booking necessary, also at **Hilton Hotel**, **Tranquility Square Lawn Tennis Club**, T6254182, and public tennis courts at **Princes Building Grounds**, Upper Frederick St, T6231121.

Tour operators

Trinidad and Tobago Tour Guide Association, president Greer Contant, T6201605.
Trinidad and Tobago Sightseeing Tours, run by Gunda Busch-Harewood, 12 Western Rd, St James, T6281051, F6229205. Speaks German, will arrange accommodation and car hire and has a representative on Tobago (Margaret Hinkson, T6397422, F6229205). Gunda offers evening tours, sightseeing tours, deep-sea fishing, panyard visits, tickets for carnival fetes, etc.
The Travel Centre Limited, Level 2, Uptown Mall, Edward St, Port of Spain, T6235096, F6235101, is an American Express Travel Service Representative.
Caribbean Discovery Tours Ltd, 9B Fondes Amandes Rd, St Ann's, T6247281, run by Stephen Broadbridge together with Merryl See Tai of the **Kayak Centre**, T6292680 (see p908). Walking tours, cave exploration, horse riding in the Northern Range, kayaking expeditions and other trips off the beaten track. Camping (in basic-luxury tents or cabins) or lodging in guesthouses arranged for longer trips, tailor-made tours.
Banwari Experience Ltd, River Rd, Bourg Mulatresse, Lower Santa Cruz, T6215893, banwari@tstt.net.tt, run by Andrew Welch, offers cultural and nature tours, hiking, birdwatching, Carnival.
Wilderness Explorers, based in Guyana, www.wilderness-explorers.com, specialize in nature and adventure travel.
Avifauna Tours, Ahie Villa, Sierra Leone Rd, Diego Martin, T6335614, www.rogerneckles.com. With wildlife photographer Roger Neckles.

Watersports

Contact Alan Davis at the **Surfing** Association of Trinidad and Tobago, T6230920, and the

Windsurfing Association of Trinidad and Tobago, T6288908. **Kayaking** (including tuition) is available at the **Chaguaramas Kayak Centre**, T6337871, run by Merryl See Tai, 500 m after the Alcoa dock, just before Pier One. You can kayak in the bay or go on excursions along the coast, up rivers (eg at Blanchisseuse on Sun) or to the Bush Bush Sanctuary in the Nariva Swamp.

● Transport

Trinidad *p885, map p886*
Air
Charter flights can be difficult to book without an accommodation package.

From North America Air Canada and Caribbean Airlines from Toronto; **American Airlines** from Miami, New York and San Juan; **Caribbean Airlines** from Miami and New York, all to Port of Spain.

From Europe Caribbean Airlines direct from London to Port of Spain; or go with **American** via Miami, or else **British Airways**, **Excel** or **Virgin Atlantic** from London Gatwick to Tobago and get a connection from there to Port of Spain. Several charters from London Gatwick to Tobago. **Martinair** from Amsterdam to Tobago, weekly.

From South and Central America To Port of Spain, **Aeropostal** from Caracas, **Conviasa** (T6274118) and **Avior** (T6238201) from Margarita, with connections to Barcelona and Bogotá; **Caribbean Airlines** and **LIAT/Caribbean Star** from Georgetown, Guyana; **Surinam Airways** and **Caribbean Airlines** from Paramaribo.

From the Caribbean Caribbean Airways, LIAT/Caribbean Star connect Trinidad and Tobago with other Caribbean islands including Antigua, Barbados, Curaçao, Grenada, Jamaica (Kingston), St Lucia, St Maarten, St Vincent, San Juan, Puerto Rico.

Boat
See Getting around, page 880, for the ferry between Trinidad and Tobago. Drug dealers and pirates operate in these waters so behave with extreme caution. Small boats are likely to be intercepted by Venezuelan or Trinidad coastguards, or both.
Pier One, Chaguaramas, T6344472 (Acosta Asociados, Güiria, T294-9821556), runs a ferry to Venezuela on Wed, check in 0700 for

0900, buy ticket in advance with passport, 3½ hrs, leaves Güiria about 1730, US$138 return, departure tax US$12, plus US$23 from Venezuela.

Bus
Express Commuter Service (ECS) every 15-30 mins, 0600-2100 Mon-Sat, every 30 mins 0700-2100 Sun, from City Gate Terminal, Port of Spain, to San Fernando, US$1, or US$0.60 to other destinations: Arima, Chaguanas, Five Rivers. PTSC (T6237872) bus from City Gate to Chaguaramas every 60-90 mins, 0500-2200, US$0.30. Bus to airport from City Gate, 4 times daily, 0630, 0700, 1515, 1700, 45 mins, return 0715, 0745, 1610, 1800.

Car
Car rental firms are numerous and include: **Auto Rentals Ltd**, Lady Young Rd, Morvant, T6757368, Piarco Airport, T6692277, www.autorentalstt.com; **Bacchus Taxi and Car Rental**; 37 Tragarete Rd, T6225588. **Kalloo**, Southern Main Rd, Caroni, also airport, and Woodbrook, T6229073, T/F6695673, helpful, check tyres. **Singh's**, 7-9 Wrightson Rd, T6230150, and at airport, T6695417, singhsautorentals@singhs.com, **Southern Sales and Service Co Ltd**, El Socorro Extension Rd, San Juan, T6752424, 24-hr service. **Autocenter Car Rentals**, 6 Ariapita Av, T6284400, friendly and helpful. **Econo Car Rentals**, 191-193 Western Main Rd, T6228074, and airport, one of the cheapest, but do not take bookings more than a couple of days in advance. International companies, Avis (T6277753), Budget (T6691635) and Hertz (T8003131) are more expensive. If you prefer a smarter car, contact **Executive Limousine Service**, 11 Tragarete Rd, Port of Spain, T6278247.

Cycle
Excellent bike shop, **Geronimo's Cycle and Sport Ltd**, 15 Pole Carew St, Woodbrook, Port of Spain, T6222453, owned and managed by former professional cyclist, Gene Samuel. **Bike Inn**, St James and 3 branches, T6455575, has new bikes from around US$140. See also pages 880 and 886.

Taxi
Maxi-taxi These are colour-coded: yellow

for Diego Martin and west, **red** for east, **green** for San Fernando, **brown** or **black** for maxis which start in San Fernando and travel south from there. The green and red ones set off mostly from the City Gate terminal; the yellow band from further west on South Quay; most Carenage and Chaguaramas maxis start from Green corner on St Vincent and Park streets (Globe cinema); Maraval maxis start from Oxford and Charlotte streets. Check route before starting, eg east taxis are either 'San Juan' or 'all the way up' the Eastern Main Rd to Arima, or 'highway', which is faster and closer to the airport but misses places like Tunapuna and Curepe. Fares start at US$0.30 and run to Arima, US$1; to Chaguanas, US$1; to San Fernando, US$1.75.

Route taxi In Port of Spain most sedan taxis (saloon cars, often rather beat up) set off from close to Independence Sq and use fast food restaurants as markers. They leave to the west from Chacon St on south side of square, for Chaguanas and San Fernando from near **KFC**, close to **Royal Castle** for Arima. Those for St Ann's and St James leave from Woodford Sq or Bell's Quay, for Carenage from Green Corner (St Vincent and Park Sts), and for Maraval, Belmont and Morvant from Duke and Charlotte Sts (also from here infrequently on to Maracas and the north coast). Fares in town US$0.50, further out US$0.75. If in a hurry you can pay for any empty seats and ask the driver to go. They will also go off-route for a little extra but this depends on how many people are in the car.

🅞 Directory

Trinidad *p885, map p886*
A lot of places, eg University of the West Indies, are listed under 'T' for 'The' in the phone book. **Banks** Republic Bank Ltd), 9-17 Park St, Port of Spain, T6254411, F6241323, Mon-Thu 0800-1400, 1200-1400, Fri 0800-1300, 1500-1700. **Royal Bank of Trinidad and Tobago (RBTT)**, 3B Chancery Lane, Port of Spain, T6234291, and Western Main Rd, Chaguaramas, not far from the marinas. **Scotia Bank**, Park and Richmond Sts, Port of Spain, T6253566. **Citibank**, Queens Park East, Port of Spain, T6251040. **Citicorp Merchant Bank**, same address,

T6233344. **Western Union Money Transfer**, Uptown Mall, Edward St, Port of Spain, T6236000, and 45 other locations in Trinidad and Tobago. Bank branches in all major centres. Many suburban or shopping mall branches open 1000-1800. **Republic Bank** branch and ATM at **Crew's Inn Marina**. **Peake's Yacht Yard** has a branch with a 24-hr cash machine and a teller from 0900-1400. **Embassies and** consulates **Australia**, High Commission, 18 Herbert St, St Clair, T6280695. **Canada**, High Commission, 3-3A Sweet Briar Rd, St Clair, T6226232. **France** Embassy, 6th floor, Tatil Bldg, 11 Maraval Rd, T6227446, F6282632. **Germany**, 7-9 Marli St, PO Box 828 (T6281630/2, F6285278). **Jamaica** High Commission, 2 Newbold St, St Clair, T6224995/7, F6289180. **Netherlands**, Life of Barbados Building, 69 Edward St, T6251210/1722, F6251704. **Suriname**, 5th floor, Tatil Bldg, Maraval Rd, T6280704. **UK** High Commission, 19 St Clair Av, St Clair, T6222748, F6224555. **USA**, 15 Queen's Park West, T6226371/6, F6285462, 0730-1600. **Venezuela**, 16 Victoria Av, T6279823/4, 0900-1700, Consulate at same address, T6279773/4, visa section only open mornings. **Internet** About 20 cafés listed in yellow pages, open and close frequently. Many in Newtown, such as **L&C Internet Café**, 26 Maraval Rd, T6226467. At Chaguaramas **Mariner's Office** (Crew's Inn Marina). **Medical services** There are hospitals in Port of Spain and San Fernando, as well as several district hospitals and community health centres. **Port of Spain General Hospital**, 169 Charlotte St, T6232951. **Mount Hope**, T6454673, has better facilities. **St Clair Medical Centre**, T6281451, is private, more comfortable, expensive, but not necessarily better equipped. **West Shore Medical**, 239 Western Main Rd, Cocorite, T6229878, is new, well-equipped and expensive. **Post** TT Post, has a Port of Spain office on west side of Chacon St, north of Independence Sq. Stamps for Europe US$0.72 upwards, USA US$0.60. Letters to/from UK can take several weeks. Express Mail usually faster, alternatively use a courier, **DHL** and **Fedex** do pickups until mid-afternoon. **Telephone** The main Telecommunications Services of Trinidad and Tobago Ltd (TSTT) offices on Chacon St and Independence Sq operate international telephone and fax. Charges for international calls are high. Independent operators offer net-based calls to public, several around Independence Sq but others elsewhere, charging US$0.16 per min. **Companion** phone cards are available for US$1.60, 4.80, 9.60, or 16 plus 15% VAT, from TSTT offices, banks, airport, etc. Can be used from any touch tone phone. **Home Direct Service** for AT&T, Sprint and MCI, also Canada Direct and UK Direct available from TSTT, cruise ship complex in Port of Spain, TTYC, TTYA and Peake's Yacht Yard, also at Penitence St, San Fernando. To activate an overseas cellphone, visit a dealer (check yellow pages under 'cellular'), or the TSTT office on Chacon St, Independence Sq, Port of Spain (Mon-Fri 0900-1700), West Mall or Trincity Mall (Mon-Fri 0900-1700, Sat 1000-1700), DSM Plaza, Chaguanas (Mon-Fri

0800-1600), St James St, San Fernando (Mon-Fri 0800-1600), Wilson Rd, Tobago (Mon-Fri 0800-1600), with passport. Allow at least 1 hr for service. The charge is US$18.40 to activate for use with prepaid cards (which then cost US$3.20-16 plus VAT). There is a 'roaming' agreement with some US and other overseas cellphone systems, but per minute costs are very high. For a 'postpaid' service you will need a credit card. Alternatively, you can visit any Digicel dealer, T6287000 (Digichat, Excellent City Centre Mall, 60 Independence Sq, T6254111; Mobile Haven, 26 Cipero St, San Fernando, T6539991; Uptown Drugs Ltd, LP1 Main Street, Scarborough T6350368, and many other locations throughout both islands) to activate an overseas cellphone: US$16 plus prepaid cards (US$3.20-80 plus VAT). For a postpaid phone you need proof of a local address (such as a utility bill).

Tobago → *Country code: 868. Colour map 5, C6.*

Tobago is not as bustling as Trinidad but the island is ideal for people in search of relaxation. The tourist area is concentrated on the southwest end and about six miles from the capital, Scarborough. There are small hotels and guesthouses scattered all around the island, however, offering peace and quiet in beautiful surroundings. The forest on the central hills is quite wild and provides a spectacular backdrop for the many horseshoe bays around the coast and there is good walking, birdwatching, sailing and diving. Tobago is 26 miles long and only nine miles wide, about the same size as Barbados, but with only a fifth of the population and a tiny fraction of the number of tourists. It is shaped like a cigar with a central 18-mile ridge of hills in the north (the Main Ridge, highest point 1890 ft), running parallel with the coast. These northeast hills are of volcanic origin and the southwest is flat or undulating and coralline. The population is concentrated in the west part of the island around Scarborough. The climate is generally cooler and drier, particularly in the southwest, than most parts of Trinidad. ▸▸ *For Sleeping, Eating and other listings, see pages 916-925.*

Ins and outs

There is a good ferry service and air shuttle from Trinidad, while many international flights come direct to Tobago. Many hotels are within walking distance of the airport and close to the beach. Scarborough is only 15-25 minutes' drive from Crown Point Airport and small enough to walk around, but for trips to the suburbs or further afield take a route taxi or hire a car. If you are driving around Tobago, maps are available from the tourist offices at the airport and at the port . Some of the minor roads are suitable only for 4WD. If you are hiking, get the three 1:25,000 sheets, not currently available in Tobago but obtainable from the Lands and Survey Division, Richmond St, Port of Spain, or from a good map shop. It is possible to walk anywhere. There is a book of trails. ▸▸ *See page 924 for further transport details.*

Scarborough

Scarborough is the capital of Tobago and the centre of all business activity on the island. Boats come into the bay bringing cargo and passengers and there is a lively market at the water's edge, with a fair degree of traffic congestion. A seafront Promenade has been developed with stalls selling food and souvenirs along the walkway heading west from the port. The town is pleasant but perhaps not worth an extended visit. There are very few places to stay or eat as tourist development has been concentrated elsewhere.

Sights

In Scarborough itself the **Botanic Gardens** on the hill behind the mall are worth a visit. There are also some interesting structures, such as the House of Assembly on James Park (built in 1825), and Gun Bridge, with its rifle-barrel railings. New development has included a new deep-water harbour and cruise ship terminal. Scarborough Mall is modern, concrete and rather tatty but most activity is around here, including the market, where you can find local varieties of fruit and vegetables, clothing, meat and fresh coconut water. There are banks on Main Street and Carrington Street.

Above the town is **Fort King George Heritage Park** ⓘ *Mon-Fri 0900-1630. US$1.60/US$2, teenagers US$0.80, children under 12 US$3.20*, which is well maintained and has good views along the coast (drive through the hospital to get to the fort). Building commenced in 1777 and continued under the French in 1786. Fort Castries was renamed Fort Liberté in 1790 after the garrison revolted, recaptured by the British in 1793, returned to France in 1801 and, after the island was ceded to Britain in 1802, named Fort King George in 1804. It was decommissioned in 1854. The gardens are attractive and well kept and there are excellent views over Scarborough. There are a number of historic buildings here including the Officers' Mess, the Barrack Guard House, the Magazine (almost hidden under an enormous silk cotton tree), the

Trinidad & Tobago Tobago

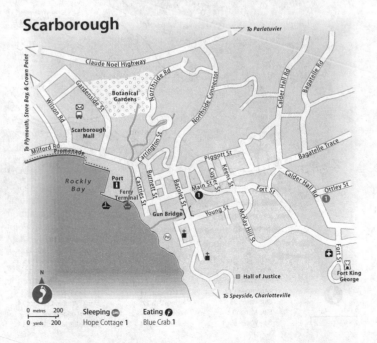

Scarborough

Sleeping 🛏 Eating 🍴
Hope Cottage 1 Blue Crab 1

Bell Tank (still with water in it and an amazing echo), and a lighthouse to guide ships around the coastal road into Scarborough harbour. A number of cannon mounted on metal garrison gun carriages can also be seen. There are two of artist Luise Kimme's huge wooden figures in the middle of the parade ground which are very attractive. (You can visit her workshop on Sunday, T6390257.) At the Officers' Mess, the **Tobago museum** has an excellent display of early Tobago history including Amerindian pottery, military relics, maps and documents from the slave era. Beautifully restored in 2006, the yellow ballast bricks look as good as new. The layout and structural design of the renovated buildings has been preserved as it was prior to the hurricane of 1847.

Around the island

East from Scarborough

Off the coastal road you can go to the **Forest Reserve** by taking a bus from Scarborough to **Mount St George** and then walking or hitching to **Hillsborough Dam**. The lake is the drinking-water supply for the island so swimming is not allowed, but you may find a man to take you out in a rowing boat. It is a lovely forest setting. A 4WD

Tobago

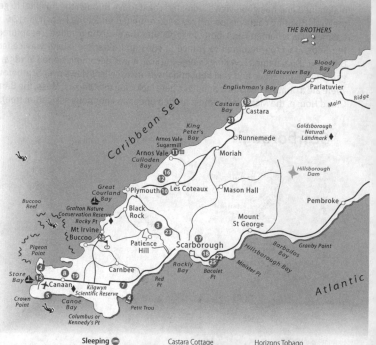

Sleeping 🛏
Ade's Domicile **22**
Adventure Eco-Villas **10**
Angel Apartments **13**
Arnos Vale **11**
Arnos Vale Vacation
 Apartments **12**
Blue Haven **25**
Blue Mango **13**
Blue Waters Inn **1**

Castara Cottage
 Apartments **13**
Cholson's Chalet **14**
Coco Reef **2**
Conrado Beach Resort **15**
Crown Point Beach **15**
Dr P's Resort **14**
Federal Villa **17**
Footprints Eco Resort **16**
Hilton Tobago **4**

Horizons Tobago
 Apartments **18**
James Holiday Resort **15**
Jetway Holiday Resort **15**
Johnston Apartments **15**
Kariwak Village **5**
Lesville's Place **19**
Man O'War Bay Cottages **14**
Manta Lodge **6**
Marshall & Michelle Jack **14**

vehicle is necessary if you want to drive but the walk there is recommended. From there continue northeast through the forest to **Castara** or **Mason Hall** on an unpaved, rough road. A guide is not necessary, as there is only one path. Birdwatching is excellent (oropendulas, mot-mots, jacamans, herons) and there are cayman in the lake, but look out for snakes (none of them poisonous). Alternatively, take a taxi to Mason Hall (ask the taxi to drop you at the road for the Hillsborough Dam) and walk to Mount St George via Hillsborough Dam, which is easier walking as the track is on the level or downhill, about nine miles. By Mount St George (Tobago's first, short-lived principal town, then called George Town) is **Studley Park House** and **Fort Granby**, which guards Barbados Bay.

The road continues through **Pembroke** and **Belle Garden** and nearby is **Richmond Great House**, now closed to the public. **Roxborough**, the island's second town, also on the Windward coast, is worth a visit. The **Argyll River** waterfalls near Roxborough ⓘ *0900-1700, US$5, children half price*, are a 10-minute walk upstream from the road. There are four beautiful falls with a big green pool at the bottom where you can swim. Guides are available but not really necessary as the path is obvious. The agile can scramble up the path from the pool to the top of the falls.

For a good walk take the road from Roxborough to Parlatuvier and Bloody Bay through the **Main Ridge Forest Reserve**. This is the oldest protected forest in the Western Hemisphere, dating from the 1760s when it was realised that the island's water supply could not be guaranteed if the forest was cut down. You go through singing forests with masses of birds including cocricos, collared trogon, mot-mots, jacamans, hummingbirds. After the 5-mile marker is a semi-circular trail in the forest called Gilpin's Trace. There are great views from the hut at the top of the road. There are several other walks in the forest and guides have their own favourites, where they know where to find particular birds. Beyond Roxborough is **King's Bay**, with waterfalls near the road In which you can swim.

Speyside and Little Tobago

From the fishing village of Speyside you can visit Little Tobago, a forested islet off the northeast coast, and a sanctuary for birds. There are wild fowl ad 58 species of other birds, including the red-billed tropic bird found here in the largest nesting colony in the north Atlantic. Boats across cost US$20 (includes a guided tour of the islet and snorkelling). There are lots of glass-bottomed boats and boatmen will find you fish and coral to see (see page 916). Go early in the morning to see the birds. If you want to camp, you are supposed to have prior permission from the **Forestry Division** ⓘ *Studley Park, T6394468.* They also

Moonlight Mountain
  Retreat **23**
Morre's **14**
Mount Irvine Bay
  & Golf Course **20**
Mrs May Williams **14**
Naturalist Beach Resort **21**
Ocean Point **7**
Palms Villa Resort **3**
Scarborough House **8**

Speyside Inn **9**
Store Bay Holiday Resort **15**
Surf Side **15**
Top Ranking Hill View
  Guest House **24**
Toucan Inn **15**

have a rudimentary camp on main ridge by the Roxborough-Parlatuvier road, which can be used by arrangement.

From Speyside you can climb **Pigeon Peak**, at about 1,900 ft the highest point on the island. There are two routes up the hill through the forest, the shorter one is steeper than the longer one, so both take about three hours. There is also a track on the Speyside Road from Charlotteville, 100 yd on the right before the turning to Flagstaff Hill. This is suitable for a 4WD to begin with. After about 30 minutes' walk you clamber down into a stream bed and up again, from which point it becomes a rough, steep path through old banana plantations and then woodland. There is no trouble following the path here, with markers cut into or painted on to trees, and there are many birds. However, when the ground becomes flatter, it becomes confusing. A guide is therefore essential. The actual summit is above the woodland, through grass and small shrubs, and has a trig point. From the top you can see the north and south coasts and offshore islets.

There are lurid, yet true, tales of tourists being lost up here for days.

Charlotteville

A trip to Charlotteville in the northeast is recommended. The easiest way to get there is by one of the seven buses a day from Scarborough (US$1.28. There are maxi-taxis from Scarborough (US$1.60, three a day but not on Saturday, when the Adventist drivers do not work; for the return journey you can arrange to be picked up). There are magnificent views on the way and the village itself is on a fine horseshoe bay with a good beach, lifeguard, good swimming and snorkelling and two dive shops. During the Second World War the Americans erected a radio tracking station on Flagstaff Hill overlooking Charlotteville (take the rough track off the main Speyside-Charlotteville road about ½ mile). There are several seats and a bandstand here. Half way along the rough road to Flagstaff Hill there is a cattle path to the right. Follow this as it descends and curves to the left. Near the bottom it meets another, wider trace (trail). Turn left and this will eventually bring you back to Charlotteville. It is a pleasant, shaded walk. From Charlotteville, it is a 15-minute walk to **Pirate's Bay**, which is magnificent and unspoilt and good for snorkelling. Also adjacent is Man O'War Bay. **Campbellton Bay** is a 30- to 40-minute walk from Charlotteville (ask for directions) through dense forest to a secluded beach, mostly used only by fishermen.

The north coast

The road between Charlotteville and L'Anse Fourmi along the Caribbean coast is partly paved and passable in dry weather with 4WD but is not recommended. However, it is a wonderful hike. The views are worth the trouble, with lots of lovely bays beneath you. Get a taxi to L'Anse Fourmi and walk (a comfortable four hours) along the track to **Corvo Point**, **Hermitage** (bush rum for sale), **Man O'War Bay** and **Charlotteville**. The terrain is undulating, bird life is plentiful, including parrots, and you may see iguanas. The stretch of road between **L'Anse Fourmi** and **Moriah** through Parlatuvier and Castara is smooth, traffic is light and it is very picturesque. Take water with you. The small fishing village of **Castara** on the coast is a pleasant place to visit or stay. The bay is hemmed in by cliffs and forest, but contains two sandy beaches separated by rocks, Big Bay and Little Bay, also known as Heavenly Bay, and a snorkelling reef. Apartments and guest houses are perched on the hillside above Little Bay, while restaurants are dotted along the beaches. A small river comes out at Big Bay, and a 10-minute walk inland will take you to an easily

There's no public transport from Plymouth to Parlatuvier; you have to go via Roxborough.

 A much-quoted attraction in Plymouth is the enigmatic tombstone of Betty Stevens (25 November 1783), which reads: "She was a mother without knowing it, and a wife, without letting her husband know, except by her kind indulgences to him."

accessible waterfall. Lifeguards are on duty daily at Big Bay at the Castara Beach Facility. Local women produce excellent bread and bakeries morning and afternoon from a traditional clay oven behind the beach at Big Bay. Watch them mixing, kneading and leaving the dough to prove on banana leaves, before baking. On the beach at Big Bay is a little wooden shack called Boboshanti's herbal steam bath and massage ① T6600005, Sun-Fri 0900-1800, where you can have a steam bath using 13 local herbs grown around the hut, a full body massage ending with reflexology, or other treatments. It is extremely rustic and a very local experience, but the therapists are all fully trained abroad and highly experienced.

The southwest

At the southwest end of the island there are many hotels and resorts, particularly in the **Crown Point** area. At **Store Bay** stand the ruins of small **Milford Fort**, and brown pelicans frequent the beautiful but crowded beach, which is a good place to watch the sunset. The fort was once Dutch (Bella Vista) but was overrun by the Indians. The British maintained a small battery here but it is now no more than a nice garden. Store Bay Beach Facility ① daily 1000-1730, lockers US$1.60, with unlimited entry to changing rooms, toilets, or US$0.16 per entry, beach chairs for rent US$6.40-9.60 per day, has a large car park and stalls for vendors of T-shirts, beach wraps and souvenirs as well as a food court for snacks, local specialities, ice cream and drinks. Vending is not allowed on the beach. **Pigeon Point** ① US$3, US$0.50 children, has the island's most beautiful beach, clean and with calm water. There are huts, tables and benches, lockers, bars, shopping, boat hire and watersports. It is another good place to watch the sunset.

From **Mount Irvine Bay**, where there is an attractive, palm-fringed championship golf course, you can walk up to **Bethel** (about two miles), the island's highest village, for excellent views across the island. Another beach well worth a visit is **Turtle Bay**.

The main town on this coast is **Plymouth**, with **Fort James** overlooking **Great Courland Bay** (site of the Courlander settlement in the 17th century). Destroyed several times, the present fort was erected in 1800. Also here is the Latvian Monument. Designed by a local artist, it was erected in 1976 and represents 'Freedom'. Plymouth is the site of an international jazz festival held on the sports field by Fort James which attracts many famous artistes including Elton John for the 2007 festival. There is also a heritage festival in the summer.

Hidden in the forest some miles from **Arnos Vale** is the **Arnos Vale Sugarmill**, dating from 1880; a recommended excursion, it is possible to hitchhike. The **Arnos Vale Waterwheel Park** has a restaurant and stage where shows are put on.

Beaches and activities

Tobago is noted for its beaches, two of the best being only minutes from the airport: **Store Bay**, popular with locals, lots of vendors, food stalls and glass-bottom boats; and **Pigeon Point**, a picture-postcard beach fringed with palms with calm, shallow water protected by **Buccoo Reef**. You have to pay to use the facilities at the beach, but you get changing space, umbrellas and beach bars. Here also there are lots of glass-bottom boats going out to Buccoo Reef and a catamaran for coastal tours and swimming in the Nylon Pool, a shallow area offshore. Other good beaches on the leeward side of the island are **Stone Haven Bay**, **Mount Irvine Bay** and **Courland Bay**, one of the longest. All have resort hotels and watersports. **Castara** is a pretty bay cut in two by rocks jutting out into the sea. The forest comes down to the water at either end and a river can be followed from the sea up to some waterfalls. **Englishman's Bay** is another lovely bay, with the forest coming down to the beach and a river running into the sea. The east coast is more rugged and windswept. **Hillsborough Bay**, just outside Scarborough, has a glorious beach, but the sea is dangerous because of rip tides. Do not swim there. **Big Bacolet Bay**, also known as Minister Bay, is great for surfing, body surfing and boogie boarding, but watch out for the currents. **Bacolet Bay**, by the Blue Haven Hotel, is a better bet for swimming as it is protected by rocks and a reef. In the northeast, **King's Bay** has a beach bar, toilets and huts for shade. There is a signpost to the beach, almost opposite the track to **King's Bay Waterfall**. **Speyside** and **Charlotteville** both have protected bays. From the former you can take glass-bottom boat trips to **Little Tobago** with birdwatching, walking and snorkelling included (about US$20) and from the latter you can walk to Pirate's Bay through the forest. Snorkelling is good on the reef here.

Diving

The waters around Tobago are known as an unspoilt diving destination and there are several reputable dive shops. Most species of hard and soft corals can be found, and there is a huge brain coral, believed to be one of the world's largest, off Little Tobago, which you can see on a glass-bottom boat tour. The parrot fish are nibbling away at it, but it is so large that they are not yet doing major damage. The Guyana current flows round the south and east shores of Tobago and supports a large variety of marine life. Dive sites are numerous and varied, with walls, caves, canyons, coral gardens and lots of fish. There is exciting drift diving but it is not recommended for novices. You are swept along the coral reef at up to five knots while, high above, manta rays flap lazily to remain stationary in the current as they sieve out the plankton. Manta rays are not as plentiful as they used to be, because of changes in the temperature of the current; they are best seen between January and March. Eagle rays and southern sting rays can also be seen. Some of the most popular sites are **Arnos Vale**, **Pirate's Bay**, **Store Bay**, **Man O'War Bay** and **Batteaux Bay**. In 1997 a new site was added, with the sinking of the *Scarlet Ibis*, renamed the *Maverick*, a 350-ft roll-on/roll-off ship. This artificial reef lies 100 ft deep on a sandy bed and coral has grown and schools of fish are living in the wreck. The deck has now collapsed but with care you can still swim through the hull. Another vessel was sunk in 100 ft of water off the point at Speyside in 2003. The aluminium hull is starting to grow hard coral and creatures are beginning to live there. **Snorkelling** is also excellent almost everywhere, with good visibility.

Buccoo Reef Glass-bottomed boats for visiting this undersea garden leave from Pigeon Point, Store Bay and Buccoo Bay. The charge is about US$15 for 2-2½ hours, with snorkel provided; wear a hat. Longer trips with barbecue cost around US$50-60, worth it if you eat and drink plenty. The dragging of anchors and greed of divers as well as temperature changes resulting in bleaching of the coral have tarnished the glory of this once marvellous reef (you may prefer to make the trip to Speyside where glass-bottomed boats make trips over a pristine reef). Elkhorn and other corals have been badly damaged by snorkellers and divers walking on them, but there is still a good variety of fish, including reef sharks and the colourful parrot fish and angel fish, while shoals of squid can be seen. Boat trips also include the **Nylon Pool**, an emerald-green pool in the Caribbean. Boats leave between 0900 and 1430, depending on the tide. Be selective in choosing which boat – and captain – you take for the trip; some are less than satisfactory.

The reef is now protected by law; it is forbidden to remove or destroy the corals or other marine life.

● Sleeping

Scarborough *p911, map p911*
LL Blue Haven, Bacolet Point, T6607400, www.bluehavenhotel.com. The nicest hotel on the island, lovely location, excellent service. Built in 1940s, its heyday was in the 1950s when movie stars like Robert Mitchum, Debra Kerr, Jack Lemmon and Rita Hayworth stayed here while making

Fire Down Below, Heaven Knows Mr Allison, or Swiss Family Robinson. The original building perched on the point has been restored and new wings with flying roofs have been built either side, one overlooking pretty Bacolet Beach and the other looking out to Scarborough and the Atlantic. All 51 rooms have a sea view, balcony and are light and bright in white with a nautical blue trim. Some rooms have a window between the bathroom and bedroom so you can watch the sunset from your tub. Eco-friendly policies for water, waste management, energy and food, local natural products in bathroom. Beach bar for lunch, restaurant up the hill for breakfast and dinner, wonderful food, glorious view.

A Horizons Tobago Apartments, 89 Bacolet Point, T/F44-(0)121 7077503, www.horizonstobago.com. 1- and 2-bedroomed open plan apartments with rattan furniture, a/c, fans, mosquito nets, TV, free local calls, laundry room, large private pool, good amenities. 2 mins from Bacolet beach where Robinson Crusoe was stranded here by his author, Daniel Defoe, on 30 Sep 1659. Airport transfers, discounts on car hire.

B Ade's Domicile, 19 Old Lighthouse Rd, Bacolet Point, T6394306, www.adesdomicil.de. Quiet, residential area, short walk to three beaches, sea view. 2 studios downstairs, a/c, fan, large room, good kitchen, all very spacious, TV, veranda with furniture under cover, 2 1-bedroom apartments upstairs, also roomy with balcony and better view. Owner, Ade, lives in house above with her dogs.

C Miriam's Bed and Breakfast, or **Federal Villa**, 1-3 Crooks River, T6393926, F6393566. 5 rooms, shared bath, shared kitchen, breakfast included, fan, modest but clean and comfortable, 7-min walk to harbour, run by friendly and helpful Miriam Edwards.

D-E Hope Cottage, Calder Hall Rd, corner of Ottley St, on the way up to the hospital and Fort King George, T6392179, F6397550. 15 rooms, 3 with private bathroom, fan, pleasant, kitchen can be used, mini-market nearby, spacious public rooms, bar, restaurant, veranda, homely, peaceful, a bit tatty, popular with students, entrance between 2 tamarind trees, brought from India and planted when original house was built in early 19th century.

Speyside and Little Tobago p913, map p912

LL-A Blue Waters Inn, Batteaux Bay, Speyside, T6604341, www.bluewatersinn.com. An isolated and delightfully unsophisticated hotel, 38 large a/c rooms and efficiencies, some interconnecting, with sea view , and 3 bungalows at the other end of the property with 1 or 2 bedrooms, caters for people who want to sit on the beach, hikers, birdwatchers and divers, also wheelchair accessible. Rate includes tax and service. Dive packages with **Aquamarine Dive** on site, tennis, games room with TV, library, table tennis. Very pretty bay, no other development, view of Little Tobago, great swimming, snorkelling and diving, the best place to stay in this area.

L-AL The Speyside Inn, Windward Rd, Speyside, T6604852, www.speysideinn.com. 18 rooms, 3 cabins, 3 bungalows, lovely airy rooms, nicely furnished, breakfast included with home-made breads, dinner by reservation only, small beach across road, pool, dive shop, view of Little Tobago, close to Jemma's restaurant.

L-A Manta Lodge, Windward Rd, Speyside, T6605268, www.mantalodge.com. 22 standard, superior, loft or attic rooms, attic has no view, a/c essential as hot under roof, superior rooms are better, with balcony, view and more air, small pool, bar, restaurant, caters mainly to divers, packages available with **Tobago Dive Experience** on site.

A-C Top Ranking Hill View Guest House, Top Hill St, Speyside, T6604904, www.caribinfo.com/toprank. 5 rooms and suites of different sizes sleeping 2-4 people, with kitchenettes, balcony or patio and view, run by Ann and Max Davidson. 10-min walk to beach and restaurants, mini-mart on site. Glass-bottom boat tours also operated by Max.

Charlotteville p914, map p912
Lots of basic places to stay in the **D-E** range, just turn up and look around, advance reservations are difficult to arrange.

AL-B Man O'War Bay Cottages, T6604327, www.man-o-warbaycottages.com. 10 cottages in a range of sizes, good for groups with lots of single beds, spacious, well-equipped kitchen, right on beach with tropical gardens behind, rustic setting, barbecue facilities, expensive shop with limited range, check your bill carefully. Great location with good swimming and beach but only basic accommodation.

A-C Cholson's Chalets, 72-74 Bay St, contact Pat Nicholson (T6398553), www.cholsonchalets.com. Across the road from the dark golden beach where fishing boats come in, looking towards Campbleton Bay with Pirates Bay to the right. Old family residence with great grandmother's wooden house in the garden; one apartment has the matrimonial bed the family was born in. 6 apartments, vary in size and character but all are green and white, spotlessly clean, bright white linens, with partition walls allowing air circulation in the roof but little privacy. Lots of rules for safety and conservation of resources. Herbs, fruits and aloe vera in the garden for guests' use. Very popular and you may need to book in advance even in low season; advance bookings of less than a week are not accepted. 4 more apartments round the corner in newer block under same management but less attractive.

C Morre's, Bellaire Rd, Charlotteville, T6604799, contact Susan Simon. 4 double rooms and a 2-bedroom self-contained apartment, all with kitchen facilities.

D Marshall and Michelle Jack (twins), 13A Pirates Bay Rd, T6605923. Shared bathroom, no soap or towels but very clean, use of good kitchen, so close to sea that you could jump in from window, so don't stay there if the noise of the sea keeps you awake.

D Mrs May Williams has ground-floor apartment, 2 rooms sleep 6, communal kitchen, bathroom, house faces jetty, between 2 shops painted blue, quite pleasant.

E Dr P's Resort, Belle Air St, T6605907. Double room or 2-room apartment, not the cleanest ever, kitchen, shower, toilet, fan, terrace, beautiful view of sea from hillside, accessible from track between Charlotteville and Pirate's Bay.

The north coast *p914, map p912*

L-A Blue Mango, 2 Bay Rd, Castara, T6392060, www.blue-mango.com. Owned by friendly Colin Ramdeholl, 2 traditional wooden cottages sleep 2 or 4, with kitchen, bathroom and fan, mosquito nets, balconies and hammocks, charming, built on cliff side between the two beaches, rustic but lovely location and views, good walking and swimming, breakfast at the Clay Kitchen included. No credit cards, no extra taxes or service charges.

L-D The Naturalist Beach Resort, Castara Bay Rd, Castara, T6395901, www.seetobago.com/tobago/resorts/natural/. 6 simple apartments for couples or families, cell phone and car hire can be included as well as breakfast, on the beach, internet café.

A-B Angel Apartments, Heavenly Bay, Castara, T6395291. www.angel-apartments.com. 4 dark a/c apartments on ground floor opening on to pool, 8 apartments on middle and upper floors with balcony and sea view, price higher for top floor. Close to beach and restaurants. Managed in the UK by Jan Marson, and in Tobago by Dexter Taylor, who also runs Cascreole restaurant along the beach.

A-B Castara Cottage Apartments, T7571044, www.castaracottage.com. 3 apartments on two floors sleep up to 11 if all booked together. Upstairs are a studio and a 2-bedroom apartment which interconnect and downstairs there is another 2-bedroom apartment. A sofabed is available for extra accommodation. Set on the point between the two beaches, the apartments have lovely views and get plenty of breeze. Good kitchens, hammocks, simply furnished.

The southwest *p915, map p912*

There are lots of guesthouses and small hotels along the road between the airport and Pigeon Point, all within walking distance of the airport. Heading east along the coast there are several all-inclusives or package holiday hotels, such as the Grafton Beach Resort and its upmarket sister hotel, Le Gran Courlan at Stonehaven Bay, Black Rock, or the older Turtle Beach, run by Rex Resorts, where 95% of the guests are British.

LL Coco Reef, eastern end of Store Bay, T6398571, www.cocoreef.com. Modelled on a Bermudan hotel, peach and white walls, red roof, 135 rooms, suites and villas on man-made beach, set in 10 acres of manicured gardens and lawns, pretty view of Pigeon Point, height of luxury with prices to match, close to airport and in main hotel area. Spa and gym for workouts and relaxation.

LL Hilton Tobago Golf Resort & Spa, T6608500, www.hiltoncaribbean.com/ tobago. All 200 rooms and suites with seaview. Part of **Tobago Plantations**, T6399377, www.tobagoplantations.com, a 750-acre development around Petit Trou Lagoon, with hotel, villas, condominiums bungalows, championship Jack Nicklaus golf course and Equilibrium Spa, T6310038. Built on a very windy bit of coast, the hotel is plagued with rust from the salty breeze, but the rooms are comfortable and well-equipped. Very remote, you need a car/taxi to go anywhere; daily shuttle to Pigeon Point where the sea isn't so rough, watersports centre at both locations.

LL The Palms Villa Resort, Signal Hill Old Road, Signal Hill, T6351010. www.thepalmstobago.com. 5 villas in gated community with security. Pretty colonial style architecture with large central gardens and play area on hilltop above Scarborough. Each villa has good-sized pool with children's section, barbecue and outdoor eating area, sleep up to 6 adults, comfortable bedrooms, lots of storage space, TV and entertainment, housekeeper can prepare meals at extra cost, car hire useful, 10 mins to beach.

LL-L Mount Irvine Bay Hotel and Golf Club, Plymouth, T6398871, www.mtirvine .com. Older-style hotel, rooms, suites or garden cottage, luxury furnishings, TV, phone, pool, beach, sauna, gym, mediocre food at **Sugar Mill** restaurant, tennis, gardens of 16 acres, pretty golf course.

LL-AL Arnos Vale Hotel, Arnos Vale, T6392881, www.arnosvalehotel.com. Rooms and cottages, meal plans available, beautiful surroundings in tropical forest, great birdwatching, mot mots and other birds come to be fed at 1600, afternoon tea-time, hospitable, dive shop, new 30-room complex at site of old water wheel.

LL-AL Footprints Eco Resort, Culloden Bay, T6600118, www.footprintseco-resort.com. Set in 62 acres of nature reserve, 2 villas, 1 honeymoon retreat, 2 suites and 8 seafront

rooms, all on stilts and made from recycled or waste timber, well-equipped, palm roofs, solar powered with a/c, jacuzzi, spa with aromatherapy, hydrotherapy and thalassotherapy, great views over sea, saltwater pools at low tide, good snorkelling on reef, very noisy cocrico birds at dawn calling across the valley. Cocoa House restaurant has retreating roof, serves seafood and healthy meals. Get to it from Golden Lane, which passes the enormous silk cotton tree that is supposed to be the grave of Gan' Gan' Sarah.

L-A Viola's Place, Birchwood Triangle, Hampden, T/F6399441, www.violasplace .com. 10 studios, 4, 1-bedroom apartments, 6 with 2 bedrooms, on 2 floors, kitchenette, basic equipment, pool, restaurant, convenience store, airport pick-up. Right by golf courses, at Mt Irvine and Tobago Plantations, 2 km to beach.

AL Kariwak Village, Store Bay Local Rd, Crown Point, T6398442, www.kariwak.com. A little oasis in main tourist area 5 mins' walk from airport and Store Bay Beach and the nicest place to stay in this area. Allan and Cynthia Clovis started the hotel in the 1970s, concentrating on guests' physical and spiritual well-being. Beautiful and aromatic gardens with flowers, fruits, herbs and vegetables, lots of birds and butterflies, hammocks and jacuzzi. Morning stretch, yoga, tai chi and other activities most days, free for guests, occasional yoga retreats with international instructors. Holistic Health Centre offers Ayurvedic body works, massage, reflexology, reiki, ozonated water baths, biophoton light therapy and other treatments to promote healing and regeneration. 18 simple but comfortable rooms around main pool, 6 more in gardens. Open air thatched restaurant serves excellent, fresh and wholesome food, with menus changed daily, vegetarian options, Tobagonian specialities for breakfast, lunch and dinner.

AL-A Crown Point Beach Hotel, T6398781, www.crownpointbeachhotel.com. Garish orange on road side but more tasteful white with orange trim on sea side. Prime position on cliffs at end of Store Bay looking down onto beach. Studios, 1-bedroom apartments and cabins, all with sea view, basic self-catering, pool, pleasant grounds, tennis, table tennis, internet access, restaurant and outdoor bar. **Royalton Casino** with **Max's Sports Bar** next door and mini-market a few steps away.

AL-B Adventure Eco-Villas, Adventure Farm & Nature Reserve, Arnos Vale Road, Plymouth, T6392839, www.adventure-ecovillas.com. Two delightful wooden cottages on stilts looking out over the forest with a shared deck, ideal for birdwatching, or a smaller, darker, cheaper apartment attached to the main building. The cottages have a double and single bed, bathroom with tub, living/dining area with louvre windows which can be opened up completely, well-equipped kitchen, cheerful, painted blue and yellow, surrounded by lush green vegetation, forest noises and birdsong.

A-B Ocean Point, Milford Rd, Lowlands, T/F6390973, www.oceanpoint.com. Studios sleep 3, suites fit 5, a bit cramped but all with kitchenettes, dive and golf packages available, a/c, TV, pool, sundeck, hammocks, 2-min walk from sea, transport needed, family-run, friendly.

A Johnston Apartments, Crown Point, T6398915, www.johnstonapartments.com. Guests have use of **Crown Point** pool, restaurant and tennis court. Spacious, 1-3 bedroom apartments scattered over clifftop garden, steps to beach, short walk to airport, good location.

A Toucan Inn, Crown Point, T6397173, www.toucan-inn.com. 20 poolside cabanas or garden rooms, rates include tax, helpful staff, short walk to beach, well-regarded small hotel, very relaxing. Good food and entertainment at **Bonkers** restaurant, 0730-2230, main courses from US$12. **R&Sea Divers** on site with dive packages.

A-B Conrado Beach Resort, Milford Extension Rd, between Store Bay and Pigeon Point, T6390145. Breakfast included, beachfront, standard or superior rooms, some small, some with balconies, some roadside view, priced accordingly although overpriced around Carnival when rates soar, restaurant on beach for breakfast, inside for night-time, good snorkelling offshore on small reef, fishing boats moored outside, family-owned, excellent service.

A-C Scarborough House, 24 Dillon St, Bon Accord, T/F6399039, www.scarboroughhousejs.com. Variety of rooms and 1-2-bedroom suites with kitchenettes or full kitchens, a/c or fan, TV, no smoking, L-shaped pool, car rental next door. Walking distance to Store Bay, Pigeon Point and bus stop on Milford Main Road. Bakery round the corner for wholewheat bread and health food. Breakfast US$10 by prior arrangement.

B Moonlight Mountain Retreat, off road to Plymouth, T6394346, www.moonlightmountainretreat.com. Perched up in the hills above Scarborough, with views to both the Caribbean and Atlantic and breezes from both oceans. Traditional but modern house with balconies and wooden fretwork set in lush gardens and forest, used for yoga retreats or just B&B. 4 bedrooms upstairs, one with en suite, the others share 2 bathrooms, self-catering apartment downstairs, simple yet stylish furnishings. Plunge pool, hammocks, very relaxing, run by Ginny (yoga teacher) and Kelly (great cook) Almann, who also know all the best places to lime, where bands are playing and where to dance. Massage and reflexology available. Local and international breakfast and evening meal by prior reservation. Meals served buffet style on the veranda, delicious smoothies with fruit from the garden.

B-C Arnos Vale Vacation Apartments, Arnos Vale Rd, Plymouth, T/F6391362, arnosvaleapts@hotmail.com. Run by hospitable, helpful Victor Forde, very spacious 1- or 2-bedroom apartments, huge open plan kitchen and living area, fully furnished and comfortable, upstairs apartment has balcony overlooking beautiful garden with fruit trees and tropical birds which come to the feeders, transport to airport, car hire available. Excellent value, very popular, dive packages with **Tobago Dive Experience**.

B-C James Holiday Resort, Crown Point, T/F6398084, jameshol@tstt.net.tt. Standard room or 3-bedroom apartment (maximum 12 people), car and jeep rental, credit cards accepted, 2-min walk from airport, TV, patio or balcony, restaurant.

B-C Jetway Holiday Resort, 100 m from airport terminal, T/F6398504. Can be noisy until after 2200, 9 pleasant self-contained units with cooking facilities, friendly, helpful, a few mins' walk to Pigeon Point and Store Bay.

B-C Lesville's Place, Canaan Feeder Rd, Canaan, T6390629, www.tobagolesville.com. Run by Lestell and Orville Moore, who live alongside this new block of rooms, studios and apartments in a quiet residential area off the beaten track. Simple accommodation, large rooms with small bathrooms and kitchens, TV, a/c or fan, tiled floors, no smoking, one of the few properties on Tobago with solar-powered hot water, fruit trees all round with produce for guests, car hire, transfers, beach trips, public transport close by.

B-C Store Bay Holiday Resort, Local Rd, Crown Point, turn right out of the airport, and take the first right, T6398810, F6399733. 5-min walk to airport or beach, do not be fooled by taxi drivers who will charge US$5 for the ride. About the cheapest in this area, but self-catering only, 16 a/c apartments, clean, well furnished, kitchen, gardens, night-time security guard, small pool, friendly, good value.

B-C Surf Side Hotel, Milford Rd Extension, Crown Point, T6390614, www.surfside tobago.com. Single or double rooms, 2-room apartments or villas, all with kitchenettes, simply furnished, a/c, pool, 10-min walk to Store Bay, 12 mins to airport.

● Eating

Watch out for extra charges such as 10% service and 15% VAT.

Scarborough *p911, map p911*
❢ **Old Donkey Cart**, Bacolet, T6393551. Dec-Apr daily 0800-2200, May-Nov closed Wed. Good food, European wines, nice shady garden setting or in old house if it is raining.
❢ **The Blue Crab**, corner of Main St with Fort St, T6392737. Mon-Fri 1100-1500, will open for breakfast and Mon, Wed, Fri evenings by reservation. Specializes in local food, very good lunch but slow service, reasonable prices, nice view over harbour.
❢ **The Salsa Kitchen**, Pump Mill Rd, T6391522. Tue-Sun 1900-2300. Small and intimate. South American tapas, home made pizzas and a dish of the day. Food cooked fresh to order so be prepared to sit over a rum punch or two. Well worth the wait or pre-order.

❢ **Jemma's Sea View**, Speyside, T6604066. Sun-Thu 0800-2100, Fri 0800-1600, closed Sat. Originally a platform on stilts above the beach, now expanded into a large restaurant but still with good view to Goat Island and Little Tobago. Good, filling lunch or dinner, fixed menu but 2 choices, slow service, nice atmosphere, no alcohol, you can get hassled here for boat trips.

Charlotteville *p914, map p912*
❢❢-❢ **Gail's**, Charlotteville, on seafront as you walk to Pirate's Bay. Breakfast and dinner, no lunch. All fresh, very tasty, delicious vegetables and salad, Gail is a genius with fish, very friendly.
❢❢-❢ **Sharon and Phebe's**, Charlotteville, T6605717. Mon-Sat 0900-2300, Sun 1100-2300. Nice view of the bay, very good and cheap meals, try the prawns if available, dumplings and curried crab also good, very friendly, Phebe also has a laundry and special prices for people on yachts.

The north coast *p914, map p912*
❢❢-❢ **The Boat House**, Heavenly Bay, Castara, T6607354. Open for breakfast, lunch and candlelit dinner. Owned by Brendan and Sharon, who did the décor, with fabric strips hanging from the ceiling all over the restaurant. Casual beach bar serving local food but a bit upmarket, very good. Pan band Wed night.

The southwest *p915, map p912*
❢❢❢-❢❢ **Café Coco**, beside Coco Reef Hotel, off Pigeon Point Rd, T6390996. Pleasant setting with lots of tiles on the walls and plants and fishponds. Open kitchen serves up regional cuisine, from Cuban and Jamaican to Tobagonian dishes, tasty, fresh, well-presented.
❢❢❢-❢❢ **Golden Star**, Crown Point, T6390873. Daily 0700-2300. Restaurant and bar, lobster thermidor and grilled king fish in Creole sauce.
❢❢❢-❢❢ **La Tartaruga**, Buccoo Bay, by the pier from where glass-bottomed boats depart, T6390940. Mon-Sat 1900-2130. Italian restaurant café-bar, excellent Italian food, pizzas, limited menu, expensive, reservations essential.

♥♥♥-♥♥ The Seahorse Inn, across the road from the beach, next to **Grafton Beach Resort**, T6390686, www.seahorseinntobago.com. Daily 1200-1530, 1830-2200, happy hr 1730-1830 for drinks. Excellent dinners, beautifully presented, lots of seafood, lobster, shrimp and catch of the day. Good portions, yummy desserts, friendly service, extensive wine menu. Style is elegant rustic, sit upstairs overlooking garden and bar downstairs. Reservations essential.

♥♥♥-♥♥ Shirvan Watermill, on Shirvan Rd, T6390000. Daily 1700-2200. Specializes in seafood and steaks, expensive and romantic, main courses from US$15, fresh open feel.

♥♥ Beach Bar, Store Bay. Daily 1000-2400. Music all day on Sat, and a barbecue from 2000-2400, for US$17 per head for drinks and small portions of fish and chicken, poor value unless you drink a lot.

♥♥ Black Rock Café on Black Rock main road, T6397625. Mon-Fri 1130-2300, Sat, Sun 1500-2300. Recommended for very good food, slow service, very busy.

♥♥ Bonkers, Store Bay Local Rd, T6397173, 0700-2200. Cheerful bar and restaurant, popular and usually full. Live music some nights. Reasonable food.

♥♥ Café Iguana, corner of Store Bay Local Rd and Main Rd, Crown Point, T6318205. Open for breakfast, lunch and dinner, closed Wed. Attractive setting, cocktail bar with good food and sometimes live bands at weekends. Art on the walls. Run by Trinidadian and German couple.

♥♥ Caribbean Chula, Shirvan Rd. Delightful, romantic setting above **Mélange**, a more sophisticated restaurant owned by the same chef. Fairy lights in the trees outside and pretty Indian artefacts inside. Food is a mix of Indian and Creole.

♥♥ Indigo, 2 Horseshoe Ridge, Pleasant Prospect, Grafton, T6310353, indigo2@ tstt.net.tt. Mon-Fri 1200-1500, plus 1900-2200 Mon-Sat. Local and foreign dishes, very good food, garden setting , also accommodation.

♥♥ Patinos, Shirvan Rd, T6399481. Lunch and dinner, daily 1830-2230. Run by Kenneth and Marcia Patino with their son as chef, excellent food, delicious West Indian platter at lunchtime, evening steel band once a week, reservations needed. Good accommodation too.

♥ D'Art Café, in the Backyard, Milford Rd, Crown Point, Mon-Fri 1200-2000, Sat 1000-1600. See the batiks and crafts. Swedish-owned, great for salads, chicken Caesar, Greek and delicious fruit smoothies. Good plate of spaghetti Bolognese too.

♥ Miss Esme, T6390163. Daily 0730-1730. Flying fish and bake.

♥ Miss Jean's, T6390211. Daily 0800-1900. US$2 and less for all kind of 'ting', a full meal with drinks for 2 costs less than US$10, crab and dumplings are a speciality but the crabs are woefully small because of overfishing.

⊙ Bars and clubs

Tobago *p910, maps p912 and p911*
Though not as lively as Trinidad, Tobago does offer dancing in its hotels and in Scarborough, at **Golden Star Entertainment Centre**, nightly.

Entertainment is available every night of **Tobago Race Week**, mostly at **Crown Point** but also at **Grafton Beach** or **Grand Courlan** hotels.

Bogos Bar, by the sea on the way to Pigeon Point, T6318487. Tue-Sun 1030-2100. Happy hour 1800-1900. Owned by Tobagonian Shirley and her British husband Bob, this bar has great atmosphere. Everything you would expect from a beach bar and more. Good roti. Live music Sun. Take mosquito repellent.

Crown Point, T6398781, 0700-0100, or until 0400 weekends/special events. Seafront location, good view of Store Bay. Outdoor bar attached to hotel restaurant. Live entertainment Fri nights.

Green Light, Store Bay, busiest Fri, Sat, 2200-0400.

Michael's Bar, Black Rock, recommended for friendly evening entertainment.

Sunday School on Buccoo Beach, a big party starting early every Sun evening with live music, followed at about 2300 by a DJ playing until early in the morning, US$0.80, 2000-0400. Don't miss.

⊙ Entertainment

Tobago *p910, maps p912 and p911*
Cinema Scarborough, is good value, US$1.10 for 2 films, but the audience can be a bit noisy.

O Shopping

Tobago *p910, maps p912 and p911*
Arts and crafts
Backyard, Milford Rd, Crown Point. Local batiks.
Batiki Point, Buccoo. A cavern of colourful local and imported crafts. Owned by Tina from Finland and her Tobagonian husband Lion. Colourful wall hangings depicting local life, beautiful Indian sari/sarongs and jewellery. In-house designs for T-shirts and batiks.
Cotton House, Bacolet St, just outside Scarborough. Excellent handicrafts, batik studio, high standard, pictures and clothes at reasonable prices. They also have an outlet at Sandy Point.
Shore Things, Lambeau, Mon-Sat 1000-1800. Locally produced artefacts. Giselle also offers light lunches with yummy desserts, sit and watch the birds and the view.

Food
Francis Supermarket, Crown Point, is not particularly well stocked but is open Mon-Sat 0800-1800, Sun and holidays 1000-1400.
Penny Savers, main road at Milford, is the main supermarket stocks a good range including pharmaceuticals, open long hrs and holidays, has ATM (blue machine).

Music
Arcade Record Store, Castries Rd, Scarborough, will make tape compilations to your specification, as will others, but check copyright status.

Shopping centre
Gulf City Lowlands Shopping Mall, on the outskirts of Scarborough. Opened in 2006 with a variety of new shops. A cinema is proposed.

▲ Activities and tours

Tobago *p910, maps p912 and p911*
Basketball
Black Rock has a basketball league in late Aug, early Sep; you can play before or after the games.

Diving
Association of Dive Operators in Tobago, T6605445, www.tobagoscubadiving.com, keeps a list of operators who meet their safety standards. There is a full list in **Discover Trinidad and Tobago**. There is a hyperbaric chamber in Roxborough, T6394354, divingsuperintendent@yahoo.com.
Aquamarine Dive Ltd (Keith and Alice Darwent) is at **Blue Waters Inn**, Speyside, T6605445, www.aquamarinedive.com (**Blue Waters Inn** tends to be full throughout the year so book early.) This is a 5-star PADI facility, dives are around Little Tobago and all escorted by at least 2 dive masters because of the currents. Full range of courses available; a single tank dive costs on average US$42, night dives US$48, PADI Open Water course US$460, rental of BCD and regulator US$7, mask, fins and snorkel US$10.
Tobago Dive Experience (owned by Sean Robinson and Mark Borrett), at **Manta Lodge**, T6604888, and at **Arnos Vale**, T6602222, offers NAUI, BSAC and PADI certification, www.tobagodiveexperience.com.

Fishing
Contact Capt Gerard 'Frothy' De Silva, Friendship Estate, Canaan, T6397108. He has a custom-built, 38-ft sports-fishing boat, *Hard Play*, and 2, 23-ft skiffs for flats fishing.

Golf
Mount Irvine Bay, T6398871: green fee US$20 per day.
Tobago Plantations, T6399377, www.tobagoplantations.com. US$78 for one round, US$136 for 2 rounds in 5 days, driving range US$5, 30-min lesson US$30, 1 hr US$50.

Sailing
Each year Tobago has a sailing week in May, sponsored by *Angostura and Yachting World* magazine; many crewing possibilities, lots of parties.

Squash
Squash at **Grafton Beach Resort**, 0800-2200, US$9.50 for 45 mins including court, ball and racket rental.

Tennis
Mount Irvine Bay, T6398871, US$3 daytime, US$6 at night.

923

Trinidad & Tobago Tobago Listings

AJM Tours at the airport, T6390610, F6398918. Day trips on Tobago and to Margarita, Angel Falls, Grenada and the Grenadines. Peter Gremli, T6398400, is a recommended tour guide, friendly, knowledgeable and popular. Taxi drivers have set rates for sightseeing tours and can be more flexible than an organized tour. **Harris Jungle Tours**, Golden Grove Rd, Canaan, T6390513/7590170, www.harris-jungle-tours.com. Harris Macdonald offers hiking and birdwatching tours in the forest, with pick-up at 0530 so you can get there as the sun is rising and see the birds at dawn. It is also cooler then. An award-winning and certified tour guide, Harris is a lifeguard, tall, fit and capable. He knows the Latin as well as the local names for the flora and fauna. Tours are US$50-100, depending on numbers, and can include the forest, beaches, Little Tobago, Charlotteville, waterfalls and snorkelling. **Johnsons Sea Tours**, Buccoo Point, T6398519. Glass bottom boat trips to the coral gardens and Nylon pool with swimming and snorkelling, daily at 1100 from the pier at Buccoo, US$14.40. An assortment of wooden glass bottom boats offering similar tours leave from different departure points. Marine police check to see no boat damages the reef with an anchor.

Watersports

World of Watersports, at Tobago Hilton and at Pigeon Point, T6607234, www.worldofwatersports.com. The main location is at the Hilton, but because of the winds, the windsurfing centre is at Pigeon Point. Other activities offered include diving, kitesurfing, wake-boarding, water-skiing, sailing and sport fishing. Hire of mask and snorkel US$5, fins US$5, the set US$9.

◉ Transport

Tobago *p910, maps p912 and p911*

Air

There are many seasonal and regular charters to Tobago in addition to the following scheduled flights: from Barbados (**Caribbean Airlines**), Grenada (**LIAT/ Caribbean Airlines**), Amsterdam (**Martinair**), London (**British Airways**, **Excel** and **Virgin**

Atlantic) and Miami (Caribbean Airlines). Other flights connect through Port of Spain, see Transport, p908.

Car

Auto Rentals Ltd, Crown Point Airport, T6390644, F6390313. **Peter Gremli Car Rental**, Crown Point, T6398400. **Rodríguez Travel**, Clark Trace, Bethany, T6398507. **Banana Rentals** at Kariwak Village, T6398441, cars and jeeps, US$21 per day, scooters US$10 per day (deposit US$60). **Suzuki Jeep Rental** and small cars, and **Cherry Scooter Rental** at Sandy Point Beach Club scooters and deposit cheaper than Banana Rentals. **Tobago Travel**, Store Bay Rd, Crown Point, T6398778, F6398786, **Baird's**, Lower Sangster Hill Rd, T6392528. **Rollock's Car Rental Service**, Lowlands, T6390328, after hrs T6397369, US$48 per day, recommended. **Hill Crest Car Rental Service**, 47 Mt Pelier Trace, Scarborough, T/F6395208. **Thrifty Car Rental**, Turtle Beach Hotel, T6398111, and other agencies.

Bus

Buses originate in Scarborough. Every hr on the hr between **Scarborough** and Crown Point (airport), US$3.20, 25 mins. Bus Scarborough-Plymouth hourly on the hr, return on the ½ hr, half-hourly at busy times, via Carnbee, Buccoo junction, Mt Irvine and Black Rock. To **Charlotteville** 7 buses a day, US$1.30, first one at 0430, 1½ hrs and then return. Also some maxis on this route. On Tobago, route taxis charge US$0.65 and leave from Republic Bank in Scarborough. The Crown Point Airport route is the best, every 15-30 mins, 0530-1830; Black Rock route is fair, every 30 mins Mon-Fri 0530-2030, every 60-75 mins Sat and Sun until 2000. **Route taxis** to **Charlotteville** start from Burnett Sq, US$1.45-1.60 depending on whether vehicle is minibus or car, 1-1½ hrs.

Cycle

Bike repairs and parts at **Numeral Uno** hardware store in Carnbee, a good contact for joining local riders for some fun road riding. Bikes for hire from **Banana Rentals**, US$4 per day, see above.

Taxi

Taxi fares are clearly displayed as you leave

the airport: to **Crown Point** US$6, **Pigeon Point** US$7, **Scarborough** US$10, **Mt Irvine**, Roxborough US$33, **Speyside** US$40, Charlotteville US$45.

❶ Directory

Tobago *p910, maps p912 and p911*
Banks On Tobago, there are no banks in the north of the island. ATMs can be found at the airport, Penny Savers Supermarket on Milford Rd, in Charlotteville and in Scarborough. They accept Visa, Plus, MasterCard and Cirrus. **Telephone** There is a TSTT telephone office in Scarborough. Home direct service for AT&T, Sprint and MCI available from TSTT office and at the airport. **Medical services** There is a hospital in Scarborough, T6392551.

Background

History

Columbus' arrival Trinidad was discovered by Columbus and he claimed it for Spain on his third voyage in 1498. Whether he named the island after the day of the Holy Trinity, or after a group of three hills that he spied from the sea is a matter of dispute. At that time there were probably seven tribes of Amerindians living on the island. It was their hostility which prevented successful colonization until the end of the 17th century when Catalan Capuchin missionaries arrived. European diseases and the rigours of slavery took their toll on the Amerindian population and by 1824 their numbers had been reduced to 893.

Spanish rule The first Spanish Governor was Don Antonio Sedeño who arrived in 1530 but who failed to establish a permanent settlement because of Indian attacks. In 1592 Governor Don Antonio de Berrio y Oruna, founded the town of San José de Oruna (now St Joseph). It was destroyed by Sir Walter Raleigh in 1595 and not rebuilt until 1606. In 1783 a deliberate policy to encourage immigration of Roman Catholics was introduced, known as the Royal Cedula of Population, and it was from this date that organized settlement began with an influx of mostly French-speaking immigrants, particularly after the French Revolution. Many also came from St Lucia and Dominica when these islands were ceded to Britain in 1784. Others came with their slaves from the French Caribbean when slavery was abolished and from Saint Domingue after the War of Independence there (including the Compte de Lopinot, whose house in Lopinot has been restored, see page 892).

> ✤ VS Naipaul's The Loss of El Dorado *is a fascinating, if pessimistic, account of the early Spanish settlement, Sir Walter Raleigh's raid, and the early years of British rule.*

British rule British rule in Trinidad began in 1797 when an expedition led by Sir Ralph Abercromby captured the island. It was formally ceded to Britain by Spain in 1802 under the Treaty of Amiens. African slaves were imported to work in the sugar fields introduced by the French, until the slave trade was abolished in 1807. After the abolition of slavery, in 1834, labour became scarce and the colonists looked for alternative sources of workers. Several thousands of immigrants from neighbouring islands came in 1834 to 1848, and some Americans from Baltimore and Pennsylvania came in 1841 and Madeiran 'Portuguese' came seeking employment and were joined by small numbers of European immigrants – British, Scots, Irish, French, Germans and Swiss. There was also immigration of free West Africans in the 1840s. In 1844 the British Government gave approval for the import of East Indian labour and the first indentured labourers arrived in 1845. By 1917, when Indian immigration ceased, 141,615 Indians had arrived for an indentured period of five years, and although many returned to India afterwards, the majority settled. The first Chinese arrived in 1849 during a lull in Indian immigration. In 1866 the Chinese Government insisted on a return passage being paid which put an end to Chinese immigration. Labour shortages led to higher wages in Trinidad than in many other islands and from emancipation until the 1960s there was also migration from Barbados, Grenada and St Vincent. In the 1980s and 1990s there has been immigration from Guyana.

Colonial Tobago Tobago is thought to have been discovered by Columbus in 1498, when it was occupied by Caribs. In 1641 James, Duke of Courland (in Latvia), obtained a grant of the island from Charles I and in 1642 a number of Courlanders settled on the north side. In 1658 the Courlanders were overpowered by the Dutch, who remained in possession of the island until 1662. In this year Cornelius Lampsius procured Letters Patent from Louis XIV creating him the Baron of Tobago under the Crown of France. After being occupied for short periods by the Dutch and the French, Tobago was ceded by France to Britain in 1763 under the Treaty of Paris. But it was not until 1802, after further invasions by the French and subsequent recapture by the British, that it was finally ceded to Britain, becoming a Crown Colony in 1877 and in 1888 being amalgamated politically with Trinidad. By some reckonings Tobago changed hands as many as 29 times and for this reason there are a large number of forts.

Dr Eric Williams The first political organizations in Trinidad and Tobago developed in the 1880s, but in the 1930s economic depression spurred the formation of labour movements. Full adult suffrage was introduced in 1946 and political parties began to develop. In 1956, the People's National Movement (PNM) was founded by the hugely influential Dr Eric Williams, who dominated local politics until his death in 1981. The party won control of the new Legislative Council, under the new constitutional arrangements which provided for self-government, and Dr Williams became the first Chief Minister. In 1958, Trinidad and Tobago became a member of the new Federation of the West Indies, but after the withdrawal of Jamaica, in 1961, the colony, unwilling to support the poorer members of the Federation, sought the same Independence rights for Trinidad and Tobago. The country became an independent member of the Commonwealth on 31 August 1962, and became a republic within the Commonwealth on 1 August 1976. Dr Williams remained Prime Minister until his death in 1981, his party drawing on the support of the ethnically African elements of the population, while the opposition parties were supported mainly by the ethnic Indians.

Contemporary politics In 1986, the National Alliance for Reconstruction (NAR) ended 30 years' rule by the PNM, which had been hit by corruption scandals and the end of the oil boom of the 1970s, winning 33 of the 36 parliamentary seats in the general election.

The 1991 elections brought another about turn in political loyalties, with Patrick Manning, of the PNM, leading his party to victory, winning 21 seats. By mid-term the Government was suffering from unpopularity and lack of confidence. In 1995 the economy began to improve and the Prime Minister took a gamble in calling early general elections to increase his majority. His tactic failed, however, when the United National Congress (UNC), led by Basdeo Panday, and the PNM both won 17 seats. Although the PNM received 48.8% of the vote compared with 45.8% for the UNC, Basdeo Panday formed an alliance with the NAR, who again won the two Tobago seats, and he was sworn in as Prime Minister on 9 November 1995. A lawyer and trade union leader, he was the first head of government of Indian descent.

Elections were held in December 2000, after a bad-tempered campaign. The opposition PNM accused the Government of large-scale corruption. With high energy prices and continuing economic growth, the UNC claimed a record of strong 'performance' and attacked the personality of Patrick Manning (PNM leader). The UNC

won 52% of the popular vote and 19 of the 36 seats. However, the PNM disputed this
result in a number of court cases, alleging electoral malpractice.

In September 2001, three cabinet ministers were fired for speaking out against alleged government corruption. Accordingly, the UNC lost its parliamentary majority, and new elections were held in December 2001, in which both PNM and UNC won 18 seats. With no constitutional mechanism for choosing a prime minister in a 'hung' parliament, both party leaders agreed after discussions that the choice should be made by President Robinson. On Christmas Eve, he appointed Mr Manning of the PNM as Prime Minister. However, the UNC then immediately said that while the President could choose, any choice other than Mr Panday was unconstitutional. With the UNC also reneging on an agreed choice of Speaker, parliament could not function. With a number of official inquiries into corruption allegations in progress, six people including a former UNC finance minister were charged formally with corruption and money laundering in March 2002. New elections in October 2002 gave the PNM a working majority, with 20 seats to 16 for the UNC. In 2006, Mr Panday was found guilty of corruption and given a prison sentence, although he remained on bail, pending an appeal. A dissatisfied faction of the UNC set up a new party, Congress of the People, in time for the 2007 elections.

Government

Trinidad and Tobago became a republic within the Commonwealth on 1 August 1976 under a constitution which provides for a President and a bicameral Parliament comprising a 31-seat Senate and a 36-seat House of Representatives. Tobago has its own 12-seat House of Assembly, which runs many local services. In 2003 the presidential election was won by Max Richards, a former principal of the University of the West Indies. The electoral college which votes for the president is made up of the House of Representatives and the Senate.

Economy

Petroleum, natural gas and their products dominate the economy, providing about 31% of GDP, 33% of government current revenue but only 3% of employment. Production is around 150,000 barrels a day. There is one refinery, at Pointe-à-Pierre. The island has substantial proven reserves of natural gas of 733 billion cu m, producing about 28 billion cu m a year. These are used as a basic raw material for the production of petrochemicals such as methanol and ammonia, to provide liquefied natural gas for export and to provide electric power throughout the country. Trinidad's mineral deposits include asphalt from the pitch lake at La Brea on the southwest coast, gypsum, limestone, sand and gravel, which are mainly used for construction. Agriculture now contributes only 0.8% of GDP and employs only 5% of the labour force. Coffee and cocoa production has fallen and the sugar industry is being phased out. A shortage of fruits and vegetables pushed up prices by 26% in 2006.

Tourism is an important source of foreign exchange, but only really in Tobago. Of 460,195 total stopover arrivals in 2005, 33%, around 154,000, were leisure tourists staying in hotels and guesthouses, most of whom go to Tobago. Business visitors made up 18% of the total and 60% are Trinidadians and visitors staying with friends and relatives. Tobago now has 2,200 hotel rooms available, following an expansion in construction, notably a 200-room Hilton hotel, while Trinidad has slightly fewer. There were 67,000 cruise ship passengers in 2005, most of them to Port of Spain but with some to Tobago. Neither island is a major cruise port.

Culture

People Trinidad has one of the world's most cosmopolitan populations. The emancipation of the slaves in 1834 and the adoption of free trade by Britain in 1846 resulted in far-reaching social and economic changes. To meet labour shortages, over

150,000 immigrants were encouraged to settle here from India, China and Madeira. Of today's population of approximately 1,276,000, about 38% are black and 40% East Indian. The rest are mixed race, white, Syrian or Chinese. French and Spanish influences dominated for a long time (Catholicism is still strong) but gradually the English language and institutions prevailed and today the great variety of peoples has become a fairly harmonious entity, despite occasional political tension between blacks and those of East Indian descent. French patois is still spoken here and there, eg in the village of Paramin, just north of Port of Spain.

Tobago's population, mainly black, numbers about 51,000. The crime rate is catching up with Trinidad's but the people are still noticeably helpful and friendly.

Religion Catholics are still the largest religious group but Hindus are not far behind. The Anglican Church and Methodists are also influential, as are many evangelical groups and the Muslim organisations. Spiritual Baptists blend African and Christian beliefs; the women wear white robes and head ties on religious occasions. They can be seen performing baptisms in the sea on the coast to the west of Port of Spain on Sunday nights. Orishas follow a more purely African tradition. Most East Indians are Hindu, some are Muslim, while others have converted to Christianity, particularly Presbyterianism (Canadian Presbyterian missionaries were the first to try converting the Indian population).

Carnival and visual arts The most exciting introduction to the culture of this republic is the Carnival, or 'De Mas', as locals refer to the annual 'celebration of the senses'. Alongside a strong oral/literary tradition goes a highly developed visual culture, reflecting the islands' racial mix. The most obvious examples are the designs for the carnival bands, which often draw on craft skills like wire bending, copper beating, and the use of fibreglass moulds. A fabled, controversial Mas' designer is Peter Minshall, who designed the opening ceremony for the 1992 Barcelona Olympic Games and for the Atlanta Games in 1996. Michel Jean Cazabon, born 1813, was the first great local artist (an illustrated biography by Geoffrey MacLean is out of print, but there is an illustrated book on the Lord Harris Collection with plenty of information). Contemporary work to look out for includes paintings and other artwork by Christopher Cozier, Irenée Shaw, Sarah Beckett, Che Lovelace, Mario Lewis, Wendy Nanan, Emheyo Bahabba (Embah), Francisco Cabral, and Anna Serrao and Johnny Stollmeyer. Other established artists include Pat Bishop, Isaiah Boodhoo, LeRoy Clarke, Kenwyn Crichlow and Boscoe Holder. A space with contemporary work on show is **CCA7** ① *Fernandes-Angostura distillery compound, T6251889, www.cca7.org, Mon, Fri, 1200-1700, Thu, 1200-2000, Sat 1000-1700, also international artist residency programme and educational programme and Thu pm films*. Commercial galleries include **Horizons** ① *37 Mucurapo Rd, T6289769*, **101 Art Gallery** ① *Art Society Building, Corner Jamaica Blvd and St Vincent Af, Federation Park, T6284081, 101arts@tstt.net.tt*, and **Art Creators** ① *de Lima Apts, St Ann's, T6244369, close to the Normandie*.

Carnival is a national obsession. It is an extraordinary spectacle and a vibrant time to be in Trinidad. Much of the country's artistic energy is poured into these heady few days. Carnival in Trinidad is considered by many to be safer, more welcoming to visitors and artistically more stimulating than its nearest rival in Rio de Janeiro. Commercialization is undermining many of the greatest Mas' traditions, but some of the historical characters like the **Midnight Robber** and the **Moko Jumbies** can be glimpsed at the Viey La Cou old-time Carnival street theatre at Queen's Hall a week before Carnival and often at **J'Ouvert** (pronounced joo-vay) on Carnival Monday morning, and in small, independent bands of players. But it's a great party, enlivened by hundreds of thousands of costumed masqueraders and the homegrown music, calypso and steel band (usually referred to as 'pan'). The traditional venue for the majority of Carnival events, Queen's Park Savannah, is likely to be replaced from 2007 because of a major construction project, see www.ncctt.org for information.

Music and theatre Calypsonians (or kaisonians, as the more historically minded call them) are the commentators, champions and sometime conscience of the people. This unique musical form, a mixture of African, French and, eventually, British, Spanish and East Indian influences, dates back to Trinidad's first 'shantwell', Gros Jean, late in the 18th century. Since then it has evolved into a popular, potent force, with both men and women (also children, of late) battling for the Calypso Monarch's crown. This fierce competition takes place at the Sunday night Dimanche Gras show, which in turn immediately precedes the official start of J'Ouvert at 0400 on the Monday morning, marking the beginning of Carnival proper. Calypsonians band together to perform in 'tents' (performing halls) in the weeks leading up to the competition and are judged in semi-finals, which hones down the list to six final contenders. The season's songs blast from radio stations and sound systems all over the islands and visitors should ask locals to interpret the sometimes witty and often scurrilous lyrics, for they are a fascinating introduction to the state of the nation. Currently, party soca tunes dominate, although some of the commentary calypsonians, like Sugar Aloes, are still heard on the radio. There is also a new breed of 'Rapso' artists, fusing calypso and rap music. Chutney, an Indian version of calypso, is also becoming increasingly popular, especially since the advent of radio stations devoted only to Indian music. Chutney is also being fused with soca, to create 'chutney soca'.

Pan music has a shorter history, developing this century from the tamboo-bamboo bands which made creative use of tins, dustbins and pans plus lengths of bamboo for percussion instruments. By the end of the Second World War (during which Carnival was banned) some ingenious souls discovered that huge oil drums could be converted into expressive instruments, their top surfaces tuned to all ranges and depths (the ping pong, or soprano pan, embraces 28 to 32 notes, including both the diatonic and chromatic scales). Aside from the varied pans, steel bands also include a rhythm section dominated by the steel, or iron men. For Carnival, the steel bands compete in the grand Panorama, playing calypsoes which are also voted on for the Road March of the Year. Biennally, the **World Steel Band Festival** highlights the versatility of this music, for each of the major bands must play a work by a classical composer as well as a calypso of their choice. On alternate years the National Schools Steel Band Festival is held, in late October/early November. A pan jazz festival is held annually in November, with solos, ensembles and orchestras all emphasizing the versatility of the steel drum, www.pantrinbago.co.tt.

Other musical forms in this music-mad nation include parang (pre-Christmas). Part of the islands' Spanish heritage, parang is sung in Spanish and accompanied by guitar, cuatro, mandolin and tambourine. The big annual **parang** competitions are at Paramin, in a natural hillside amphitheatre, and at Lopinot. For the Hindu and Muslim festivals, there are East Indian drumming and vocal styles such as chowtal, which is particularly associated with Phagwa in early March.

Throughout the year, there are regular performances of plays and musicals, often by Caribbean dramatists, and concerts by fine choirs such as the **Marionettes Chorale** and the **Lydian Singers**, often accompanied by a steel band. There is a lot of comedy and some serious plays too, see press for details. Theatres include the **Little Carib Theatre** (T6224644), the **Central Bank Auditorium** (T6230845) and **Queen's Hall** (T6241284) and the **Naparima Bowl** (T6524704) in southern Trinidad. Occasional performances at **Under the Trees at Normandie** (T6241181).

Flora and fauna
The rainforests of the **Northern Range** running along the north coast and the wetlands

929

Trinidad & Tobago Background

on the east and west coast are more extensive, more dense and display a greater diversity of fauna and flora than any other ecosystems in the Caribbean. The **Forestry Division** ⓘ *Long Circular Rd, St James, Port of Spain, T6224521*, information on guided tours and hikes) has designated many parts of Trinidad and Tobago as national parks, wildlife reserves and protected areas. On Trinidad, the national parks are the Caroni and Nariva Swamps, Matura and Chaguaramas.

❢ *Trinidad combines the species of the Caribbean chain from Jamaica to Grenada with the species of the continental rainforests of South America.*

Many flowering trees can be seen on the islands: pink and yellow poui, frangipani, cassia, pride of India, immortelle, flamboyant, jacaranda. Among the many types of flower are hibiscus, poinsettia, chaconia (wild poinsettia – the national flower), ixora, bougainvillea, orchid, ginger lily and heliconia. The **Horticultural Society of Trinidad and Tobago** (PO Box 252) has its office on Lady Chancellor Road, Port of Spain, T6226423.

The islands are home to 60 types of bat, and other mammals include the Trinidad capuchin and red howler monkeys, brown forest brocket (deer), collared peccary (quenk), manicou (opossum), agouti, rare ocelot and armadillo. A small group of manatees is being protected in a reserve in the Nariva Swamp. Other reptiles include iguanas and 47 species of snakes, of which few are poisonous: the fer-de-lance (locally, *mapipire*), bushmaster and two coral snakes. The variety of fauna on Tobago is larger than on other similar-sized islands because of its one-time attachment to South America. It is home to 210 different bird species, 123 different butterfly species, 16 types of lizards, 14 kinds of frogs, 24 species of snakes (all of them harmless), and it has some spectacled caymans at Hillsborough Dam.

Trinidad and Tobago together have more species of birds than any other Caribbean island, although the variety is South American, not West Indian. No species is endemic, but Tobago has 13 species of breeding birds not found on Trinidad. Some estimates say that there are 433 species of bird, including 41 hummingbirds, parrots, macaws, the rare red-breasted blackbird, the nightingale-thrush and the mot mot. There are also 622 recorded species of butterfly. The most accessible birdwatching sites are the **Caroni Bird Sanctuary**, the **Asa Wright Centre**, the Caurita Plantation and the **Wild Fowl Trust**.

Each October Trinidad and Tobago hold **Natural History Festivals** to foster understanding of the islands' flora and fauna. The **Trinidad Field Naturalists Club** ⓘ *PO Box 642, Port of Spain, T6248017 (evenings only)*, organizes walks on Sunday.

Wetlands Trinidad has mangrove swamps, fresh swamps, grassy freshwater marshes, palm marshes and water-logged savannah land, covering 7,000 acres of the Central Plain. A permit from the Wildlife Section of the Forestry Division (T6625114) is necessary for trips into restricted areas such as the Nariva Swamp and Bush Bush Island in the Aripo Scientific Reserve; 72 hours' notice is required; visit with a guide who can arrange it for you. The **Nariva Swamp**, the largest freshwater swamp in Trinidad, is a Wetland of International Importance under the Ramsar Convention. It contains hardwood forest and is home to red howler monkeys and the weeping capuchin as well as 55 other species of mammal of which 32 are bats. Birds include the savannah hawk and the red-breasted blackbird. A tour by kayak is recommended (**Caribbean Discovery Tours**, T6247281) as you will see more than you would on a motor boat. You paddle silently across fields of giant water lilies, through channels in the thick forest of mangroves and towering silk cotton trees, with monkeys and parrots chattering overhead. The **Caroni Swamp** is usually visited in the late afternoon as it is the roosting place of scarlet ibis and egrets.

Rainforests The **Northern Range Sanctuary**, Maracas, or **El Tucuche Reserve**, is a forest on the second-highest peak, at 3072 ft, covering 2313 acres. The slopes are covered with forest giants such as the silk cotton trees, which carry creepers and vines. The thick forest canopy of mahogany, balata, palms and flowering trees like the poui and immortelle provides cover and maintains a cool, damp environment no matter the heat of the day. The interesting flora and fauna include giant bromeliads and orchids, the golden tree frog and the orange-billed nightingale-thrush. There are several hiking trails, the most popular of which is from Ortinola estate (Maracas, St Joseph valley, which is on other side of mountains from Maracas beach; guides can be hired. The seven-mile trek to the peak takes five hours through dense forest; the views from the top are spectacular; for information on hiking contact the **Field Naturalists' Club** (see above). Much easier is the three-hour trail to Maracas beach from Gasparillo village in Santa Cruz, not to be confused with Gasparillo near San Fernando. The trail is kept clear by a job-creation scheme and is easy to follow.

> ♣ Walking alone is not recommended in the northern hills; join a group or go with someone who knows the trails well.

The **Trinity Hills Wildlife Sanctuary** lies west of Guayaguayare and was founded in 1934. Its forests are home to a large variety of birds, monkeys, armadillos and opossums. Permits can be obtained from the Wildlife Section of the Forestry Division (T6625114).

The **Valencia Wildlife Sanctuary** has mostly been destroyed due to extensive quarrying in the area. No permit needed. The **Arena Forest**, is one of about 10 recreation parks, while five areas have been designated scenic landscapes (Blanchisseuse, Maracas and Toco-Matelot on the north coast, Cocos Bay on the Atlantic, and Mount Harris on the Southern Road, south of Sangre Grande). Permission to visit certain forests and watershed areas must be obtained from the **Water and Sewerage Authority (WASA)** ① *Farm Rd, Valsayn, St Joseph*. Although about 31% of the island remains forested, there is concern about the loss of wildlife habitats, with damage from hunting, illegal logging and quarrying and clearing of wetland for rice cultivation.

On Tobago, apart from two reserves (Buccoo Reef and the virgin and secondary forests of east Tobago), there are the **Goldsborough** natural landmark, the **Kilgwyn** wetland, which it is hoped will be designated a scientific reserve, the **Grafton** nature conservation area, the **Parlatuvier-Roxborough** scenic landscape, and three recreation parks (including Mount Irvine). The Main Ridge Rainforest is the oldest rainforest reserve in the Western Hemisphere but has not yet been made a national park. At the **Grafton Bird Sanctuary** some of the world's most beautiful birds, the blue crowned mot mots, are fed at 0800 and 1600 at the Old Copra House. They are not tame enough to be hand-fed but it is still a spectacular sight. Many of the small islands (Saut d'Eau, Kronstadt Island and Soldado Rock off Trinidad, and Little Tobago, St Giles and Marble Islands off Tobago) are reserves for wildlife with the largest seabird colonies in the southern Caribbean. They are important breeding grounds for red-billed tropic birds, frigate birds, man-o-war and other seabirds. A permit is needed to visit these areas, usually arranged through a tour guide.

> ♣ It is possible to do voluntary work with Environment Tobago, Robinson St, Rollocks Building, Scarborough, T6607462.

Books

Some authors to investigate are CLR James, Samuel Selvon, Shiva Naipaul, all now deceased, as well as Shiva's more famous brother, VS Naipaul, who in 2001 won the Nobel Prize for Literature. Another Nobel winner, the St Lucian Derek Walcott, spent many years with the Trinidad Theatre Workshop. Also, look out for works by the historian and past prime minister Dr Eric Williams, Earl Lovelace and Valerie Belgrave (whose Ti Marie has been described as the 'Caribbean *Gone with the Wind*'). Although the tradition of performance poetry is not as strong here as in, say, Jamaica (calypso fulfils some of its role), the monologues of Paul Keens-Douglas, some of which are on album or cassette, are richly entertaining and a great introduction to the local dialect or patois (if now somewhat dated).

Barrow, Russel *Birds of Trinidad and Tobago – A Photographic Atlas* (MEP Trinidad, 1994, out of print). Has clear and striking pictures.

Comeau, P, L Guy, E Heesterman, and H Clayton The Trinidad and Tobago Field Naturalists' Club Trail Guide (1992). 288 pages on 48 trails, difficult to obtain.

Ffrench, Richard *A Guide to the Birds of Trinidad and Tobago* (Cornell University Press), Introductory information on rainfall, the environment and vegetation as well as birds. Recommended.

Ffrench, Richard *Birds of Trinidad and Tobago* (Macmillan Caribbean Pocket Natural History Series). A shorter guide with colour photos of 83 of the more common species.

Ffrench and Bacon *Nature Trails of Trinidad*, First published in 1982, has been revised by Dr Victor Quesnel and reissued by SM Publications Ltd under the auspices of the Asa Wright Nature Centre.

Kenny, Julian *Views from the Ridge* (Prospect Press). This beautifully produced and illustrated work by a respected local biologist is now out of print, but *Flowers of Trinidad and Tobago* came out in 2006 and can be found in Nigel Khan bookshops.

Smailes, Alex *Trinidad and Tobago* (Macmillan, 2006). A beautiful book of photographs with introduction by Jeremy Taylor.

★ Don't miss...

1 Washington/Slagbaai National Park Occupying the northern part of Bonaire, this park is a haven for around 190 species of bird. Visitors can drive on trails through the bush and past deserted beaches and bays, page 940.

2 Salt works Bonaire's salt pans are a stunning pink/purple colour while the piles of salt are a brilliant white, looking like mountains of snow. Thousands of flamingos build their conical nests here, page 940.

3 Willemstad One of the most attractive capital cities in the Caribbean, a model of Dutch colonial architecture with tall pastel-painted buildings, page 949.

4 Christoffel Park The park includes an array of fauna and flora, including tiny Curaçao deer, with a network of trails for a stroll or a hike, page 955.

5 Fisherman's Huts Aruba is popular with windsurfers and kitesurfers and this area guarantees high speeds and strong offshore winds, page 973.

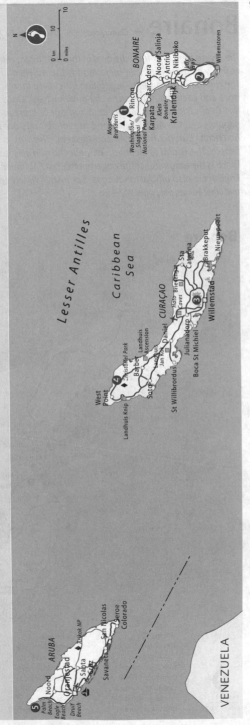

Bonaire → *Country code: 599. Colour map 5, B2. Population: 12,000.*

The diving here is among the best in the Caribbean, with pristine reefs and wonderful visibility as there is no run-off to muddy the waters and it is out of the hurricane belt. The climate is dry and the vegetation little more than scrub, slow-growing hardwood trees and cactus but it is prized by birdwatchers. Once important as a salt producer, this Dutch island now makes its living out of tourism. Bonaire is the least densely populated of the ABC islands and the inhabitants are mostly of mixed native South American, European and African descent. They are a very friendly and hospitable people. The island is clean, quiet, peaceful and very safe. As in Curaçao and Aruba, Dutch is the language of the government, but Papiamentu, the colloquial tongue, and English are also official languages. Spanish is widely spoken too. ▸▸ *For Sleeping, Eating and other listings, see pages 942-948.*

Netherlands Antilles, ABC Islands Bonaire

Bonaire

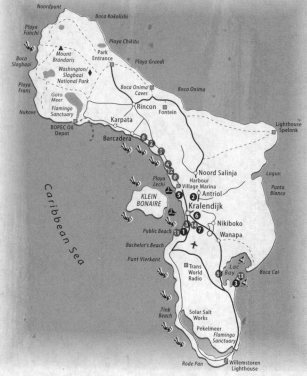

N

0 km 2
0 miles 2

Sleeping 🛏
Black Durgon Inn & Pilot
  Fish Apartments **2**
Bruce Bowker's Carib Inn **3**
Buddy Beach & Dive Resort **4**
Captain Don's Habitat **5**
Caribbean Club Bonaire **6**
Eden Beach Resort **8**

Lac Bay Resort &
  Kontiki Beach Club **9**
Palm Studios **14**
Plaza Resort Bonaire **11**
Port Bonaire Resort **11**
Sand Dollar Condominium
  Resort **12**
Sorobon Beach Resort **13**

Eating 🍴
Casablanca **1**
Garden Café **5**
Hang Out **3**
Lost Penguin **6**
Papaya Moon **2**
Swiss Chalet **7**

Touching down

Departure tax Departure Tax for all international destinations is US$32 per person, payable in cash or debit/credit card (MC, Visa, Discover, Maestro, Kompa Leon all accepted, but American Express is not) at the airport prior to check-in. Departure tax to Curaçao and Aruba is lower.

Hours of business Shops: Mon-Sat 0800-1200, 1400-1800, although about half the stores close Sat pm and nearly everything is closed Sun and holidays. **Supermarkets**: 0800-1900, and some on Sun 0900-1400. **Banks**: are normally open Mon-Fri 0800-1530.

Media Newspapers: The *Bonaire Reporter* is the island's weekly English- language newspaper full of information of interest to visitors and is available free on Bonaire or on the internet at www.bonairereporter .com. **Radio**: The news is broadcast in Dutch on Voz di Bonaire, FM 94.7 MHz, Mon-Sat on the hour 0700-1800. Transworld Radio broadcasts in English on 800 KHz MW daily 0700-0830, 2200- 2400, news Mon-Fri 0700, daily 0800 and 2200, Sat and Sun 2300; Caribbean weather forecast Mon-Fri 0730, Sat and Sun 0800. Radio Nederland, 6020 KHz at 0630, 6165 and 15315 KHz at 2030, 9590 and 11720 KHz at 2330. The Papiamento broadcast is on 97.1 and 102.5 FM.

Public holidays New Year's Day, Good Fri, Easter Mon, Queen's Birthday and Rincon Day (30 Apr), Labour Day (1 May), Ascension Day, Bonaire Day (6 Sep), Christmas Day and Boxing Day.

Tourist information Bonaire **Tourist Office**, Kaya Grandi 2, Kralendijk, T7178322, www.InfoBonaire.com. The **Bonaire Hotel and Tourism Association (Bonhata)** is at T7175134, info@bonhata.org. The Bonaire tourist map shows all the dive and snorkelling sites.

Tourist offices overseas
Netherlands: Basis Communicatie BV, Wagenweg 252, PO Box 472, NL-2000 AL Haarlem, T31-23 5430705, Europe@tourismbonaire .com. **USA**: Adams Unlimited, 80 Broad St, 32nd floor, Suite 3202, New York, NY 10004, T212-9565912, usa@tourismbonaire.com.
Venezuela: Flamingo Representaciones, Av Humboldt, Edif Humboldt, Piso 1 Apt 5, urb Bello Monte, Caracas, T58-212 9534653, southamerica@tourismbonaire.com.
Voltage 127 volts, 50 cycles. 220 volts available at some resorts.

Netherlands Antilles, ABC Islands Bonaire

Ins and outs

Getting there Long-distance regular direct flights come from Amsterdam, Houston and New York, while additional connecting flights from the USA and Europe come via Aruba, Curaçao, Montego Bay, Jamaica and San Juan, Puerto Rico, and there are charter flights from other destinations in season. ▶ *See Transport, page 947 for further details.*

Getting around There is no scheduled bus service, but so-called *autobuses* (AB on the licence plate) pass at certain places in town and take you where want to go for a few guilders. There are taxis at the airport but they are difficult to find around the island. Taxis do not 'cruise' so you must telephone for one, T7178100. The best way of getting about is to hire a car, scooter or mountain bike. Distances are not great but the heat can be. Some hotels have a free shuttle service to town. Hitching is fairly easy and safe.

Kralendijk → *Population: 1,690.*

Kralendijk, meaning coral dike, the capital of Bonaire, is a small, sleepy town with colourful buildings most one or two storeys high. However, some newer buildings near the shore are four storeys. It is often referred to locally as simply *Playa*, because of its historic position as the main beach landing place. The town is just a few blocks long with several streets projecting inland. A 1.5-km seaside promenade extends from the northern end of Kralendijk, south to the **Divi Flamingo** hotel. Most of the shops are in the small **Harbourside Shopping Mall** and on the main street, the name of which changes from J A Abraham Boulevard to Kaya Grandi to Kaya Gobornador Debrot. The **Museum** ① *(Department of Culture) Kaya J van der Ree 7, or Kaya Sabana 14, T7178868, Mon-Fri 0800-1200, 1300-1700, small donation requested*, tucked away on a side street near the big Catholic church with the clock tower, houses snippets of folklore, art, archaeology, old photographs and a shell collection. Small enough for you to get personal attention if you want it. **Fort Oranje** has been renovated and now houses the Bonairean Court of Justice as well as a permanent archaeological collection with items found during the renovation. The shorefront plaza, **Wilhelminaplein**, has a monument to the Bonaireans who were killed in the Merchant Marine in the Second World War, and a **vegetable market** built like a Greek temple.

Around the island

The island can be toured in a day if you start early but it is more pleasant to do a north tour on one day and a south tour another. Take food and drinks, there are rarely any

Kralendijk

Not to scale

Sleeping 🛏
Dive Inn 2

Divi Flamingo Beach
Resort & Casino 1
Rochaline 3

Eating 🍴
Mona Lisa 3
Zeezicht 5

La Dania's Leap

Divers and snorkellers can have a thrilling, yet safe, experience by doing a drift dive from shore. First drive north on the 'tourist road' to the La Dania's leap dive site. Bonaire's best sites are identified by a painted yellow rock with the site's name. Unload your gear. Have the driver continue another 1 km and park the car at the Karpata dive site. After he/she walks back to the group, proceed to the edge of the cliff. Don your gear and jump into the sea. It's less than a 2 m drop. Turn right and head north. The coral here is especially beautiful and massive. Swim slowly because the slight current will push you along. You will know you are coming to your exit point when you pass a huge, old ship's anchor. The exit at Karpata has an old concrete pier and steps carved in the cliff. Your car is a five-ten minute walk back. This adventure should take about 45 minutes.

available along the way, and aim to picnic somewhere you can swim to cool off. Dominating the skyline outside Kralendijk is a long hill or **Seru Largu**. A good paved road leads to the top for spectacular views of the town, the small island of Klein Bonaire, the salt hills and the surrounding sea and farmland. It's quiet and undeveloped except for a few benches, and is a favourite spot for a picnic.

North of Kralendijk

North of Kralendijk the road passes most of the hotels, past the Power and Water Distillation Plant along the 'scenic' road, which offers several descents to the sea and some excellent spots for snorkelling along the rocky coastline. The first landmark is the Radio Netherlands station which has masses of aerials. Note that the road becomes one-way after the radio station, do not turn round. At the abandoned Karpata Landhuis, if you turn right you go directly to Rincon, climbing to the top of the hill for a steep descent and a good view of Rincon and the Windward coast. Alternatively, continue along to the Bonaire Petroleum Company Tank Farm (BOPEC) where the road turns inland to **Goto Meer Lake**, the best place to see flamingos close up, and another road to Rincon.

The road is new and smooth but narrow; watch out for the sunbathing iguanas and lizards.

Every Saturday the sleepy village of **Rincon**, Bonaire's oldest settlement where the slaves' families lived, comes alive with a street market, the *Marshé Rincon*. It wasn't intended as a tourist attraction but has become one for the visitors lucky enough to find out about it. Dozens of stands are set up to sell fresh produce, plants, handicrafts, pastries, local foods, clothing and assorted goods. It is the only scheduled time for the **Soldachi (hermit crab) tours** ① *T7172670 or 7176435, wilmari@bonairelive.com, walking tour 0900-1000, US$5.60; bus tour 1030-1200, US$10*. The tours leave from the Marshé centre and are either on foot, with a guide who explains the architecture, history and culture of Rincon, or by bus, around Rincon, the Lourdes Grotto, the Altamira overlook, Ita's Garden and the museum at Washington Park.

East of Rincon is a side road to the **Boca Onima** caves with their Arawak Indian inscriptions. Inscriptions can still be seen in several caves around the island. The springs of **Fontein** are unique on the island. On Bonaire it's very unusual to see fresh water pouring through the walls of a cave and flowing freely down the hill. The water has nurtured huge trees and tropical fruit groves along its path. You can tour the area, picnic and cool off in one of three pools fed by the spring water. Fontein is open on an irregular schedule and you must pass by to see if it is open. Fortunately, it is a few minutes off the main Kralendijk to Rincon road and is well marked.

Bonaire Sky Park

Bonaire's skies are usually clear and always free of pollution. Residents like to call the heavens at night the Sky Park; a place where there's no admission fee and nature holds sway. One of the best features of the Sky Park is the fact that it holds both northern and southern hemisphere stars. During the winter peak tourist season, just after dark, you'll see two bright stars winking emerald and white light at you. The brighter, although not by much, is Sirius, the Dog Star, the eye of Canis Major, familiar to those who live in the north. But the other is a true southern star, the wonderful Canopus, that bright star that most northerners have never seen. In fact it's the second brightest star visible from Earth. If you wait until midnight you'll easily spot the Southern Cross low in the southern sky. And if you can stay awake for a couple more hours you can spot Alpha Centauri, the star closest to Earth, rising just as Canopus sets. The dark east side of Bonaire has the best viewing.

Washington/Slagbaai National Park

ⓘ *Daily 0800-1700 (no entry after 1500). NAf17.50, US$10, children up to 15, NAf 5, US$3. Mountain bikes are welcome, but make sure they are in top condition; other 2-wheeled transport is not permitted. Toilets at the entrance. Bring food and plenty of water.*

The road leading north from Rincon takes you to Washington/Slagbaai National Park, established in 1969, which occupies the north portion of the island, about 5,460 ha, and contains more than 190 species of birds.

There is a small store selling food, drinks and souvenirs at the entrance. Behind the shop there are displays of traditional crafts of lime and charcoal making, a walking trail and an outstanding museum of local historical items plus a room with geological explanations, bird pictures, the reconstruction of a huge whale (the largest in the Caribbean) and a shell collection. Several easy to challenging hiking trails begin behind the entrance. You can choose to drive a 34-km or a 24-km tour, the roads being marked by yellow or green arrows. You will get a route map when you pay to get in. The road is dirt, rough in parts, and the long route, which passes lovely beaches (including Playa Cocolishi, almost paved in tiny shells), can be hot and tiring but is less hilly. It is possible to drive round in an ordinary car but many car rental agencies discourage the use of their normal cars, especially after rain, and a pick-up or 4WD is preferable. Once you have chosen your route you have to stick to it. Even the short route takes a minimum of two hours. There are guided hiking excursions up **Mount Brandaris**, Bonaire's highest hill, or you can do it on your own; hiking trails have been marked. An area has been set aside for rappelling. You can drive to view Goto Meer on the longer route but the view is better from the observation point outside the park. The return to Kralendijk is inland through the villages of **Noord Salinja** and **Antriol**.

South of Kralendijk

The tour south passes the airport and Trans World Radio's towering 213-m antenna. The salt pier dominates the view along the coastal road and the **salt pans** are a stunning pink/purple colour. Further on are the snow-white salt piles and the three obelisks which guided the sailing ships coming to load salt: blue, white, and orange, dating from 1838, with the tiny huts that sheltered the slaves who worked the salt pans. Thousands of flamingos build their conical nests here.

‡ *The flamingos are easily frightened, so move quietly if near them.*

At the southern tip of the island is **Willemstoren**, one of Bonaire's three main lighthouses, which dates from 1837. Pass Sorobon Beach and the mangrove swamps to **Boca Cai** at landlocked **Lac Bay**, with its clear water excellent for underwater exploration. The extensive sea grass beds and surrounding mangroves are an important nursery for marine creatures. Near the Sorobon Resort is the Sea Hatch Bonaire shrimp farming project. Tours can be arranged. Stop at the office to check. Take the road back to Kralendijk through the village of **Nikiboko,** or a straight route west to the airport area. There is a **Donkey Sanctuary** ① *T5607607, donkeyshelp@ bonairelive.com, Tue-Sun 1000-1600, US$10*, just south of the airport, founded in the mid-1990s by a Dutch woman, Marina Melis. She is mother to hundreds of donkeys which were penned in after island residents became tired of hitting them on the roads. However many donkeys are still free, so exercise extra caution after dark. It is a well-organized facility and visitors are encouraged. A drive-through safari park is part of the attraction, but most of the 'action' is at the entrance.

Beaches and activities

Bonaire is not noted for its beaches; the sand is usually full of coral and rather hard on the feet, and those on the west coast are narrow, although beaches in front of some hotels have been helped with extra sand. They do offer peace and quiet, though, and you will not get pestered by people trying to sell you things. **Pink Beach**, at the southern tip of the island is popular, the water is shallow and good for swimming, but the sand is gritty. **Sorobon Beach** is a private, family-oriented nudist resort where non-guests pay US$15 for daily admission. Kai at **Lac Bay** has an area of mangroves at the north end of the bay and a sheltered beach ideal for toddlers. In the northeast **Playa Chiquitu** is pleasant for sunbathing but has strong surf. In Washington-Slagbaai National Park are two attractive bays: **Playa Funchi**, which is good for snorkelling, but has no sand and **Boca Slagbaai**, where the restored colonial buildings are available for overnight stays and you can see flamingoes wading in the salt pans behind the beach.

> ⁝ *Be careful at east coast beaches; the surf is strong and it is dangerous to swim everywhere except within Lac Bay.*

Diving Bonaire's combination of low rainfall, little run-off, fringing reef and gin-clear water with visibility of 30 m or more makes for diving that is unsurpassed in the Caribbean. Bonaire's reefs have been protected since 1971. Surrounding the island are corals harbouring over a thousand different species of marine creatures. Ranked as one of the top dive spots in the world, Bonaire led the movement for preservation of underwater resources. Surrounding the whole island is a protected marine park from the high water mark down to 60 m. Two areas have been designated marine reserves, with no diving allowed along Playa Frans, north to Boca Slagbaai, and west of Karpata. Lac Bay, a natural nursery for fish, is also part of the Marine Park because of its extensive mangroves and seagrass beds. Stringent laws passed in 1971 ban spearfishing and the removal of any marine life from Bonaire's waters. It is a serious offence to disturb the natural life of the coral reefs. Permanent anchors have been placed in all dive sites to avoid doing any unwarranted damage. Do not: touch the coral or other underwater life, such as sea horses; move anything to create a better photo; feed the fish, as it is not natural and encourages more aggressive species; or drop litter. A US$25 per person levy for maintenance of the Marine and Land Park has to be paid only once every calendar year. You will be given a Park tag to wear on your gear when scuba diving and a receipt to show for free entrance to Washington Park. If you do not scuba dive the cost of the tag is US$10.

On the east side of the island there is a shelf and a drop-off about 12 m from the shore down to a 30-m coral shelf and then another drop down to the ocean floor. The sea is rather rough on that side for most of the year although it sometimes calms down in October or November. Along the built-up 'hotel' west side of the island the sea is calm and there are numerous snorkel and dive sites of varying depths with wrecks as well as reefs. The most frequently dived sites include **Rappel, Pink Beach,**

Small Wall, **Angel City** and the **Town Pier**. There are also dozens of sites for boat dives off the island Klein Bonaire, just 1½ km from Kralendijk. *Bonaire Diving Made Easy* is recommended for divers and snorkelers who will be diving from shore and can be obtained from dive shops for US$12.

Sea turtles can be seen at numerous sites around Bonaire and Klein Bonaire. Turtle spotters can report sightings to the **Sea Turtle Conservation Bonaire** (**STCB**) ① *T7172225 or T7900433*, via a form available in all dive shops, or contact the **Bonaire Marine Park** ① *T7178444, www.bmp.org*. During the sea turtle nesting season transmitters are attached to selected male and female turtles to track their movements. After mating and birthing Bonaire's turtles have been recorded swimming thousands of kilometres to feed in remote corners of the Caribbean. In January, after the hatching season, the island's year-round resident turtles are tagged. Visitors are invited to accompany the biologists during both of these activities free of charge. Contact the **STCB** (see above) to arrange it.

All dive operations are well equipped and well staffed with excellent safety records. If booking a package deal check whether their week-long dive packages include nightly night dives, or only one a week. For less experienced divers it is worth choosing a dive boat which keeps staff on board while the leader is underwater, in case you get into difficulties. Shore diving is available nearly everywhere, weather and sea conditions permitting. The guide book *Bonaire Diving Made Easy* details the entry and dive site conditions. There is a recompression chamber at the San Francisco Hospital Emergency Room and doctors trained in hyperbaric medicine.

Windsurfing Conditions are ideal for windsurfing with winds of 15-25 knots in December to August and 12-18 knots in September to November. On the leeward side, offshore winds allow you to windsurf in protected water. At Lac Bay on the windward side of the island, where the water is calm and shallow, there is a constant onshore wind making it safe and easy to learn the sport. The bay is about 8 sq km but a coral reef just outside the bay breaks up the waves. However, the adventurous can get out of the bay at one end where long, high waves enable you to wave ride, jump or loop. Kitesurfing is also increasingly popular and there is a kite school at the Atlantis dive site on the southwest coast.

● Sleeping

A US$5.50-6.50 per person per night government tax and 10-15% service charge must be added. Anyone who doesn't charge the tax is unregistered, unregulated and therefore illegal. High season rates (16 Dec to 2 weeks after Easter) are roughly double low-season rates in the more expensive hotels; the cheaper ones tend to charge the same all year round. Aug is 'family month' with lots of good deals. All the hotels with on-site dive shops, and some others besides, offer dive packages which give better value than the rack rates listed here. In addition there are lots of apartments and condos for rent, not mentioned here. Ask at the tourist office for details.

Kralendijk *p938, map p938*
AL-A Dive Inn, Kaya CEB Hellmund 27,

T7178761, www.diveinnbonaire.com. 7 basic studios, kitchenettes. Next to Dive Inn dive shop, own pier across the road. Owner operated, voted second best value in the Caribbean by German dive magazine.
A Blue Divers Apartments attached to Blue Divers Diveshop, Kaya Norwega 1, T7176860, www.bluedivers-bonaire.com. 10 studios sleep 2 or 3, a/c, kitchen, big garden, clean, cosy, pool, recommended for budget travellers/divers, popular and often full.
A Hotel Rochaline, Kaya Grandi 7, T7178286, www.hotelrochalinebonaire.com. Renovated 2006, 17 rooms on first floor overlooking sea or street, new beds, a/c, TV, phone, bar facing sea, City restaurant and café next door for breakfast, lunch and dinner, café open until 0200, cybercafé. On site WannaDive dive shop is top notch.

North of Kralendijk *p939, map p936*

LL-L Sand Dollar Condominium Resort, Kaya Gobernador N Debrot 79, T7178738, www.divesanddollar.com. 76 somewhat gloomy seaside apartments, all privately owned and rented via the resort, a/c, rocky shoreline, tennis, pool, day spa.

LL-AL Captain Don's Habitat, Kaya Gob N Debrot 103, T7178290. www.habitatdiveresorts .com. 93 nicely furnished sea view rooms, studios, suites, villas, well laid out seafront bar and restaurant, dive packages, family packages, pool, Bonaire's pioneer dive shop.

L-AL Buddy Beach and Dive Resort, Kaya Gob N Debrot 85, T7175080, www.buddydive .com. Rooms and 1-3 bedroom apartments with garden or sea views, a/c, kitchen, 3 pools, restaurant and bar, hammocks, **Buddy Watersports Center**. Enthusiastic staff and management. Especially good value for groups, with 7-day drive and dive packages of accommodation, double cabin pick-up truck, unlimited air fills, 6 boat dives and breakfast.

L-AL Eden Beach Resort, Kaya Gobernador N Debrot 74, T7176720. Good value rooms, studios and apartments, pool, well-equipped, **WannaDive** dive shop and **Bongos Restaurant** on the premises.

L-A Caribbean Club Bonaire, Blvd Santa Barbara 50, T7177901, www.caribbeanclubbonaire.com. Rooms, bungalows and villas, good value, cosy, secluded, nice bar and snack restaurant, internet lounge, pool.

AL-A Black Durgon Inn, Kaya Gobernador N Debrot 145, T7175/36, rona@blackdurgon.com. 10-room bed and breakfast inn, simple facilities, 1-bedroom apartments, 2/3-bedroom villa, with view of Klein Bonaire, common cooking facilities, guest fridges, a laid-back dive shop, shore dives only but unlimited air refills for guests, good gear storage, excellent diving and snorkelling offshore, very friendly and popular.

South of Kralendijk *p940, map p936*

LL-L Divi Flamingo Beach Resort & Casino, J A Abraham Blvd 40, T7178285, www.divibonaire.com. Large and colourful hotel, standard rooms, suites or more luxurious, is on a small artificial beach, snorkelling or diving just off the beach is excellent, dive shop, 2 pools, jacuzzi, 2 restaurants, casino, beauty salon and spa.

LL-L Port Bonaire Resort, Kaya International, T7172450, www.portbonaire .com. Part of the **Plaza Resort**, a condo-resort, villas and apartments, on waterfront, no beach, pool, dock.

LL-L Sorobon Beach Resort, at Lac Bay, T7178080, www.sorobonbeachresort.com. Naturist resort, 30 spacious a/c chalets on the beach, restaurant for hotel guests, small shop for self-catering, free trips to town for shopping daily, free snorkelling, kayaks, windsurfing. Internet facility, no TV anywhere. Ultra relaxed ambiance with rustic luxury.

LL-AL Lac Bay Resort and Kontiki Beach Club, Kaminda Sorobon 64, T7175369, www.kontikibonaire.com. In protected nature area, studios, apartments and 3-bedroom villa, good view from **Kon Tiki** restaurant and bar, playground, run by couple with young children, family friendly.

LL-AL Plaza Resort Bonaire, J A Abraham Blvd 80, T7172500, www.plazaresortbonaire.com. 200 rooms, suites and villas, diving, tennis, volley ball, watersports, casino, pool, beach, striving to be 5-star resort.

L-AL Bruce Bowker's Carib Inn, J A Abraham Blvd 46, T7178819, www.caribinn.com. Rooms, apartments and 3-bedroom house, a/c, cable TV, pool with Wi-Fi internet access, dive shop. Owner-operated, plain but complete accommodations, usually hard to book at short notice.

🍴 Eating

A 10-15% tip is often added automatically to the bill. Food is imported, so market fruit and veg are pricey. Try local dishes such as salt fish, goat stew or funchi (corn meal polenta). International food at the major hotels varies on different nights of the week with barbecues, Italian or Indonesian nights, etc. There are over 80 restaurants on this small island including lots of good-value Chinese restaurants open for lunch and dinner. Main courses in the upper-priced restaurants are about US$12-25, but several do bar snacks, 'Bar Hap', if you want to economize.

Water comes from a desalinization plant, has an excellent taste and is safe to drink. Take water with you on excursions. Do not, however, wash in or drink water from outside taps. This is often *sushi* (dirty) water, treated sufficiently for watering plants but nothing more.

Kralendijk *p938, map p936*

Mona Lisa, on Kaya Grandi, T7178718. Mon-Fri 1700-2200. Bar and restaurant, interesting, imaginative food, Dutch brown bar atmosphere. Friendly service, popular with Europeans but all welcome.

Papaya Moon, Kaya Grandi 48, T7175025. Tue-Sun, dinner only. Modern Tex Mex and ranch cuisine, in historic town house, a/c dining room or garden dining.

Richard's Waterfront Dining, J A Abraham Blvd 60, south of town, just past **Carib Inn**, T7175263. Dinner 1830-2230, happy hour 1700-1900, closed Mon. American owner, seafood and steak specialities. A divers' favourite.

Casablanca, J A Abraham Blvd 12, T7174433. Daily 1700-2300. Named 'Diver's Favourite Caribbean Restaurant' in *Rodale Scuba Diver* magazine poll. Huge portions, Argentine steaks, attentive service.

The Garden Café, Kaya Gob Debrot 11, T7173410. Mon-Sat 1700-2200. Features Middle Eastern and South American meals. The owner/manager is a dead ringer for Santa Claus.

The Swiss Chalet, Kaya Simon Bolivar 21, T7173366. Mon-Sat 1700-2200. A bit out of the way but only 2 mins' walk from the main street. International food and Swiss specialities, raclette, fondue, rostis. Homely atmosphere.

Zeezicht, Kaya JNE Craane 12, T7178434. Breakfast, lunch and dinner daily. On the waterfront, Bonaire's oldest restaurant, sandwiches and omelettes as well as fish, steak, pasta and some Indonesian.

The Lost Penguin, town centre. Breakfast, lunch and early dinner. Street-side bistro-style restaurant, with sandwiches, cakes, coffee and juices. Eggs Benedict a speciality.

North of Kralendijk *p939, map p936*

The Lion's Den, at the Buddy Dive Resort, T7173400. Daily 1700-2200. One of the most spectacular views and a stylish menu.

The Rose Inn, in the heart of the village of Rincon, T7176420. Sat-Sun 1200-2000. An authentic Bonaire weekend dining experience run by the head of the Bonaire Chef's team and his family. Local dishes superbly prepared.

Rum Runners at the Reef at Captain Don's Habitat, T7177303. Breakfast, lunch and dinner. Theme nights, eg Bonairean, Mexican or barbecue, with live music some nights.

Vesuvio Restaurant, at the Harbour Village marina, T7177500. Daily 1700-2200. Italian specialities and you can use the cascade pool and outdoor pool table.

South of Kralendijk *p940, map p936*

Kontiki Beachclub, next to the Lac Bay Resort, T7175369, www.kontikibonaire.com. Tue-Sun 1200-1500, 1830-2200. Seafood, steaks, salads and a wide variety of international cuisine, friendly, casual, beautiful view, Caribbean decor.

Old Inn, on J A Abraham Blvd opposite Plaza Resort, T7176666. Dinner only, Thu-Tue. Indonesian *rijsttafel* a speciality, also steak, fish and children's menu.

Hang Out, the beach bar at Jibe City. Daily 1100-1500. Recommended for terrific sandwiches, drink, shade, rest and regaining energy for windsurfing.

🎭 Entertainment

Bonaire *p936*

Very little contrived typically Caribbean entertainment and gambling, but Bonaire's real nightlife revolves around free slide and video shows at hotels and dive shops. Check schedule of Bonaire's *Weekly Happenings* update at tourist office, or in the free English language weekly, *The Bonaire Reporter*.

Casino

Divi Flamingo Beach Resort, T7178285. Open from 2000.

Cinema

The Movies Bonaire, on Kaya Prinses Marie, T7172400, www.InfoBonaire.com/cinema. Usually closed Mon. Shows change on Fri and there are children's movies on Sat and Sun.

Music

Most restaurants offer live Caribbean music at least once a week during the dinner hour. **Karel's Beach Bar**, Kaya K Craane 12. Has a

live band from 2200 Fri and Sat.
Little Havana Jazz Club, just off the promenade down town. Spins vinyl jazz tunes in the evening and occasionally hosts live jazz groups. Most popular with the over 30s.

✱ Festivals and events

Bonaire *p936*
Jan-Mar Maskarada begins on New Year's Day and continues for several weekends with masked and costumed dancers performing at outdoor venues around the island. The dancers act out traditional activities of rural Bonaire. Performances are free and last about an hour. **Carnival** takes place over about 6 weeks from the end of Jan to the beginning of Mar, with parades, jump-ups and the election of King and Queen of the Carnival and 'Prince and Pancho'. Several days are devoted to the Tumba festival, a Tumba being a winning song. Carnival is organized by the Fundashon Karnival Boneiru (Fukabo). The Grand Carnival Parade is always on the Sun preceding Ash Wed.
End Mar Annual Bonaire International Fishing Tournament.
May A lead-off event of the **World Freestyle Windsurfing Championship** is held in Lac Bay, contact Elvis Martinus, T7172788,
Jun Annual Dive Festival.
Early Oct Annual Bonaire Sailing Regatta. This has grown into a world-class event with races for seagoing yachts, catamarans, sunfishes, windsurfers and local fishing boats. All craft compete in Kralendijk Bay, while the larger boats race round Bonaire and Klein Bonaire. Held over 5 days, the event attracts crowds and hotel reservations need to be made well in advance. For information call the Regatta office, T7177425, F7175576. There are also monthly regattas for several classes of small boats.
Nov Competitive swim.

✥ Shopping

Bonaire *p936, map p936*
Bonaire is not a major shopping centre, though some shops do stock high quality, low duty goods. Sales tax is 5%.

Arts and crafts
Local arts and crafts are largely sea-based and fabrics.
Fundashon Arte Industri Bonairano, in Kralendijk, is good for souvenirs.
Palu Wiri, a band which plays local, native instruments, has recorded 3 CDs, available locally, of Bonairean and Antillean songs.

Food
The largest supermarkets are **Cultimara**, T7178278, and **Bonaire Warehouse**, on Kaya Industeria, T7178700, with American and Dutch brand groceries and some household goods. There are also several minimarkets. **Sand Dollar Grocery**, open daily, is located in a small plaza in front of the Sand Dollar Beach Club along with **Lovers Ice Cream Parlour**. Near the Divi Flamingo, a turning opposite leads to **Joke's** grocery and minimarket.

Shopping mall
Harbourside Shopping Mall contains small boutiques, KFC and an internet café.

▲▲ Activities and tours

Bonaire *p936*
Cycling
Cycling is popular and tours are organized or there is a cycling trails map if you want to go it alone. Bikes and mountain bikes can be rented at several hotels and outlets.

Diving
According to the latest Reader Survey (2005/2006) carried out by **Rodale's Scuba Diving Magazine**, Bonaire was again rated top dive destination in the Caribbean. For above and underwater images of the reef, see www.BonaireWeb-Cams.com, updated every 2 mins.
Buddy Dive, T7175080, www.buddydive.com, and **Toucan Diving**, T7172500 at the **Plaza Resort Bonaire**, received top ratings from Rodale's.
The Dive Inn, T7178761, was rated the No 2 resort in the Caribbean by the German magazine *Tauchen*.
The other main schools are:
Blue Divers, T7176860, www.bluedivers.com.
Dive Bonaire, at the Divi Flamingo, T7178285.

Habitat Dive Center, T7178290.
Larry's Wildside Diving, T7909156,
www.larryswildsidediving.com. A dive
operation emphasizing safe diving on the
rough east side. A 2-tank dive costs US$100.
Photo Tours Divers, at the Caribbean Court
Resort, T7175353, ext 328,
www.bonairephototours.com.
WannaDive, at the Eden Beach Resort, City
Café/Hotel Rochaline and at the Wannadive
Hut, between the two (accommodation
available B), T7178884, www.wannadive.com.

All dive schools can conduct lessons in
English, Dutch, German, Spanish and
sometimes other tongues. Prices are
competitive, ranging from US$30-60 for a
2-tank dive if you have your own equipment.
Add a 10% service charge on most diving and
5% sales tax on all training courses and
rentals. All packages include tank, air, weights
and belt; equipment rental varies, US$8-12 for
a BC jacket, US$7-12 for a regulator, US$6-10
for mask, snorkel and fins. Camera and other
equipment rental widely available.

You can have a video made of yourself or
your group while diving. For US$85 Hendrik
Wuyts, T7862844, acclaimed underwater
filmmaker for The World of Ocean Films and
Eye On ... series, will custom produce a DVD
or tape for you to bring home.

Fishing

You can charter a fishing boat through your
hotel and arrange half- or full-day trips with
tackle and food included. Bonaire has good
bonefishing and also deep-sea fishing.
Big Game, T7176500, www.bonairenet.com
.Biggame/indexbgs.htm. A 30-ft Bertram
sport fisherman run by Captain Cees and his
son Thomas, US$325 half day, US$450 full
day for up to 5 people.
Blonk Boatworks, T7176800, 5670871.
Charter a wonderful motor sloop, The Green
Parrot, for US$140 per day, all-inclusive.
Nautico Bonaire, Kaya Jan NE Craane 24,
T7175800, F7175850. Charter recreational
boats.
Piscatur, T7178774, F7174784. An
independent company run by Captain Chris
Morkos. Half day US$275 for 4 people,
US$425 full day in 38-ft diesel boat, or
US$125 half day for 2 people, US$225 full
day in 15-ft skiff.

Hiking

Walking and birdwatching are popular
in the Washington/Slagbaai National Park,
particularly climbing up Mt Brandaris, the
highest point on the island.

Horse riding

Kunuku Warahama, Kaya Guwanare 11,
T7175558. Has horses and playgrounds for
the children as well as lots of other animals.
Lunch and dinner also available, not always
open, so phone ahead.

Kayaking

A few dive shops rent kayaks, quite a good
way of getting to Klein Bonaire without a
boatload of other people, but remember
that it is about 1 km back paddling into the
wind.
Jibe City, see Windsurfing, below, rents
kayaks in Lac Bay for a whole (US$30 single
kayak, US$35 double) or half day (US$20/25)
or a couple of hrs (US$10/15).

Parasailing

Parasail, T7174998. Has waterskiing and
banana boat rides in addition to parasailing.

Sailing

The Marina at Harbour Village is the only
full-service marina in Bonaire. There are 60
slips for boats up to 110 ft with showers,
laundry, fuel, water, chandlery, etc, and a
shop for repairs. Sailing trips with snorkelling
and beach barbecue, often on Klein Bonaire,
or sunset booze cruises, from US$38 per
person plus 10% service, are offered on
Samur, T7175592, samur@bonairelive.com,
a 56-ft Siamese junk built in Bangkok in
1968, based at Captain Don's Habitat, with
pick-up service from most resorts.
Others include:
Mushi Mushi, T7905399. A 42-ft catamaran
offering trips to the nearby Klein Bonaire and
Slagbaai as well as day sailing.
Skiffy Water Taxi, T5607254. Run by the
amiable Henk Ram, offers a water taxi service
to Klein Bonaire from Nautico Bonaire and
most hotels, US$14. Cruises Tue, Fri, Sat, and
snorkel trips.
Woodwind, T5607055. A 37-ft trimaran
offering sailing and guided snorkelling
around Bonaire and Klein Bonaire.

Snorkelling

Snorkelling is excellent at **The Andreas, Oil Slick Leap, Tori's Reef, Windsock Steep** and along the east side of **Klein Bonaire**. Dive boats usually take snorkellers along for about US$12. The **Sea and Discover** marine education service, T7175322, seaandis@bonairelive.com, offers snorkelling excursions with a guide for US$30 per person. The **Skiffy** water taxi provides round trips to Klein Bonaire for US$12. There is a glass-bottomed sailboat **Aquaspace**, T7172568, US$35. Tickets available at local hotels.

Tennis

Tennis courts at the **Divi Flamingo Beach** Resort, T7178285, open 0800-2200, and the **Harbour Village Beach Resort** and **Sand Dollar Condominium Resort**, T7178738, open 0900-2100.

Tour operators

Taxis have fixed prices for sightseeing tours. **Bonaire Tours**, T7178778, head office at the Harbour Village Marina, for large or small groups. 2-hr north or south tour, half- or full-day Washington Park tour, day trip to Curaçao.
Discover Bonaire, Kaya Gob N Debrot 79, T7175252, www.discover bonaire.com. For kayaking, nature tours, guided snorkelling and mountain biking, tours. Also tours through the *kunuku* (farm) areas and Washington/Slagbaai National Park.

Windsurfing

Jibe City, T7175233, www.jibecity.com (closed Sep), run by Ernst Van Vliet. This BIC/TIGA Centre and has the latest models and Gaastra sails with retail shop and **Hangout Bar**. Lessons from US$45 per hr, rentals from US$55 per day, US$265 per week.
The Place, Lac Bay, T7172288. Managed by Elvis Martinus and Bonaire's first Olympian, Patun Sargosa, features top-notch gear. Windsurfing rentals and instruction are available along with kayak, sunfish, mini speed boats, waterskiing, sea sausage rides, small Hobie cat, waterskiing, hydrosliding and paddle boats.

⊙ Transport

Bonaire *p936, maps p936 and p938*

Air

Flamingo Airport (**BON**) can accommodate 747 jumbo jets with a runway of over 4 km. KLM flies non-stop from Amsterdam and on to Quito or Lima. Arkefly has a weekly service from Amsterdam in high season.
Continental flies from Houston and Newark. **Air Jamaica** flies from 9 American cities via Montego Bay. **American Eagle** flies from San Juan, Puerto Rico, where you can make connections with major US cities. Several other international airlines fly to Curaçao, 48 km away, or Aruba, from where frequent daily flights are available to Bonaire. **Dutch Antilles Express (DAE)**, flies to Aruba, Curaçao and Sint Maarten. Other airlines flying the Bonaire-Curaçao route include Divi Divi and Insel Air. From Venezuela, Transaven flies from Caracas or Valencia. Other flights from South America connect through Aruba.

Airlines DAE, at the airport, T7170707, 0600-2130, or at their call centre, T7170808, Mon-Fri 0900-1800, reservations can also be made online, www.flydae.com. **KLM, Air Jamaica, American Eagle**, T7178300. **Divi Divi** is in Curaçao, T599-9-8881050, www.baibini.com, as is **Insel Air**, T599-9-7331521, www.fly-inselair.com.

Bicycle

The roads in the south are flat and in good condition but there is no shade and you would need lots of water and sun screen. In the north it is hilly and the roads are not as good. For mountain bikers there are lots of unpaved trails and goat paths. Bicycles are available to rent from most hotels' front desks (see above).
Cycle Bonaire/Discover Bonaire, has Trek mountain bikes and offers rentals, repairs and guided tours. Bike rental is US$15 per day or US$75 per week, while guided excursions are US$40 half day including drinks and US$65 whole day with lunch but not including bike rental.
De Freeweiler, on Kaya Grandi downtown, T7178545. Sells, rents and repairs touring and Giant mountain bikes. Bike hire from US$10 per day, US$40 per week.

The speed limit in built-up areas is 40 kmph, outside towns it is 60 kmph unless otherwise marked. Several of the streets in Kralendijk and the tourist road north of the Radio Netherlands towers are 1-way. There are 4 filling stations, open Mon-Sat 0700-2100. The Kralendijk stations are also open Sun 0900-1530.

Car hire You must have a valid driver's licence. Minimum age for car rental varies between agencies from 21-26. A few agencies will not rent to people over 70. Some companies prohibit the use of ordinary cars on unpaved roads and in Washington/Slagbaai Park. There is a government tax of US$4 per day plus 2% of the rental fee. At the busiest times of the year, it is best to reserve a car in advance. 4WD vehicles are not easy to find, and it is best to reserve one in advance. Most cars are manual shift. **A B Car Rental** at the airport, T7178980, F7175034. **Budget**, T7174700, F7173325. **Trupial Car Rental**, Kaya Grandi No 96, T7178487. **Avis**, J A Abraham Blvd 4, Kralendijk, T7175795, F7175793. There are nearly a dozen other companies not listed here, plenty of choice, and many have offices in the hotels. There are lots of pick-ups and minivans for divers wanting to carry gear around for shore diving.

Motorcycle

Motorcycles and quad bikes can be rented from US$18 a day; shop around as there are several new scooter shops and rates are competitive: **Rent-O-Fun Drive**, T7173708; **De Freeweiler**, T7178545; **Macho Scooter Rentals**, T7172500; **Orlando's Bonaire Motorcycle Shop**, T7178429, 7904409, rent Harleys or other interesting motorcycles for US$50 and up a day.

Taxi

Drivers carry a list of officially approved rates, including touring and waiting time. The short trip from the airport to the Divi Flamingo Beach Resort is the minimum fare of US$7, To Buddy Dive Resort US$11 and to Sorobon US$18, add 20% per additional passenger, maximum 4 passengers; fares increase by 20% after 1900 and by 50% from midnight-0700. Taxis have TX on their licence plates, they are available at the

airport but do not cruise for business elsewhere. Any hotel will call a taxi for you. To call a taxi yourself, T7178100, for the taxi stand at the airport.

● Directory

Bonaire *p936, map p938*
Banks Mon-Fri 0800 or 0830-1530 or 1600. All have ATMs. TCs and credit cards are widely accepted. **Royal Bank of Trinidad & Tobago**, T7178417, F7178469. **Maduro & Curiel's Bank (Bonaire) NV**, T7177249, F7172645, is a full-service Antillean bank, affiliated with Scotiabank of Canada, with a branch in Rincon, T7176266. **Emergency** T911.
Government T7175300.
Immigration T7178000. **Internet** Chat n' Browse, at Kaya Gob. Debrot 79, near Sand Dollar, T7172281, is a 'barefoot internet centre'. City Cybercafé, offers high-speed internet access at downtown locations. Several hotels offer internet access and wireless hot spots to their guests as well. **Medical services** The Hospitaal San Francisco in Kralendijk, T911 or T7178000, has 60 beds. There is an air ambulance for emergency evacuation and a recompression chamber. **Park authorities** Stinapa and Bonaire Marine Park, T7178444.
Police T7178000 or T911. **Post** Niew Post, J A Abraham Blvd, Kralendijk, on the corner of Plaza Reina Wilhelmina opposite the TCB Office, 0730-1200, 1330-1700 for stamps and postage, 1330-1600 for money orders, etc. Airmail to the USA and Canada is NAf1.75 for letters, NAf0.90 for postcards. There is also **Express Mail** and **Federal Express. Rocargo Services**, T7178922, F7175791, is the FedEx and cargo agent.
Telephone The international code for Bonaire is 599, followed by a 7-digit number. Avoid the 'blue' long-distance credit card phones; even short conversations can cost US$25. For information on services, contact **Telbo**, T7177000, F7175007. You can dial most US 800 numbers from Bonaire, T0101001, then 300 instead of the 800. You may be charged for the international portion of the call. Some firms, especially credit card companies, can be reached toll free by dialling the international access code 00, followed by the normal 1-800 number. You can rent cellular phones at several places at low rates. European GSM phones and USA GSM tri-band phones will work in Bonaire.

Netherlands Antilles, ABC Islands Bonaire Listings

Curaçao → *Country code: 599. Colour map 5, B1. Population: 170,000.*

Curaçao is the largest of the Netherlands Antilles and its capital, Willemstad, has some very fine Dutch colonial architecture painted in a variety of pastel colours, while in the countryside there are several beautiful plantation houses, called landhuisen. *It also has one of the most important historical sites in the Caribbean: a synagogue dating back to 1732, which is the oldest in continuous use in the Western Hemisphere. For most of the 20th century the island's fortunes, like Aruba, depended on its oil refinery, which processes Venezuelan crude oil, but more recently tourism has increased in importance. Diving has grown very popular since the establishment of an underwater park to preserve the reef and there are dive sites all along the Leeward side of the island.* ▸▸ *For Sleeping, Eating and other listings, see pages 959-967.*

Ins and outs

Getting there There are daily, non-stop flights to Amsterdam, the USA and Venezuela. There are also direct flights from Suriname, Colombia, Puerto Rico, Jamaica, Trinidad & Tobago, the Dominican Republic, Bonaire, Aruba and St Maarten. Other flights connect in Miami or San Juan. Curaçao has good links with South America and it is easy to get to from Venezuela, Colombia and Ecuador. The **Curaçao International Airport** at Hato is about 12 km from Willemstad and if you don't want to pay for a taxi there are buses to Punda and Otrobanda. For US military reasons, the airport has the biggest runway in the Caribbean at 3,410 metres in length and 60 meters in width, capable of handling almost any type of aircraft.

> ⁂ *Airlines and their routes change frequently so check the latest flight guides.*

Getting around Willemstad is a great place to walk around and there are tours if you want a guide who can explain all the architecture and history to you. The two halves of the city are connected with a pontoon bridge, the **Queen Emma Bridge**, which you can walk across when it is not open for shipping. Collective taxis and buses will take you further afield to most parts of the island; alternatively rent a car and explore on your own. There are about four car rental agencies at the airport, all the offices are together so it is easy to pick up price lists for comparison. One or two companies usually have desks in each of the major hotels. Look in local tourist literature or newspapers for news of special deals on offer, there is lots of choice. Taxis are easily identified by the signs on the roof and TX before the licence number. There are taxi stands at all hotels and at the airport, as well as in principal locations in Willemstad. ▸▸ *See Transport, page 965, for further details.*

Willemstad → *Population: 140,000.*

Willemstad, capital of the Netherlands Antilles and of the island of Curaçao, is full of charm and colour. The architecture is a tropical adaptation of 17th-century Dutch, painted in storybook colours. Pastel shades are used for homes, shops and government buildings alike. Fanciful gables and bulging columns evoke the spirit of the Dutch colonial burghers. The earliest buildings in Willemstad were exact copies of Dutch buildings of the mid-17th century, high-rise and close together to save money and space. Not until the first quarter of the 18th century did the Dutch adapt their northern ways to the tropical climate and begin building galleries on to the façades of their houses, to give shade and more living space. The chromatic explosion is attributed to a Governor-General of the islands, the eccentric Vice-Admiral Albert Kikkert ('Froggie' to his friends), who blamed his headaches on the glare of white

Touching down

Business hours Shops: Mon-Sat 0830-1200, 1400-1800; Sun am and lunchtime if cruise ships are in port.

Departure tax There is an airport tax of US$10 on departure to the Netherlands Antilles or US$23 to Aruba or other destinations.

Documents Most nationalities (including US and Canadian citizens) need a passport and onward/return ticket. Visas are needed by citizens of Colombia, Cuba, Dominican Republic, Haiti, India, Peru, South Africa and others. Transit visitors and cruise ship passengers must have proof of identity for a 24-hour, or less, stay on the island. Immigration procedures at the airport are quick and easy.

Health The climate is healthy and non-malarial; epidemic incidence is slight. Rooms without a/c or window and door screens may need mosquito nets during the wetter months of Nov and Dec and sometimes May and Jun, and, although some spraying is done in tourist areas, mosquitoes are a problem. Some anti-mosquito protection is recommended if you are outdoors any evening. Beware of a tree with small, poisonous green apples that borders some beaches. This is manchineel (*manzanilla*) and its sap causes burns on exposed skin.

Money The currency is the guilder, divided into 100 cents. Old and new coins are in circulation. Exchange The exchange rate is US$1=NAf1.77 for bank notes, NAf1.79 for cheques, although the rate of exchange offered by shops and hotels ranges from NAf1.75-1.80. Credit cards and US dollars are widely accepted.

Official time Atlantic Standard Time, 4 hrs behind GMT, 1 hr ahead of EST.

Safety Curaçao is not as safe as it used to be and robbery and muggings have been reported. You should take care with your personal possessions and watch out for potential security risks. There is a drugs problem in Willemstad and you are advised to be careful in Otrobanda at night and avoid the outer stretches of Pietermaai even by day (crack houses). If strangers stop you on the street asking '*alles goed?*' (everything OK?) be assured that they are not enquiring after your health.

houses and decreed in 1817 that pastel colours be used. Almost every point of interest in the city is in or within walking distance of the shopping centre in **Punda**, which covers about five blocks. Some of the streets here are only 5 m wide, but attract many tourists with their myriad shops offering international goods at near duty-free prices. The numerous jewellery shops in Willemstad have some of the finest stones to be found anywhere.

There is a red and white trolley train which takes 60 passengers around the streets of Punda several times a day.

The **Floating Market**, a picturesque string of visiting Venezuelan, Colombian and other island schooners, lines the small canal leading to the Waaigat, a diminutive yacht basin. Fresh fish, tropical fruit, vegetables and a limited selection of handicrafts are sold with much haggling. In the circular, concrete, public market building nearby there are straw hats and bags, spices, butcheries, fruit and vegetables for sale, while in the old market building behind, local food is cooked over charcoal and sold to office workers .

Nearby on Hanchi Snoa, is one of the most important historical sites in the Caribbean, the **Mikvé Israel-Emanuel synagogue** ① *normally Mon-Fri 0900-1145 and 1430-1645, free, services Fri 1830 and Sat 1000*, which dates back to 1732, making it the oldest in continuous use in the Western Hemisphere. In the 1860s, several families broke away from the Mikvé Israel congregation to found a Sephardi Reform congregation which was housed in the **Temple Emanuel** (1867-1964) on the Wilhelminaplein. In 1964, however, they reunited to form the Mikvé Israel-Emanuel

Public holidays New Year's Day, Carnival Mon (Feb), Good Fri, Easter Mon, Queen's Birthday (30 Apr), Labour Day (1 May), Ascension Day, Flag Day (2 Jul), Antillean Day (21 Oct), Christmas on 25 and 26 Dec, half day holiday 31 Dec.

Tourist information Curaçao Tourism Development Bureau, Pietermaai 19, Willemstad, PO Box 3266, T4348200, info@curacao.com, www.curacao-tourism.com, www.gaycuracao.com. There are information offices on Breedestraat, east of Hendrikplein, and at the airport. The **Curaçao Hotel and Tourism Association (CHATA)**, Kaya Junior Salas 1, Punda, T4651005, offers information, maps and assistance in finding a hotel. Several visitor information centres and booths are dotted round Willemstad. **Maps** A road map (Curoil) with a satellite photo of the island and superimposed information, town street plans and index is available in bookshops. For maps on the web, www.cartocaribe.com.

Tourist offices overseas

Netherlands: Vasteland 82-84, 3011 BP Rotterdam, PO Box 23227, T3110-4142639, info@ctbe.nl. **UK**: Axis Sales and Marketing, 421a Finchley Rd, London NW3 6HJ, T0207-4314045, curacao@axissm. com **US**: 5810 Biscayne Blvd, Miami, Florida 33137, T305-2850511, northamerica@curacao.com.

Colombia: Calle 7D 43 A-99, Torre Almagran Of 402, Medellín, T4-3118677, tmocurazaocol@epm.net.co.

Germany: Bayerstr 16a, 80335 Munich, T49-0-8951703296, info@curacao.de. **Sweden**: Gökärtsvägen 8, 434 45 Kungsbacka, T46-300 74217, info@abcisislands.se.

Venezuela: Av Mohedano con Av Tamanaco, Torre Atlantic, Piso 7, Of 7-C, El Rosal, Caracas, T58-212-9533412, curacaoturismo@cantv.net.

Voltage 127/120 volts AC, 50 cycles. US appliances at 60 cycles work well and you do not need an adapter. Visitors from Europe need an adapter, which most hotels keep in stock.

Weights and measures Metric.

congregation, which is affiliated with both the Reconstructionist Foundation and the World Union for Progressive Judaism. The big brass chandeliers are believed to be 300 years older than their synagogue, originating in Spain and Portugal, their candles are lit for Yom Kippur and special occasions. The names of the four mothers, Sara, Rebecca, Leah and Rachel are carved on the four pillars and there are furnishings of richly carved mahogany with silver ornamentation, blue stained-glass windows and stark white walls. The traditional sand on the floor is sprinkled there daily, some say, to symbolize the wandering of the Israelites in the Egyptian desert during the Exodus. Others say it was meant to muffle the sound of the feet of those who had to worship secretly during the Inquisition period. Dress code for men is coat and tie and ladies equally conventional.

In the courtyard is the **Jewish Cultural Historical Museum** ① *Hanchi di Snoa 29, T4611633, www.snoa.com, open the same hours as the Synagogue, closed Jewish and public holidays, US$2, children US$1,* occupying two restored 18th-century houses, which harbours an excellent permanent exhibition of religious objects, most of which have been donated by local Jewish families. There are scrolls, silver, books, bibles, furniture, clothing and household items, many 18th-century pieces and family bequeathments. Outside are some tombstones and a ritual bath excavated during restoration work. A small shop sells souvenirs, the *Synagogue Guide Book* and *Our Snoa*, Papiamento for synagogue, produced for the 250th anniversary in 1982.

West of the city, on the Schottegatweg Nord, is one of the two **Jewish cemeteries**, Bet Chayim (or Beth Haim), consecrated in 1659 and still in use. There are more than 1,700 tombstones from the 17th and 18th centuries, with bas-relief sculpture and inscriptions, many still legible. It is a little out of the way but well worth a visit. It is also a fine example of what atmospheric pollution can do, as the tombstones have suffered from the fumes from the surrounding oil refinery.

Fortkerk ① *T4611139, bupha@cura.net, Mon-Fri 0900-1200, 1400-1700, tours from 1000-1200, US$2/NAf3, children US$1,* an 18th-century Protestant church at the back of the square behind **Fort Amsterdam**, the Governor's palace, still has a British cannonball embedded in its walls. You get a guided tour of the church and the associated museum. The church is not as large as the synagogue museum, but the museum is well laid out, with some interesting items, like original church silver and reproductions of old maps and paintings of Curaçao. Note the clock in the ceiling of the church and the still-functioning rainwater cistern inside the church. It was once the main source of fresh water for the garrison.

Two forts, **Rif Fort** and **Water Fort** were built at the beginning of the 19th century to protect the harbour entrance and replace two older batteries. All that is left of Rif Fort is a guard house dating from about 1840, but you can walk on the walls and eat at the restaurants in the vaults. The Water Fort Arches have been converted to house shops, bars and restaurants.

The **Philatelic Museum** ① *corner of Keukenstraat and Kuiperstraat, T4658010, F4617851, Mon-Fri 0900-1200, 1330-1700, Sat 1000-1500, US$2/NAf3.50, chidren NAf1.75,* is in a recently restored building which is the oldest in Punda (1693). There is a permanent display of Dutch Caribbean stamps, plus temporary exhibitions.

Heading east from the centre along Breedestraat, you get to the **Octagon Simón Bolívar Museum** ① *Penstraat 100,* now part of the ever-expanding Avila Hotel,

Willemstad orientation

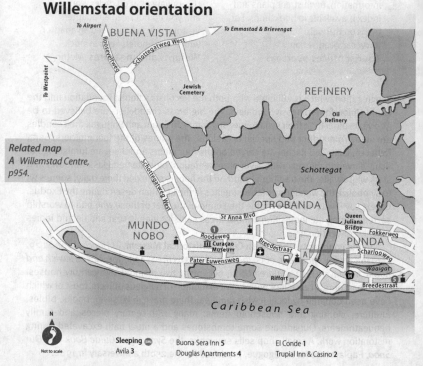

Related map
A Willemstad Centre,
p954.

N
Not to scale

Sleeping
Avila **3**

Buona Sera Inn **5**
Douglas Apartments **4**

El Conde **1**
Trupial Inn & Casino **2**

T4614377, www.avilahotel.com. Open Mon, Wed, Sun, housing an exhibition of the 953
life and works of the liberator of South America and his associations with Curaçao,
where he lived for a time. The Octagon is also used for wedding ceremonies.

The swinging **Queen Emma Bridge** spans St Anna Bay, linking the two parts of the
city, Punda and Otrobanda (the latter means 'the other side' in Papiamento, and
people tend to refer to 'Punda' and 'Otrobanda' rather than 'Willemstad'). Built on 16
great pontoons, it is swung aside some 30 times a day to let ships pass in and out of
the harbour. The present bridge was built in 1939; while it is open, pedestrians are
shuttled across for free by small ferry boats. The bridge is closed to vehicular traffic.

The new **Queen Juliana** fixed bridge vaults about 50 m over the bay and connects
Punda and Otrobanda by a four-lane highway. Taxis will often offer to stop at the
bridge so you can get a panoramic view and photo of Willemstad on one side and the
oil refinery on the other. Although you can reach it on foot it is not open for
pedestrians; the wind and the way it shakes will explain why.

Parts of **Otrobanda** are being restored and there are many old houses here, both
small, tucked away down alleys, and mansions or town houses. Breedestraat is the
main shopping street. The **Basilica Santa Ana**, founded in 1752 and made a Basilica in
1975 by Pope Paul VI, is just off here. The houses fronting on to the Pater Euwensweg,
once overlooked the Rifwater lagoon, now reclaimed land. Along St Anna Bay, past
the ferry landing, is **Porto Paseo**, a restored area with bars and restaurants. The old
hospital has been restored into the **Hotel and Casino Porto Paseo**. A cruise ship pier
has been built at Otrobanda for liners too big to reach the existing terminal in
Willemstad harbour.

The **Central Bank of the Netherlands Antilles** owns and operates a **Numismatic
Museum** ① *De Rouvilleweg 7, Otrobanda, T4625912, museum@centralbank.an, Mon-Fri
0830-1130, 1330-1630, free*, with a collection of coins and notes from the Netherlands
Antilles, as well as a display of precious
and semi-precious gemstones.

A good museum in this area, opened
in 1999, relates to Willemstad's maritime
and trading history. The **Kurá Hulanda
Museum** ① *Klipstraat 9, T4347765,
www.kuruhulanda.com, daily 1000- 1700,
US$6, children US$3 (audio cassettes for
rent; guided tours, photography and group
rates available on request)*, has exhibits of
the slave trade, tracing it back to the
capture of slaves in Africa, their
transatlantic crossing and eventual sale as
commercial goods. Other exhibitions are
on the predominant cultures of the island,
the origin of man, West African empires,
pre-Columbian gold, Mesopotamian relics
and Antillean art. There's a gift shop.

On the outskirts of Otrobanda, on
van Leeuwenhoekstraat, is the **Curaçao
Museum** ① *T4623873, curmuseum@
yahoo.com, Mon-Fri 0830-1630, Sun
1000- 1600. US$2.25/NAf5.30, children
under 14 US$1.25/ NAf2.60*, founded in
1946 (housed in an old quarantine
station built in 1853) with a small
collection of artefacts of the Caiquetio
Indian culture, as well as 19th- and

Netherlands Antilles, ABC Islands Curaçao

20th-century paintings, antique locally made furniture, and other items from the colonial era. In the basement there is a children's **museum of science**. On the roof is a 47-bell carillon, named The Four Royal Children after the four daughters of Queen Juliana of the Netherlands.

Another area within walking distance of Punda and worth exploring, is **Scharloo**, across the Wilhelmina bridge from the floating market. A former Jewish merchant housing area, now under renovation, there are many substantial properties with all the typical architectural attributes; note the green house with white trimmings known as the **Wedding Cake House** ① *Scharlooweg 77*.

The **Maritime Museum** ① *Van der Brandhofstraat 7 Scharloo Abou, T4652327, www.curacaomaritime.com, Mon-Sat 0900-1600. US$8.50, US$4.50 for students and children under 12*, opened in 1998 in a 1729 colonial mansion on the Waaigat inlet near the Floating Market. It has permanent and temporary exhibitions of marine history relating to Curaçao and the Caribbean, with video presentations and multimedia displays. The museum has its own boat for tours of the harbour Wed and Sat and ferrying cruise ship passengers. Call for reservations for the tour of the museum, the harbour through the Annabaai, the Brionwerf and the refinery. Harbourside café and gift shop.

The **Mongui Maduro Library** is at the **Landhuis Rooi Katootje** ① *T7375119, info@madurolibrary.org, open by appointment*, the site, in 1954, of the Round Table Conferences which led to the Statuut between the Dutch Kingdom and its Caribbean territories. The library, in the beautifully restored *landhuis* (country estate house), contains all manner of things Caribbean and the conference table still stands in the dining room. To get there, take the Rond minibus from Punda and ask to be let off next to the chicken factory.

> ❖ Country estate houses, or landhuizen, emerge here and there in the parched countryside.

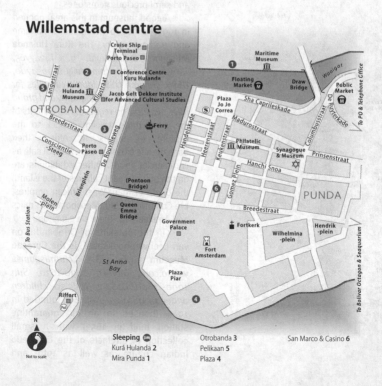

Willemstad centre

Cruise Ship Terminal
Porto Paseo
Maritime Museum ①
Conference Centre Kuru Hulanda ②
Floating Market
Draw Bridge
Public Market
Kurá Hulanda Museum ⑤
Jacob Gelt Dekker Institute for Advanced Cultural Studies
OTROBANDA
Langestraat
Klipstraat
Breedestraat
Conscientie-Steeg
Porto Paseo ③
De Rouvilleweg
Ferry
Plaza Jo Jo Correa ⓢ
Sha Caprileskade
Handelskade
Heerenstraat
Keukenstraat
Madurostraat
Philatelic Museum ⑪
Synagogue & Museum ✡
Prinsenstraat
Hanchi Snoa
Gomez Plein
(Pontoon Bridge)
⑥
PUNDA
Breedestraat
Brionplein
Queen Emma Bridge
Government Palace
Fortkerk ✝
Wilhelmina-plein
Hendrik-plein
Molen-plein
To Bus Station
St Anna Bay
Fort Amsterdam ⌂
Plaza Piar
④
Riffort (Pol)
Waaigat
To PO & Telephone Office
De Ruyterkade
Columbusstraat
To Bolivar Octagon & Seaquarium

N
Not to scale

Sleeping 🛏
Kurá Hulanda **2**
Mira Punda **1**

Otrobanda **3**
Pelikaan **5**
Plaza **4**

San Marco & Casino **6**

Set in 503 ha in the east part of the island is **Brievengat** ① T6914961, daily 0915-1215, 1500-1800, US$2, children half price. Its exact date of construction is unknown, but it is believed to date from about 1750 when it was the centre of a 500-ha plantation, one of the largest. It was used in the 19th century to produce cattle, cochineal and aloe, but a hurricane in 1877 devastated the plantation and the house was gradually abandoned. Shell later took over the property to extract water from the subsoil, but in 1954 when it was in a state of ruin Shell donated it to the Government who restored it to its former grandeur. The windows and the roof are typical of the local style but unusual are the arches extending the length of the house and the two towers at either side, which were once used to incarcerate slaves. Bar and snacks are served and there's live music at weekends, check beforehand. On Sunday (1000-1500) it's open house with folklore show at 1700 on the last Sunday of the month. To get there, take the bus marked Punda-Hato from Punda at 15 minutes past the hour and get off at the Sentro Deportivo Korsou.

Chobolobo ① *Salinja, T4613526, Mon-Fri 0800-1200, 1300-1700, free and visitors may taste the liqueur,* came into the Senior family in 1948 and **Senior & Co** make the Curaçao liqueur here, using a copper still dating from 1896 and the original Valencia orange known locally as Laraha. The clear, orange, amber, red, green and blue are for cocktails and all taste the same; others are chocolate, coffee, rum and raisin. Chobolobo is worth visiting, but if you resist the temptation to buy **Senior & Co's** products you will find them cheaper in the duty-free lounge at Hato Airport although they occasionally run out of some flavours. The original *Curaçao Liqueur* can only be purchased on the island. Copy cats are exported from Holland, etc.

Near the Hato International Airport on Rooseveltweg, are the **Hato Caves** ① *T8680379, caves@cura.net, 1000-1700, guided tours every hour, the last at 1600, US$6.25, children US$4.75,* which contain stalactites and stalagmites, a colony of long-nose bats and pools among spectacular limestone formations. There are also some **Caquetio rock drawings** believed to be 1,500 years old.

Jan Kok ① *T8648087, high season 1100-2100, low season Sun 1100-1900, guided tour Tue, Thu 0900-1300,* is the oldest landhouse on the island, dating from 1654 and overlooking the salt flats where flamingoes gather. There's a bar and restaurant, and you can take a guided tour through the salt pans and the landhouse. To get there, take the bus marked Lagun and Knip from the Riffort, Otrobanda, at half past the even hour in the morning or half past the odd hour in the afternoon. **Santa Martha** ① *T8641323, www.tsoshal.org, Mon-Thu 0900-1200, 1300-1500, Fri 0900-1200,* built in 1700 and restored in 1979, is used as a day-care centre for the physically and mentally disabled, but is open to visitors if you call in advance. **Ascension** ① *T8641950, first Sun of the month 1000-1400 only,* built in 1672 and restored in 1963, is used by Dutch marines stationed on the island. You can find local music, handicrafts and snacks. To get there, take bus marked Westpunt from Otrobanda (see below). **Kas Di Pali Mashl** ① *Dokterstuin 27, Ascension, T8642742, museacur@hotmail.com, Mon-Fri 0900-1600, Sat, Sun 0900-1800,* is a traditional adobe house with a thatched roof built at the end of the 19th century, although the method of construction was typical of that in use by Afro-Curaçaoan plantation workers since the end of the 17th century. There is a small museum inside with typical household artefacts and outside at the back local food is served at lunchtime. **Landhuis Kenepa** or **Knip** ① *T8640244, F640385,* near the beach of the same name, is a restored 17th-century landhouse where there was a slave rebellion in 1795. It has a collection of antique furniture and an exhibition about the Kenepa people. It's on the same bus route as Jan Kok, see above.

Christoffel Park ① *T8640363, www.carmabi.org, Mon-Sat 0800-1600, Sun*

0600-1500 (Mon-Sat admission to the mountain side closes at 1400 and to the ocean side at 1500, although you can stay in until later; on Sun no admittance after 1300 and 1400 for inland or sea routes, US$9; guided walking tours US$15, Christoffel mountain climb (Sun 0700 US$30, reservations required), Savonet history tour (Tue, Wed, Sun 1000 US$20, reservations required), deer watching (Thu 1600-1830 US$30, reservations required), pick-up truck safari tours (0800-1200 daily except Sat US$30, reservations required), covers an area of 1,860 ha in the west of the island, including Mount Christoffel at 375 m, which was formerly three plantations. These plantations, Savonet, Zorgvlied and Zevenbergen, are the basis for a system of well-marked trails, blue (9 km), green (7½ km or 12 km) and yellow (11 km), and there is a red walking trail up Mount Christoffel which takes about four to five hours there and back. You can see a wide range of fauna and flora, including orchids, the indigenous wayacá (lignum vitae) plant, acacias, aloe, many cacti, calabash and the tiny Curaçao deer. The ruins of the Zorgvlied landhouse can be seen off the green route. The Savonet route takes you to the coast and along to Amerindian rock drawings, painted between 500 and 2,000 years ago in terracotta, black and white. In this area there are also two caves, one of which is about 125 m long and you have to crawl in before you can stand up and walk to the 'white chamber' (stalactites and stalagmites) and the 'cathedral'.

The 17th-century **Savonet Plantation House** is at the entrance to the park on the Westpoint Road. It is not open to the public but several outbuildings are used. There is a small museum with archaeological exhibits. Guided tours are available, special walks at dawn or dusk are organized at random, check in the newspapers, evening walking tours to see the Curaçao deer, maximum eight people, reservations essential. Stinapa publishes an excellent *Excursion Guide to the Christoffel Park, Curaçao*, by Peer Reijns, 1984, which is available at the Park administration. A basic map of the trails is also provided. **Rancho Alfin** ① *T8640535*, at the park also does

Curaçao

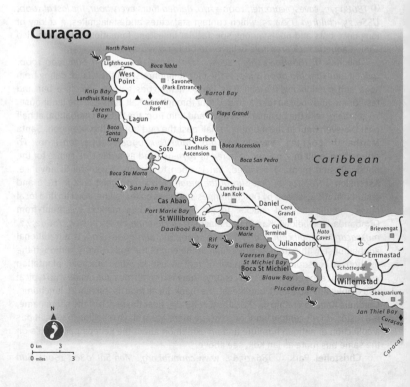

tours, walking, mountain biking or horse riding, including night trips, sunrise trips and a romantic package for honeymooners. The Otrobanda-Westpunt bus passes the entrance to the park.

Seaquarium

ⓘ T4616666, www.curacao-sea-aquarium.com, 0830-1730, US$15, children under 5-12 US$7.50; there is a restaurant, snack bar and shops selling shells and coral, in marked contrast to the conservation efforts of the Underwater Park administration.

The Seaquarium, southeast of Willemstad, just beyond the **Lions Dive Hotel**, has a collection of underwater creatures and plants found around the island, which live in channelled sea water to keep them as close as possible to their natural environment. The Seaquarium was built in 1984, the lagoons and marina being excavated so as to leave the original coastline untouched and do minimal damage to the reef offshore. There is a shark (lemon and nurse) and animal (turtles, stingrays) encounter programme, where you get in the water with them to feed them, good for photography, poor for animal welfare, US$54 for diving (no previous experience necessary), US$34 snorkelling. An even more controversial attraction has been the recent introduction of a swim with the dolphins programme, where dolphins caught in the wild are kept in tanks for visitors' amusement. The Seaquarium can be reached by bus marked Dominguito from the post office at 35 minutes past the hour (except for 1335), which passes the **Avila Beach Hotel**.

Beaches and activities

There are several good beaches on Curaçao. The northwest coast is rugged and rough, but the southwest coast has some sheltered bays and beaches with excellent swimming and snorkelling. Windsurfing, waterskiing, yachting and fishing are available at resorts. Many of the beaches are private and make a charge per car (amount depends on day of the week and popularity, US$3-6) but in return you usually get some changing facilities, toilets and refreshments. Public beaches are free but most have no facilities and some are rather dirty and smelly.

Heading south out of Willemstad are the two small, artificial beaches at the **Avila Beach Hotel**, where non-residents pay an entrance fee. The sand is imported and the sea is often not calm enough to see much if you snorkel but the breakwaters make it pleasant for swimming. You can get to the beach at **Piscadera Bay** near the **Sheraton** hotel by catching one of their shuttle buses from beside the Rif Fort in Otrobanda. Southeast of Willemstad, by the **Princess Beach Hotel**, the **Lions Dive Hotel** and the Seaquarium (see below), is a 450-m, man-made **beach and marina** ⓘ 0830-1800, entrance to the beach US$2.25, showers and toilets, with all watersports available and the **Mambo Beach Club** for

> ☺ Topless sunbathing is prohibited on public beaches but is tolerated on a few private beaches.

night-time entertainment. The beach can be crowded and noisy with music; motorized watersports are all down one end. Past the Seaquarium is a residential area and private beach on **Jan Thiel Bay** ① *entrance NAf6 per car, changing facilities, drinks and snacks*, which has good swimming and snorkelling. **Santa Barbara** ① *0800-1800, entrance US$2.25 per person, changing rooms, toilets and snack bars*, located at the mouth of Spanish Water Bay on the Mining Company property, is a favourite with locals. Behind Spanish Water Bay rises **Mount Tafelberg**, where phosphate mining used to take place. To get to Santa Barbara you can take a bus from the post office, get off at the Mining Company gate and hitch down to the beach, or take a taxi. Across the bay, which is one of the island's beauty spots, is the **Curaçao Yacht Club**. There are four yacht clubs in Spanish Water. **Caracas Bay Island** offers biking, horse riding, a tour of the fort and watersports such as kayaking, canoeing, guided snorkelling tours, windsurfing and jet skis. The **Baya Restaurant on the Beach** ① *1200-2300*, has French Oriental cuisine, while there is also the **Baya Beach Club** ① *T7470777, www.bayabeach.com*, for a daytime drinking spot or night-time entertainment. The new **Curaçao Howard Johnson** hotel in Willemstad has an agreement for its guests to be shuttled to **Baya Beach Club** for beach activities.

Travelling northwest from Willemstad heading towards Westpoint, there are lots of coves and beaches worth exploring. A left turn soon after leaving town will take you to **St Michiel's Bay** ① *free*, a fishing village and tanker-clearing harbour. **Daaibooibaai**, south of St Willibrordus is a public beach and gets very crowded on Sundays. Further up the coast, **Porto Marie** ① *Mon-Sat US$2, Sun US$2.50, including soft drink, 0930-1830*, is private and sandy and there are umbrellas for shade. There's a restaurant and dive area to change, rinse off equipment, etc. A double reef here gives good snorkelling and diving. **Cas Abao Beach** ① *changing facilities, showers, shade huts, lounge chairs cost US$3, US$3 per car per day, US$5 at weekends and holidays, snacks and beverages*, is pretty with good snorkelling and diving from shore in beautiful clear water. **San Juan** ① *entrance fee charged*, a private beach with lots of coral is off to the left of the main Westpoint road down a poor track. **Boca Santa Martha** ① *beach entrance US$4.50 for non-residents, no pets or food allowed on the beach, some shade provided*, where the **Coral Cliff Resort** is located, is quiet with nice sea. **Lagun** is a lovely secluded beach in a small cove with cliffs surrounding it and small fishing boats pulled up on the sand. It is safe for children and good for snorkelling. There are facilities and some shade from trees. Some buses pass only 50 m from the beach. **Jeremi**, a public beach with no charge, is of the same design, a slightly larger sandy beach with a steep drop to deep water and boats moored here, protected by the cliffs. Further up the coast, **Knip** is a more open, larger, sandy beach again with cliffs at either end. Many people rate this the best beach on the island. There are some facilities here and it is very popular at weekends when there is loud music and it gets crowded and noisy. **Playa Abau** is big, sandy, with beautiful clear water, surrounded by cliffs. There are toilets, some shade is provided, it's well organized, popular at weekends and busy. Nearing the west tip, **Playa Forti** has good swimming. There is a restaurant on the clifftop overlooking the sea. The beach at **Westpoint** below the church is stoney, the only shade comes from the poisonous manchineel trees. Fishing boats tie up at the pier but bathers prefer to go to Playa Forti. Beyond Westpoint is **Kalki Beach** which is good for snorkelling and diving as well as bathing. Westpoint is the end of the road, about 45 minutes by car or one hour by bus from Otrobanda (US$1).

Diving The waters around Curaçao contain a wide variety of colourful fish and plant life and several wrecks (*Superior Producer*, near the water distillation plant, and a tugboat in Caracas Bay), which have foundered on the coral reef just offshore. The reef surrounds

 One of the most bizarre sights of Curaçao, not dealt with in the tourist brochures, is the government-operated red-light area. Close to the airport, it resembles a prison camp and is guarded by a policeman.

the island and consists generally of a gently sloping terrace to a depth of about 10 m, then a drop-off and a reef slope with an angle of about 45°. The coral formations are spectacular in places and there are many huge sponges; one in Boca Santa Martha is so big it is known as 'the double bed'. There are lots of fish and you are likely to see barracuda, moray eels, spiny lobsters, turtles, manta rays and maybe sharks. Underwater visibility averages 24 m and water temperature varies between 24°C and 27°C. There are lots of opportunities for successful underwater photography.

Many of the large resort hotels have dive shops on site. They have been encouraged by the establishment in 1983 of the **Curaçao Underwater Park** managed by the **Netherlands Antilles National Parks Foundation (Stinapa)**, which stretches from the **Princess Beach Hotel** to East Point. The park extends out from the shore to a depth of 60 m and covers 600 ha of reef and 436 ha of inner bays.

Over 40 permanent mooring buoys for boats have been placed at dive sites along the south coast as part of Stinapa's programme for sustained utilization of the reef. A few of the sites can be dived from the shore (West Point, Blauwbaa, Port Marie, Daaibooi, Vaersen Bay, San Juan, Playa Kalki), but most of the coastal strip is private property and boat dives are necessary. The *Guide to the Curaçao Underwater Park*, by Jeffrey Sybesma and Tom van't Hof (published in 1989 by Stinapa and available locally), describes the sites and discusses conservation. For independent divers and snorkellers without a boat there is the *Complete Guide to Landside Diving and Snorkelling Locations in Curaçao*, by Jeffrey Sybesma and Suzanne Koelega. No harpoons or spear guns are allowed and do not damage or remove coral or any other sea creatures.

⬤ Sleeping

There is a 7% government tax and 12% service charge to be added to any quoted room rate.

New hotels, villas or timeshare developments are springing up all over Curaçao and the number of hotel rooms is around 5,000. Be prepared for construction work. We have not included here the international chain hotels such as **Marriott**, **Hilton** or **Breezes**, for contact details see www.curacao-tourism.com. Several small hotels have organized themselves into the **Curaçao Apartments and Small Hotel Association (CASHA)**, www.curacaoweb.com/casha.

Many hotels have no hot water taps, only cold because the water pipes are laid overground, so the water in them is warmed by the sun during the day and is cold at night. Time your shower accordingly.

Willemstad *p949, maps p952 and p954*
LL Kurá Hulanda Spa & Casino, Langestraat 8, Otrobanda, T4347700, www.kurahulanda .com. The most luxurious hotel in town, 100 rooms and suites close to the Queen Emma bridge, in restored 18th- and 19th-century colonial buildings around several courtyards on a former slave trading site, marble bathrooms,

a/c, fans, cable TV, phone with modem, spa and fitness centre, 2 pools, several restaurants and cafés, casino, business centre, anthropological museum on site and conference centre and **Institute for Advanced Cultural Studies** across the road. The **Lodge Kurá Hulanda and Beach Club**, at the west end of the island, has 74 villas, suites and guest rooms, most with kitchens, massage, scuba diving and watersports, horse riding, tennis, hiking and biking trails, shuttle service to Willemstad to the hotel, museum and casino.
LL-L Avila, Penstraat 130, 15 mins' walk east of the centre, T4614377, www.avilahotel.com. Built in 1811 as Governor's residence, the first hotel rooms were in an old hospital wing, small and with no sea view. However, all that has changed with frequent expansions and makeovers and the hotel's various sections now stretch down the coast to include the Bolívar Octagon museum. All new rooms and suites with sea view, both the beaches are protected by breakwaters and have imported sand for pleasant swimming.
LL-AL Plaza Hotel and Casino, on Punda seafront, T4612500, www.plazahotelcuracao .com. Very central, huge tower dominates the skyline by the fortress walls, 252 rooms

and suites, most with sea or harbour view, price per room includes service, tax, bargain for a cheaper rate for several nights, popular with the Dutch, good food, shops, restaurants, diving, boat excursions, pool, child care.

AL Otrobanda Hotel & Casino, Breedestraat, just by the bridge in Otrobanda, T4627400, www.otrobandahotel .com. Excellent location, good for business travellers, rooms small but comfortable, suites and single, double, triple or quad rooms available, some interconnecting, coffee shop and restaurant with good view of Punda and floating bridge, pool.

AL-A Trupial Inn and Casino, Groot Davelaarweg 5, T7378200, www.trupialinn .com. In residential area, 74 rooms, a/c, pool with waterfall, restaurant, tennis for day and night time play, open-air bar, entertainment, shuttle bus to downtown, suites available, Wi-Fi hotspot.

A Hotel San Marco and Casino, Columbusstraat 5, Punda, T4612988, www.sanmarcocuracao.com. 82 rooms, completely renovated, a/c, TV, breakfast included.

A-B Pelikaan Hotel, Lange Straat 78, T4623555, www.hotelpelikaan.com. In the heart of Otrobanda, newly rebuilt, clean and smart, 62 good value rooms, a/c, TV, internet access, casino, restaurant.

B Douglas Apartments, Salinja 174, T4614549, lizac@interneeds.net. A/c, cots available, towels and linen provided, kitchenettes, phone, fax facilities, on 1st floor of shopping gallery, bus stop outside.

B El Conde Hotel, Roodeweg 74, near hospital, T4627875, F4627611. Some rooms noisy, basic, 7 rooms, a/c.

B-C Mira Punda, Van de Brandhofstraat 12, T4613995, joserosales@cura.net. Near floating market, 11 rooms, fan, cold water, clean, private bath, in restored mansion, bar.

C Buona Sera (Bonacera) Inn, Kaya Wilson Godett (Pietermaai)104, T4658565, F4658344. A good small hotel, 16 rooms, sleep 1-4, a/c, private bathroom, seaview restaurant and bar, English, Dutch, Spanish, French and Papiamento spoken.

Around the island p955, map p956

LL-L Floris Suite, Piscadera Bay, T4626111, www.florissuitehotel.com. Designer hotel with 72 suites of varying sizes, lots of white with splashes of colour, very tasteful. Plenty of facilities, tennis, pool, spa treatments, dive centre close by.

LL-L Lion's Dive, Dr Martin Luther King Blvd, east of Willemstad, T4348888, www.lionsdive.com. Attractive Green Globe hotel on private beach next to Seaquarium (free entry), 72 rooms, breakfast included, a/c, fan, TV, pool, dive shop on site, dive packages, health club and fitness centre, windsurfing, **Nemo** restaurant, friendly staff, caters for hard-core diving fraternity, courtesy bus to town, internet access.

LL-AL Habitat Curaçao, linked to **Captain Don's Habitat** in Bonaire, at Rif St Marie, Willibrordus, T8648800, www.habitatdiveresorts.com. Suites with garden or ocean view and 2-bedroom cottages around sea- water pond, with meeting rooms, pool, restaurant, bar, beach, spa for massages, free town shuttle bus, dive centre, lots of dive packages available for shore or boat diving.

L-A Seru Coral Resort, Koral Partier 10, T7678499, www.serucoralresort.com. In the eastern part of the island, in the middle of nowhere but great restaurant, nice pool, studios, apartments and villas, 5 km from beach, 29 km from airport, 22 km from town.

A All West Apartments, Westpoint, T4612310, www.allwestcuracao.com. Studios are older, basic, but with sea view and terrace, newer 1-bedroom apartments are more upmarket, also with terrace and sea view, a/c, caters to individuals, dive shop attached, adventure diving, PADI courses, boat and shore diving, small scale, car hire and pick-ups, dive packages.

A Art and Nature Inn, 17 Valkenweg, Julianadorp, T8682259, www.curacao accommodations.com. 10 mins' drive from Willemstad, bungalow with kitchenette and bathroom, each of 14 studio apartments is decorated with murals, mosaics and paintings by the proprietor, Geerdine Kuijpers, an internationally known artist, speaks 6 languages, 5-min drive to supermarket, 1 week minimum stay.

A Bahia Apartments & Diving, Lagun 208, above Lagun beach, T8641000, www.bahia-apartments.com. 8 apartments sleep 3-4 or 4-5 with sofabed in living room, kitchen, balcony or terrace, in blocks painted bright trupial yellow, steps down to beach where fishermen bring their catch, good snorkelling, nice beach for families. Owners live on site, can help with travel arrangements and excursions, cleaning and linen change once a week.

A Holland, 2 mins from the airport, T8688044. 45 rooms, a/c, TV, phone, business services, restaurant, pool, car rental, casino, diving.

A-B Wayaca Apartments and Bungalows, Gosieweg 153, outside town to the north, T7375589, wimgonny@cura.net. A/c, TV, phone, supermarket, launderette, tennis, minimum 1 week, car rental can be included; houses also available usually on weekly basis or longer.

A-C Landhuis Daniel, weg naar Westpunt, T/F8648400, www.landhuisdaniel.com. Another *landhuis* guesthouse, built by Daniel Ellis in 1711 on extensive property leading to sea, used as an inn for travellers on the east-west route for centuries, renovated 1997, 4 rooms in plantation house, 4 more in small row house (former slave quarters) by pool, breezy French Caribbean restaurant for breakfast, lunch, dinner and snacks (also Dutch pancakes, 25 varieties), home grown organic vegetables in season, diving can be arranged with Aqua Diving nearby.

B-C Bulado Inn, in Boca St Michiel fishing village, Red A'Weg, T8695731, buladoinn@attglobal.net. Family-run, very nice, good value, call and check for deals, 17 a/c rooms, all ocean view, more planned, restaurant, bar, pool, dive centre, nicely landscaped, tennis, meeting rooms, car rental, parking, 10 mins' walk from beach.

❶ Eating

5% sales tax and 10% service is added to the bill in restaurants but an extra 5% is appreciated.

Native food is filling and the meat dish is usually accompanied by several different forms of carbohydrate, one of which may be *funchi*, a cornmeal bread in varying thickness but usually looking like a fat pancake (the same as *cou-cou* in the Eastern Caribbean). Goat stew (*stoba di kabritu*) is popular, slow cooked and mildly spicey (milder and tastier than Jamaican curry goat), recommended. Soups (*sopi*) are very nourishing and can be a meal on their own, grilled fish or meat (*la*

paria) is good although the fish may always be grouper, red snapper or conch (*karkó*), depending on the latest catch; meat, chicken, cheese or fish-filled pastries (*pastechi*) are rather like the *empanadas* of South America or Cornish pasties.

While in the Netherlands Antilles, most visitors enjoy trying a *rijsttafel* (rice table), a sort of Asian *smørgasbørd* adopted from Indonesia, and delicious. Because *rijsttafel* consists of anywhere from 15 to 40 separate dishes, it is usually prepared for groups of diners, although some Curaçao restaurants will do a modified version of 10 or 15 dishes.

There is plenty of fast food to cater for most tastes, including pancake houses. Late night fast food, local fashion, can be found at truk'i pans, bread trucks which stay open until 0400-0500 and sell sandwiches filled with conch, goat stew, salt fish and other Antillean specialities.

You can get great fruit shakes at **Trax's**, a van at the Otrobanda side of the Queen Emma bridge. Wonderful home-made ice cream, large variety, is on offer at **Vienna Ice Café**, on Handelskade in Punda.

A selection of European, South American (mostly Chilean) and Californian wines is usually available in restaurants. Curaçao's gold-medal-winning *Amstel* beer, the only beer in the world brewed from desalinated sea water, is very good indeed and available throughout the Netherlands Antilles. *Amstel* brewery tours are held on Tue and Thu at 1000, T4612944 for information. Some Dutch and other European beers can also be found. Fresh milk is difficult to get hold of and you are nearly always given evaporated milk with your tea or coffee. Curaçao's tap water is excellent; also distilled from the sea.

Willemstad *p949, map p954*
The best place to try local food in Willemstad is the old market building beyond the round concrete market tower by the floating market, Mon-Fri 1100-1430. Here many cooks offer huge portions of good, filling local food cooked in vast pots on charcoal fires, at reasonable prices, choose what you want to eat and sit down at the closest bench or one of the nearby tables having first ordered, takeaway available, very busy at lunchtimes, the best

dishes often run out, make sure you have the right money available.

There are several restaurants in the Arches, good for a meal or just drinks.

ⓉⓉⓉ **Bistro Le Clochard**, in the Rif Fort walls overlooking the harbour, T4625666, www.bistroleclochard.com. Mon-Fri 1200-1400, 1830 onwards, Sat evenings only, open Sun Dec-Mar. French and Swiss cuisine, choose fresh local fish rather than imported. Very expensive for what you get but the location is spectacular, go for sunset drinks if not to eat.

ⓉⓉⓉ **Fort Nassau**, T4613450. Mon-Fri 1200-1400, Mon-Sun 1830-2300. Spectacular location with a panoramic view from the 200-year-old fort, no shorts, sandals or sneakers.

ⓉⓉⓉ **Grill King**, in the Waterfort Arches, T4616870. Mon-Sat 1100-2300, Sun 1700-2300. Friendly and has good international food.

ⓉⓉⓉ **La Pergola**, in the Waterfort Arches, T4613482. Mon-Sat 1200-1400, daily 1830-2230 daily. Italian food, fish, pizza, terrace or a/c dining.

ⓉⓉⓉ **Larousse**, in an old house on Penstraat 5, almost opposite the **Avila Beach**, T4655418. Tue-Sun 1800-2400. French menu with local and imported North Sea fish, quiet, no shorts or sandals.

ⓉⓉⓉ **The Wine Cellar**, Concordiastraat, T4612178. Mon-Sat. Owned by chef Nico Cornelisie, a master rotisseur, one of the most highly regarded restaurants in Willemstad, in small old house, only 8 tables, chilly a/c, very good food but unexciting wine list, local fish and meat (ostrich) particularly good, no shorts or sandals, reservations recommended.

ⓉⓉⓉ-ⓉⓉ **Sawasdee**, Eyck Van Voorthuyzenweg 5, near Curaçao Museum, T4626361. 1830-2200. Thai restaurant, takeaway available.

ⓉⓉ **Fort Waakzaamheid**, Seru Domi, T4623633, www.fort-waakzaamheid.net. 1200-1400, 1800-2230. Lovely sunset views from the terrace on top of the fort, which is on a hill above Otrobanda, restaurant and tavern, good food and menu, reservations suggested.

ⓉⓉ **Green Mill**, Salinja Galleries, T4658821. Lunch or dinner, happy hour Mon-Thu 1800-1900, Fri 1700-1830. Menu with good variety.

ⓉⓉ **Hook's Hut**, T4626575, between **Marriott** and **Hilton** hotels. Thatched tiki hut bar and restaurant next to the sea, good drinks, food OK, evening entertainment at weekends, insect repellent advised.

ⓉⓉ **The Indonesia**, Mercuriusstraat 13, T4612606. Mon-Sat 1200-1400, daily 1800-2130. Wonderful Javanese food specializing in 16 or 25-dish *rijsttafel*, essential to book, often several days ahead, no shorts.

ⓉⓉ **Mambo Beach**, at the Seaquarium, T4618999. 1000-2200. Check what's on offer, special nights, such as barbecues, on the beach, sometimes live music.

Ⓣ **Downtown Terrace**, Gomezplein 4, T4616722. For drinks, snacks or cheap lunches and dinner. You can hear the chimes from the Spritzer and Fuhrmann bells, great selection of Belgian beers.

Ⓣ **The Golden Star**, Socratesstraat 2, T4654795. Daily 1200-2300, live music Sat 1900-2300, takeaway available. The best restaurant for local food. Informal, friendly, plastic table cloths, fun, TV showing American sport, home cooking, very filling, goat stew washed down by a couple of *Amstels* recommended, popular with locals and tourists.

Around the island *p955, map p956*

ⓉⓉ **El Marinero**, Schottegatweg Noord 87B, T7379833. Lunch 1200-1500, dinner 1830-2330. A good fish and seafood restaurant.

ⓉⓉ **Fisherman's Wharf**, Dr Martin Luther King Blvd 91-93, T4657558. Very good seafood, lunch and dinner.

ⓉⓉ **Jaanchie's**, Westpoint 15, T8640126. Popular, huge, filling portions, good catch of the day, see the bananaquits (kind of honeycreeper) eating sugar, parties catered for, takeaway service, no reservations, bus stops outside for return to Willemstad.

ⓉⓉ **Oasis**, Savonet 79, on the Westpoint road, opposite the entrance to the Christoffel Park, T8640085. Mon-Fri 1200-2400, Sat and Sun 1030-0300, dinner served until 2100, dancing afterwards. Seafood and Creole dishes but also offering chicken and ribs.

ⓉⓉ **Octopus**, Marinebadplaats, St Michielsbay, T8881244, susernv@cura.net. Fresh fish, local food, bar, restaurant and terrace by the sea.

Bars and clubs

Willemstad *p949, map p954*
K-Pasa is a weekly dining and entertainment guide, widely available, check for happy hours, www.k-pasa.com.

All the large hotels have **casinos**, with gaming tables and rows and rows of fruit machines, open virtually all hours, but usually 1400-0500. There are plenty of nightclubs and discos, several of which are in the **Salinja** area.

Façade, Lindberghweg 32-34, T4614640, Tue and Wed, Fri-Sun 2200-0400, happy hour Fri from 1800, and **Studio 99**, Lindberghweg, are favoured by wealthy locals of all ages; you will not be let in wearing jeans or trainers.

The Living Room, Salinja 129, T4614433, thelivingroom@cura.net. Has a restaurant, dance floor and lounge, DJ playing latest hits. Latin music and dance is very popular here.

Lyric's Gay Café, Waterfort Arches. 2200-0300 Thu, Fri, 2200-0400 Sat. Popular gay club.

The Music Factory, Salinja 131, T4610631. Mon-Sat 1700-0300. Fri live music, Sat DJ, special drinks nights with half-price brand names 2200-2400.

Salsipuedes, at De Ruyterkade 55, Punda, T461090. Salsa dancing, classes, concerts.

Tututango, at Plaza Mundo Merced, T4654633. Latin music and dancing. Fri open until 0400, gay friendly.

Around the island *p955, map p956*
Baya Beach Club, Caracas Bay Island, T470777. Latin night Fri, best on Sat night, disco and drinking spot.

Mambo Beach Club, on the Seaquarium beach, T4618999, see p957, above. A good nightspot with happy hour and dancing weekends until 0400, gay friendly, restaurant during the week.

Octopus, see Eating, above. Live music and dancing most nights at happy hour 1800-1900.

Entertainment

Curaçao *p949, maps p952 and p956*
Cinema
The Movies Curaçao, T4651000, www.themoviescuracao.com.

Dance

If you want to improve your salsa or merengue, you can take lessons at **Salsa City**, T5610782; at the **Danzarte Academy**, T6674616; at **Landhuis Brievengat**, T5603645, 1900, Wed, Thu; or at **Salsipuedes**, see Bars and clubs, above.

Festivals and events

Curaçao *p949, maps p952 and p956*
Feb Curaçao, Aruba and Bonaire all hold the traditional **pre-Lent Carnival**. On the Sun, a week before, is the children's parade. Curaçao's main parade is on the Sun at 1000 and takes 3 hrs to pass, starting at Otrobanda. The following Mon most shops are closed. On the Mon at 1500 there is a children's farewell parade and there is a Farewell Grand Parade on the Tue evening when the Rey Momo is burned. **Curaçao Carnival Foundation**, T4612717. You can hear *tumba* around carnival time and a **Tumba Competition** is held at the Festival Center, T7376343.

Mar/Apr Kite Festival with kite-flying competitions, is held around Easter when the winds pick up, T7331127, kasdicultura@curinfo.an.

May May Jazz Festival, contact the Curaçao Jazz Foundation, T4658043, www.curacaojazz.com, for details. **Merengue Festival**, contact the Festival Center, T7376343, for details.

Aug Salsa Festival, contact the Festival Center, T7376343, for details.

Oct Golden Artists Music Festival, T4655777.

Nov Jazz Festival, contact the Curaçao Jazz Foundation, T4658043, www.curacaojazz.com, for details.

Shopping

Curaçao *p949*
Willemstad's jewellery shops are noted for the quality of their stones. The main tourist shopping is in Punda where you can pick up all sorts of duty-free bargains in fashion, china, etc.

Art and crafts
Arawak Craft Products, Mattheywerf 1, Otrobanda, T4627249, F4628394, near

cruise ship dock and ferry. Tiles, reliefs of Dutch-style houses and other ceramics, you can watch the potters and artists and even make your own, **Arawak Art Gallery** upstairs, Mon-Sat 0900-1800, Sun too if cruise ship in dock.

Bookshops
Boekhandel Mensing, Punda. Has a limited selection of guide books and maps. Larger and better stocked bookshops are out of the centre of Willemstad.

Mensings' Caminada and **Schottegatweg and Van Dorp** in the Promenade Shopping Centre, good maps and guide book section. **Van Dorp** shops are also located in most large hotels; they stock *Footprint* guides.

▲ Activities and tours

Curaçao *p949, maps p952 and p956*
Bowling
Curaçao Bowling Club, Chuchubiweg 10, T7379275. 6 lanes, US$11 per hr, reservations advised.

Cycling
Rancho Alfin, T8640535. Guided mountain bike rides through the Christoffel Park, or you can go alone.

Biking is also available at Caracas Bay Island.

Diving
There are many dive operators, not all of which are mentioned here, and it is worth shopping around before booking a package deal. Most operators offer a single-tank boat dive for around US$40, a 2-tank dive for US$65-70 and snorkelling trips including equipment for about US$20-25, but check when booking whether 10% service is included in the quoted price.
All West Diving, Westpoint and Playa Kalki, T8640102, www.allwestcuracao.com. Courses, boat dives, kayaks for diving and equipment for rent. Students are given preferential rates.
Dive School Wederfoort, Marine Beach Club, St Michielsbaai, T8884414, www.divewederfoort.com. Contact Eric and Yolanda Wederfoort. Has been in operation since 1966, very friendly, reputable, mostly shore dives, the drop starts 25 m from dive

centre; a PADI open-water course is US$300, accommodation and restaurant available.
Habitat Curaçao, T8648200, curacao@habitatdiveresort.com. An offshoot of **Captain Don's Habitat** in Bonaire, at Rif St Marie, offering PADI, NAUI and SSI courses, boat dives, shore dives, snorkelling, photography, all equipment available for rent, lots of package deals.
Ocean Encounters, at the Lions Dive Hotel next to the Seaquarium, T4618131, www.oceanencounters.com. A PADI 5-star Gold Palm Resort and one of the larger operations. Dive boats are fully equipped for emergencies and take no more than 16 divers each. It has a large air station, equipment rental, a retail shop and offers several courses.

Fishing
The **International Blue Marlin** tournament is held in Mar.
Hemingway Fishing Charters, T5630365. One of several companies offering deep-sea fishing charters.

Golf
Blue Bay Golf and Beach Resort, T7373590, www.bluebaygolf.com. 18-hole championship course opened in 2000.
Curaçao Golf and Squash Club, Wilhelminalaan, Emmastad. A 9-hole sand golf course open 0800-1230, green fee US$15 for 18-hole round. There are also 2 **squash** courts, US$7, open 0800-1800, T7373590.

Horse riding
Ashari's Ranch, Groot Piscadera Kaya A-23, T8690315. 1000-1900. Offers horses for hire by the hour inland (US$20), or 1½ hrs including a swim at the beach (US$30). Beginners as well as experienced riders, playground for children.
Rancho Alegre, T8681181. Does horse riding for US$20 per hr, including transport.
Rancho Alfin, T8640535. Has guided rides through the Christoffel Park, no experience necessary.

Running
For information about running, particularly for the marathon, half marathon and 10-km run in Nov, contact **Road Runners Club**, T8682317. Triathlons are sometimes organized, with sea

swimming, mountain biking and trail running, contact **Vista Bike and Body Beach**, Boca Sint Michiel, T8682576.

Sailing

Many charter boats and diving operators go to Klein Curaçao, a small, uninhabited island off East Point which has sandy beaches and is good for snorkelling and scuba diving, a nice day trip with lunch provided for about US$65. Sailing boats include *Mermaid*, T5601530, www.mermaidboattrips.com, and *Bounty*, T5601887, www.bountyadventures .com. There are snorkel, snorkel-picnic and sunset trips; also day sailing trips from Willemstad up the coast with barbecue lunches at, for example, **Port Marie**, for about US$65, to the **East End** with lunch at Santa Barbara, and weekend sailing trips to Bonaire, accommodation on board. 1 such sailing ship is the 120-ft *Insulinde*, T5601340, www.insulinde.com, beautiful trip, including lunch but not drinks. You can also go on **hovercraft** excursions to various beaches for snorkelling or for sunset tours, with **Neptune Hovercraft Tours**, T8641500.

The Curaçao International Sailing Regatta is held end-Jan with competitions in 3 categories, short distance (windsurfers, hobie cats, sunfish, etc), long distance and open boat (trimarans, catamarans, etc, race 32 km to Spanish Water and back), all starting from the Santa Barbara Beach Resort. For details, T5619292, www.curacaoregatta.com.

The **Sami Sail Regatta** in Apr is organized by the village of Boca Sami, accompanied by local food and live music, T5618090.
Yacht Club, Brakkeput Ariba, z/n, T7673038, or contact Mr B van Eerten, T7675275.
Sail Curaçao, T7676003. Has sailing courses, rentals and boat trips, also surfing lessons.

Tennis

The large hotels have tennis courts and some have a pro.
Santa Catharina Sport and Country Club, T7677028, F7677026. 6 hard courts, a swimming pool, bar and restaurant.

Tour operators

Casper Tours, T5100721/4653010. One of the best island tours, informative, fun, covers east to west, 0900-1600 including lunch at a local restaurant for US$35 (cruise ships' tours

from US$15) in a/c minibuses, English, Dutch and Spanish spoken.
Dornasol Tours, T8682735. Highly recommended local guide with minibus, full- or half-day eco-tours by biologist and historian Lies van de Kar, English, Dutch, German and Spanish spoken, also tours of Jewish sites.
Old City Tours, T4613554. Walking tour of Otrobanda, 1715-1900, US$5.55 including a drink.
Taber Tours, T7376637, http://curacao.com /tabertours (branch at airport and at many hotels). A variety of tours, usually in large Greyhound-type buses.
Tour Guide Curaçao, T5268930, tourguidecuracao@hotmail.com. Michel Brouwer offers guided tours with city walks and hiking trails.

⊙ Transport

Curaçao *p949, maps p952 and p954*
Air
From Europe KLM and Arkefly fly direct from Amsterdam several times a week and KLM has connecting flights to Guayaquil and Quito.

From North America There are flights from Miami with **American Airlines** and from Atlanta with **Delta**; connecting flights from other US cities generally go through Miami, San Juan or Montego Bay (**Air Jamaica**).

From South America There are lots of flights from Colombia, Venezuela and Suriname but airlines tend to change frequently.

From the Caribbean DAE, Divi Divi and **Insel Air** connect Curaçao with the other Dutch islands of Aruba, Bonaire and Sint Maarten. **Air Jamaica** from Kingston, Montego Bay. **American Eagle** from San Juan.
Airlines KLM, Promenade Shopping Centre, Schottegatweg Oost, T7361422; Insel Air, Dokweg 19, Maduro Plaza, T7331521.

At the airport are: Aeropostal Alas de Venezuela, T8882808; Aerovías de Integración Regional (AIRES), T8883431; Air Jamaica, T8881919; American Airlines/American Eagle, T8695707, T800-4337300; Arkefly, T8686811; Aserca, T8680778; Avior, T8681912; Avianca, T8680122; Delta, T8886644; Divi Divi, T8881050; Dutch Antilles Express, T8682233, call centre T07170808; **Surinam Airways**, T8689600.

Bus

There are collective taxis taking 9 passengers, called 'bus', and identified by an BUS on their licence plates. *Konvoois* are big yellow or blue buses which run to a schedule and serve outlying areas of Curaçao. The fare for the Konvooi is NAf1 for rides within the city and to the east, or NAf1.50 for rides to the west. There is a terminal at the post office by the circular market in Punda and another near the Rif Fort in Otrobanda. At the bus station at Otrobanda a schedule (Buki di Bus) is available. The small buses go more often than the Konvooi but have no schedule. The price fluctuates between NAf1.25-1.75, depending on where you're heading. To the **airport** get a bus marked Hato from Punda at 15 mins past the hr from 0615 to 2315, or from Otrobanda at 15 mins past the hr from 0615 to 2320, returning on the hr, usually full. Buses to **Westpunt** leave from Otrobanda on the odd hr, last bus 2300, return on the even hr. Buses and minibuses to **Dominguito** (the Seaquarium) and **Caracas Bay** run from Punda. A bus marked Schottegat runs from Punda via the Trupial Inn and Casino, the Curaçao Golf and Squash Club, the Jewish cemetery and the Curaçao Museum to **Otrobanda**. The **Lagun** and **Knip** bus route leaves Otrobanda at half past the even hr in the mornings and on the odd hr in the afternoons via the Curaçao Museum, the University, Landhuis Jan Kok, Santa Cruz beach, Jeremi beach, Lagun Beach and Bahia beach, returning from Knip on the alternate hr. While the service in and around Willemstad is efficient, the service to **Westpunt** is erratic and planning is needed to avoid getting stranded. The standard city bus fare is NAf1 with no apparent timetables or bus stops. Outside town you may get charged a variety of fares, particularly on minibuses. Check beforehand or ask what others are paying.

Car

Traffic circulates on the right.
Car hire Foreign and international driving licences are accepted. Companies include: Avis, T4611255, www.avis.com; **Budget**, best rates, ask for specials or coupons, T8683466, www.curacao-budgetcar.com; **Europcar/ National**, T8694433, www.nationalcuracao .com; **Star Rent a Car**, T4627444; **Vista**

Rent-a-Car, T7378871. Prices start at about US$30 daily, US$180/week; jeeps, minimokes, buggies, scooters and bikes also available.

Motorcycles/Scooters/Bicycles
American Scooter, T4650772, www.american-scooter.com. Tours, rentals and sales of scooters.
The Bike Shop, T5603882, jackbikeshop@hotmail.com. Motorbike rental and ATV tours.
Bon Bini Brommie, T5236203. For motorbike rental and tours.
Scooby's Rental Scooters, T5238618, www.scooterscuracao.com. Rentals and tours.
Wanna Bike Curaçao, T5273720, info@wannabike.net. Mountain bike tours.

Taxi
It is not always possible to get a taxi to the airport early in the morning or late at night so if you are going to a night club arrange your taxi in advance (sometimes the driver will turn up a little early and join you on the dance floor).

Taxi fares are fixed. Fares from the airport to **Van der Valk Plaza** or **Avila Beach**, US$22-24; **Lion's Dive**, US$27-29; **Habitat Dive Resort**, US$38-40. Rates are for 4 passengers, each additional passenger pays an additional 25% each. Fares increase by 25% 2300-0600. Airport displays taxi fares to main hotels. Try and pay in guilders as taxi drivers do not always have the right change for dollars. Fares for sightseeing trips should be established at beginning of trip, the usual price is US$20 for the 1st hr and US$5 for each subsequent 15 mins. Tipping is not strictly obligatory. The high price of taxis is a common complaint. Taxis do not always go looking for business and it can be difficult to hail one. Best to telephone from a hotel lobby or restaurant/bar, one will arrive in a couple of mins, or go to a taxi stand and just get into an empty car, the driver will then turn up. Taxi stands are outside hotels, in Punda and Otrobanda, or at the airport. Drivers do not always know the area as well as they should, even restaurants can sometimes be tricky for them to find. Courtesy vans operated by the hotels can be more comfortable. For taxi fares or complaints T163.

● Directory

Curaçao *p949, maps p952 and p956*
Banks ABN-AMRO Bank; Antilles Banking
Corp; Maduro & Curiel Bank, Plaza Jojo
Correa, T4611100; **Banco di Caribe**,
Schottegatweg Oost, T4616588. Banking
hours are 088-1530 Mon-Fri. At the airport the
bank is open Mon-Sat 0800-2000, Sun
0900-1600. ATMs at **ABN-AMRO Bank** and
Maduro & Curiel Bank (Visa, Mastercard and
Cirrus, issuing either US$ or Naf).
Internet There are lots of internet cafés in
Willemstad, offering internet access,
international phone calls, scanners, printers,
photocopying, CD burning and fax. In
addition, the **public library**, Chumaceiro Blvd
17, T4345200, has public internet terminals.
Wireless hotspots can be found at the airport,
cafés and many hotels. **Telephone** Local
companies are UTS (United
Telecommunication Services), Rigelweg 2,
T7770101, and CT (Curaçao Telecom),
Schottegatweg Oost 19, T7361056.

International roaming is available for mobile
phones in Curaçao, but if it is not available
with your local network, you can either opt
for a rental cellular phone, or buy a pre-paid
chip and number for your own phone from
UTS or CT. **Library** The public library,
T4617055, is a modern building in Scharloo,
cross the bridge by the floating market, turn
right along the water and it is on your left.
The Reading Room has books in Dutch,
English, Spanish, French and Papiamento.
Medical services The 550-bed **St
Elisabeth Hospital** is well equipped and
modern with good facilities including a
coronary unit and a recompression chamber
(T4624900). For **emergencies**, T910
(hospital), T912 (ambulance). The **Sentro
Mediko Santa Rosa**, at Santa Rosaweg 329,
daily 0700-0000, laboratory on the premises.
For minor complaints, over-the-counter
medicines can be bought at a local
pharmacy (botika). Most are open all day
until 1900 and some stay open 24 hours on a
rotating schedule. **Police and fire** T911.

Aruba → *Country code: 297. Colour map 5, B1.*

*Aruba is the smallest of the 'ABC' group of islands, only 25 km north of Venezuela. It
has been closely linked with the Venezuelan oil industry for most of the 20th century,
but when times were hard, a decision was made to diversify into mass tourism. The
coastal strip on the Leeward side of the island with the best beaches is now
wall-to-wall hotels, with all those of more than 300 rooms allowed to have a casino. A
wide range of watersports is on offer, including excellent windsurfing, which is world
class. On land there is a golf course among the sand dunes in the north.* ► *For Sleeping,
Eating and other listings, see pages 973-982.*

Ins and outs

Getting there Like the other Dutch islands, there is a scheduled flight from Amsterdam
with **KLM**, but otherwise poor connections with Europe. More flights, bringing
sun-worshippers, honeymooners and gamblers, come from North and South America.

Getting around There are buses and taxis, otherwise you can hire a car, motorcycle
or bicycle. Most people don't bother and simply book a seat on a tour bus if they want
to get away from the beach and hotel for a while but a car is useful for dining at
restaurants away from your hotel. The airport is only 3.5 km south of Oranjestad, the
capital, but nearly all the hotels hug the coast north of town; there are buses on the
route from Oranjestad to San Nicolas in the extreme southeast, and taxis, which have
a set charge for each hotel based on distance. ► *See Transport, page 980, for further details.*

Oranjestad → *Population: 21,000*

Oranjestad, the capital of Aruba, is a busy little town where 'duty-free' generally implies a discount rather than a bargain. The main shopping area is on **Caya G F (Betico) Croes**, and streets off it. Many of the buildings in the colourful Antillean style are actually modern and do not date from colonial times as in Willemstad, Curaçao. The former fruit market area on the harbour opposite the Royal Plaza Mall is now a **Plaza Cultural**, a market place for arts, crafts and food, with performance artists.

The small museum in the restored 17th-century **Fort Zoutman/Willem III Tower**, Zoutmanstraat, is closed and due to move to a newly renovated historical building on Schelpstraat in 2008. The fort, next to the Parliament buildings, opposite the police station, dates from 1796 and marks the beginning of Oranjestad as a settlement. Built with four guns to protect commercial traffic, in 1810-1911 it sheltered the government offices. The tower was added around 1868 with the first public clock and a petrol lamp in the spire; the lamp was first lit on King Willem III's birthday in 1869 and served as a lighthouse. The Fort was restored in 1974 and the tower in 1980-1983. The **Archaeological Museum** ⓘ *J E Irausquin 2-A, T5828979, Mon-Fri 0800-1200 1300-1600*, is small, but recommended as the best museum in the ABCs. It is cleverly laid out in three parts, Preceramic, Ceramic (from AD 500) and Historic (from AD 1500-1800 when the Amerindians used European tools). The two main sites excavated are Canashitu and Malmok and most objects come from these. There are some interesting publications available in English. A numismatic museum, **Mario's Worldwide Coin Collection**, also known as the **Museo Numismático** ⓘ *Weststraat, next to the bus station by the cruise dock, www.museumaruba.org. Mon-Thu 0900-1600, Fri 0900-1300, Sat 0900-1200*

Aruba

donations welcomed, not far from Fort Zoutman and the **Central Bank of Aruba**, has a collection of over 40,000 coins from over 400 countries and from ancient Greece, Rome, Syria and Egypt. A bit cramped, but with a lot of fascinating material, the museum is run by the daughter of the collector, Mario Odor. The **Aloe Museum** ① *Pitastraat 115, Hato, T5883222, www.arubaaloe.com, Mon-Fri 0800-1600*, is a factory tour of aloe and its products in Hato. Aloe has long been important in Aruba, where growing conditions are ideal, and the plant even figures in the national coat of arms. Cosmetics and other products are for sale.

Around the island

Aruba is the smallest and most westerly of the ABC group lying 25 km north of Venezuela and 68 km west of Curaçao. Like Curaçao and Bonaire, Aruba has scant vegetation, its interior or *cunucu* is a dramatic landscape of scruffy bits of foliage, mostly cacti, the weird, wind-bent divi divi (*watapana*) trees and tiny bright red flowers called *fioritas*, plus huge boulders, caves and lots of dust. Flashes of colour are provided by bougainvillea, oleanders, flamboyant, hibiscus and other tropical plants. You will need a couple of days to see everything on offer inland without rushing. The Esso Road Map marks all the sites worth seeing and it is best to hire a car (4WD if possible) as you have to go on dirt roads to many of them and there is no public transport.

In the hotel strip, across the road from the Westin and Phoenix hotels is the **Butterfly Farm** ① *www.thebutterflyfarm.com, open daily 0900-last tour at 1600, US$13 adults, US$6 children 4-16, unlimited entries during your stay on the island, 25-min tours every 10-15 mins, gift shop*, where you can see the eggs, caterpillars, pupae and over 40 species of butterfly. In the morning there is lots of activity, but in the afternoon the butterflies are sleepy and photography is easier. They are attracted by brightly-coloured clothing and also by citrus-based perfume.

The village of **Noord** is known for the **Santa Anna Church** ① *services are held Mon, Wed and Fri at 1830, Sat at 1900 and Sun at 0730 and 1800*, founded in 1766, rebuilt in 1831 and 1886, the present stone structure was erected in 1916 by Father Thomas V Sadelhoff, whose portrait is on the twelfth Station of the Cross. It has heavily carved neo-Gothic oak altar, pulpit and communion rails made by the Dutchman, Hendrik van der Geld, which were the prize work shown at the Vatican Council exhibition in 1870. They were then housed in St Anthony's Church at Scheveningen in Holland, before being given to Aruba in 1928. The church is popular for weddings, being light and airy with a high vaulted ceiling and stained-glass windows. Not far from Noord on the north coast is the tiny **Chapel of Alto Vista**, dating from 1952 but on the site of the chapel built by the Spanish missionary, Domingo Antonio Silvester in 1750. It is in a spectacular location overlooking the sea and is so small that stone pews have been built in semi circles outside the chapel.

Also on the north coast are the ruins of a gold mine at **Seroe Gerard** and a refinery at **Bushiribana** in a particularly bleak and sparsely vegetated area. The machinery at the mill, right on the coast, was damaged by sea spray and moved to Frenchman's Pass in 1824. A partly paved road leads to the **natural bridge** where long ago the roof of a cave collapsed, leaving only the entrance standing. It is actually fairly low and not as spectacular as tourist brochures would have you believe. There is a souvenir shop. On the road to the natural bridge there is an **Ostrich Farm** ① *T5859630, greatoutdoors@setarnet.aw, open daily for guided tours 0900-1600, US$12 adults, US$6 children 4-16*, where you can hand feed the birds and see their eggs in the incubator. These African birds seem to be ideally suited to the arid terrain and rugged landscape of Aruba.

Inland, extraordinary rock formations can be seen at **Casibari** and **Ayó**, where huge, diorite boulders have been carved into weird shapes by the wind. At Casibari

⁚ Touching down

Documents All nationalities need a passport and some, such as citizens of former Communist bloc countries, need a visa, unless they are legally residing in a country whose citizens do not need a visa. A return or onward ticket and proof of adequate funds are also required for all visitors. Dogs and cats are permitted entry if they have a valid rabies and health certificate; no pets are allowed from South or Central America.

Customs People over 18 are allowed to bring in one-fifth of liquor, 200 cigarettes, 50 cigars and 250 grammes of tobacco.

Currency Aruba has its own currency, the Aruban florin, not to be confused with the Antillean guilder, which is not accepted in shops and can only be exchanged at banks. The exchange rate is Afl1.77=US$1, but shops' exchange rate is Afl1.80. US dollars are widely accepted, even on buses.

Departure tax US$37, usually included in the price of your flight ticket, or US$10 to Bonaire, but a general usage tax of US$7 still has to be paid. If flying out to the USA, you will clear US customs and immigration in Aruba (US Immigration, T5831316).

Clothing Swimsuits are not permitted in the shopping area. Most casinos require men to wear jackets, and smart clothes (but no ties) are expected at expensive restaurants; otherwise casual summer clothes worn all year. Nudity of any kind is illegal although topless sunbathing is tolerated on most resort beaches.

Public holidays New Year's Day, GF Betico Croes Day (25 Jan), Carnival Mon (early Feb), Flag Day (18 Mar), Good Fri, Easter Sun and Mon, Queen's Birthday (30 Apr), Labour Day (1 May), Ascension Day (May), Christmas Day, Boxing Day.

Tourist information Aruba Tourism Authority, L G Smith Blvd 172, Oranjestad, near the harbour,

steps have been made so that you can climb to the top, from where you get a good view of the island and the Haystack. There is a snack bar and souvenir shop. Ayó does not have steps, you have to clamber up, but a wall is being built up around the rocks to keep out the goats. There are some Indian inscriptions. Toilets, a snack bar and souvenir shop are planned. The 541 ft **Hooiberg**, or Haystack, has steps all the way up. It's very safe, even with children, and the view is worth the effort.

At the village of **Santa Cruz**, just southeast of the Haystack, a cross on top of a boulder marks the first mission on the island. Travelling east from here you pass the **Arikok National Park**, where there are some well-laid-out trails for easy, but hot, walking. There are some interesting rock formations, indigenous fauna and flora (see page 985) and Amerindian art. The road leads to **Boca Prins** (dune sliding) and the **Fontein** cave. Work has been completed to restore the Amerindian drawings in the cave, clean up the more recent graffiti and install a car park and picnic benches. The cave is open to visitors during daylight hours only. There is a large chamber at the entrance, with natural pillars, and a 100-m tunnel leading off, halfway down which are Indian paintings. Despite the desolation of the area, there is a well near the caves with brackish water, which a Japanese man uses to cultivate vegetables for the Chinese restaurants on the island. Further along the coast are the **Guadirikiri** caves, two large chambers lit by sunlight, connected by passages and pillars, with a 100 m tunnel, for which you need a torch. Bats live in this cave system. The road around the coast here is very bumpy and dusty, being used by quarry trucks. A third cave, **Huliba**, is known as the Tunnel of Love (no entry fee but helmets, US$7, and torches available). The walk through the tunnel takes 20-30 minutes with a 10-minute return walk overground. Be prepared for a certain amount of scrambling and rock climbing in the dark, you are told to follow the arrows.

T5823777, www.aruba.com. Also at airport (open daily until about 1900) and cruise dock. Another very good site on Aruba is www.visitaruba.com.
Tourist offices overseas Canada, 5875 Highway 7, Suite 201, Woodbridge, Ontario, L4L 1T9, T905-2643434, ata.canada@ aruba.com. **Germany**, Postfach 1204, D064333 Seeheim, T49-6257-962921, ata.germany@aruba.com.
Netherlands, Schimmelpenninncklaan 1, 2517 JN, Den Haag, T31-70-3028040, ata.europe@aruba.com. **Spain**, Capitán Haya 16.9B, 28020 Madrid, T34-91-5560040, ata.spain@aruba.com. **Sweden**, c/o NBTC, Box 15021, SE-104 65 Stockholm, T46 (0)8-55600759, mprinselaar@holland.com. **UK**, The Saltmarsh Partnership, The Copperfield, 25 Copperfield St, London SE1 0EN, T44-(0)20-79281600, geoff@saltmarshpr.co.uk. **USA**, 1001 Garden View Drive 418, Atlanta, GA 30309-3688, T404-8927822, ata.atlanta@aruba.com; I Financial Plaza, Suite 136, Fort Lauderdale, FL 33394, T954-7676477, ata.florida@aruba.com; 5901 N Cicero, Suite 301, Chicago, Il 60646, T773-2025054, ata.chicago@ aruba.com; 2344 Salzedo St, Miami, FL 33144-5033, T305-5672720; North Freeway Suite 138, Houston, TX 77060-1234 T281-8727822, ata.houston@aruba.com; 1000 Harbor Blvd, Weehawken, NJ 07087, T201-3300800, ata.newjersey@ aruba.com. **Venezuela**, Centro Ciudad Comercial Tamanaco, Torre C, Piso 8, Oficina C-805, Chuao, Caracas, T0602-9599166, ata.venezuela@ aruba.com.
Voltage 110 volts 60 cycle AC same as USA.
Weights and measures Metric.

The road then takes you to **San Nicolas** where there is a strong smell of oil. The Lago Oil Refinery (Exxon) was built in 1928 and was the largest refining plant in the world during the Second World War, when it supplied the allies. The effect on San Nicolas was dramatic. It drew immigrant workers from 56 countries and the community thrived. However, after the war a steady decline set in, and after the closure of the oil refinery in 1985 San Nicolas was a ghost town. But since Coastal Oil took over the refinery, activity has picked up. Old wooden houses have been demolished and new concrete houses built instead. A landmark is **Charlie's Bar**, which has been in operation since 1941 and is a good place to stop for refreshment to see the souvenirs hanging everywhere. Efforts are being made to rejuvenate the town and attract tourism.

Returning northwest towards Oranjestad you pass through Savaneta, where the Dutch marines have a camp. Turn off to the left to **Brisas del Mar**, a good seafood restaurant open to the sea and very popular. At **Pos Chiquito**, a walkway leads through mangroves to **Isla di Oro**, a restaurant built like a ship where there is dancing at weekends and pedalos and watersports. A little further on, a bay with shallow water and mangroves is ideal for snorkelling beginners. The view is not spectacular but you can see many colourful fish. **Spanish Lagoon**, once a pirates' hideout, is a seawater channel, at the mouth of which is the **Aruba Nautical Club** and the water desalination plant. At the other end is a bird sanctuary where parakeets breed, and the ruins of the Balashi gold mill dating from 1899, where the machinery is better preserved than at Bushiribana. There is quicksand in the area around the bird sanctuary, so it is not advisable to walk there. Nearby is **Frenchman's Pass** where the French attacked the Indians in 1700. From here you can turn east again to drive up **Jamanota**, which, at 189 m, stands as the highest elevation on the island.

There are good, sandy beaches on both sides of the island although fewer on the east side which is rough and not so good for swimming. Travelling north along the west coast from Oranjestad an excellent road takes you to the main resort areas where nearly all the hotels are gathered. **Druif Beach** starts at the **Tamarijn Aruba Beach Resort**, extending and widening along the coast to the sister hotel, the **Divi Aruba**, with good windsurfing. At the **Manchebo** there is a huge expanse of sand, often seen in advertisements. North of here is **Eagle Beach** where the 'low rise' hotels are separated from the beach by the road, and then **Palm Beach** where the 'high rise' hotels front directly on to the beach. These three sandy beaches extend for several kilometres, the water is calm, clear and safe for children, although watch out for watersports and keep within markers where provided.

A residential area and the new golf course stretches up from Arashi to the **lighthouse** and the coast is indented with tiny rocky bays and sandy coves, the water is good for snorkelling, while shallow and safe for children. It is also a fishing ground for the brown pelicans. There is a blow hole, where water sometimes spouts up more than 5 m.

At the other end of the island is **Seroe Colorado**, known as 'the colony', which used to be a residential area for Exxon staff. You have to enter the zone through a guard post, but there is no entrance fee and no hindrance. There are two west-facing beaches here worth visiting. **Rodgers Beach** has a snack bar, showers, yachts and is protected by a reef but is in full view of the refinery. **Baby Beach**, on the other hand, is round the corner, out of sight of the refinery, in a lovely sandy bay, protected by the reef, nice swimming and snorkelling, very busy on Sunday, with toilets but little shade. **Sea Grape Grove** and **Boca Grandi**, on the east coast of the south tip has good snorkelling and swimming, being protected by a reef, and is popular with tours which come to see the largest elkhorn coral. Experienced windsurfers come here to wave jump. The prison is near here, remarkable for the pleasant sea view from the cells. Other beaches on the east side of the island are **Boca Prins**, where there are sand dunes, and further north from there, reached by a poor road, is **Dos Playa** where there is good surf for body surfing. The beach here is closed to vehicles because of nesting turtles. **Andicouri** is also popular with surfers, note that you may not approach it through the coconut grove which is private property.

‣ The California Lighthouse area was originally called Hudishibana, but acquired this name after the California steamship was wrecked here one stormy night in 1891.

Diving Visibility in Aruban waters is about 30 m in favourable conditions and snorkelling and scuba diving are very good, although not as spectacular as in the waters around Bonaire. A coral reef extends along the west side of the island from California reef in the north to Baby Beach reef in the south, with dives varying in depth from 5 m to 45 m. There are lots of dive sites suitable for beginners where you can see morays, grouper, eagle rays, manta rays and sting rays, as well as lobsters, parrot fish, angel fish and others. The northwest of the island has fields of seagrass which attract leatherback turtles during the nesting season and are home to hawksbill, green and loggerhead turtles all year. The other side of the island is only for experienced divers as there are strong currents. Organized boat trips regularly visit two wrecks worth exploring, although they can get a bit crowded and then visibility deteriorates. One is a German freighter, the *Antilla*, which was scuttled just after the Second World War was declared in 20 m of water off Malmok beach on the west coast. You can see quite a lot just snorkelling here as parts of the wreck stick up above the water. Snorkelling boat trips usually combine Malmok beach and the wreck. The other wreck is nearby in 10 m of water, the *Pedernales*, a flat-bottomed oil tanker which was hit in a submarine attack in May 1941, while ferrying crude oil from Venezuela to Aruba. The **Aruba Watersports Association** recently sunk a DC-3 aeroplane near the *Pedernales*, to be another wreck dive site only 10 m deep, and the *Star Gerren* tanker was sunk in 2000 at a similar depth for snorkellers and divers opposite the hotel strip by Hadicurari. Be careful not to touch anything underwater; not all the dive masters warn you of the dangers of fire coral and hydroids. An annual **Aruba Perrier Reef Care Project** takes place over a weekend in June or July when everyone gets together to clean up debris and pollution from the main dive sites and beaches.

Windsurfing For excellent windsurfing, head north of Palm Beach to an area of shallow water, known as **Fisherman's Huts** (next to the **Marriott**). Although speeds are high and there is a strong offshore wind, surfing is safe and there are several rescue boats. **Kitesurfing** can also be arranged at Fisherman's Huts, but is done before 1000 and after 1630 so as not to conflict with windsurfers. This beach is called **Malmok** (south end) or **Arashi** (north end) and there are many villas and guesthouses around. There are several high-quality operators offering windsurf packages, boards, sails and accommodation. For

> *Of the three ABC islands, Aruba stands out as having the best beaches, all of which are public and free.*

information about the **Aruba Hi-Winds Pro/Am** competitions, contact **ATA Special Events** ① *T5860440, www.aruba-hiwinds.org*. They usually take place in June. At the same time a **Windsurfing Festival** combines a consumer trade show, with all the latest gear, and music and food on the beach.

🔴 Sleeping

Anything up to 21% tax/service charge is added; some hotels also add a US$1.50-8.25 per day energy surcharge.

If you arrive at a weekend the tourist office in town will be shut and you cannot get any help except at the airport.

Glittering luxury hotels jostle for space along Druif Bay, and Eagle and Palm beaches, many of them all-inclusive, some of them massive, with up to 800 rooms. Hotels with over 300 rooms have casinos. The low-rise resort hotel development starts on **Punta Brabo Beach**, Druif Bay, all hotels are on the beach and offer swimming pools, tennis, watersports, shops, restaurants, etc. The road curves round **Palm Beach** where all the high-rise luxury hotels are. All have at least 1 smart restaurant and another informal bar/restaurant, some have about 5, all have shops, swimming pools, watersports, tennis and other sports facilities on the premises and can arrange anything else. Several are managed by **Divi**, while **Radisson**, **Holiday Inn**, **Best Western**, **Wyndham**, **Hyatt** and **Marriott** are also represented, but not described here. Decent, cheap accommodation is now very difficult to find unless you rent an apartment and share with friends. The **Aruba Tourism Authority** publishes a list of apartments and guesthouses. Weekly or monthly rates are more advantageous. The **Aruba Apartment**

Resort and Small Hotel Association (ARASA) members offer accommodation at less than US$100 but to get a double room at that price at one of the large hotels you will have to negotiate a package deal in advance. Summer rates are substantially less, sometimes half high-season winter rates (16 Dec-15 Apr).

Oranjestad *p968, map p974*
LL Renaissance Aruba Beach Resort & Casino, at L G Smith Blvd 82, T5836000, www.renaissancearubaresort.com. 560 rooms, Seaport Village shops and Crystal casino, on the waterfront. Private island with Aruba's only private beaches, kids club, spa, watersports.
LL-A Aruba Harmony Apartments, Palmitastraat 9, Ponton, T5886787, www.arubaharmony.com. In residential area, Dutch management, good value, rooms, suites, apartments and villas, tiled floors, kitchen, TV, quiet a/c, daily maid service, good beds, free-form pool in garden, Wi-Fi internet, car rental, parking.
A-B A1 Apartments, Pagaaistraat 5, T5828963, www.a1apartmentsaruba.com. Stanley and Ingrid Kemp have fully furnished a/c rooms of different sizes with kitchenette, 10 mins' walk from main shopping centre, TV, well-stocked fridge, car hire arranged, laundry and internet services, friendly, homely.

B Andicuri Inn, De LKA Sallestraaat 13, T5821539, www.aruba.com/exthotel/andicuri.htm. Apartments with a/c bedroom, living room, kitchenette, TV, balcony, sleep 2 plus 1 child, pool, convenient for nightlife but nothing special.

Around the island *p969, maps p968*
LL **Bucuti Beach Resort & Tara Beach Suites**, J E Irausquin Blvd 55-B, T5831100, www.bucuti.com. On 14 acres with a huge sweep of pristine beach. Attractive design, pleasant resort, rooms, beach suites and penthouse suites, tastefully decorated in muted colours and furnished with dark woods, fitness centre, spa, tennis, pool, fine dining in **Pirates' Nest** restaurant, a replica 16th century Dutch galleon, business centre, Wi-Fi internet access.

LL **Casa del Mar**, J E Irausquin Blvd 51, Punta Brabo Beach, T5827000, www.casadelmar-aruba.com. 147 luxury 2-bedroom (time-share) apartments on the beach and 1-bedroom suites not on the beach, children's play area, tennis, pool, minimarket, laundromats. Beware additional charges for tax, service and energy, which really mount up here.

LL **Playa Linda Beach Resort**, J E Irausquin

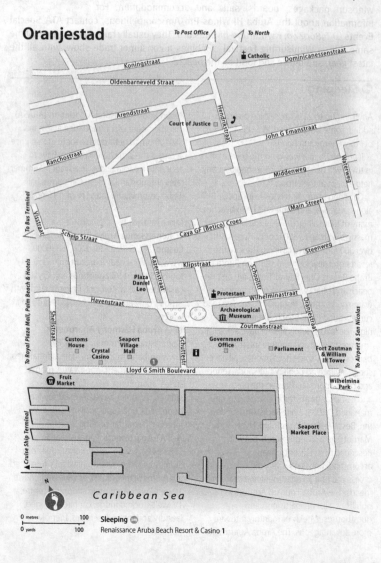

Oranjestad

Netherlands Antilles, ABC Islands Aruba Listings

Sleeping
Renaissance Aruba Beach Resort & Casino 1

Blvd 87, T5861000, www.playalinda.com. A time-share resort of suites and efficiencies, health club, games room, **Spa del Sol** in lobby area for lots of treatments, 0900-1800.

LL-L Amsterdam Manor, J E Irausquin Blvd 252, T5871492, www.amsterdammanor.com. Low-rise, pleasant, painted Dutch colonial-style, 72 studios and apartments with sea view, kitchen, pool, bar and restaurant.

LL-L Manchebo Beach Resort & Spa, J E Irausquin Blvd 55, Manchebo, T5823444, www.manchebo.com. 71 rooms with balcony or terrace in 2 curved wings on huge expanse of sandy beach, meal plans available, fridge, microwave oven, TV, phone, 3 restaurants.

LL-AL Aruba Beach Club, JE Irausquin Blvd 53, T5823000, mshipabccdm@setarnet.aw. 131 rooms with kitchenette, for up to 4 people, functional, members pay lower rates than transient guests. Olympic size pool, lit tennis courts, kids activities, spa, internet café, Wi-Fi internet access.

LL-AL Boardwalk Vacation Retreat, Bakval 20, Noord, T5866654, www.theboardwalk-aruba.com. Right by the **Marriott**, 150 m to the beach, 1 or 2-bedroom *casitas* with living room and kitchen, hammocks, fans, a/c, well equipped, nice furnishings, mini market, pool with jacuzzi, gardens with flowering plants, palm trees and hummingbirds.

LL-AL La Quinta, J E Irausquin Blvd 228, T5875010, www.webnova.com/laquinta. Time-share with rentals, 54 apartments with kitchenette, pools, tennis, across the road from the beach.

LL-AL The Mill Resort, J E Irausquin Blvd 330, T5867700, www.millresort.com. 200 rooms and suites with kitchens, restaurant, sauna, exercise room, tennis, 2 pools, 5-min walk to beach, transport offered.

LL-A Aruba Beach Villas (Sailboard Vacations), 462 LG Smith Blvd, ½ mile north of **Marriott**, T5862527, www.arubasailboardvacations.com. Windsurfing resort with large board and sail shop, 31 villas with 1-2 bedrooms across the road from the sea at Fishermen's Huts, breakfast included, pool, sundeck, jacuzzi, kayaks, beach towels, internet, multilingual staff.

L-A Aruba Millennium Resort, Palm Beach Rd, T5861120, www.arubamillennium resort.com. 12 studios and 10, 1-bedroom time-share apartments, price difference reflects 50% cut in summer. Light, bright, nice furnishings, kitchen, TV, whirlpool outside suite, also pool, sundeck, minimarket, car rental arranged, 2 mins' walk from beach.

AL-A Coconut Inn, Noord 31, T5866288, www.coconutinn.com. Walking distance from supermarket, banks and restaurants, 40 a/c studios and 1-bedroom apartments, TV, balcony, kitchenette, pool, near beach.

AL-A Vistalmar, Bucutiweg 28, T5828579, www.arubavistalmar.com. 1-bedroom apartments with car run by Alby and Katy Yarzagaray, friendly, wooden jetty for swimming and sunbathing, near airport, laundry facilities.

A Arubiana Inn, T5877700, www.arubianainn.com. 12-min walk to Eagle Beach, 18 ground floor studios around pool with fridge and microwave, TV, phone, small living room, beach towels, mini-market, cocktail lounge.

A-B Seabreeze Apartments, Malohistraat 5, Pos Chiquito, 8 km southeast of Oranjestad, T/F5857140, www.sea-breezeappartments.com. Well away from tourist conglomeration, 9 studios and 1-bedroom suites, a/c, kitchenette, patio, TV, clean and smart, dive packages available, snorkelling offered on owner's boat, free airport pick-up, cool boxes provided for picnics, special deals on car hire, short walk to beach, supermarket or **Marina Pirata** restaurant.

Camping

Permit needed from police station, on Arnold Schuttrstraat, Oranjestad. It can take 10 days to get a permit and you must have a local address (ie hotel room).

⊙ Eating

Drinking water is distilled from sea water and is safe to drink.

With few exceptions, meals on Aruba are expensive and generally of the beef-and-seafood variety, but you can get some excellent food. The hotels have some very good gourmet restaurants. Service charge on food and drinks is 15% at the hotels but at other places varies from 10% to 15%. The Aruba Gastronomic Association (AGA), www.arubadining.com, has a dine around programme at 27 restaurants, but there is a surcharge on many items you might want to eat.

Try Balashi beer, brewed by the award

winning Brouwerij Nacional Balashi. It is the island's first fully-automated brewery and uses no artificial additives.

Oranjestad *p968, map p974*

The white trucks (mobile restaurants) located at **Wilhelmina Park**, the post office and the courthouse serve local food and snacks from 2100-0500 at around US$5.

El Gaucho, Wilhelminastraat 80, T5823677, www.elgaucho-aruba.com. Mon-Sat, 1130-1430, 1800-2300. Some say this is the best steak restaurant, with excellent Argentine tenderloin, others complain about crowding and noise, go early for best service. Children's playroom with arcade games, videos, lego etc. Have an aperitif beforehand at the **Garufa Cigar & Cocktail Lounge** across the street and they will page you when your table is ready.

Mathilde/M, Havenstraat 23, T5839200, www.matildearuba.com. Matilde: 1800-2300, occasional Sun brunch; M: 1130-1500, 1800-2300, 2300-0100 Fri, Sat. Now in two parts, with the casual **'M' Bistro Lounge**, a modern restaurant with artwork and TV screens in front of the more formal French restaurant, Matilde. Service can be slow and the atmosphere a bit pretentious, but good food and extensive wine cellar you can wander through. While recently renovated and redesigned with a new manager, the building has been in the Oduber family since the 19th century.

Sake House, Caya Betico Croes 9, T5830405, 1200-2300. Japanese.

Cuba's Cookin', Wilhelminstraat 27, T5880627. Mon-Sat 1130-2230, Sun 1700-2200. Cuban cuisine, accompanied by a live trio playing Cuban music, a cigar salon where you can enjoy a *cohiba*.

Driftwood, Lipstraat 12, Oranjestad, T5832515, www.driftwoodaruba.com. 1700-2300. Good fresh sea food, served Aruban style. Fish caught daily by the owner.

Le Petit Café, at Royal Plaza Mall, second floor overlooking cruise ship dock, T5823166. Cook your own steak on hot coals, reasonable prices.

Qué Pasa?, centre of Oranjestad, T5834888. 1800-0100. A good, intimate restaurant, Italian/international.

Sakura, Wilhelminastraat 4, T5824088. 1200-2300 Mon-Sat. For Japanese food, also Thai.

Café The Plaza, Seaport Market Place, T5838826. Food 1000-2400, but open until 0200. Nice terrace and you can get a good, reasonably priced meal there, daily specials.

Villa Germania, Seaport Market Place, T5836161. 0800-2200. German food for breakfast, lunch and dinner.

Eetcafé The Paddock, L G Smith Blvd 13, T5832334, www.paddock-aruba.com. 1000-0200. Outside or indoor seating, sea view, very good, great saté, inexpensive for Aruba, Amstel on draught and the *daghap* (dish of the day), live music on Sun.

Around the island *p969, map p968*

Amazônia, JE Irausquin Blvd 374, Palm Beach, T5864444, www.amazonia-aruba.com. Mon-Sat 1800-2300, Sun, 1600-2300. Meat and more meat, waiters bring it round all the tables as they do in Brazil, huge salad bar to die for, all you can eat price, but go there really hungry.

The Buccaneer, Gasparito 11 C, T5866172, www.arubadining.com /buccaneer. Mon-Sat 1730-2300. Seafood, giant aquariums, no reservations.

Flying Fishbone, Savaneta 344, south of the airport off the road to San Nicolas, T5842506, www.flyingfishbone.com. 1230-2200. Tables on the beach, some seating on deck, an excellent seafood restaurant, lobster tank, reserve well in advance as very popular.

Gasparito, Gasparito 3, T5867044, www.gasparito.com. Daily except Wed 1730-2200. Aruban specialities and seafood, wins awards for cuisine, art gallery attached exhibiting Aruban works.

Le Dôme, J E Irausquin Blvd 224, Eagle Beach, T5871517, http://ledome-aruba.com. Mon-Fri 1200-1500, daily 1800-2230, Sun brunch 1100-1500. Belgian restaurant with indoor and outdoor seating, open for lunch and dinner, fine dining, 3-course dinner with wine and coffee around US$130-140 for 2. Sun brunch recommended, fixed price, order from menu for breakfast dishes, hot or cold appetizers, entrées and desserts, in any order, as many helpings as you want, better than a buffet. Champagne and mimosas included.

Texas de Brazil, J E Irausquin Blvd, Palm Beach, upstairs above **Amici's**, T5864686. Mon-Sat 1800-2300, Sun 1700-2300, Fri lunch 1100-1500, bar open late. Part of a US chain of steak restaurants, Brazilian-style. Lots of meat like at **Amazonia**, great salad bar and good wine list.

TTT-TT Blossom's, at the **Wyndham Hotel**. Japanese food on 1 side and Chinese on the other, also excellent sushi bar, early-bird special US$16 1730-1830, good value.

TTT-TT Charlie's Bar, Zeppenfeldtstraat 56, San Nicolas, T5845086, www.charliesbararuba .com. 1200-2130, bar until 2200, but could open earlier or later, kitchen closed Sun. International, Aruban and seafood, in operation since 1941.

TTT-TT La Nueva Marina Pirata, at Spanish Lagoon, T5857150. Mon and Wed-Sat 1800-2300, Sun 1200-2300. Seafood and Aruban dishes, follow the main road to San Nicolas, turn right at **Drive Inn**.

TTT-TT Madame Janette, 5 mins east of the high-rise hotels, T5870184. Tenderloin good, also fish, garden dining, one of the in places to eat and very romantic when the torches are lit at night and the musicians start to play, reservations needed.

TT Benihana, Sasakiweg, T5826788, 1200-2300. Japanese, meals around US$20.

TT Brisas del Mar, Savaneta 222A, T5847718. Tue-Sun 1200-1500, Tue-Sat 1700-2300, Sun 1800-2200. Seafood specialities, on deck right on the sea, cool and airy, reasonable prices, catch of the day US$12.

TT French Steak House, in the Tam complex by the **Manchebo**, T5823444, www.manchebo.com/steakhouse. 1730-2300. A relaxed atmosphere, very good steak and piano player, US$32.95 for 5-course steak dinner.

TT The Green House, Palm Beach 29, T5865241. 1100-1400. Most restaurants have vegetarian options on the menu, but this is only vegetarian restaurant. Fairly cheap at around US$15 but only open for lunch.

TT The Old Cunucu House, Palm Beach 150, T5861666. Mon-Sat, 1800-2230. In a typical, low Aruban house, serving Aruban and international food.

TT Promenade, San Nicolas, 2 blocks from Charlie's, T5843131, www.promenadearuba .com. Lunch from 1130, dinner from 1800. Sun brunch from 1130 is good, unlimited amount of food, good choice of appetizers and entrées, live music.

TT Twinkletone's, Turibana Plaza, Noord 124, T5869806. Mon-Sat 1600-2300. For

surf'n'turf, prices around US$18 for main course, prime rib, great lobster and shrimp, singing chefs and waiters.

TT Warung Djawa, Wilhelminastraat 2, T5834888. Mon-Fri 1130-1400 for weekday *rijsttafel* buffet lunch, and Wed-Mon 1800-2300, all you can eat. Serves Indonesian and Surinamese food.

T Freddy's Snack, Mauritsstraat 4A, San Nicolas, T5847888. 0730-2330. Good, if you are in San Nicolas and want to try a local Aruban establishment serving Creole food, main dishes around US$6, nothing fancy, no credit cards.

Bars and clubs

Aruba *p967, map p968*
The legal age for consumption of alcohol and entry to nightclubs is 18.

Most action takes place in Oranjestad and doesn't get going until around midnight.

Start the night at **Carlos'n'Charlies**, www.carlosandcharlies.com. **Mexican**, the hottest place at the moment, then when they close, 0100 weekdays, 0300 weekends, move on to **Mambo Jambo**, for Latin, salsa and merengue. **Club 2000**, has lots of dance music and techno.

Cellar Bar, close to Benetton, behind **Renaissance**, is a small, cosy bar downstairs but upstairs it is **The Music Factory** (TMF), popular with gays at weekends (gets going after 0100), empty weekdays, trance, club, house music, also salsa and merengue. **Choose A Name**, behind Royal Plaza Mall, is the cool place for the more sophisticated crowd, with a bar/restaurant and live music.

Dancing spots include **La Bahia**, Weststraat, Oranjestad; **Club City One**, Sasakiweg, Eagle Beach; **E-Zone**, Weststraat, Oranjestad; **La Fiesta**, Aventura Mall, Oranjestad, and plenty of others in hotels or elsewhere. **Garufa Cigar & Cocktail Lounge** Wilhelmina-straat 63, Oranjestad, T5823677, catches the clientele of **El Gaucho** before and after their meal for aperitifs or coffee and cigars.

Places open late for drinking include **Café The Plaza**, in Seaport Market Place, and **Eetcafé The Paddock**, LG Smith Blvd 13, see Eating, above, both open until 0200.

If you want to bar hop book a seat on **Kukoo Kunuku** (Aruba Adventures, Turibana Plaza 124, T5862010) an open-sided bus, which takes you to 5 stops including an Aruban dinner and a champagne beach halt, US$55, Mon-Sat 1800-2400. Another party bus is **Yabbadabbadoo** (T5870115) which starts with a barbecue at **Monte Blanco Ranch** and carries on with carnival music, dancing, free draft beer and snacks, 1900-2400, US$55.

Tattoo, T5862010, www.arubaadventures .com. Is a floating nightclub, a double-deck boat with rope swing, sunset and dinner-dance cruise, US$55, all drinks US$1, 2 and 3.

◉ Entertainment

Aruba *p967, map p968*
Casinos
A major attraction is gambling and there are 11 casinos on the island. Hotels must have 300 rooms before they can build one; those that do usually start at 1100 and operate 2 shifts. A few are open 24 hrs.

Cinema
Seaport Cinema, Oranjestad. Has 6 screens showing US films.
Drive-In Theatre, Balashi. Occasionally shows European or Latin American films.

◉ Festivals and events

Aruba *p967, map p968*
Throughout the year there are several different music and dance festivals. The **International Theatre Festival** takes place every other year; for information contact CCA, Vondellaan 2, T5821758.
Feb The most important festival of the year, the **Pre-Lenten Carnival** gets earlier every year with supplementary parades and festivities preceding the event itself. There are colourful parades and competitions for best musician, best dancer, best costume, etc. The culmination is the Grand Parade on the Sun preceding Lent.
18 Mar National Anthem and Flag Day, when there are displays of national dancing and other folklore.
24 Jun St John's Day is another folklore day: 'Derramento di Gai'.
Oct Music Festival held over 2 days, with R&B, rock, Latin musicians, T5823777. Local dance music, such as the fast, lively *tumba* is very influenced by Latin America. Arubans are also fond of *merengue*.

Dec New Year's Eve, when fireworks are let off at midnight and musicians and singers go round from house to house (and hotel to hotel).

◯ Shopping

Aruba *p967, map p968*
A wide range of luxury items are imported from all over the world for resale to visitors at cut-rate prices. Liquor rates are good, but prices for jewellery, silverware and crystal are only slightly lower than US or UK prices. There is no sales tax.

In addition to **Caya G F (Betico) Croes** shopping areas include the **Port of Call Market Place**, **Seaport Village Mall**, **Royal Plaza Mall**, **Harbour Town**, **The Galleries**, **Strada I and II** and the **Holland Aruba Mall**.

Arts and crafts
There are local handicrafts such as pottery and artwork.
Artesanía Arubiano, LG Smith Blvd 178, opposite **Tamarijn Hotel**, T5837494, or ask the **Institute of Culture**, T821010, or the **Aruba Tourism Authority**, T823777, for more information.
Galería Harmonia, Main St, St Nicolas, T5842969. Exhibits and sells local artists' work.

Bookshops
Many bookshops in the hotels have some paperbacks.
Van Dorp, Caya G F (Betico) Croes. The main town centre bookshop.
Captains Log, in the new Harbour Town development. Light and airy with a few books and reading material but mostly souvenirs.

▲ Activities and tours

Aruba *p967, map p968*
Bowling
There is an international bowling tournament in Apr, T5826443 for details, and an international youth tournament in Jul.
Eagle Bowling Palace, Pos Abou, T5835038. 16 lanes, 6 of which are for reservation, 1000-0200, US$9 from 1000-1500, US$10.50 from 1500-0200, US$1.20 shoe rental; also 3 racquetball courts.

Diving

For further information on diving and marine news contact the Aruba Tourism Authority. Prices start from about US$45 for a single-tank dive.

Aruba Pro Dive, at about 5 resorts, T5825520. Tries to keep groups small at an average of 6 divers.

Atlantis Submarines, T5836090, operate a US$75, 2-hour trip, including the boat ride to the *Atlantis VI*, which descends to 30 m and explores the *MI Dushi I* and *Morgenster* shipwrecks or the *Sonesta* aeroplane wreck.

Seaworld Explorer, T5862416. A semi-submersible offering a tour along the Arashi Reef and the *Antilla* wreck, at 1130, 1330 and 1630 daily.

Red Sail Sports, L G Smith Blvd 83, T5861603, and at hotels. Sailing, snorkelling, diving with PADI, SSI, IDEA, HSA certification courses, windsurfing, waterskiing, hobie cats, etc, accommodation packages available, this is a large, reputable but expensive international operation.

Other dive operators include **Pelican** (PADI, NAUI, SSI, T5872302); **Unique Sports of Aruba** (PADI, T/F5860096, uniquesports@visitaruba.com); **SEAruba** (T/F5838759), who offer diving in the southeast and to Venezuela; **Native Divers** (IDD, PADI, T/F5864763); **Dax Divers** (PDIC, T/F5851270); and **Dive Aruba** (PADI, T5827337, www.divearuba.com).

Snorkelling from a dive boat varies from US$20-30, although a longer trip with lunch will cost from US$40-65. On these trips you will visit around 3 sites, usually including the *Antillia*, and snuba is often available for 1 of these stops.

Fishing

Many charter boats are available for deep-sea fishing. **Driftwood Fishing Charters**, from Seaport Marina, T5832515, and others. The tourist office has a list so you can contact the captain direct, or else go through **De Palm Tours**. Whole-day trips including meals range from US$350-500, half days around US$250-300, depending on the number of people on board. A deep-sea fishing tournament is held in Oct at the **Aruba Nautical Club**, T5853022 for information.

Golf

Tierra del Sol Golf Course, near the lighthouse, T5860978, www.tierradelsol.com. 18-hole, par 71 course, designed to fit in with the natural landscape and with the sea. A community of homes and villas has also been designed to blend in with the surrounding vegetation with a full-service clubhouse, swimming pool, golf practice range and tennis and fitness complex. One of the best golf courses in the Caribbean. Many hotels are signing up for preferential rates for their guests. Green fees US$68-133 depending on time of day and time of year.

Aruba Golf and Leisure, Sasakiweg just east of **The Mill Resort**, T5864590. A golf driving range, daily 0700-2300, with pro-shop, family centre, Chinese restaurant and café with internet.

There is a 9-hole golf course with oiled sand greens and goats near **San Nicolas**, T842006, golf clubs for rent US$6, green fee US$10 for 18 holes, US$7.50 for 9 holes, Sat and Sun members only, daily 0800-1700; **Divi Aruba**, www.divigolf.com, has a 9-hole golf course; **Adventure Golf** has an 18-hole mini-golf course.

Riding

Rancho El Paso, Washington 44, near Santa Ana Church, T5873310, daily rides except Sun, 1 hr through countryside, US$15, or 2 hrs part-beach, part-*cunucu*, US$30, special trips on paso fino horses for experienced riders. The **National Horse Fair**, a 3-day international competition for paso fino horses is held here in Apr.

Rancho Daimari, T5860239. Also has paso fino horses and offers 2½-hr rides with snorkelling, daily at 0900 and 1500, a/c transport from your hotel included.

Rancho del Campo, T5850290. Takes riders into the national park or to the natural bridge, 2½ hrs, 0930 or 1530, US$45 including transport and snorkelling.

Rancho Notorious, T5860508. Has a choice of 3 trails, to the Alto Vista chapel, the California Lighthouse or a sunset beach ride.

Running

Triathlons and marathons are held periodically, contact the tourist office for details or **IDEFRE**, JG Emanstraat, Oranjestad, T5824987.

Aruba Nautical Club complex, near Spanish Lagoon, T5853022. Pier facilities offering safe, all-weather mooring for almost any size of yacht, plus gasoline, diesel fuel, electricity and water. For information, write to PO Box 161. They also organize an annual 'catch and release' deap-sea fishing tournament every Oct. **Bucuti Yacht Club**, a short sail downwind from the **Aruba Nautical Club**. With clubhouse and storm-proofed pier providing docking, electricity, water and other facilities. Write to PO Box 743.
Catamaran Regatta is held annually in Nov in front of the Palm Beach hotels, with competitors from the USA, Europe and Venezuela. For information contact the *Aruba Tourism Authority*, T5823777.
Seaport Yacht Race, also in Nov, with races from Havana to Seaport Marina, around the island and from Punto Fijo in Venezuela. For details contact Mr Henk Grim at the Seaport Marina, T5839190.

Cruises Several yachts and catamarans offer cruises along the coast with stops for snorkelling and swimming. A morning cruise often includes lunch (about US$40-50), an afternoon trip will be drinks only – and then there are the sunset booze cruises (about US$20-30). The largest catamaran is **Red Sail Sports** (see above), *Fiesta*, which carries 90 passengers, while its sister ship, *Balia*, a 53-ft racing catamaran, does all the usual cruises, T5864500; *Pelican I* is a 50-ft catamaran running along the west coast from Pelican pier, T5872302; *Wave Dancer*, another catamaran, departs from **Holiday Inn** beach, T5825520; *Octopus* is a 40-ft trimaran, departing from **Holiday Inn** pier, also available for private charter, snorkelling and sailing cruises, T5833081; *Mi Dushi* is an old sailing ship built in 1925 which starts cruises from the **Aruba Grand Beach Resort** pier, T5823513.

Tennis
There are tennis courts at most major hotels. **Aruba Racquet Club**, Rooi Santo 21, Palm Beach area, T5860215. 8 lit courts, an exhibition centre court, pro-shop, pool, aerobics classes, fitness centre, bar and restaurant. 0800-2300. There is usually an international tennis tournament in Sep.

Tour operators
De Palm Tours, L G Smith Blvd 142, T5824400, www.depalm.com, also with offices in many hotels. Sightseeing tours of the island and excursions to nearby islands or Venezuela. An excursion to private **De Palm Island** is popular, with good snorkelling, snuba and sea trek offered, sandy beaches along the cay, refreshments, reached by 5-min ferry, leaves every half hr.
Corvalou Tours, T5821149. Julio Maduro, specializes in archaeological, geological, architectural, botanical and wildlife tours.

For a combination 6-hr tour with lunch, US$35, call archaeologist **Egbert Boerstra**, T5841513, or **Julio Maduro**, or **Private Safaris** educational tour, T834869. Mr Boerstra has been involved in excavation work at Ser'l Noka, Malmok, Savaneta, Tanki Flip and Canashito and has worked with the project to establish the Arikok National Park.

There are lots of companies offering tours of the island by minibus with a swimming and snorkelling stop at Baby Beach, about US$35.

Watersports
Virtually every type of watersport is available and most hotels provide extensive facilities. Activities which are not offered on site can be arranged through several tour agencies such as **De Palm Watersports**, T5824545, **Pelican Watersports**, T5831228, and **Red Sail Sports**, T5824500. You can hire jetskis, waterskis, wave runners, banana boats, snorkelling equipment and other toys. Parasailing can be done from the high-rise hotels. Glass-bottomed-boat trips from various locations are around US$20-25, but can be more for a sunset cruise.

⊝ Transport

Aruba *p967, map p968*
Air
From Europe KLM has direct flights from Amsterdam, going on to Lima. **Arkefly** has a flight from Amsterdam. **First Choice** has charters from Gatwick and Manchester (scheduled flights from the UK overnight in New York), while **Air Pullmantur** runs charters from Barcelona.

From North America Atlanta (Delta), Boston (**American Airlines**), Charlotte (US

Airways), Chicago (**United Airlines**), Detroit (**Funjet Vacations**), Houston (**Continental**), Miami (**American Airlines, Martinair**), New York (**American Airlines, Continental**), Philadelphia (**US Airways**). There are also charter services. Scheduled services from Canada involve a change of plane in Miami. Charter service from Canada is available through **My Travel/Skyservice** on a seasonal basis.

From South America Lots of flights from Venezuela with **Avior, Aeropostal, Aserca**. From Colombia, **Avianca** fly from Bogotá and **Aires** from Barranquilla. **KLM** from Lima, Sao Paulo and Quito, **Aerolíneas Argentinas** from Buenos Aires.

From the Caribbean From San Juan with **DAE, Insel Air and Divi Divi** have flights from Bonaire and Curaçao. From Santo Domingo with **Aeropostal**, as well as with **DAE**.

Airline offices Airline offices for all airport lines T5824800. **American Airlines**, T5822700. **Avianca/SAM**, T5826277. **KLM**, T5823546/7. **Viasa**, T5836526. **Aeropostal**, T5837799.

Boat
The harbour is 5 mins' walk from the town, there is a tourist information centre and some souvenir shops which open if a cruise ship is in.

Bus
The bus station is behind the Public Works Department and the Royal Plaza Mall. **Route 1** starts in San Nicolas and runs through Oranjestad via the hospital to Malmok, Mon-Sat, 0455-2255 hourly, returning from Malmok on the hr, journey time 55 mins. **Route 2** also runs from San Nicolas on a slightly different route to Oranjestad and Palm Beach, more or less hourly, 0525-2200. **Route 3** runs between Oranjestad and San Nicolas, 0550-2030 and **Route 4** runs from Oranjestad through Noord to Palm Beach almost hourly on the ½ hr. There are also extra buses running between Oranjestad and the Holiday Inn (schedules available at the hotels and the tourist office). One-way fare is US$1. Otherwise there are 'jitney cars' which operate like *colectivos*; the fare is US$1.25. A jitney or bus from Oranjestad to San Nicolas will drop you at the airport.

Car
Driving is on the right and all traffic, except bicycles, coming from the right should be given right of way, except at T-junctions.
Car hire You must have a valid foreign (held for at least 2 yrs) or international driver's licence and be at least 21 to rent a car. Requirements vary between companies with a minimum age of 21-25 and a maximum of 65-70. There are some 23 car hire companies. **Airways** (Sabana Blanco 35, T5821845, airport T5829112); **Hertz** (L G Smith Blvd 142, T5824545, airport T5824886); **Avis** (Kolibristraat 14, T5828787, airport T5825496); **Budget** (Kolibristraat 1, T5828600, airport T5825423); **Dollar** (Grenedaweg 15, T5822783, airport T5825651) and **Toyota** (L G Smith Blvd 114, T5834832, airport, T5834902, toyota.rentacar@setarnet.aw) have offices in Oranjestad and at the airport. Many companies also have desks in the hotels. Prices begin at US$35 daily, US$215 weekly, with unlimited mileage. Often when you rent a 4WD vehicle you cannot take out all risks insurance.

Motorcycles and bikes
A rental 50cc moped or scooter costs around US$30 a day, a 250cc motorcycle US$40, a Harley Davidson SP1100 US$90 and insurance is US$8-15 a day, depending on the size of engine. **Big Twin** rents Harley Davidson, T5839322. **Pablito's Bikes Rental**, L G Smith Blvd 228, T5878300, at La Quinta Beach Resort, Eagle Beach, men's, ladies', children's **bicycles**, US$3 per hr, US$8 half day, US$12 per 24 hrs. Other companies include **Donata**, T5878300, **Dream Cycles**, T5824329, **George**, T5825975, **Nelson**, T5866801, **New York**, T5863885, **Semver**, T5866851, and **Ron's** T5862090.

Taxi
Telephone the dispatcher at Pos Abao 41 behind the **Eagle Bowling Palace** on the Sasaki road, T5822116. Drivers speak English and individual tours can be arranged. Taxis do not have meters; rates are set by the government. From the airport to Oranjestad is US$13, to the low-rise hotels US$17 and to the high-rise hotels US$20 per taxi, not per person, maximum 5 passengers. On public holidays and after midnight a surcharge of US$1 is added.

❶ Directory

Aruba *p967, map p968*

Banks ABN/AMRO Bank, Caya G F (Betico) Croes 89, T5821515, at the Port of Call shopping centre on L G Smith Blvd; ATMs at these offices and at Sun Plaza Building, LG Smith Blvd 160 and Dr Horacio Oduber Hospital, for Cirrus or Mastercard. Aruba Bank NV, Caya G F (Betico) Croes 41, T5821550, and at L G Smith Blvd 108, T5831318. **Banco di Caribe NV**, Caya G F Croes 90-92, T5832168. **Caribbean Mercantile Bank NV**, Caya G F (Betico) Croes 51, T5823118, ATM for Cirrus or Mastercard here and also at Palm Beach 48 (Noord), Zeppenfeldstraat 35 (San Nicolas), Santa Cruz 41 (Santa Cruz), LG Smith Blvd 17, Seaport Village Mall. **Interbank**, Caya G F (Betico) Croes 38, T5831080. **First National Bank**, Caya G F (Betico) Croes 67, T5833221. **Western Union Money Transfer Service**, T5824400. **American Express** representative for refunds, exchange or replacement of cheques or cards is **SEL Maduro & Sons**, Rockefellerstraat 1, T5823888, open Mon-Fri 0800-1200, 1300-1700. **Aruba Bank**, **Caribbean Mercantile Bank** and **Interbank** are Visa/Mastercard representatives with cash advance. Aruba Bank at the airport is open daily 0800-1600. **Embassies and consulates** Denmark, L G Smith Blvd 82, T5824622. **Dominican Republic**, J G Emanstraat 79, T5836928. **Germany**,

Scopetstraat 13, T5821767. **Italy**, Caya G F Betico Croes 7, T5822621. **Spain**, Madurostraat 9, T5823163. **Sweden**, Havenstraat 33, T5821821. **Venezuela**, Adriane Lacle Blvd 8, T5821078.

Internet There is an internet café at **Royal Plaza Mall**, Oranjestad, with access for US$7 per 30 mins. Email services at some hotels are complimentary for guests and many of them now offer Wi-Fi internet access.

Medical services All the major hotels have a doctor on call. **Dr Horacio Oduber Hospital**, L G Smith Blvd, T5874300, 280-bed hospital near the main hotel area. **Post** The post office at JE Irausquinplein is open 0730-1200, 1300-1630. Postal rates to the USA, Canada and the Netherlands are Afl 1.40 for letters and Afl0.60 for postcards. Letters to Europe Afl 1.50, postcards Afl 0.70. Collectors can subscribe for new issues by contacting the Philatelic Service, T5821900.

Telephone Modern telephone services with direct dialling are available. Phone numbers have 7 digits, all beginning with 5. Mobile phone numbers also have 7 digits, beginning with 9. Hotels add a service charge on to international calls. The **ITT** office is on Boecoetiweg 33, T5821458. Phone and fax calls, email and mariphone calls at **Servicio di Telecommunicacion di Aruba (Setar)**, at Palm Beach opposite Hyatt Regency Aruba Beach Resort, in Oranjestad just off the Plaza and next to the Post Office Building at Irausquinplein, Oranjestad.

Background

History

The first known settlers of the islands were the Caiquetios, a tribe of peaceful Arawak Indians. They survived principally on fish and shellfish and collected salt from the Charoma saltpan to barter with their mainland neighbours for supplements to their diet. There are remains of Indian villages on Curaçao at Westpunt, San Juan, de Savaan and Santa Barbara, and on Aruba near Hooiberg. The Arawaks in this area had escaped attack by the Caribs but soon after the arrival of the Spaniards most were transported from Curaçao to work on Hispaniola. Although some were later repatriated, more fled when the Dutch arrived. The remainder were absorbed into the black or white population, so that by 1795, only five full-blooded Indians were to be found on Curaçao. On Aruba and Bonaire the Indians maintained their identity until about the end of the 19th century, but there were no full-blooded Indians left by the 20th century.

The islands were encountered in 1499 by a Spaniard, Alonso de Ojeda, accompanied by the Italian, Amerigo Vespucci and the Spanish cartographer Juan de la Cosa. The Spanish retained control over the islands throughout the 16th century, but because there was no gold, they were declared 'useless islands'. After 1621, the Dutch became frequent visitors looking for wood and salt and later for a military foothold. Curaçao's strategic position between Pernambuco and New Amsterdam within the Caribbean setting made it a prime target. In 1634, a Dutch fleet took Curaçao, then in 1636 they took Bonaire, which was inhabited by a few cattle and six Indians, and Aruba which the Spanish and Indians evacuated. Curaçao became important as a trading post and as a base for excursions against the Spanish. After 1654, Dutch refugees from Brazil brought sugar technology, but the crop was abandoned by 1688 because of the dry climate. About this time citrus fruits were introduced, and salt remained a valuable commodity. Much of Curaçao's wealth came from the slave trade. From 1639-1778 thousands of slaves were brought to Willemstad, and sold to the mainland and other colonies. The Dutch brought half a million slaves to the Caribbean, most of which went through Curaçao.

Wars between England and the Netherlands in the second half of the 17th century led to skirmishes and conquests in the Caribbean. The Peace of Nijmegen in 1678 gave the Dutch Aruba, Curaçao, Bonaire and the three smaller islands in the Leeward group, St Eustatius, Saba and half of St Martin. Further conflicts in Europe and the Americas in the 18th century led to Curaçao becoming a meeting place for pirates, American rebels, Dutch merchants, Spaniards and Creoles from the mainland. In 1800 the English took Curaçao but withdrew in 1803. They occupied it again from 1807 until 1816 (when Dutch rule was restored), during which time it was declared a free port. From 1828 to 1845, all Dutch West Indian colonies were governed from Surinam. In 1845 the Dutch Leeward Islands were joined to Willemstad in one colonial unit called Curaçao and Dependencies. The economy was still based on commerce, much of it with Venezuela, and there was a ship building industry, some phosphate mining and the salt pans.

In the 20th century oil was discovered in Venezuela and the Dutch-British Shell Oil Company set up a refinery on Curaçao because of its political stability, its port facilities and its better climate. The Second World War was another turning point as demand for oil soared and British, French and later US forces were stationed on the islands. The German invasion of Holland encouraged Dutch companies to transfer their assets to the Netherlands Antilles leading to the birth of the offshore financial centre.

Government

The organization of political parties began in 1936 and by 1948 there were four parties on Curaçao and others on Aruba and the other islands, most of whom endorsed autonomy. In 1948, the Dutch constitution was revised to allow for the transition to complete autonomy of the islands. In 1954 they were granted full autonomy in domestic affairs and became an integral part of the Kingdom of the Netherlands. The Crown continued to appoint the Governor. Nevertheless, a strong separatist movement developed on Aruba and the island finally withdrew from the Netherlands Antilles in 1986, becoming an autonomous member of the Kingdom of the Netherlands.

The Netherlands Antilles then formed two autonomous parts of the Kingdom of the Netherlands. The main part, comprising all the islands except Aruba, was a parliamentary federal democracy, the seat of which was in Willemstad, Curaçao, and each island had its own Legislative and Executive Council. Parliament (Staten) was elected in principle every four years, with 14 members from Curaçao, three from Bonaire, three from Sint Maarten and one each from Saba and St Eustatius. However, all this changed in 2007.

Separate status for some or all of the islands has been a political issue with a breakaway movement in Curaçao and Sint Maarten. Referenda were held in 1993 and 1994 which supported the status quo, but in 2000 Sint Maarten voted for 'status aparte'. In 2004 referenda were held on Bonaire, Sint Eustatius and Saba asking the electorate to choose between a new constitutional status or to remain part of the

Netherlands Antilles. Bonaire and Saba chose to establish closer ties with Holland and no longer be a member of the Netherlands Antilles. Sint Eustatius later chose to follow suit. Subsequent negotiations resulted in the three voting islands becoming a municipality of the Netherlands on 1 July 2007, phasing into the Dutch mainstream within five years. As we went to press it was still undecided which currency would be used and other details were still being ironed out. Changes for St Maarten, which wants a status similar to Aruba's, and Curaçao, which has not yet agreed to Dutch proposals for their status, will come later. The Netherlands Antilles as an overseas territory of Holland will disappear, but the individual islands will continue their association with the Dutch Kingdom either as semi-autonomous entities or integrated into the Dutch provincial/municipal structure.

Economy

Bonaire Bonaire's economy is heavily dependent on tourism, with small operations for solar salt mining, oil trans-shipment and radio communications industry. Cargill Corporation, the world's largest private company, operates the salt industry, which benefits so greatly from the constant sunshine (with air temperatures averaging 27°C and water 26°C), scant rainfall, and refreshing trade winds. A shrimp farm started operations in 1999; **Sea Hatch Bonaire** is near Sorobon and offers tours.

Tourism is specialized and most visitors are divers. The USA is the largest single market, followed by the Netherlands, Venezuela and Germany. Accommodation for tourists is split fairly evenly between hotels and condominiums or villas, amounting to about 1,100 rooms and still growing. Financial assistance for the development of tourism has been provided by the EU and Holland, which have financed the expansion of the airport and development of other infrastructure.

Curaçao Curaçao has a more diversified economy than the other islands, yet even so, it suffered severe recession in the 1980s and unemployment is around 13% of the labour force. The major industry is the oil refinery dating back to 1917, now one of the largest in the world, to which the island's fortunes and prosperity are tied. Imports of crude oil and petroleum products make up two-thirds of total imports, while exports of the same are 95% of total exports. That prosperity was placed under threat when Shell pulled out of the refinery in 1985, but the operation was saved when the island government purchased the plant, and leased it to Venezuela for US$11 mn a year. Despite the need for a US$270 mn reconstruction, principally to reduce pollution, the Venezuelan company, **PDVSA**, signed a 20-year lease agreement which came into effect in 1995, ending its previous system of short-term operating leases. Bunkering has also become an important segment of the economy, and the terminal at Bullenbaai is one of the largest bunkering ports in the world. The island's extensive trade makes it a port of call for a great many shipping lines.

Coral reefs surrounding the island, constant sunshine, a mean temperature of 27°C (81°F), lure visitors. Curaçao used to be a destination for tourists from Venezuela, but a devaluation of the bolívar in 1983 caused numbers to drop by 70% in just one year. A restructuring of the industry has led to a change of emphasis towards attracting US and European tourists, as well as South Americans, and numbers have now increased. Cruise visitor numbers have been boosted by the arrival of the megaship *Rhapsody of the Seas*, which carries 2,000 and calls 26 times a year. The single largest market for visitors to Curaçao is Holland, with 30% of stayover arrivals, followed by the USA with 15% and Venezuela with 14%. Diving has been promoted and Curaçao now registers about 10,000 visiting divers a year. A major foreign currency earner, the offshore financial sector, is seeking new areas of business, including captive insurance and mutual funds, in a highly competitive market.

Aruba Gold was discovered in 1825, but the mine ceased to be economic in 1916. In

1929, black gold brought real prosperity to Aruba when **Lago Oil and Transport Co,** a subsidiary of **Exxon,** built a refinery at San Nicolas at the east end of the island. At that time it was the largest refinery in the world, employing over 8,000 people. In March 1985 **Exxon** closed the refinery, a serious shock for the Aruban economy, and one which the Government has striven to overcome. In 1989, **Coastal Oil of Texas** signed an agreement with the Government to reopen part of the refinery by 1991, with an initial capacity of 150,000 barrels a day, but despite plans to increase it, present capacity is only about 140,000 b/d.

The economic crisis of 1985 forced the Government to turn to the IMF for help. The fund recommended that Aruba promote tourism and increase the number of hotel rooms by 50%. The Government decided, however, to triple hotel capacity to 6,000 rooms, which it was estimated would provide employment for 20% of the population. In 1995 the opening of the **Marriott** raised the total to 6,626 rooms in hotels, a figure which had risen to 7,103 by 1996. Total employment in tourism absorbs 35% of the workforce. The economy is dependent on tourism for income and in 2000 combined stayover and cruise ship passengers exceeded 1 million for the first time with more than 25 cruise lines visiting each month and even more airlines adding Aruba to their routes from the USA.

Efforts are being made to diversify away from a single source of revenues into areas such as re-exporting through the free trade zone, and offshore finance. Aruba is still dependent on the Netherlands for budget support and aims to reduce financial assistance.

Unemployment is rare on Aruba and labour is imported for large projects such as the refinery and construction work. The Government is encouraging skilled Arubans to return from Holland but is hampered by a housing shortage.

Flora and fauna

Bonaire An environmental awareness for preservation of the reefs and the island's natural state pervades society here like no other Caribbean destination. Nature and the environment is even a subject for study in the primary and secondary school systems thanks to grants given on a regular basis by the **World Wildlife Fund** and the **Dutch Lottery Fund.** It is a **United Nations Environmental Project (UNEP)** demonstration location and a candidate for a UN World Heritage Site. All of the waters to 60 m deep and much of the countryside, fauna and flora of Bonaire is protected.

Bonaire has one of the largest Caribbean flamingo colonies in the Western Hemisphere (between 3,500 and 11,000 depending on the season).These birds build their conical mud nests in the salt pans. The **Salt Company** has set aside an area of 56 ha for a flamingo sanctuary, with access strictly prohibited. The birds have settled into a peaceful co-existence, so peaceful in fact that they are now laying two eggs a year instead of one. They can be seen from the roads in the south and in Goto Meer Bay in the northwest, in the salt lake near Playa Grandi, and in Lac Bay on the southeast coast of Bonaire, feeding on algae and the crustaceans that give them their striking pink colour. Air traffic over the flamingo sanctuary is prohibited.

There are also two smaller bird sanctuaries at the **Solar Salt Works** and Goto Meer. At Pos'i Mangel, in Washington Park, thousands of birds gather in the late afternoon. Bronswinkel Well, also in the park, is another good place to see hundreds of birds and giant cacti. The indigenous Bonaire green parrot (a conjure rather than a parrot) and the endangered yellow-shouldered Amazon (*Amazona barbarebdis rothschildi*) can be seen in the park and at other locations around the island. In the dry season they spend part of their day in the main city. About 190 species of bird have been found on Bonaire in addition to the flamingos.

There are lots of iguanas and lizards of all shapes and sizes. The big blue lizards are endemic to Bonaire, while the Anolis, a tree lizard with a yellow dewlap, is related to the Windward Islands Anolis species rather than to the neighbouring Venezuelan species. The most common mammals you are likely to see are feral goats and donkeys. Try to resist feeding the friendly donkeys because this attracts them to the roadside where they are hit by vehicles too frequently. Bonaire's only native mammal is the bat, of which eight species have been identified.

Aruba Aruba has 48 different types of native trees, 11 of which are now very scarce and in some cases have only five examples left. The loss of native trees is due to wood cutting, changing weather and marauding goats. A tree-planting programme is under way and negotiations with goat owners are in progress to keep them out of protected areas. About 170 species of bird can be found on Aruba, and about 50 species breed on the island but if you include the migratory birds which come in November to January the total rises to around 300 species. The most common birds are the *trupiaal* (bright orange), the *chuchubi*, the *prikichi* (a little parrot) and the *barika geel* (the little yellow-bellied bird you will find eating the sugar on the table in your hotel). The *shoco*, a burrowing owl, is endangered. An interesting place to see waterfowl is the Bubali Plassen, opposite the Olde Molen. Here you can often find cormorants, herons and fish eagles. Brown pelicans can be seen along the south shore. Two kinds of snake can be found on Aruba: the harmless little Santanero (however, be careful when you pick it up, because it defecates in your hand) and the not-so-harmless rattle snake. Aruba's rattle snake, the cascabel, is a nearly extinct subspecies that does not use its rattle. Rattle snakes live in the triangular area between the Jamanota, Fontein and San Nicolas. The best place to go looking for rattle snakes, if you really want to, is the area south of the Jamanota mountain. In the unlikely event that you get bitten, go immediately to the hospital; they have anti-serum.

As well as various kinds of lizards, Aruba has large iguanas, that are hunted to prepare a typical Arubian soup.

The **Arikok National Park** ① *www.arubanationalparks.com*, covers a triangle of land between Boca Prins and San Fuego and bounded on the east by the sea as far as Boca Keto. After decades of discussion the plan converts 17% of the island into a protected park area. Work is continuing to provide trails, clean up and upgrade the park, clearing litter and reconstructing benches and a stairway built at Fuerte Prins in the 1960s. The three centres will be linked by trails for cars and walkers. Arikok Centre contains the 184.5 m Arikok hill, the second highest point in Aruba. **Prins Centre** in the northeast includes the former Prins Plantation, the functioning Fontein Plantation and the Fontein Cave. The **Jamanota Centre** in the south includes the 189 m Jamanota hill, the highest point of the island, and the old gold-mining operation at Miralamas. The Spanish Lagoon area is also included.

Footnotes

Index → *Entries in bold refer to maps.*

Footnotes

Advertisers' index

Complete title listing

Footprint publishes travel guides to over 150 destinations worldwide. Each guide is packed with practical, concise and colourful information for everybody from first-time travellers to travel aficionados. The list is growing fast and current titles are noted below.

(P) denotes pocket guide

Latin America & Caribbean
Antigua & Leeward Islands (P)
Argentina
Barbados (P)
Bolivia
Brazil
Caribbean Islands
Chile
Costa Rica
Cuba
Cuzco & the Inca heartland
Discover Belize, Guatemala & Southern Mexico
Discover Patagonia
Discover Peru, Bolivia & Ecuador
Dominican Republic (P)
Ecuador & Galápagos
Mexico & Central America
Nicaragua
Peru
South American Handbook

North America
Discover Western Canada
Vancouver (P)

Africa
Cape Town (P)
Egypt
Kenya
Morocco
Namibia
South Africa
Tanzania

Middle East
Dubai (P)
Jordan

Australasia
Australia
Discover East Coast Australia
New Zealand
Sydney (P)

Asia
Borneo
Cambodia
Discover Vietnam, Cambodia & Laos
India
Laos
Malaysia & Singapore
Rajasthan
South India
Sri Lanka
Thailand
Vietnam

Europe
Andalucía
Antwerp & Ghent (P)
Barcelona (P)
Bilbao & the Basque country (P)
Bologna (P)
Cardiff (P)
Copenhagen (P)
Costa de la Luz (P)
Croatia
Dublin (P)
Lisbon (P)
London
London (P)
Madrid (P)
Naples & the Amalfi Coast (P)
Northern Spain
Paris (P)
Reykjavík (P)
Scotland Highlands & Islands
Seville (P)

Siena & the heart of Tuscany (P)
Tallinn (P)
Turin (P)
Valencia (P)
Verona (P)

Lifestyle & activity guides
Body & Soul escapes
Diving the World
European City Breaks
Snowboarding the World
Surfing Britain
Surfing Europe
Surfing the World
Wine Travel Guide to the World

Also available
Traveller's Handbook (WEXAS)
Traveller's Healthbook (WEXAS)
Traveller's Internet Guide (WEXAS)

**Footprint guides are
available from all good
bookshops and online at
www.footprintbooks.com**

Credits

Footprint credits
Editor: Alan Murphy
Map editor: Sarah Sorensen
Picture editor: Kevin Feeney

Publisher: Patrick Dawson
Editorial: Sophie Blacksell, Alan Murphy,
Nicola Gibbs, Jo Williams
Cartography: Robert Lunn, Kevin Feeney
Design: Mytton Williams
Sales and Marketing: Andy Riddle,
Zoë Jackson, Hannah Bonnell
Advertising: Debbie Wylde
Finance and administration:
Elizabeth Taylor

Photography credits
Front cover: Grand Piton – Stone/Getty
Back cover: Colourful shells – age
fotostock/Superstock

Inside colour section: Superstock, age
fotostock/Superstock, Angelo
Cavalli/Superstock, Alamy' Robert Harding
Picture Library Ltd/Alamy, SC Photos/Alamy,
Nick Hanna/Alamy, Dave Saunders, Cayman
Islands Department of Tourism, Maca Bana,
St Lucia Tourist Board, Commonwealth of
Puerto Rico Tourist Company.

Print
Manufactured in India by Nutech
Photolithographers, Delhi
Pulp from sustainable forests

Footprint feedback
We try as hard as we can to make each
Footprint guide as up to date as possible
but, of course, things always change.
If you want to let us know about your
experiences – good, bad or ugly – then don't
delay, go to www.footprintbooks.com
and send in your comments.
    Hotel and restaurant price codes should
only be taken as a guide to the prices and
facilities offered by the establishment. It is at
the discretion of the owners to vary them
from time to time.

Publishing information
Footprint Caribbean Islands
17th edition
© Footprint Handbooks Ltd
August 2007

ISBN: 978 1 904777 97 7
CIP DATA: A catalogue record for this
book is available from the British Library

® Footprint Handbooks and the Footprint
mark are a registered trademark of
Footprint Handbooks Ltd

Published by Footprint
6 Riverside Court
Lower Bristol Road
Bath BA2 3DZ, UK
T +44 (0)1225 469141
F +44 (0)1225 469461
discover@footprintbooks.com
www.footprintbooks.com

Every effort has been made to ensure that
the facts in this guidebook are accurate.
However, travellers should still obtain
advice about travel and visa requirements
before travelling. The authors and publishers
cannot accept responsibility for any loss,
injury or inconvenience however caused.

Map symbols

Administration

- □ Capital city
- ○ Other city, town
- International border
- Regional border
- Disputed border

Roads and travel

- Motorway
- Main road (National highway)
- Minor road
- Track
- Footpath
- Railway with station
- ✈ Airport
- Bus station
- Ⓜ Metro station
- Cable car
- Funicular
- ⚓ Ferry

Water features

- River, canal
- Lake, ocean
- Seasonal marshland
- Beach, sandbank
- Waterfall
- Reef

Topographical features

- Contours (approx)
- ▲ Mountain, volcano
- Mountain pass
- Escarpment
- Gorge
- Glacier
- Salt flat
- Rocks

Cities and towns

- Main through route
- Main street

- Minor street
- Pedestrianized street
- Tunnel
- One-way street
- Steps
- Bridge
- Fortified wall
- Park, garden, stadium
- Sleeping
- Eating
- Bars & clubs
- Building
- Sight
- Cathedral, church
- Chinese temple
- Hindu temple
- Meru
- Mosque
- Stupa
- Synagogue
- Tourist office
- Museum
- Post office
- Police
- Bank
- Internet
- Telephone
- Market
- Medical services
- Parking
- Petrol
- Golf
- Detail map
- Related map

Other symbols

- Archaeological site
- National park, wildlife reserve
- Viewing point
- Campsite
- Refuge, lodge
- Castle, fort
- Diving
- Deciduous, coniferous, palm trees
- Hide
- Vineyard, winery
- Distillery
- Shipwreck
- Historic battlefield

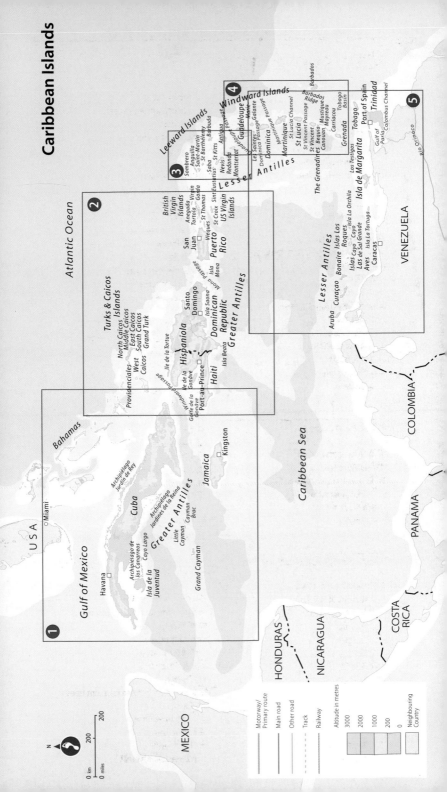

Caribbean Islands

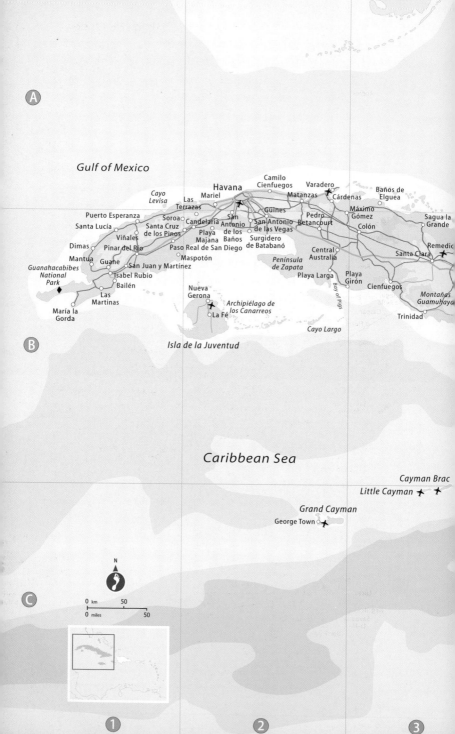

Map 1 Cuba, Jamaica & the Cayman Islands

USA

Gulf of Mexico

Havana

Camilo Cienfuegos

Varadero

Baños de Elguea

Cayo Levisa
Mariel
Las Terrazas
Matanzas
Cárdenas

Puerto Esperanza
Soroa
Candelaria
Güines
Pedro Betancourt
Máximo Gómez
Sagua la Grande

Santa Lucía
Santa Cruz de los Pinos
San Antonio de los Baños
San Antonio de las Vegas
Colón

Dimas
Playa Majana
Surgidero de Batabanó
Central Australia
Remedios

Pinar del Río
Paso Real de San Diego
Santa Clara

Mantua
San Juan y Martínez
Maspotón
Península de Zapata

Guanahacabibes National Park
Guane
Playa Larga
Playa Girón
Montañas Guamuhaya

Isabel Rubio
Bailén
Nueva Gerona
Cienfuegos

Las Martinas
La Fé
Archipiélago de los Canarreos
Trinidad

María la Gorda
Bay of Pigs

Isla de la Juventud
Cayo Largo

Caribbean Sea

Cayman Brac
Little Cayman

Grand Cayman
George Town

N

0 km 50
0 miles 50

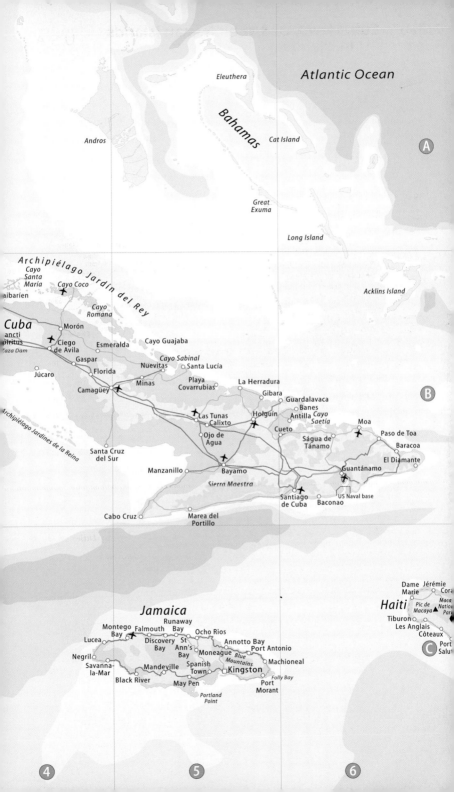

Map 2 Hispaniola, Puerto Rico, Turks & Caicos Islands & the Virgin Islands

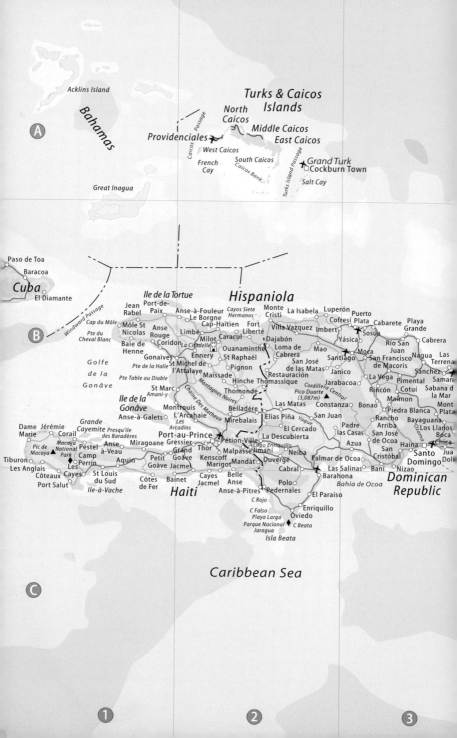

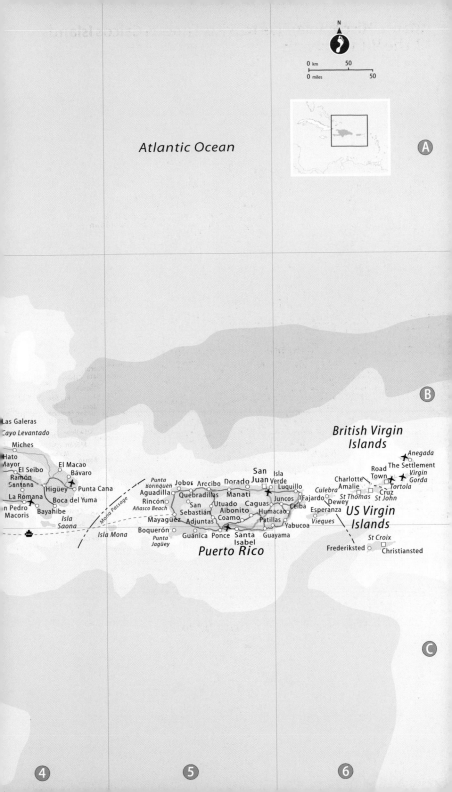

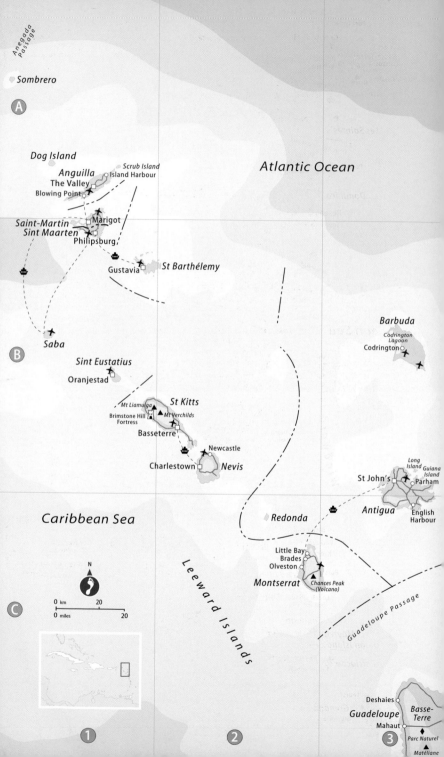
Map 3 Leeward Islands

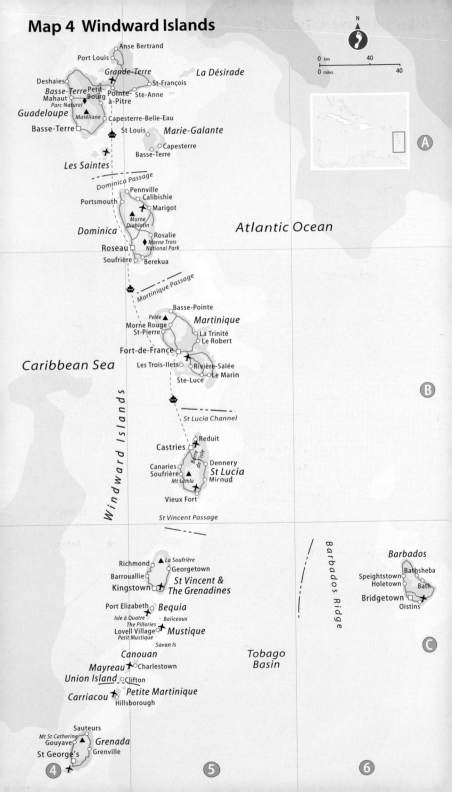

Map 4 Windward Islands

N

| 0 km | 40 |
| 0 miles | 40 |

A

Anse Bertrand
Port Louis
Grande-Terre   *La Désirade*
Deshaies   St-François
Basse-Terre Petit- Pointe- Ste-Anne
Mahaut Bourg à-Pitre
Parc Naturel
Guadeloupe Matéliane Capesterre-Belle-Eau
Basse-Terre St Louis *Marie-Galante*
Capesterre
Les Saintes Basse-Terre

Dominica Passage

Pennville
Calibishie
Portsmouth Marigot
Morne
Diablotin
Dominica Rosalie
Morne Trois
Roseau *National Park*
Soufrière Berekua

Atlantic Ocean

Martinique Passage

Basse-Pointe
Pelée
Morne Rouge *Martinique*
St-Pierre La Trinité
Le Robert
Fort-de-France
Les Trois-Ilets Rivière-Salée
Le Marin
Ste-Luce

Caribbean Sea

B

St Lucia Channel

Reduit
Castries
Barre
Canaries *de l'Isle* Dennery
Soufrière *St Lucia*
Mt Gimie Miroud
Vieux Fort

St Vincent Passage

Windward Islands

Richmond *La Soufrière*
Georgetown
Barrouaille *St Vincent &*
Kingstown *The Grenadines*

Port Elizabeth *Bequia*
Isle à Quatre Baliceaux
The Pillories
Lovell Village *Mustique*
Petit Mustique
Savan Is
Canouan
Mayreau Charlestown
Union Island Clifton
Carriacou *Petite Martinique*
Hillsborough

Tobago
Basin

Barbados Ridge

C

Barbados
Bathsheba
Speightstown
Holetown Bath
Bridgetown
Oistins

Sauteurs
Mt St Catherine
Gouyave *Grenada*
St George's Grenville

4   **5**   **6**

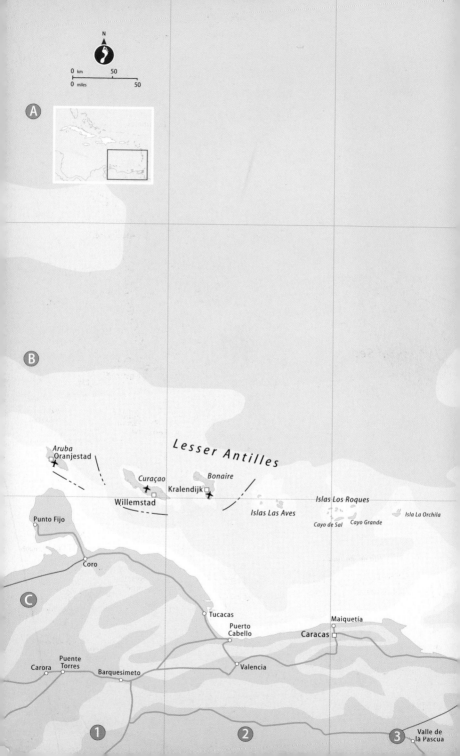

Map 5 Lesser Antilles & Trinidad

N

0 km 50
0 miles 50

A

B

Lesser Antilles

Aruba
□Oranjestad

Curaçao
□
Willemstad

Bonaire
Kralendijk □

Islas Los Roques

Islas Las Aves

Isla La Orchila

Cayo de Sal *Cayo Grande*

Punto Fijo

Coro

C

Tucacas

Maiquetía

Puerto
Cabello

Caracas □

Carora
Puente
Torres

Barquesimeto

Valencia

1

2

3 Valle de
la Pascua